D0086390

Making America

Making America

A HISTORY OF THE UNITED STATES

SEVENTH EDITION

[**VOLUME 2: SINCE 1865**]

Carol Berkin
Baruch College, City University of New York

Christopher L. Miller
The University of Texas–Pan American

Robert W. Cherny
San Francisco State University

James L. Gormly
Washington and Jefferson College

Australia • Brazil • Canada • Mexico • Singapore • United Kingdom • United States

CENGAGE

Making America: A History of the United States, Volume 2: Since 1865, Seventh Edition

Carol Berkin, Christopher L. Miller, Robert W. Cherny, James L. Gormly

Product Director: Suzanne Jeans

Senior Product Manager: Ann West

Content Coordinator: Megan Chrisman

Product Assistant: Liz Fraser

Media Developer: Kate MacLean

Marketing Brand Manager: Melissa Larmon

Senior Content Project Manager:
Carol Newman

Senior Art Director: Cate Rickard Barr

Manufacturing Planner: Sandee Milewski

Senior Rights Acquisition Specialist:
Jennifer Meyer Dare

Production Service/Compositor:
S4Carlisle Publishing Services

Text Designer: Cia Boynton/Boynton Hue Studio

Cover Designer: Cassandra Chu

Cover Image: Detroit Industry, north wall, 1933 (fresco) (detail), Rivera, Diego (1886-1957)/ Detroit Institute of Arts, USA/The Bridgeman Art Library/©2013 Banco de México Diego Rivera Frida Kahlo Museums Trust, Mexico, D.F./Artists Rights Society (ARS), New York

Feature Photo Credits: In the Wider World: NASA/SCIENCE Photo Library/Getty Images; It Matters Today: Keith Bedford/ Stringer/Getty Images

Brief Contents

15 Reconstruction: High Hopes and Shattered Dreams, 1865–1877 369

16 The Nation Industrializes, 1865–1900 397

17 Life in the Gilded Age, 1865–1900 433

18 Politics and Foreign Relations in a Rapidly Changing Nation, 1865–1902 466

19 The Progressive Era, 1900–1917 503

20 The United States in a World at War, 1913–1920 536

21 Prosperity Decade, 1920–1928 565

22 The Great Depression and the New Deal, 1929–1939 597

23 America's Rise to World Leadership, 1929–1945 632

24 Truman and Cold War America, 1945–1952 664

25 Quest for Consensus, 1952–1960 690

26 Great Promises, Bitter Disappointments, 1960–1968 716

27 America Under Stress, 1967–1976 741

28 New Economic and Political Alignments, 1976–1992 766

29 Entering a New Century, 1992–2013 793

Brief Contents

13   Reconstruction: High Hopes and Shattered Dreams, 1865–1877   350

14   The Nation Industrializes, 1865–1900   397

15   Life in the Gilded Age, 1865–1900   733

16   Politics and Foreign Relations in a Rapidly Changing Nation, 1865–1901   800

17   The Progressive Era, 1900–1917   809

18   The United States in a World at War, 1913–1920   556

19   Prosperity Decade, 1920–1928   515

20   The Great Depression and the New Deal, 1929–1939   747

21   America Rises to World Leadership, 1929–1945   632

22   Truman and Cold War America, 1945–1952   604

23   Quest for Consensus, 1952–1960   690

24   Great Promises, Bitter Disappointments, 1960–1968   716

25   America Under Stress, 1967–1973   741

26   New Economic and Political Alignments, 1970–1992   768

27   Entering a New Century, 1992–2015   733

Contents

Maps **xiv**

Features **xv**

Preface **xvii**

A Note for the Students: Your Guide
to *Making America* **xxvii**

About the Authors **xxix**

[15] Reconstruction: High Hopes and Shattered Dreams, 1865–1877 369

INDIVIDUAL CHOICES: Joseph Rainey **369**

Presidential Reconstruction **371**

Republican War Aims **371**

Lincoln's Approach to Reconstruction: "With Malice Toward None" **372**

Abolishing Slavery Forever: The Thirteenth Amendment **372**

Andrew Johnson and Reconstruction **373**

IN THE WIDER WORLD: Abolition of Slavery Around the World **374**

The Southern Response: Minimal Compliance **375**

Freedom and the Legacy of Slavery **375**

Defining the Meaning of Freedom **376**

Creating Communities **376**

Land and Labor in the Postwar South **377**

The White South: Confronting Change **378**

Congressional Reconstruction **380**

Challenging Presidential Reconstruction: The Civil Rights Act of 1866 **380**

Defining Citizenship: The Fourteenth Amendment **381**

IT MATTERS TODAY: The Fourteenth Amendment **382**

Radicals in Control **382**

Political Terrorism and the Election of 1868 **383**

TOWARD A MORE PERFECT UNION: Constitutional Revolution **384**

Voting Rights and Civil Rights **384**

Black Reconstruction **385**

The Republican Party in the South **386**

Creating Public Education, Fighting Discrimination, and Building Railroads **387**

The End of Reconstruction **388**

The "New Departure" and the 1872 Presidential Election **388**

The Politics of Terror: The "Mississippi Plan" **390**

The Troubled Presidential Election of 1876 **390**

A DEEPER UNDERSTANDING OF HISTORY: When Historians Disagree **392**

After Reconstruction **393**

INDIVIDUAL VOICES: Congressman Joseph Rainey, from a Speech Supporting the Ku Klux Klan Act **394**

STUDY TOOLS: Summary │ Chronology │ Focus Questions │ Key Terms │ Suggested Resources **395–396**

[16] The Nation Industrializes, 1865–1900 397

INDIVIDUAL CHOICES: John D. Rockefeller **397**

Foundation for Industrialization **398**

Resources, Skills, Capital, and New Federal Policies **398**

The Transformation of Agriculture **400**

The Dawn of Big Business **401**

Railroads: The First Big Business **401**

Railroads, Investment Bankers, and "Morganization" **405**

Andrew Carnegie and the Age of Steel **405**

IT MATTERS TODAY: Vertical Integration **407**

Survival of the Fittest? **407**

A DEEPER UNDERSTANDING OF HISTORY: Memoirs and Autobiographies **408**

Expansion of the Industrial Economy **409**

Standard Oil: Model for Monopoly **409**

Thomas Edison and the Power of Innovation **410**

IN THE WIDER WORLD: Cartels **411**

Selling to the Nation **412**

Economic Concentration in Consumer-Goods Industries **413**

TOWARD A MORE PERFECT UNION: Corporate Personhood **413**

Seeking a New South   414

Incorporating the West into the National Economy   415

    War for the West   415

    Transforming the West: Railroads, Cattle, and Mining   420

    Transforming the West: Farming and Lumbering   422

    Water and Western Development   426

Boom and Bust: The Economy from the Civil War to World War I   426

    Growth and Depression in the 1870s and 1880s   426

    Economic Collapse and Depression in the 1890s   428

    The "Merger Movement"   428

    INDIVIDUAL VOICES: John D. Rockefeller Explains the Inevitability of Big Business   430

STUDY TOOLS: Summary | Chronology | Focus Questions | Key Terms | Suggested Resources   431–432

[17] Life in the Gilded Age, 1865–1900   433

    INDIVIDUAL CHOICES: The Tape Family   433

The New Urban America   434

    The New Face of the City   435

    The New Urban Middle Class   438

    Redefining Gender Roles   439

    Emergence of a Gay and Lesbian Subculture   441

    "How the Other Half Lives"   442

    IT MATTERS TODAY: Urban Building Codes   443

New South, Old Problems   444

    Social Patterns in the New South   444

    The Second Mississippi Plan and the Atlanta Compromise   445

    IN THE WIDER WORLD: South Africa Establishes Racial Separation   446

Ethnicity and Race in the Gilded Age   447

    A Flood of Immigrants from Europe   447

    Nativism   449

    Immigrants to the Golden Mountain   450

    A DEEPER UNDERSTANDING OF HISTORY: Reconstructing Past Social Patterns   451

    TOWARD A MORE PERFECT UNION: Defining the Meaning of the Fourteenth Amendment   452

    Forced Assimilation   452

    Mexican Americans in the Southwest   454

Workers Organize   455

    Workers for Industry   455

The Origins of Unions and Labor Conflict in the 1870s   457

Competing Labor Organizations in the 1880s   459

Labor on the Defensive in the 1890s   461

    INDIVIDUAL VOICES: Mary Tape Challenges the San Francisco Board of Education   463

STUDY TOOLS: Summary | Chronology | Focus Questions | Key Terms | Suggested Resources   464–465

[18] Politics and Foreign Relations in a Rapidly Changing Nation, 1865–1902   466

    INDIVIDUAL CHOICES: Carl Schurz   466

Parties, Spoils, Scandals, and Stalemate, 1865–1880   467

    Parties, Conventions, and Patronage   467

    Republicans and Democrats   469

    Grant's Troubled Presidency   470

    The Politics of Stalemate, 1876–1889   471

    Harrison and the Fifty-First Congress   472

Challenges to Politics as Usual   474

    Grangers, Greenbackers, and Silverites   474

    IT MATTERS TODAY: The Defeat of the Lodge Bill   475

    TOWARD A MORE PERFECT UNION: The Meaning of the Commerce Clause   476

    Reforming the Spoils System   477

    Challenging the Male Bastion: Woman Suffrage   478

    Structural Change and Policy Change   479

    IN THE WIDER WORLD: Woman Suffrage   480

Political Upheaval in the 1890s   481

    The People's Party: Revolt of the West and South   481

    The Elections of 1890 and 1892   482

    Failure of the Divided Democrats   483

    The 1896 Election and the New Republican Majority   484

Standing Aside from World Affairs, 1865–1889   486

    Alaska, Canada, and the *Alabama* Claims   486

    The United States and Latin America   487

    Eastern Asia and the Pacific   487

Stepping into World Affairs: Harrison and Cleveland, 1889–1897   489

    Building a Modern Navy   489

    A New American Mission?   490

    Revolution in Hawai'i   490

    Crises in Latin America   491

Striding Boldly in World Affairs: McKinley, War, and Imperialism, 1898–1902   492

    McKinley and War   492

The "Splendid Little War"   493
The Treaty of Paris   494
The New American Empire   496
The Open Door and the Boxer Rebellion in China   497
A DEEPER UNDERSTANDING OF HISTORY: The Decision to Annex the Philippine Islands   498
INDIVIDUAL VOICES: Carl Schurz Comments on America's Changing Role in World Affairs, 1896–1899   500
STUDY TOOLS: Summary | Chronology | Focus Questions | Key Terms | Suggested Resources   501-502

[19] The Progressive Era, 1900–1917   503

INDIVIDUAL CHOICES: Jane Addams   503
Organizing for Change   504
The Changing Face of Politics   505
"Spearheads for Reform": The Settlement Houses   505
Women and Reform   506
Moral Reform   507
Organizing Against Racism   508
Challenging Capitalism: Socialists and Wobblies   509
The Reform of Politics, the Politics of Reform   510
Exposing Corruption: The Muckrakers   511
Reforming City Government   512
Reforming State Government   513
The Weakening of Parties and Rise of Organized Interest Groups   514
Roosevelt, Taft, and Republican Progressivism   515
Roosevelt: Asserting the Power of the Presidency   516
The Square Deal in Action: Creating the Regulatory State   516
A DEEPER UNDERSTANDING OF HISTORY: The Reductive Fallacy   517
Regulating Natural Resources   518
Taft's Troubles   519
"Carry a Big Stick": Roosevelt, Taft, and World Affairs   519
TOWARD A MORE PERFECT UNION: The Sixteenth and Seventeenth Amendments   520
Taking Panama   520
Making the Caribbean an American Lake   521
Roosevelt and Eastern Asia   522
The United States and World Affairs, 1901–1913   523
IN THE WIDER WORLD: The Scramble for the Last Colonies   524
Wilson and Democratic Progressivism   524
Debating the Future: The Election of 1912   524

Wilson and Reform, 1913–1916   526
IT MATTERS TODAY: The Federal Reserve Act   527
New Patterns in Cultural Expression   528
Realism, Impressionism, and Ragtime   528
Mass Entertainment in the Early Twentieth Century   529
Celebrating the New Age   530
Progressivism in Perspective   530
INDIVIDUAL VOICES: Jane Addams Explains Her Participation in the 1912 Presidential Campaign   532
STUDY TOOLS: Summary | Chronology | Focus Questions | Key Terms | Suggested Resources   533-535

[20] The United States in a World at War, 1913–1920   536

INDIVIDUAL CHOICES: Charles Young   536
Inherited Commitments and New Directions   537
Anti-Imperialism, Intervention, and Arbitration   538
Wilson and the Mexican Revolution   538
The United States and the Great War, 1914–1917   539
The Great War in Europe   540
American Neutrality   542
Neutral Rights and German U-Boats   542
The Election of 1916   543
The Decision for War   544
A DEEPER UNDERSTANDING OF HISTORY: A History Detective at Work   545
The Home Front   546
Mobilizing the Economy   546
Mobilizing Public Opinion   547
Civil Liberties in Time of War   549
The Great Migration and White Reactions   549
TOWARD A MORE PERFECT UNION: Civil Liberties in Wartime   549
Planning for Peace in the Midst of War   550
Mobilizing for Battle   550
Americans "Over There"   551
Bolshevism, the Secret Treaties, and the Fourteen Points   552
The Peace Conference and the Treaty   553
The World in 1919   553
IN THE WIDER WORLD: Civil War in Russia, 1918–1920   554
Wilson at Versailles   554
IT MATTERS TODAY: Redrawing the Map of the Middle East   556
The Senate and the Treaty   556
Legacies of the Great War   557
America in the Aftermath of War, November 1918–November 1920   557
"HCL" and Strikes   557

Red Scare 558

Race Riots and Lynchings 559

Amending the Constitution: Prohibition and Woman Suffrage 560

The Election of 1920 561

INDIVIDUAL VOICES: Woodrow Wilson Proposes His Fourteen Points 562

STUDY TOOLS: Summary | Chronology | Focus Questions | Key Terms | Suggested Resources 563–564

[21] Prosperity Decade, 1920–1928   565

INDIVIDUAL CHOICES: Clara Bow 565

The Bullish Decade 566

The Economics of Prosperity 567

Targeting Consumers 567

The Automobile: Driving the Economy 568

Changes in Banking and Business 569

"Get Rich Quick" 570

Agriculture: Depression in the Midst of Prosperity 571

The "Roaring Twenties" 571

A People on Wheels: The Automobile and American Life 571

Los Angeles: Automobile Metropolis 572

A Homogenized Culture Searches for Heroes 572

Alienated Intellectuals 574

Renaissance Among African Americans 574

"Flaming Youth" 576

Traditional America Roars Back 577

TOWARD A MORE PERFECT UNION: The Eighteenth and Nineteenth Amendments 577

Prohibition 577

Fundamentalism and the Campaign Against Evolution 578

IT MATTERS TODAY: Teaching Evolution in Public Schools 579

Nativism, Immigration Restriction, and Eugenics 579

The Ku Klux Klan 580

New Social Patterns in the 1920s 580

Ethnicity and Race: North, South, and West 580

Beginnings of Change in Federal Indian Policy 581

Mexican Americans 582

Labor on the Defensive 583

Changes in Women's Lives 583

A DEEPER UNDERSTANDING OF HISTORY: Using Statistics in Historical Analysis 584

Development of Gay and Lesbian Subcultures 585

The Politics of Prosperity 585

Harding's Failed Presidency 585

The Three-Candidate Presidential Election of 1924 586

The Politics of Business 587

The 1928 Campaign and the Election of Hoover 588

The Diplomacy of Prosperity 589

The United States and Latin America 589

America and Europe 591

IN THE WIDER WORLD: Hyperinflation in the Weimar Republic 592

Encouraging International Cooperation 592

INDIVIDUAL VOICES: Sexuality and Innuendo in Movie Advertising 594

STUDY TOOLS: Summary | Chronology | Focus Questions | Key Terms | Suggested Resources 595–596

[22] The Great Depression and the New Deal, 1929–1939   597

INDIVIDUAL CHOICES: Frances Perkins 597

The Economic Crisis 598

The Crash and the Great Depression 598

IT MATTERS TODAY: Preventing Another Great Depression 600

Hoover's Response to Crisis 600

A Rising Tide of Discontent 602

The Roosevelt Landslide 603

A DEEPER UNDERSTANDING OF HISTORY: Finding New Archival Sources 604

The New Deal 605

1933—The First Hundred Days 605

1934—Year of Turmoil 609

IN THE WIDER WORLD: The Spanish Civil War 610

1935—The Second Hundred Days 611

The Election of 1936 and the Waning of the New Deal 612

TOWARD A MORE PERFECT UNION: The "Judicial Revolution" of 1937 613

Changing the Face of America: The New Deal in Action 614

PWA and WPA 614

The Wagner Act and the Growth of Organized Labor 616

The New Deal and Agriculture 617

Americans Grapple with the Depression 619

"Making Do" 619

Changing Women's Roles 620

Race and Depression: South and West 621

A New Deal for All? 622

Cultural Expression in the Midst of Depression 625

The Great Depression and New Deal in Perspective 627

   INDIVIDUAL VOICES: Frances Perkins Explains the Social Security Act 628

STUDY TOOLS: Summary | Chronology | Focus Questions | Key Terms | Suggested Resources 629–631

[23] America's Rise to World Leadership, 1929–1945 632

   INDIVIDUAL CHOICES: Minoru Kiyota 632

The Road to War 634

   Diplomacy in a Dangerous World 634

   Roosevelt and Isolationism 634

   IN THE WIDER WORLD: Aliens in Their Own Land 636

   War and American Neutrality 638

   The Battle for the Atlantic 639

   Pearl Harbor 640

America Responds to War 641

   Japanese American Internment 642

   IT MATTERS TODAY: Internment 644

   Mobilizing the Nation for War 644

   TOWARD A MORE PERFECT UNION: War and Governmental Power 645

   A People at Work and War 647

   New Opportunities and Old Constraints 647

   Wartime Politics 651

Waging World War 651

   Halting the Japanese Advance 651

   Roads to Berlin 652

   Stresses in the Grand Alliance 655

   The Holocaust 656

   Closing the Circle on Japan 657

   Entering the Nuclear Age 658

   A DEEPER UNDERSTANDING OF HISTORY: Choosing Targets for the Atomic Bomb 659

   INDIVIDUAL VOICES: Justice Hugo Black Explains the Majority View in *Korematsu v. United States* 661

STUDY TOOLS: Summary | Chronology | Focus Questions | Key Terms | Suggested Resources 662–663

[24] Truman and Cold War America, 1945–1952 664

   INDIVIDUAL CHOICES: Jackie Robinson 664

The Cold War Begins 666

   Truman and Paths to Peace 666

   The Division of Europe 667

   The U.S. Presence in Latin America and the Middle East 671

The Cold War in Asia 671

   The Chinese Civil War 672

   Halting Communist Aggression in Korea 672

   Seeking to Liberate North Korea 672

   A DEEPER UNDERSTANDING OF HISTORY: Deciding on War in Korea 674

Postwar Politics 675

   Truman and Liberalism 675

   The 1948 Election 677

Cold War Politics 678

   The Red Scare 679

   TOWARD A MORE PERFECT UNION: The Cold War and Freedom of Speech 679

   Joseph McCarthy and the Politics of Loyalty 680

Homecoming and Social Adjustments 681

   Rising Expectations 681

   IT MATTERS TODAY: The G.I. Bill 683

   From Industrial Worker to Homemaker 683

   IN THE WIDER WORLD: The Condition of Women 684

   Latinos and African Americans: Restrained Expectations 685

   INDIVIDUAL VOICES: The *Sporting News* Editorializes on African Americans in Baseball 687

STUDY TOOLS: Summary | Chronology | Focus Questions | Key Terms | Suggested Resources 688–689

[25] Quest for Consensus, 1952–1960 690

   INDIVIDUAL CHOICES: Alan Freed 690

Politics of Consensus 692

   Eisenhower Takes Command 692

   Dynamic Conservatism 693

   The Problem with McCarthy 694

Eisenhower and World Affairs 694

   The New Look 694

   The Third World 696

   Turmoil in the Middle East 696

   A Protective Neighbor 698

   The New Look in Asia 699

   IN THE WIDER WORLD: The Great Leap Forward 700

   The Soviets and Cold War Politics 700

The Best of Times 701

   The Web of Prosperity 702

   Suburban Culture and Consumerism 703

   A DEEPER UNDERSTANDING OF HISTORY: Television Pictures the American Family 704

   Working Wives and Rocking Kids 706

   Rejecting Consensus 707

   Outside Suburbia 708

The Civil Rights Movement 708

Integrating Schools 708

IT MATTERS TODAY: The *Brown* Decision 709

The Montgomery Bus Boycott 710

TOWARD A MORE PERFECT UNION: Desegregation and the Supreme Court 712

Ike and Civil Rights 712

INDIVIDUAL VOICES: *Pageant* Magazine Examines "Rock 'n' Roll Alan Freed" (July 1957) 713

STUDY TOOLS: Summary | Chronology | Focus Questions | Key Terms | Suggested Resources 714-715

[26] Great Promises, Bitter Disappointments, 1960–1968 716

INDIVIDUAL CHOICES: Eunice Kennedy Shriver 716

The Politics of Action 718

The 1960 Campaign 718

The New Frontier 719

Kennedy and Civil Rights 719

IT MATTERS TODAY: Food Stamps 720

Flexible Response 723

Confronting Castro and the Soviets 724

Vietnam 725

Death in Dallas 726

Defining a New Presidency 726

Old and New Agendas 726

Implementing the Great Society 728

TOWARD A MORE PERFECT UNION: The Twenty-Fourth Amendment to the Constitution 730

New Voices 732

Urban Riots and Black Power 732

Rejecting the Feminine Mystique 733

A DEEPER UNDERSTANDING OF HISTORY: Using Political Cartoons: The 1960s Urban Riots 734

Rejecting Gender Roles 735

IN THE WIDER WORLD: Prague Spring, 1968 736

The Youth Movement 736

The Counterculture 737

INDIVIDUAL VOICES: Eunice Kennedy Shriver Champions New Perspectives 738

STUDY TOOLS: Summary | Chronology | Focus Questions | Key Terms | Suggested Resources 739-740

[27] America Under Stress, 1967–1976 741

INDIVIDUAL CHOICES: Dolores Huerta 741

Johnson and the War 742

Americanization of the Vietnam War 743

The Antiwar Movement 745

A DEEPER UNDERSTANDING OF HISTORY: Opposing the War in Vietnam: Public Opinion—Who and When 746

Tet and the 1968 Presidential Campaign 747

The Tet Offensive 747

Changing of the Guard 748

The Election of 1968 748

Defining the American Dream 749

The Emergence of *La Causa* 749

Native American Activism 751

Nixon and the World 753

Vietnamization 753

Modifying the Cold War 755

Nixon and the Domestic Agenda 756

IN THE WIDER WORLD: The Sino–Soviet Split 757

Nixon as Pragmatist 757

IT MATTERS TODAY: Banning DDT 758

TOWARD A MORE PERFECT UNION: The Twenty-Sixth Amendment to the Constitution 759

Building the Silent Majority 759

An Embattled President 760

An Interim President 761

INDIVIDUAL VOICES: Dolores Huerta on Winning Rights for Farm Workers 763

STUDY TOOLS: Summary | Chronology | Focus Questions | Key Terms | Suggested Resources 764-765

[28] New Economic and Political Alignments, 1976–1992 766

INDIVIDUAL CHOICES: Phyllis Schlafly 766

The Carter Presidency 768

New Directions in Foreign Policy 768

Domestic Priorities 771

TOWARD A MORE PERFECT UNION: The Twenty-Seventh Amendment to the Constitution 772

Resurgent Conservatism 773

The New Right 773

Reaganism 775

A Society and Economy in Transition 776

A Shifting Economy 776

IN THE WIDER WORLD: The European Union and the Euro 778

New Immigrants 778

A DEEPER UNDERSTANDING OF HISTORY: Immigration Since 1965: Unintended Consequences 779

IT MATTERS TODAY: Illegal Immigrants 780

Asserting World Power 781

Cold War Renewed 781

The Middle East and Terrorism 782

Reagan and Gorbachev 783

In Reagan's Shadow   784

Bush Assumes Office   784
Bush and a New International Order   784
The Election of 1992   788

INDIVIDUAL VOICES: Phyllis Schlafly Opposes the Equal Rights Amendment   790

STUDY TOOLS: Summary | Chronology | Focus Questions | Key Terms | Suggested Resources   791–792

[29] Entering a New Century, 1992–2013   793

INDIVIDUAL CHOICES: Evan Williams   793

The Clinton Years   795

The Opening Round   795
The Comeback   796
Clinton's Second Term   797
Clinton's Foreign Policy   797

Economy and Society in the 1990s   798

A Revitalized Economy   799
Rich, Poor, and in Between   800
Women, Family, and the Culture War   800
The Judicial Arena   801

New Agendas and Challenges   802

The 2000 Election   803

TOWARD A MORE PERFECT UNION: Federalism and the Supreme Court   803

The Bush Agenda   803
Charting New Foreign Policies   804
An Assault Against a Nation   804

War and Politics   805

The War on Terrorism   805

IT MATTERS TODAY: Islamic Fundamentalism   806

Iraq and Politics   807
Bush's Second Term   809
Economic Crises and Obama   811

Obama's Presidency   812

Shifts in Foreign Policy   813

IN THE WIDER WORLD: The Arab Spring   814

Change and the Politics of Filibuster   814

A DEEPER UNDERSTANDING OF HISTORY: Evaluating *The National Federation of Independent Business v. Sebelius Case*   816

Republican Resurgence   817
Gridlock and the Election of 2012   817

INDIVIDUAL VOICES: Nicholas Carr Asks, "Is Google Making Us Stupid?"   821

STUDY TOOLS: Summary | Chronology | Focus Questions | Key Terms | Suggested Resources   822–824

DOCUMENTS   A-1

Declaration of Independence in Congress, July 4, 1776   A-1
Articles of Confederation   A-3
Constitution of the United States of America and Amendments   A-7
Presidential Elections   A-16

INDEX   I-1

Maps

MAPS

15.1 African American Population and the Duration of Reconstruction **386**

15.2 Popular Vote for President in the South, 1872 **389**

15.3 Election of 1876 **391**

16.1 Expansion of Agriculture, 1860–1900 **400**

16.2 Railroad Expansion and Railroad Land Grants **403**

16.3 The West in the Late Nineteenth Century **416**

16.4 Indian Reservations **418**

16.5 Rainfall and Agriculture, ca. 1890 **423**

17.1 Cities, Industry, and Immigration **436**

18.1 Popular Vote for President, 1892 **483**

18.2 Election of 1896 **486**

18.3 American Involvement in the Caribbean and Pacific **495**

19.1 The United States and the Caribbean, 1898–1917 **521**

19.2 Election of 1912, by Counties **526**

20.1 The United States and the Mexican Revolution **539**

20.2 The War in Europe, 1914–1918 **541**

20.3 The War at Sea **543**

20.4 Postwar Boundary Changes in Central Europe and the Middle East **555**

21.1 Election of 1924, by County **587**

21.2 The United States and Latin America Between the Wars **590**

22.1 Presidential Election, 1932, Popular Vote by County **603**

22.2 The Tennessee Valley Authority **607**

22.3 Unemployment Relief, 1934 **608**

22.4 The Dust Bowl **618**

23.1 German and Italian Expansion, 1933–1942 **637**

23.2 Japanese Advances, December 1941–1942 **641**

23.3 Internment Camps **643**

23.4 Closing the Circle on Japan, 1942–1945 **653**

23.5 The Fall of the Third Reich **655**

24.1 Cold War Europe **668**

24.2 Cold War Germany **670**

24.3 The Korean War, 1950–1953 **673**

24.4 Election of 1948 **678**

24.5 Postwar Affluence **682**

25.1 Election of 1952 **693**

25.2 Cold War Confrontation **697**

25.3 Movement Across America, 1950–1960 **703**

26.1 Election of 1960 **719**

26.2 The Struggle for Civil Rights, 1960–1968 **722**

26.3 African Americans and the Southern Vote, 1960–1971 **731**

27.1 Southeast Asia and the Vietnam War **744**

27.2 Election of 1968 **749**

27.3 Changing Latino Population **750**

27.4 American Indian Reservations **751**

28.1 The Middle East **769**

28.2 The United States and Central America and the Caribbean **782**

28.3 The End of the Cold War Changes the Map of Europe **785**

28.4 The Gulf War **788**

28.5 Election of 1992, by State **789**

29.1 Election of 2000 **804**

29.2 The Middle East and Afghanistan **807**

29.3 Second Iraq War **808**

29.4 Election of 2008, by State **812**

29.5 The Arab Spring and Change **815**

29.6 Election of 2012, by State **820**

Features

INDIVIDUAL CHOICES

Joseph Rainey   369
John D. Rockefeller   397
The Tape Family   433
Carl Schurz   466
Jane Addams   503
Charles Young   536
Clara Bow   565
Frances Perkins   597
Minoru Kiyota   632
Jackie Robinson   664
Alan Freed   690
Eunice Kennedy Shriver   716
Dolores Huerta   741
Phyllis Schlafly   766
Evan Williams   793

INDIVIDUAL VOICES

Congressman Joseph Rainey, from a Speech
    Supporting the Ku Klux Klan Act   394
John D. Rockefeller Explains the Inevitability of Big
    Business   430
Mary Tape Challenges the San Francisco Board of
    Education   463
Carl Schurz Comments on America's Changing Role in
    World Affairs, 1896–1899   500
Jane Addams Explains Her Participation in the 1912
    Presidential Campaign   532
Woodrow Wilson Proposes His Fourteen Points   562
Sexuality and Innuendo in Movie Advertising   594
Frances Perkins Explains the Social Security
    Act   628
Justice Hugo Black Explains the Majority View in
    Korematsu v. United States   661
The Sporting News Editorializes on African Americans in
    Baseball   687
Pageant Magazine Examines "Rock 'n' Roll Alan Freed"
    (July 1957)   713
Eunice Kennedy Shriver Champions New
    Perspectives   738
Dolores Huerta on Winning Rights for Farm
    Workers   763
Phyllis Schlafly Opposes the Equal Rights
    Amendment   790
Nicholas Carr Asks, "Is Google Making Us
    Stupid?"   821

IT MATTERS TODAY

The Fourteenth Amendment   382
Vertical Integration   407
Urban Building Codes   443
The Defeat of the Lodge Bill   475
The Federal Reserve Act   527
Redrawing the Map of the Middle East   556
Teaching Evolution in Public Schools   579
Preventing Another Great Depression   600
Internment   644
The G.I. Bill   683
The *Brown* Decision   709
Food Stamps   720
Banning DDT   758
Illegal Immigrants   780
Islamic Fundamentalism   806

A DEEPER UNDERSTANDING OF HISTORY

When Historians Disagree   392
Memoirs and Autobiographies   408
Reconstructing Past Social Patterns   451
The Decision to Annex the Philippine Islands   498
The Reductive Fallacy   517
A History Detective at Work   545
Using Statistics in Historical Analysis   584
Finding New Archival Sources   604
Choosing Targets for the Atomic Bomb   659
Deciding on War in Korea   674
Television Pictures the American Family   704
Using Political Cartoons: The 1960s Urban
    Riots   734
Opposing the War in Vietnam: Public Opinion—Who
    and When   746
Immigration Since 1965: Unintended
    Consequences   779
Evaluating *The National Federation of Independent
    Business v. Sebelius Case*   816

TOWARD A MORE PERFECT UNION

Constitutional Revolution   384
Corporate Personhood   413
Defining the Meaning of the Fourteenth
    Amendment   452
The Meaning of the Commerce Clause   476

The Sixteenth and Seventeenth Amendments   **520**

Civil Liberties in Wartime   **549**

The Eighteenth and Nineteenth Amendments   **577**

The "Judicial Revolution" of 1937   **613**

War and Governmental Power   **645**

The Cold War and Freedom of Speech   **679**

Desegregation and the Supreme Court   **712**

The Twenty-Fourth Amendment to the
Constitution   **730**

The Twenty-Sixth Amendment to the
Constitution   **759**

The Twenty-Seventh Amendment to the
Constitution   **772**

Federalism and the Supreme Court   **803**

IN THE WIDER WORLD

Abolition of Slavery Around the World   **374**

Cartels   **411**

South Africa Establishes Racial Separation   **446**

Woman Suffrage   **480**

The Scramble for the Last Colonies   **524**

Civil War in Russia, 1918–1920   **554**

Hyperinflation in the Weimar Republic   **592**

The Spanish Civil War   **610**

Aliens in Their Own Land   **636**

The Condition of Women   **684**

The Great Leap Forward   **700**

Prague Spring, 1968   **736**

The Sino–Soviet Split   **757**

The European Union and the Euro   **778**

The Arab Spring   **814**

The authors of this book were once students themselves. We remember groaning when we opened a textbook, our heads filled with images of underlining, highlighting, memorizing facts and dates—at least until the exam was over. Because these memories are still vivid for us, we have worked hard to produce a history book that is different. We wanted it to convey the excitement, the drama, the surprising twists and turns, the individual and collective tales of success and failure that are the real story of our American past. It is a complex story, of course, and it introduces us to women and men we have never met, to a world very different from the one we live in today, and to ideas and behaviors that may strike us as odd or foolish or simply wrong. We have found this story endlessly interesting and we hope to stimulate that interest in others.

Many of the textbooks we read only allowed us to be passive recipients of history. We were told what happened but never how the authors knew what happened. We decided therefore to invite students to "do history," as well as simply read it, by including special features that ask our readers to consider where evidence can be found, why some stories are easier to tell than others, and what questions we might never be able to answer fully. Providing a textbook that both challenges students to try new ways of thinking and sparks curiosity about the past has been, and remains, the guiding principle behind *Making America*.

Our own teaching experience has played a role in shaping this book. Three of us teach in large public universities located on our nation's borders—the Pacific Ocean, the Atlantic, and the Rio Grande—while one teaches in a small college in Pennsylvania. We know that every student body today is culturally diverse, with a mix of recent immigrants and U.S.-born students. For some, English is a first language but for others it is a second or even a third tongue. Many of our serious-minded students do not have the formal skills to match their enthusiasm for learning. Thus, from its first edition to this, its seventh, we have made certain that our textbook meets the needs of the modern student.

For example, *Making America* offers a chronological narrative that does not assume or demand a lot of prior knowledge about the American past. It does not rely solely on words to tell this story, for we know that people, places, and events can be brought to life through maps, paintings, photos, and cartoons as well as the written word. Above all, our book speaks in a voice intended to communicate with rather than impress. We want to encourage our readers to draw their own conclusions about the causes and consequences of individual choices, public policies, political decisions, protest, and reform, and we provide them with primary source materials on which to build their own interpretations. Finally, our book offers a full array of integrated and supportive learning aids to help students at every level of preparedness comprehend what they read.

Over the years we have remained learners as well as teachers. In each edition of *Making America* we have listened to readers, both professors and students, and made changes to improve the book. Thus, this seventh edition has eliminated elements that did not prove effective and added features that we believe will help us convey the pleasure and value of understanding the people of the past and their role in making America.

The Approach

Professors and students who have used the previous editions of *Making America* will recognize immediately that we have preserved many of its central features. We have again set the nation's complex story within an explicitly political chronology, relying on a basic and familiar structure that is nevertheless broad enough to accommodate generous attention to social, economic, and diplomatic aspects of our national history. Because our own scholarly research often focuses on the experiences of women, working people, immigrants, African Americans, and Native Americans, we would not have been content with a framework that marginalized their history. *Making America* continues to be built on the premise that *all* Americans have been historically active figures, playing significant roles in creating the history of our nation's development. We have also continued the tradition in *Making America* of providing pedagogical tools for students that allow them to master complex material and enable them to develop analytical skills.

Themes

The seventh edition continues to weave five central themes through the narrative. The first of these themes, the political development of the nation, is evident in the text's coverage of the creation and revision of the federal and local governments, the contests waged over domestic and diplomatic policies, the internal and external crises faced by the United States and its political institutions, and the history of political parties and elections.

The second theme is the diversity of a national citizenry created by both Native Americans and immigrants. To do justice to this theme, *Making America* explores the full array of groups that have immigrated to the North American continent. The text attends to the tensions and conflicts that arise in a diverse population, but it also examines the shared values and aspirations that define middle-class and working-class American lives.

Making America's third theme is the significance of regional subcultures and economies. This regional theme is developed for societies in North America before European colonization and for the colonial settlements of the seventeenth and eighteenth centuries. It can be seen in our attention to the striking social and cultural divergences that existed between the American Southwest and the Atlantic coastal regions and between the antebellum South and North, as well as significant differences in social and economic patterns in the West.

A fourth theme is the rise and impact of large social movements, from the Great Awakening in the 1740s to the rise of youth cultures in the post–World War II generations, movements prompted by changing material conditions or by new ideas challenging the status quo.

The fifth theme is the relationship of the United States to other nations. In *Making America* we explore in depth the causes and consequences of this nation's role in world conflict and diplomacy, whether in the era of colonization of the Americas, the eighteenth-century independence movement, the removal of Indian nations from their traditional lands, the rhetoric of manifest destiny, American policies of isolationism and interventionism, or the modern role of the United States as a dominant player in world affairs. Viewing American history in a global context, we point out the parallels and the contrasts between our society and those of other nations.

Learning Features

Making America provides students with several ways to engage with the content. Each chapter begins with an absorbing story, **Individual Choices,** which spotlights a woman or man whose experiences provide a window on the major events and themes of the chapter and whose own words or deeds, whether public or private, are part of the record of the era relied on by historians. Whether historical figures or lesser-known individuals, these people demonstrate the importance of individual agency, or the ability to make choices and act on them. At the end of the chapter, **Individual Voices** offers a primary source related to that person with thought-provoking questions and comments about that source. The primary sources allow the individuals profiled to speak for themselves and encourage students to engage directly in historical analysis. An introduction to each source explains how the source can aid historians in understanding the era and its events.

Each chapter concludes with a **Study Tools** section, which includes a summary that reinforces the most important themes and information covered in the chapter; a chronology that lists key events discussed in the chapter; a restatement of the focus questions; a list of the glossary terms that are highlighted as key study terms in the on-page glossary, with page numbers provided for review; and a group of annotated suggested resources. These tools can help students gain a firmer understanding of the material they have just read.

Within each chapter students will encounter several distinctive features that will help them get the most out of their reading. To help students focus on the broad questions and themes throughout the text, we provide **focus questions** at the beginning of each major chapter section. Students can use these critical thinking questions as guideposts to prepare for reading and also as review prompts to help remember the important points to take from a section. *Making America* provides a unique on-page glossary that defines two types of words for students. The first type is basic vocabulary—words that might trip up some students. The glossary defines words such as "allegory," "impeach," and "dividend" and each provides the word's historical context to ensure that students understand the full meaning of a discussion. The second type of term highlighted and defined includes major historical events, people, phrases, and documents. These historical key terms appear with a color bullet to emphasize their importance to the historical narrative. We believe that this approach will help students simultaneously build their vocabularies and review for tests; it reflects our concern about communicating fully with student readers without sacrificing the complexity of the history we are relating.

The seventh edition also retains the popular feature **It Matters Today,** which points out critical connections between current events and past ones. This feature includes discussion and reflection questions that challenge students to examine and evaluate these connections. We hope that these brief essays will also stimulate faculty and students to generate their own additional "It Matters Today" discussions on other key issues within the chapter. We have also retained the **In the Wider World** feature, which introduces a global perspective on the era covered in each chapter. It reminds students that, no matter how significant or how unique to American society an event or development may be, it always exists within the context of a world in motion around it.

Finally, the illustrations in each chapter were chosen carefully to provide a visual connection to the past that is useful rather than simply decorative. The captions that accompany these illustrations analyze the subject of the painting, photograph, or artifact—and relate it to the narrative. For this edition we have selected many new illustrations to reinforce or illustrate the themes of the narrative.

New to This Edition

In this new edition we have preserved what our colleagues and their students considered the best and most useful aspects of *Making America*, including the strong narrative voice, the respect for chronology, and features such as Individual Choices, Individual Voices, and focus questions. We have replaced what was less successful, revised what could be improved, and added new elements to strengthen the book.

The seventh edition includes two new features. The first, **A Deeper Understanding of History**, introduces students to the processes historians use as they work, actively engaging students in methods of historical investigation and critical thinking. Each of these features includes a visual component, and many of them make use of graphs and maps to help students learn how to read and interpret visual data as well as primary sources. Following are selected examples of the content in this new feature:

Chapter 2
- "Cowboy and Indian Movies Got It All Wrong": Explains the importance of cross-disciplinary study in understanding the true complexity and sophistication of Native American societies.

Chapter 3
- "Who's Telling the Story? And Whose Voice Is Silent?": Guides students in interpreting a primary source, in this case, an artifact from Jamestown.

Chapter 7
- "The Maze of History": Walks students through analysis of how historical actors arrived at a particular choice (the Electoral College).

Chapter 9
- "Charting the Growth of Cotton and Slavery": Explains that there are various ways to visualize historical information and shows how different methods (a graph and a county map) can answer different questions.

Chapter 11
- "Immigration: Visualizing the Numbers": Shows how use of a graph-enhanced map can make historical information manageable.

Chapter 15
- "When Historians Disagree": Explains the process of historical interpretation, using the contrasting assumptions and conclusions of W. E. B. Du Bois and William A. Dunning to illustrate.

Chapter 17
- "Reconstructing Past Social Patterns": Walks students through analysis of an excerpt from the 1880 manuscript census and one from the Sanborn insurance maps of the late 1890s to make conclusions about the life of individuals featured in the chapter's Individual Choices/Voices features.

Chapter 20
- "A History Detective at Work": As an example of the need to approach sources critically, we give a step-by-step account of how historian Jerald Auerbach arrived at his persuasive argument that a widely cited conversation between Woodrow Wilson and *New York World* editor Frank Cobb never took place.

Chapter 25
- "Television Pictures the American Family": Guides students in analyzing a primary source, in this case a Motorola television ad picturing the "typical" American family.

Chapter 28
- "Immigration Since 1965: Unintended Consequences": Leads students into an analysis of immigration since the Immigration Act of 1965, illustrated by a graph showing country of origin, as an example of an unintended consequence.

The second new feature, **Toward a More Perfect Union,** appears in most chapters of Volume 1 and all chapters of Volume 2. Each instance of this feature briefly explains how a constitutional issue was addressed by an amendment or a Supreme Court decision. In pre-Constitution chapters where the feature appears, it offers background on matters related to the Constitution, such as the Magna Carta (Chapter 1) and direct versus virtual representation (Chapter 5). Following are some other examples of the content in this new feature:

Chapter 3
- "The Case of the Vanishing Women," on coverture

Chapter 10
- "Establishing Federal Supremacy over Commerce" (*Gibbons v. Ogden*, etc.)

Chapter 13
- "*Dred Scott v. Sandford*"

Chapter 16
- "Corporate Personhood," on the Supreme Court's endorsement of this concept

Chapter 22
- "The 'Judicial Revolution' of 1937," on Harlan Fiske Stone's footnote in the *U.S. v. Carolene Products* opinion

Chapter 25
- "Desegregation and the Supreme Court" (*Brown, Cooper,* and circuit court *Gayle v. Browder* decisions).

We have also introduced several new Individual Choices and Individual Voices profiles and primary sources. Selected examples are Charles Cotesworth Pinckney and the XYZ affair, in Chapter 8; Jarena Lee, an African American woman who became a licensed preacher, in Chapter 11; Mary Ashton Rice Livermore, a reformer who became a Sanitary Commission leader and feminist activist, in Chapter 14; the middle-class Chinese American family of Mary Tape, who challenged the San Francisco School Board on segregated schools for Chinese American children, in Chapter 17; reformer and settlement house leader Jane Addams in Chapter 19; Alan Freed, rock 'n' roll's "Moondog," in Chapter 25; and STOP-ERA leader Phyllis Schlafly in Chapter 28.

In addition, a new element, **Suggested Resources**, has been added to the Study Tools section at the end of each chapter and directs students to Internet, print, and film sources where they can gain further insight into topics in each chapter and conduct research on their own.

We have also made important changes in the text itself. Many are based on feedback from instructors, and all reflect our commitment to incorporating the newest scholarship and producing a coherent narrative, rather than an oversimplified one. Selected examples follow:

Chapter 1
- Expanded discussion of slavery in West Africa and how slavery worked there among Africans. Reorganized treatment of the Columbian Exchange.

Chapters 3 and 4
- An explanation and discussion of mercantilism has been added. An addition has been made on the Carolina-Barbados connection. The section on colonial politics has been revised, with examples added, to liven up the discussion.

Chapter 7
- The Articles of Confederation section has been reworked and expanded, with more analysis of why the Articles were framed as they were.

Chapter 10
- Coverage of the Peggy Easton affair has been added. Coverage of Denmark Vesey has been moved into this chapter from Chapter 9 for better chronology.

Chapter 12
- Two new subsections have been created, one on labor and one on slavery, and all information on each topic has been consolidated in its new section.

Chapter 13
- For better chronology, the subsection "Politicizing Slavery in the 1840s" has been moved to precede the section on the Mexican war, and the discussion of the Gold Rush has been moved from Chapter 11 to the wrap-up discussion of the Mexican war.

Chapter 18
- Coverage of the political landscape after the 1896 election has been reorganized to improve flow.

Chapter 21
- Coverage of Frederick W. Taylor has been added in the discussion of manufacturing efficiency.

Chapter 22
- Significantly reorganized to bring more attention to some topics and to consolidate coverage of closely related topics.

Chapter 23
- Added details on the coverage of Latin America and the Good Neighbor Policy. Additions on the patriotism of Japanese American internees and on Higgins Industries (Louisiana) and Higgins Boats.

Chapter 26
- Coverage of Young Americans for Freedom and of *Baker v. Carr* has been added.

Chapter 28
- Expanded discussion of Reagan's first budget to add emphasis on the deficit. Coverage of immigration has been expanded.

Chapter 29
- Fully updated with new material on the Obama administration, Afghanistan, the Affordable Care Act and Court decision, the 2012 election, and the fiscal crises.

We, the authors of *Making America,* believe that this new edition will be effective in the history classroom. Please let us know what you think.

Making America Versions and Platforms

Making America is available in a number of different versions and formats, so you can choose the version and format that makes the most sense for you and your students. The options include eBooks, Aplia™ online homework, and MindTap™, a personalized, fully online digital learning platform that contains the eBook and homework all in one product. In addition, a number of useful teaching and learning aids are available to help you with course management/presentation and to help students get the most from their course studies.

eBook for *Making America* An eBook version of *Making America* in pdf format and individual eChapters are availablurchase at www.cengagebrain.com. Students can also purchase the eBook from our partner, CourseSmart, at www.CourseSmart.com.

MindTap Reader for *Making America* This eBook is specifically designed to e for paddress the ways students assimilate content and media assets. The MindTap Reader for *Making America* combines thoughtful navigation, advanced student annotation, note-taking, search tools, embedded media assets such as video and MP3 chapter summaries, primary source documents with critical thinking questions, and interactive (zoomable) maps. Students can use the eBook as their primary text or as a multimedia companion to their printed book. The MindTap Reader eBook is available within the MindTap and Aplia online offerings found at www.cengagebrain.com.

MindTap™: The Personal Learning Experience MindTap for Berkin's *Making America* is a personalized, online digital learning platform providing students with the *Making America* content and related interactive assignments and app services—while giving you a choice in the configuration of coursework and curriculum enhancement. Through a carefully designed chapter-based learning path, students can access the *Making America* eBook (**MindTap Reader**, see description below); Aplia™ assignments developed for the most important concepts in each chapter (see **Aplia** description below); brief quizzes written by Trent Booker of Northwest Mississippi Community College; and a set of Web applications known as MindApps to help you create the most engaging course for your students. The MindApps range from ReadSpeaker (which reads the text out loud to students) to Kaltura (allowing you to insert inline video and audio into your curriculum) to ConnectYard (allowing you to create digital "yards" through social media—all without "friending" your students). To learn more, ask your Cengage Learning sales representative to demo it for you—or go to www.Cengage.com/MindTap.

Aplia™ This online homework product improves comprehension and outcomes by increasing student effort and engagement. Founded by a professor to enhance his own courses, Aplia provides automatically graded assignments with detailed, immediate explanations on every question. The assignments developed for *Making America* address the major concepts in each chapter and are designed to promote critical thinking and engage students more fully in their learning. Question types include questions built around animated maps, primary sources such as newspaper extracts and cartoons, or imagined scenarios, like engaging in a conversation with Benjamin Franklin; images, video clips, and audio clips are incorporated into many of the questions. More in-depth primary source question sets built around larger topics, such as "Native American and European Encounters" or "The Cultural Cold War," promote deeper analysis of historical evidence. Students get immediate feedback on their work (not only what they got right or wrong, but *why*), and they can choose to see another set of related questions if they want to practice further. A searchable **MindTap Reader eBook** (see description below) is available inside the course as well, so that students can easily reference it as they are working. Aplia's simple-to-use course management interface allows you to post announcements, upload course materials, and manage the gradebook. Personalized support from a knowledgeable and friendly support team also offers assistance in customizing assignments to the instructor's course schedule. For a more comprehensive, all-in-one course solution, Aplia assignments may be found within the **MindTap Personal Learning platform** (see above). To learn more, ask your Cengage Learning sales representative to provide a demo—or view a specific demo for this book, at www.aplia.com.

Instructor Resources

Instructor Companion Site Instructors will find here all the tools they need to teach a rich and successful U.S. history survey course. The protected teaching materials include the Test Bank and Cognero® online testing program, Instructor's Resource Manual, and customizable Microsoft® PowerPoint® slides of both lecture outlines and images from the text. Go to login.cengage.com to access this site.

Instructor's Resource Manual Prepared by Kelly Woestman of Pittsburg State University, this manual includes instructional objectives, chapter outlines and summaries, lecture suggestions, suggested debate and research topics, cooperative learning activities, and suggested readings and resources. Available on the instructor's companion website.

CourseReader CourseReader lets you create a customized electronic reader in minutes. With our easy-to-use interface and assessment tool, you can choose exactly what your students will be assigned—simply search or browse Cengage Learning's extensive document database to preview and select your customized collection of readings.

Once you've made your choices, students will always receive the pedagogical support they need to succeed with the materials you've chosen: each source document includes a descriptive head note that puts the reading into context, and every selection is further supported by both critical thinking and multiple-choice questions designed to reinforce key points. Contact your local Cengage Learning sales representative for more information and packaging options.

Test Bank and Cognero Online Testing. The Test Bank for *Making America*, authored by Steven J. Rauch of Georgia Regents University and Trent Booker of Northwest Mississippi Community College, includes between 65 and 75 multiple-choice questions plus five essay questions with model responses for each chapter. It is available in Word format on the instructor's companion site and through Cognero®, a flexible online system that allows you to author, edit, and manage the content. You can create multiple test versions instantly and deliver them through your learning management system from your classroom, or wherever you may be, with no special installations or downloads required.

Student Resources

cengagebrain.com Save your students time and money. Direct them to www.cengagebrain. com for choices of formats and savings and a better chance to succeed in class. Students have the freedom to purchase or rent à la carte exactly what they need when they need it, including a downloadable eBook or access to MindTap and Aplia course products. Here students will also be able to access study and review tools developed specifically for *Making America* and additional U.S. history study materials such as eAudio modules from *The History Handbook* (see below). Students can save 50 percent on the electronic textbook and can pay as little as $1.99 for an individual eChapter.

The History Handbook, **2e** [ISBN: 9780495906766] Written by Carol Berkin of Baruch College, City University of New York, and Betty Anderson of Boston University, this book teaches students both basic and history-specific study skills such as how to take notes, get the most out of lectures and readings, read primary sources, research historical topics, and correctly cite sources. Substantially less expensive than comparable skill-building texts, *The History Handbook* also offers tips for Internet research and evaluating online sources. Additionally, students can purchase and download the **eAudio** version of *The History Handbook* or any of its eighteen individual units at www.cengagebrain.com to listen to on the go.

Doing History: Research and Writing in the Digital Age, **2e** [ISBN: 9781133587880] Prepared by Michael J. Galgano, J. Chris Arndt, and Raymond M. Hyser of James Madison University. This text's "soup to nuts" approach to researching and writing about history addresses every step of the process, from locating sources and gathering information, to writing clearly and making proper use of various citation styles to avoid plagiarism.

Rand McNally Atlas of American History, **2e** [ISBN: 9780618842018] This comprehensive atlas features more than eighty maps, with new content covering global perspectives, including events in the Middle East from 1945 to 2005, as well as population trends in the United States and around the world. Additional maps document voyages of discovery; the settling of the colonies; major U.S. military engagements, including the American Revolution and World Wars I and II; and sources of immigrations, ethnic populations, and patterns of economic change.

Reader Program Cengage Learning publishes a number of readers, some containing only primary sources, some with essays only, and others with a combination of primary and secondary sources; all are designed to guide students through the process of historical inquiry. Visit www.Cengage.com/history for a complete list of readers or ask your sales representative to recommend a reader that would work well for your specific needs.

Custom Options

Nobody knows your students like you, so why not give them a text that is tailor-fit to their needs? Cengage Learning offers custom solutions for your course—whether it's making a small modification to *Making America* to match your syllabus or combining multiple sources to create something truly unique. You can pick and choose chapters, include your own material, and add additional map exercises along with the Rand McNally Atlas (including questions developed around the maps in the atlas) to create a text that fits the way you teach. Ensure that your students get the most out of their textbook dollar by giving them exactly what they need. Contact your Cengage Learning representative to explore custom solutions for your course.

Acknowledgments

The authors of *Making America* have benefited greatly from the critical reading of this edition of the book by instructors from across the country. We would like to thank these scholars and teachers who provided feedback for this current revision:

Tom Angle, Metropolitan Community College

Anthony Beninati, Valencia Community College

Martha Bonte, Clinton Community College, Eastern Iowa
    Community College District

Trent Booker, Northwest Mississippi Community College

Scott Buchanan, South Plains College

Thomas Clarkin, San Antonio College

Robert Cray, Montclair State University

Latangela Crossfield, Paine College

Mary Ellen Curtin, American University

Jeffrey Davis, Bloomsburg University of Pennsylvania

Julian DelGaudio, Long Beach City College

Gretchen Eick, Friends University

Ronald Feinman, Florida Atlantic University

George Frode, Mass. Bay Community College

Jennifer Fry, King's College

Michael Gabriel, Kutztown University

John Glen, St. Louis Community College

Leah Hagedorn, Tidewater Community College

Jillian Hartley, Arkansas Northeastern College

Stephen Katz, Community College of Philadelphia

Eileen Kerr, Modesto Junior College

Kurt Kortenhof, Saint Paul College

Mark Kuss, Our Lady of Holy Cross College

Margaret Lowe, Bridgewater State College

Mark McCarthy, Southern New Hampshire
    University Online

Richard McCaslin, University of North Texas

Suzanne McCormack, Community College of Rhode Island

Todd Menzing, Saddleback College

Rebecca Montgomery, Texas State University

Bryant Morrison, South Texas College

David Parker, California State University–Northridge

Laura Perry, The University of Memphis

Mark Quintanilla, Hannibal-LaGrange University

Steven Rauch, Augusta State University

Kathryn Rokitski, Old Dominion University

James Seaman, Saddleback College

Carey Shellman, Armstrong Atlantic State University

Bruce Way, University of Toledo

Carol Berkin, who is responsible for Chapters 3 through 7, wants to acknowledge the colleagues and students who suggested interesting new Individual Choices subjects and primary sources for her chapters. She thanks the many teachers she met through Teaching American History grant programs for their excellent ideas about what makes a textbook useful in the classroom. She has gained valuable insights from her work as editor of the online journal for teachers, *History Now,* and through her Gilder Lehrman Summer Institutes with teachers from across the country. Finally she thanks the wonderful team of historians, editors, and Cengage staff who make working on this book such a pleasure.

Christopher L. Miller, who is responsible for Chapters 1 and 2 and 8 through 14, is indebted to the community at the University of Texas–Pan American for providing the constant inspiration to innovate. Colleagues, including Tamer Balci, Robert Hoppins, and Kristine Wirts, were particularly helpful in identifying events to include in the In the Wider World features. Colleagues on various H-Net discussion lists as always were generous with advice, guidance, and often abstruse points of information. As in each of our collaborative projects, thanks are owed to Carol Berkin, Bob Cherny, and Jim Gormly, and to Kelly Woestman and Doug Egerton.

Robert W. Cherny, who is responsible for Chapters 15 through 22, wishes to thank his students who, over the years, have provided the testing ground for much that is included in these chapters, and especially to thank his colleagues and research assistants who have helped with the previous editions. The staff of the Leonard Library at San Francisco State has always been most helpful. Rebecca Marshall Cherny, Sarah Cherny, and Lena Hobbs Kracht Cherny have been unfailing in their encouragement, inspiration, and support.

James L. Gormly, who is responsible for Chapters 23 through 30, would like to acknowledge the support and encouragement he received from Washington and Jefferson College. He wants to gives a special thanks to Sharon Gormly, whose support, ideas, advice, and critical eye have helped to shape and refine his chapters.

Kelly Woestman has been involved with *Making America* from the First Edition and has continued her substantive role in the seventh edition. We suspect that no other supplements author has been so well integrated into the author team as Kelly has been with our team, and we know that this adds significantly to the value of these resources.

As always, this book is a collaborative effort between authors and the editorial staff of Wadsworth, Cengage Learning. We would like to thank Ann West, senior product manager; Megan Chrisman, associate content developer: Carol Newman, senior content project manager; Pembroke Herbert and Reba Fredericks, who helped us fill this edition with remarkable illustrations, portraits, and photographs; and Charlotte Miller, who helped us improve the maps in the book. Finally, but far from least, we thank Jan Fitter, our always patient and tactful text editor, who made our prose clearer and more concise in every chapter. These talented, committed members of the publishing world encouraged us and generously assisted us every step of the way.

A Note for the Students

☆ **Your Guide to *Making America*** ☆

Dear Student:

History is about people—brilliant and insane, brave and treacherous, lovable and hateful, murderers and princesses, daredevils and visionaries, rule breakers and rule makers. It has exciting events, major crises, turning points, battles, and scientific breakthroughs. We, the authors of *Making America*, believe that knowing about the past is critical for anyone who hopes to understand the present and chart the future. In this book, we want to tell you the story of America from its earliest settlement to the present and to tell it in a language and format that helps you enjoy learning that history.

This book is organized and designed to help you master your American History course. The narrative is chronological, telling the story as it happened, decade by decade or era by era. We have developed special tools to help you learn. Here, we'll introduce you to the unique features of this book that will not only help you understand the complex and fascinating story of American history but also provide you the tools to "do" history yourself.

At the back of the book, you will find some additional resources. The Appendix provides reprints of three of the most important documents in American history: the Declaration of Independence, the Articles of Confederation, and the Constitution. Here, too, a table gives you quick access to important data on presidential elections. Finally, you will see the index, which will help you locate a subject quickly if you want to read about it. Terms that appear in the on-page glossary are boldfaced in the index.

In addition, you will find a number of useful study tools on the *Making America* companion website. Go to cengagebrain.com to access these tools. If your instructor has adopted one of the digital products available with *Making America* (for instance, Aplia or MindTap) be sure to take advantage of all they have to offer! These products offer numerous avenues for engaging with the content in meaningful ways, and they can provide not just additional opportunity for further study and practice, but multiple opportunities to make your learning deeper and longer lasting. Here, now, is some additional advice on how to approach your learning experience.

How to Succeed in Your History Course

We know that, at first glance, a history textbook can seem overwhelming. There is so much to learn, so much to remember, so much to think about. The features of *Making America* are all designed to help you conquer your anxiety and enjoy your journey through the American past. Here are a few tips to make this a smoother trip:

☆ *Follow all the clues the authors provide.*

What are the important issues raised in the Individual Choices story? How many of the key topics in the chapter outline are familiar to you—and which ones are new? Don't just pay attention to the unfamiliar material; read carefully how the authors describe those events you have encountered before. Surprises may be in store. Use the focus questions as your guide to each major section of the chapter. Don't highlight everything. Read the whole section once; then read it again to find the answers to the focus questions. They are there because they point to the most important issues in the section.

☆ *Don't skip over unfamiliar words in the text.*

Use the glossary to help you understand the reading—and to increase your vocabulary. That vocabulary will come in handy if you are asked to write an exam essay.

⭐ *Use the study tools feature to test your own strengths and weaknesses as you prepare for an exam.*

Would your own summary of the chapter be similar to the summary the authors provide? Can you remember the context for the events that appear in the chapter chronology? Can you answer the focus questions now that you have read and taken notes on the chapter? Would you be able to identify and explain the significance of the key terms if your professor required you to do so? If not, page numbers will help you review and strengthen your command of the material.

Working with Primary Sources

This book gives you multiple opportunities to practice doing what historians do. The Deeper Understanding of History feature inside each chapter, gives you a chance to see historical investigation in action, showing you how to read and interpret primary sources and visual data, including graphs and maps.

The Individual Voices feature at the end of each chapter lets you try your hand at doing the work of a historian. This feature gives you a primary source document that we have annotated to show you what kinds of questions historians hope the source can answer. We call this process "interrogating the source," much as a detective interrogates a witness. Often the questions historians ask cannot be answered by a single source, and so we turn to other sources to help us piece together the puzzle of the past. Any public, official, or private document, any illustration or portrait, even any artifact that was created during the era we are examining is a primary source. You can find them in books, in historical societies, in libraries, and sometimes in your own attic.

In addition to those in the book, *Making America* offers a wealth of primary sources online and inside its digital products. Your professor may distribute some in class or point you to others online. Practice analyzing some primary sources, asking questions such as: Who was the person who created this source? Under what circumstances was it created? What prompted this person to write this document or to paint this portrait or to build this house or make this piece of clothing or this tool or weapon? Was the author a reliable witness or was he or she a participant in the event being described? Does this source agree with or contradict other sources you have found? Does it challenge the interpretations you have read in history books?

This type of analysis is not only useful for success in a history class. It will also benefit you as you read the newspaper, watch today's news on the Web or TV, or listen to the critical arguments of your own day. It will help you form your own independent judgments about the world around you.

We hope that our textbook conveys to you our own fascination with the American past and sparks your curiosity about the nation's history. We invite you to share your feedback with your instructor and with us.

CAROL BERKIN, CHRIS MILLER,
BOB CHERNY, *and* JIM GORMLY

CAROL BERKIN

Born in Mobile, Alabama, Carol Berkin received her undergraduate degree from Barnard College and her Ph.D. from Columbia University. Her dissertation won the Bancroft Award. She is now Presidential Professor of history at Baruch College and the Graduate Center of City University of New York. She has written *First Generations: Women in Colonial America* (1996); *A Brilliant Solution: Inventing the American Constitution* (2002); *Revolutionary Mothers: Women in the Struggle for America's Independence* (2005); *Civil War Wives: The Lives and Times of Angelina Grimke Weld, Varina Howell Davis, and Julia Dent Grant* (2009); and *Wondrous Beauty: The Extraordinary Life of Elizabeth Patterson Bonaparte* (2014). She has edited *Women of America: A History* (with Mary Beth Norton, 1979); *Women, War and Revolution* (with Clara M. Lovett, 1980); *Women's Voices, Women's Lives: Documents in Early American History* (with Leslie Horowitz, 1998); *Looking Forward/Looking Back: A Women's Studies Reader* (with Judith Pinch and Carole Appel, 2005); and *Clio in the Classroom: A Guide to Teaching U.S. Women's History* (with Margaret Crocco and Barbara Winslow, 2009). Professor Berkin edits *History Now*, an online journal for teachers sponsored by the Gilder Lehrman Institute of American History. She has appeared in the PBS series *Liberty! The American Revolution; Ben Franklin;* and *Alexander Hamilton;* and The History Channel's *Founding Fathers*. She has served on the Planning Committee for the U.S. Department of Education's National Assessment of Educational Progress, and chaired the CLEP Committee for Educational Testing Service. She currently serves on the Board of Trustees of the Gilder Lehrman Institute of American History and is an elected member of the American Antiquarian Society and the Society of American Historians.

CHRISTOPHER L. MILLER

Born and raised in Portland, Oregon, Christopher L. Miller received his bachelor of science degree from Lewis and Clark College and his Ph.D. from the University of California, Santa Barbara. He is currently associate professor of history at the University of Texas–Pan American. He is the author of *Prophetic Worlds: Indians and Whites on the Columbia Plateau* (1985), which was republished (2003) as part of the Columbia Northwest Classics Series by the University of Washington Press and co-editor with Tamer Balci of *The Gülen Hizmet Movement: Circumspect Activism in Faith-Based Reform* (2012). His articles and reviews have appeared in numerous scholarly journals and anthologies as well as standard reference works. He has been a research fellow at the Charles Warren Center for Studies in American History at Harvard University and was the Nikolay V. Sivachev Distinguished Chair in American History at Lomonosov Moscow State University (Russia).

ROBERT W. CHERNY

Born in Marysville, Kansas, and raised in Beatrice, Nebraska, Robert W. Cherny received his B.A. from the University of Nebraska and his M.A. and Ph.D. from Columbia University. He is professor of history at San Francisco State University. His books include *Competing Visions: A History of California* (with Richard Griswold del Castillo and Gretchen Lemke Santangelo, 2005, 2014); *American Politics in the Gilded Age, 1868–1900* (1997); *San Francisco, 1865–1932: Politics, Power, and Urban Development* (with William Issel, 1986); *A Righteous Cause: The Life of William Jennings Bryan* (1985, 1994); and *Populism, Progressivism, and the Transformation of Nebraska Politics, 1885–1915* (1981). He is co-editor of *California Women and Politics from the Gold Rush to the Great Depression* (with Mary Ann Irwin and Ann Marie Wilson, 2011) and of *American Labor and the Cold War: Unions, Politics, and Postwar Political Culture* (with William Issel and Keiran Taylor, 2004). In 2000, he and Ellen Du Bois co-edited a special issue of the *Pacific Historical Review* that surveyed woman suffrage movements in nine locations around the Pacific Rim. Most of his thirty-some articles in journals and anthologies have dealt with politics and labor in the late nineteenth and early twentieth centuries and with California and the West. He has been an NEH Fellow, Distinguished Fulbright Lecturer at Lomonosov Moscow State University (Russia), Visiting Research Scholar at the University of Melbourne (Australia), and Senior Fulbright Scholar at the Heidelberg Center for American Studies, University of Heidelberg (Germany). He has served as president of H-Net (an association of more than one hundred electronic networks for scholars in the humanities and social sciences), the Society for Historians of the Gilded Age and Progressive Era, and the Southwest Labor Studies Association; as treasurer of the Organization of American Historians; and as a member of the council of the American Historical Association, Pacific Coast Branch.

JAMES L. GORMLY

Born in Riverside, California, James L. Gormly received a B.A. from the University of Arizona and his M.A. and Ph.D. from the University of Connecticut. He is now professor of history at Washington and Jefferson College. He has written *The Collapse of the Grand Alliance* (1970) and *From Potsdam to the Cold War* (1979). His articles and reviews have appeared in *Diplomatic History, The Journal of American History, The American Historical Review, The Historian, The History Teacher,* and *The Journal of Interdisciplinary History.*

Making America

15

Reconstruction: High Hopes and Shattered Dreams, 1865–1877

CHAPTER OUTLINE

Presidential Reconstruction

Republican War Aims

Lincoln's Approach to Reconstruction: "With Malice Toward None"

Abolishing Slavery Forever: The Thirteenth Amendment

Andrew Johnson and Reconstruction

The Southern Response: Minimal Compliance

Freedom and the Legacy of Slavery

Defining the Meaning of Freedom

Creating Communities

Land and Labor in the Postwar South

The White South: Confronting Change

Congressional Reconstruction

Challenging Presidential Reconstruction: The Civil Rights Act of 1866

Defining Citizenship: The Fourteenth Amendment

Radicals in Control

Political Terrorism and the Election of 1868

Voting Rights and Civil Rights

Black Reconstruction

The Republican Party in the South

Creating Public Education, Fighting Discrimination, and Building Railroads

The End of Reconstruction

The "New Departure" and the 1872 Presidential Election

The Politics of Terror: The "Mississippi Plan"

The Troubled Presidential Election of 1876

After Reconstruction

INDIVIDUAL VOICES: *Congressman Joseph Rainey, from a Speech Supporting the Ku Klux Klan Act*

Study Tools

INDIVIDUAL CHOICES

Joseph Rainey

On December 12, 1870, Joseph Rainey became the first African American to serve in the House of Representatives. Rainey had come a long way since he was born into slavery in 1832 in Georgetown, South Carolina. Growing up, he had a relatively privileged life compared to most slaves. His father, also a slave, was a barber, and as the law required, he kept part of what he earned. Rainey's father eventually saved enough to buy freedom for his family.

Rainey learned the barber's skills from his father, but his trade was interrupted by the Civil War. The Confederate Army put him to work building fortifications, then crewing on a blockade runner (a ship that carried goods through the Union navy's blockade from Bermuda, the closest British port). Rainey and his wife, Susan, managed to escape to Bermuda, where slavery was illegal. There he resumed his trade as a barber, and Susan opened a dress shop. They saved their earnings and returned to South Carolina at the end of the war with considerable savings.

Rainey soon chose to enter Republican politics. He held several party offices and appointed positions before winning elections to the state constitutional convention in 1868, to the state legislature in 1870, and later that same year to the U.S. House of

Library of Congress.

Representatives. He was reelected to Congress in 1872 with no opposition. In 1874 and 1876, however, when he ran for reelection, he faced increasing, and increasingly violent, opposition—even threats to his life—but he won both times. By then, it took courage for a black man to run for office in many parts of the South. In some places, African American candidates were assassinated by those seeking to restore white supremacy. In most places, black candidates and voters faced intimidation or violence. Defeated in 1878 as Reconstruction was collapsing throughout the South, Rainey left office in early 1879.

As a member of the House of Representatives, Rainey spoke forcefully in support of the Ku Klux Klan Act of 1871; an excerpt appears in the Individual Voices feature at the end of this chapter. The act was intended to use federal authority to end the reign of terror against African Americans that was being carried out by the Klan and similar organizations. He also worked tirelessly for the passage of the Civil Rights bill, and was especially committed to desegregating public schools. In his speech to Congress in support of the bill, he vividly described the widespread segregation in many aspects of southern life. The bill passed in early 1875, but without provisions on school segregation or equality for segregated schools. Rainey's efforts were not limited to matters affecting African Americans. He also supported legislation to grant amnesty to many former Confederates, seeing it as a balance to the Civil Rights Act, and he opposed efforts to restrict immigration from China.

Rainey was not the only African American who escaped to freedom while the war was raging. That experience was repeated time and time again, with many variations, all across the South. Those many individual decisions were made legal by the Emancipation Proclamation, enforced by the presence of Union armies, and made permanent by the Thirteenth Amendment to the Constitution. Like Rainey, African Americans often had their own ideas about what they wanted most from freedom.

After four long, bloody years of civil war, Union armies had smashed across the South, leaving wreckage in their wake: shelled buildings, ravaged farms, twisted railroad tracks. Slavery—the dominant economic and social institution in many parts of the South—collapsed. As white southerners grieved for their dead and were dismayed by their ravaged countryside, many were also deeply troubled by the **emancipation** of 4 million slaves. The end of slavery forced southerners of both races to develop new social, economic, and political patterns. The years following the war were a time of physical rebuilding throughout the South, but historians use the term **Reconstruction** to refer primarily to the rebuilding of the federal union and to the political, economic, and social changes that came to the South. Reconstruction involved some of the most momentous questions in American history: How was the defeated South to be treated? What was to be the future of the former slaves? Should key decisions be made by the federal government or in state capitols and county courthouses throughout the South? Which branch of the government was to establish policies? What would happen to those who had supported the Confederacy? Thousands of voices across the nation proposed very different answers.

As the dominant Republicans turned their attention from waging war to reconstructing the Union, they wrote into law and the Constitution new definitions of the Union itself. They also defined the rights of the **freed people** and the terms on which the South might rejoin the Union. And they permanently changed the definition of American citizenship.

emancipation Release from slavery.

■ **Reconstruction** Term applied by historians to the years 1865–1877, when the Union was restored after the Civil War; important changes were made to the federal Constitution, and relations between the races were transformed in the South.

freed people Former slaves; *freed people* is the term used by historians to refer to former slaves, whether male or female.

Most white southerners disliked the new rules emerging from Washington, and some resisted. Disagreement over the future of the South and the status of the former slaves led to conflict between the president and Congress. A temporary result of this conflict was a more powerful Congress and a less powerful executive. A lasting outcome of these events was a significant increase in the authority of the federal government and new limits on local and state governments.

Reconstruction significantly changed many aspects of southern life. In the end, however, Reconstruction failed to fulfill many African Americans' hopes for their lives as free people.

PRESIDENTIAL RECONSTRUCTION

☆ *What did Presidents Lincoln and Johnson seek to accomplish for the South? How did white southerners respond to those efforts?*

On New Year's Day, 1863, the Emancipation Proclamation took effect. At the time, however, the proclamation did not affect any slaves because it abolished slavery only in territory under Confederate control and was, therefore, unenforceable. But every advance of a Union army after January 1, 1863, brought emancipation to the slaves of the Confederacy.

Republican War Aims

For **Abraham Lincoln** and the Republican Party, freedom for the slaves became a central concern partly because **abolitionists** were influential within the party. During its 1860 electoral campaign, the Republican Party had promised only to prohibit slavery in the territories, and Lincoln initially defined the war as one to maintain the Union. Some leading Republicans, however, wanted to abolish slavery everywhere. As Union troops moved into the South, some slaves simply walked away from their owners. Many sought safety with the Union army. Soon former slaves became Union soldiers as well. Abolitionists throughout the North—including **Frederick Douglass**, an escaped slave and an important leader of the abolition movement—now argued that emancipation would be meaningless unless the government guaranteed the civil and political rights of the former slaves. Thus some Republicans expanded their definition of war objectives to include abolishing slavery, extending citizenship for the former slaves, and guaranteeing the equality of all citizens before the law. At the time, these were extreme views on abolition and equal rights, and the people who held them were called **Radical Republicans**, or simply Radicals.

Thaddeus Stevens, 73 years old in 1865, was the leading Radical in the House of Representatives. He

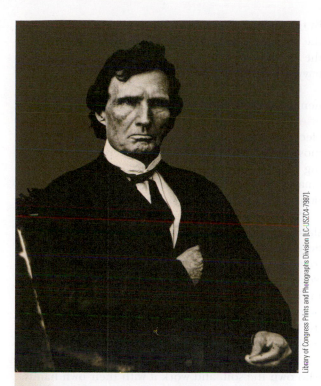

Library of Congress Prints and Photographs Division [LC-USZ04-7987].

Thaddeus Stevens, seen here at the height of his power, was the leader of the Radical Republicans in the House of Representatives. He died in 1868. He requested that he be buried in a cemetery that did not discriminate on the basis of race.

had made a successful career as a Pennsylvania lawyer and iron manufacturer before winning election to Congress in 1858. Born with a clubfoot, he identified with those outside the social mainstream. He became a compelling spokesman for abolition and an uncompromising advocate of equal rights for African Americans. A masterful parliamentarian, he was known for his honesty and sarcastic wit. From the beginning of the war, Stevens urged that the slaves not only be freed but also be armed to fight the Confederacy.

■ **Abraham Lincoln** (1809–1865) Sixteenth president of the United States, who presided over the Union during the Civil War, issued the Emancipation Proclamation, initiated Reconstruction, and was assassinated shortly after beginning his second term as president.

abolitionist Individual who condemns slavery as morally wrong and seeks to abolish (eliminate) slavery.

■ **Frederick Douglass** (c. 1818–1895) Escaped slave who became a leader of the abolition movement and later an important African American leader and Republican politician.

■ **Radical Republicans** Group within the Republican Party during the Civil War and Reconstruction that advocated for abolition of slavery, citizenship for the former slaves, and sweeping alteration of the South.

By the end of the war, some 180,000 African Americans, the great majority of them freedmen, had served in the Union army and a few thousand in the Union navy. Many more worked for the army as laborers.

Charles Sumner of Massachusetts, a prominent Radical in the Senate, had argued for **racial integration** of Massachusetts schools in 1849 and won election to the U.S. Senate in 1851. The Senate's foremost champion of abolition, he suffered a severe beating in 1856 because of an antislavery speech. After emancipation, Sumner, like Stevens, fought for full political and civil rights for the freed people.

Stevens, Sumner, and other Radicals opposed slavery both on moral grounds and because they believed free labor was more productive. Slaves worked to escape punishment, they argued, but free workers worked to benefit themselves. Eliminating slavery and instituting a free-labor system, they claimed, would benefit everyone by increasing the nation's productivity. In this view, free labor not only contributed centrally to the dynamism of the North's economy, but was crucial to democracy itself. "The middling classes who own the soil, and work it with their own hands," Stevens once proclaimed, "are the main support of every free government."

Not all Republicans agreed with the Radicals. All Republicans objected to slavery, but not all Republicans were abolitionists. Similarly, not all Republicans wanted to extend full citizenship rights to the former slaves. Some favored rapid restoration of the South to the Union so that the federal government could concentrate on stimulating the nation's economy and developing the West. Such Republicans are usually referred to as **moderates**.

Lincoln's Approach to Reconstruction: "With Malice Toward None"

After the Emancipation Proclamation, President Lincoln and the congressional Radicals agreed that abolition of slavery had to be a condition for the return of the South to the Union. Major differences soon appeared, however, over other terms for reunion and the roles of the president and Congress in establishing those

terms. In his second inaugural address, a month before his death, Lincoln defined the task facing the nation:

> With malice toward none; with charity for all; with firmness in the right, as God gives us to see the right, let us strive on to finish the work we are in: to bind up the nation's wounds; to care for him who shall have borne the battle, and for his widow and orphan, to do all which may achieve and cherish a just and lasting peace among ourselves, and with all nations.

Lincoln began to rebuild the Union on the basis of these principles. As soon as Union armies occupied portions of southern states, he appointed temporary military governors for those regions and tried to restore civil government as quickly as possible.

Drawing on the president's constitutional power to issue **pardons** (Article II, Section 2), Lincoln issued a Proclamation of **Amnesty** and Reconstruction in December 1863. Called the "Ten Percent Plan," it promised a full pardon and restoration of rights to those who swore their loyalty to the Union and accepted the abolition of slavery. Only high-ranking Confederate leaders were not eligible. Once those who had taken the oath in a state amounted to 10 percent of the votes cast by that state in the 1860 election, the pardoned voters were to write a new state constitution that abolished slavery, elect state officials, and resume self-government.

Some Radicals considered Lincoln's approach too lenient. When they tried to set more stringent standards, Lincoln blocked them, fearing their plan would slow restoration of civil government and perhaps lengthen the war.

Under Lincoln's Ten Percent Plan, new state governments were established in Arkansas, Louisiana, and Tennessee during 1864 and early 1865. In Louisiana, the new government denied voting rights to men who were one-quarter or more black. Radicals complained, but Lincoln urged patience, suggesting the reconstructed government in Louisiana was "as the egg to the fowl, and we shall sooner have the fowl by hatching the egg than by smashing it." Radicals, however, concluded that freed people were unlikely to receive equitable treatment from state governments formed under the Ten Percent Plan. Some moderates agreed and moved toward the Radicals' position that only **suffrage** could protect the freedmen's rights and that only federal action could guarantee black suffrage.

Abolishing Slavery Forever: The Thirteenth Amendment

Amid questions about the rights of freed people, congressional Republicans prepared for the final destruction of slavery. The Emancipation Proclamation had been a wartime measure, justified partly by military necessity. It never applied in Union states. State legislatures or conventions abolished slavery in West

---

racial integration Equal opportunities to participate in a society or organization by people of different racial groups; the absence of race-based barriers to full and equal participation.

moderates People whose views are midway between two extreme positions; in this case, Republicans who favored some reforms but not all the Radicals' proposals.

pardon Governmental directive canceling punishment for a person or people who have committed a crime.

amnesty General pardon granted by a government, especially for political offenses.

suffrage The right to vote.

These Union soldiers and officers in 1865 are administering the oath of allegiance to the United States to white southerners as part of the process of restoring civil government in the South.

Virginia, Maryland, Missouri, and the reconstructed state of Tennessee. In early 1865, slavery remained legal in Delaware and Kentucky, and prewar state laws—which might or might not be valid—permitted slavery in the states that had seceded. To destroy slavery forever, Congress in January 1865 approved the **Thirteenth Amendment**, which read simply, "Neither slavery nor involuntary servitude, except as a punishment for crime whereof the party shall have been duly convicted, shall exist within the United States, or any place subject to their jurisdiction."

The Constitution requires any amendment to be ratified by three-fourths of the states—then twenty-seven of thirty-six states. By December 1865, only nineteen of the twenty-five Union states had ratified the amendment. The measure passed, however, when eight of the reconstructed southern states approved it. In the end, therefore, the abolition of slavery hinged on action by reconstructed state governments in the South.

Andrew Johnson and Reconstruction

In April 1865, shortly after the surrender of the main Confederate army, Lincoln was assassinated by a supporter of the Confederacy. Vice President **Andrew Johnson** became president. Johnson had never had an opportunity to attend school and spent his early life struggling against poverty. As a young man in Tennessee, he worked as a tailor, then turned to politics. His wife, Eliza McCardle Johnson, tutored him in reading, writing, and arithmetic. A Democrat, Johnson was elected to Congress and later as governor before winning election to the U.S. Senate in 1857. His political support came primarily from small-scale farmers and working people. The state's elite of plantation owners usually opposed him. Johnson, in turn, resented their wealth and power, and blamed them for secession and the Civil War.

■ **Thirteenth Amendment** Constitutional amendment, ratified in 1865, that abolished slavery in the United States and its territories.

■ **Andrew Johnson** (1808–1875) Seventeenth president of the United States; elected vice president in 1864, became president after Lincoln's assassination, and was impeached, but not removed from the presidency.

In the Wider World

Abolition of Slavery Around the World

By abolishing slavery, the United States followed the lead of most of the nations of Europe and Latin America. Slavery had existed throughout human history, but in the eighteenth century, Enlightenment thinkers began to criticize slavery as violating human rights. At the same time, some religious groups, notably the Quakers, began to work for abolition. The following list summarizes general patterns in the abolition of slavery around the world; space does not permit listing all nations.

Though illegal, chattel slavery still exists in parts of Africa and the Middle East, notably Mauritania and Sudan. In other places, people work in conditions approaching slavery, through forced prostitution, debt bondage, and forced-labor camps.

1587	Slave trade abolished in Japan
1772	Slavery abolished in England and Wales
1794	Slavery abolished in France
1807	British navy begins operations to end the international slave trade
1808	United States prohibits importation of slaves
1820s	Slavery abolished in most Spanish-speaking Latin American nations
1833	Slavery abolished within the British Empire
1848	Slavery abolished within the French Empire
1861	Abolition of serfdom in Russia
1863	Emancipation Proclamation (United States); slavery abolished within the Dutch Empire
1865	Thirteenth Amendment (United States)
1876	Slavery abolished within the Ottoman Empire
1888	Slavery abolished in Brazil
1910	Slavery abolished in China
1926	Thirty-five nations sign a Convention to Suppress the Slave Trade and Slavery
1948	United Nations adopts the Universal Declaration of Human Rights, including calls to abolish slavery and the slave trade
1962	Slavery abolished in Saudi Arabia

Johnson was the only southern senator who rejected the Confederacy. Early in the war, Union forces captured Nashville, the capital of Tennessee, and Lincoln appointed Johnson as military governor. Johnson dealt harshly with Tennessee secessionists, especially wealthy planters. Radical Republicans approved. Johnson was elected vice president in 1864, receiving the nomination in part because Lincoln wanted to appeal to Democrats and Unionists in border states.

chattel slavery Condition in which one person is legally defined as the personal property of another person.

states' rights Political position favoring limitation of the federal government's power and maximum self-government by individual states.

empower To increase the power or authority of some person or group.

When Johnson became president, Radicals hoped he would join their efforts to transform the South. Johnson, however, was strongly committed to **states' rights** and opposed the Radicals' objective of a powerful federal government. "White men alone must manage the South," Johnson announced, although he recommended limited political roles for the freedmen. Self-righteous and uncompromising, Johnson saw the major task of Reconstruction as **empowering** the region's white middle class and excluding wealthy planters from power.

Like Lincoln, Johnson relied on the president's constitutional power to grant pardons. He wanted a quick restoration of the southern states to the Union and granted amnesty to most former Confederates who pledged loyalty to the Union and support for emancipation. In one of his last actions as president, he granted full pardon and amnesty to all southern rebels—unlike Lincoln who exempted high-ranking

The Metropolitan Museum of Art/Art Resource, NY.

Before emancipation, slaves typically made their own clothing or received the used outfits of their owners and overseers. With emancipation, freed people with an income could afford to dress more fashionably. The Harry Stevens family probably put on their best clothes for a visit to the photographer in 1866.

Confederates from his pardons—although the Fourteenth Amendment (discussed later in this chapter) prevented him from restoring their right to hold office.

Johnson appointed **provisional** civilian governors for the southern states not already reconstructed. He instructed them to reconstitute state government and to call constitutional conventions of delegates elected by pardoned voters. Some provisional governors, however, appointed former Confederates to state and local offices, outraging those who expected Reconstruction to bring to power loyal Unionists committed to a new southern society.

The Southern Response: Minimal Compliance

Johnson expected the state constitutional conventions to abolish slavery, ratify the Thirteenth Amendment, renounce secession, and **repudiate** their state's war debts. The states were then to hold elections and resume their places in the Union. State conventions during the summer of 1865 usually complied with these requirements, some grudgingly. Every state, however, rejected black suffrage.

By April 1866, a year after the close of the war, all the southern states had fulfilled Johnson's requirements for rejoining the Union and had elected legislators, governors, and members of Congress. Johnson had hoped for the emergence of new political leaders in the South but was dismayed at the number of rich planters and former Confederate officials who won elections.

Most white southerners, however, viewed Johnson as their protector, standing between them and the Radicals. His support for states' rights and his opposition to federal determination of voting rights led white southerners to expect that they would shape the transition from slavery to freedom—that they, and not Congress, would define the status of the former slaves.

FREEDOM AND THE LEGACY OF SLAVERY

★ *What seem to have been the leading objectives among freed people as they explored their new opportunities?*

★ *How do the differing responses of freed people and southern whites show different understandings of the significance of emancipation?*

As state conventions wrote new constitutions, African Americans throughout the South set about creating new, free lives for themselves. In the antebellum South, all slaves and most free African Americans had led lives tightly constrained by law and custom. They were permitted few social organizations of their own. Not surprisingly, the central theme of the black response to emancipation was a desire for freedom from white control, for **autonomy** as individuals and as a community. The prospect of autonomy touched every aspect of life—family, churches, schools, newspapers, and a host of other social institutions. From this ferment of freedom came new, black institutions that provided

provisional Temporary.

repudiate The act of rejecting the validity or authority of something; to refuse to pay.

autonomy Control of one's own affairs.

the basis for southern African American communities. At the same time, the economic life of the South had been shattered by the Civil War and was being transformed by emancipation. Thus white southerners also faced drastic economic and social change.

Defining the Meaning of Freedom

At the most basic level, freedom came every time an individual slave stopped working for a master and claimed the right to be free. Thus freedom did not come to all slaves at the same time or in the same way. For some, freedom came before the Emancipation Proclamation when they walked away from their owners, crossed into Union-held territory, and asserted their liberty. Toward the end of the war, as civil authority broke down throughout much of the South, many slaves declared their freedom and left the site of their bondage. Some left for good, but many remained nearby, though with a new understanding of their relationship to their former masters. For some, freedom did not come until ratification of the Thirteenth Amendment.

Across the South, the approach of Yankee troops set off a joyous celebration—called a Jubilee—among those who knew their enslavement was ending. As one Virginia woman remembered, "Such rejoicing and shouting you never heard in your life." Once the celebrating was over, however, the freed people had to decide how best to use their freedom.

The freed people expressed their new status in many ways. Some chose new names to symbolize their new beginning. Many freed people changed their style of dress, discarding the cheap clothing provided to slaves. Some acquired guns. A significant benefit of freedom was the ability to travel without a pass and without being checked by the **patrollers** who had enforced the **pass system**.

Many freed people took this new opportunity to travel. Some felt they had to leave the site of their enslavement to experience full freedom. One freed man later recalled that he refused to work for his last owner, not because he had anything against him but because he wanted "to take my freedom." A freed woman said, "If I stay here I'll never know I'm free." Most traveled only short distances, to find work or land to farm, to

seek family members separated from them by slavery, or for other well-defined reasons.

The towns and cities of the South attracted some freed people. The presence of Union troops and federal officials promised protection from the random violence against freed people that occurred in rural areas. In March 1865, Congress created the **Freedmen's Bureau** to assist the freed people in their transition to freedom. In cities and towns, this agency offered assistance with finding work and necessities. Cities and towns also held black churches, newly established schools, and other social institutions, some begun by free blacks before the war. Some African Americans came to towns and cities looking for work. Little housing was available, however, so freed people often crowded into hastily built shanties. Sanitation was poor and disease a common scourge. Such conditions improved only very slowly.

Creating Communities

During Reconstruction, African Americans created their own communities with their own social institutions, beginning with family ties. Joyful families were sometimes reunited after years of separation caused by the sale of a spouse or children. Other people spent years searching for lost family members.

The new freedom to conduct religious services without white supervision was especially important. Churches quickly became the most prominent social organizations in African American communities. Churches were, in fact, among the very first social institutions that African Americans fully controlled. During Reconstruction, black denominations grew rapidly in the South, including the African Methodist Episcopal, African Methodist Episcopal Zion, and several Baptist groups (all founded before the Civil War). Black ministers helped congregation members adjust to the changes that freedom brought, and ministers often became key leaders within developing African American communities.

Throughout the cities and towns of the South, African Americans created schools. Setting up a school, said one, was "the first proof" of independence. Many new schools were for both children and adults, because laws had prohibited education for slaves. The desire to learn was widespread and intense. One freedman in Georgia wrote to a friend: "The Lord has sent books and teachers. We must not hesitate a moment, but go on and learn all we can."

When African Americans set up schools, they faced severe shortages of teachers, books, and schoolrooms—everything but students. As abolitionists and northern reformers tried to assist the transition from slavery to freedom, many of them also focused on education. The Freedmen's Bureau played an important role in organizing and equipping schools. Freedmen's

patrollers During the era of slavery, white guards who made the rounds of rural roads to make certain that slaves were not moving about the countryside without written permission from their masters.

pass system Laws that forbade slaves to travel without written authorization from their owners.

■ **Freedmen's Bureau** Agency established in 1865 to aid former slaves in their transition to freedom, especially by administering relief and sponsoring education.

Faith Memorial Church, seen here in a photo from 1915, was built by the Rev. Mr. Guerry during reconstruction. The location was not specified in the book where the photograph originally appeared.

black man has the ballot." In 1865, political conventions of African Americans attracted hundreds of leaders of the emerging black communities. They called for equality and voting rights, and pointed to black contributions in the American Revolution and the Civil War as evidence of patriotism and devotion. They also appealed to the nation's republican traditions, in particular the Declaration of Independence and its dictum that "all men are created equal."

Land and Labor in the Postwar South

Few white southerners welcomed the end of slavery. Only a few former slave owners provided financial assistance to their former slaves, and some tried to keep their slaves from learning of their freedom.

Many freed people looked to Union troops for assistance. When General William T. Sherman led his victorious army through Georgia in the closing months of the war, thousands of African American men, women, and children claimed their freedom and followed in the Yankees' wake. Their leaders told Sherman that they wanted to "reap the fruit of our own labor." In January 1865, Sherman issued Special Field Order No. 15, setting aside the Sea Islands and land along the South Carolina coast for freed families. Each family, he specified, was to receive 40 acres and the loan of an army mule. By June, the area had filled with forty thousand freed people settled on 400,000 acres of "Sherman land."

Sherman's action encouraged African Americans to expect that the federal government would redistribute land throughout the South. "Forty acres and a mule" became a rallying cry. Only land, Thaddeus Stevens proclaimed, would give freed people control of their own labor. "If we do not furnish them with homesteads," Stevens said, "we had better left them in bondage."

By the end of the war, the Freedmen's Bureau controlled some 850,000 acres of land abandoned by former owners or confiscated from Confederate leaders. In July 1865, General Oliver O. Howard, head of the bureau, directed that this land be divided into 40-acre plots to be given to freed people. However, President Johnson ordered Howard to halt **land redistribution** and to return to its former owners land already handed over. Johnson's order displaced thousands of African Americans who had already taken their 40 acres. Those who had expected land of their

Aid Societies sprang up in most northern cities and, along with northern churches, collected funds and supplies for the freed people. Teachers—mostly white women, often from New England, and often acting on religious impulses—came from the North. Northern aid societies and church organizations, together with the Freedmen's Bureau, established schools to train black teachers. Some of those schools evolved into black colleges. By 1870, the Freedmen's Bureau supervised more than four thousand schools, with more than nine thousand teachers and 247,000 students. Still, in 1870, only one-tenth of school-age black children were in school.

African Americans created other social institutions in addition to churches and schools, including **fraternal orders**, **benevolent societies**, and newspapers. By 1866, the South had ten black newspapers, led by the *New Orleans Tribune*. These newspapers played important roles in shaping African American communities.

In politics, African Americans' first objective was recognition of their equal rights as citizens. Frederick Douglass insisted, "Slavery is not abolished until the

fraternal order A men's organization, often with a ceremonial initiation, that typically provided rudimentary life insurance.

benevolent society Organization dedicated to some charitable purpose.

land redistribution Division of land held by large landowners into smaller plots that are turned over to landless people.

During Reconstruction, freed people gave a high priority to schools, often with the assistance of the Freedmen's Bureau and northern missionary societies. This teacher and her barefoot pupils were photographed in the 1870s, in Petersburg, Virginia. In such schools, one teacher typically taught grades 1 through 8.

Clayton Lewis, William L. Clements Library, University of Michigan.

own felt betrayed. One later recalled that they had expected "a heap from freedom dey didn't git."

The Freedmen's Bureau also assisted white refugees. In a few places, white recipients of aid outnumbered the freed blacks. Many southern whites had never owned slaves, and now feared they would have to compete with the freed people for farmland or wage labor. Like the freed people, many southern whites lacked the means to farm on their own. When the Confederate government collapsed, Confederate money became worthless. This sudden reduction in the amount of money in circulation, together with the failure of southern banks and the devastation of the southern economy, meant that the entire region was short of **capital**.

Sharecropping slowly emerged across much of the South, derived from the central realities of southern agriculture. Much of the land was in large holdings, but the landowners had no one to work it. Capital was scarce. Many landowners lacked cash to hire farm workers. Many families, both black and white, wanted their own farm but had no land, no supplies, and no money. Under sharecropping, an individual—usually a family head—signed a contract with a landowner to rent land as home and farm, paying a share of the

harvest as rent. The landlord's share might amount to half or more of the crop if the landlord provided mules, tools, seed, and fertilizer as well as land. Many landowners thought that sharecropping encouraged tenants to be productive, to get as much value as possible from their shares of the crop.

Southern farmers—black or white, sharecroppers or owners of small plots—often found themselves in debt to a local merchant who advanced supplies on credit. In return for credit, the merchant required a lien (a legal claim) on the growing crop. Many landlords ran stores that they required their tenants to patronize. Often the share paid as rent and the debt owed the store exceeded the value of the entire harvest. Furthermore, many rental contracts and **crop liens** were automatically renewed if all debts were not paid at the end of a year. Thus, in spite of their efforts to achieve greater control over their lives and labor, many southern farm families, black and white alike, found themselves trapped by sharecropping and debt. Still, sharecropping gave freed people more control over their daily lives than had slavery.

Landlords could exercise political as well as economic power over their tenants. Until the 1890s, voting was an open process, and any observer could see how an individual voted (as illustrated on page 385). Thus, when a landlord or merchant advocated a particular candidate, the unspoken message was often an implicit threat to cut off credit at the store or to evict a sharecropper if he did not vote accordingly. Such forms of economic **coercion** could undercut voting rights.

The White South: Confronting Change

The Civil War and the end of slavery transformed the lives of white southerners as well as black southerners.

capital Money, especially the money invested in a commercial enterprise.

sharecropping System for renting farmland in which tenant farmers—the sharecroppers—give landlords a share of their crops, rather than cash, as rent.

crop lien Legal claim to a farmer's crop, similar to a mortgage, based on the use of crops as collateral for extension of credit by a merchant.

coercion Use of threats or force to compel action.

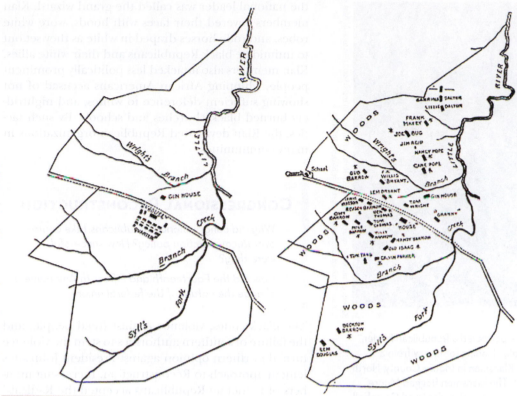

David C. Barrow, Jr. "A Georgia Plantation." *Scribner's Monthly*, vol. 21 issue 5 March 1881.

These maps of a plantation in Georgia appeared in *Scribner's Monthly* in 1881. On the left, the pre-war plantation, had one center for plantation activities—the owner's house, the slave quarters, and the various buildings for work and storage. The map on the right shows the same plantation in 1881, with a large number of small, family farms operated by sharecroppers.

For some, the changes were nearly as profound as those experienced by freed people. Savings vanished. Some homes and other buildings were destroyed. Thousands left the South.

Before the war, few white southerners had owned slaves, and very few owned large numbers. Distrust or even hostility had always existed between the privileged planter families and the many whites who farmed small plots. Some regions populated by small-scale farmers had resisted secession, and some welcomed the Union victory and supported the Republicans during Reconstruction. Some southerners also welcomed the prospect of the economic transformation that northern capital might bring.

Most white southerners, however, shared what one North Carolinian described in 1866 as "the bitterest hatred toward the North." Even people with no attachment to slavery detested the Yankees who so profoundly changed their lives. During the early phases of Reconstruction, most white southerners apparently expected that, except for slavery, things would soon be put back much as they had been before the war. For many, the "lost cause" of the Confederacy came to symbolize their defense of their prewar lives, not an attempt to break up the nation or protect slavery.

In late 1865 and 1866, the newly organized state legislatures passed **black codes** defining the new legal status of African Americans. These regulations varied from state to state, but every state placed significant restrictions on black people. Various black codes required African Americans to have an annual employment contract, limited them to agricultural work, forbade them from moving about the countryside without permission, restricted their ownership of land, and provided for forced labor by those guilty of **vagrancy**—which usually meant anyone without a job. Taken together, the black codes represented an effort by white southerners to define a legally subordinate place for African Americans and significantly restrict their new freedom.

black codes Laws passed by the southern states after the Civil War limiting the civil rights of freed people and defining their status as subordinate to whites.

vagrancy Legal condition of having no fixed place of residence or means of support.

Planning the contemplated murder of John Campbell in North Carolina (engraving). English School, (19th century)/Private Collection/© Look and Learn/Rosenberg Collection/The Bridgeman Art Library.

THE KU-KLUX-KLAN AGAIN.—PLANNING THE CONTEMPLATED MURDER OF JOHN CAMPBELL IN NORTH CAROLINA.

In this picture, the artist has portrayed a Republican leader, white grocer John Campbell, pleading for mercy from a group of bizarrely dressed Klansmen in Moore County, North Carolina, on August 10, 1871. The Klansmen flogged Moore before releasing him. Curiously, the artist depicted Campbell as an African American.

Some white southerners used violence to coerce freed people into accepting a subordinate status. Violence and terror became closely associated with the **Ku Klux Klan**, a secret organization formed in 1866 and led by a former Confederate general. The turn to terror suggests that Klan members felt themselves largely powerless through normal politics, and used terror to create a climate of fear among their opponents. Most Klan members were small-scale farmers and workers, but the leaders were often prominent within their own communities—one Freedmen's Bureau agent observed, "The most respectable citizens are engaged in it." Klan groups existed throughout the South, but operated with little central control. Their major goals were to restore **white supremacy** and to destroy the Republican Party. Other, like-minded organizations also formed and adopted similar tactics.

Klan members were called ghouls. Officers included cyclops, night-hawks, and grand dragons, and

the national leader was called the grand wizard. Klan members covered their faces with hoods, wore white robes, and rode horses draped in white as they set out to intimidate black Republicans and their white allies. Klan members also attacked less politically prominent people, whipping African Americans accused of not showing sufficient deference to whites, and nightriders burned black churches and schools. By such tactics, the Klan devastated Republican organizations in many communities.

CONGRESSIONAL RECONSTRUCTION

☆ *Why did congressional Republicans take control over Reconstruction policy? How successful were they?*

☆ *How did the Fourteenth and Fifteenth Amendments change the nature of the federal union?*

The black codes, violence against freed people, and the failure of southern authorities to stem the violence turned northern opinion against President Johnson's lenient approach to Reconstruction. Increasing numbers of moderate Republicans accepted the Radicals' arguments that the freed people required greater federal protection, and congressional Republicans moved to take control of Reconstruction. When stubborn and uncompromising Andrew Johnson ran up against stubborn and uncompromising Thaddeus Stevens, the nation faced a constitutional crisis.

Challenging Presidential Reconstruction: The Civil Rights Act of 1866

In December 1865, the Thirty-Ninth Congress (elected in 1864) met for the first time. Republicans outnumbered Democrats by more than three to one. President Johnson proclaimed Reconstruction complete and the Union restored, but few Republicans agreed. Events in the South had convinced most moderate Republicans of the need to protect free labor in the South and establish basic rights for freed people. Most also agreed that Congress could withhold representation from the South until reconstructed state governments met these conditions.

On the first day of the Thirty-ninth Congress, moderate Republicans joined Radicals to exclude newly elected congressmen from the South. Citing Article I, Section 5, of the Constitution (which makes each house of Congress the judge of the qualifications of its members), Republicans set up a Joint Committee on Reconstruction to evaluate whether electees from southern states were entitled sit in Congress. In the meantime, the former Confederate states had no representation in Congress.

■ **Ku Klux Klan** Secret society organized in the South after the Civil War to restore white supremacy by means of violence and intimidation.

white supremacy Racist belief that whites are inherently superior to other races and entitled to rule over them.

Congressional Republicans also moved to provide more assistance to the freed people. Moderates and Radicals approved a bill extending the Freedmen's Bureau and giving it more authority against racial discrimination. When Johnson vetoed it, Congress passed a slightly revised version. Republicans also produced a **civil rights** bill, a far-reaching measure extending citizenship to African Americans and guaranteeing certain rights to all citizens. Johnson vetoed both the civil rights bill and the revised Freedmen's Bureau bill, but Congress passed both over his veto. With creation of the Joint Committee on Reconstruction and passage of the Civil Rights and Freedmen's Bureau acts, Congress took control of Reconstruction.

For the first time, the Civil Rights Act of 1866 defined all persons born in the United States (except Indians not taxed) as citizens and listed certain rights of all citizens, including the right to testify in court, own property, make contracts, bring lawsuits, and enjoy "full and equal benefit of all laws." It restricted state authority on the grounds that the rights of national citizenship took precedence over state actions. The law expanded federal powers in unprecedented ways and challenged traditional concepts of states' rights. Though the law applied to all citizens, its most immediate consequence was to benefit African Americans.

Debate in Congress focused on the freed people. Some supporters saw the Civil Rights Act as a way to secure freed people's basic rights. For other Republicans, the bill carried broader implications because it empowered the federal government to force states to abide by the principle of equality before the law. They applauded its redefinition of federal-state relations. Senator Lot Morrill of Maine described it as "absolutely revolutionary" but added, "Are we not in the midst of a revolution?"

When President Johnson vetoed the bill, he argued that it violated states' rights. He may have hoped to generate enough political support to elect a conservative Congress in 1866 and to win the presidency in 1868. He probably expected his veto to turn voters against the Radicals. Instead, the veto led most moderate Republicans to abandon hope of cooperating with him. In April 1866, when Congress passed the Civil Rights Act over Johnson's veto, it was the first time that Congress had overridden a presidential veto of major legislation.

Defining Citizenship: The Fourteenth Amendment

Leading Republicans worried that the Civil Rights Act could be amended or repealed by a later Congress or declared unconstitutional by the Supreme Court. Only a constitutional amendment, they concluded, could permanently safeguard the freed people's rights as citizens.

The **Fourteenth Amendment** began as a Radical proposal for a constitutional guarantee of equality before the law. However, the final wording—the longest of any amendment—resulted from many compromises. Section 1 of the amendment defined American citizenship in much the same way as the Civil Rights Act of 1866, then specified that

> No State shall make or enforce any law which shall abridge the privileges or immunities of citizens of the United States; nor shall any State deprive any person of life, liberty, or property, without due process of law; nor deny to any person within its jurisdiction the equal protection of the laws.

The Constitution and Bill of Rights prohibit federal interference with basic civil rights. The Fourteenth Amendment extends this protection against action by state governments.

The amendment was vague on some points. For example, it penalized states that did not **enfranchise** African Americans by reducing their congressional representation, but it did not specifically guarantee to African Americans the right to vote.

Not everyone approved of the final wording. Charles Sumner condemned the provision that permitted a state to deny suffrage to male citizens if it accepted a penalty. Woman suffrage advocates, led by **Elizabeth Cady Stanton** and **Susan B. Anthony**, complained that the amendment, for the first time, introduced the word *male* into the Constitution in connection with voting rights.

Despite such concerns, Congress approved the Fourteenth Amendment by a straight party vote and sent it to the states for ratification. Tennessee promptly ratified the amendment, became the first reconstructed state government to be recognized by Congress, and was exempted from most later Reconstruction legislation.

Although Congress adjourned in the summer of 1866, the nation's attention remained fixed on Reconstruction. In May and July, in Memphis and New Orleans, bloody riots aimed at

civil rights Rights, privileges, and protections that are part of citizenship.

■ **Fourteenth Amendment** Constitutional amendment, ratified in 1868, defining American citizenship and rights and restricting state authority and the political activities of former Confederates.

enfranchise To grant the right to vote to an individual or group.

■ **Elizabeth Cady Stanton** Founder and leader of the American woman suffrage movement from 1848 (Seneca Falls Convention) until her death in 1902.

■ **Susan B. Anthony** Tireless campaigner for woman suffrage and close associate of Elizabeth Cady Stanton.

It Matters Today

The Fourteenth Amendment

The Fourteenth Amendment is one of the most important sources of Americans' civil rights, next to the Bill of Rights (the first ten amendments). One key provision in the Fourteenth Amendment is the definition of American citizenship. Previously, the Constitution did not address that question. The Fourteenth Amendment cleared up any confusion about who was, and who was not, a citizen.

The amendment also specifies that no state could abridge the liberties of a citizen "without due process of law." Until this time, the Constitution and the Bill of Rights restricted action by the *federal* government to restrict individual liberties. The Supreme Court has interpreted the Fourteenth Amendment to mean that the restrictions placed on the federal government by the First Amendment also limit state governments—that no *state* government may abridge freedom of speech, press, assembly, and religion.

The Supreme Court continues to interpret the Fourteenth Amendment when it is presented with new cases involving state restrictions on the rights of citizens. For example, in *Roe v. Wade* (1973), the Supreme Court cited the due process clause among other provisions of the Constitution to conclude that state laws may not prevent women from having abortions. In *Lawrence v. Texas* (2003), the Court cited the Fourteenth Amendment to conclude that states may not punish adults for engaging in consensual sexual activities. Current arguments over same-sex marriage often focus on the equal-protection clause of the Fourteenth Amendment.

- Look up the Fourteenth Amendment in the back of this book. How does the Fourteenth Amendment define citizenship? Using an online newspaper, can you find recent proposals to change the definition of American citizenship?
- What current political issues might lead to court cases in which the Fourteenth Amendment is likely to be invoked?

African Americans turned more moderates against Johnson's Reconstruction policies. Some interpreted congressional elections that fall as a referendum on Reconstruction and the Fourteenth Amendment, pitting Johnson against the Radicals. Republicans swept the 1866 elections, outnumbering Democrats 143 to 49 in the new House of Representatives, and 42 to 11 in the Senate. Lyman Trumbull, senator from Illinois and a leading moderate, voiced the consensus of congressional Republicans: Congress should now "hurl from power the disloyal element" in the South.

Radicals in Control

As congressional Radicals struggled with President Johnson over control of Reconstruction, it became clear that the Fourteenth Amendment might fall short of ratification. Rejection by ten states could prevent its acceptance. By March 1867, the amendment had been rejected by twelve states—Delaware, Kentucky, and all former Confederate states except Tennessee. Moderate Republicans who had expected the Fourteenth Amendment to be the final Reconstruction measure now became receptive to other proposals by the Radicals.

On March 2, 1867, Congress overrode Johnson's veto of the Military Reconstruction Act, which divided the Confederate states (except Tennessee) into five military districts. Each district was to be governed by a military commander authorized by Congress to use military force to protect life and property. These ten states were to elect delegates and hold constitutional conventions, and all adult male citizens were to vote, except former Confederates who were barred from office under the proposed Fourteenth Amendment. The constitutional conventions were then to create new state governments that permitted black suffrage, and the new governments were to ratify the Fourteenth Amendment. Congress would then evaluate whether those state governments were ready to regain representation in Congress.

Congress had wrested a major degree of control over Reconstruction from the president, but it was not finished. The Command of the Army Act specified that the president could issue military orders only through the General of the Army—Ulysses S. Grant,

Library of Congress.

Tickets such as these were in high demand, for they permitted the holder to watch the proceedings as the Radical leaders presented their evidence to justify removing Andrew Johnson from the presidency.

considered an ally of Congress—and that the General of the Army could not be removed without Senate permission. Congress thereby blocked Johnson from direct communication with military commanders in the South. The Tenure of Office Act specified that officials appointed with the Senate's consent were to remain in office until the Senate approved a successor, thereby preventing Johnson from removing federal officials who opposed his policies. Johnson understood both measures as invasions of presidential authority.

Early in 1867, some Radicals began to consider impeaching President Johnson. The Constitution (Article I, Sections 2 and 3) gives the House of Representatives exclusive power to **impeach** the president—that is, to charge the chief executive with misconduct. The Constitution specifies that the Senate shall hold a trial on those charges, with the chief justice of the Supreme Court presiding. If found guilty by a two-thirds vote of the Senate, the president is removed from office.

When Johnson directly challenged Congress over the Tenure of Office Act by removing Edwin Stanton as secretary of war, Johnson's opponents now claimed he had violated the law. When the House Judiciary Committee failed to bring impeachment charges, the Joint Committee on Reconstruction, led by Thaddeus Stevens, took over. On February 24, 1868, the House adopted eleven articles, or charges, nearly all based on the Stanton affair. The actual reasons the Radicals wanted Johnson removed were clear to all: they disliked him and his actions.

To convict Johnson and remove him from the presidency required a two-thirds vote by the Senate. Johnson's defenders argued he had done nothing to warrant impeachment. The Radicals' legal case was weak, but they urged senators to vote on whether they wished Johnson to remain as president. Some moderates, fearing the precedent of removing a president for such flimsy reasons, joined with Democrats to defeat the Radicals. The vote was 35 in favor of conviction and 19 against, one vote short of the required two-thirds. By this tiny margin, Congress endorsed the principle that it should not remove the president from office simply because members of Congress disagree with or dislike the president.

Political Terrorism and the Election of 1868

The Radicals' failure to unseat Johnson left him with less than a year remaining in office. As the election approached, the Republicans nominated Ulysses S. Grant for president. A war hero, popular throughout the North, Grant committed himself to the congressional view of Reconstruction. The Democrats nominated Horatio Seymour, a former governor of New York, and denounced Reconstruction.

In the South, the campaign stirred up fierce activity by the Ku Klux Klan and similar groups. **Terrorists** assassinated an Arkansas congressman, three members of the South Carolina legislature, and several other Republican leaders. Throughout the South, mobs attacked Republican offices and meetings, and sometimes attacked any black person they could find. Such coercion had its intended effect at the ballot box.

Despite such violence, many Americans may have anticipated a calmer political future. In June 1868 Congress had readmitted seven southern states that met the requirements of congressional Reconstruction.

impeach To charge a public official with improper, usually criminal, conduct.

terrorists Those who use threats and violence to achieve ideological or political goals.

Constitutional Revolution

Senator Lot Morrill described what they were doing as "revolutionary," and historians have agreed that the constitutional changes of the Civil War and Reconstruction were a constitutional revolution or even "the second American revolution." Before the Civil War, some Americans had argued that the Union was voluntary and states could secede or nullify federal laws. Now it was clear that the United States was one nation, indivisible—and that secession constituted insurrection and would be met by force.

Defenders of slavery had long argued that Congress had no constitutional authority to limit, much less abolish, slavery. The Thirteenth Amendment changed that forever.

Previously, states had their own definitions of citizenship, and the *Dred Scott* decision of the U.S. Supreme Court (1857) stated that African Americans could not be citizens. The Fourteenth Amendment now defined an American citizenship that took precedence over state definitions and significantly limited state authority. The Fifteenth Amendment similarly limited state authority over voter eligibility.

Overall, the constitutional revolution of the Civil War and Reconstruction significantly enhanced federal authority at the expense of the states.

In July, the secretary of state declared the Fourteenth Amendment ratified. In November, Grant easily won the presidency, carrying twenty-six of the thirty-four states and 53 percent of the vote.

Voting Rights and Civil Rights

With Grant in the White House, Radical Republicans moved to secure voting rights for all African Americans. The states still defined voting rights. Congress had required southern states to enfranchise black males as the price of readmission to the Union, but only seven northern states had taken that step. Further, any state that had enfranchised African Americans

◾ **Fifteenth Amendment** Constitutional amendment, ratified in 1870, that prohibited states from denying the right to vote because of a person's race or because a person had been a slave.

disfranchisement Taking away the right to vote.

nativity Place of birth.

discrimination Denial of equal treatment based on prejudice or bias.

could change its law at any time. In addition to the principled arguments of Douglass and other Radicals, many Republicans concluded that they needed to guarantee black suffrage in the South if they were to continue to win presidential elections and enjoy majorities in Congress.

To secure suffrage rights for all African Americans, Congress approved the **Fifteenth Amendment** in February 1869. The amendment prohibited both federal and state governments from restricting the right to vote because of "race, color, or previous condition of servitude." Like the Fourteenth Amendment, the Fifteenth marked a compromise between moderates and Radicals. Some African American leaders argued for language guaranteeing voting rights to all male citizens, because prohibiting some grounds for **disfranchisement** might imply the legitimacy of other grounds. Some Radicals tried, unsuccessfully, to add "**nativity**, property, education, or religious beliefs" to the prohibited grounds. Democrats condemned the Fifteenth Amendment as a "revolutionary" attack on states' authority to define voting rights.

Elizabeth Cady Stanton, Susan B. Anthony, and other advocates of woman suffrage opposed the amendment because it ignored restrictions based on sex. For nearly twenty years, efforts to secure women's rights and black rights had marched together. Once black male suffrage came under discussion, however, this alliance began to fracture. The break was eventually papered over, but the wounds never completely healed.

Despite such opposition, within thirteen months the proposed amendment received the approval of enough states to take effect. Success came in part because Republicans, who might otherwise have been reluctant to impose black suffrage in the North, concluded that the future success of their party required black suffrage in the South.

The Fifteenth Amendment did not reduce the violence—especially at election time—that had become almost routine in the South. When Klan activity escalated in the elections of 1870, southern Republicans looked to Washington for support. In 1870 and 1871, Congress adopted several Enforcement Acts—often called the Ku Klux Klan Acts—to enforce the Fourteenth and Fifteenth Amendments.

Despite obstacles, the prosecution of Klansmen began in 1871. Across the South hundreds were indicted, and many were convicted. In South Carolina, President Grant declared martial law. By 1872, federal intervention had broken much of the strength of the Klan.

Congress passed one final Reconstruction measure. Charles Sumner introduced a bill prohibiting **discrimination** in 1870 and in each subsequent session of Congress until his death in 1874. On his deathbed, Sumner urged his visitors to "take care of the civil-rights bill," begging them, "Don't let it fail."

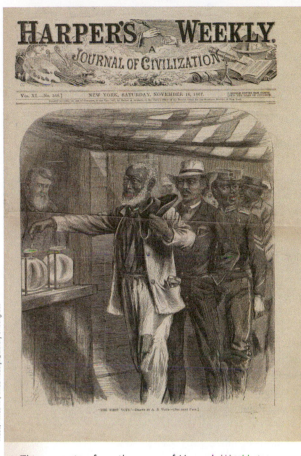

Waud, Alfred R. (Alfred Rudolph)/Library of Congress

This engraving, from the cover of *Harper's Weekly* in November 1867, shows black men lined up to vote. The artist has shown first an older workingman, with his tools in his pocket; next a well-dressed, younger man, probably a city-dweller and perhaps a leader in the emerging black community; next a Union soldier. Voters received a ballot (a "party ticket") from a party campaigner and deposited that ballot in a ballot box, in full sight of all. Voting was not secret until much later.

Approved after Sumner's death, the **Civil Rights Act of 1875** prohibited racial discrimination in the selection of juries and in public transportation and **public accommodations**.

BLACK RECONSTRUCTION

☆ *What major groups made up the Republican Party in the South during Reconstruction? Compare their reasons for being Republicans, their relative sizes, and their objectives.*

☆ *What were the most lasting results of the Republican state administrations?*

Congressional Reconstruction set the stage for new developments at state and local levels throughout the South. African Americans never completely

© Cengage Learning

This lithograph from 1883 depicts African American men, most of whom had leading roles in Black Reconstruction: Frederick Douglass is in the center. Joseph Rainey is in the lower right.

controlled any state government but did form a significant element in the governments of several states. The time when African Americans participated prominently in state and local politics is usually called **Black Reconstruction**. It began with efforts by African Americans to take part in politics as early as 1865 and lasted for more than a decade. A few African Americans continued to hold elective office in the South after 1877, but by then they could do little to bring about significant political change. Map 15.1 indicates the proportion of African Americans in each of the southern states, and also the years when each state was under a Reconstruction state government.

■ **Civil Rights Act of 1875** Law passed by Congress in 1875 prohibiting racial discrimination in selection of juries and in businesses open to the general public.

public accommodations Hotels, bars and restaurants, theaters, and other places set up to do business with anyone who can pay the price of admission.

■ **Black Reconstruction** The period of Reconstruction when African Americans took an active role in state and local government.

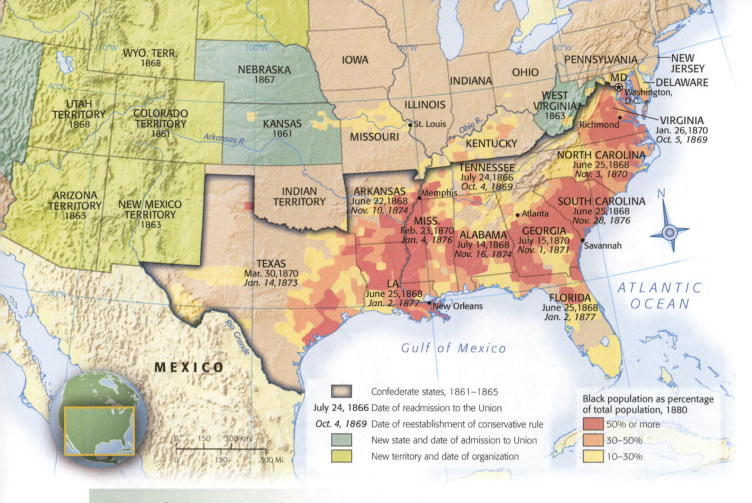

MAP 15.1 **African American Population and the Duration of Reconstruction**
This map shows the proportion of African Americans in the South and the dates when each former Confederate state was under a Reconstruction state government. Does the map suggest any relationship between the proportion of a state's population that was African American and the time that the state spent under a Reconstruction state government? © Cengage Learning.

The Republican Party in the South

Nearly all African Americans who participated in politics did so as Republicans, and they formed the majority of the Republican Party in the South. Nearly all black Republicans were new to politics, and they often braved considerable personal danger by participating in a party that many white southerners equated with the conquering Yankees.

Suffrage made politics centrally important for African American communities. The state constitutional conventions that met in 1868 included 265 black delegates, but only in Louisiana and South Carolina were half or more of the delegates black. With suffrage established, southern Republicans began to elect African Americans to public office. Between 1869 and 1877, fourteen black men (including Joseph Rainey) served in the national House of Representatives, and Mississippi sent two African Americans to the U.S. Senate.

Across the South, six African Americans served as lieutenant governors, and one of them, P. B. S. Pinchback, succeeded briefly to the governorship of

Louisiana. More than six hundred black men served in southern state legislatures, but only in South Carolina did African Americans ever have a majority in the state legislature. Elsewhere they formed part of a Republican majority but rarely held key legislative positions. Only in South Carolina and Mississippi did legislatures elect black presiding officers. Although politically inexperienced, most African Americans who held office during Reconstruction had some education. Of the eighteen who served in statewide offices, all but three are known to have been born free. P. B. S. Pinchback, for example, was educated in Ohio and served in the army as a captain before entering politics in Louisiana. Most black politicians first achieved prominence through service with the army, the Freedmen's Bureau, the new schools, or the religious and civic organizations of black communities.

Republicans gained power in southern states only by attracting some white voters. These white Republicans are usually remembered by the names fastened on them by their political opponents: "carpetbaggers" and "scalawags." Both groups included idealists who

Bags made of carpeting, like this one, were inexpensive luggage. Southern opponents of Reconstruction fastened the label "carpetbaggers" on northerners who came south to participate in Reconstruction, suggesting that they were cheap opportunists. Collection of Picture Research Consultants and Archives.

hoped to create a new southern society, but both also included opportunists expecting to exploit politics for personal gain.

Southern Democrats applied the term **carpetbagger** to northern Republicans who came to the South after the war, regarding them as second-rate schemers—outsiders with their belongings packed in a cheap carpet bag. In fact, most northerners who came south were well-educated men and women from middle-class backgrounds. Most men had served in the Union army and moved south before blacks could vote. They included lawyers, newspaper editors, and investors in agricultural land, as well as teachers in the new schools, or agents of the Freedmen's Bureau, and most hoped to transform the South by creating new institutions based on northern models, especially free labor and free public schools. Few in number, transplanted northerners nonetheless took leading roles in state constitutional conventions and state legislatures. Some were also prominent advocates of economic modernization.

Southern Democrats reserved their greatest contempt for those they called **scalawags**, slang for someone unscrupulous and worthless. Scalawags were white southerners who became Republicans. They included many southern Unionists, who had opposed secession, and others who thought the Republicans offered the best hope for economic recovery. Scalawags included merchants, artisans, and professionals who favored a modernized South. Others were small-scale farmers who saw Reconstruction as a way to end political domination by the plantation owners.

The freedmen, white newcomers from the North, and white southerners who made up the Republican Party in the South hoped to inject new ideas into that region. They tried to modernize state and local governments and make the postwar South more like the North. They repealed outdated laws and established or expanded schools, hospitals, orphanages, and penitentiaries.

Creating Public Education, Fighting Discrimination, and Building Railroads

Free public education was perhaps the most enduring legacy of Black Reconstruction, because Reconstruction constitutions required tax-supported public schools. Implementation, however, was expensive and proceeded slowly. By the mid-1870s, only half of southern children attended public schools.

In creating public schools, Reconstruction state governments faced a central question: Would white and black children attend the same schools? Many African Americans favored racially integrated schools. Southern white leaders, including many southern white Republicans, argued that integration would destroy the fledgling public school system by driving whites away. In the end, no state required school integration. Southern states also created separate black normal schools (to train schoolteachers) and colleges. On balance, most blacks probably agreed with Frederick Douglass that separate schools were "infinitely superior" to no public education at all. Some found other reasons to accept **segregated** schools—separate black schools gave a larger role to black parents, and they hired black teachers and administrators.

Creating and operating two educational systems, one white and one black, was costly, and funds were always limited. Black schools almost always received fewer dollars per student than white schools. Despite their accomplishments, the segregated schools institutionalized discrimination.

Reconstruction state governments moved toward protection of equal rights in other areas. Southern Republicans often wrote into their new state constitutions prohibitions against discrimination and protections for civil rights. Some Reconstruction state

carpetbagger Derogatory term for the northerners who came to the South after the Civil War to take part in Reconstruction.

scalawag Derogatory term for white southerners who aligned themselves with the Republican Party during Reconstruction.

segregated Separated on account of race or class, such as the separation of blacks from whites in most southern school systems.

governments enacted laws guaranteeing **equal access** to public transportation and public accommodations. Elsewhere, efforts to pass equal access laws foundered on the opposition of southern white Republicans, who often joined Democrats to favor segregation. Such conflicts pointed up the internal divisions within the southern Republican Party. Even when equal access laws were passed, they were often not enforced.

Republicans everywhere—North, South, and West—sought to use government authority to encourage economic growth and development. Promoting economic development often meant encouraging railroad construction. In the South, as elsewhere, some state governments granted land to railroads, or lent them money, or committed the state's credit to **underwrite** bonds for construction. Sometimes they subsidized railroads without planning adequately or determining whether companies were financially sound. Some projects failed as companies squandered funds without building rail lines. During the 1870s, only 7,000 miles of new track were laid in the South, compared with 45,000 miles elsewhere in the nation. Even that was a considerable accomplishment for the South, given its dismal economic situation.

Railroad companies and other corporations sometimes sought favorable treatment by bribing public officials. All too many officeholders—South, North, and West—accepted their offers. Given the excessive favoritism that most public officials showed to corporations, revelations and allegations of corruption became common from New York to Mississippi to California.

Southern politics proved especially ripe for corruption as government responsibilities expanded rapidly and created new opportunities for scoundrels. Too many Reconstruction officials—white and black— saw politics as a way to improve their own finances. One South Carolina legislator bluntly described his attitude toward electing a U.S. senator: "I was pretty hard up, and I did not care who the candidate was if I got two hundred dollars." Corruption was usually nonpartisan, but it seemed more prominent among Republicans because they held the most important offices.

William Mahone, shown here at about the time he served in the U.S. Senate from Virginia, had been a railroad developer in Virginia before the Civil War. A major general in the Confederate army, he again became head of a railroad company after the war. He organized a political coalition of African Americans, white Republicans, and conservative Democrats that took control of state government and elected Mahone to the U.S. Senate, where he usually caucused with the Republicans.

Library of Congress Prints and Photographs Division[LC-BH832- 2462].

THE END OF RECONSTRUCTION

★ *What major factors brought about the end of Reconstruction? Evaluate their relative significance.*

From the beginning, most white southerners resisted the new order that the conquering Yankees imposed on them. Initially, resistance took the form of black codes and the Klan. Later, some southern opponents of Reconstruction developed new strategies, but terror remained an important instrument of resistance.

The "New Departure" and the 1872 Presidential Election

By 1869, some leading southern Democrats had abandoned their resistance to change, deciding instead to accept some Reconstruction measures and African American suffrage. At the same time, they also tried to secure restoration of political rights for former Confederates. Behind this **New Departure** for southern Democrats lay the belief that continued resistance

equal access Right of any person to make the same use of a public facility, such as streetcars, as any other person.

underwrite To assume financial responsibility for; here, to guarantee the purchase of bonds.

▫ **New Departure** Strategy adopted by some leading southern Democrats of cooperating with some Reconstruction measures in the hope of winning compromises favorable to their party.

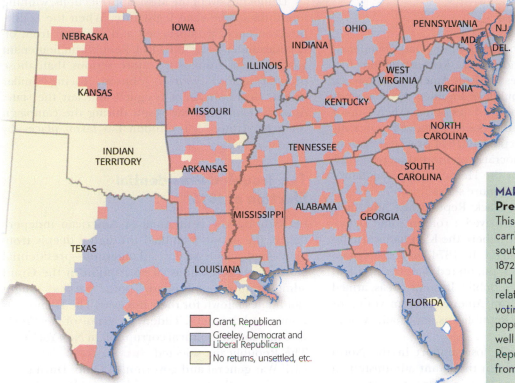

MAP 15.2 Popular Vote for President in the South, 1872 This map shows which candidate carried each county in the southeastern United States in 1872. Looking at both this map and Map 15.1, you can see the relationship between Republican voting and African American population in some areas, as well as where the southern Republican Party drew support from white voters. © Cengage Learning.

Legend:
- Grant, Republican
- Greeley, Democrat and Liberal Republican
- No returns, unsettled, etc.

would only cause more regional turmoil and prolong federal intervention.

Sometimes southern Democrats supported conservative Republicans for state and local offices instead of members of their own party, hoping to defuse concern in Washington and dilute Radical influence in state government. This strategy appeared first in Virginia, where William Mahone forged a broad political **coalition** that accepted black suffrage and in 1869 elected as governor a northern-born banker and moderate Republican. Virginia thereby avoided Radical Republican rule.

Coalitions of Democrats and moderate Republicans won in Tennessee in 1869 and in Missouri in 1870. Elsewhere leading Democrats grudgingly accepted black suffrage but attacked Republicans for raising taxes, increasing state spending, and being corrupt. Such campaigns brought a positive response from many taxpayers because southern tax rates had risen significantly to support the new schools, railroad subsidies, and other modernizing programs. Several victories by so-called **Redeemers** and New Departure Democrats in the early 1870s also coincided with renewed terrorist activity aimed at Republicans. The worst single incident occurred in 1873. A group of armed freedmen fortified the town of Colfax, Louisiana, to hold off Democrats who were planning to seize the county government. After a three-week siege, well-armed whites overcame the black defenders and killed 280 African Americans. Leading

Democrats rarely endorsed such bloodshed, but they reaped political advantages from it.

The New Departure movement coincided with a nationwide division within the Republican Party. The Liberal Republican movement attracted moderates, concerned that the Radicals had gone too far. Others opposed Grant on issues unrelated to Reconstruction, especially growing evidence of corruption.

Horace Greeley, editor of the *New York Daily Tribune*, won the Liberal nomination for president in 1872. An opponent of slavery before the Civil War, Greeley had given strong support to the Fourteenth and Fifteenth Amendments. But he had sometimes taken puzzling positions, including a willingness to let the South secede. One political observer described him as "honest, but . . . conceited, fussy, and foolish." Greeley had long ripped the Democrats in his newspaper columns, but the Democrats nonetheless nominated him in an effort to defeat Grant. Grant won convincingly, carrying 56 percent of the vote and winning every northern state and ten of the sixteen southern and border states (see Map 15.2).

---

coalition An alliance, especially a temporary one of different people or groups.

■ **Redeemers** Southern Democrats who hoped to bring the Democratic Party back into power and to suppress Black Reconstruction.

The Politics of Terror: The "Mississippi Plan"

By 1872, nearly all southern whites had abandoned the Republicans, and Black Reconstruction had ended in several states. African Americans, however, maintained their Republican loyalties. As Democrats worked to unite southern whites behind their banner of white supremacy, the South polarized politically along racial lines. Elections in 1874 proved disastrous for Republicans: Democrats won more than two-thirds of the South's seats in the House of Representatives and "redeemed" several more states.

Terrorism against black Republicans and their remaining white allies played a role in some Democratic victories in 1874. Where the Klan had worn disguises and ridden at night, by 1874 Democrats often formed rifle companies, put on red-flannel shirts, and marched and drilled in public. In some areas, armed whites prevented African Americans from voting or terrorized prominent Republicans, especially African American Republicans.

Republicans in 1874 lost support in the North because of scandals within the Grant administration and because a major economic depression was producing high unemployment. In the 1874 elections, Democrats won control of the House of Representatives for the first time since the 1850s and could block any new Reconstruction proposals.

During 1875 in Mississippi, political violence reached such levels that the use of terror to overthrow Reconstruction became known as the Mississippi Plan. Democratic rifle clubs broke up Republican meetings and attacked Republican leaders. One black Mississippian described the election as "the most violent time we have ever seen." When Mississippi's carpetbagger governor, Adelbert Ames, requested federal help, President Grant declined. Grant feared that the southern Reconstruction governments had become so discredited that further federal military intervention might endanger the election prospects of Republican candidates in the North.

depression Period of economic contraction, characterized by decreasing business activity, falling prices, and high unemployment.

■ Mississippi Plan Use of threats, violence, and lynching by Mississippi Democrats in 1875 to intimidate Republicans and bring the Democratic Party to power.

■ Rutherford B. Hayes (1822–1893) Seventeenth president of the United States; Ohio governor and former Union general, president when Reconstruction ended.

■ Compromise of 1877 Name applied by historians to discussions around the disputed presidential election of 1876; in the end, Republicans gained the presidency, and southern Democrats received some concessions.

Democrats swept the Mississippi elections, winning four-fifths of the state legislature. When the legislature convened, it impeached and removed from office Alexander Davis, the black Republican lieutenant governor, on grounds no more serious than those brought against Andrew Johnson. Facing similar action, Governor Ames resigned and left the state. Ames had foreseen the result during the campaign when he wrote, "A revolution has taken place—by force of arms."

The Troubled Presidential Election of 1876

In 1876, on the centennial of American independence, the nation stumbled through a deeply troubled—and potentially dangerous—presidential election. As revelations of corruption in the Grant administration multiplied, both parties sought candidates known for their integrity. The Democrats nominated Samuel J. Tilden, governor of New York, who had fought political corruption in New York City. The Republicans selected Rutherford B. Hayes, a Civil War general and governor of Ohio. During the campaign in the South, intimidation of Republicans, both black and white, continued in many places.

Early election reports indicated a victory for Tilden (see Map 15.3). In addition to the border states and South, he also carried New York, New Jersey, and Indiana. Tilden received 51 percent of the popular vote versus 48 percent for Hayes.

State Republican officials still controlled the counting and reporting of ballots in South Carolina, Florida, and Louisiana. Charging voting fraud, Republican election boards in those states rejected enough ballots so that the official count gave Hayes narrow majorities and thus a one-vote margin of victory in the Electoral College. Crying fraud in return, Democratic officials in those states submitted their own versions of the vote count. Angry Democrats vowed to see Tilden inaugurated, by force if necessary. Some Democratic newspapers ran headlines that read "Tilden or War."

For the first time, Congress faced the problem of disputed electoral votes that could decide the outcome of an election. To resolve the challenges, Congress created a commission of five senators, five representatives, and five Supreme Court justices. The Republicans had a one-vote majority on the commission.

As commission hearings droned on through January and into February 1877, informal discussions took place among leading Republicans and Democrats. The result has been called the Compromise of 1877.

Southern Democrats demanded an end to federal intervention in southern politics but insisted on federal subsidies for railroad construction and waterways in the South. And they wanted one of their own

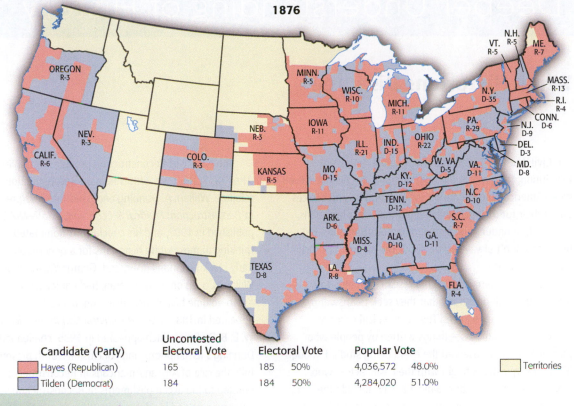

1876

Candidate (Party)	Uncontested Electoral Vote	Electoral Vote		Popular Vote	
Hayes (Republican)	165	185	50%	4,036,572	48.0%
Tilden (Democrat)	184	184	50%	4,284,020	51.0%

Territories

MAP 15.3 Election of 1876
The end of Black Reconstruction in the South combined with Democratic gains in the North to give a popular majority to Samuel Tilden, the Democratic candidate. The disputed electoral vote was ultimately resolved in favor of Rutherford B. Hayes, the Republican. © Cengage Learning.

as postmaster general because that office held the key to most federal patronage. In return, southern Democrats seemed willing to abandon Tilden's claim to the White House. The Compromise of 1877, however, was never set down in one place or agreed to by all parties.

By a straight party vote, the commission confirmed the election of Hayes. Soon after his inauguration, the new president ordered the last of the federal troops withdrawn from the South. The era of a powerful federal government pledged to protect "equality before the law" for all citizens was over. The last three Republican state governments fell in 1877, giving the Democrats, the party of white supremacy, control in every southern state. One Radical journal bitterly concluded that African Americans had been forced "to relinquish the artificial right to vote for the natural right to live." In parts of the South thereafter, election fraud and violence became routine. A Mississippi judge acknowledged in 1890 that "since 1875 . . . we have been preserving the ascendancy of the white people by . . . stuffing ballot boxes, committing perjury and here and there in the state carrying the elections by fraud and violence."

Reconstruction was over. The Civil War was more than ten years in the past. Many moderate Republicans had hoped that the Fourteenth and Fifteenth Amendments and the Civil Rights Act would guarantee black rights without a continuing federal presence in the South. Southern Democrats persistently argued—on paltry evidence—that carpetbaggers and scalawags were all corrupt, that they manipulated black voters, that African American officeholders were ignorant and illiterate, and that southern Democrats wanted only honest self-government. The truth of the situation made little difference.

Northern Democrats had always opposed Reconstruction and readily adopted the southern Democrats' version of reality. Such portrayals found growing acceptance among other northerners too, for many had shown their own racial bias when they resisted black suffrage and kept their public schools segregated. In 1875, when Grant refused to use federal troops to protect black rights, he declared that "the whole public are tired out with these . . . outbreaks in the South." He was quoted widely and with approval throughout the North. In addition, a major depression in the mid-1870s, unemployment and labor disputes,

When Historians Disagree

The Civil War and Reconstruction, like the American Revolution, form a dividing point in American history, a time when Americans made important and long-lasting choices about their future. Such dividing points attract historians, who seek to understand such momentous decisions. But historians don't always agree about the meaning of such important events.

When historians approach a research project, they often begin with questions that they seek to answer by examining primary sources. The most typical primary sources are documents—things written by people who participated in or observed the event being studied. Though historians' questions begin with the basic facts—who, what, when, where—they almost always include the more difficult questions of causation and motivation: Why did events unfold as they did? What motivated individuals and groups to make the decisions they made? While historians tend to agree on the facts, they may disagree on causation and motivation, because those questions require judgments about the meaning of documents, the resolution of conflicting sources, and the relative importance of documents. Historians must also decide what weight to give to the views of those on differing sides of an issue; for example, how much weight to give to the perspectives of black leaders of Reconstruction compared to those of their white opponents. Though historians seek to be objective and to understand the past on its own terms, they may unconsciously view the past through the biases and prejudices of their own time.

The history of Reconstruction provides examples. After 1877, southern whites held up Reconstruction as a failure. William A. Dunning endorsed that interpretation in *Reconstruction: Political & Economic, 1865–1877*, published in 1907, and his conclusions dominated the thinking of most white historians for a generation. Early black historians disagreed. George Washington Williams, a Union army veteran, had earlier written a two-volume history of African Americans that appeared in 1882. *Black Reconstruction in America,* by W. E. B. Du Bois, which appeared in 1935, challenged Dunning's assumptions and conclusions. Both presented fully the role of African Americans in Reconstruction and pointed to the accomplishments of Reconstruction state governments and black leaders. Beginning in the 1940s and continuing into the 1960s, as the racial attitudes of many white Americans were challenged and often changed by the civil rights movement (covered in Chapters 25 and 26), white historians increasingly questioned Dunning's views and began to give more attention to the perspectives of the African Americans who had taken part in Reconstruction. Historians today recognize that Reconstruction produced significant changes in southern life and in the life of the nation, and that Reconstruction collapsed partly because of internal flaws, partly because of divisions within the Republican Party, and partly because of the political terrorism unleashed in the South and the refusal of the North to commit the force required to protect the constitutional rights of African Americans.

William Archibald Dunning taught in the history department of Columbia University from 1886 to his death in 1922, and was honored by the presidency of the American Historical Association in 1913 and the presidency of the American Political Science Association in 1921.

Butler Library, Columbia University in the City of New York.

W. E. B. Du Bois combined the life of a scholar with that of an activist for black rights. From 1910 to 1933, in addition to his scholarly writing, he also edited *The Crisis*, the monthly magazine of the National Association for the Advancement of Colored People. *Black Reconstruction* was published in 1935, shortly after he returned to college teaching.

Schomburg Center/Art Resource, NY.

the growth of industry, the emergence of big business, and the development of the West focused the attention of many Americans, including many members of Congress, on economic issues.

Some Republicans, to be certain, kept the faith of their abolitionist and Radical forebears and hoped the federal government might again protect black rights. But though Republicans routinely condemned violations of black rights after 1877, few Republicans showed much interest in using federal power to prevent such outrages.

After Reconstruction

After 1877, southern Democrats moved to establish new systems of politics and race relations. They worked to reduce taxes, dismantle Reconstruction legislation and agencies, and eliminate meaningful black participation in politics. They also began the process of turning the South into a one-party region, a situation that reached its fullest development around 1900 and persisted through the 1950s.

Voting and officeholding by African Americans did not cease in 1877, but without federal enforcement of black rights, the threat of violence and the potential for economic retaliation by landlords and merchants sharply reduced meaningful political involvement. Efforts to mobilize black voters posed dangers to candidates and voters, and many black political leaders concluded that their political survival depended on favors from influential white Republicans or even from Democratic leaders. The public schools survived, segregated and underfunded, but

nonetheless presenting important opportunities. Many Reconstruction-era laws remained on the books, and for a time many theaters, bars, restaurants, hotels, streetcars, and railroads continued to serve African Americans without discrimination. White supremacy had been established by force of arms, however, and blacks exercised their rights at the sufferance of the dominant whites.

After 1877, Reconstruction was held up as a failure. Although far from accurate, the southern whites' version of Reconstruction—that conniving carpetbaggers and scalawags had manipulated ignorant freedmen—appealed to many white Americans throughout the nation, and it gained widespread acceptance among many novelists, journalists, and historians. Thomas Dixon's popular novel *The Clansman* (1905) inspired the highly influential film *The Birth of a Nation* (1915). Historically inaccurate and luridly racist, the book and the movie portrayed Klan members as heroes who rescued the white South, and especially white southern women, from domination and debauchery at the hands of depraved freedmen and carpetbaggers. (For the response of historians, see the A Deeper Understanding of History feature.)

Today we recognize that Reconstruction produced many positive changes both in the South and elsewhere. The creation of public schools was among the important changes in southern life produced by the Reconstruction state governments. The Fourteenth and Fifteenth Amendments eventually provided the constitutional leverage to restore the principle of equality before the law that so concerned the Radicals.

Individual Voices

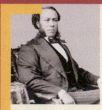

CONGRESSMAN JOSEPH RAINEY,
from a Speech Supporting the Ku Klux Klan Act

In the House of Representatives, Joseph Rainey was a consistent defender of African Americans and a strong proponent for federal protection for all those southerners who were attacked because they were Republicans. These are excerpts from his speech in support of the Ku Klux Klan act.
Library of Congress.

1 Where does Rainey fix the blame for the crimes he describes?

2 How does Rainey respond to arguments that military rule has no place in a republic? How does he indicate that he is not just appealing for protection of African Americans?

3 How does Rainey define the problem as one that goes to the very center of what it means to be an American?

A remedy is needed to meet the evil now existing in most of the southern States, but especially in that one which I have the honor to represent in part, the State of South Carolina. The enormity of the crimes constantly perpetrated there finds no parallel in the history of this Republic in her very darkest days. . . . The prevailing spirit of the Southron [white southerner] is either to rule or to ruin. Voters must perforce succumb to their wishes or else risk life itself. . . . **1**

Daily reports come to us of men throughout the country being whipped; of school-houses for colored children being closed, and of parties being driven from their houses and their families. . . . The law affords no protection for life and property in this county, and the sooner the country knows it and finds a remedy for it, the better it will be. Better a thousand times the rule of the bayonet than the humiliating lash of the Ku Klux and the murderous bullet of the midnight assassin. . . . This protection is equally desired for those loyal whites . . . who are now undergoing persecution simply on account of their activity in carrying out Union principles and loyal sentiments in the South. . . . **2**

In the dawn of our freedom our young Republic was widely recognized and proudly proclaimed to the world the refuge, the safe asylum of the oppressed of all lands. Shall it be said that at this day, through mere indifference and culpable neglect, this grand boast of ours is become a mere form of words, an utter fraud? I earnestly hope not! And yet, if we stand with folded arms and idle hands, while the cries of our oppressed brethren sound in our ears, what will it be but a proof to all men that we are utterly unfit for our glorious mission, unworthy of our noble privileges, as the greatest of republics, the champions of freedom for all men? **3**

Study Tools

SUMMARY

At the end of the Civil War, the nation faced difficult choices regarding the restoration of the defeated South and the future of the freed people. Committed to ending slavery, President Lincoln nevertheless chose a lenient approach to restoring states to the Union, partly to persuade southerners to abandon the Confederacy and accept emancipation. When Johnson became president, he took an even more lenient approach.

The end of slavery brought new opportunities for African Americans, whether or not they had been slaves. Taking advantage of the opportunities that freedom opened, they tried to create independent lives for themselves, and they developed social institutions that helped to define black communities. Because few managed to acquire land of their own, most became either sharecroppers or wage laborers. White southerners also experienced economic dislocation, and many also became sharecroppers. Most white southerners expected to keep African Americans in a subordinate role and initially used black codes and violence toward that end.

In reaction against the black codes and violence, Congress took control of Reconstruction and passed the Civil Rights Act of 1866, the Fourteenth Amendment, and the Reconstruction Acts of 1867. An attempt to remove Johnson from the presidency was unsuccessful.

Additional federal Reconstruction measures included the Fifteenth Amendment, laws against the Ku Klux Klan, and the Civil Rights Act of 1875. Several of these measures strengthened the federal government at the expense of the states.

Enfranchised freedmen, white and black northerners who moved to the South, and some southern whites created a southern Republican Party that governed most southern states for a time. The most lasting contribution of these state governments was the creation of public school systems. Like government officials elsewhere, however, some southern politicians fell prey to corruption.

In the late 1860s, many southern Democrats chose a "New Departure": they grudgingly accepted some features of Reconstruction and sought to recapture control of state governments. By the mid-1870s, however, southern politics turned almost solely on race. The 1876 presidential election was very close and hotly disputed. In the end, Hayes took office and ended Reconstruction. Without federal protection for their civil rights, African Americans faced terrorism, violence, and even death if they challenged their subordinate role. With the end of Reconstruction, the South entered an era of white supremacy in politics and government, the economy, and social relations.

CHRONOLOGY
Reconstruction

1863	Emancipation Proclamation
1864	Lincoln reelected
1865	Freedmen's Bureau created
	Civil War ends
	Andrew Johnson becomes president
	Thirteenth Amendment (abolishing slavery) ratified
1866	Ku Klux Klan formed
	Congress takes control over Reconstruction
1867	Military Reconstruction Act
1868	Impeachment and acquittal of President Johnson
	Fourteenth Amendment (defining citizenship) ratified
	Grant elected president
1869–1870	Victories of "New Departure" Democrats in some southern states
1870	Fifteenth Amendment (guaranteeing voting rights) ratified
1870–1871	Ku Klux Klan Acts
1872	Grant reelected
1875	Civil Rights Act of 1875
	Mississippi Plan ends Reconstruction in Mississippi
1876	Disputed presidential election
1877	Compromise of 1877; Hayes becomes president
	End of Reconstruction

Study Tools

FOCUS QUESTIONS

If you have mastered this chapter, you should be able to answer these questions and to explain the terms that follow the questions.

1. What did Presidents Lincoln and Johnson seek to accomplish for the South? How did white southerners respond to those efforts?

2. What seem to have been the leading objectives among freed people as they explored their new opportunities?

3. How do the differing responses of freed people and southern whites show different understandings of the significance of emancipation?

4. Why did congressional Republicans take control over Reconstruction policy? How successful were they?

5. How did the Fourteenth and Fifteenth Amendments change the nature of the federal union?

6. What major groups made up the Republican Party in the South during Reconstruction? Compare their reasons for being Republicans, their relative sizes, and their objectives.

7. What were the most lasting results of the Republican state administrations?

8. What major factors brought about the end of Reconstruction? Evaluate their relative significance.

KEY TERMS

Reconstruction   *p. 370*

Abraham Lincoln   *p. 371*

Frederick Douglass   *p. 371*

Radical Republicans   *p. 371*

Thirteenth Amendment   *p. 373*

Andrew Johnson   *p. 373*

Freedmen's Bureau   *p. 376*

Ku Klux Klan   *p. 380*

Fourteenth Amendment   *p. 381*

Elizabeth Cady Stanton   *p. 381*

Susan B. Anthony   *p. 381*

Fifteenth Amendment   *p. 384*

Civil Rights Act of 1875   *p. 385*

Black Reconstruction   *p. 385*

New Departure   *p. 388*

Redeemers   *p. 389*

Mississippi Plan   *p. 390*

Rutherford B. Hayes   *p. 390*

Compromise of 1877   *p. 390*

SUGGESTED RESOURCES

W. E. B. Du Bois. *Black Reconstruction in America* (1935; reprint ed., Oxford University Press, 2007). This 2007 edition of Du Bois's classic includes an introduction that places Du Bois's work into the context of work by subsequent historians.

Eric Foner. *Reconstruction: America's Unfinished Revolution, 1863–1877* (1988; reprint ed., Harper, 2002). Still the standard account after nearly a quarter century; thorough and detailed (700-plus pages).

Gilder Lehrman Institute of American History. "Reconstruction," http://www.gilderlehrman.org/history-by-era/civil-war-and-reconstruction-1861-1877/reconstruction. Includes essays by prominent historians, primary sources, and suggestions for additional reading.

Michael Perman. *Emancipation and Reconstruction*, 2nd ed. (Harlan Davidson, 2003). A good, brief, and well-written introduction to the topics.

Public Broadcasting System. "Reconstruction: The Second Civil War," *The American Experience*, http://www.pbs.org/wgbh/amex/reconstruction/index.html. A large collection of primary sources and photographs, intended to accompany the PBS program of the same name. The film itself is not available online.

16

The Nation Industrializes, 1865–1900

CHAPTER OUTLINE

Foundation for Industrialization

Resources, Skills, Capital, and New Federal Policies
The Transformation of Agriculture

The Dawn of Big Business

Railroads: The First Big Business
Railroads, Investment Bankers, and "Morganization"
Andrew Carnegie and the Age of Steel
Survival of the Fittest?

Expansion of the Industrial Economy

Standard Oil: Model for Monopoly
Thomas Edison and the Power of Innovation
Selling to the Nation
Economic Concentration in Consumer-Goods Industries
Seeking a New South

Incorporating the West into the National Economy

War for the West
Transforming the West: Railroads, Cattle, and Mining
Transforming the West: Farming and Lumbering
Water and Western Development

Boom and Bust: The Economy from the Civil War to World War I

Growth and Depression in the 1870s and 1880s
Economic Collapse and Depression in the 1890s
The "Merger Movement"

INDIVIDUAL VOICES: *John D. Rockefeller Explains the Inevitability of Big Business*

Study Tools

INDIVIDUAL CHOICES

John D. Rockefeller

For a generation of Americans, the name Rockefeller was synonymous with aggressive competition and monopoly. John D. Rockefeller was born in upper New York State in 1839 and educated in Cleveland, Ohio. After working as a bookkeeper, he became a partner in a grain and livestock business in 1859 and earned substantial profits during the Civil War. He soon shifted his attention to the oil-refining business, a major new enterprise in Cleveland.

The refining business was uncertain and highly competitive, and Rockefeller set out to stabilize his operations by reducing the competition. He joined with others to create a **cartel**, and then negotiated an astounding deal with the railroads that served Cleveland. Because the three major railroads serving Cleveland were highly competitive among themselves, Tom Scott, head of the Pennsylvania Railroad, proposed a plan that would have guaranteed each railroad a stable share of the shipping by the Rockefeller cartel, called the South Improvement Company. Scott proposed that the three railroad companies would double

Photo by Time Life Pictures/Mansell/Time Life Pictures/Getty Images.

their prices for carrying petroleum products to $2.56 per barrel, but would give the South Improvement Company a rebate of $1.06 per barrel and also pay the South Improvement Company $1.06 per barrel for petroleum products that any other petroleum refining company shipped on the railroads! The railroads were also to provide the South Improvement Company with complete information on all petroleum products shipped by its competitors. In return, the South Improvement Company would divide its business among the three railroads, with the Pennsylvania Railroad getting a double share.

When news of this leaked out in 1872, other refining companies raised a great outcry, which led the railroad companies to promise to treat all shippers equally. Rockefeller pursued other means to reduce competition. Soon, though, Rockefeller's Standard Oil still managed to receive favorable treatment from the railroads and also controlled 90 percent of the refining capacity in the entire country, making it one of a few genuine monopolies of the era (see the Individual Voices feature at the end of this chapter). Rockefeller emerged as the first American billionaire. After his retirement in the mid-1890s, he devoted much of his attention to giving away his fortune, especially for research.

Rockfeller's rise to wealth came amidst an economy that was being dramatically and profoundly transformed. In 1865 many Americans probably anticipated economic growth, but few imagined that steel production could increase a thousand times by 1900, or that railroads could operate nearly six times as many miles of track, or that farmers could triple their harvests. These economic changes and many others were the result of decisions by many individuals—where to invest, whether to expand production, how to react to a business competitor, whom to trust.

Americans also made choices about competition and cooperation. As the industrial economy took off, many people found themselves in a love–hate relationship with competition. Andrew Carnegie, leader of the new steel industry, loved it, arguing that competition "insures the survival of the fittest" and "insures the future progress of the race" by producing the highest quality, largest quantity, and lowest prices. Other entrepreneurs saw competition as the most unpredictable factor they faced and a serious constraint on economic progress. Carnegie's zeal for competition was unusual. Although many entrepreneurs publicly applauded the idea of the "survival of

the fittest," most loved competition only in the abstract and preferred to find alternatives to it in their own business affairs.

Other Americans also found themselves making choices regarding cooperation. Individualism was deeply entrenched in the American psyche, yet the increasing complexity of the economy presented repeated opportunities for cooperation. Railroad executives, as in the example of the South Improvement Company, sometimes cooperated by dividing a market rather than competing in it. Wage earners sometimes joined together to demand better wages or working conditions. The result of these many decisions was the industrialization of the nation and the transformation of the economy.

FOUNDATION FOR INDUSTRIALIZATION

☆ *What factors encouraged economic growth and industrial development after the Civil War?*

By 1865, conditions in the United States were ripe for rapid industrialization. Abundant natural resources, a capable workforce, an agricultural base that produced enough food for a large urban population, and favorable governmental policies combined to lay the foundation.

Resources, Skills, Capital, and New Federal Policies

At the end of the Civil War, entrepreneurs could draw on vast and virtually untapped natural resources.

◼ **cartel** A group of separate companies within an industry that cooperate to control the production, pricing, and marketing of goods within that industry; also called a pool.

entrepreneur A person who takes on the risks of creating, organizing, and managing a business enterprise.

Americans had long since plowed the fertile farmland of the Midwest (where corn and wheat dominated) and the South (where cotton was king). They had just begun to farm the rich soils of Minnesota, Nebraska, Kansas, Iowa, and the Dakotas, as well as the productive valleys of California and Oregon. Through the central part of the nation stretched vast grasslands that received too little rain for most farming but were well suited for grazing. The Pacific Northwest, the western Great Lakes region, and the South all held extensive forests untouched by the lumberman's saw.

The nation was also rich in mineral resources. Before the Civil War, the iron **industry** had developed in Pennsylvania, where there was easy access to iron ore and coal. Pennsylvania was also the site of early efforts to tap underground pools of crude oil. The California gold rush, beginning in 1848, had drawn many people west, and some of them found great riches. At the end of the war, other minerals lay unused or undiscovered across the country, including iron ore, coal, oil, gold and silver, and copper. Many of these natural resources were far from population centers, and their use awaited adequate transportation facilities. Exploitation of some of these resources also required new technologies.

A skilled and experienced workforce was essential for economic growth. In the 1790s and early 1800s, New Englanders had developed manufacturing systems based on **interchangeable parts** (first used for guns and clocks) and factories for making cotton cloth. These accomplishments gave them a reputation for "Yankee ingenuity"—a talent for devising new tools and inventive methods. Such skills and problem-solving abilities were key ingredients in nearly all large-scale manufacturing because early factories usually relied on skilled **artisans** to supervise less-skilled workers in assembling products. Some of the early artisans and factory owners came from Great Britain, the world's first industrial nation.

Another crucial element for industrialization was capital. Before the Civil War, capital became centered in the seaport cities of the Northeast—Boston, New York, and Philadelphia, especially—where prosperous merchants invested their profits in banks and factories. Banks were important instruments for mobilizing capital. Before the war, some bankers had begun to specialize in arranging financing for large-scale enterprises, and some had opened offices in Britain to tap sources of capital there. **Stock exchanges** had also developed long before the Civil War as important institutions for raising capital for new ventures.

Still another important element for rapid economic development was favorable governmental policies. When Republicans took command of the federal government in 1861, they were immediately faced with the need to wage war against the Confederacy.

At the same time, however, they forged new policies to stimulate economic growth, beginning with a new **protective tariff** in 1861. The tariff increased the price of imports to equal or exceed the price of American-made goods, thereby protecting domestic products from foreign competition and encouraging investment in manufacturing. Tariff rates changed periodically, but the protective tariff remained central to federal economic policy for more than a half-century. Republicans also passed a series of measures to stabilize and centralize the banking and currency systems.

New federal land policies, too, stimulated economic growth. Before the Civil War, the federal government claimed a billion acres of land—half of the land area of the nation—as federal property, or the **public domain**. Republicans used the public domain to encourage economic development. The **Homestead Act** (1862) provided that any person could receive free as much as 160 acres (a quarter of a square mile) of government land by building a house, living on the land for five years, and farming it. The **Land-Grant College Act** (1862)—often called the Morrill Act for its sponsor, Senator Justin Morrill of Vermont—gave land to each state to fund a public university, which was required to provide education in engineering and agriculture. Also in 1862, Congress approved land grants for the first transcontinental railroad, and more land grants to railroads followed.

industry A basic unit of business activity in which the various participants do similar activities; for example, the railroad industry consists of railroad companies and the firms and factories that supply their equipment.

interchangeable parts Identical mechanical parts that can be substituted for one another.

artisan A skilled worker, whether self-employed or working for wages.

stock exchange A place where people buy and sell stocks (shares in the ownership of companies); stockholders may participate in election of the company's directors and share in the company's profits.

■ **protective tariff** A tax placed on imported goods for the purpose of raising the price of imports as high as or higher than the prices for the same item produced within the nation.

public domain Land claimed by the federal government.

■ **Homestead Act** Act of Congress in 1862 offering 160 acres of designated public lands to any citizen or any immigrant who declared his or her intent to become a citizen and who lived on and improved the land for five years.

■ **Land-Grant College Act** Act of Congress in 1862 that gave land to states to be used to fund public universities that were to offer courses in engineering and agriculture and to train military officers.

© Cengage Learning.

MAP 16.1 Expansion of Agriculture, 1860–1900
The amount of improved farmland more than doubled during these years as western lands were brought under cultivation and other land was cultivated more intensely.

The Transformation of Agriculture

The expanding economy rested on a highly productive agricultural base. Improved transportation—canals early in the nineteenth century and railroads later—speeded the expansion of agriculture by making it possible to move agricultural produce over long distances. Before the Civil War, farmers had developed 407 million acres into productive farmland. During the next forty years, this figure more than doubled, to 841 million acres. Map 16.1 indicates where this growth occurred.

The Homestead Act contributed to the rapid settlement of Kansas, Nebraska, the Dakotas, and Minnesota. Between 1862 and 1890, 48 million acres passed from government ownership to private hands in this way. Other federally owned land could be purchased for as little as $1.25 per acre, and much more was obtained at this bargain price than was acquired free under the Homestead Act.

Production of leading commercial crops increased rapidly. Though the total number of acres in farmland doubled, the number of acres planted in corn, wheat, and cotton more than tripled. New farming methods increased harvests even more—corn by 264 percent, wheat by 252 percent, and cotton by 383 percent. Through these years, farm output grew more than twice as much as the population.

As production of major crops rose, prices for them fell. Though several factors contributed to this situation, the most obvious was that supply outpaced demand. Production increased more rapidly than the population (which determined the demand within the nation) and the demand from other countries. When American farmers received less for their crops, they often raised *more* in an effort to maintain the same level of income. To increase their harvests, they bought fertilizers and elaborate machinery. And the more the farmers raised, the lower prices fell—and with them, the economic well-being of many farmers.

New machinery greatly increased the amount of land one person could farm. A single farmer with a hand tool could harvest 2 acres of wheat in a day. Using the McCormick reaper (first produced in 1849), a single farmer and a team of horses could harvest 2 acres in an hour. For other crops too, a person with modern machinery could farm two or three times as much land as a farmer fifty years before.

Agricultural expansion also stimulated the farm equipment industry and, in turn, the iron and steel industry. Agricultural exports—cotton, tobacco, wheat, meat—spurred oceanic shipping and shipbuilding, and increased shipbuilding meant a greater demand for iron and steel. Railroads played a crucial role in the expansion and commercialization of agriculture by carrying farm products to distant markets and transporting fertilizer and machinery from factories to farming regions.

THE DAWN OF BIG BUSINESS

☆ *What was the significance of the railroad and steel industries in the new industrial economy that emerged after the Civil War?*

☆ *How did investment bankers such as J. P. Morgan contribute to the new industrial economy?*

To many Americans of the late nineteenth century, nothing symbolized economic growth so effectively as a locomotive—a huge, powerful, noisy, smoke-belching machine barreling forward at great speed. Railroads set much of the pace for economic expansion after the Civil War. Growth of the rail network stimulated industries that supplied materials to the railroads—especially steel and coal—and industries that relied on railroads to connect them to the emerging national economy. Railroad companies also came to symbolize "big business"—companies of great size, employing thousands of workers, operating over large geographic areas—and some Americans began to fear their power.

Railroads: The First Big Business

Before the Civil War, much of the nation's commerce moved on rivers, canals, and coastal waterways. At the end of the Civil War, the nation still lacked a

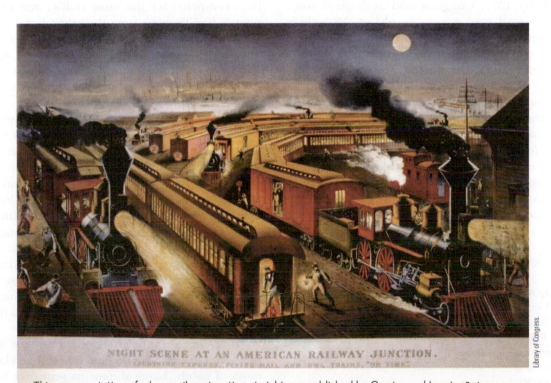

NIGHT SCENE AT AN AMERICAN RAILWAY JUNCTION.

Library of Congress.

This representation of a busy railway junction at night was published by Currier and Ives in 1876. By then, such scenes were increasingly common in larger towns and cities. Also by then, many Americans were coming to equate the locomotive—a huge, powerful, noisy, smoke-belching machine—with economic growth and progress.

comprehensive national transportation network. Railroads clearly had that potential, but railway companies operated on tracks of varying **gauges**, which made the transfer of railcars from one line to another impossible. Few railway bridges crossed major rivers. Until 1869, no railroad connected the eastern half of the country to the booming Pacific Coast region.

By the mid-1880s, the elements were in place for a national rail network. The first transcontinental rail line was completed in 1869, connecting California to Omaha, Nebraska, and ultimately to eastern cities. Within the next twenty-five years, four more rail lines linked the Pacific Coast to the eastern half of the nation. Between 1865 and 1890, railroads grew from 35,000 miles of track to 167,000 miles (see Map 16.2). Major rivers were bridged, and new inventions increased the speed, carrying capacity, and efficiency of trains. In 1886 the last major lines converted to a standard gauge, making it possible to transfer railcars from one line to another simply by throwing a switch. Entrepreneurs could now plan in terms of a national economic system in which raw materials and finished products moved easily from one region to another. Railroads, especially in the West, expanded with generous governmental assistance. In the **Pacific Railway Act** of 1862, Congress provided the Union Pacific and Central Pacific companies not only with sizable loans but also with 10 square miles of the public domain for every mile of track laid—an amount soon doubled. By 1871, Congress had authorized some seventy railroad land grants, involving 128 million acres—approximately equal in size to Colorado and Wyoming together—though not all companies qualified to claim their entire grants. Most railroads sold their land to raise capital for railroad operations. By encouraging farmers, businesses, or organizations to develop the land, railroad companies tried to build up the economies along their tracks and thereby boost demand for their freight trains to haul supplies to new settlers and carry settlers' products (wheat, cattle, lumber, ore) to market.

The expansion of railroads created the potential for a nationwide market, stimulated the economic development of the West, and created a demand for iron, steel, locomotives, and similar products. Railroad companies also provided an organizational model for newly developing industrial enterprises.

Because they spanned such great distances and managed so many employees and so much equipment, railroads encountered problems of scale that few companies had faced before but that other industrial entrepreneurs soon had to address. Railroad companies also required a higher degree of coordination and long-range planning than most previous businesses. Earlier companies typically operated at a single location, but railroads functioned over long distances and at multiple sites. Financial transactions carried on over hundreds of miles by scores of employees required a centralized accounting office. One result was development of a company bureaucracy of clerks, accountants, managers, and agents. Railroads became training grounds for administrators, some of whom later entered other industries. Indeed, the experience of the railroads was central in defining the subject of business administration when it began to be taught in colleges.

Railroads faced higher **fixed costs** than most previous companies. These costs included payments on debts and the expense of maintaining and protecting far-flung equipment and property. To pay fixed costs and keep profits high, railroad companies tried to operate at full capacity whenever possible. Doing so, however, often proved difficult. Where two or more lines competed for the same traffic, one might cut rates to lure business from the other. But if the other company responded with cuts in its rates, neither stood to gain significantly more business, and both took in less income. Competition between railroad companies sometimes became so intense that no line could show a profit.

Some railroad operators chose to defuse intense competition by forming a **pool**. In a pool, the railroads agreed to divide the existing business and not to compete on rates. The most famous was the Iowa Pool, made up of railroads running between Chicago and Omaha, across Iowa. Formed in 1870, the Iowa Pool operated until 1874, and some pooling continued until the mid-1880s. Few pools lasted very long. Often one or more pool members tired of a restricted market share and broke the pool arrangement in an effort to expand, thereby setting off a new price war. When a pooling arrangement became known, it brought loud complaints from customers, who concluded that they paid higher rates because of the pool.

To compete more effectively, railroads adjusted their rates to attract companies that shipped large volumes of goods. Large shipments sent over long distances cost the railroad companies less per mile than small shipments sent over short distances, so companies developed different rate structures for long hauls and short hauls. Thus the largest shippers, with

gauge In this usage, the distance between the two rails making up railroad tracks.

▫ **Pacific Railway Act** Act of Congress in 1862 that gave loans and land to the Central Pacific and Union Pacific Railroad companies to subsidize construction of a rail line between Omaha and the Pacific Coast.

fixed costs Costs that a company must pay even if it closes down all its operations—for example, interest on loans, debt payments, and property taxes.

pool An agreement among businesses in the same industry to divide up the market and charge equal prices instead of competing; another name for a cartel.

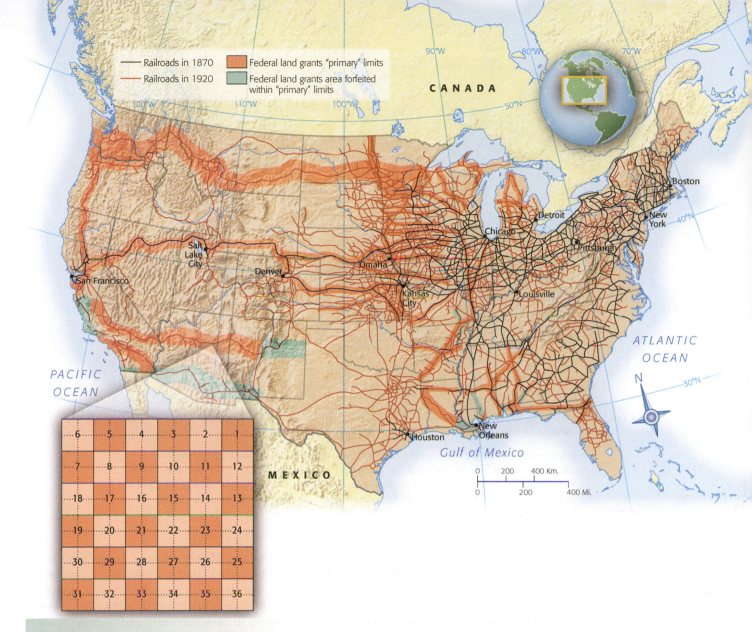

MAP 16.2 **Railroad Expansion and Railroad Land Grants**
Railroad expansion produced the transportation base for an industrial economy. Note the high density of rail lines in the Northeast and Midwest. This map also shows federal land grants to railroads. The map at lower left shows a typical survey township within the area of a railroad land grant. The railroad company typically received every odd-numbered section (one square mile). Within the land grant, the price of the remaining federal land was doubled. Thus, the total income to the federal government was only slightly affected by the land grant. © Cengage Learning

the power to secure low rates, could often ship more cheaply than small businesses and individual farmers. Railroad companies defended the differences on the basis of differences in costs, but small shippers who paid high prices saw themselves as victims of rate discrimination.

Railroads viewed state and federal governments as sources of valuable subsidies. At the same time, they constantly guarded against efforts by their customers to use government to restrict or regulate their enterprises—by outlawing rate discrimination, for example. Companies sometimes campaigned openly to secure

the election of friendly representatives and senators and to defeat unfriendly candidates. They maintained well-organized operations to **lobby** public officials in Washington, D.C., and in state capitals. Most railroad companies issued free passes to public officials— a practice that reformers attacked as bribery. Some railroads won reputations as the most influential

lobby To try to influence the thinking of public officials for or against a specific cause.

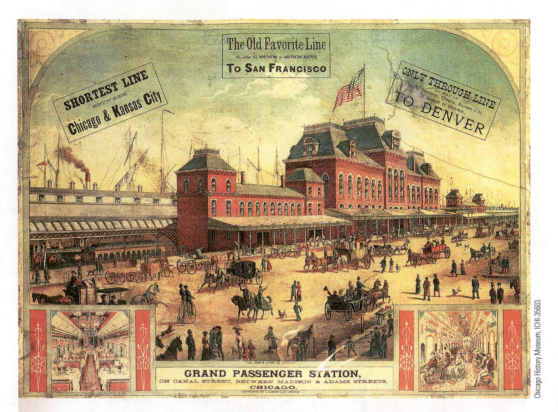

Chicago was perhaps the most important single center for the nation's rail traffic in the late nineteenth century. This lithograph shows Chicago's Grand Passenger Station in 1880 and advertises some of the many rail connections possible through this station—to Kansas City, Denver, and San Francisco. Note also the many forms of street transportation in front of the station, including a coach, several varieties of carriages, and bicycles.

political power in entire states—the Southern Pacific in California, for example, or the Santa Fe in Kansas.

Stories of railroad officials bribing politicians became commonplace after the Civil War. The Crédit Mobilier scandal (discussed in Chapter 18) touched some of the most influential members of Congress in the 1870s. A decade later, Collis P. Huntington of the Southern Pacific Railroad candidly explained his expectations regarding public officials: "If you have to pay money to have the right thing done, it is only just and fair to do it." For Huntington, "the right thing" meant favorable treatment for his company.

Politically powerful or not, railroads produced significant change. Between 1850 and 1890, railroads transformed Chicago from a town of thirty thousand residents to the nation's second-largest city. Chicago emerged as the rail center not just of the Midwest but of much of the nation. By 1880, more than twenty

railroad lines and 15,000 miles of tracks connected Chicago with nearly all of the United States and much of Canada. The boom in railroad construction during the 1880s only reinforced the city's prominence. Entrepreneurs in manufacturing and commerce soon developed new enterprises based on Chicago's unrivaled location at the hub of a great transportation network.

Chicago's rail connections made it the logical center for the new business of **mail-order sales**. Central location and rail connections also made Chicago a major manufacturing center. By the 1880s, Chicago's factories produced more farm equipment than those of any other city, and its iron and steel production rivaled that of Pittsburgh. Other leading Chicago industries produced railway cars and equipment, metal products, a wide variety of machinery, and clothing. The city also claimed the title of the world's largest grain market.

Location and rail lines also made Chicago the nation's largest center for **meatpacking**. Livestock from across the Midwest and as far as southern Texas was unloaded in Chicago's Union Stockyards—400 acres of railroad sidings, chutes, and pens filled with cattle, hogs, and sheep. Huge slaughterhouses flanking the stockyards received a steady stream of live animals

mail-order sales The business of selling goods using the mail; mail-order houses send out catalogs, customers submit orders, and products are delivered, all by mail.

meatpacking The business of slaughtering animals and preparing their meat for sale as food.

and disgorged a steady stream of fresh, canned, and processed meat. The development in the 1870s of refrigeration for railroad cars and ships permitted fresh meat to be sent throughout the nation and to Europe.

Railroads, Investment Bankers, and "Morganization"

Railroads expanded significantly in the 1880s, but some lines earned little profit. Some traversed sparsely populated areas of the West. Others spread into areas already saturated by rail service. In the 1880s, a few ambitious, talented, and occasionally unscrupulous railway executives maneuvered to produce great regional railway systems. The Santa Fe and the Southern Pacific, for example, came to dominate the Southwest, and the Great Northern and the Northern Pacific held sway in the Northwest. The Pennsylvania and the New York Central controlled much of the shipping in the Northeast. By consolidating lines within a region, railway executives tried to create more efficient systems with less duplication, fewer price wars, and more dependable profits.

Railroads required far more capital than most manufacturing concerns. Even railroads that received government subsidies required large amounts of private capital. The railroads' huge appetite for capital made them the first American businesses to seek investors on a nationwide and international scale. Those who invested their money could choose to buy either stocks or **bonds**. Sales of railroad stocks provided the major activity for the New York Stock Exchange through the second half of the nineteenth century.

To raise the enormous amount of capital necessary for construction and consolidation, railroad executives turned increasingly to **investment banks**. By the late 1880s, **John Pierpont Morgan** had emerged as the nation's leading investment banker. Born in Connecticut in 1837, son of a successful merchant turned banker, young Morgan attended schools in Switzerland and Germany, then began working in his father's bank in London. In 1857 he moved to New York, to a banking position arranged by his father.

Morgan's experience and growing stature in banking gave him access to capital within the United States and abroad in London and Paris. Investors wanted to put their money where it would be safe and give them a reliable **return**. Morgan therefore tried to stabilize the railroad business, especially the cutthroat rate competition that resulted when several companies served one market. Railroad companies that turned to Morgan for capital found that Morgan wanted a say in their management. He insisted that companies seeking his help reorganize to simplify corporate structures and to combine small lines into larger, centrally controlled systems. He often demanded a seat on the board of directors as well, to guard against

J. P. Morgan, Sr., was at the pinnacle of his power when this photograph was taken around 1900. Morgan seems to exude both power and anger. The anger may reflect his anxiety over being photographed. Morgan was very sensitive about his appearance, especially his nose. He suffered from *acne rosacea*, which made his nose large and misshapen.

Museum of the City of New York/Getty Images.

risky decisions in the future. Some began to refer to this process as "Morganization," and "Morganized" lines soon included some of the largest in the country. A few other investment bankers followed similar patterns.

Andrew Carnegie and the Age of Steel

The new industrial economy rode on steel rails, propelled by steel locomotives. Steel plows broke the

bonds A certificate of debt issued by a government or corporation guaranteeing payment of the original investment plus interest at a specified future date.

investment bank An institution that acts as an agent for corporations issuing stocks and bonds.

■ **John Pierpont Morgan** The most prominent and powerful American investment banker in the late nineteenth century.

return The yield on money that has been invested in an enterprise. Today, companies typically pay a dividend (a proportionate share of the profits) to their stockholders each quarter.

This photograph shows the Carnegie steel works at Homestead, Pennsylvania, about 1905. One of the largest industrial plants in the world, this plant was also the largest producer of pig iron and steel rails in the world in the late nineteenth century.

tough sod of the western prairies. The new skyscrapers relied on steel frames as they boldly shaped urban skylines. Steel defined the age.

Made by combining carbon and molten iron and then burning out impurities, steel has greater strength, resilience, and durability than iron. However, steel was difficult and expensive to make until the 1850s, when Henry Bessemer in England and William Kelly in Kentucky independently discovered ways to make steel in large quantities at a reasonable cost. Even so, the first Bessemer or Kelly process plants did not begin production in the United States until 1864. That year, the entire nation produced only 10,000 tons of steel.

In 1875, just south of Pittsburgh, Pennsylvania, **Andrew Carnegie** used a loan from J. P. Morgan's father's bank to construct the nation's largest steel plant, employing fifteen hundred workers. From then until 1901 (when the plant had grown to more than eight thousand workers), Carnegie held the central place in the steel industry.

Born in Scotland in 1835, Carnegie and his penniless parents came to the United States in 1848. Young Andrew worked in a textile mill, then as a messenger in a **telegraph** office. He soon became a telegraph operator, then personal telegrapher for a high official of the Pennsylvania Railroad, then a superintendent (a high management position) at the age of 25. At the end of the Civil War, he devoted his full attention to iron and steel and quickly applied to his own companies the management lessons he had learned with the railroad.

Carnegie's basic rule was "Cut the prices; scoop the market; run the mills full." An aggressive competitor, he repeatedly cut costs so that he might show a profit while charging less than his rivals. He usually chose to undersell competitors rather than cooperate with them. In 1864, steel rails sold for $126 per ton; by 1875, Carnegie was selling them for $69 per ton. Driven by improved technology and Carnegie's competitiveness, prices fell to $29 a ton in 1885 and less than $20 in the late 1890s. Carnegie was the largest steel manufacturer in the United States, though his company accounted for only a quarter of the nation's production. By 1900, the nation produced nearly 10 million tons of steel each year, more than any other nation.

Carnegie's company was larger and more complex than any manufacturing enterprise in pre–Civil War America. In its own day, however, other companies were as complex, and several challenged it in size. By 1880, five steel companies each had more than fifteen hundred employees, as did several textile mills and a locomotive factory. The size of such operations continued to grow. In 1900 the three largest steel plants each employed eight to ten thousand workers, and seventy other factories employed more than two thousand, producing everything from watches to locomotives, from cotton cloth to processed meat.

Carnegie and other entrepreneurs transformed the organizational structure of manufacturing. They often joined a range of operations formerly conducted by separate businesses—acquisition of raw materials, processing, distribution of finished goods—into one company, achieving **vertical integration**. Companies

■ **Andrew Carnegie** Scottish-born industrialist who made a fortune in steel and believed the rich had a duty to act for the public benefit.

telegraph Apparatus used to communicate at a distance using electrical impulses sent over a wire, usually using Morse code.

It Matters Today

Vertical Integration

Since Rockefeller's day, vertical integration has been a central feature of American manufacturing. Many manufacturing companies have sought a competitive advantage by controlling raw materials and other components of manufacturing (like Carnegie), or distribution and marketing of finished products (like automobile makers in the 1920s), or both (like Rockefeller). More recently, however, many American manufacturers have closed their plants in the United States and contracted with factories in other parts of the world to make their products.

An exception is American Apparel, which proudly calls itself a vertically integrated and sweatshop-free company that designs, produces, and distributes clothing; does its own advertising often without professional models, sometimes using its own employees in its ads; and operates some 250 retail stores worldwide. Through vertical integration, American Apparel argues that it is able to convert a design to a product ready for distribution within a week. All design and production is done in Los Angeles.

- Use an online newspaper to research why some American manufacturers prefer to contract out their manufacturing today rather than follow the nineteenth-century model of vertical integration.
- Why might vertical integration be disadvantageous in the computer industry?

usually developed vertical integration to ensure steady operations and to gain a competitive advantage. Control over the sources and transportation of raw materials, for example, guaranteed a reliable flow of crucial supplies at predictable prices. Such control may also have denied materials to a competitor.

Steel plants stood at one end of a long chain of operations that Carnegie owned or controlled through partnerships: iron ore mines in Minnesota, a fleet of ships that transported iron ore across the Great Lakes, hundreds of miles of railway lines, tens of thousands of acres of coal lands, ovens to produce coke (coal treated to burn at high temperatures), and plants for turning iron ore into bars of crude iron. Carnegie Steel was vertically integrated from the point where the raw materials came out of the ground through the delivery of steel rails and beams.

Survival of the Fittest?

The concentration of power and wealth during the late nineteenth century generated extensive comment and concern. One prominent view on the subject was known as **Social Darwinism**, reflecting its roots in Charles Darwin's work on evolution. In his book *On the Origin of Species* (published in 1859), Darwin concluded that creatures compete with one another for survival in an often inhospitable environment, and the survivors are those that have, through mutation and inheritance, developed traits best adapted to their surroundings. Such adaptation, he suggested, leads to the evolution of different species, each uniquely suited to a particular ecological niche.

Two philosophers, Herbert Spencer, writing in England after 1850, and William Graham Sumner, in the United States after 1874, put their own interpretations on Darwin's reasoning and applied it to the human situation, producing Social Darwinism (a philosophical perspective that bore little relation to Darwin's original work). Social Darwinists contended that competition among people, and by extension among powerful entrepreneurs, produced "progress" through "survival of the fittest" and that unrestrained competition provided the best route for improving humankind and advancing civilization. Further, they argued that efforts to ease the harsh impact of competition only protected the unfit and thereby worked to the long-term disadvantage of all. When applied to government, this notion became a form of **laissez faire**.

The wealthiest entrepreneurs, though, could be inconsistent. Carnegie, for example, embraced Spencer's

vertical integration The process of bringing together into a single company several of the activities involved in creating a manufactured product, such as acquiring raw materials, manufacturing products, and marketing, selling, and distributing finished goods.

◻ **Social Darwinism** The philosophical argument, inspired by Charles Darwin's theory of evolution, that competition in human society produced "the survival of the fittest" and therefore benefited society as a whole; Social Darwinists opposed efforts to regulate competitive practices.

laissez faire The principle that the government should not interfere in the workings of the economy.

A Deeper Understanding of History

Memoirs and Autobiographies

John D. Rockefeller and Andrew Carnegie both wrote books recounting their own lives: Rockefeller's *Random Reminiscences of Men and Events* (as noted in the Individual Voices feature) and Carnegie's *The Autobiography of Andrew Carnegie*.

A person's own account of his or her life is called a *memoir* or an *autobiography*. An autobiography typically recounts a person's entire life, but a memoir may focus on just one or a few topics; a *biography* is a life story written by another person.

Historians are always interested in memoirs and autobiographies. When they examine such sources, they do so critically; that is, they are interested in both finding new information and identifying questionable statements. For example, if a 70-year-old person writes about his childhood—as Carnegie did—there's a possibility that he may not remember the details accurately. Historians are always skeptical when someone presents a long conversation, word for word, in quotation marks, even though it occurred fifty years before—as Carnegie did—because remembering the exact words after such a long period of time is highly unlikely. Problematic statements can stem from one's perspective—describing one's own involvement in an event may involve making assumptions about others' participation, and those assumptions may

not be accurate. So the historian typically looks for as many other primary sources as possible, preferably from the time of the event, to corroborate information from a memoir or autobiography.

Historians once thought of memory as being like a computer's hard disk, on which one might find, or fail to find, a given record, or on which records might become mixed together or truncated. Cognitive psychologists, however, think of memory differently. As historians have learned from psychologists, a new understanding of memory has emerged: the memory of an event is actually constructed with the first telling of the story and that memory is reconstructed each time the story is told. Individuals define and redefine themselves and their relation to other people as they construct and reconstruct their memories of events. Stories—memories—may grow and take on new meanings through frequent repetition.

A person's construction of a memory therefore involves telling a story. Stories are told for different purposes, and psychologists assure us that storytellers fit their story to their audience. Is the storyteller using his or her own life experience to teach a moral lesson to the reader? Carnegie frequently draws moral lessons from his experiences, devoting an entire chapter to promoting his "Gospel of Wealth" (Chapter 19 of *Autobiography*). Is the storyteller trying to put a favorable spin on some event for which he or she was criticized? Carnegie devotes an entire chapter of his autobiography to justifying his behavior during the Homestead strike (page 461); Rockefeller, in his memoirs, tells his version of the formation of Standard Oil (page 409). Is the storyteller using the story to create a particular image of himself or herself for future readers? Historians therefore must not only pay careful attention to a person's telling of his or her life, but also carefully evaluate the storyteller's purpose for the story and compare the person's account to evidence from other primary sources.

A CABINET THAT COULD AFFORD IT.

Library of Congress.

arguments but also preached what he called the **Gospel of Wealth**: the idea that the wealthy should return their riches to the community. Carnegie spent his final eighteen years giving away his fortune. He funded three thousand public library buildings, gave gifts to universities, built Carnegie Hall in New York City, and created several foundations. Like Carnegie and Rockefeller, other great entrepreneurs of that time gave away vast sums to promote learning and research—even as some of them also built ostentatious mansions, threw extravagant parties, and otherwise flaunted their wealth.

Although many Americans subscribed to the vision of Social Darwinism propounded by Spencer and Sumner, many others did not. Entrepreneurs themselves sometimes welcomed some forms of government intervention in the economy—from railroad land grants to the protective tariff to suppression of strikes—although most agreed with the Social Darwinists that government should not assist the poor and destitute.

Other Americans disagreed with the Social Darwinists' equating of laissez faire with progress. Henry George, a San Francisco journalist, pointed out in *Progress and Poverty* (1879) that "amid the greatest accumulations of wealth, men die of starvation," and concluded that "material progress does not merely fail to relieve poverty—it actually produces it." Lester Frank Ward, a sociologist, in 1886 posed a carefully reasoned refutation of Social Darwinism, suggesting that biological competition produces bare survival, not civilization. Civilization, he argued, derived not from "aimless competition" but from rationality and cooperation.

EXPANSION OF THE INDUSTRIAL ECONOMY

★ *How and why did companies expand their operations and control within an industry?*

★ *In what ways was the economy of the South distinctive? What direction did development efforts take in the South?*

Innovative technologies and the integrated railway network began to change the ways that Americans shopped for goods from clothing to food, from tools to home lighting products. John D. Rockefeller took the lead in bringing vertical and horizontal integration to the production of kerosene and other petroleum products, and other entrepreneurs created similar corporate structures in other consumer-goods industries.

Standard Oil: Model for Monopoly

Just as Carnegie provided a model for other steel companies and for heavy industry in general, John D. Rockefeller revolutionized the petroleum industry and provided a model for other consumer-goods industries. The major product of oil refining was kerosene, which transformed home lighting as kerosene lamps replaced candles and oil lamps.

During the Civil War, Rockefeller sold supplies to the Union Army. In 1863, he invested his profits in a **refinery**. After the war, he bought control of more refineries and incorporated them as Standard Oil in 1870. The refining business was relatively easy to enter and highly competitive, and aggressive competition came to define Standard Oil. Recognizing the competitive advantage technology could bring, Rockefeller recruited experts to make Standard the most efficient refiner. He secured favorable treatment from railroads by offering a heavy and predictable volume of traffic. He usually sought to persuade his competitors to join the cartel he was creating. If they refused, he sometimes tried to drive them out of business.

By 1881, following a strategy of **horizontal integration**, Rockefeller and his associates controlled some forty refineries, with about 90 percent of the nation's refining capacity. Standard also moved toward vertical integration by gaining control of oil fields, building transportation facilities (including pipelines and oceangoing tanker ships), and creating retail marketing operations (see Figure 16.1). By the early 1890s, Standard Oil had achieved almost complete vertical and horizontal integration of the American petroleum industry—a virtual **monopoly** over an entire industry.

Between 1879 and 1881, Rockefeller and his associates centralized decision making among all their companies by creating the Standard Oil **Trust**, a new organizational form designed to get around state laws that prohibited one company from owning stock in another. Rockefeller and others who held shares in the individual companies exchanged their stock for trust certificates issued by Standard Oil. Standard Oil

□ **Gospel of Wealth** Andrew Carnegie's idea that possessors of great wealth should spend or otherwise disburse their money to help people help themselves.

refinery An industrial plant that transforms raw materials into finished products; a petroleum refinery processes crude oil to produce a variety of products for use by consumers.

horizontal integration Merging one or more companies doing the same or similar activities as a way of limiting competition or enhancing stability and planning.

monopoly Exclusive control by an individual or company of the production or sale of a product.

trust A legal arrangement in which an individual (the trustor) gives control of property to a person or institution (the trustee); in the late nineteenth century, a legal device to get around state laws limiting the activities of companies chartered in that state, and often synonymous in common use with *monopoly*; first used by John D. Rockefeller to consolidate Standard Oil.

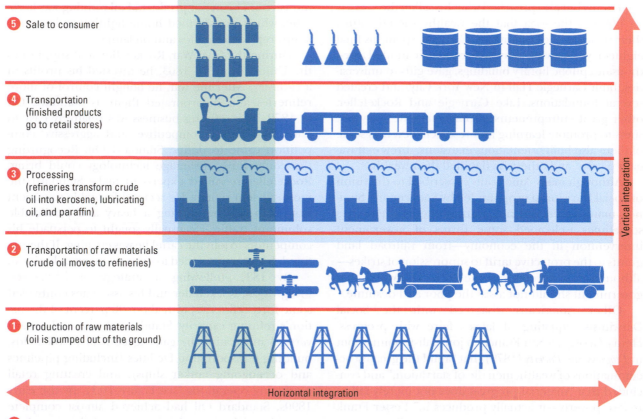

FIGURE 16.1 Vertical and Horizontal Integration of the Petroleum Industry
This diagram represents the petroleum industry before Standard Oil achieved its dominance. The symbols represent different specialized companies, each engaged in different steps in the production of kerosene. Rockefeller entered the industry by investing in a refinery, and first expanded *horizontally* by absorbing several other refineries (indicated by the blue band). His Standard Oil Company then practiced *vertical integration* (indicated by the green band) by acquiring oil leases, oil wells, pipelines, advantageous contracts with railroads, and eventually retail stores. For a time, Standard Oil controlled nearly 90 percent of the industry. © Cengage Learning.

thus controlled all the individual companies, though technically it did not own them. Eventually, new laws in New Jersey made it legal for corporations chartered in New Jersey to own stock in other companies. So Rockefeller set up Standard Oil of New Jersey as a **holding company** for the companies in the trust.

Once Standard Oil achieved its near-monopoly, it consolidated its operations by closing older refineries and building larger plants based on the newest technology. Such innovations reduced the cost of producing petroleum products by more than two-thirds, leading to a decline by more than half in the price paid by consumers. Standard also took a leading role in world markets, producing nearly all American petroleum products sold in Asia, Africa, and Latin America during the 1880s. Rockefeller retired from active participation in business in the mid-1890s.

Standard's monopoly was short lived because of the discovery of new oil fields in Texas and elsewhere at the turn of the century. New companies tapped those fields and quickly followed their own paths to vertical integration. Nonetheless, the "Rockefeller interests" (companies dominated by Rockefeller or his managers) steadily gained in power. They included the National City Bank of New York (an investment bank second only to the House of Morgan), railroads, mining, real estate, steel plants, steamship lines, and other industries.

Thomas Edison and the Power of Innovation

By the late nineteenth century, many American entrepreneurs had joined Rockefeller and Carnegie in viewing technology as a powerful competitive device.

holding company A company that exists to own other companies, usually through holding a controlling interest in their stocks.

In the Wider World

Cartels

Though American entrepreneurs sometimes cooperated through pools or cartels, such efforts rarely lasted very long, unless they took legal form as a trust or holding company. In contrast, cartels emerged as a more typical form of business cooperation in Germany, which was also undergoing rapid industrialization in the late nineteenth century.

By 1905, nearly four hundred industrial cartels were operating in Germany and were especially prominent in the coal, iron, and steel industries and in chemicals. By then, there were also at least forty international cartels, typically including companies from neighboring European countries. The first attempt at a global cartel, initiated by a French company in 1887 in an effort to monopolize worldwide production of copper, included participation by companies in France, Germany, Spain, and the United States. It briefly controlled three-quarters of the world's supply of copper but lasted only until 1889.

Railroads wanted more powerful locomotives, roomier freight cars, and stronger rails so they could carry more freight at a lower cost. Steel companies demanded larger and more efficient furnaces to make more steel more cheaply. Ordinary citizens as well as famous entrepreneurs seemed infatuated with technology. One invention followed another: an ice-making machine in 1865, the vacuum cleaner in 1869, the telephone in 1876, the phonograph in 1878, the electric light bulb in 1879, an electric welding machine in 1886, and the first American-made gasoline-engine automobile in 1895, to name only a few. By 1900, many Americans had come to expect a steady flow of ever more astounding creations, especially ones that could be purchased by the middle and upper classes.

Many new inventions relied on electricity, and there one person stood out: **Thomas A. Edison**. Born in 1847, he secured the first of his thousand-plus **patents** at age 22. In 1876 Edison set up the first modern research laboratory, and he opened a new and improved facility in 1887. Edison promised "a minor invention every ten days and a big thing every six months," and he backed up his words with results. His laboratories invented or significantly improved electrical lighting, electrical motors, the storage battery, the electric locomotive, the phonograph, the microphone, and many other products. Research and development by Edison's laboratories and others quickly translated into production and sales. Nationwide, sales of electrical equipment were insignificant in 1870 but reached nearly $2 million ten years later and nearly $22 million in 1890.

Library of Congress.

This photograph from 1893 shows Thomas A. Edison in his laboratory, the world's leading research facility when it opened in 1876. By creating research teams, the Edison laboratories could pursue several projects at once. They developed a dazzling array of new products, most based on electrical power.

Thomas A. Edison American inventor, especially of electrical devices, among them the phonograph and the light bulb.

patent A government statement that gives the creator of an invention the sole right to produce, use, or sell that invention for a set period of time.

Such sales meant that generating and distribution systems had to be constructed, and wires to carry electrical current had to be installed along city streets and in homes. The pace of this work picked up appreciably after Nikola Tesla demonstrated the superiority of alternating current (AC) over direct current (DC) for transmitting power over long distances. Edison's distribution networks had relied on DC, which had limited their range.

Early developers of electrical devices and electrical distribution systems needed major financial assistance, and investment bankers came to play an important role in public utilities industries. General Electric, for example, developed out of Edison's company through a series of **mergers** arranged by J. P. Morgan.

Selling to the Nation

The expansion of manufacturing accelerated earlier trends toward new and more affordable consumer goods. Large, vertically integrated manufacturers of consumer products often competed to sell items that differed little from one another and that cost virtually the same. Such companies frequently competed not on the basis of price but through advertising.

By the late nineteenth century, advertisements in newspapers and magazines had become large and complex as manufacturers relied on advertising to promote many mass-produced consumer goods, including **patent medicines**, clothing, books, packaged foods, soap, and petroleum products. In some cases—notably cigarettes—advertising greatly expanded the market for the product. After the federal Patent Office registered the first **trademark** in 1870, companies rushed to develop brands and logos that they hoped would distinguish their products from nearly identical rivals.

Along with advertising came new ways of selling. Previously, most people expected to purchase goods from artisans who made items on order (shoes, clothes, furniture), or from door-to-door peddlers (pots and pans), or in small specialty stores (hardware, dry goods) or general stores. In urban areas following the Civil War, the first American **department stores** appeared and flourished, offering many types of ready-made products—fashionable clothing, shoes, household goods, and much more. Department stores' products, unlike those in most previous retail outlets, not only had clearly marked prices but also could be returned or exchanged if the customer were dissatisfied. R. H. Macy's in New York City, Jordan Marsh in Boston, Marshall Field in Chicago, and similar stores relied heavily on newspaper advertising to attract throngs of customers, especially women, from throughout the city and its suburbs. They targeted middle- and upper-class women but also appealed to young single women who worked for wages and could afford the current fashions. Young single women also often found white-collar jobs as clerks in the new department stores.

The variety presented by department stores paled when compared with the array of goods available through the new mail-order catalogs. Led by two Chicago companies, Montgomery Ward (which issued its first catalog in 1872) and Sears, Roebuck and Co.

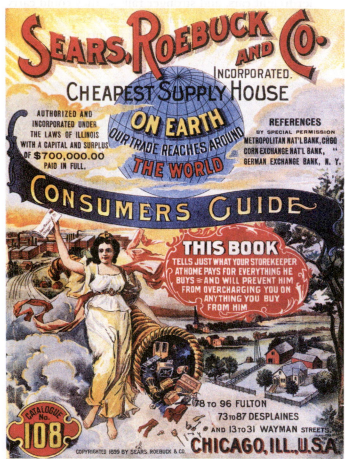

The Granger Collection, New York.

This 1899 catalog for Sears and Roebuck proudly proclaimed that company to be the "Cheapest Supply House on Earth." The classically garbed woman holds a cornucopia, an ancient symbol of abundance, and Sears's cornucopia is filled to overflowing with a vast array of consumer goods available through the catalog.

merger The joining together of two or more organizations.

patent medicine A medical preparation that is advertised by brand name and available without a physician's prescription.

trademark A name or symbol that identifies a product and is officially registered and legally restricted for use by the owner or manufacturer.

department store Type of retail establishment that developed in cities in the late nineteenth century and featured a wide variety of merchandise offered for sale in separate departments.

(whose first general catalogs appeared in 1893), mail-order houses aimed at rural America. They offered a wider range of choices than most rural-dwellers had ever before seen—from hams to hammers, handkerchiefs to harnesses.

Department stores and mail-order houses became feasible because manufacturers were now producing many types of consumer goods in large volumes. Mail-order houses depended on railroads and the U.S. mail to deliver their catalogs and products across great distances, and department stores relied on railroads to bring goods from distant factories. Together, advertising, mail-order catalogs (in rural areas), and department stores (in urban areas) began to change Americans' buying habits.

Economic Concentration in Consumer-Goods Industries

Carnegie, Rockefeller, Edison, Morgan, and a few others redefined the expectations of American entrepreneurs and provided models for their activities. In a number of consumer-goods industries, massive, complex companies—vertically integrated, sometimes horizontally integrated, often employing extensive advertising—appeared relatively suddenly in the 1880s.

The American Sugar Refining Company, created in 1887, imitated Rockefeller's organization to control three-quarters of the nation's sugar-refining capacity by the early 1890s. James B. Duke used efficient machinery, extensive advertising, and vertical integration to become the largest manufacturer of cigarettes. In 1890 he merged with his four largest competitors to create the American Tobacco Company, which dominated the cigarette industry. Gustavus Swift in the early 1880s began to ship fresh meat from his slaughterhouse in Chicago to markets in the East, using his own refrigerated railcars. He eventually added refrigerated storage plants in several cities, along with a sales and delivery staff. Other meatpacking companies followed Swift's lead. By 1890, half a dozen firms dominated meatpacking. Such a market, in which a few firms dominate an industry, is called an **oligopoly**. Oligopolies were (and are) more typical than monopolies.

Some of the new manufacturing companies did not sell stock or use investment bankers to raise capital. Standard Oil, like Carnegie Steel, never "went public"—that is, Rockefeller never used the stock exchange to raise capital. Instead, he expanded either through mergers or by making purchases capitalized by his profits. Rockefeller and his associates, like Carnegie and his partners, concentrated ownership and control in their own hands. So did many others among the new manufacturing companies. As late as 1896, the New York Stock Exchange sold stock in only twenty manufacturing concerns.

TOWARD A MORE PERFECT UNION

Corporate Personhood

Section 1 of the Fourteenth Amendment (see page 381) states in part: "No State shall . . . deprive any person of life, liberty, or property, without due process of law; nor deny to any person within its jurisdiction the equal protection of the laws." In 1819, long before the Fourteenth Amendment was adopted, the Supreme Court specified that corporations have the same rights regarding contracts as persons. With the rise of large and powerful corporations after the Civil War, more and more cases involving corporations began to come before the Supreme Court. In 1888, in *Pembina Silver Mining Co. v. Pennsylvania*, the Supreme Court ruled on the meaning of the Fourteenth Amendment: "Under the designation of 'person' there is no doubt that a private corporation is included. Such corporations are merely associations of individuals united for a special purpose and permitted to do business under a particular name and have a succession of members without dissolution." While the Supreme Court has continued to define the meaning of the Fourteenth Amendment, there has been no successful challenge to the ruling that a corporation is legally a person, with constitutional rights to "due process" and "equal protection" under state laws.

Gradually, however, with the passing of the first generation of industrial empire builders, ownership grew apart from management. Many new business executives were professional managers. Ownership rested among hundreds or thousands of stockholders, all of whom wanted a reliable return on their investment, even though the vast majority remained uninvolved with business operations. The huge size of the new companies also meant that most managers rarely saw or talked with most of their employees. Careful **cost analysis**, the desire for efficiency, and the need to pay shareholders regular **dividends** led many companies to treat most of their employees as expenses to be increased or cut as necessary, with little regard to the effect on individuals.

oligopoly A market or industry dominated by a few firms (from Greek words meaning "few sellers"); more common than a *monopoly* (from Greek words meaning "one seller").

cost analysis Study of the cost of producing manufactured goods to find ways to cut expenses.

dividend A share of a company's profits received by a stockholder.

This engraving from 1887 presents Atlanta as a modern city, with a bustling train station, arriving trains trailing clouds of smoke, and up-to-date, multi-story buildings.

Seeking a New South

The term **New South** usually refers to efforts by some southerners after Reconstruction to modernize their region. Some New South advocates promoted a more diverse economic base, with more manufacturing and less reliance on a few staple agricultural crops, as a way to strengthen the southern economy and integrate it into the emerging national economy.

Foremost among proponents of the New South was **Henry Grady**, who built the *Atlanta Constitution* into a powerful regional newspaper in the 1880s. Like Chicago, Atlanta grew as a railroad center. Though destroyed by Sherman's troops in 1864, Atlanta rebuilt quickly. It became the capital of Georgia in 1877. Thanks in part to Grady's skillful journalism, the city emerged as a symbol of the New South—a center for transportation, industry, and finance.

The importance of railroads in spurring Atlanta's growth was no coincidence. After the Civil War, inadequate transportation, especially railroads, posed a critical limit on the South's economic growth. During the 1880s, however, southern railroads more than doubled their miles of track. In the 1890s,

■ **New South** Late-nineteenth-century term used by some southerners to promote the idea that the South should become industrialized, have a more diverse agricultural focus, and be thoroughly integrated into the economy of the nation.

■ **Henry Grady** Prominent Atlanta newspaper publisher and leading proponent of the concept of a New South.

J. P. Morgan led the efforts to reorganize southern railroads into three large systems, dominated by the Southern Railway. With the emergence of better rail transportation, some entrepreneurs began to consider introducing new industries.

Some southerners had long advocated that their cotton be manufactured into cloth in the South, rather than in the New England textile mills that had been using southern cotton since early in the century. The southern cotton textile industry boomed during the 1880s and 1890s. The South counted 161 textile mills in 1880 and 400 in 1900. The new mills had more modern equipment and were larger and more productive than the mills of New England. They also had cheaper labor costs, partly because they relied on child labor. Similar patterns characterized the emergence of cigarette manufacturing as another new southern industry. In the end, these enterprises did little to improve the lives of many southerners. Most of the new companies paid low wages, and some chose locations in the South specifically to take advantage of its cheap, unskilled, nonunion labor.

Other southerners tried to diversify the region's agriculture and to reduce its dependence on cotton and tobacco. Such efforts, however, ran up against the cotton textile and cigarette industries, both of which built factories in the South to be near their raw materials. Thus southern agriculture changed little: owners and sharecroppers farmed small plots, obligated by their rental contracts or crop liens to raise cotton or tobacco. In parts of the South, farmers became even more dependent on cotton than they had been before the Civil War. Parts of Georgia, for example, produced almost 200 percent more cotton in 1880 than in 1860.

Of greater potential to transform part of the South was the iron and steel industry that emerged in northern Alabama. Dominated by the Tennessee Coal, Iron, and Railroad Company, the industry drew on coal from Tennessee and Alabama mines and iron ore from northern Alabama. In 1897, the first southern steel mill opened in Ensley, Alabama, and soon established itself as a serious rival to those of the North. Soon Birmingham, Alabama, emerged as one of the world's largest producers of pig iron. In 1907, J. P. Morgan arranged the merger of the Tennessee Company into his United States Steel Corporation.

The turn of the century also saw the beginning of a southern oil industry near Beaumont, Texas, with the tapping of the Spindletop Pool—so productive the press labeled it "the world's greatest oil well." The center of petroleum production now shifted from the Midwest to Texas, Oklahoma, and Louisiana, where important discoveries also came in 1901. In addition to attracting attention from Standard Oil, the new discoveries prompted the growth or creation of new companies, notably Gulf and Texaco.

INCORPORATING THE WEST INTO THE NATIONAL ECONOMY

★ What were the causes and outcomes of the Indian wars of the late nineteenth century? Could they have been avoided?

★ What were the major ways in which the West was incorporated into the national economy?

As Rockefeller was monopolizing the petroleum industry and Edison was perfecting the light bulb, the U.S. Army was subduing the last Indian resistance in the West. Before the Civil War, the issue of slavery had blocked economic development efforts in the West. The secession of the southern states permitted the Republicans who took over the federal government to open the West to economic development, through such measures as the Pacific Railway Act and the Homestead Act. The end result was the incorporation of the West into the emerging national industrial economy.

War for the West

When Congress decided to use the public domain—western land—to encourage economic development, most Americans considered the West to be largely vacant. In fact, American Indians lived throughout most of the West. The most tragic outcome of the development of the West was the upheaval in the lives of the Native Americans who lived there.

Long before, the acquisition of horses and guns had transformed the lives of western Native Americans. The transformation was most dramatic among tribes living on or near the **Great Plains** (see Map 16.3). This vast, relatively flat, and treeless region was the rangeland of huge herds of buffalo. Horses found their way onto the Great Plains slowly, trickling northward from Spanish settlements in what is now New Mexico and reaching the upper plains in the mid-eighteenth century. By that time, French and English traders working northeast of the plains had begun to provide guns to the Indians in return for furs. Together, horses and guns transformed the culture of some Plains tribes.

Although the possession of horses might confer status, among most of the Plains Indians a person achieved high social standing not by accumulating possessions but by sharing. Francis La Flesche, son of an Omaha leader, learned from his father that "the persecution of the poor, the sneer at their poverty is a wrong for which no punishment is too severe." His mother reinforced the lesson: "When you see a boy barefooted and lame, take off your moccasins and give them to him. When you see a boy hungry, bring him to your home and give him food."

The Native American peoples of the plains included both farmers and nomadic hunters. The farmers lived most of the year in large permanent villages. Women raised corn, squash, pumpkins, and beans, and gathered wild fruit and vegetables. Men hunted and fished near their villages and cultivated tobacco. Before the arrival of horses, twice a year entire villages went, on foot, on extended hunting trips for buffalo. During these hunts, the people lived in **tipis**, cone-shaped tents of buffalo hide that were easy to move. Acquisition of horses changed the culture of these Indians only slightly.

The horse revolutionized the lives of other Plains Indians. Because a hunter on horseback could kill twice as many buffalo as one on foot, the horse substantially increased the number of people the plains could support. The horse also increased mobility, permitting a band to follow the buffalo as they moved across the grasslands. Some groups abandoned farming and became nomadic, living in tipis year-round and following the buffalo herds. By the early nineteenth century, the **horse culture** existed throughout the Great Plains.

Great Plains High grassland of western North America, stretching north to south across the center of the nation; it is generally level, treeless, and fairly dry.

tipis Conical tents made from buffalo hide and used as a portable dwelling by Indians on the Great Plains.

◾ **horse culture** The nomadic way of life of those American Indians, mostly on the Great Plains, for whom the horse brought significant changes in their ability to hunt, travel, and make war.

The **Lakotas**, largest of all the groups who adopted the horse culture, were the westernmost members of a group of Native American peoples often called Sioux—a name applied to them by the French. Their name for themselves can be translated as *allies*, reflecting their organization as a **confederacy**. The Lakotas shared a common language, but the northern Cheyenne were generally considered members of the Lakota confederacy by the mid-nineteenth century.

Before 1851, federal policymakers had considered the region west of Arkansas, Missouri, Iowa, and Minnesota and east of the Rocky Mountains to be a permanent Indian country. But farmers bound for Oregon and gold seekers on their way to California carved trails across the central plains, and in 1851 Congress approved a new policy, designed in part to open the central plains as a railroad route to the Pacific. The new policy promised each tribe a definite territory "of limited extent and well-defined boundaries," within which the tribe was to live. The government was to supply whatever needs the tribes could not meet themselves. Federal officials first planned large reservations taking up much of the Great Plains.

With the end of the Civil War in 1865, railroad construction crews prepared to build westward. Federal policymakers tried to head off hostilities with the tribes by carving out a few great western reservations. The remainder of the West was to be opened for development—railroad building, mining, and farming. Native Americans on the reservations were to be given food and shelter by the federal government, and agents were to teach them how to farm and raise cattle.

Treaties were negotiated in 1867 and 1868 in fulfillment of the new policy. In 1867 a conference at Medicine Lodge Creek produced treaties by which

MAP 16.3 The West in the Late Nineteenth Century

This map indicates major geographic features of the West in the late nineteenth century, including topography, major cities, subregions, cattle trails, and the major transcontinental railroads that had been completed by the 1890s. Mining areas for three important metals are also shown. © Cengage Learning.

John Mix Stanley painted this buffalo hunt in 1845, dramatically illustrating how the horse increased the ability of Native American hunters to kill buffalo. A hunter on foot could not have approached closely enough to drive a lance into a buffalo's heart.

the major southern Plains tribes accepted reservations in what is now western Oklahoma (see Map 16.4). In April 1868, many members of the northern Plains tribes met at Fort Laramie and signed treaties creating a Great Sioux Reservation on the northern plains. They believed that they retained "unceded lands" for hunting in the Powder River country—present-day northeastern Wyoming and southeastern Montana. In May 1868 the Crows agreed to a reservation in Montana. In June 1868 the Navajos accepted a large reservation in the Southwest. Given the fluid structure of authority among most Indian peoples, however, those who signed the treaties did not necessarily obligate those who did not.

As some federal officials were negotiating these treaties, other federal officials were permitting and even encouraging white hunters to kill the buffalo—for sport, for meat, and for hides purchased by **tanneries** in the East. In the mid-1870s more than 10 million buffalo were killed and stripped of their hides, which sold for a dollar or so. The southern herd was wiped out by 1878, the northern herd by 1883. Only two thousand survived, the remnant of a species whose numbers once seemed as vast as the stars. Given the importance of the buffalo in the lives of the Plains Indians, their way of life was doomed once the slaughter began.

Some members of the southern Plains tribes refused to accept the terms of the Medicine Lodge Creek treaties and continued to live in their traditional territory. Resisting efforts to move them onto the reservations, they occasionally attacked stagecoach stations, ranches, travelers, and military units. After a group of southern Cheyennes inflicted heavy losses on an army unit, General William Tecumseh Sherman, the Civil War general and now head of the army, decreed that all Native Americans not on reservations "are hostile and will remain so till killed off."

Sherman's response was the usual reaction of a conventional military force to **guerrilla warfare**: concentrate the friendly population in defined areas (in this case, reservations) and then open fire on anyone outside those areas. In the winter of 1868–1869, the army launched a southern campaign under the command of General Philip Sheridan, another Union army veteran, who directed his men to "destroy their

■ **Lakota** A large confederation of Siouan-speaking Indian peoples, nomadic buffalo hunters, who lived on the northern Great Plains.

confederacy An organization of separate groups that have become allies for mutual support or joint action.

tannery An establishment where animal skins and hides are made into leather.

guerrilla warfare A method of warfare in which small bands of fighters in occupied territory harass and attack their enemies.

villages and ponies, to kill and hang all warriors, and bring back all women and children." The brutality that ensued convinced most southern Plains tribes to abandon further resistance.

In the early 1870s, sizable buffalo herds still roamed west and south of Indian Territory, in the Red River region of Texas. Though this was not reservation land, the Medicine Lodge Creek treaties permitted Indians to hunt there. When white buffalo hunters began work there in 1874, young men from the Kiowa, Comanche, and southern Cheyenne tribes attacked them. Sheridan responded with another **war of attrition**, destroying tipis, food, and animals. When winter came, the cold and hungry Indians surrendered to avoid starvation. War leaders were imprisoned in Florida, far from their families. Buffalo hunters then quickly exterminated the remaining buffalo on the southern plains.

On the northern plains, many Lakotas and some northern Cheyennes, led by **Crazy Horse** and **Sitting Bull**, lived on unceded hunting lands in the Powder River region. Complicating matters further, gold was discovered in 1874 in the Black Hills, in the heart of the Great Sioux Reservation, touching off an invasion of Indian land by miners. As the Northern Pacific Railroad prepared to lay track in southern Montana, federal authorities determined to force all Lakota and Cheyenne people onto the reservation, triggering a conflict sometimes called the **Great Sioux War**.

Military operations in the Powder River region began in the spring of 1876. Sheridan ordered troops to enter the area from three directions and converge on the Lakotas and Cheyennes. The offensive went dreadfully wrong when Lieutenant Colonel George A. Custer, without waiting for the other units, sent his Seventh Cavalry against a major village that his scouts had located. The encampment, on the **Little Bighorn River**, proved to be one of the largest ever on the northern plains. Custer unwisely divided his force, and more than two hundred men, including Custer, met their deaths.

MAP 16.4 Indian Reservations

This map indicates the location of most western Indian reservations in 1890, as well as the Great Sioux Reservation before it was broken up and severely reduced in size. Note how development of reservations on the northern plains and others on the southern plains opened the central plains for railroad construction and agricultural development. © Cengage Learning.

This photo shows the insensitive treatment of the Lakotas who died at Wounded Knee, having fled the reservation following Sitting Bull's death. They were buried in a mass grave, still frozen as they had fallen.

Library of Congress.

That winter, U.S. soldiers unleashed another campaign of attrition on the northern plains. Troops defeated some Indian bands. Hunger and cold drove others to surrender. Crazy Horse and his band held out until spring and surrendered only when told that they could live in the Powder River region. A few months later, Crazy Horse was killed when he resisted being put into an army jail. Sitting Bull and his band escaped to Canada and remained there until 1881, when he finally surrendered. The government cut up the Great Sioux Reservation into several smaller units and took away the Powder River region, the Black Hills (which the Lakotas considered sacred), and other lands. After the Great Sioux War, no Native American group could muster the capacity for sustained resistance.

In 1877 an effort to move the Nez Perces to a new reservation in western Idaho led to a battle in which a small group of Nez Perces defeated a larger group of U.S. troops and local civilian volunteers. Led by **Chief Joseph**, the Nez Perces then attempted to flee to Canada. Between July and early October, they evaded the army as they traveled east and north. More than two hundred members of the band died along the way. In the end, Joseph surrendered on the condition that the Nez Perces be permitted to return to their previous home. Federal officials instead sent the Nez Perces to faraway Indian Territory, where, in an unfamiliar climate, many died of disease.

The last sizable group to resist confinement was Geronimo's band of Chiricahua Apaches, who long managed to elude the army in the mountains of the Southwest. They finally gave up in 1886, and the men were sent to prison in Florida.

The last major confrontation between the army and Native Americans came in 1890, in South Dakota. Some Lakotas had taken up a new religion, the **Ghost Dance**, which promised to restore the buffalo and sweep away the whites. Fearing an uprising, federal authorities ordered the Lakotas to stop the ritual and, concerned that Sitting Bull might encourage defiance, ordered his arrest. He was killed when some of his followers resisted. A small band of Lakotas fled but was

war of attrition A form of warfare based on deprivation of food, shelter, and other necessities; if successful, it drives opponents to surrender out of hunger or exposure.

■ **Crazy Horse** Lakota war leader who resisted white encroachment in the Black Hills and fought at the Little Bighorn River in 1876.

■ **Sitting Bull** Lakota war leader and holy man; also fought at Little Bighorn.

■ **Great Sioux War** War between the U.S. Army and the tribes that took part in the Battle of Little Bighorn; it ended in 1881 with the surrender of Sitting Bull.

■ **Little Bighorn River** River in Montana where in 1876 Lieutenant Colonel George Custer attacked a large Indian encampment; Custer and most of his force died in the battle.

■ **Chief Joseph** Nez Perce chief who led his people in an attempt to escape to Canada in 1877; after a grueling journey they were forced to surrender and were exiled to Indian Territory.

■ **Ghost Dance** Indian religion centered on a ritual dance; it held out the promise of an Indian messiah who would banish the whites, bring back the buffalo, and restore the land to the Indians.

surrounded by the Seventh Cavalry near **Wounded Knee Creek**. When one Lakota refused to surrender his gun, both Indians and soldiers fired their weapons. The soldiers, with their vastly greater firepower, quickly prevailed. As many as 250 Native Americans died, as did 25 soldiers.

The events at Wounded Knee marked the symbolic end of armed conflict on the Great Plains. Once the federal government began to encourage rapid economic development in the West, displacement of the Indians was probably inevitable. From the beginning, the Indians faced overwhelming odds—they had a superior knowledge of the terrain, superior horsemanship and mobility, and great courage, but the U.S. Army had superior numbers and superior technology. The Army was also often able to find allies among Native American groups who were traditional enemies of the defiant tribes.

Transforming the West: Railroads, Cattle, and Mining

Long before the last battles between the army and the Indians, the incorporation of the West into the national economy was well under way. Railroad construction played a major role. In the eastern United States, railroad construction usually meant connecting established population centers. Eastern railroads moved through areas with developed economies, connected major cities, and hauled freight to and from the many towns along their lines. At the end of the Civil War, this situation existed almost nowhere in the West.

Most western railroads were built first to connect the Pacific Coast to the eastern half of the country. Railroad promoters understood that a transcontinental line was unlikely at first to carry enough freight to justify the high cost of construction. Thus they turned to the federal government for assistance. The Pacific Railway Act of 1862 provided loans and 10 square miles (later increased to 20) of the public domain for every mile of track laid. In this way, federal lawmakers sought to tie California and Nevada, with their rich deposits of gold and silver, to the Union and to stimulate the rapid economic development of other parts of the West.

Two companies received this federal support: the Union Pacific, which began laying tracks westward from Omaha, Nebraska Territory, and the Central Pacific, which began building eastward from Sacramento, California. Construction began slowly, partly because crucial supplies—rails and locomotives—had to be brought to each starting point from the eastern United States, either by ship around South America to California or by riverboat to Omaha. Both companies experienced labor shortages. The Union Pacific solved its labor shortages only after the end of the Civil War, when former soldiers and construction workers flooded west. Many were Irish immigrants. The Central Pacific filled its work gangs earlier by recruiting Chinese immigrants. By 1868, Central Pacific construction crews totaled six thousand workers, Union Pacific crews five thousand.

The sheer cliffs and rocky ravines of the Sierra Nevada slowed construction of the Central Pacific. Chinese laborers sometimes dangled from ropes to create a roadbed by chiseling away the solid rock face of a mountain. Because the companies earned their federal subsidies based on miles of track laid, construction became a race in which each company tried to build faster and farther than the other. In 1869, with the Sierra Nevada far behind, the Central Pacific boasted of laying 10 miles of track in a single day. The tracks of the two companies finally met at Promontory Summit, north of Salt Lake City, on May 10, 1869 (see Map 16.3). Other lines followed during the next twenty years, bringing most of the West into the national market system.

Westerners greeted the arrival of a railroad in their communities with joyful celebrations, but some soon wondered if they had traded isolation for dependence on a greedy monopoly. The Southern Pacific, successor to the Central Pacific, became known as the "Octopus" because of its efforts to establish a monopoly over transportation throughout California. It had a reputation for charging the most that a customer could afford. James J. Hill of the Great Northern, in contrast, was called the "Empire Builder" for his efforts to build up the economy and prosperity of the region alongside his rails, which ran west from Minneapolis to Puget Sound. Whether "Octopus" or "Empire Builder," railroads provided the crucial transportation network for the economic development of the West. In their wake, cattle raising, mining, farming, and lumbering all expanded rapidly.

Cattle were first brought into south Texas—then part of New Spain (Mexico)—in the eighteenth century. The environment encouraged the herds to multiply, and Mexican ranchers developed an **open-range** system. The cattle grazed on unfenced grasslands, and *vaqueros* (cowboys) herded the half-wild longhorns from horseback. Many practices that developed in south Texas were subsequently transferred to the range-cattle industry, including **roundups** and **branding**.

At the end of the Civil War, 5 million cattle ranged across Texas. And in the slaughterhouses of Chicago,

■ **Wounded Knee Creek** Site of a conflict in 1890 between a band of Lakotas and U.S. troops, sometimes characterized as a massacre because the Lakotas were so outnumbered and overpowered; the last major encounter between Indians and the army.

open range Unfenced grazing lands on which cattle ran freely and cattle ownership was established through branding.

Denver Public Library, Western History Division.

When the Central Pacific and Union Pacific companies raced to build their part of the first transcontinental railroad, Chinese laborers were responsible for some of the most dangerous construction on the Central Pacific route through the Sierra Nevadas. This photograph was apparently taken by a photographer for the Union Pacific when the two lines joined near Promontory Summit, in Utah Territory.

cattle brought ten times or more their price in Texas. To get cattle from south Texas to Midwestern markets, Texans herded cattle north through Indian Territory (now Oklahoma) to the railroads being built westward. Half a dozen cowboys, a cook, and a foreman (the trail boss) could drive one or two thousand cattle. Between 1866 and 1880, some 4 million cattle plodded north from Texas. As railroad construction crews pushed westward, cattle towns sprang up—notably Abilene and Dodge City, Kansas. In cattle towns, the trail boss sold his herd and paid off his cowboys, most of whom quickly headed for the saloons, brothels, and gambling houses. Eastern journalists and writers of **dime novels** discovered and embroidered the exploits of town marshals like James B. "Wild Bill" Hickok and Wyatt Earp, giving them national reputations—deserved or not—as "town-tamers" of heroic dimensions. In fact, the most important changes in any cattle town came when middle-class residents—especially women—organized churches and schools, and were determined to create law-abiding communities like those from which they had come.

Most Texas cattle were loaded on eastbound trains, but some continued north to where cattlemen had virtually free access to vast lands still in the public domain. One result of these "long drives" was the extension of open-range cattle raising from Texas into the northern Great Plains. By the early 1870s, the profits in cattle raising on the northern plains attracted attention in the East, England, and elsewhere among investors eager to make a fortune. Some brought in new breeds of cattle, which they bred with Texas longhorns, producing hardy range cattle that yielded more meat.

By the early 1880s so many cattle ranches were operating that beef prices began to fall. Then, in the severe winter of 1886–1887, uncounted thousands of cattle froze or starved to death on the northern plains. Many investors went bankrupt. Cattle raising lost some of its romantic aura and afterward became more of a business than an adventure. Surviving ranchers fenced their ranges and made certain that they could feed their herds during the winter.

roundup A spring event in which cowboys gathered together the cattle herds, branded newborn calves, and castrated most of the new young males.

branding Burning a distinctive mark into an animal's hide using a hot iron as a way to establish ownership.

dime novel A cheaply produced novel of the mid-to-late nineteenth century, often featuring the dramatized exploits of western gunfighters.

Collection of William Gladstone.

At some time in the 1870s, these cowboys put on good clothes and sat for a photographer before a painted background. They probably worked together and were friends. Most cowboys were young African Americans, Mexican Americans, or poor southern whites.

As the cattle industry grew, the cowboy became a popular **icon**. Fiction after the 1870s and motion pictures later created the cowboy image: a brave, white, clean-cut hero who outwitted scoundrels and rescued fair-haired white women from snarling villains. In fact, most real cowboys were young and unschooled; many were African Americans or of Mexican descent, and others were former Confederate soldiers. On a cattle drive, they worked long hours (up to twenty a day), faced serious danger if a herd stampeded, slept on the ground, and ate biscuits and beans. They earned about a dollar a day and spent much of their working time in the saddle with no human companionship.

Just as railroads made possible the cattle drives, so too did railroad construction advance the expansion of mining. Discoveries of precious metals and valuable minerals in western mountains inevitably prompted the construction of rail lines to the sites of discovery, and the rail lines in turn permitted rapid exploitation of the mineral resources by bringing in supplies and heavy equipment.

The mining industry changed rapidly. Solitary prospectors panning for gold in mountain streams gave way to corporations and wage workers. Mining operations quickly became vertically integrated, including mines, ore-crushing mills, railroads, and companies that supplied fuel and water for mining. In most parts of the West, the exhaustion of surface deposits led to construction of underground shafts and tunnels. Such operations required elaborate machinery to move men and equipment thousands of feet into the earth and to keep the tunnels cool, dry, and safe. By the mid-1870s, some Nevada silver mines boasted the most advanced mining equipment in the world. There, temperatures soared to 120 degrees in shafts more than 2,200 feet deep. Mighty air pumps circulated air from the surface to the depths, and ice was used to reduce temperatures. Massive water pumps kept the shafts dry. Powerful drills speeded the removal of ore, and enormous ore-crushing machines operated day and night on the surface. In Butte, Montana, a gold discovery in 1864 led to discoveries of copper, silver, and zinc in what has been called the richest hill on earth. Mine shafts there reached depths of a mile and accessed 2,700 miles of tunnels.

Western miners organized too, forming strong unions. Beginning in Butte and spreading throughout the major mining regions of the West, miners' unions secured wages five to ten times higher than what miners in Britain or Germany earned.

Transforming the West: Farming and Lumbering

Railroad construction also facilitated the expansion of western farming. After the Civil War, the land most easily available for new farms stretched from what is now North Dakota southward through the current state of Kansas. Mapmakers in the early nineteenth century had labeled this region the Great American Desert. It was not a desert—some parts were very fertile—but west of the line of **aridity**, roughly the 98th or 100th **meridian** (see Map 16.5), sparse rainfall limited farming. Farmers who followed traditional farming practices risked not only failing but also damaging a surprisingly fragile **ecosystem**.

After the Civil War, farmers pressed steadily westward, spurred by the offer of 160 acres of free land under the Homestead Act or lured by railroad advertising that promised fertile and productive land at little cost. Those who came to farm were as diverse as the nation itself. Thousands of African Americans left the South, seeking farms of their own. Immigrants from

icon A symbol, usually one with virtues considered worthy of imitating.

aridity Dryness; lack of enough rainfall to support trees or woody plants.

meridian One of the imaginary lines representing degrees of longitude that pass through the North and South Poles and encircle the Earth.

ecosystem A community of animals, plants, and microorganisms, considered together with the environment in which they live.

MAP 16.5 Rainfall and Agriculture, ca. 1890
The agricultural produce of any given area depended on the type of soil, the terrain, and the rainfall. Most of the western half of the nation received relatively little rainfall. The line of aridity, beyond which many crops require irrigation, lies between 28 inches and 20 inches of rain annually. © Cengage Learning.

Europe—especially Scandinavia, Germany, **Bohemia**, and Russia—also flooded in. Most homesteaders, however, moved from areas a short distance to the east, where farmland had become too expensive for them to buy.

Single women could and did claim their own land. Sometimes the wife of a male homesteader did the same, claiming 160 acres in her own name next to the claim of her husband. By one estimate, one-third of all homestead claims in Dakota Territory were held by women in 1886. Some single women seem to have seen homesteading as a speculative venture, intending to sell the land and use the money for such purposes as starting a business, paying college tuition, or creating a nest egg for marriage.

The Homestead Act had clear limits. The 160 acres that it provided were sufficient for a farm east of the line of aridity. West of that line, it was often possible to raise wheat, but most land required irrigation for other crops or was suitable only for cattle raising, which required much more than 160 acres.

Federal officials were sometimes lax in enforcing the Homestead Act's requirements. Some cattle ranchers manipulated the law by having their cowboys file claims and then transfer the land to the rancher after they received title to it. Or ranchers claimed the land along both sides of streams, knowing that surrounding land was worthless without access to water, and thus they could control the whole watershed without establishing ownership.

Those who complied with the requirement to build a house and farm the land often faced an unfamiliar environment. The plains were virtually barren of trees. The new plains settlers, therefore, scavenged for substitutes for construction material and fuel that eastern pioneers obtained without cost from trees on their land. Initially, many families carved homes out of the land itself. Some tunneled into the side of a low hill to make a cavelike dugout. Others cut the tough prairie **sod** into blocks and laid them like

Bohemia A region of central Europe now part of the Czech Republic.

sod A piece of earth on which grass grows; the dense sod of the plains was tough and fibrous with roots, dead grass from previous growing seasons, and hard-packed soil.

Omer M. Kem (standing, slicing watermelon) posed for the photographer with his children and aged father outside his sod house in Custer County, Nebraska, in 1886. Four years later, Kem was elected to the U.S. House of Representatives as a Populist, representing the grievances of western farmers. The photographer, Solomon Butcher, compiled pictures illustrating the nature of life on what one historian termed "the sod-house frontier."

bricks to make the walls of a house. Many combined dugout and sod construction. "Soddies" became common throughout the plains but seldom made satisfactory dwellings. For fuel to use in cooking or heating, women burned dried cow dung or sunflower stalks.

Plains families looked to technology to meet many of their needs. Barbed wire, first patented in 1874, provided a cheap and easy alternative to wooden fences. The barbs effectively kept ranchers' cattle off farmland. Ranchers eventually used it, too, to keep their herds from straying. Much of the plains had abundant groundwater, but the **water table** was deeper than in the East, so settlers used windmills to pump the water. Because the sod was so tough, special plows were developed to make the first cut through it.

The most serious problem for pioneers on the Great Plains was a much-reduced level of rainfall compared with eastern farming areas. During the late

1870s and into the 1880s, when the central plains were farmed for the first time, the area received unusually heavy rainfall. Then, in the late 1880s, rainfall fell below normal, and crop failures drove many homesteaders off the plains. By one estimate, half of the population of western Kansas left between 1888 and 1892. Only after farmers learned better techniques of dry farming, secured improved strains of wheat, and began to practice irrigation did agriculture become viable. Even so, farming practices in some western areas failed to protect soil that had formerly been covered by natural vegetation. This exposed soil became subject to severe wind erosion in years of low rainfall.

Throughout the Northeast and Middle West, the family farm was the typical agricultural unit. In the South after the Civil War, family-operated farms, whether run by owners or by sharecroppers, also became typical. Very large farming operations in those areas tended to be exceptions. In California and some other parts of the West, however, agriculture sometimes involved huge areas, the intensive use of heavy equipment, and wage labor. Today agriculture on such a large scale is known as **agribusiness**.

Wheat was the first major crop for which farming could be entirely mechanized. By 1880, in the Red River Valley of what is now North Dakota and in the

water table The depth at which the ground is completely saturated with water.

agribusiness A large-scale farming operation typically involving considerable land-holdings, hired labor, and extensive use of machinery; may also involve processing and distribution as well as growing.

Picture Research Consultants & Archives.

The Advance Thresher Company issued this advertisement for its farm equipment around 1900. On the left is a tractor powered by a steam engine. On the right is a thresher that is operated by the steam engine. Similar equipment was in use as early as the late 1870s on some of the large wheat farms in California, significantly reducing the amount of human labor needed to raise wheat.

San Joaquin Valley in central California, wheat farms were as large as 100 square miles. Such farming businesses, often called "bonanza farms" in Dakota Territory, required major capital investments in land, equipment, and livestock. One Dakota farm required 150 workers during spring planting and 250 or more at harvest time. By the late 1880s, some California wheat growers were using huge steam-powered tractors and **combines**.

Most of the great Dakota wheat farms had been broken into smaller units by the 1890s, but in some parts of California agriculture flourished on a scale unknown in most parts of the country. One California company, Miller and Lux, held more than a million acres, scattered throughout three states. Though California wheat raising declined in significance by 1900, large-scale agriculture employing many seasonal laborers became established for several other crops.

Growers of fruits and similar crops tended to operate small farms, but they still required a large workforce at harvest time to pick the crops quickly so that they could be shipped to distant markets while still fresh. Fruit raising spread rapidly as California growers took advantage of refrigerated railroad cars and ships. By 1892, fresh fruit from California was for sale in London.

The coastal areas of the Pacific Northwest (see Map 16.5) are very different from other parts of the West. There, heavy winter rains and cool, damp,

summer fogs nurture thick stands of evergreens, especially tall Douglas firs and coastal redwoods. The growth of California cities and towns required lumber, and it came first from the coastal redwoods of central and northern California. When the most accessible stands of timber had been cut, loggers moved north to Oregon and Washington. Seattle developed as a lumber town from the late 1850s onward, as companies in San Francisco helped to finance an industry geared to providing lumber for California cities. By the late nineteenth century, some companies had become vertically integrated, owning **lumber mills** along the northwest coast, a fleet of schooners that hauled rough lumber down the coast to California, and lumberyards in the San Francisco Bay area.

As railroads extended into the Pacific Northwest (see Map 16.3), they promoted the development of the lumber industry by offering cheap rates to transport logs. Lumber production in Oregon and Washington boomed, leaving behind treeless hillsides subject to severe erosion during heavy winter rains. Westerners

combine A large harvesting machine that both cuts and threshes grain.

lumber mill A factory or place where logs are sawed into rough boards.

committed to rapid economic development seldom thought about ecological damage, for the long-term cost of such practices was not immediately apparent.

Water and Western Development

It has been said that, in the West, "whiskey is for drinking, water is for fighting over." Throughout much of the West, water was scarce but crucial to economic development. Mining used large amounts of water for cooling the mines and separating valuable ore from worthless rock. On the Great Plains, a cattle rancher claimed grazing land by controlling a stream. In the West, competition for water sometimes produced conflict—usually in the form of courtroom battles.

In many parts of the West, irrigation was vital to the success of farming. As early as 1899, irrigated land in the eleven westernmost states produced $84 million in crops. Although individual entrepreneurs and companies undertook significant irrigation projects, the magnitude of the task led many westerners to look for federal assistance, just as they had sought federal assistance for railroad development. "When Uncle Sam," wrote one irrigation proponent, "waves his hand toward the desert and says, 'Let there be water!' we know that the stream will obey his commands." The National Irrigation Association, created in 1899, organized lobbying efforts, producing the **Reclamation Act** in 1902. Under that law, the Reclamation Service became a major power in the West as it moved the region's water to areas where it could be used for irrigation. Reclamation projects sometimes drew criticism, however, for disproportionately benefiting large landowners.

Lack of water potentially posed stringent limits on western urban growth. Beginning in 1901, San

Francisco sought federal permission to create a reservoir by damming the Hetch Hetchy Valley, on federal land adjacent to Yosemite National Park in the Sierra Nevadas. Opposition came from the **Sierra Club**, formed in 1892 and dedicated to preserving Sierra Nevada wilderness. Congress finally approved the project in 1913, and the enormous construction task took more than twenty years to complete. Los Angeles resolved its water problems in a similar way, by diverting the water of the Owens River to its use—even though Owens Valley residents resisted by trying to dynamite the **aqueduct**.

Despite potential water worries, between the end of the Civil War and 1900, San Francisco emerged as the **metropolis** of the West—the commercial, financial, and manufacturing center for much of the region west of the Rockies. Building on the city's role as the major port on the Pacific Coast, San Francisco bankers played key roles in development in the West, channeling profits from gold and silver mining into railroad and steamboat lines and manufacturing enterprises. By the 1880s, San Francisco was home to foundries that produced locomotives, technologically advanced mining equipment, agricultural implements for large-scale farming, and ships. Not until 1900 did a few other western cities—Denver, Salt Lake City, Seattle, Portland, and especially Los Angeles—seriously challenge the economic dominance of San Francisco.

BOOM AND BUST: THE ECONOMY FROM THE CIVIL WAR TO WORLD WAR I

☆ *What were the major changes in the U.S. economy from the Civil War to World War I?*

The nation grew dramatically in the late nineteenth and early twentieth centuries. Between 1865 and 1920, the population increased by nearly 200 percent, from 36 million to 106 million. During the same years, railroad mileage increased by more than 1,000 percent. The output of manufacturing increased by a similar margin. Agricultural production grew far faster than the population. Perhaps most significantly, the total domestic product, per capita, in constant dollars, nearly tripled. (Figure 16.2 presents some of these patterns.)

Growth and Depression in the 1870s and 1880s

Much of this growth was sporadic. Economic historians think of the economy as developing through a cycle in which periods of **expansion** (growth) alternate with times of **contraction** (**recession** or **depression**,

---

□ **Reclamation Act** Law passed by Congress in 1902 that provided funding for irrigation of western lands and created the Reclamation Service to oversee the process.

Sierra Club Environmental organization formed in 1892; now dedicated to preserving and expanding parks, wildlife, and wilderness areas.

aqueduct A pipe or channel designed to transport water from a remote source, usually by gravity.

metropolis The dominant city within a region.

□ **expansion** In the economic cycle, a time when the economy is growing, characterized by increased production of goods and services and usually by low rates of unemployment.

□ **contraction** In the economic cycle, a time when the economy has ceased to grow, characterized by decreased production of goods and services and often by high rates of unemployment.

□ **recession/depression** A recession is an economic contraction of relatively short duration; a depression is an economic contraction of longer duration.

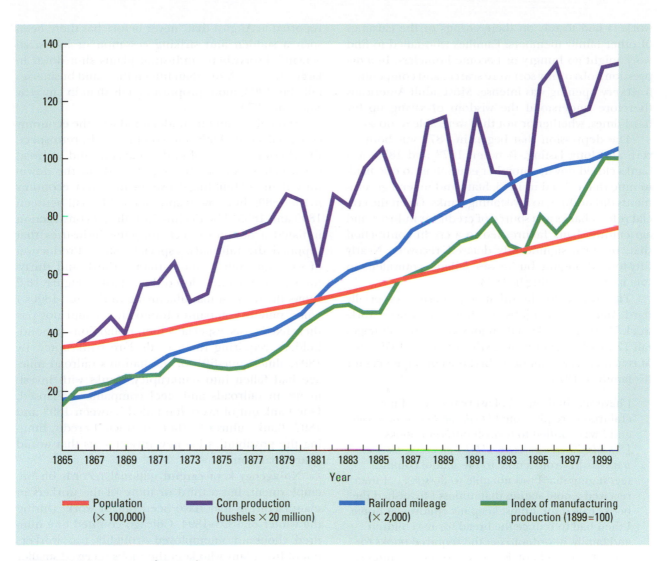

FIGURE 16.2 Measures of Growth, 1865–1900

Though many measures of economic productivity are related to population size, this graph shows how several measures of economic productivity grew more rapidly than did the population.

Source: U.S. Department of Commerce, Bureau of the Census, *Historical Statistics of the United States, Colonial Times to 1970,* Bicentennial edition, 2 vols. (Washington: Government Printing Office, 1975), I: 8, 510–512; 2: 667, 727–731.

characterized by high unemployment and low productivity). Though this alternation between expansion and contraction is predictable, there is no predictability or regularity to the duration of any given up or down period. During the late nineteenth century, contractions were sometimes severe, producing widespread unemployment and distress. After 1865, a postwar recession lasted until late 1867, reflecting sharp dislocations as the economy shifted from wartime production to other ventures. After several short expansions and contractions, a major depression began in October 1873 and lasted until March 1879. The period from 1879 to 1893 was generally one of expansion (105 months of growth), spurred in particular by railroad construction, but growth was interrupted three times by contractions (totaling 61 months), two of them quite short.

During boom periods, companies advertised for workers and ran their operations at full capacity. When the demand for manufactured goods fell, companies reduced production, cutting hours of work or dismissing employees as they waited for business to pick up. Some businesses shut down temporarily; others closed permanently.

Thus Americans living in the late nineteenth and early twentieth centuries came to expect that hard times were likely in the future, regardless of how prosperous life seemed at the moment. Until the early twentieth century, federal intervention in the economy was limited largely to stimulating growth through the protective tariff and land distribution programs. State and federal governments provided no unemployment benefits. Though churches and charity organizations sometimes gave out food, unemployed workers had to rely on their savings or the earnings of other family members. Families who failed to find work might go hungry or become homeless. In a depression, jobs of any sort were scarce, and competition for every opening was intense. Most adult Americans therefore understood the wisdom of saving up for hard times, whether or not they were able to do so.

The depression that began in 1873 was both severe and long lasting. Between 1873 and 1879, 355 banks closed down, a number equivalent to one bank in nine that existed in 1873. State and federal governments did nothing to save failing banks. Given the crucial role of banks as a source of credit for industry and agriculture, bank failures led to a credit contraction that, in turn, significantly delayed recovery. Nearly fifty-four thousand businesses failed—equivalent to one in nine operating in 1873.

The contraction hit urban wage earners especially hard. Many lost their jobs or suffered a reduced workweek. Workers who kept their jobs saw their daily wages fall 17 to 18 percent from 1873 to 1878 or 1879. One Massachusetts worker described the consequences for his family in 1875:

> I have six children . . . . Last year three of my children were promoted [*to the next grade in school*], and I was notified to furnish different books. [*Schoolchildren were responsible for providing their own textbooks.*] I wrote a note to the school committee, stating that I was not able to do so . . . . I then received a note stating that, unless I furnished the books called for, I must keep my children at home. I then had to reduce the bread for my children and family, in order to get the required books to keep them at school. Every cent of my earnings is consumed in my family; and yet I have not been able to have a piece of meat on my table twice a month for the last eight months.

Thus, though long-term economic trends reflect dramatic growth, the short-run boom-and-bust nature of the economy repeatedly claimed its victims.

Economic Collapse and Depression in the 1890s

Another major depression began in January 1893 and lasted (despite a brief upswing) until June 1897. It began when the Reading Railroad declared bankruptcy. A financial panic quickly set in. One business journal

financial panic Widespread anxiety about financial and commercial matters; in a panic, investors often sold large amounts of stock to cut their own losses, which drove prices much lower. Banks often called in their loans, forcing investors to sell assets at reduced prices, further driving down stock prices.

reported in August that "never before has there been such a sudden and striking cessation of industrial activity." Everywhere, industrial plants shut down in large numbers. More than fifteen thousand businesses failed in 1893, more proportionately than in any year since the 1870s.

At the time, no one understood why the economy collapsed so suddenly and completely. In retrospect, the slowing of agricultural expansion and railroad construction contributed significantly to the downturn. Railroad building drove the industrial economy in the 1880s, but slowed and then fell by half between 1893 and 1895. The decline in railroad construction initiated a domino effect, toppling industries that supplied the railroads, especially steel. Production of steel rails fell by more than a third, and thirty-two steel companies closed their doors. (Figure 16.2 shows the drop in manufacturing in the mid-1890s.) Some railway companies found they could not pay their fixed costs, especially their obligations to bondholders, requiring them to declare bankruptcy. By 1894, almost one-fifth of the nation's railroad mileage had fallen into bankruptcy. Banks with investments in railroads and steel companies collapsed. One bank out of every ten failed between 1893 and 1897. Bank failures further contracted credit, limiting the possibilities for new investments that would spur expansion.

No agency kept careful national records on unemployment, but a third or more of the workers in manufacturing may have been out of work. During the winter of 1893–1894, Chicago counted one hundred thousand unemployed—roughly two workers out of five. Many who kept their jobs received smaller paychecks as employers cut wages and hours.

The depression produced widespread suffering. Many who lost their jobs had little to fall back on except charity. Newspapers told of people who chose suicide when faced with the dire options of starving to death or stealing food. Many men and some women left home desperate to find work, hoping to send money to their families as soon as they could. Some walked the roads, and others hopped on freight trains, riding in boxcars.

The "Merger Movement"

As the economy finally revived in the late 1890s, Americans witnessed an astonishing number of mergers in manufacturing and mining—a "merger movement" that lasted from 1898 until 1902. The high point came in 1899, with 1,208 mergers involving $2.3 billion in capital. The merger movement resulted partly from economic weaknesses revealed by the railroad companies. The threat of vicious competition among reviving manufacturing companies prompted reorganization there too.

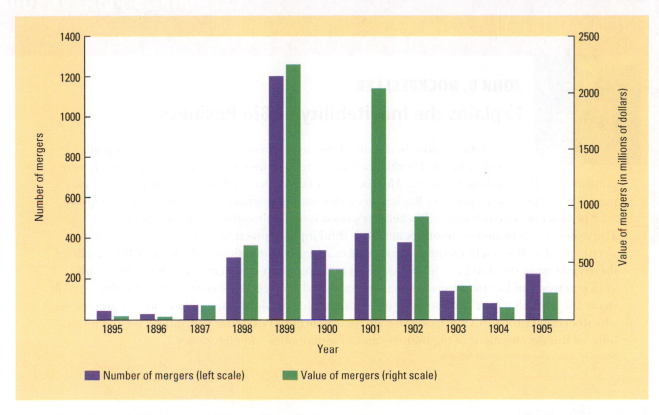

FIGURE 16.3 Recorded Mergers in Mining and Manufacturing, 1895–1905
The last few years of the 1890s and early 1900s witnessed the "merger movement," a restructuring of significant parts of corporate America. Note how the creation of United States Steel, the first "billion-dollar corporation," affects the bar for value for 1901.
© Cengage Learning.

The most prominent of the new corporations was United States Steel. As the economy edged out of the depression, J. P. Morgan began combining separate steel-related companies to create a vertically integrated operation. Andrew Carnegie had never carried vertical integration to the point of manufacturing final steel products such as wire, barrels, or tubes. By vertically integrating to include that last step, Morgan threatened to close off a significant part of Carnegie's market. Faced with the formidable prospect of having to build his own manufacturing plants for finished products, Carnegie sold all his holdings to Morgan for $480 million (equivalent to $1.2 billion today). In 1901 Morgan combined Carnegie's company with his own to create United States Steel, the first corporation capitalized at over a billion dollars (see Figure 16.3).

As with railroad reorganization in the 1880s, investment bankers sought two objectives in reorganizing an industry: first, to make the industry stable so that investments would yield predictable dividends, and second, to make the industry efficient and productive so that dividends would be high. Toward that end, investment bankers not only drove the mergers but also placed their representatives on the boards of directors of the newly created companies, to

guarantee that those two objectives were top priority. By 1912, the three leading New York banking firms together occupied 341 directorships in 112 major companies. Investment bankers argued that benefits from their activities extended far beyond the dividends that shareholders received. One of Morgan's associates predicted in 1901 that as a result of mergers and restructuring, "production would become more regular, labor would be more steadily employed at better wages, and panics caused by over-production would become a thing of the past."

In fact, the new industrial combinations failed to produce long-term economic stability. The economy continued to alternate between expansion and contraction. After the severe depression of 1893–1897, for example, a period of general expansion was interrupted by downturns in 1903, 1907–1908, 1910–1911, and 1913–1914. Morgan's hopes for stability through centralized control failed to be realized, but his activities and those of his contemporaries created many of the characteristics of modern business. Many industries were oligopolistic, dominated by a few vertically integrated companies, and the stock market had moved beyond the sale of railroad securities to play an important role in raising capital for industry.

Individual Voices

JOHN D. ROCKEFELLER
Explains the Inevitability of Big Business

Rockefeller retired in the mid-1890s and devoted much of his time thereafter to philanthropy. He also took the time to write some reminiscences, which were published as *Random Reminiscences of Men and Events* (see A Deeper Understanding of History, page 408). This excerpt provides Rockefeller's view on the origins of Standard Oil's monopoly over petroleum. The full text of Rockefeller's book is available online in several places. The excerpt tells us much about Rockefeller's thinking and practices. Efficiency and economy were central to Rockefeller's vision for success in a highly competitive industry. For Rockefeller, these goals were often to be achieved through technology. In significant part, it was Standard Oil's extension of its operations to the retail level, and the aggressive competitiveness displayed at the retail level, that gave the company its reputation for ruthlessness, and here we get an idea of why Rockefeller took this approach. We also learn part of Rockefeller's argument for the inevitability of the development of big business and of monopolies and oligopolies.

Photo by Time Life Pictures/Mansell/Time Life Pictures/Getty Images.

1 Here Rockefeller lays out a classic case of overproduction. What does the law of supply and demand, from basic economics, suggest for such a situation?

2 This is Rockefeller's explanation for the origins of the cartel that became Standard Oil. How does he explain the willingness of other petroleum refiners to join him? How does this compare with Rockefeller's reputation as an aggressive competitor?

3 Compare Rockefeller's use of technology as a competitive device with the practices of other entrepreneurs, especially Carnegie and Edison.

4 Having brought former competitors together in a cartel, and having constructed technologically advanced refineries, Standard Oil now faced what problem? How did they solve the problem?

The cleansing of crude petroleum was a simple and easy process, and at first the profits were very large. Naturally, all sorts of people went into it: the butcher, the baker, and the candlestick-maker began to refine oil, and it was only a short time before more of the finished product was put on the market than could possibly be consumed. The price went down and down until the trade was threatened with ruin **1**

This great depression [of the 1870s] led to consultations with our neighbors and friends in the business in the effort to bring some order out of what was rapidly becoming a state of chaos. To accomplish all these tasks of enlarging the market and improving the methods of manufacture in a large way was beyond the power or ability of any concern as then constituted. It could only be done, we reasoned, by increasing our capital and availing ourselves of the best talent and experience. **2**

It was with this idea that we proceeded to buy the largest and best refining concerns and centralize the administration of them with a view to securing greater economy and efficiency. **3** . . . To get the advantage of the facilities we had in manufacture, we sought the utmost market in all lands—we needed volume. **4** To do this we had to create selling methods far in advance of what then existed; we had to dispose of two, or three, or four gallons of oil where one had been sold before . . . .

It is too late to argue about advantages of industrial combinations. They are a necessity. And if Americans are to have the privilege of extending their business in all the states of the Union, and into foreign countries as well, they are a necessity on a large scale, and require the agency of more than one corporation. **5**

5 Does it seem likely that the improved quality and quantity of consumer goods in the late nineteenth century could have been possible without the development of large corporations? Why or why not?

Study Tools

SUMMARY

After 1865, large-scale manufacturing developed quickly in the United States, built on a foundation of abundant natural resources, a pool of skilled workers, expanding harvests, and favorable government policies. The outcome was the transformation of the U.S. economy.

Entrepreneurs improved and extended railway lines, creating a national transportation network. Manufacturers and merchants now began to think in terms of a national market for raw materials and finished goods. Railroads were the first businesses to grapple with the many problems related to size, and they made choices that other businesses imitated. Investment bankers, notably J. P. Morgan, led in combining separate rail companies into larger and more profitable systems. Steel was the crucial building material for much of industrial America, and Andrew Carnegie revolutionized the steel industry. He became one of the best known of many entrepreneurs who developed manufacturing operations of unprecedented size and complexity.

What Carnegie did in steel, John D. Rockefeller did in oil. Others followed their lead, producing oligopoly and vertical integration in many industries. Technology and advertising emerged as important competitive devices. One important result was the introduction of both a wide range of new consumer goods and new ways for consumers to purchase. Some southerners promoted the creation of a New South through industrialization and a more diversified agricultural base. The outcome was mixed—the South did acquire significant industry, but the region's poverty was little reduced.

Federal policymakers hoped for the rapid development of the West and often used the public domain to accomplish that purpose. Native Americans, especially those of the Great Plains, seemed to pose an obstacle to industrial development, but most were defeated by the army and relegated to reservations. Throughout the West, railroad construction overcame the vast distances, making possible cattle raising on the western Great Plains, farming in the central part of the nation, extensive mining, and lumbering. In California especially, landowners transformed western agriculture into a large-scale commercial undertaking. Water posed a significant constraint on economic development in many parts of the West, prompting efforts to reroute natural water sources.

Throughout the late nineteenth century, the economy moved through cycles of expansion and contraction, with especially severe depressions in the 1870s and 1890s. At the end of the 1890s, a large number of mergers in mining and manufacturing were seen as having the potential to stabilize the economy, but ultimately failed to do so.

CHRONOLOGY
The Nation Industrializes

1850s	Development of Bessemer and Kelly steel-making processes
1861	Protective tariff
1862	Land-Grant College Act, Homestead Act, Pacific Railway Act
1865	Civil War ends
1866–1880	Cattle drives north from Texas
1867–1868	Treaties establish major western reservations
1869	First transcontinental railroad completed
1870	Standard Oil incorporated
1870s–1880s	Extension of farming to Great Plains
1872	Montgomery Ward opens first U.S. mail-order business
1873–1879	Depression
1874	American Indian resistance ends on southern plains
1875	Andrew Carnegie opens nation's largest steel plant
1876	Alexander Graham Bell invents the telephone Indian victory in Battle of Little Bighorn; American Indian resistance ends on northern plains
1879	Invention of the incandescent light bulb
1880s	Railroad expansion and consolidation Standard Oil Trust organized
1882–1885	Recession
1883	Northern Pacific Railroad completed to Portland
1887	American Sugar Refining Company formed
1890	Conflict at Wounded Knee Creek
1902	Reclamation Act

Study Tools

FOCUS QUESTIONS

If you have mastered this chapter, you should be able to answer these questions and to identify the terms that follow the questions.

1. What factors encouraged economic growth and industrial development after the Civil War?

2. What was the significance of the railroad and steel industries in the new industrial economy that emerged after the Civil War?

3. How did investment bankers such as J. P. Morgan contribute to the new industrial economy?

4. How and why did companies expand their operations and control within an industry?

5. In what ways was the economy of the South distinctive? What direction did development efforts take in the South?

6. What were the causes and outcomes of the Indian wars of the late nineteenth century? Could they have been avoided?

7. What were the major ways in which the West was incorporated into the national economy?

8. What were the major changes in the U.S. economy from the Civil War to World War I?

KEY TERMS

cartel   *p. 397*

protective tariff   *p. 399*

Homestead Act   *p. 399*

Land-Grant College Act   *p. 399*

Pacific Railway Act   *p. 402*

mail-order sales   *p. 404*

John Pierpont Morgan   *p. 405*

Andrew Carnegie   *p. 406*

Social Darwinism   *p. 407*

Gospel of Wealth   *p. 409*

department store   *p. 412*

New South   *p. 414*

Henry Grady   *p. 414*

horse culture   *p. 415*

Lakota   *p. 416*

Crazy Horse   *p. 418*

Sitting Bull   *p. 418*

Great Sioux War   *p. 418*

Little Bighorn River   *p. 418*

Chief Joseph   *p. 419*

Ghost Dance   *p. 419*

Wounded Knee Creek   *p. 420*

Reclamation Act   *p. 426*

expansion   *p. 426*

contraction   *p. 426*

recession/depression   *p. 426*

SUGGESTED RESOURCES

Edward L. Ayers. *The Promise of the New South: Life After Reconstruction* (1992; New York: Oxford University Press, 2007). A comprehensive survey of developments in the South in the late nineteenth century.

Gilder Lehrman Institute of American History. *"The Rise of Industrial America, 1877–1900,"* http://www.gilderlehrman.org/history-by-era/rise-industrial-america-1877-1900. A collection of primary sources and essays by prominent historians; look especially at the sections on the Gilded Age and the development of the West.

Glenn Porter. *The Rise of Big Business, 1860–1910,* 3rd ed. (Hoboken, NJ: Wiley-Blackwell, 2006). A brief and well-written introduction to the subject, surveying the role of the railroads, vertical and horizontal integration, and the merger movement.

Elliott West. *The Last Indian War: The Nez Perce Story* (New York: Oxford University Press, 2009). A masterful retelling of a pivotal and poignant moment in U.S. history, based on extensive archival research and placing western events into the national context of Reconstruction and industrialization.

Richard White. *"It's Your Misfortune and None of My Own": A History of the American West* (1991; Norman: University of Oklahoma Press, 1993). White reconsiders the history of the West, from the first European contact to the late 1980s.

17

Life in the Gilded Age, 1865–1900

CHAPTER OUTLINE

The New Urban America

The New Face of the City

The New Urban Middle Class

Redefining Gender Roles

Emergence of a Gay and Lesbian Subculture

"How the Other Half Lives"

New South, Old Problems

Social Patterns in the New South

The Second Mississippi Plan and the Atlanta Compromise

Ethnicity and Race in the Gilded Age

A Flood of Immigrants from Europe

Nativism

Immigrants to the Golden Mountain

Forced Assimilation

Mexican Americans in the Southwest

Workers Organize

Workers for Industry

The Origins of Unions and Labor Conflict in the 1870s

Competing Labor Organizations in the 1880s

Labor on the Defensive in the 1890s

INDIVIDUAL VOICES: *Mary Tape Challenges the San Francisco Board of Education*

Study Tools

INDIVIDUAL CHOICES

The Tape Family

Born in China in 1857 and orphaned shortly after in California, the little girl took the name Mary McGladery when she lived in the orphanage run by the San Francisco Ladies' Protection and Relief Society. There Mary learned English, other school subjects, how to play the piano, and how to be a proper middle-class lady. In 1875, she married Jeu Dip. Born in China in 1852, he had emigrated to San Francisco in 1869, learned English, operated a successful business, and Americanized his name to Joseph Tape.

The Tapes moved to a house outside Chinatown where their first child, Mamie, was born in 1876. Three more children followed. In 1884, the Tapes tried to enroll Mamie in the school nearest their home, but the San Francisco school board had long denied admission to children of Chinese parentage. The Tapes filed a lawsuit to permit Mamie to attend school, and the court ruled in their favor, as did the state supreme court. However, the San Francisco school superintendent persuaded the legislature to amend state law to permit separate schools for children of Chinese descent. Mamie was again denied admission to her neighborhood school (see the Individual Voices feature at the end of this chapter).

Courtesy of Alisa J. Kim and Mitchell C. Kim.

433

Mamie and her brother were the first to enroll at the new Chinese school. There Mamie and her siblings learned Cantonese and other Chinese cultural patterns. In 1895, the Tapes moved to Berkeley, where the younger children could attend the regular public schools. While still in San Francisco, Mary had become an award-winning and technologically innovative amateur photographer. In Berkeley, Joseph's businesses continued to prosper, and the Tapes invested in real estate and eventually owned two ranches, where Joseph enjoyed hunting.

Mary and Joseph Tape provide examples of those whom historians of immigration have called "rapid assimilators"—those who quickly learn English and adopt many aspects of the majority lifestyle. Joseph's successful business enterprises permitted them to live in middle-class, white neighborhoods. Mae Ngai, a historian who has researched the Tape family, describes them as "highly unusual" among the immigrants of their time, but as "archetypical members of the first Chinese American middle class."

The Tapes' experiences as immigrants, city-dwellers, and westerners all involve major areas of change in American life following the Civil War. American cities grew rapidly, and technology made cities ever more exciting places, with skyscrapers, self-propelled streetcars, and electric lights. Technology joined with industry to produce new marvels for urban consumers like telephones, phonographs, and cameras such as those Mary Tape used to take her award-winning photographs.

Historians often call the late nineteenth century the Gilded Age, after *The Gilded Age: A Tale of Today,* a novel by Samuel L. Clemens and Charles Dudley Warner, published in 1873. In the novel—the first for either writer—Clemens and Warner satirized the business and politics of their day. (Clemens used the pen name Mark Twain as the author of *Tom Sawyer, Huckleberry Finn,* and other classics.) Using "the Gilded Age" to refer to the years from the late 1860s through the 1890s suggests the gleam of a surface gilded with a thin coating of gold that covers a cheap base metal underneath. Among the aspects of late-nineteenth-century life that might justify the label "gilded" were the dramatic expansion of the economy, the spectacular accomplishments of new technologies, the extravagant wealth and great power of the new industrial entrepreneurs, and the rapid economic development of the West. Just below that glittering surface, however, lay the grim realities of life for most industrial workers, the crowded and unsanitary tenements of the cities, and discrimination against racial and ethnic minorities. In turning to the courts, the Tapes were among the significant numbers of Chinese Americans who sought judicial redress when local or state laws violated their legal and constitutional rights, thereby helping to break down racial segregation and discrimination.

THE NEW URBAN AMERICA

☆ *What were the key factors in the transformation of American cities in the late nineteenth century?*

☆ *What important new social patterns emerged in urban areas in the late nineteenth century?*

During the late nineteenth century, American cities boomed in size. Chicago doubled to take second rank, behind New York. In just ten years, Brooklyn grew by more than 40 percent, St. Louis by nearly 30 percent, and San Francisco by almost as much. Cities not only added more people but also expanded upward and outward, and became more complex, both socially and economically. The burgeoning cities presented new opportunities for some, especially the middle class. In the new urban environments, some women questioned traditionally defined gender roles, as did gays and lesbians. But as cities grew, so did the population of their most disadvantaged residents.

walking city Term describing cities before changes in urban transportation permitted cities to expand beyond the distance that a person could easily cover on foot.

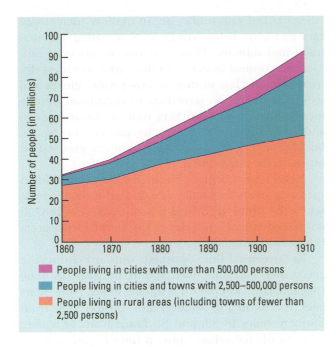

FIGURE 17.1 Urban and Rural Population of the United States, 1860–1910

Although much of the population increase between 1860 and 1910 came in urban areas, the number of people living in rural areas increased as well. Notice that the largest increase was in towns and cities between 2,500 and 500,000 people.

Source: U.S. Bureau of the Census, Department of Commerce, *Historical Statistics of the United States,* 2 vols. (Washington, D.C.: U.S. Government Printing Office, 1975), Series A-58, A-59, A-69, A-119.

The New Face of the City

Many Americans were fascinated by their burgeoning cities. Cities boasted technological innovations that many equated with progress, but the lure of the city stemmed from more than telephones, streetcars, and technological gadgetry. Samuel Lane Loomis in 1887 listed the many activities found in cities: "The churches and the schools, the theatres and concerts, the lectures, fairs, exhibitions, and galleries…and the mighty streams of human beings that forever flow up and down the thoroughfares." Not every urban vista was so appealing. Some visitors were shocked and repulsed by the poverty, crime, and filth that cluttered the urban landscape.

Filled with glamour and destitution, cities grew rapidly. Cities with more than fifty thousand people grew almost twice as fast as rural areas (see Figure 17.1). The nation had twenty-five cities that large in 1870. By 1890, fifty-eight cities—nearly all in the Northeast and Great Lakes region—had reached that size and held nearly 12 million people. The mechanization of American agriculture meant that farming required fewer workers, so newcomers from America's farmlands contributed to the growth of the cities, along with immigration from outside the United States, especially Europe.

The growth of manufacturing went hand in hand with urban expansion. By the late nineteenth century, the nation had developed a manufacturing belt. This region, which included nearly all the largest cities as well as the bulk of the nation's manufacturing, may be thought of as the nation's urban-industrial "core" (see Map 17.1). Some of the cities in this region—notably Boston, New York, Baltimore, Buffalo, and St. Louis—had long been among the busiest ports in the nation. Now manufacturing also flourished there. Other cities developed as industrial centers from their beginnings. Some cities became known for a particular product—iron and steel in Pittsburgh, clothing in New York City, meatpacking in Chicago. A few cities, especially New York, stood out as major centers for finance.

As the urban population swelled and the urban economy grew more complex, cities expanded upward and outward. In the early 1800s, most cities measured only a few miles across, and most residents got around on foot. Historians call such places "**walking cities**." In the late nineteenth century, new technologies for construction and transportation transformed the cities.

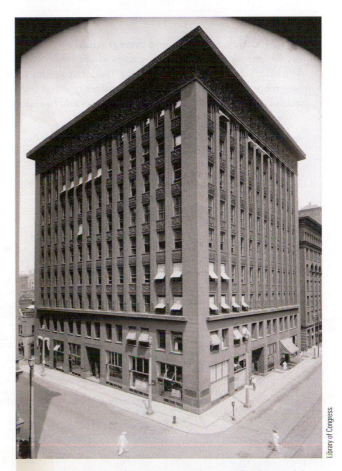

Louis Sullivan, one of the Chicago architects who designed the early skyscrapers, designed the Wainwright Building (St. Louis, 1890) with the intention of creating what he called a "proud and soaring thing." He also tried to design exteriors that reflected interior functions, in keeping with his rule that "form follows function." The building was widely acclaimed and often imitated.

Until the 1880s, construction techniques restricted building height because the walls carried the structure's full weight. William LeBaron Jenney designed the first skyscraper—ten stories high, erected in Chicago in 1885. Chicago architects, adapting Jenney's approach by using a steel frame to carry the weight instead of the walls, took the lead in designing other tall buildings. Economical and efficient, skyscrapers created unique city skylines.

Just as steel-frame buildings allowed cities to grow upward, so new transportation technologies led cities to expand outward. In the 1850s, horses pulled the first streetcars over iron rails laid in city streets. By the 1870s and 1880s, some cities boasted streetcars powered by underground moving cables. Electricity, however, revolutionized urban transit. Frank Sprague designed a streetcar driven by an electric motor that drew power from an overhead wire; he installed his first system in Richmond, Virginia, in 1888. Within a dozen years, electric streetcars replaced nearly all horse and cable cars. In the early 1900s, some large

cities, choked with traffic, began to move their streetcars above or below street level, creating elevated trains and subways. Thus elaborate networks of rails came to connect **suburbs** to downtown business districts. Middle-class women wearing white gloves and stylish hats rode on streetcars to downtown department stores. Skilled workers took streetcar lines to and from their jobs. Streetcars carried the typists, bookkeepers, and corporate executives who staffed offices in the city's center.

New construction technologies launched bridges spanning rivers that had once limited urban growth. When the Brooklyn Bridge was completed in 1883, it was hailed as a new wonder of the world. Other great bridges soon followed.

As streetcar lines pushed outward from the city center, cities annexed suburban areas. In 1860 Chicago had occupied 17 square miles; forty years later, it took in 190 square miles. Boston grew from 5 square miles to 39, and St. Louis from 14 square miles to 61. Suburban railroad lines began to bring

MAP 17.1 Cities, Industry, and Immigration

This map presents major U.S. cities, areas where immigrants lived, and the urban-industrial core region that included most cities and manufacturing. Western counties are much larger than eastern counties but were much more sparsely populated, so the western counties that show large *proportions* of immigrants did not necessarily have *numbers* of immigrants comparable to eastern cities. © Cengage Learning

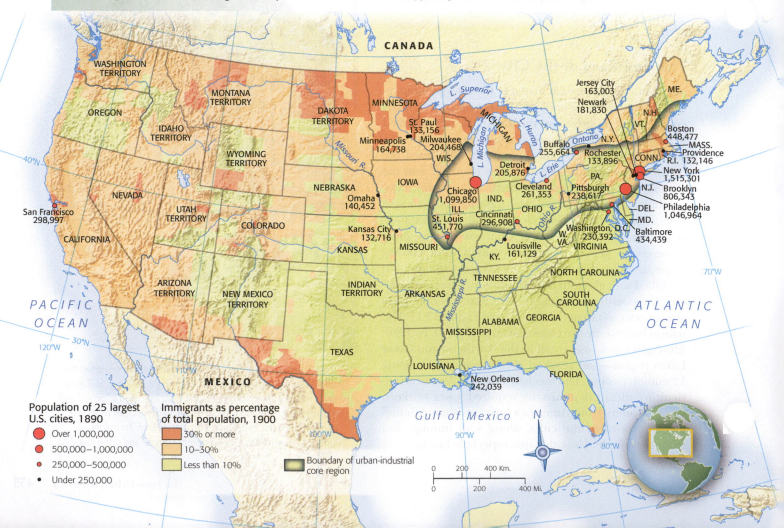

STATE STREET, CHICAGO

Photo by Lake County Museum/Getty Images.

This postcard shows the heart of the Chicago shopping district about 1910. Streetcars made it possible for the city to expand dramatically, from 17 square miles in 1860 to 170 square miles in 1900. "Streetcar suburbs" took in even more territory. This postcard also shows some of the skyscrapers, a term and a technology that originated in Chicago.

more distant villages within commuting distance of urban centers. Wealthier residents could now afford to leave the city at the end of the workday. By about 1890 seventy thousand suburbanites were pouring into Chicago each day, and commuter lines brought more than a hundred thousand workers daily into New York City just from its northern suburbs.

New suburbs ranged outward from the city center in order of wealth. Those who could afford to travel the farthest could also afford the most expensive homes. Those too poor to ride the new transportation lines lived in densely populated and deteriorating neighborhoods in the center of the city or clustered around industrial plants. Much of the burgeoning urban middle class lived between the two extremes, far enough from the central business district that many residents rode streetcars downtown to work or shop.

Caught up in headlong growth, cities and their **infrastructure** developed with minimal planning. Local governments did little to regulate expansion or create building standards, leaving landowners, developers, and builders to make decisions about land use and construction practices. Everywhere, builders and owners sought to construct the most space for the least cost. Such profit calculations rarely left room for amenities like varied designs or open space. Most of the great urban parks that exist today, including Central Park in New York City, Prospect Park in Brooklyn, and Golden Gate Park in San Francisco, were established on the outskirts of their cities, before the surrounding areas were developed.

Given the rapid and largely unplanned nature of most urban growth, city governments often had difficulty meeting the demands for expanded municipal utilities and services—fire and police protection, schools, sewage disposal, street maintenance, water supply.

The quality and quantity of the water supply varied greatly from city to city. Some cities spent enormous sums to transport water over long distances, but water quality remained a problem in most locales. As city officials learned that germs caused diseases, some cities introduced filtration and **chlorination** of their water, but change came slowly—only 6 percent of urban residents received filtered water by 1900.

City residents faced major obstacles in disposing of sewage, cleaning streets (especially given the ever-present horses), and removing garbage. Not all cities had sewer lines, and those that did usually dumped untreated sewage into a nearby body of water. The disgusted mayor of Cleveland in 1881 called the Cuyahoga River "an open sewer through the center of the city"; similar situations existed in most large cities.

■ **suburb** A residential area lying outside the central city; many residents of suburbs work and shop in the central city though living outside it.

infrastructure Basic facilities that a society needs to function, such as transportation systems, water and power lines, and public institutions such as schools, post offices, and prisons.

chlorination The treatment of water with the chemical chlorine to kill germs.

Few city streets were paved, so most became mud holes in the rain, threw up dust clouds in dry weather, and froze into deep ruts in the winter. Chicago in 1890 included 2,048 miles of streets, but only 629 miles were paved, typically with wooden blocks. Only in the late nineteenth century did cities begin using asphalt paving. Street cleaning was often minimal—clearing garbage from a street in the 1890s, one Chicagoan discovered pavement under 18 inches of trash.

City utilities, including gas, public transit, sometimes water, and later electricity and telephone service, were typically provided by private companies operating under **franchises** from the city. Entrepreneurs eagerly competed for such franchises, sometimes bribing city officials to secure them. As a result, new residential areas sometimes had gas lines before sewers, and streetcars before paved streets.

Despite such growing pains, most city utilities and services improved between 1870 and 1900. New York City created the first uniformed police force in 1845, and other cities followed. By 1871, major cities had switched from volunteer fire companies to paid, professional firefighters. The new system proved inadequate, however, in the Great Chicago Fire of 1871, which devastated 3 square miles, including much of the downtown, killed more than 250 people, and left 18,000 homeless. Such disasters spurred efforts to improve fire protection by better training and equipping firefighters and by regulating construction so that buildings were more fire resistant. By 1900, most American cities had impressive firefighting forces. Chicago had more firefighters and fire engines than London, a city three times its size.

The New Urban Middle Class

The Gilded Age brought significant changes to the lives of many middle-class Americans, especially those in the army of accountants, lawyers, secretaries, agents, and managers who staffed developing corporate headquarters and professional offices in the rising central business districts. Streetcar lines allowed this growing middle class to live in expanding suburbs distinct from both the neighborhoods of the industrial working class and the enclaves of the wealthy.

Single-family houses set amid carefully tended lawns were common in many new middle-class neighborhoods or suburbs in the late nineteenth century. Such developments accelerated the tendency of American urban and suburban areas to sprawl for miles. Owning property had long been central to the American dream. In the late nineteenth century, the

· A ·Twelve· Hundred· Dollar· Cottage·

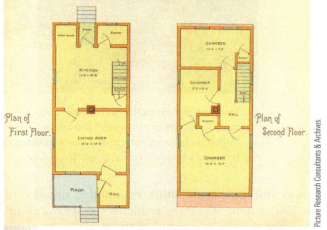

Plan of First Floor.

Plan of Second Floor.

Picture Research Consultants & Archives.

As streetcars permitted some Americans to move to the new, streetcar suburbs, developers and building contractors depicted new homes set amidst green trees and lawns where children could play. This design for a middle-class suburban house appeared in *Scientific American: Architects and Builders Edition,* in June 1887. The floor-plan indicates just how modest this house was: it had no dining room, no bathroom, and only one closet. The price, $1,200 not including the land, was equivalent in purchasing power to about $30,000 in 2012, but it was still far beyond the reach of the average blue-collar worker.

single-family house became the realization of that dream for many middle-class families. Many members of the middle class found it especially attractive to acquire a house in a suburb with streetcar or commuter rail connections to the city. Such suburbs allowed the urban middle class to avoid the congestion of the slums, the violence of labor conflicts, and the higher property taxes that funded city governments.

In new middle-class neighborhoods, many families employed a domestic servant to assist with household chores, and middle-class women often participated in social organizations outside the home. Unlike many working-class families, middle-class parents rarely expected their children to contribute to the family's finances.

franchise Government authorization allowing a company to provide a public service in a certain area.

Middle-class families provided the major market for an expansion of daily newspapers, which began to include sections designed to appeal to women—household hints, fashion advice, and news of women's organizations—along with sports sections aimed at men, and comics for the children. Such families were also likely to subscribe to magazines such as the *Ladies' Home Journal* and the *Saturday Evening Post*. Much of the advertising in such publications was aimed at the middle class, fostering what historians have called a consumer culture among middle-class women, who became responsible for nearly all their family's shopping.

Middle-class parents' concern for their children's education combined with other factors to bring important changes to American education. Between 1870 and 1900, most northern and western states and territories established school attendance laws, requiring children between certain ages (usually 8 to 14) to attend school for a minimum number of weeks each year, typically twelve to sixteen.

A bigger change came at the secondary level. There were fewer than eight hundred high schools in the entire nation in 1878, but fifty-five hundred by 1898. The proportion of high school graduates in the population tripled. By 1890, four-year, public high schools were to be found in urban areas except in the South (see page 444). The new high school curriculum included science, civics, business, and home economics, as well as skills needed by industry, such as drafting, woodworking, and the mechanical trades. From 1870 onward, women outnumbered men among high school graduates. High schools, however, remained largely an urban, middle-class phenomenon. In rural areas, few students continued beyond the eighth grade, and urban working-class youth often started working full time at about the same age.

College enrollments also grew, especially the state universities created under the Land-Grant College Act of 1862, but college students came disproportionately from middle- and upper-class families and rarely from farms. The college curriculum changed dramatically, from a few courses required of all students (Latin, Greek, mathematics, rhetoric, and religion) to a system in which students focused on a major and took additional electives. Land-grant universities all provided instruction in engineering and agriculture, and other new college subjects included economics, political science, modern languages, laboratory sciences, business administration, and teacher preparation. In 1870 most colleges' curricula still resembled those of a century before. By 1900, curricula looked much like those today.

Far fewer women than men marched in college graduation processions. Only one college graduate in seven was a woman in 1870, and this improved only to one in four by 1900 (see Figure 17.2). In 1879 fewer than half of the nation's colleges admitted women, although most public universities did so. Twenty years

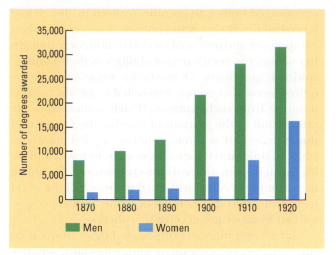

FIGURE 17.2 Number of First Degrees Awarded by Colleges and Universities, 1870–1920
This figure shows the change in the number of people receiving B.A., B.S., or other first college degrees, at ten-year intervals from 1870 to 1920. Notice that, after 1890, the number of women increased more rapidly than the number of men.

Source: Bureau of the Census, Historical Statistics of the United States, Colonial Times to 1970, Bicentennial edition (Washington, D.C.: U.S. GPO, 1975), 1: 385–386.

later, four-fifths of all colleges, universities, and professional schools enrolled women.

Nonetheless, some colleges remained all-male enclaves, especially prestigious private institutions such as Harvard and Yale. Colleges exclusively for women began to appear after the Civil War, partly because so many colleges refused to admit women and partly owing to the notion that men and women should occupy "separate spheres." Such institutions also provided opportunities for women as faculty members and administrators. The initial faculty of Vassar College, chartered in 1861, consisted of eight men and twenty-two women, including Maria Mitchell, a leading astronomer and the first female member of the American Academy of Arts and Sciences.

Redefining Gender Roles

Greater educational opportunities for women marked one part of a major reconstruction of gender roles. Throughout the nineteenth century, most Americans defined women's roles as those of wife and mother, responsible for the family's moral, spiritual, and physical well-being. This emphasis on domesticity also

■ **consumer culture** A consumer buys products for personal use; a consumer culture emphasizes the values and attitudes that derive from the participants' roles as consumers.

■ **domesticity** The notion common throughout much of the nineteenth century that women should focus on the home, nurture of children, church, and school.

encouraged women to become involved in church and school affairs. Business and politics, however, with their competition and potential for corruption, were thought to endanger women's responsibilities as their families' spiritual guardians. Domesticity, some argued, required women to occupy a so-called **separate sphere**, immune from such dangers. Widely touted from the pulpits and in the journals of the day, the concepts of domesticity and separate spheres applied mostly to white middle- and upper-class women in towns and cities. Farm women and working-class women (including most women of color) witnessed too much of the world to fit easily into the patterns of dainty innocence prescribed by advocates of separate spheres.

Increasing numbers of people began to question the concepts of domesticity and, especially, separate spheres in the late nineteenth century. One challenge came through education. As more and more women finished college, some entered the professions. By 1900, teaching had come to be dominated by women, and some women were succeeding as journalists, authors, and artists. As early as 1849, Elizabeth Blackwell became the first woman to complete medical school, and she helped to open a medical school for women in 1868. By the 1880s, some twenty-five hundred women held medical degrees. After 1900, however, new admission practices sharply reduced the number of female medical students. In 1869, Arabella Mansfield became the first woman admitted to practice law, but only sixty women practiced law, nationwide, ten years later. Most law schools refused to admit women until the 1890s. Other professions also yielded, sometimes very slowly, to women seeking admission.

Professional careers attracted a few women, but many middle- and upper-class women in towns and cities became involved in other women's activities, especially women's clubs, which claimed one hundred thousand members nationwide by the 1890s. Such clubs often began within the separate women's sphere as forums for discussing literature or art, but they sometimes led women into reform activities in the public sphere. (Of course, women had publicly participated in reform before, especially in the movement to abolish slavery.) Ida Wells-Barnett, a crusader for black civil rights, actively promoted the development of black women's clubs.

Women who regarded alcohol as the chief reason for men's neglect and abuse of their families organized the **Woman's Christian Temperance Union** (WCTU) in 1874. WCTU members committed themselves to total abstinence from all alcohol and sought to protect the home and family by converting others to abstinence and promoting the legal prohibition of alcohol. The organization typically operated through Protestant churches—especially the Methodists, Presbyterians, Congregationalists, and Baptists. Frances Willard was the driving force in the organization from 1879 until her death in 1898. Her motto was "Do everything," and she was untiring in her work for temperance. By the early 1890s, the WCTU claimed 150,000 members, making it the largest women's organization in the nation. For Willard as for many of its members, the organization rested squarely on the ideals of domesticity. She once offered a simple statement of purpose for the WCTU: "to make the whole world homelike."

Women's church organizations, clubs, and reform societies all provided experience in working together toward a common cause and sometimes in seeking changes in public policy. Through them, women cultivated leadership skills. These experiences and contacts contributed to the growing effectiveness of women's efforts to establish their right to vote. In 1882 the WCTU endorsed woman suffrage, the first support for that cause from a major women's organization other than those formed specifically to advocate woman suffrage. Thus domesticity—the guiding principle of the WCTU—led its members to challenge the notion of separate spheres.

Just as women's gender roles were undergoing reconstruction in the late nineteenth century, so too were those of men. In the early nineteenth century, manliness was defined largely in terms of "character," which included courage, honor, independence, duty, and loyalty (including loyalty to a political party), along with providing a good home for a family. With the growth of the urban industrial society, fewer men were self-employed (and thus no longer "independent"), and fewer men had opportunities to demonstrate courage or boldness. The rise of big-city political organizations dominated by saloonkeepers and working-class immigrants caused some middle- and upper-class males to question older notions of party loyalty.

In response, some middle-class men turned to activities that emphasized male bonding or masculinity. Fraternal organizations modeled on the **Masons** multiplied in the late nineteenth century, providing a ritualistic affirmation of traditional values and modest insurance benefits for widows and orphans. Professional athletics, especially baseball and boxing, began to attract male spectators of all classes. The

□ separate spheres The notion that men should engage in the public sphere of business and politics but women should limit themselves to the private, domestic sphere. Some women and men challenged this idea in the late nineteenth century.

□ Woman's Christian Temperance Union (WCTU) Woman's organization founded in 1874 that opposed alcoholic beverages and supported reforms such as woman suffrage.

Masons The Ancient Free and Accepted Masons is one of the largest secret fraternal societies. The order uses allegorical rituals, open only to members, to teach moral values. It is limited to men but has auxiliaries open to women.

The WCTU developed out of activities by women in various locations in the early 1870s. These early temperance advocates gathered outside saloons, sang hymns, and urged men to come out or not go in. This group of temperance workers was photographed in Mount Vernon, Ohio, around 1873 or 1874.

Young Men's Christian Association (YMCA) spread rapidly in American cities after the Civil War, emphasizing Christian values, physical fitness, and service. Wilderness camping and hunting—once necessities for many Americans—now became a middle- and upper-class sport, a demonstration of masculinity. Theodore Roosevelt claimed that hunting big game promoted the manly virtues of "nerve control" and "cool-headedness."

Emergence of a Gay and Lesbian Subculture

Urbanization and economic change contributed to the social redefinition of gender roles for middle-class women and men, but a quite different redefinition occurred at the same time, as burgeoning cities provided a setting for the development of gay and lesbian subcultures.

Homosexual behavior was illegal everywhere. At the same time, however, men and women engaged in a wide variety of socially acceptable same-sex relationships. The concept of separate spheres and the tendency for most schools and workplaces to be segregated by sex meant that many men and women spent much of their time with others of their own sex. Same-sex relationships may not have involved physical contact, although kisses and hugs—and sleeping in the same bed—were common expressions of affection among young women. Participants did not consider themselves to be committing what the laws called "an unnatural act," and most married partners of the opposite sex.

Same-sex relationships that involved genital contact violated the law and the expectations of society. In rural communities, where most people knew one another, people physically attracted to those of their own sex either suppressed those desires or exercised them discreetly, but the record of convictions for **sodomy** indicates that some failed to do so. A few men and somewhat more women changed their dress and behavior and passed for a member of the other sex; some even married someone of their own sex.

sodomy Varieties of sexual intercourse prohibited by law in the nineteenth century, typically including intercourse between two males.

This photograph from Jacob Riis's book *How the Other Half Lives* shows an interior court on the Lower East Side of New York City, open to the sky above. As the photograph suggests, such places were often the playgrounds for children of the poor residents. On the far right is a water pump, probably the source of water for the residents. Adding such powerful visual images—possible because of new printing technologies—greatly increased the effectiveness of Riis's book in mobilizing reform.

The Museum of the City of New York/Art Resource, NY.

The burgeoning cities of the late nineteenth century permitted an anonymity not possible in rural societies. Homosexuals and lesbians gravitated toward the cities and began to create distinctive **subcultures**. By the 1890s, one researcher reported that "perverts of both sexes maintained a sort of social set-up in New York City, had their places of meeting, and [the] advantage of police protection." Reports of homosexual meeting places—clubs, restaurants, steam baths, parks, streets—also issued from Boston, Chicago, New Orleans, St. Louis, and San Francisco. Although most participants in these subcultures were secretive, some flaunted their sexuality.

In the 1880s, physicians began to study members of these emerging subcultures and created medical names

for them, including "homosexual," "lesbian," "invert," and "pervert." Earlier, law and religion had defined particular *actions* as illegal or immoral. The new, clinical definitions emphasized not the actions but instead the *persons* taking the actions. As medical and legal definitions shifted from actions to persons, the nature of same-sex relationships also changed. Once-acceptable behavior, including expressions of affection between heterosexuals of the same sex, became less common as many individuals tried to avoid any suggestion that they were anything but heterosexual.

"How the Other Half Lives"

In 1890 Jacob Riis shocked many Americans with the revelations in *How the Other Half Lives*.* Of New York City's million and a half inhabitants, Riis claimed, half a million had begged for food at some time over the preceding eight years. Of these, more than half were

subculture A group whose members share most values and interests with the dominant culture but differ from it in some values or interests.

*Jacob A. Riis, How the Other Half Lives: Studies Among the Tenements of New York (New York: Charles Scribner's Sons, 1890), Ch. 2.

It Matters Today

Urban Building Codes

Nineteenth-century cities grew with little regulation or planning. As Jacob Riis revealed, housing was often poorly constructed, with little attention paid to health or safety. Riis's book led to new regulations for tenement buildings, notably a requirement that rooms must have a window. A later regulation required that the window open to the outside to provide fresh air for the inhabitants. Devastating fires, such as the Chicago fire of 1871, led to regulations intended to prevent or restrict fire. Today, cities typically have highly detailed building codes intended to protect the health and safety of those who live and work in buildings, to prevent or restrict fires, and to prevent overcrowding. Today, the International Code Council, a nongovernmental, nonprofit body develops model building codes that are often adopted by cities and other governmental bodies.

- Building codes can spark local political controversies. Use the Internet to find recent examples of controversies over building codes. What are the issues? Do they reflect the origins of building codes?
- Use the Internet to investigate the International Code Council. Who belongs to it? What authority does it have? Is it related to the origins of building codes?

---

unemployed, but only 6 percent were physically unable to work. Most of Riis's book described the appalling conditions of **tenements**—home, he claimed, to three-quarters of the city's population.

Strictly speaking, a tenement is a building occupied by three or more families, but the term came to imply overcrowded and poorly maintained housing that was hazardous to the health and safety of its residents. Riis described the typical, cramped New York tenement of his day as

> a brick building from four to six stories high on the street, frequently with a store on the first floor....Four families occupy each floor, and a set of rooms consists of one or two dark closets, used as bedrooms, with a living room twelve feet by ten. The staircase is too often a dark well in the center of the house...no direct through ventilation is possible.

Such buildings, Riis insisted, "are the hotbeds of the epidemics that carry death to rich and poor alike; the nurseries of pauperism and crime that fill our jails and police courts....Above all, they touch the family life with deadly moral contagion." He especially deplored the harmful influence of poverty and miserable housing conditions on children and families.

Crowded conditions in working-class sections of large cities developed in part because so many of the poor needed to live within walking distance of sources of employment for various family members. By dividing buildings into small rental units, landlords packed in more tenants and collected more rent. To pay the rent, many tenants took in lodgers. Such practices produced shockingly high population densities in lower-income urban neighborhoods.

No other city was as densely populated as New York, but nearly all urban, working-class neighborhoods were crowded. Most Chicago stockyard workers, for example, lived in small row houses near the slaughterhouses. Though some owned their homes, a survey in 1911 revealed that three-quarters of the houses were subdivided into two or more living units, typically of four rooms each, and that a small shanty often sat in the backyard. More than half of all families took in lodgers, and lodgers who worked different shifts at the stockyards sometimes took turns sleeping in the same bed.

Few agreed on the causes of urban poverty, still fewer on its cure. Riis divided the blame among greedy landlords, corrupt officials, and the poor themselves. In *Progress and Poverty* Henry George, a San Francisco journalist, pointed to the ever increasing value of urban real estate, which made it difficult or impossible for many to afford a home of their own. In contrast, the Charity Organization Society (COS), with chapters in a hundred cities by 1895, claimed that, in most cases, individual character defects produced poverty and that assistance for such people only rewarded immorality or laziness. The COS insisted that assistance should be given only after careful investigation and only until the person secured work. COS officials also required recipients of aid to be moral, thrifty, and hardworking.

tenement A multifamily apartment building, often unsafe, unsanitary, and overcrowded.

In 1908, Lewis Hine, a photographer working for the National Child Labor Committee, documented the exploitation of American children. His work—including some of the most famous photographs ever taken—made clear that violations of child labor laws were widespread, and that child labor was robbing children of their youth, education, and opportunities for a better life. Hine recorded this information about the photo on the left: "Furman Owens, 12 years old. Can't read. Doesn't know his A, B, C's. Said, 'Yes I want to learn but can't when I work all the time.' Been in the mills 4 years, 3 years in the Olympia Mill. Columbia, South Carolina." For the photo on the right, Hine wrote, "The overseer said apologetically, 'She just happened in.' She was working steadily. The mills seem full of youngsters who 'just happened in' or 'are helping sister.' Newberry, S.C."

New South, Old Problems

★ *What new social patterns appeared in the South after Reconstruction?*

★ *How did southern racial relations develop after Reconstruction?*

The South experienced less urban growth than the Northeast. Some southerners worked to promote a New South based on a more diverse economy, with more manufacturing and less reliance on staple agricultural crops (see page 414). They and their neighbors—white and black alike—grappled, too, with the legacy of slavery, Civil War, Reconstruction, and poverty. In the end, white southerners created a racially segregated social structure that persisted with little change for more than a half-century.

Social Patterns in the New South

Of the nation's twenty-five largest cities in 1890, only New Orleans was located in the South, and no other southern city came close to its 242,000 people. Atlanta, which prided itself as the center of the New South and had nearly doubled in size between 1880 and 1890, counted nearly 81,000 people in 1890 but ranked only forty-first among the nation's cities. Birmingham, center of the developing southern iron and steel industry, grew by ten times between 1880 and 1900, but ranked only one-hundredth in the nation in size as late as 1900. Thus, while an urban middle class did develop and grow in the South, it was significantly smaller than

its counterpart to the north—and was sharply divided by the lines of race.

Education lagged throughout most of the South, especially in rural areas. Compared with the rest of the nation, fewer children attended school in the South, where the school term was often just a few months, and school facilities were often inadequate. Few southern states had compulsory school attendance laws. Southerners were slow to create public high schools—as late as 1903, the entire state of Georgia had only four 4-year, public high schools. Instead, most public schools stopped at the eighth grade, and private academies educated the children of the wealthy. Some industries of the New South, especially textiles and cigarettes, were built on child labor, so many children worked instead of attending school. Seventy percent of southern cotton-mill workers were younger than 21, and many were under 14. Mostly girls, they worked 70-hour weeks and earned 10 to 20 cents a day. Not surprisingly, as late as 1900, 10 percent of the southern white population was illiterate, compared with fewer than 4 percent elsewhere in the country. Illiteracy among African Americans was significantly higher—35 percent in the South, and 19 percent elsewhere.

Despite repeated backing for the idea of a New South by some southern leaders, and despite growth of some industry in the South, the late nineteenth century was also the time when the myths of the **Old South** and the **Lost Cause** reached deeply into white southern life. Popular fiction and song, North and South, romanticized the pre–Civil War "Old South" as a place of gentility and gallantry, where "kindly"

444   CHAPTER 17   Life in the Gilded Age, 1865–1900

plantation owners cared for "loyal" slaves. The "Lost Cause" myth portrayed the Confederacy as a heroic, even noble, effort to retain the life and values of the Old South. Leading southerners—especially Democratic Party leaders—promoted the myth. Hundreds of statues of Confederate soldiers appeared on courthouse lawns, and gala commemorative events and organizations reflected devotion to the myth among many white southerners. One of the few dissenting voices was that of Samuel Clemens (Mark Twain).

The Second Mississippi Plan and the Atlanta Compromise

Although Reconstruction ended in 1877, the Civil Rights Act of 1875 should have protected African Americans against discrimination in public places. Some state laws required racial separation—for example, most states prohibited racial intermarriage. Throughout the South and in some places outside the South, state or local law, or local practice, had produced racially separate school systems, churches, hospitals, cemeteries, and other voluntary organizations. Segregation existed throughout the South, driven by local custom and the ever-present threat of violence against any African American who dared to challenge it. Restrictions on black political participation were also extralegal, enforced through coercion or intimidation.

In the **Civil Rights Cases** of 1883, the U.S. Supreme Court ruled the Civil Rights Act of 1875 unconstitutional. The Court said that the "equal protection" promised by the Fourteenth Amendment applied only to state governments, not to individuals or companies. Though state governments were obligated to treat all citizens as equal before the law, private businesses need not do the same. Southern lawmakers soon began to require businesses to practice segregation. In 1887 the Florida legislature ordered separate accommodations on railroad trains. Mississippi passed a similar law the next year, and other southern states soon followed.

Mississippi whites took a more brazen step in 1890, holding a state constitutional convention to eliminate African Americans' participation in politics. The new provisions did not mention the word *race*. Instead, they imposed a **poll tax**, a literacy test, and other requirements for voting. Everyone understood that these measures were designed to **disfranchise** black voters. Men who failed the literacy test could vote if they could understand a section of the state constitution or law when a local (white) official read it to them. The typical result was that the only illiterates who could vote were white. Most of the South watched this so-called Second Mississippi Plan unfold with great interest.

In 1895 a black educator signaled his apparent willingness to accept disfranchisement and segregation, at least for the moment. Born into slavery in

Booker T. Washington posed for this formal portrait around the time of his Atlanta address.

1856, **Booker T. Washington** worked as a janitor while studying at Hampton Normal and Agricultural Institute in Virginia, a school that combined preparation for elementary school teaching with vocational education in agriculture and industrial work. Washington then taught at Hampton. In 1881 the Alabama legislature authorized a black **normal school** at Tuskegee. Washington became its principal, and he made Tuskegee Normal and Industrial Institute into a leading black educational institution.

Old South Term for a romanticized view of the pre–Civil War South as a place of gentility and gallantry.

Lost Cause Term for a romanticized view of the Confederate struggle in the Civil War as a noble but doomed effort to preserve a way of life.

■ **Civil Rights Cases** Supreme Court decisions in 1883 specifying that private companies could legally discriminate against individuals based on race.

■ **poll tax** Annual tax imposed on each citizen; used in some southern states to disfranchise black voters, because the only penalty for not paying was loss of voting rights.

disfranchise To take away the right to vote.

■ **Booker T. Washington** Former slave who became an educator and founded Tuskegee Institute, a leading black educational institution; known as an advocate of accommodation with white southerners.

normal school Two-year school for training teachers for grades 1–8.

Library of Congress.

In the Wider World

South Africa Establishes Racial Separation

As southern states legislated disfranchisement and segregation, similar changes occurred in the British colonies and Boer (descendants of Dutch colonists) republics of South Africa. In the British colonies, a law in 1892 limited black voting, and another law in 1894 disfranchised migrants from India. In 1905 the General Pass Regulations Bill completely disfranchised blacks and restricted where they could live and their freedom of movement. In 1910 the British and Boer areas combined in the Union of South Africa. New legislation gave whites complete political control over all other racial groups. Subsequent laws limited black and Indian land ownership and required residential segregation. The American South and South Africa followed diverging paths after World War II, when segregation and disfranchisement began to break down in the American South, but adoption of apartheid in South Africa brought even more rigid racial separation until 1994.

In 1895 Atlanta hosted the Cotton States and International Exposition. The exposition directors invited Washington to speak, hoping he could reach out to southern whites, southern blacks, and northern whites. Washington did not disappoint. In his speech, he seemed to accept an inferior status for blacks for the present: "No race can prosper till it learns that there is as much dignity in tilling a field as in writing a poem. It is at the bottom of life we must begin, and not at the top." Implying that equal rights had to be earned, Washington seemed to condone segregation: "In all things that are purely social, we can be as separate as the fingers, yet one as the hand in all things essential to mutual progress."

The speech—soon dubbed the **Atlanta Compromise**—won great acclaim. Southern whites were pleased to hear a black educator urge his race to accept segregation and disfranchisement. Northern whites too were receptive to the notion that the South would work out its race relations by itself. Until his death in 1915, Washington was the most prominent black leader in the nation, at least among white Americans.

■ **Atlanta Compromise** Name applied by Booker T. Washington's critics to his 1895 speech urging African Americans to temporarily accept segregation and disfranchisement.

grandfather clause Louisiana rule that permitted a man to vote if his father or grandfather was eligible in 1867, allowing white men to circumvent rules disfranchising blacks; now refers to any law that exempts some people from current regulations based on past practice.

■ **Plessy v. Ferguson** Supreme Court decision in 1896 upholding a Louisiana law requiring segregation of railroad facilities; argued that "separate but equal" facilities were constitutional under the Fourteenth Amendment.

Among African Americans, Washington's message found a mixed reception. Some accepted his approach as appropriate for the moment. Others criticized him for sacrificing black rights. Henry M. Turner, bishop of the African Methodist Episcopal Church in Atlanta, declared that Washington "will have to live a long time to undo the harm he has done our race." Privately, however, Washington never accepted disfranchisement and segregation as permanent fixtures in southern life.

Even as African Americans debated Washington's Atlanta speech,* southern lawmakers were redefining the legal status of African Americans. State after state followed the lead of Mississippi and disfranchised black voters. Louisiana, in 1898, added the infamous **grandfather clause**, specifying that men who failed to meet new requirements could vote if their fathers or grandfathers had been eligible to vote in 1867 (before the Fourteenth Amendment extended the suffrage to African Americans). Thus poor or illiterate whites could vote. Methods varied, but each southern state set up barriers to voting, then carved holes through which only whites could pass. Southern Democrats, who had long defined themselves as the "white man's party" or the party of white supremacy, restricted their primaries and conventions to whites only. South Carolina took this step first, in 1896, and other states followed.

Southern lawmakers began to extend segregation by law, especially after the U.S. Supreme Court's decision in **Plessy v. Ferguson** (1896), involving a Louisiana law requiring segregated railroad cars. When the Court ruled that "separate but equal" facilities did not violate the equal protection clause of the Fourteenth Amendment, southern legislators applied that reasoning elsewhere, requiring segregation of almost everything—and especially public places such as parks and restaurants.

---

*Booker T. Washington from Atlanta Compromise speech.

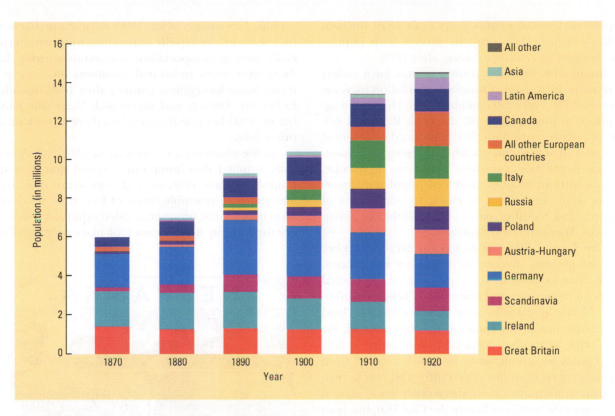

FIGURE 17.3 Foreign-Born Population of the United States, 1870–1920
This graph shows the largest foreign-born groups living in the United States at the time of the census (every ten years). The number of foreign-born increased dramatically during these fifty years, and the foreign-born were increasingly diverse by country of origin.

Source: Bureau of the Census, *Historical Statistics of the United States, Colonial Times to 1970,* Bicentennial edition (Washington, D.C.: U.S. GPO, 1975), 1: 116–117.

Violence against African Americans accompanied the new laws, providing an unmistakable lesson in the consequences of resistance. From 1885 to 1900, when the South was redefining relations between the races, the region witnessed more than twenty-five hundred deaths by lynching—about one every two days. The victims were almost all African Americans, and the largest numbers were in the states with the most black residents.

ETHNICITY AND RACE IN THE GILDED AGE

☆ *How did the expectations of European immigrants differ from their experiences?*

☆ *Compare the experiences of Chinese Americans, American Indians, Mexican Americans, and African Americans in the Gilded Age.*

By 1890, immigrants made up more than 40 percent of the population of New York, San Francisco, and Chicago, and more than a third of the population in several other major cities. The United States has always attracted large numbers of immigrants but never before experienced a flood like that between the Civil War and World War I. Nearly all these immigrants came from Europe, and many settled in cities. Significant numbers of immigrants also came from Asia, nearly all of whom settled in the West. At the same time, American Indians and Latinos in the Southwest faced new constraints on their choices and opportunities.

A Flood of Immigrants from Europe

The numbers of immigrants varied from year to year—higher in prosperous years, lower in depression years—but the trend was upward. Nearly a quarter of a million arrived in 1865, two-thirds of a million in 1881, and a million in 1905. In the 1870s and 1880s, most came from Great Britain, Ireland, **Scandinavia**, Germany, and Canada, but after about 1890 increasing numbers arrived from southern and eastern Europe. By 1910, immigrants and their children made up more than 35 percent of the total population. Figure 17.3 shows the place of birth of the foreign-born

Scandinavia The region of northern Europe consisting of Norway, Sweden, Denmark, and Iceland.

population for the census years from 1870 through 1920. Note especially how the foreign-born population became increasingly diverse after 1890.

Immigrants left their former homes for a variety of reasons. In Ireland, a fourfold population increase between 1750 and 1850 combined with changes in agriculture to push people off the land. Repeated failure of potato crops after 1845 produced widespread **famine** and starvation, greatly increasing migration. Similar population pressures elsewhere in Europe, though without famine, produced population movements from rural areas to cities, to other parts of Europe, and to other parts of the world, including Canada, Argentina, and Australia.

The United States attracted the largest number and the greatest diversity of European immigrants. Some came because of the reputation of the United States for democracy and toleration of religious difference. Nearly all came because America was the "land of opportunity." They came, as one bluntly said, for "jobs" and, as another declared, "for money." In fact, the reasons for immigrating to America varied from person to person, country to country, and year to year.

Irish immigrants, many desperately poor, arrived in the greatest numbers before the Civil War, but Irish immigration continued at high levels until the 1890s. Many Irish settled in the cities of the Northeast, making up a quarter of the population in New York City and Boston as early as 1860. Many immigrants who came in the 1870s and 1880s found that good farmland was available in the north-central states at reasonable prices or even free under the Homestead Act. One woman recalled that, in rural Nebraska in the 1880s, her family could attend Sunday church services in Norwegian, Danish, Swedish, French, Czech, or German, as well as English. Scandinavians, Dutch, Swiss, Czechs, and Germans were most likely to be farmers, but all those groups were also to be found in cities, especially in the Midwest. Map 17.1 shows clearly that immigrant communities were not limited to cities or industrial areas.

Patterns of settlement reflect in part the opportunities immigrants found when they arrived. After 1890, farmland was more difficult to obtain. The 1890s also marked a shift in the sources of immigration, with proportionately more coming from southern and eastern Europe and arriving with little or no capital. Newcomers after 1890 were more likely to find work in the rapidly expanding industries, especially mining, transportation, and manufacturing, but there were many individual variations on these patterns. Some immigrants coming after 1890 intended to become farmers and succeeded. Many who came before 1890 became industrial workers or took other urban jobs.

In the nineteenth century, most **old-stock** Americans assumed that immigrants should quickly learn English, become citizens, and restructure their lives and values to resemble those of long-time residents. Most immigrants, however, resisted rapid **assimilation**. For the majority, assimilation took place over a lifetime

Nebraska State Historical Society

Railroad companies, seeking to sell their land grants, advertised in Europe for immigrants to buy farmland in the West. This poster, issued by the Burlington and Missouri Railroad, is in Czech, but the same poster was issued in German and Swedish. The sequence of drawings shows a six-year transition from bare prairie to prosperous farm. Such advertising helped to attract European immigrants to the north-central states (see Map 17.1).

famine A serious and widespread shortage of food.

old stock Those who were born in the United States of parents born in the United States; more generally, those Americans several generations removed from immigration. Foreign stock refers to those of foreign birth or parentage.

assimilation Among culturally distinct groups, the process of adopting the behaviors and values of the dominant society and its culture.

or even over generations. Most retained elements of their own cultures even as they embraced their new lives in America. For many, their sense of identity came to reflect where they came from and where they lived now—that is, they came to think of themselves as hyphenated Americans: German-Americans, Irish-Americans, Norwegian-Americans.

On arriving in America, with its strange language and customs, many immigrants sought others who shared their cultural values, practiced their religion, and especially, spoke their language. Ethnic communities emerged wherever there were large numbers of immigrants. These communities played a significant role in newcomers' transition to America, giving new immigrants a chance to learn about their new home with assistance from those who had come earlier. At the same time, newcomers could, without apology or embarrassment, retain cultural values and behaviors from their homelands. Foreign-language newspapers helped to connect the old country to the new, for they provided news from the old country as well as from other similar communities in the United States.

For members of nearly every **ethnic group**, religious institutions provided important elements of ethnic group identity. Protestant immigrant groups created new church organizations based on both theology and language. Catholic parishes in immigrant neighborhoods often took on the ethnic characteristics of the community, with services in the immigrants' language and special observances transplanted from the old country. Jewish congregations, too, often differed according to the ethnic background of their members.

Nativism

Though most immigrants changed their behavior, many old-stock Americans (even some only a generation removed from immigrant forebears) expected immigrants to lay aside their previous identities and blend into prevailing cultural patterns. Some old-stock Americans fretted over the multiplication of German and Italian newspapers, feared to go into neighborhoods where they rarely heard an English sentence, and shuddered at the sprouting of Catholic schools. Such fears and misgivings fostered the growth of **nativism**. Nativists argued that only their values and institutions were genuinely American, and they feared that immigrants threatened those traditions.

Nativism was often linked to anti-Catholicism. Irish and German immigrant groups, and later Italian and Polish groups, included large numbers of Catholics, and many old-stock Americans came to identify the Catholic Church as an immigrant church. The **American Protective Association (APA)**, founded in 1887, loudly proclaimed itself the voice of anti-Catholicism.

Its members pledged not to hire Catholics, not to vote for them, and not to strike with them. A half-million strong by 1894, APA members often tried to dominate the Republican Party—and succeeded in parts of the Midwest—before they died out by the late 1890s.

Jews, too, faced religious antagonism. In the 1870s, increasing numbers of organizations and businesses began to discriminate against Jews. Some employers refused to hire Jews. After 1900, such discrimination intensified. Many social organizations barred Jews from membership, and **restrictive covenants** kept them from buying homes in certain neighborhoods.

During the 1890s, a diverse political coalition emerged aimed at reducing immigration. Labor organizations began to look at immigrants as potential threats to jobs and wage levels. Some employers now connected immigrants with unions and radicalism and charged that unions represented foreign, un-American influences. Foreign-born radicals and **anarchists** were a special target, as newspapers claimed that "there is no such thing as an American anarchist." In 1901 Leon Czolgosz, an American-born anarchist with a foreign-sounding name, assassinated President William McKinley, and Congress promptly passed a bill barring anarchists from immigrating to the United States.

During the 1890s, nativism grew as the sources of European immigration shifted from northwestern Europe to southern and eastern Europe, bringing larger numbers of Italians, Poles and other Slavs, and eastern European Jews. Anti-Catholicism and anti-Semitism combined to create a sense that these "**new immigrants**" were less desirable than "**old immigrants**" from northwestern Europe.

The arrival of many "new immigrants" after 1890 coincided with a growing tendency to glorify Anglo-Saxons (ancestors of the English) and accomplishments by the English and English Americans.

ethnic group A group that shares a racial, religious, linguistic, cultural, or national heritage.

■ **nativism** The view that old-stock values and social patterns were preferable to those of immigrants.

■ **American Protective Association (APA)** An anti-Catholic organization founded in Iowa in 1887 and active during the next decade.

restrictive covenant Provision in a property title restricting subsequent sale or use of the property, often specifying sale only to a white Christian.

anarchist A person who believes that all forms of government are oppressive and should be abolished.

"new immigrants" Newcomers from southern and eastern Europe who began to arrive in the United States in significant numbers during the 1890s and after.

"old immigrants" Newcomers from northern and western Europe who made up much of the immigration to the United States before the 1890s.

Proponents of Anglo-Saxonism took alarm from statistics showing old-stock Americans having fewer children than immigrants. Some voiced fears of "race suicide" in which Anglo-Saxons allowed themselves to be bred out of existence. Some nativists now became blatant racists. By the 1890s, these economic, political, religious, and racist strains converged in demands that the federal government restrict immigration from Europe.

Immigrants to the Golden Mountain

The West has long had greater ethnic diversity than the rest of the nation (as illustrated in Figure 17.4). In 1900 the western half of the United States included more than 80 percent of all Native Americans, Mexican Americans, and Asian Americans. Between 1854 and 1882, some three hundred thousand Chinese immigrants entered the United States. Most came from southern China, which in the 1840s and 1850s suffered from political instability, economic distress, and famine. Among Chinese immigrants who came during the California gold rush, California became known as *gam saan*, or "gold mountain." Many Chinese worked in mining or construction, especially western railroad building. Others worked as agricultural laborers and farmers, notably in California. Some made important contributions to crop development, especially fruit growing.

In San Francisco and elsewhere in the West, Chinese immigrants established Chinatowns—relatively autonomous and largely self-contained Chinese communities. In San Francisco's Chinatown, immigrants formed kinship organizations and district associations (whose members had come from the same part of China) to assist and protect each other. A confederation of such associations, the Chinese Consolidated Benevolent Association (often called the "Six Companies"), eventually dominated the social and economic life of Chinese communities in much of the West. Such communities were largely male, partly because immigration officials permitted only a few Chinese women to enter the country, apparently to prevent an American-born generation. As was true in many largely male communities, gambling and prostitution flourished, giving Chinatowns reputations as centers for vice.

Almost from the beginning, Chinese immigrants encountered discrimination and violence. During the Gold Rush, a California state tax on foreign-born miners posed a significant burden on Chinese (and also Latino) gold seekers. During the 1870s, many white workers blamed the Chinese for driving wages down

Chinatown A section of a city inhabited chiefly by people of Chinese birth or ancestry.

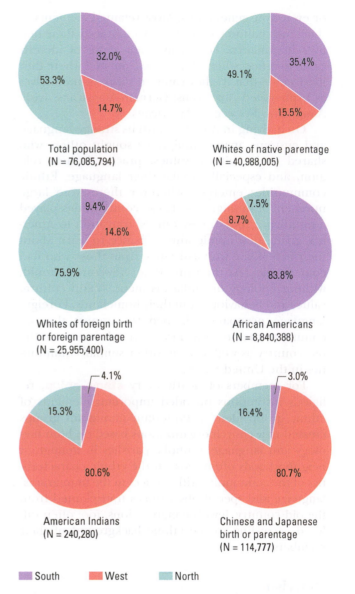

FIGURE 17.4 Regional Distribution of Population, by Race, 1900
These pie charts indicate the distinctiveness of the West with respect to race and ethnicity. Note that the West held about 15 percent of the nation's total population and about the same proportion of the nation's white population (including whites of foreign birth or parentage) but included more than four-fifths of American Indians and those of Chinese and Japanese birth or parentage.

Source: Data from *Twelfth Census of the United States: 1900* (Washington, D.C., 1901), *Population Reports*, vol. 1, p. 483, Table 9.

and unemployment up. In fact, different economic factors depressed wage levels and brought unemployment, but white workers seeking a scapegoat instigated anti-Chinese riots in Los Angeles in 1871 and in San Francisco in 1877. In these riots, the message was usually the same: "The Chinese Must Go."

In 1882 Congress responded to repeated pressures from Pacific Coast labor organizations by passing

Reconstructing Past Social Patterns

When historians seek to understand the lives of ordinary people in past times, they rarely find memoirs or autobiographies like those discussed in A Deeper Understanding of History in Chapter 16. Few past Americans left such records. Historians have instead used a variety of primary sources to reconstruct the social and economic patterns of past communities. Two valuable sources for that purpose are the manuscript census and the Sanborn insurance maps.

For much of American history, the census was taken by people who went door to door, talking to someone at each household to collect information about the people who lived there. The census-takers recorded information on large printed forms. These forms still exist. Historians can review them through 1940; those after 1940 are closed to protect the privacy of living persons.

The 1880 manuscript census (the excerpt shown here is part of a larger page) records that the Tape family lived at 1771 Green Street in San Francisco. Their neighbors were all white and mostly born in the United States; a few were from Ireland or Germany. Neighboring households included a physician, a railway conductor, a contractor, two carpenters, an engineer, and a lawyer. Joseph Tape's occupation appears as expressman. All the adults in their neighborhood were literate. Only a few families took in boarders. All this information points to this as a middle-class neighborhood, with a mix of professionals, small business owners, skilled artisans, and a few blue-collar boarders. The 1900 census records that the Tape family, by then, was living in a similar neighborhood in Berkeley. This evidence reinforces the conclusion that the Tapes were well assimilated, living in white, middle-class neighborhoods.

The Sanborn insurance maps made for insurance agents to determine how much to charge people for fire insurance. The maps plotted the configuration, construction material, and uses of all properties, identifying potential sources of fire. Historians use the Sanborn maps to reconstruct neighborhoods. The 1885 city directory provides the address of Joseph Tape's express company as 704 Dupont Street

(now Grant Avenue), in the midst of Chinatown. A Sanborn map from a few years later (shown here in part) shows 704 Dupont Street as part of a densely packed area of small stores, shops, small apartments or sleeping rooms, and small factories making shoes, clothing, and cigars.

Comparing the Sanborn maps with the census information makes clear that the Tape family lived very different lives than those who lived in Chinatown.

One city block in San Francisco's Chinatown, from the 1899 insurance map published by the Sanborn-Perris Company.

Part of the 1880 census manuscript containing the entry for the Tape family.

Defining the Meaning of the Fourteenth Amendment

The Fourteenth Amendment (see page 381) states in Section 1 that "No State shall... deny to any person within its jurisdiction the equal protection of the laws." In the 1880s, the city of San Francisco adopted a number of city ordinances that discriminated against Chinese immigrants. In the case of *Yick Wo v. Hopkins* (1886), the Supreme Court ruled that the Fourteenth Amendment guaranteed equal protection to a person who was not a citizen.

Section 1 also reads in part: "All persons born or naturalized in the United States, and subject to the jurisdiction thereof, are citizens of the United States." In the late nineteenth century, several people born in the United States to Chinese immigrant parents faced challenges to their citizenship. In *U.S. v. Wong Kim Ark* (1897), the Supreme Court ruled that Wong was a citizen because he was born in the United States to parents who, though not citizens, were living in the country and were not employees of a foreign government.

the **Chinese Exclusion Act**, prohibiting entry to all Chinese people except teachers, students, merchants, tourists, and officials. This was the first significant restriction on immigration. The law reaffirmed that Asian immigrants were not eligible to become naturalized citizens. Soon after, in 1885 anti-Chinese riots swept through much of the West. In Rock Springs, Wyoming Territory, white coal miners burned the Chinatown and killed twenty-eight Chinese. In response, many Chinese retreated to the largest Chinatowns, and some returned to China.

In some parts of the West, the Chinese were subjected to segregation similar to that imposed on African Americans in the South, including residential and occupational segregation rooted in local custom rather than law. In 1871 the San Francisco school board barred Chinese students from that city's public schools. When the the courts ordered the city to provide education for Mamie Tape, they school board set up a segregated school for Chinese children. A few other places in the West set up segregated schools for Chinese American children, but school segregation began to break down in the 1910s and 1920s.

◻ **Chinese Exclusion Act** Act of Congress (1882) prohibiting Chinese laborers from entering the United States; extended periodically until World War II.

Chinese organizations sometimes fought anti-Chinese legislation through the courts. When a San Francisco law restricted Chinese laundry owners, they brought a court challenge. In *Yick Wo v. Hopkins* (1886), the U.S. Supreme Court for the first time declared a licensing law unconstitutional because local authorities had used it to discriminate on the basis of race. The decision also established that the Fourteenth Amendment applied to immigrants who were not citizens.

When other immigrants began to arrive from Asia, they too concentrated in the West. Japanese immigrants started coming in significant numbers after 1890. From 1891 through 1907, nearly 150,000 arrived, most through Pacific Coast ports. Whites in the West, especially organized labor, viewed Japanese immigrants much as they had earlier immigrants from China—with hostility and scorn. Pushed by western labor organizations, President Theodore Roosevelt in 1907 negotiated an agreement with Japan to halt immigration of Japanese laborers.

Forced Assimilation

As headlines about the Great Sioux War, the Nez Perces, and Geronimo faded from the nation's newspapers (see page 417), many Americans began to describe American Indians as a "vanishing race." But Indian people did not vanish. With the end of armed conflict, relations between Native Americans and the rest of the nation entered a new phase.

Well before the end of the Indian wars, federal policymakers began to implement plans to assimilate Native Americans into white society. They were influenced by leading scholars, notably Lewis Henry Morgan of the Smithsonian Institution, who viewed culture as an evolutionary process. All peoples, they thought, were evolving toward "higher" cultural types. Most white Americans probably agreed that western Europeans and their descendants around the world had reached the highest level of development. Public support for changes in federal policy grew in response to speaking tours by American Indians and white reformers and publication of several exposés, notably Helen Hunt Jackson's *A Century of Dishonor* (1881) and *Ramona* (a novel, 1884). Federal policymakers now accepted reformers' arguments for speeding up the evolutionary process for Native Americans. Apparently no reformers or federal policymakers understood that American Indians had complex cultures that were very different from—but not inferior to—the culture of Americans of European descent, and not until the 1890s did Morgan's evolutionary perspective come under challenge, notably from Franz Boas, an anthropologist who held that every culture develops and should be understood on its own, rather than as part of an evolutionary chain.

Education was an important element in the reformers' plans for "civilizing" the Indians. Federal

Nebraska State Historical Society.

Susan La Flesche was the first Indian woman to graduate from medical college. Her sister, Susette, was a prominent advocate for Indian rights, and her brother, Francis, was a leading ethnologist.

Library of Congress.

Luther Standing Bear was called Ota K'te when he was born in 1868, son of a chief who fought against Custer at the Battle of Little Bighorn. Standing Bear attended the Carlisle Indian School in Pennsylvania, toured with a Wild West Show, became an actor, and belonged to the Actors' Guild (a union). He was also a hereditary chief of the Oglala Lakota.

officials worked with churches and philanthropic organizations to establish schools distant from the reservations, where many Native American children were sent to live and study. Intending to assimilate these students into white society, teachers forbade Indian students to speak their languages, practice their religion, or otherwise follow their own cultural patterns. Other educational programs aimed to train adult Indian men as farmers or mechanics. Federal officials also tried to prohibit some religious observances and traditional practices on reservations.

The **Dawes Severalty Act** (1887) was an important element in the "civilizing" effort. Its objective was to make the Indians into self-sufficient, property-conscious, profit-oriented, individual farmers—model citizens of nineteenth-century white America. The law created a governmental policy of severalty—that is, individual ownership of land by Native Americans. Reservations were to be divided into individual family farms of 160 acres. Once each family received its allotment, the government would sell surplus reservation land and use the proceeds for Indian education. This policy found enthusiastic support among both reformers urging rapid assimilation and westerners who coveted Indian lands.

Individual landownership, however, violated traditional Native American views that land was for the use of all and that sharing was a major obligation. Though some Indian leaders favored the Dawes Act, others urged Congress to defeat it. Delegates from the Cherokee, Creek, and Choctaw Nations bluntly told Congress, "Our people have not asked for or authorized this....Our own laws regulate a system of land tenure suited to our condition."

Nonetheless, Congress approved the Dawes Act. The result bore out the warning of Senator Henry Teller of Colorado, who called it "a bill to despoil the Indians of their land." Once allotments to Indian families were made, about 70 percent of the reservation lands remained, and much of it was sold. In the end, the Dawes Act did not end the reservation system, nor did it reduce the Indians' dependence on the federal

■ **Dawes Severalty Act** Act of Congress (1887) intended to break up Indian reservations to create individual farms (holding land in severalty, that is, individually) rather than maintaining common ownership of the land.

government. It did, however, separate the Indians from a good deal of their land.

Native Americans responded to their situation in various ways. Some tried to cooperate with the assimilation programs. Susan La Flesche, daughter of an Omaha leader, graduated from medical college in 1889 at the head of her class. But she disappointed her teachers, who wanted her to abandon Indian culture, when she set up her medical practice near the Omaha Reservation, treated both white and Omaha patients, took part in tribal affairs, and also participated in the local white community through the temperance movement and sometimes by preaching in the local Presbyterian church.

Dr. La Flesche seems to have moved easily between two cultures. Some Native Americans preferred the old ways, keeping their children out of school and secretly practicing traditional religious ceremonies. Native American peoples' cultural patterns changed, but not always in the way federal officials intended. In Oklahoma, where groups with different traditional cultures lived in proximity, people began to borrow cultural practices from others. In some places, Indians became part of the wage-earning workforce near their reservations, sometimes against the wishes of reservation officials. In the late nineteenth century, the **peyote cult**, based on the hallucinogenic properties of the peyote cactus, emerged as an alternative religion. It evolved into the Native American Church, combining elements of traditional Indian culture, Christianity, and peyote use.

Mexican Americans in the Southwest

The United States annexed Texas in 1845 and soon after acquired vast territories from Mexico at the end of the Mexican War. Large numbers of people who lived there spoke Spanish; many were **mestizos**—of mixed Spanish and Native American ancestry. The treaties by which the United States acquired those territories specified that Mexican citizens living there automatically became American citizens.

Throughout the Southwest during the late nineteenth century, many Mexican Americans lost their land as the region attracted English-speaking whites (often called **Anglos** by those whose first language was Spanish). The Treaty of Guadalupe Hidalgo, which ended the war with Mexico, guaranteed Mexican Americans' landholdings, but the vagueness of Spanish and Mexican land grants encouraged legal challenges. Sometimes Mexican Americans were cheated out of their land through fraud.

The California gold rush, beginning in 1849, attracted fortune seekers from around the world, most from the eastern United States and Europe. A hundred thousand gold seekers inundated the few thousand Mexican Americans in northern California. People from Latin America who came to California as gold seekers were often driven from the mines by racist harassment and a tax on foreign miners. Fewer Anglos came to southern California until late in the nineteenth century. There, **Californios** won election to local and state office, including Romualdo Pacheco, who served as state treasurer and lieutenant governor and succeeded to the governorship in 1875.

By the 1870s, many of the pueblos (towns created under Mexican or Spanish governments) had become **barrios**—some rural, some in inner cities. Like the ethnic neighborhoods created by European immigrants, barrios had mutual benefit societies, political associations, and newspapers published in the language of the community, and the cornerstone of both immigrant neighborhoods and barrios was often a church. There was an important difference, however. European immigrants had come to a new land where they anticipated making changes in their own lives. Barrio residents, in contrast, lived where Mexicans had lived for generations but now found themselves surrounded by English-speaking Americans who hired them for cheap wages, sometimes scorned their culture, and pressured them to assimilate.

In Texas, as in California, some **Tejanos** had welcomed the break with Mexico. Lorenzo de Zavala, for example, served as vice president of the Texas Republic. By 1900, though, much of the land in south Texas had passed out of Tejano hands—sometimes legally, sometimes fraudulently—but the new Anglo ranch owners usually maintained the social patterns characteristic of Tejano ranchers.

A large section of south Texas remained culturally Mexican, home to Tejanos and two-thirds of all Mexican immigrants who came to the United States before 1900. In the 1890s, one journalist described the area as "an overlapping of Mexico into the United States." During the 1860s and 1870s, conflict sometimes broke out as Mexican Americans challenged the political and economic power of Anglo newcomers. In social relations and in politics, all but a

peyote cult A religion that included ceremonial use of the hallucinogenic peyote cactus, native to Mexico and the Southwest.

mestizos Persons of mixed Spanish and Indian ancestry.

Anglos A term applied in the Southwest to English-speaking whites.

Californios The Spanish-speaking settlers of California and their descendants.

barrio A Spanish-speaking community, often a part of a larger city.

Tejanos Spanish-speaking people born in Texas.

Throughout the Southwest during the late nineteenth and early twentieth centuries, many Mexican American men found work as railway maintenance workers, called section hands. These Mexican American section hands were photographed in Arizona in 1904, traveling on a hand-truck to repair track.

Denver Public Library, Western History Collection.

few wealthy Tejanos came to be subordinate to the Anglos, who dominated the regional economy and the professions.

In New Mexico Territory, **Hispanos** were the majority throughout the nineteenth century. They made up a majority in the territorial legislature and were frequently elected as territorial delegates to Congress (the only territorial position elected by voters). Anglos began to arrive in significant numbers with the first railroad in 1879. Although Hispanos were the majority, many lost their landholdings in ways similar to patterns in California and Texas—except that some who enriched themselves were wealthy Hispanos.

Until 1910, the Latino population in the Southwest grew more slowly than the Anglo population. After 1910, that situation reversed as political and social upheavals in Mexico prompted massive migration to the United States. Probably a million people—equivalent to one-tenth of the population of Mexico in 1910—arrived over the next twenty years. More than half stayed in Texas, but significant numbers settled in southern California and elsewhere in the Southwest. Inevitably, this new stream of immigrants changed some of the patterns of ethnic relations that had characterized the region since the mid-nineteenth century.

WORKERS ORGANIZE

★ *How did industrialization affect workers in the new industries?*

★ *How did the various labor organizations define their membership and purpose? Does this help explain their successes and shortcomings?*

The rapid expansion of railroads, mining, and manufacturing created a demand for labor to lay the rails, dig the ore, tend the furnaces, and carry out a thousand other tasks. America's new workers—men, women, and children from many ethnic groups—came from across the nation and around the world. Despite hopes for a rags-to-riches triumph such as Andrew Carnegie's, very few rose from shop floor to manager's office.

Workers for Industry

The labor force more than doubled in size between 1870 and 1900. The largest increases occurred in

Hispanos The Spanish-speaking settlers of New Mexico and their descendants.

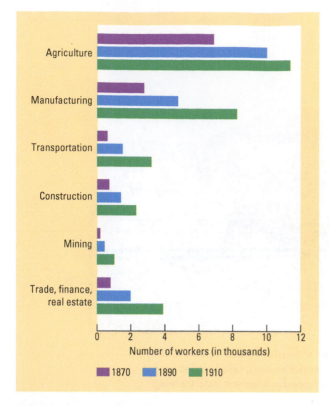

FIGURE 17.5 Industrial Distribution of the Workforce, 1870, 1890, 1910
The number of workers in every industry grew significantly after the Civil War. Though agriculture continued to employ more workers than any other industry, other industries were growing more rapidly than agriculture. © Cengage Learning.

industries undergoing the greatest changes (see Figure 17.5). Agriculture continued to employ the largest share of the labor force, ranging downward from more than half in 1870 to two-fifths in 1900, but the agricultural workforce grew the least, proportionately, of all major categories of workers.

Some new industrial workers came from rural areas. At the same time that mechanization was reducing the number of farm workers needed, farm birth rates remained high. Thus, throughout rural parts of New England and the Middle Atlantic states, many people found it difficult to make a living from agriculture and moved to urban or industrial areas.

The expanding economy, however, needed many more workers than the nation itself could supply. The large-scale immigration of the time contributed many adult males to the workforce—especially in mining, manufacturing, and transportation. The expanding economy also pulled women and children into the industrial workforce. A study in 1875 showed that the average male factory worker in Lawrence, Massachusetts,

piecework Work for which someone is paid for the number of items turned out, rather than by the hour.

earned $500 per year, and that the average family in Lawrence required a minimum annual income of $600 to provide sufficient food, clothing, and shelter. Since Lawrence was fairly typical of much of the new industrial economy, this study and others like it indicate why workers' families often required two or more incomes.

By 1880, a million children (those under the age of 16) worked for wages, the largest number in agriculture. Children worked in the fields and mills of the South, operated sewing machines in New York, and sorted vegetables in Delaware canneries. Others worked as newsboys, bootblacks, or domestic servants. Still others worked at home, alongside their parents who brought home **piecework**. Most working children turned over their wages to their parents.

Most women who worked outside the home were unmarried. In 1890, 40 percent of all single women worked for wages, along with 30 percent of widowed or divorced women. Among married women, only 5 percent did so. Black women were employed at higher proportions in all categories. Some occupations came to be filled mainly by women. By 1900, females made up more than 70 percent of the workforce in clothing factories, knitting mills, and other textile operations. Women dominated certain types of office work; for example, they made up more than 70 percent of secretaries and typists and 80 percent of telephone operators. However, as women moved into office work, displacing men, wage levels fell, along with the likelihood of promotion from clerical worker to managerial status. For women, office work usually paid less than factory work but was safer and of higher status.

Women and children workers almost always earned less than their male counterparts. In most industries, work was separated by age and gender, and adult males usually held the more skilled jobs commanding the best pay. Even when men and women did the same work, they rarely received the same pay (see Figure 17.6). This wage differential was often explained by the argument that a man had to support a family, whereas a woman worked to supplement the income of her husband or father.

Some women were self-employed. For example, they made and sold women's hats or dresses. In urban working-class neighborhoods, married or widowed women often rented a room to a boarder or charged to do other people's laundry or sewing. In rural areas, married women often kept chickens and sold eggs to supplement their family's income.

Because so many of the new industrial workers had been born into a rural society, either in the United States or in Europe, they found industrial work quite different from their previous work. Farm families worked from sunrise to sunset, but they did so at their own pace, taking a break when they felt the need and managing their work to avoid exhaustion. Self-employed blacksmiths, carpenters, dressmakers, and other skilled workers also controlled

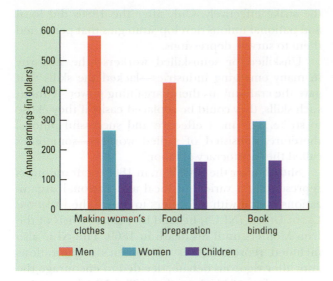

FIGURE 17.6 *Average Annual Earnings for Men, Women, and Children, in Selected Industries, 1890*
© Cengage Learning.

the speed and intensity of their work, although, like the farmer, they might work long hours. Such artisans often considered this autonomy part of the dignity of labor. In many early factories, skilled workers often set the pace of work around them. They also earned more than other workers and were difficult to replace.

In the late nineteenth century, the workday in most industries averaged ten or twelve hours, six days a week. People expected to work long hours but found that industrial work controlled them, rather than the other way around. In many factories, the speed of the machines set the pace of the work, and machine speeds were often centrally controlled. If managers ordered a **speed-up**, workers worked faster. Ten- or twelve-hour days at a constant, rapid pace drained the workers. A woman textile worker in 1882 said, "I get so exhausted that I can scarcely drag myself home when night comes."

The pace of industrial work, together with inadequate safety precautions, contributed to a high rate of accidents, injuries, and deaths. The first thorough study of workplace fatalities was not conducted until 1913, when the Bureau of Labor Statistics found 23,000 industrial deaths among a workforce of 38 million, equivalent to 61 deaths per 100,000 workers. (Today there are about 4 deaths per 100,000 workers.) Injuries and disabilities were even more numerous. Those disabled by industrial accidents received no benefits from the federal government and rarely received anything from state or local government or from their employers. Many businesses considered an on-the-job injury to be due to carelessness by the employee and grounds for firing.

Despite rags-to-riches success stories, extreme mobility was highly unusual. Nearly all successful business leaders, in fact, came from middle- or upper-class

families. Few workers moved more than a step or so up the economic ladder. An unskilled laborer might become a semiskilled worker, or a skilled worker might become a foreman, but few wage earners moved into the middle class. If they did, it was usually as the owner of a small and often struggling business.

The Origins of Unions and Labor Conflict in the 1870s

Just as the entrepreneurs of the late nineteenth century faced choices between competition and cooperation, so too did their employees. Some workers reacted to the far-reaching changes in the nature of work by joining with other workers in efforts to maintain or regain control over their working conditions.

Skilled workers remained indispensable in many fields. Only a skilled iron molder could set up the molds and know exactly when and how to pour molten iron into them. Only an experienced carpenter could build stairs or hang doors properly. Only a skilled typesetter could quickly transform handwritten copy into lines of lead type. Such workers took pride in the quality of their work and knew that their skill was crucial to their employer's success. One union leader was referring to such workers when he said, "The manager's brains are under the workman's cap."

Skilled workers formed the first unions, called **craft unions** or **trade unions** because membership was limited to skilled workers in a particular craft or trade. Before the Civil War, workers in most American cities created local trade unions in attempts to regulate the quality of work, wages, hours, and working conditions within their craft. Such unions often limited their membership not just to workers with particular skills but to white males with those skills. Local unions eventually formed national trade organizations—twenty-six by 1873, thirty-nine by 1880. They sometimes called themselves brotherhoods—for example, the United Brotherhood of Carpenters and Joiners, formed in 1881—and they drew on their craft traditions to forge bonds of unity.

The skills that defined craft union membership also provided the basis for their success. Skills that sometimes took years to develop made craft workers difficult to replace. If most craft workers within a city belonged to the local union, a strike could badly disrupt or shut down the affected businesses. The strike, therefore, was a powerful weapon for skilled workers. Strikes most often succeeded in times of prosperity,

speed-up An effort to make employees produce more goods in the same time or for the same pay.

■ **craft union, trade union** Labor union that organizes skilled workers engaged in a specific craft or trade.

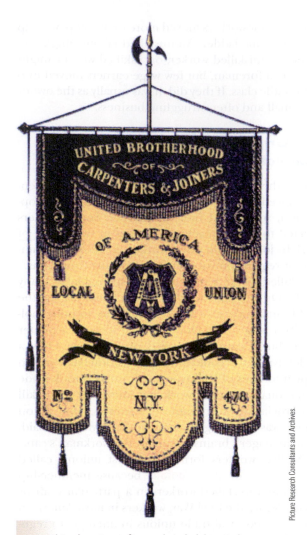

Local trade unions often ordered elaborate banners, such as this one, to hang in their union hall during their meetings and carry in parades or display at funerals of members. Such organizations sometimes styled themselves as brotherhoods, symbolizing not only the solidarity of the organization but also its masculine nature.

Picture Research Consultants and Archives.

when employers wanted to continue operating and were financially able to make concessions to workers. When the economy turned down and employers reduced work hours or laid off workers, craft unions sometimes disintegrated because they could not use

■ **National Labor Union** (NLU) Federation of trade unions and reform societies organized in 1866; it lasted only six years but helped push through a law limiting government employees to an eight-hour workday.

militia A volunteer military force, organized by state governments, consisting of civilians who agree to be mobilized in times of emergency; now superseded by the National Guard.

general strike A strike by members of all unions in a particular region.

the strike effectively. Only after the 1880s did local and national unions develop strategies that permitted them to survive depressions.

Unskilled or semiskilled workers—the majority in many emerging industries—lacked the skills that gave the craft unions their bargaining power. Without such skills, they could be replaced easily if they chose to strike. The most effective and successful unions, therefore, consisted of skilled workers—sometimes called the "aristocracy of labor."

Shortly after the Civil War, in 1866, craft unionists representing a variety of local and national organizations joined with reformers to create the **National Labor Union** (NLU), headed by William Sylvis of the Iron Molders until his death in 1869. The NLU also included representatives of women's organizations and, after vigorous debate, decided to encourage the organization of black workers. The NLU's most important objective was to establish eight hours as the proper length for a day's work. In 1870 the NLU divided itself into a labor organization and a political party, the National Labor Reform Party. In 1872 that party nominated candidates for president and vice president, but the campaign was so unsuccessful and divisive that neither the NLU nor the party met again.

In 1877, for the first time, the nation witnessed widespread labor strife. After the onset of depression in 1873, railroad companies reduced costs by repeatedly cutting wages. Railroad workers' pay fell by more than a third from 1873 to 1877. Union leaders talked about striking but failed to act. Railway workers took matters into their own hands when companies announced additional pay cuts. On July 16, 1877, firemen and brakemen on the Baltimore & Ohio Railroad stopped work in Maryland. The next day, in West Virginia, railway workers refused to work until the company restored their wages. Members of the local community supported the strikers. The governor of West Virginia sent in the state **militia**, but strikers still prevented the trains from moving. The governor then requested federal troops, and President Rutherford B. Hayes sent them.

Federal troops restored service on the Baltimore & Ohio, but the strike spread to other lines. Strikers shut down trains in Pittsburgh. The local militia refused to act against the strikers, so the governor of Pennsylvania sent militia units from Philadelphia. When the militia killed twenty-six people, strikers and their sympathizers fought back, forced the troops to retreat, and burned and looted railroad property throughout Pittsburgh.

Strikes erupted across Pennsylvania and New York and throughout the Midwest. Strikers everywhere drew support from their local communities. In various places, coal miners, factory workers, small business owners, farmers, black workers, and women demonstrated their solidarity with the railroad workers.

This engraving depicts striking railroad workers in Martinsburg, West Virginia, as they stopped a freight train on July 17, 1877, in the opening days of the Great Railway Strike. Engravings such as this, showing strikers as heavily armed, may not have been accurate depictions of events. The technology of the day could not reproduce photographs in newspapers, so the public's understanding of events such as the 1877 strike was formed largely through artists' depictions.

Unions in St. Louis declared a **general strike** to secure the eight-hour workday and end child labor. Eventually state militia, federal troops, and local police broke up the strikes. By the strikes' end, dozens of people had lost their lives and damage to railroad property reached $10 million, half of the losses in Pittsburgh.

The **Great Railway Strike of 1877** revealed widespread dislike for the railroad companies and significant community support for strikers. However, the strike alarmed many other Americans. Some considered the use of troops only a temporary expedient and, like President Hayes, hoped for "education of the strikers," "judicious control of the capitalists," and some way to "remove the distress which afflicts laborers." Others saw in the strike a forecast of future labor unrest, and they called for better means to enforce law and order.

Competing Labor Organizations in the 1880s

The Great Railway Strike of 1877 suggested that working people could unite across lines of occupation,

race, and gender, but no organization drew on that potential until the early 1880s, when the **Knights of Labor** emerged as an alternative to craft unions.

The Knights grew out of an organization of Philadelphia garment workers formed in 1869. Abandoning their craft union origins, they proclaimed that labor was "the only creator of values or capital" and recruited members from what they considered "the producing class"—those who, by their labor, produced value. Anyone joining the Knights was required to have worked for wages at some time, but the organization specifically excluded only professional gamblers, stockbrokers, lawyers, bankers, and liquor dealers.

The Knights accepted African Americans as members, and some sixty thousand joined by 1886. The

- **Great Railway Strike of 1877** Largely spontaneous strikes by railroad workers, triggered by wage cuts.
- **Knights of Labor** Organization founded in 1869, open to all workers; membership peaked in 1886; members favored a cooperative alternative to capitalism.

Terence Powderly, in the center, advocates arbitration. The Knights of Labor urged that labor and management (identified here as "capital") should settle their differences this way, rather than by striking. Note how the cartoonist has depicted labor and management as of equal size, and given both of them a large weapon; management's club is labeled "monopoly" and labor's hammer is called "strikes." In fact, labor and management were rarely equally matched when it came to labor disputes in the late nineteenth century.

Picture Research Consultants & Archives.

Knights also opened their ranks to women and enrolled about fifty thousand by 1886. Some women and African Americans held local and regional leadership positions, and the Knights briefly appointed a woman as a national organizer. Through their activities, the Knights provided both women and African Americans with experience in organizing.

Terence V. Powderly, a machinist, led the Knights from 1879 to 1893. Under his leadership, they focused on organization, education, and cooperation as their chief objectives. The Knights favored political action to accomplish such labor reforms as health and safety regulations, the eight-hour workday, prohibition of child labor, equal pay for equal work regardless of gender, and the graduated income tax. They also endorsed government ownership of the telephone, telegraph, and railroad systems. In 1878, 1880, and 1882, Powderly won election as mayor of Scranton, Pennsylvania, as the candidate of a labor party. Local

labor parties often appeared in other cities where the Knights were strong.

A major objective of the Knights was "to secure to the workers the full enjoyment of the wealth they create." They committed themselves in 1878 to promote producers' and consumers' **cooperatives**, which they hoped would "supersede the wage-system." They had established some 135 cooperatives by the mid-1880s, but few lasted very long. Most failed because of lack of capital, opposition from rival businesses, or poor organization.

Before problems developed with their cooperatives, the Knights became the largest labor organization in the country, expanding from 9,000 members in 1879 to 703,000 in 1886. This meteoric growth suggested that many working people were seeking ways to challenge emerging corporate power or to regain control over their own working lives. Though the rise of the Knights of Labor seemed to signal a growing sense of common purpose among many working people, labor organizations soon found themselves divided and on the defensive.

On May 1, 1886, some eighty thousand unionists and radicals marched through Chicago's streets in support of an eight-hour workday. Three days later,

■ **Terence V. Powderly** Leader of the Knights of Labor from 1879 to 1893; three-term mayor of Scranton, Pennsylvania.

cooperative A business enterprise in which workers and consumers share in ownership and take part in management.

Chicago police killed several strikers at the McCormick Harvester Works. Hoping to build on the May Day unity, a group of anarchists called a protest meeting at Haymarket Square. When police tried to break up the rally, someone threw a bomb at the officers. The police then opened fire on the crowd, and some protesters fired back. Eight policemen died, along with an unknown number of demonstrators, and a hundred people suffered injuries.

The Haymarket bombing sparked public anxiety and anti-union feelings. Employers who had previously opposed unions now tried to discredit them by playing on fears of terrorism. Some people who had supported union goals of better wages and working conditions now shrank back in horror. In Chicago, amid widespread furor over the violence, eight leading anarchists stood trial for inciting the bombing and, on flimsy evidence, were convicted. Four were hanged, one committed suicide, and three remained in jail until a sympathetic governor, John Peter Altgeld, released them in 1893.

Two weeks after the Haymarket bombing, trade union leaders met to discuss the inroads that the Knights of Labor were making among their members. They proposed an agreement with the Knights: trade unions would recruit skilled workers, and the Knights would organize only unskilled workers. The Knights refused, so the trade unions organized the **American Federation of Labor** (AFL). Membership in the AFL was limited to national trade unions. The combined membership of the thirteen founding unions amounted to about 140,000—only one-fifth of the number claimed by the Knights at the time.

Samuel Gompers became the AFL's first president. Born in London in 1850 to Dutch Jewish parents, he learned the cigarmaker's trade before coming to the United States in 1863. He joined the Cigarmakers' Union and became its president in 1877. Except for one year, Gompers continued as president of the AFL until his death in 1924. As AFL president, Gompers opposed labor involvement with radicalism or politics, and favored "pure and simple" unionism: higher wages, shorter hours, and improved working conditions for union members, achieved not through politics but through the power of their organizations in relation to their employers. Though most AFL unions did not challenge capitalism, they repeatedly used strikes and sometimes engaged in long and bitter struggles with employers.

After the 1880s, the AFL suffered little competition from the Knights of Labor. The decline of the Knights came swiftly: 703,000 members in 1886; 260,000 in 1888; 100,000 in 1890. The failure of several strikes involving the Knights in the late 1880s cost them many supporters. Some who left were probably disappointed that the "cooperative commonwealth" failed to materialize. Some units of the Knights were organized like trade unions, and these groups often preferred the more kindred AFL. The United Mine Workers of America switched from the Knights to the AFL in 1890 but retained some central principles of the Knights, including commitments to include both whites and African Americans and to organize all workers in coal mining, not just the most skilled.

Labor on the Defensive in the 1890s

In the 1890s, workers often found that even the strongest unions could not withstand the power of the new industrial titans. A major demonstration of this power came in 1892 in Homestead, Pennsylvania, at the giant Carnegie Steel plant managed by Henry Clay Frick, Carnegie's partner. The union there had a contract with Carnegie Steel. When Frick proposed major wage cuts and the union balked, Frick locked out the union members and prepared to bring in replacements.

Frick hired the Pinkerton National Detective Agency to protect strikebreakers. Three hundred armed "Pinkertons" arrived by riverboat, but ten thousand strikers and community supporters resisted when the private army tried to land. Shots rang out. In the ensuing battle, seven Pinkertons and nine strikers were killed, and sixty people were injured. The Pinkertons surrendered, leaving the strikers in control. The governor of Pennsylvania then sent in the state militia, who patrolled the city and successfully protected the strikebreakers. The union never recovered. This crushing defeat suggested that no union could stand up to America's industrial giants, especially when they could call on the government for assistance.

A similar fate befell the most ambitious new union of the 1890s. In 1893, under the leadership of **Eugene V. Debs**, railway workers launched the American Railway Union (ARU). Previously, railway workers had organized separate unions for engineers, locomotive firemen, switchmen, and conductors, but Debs—a former officer of the firemen's union—hoped to bring all railway workers, skilled and unskilled, together into one union, thereby creating an **industrial union**. Success came quickly. Within a year, the ARU claimed 150,000 members, making it the largest single union in the nation.

■ **American Federation of Labor** (AFL) National organization of trade unions founded in 1886; such unions typically used strikes and boycotts to improve the lot of craft workers.

■ **Samuel Gompers** First president of the AFL; sought to divorce labor organizing from politics and stressed practical demands involving wages and hours.

■ **Eugene V. Debs** American Railway Union leader who was jailed for his role in the Pullman strike; later became a leading socialist and ran for president.

■ **industrial union** A union that includes all of the workers, both skilled or unskilled, in a particular industry.

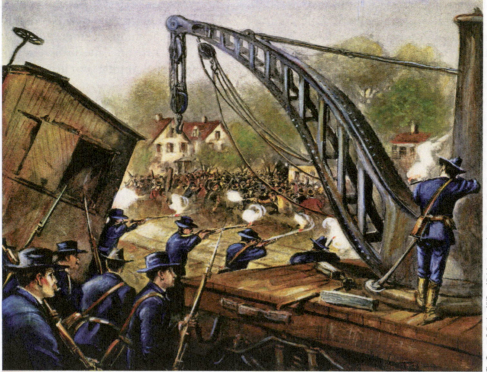

The Granger Collection, NYC — All rights reserved.

This drawing depicts U.S. troops firing on striking railroad workers in Chicago on July 7, 1894, during the Pullman strike. Because of Chicago's position as the center of so much of the nation's rail traffic, and because of the strength of the unions in that area, the Chicago area was the site of much of the violence of that strike. The intervention of U.S. troops, federal marshals, and the Illinois national guard effectively broke the strike by protecting strikebreakers.

The twenty-four railway companies whose lines entered Chicago had formed the General Managers Association (GMA) to address common problems. Alarmed at the rise of the ARU, they found an opportunity to challenge the new union in 1894. Striking workers at the Pullman Palace Car Company, which manufactured luxury railway cars, asked the ARU to boycott Pullman cars—to disconnect them from trains and proceed without them. When the ARU agreed, the GMA promised to fire any worker who observed the boycott. Their real purpose, as expressed by the GMA chairman, was to eliminate the ARU and "wipe him [Debs] out."

Within a short time, all ARU members were on strike. Rail traffic in and out of Chicago ground to a halt, affecting railways from the Pacific Coast to New York. U.S. Attorney General Richard Olney, a former railroad lawyer, obtained an **injunction** against the strikers on the grounds that the strike prevented delivery of the mail and violated the Sherman Anti-Trust Act (discussed in the next chapter). President Grover Cleveland assigned thousands of **U.S. marshals** and federal troops to protect trains operated by strikebreakers. In response, mobs attacked railroad property, especially in Chicago, burning trains and buildings. ARU leaders condemned the violence, but a dozen people died before the strike finally ended. Union leaders, including Debs, were jailed, and the ARU was destroyed.

The depression that began in 1893 further weakened the unions. In 1894 Gompers acknowledged that nearly all AFL affiliates "had their resources greatly diminished and their efforts largely crippled" through lost strikes and unemployment. Nevertheless, the AFL hung on. By 1897, the organization claimed fifty-eight national unions with a combined membership of nearly 270,000.

injunction A court order requiring an individual or a group to do something or to refrain from doing something.
U.S. marshal A federal law-enforcement official.

Individual Voices

MARY TAPE

Challenges the San Francisco Board of Education

In this letter, published in the *Alta California* (a San Francisco newspaper) on April 16, 1885, Mary Tape challenges the decision of the school board to deny her daughter, Mamie, the right to attend the public school in her neighborhood and to require her instead to travel a long distance to attend a new, segregated school created for Chinese American children. (The letter has been edited and slightly rearranged here.)

Courtesy of Alisa J. Kim and Mitchell C. Kim.

❶ One prejudice against Chinese immigrants was that they were "heathen" (not Christian). How does Mary Tape appeal to religious values in this part of her letter?

❷ Another argument against Chinese immigrants was that they were not interested in assimilation and could not be assimilated. How does Mary Tape challenge that argument?

❸ Here Mary Tape, having addressed other arguments against permitting Mamie to attend her neighborhood school, flatly accuses the school board members and administrators of racial prejudice. What is the implication of her final sentence? How is she defining the meaning of being an American?

I see that you are going to make all sorts of excuses to keep my child out of the public schools. Dear sirs, will you please to tell me, is it a disgrace to be born a Chinese? Didn't God make us all? What right have you to bar my child out of the school because she is of Chinese descent? There is no other worldly reason that you could keep her out, except that. I suppose you all go to churches on Sundays. Do you call that a Christian act to compel my little children to go so far to a school that is made on purpose for them? **❶** My children don't dress like the other Chinese. They look just as funny amongst them as the Chinese dressed in Chinese [clothes] look amongst you Caucasians....[Mamie's] playmates are all Caucasians ever since she could toddle around. If she is good enough to play with them, then is she not good enough to be in the same room and study with them? You had better come and see for yourselves. See if the Tapes are not [the same] as other Caucasians, except in features. It seems no matter how a Chinese may live and dress so long as you know they are Chinese, then they are hated as one. There is not any right or justice for them.... **❷** I will let the world see, sir, what justice there is when it is governed by the race prejudiced men!...Just because she is descended of Chinese parents that is going to prevent her being educated. I guess she is more of an American than a good many of you. **❸**

Source: Mrs. M. Tape.

Study Tools

SUMMARY

In the Gilded Age, as industrialization transformed the economy, immigration and urbanization challenged many established social patterns. As rural Americans and European immigrants sought better lives in the cities, urban America changed dramatically. New technologies in construction, transportation, and communication produced a new urban geography with residential neighborhoods defined by economic status. Urban growth brought a new urban middle class. Education underwent far-reaching changes. Socially defined gender roles began to change as some women chose professional careers and took active roles in reform. Some men responded by redefining masculinity through organizations and athletics. Urbanization offered new choices to gay men and lesbians by making possible the development of distinctive urban subcultures.

The South shared in some of the changes of the Gilded Age, but lagged in others, notably education. The myths of the Old South and the Lost Cause obscured for some southerners the real source of their difficulties. Changes in state laws disfranchised black voters and other new laws legalized and extended racial segregation.

Many Europeans immigrated to the United States because of economic and political conditions in their homelands and their expectations of better opportunities in America. Immigrants often formed distinct communities, frequently centered on a church. The flood of immigrants spawned nativist reactions among some old-stock Americans. The West included immigrants from Asia, American Indians, and Latino peoples in substantial numbers. White westerners used politics and sometimes violence to exclude and segregate Asian immigrants. Federal policy toward American Indians proceeded from the expectation that they could and should be rapidly assimilated, but such policies largely failed. Latinos—descendants of those living in the Southwest before it became part of the United States and those who came later from Mexico or elsewhere in Latin America—often found their lives and culture under challenge.

Industrial workers had little control over the pace or hours of their work and often faced difficult or dangerous working conditions. Even so, people in both the United States and other parts of the world chose to migrate to expanding industrial centers from rural areas. The new workforce included not only adult males but also women and children. Some workers formed labor organizations to seek higher wages, shorter hours, and better conditions. Trade unions, based on craft skills, were the earliest and most successful of such organizations. The Great Railway Strike of 1877 was the first indication of what widespread industrial strife could do to the nation's new transportation network based on railroads. Public officials resorted to federal troops to suppress the strike.

CHRONOLOGY
Life in the Gilded Age

1862	Land-Grant College Act
1865	Civil War ends
1866	National Labor Union organized
1870	Populations in 25 cities exceed 50,000
1871–1885	Anti-Chinese riots across the West
1871	Great Chicago Fire
1872	Montgomery Ward opens first U.S. mail-order business
1873–1879	Depression
1874	Women's Christian Temperance Union founded
1877	Great Railway Strike
1881	669,431 immigrants enter United States Publication of Helen Hunt Jackson's *A Century of Dishonor*

1886	Knights of Labor reaches peak membership Haymarket Square bombing American Federation of Labor founded
1887	American Protective Association founded Dawes Severalty Act
1888	First electric streetcar system
1890	Populations in 58 cities exceed 50,000 Second Mississippi Plan
1892	Homestead strike
1893–1897	Depression
1894	Pullman strike
1895	Booker T. Washington delivers Atlanta Compromise
1896	*Plessy v. Ferguson*

Study Tools

Espousing cooperatives and reform, the Knights of Labor opened its membership to the unskilled, to African Americans, and to women—groups usually not admitted to craft unions. The Knights died out after 1890. The American Federation of Labor was formed by craft unions, and its leaders rejected radicalism and sought instead to work within capitalism to improve wages, hours, and conditions for its members. Organized labor suffered two dramatic defeats in the 1890s, one at the Homestead steel plant in 1892 and the other over the Pullman car boycott in 1894.

FOCUS QUESTIONS

If you have mastered this chapter, you should be able to answer these questions and to explain the terms that follow the questions.

1. What were the key factors in the transformation of American cities in the late nineteenth century?

2. What important new social patterns emerged in urban areas in the late nineteenth century?

3. What new social patterns appeared in the South after Reconstruction?

4. How did southern racial relations develop after Reconstruction?

5. How did the expectations of European immigrants differ from their experiences?

6. Compare the experiences of Chinese Americans, American Indians, Mexican Americans, and African Americans in the Gilded Age.

7. How did industrialization affect workers in the new industries?

8. How did the various labor organizations define their membership and purpose? Does this help explain their successes and shortcomings?

KEY TERMS

suburb   *p. 436*

consumer culture   *p. 439*

domesticity   *p. 439*

separate spheres   *p. 440*

Woman's Christian Temperance Union   *p. 440*

Civil Rights Cases   *p. 445*

poll tax   *p. 445*

Booker T. Washington   *p. 445*

Atlanta Compromise   *p. 446*

Plessy v. Ferguson   *p. 446*

nativism   *p. 449*

American Protective Association (APA)   *p. 449*

Chinese Exclusion Act   *p. 452*

Dawes Severalty Act   *p. 453*

craft union, trade union   *p. 457*

National Labor Union   *p. 458*

Great Railway Strike of 1877   *p. 459*

Knights of Labor   *p. 459*

Terence V. Powderly   *p. 460*

American Federation of Labor   *p. 461*

Samuel Gompers   *p. 461*

Eugene V. Debs   *p. 461*

industrial union   *p. 461*

SUGGESTED RESOURCES

Melvyn Dubofsky. *Industrialism and the American Worker, 1865–1920*, 3rd ed. (Wheeing, IL: Harlan Davidson, 1996). A brief and highly readable introduction to the topic, organized chronologically.

Alan M. Kraut. *The Huddled Masses: The Immigrant in American Society, 1880–1921*, 2nd ed. (Wheeling, IL: Harlan Davidson, 2001). A brief and well-written introduction to immigration in the Gilded Age, especially the so-called "new immigrants."

Raymond A. Mohl. *The New City: Urban America in the Industrial Age, 1860–1920* (Wheeling, IL: Harlan Davidson, 1985). Still probably the best brief introduction to nearly all aspects of the growth of the cities in the Gilded Age.

Mae Ngai. *The Lucky Ones: One Family and the Extraordinary Invention of Chinese America* (Boston: Houghton Mifflin Harcourt, 2010). The fascinating story of Joseph and Mary Tape and their children.

"Illinois in the Gilded Age," http://lincoln.lib.niu.edu/fimage/gildedage/search.php. Though focused on Illinois, this website has a wealth of materials on life in the Gilded Age more generally.

18

Politics and Foreign Relations in a Rapidly Changing Nation, 1865–1902

CHAPTER OUTLINE

Parties, Spoils, Scandals, and Stalemate, 1865–1880
Parties, Conventions, and Patronage
Republicans and Democrats
Grant's Troubled Presidency
The Politics of Stalemate, 1876–1889
Harrison and the Fifty-First Congress

Challenges to Politics as Usual
Grangers, Greenbackers, and Silverites
Reforming the Spoils System
Challenging the Male Bastion: Woman Suffrage
Structural Change and Policy Change

Political Upheaval in the 1890s
The People's Party: Revolt of the West and South
The Elections of 1890 and 1892
Failure of the Divided Democrats
The 1896 Election and the New Republican Majority

Standing Aside from World Affairs, 1865–1889
Alaska, Canada, and the *Alabama* Claims
The United States and Latin America
Eastern Asia and the Pacific

Stepping into World Affairs: Harrison and Cleveland, 1889–1897
Building a Modern Navy
A New American Mission?
Revolution in Hawai'i
Crises in Latin America

Striding Boldly in World Affairs: McKinley, War, and Imperialism, 1898–1902
McKinley and War
The "Splendid Little War"
The Treaty of Paris
The New American Empire
The Open Door and the Boxer Rebellion in China

INDIVIDUAL VOICES: *Carl Schurz Comments on America's Changing Role in World Affairs, 1896–1899*

Study Tools

INDIVIDUAL CHOICES

Carl Schurz

Born in what is now Germany, Carl Schurz became involved in politics as a student at the University of Bonn, in 1848, when he joined a failed revolution in support of greater democracy. Like other "48ers," he fled to the United States. Immediately drawn to the antislavery movement, he soon began campaigning for the new Republican Party, especially among German Americans. Schurz fought in the Union Army, reaching the rank of major general by the end of the Civil War. He served in the U.S. Senate from Missouri from 1869 to 1875, the first German American in that body, and President Rutherford B. Hayes appointed him secretary of the interior, a post he held from 1877 to 1881. Thereafter, as a nationally prominent journalist, he worked for civil service reform and, after 1898, against American acquisition of the Philippines and imperialism more generally.

In 1887, Hayes encouraged Schurz to write something to explain his political career because many politicians considered him an "enigma" and a "mystery." Hayes continued that "[T]he common explanation is, 'Well he is a German'—or 'He is a Free Trader.' 'He is a good man—an honest man—a man of extraordinary talents, but not a practical man in

akg-images/The Image Works.

his political conduct.'" In what way was Schurz not "practical"? Hayes specified that it was because Schurz was so lacking in "the strength of the tie which binds the average...American to his party. To break it is almost a crime."

Schurz entered American politics at a time when political parties were at their strongest, controlling nearly every aspect of political decision making. It was a time when all men were expected to have strong and continuing loyalty to a political party, and to "vote the party ticket straight"—that is, unquestioningly support their party's candidates. Those who broke with their party drew the contempt of mainstream politicians, who called them "political hermaphrodites," "eunuchs," and "man-milliners" (men who made women's hats), reflecting the extent to which being a loyal party member was closely tied to men's gender role.

For Schurz, however, loyalty to principles was more important than loyalty to party. During the presidency of U.S. Grant, Schurz broke with the Republican Party and led the Liberal Republican movement, which opposed Grant's reelection. He later returned to Republican ranks, but refused to support the Republican presidential candidate in 1884. He then became the nation's best known independent, dividing his support for candidates on the basis of issues, especially civil service reform and, later, foreign policy (see the Individual Voices feature at the end of this chapter). His principled independence brought him many admirers, but he made even more enemies by his scathing criticism of those he considered unprincipled.

Schurz's political career came during a time when the nation's economy was changing at a breakneck pace, but when politics seemed to change very little. Americans expected that politics meant *party* politics and that all meaningful political choices came through the major parties. Yet from 1874 until the 1890s, there were few innovations in federal policies as the two major parties deadlocked. In foreign relations, too, things changed very little.

All that began to change in the 1890s, when political discontent in the West and South erupted into a new party, the People's Party, soon called the Populists. Politics crackled with new ideas and new alignments, shooting sparks in all directions. The 1896 presidential election was one of the most hard fought in the nation's history. That election brought an end to the long political logjam. Republicans emerged victorious and dominated politics for the next thirty-four years. And the 1890s ended with a war that ushered in a new role for the United States in world affairs, including the acquisition of new territorial possessions stretching nearly halfway around the world.

PARTIES, SPOILS, SCANDALS, AND STALEMATE, 1865–1880

★ What was the significance of political parties in the late nineteenth century?

★ Compare the presidencies from Grant through Cleveland. Which do you consider successful? Why?

Political parties were central to politics and government throughout most of the nineteenth century, but they were organized and behaved very differently from their counterparts today. Any understanding of politics in this period, therefore, must begin with political parties—what they were, what they did, what they stood for, and what choices they offered to voters.

Parties, Conventions, and Patronage

After the 1830s, nominations for political offices came from **party conventions**. The process of selecting

party convention Party meeting to nominate candidates for elective offices and adopt a platform.

convention delegates began when neighborhood voters gathered in party caucuses to choose delegates to local conventions. Conventions took place at county, state, and national levels and for congressional districts and state legislative districts. At most conventions, the delegates listened to long-winded speakers glorifying their party and denouncing the opposition. They nominated candidates for elective offices or chose delegates to another convention further up the federal ladder. And they adopted a platform. Party leaders worked to negotiate compromises among major groups within their party, on both candidates and platform language, and such deal-making sometimes occurred in informal settings—perhaps hotel rooms thick with cigar smoke and cluttered with whiskey bottles. Such behind-the-scenes deal making reinforced the notion of political parties as all-male bastions into which no self-respecting women would venture.

After choosing their candidates, parties launched their campaigns. Campaigns focused on party identity. Newspapers were the major source of news, and nearly every newspaper identified closely with a political party. The parties subsidized sympathetic newspapers, and the newspapers delivered both effusive support for their party and scathing attacks on the opposition. Before an election, local party organizations whipped up enthusiasm among party loyalists and tried to recruit new or undecided voters through parades, barbecues, and rallies capped by hours of speechmaking.

On election day, each party tried to mobilize all its supporters and make certain that they voted. This produced very high levels of voter participation—more than 80 percent of eligible voters cast their ballots in 1876. At polling places, party workers distributed lists, or "tickets," of their party's candidates, which voters used as ballots. Voting was not secret until the 1890s. Before then, everyone could see which party's ticket a voter turned in (illustrations of voting appear on pages 385 and 479). The voting process discouraged voters from crossing party lines.

Once the votes were counted, newly elected presidents or governors or mayors began appointing their supporters to government jobs, which were widely considered appropriate rewards for hard work during a winning campaign. Those appointed to such jobs were also expected to return part of their salaries to the party. This was called the patronage system or spoils system, after a statement by Senator William Marcy in 1831: "To the victor belong the spoils." Its defenders were labeled spoilsmen.

Party loyalists inevitably outnumbered available jobs, so fierce competition raged over appointments. When James Garfield became president in 1881, he was so overwhelmed with demands for jobs that he exclaimed in disgust, "My God! What is there in this place that a man should ever want to get into it?" Jobs in highest demand often involved purchasing or government contracts, another form of spoils, awarded to businessmen who supported the party. This system invited corruption. One post office official, for example, pressured postmasters to buy clocks from one of his political associates. Such opportunities were limited only by the imagination of the spoilsmen. Some critics, including Carl Schurz, argued that, by concentrating so much on patronage, politics ignored principles and issues and revolved instead around greed for office. The spoils system had many defenders, however. George W. Plunkitt, a long-time participant in New York City politics, explained, "You can't keep an organization together without patronage. Men ain't in politics for nothin'." Plunkitt described the reality: given the many party workers needed to identify supporters and mobilize voters, politics required rewards.

In 1905, a newspaper reporter published a series of conversations with Plunkitt. His observations provide insights into the nature of urban politics and its relation to urban poverty. Born in a poor Irish neighborhood of New York City, Plunkitt left school early, entered politics, and eventually became a district leader of Tammany Hall, the organization that dominated the city's Democratic Party. Between 1868 and 1904, he served in state and city government. Plunkitt explained how he kept the loyalty of his neighborhood voters:

> Go right down among the poor families and help them in the different ways they need help.... It's philanthropy, but it's politics, too—mighty good politics.... The poor are the most grateful people in the world, and, let me tell you, they have more friends in their neighborhoods than the rich have in theirs.... The consequence is that the poor look up to George W. Plunkitt* as a father, come to him in trouble—and don't forget him on election day.

Plunkitt typified many big-city politicians across the country. Throughout the late nineteenth century,

caucus A meeting of people with a common political interest—for example, to choose delegates to a party convention.

platform A written statement of the principles, policies, and promises on which a political party appeals to voters.

▫ patronage system System that lets the winning party distribute appointive government jobs to loyal party members; also called the spoils system.

spoilsmen Derogatory term for defenders of the patronage or spoils system.

postmaster An official appointed to manage a local post office.

Tammany Hall New York City political organization that often dominated city and sometimes state politics by controlling the Democratic Party in New York City.

Plunkitt of Tammany Hall: A Series of Very Plain Talks on Very Practical Politics, Delivered by Ex-Senator George Washington Plunkitt, the Tammany Philosopher, from His Rostrom—the New York County Court House Bootblack Stand – and Recorded by William L. Reardon (New York: McClure, Phillips & Co., 1905), pp. 51–52.

urban politicians cultivated lower-income voters by addressing their needs directly and personally. They tried to build a personal rapport with voters, and responded to the needs of the poor by providing an occasional basket of food or a job in some city department. In return, they wanted political loyalty. Such urban political organizations flourished during the years 1870–1910, and some survived long after that. Similar organizations—sometimes Republican but more often Democratic—emerged in nearly all large cities, based among lower-income voters, usually led by recent immigrants. Where they amassed great power, their rivals denounced the leader as a boss and the organization as a **machine**.

Everywhere, opponents of such organizations charged corruption. Some bosses accumulated sizable fortunes—sometimes through gifts or retainers from companies seeking franchises or city contracts (their critics called these bribes), sometimes through advance knowledge of city planning. Richard Croker, the boss of Tammany in the 1890s, accumulated an immense personal fortune, but he always insisted that he had never taken a dishonest dollar.

Above all, the bosses centralized political decision making. "There's got to be in every ward somebody that any bloke can come to," a Boston politician insisted, "to get help." If a pushcart vendor needed a permit to sell tinware, or a railroad president needed permission to build a bridge, or a saloonkeeper wanted to stay open on Sunday despite state law, the machine could help them all—if they showed the proper gratitude in return.

Republicans and Democrats

Beneath the hoopla and interminable speeches, important differences characterized the major parties. Republicans pointed to their defense of the Union during the Civil War and claimed a monopoly on patriotism, arguing that Democrats—especially southern Democrats—had proven themselves disloyal. "Every man that shot a Union soldier," one Republican orator proclaimed, "was a Democrat." Such rhetoric was often called "waving the bloody shirt." Republicans in Congress voted generous pensions to disabled Union army veterans and the widows and orphans of those who died, and Republican leaders cultivated the Grand Army of the Republic (GAR), the organization of Union veterans, attending their meetings and urging them to "vote as you shot." Republican presidential candidates were usually Union veterans, as were many state and local officials throughout the North.

Republicans proudly claimed responsibility for prosperity, insisting that postwar economic growth resulted from their policies, especially the protective tariff. Republicans boasted that they were the party of decency and morality, and portrayed as typical Democrats "the old slave-owner and slave-driver, the saloon-keeper, the ballot-box-stuffer, the Kuklux [Klan], the criminal class of the great cities, the men who cannot read or write."

Where Republicans defined themselves in terms of what their party did and who they were, Democrats typically focused on what they opposed. Most leading Democrats stood against the protective tariff and land grants, equating government activism with privileges for a favored few. The protective tariff, they charged, protected manufacturers from international competition at the expense of consumers who paid higher prices. The public domain, they argued, should provide farms for citizens, not subsidies for railroad corporations. In general, Democrats favored a strictly limited role for the government in the economy.

Just as the Democrats opposed governmental interference in the economy, so too did they oppose governmental interference in social relations and behavior. In the North, especially in Irish and German communities, they condemned **prohibition**, which they called a violation of personal liberty. In the South, Democrats rejected federal enforcement of equal rights for African Americans, which they denounced as a violation of states' rights. There, Democrats stood for white supremacy. Most voters developed strong loyalties to one party or the other, often based on ethnicity, race, or religion. Nearly all Catholics and many Irish, German, and other immigrants supported the Democrats. Most southern whites supported the Democrats as the party of white supremacy. The Democrats' opposition to the protective tariff attracted entrepreneurs with interests in international commerce. The Democrats, all in all, comprised a diverse coalition, holding together primarily because their various components opposed government action on social or economic matters.

Outside the South, most old-stock Protestants voted Republican, as did most Scandinavian and British immigrants. Nearly all African Americans supported the Republicans as the party of emancipation, as did most veterans of the abolition movement. So many Union veterans supported the Republicans that someone suggested GAR stood for "generally all Republicans." Republicans usually carried New England, Pennsylvania, and much of the Midwest.

machine When applied to urban political organizations, a derogatory term implying that the organization concentrated on patronage and graft to the exclusion of issues and principles.

prohibition A legal ban on the manufacture, sale, and use of alcoholic beverages.

Thomas Nast, the most influential cartoonist of the 1870s, began using an elephant to symbolize the Republicans and a donkey for the Democrats. At the time, however, Republicans often preferred an eagle, and Democrats usually chose a rooster.

Republicans comprised the more coherent political organization, united around policies that involved action by the federal government to foster economic growth and protect blacks' rights. The protective tariff and use of the public domain to encourage economic development both involved positive governmental action. During Reconstruction, the dominant Republicans had changed the very nature of the federal government, redefining citizenship and relations between the federal government and the states. As one leading Republican put it, "The Republican party does things, the Democratic party criticizes." Neither party, however, proposed to regulate, restrict, or tax the new industrial corporations.

Grant's Troubled Presidency

Despite success as a general, Ulysses S. Grant seemed unprepared when he won the presidency in 1868. During his two terms (1869–1877), he usually deferred to Congress for domestic policymaking. Too often he appointed friends or acquaintances to posts for which they possessed few qualifications, and too often

■ **Crédit Mobilier** Company created to build the Union Pacific Railroad; in a scandalous deal uncovered in 1872–1873, it sold shares cheaply to congressmen who approved federal subsidies for railroad construction.

he believed their denials of wrongdoing. He failed to form a competent cabinet and faced constant turnover among his advisers. He did choose a highly capable secretary of state, Hamilton Fish, and eventually found in Benjamin Bristow a secretary of the treasury who vigorously combated corruption.

Congress supplied its full share of scandal. Visiting Washington in 1869, Henry Adams was surprised to hear a cabinet member bellow, "You can't use tact with a Congressman! A Congressman is a hog! You must take a stick and hit him on the snout!" Too many members of Congress behaved in ways that confirmed such cynical views. In 1864, the chief shareholders in the Union Pacific Railroad set up the **Crédit Mobilier** as a construction company and then gave it a generous contract, thereby paying themselves handsomely, using stockholder funds, to build their own railroad! To prevent congressional scrutiny, they sold shares at cut-rate prices to key congressmen. Revelation of these arrangements in 1872–1873 scandalized the nation. No sooner did that furor pass than Congress voted itself a 50 percent pay raise and made the increase two years retroactive. Only after widespread public protest did Congress repeal its "salary grab."

Public disgrace was not limited to the federal government nor to Republicans. In New York City, the **Tweed Ring** scandal involved city and state officials accused of using bribery, **kickbacks**, and padded accounts to steal money from New York City and the state. At the center was **William Marcy Tweed**, whose name became synonymous with urban political corruption. Tweed entered New York City politics in the 1850s and became head of Tammany Hall in 1863. Labeled "Boss Tweed" by opponents, he and his associates built public support by spending tax funds on charities and giving to the poor from their own pockets—pockets filled with ill-gotten gains.

Under Tweed's direction, city government launched major construction projects: public buildings, streets, parks, and sewers. Between 1868 and 1871, the Tweed Ring may have plundered $200 million from the city, mostly by giving bloated construction contracts to businesses that returned a kickback to the ring. In 1871 evidence of corruption led to Tweed's indictment and ultimately his conviction and imprisonment.

Grant easily won reelection in 1872, but the midterm elections of 1874 were a different story. The congressional scandals alienated some voters. Moreover, the depression that began in 1873 undercut Republicans' claim to have produced prosperity. Throughout the South, political terrorism suppressed the Republican vote. As a result, Democrats took control of the House of Representatives. For twenty years, from 1874 until 1894, Democrats usually kept their majority in the House of Representatives. Though Republicans usually won the presidency, Democratic control of the House made it difficult or impossible for the Republicans to enact major legislation.

More scandals were to come. In 1875 Treasury Secretary Bristow revealed that a **Whiskey Ring** of federal officials and distillers, centered in St. Louis, had defrauded the government of millions of dollars. The 230 men indicted included several of Grant's appointees and even his private secretary. The next year, William Belknap, Grant's secretary of war, resigned shortly before he was impeached for accepting bribes.

The Politics of Stalemate, 1876–1889

From the mid-1870s through the 1880s, as the nation's economy and social patterns changed with astonishing speed, American politics seemed frozen in place. From the end of the Civil War to the mid-1870s, politics had revolved largely around issues of war and Reconstruction. By the late 1870s, other issues became central, notably the economy and political corruption. After the mid-1870s, however, voters divided almost evenly between the two major political parties, beginning a long political **stalemate** during which neither party could enact its proposals.

Republican Rutherford B. Hayes became president after the closely contested election of 1876 (discussed in Chapter 15). His personal integrity and principled stand on issues helped restore his party's reputation after the embarrassments of the Grant administration. However, Democrats held the majority in the House of Representatives. Moreover, Roscoe Conkling, a flamboyant senator and leader of New York's powerful and patronage-hungry Republican organization, scathingly attacked Hayes after Hayes refused Conkling's patronage demands. Hayes even estranged reformers by not seeking reform of the spoils system. He did not seek reelection in 1880.

In 1880, the Republican nominating convention deadlocked between supporters of James G. Blaine of Maine, a spellbinding orator who attracted loyal supporters and bitter enemies, and Conkling and his followers, who called themselves **Stalwarts** and wanted to nominate former president Grant. Eventually the convention compromised, choosing James A. Garfield, a congressman from Ohio. Born in a log cabin, Garfield had grown up in poverty. A minister, college president, and lawyer before the Civil War, he became the Union's youngest major general. For vice president, the delegates nominated Conkling's chief lieutenant, Chester A. Arthur.

Garfield won the popular vote by half a percentage point but won a secure electoral majority. He brought to the presidency a solid understanding of Congress and a studious approach to issues. He appointed Blaine as secretary of state, the most prestigious cabinet position, but also tried to cooperate with the Stalwarts. When Conkling arrogantly demanded his supporters be appointed to key positions, Garfield outmaneuvered him. Humiliated, Conkling resigned from the Senate, and Garfield scored a victory for a stronger presidency.

On July 2, 1881, four months after taking office, Garfield was shot while walking through a Washington railroad station. His assassin, Charles Guiteau, a mentally unstable religious fanatic and disappointed

■ **Tweed Ring** Name applied to the political organization of William Marcy Tweed. *Ring*, in this context, means a group of people who act together to exercise control over politics.

kickback An illegal payment by a contractor to the official who awarded the contract.

William Marcy Tweed New York City political boss who used the Tammany organization to control city and state government from the 1860s until his downfall in 1871.

Whiskey Ring Distillers and federal revenue officials in St. Louis who were revealed in 1875 to have defrauded the government of millions of dollars in whiskey taxes.

stalemate In chess, a situation where neither player can move, and therefore neither can win. Thus, any situation where neither side can gain an advantage.

Stalwarts Faction of the Republican Party led by Roscoe Conkling of New York; Stalwarts claimed to be the genuine Republicans.

office-seeker, claimed he had acted to save the Republican Party. Two months later, Garfield died—owing to incompetent medical care.

Chester A. Arthur now became president. Probably best known as a member of the Conkling organization and a dapper dresser, Arthur soon showed, as a former associate said, that "He isn't 'Chet' Arthur any more; he's the President." In 1882 doctors diagnosed him with Bright's disease, a kidney condition that produced fatigue, depression, and eventually death. Arthur kept the news secret from all but his family and closest friends. Despite political liabilities and his own physical limitations, Arthur proved more capable than anyone might have predicted.

In 1884, Blaine—charming and quick witted—finally secured the Republican nomination. Democrats chose Grover Cleveland, governor of New York, whose reputation for integrity and political courage had come partly from attacking Tammany Hall. Seeking to tarnish that reputation, Republicans chanted "Ma! Ma! Where's my pa?" to trumpet that Cleveland had fathered a child outside marriage. The election hinged on New York State, where many Irish voters—a large component in Tammany—seemed attracted to Blaine. A few days before the election, however, Blaine was present when a preacher in New York City called Democrats the party of "rum, Romanism [Catholicism], and rebellion." Blaine was slow to respond to this insult to Irish Catholics. Cleveland won New York by a tiny margin, and New York's electoral votes gave him victory.

Cleveland enjoyed support from many who opposed the spoils system, and he insisted on demonstrated ability in those he appointed to office. Staunchly committed to minimal government and cutting federal spending, Cleveland vetoed 414 bills—most granting pensions to individual Union veterans—twice as many vetoes as all previous presidents *combined*. Cleveland deferred to Congress regarding policymaking and approved several important measures produced by the Democratic House and Republican Senate, including the Dawes Severalty Act (discussed in Chapter 17) and the Interstate Commerce Act.

The Interstate Commerce Act grew out of political pressure from farmers and small businesses. In the early 1870s, several midwestern states passed "Granger laws," regulating railroad freight rates (discussed later in this chapter). In 1886, however, the Supreme Court limited states' power to regulate railroad rates. In response, amid growing protests over railroad rate discrimination, Congress passed the Interstate Commerce Act in 1887. The new law created the **Interstate Commerce Commission** (ICC), the first federal regulatory commission. Though the law prohibited pools and rebates and required that rates be "reasonable and just," the ICC had little real regulatory power until the Hepburn Act strengthened it in 1906.

Cleveland considered the nation's greatest problem to be the federal budget surplus. After the Civil War, the tariff usually generated more income than the country needed (see Figure 18.1). Worried that the surplus encouraged wasteful spending and that tariffs reduced competition and led to monopolies, Cleveland demanded in 1887 that Congress cut tariff rates. His action divided Democrats, but Cleveland provided little leadership. The House and Senate deadlocked, each writing a quite different version of tariff reform. Congress then adjourned without taking action. Cleveland's call for tariff reform came to nothing.

In the 1888 presidential election, Democrats renominated Cleveland, but he avoided the tariff issue and did little campaigning. Republicans nominated Benjamin Harrison, senator from Indiana and former Civil War general. Thoughtful and cautious, Harrison impressed many as cool and distant. Republicans campaigned vigorously in defense of the protective tariff, raising unprecedented amounts of campaign money from business leaders and issuing record amounts of campaign materials. Harrison received fewer votes than Cleveland (47.9 percent to Cleveland's 48.7 percent) but won in the Electoral College. As important for the Republicans as their narrow presidential victory, however, were the majorities they secured in the House and Senate.

Harrison and the Fifty-First Congress

With Harrison in the White House and Republican majorities in Congress, the Republicans set out to do a lot and to do it quickly. When the fifty-first session of Congress opened late in 1889, Harrison worked more closely with congressional leaders of his own party than any other president in recent memory. Democrats in the House of Representatives tried to delay, but Speaker Thomas B. Reed—an enormous man renowned for his wit—imposed new rules designed to speed up House business.

Republicans first turned to tariff revision to cut the troublesome federal surplus without reducing protection. Led by **William McKinley** of Ohio, the House approved a bill that moved some items to the

▫ **Interstate Commerce Commission** (ICC) The first federal regulatory commission, created in 1887 to regulate railroads and require that rates be "reasonable and just."

▫ **William McKinley** (1843–1901) Twenty-fifth president. Served in the House of Representatives and as governor of Ohio before winning the presidency in 1896. Assassinated in 1901.

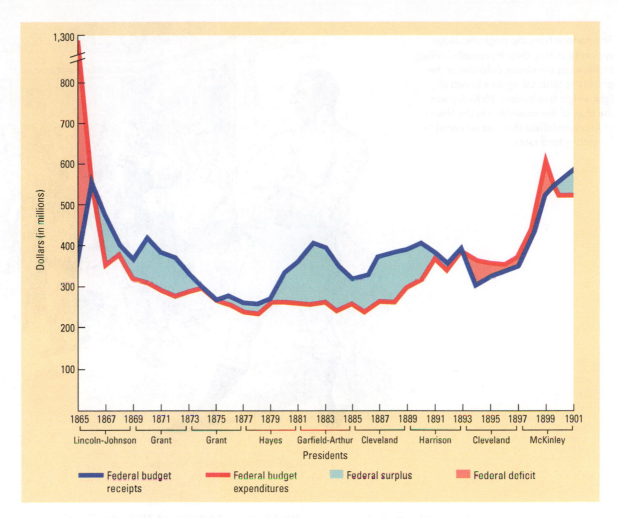

FIGURE 18.1 Federal Receipts and Expenditures, 1865–1901
The federal surplus usually shrank during economic downturns (mid-1870s and mid-1890s) and grew in more prosperous periods (1880s). During the Harrison administration, however, the surplus virtually disappeared, reflecting efforts to reduce income and increase expenditures.

Source: U.S. Department of Commerce, Bureau of the Census, *Historical Statistics of the United States, Colonial Times to 1970*, Bicentennial edition, 2 vols. (Washington, D.C.: U.S. Government Printing Office, 1975), 1: 1104.

free list (notably sugar, a major source of tariff revenue) but raised tariffs on other items. Called the **McKinley Tariff**, the bill was sent to the Senate. The House also approved a federal elections bill, sponsored by Representative Henry Cabot Lodge of Massachusetts. The bill proposed federal supervision over congressional elections in the South to protect the voting rights of African Americans. Democrats called it a "force bill," evoking memories of Reconstruction. After passing the House, the measure went to the Senate, where approval by the Republican majority seemed likely.

Harrison wanted the two bills passed as a party package, but Republicans feared that a Democratic **filibuster** against the elections bill would prevent passage of both measures. Despite protests by Lodge and others, a compromise emerged—Republicans would table the elections bill, and Democrats would not delay the tariff bill. Thus Republicans sacrificed

African Americans' voting rights to gain the revised tariff. Harrison signed the McKinley Tariff on October 1, 1890, and the revised tariff soon produced the intended result: it reduced the surplus by cutting tariff income.

The Senate, meanwhile, had been laboring over two measures named for Senator John Sherman of Ohio: the Sherman Silver Purchase Act (discussed shortly)

■ **McKinley Tariff** Tariff passed by Congress in 1890 that sought not only to protect established industries but by prohibitory duties to stimulate the creation of new industries.

filibuster A speech by a bill's opponents to delay legislative action; usually applies to extended speeches in the U.S. Senate, which has no time limit on speeches and where a minority may therefore "talk a bill to death" by holding up all other business.

This cartoon from the magazine *Judge* appeared in May 1890. It presents William McKinley as the strong defender of the protective tariff, taking on a bunch of light-weight free traders. McKinley was the chair of the committee in the House of Representatives that was responsible for setting tariff rates.

CHAMPION McKINLEY OPENS THE TARIFF BATTLE.
An unequal match between the heavy and the light weights.

and the **Sherman Anti-Trust Act**. The Anti-Trust Act, drafted by several Republican senators working with Harrison, was Republicans' response to public concern about monopolies. Approved overwhelmingly, the law declared that "every contract, combination in the form of trust or otherwise, or conspiracy, in restraint of trade or commerce among the several states, or with foreign nations, is hereby declared to be illegal." The law made the United States the first industrial nation to attempt to prevent monopolies, but it proved difficult to interpret and had little initial effect.

In ten months the Republicans passed what one Democrat called "a raging sea of ravenous legislation." In addition to the McKinley Tariff, the Sherman Anti-Trust Act, and the Silver Purchase Act, the record number of new laws included appropriations to create a modern navy, a major increase in pension eligibility for disabled Union veterans and their dependents, statehood for North and South Dakota, Montana,

Washington, Idaho, and Wyoming, and creation of a territorial government in Oklahoma. Republicans hoped they had finally broken the political logjam that had clogged politics since 1875.

CHALLENGES TO POLITICS AS USUAL

☆ *What were the major goals of the various reform groups?*

☆ *Why were some reformers more successful than others?*

Though political change seemed to move at a glacial pace in the Gilded Age, several groups challenged mainstream politics and sought new policies and new political procedures. Given the large number of Americans engaged in agriculture, it is not surprising that farmers were prominent in several significant movements.

Grangers, Greenbackers, and Silverites

Crop prices fell steadily after the Civil War as production of wheat, corn, and cotton grew much faster

◼ **Sherman Anti-Trust Act** Law passed by Congress in 1890 authorizing the federal government to prosecute any "combination... in restraint of trade"; because of adverse court rulings, it had little initial effect.

It Matters Today

The Defeat of the Lodge Bill

The failure of the Fifty-First Congress to approve the Lodge bill marked a long-term retreat from federal enforcement of voting rights, and southern states systematically disfranchised African Americans. Many African Americans and a few white allies continued to challenge this situation, but their efforts did not succeed until the 1960s.

Serious federal enforcement of voting rights came only with the Voting Rights Act of 1965, which included features similar to those in the Lodge bill. The 1965 act has since been amended, interpreted by the courts, and periodically extended. In 2006, the Republican leadership in Congress pushed through a twenty-five-year renewal of the Voting Rights Act a year ahead of schedule. In 2012, the Texas Republican party proposed repealing the Voting Rights Act.

- Go online and read newspapers from 1965 when the original Voting Rights Act was being discussed in Congress. How is the Voting Rights Act similar to the Lodge bill? What were the arguments against the Voting Rights Act?
- Go online and find recent newspaper accounts that deal with the Voting Rights Act. What arguments are being made against the law? What are the arguments being made to retain it?

than the population. Some farmers, however, denied that prices were falling because of overproduction, pointing to the hungry and ragged residents of urban slums. Farmers condemned the monopolistic practices of **commodity markets** in Chicago and New York that determined crop prices. When they brought their crops to market, farmers accepted the price that was offered because they needed cash to pay their debts and could not store their crops for later sale at a higher price. But they knew that the bushel of corn they sold for 10 or 20 cents in October brought three or four times that amount in New York in December.

Many farmers borrowed heavily to establish new farms after the Civil War. Falling prices magnified their indebtedness. Because crop prices sank lower and lower, farmers raised more and more just to pay their mortgages and buy necessities. Given the relation between supply and demand, the more they raised, the lower prices fell. As they ran faster and faster just to stay in the same place, many found they could not keep up.

The railroads, too, seemed to be greedy monopolies that charged as much as possible to deliver supplies to rural America and carry farm crops to market. It sometimes cost four times as much to ship freight in the West or South as in the East. Farmers also protested that railroads dominated politics in many western and southern states and distributed free passes to politicians in return for favorable treatment.

Soon organizations began to address the scourges of falling prices and high railroad freight rates. The first, officially called the Patrons of Husbandry but usually known as the **Grange**, was

formed in 1867 and extended full participation to women as well as men.

Initially intended as a social outlet for farm families and a way to educate them in new farming methods, the Grange grew rapidly, especially in the Midwest and central South. In the 1870s, many local Granges set up cooperative stores (consumers' cooperatives), where members did their shopping and divided any profits among themselves. Some formed producers' cooperatives, in which farmers agreed to hold their crops back from market and jointly negotiate over prices. Two state Granges began manufacturing farm machinery, and Grangers planned for cooperative factories producing everything from wagons to sewing machines. Some Grangers formed mutual insurance companies, and a few experimented with cooperative banks.

The Grange defined itself as nonpartisan. However, as Grange membership boomed in the 1870s, midwestern and western Grangers moved toward political action. New political parties emerged in eleven states, usually called "Granger Parties." They demanded state legislation to prohibit railroad rate discrimination. Other groups, especially merchants, also

commodity market Financial market in which brokers buy and sell agricultural products in large quantities, thus determining the prices paid to farmers for their harvests.

■ **Grange** Organization for farmers that combined social activities with education about improved farming methods and cooperative economic efforts; formally called the Patrons of Husbandry.

TOWARD A MORE PERFECT UNION

The Meaning of the Commerce Clause

The Sherman Anti-Trust Act reads, in part, "Every person who shall monopolize, or attempt to monopolize, or combine or conspire with any other person or persons, to monopolize any part of the trade or commerce among the several States… shall be deemed guilty of a felony"; the law was widely understood at the time as outlawing such monopolies as Standard Oil. By referring to "commerce among the several States," the law was citing the constitutional authority of Congress to "regulate Commerce… among the several States" (Article I, Section 8).

The American Sugar Refining Company challenged the law. In *U.S. v. E.C. Knight* (1895), the Supreme Court specified that manufacturing (such as sugar refining) took place entirely within one state and was therefore immune from federal law. This decision significantly limited federal regulatory authority until 1905, when the Supreme Court defined manufacturing as part of a "stream of commerce" that crossed state lines and was therefore subject to federal regulation. The "stream of commerce" doctrine underlies most federal economic regulations of subsequent years, but has recently been questioned by the Supreme Court.

■ **Granger laws** State laws regulating railroads, passed in several states in the 1870s in response to lobbying by the Grange and other groups.

monetary policy Now, the regulation of the money supply and interest rates by the Federal Reserve. Before 1913, federal monetary policy was largely limited to defining the medium of the currency (gold, silver, or paper) and the relations between the types of currency.

deflation Falling prices; a situation in which the purchasing power of the dollar increases. The opposite of deflation is inflation, when prices go up and the purchasing power of the dollar declines.

greenbacks Paper money, not backed by gold, that the federal government issued during the Civil War.

graduated income tax Tax based on income, such that the percentage of income paid as tax increases with income level, so that those with the lowest income pay the lowest percentage and those with higher incomes pay a larger percentage.

■ **gold standard** A monetary system based on gold, under which legal contracts typically called for the payment of all debts in gold, and paper money could be redeemed for gold at a bank.

sought such laws, but the resulting state laws, most dating to 1872–1874, were usually called **Granger laws**. When the constitutionality of such regulation was challenged, the Supreme Court ruled, in *Munn v. Illinois* (1877), that businesses with "a public interest," including warehouses and railroads, "must submit to be controlled by the public for the common good."

The Grange reached its zenith in the mid-1870s. Hastily organized cooperatives soon encountered financial problems that were compounded by the national depression. As cooperatives collapsed, they often pulled down Grange organizations. Political activity brought some successes but also generated bitter internal disputes. The organization lost many members, and surviving Granges generally avoided both cooperatives and politics.

With the decline of the Grange, some farmers looked to **monetary policy** for relief. After the Civil War, most prices fell (a situation called **deflation**) because of increased production, more efficient techniques in agriculture and manufacturing, and the failure of the money supply to grow as rapidly as the economy. Deflation injures debtors because it means that the money to pay off a loan has greater purchasing power (and so is harder to come by) than the money of the original loan. The Greenback Party argued that printing more **greenbacks**, the paper money issued during the Civil War, would increase the supply of money and thereby stabilize prices. They found a receptive audience among farmers in debt.

In the congressional elections of 1878, the Greenback Party received nearly a million votes and elected fourteen congressmen. In the 1880 presidential election, Greenbackers tried to attract urban workers by supporting the eight-hour workday, legislation to protect workers, and the abolition of child labor. They also called for regulation of transportation and communication, a **graduated income tax** (which they considered the fairest form of taxation), and woman suffrage. For president, they nominated James B. Weaver of Iowa, a Greenback congressman and former Union army general. He got only 3.3 percent of the vote. The prevalent currency deflation also motivated those who wanted the government to resume issuing silver dollars. In 1873 Congress dropped the silver dollar from the list of approved coins, following the lead of Britain, Germany, and other European nations, which had specified that only gold was to serve as money. Some Americans believed that adhering to this **gold standard** was essential if American businesses were to compete effectively in international markets for capital and goods.

Given major silver discoveries in the West, resuming silver coinage seemed a way to counteract deflation without resorting to greenbacks. Silver

This lithograph was likely inspired by the Granger movement, which issued a similar poster with the title, "I Pay for All." Here the farmer says, instead, "I feed you all." Around the edges are, clockwise from top left, a lawyer ("I Plead for All"); a seated President Ulysses S. Grant ("I Rule for All"); an army officer leading a charge ("I Fight for All"); a clergyman ("I Preach for All"); a ship owner ("I Sail for All"); a shopkeeper ("I Buy & Sell for All"); a doctor ("I Physic You All"); a general broker ("I Fleece You All"); a stock trader ("I Bull & Bear for All"); and a railroad owner ("I Carry for All"). The underlying message here is that the farmer is the only one of these who actually produces something of value, and the others are living off the value that the farmer produces.

coinage quickly found support not just among farmers but also among silver mining interests. Members of this farming-mining coalition were soon called "silverites." In 1878, over Hayes's veto, Congress passed the **Bland-Allison Act** authorizing a limited amount of silver dollars. The act failed to counteract deflation, and satisfied neither silverites nor gold supporters. The **Sherman Silver Purchase Act** of 1890 increased the amount of silver to be coined, but both silverites and advocates of the gold standard still found it unsatisfactory.

Reforming the Spoils System

A very different set of reformers challenged the spoils system. Called **Mugwumps** by their contemporaries and centered in Boston and New York, most were Republicans of high social status. Like Carl Schurz, they blamed many of the defects in politics on the spoils system, argued that eliminating patronage would drive out the opportunists, and advocated a merit system based on the ability to pass a comprehensive examination. As they did with others who broke with

their party, party politicians sometimes questioned the Mugwumps' manhood.

The assassination of President Garfield by a disappointed office seeker spurred efforts to reform the patronage system. Sponsored by Senator George Pendleton (an Ohio Democrat), the **Pendleton Act** of 1883 created a merit system for filling federal

Bland-Allison Act An 1878 law providing for federal purchase of limited amounts of silver to be coined into silver dollars.

■ **Sherman Silver Purchase Act** An 1890 law requiring the federal government to increase its purchases of silver to be coined into silver dollars.

■ **Mugwumps** Reformers, mostly Republicans, of the 1880s and 1890s who opposed political corruption and campaigned for reform, especially civil service reform, sometimes crossing party boundaries to achieve their goals.

■ **Pendleton Act** An 1883 law that created the Civil Service Commission and instituted a merit system of competitive examinations for federal hiring and jobs.

The Grange tries to awaken the public to the approaching locomotive (a symbol of monopoly power) that is bringing consolidation (mergers), extortion (high prices), bribery, and other evils. Railroad ties (the wooden pieces on which the rails rested) are sometimes called sleepers.

positions. The new law designated certain federal positions, about 15 percent of the total, as "classified" and required **classified civil service** positions to be filled only through competitive examinations. The law authorized the president to add positions to the classified list. Within twenty years, the law applied to 44 percent of federal employees. State and local governments eventually adopted merit systems as well.

Challenging the Male Bastion: Woman Suffrage

In the masculine political world of the Gilded Age, men were expected to display strong loyalty to a political party, but men considered women—who could not vote—to stand outside politics. The concepts of

classified civil service Federal jobs filled through the merit system instead of by patronage.

■ **National Woman Suffrage Association** (NWSA) Women's suffrage organization formed in 1869 and led by Elizabeth Cady Stanton and Susan B. Anthony; accepted only women as members and worked for suffrage and related issues such as unionizing female workers.

■ **American Woman Suffrage Association** (AWSA) Boston-based women's suffrage organization formed in 1869; it welcomed men and worked solely to win the vote for women.

domesticity and separate spheres dictated that women avoid politics, especially party politics. Some women nonetheless involved themselves in reform efforts, a few took part in party activities, and some pushed for full political participation including the right to vote.

The struggle for woman suffrage was of long standing. In 1848 Elizabeth Cady Stanton and four other women organized the world's first Woman's Rights Convention, held at Seneca Falls, New York. Their Declaration of Principles announced, in part, "It is the duty of the women of this country to secure to themselves their sacred right to the elective franchise." Stanton and Susan B. Anthony became the most prominent advocates for women's rights, especially voting rights, for the next fifty years. They secured changes in some laws that discriminated against women, and women came increasingly to participate in public affairs: in movements to abolish slavery, mobilize support for the Union, improve educational opportunities, end child labor, and more.

In 1866 Stanton and Anthony unsuccessfully opposed inclusion of the word *male* in the Fourteenth Amendment. In 1869 they formed the **National Woman Suffrage Association** (NWSA), open only to women, and sought an amendment to the federal Constitution as the only sure route to woman suffrage. NWSA built alliances with other reform and radical organizations and worked to improve women's status, promoting women's trade unions and lobbying for easier divorce laws and access to birth-control information. In contrast, the **American Woman Suffrage Association** (AWSA), organized by Lucy Stone and other suffrage advocates, also in 1869, concentrated strictly on winning the vote and avoided other issues. The two merged in 1890 to become the National American Woman Suffrage Association.

The first victories for suffrage came in the West. In 1869, in Wyoming Territory, the territorial legislature extended the franchise to women. Wyoming women had forged a well-organized suffrage movement and persuaded male legislators to support their cause. Some legislators also hoped that woman suffrage would attract women to Wyoming, where men outnumbered women by 7 to 2. Thereafter, women in Wyoming Territory voted, served on juries, and held elective office. In 1889, when Wyoming asked for statehood, some congressmen balked at admitting a state with woman suffrage. Wyoming legislators, however, bluntly stated, "We will remain out of the Union a hundred years rather than come in without the women." Congress finally voted to approve Wyoming statehood—with woman suffrage—in 1890.

Library of Congress.

This sketch of women voting in Cheyenne, Wyoming Territory, appeared in 1888. In 1869, Wyoming became the first state or territory to extend suffrage to women. This drawing appeared shortly before Wyoming requested statehood, a request made controversial by the territory's acceptance of woman suffrage.

Utah Territory adopted woman suffrage in 1870. There Mormon men formed the majority of voters, and Mormon women far outnumbered non-Mormon women. Mormons thereby strengthened their voting majority and may have hoped to silence those who claimed that polygamy degraded women. However, Congress outlawed polygamy in 1887 and simultaneously disfranchised Utah women. Not until Utah became a state, in 1896, did its women regain the vote. In 1893, Colorado voters (all male) approved woman suffrage, making Colorado the first state to adopt woman suffrage through a popular vote. In addition to a well-organized campaign by Colorado women, their cause was assisted by support from the new Populist Party (discussed in the next section). In Idaho, where both Mormon and Populist influences were strong, male voters approved woman suffrage in 1896. These western states and territories were among the first places in the world to extend equal voting rights to women.

Several states also began to extend limited voting rights to women, especially for school-related elections, reflecting perhaps the widespread assumption that women's gender roles included child rearing. By 1890, women could vote in school elections in nineteen states.

Structural Change and Policy Change

Grangers, Greenbackers, local labor parties, the Woman's Christian Temperance Union (WCTU), Mugwumps, and advocates of woman suffrage all challenged basic features of the party-bound political system of the Gilded Age. They and other groups advocated changes that the major parties ignored: abolition of the spoils system, woman suffrage, prohibition, the secret ballot, regulation of business, an end to child labor, changes in monetary policy, and more.

Most of these groups called themselves reformers, meaning that they wanted to change the *form* of politics, either by *structural* change or *policy* change. Structural reform modifies the *structure* or procedures of the political system. Advocates of woman suffrage, for example, wanted to change eligibility for voting, and the Mugwumps sought a new system for filling appointive offices.

Policy issues, in contrast, have to do with the way that government uses its powers. The debate over federal economic policy in the Gilded Age provides an array of contrasting positions. Most Democrats believed that federal interference in the economy created a privileged class. Republicans used land grants and the protective tariff to encourage economic growth. Grangers wanted the government to regulate railroads. Greenbackers wanted monetary policy to benefit debtors—or, as they would have put it, to stop benefiting lenders.

Groups seeking change may find they have little in common with other groups or may seek to cooperate with them. Frances Willard of the WCTU embraced a wide range of reforms. One key distinction between the National Woman Suffrage Association and the American Woman Suffrage Association was that the NWSA welcomed political alliances with groups who supported suffrage for all citizens. The AWSA feared such alliances might lose more support than they gained and focused narrowly on suffrage.

The tiny Prohibition Party wanted government to eliminate alcohol but also favored woman suffrage in part because they assumed that women voters would oppose alcohol. Thus, they promoted a structural reform, woman suffrage, in part to accomplish

polygamy The practice of a man having more than one wife; Mormons practiced polygamy, which they referred to as plural marriage, until 1890.

policy A course of action adopted by a government, usually pursued over a period of time and potentially involving several laws and agencies.

In the Wider World

Woman Suffrage

Table 18.1 presents the dates when women achieved voting rights for various nations and parts of nations. Space does not a permit a complete list. Some places had restricted forms of woman suffrage before the dates indicated; for example, women could vote for school board members but not in any other elections in some American states. In New Jersey, women were accidentally granted the suffrage in 1776 through the use of the word "people" rather than "men," but this grant of suffrage was removed in 1807.

TABLE 18.1   Woman Suffrage Around the World

Year	Place	Year	Place
1838	Pitcairn Island	1928	United Kingdom
1869	Wyoming Territory	1932	Thailand, Brazil, Uruguay
1870	Utah Territory (lost in 1887)	1934	Turkey, Cuba
1890	Wyoming (state)	1940	Quebec (completing full suffrage in all of Canada)
1893	Colorado, New Zealand		
1894	South Australia (limited voting since 1861)	1945	France, Italy
		1946	Japan
1896	Idaho, Utah	1948	Belgium, Chile, Israel, Republic of Korea
1899	Western Australia	1950	India
1902	New South Wales (Australia)	1952	*United Nations Covenant on Political Rights calls for woman suffrage*
1906	Finland		
1908	Australia (all states; federal voting in 1902)	1952	Greece
		1953	Bolivia
1910	Washington (state)	1954	Colombia, Ghana
1911	California	1956	Egypt, Pakistan
1912	Arizona, Kansas, Oregon	1958	Mexico
1913	Alaska Territory, Illinois, Norway	1962	Algeria
1914	Montana, Nevada	1963	Iran, Morocco
1915	Denmark, including Iceland	1964	Afghanistan, Sudan
1916	Alberta, Manitoba, Saskatchewan (Canada)	1971	Switzerland (all but one canton)
1917	New York, North Dakota, Nebraska, Rhode Island, British Columbia and Ontario (Canada), Russia	1973	Syria (first gained in 1953 and lost soon after)
		1974	Jordan, Portugal
1918	Michigan, Oklahoma, South Dakota, Austria, Germany, Poland	1976	Spain (gained in 1931 but lost following the Spanish civil war)
1919	Indiana, Maine, Missouri, Iowa, Minnesota, Ohio, Wisconsin, Tennessee, Netherlands	1977	Libya
		1980	Iraq
		1990	Last Swiss canton implements full suffrage
1920	**United States of America,** Czechoslovakia	2005	Kuwait
1921	Sweden	2010	United Arab Emirates
1922	Irish Free State (Ireland)	2011	Saudi Arabia (limited)

© Cengage Learning 2013.

a policy reform, prohibition of alcohol. Advocates of woman suffrage also argued that enfranchising women would lead to new approaches to politics and new policies.

One important structural change received widespread support. The **Australian ballot**—printed and distributed by the government, not by political parties, listing all candidates of all parties, and marked in a private voting booth—was first adopted by Massachusetts in 1888. The idea quickly spread to all states and carried important implications for political parties. Now voters could easily cross party lines. No longer could party activists see which party's ballot a voter dropped into the ballot box. The switch to the Australian ballot and the Pendleton Act marked significant early efforts to limit parties' power and influence.

POLITICAL UPHEAVAL IN THE 1890S

☆ Which groups and issues led to the formation of the Populist Party?

☆ What were the issues in the 1896 presidential election, and what were the short-term and long-term results?

In 1890–1891, farmers who felt hard-pressed by debts, low prices for their crops, and the monopoly power of the railroads formed the People's Party, or **Populists**, and won elections in several western and southern states. The Depression that began in 1893 set the stage for more political change, culminating in the 1896 presidential election, which made the Republicans the majority party for a generation.

The People's Party: Revolt of the West and South

Populism grew out of the economic problems of farmers, especially falling prices for crops, the economic power of the railroads, and currency issues. The Grange, the Greenback Party, and the silver movement in the late 1870s had expressed farmers' grievances, but those movements faded during the relatively prosperous 1880s. By 1890, however, falling crop prices and widespread indebtedness brought renewed concern among farmers.

In the 1880s, three new organizations emerged, all called **Farmers' Alliances**. One was centered in the north-central states. Another, the Southern Alliance, began in Texas in the late 1870s and spread eastward across the South. The Southern Alliance limited its membership to whites, but a third group, the Colored Farmers' Alliance, recruited black farmers. Like the Grange and Knights of Labor, the Alliances defined themselves as organizations of the "producing classes" and looked to cooperatives as partial solutions to their problems. Alliance stores were most common. The Texas Alliance experimented with cooperative cotton selling, and some midwestern local Alliances tried cooperative grain storage and selling.

Local Alliance meetings featured social and educational activities. By the late 1880s, a host of weekly newspapers across the South and West presented Alliance views. One Kansas woman described the result: "People commenced to think who had never thought before, and people talked who had seldom spoken.... Thoughts and theories sprouted like weeds after a May shower."

The Alliances defined themselves as nonpartisan and expected members to work within the major parties. This was especially important in the South, where any white person who challenged the Democratic Party risked being condemned as a traitor to both race and region. Many Midwestern Alliance leaders, however, had been in the Granger or Greenback parties. During the winter of 1889–1890, corn prices had fallen so low that some farmers found it cheaper to burn their corn than to sell it and buy fuel. More and more Alliance members talked of political action.

Through the hot summer of 1890, Alliance members in Kansas, Nebraska, the Dakotas, Minnesota, and surrounding states formed new political parties to contest state and local elections. One explained that the political battle they waged was "between the insatiable greed of organized wealth and the rights of the great plain people." Women took a prominent part in Populist campaigning, especially in Kansas and Nebraska.

Populists emphasized three elements in their campaigns: **antimonopolism**, government action on behalf of farmers and workers, and increased popular control of government. Their antimonopolism drew on their unhappy experiences with railroads, grain buyers, and manufacturing companies. It also derived from a long American tradition of opposition to concentrated economic power. Populists quoted Thomas

■ **Australian ballot** A ballot printed by the government, rather than by political parties, and marked privately.

■ **Populists** Members of the People's Party; held their first presidential nominating convention in 1892; called for federal action to control big business and assist farmers and workers. The more general term **populist** refers to a politician who attacks, and seeks to mobilize people against, the existing power structure.

■ **Farmers' Alliances** Organizations of farm families in the 1880s and 1890s, similar to the Grange.

■ **antimonopolism** Opposition to great concentrations of economic power such as large corporations, as well as to actual monopolies.

VOL. 20 NO. 50.   JUNE 6 1891   PRICE 10 CENTS.

Judge

A PARTY OF PATCHES.
Grand Balloon Ascension—Cincinnati, May 20th, 1891.

When the Populists launched their new party, one cartoonist depicted them as a hot-air balloon of political malcontents. This cartoon may have inspired Frank Baum, author of *The Wizard of Oz*, whose wizard arrived in Oz in a hot-air balloon launched from Omaha, site of the Populists' 1892 nominating convention.

Jefferson on the importance of equal rights for all, and they compared themselves to Andrew Jackson in his fight against the Bank of the United States.

"We believe the time has come," Populists proclaimed in 1892, "when the railroad companies will either own the people or the people must own the railroads." Their solution to the dangers of monopoly was governmental action on behalf of farmers and workers, including federal ownership of the railroads and the telegraph and telephone systems, and government alternatives to private banks. Currency expansion, through greenbacks, silver, or both, figured prominently in the Populists' platform, along with a graduated income tax. Through such measures, they hoped, in the words of their 1892 platform, that "oppression, injustice, and poverty shall eventually cease in the land." They sought support among urban and industrial workers by calling for the eight-hour workday and opposing companies' use of private armies in labor disputes.

Finally, the People's Party favored structural changes to make government more responsive to the people, including expansion of the merit system for government employees, election of U.S. senators by voters instead of

state legislatures, a one-term limit for the president, and the secret ballot. Many favored woman suffrage. In the South, Populists posed a serious challenge to the prevailing patterns of politics by seeking to forge a political alliance of the disadvantaged of both races. Populists usually opposed disfranchisement of black voters.

Thus Populists advocated government regulation or ownership of the corporate behemoths that had evolved in their lifetimes. They deeply distrusted the old parties and wanted to increase the power of the individual voter.

The Elections of 1890 and 1892

Despite Republicans' hopes for breaking the political logjam during the Fifty-first Congress, they immediately found themselves on the defensive. Issues in the 1890 elections for the House of Representatives and state and local offices varied by region. In the West, the Populists lambasted both major parties for ignoring the needs of the people. In the South, Democrats held up Lodge's "force bill" as a warning of the potential dangers if southern whites should bolt the party of white supremacy. There, the Southern Alliance worked within the Democratic Party to secure candidates committed to the farmers' cause. In the Northeast, Democrats attacked the McKinley Tariff for producing higher prices for consumers. In the Rocky Mountain region, nearly all candidates pledged their support for unlimited silver coinage.

The Populists scored several victories, making them the most successful new party since the Republicans in the 1850s. Kansas Republican Senator John J. Ingalls had dismissed Populists as "a sort of turnip crusade," but Populists won control of the Kansas legislature and elected a Populist to replace Ingalls in the Senate. Elsewhere Populists elected state legislators, members of Congress, and one other U.S. senator. Across the South, the Alliance claimed that successful candidates owed their victories to Alliance voters.

Everywhere Republicans suffered defeat, losing nearly half their seats in the House of Representatives and many state and local offices. Such losses bred dissension within the party, and President Harrison could not maintain party unity.

For the 1892 presidential election, the Republicans renominated Harrison though he aroused little enthusiasm among many party leaders. The Democrats again chose Grover Cleveland. Southern Alliance activists joined western Populists to form a national People's Party and nominated James Weaver, the Greenback presidential candidate in 1880. Democrats and Populists scored the most impressive victories. Cleveland became the only president in American history to win two nonconsecutive terms. Democrats kept control of the House of Representatives and won a majority in

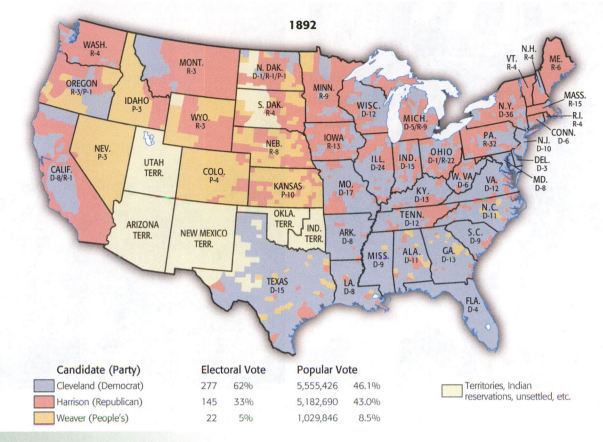

1892

Candidate (Party)	Electoral Vote		Popular Vote	
Cleveland (Democrat)	277	62%	5,555,426	46.1%
Harrison (Republican)	145	33%	5,182,690	43.0%
Weaver (People's)	22	5%	1,029,846	8.5%

Territories, Indian reservations, unsettled, etc.

MAP 18.1 Popular Vote for President, 1892
Support for the Populist Party's presidential candidate, James B. Weaver, was concentrated in the West and South. Nationwide, he received 8.5 percent of the vote. © Cengage Learning.

the Senate. Populists showed strength across the West and South (see Map 18.1). The Democrats now found themselves where the Republicans had stood four years before: in control of the presidency and Congress.

Failure of the Divided Democrats

When Congress met in 1893, Democrats faced several controversial issues, especially silver coinage and tariff reform. A major depression had begun earlier that year (discussed in Chapter 16) and rising unemployment also demanded attention. President Cleveland, holding to Democrats' traditional commitment to minimal government and laissez faire, opposed federal assistance to those in need. And, amidst national economic crisis, Cleveland suffered a personal crisis—doctors detected cancer in his mouth. Fearing this news might lead to further financial panic, the president kept his surgery and recuperation secret.

Many business leaders argued that the Sherman Silver Purchase Act of 1890 had caused a gold drain that set off the depression, but many western and southern Democrats found it preferable to no silver

coinage at all. Convinced that silver coinage had contributed to the economic collapse, Cleveland asked Congress to repeal the act. In the House of Representatives, most Republicans voted for repeal, but more than a third of the Democrats opposed. In the Senate, Republicans supported Cleveland by 2 to 1, but Democrats divided almost evenly. Cleveland won but divided his own party, pitting the Northeast against the West and much of the South.

After the Democrats' harsh condemnation of the McKinley Tariff during the 1892 elections, they now had to do better. The tariff bill produced by the House reduced duties, tried to balance sectional interests, and created an income tax to replace lost federal revenue. Senate Democrats, however, loaded on many amendments. Cleveland characterized the result as "party dishonor" and refused to sign it. It became law without his signature in 1894. (The Supreme Court soon declared the income tax unconstitutional.)

By 1894, many Americans were becoming anxious over social disorders. Early that year, Jacob S. Coxey, an Ohio Populist, announced a march on Washington to promote public works programs to provide jobs for the unemployed. The response

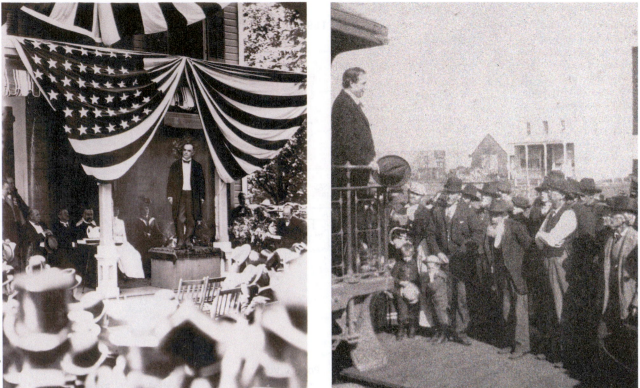

The Granger Collection, NYC.

Kean Collection/Archive Photos/Getty Images.

In 1896, William Jennings Bryan (*right*), candidate for the Democratic, Populist, and Silver Republican parties, traveled eighteen thousand miles in three months. William McKinley (*left*), the Republican, stayed home in Canton, Ohio, greeting thousands of well-wishers.

electrified the nation—by April, six thousand people were camped outside Washington. Soon after, the Pullman Strike shut down many of the nation's railroads until Cleveland deployed U.S. troops and marshals against the strikers.

Voters recorded their disgust with the disorganized Democrats in the 1894 elections. Democrats lost everywhere but in the Deep South, giving up 113 seats in the House of Representatives. Populists made few gains and suffered some losses. Republicans added 117 House seats, their biggest gain ever, and looked forward eagerly to the 1896 presidential election.

The 1896 Election and the New Republican Majority

Republicans confidently anticipated victory in the 1896 presidential election. They nominated William McKinley, a Union veteran who had risen to the rank of major. McKinley had served fourteen years in Congress (where he had specialized in the

■ **William Jennings Bryan** Nebraska Democrat who advocated silver coinage, opposed imperialism, and ran for president unsuccessfully three times.

tariff) and two terms as governor of Ohio. Calm and competent, McKinley billed himself as the "Advance Agent of Prosperity." The Republican platform supported the gold standard and opposed silver, but McKinley preferred to focus on the tariff. When the convention voted against silver, several western Republicans walked out of the convention and out of the party.

When the Democratic convention met, silverites held the majority but were split among several candidates. Then the platform committee chose **William Jennings Bryan** of Nebraska to speak in a debate on silver. Blessed with a commanding voice, Bryan had won election to the House of Representatives in 1890 and 1892 and gained national attention for his eloquent defense of silver. His speech was masterful. Defining the issue as a conflict between "the producing masses" and "the idle holders of idle capital," he argued that the first priority of federal policy should be "to make the masses prosperous," rather than to benefit the rich in the hope that "their prosperity will leak through on those below." His closing rang defiant: "We will answer their demand for a gold standard by saying to them: You shall not press down upon the brow of labor this crown of thorns. You shall not crucify mankind upon a cross of gold." The speech provoked an enthusiastic demonstration for silver—and

Janice L. and David J. Frent.

Political buttons with pins on the back were patented shortly before the 1896 presidential campaign and were in great abundance that year. The Bryan-Sewall button pictured shows a clock at 16 minutes to 1:00, a reference to the Democratic commitment to increase the coinage of silver dollars, with a ratio of 16:1—meaning that the amount of silver in a silver dollar would weigh 16 times the amount of gold in a gold dollar. The McKinley button depicts a bicycle wheel to proclaim support for McKinley by a wheelmen's club (bicyclists).

Bryan. Only 36 years old, Bryan soon won the presidential nomination.

The Populists and defecting Republicans (quickly dubbed Silver Republicans) held nominating conventions next, amid frustration that the Democrats had stolen their thunder. Bryan favored silver, the income tax, and other reforms that Populists favored, and had worked closely with Populists. Populists gave him their nomination too, and Silver Republicans did the same. Subsequently, a group of Cleveland supporters nominated a Gold Democratic candidate.

Bryan and McKinley fought all-out campaigns but used sharply contrasting tactics. Bryan, vigorous and young, used his speaking voice as his greatest campaign tool. He spoke directly to the voters in four grueling train journeys through twenty-six states and more than 250 cities. Speaking to perhaps 5 million people in all, he stressed over and over that silver was the most important issue and that other reforms would follow once it was settled. Large crowds of excited and enthusiastic supporters greeted him nearly everywhere.

While McKinley himself campaigned from his home in Canton, Ohio, the Republicans flooded the country with speakers, pamphlets, and campaign paraphernalia. They also chartered trains that brought thousands of supporters to hear McKinley speak. Many business leaders feared that Bryan and silver coinage would bring financial collapse and opposed Bryan's other proposals, especially the income tax and lower tariff rates. McKinley's campaign played on such fears to secure a fund more than double any previous effort and many times what Bryan could raise.

McKinley won by the largest margin since 1872. As Map 18.2 shows, Bryan carried the South and most of the West. McKinley prevailed in the urban, industrial Northeast, and he carried nearly every major city.

The crucial battleground was the Midwest, where McKinley carried not only the urban industrial regions but also many farming areas.

Bryan's defeat spelled the end of the Populist Party. Some Populists moved into Bryan's Democratic Party, but others tried to maintain the tattered remnants of Populism. A few joined the Socialist Party, some returned to the Republicans, and a few simply ignored politics. The issues they had raised—control of huge corporations, the extension of democratic processes, a fair monetary system—lived on in politics. Their influence remained especially prominent in Bryan's wing of the Democratic Party.

Bryan had appealed most to debt-ridden farmers, western miners, and traditional Democrats in the South and big cities. McKinley forged a broader appeal by emphasizing the gold standard and protective tariff as keys to economic recovery. For many urban residents—workers and the middle class alike—silver seemed to promise only higher prices, but the protective tariff meant manufacturing jobs. McKinley also won, in part, by restraining his party's nativist tendencies and denouncing the anti-Catholic American Protective Association, thereby solidifying support among those immigrants who approved of his stand on gold and the tariff.

American politics in 1888 looked much like American politics in 1876 or even 1844. But in the 1890s, American politics changed. Whether Republican or Democrat, many voters now held their party commitments less intensely than before. For most voters before 1890, ethnicity and party went hand in hand. Now voters sometimes felt pulled toward one party by their economic situation and toward the other party by their ethnicity. Such voters sometimes supported Republicans for some offices and Democrats for others, choices now much easier to make because of the Australian ballot.

The political role of newspapers also changed. In the 1890s, William Randolph Hearst and Joseph Pulitzer took the lead in transforming urban newspapers into mass circulation dailies, competing for readership through eye-catching headlines and sensational stories. As they focused on increasing their circulation and advertising, they also played down their ties to political parties. Some journalists began to develop the idea of providing balanced political coverage.

Bryan led the Democrats over much of the next sixteen years, and he and his allies moved the party away from its traditional commitment to minimal government. Bryan and other new Democratic leaders agreed that the solution to the problems of economic concentration lay in a more active government. "A private monopoly," Bryan never tired of repeating, "is indefensible and intolerable." Democrats nonetheless clung to their version of states' rights, which permitted southern Democrats to perpetuate

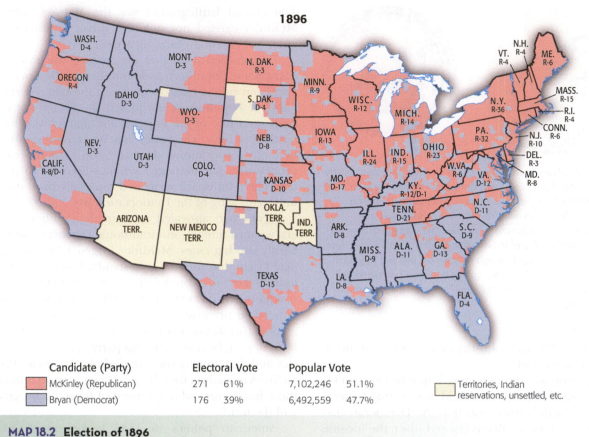

1896

Candidate (Party)	Electoral Vote		Popular Vote	
McKinley (Republican)	271	61%	7,102,246	51.1%
Bryan (Democrat)	176	39%	6,492,559	47.7%

Territories, Indian reservations, unsettled, etc.

MAP 18.2 Election of 1896
Bryan could not win with just the votes of the South and West, for they had few electoral votes. McKinley won in the urban, industrial core region and the more prosperous farming areas of the Midwest (compare Map 18.2 with Map 17.1 on page 436). © Cengage Learning.

white-supremacist regimes. And most northern Democrats continued to oppose nativism and such moral reforms as prohibition.

As president, McKinley provided strong executive leadership and worked closely with congressional leaders of his party to develop new policies including the gold standard and a sharply higher protective tariff. The surplus disappeared as an issue partly because of large naval expenditures. McKinley's victory in 1896 ushered in a new generation of Republican dominance of national politics. Republicans had majorities in the House of Representatives for twenty-eight of the thirty-six years after 1894, and in the Senate for thirty of those thirty-six years. Republicans won seven of the nine presidential elections between 1896 and 1932, and similar patterns of Republican dominance appeared in state and local government.

■ **William H. Seward** U.S. secretary of state under Lincoln and Johnson (1861–1869), a former abolitionist who had expansionist views and arranged the purchase of Alaska from Russia.

STANDING ASIDE FROM WORLD AFFAIRS, 1865–1889

★ How did American policymakers define the role of the United States in North America and other parts of the world during 1865–1889?

During the years of deadlocked domestic politics, little changed in the nation's slight role in world affairs. Most Americans expected their nation to follow George Washington's advice to "steer clear of permanent alliances with any portion of the foreign world." The effect of America's economic transformation on its foreign relations was slow in appearing.

Alaska, Canada, and the *Alabama* Claims

William H. Seward, a highly capable secretary of state, often voiced his belief in America's destiny to expand across the North American continent. When he learned that Tsar Alexander II might sell Russian holdings in North America if the price were right, Seward made an offer, and in 1867, for slightly over $7 million, Alaska was in U.S. hands.

Some journalists derided Alaska as a frozen waste-land and branded it "Seward's Folly." Charles Sumner, chairman of the Senate Foreign Relations Committee, voiced more enthusiasm, looking on the purchase of Alaska as a first step toward acquiring Canada. Sumner thought a second step might lie in claims against Great Britain arising out of the Civil War. Confederate warships, notably the *Alabama* and *Florida*, built in British shipyards and given refuge and repairs in British ports, had badly disrupted northern shipping. The United States claimed that Britain owed compensation for the damage done by the Confederate cruisers, and Sumner unrealistically suggested that Britain could meet this obligation by ceding all its North American possessions, including Canada, to the United States. Ultimately, however, the two countries agreed to arbitration, and the 1872 arbitration decision set $15.5 million as damages to be paid to the United States.

The United States and Latin America

After the Civil War, American diplomats took new interest in Latin America, partly because European powers were starting to exert influence there and partly because some Americans wanted a more prominent role there. In 1823 President James Monroe had announced that the United States would consider any attempt by a European power to colonize in North and South America to be a threat to the United States, but that the United States would neither interfere with existing colonies nor involve itself in European politics. Though later a linchpin of American policy, the Monroe Doctrine was rarely mentioned by presidents until the 1890s.

In 1861, as the United States lurched into civil war, France, Spain, and Britain sent a joint force to Mexico to collect debts that Mexico could not pay. Spain and Britain withdrew, but French troops remained despite resistance led by Benito Juarez, president of Mexico. Political opponents of Juarez cooperated with the French emperor, Napoleon III, to name Archduke Maximilian of Austria as emperor of Mexico. Maximilian, a young idealist, apparently believed the Mexican people genuinely wanted him as their leader. However, he antagonized conservative supporters with talk of reform but failed to win other support. In reality, Maximilian held power only because of the French troops.

Involved in its own civil war, the U.S. government recognized Juarez as president but could do little else. When the Civil War ended, Seward demanded that Napoleon III withdraw his troops, and fifty thousand battle-hardened U.S. troops were ordered to the Mexican border. Napoleon III brought the French soldiers home. Maximilian remained behind, where he was defeated in battle by Juarez and then executed. The withdrawal of French troops in the face of American military force renewed respect in Europe for the role of the United States in Latin America.

Eastern Asia and the Pacific

Americans had long-standing commercial interests in eastern Asia. The China trade dated to 1784, and the first treaty between China and the United States, in 1844, included a provision granting most-favored-nation status to the United States. Goods from Asia and the Pacific accounted for 8 percent of U.S. imports after the Civil War, but exports lagged, even though some Americans dreamed of selling manufactured goods to the millions of Chinese.

Japan and Korea had refused to engage in trade, their way of deflecting Western influences and avoiding European power rivalries. In 1854 an American naval force convinced the Japanese government to open its ports to foreign trade. A similar navy action opened Korea in 1882.

Growing trade between eastern Asia and the United States fueled American interest in the Pacific. American ships needed ports in the Pacific for supplies and repairs, and interest focused especially on Hawai'i. Hawai'i had attracted Christian missionaries from New England as early as 1819, shortly after King Kamehameha united the islands into one nation. First concerned with preaching the Gospel and convincing the unabashed Hawaiians to wear clothes, some missionaries and their descendants later exercised great influence over several Hawaiian monarchs.

Ideally located for resupply of ships traveling the Pacific, after 1848 Hawai'i became a routine stop for ships sailing from New York around South America to San Francisco. As early as 1842, President John Tyler announced that the United States would not allow the

Senate Foreign Relations Committee A standing committee of the Senate; its chairman often wields considerable influence over foreign policy.

arbitration Process by which parties to a dispute submit their case to the judgment of an impartial person or group (the arbiter) and agree to accept the arbiter's decision.

■ **Monroe Doctrine** Pronouncement by President James Monroe in 1823 that the Western Hemisphere was off limits for future European colonial expansion.

■ **Benito Juarez** President of Mexico who led resistance to French troops occupying his country in 1864–1867; the first Mexican president of Indian ancestry.

Maximilian Austrian archduke appointed emperor of Mexico by Napoleon III, emperor of France; later executed by Mexican republicans.

most-favored-nation status In a treaty between nation A and nation B, the provision that commercial privileges extended by A to other nations automatically become available to B.

The Bancroft Library, University of California, Berkeley.

THE NEW CALIFORNIA SUGAR REFINERY, SAN FRANCISCO.

Claus Spreckels accomplished the vertical integration of the sugar industry. His operations began with sugar cane fields on the island of Maui and ended in San Francisco, at this sugar refinery, where his employees unloaded the raw sugar from Spreckels's ships and processed it into refined sugar for sale in the American market. A similar chain of vertical integration exists today.

islands to pass under the control of another power, but Britain and France continued to take a keen interest in them.

After David Kalakaua became king of Hawai'i in 1874, relations with the United States became much closer. In 1875 he approved a treaty that gave Hawaiian sugar free access to the United States. The Hawaiian sugar industry then expanded rapidly as descendants of missionaries joined American companies in developing huge plantations. Soon Hawaiian sugar spawned a vertically integrated industry that included American-owned plantations, ships to carry raw sugar to the mainland, and sugar refineries in California—and the economies of the two nations became closely linked.

Despite these economic ties, relations between Kalakaua and the **haole** community of Hawai'i were never comfortable. Kalakaua wanted to preserve political power for **indigenous** Hawaiians, but *haoles* charged him with ignoring the needs of business and the sugar plantations. In 1887, leaders of the *haole* community forced a constitution on Kalakaua, reducing his power. *Haoles* soon dominated much of the government. That same year, Kalakaua approved an extension of the treaty of 1875 that added exclusive rights for the U.S. Navy to use Pearl Harbor. Among some members of the royal family, resentment festered over the new constitution, the Pearl Harbor provision, and especially the extent of *haole* control. Those resentments boiled over after Kalakaua's death in 1891.

haole Hawaiian word for persons not of native Hawaiian ancestry, especially whites.

indigenous Original to an area.

This engraving shows the launching of the battleship *Maine* at the New York Navy Yard in 1889. The *Maine* was the nation's first modern battleship and the prototype for those that followed.

STEPPING INTO WORLD AFFAIRS: HARRISON AND CLEVELAND, 1889–1897

☆ *How and why did some Americans' attitudes about the U.S. role in world affairs begin to change between 1889 and 1897?*

During the 1890s, America's involvement outside its borders changed in important ways. New concepts of America's role in world affairs emerged and won acceptance. One element of this involved a new role for the U.S. Navy and the commissioning of modern ships to carry it out.

Building a Modern Navy

Most presidents of the Gilded Age paid little attention to the army and navy. After the last Indian wars, the army was limited to a few garrisons, most near Indian reservations. Most federal decision makers understood the role of the navy as limited to protecting America's coasts. The navy's wooden sailing vessels deteriorated so badly that some ridiculed them as fit

only for firewood. Congress finally authorized construction of two steam-powered cruisers in 1882 —the first new ships in almost twenty years—and four more ships in 1883. Still, Secretary of the Navy William C. Whitney announced in 1885 that "we have nothing which deserves to be called a navy," and persuaded Congress to fund several more cruisers and the first two modern battleships.

Alfred Thayer Mahan played a key role in developing a modern navy. President of the Naval War College, Mahan exerted a powerful influence through lectures to navy officers, a book, *The Influence of Sea Power upon History* (1890), and articles in the press. Mahan argued that sea power had determined the outcome of European power struggles for the previous 150 years, and he explored the significance of geography, population, and government for establishing sea power. He advocated a large, modern navy centered on huge

---

■ **Alfred Thayer Mahan** Naval officer and historian who stressed the importance of sea power in international politics and diplomacy.

battleships capable of carrying American power to distant seas. He also stressed the need to establish and control a canal through Central America, command the Caribbean, dominate strategic locations in the Pacific, and create naval bases at key points.

In 1889, with Harrison in the White House and Republican majorities in both houses of Congress, Secretary of the Navy Benjamin F. Tracy urged Congress to modernize and significantly expand the navy. Tracy's ambitious proposal might have eliminated the federal budget surplus all by itself! Congress did not give him all he wanted but did vote funds for a modern navy centered on battleships. With construction under way on three battleships, Tracy happily announced that "we shall rule [the sea] as certainly as the sun doth rise!"

A New American Mission?

Mahan's strategic arguments and Tracy's battleship launchings came as some Americans began, in Mahan's phrase, to "look outward." Advocacy came from many sources: Protestant ministers, scholars, business figures, historians, politicians. Together they redefined the way many Americans, including many policymakers, viewed the nation's role in world affairs. Josiah Strong, a Protestant missionary, argued that expansion of American Protestant ideals to the world constituted a Christian duty. "The world is to be Christianized and civilized," he predicted, adding that "commerce follows the missionary."

Social Darwinism and the notion of "progress" merged with a belief in the superiority of Anglo-Saxons—the English people and their descendants. Popular books claimed that Anglo-Saxons had demonstrated a unique capacity for civilization and had a duty to enlighten and uplift other peoples. Albert Beveridge, Republican senator from Indiana, blended some of these ideas with American nationalism when he proclaimed, "[God] has made us the master organizers of the world to establish system where chaos reigns." Rudyard Kipling, an English poet, in 1899 urged the United States to "take up the white man's burden," a phrase that came to describe a self-imposed obligation to go into distant lands, bring the supposed blessings of Anglo-Saxon civilization to their peoples, Christianize them, and sell them manufactured goods.

Today historians understand Anglo-Saxonism and the "white man's burden" as imbued with racism. Such views assumed that some people, by virtue of race, possessed a superior capability for self-government

Bettmann/CORBIS.

This undated photograph of Hawai'i's Queen Lili'uokalani was taken during her relatively short reign, from 1891 to 1893. Lili'uokalani was an accomplished musician; "Aloha 'Oe," the best known of her songs, is still performed today.

and cultural accomplishment. This thinking elevated only one cultural pattern as "civilization," dismissing all others as inferior and ignoring their cultural accomplishments.

Revolution in Hawai'i

New views on the strategic significance of the Pacific focused the attention of many Americans on Hawai'i when revolution broke out there in 1893. The revolution stemmed in part from changes in American tariff rates on sugar. In 1890, the McKinley Tariff provided that all sugar could enter the United States without paying a tariff. Previously only Hawaiian sugar had this privilege. Now it faced new competition, notably from Cuban sugar. Facing economic disaster, many Hawaiian planters began to discuss annexation to the United States.

In 1891 King Kalakaua died and was succeeded by his sister, Lili'uokalani, who hoped to restore Hawai'i to the indigenous Hawaiians and return political power to the monarchy. Some *haole* entrepreneurs feared that they might lose their political clout and economic

□ **Lili'uokalani** Last queen of Hawai'i, whose desire to restore land to the Hawaiian people and strengthen the monarchy prompted *haole* planters to remove her from power in 1893.

holdings. On January 17, 1893, they proclaimed a republic and asked for annexation by the United States. John L. Stevens, the U.S. minister to Hawai'i, promptly ordered the landing of 150 U.S. Marines. Lili'uokalani surrendered, as she put it, "to the superior force of the United States." Stevens immediately recognized the new republic, declared it a **protectorate** of the United States, and raised the American flag.

The Harrison administration **repudiated** Stevens's overzealous deeds but opened negotiations with representatives of the new republic. The Senate received a treaty of annexation shortly before Cleveland became president. Cleveland was willing to consider annexing Hawai'i if the Hawaiian people requested it. However, he withdrew the annexation treaty temporarily, then learned the revolution would have failed had the marines not intervened. He asked the new officials to restore the queen. They refused, and Hawai'i continued as an independent republic, dominated by its *haole* business and planter community.

Crises in Latin America

Harrison and Cleveland disagreed regarding Hawai'i, but both presidents extended American involvement in Latin America.

In 1891 a mob in Chile set upon several American sailors on shore leave and beat them, injuring several and killing two. When the Chilean government gave no sign of apologizing, Harrison threatened "such action as may be necessary." When the Chilean government would not back down, Harrison responded with plans for a naval war. Chile then gave in, apologized, and promised to pay damages.

In 1895 and 1896, Cleveland also took the nation to the edge of war. At issue was an old boundary dispute between Venezuela and British Guiana. Venezuela proposed arbitration, which Cleveland also favored, but Britain refused. In July 1895, Secretary of State Richard Olney cited the Monroe Doctrine, demanded Britain submit to arbitration, and bombastically declared the United States preeminent throughout the Western Hemisphere. When Britain still refused, Cleveland asked Congress for authority to determine the boundary and enforce it. Now facing the possibility of conflict with the United States—at a time when the British were concerned about the rising power of Germany and facing possible war in South Africa—Britain agreed to arbitration.

Both presidents behaved forcefully, but Harrison's heavy-handed threats toward Chile discouraged closer relations with Latin America. Cleveland, however, may have helped to persuade European imperial powers that the Western Hemisphere was off-limits in the ongoing scramble for colonies.

Cuba presented a very different situation. Cuba and Puerto Rico were all that remained of the once-mighty Spanish empire in the Americas, and Cubans had repeatedly rebelled against Spain. In the early 1890s, when the McKinley Tariff permitted Cuban sugar to enter the United States without charge, the Cuban sugar industry boomed. In 1894, though, the new tariff law restored a duty on Cuban sugar and depressed the island's economy. Fueled by economic distress, a new insurrection erupted against Spanish rule. Advocates of *Cuba libre* ("free Cuba") received support from sympathizers in the United States. In 1896, in response to the **insurgents'** guerrilla warfare, the Spanish commander, General Valeriano Weyler, established a **reconcentration** policy. The civilian population was ordered into fortified towns or camps. Everyone outside these fortified areas was considered an insurgent, subject to military action. Disease and starvation swept through the camps, killing many.

American newspapers—especially **Joseph Pulitzer's** *New York World* and **William Randolph Hearst's** *New York Journal*—presented Spanish atrocities in screaming headlines, sometimes exaggerating and sensationalizing their reporters' stories (a practice called **yellow journalism**). In response, many Americans began clamoring to rescue the Cubans.

Intent on avoiding American involvement, Cleveland proclaimed U.S. neutrality and warned Americans not to support the insurrection. When members of Congress pushed Cleveland to seek Cuban independence, he urged Spain to grant concessions to the insurgents. Just as he had earlier opposed annexation of Hawai'i, Cleveland now resisted intervention in Cuba, fearing it might lead to annexation regardless of the will of the Cuban people. Nonetheless, by the time he left the presidency in early 1897, he suggested possible American intervention.

---

protectorate A country partially controlled by a stronger power and dependent on that power for protection from foreign threats.

repudiate To reject as invalid or unauthorized.

insurgent Rebel or revolutionary; one involved in an insurrection or rebellion against constituted authority.

■ **reconcentration** Spanish policy in Cuba in 1896 that ordered the civilian population into fortified areas so as to isolate and annihilate the revolutionaries who remained outside.

Joseph Pulitzer Hungarian-born newspaper publisher whose *New York World* printed sensational stories about Cuba that helped precipitate the Spanish-American War.

William Randolph Hearst Publisher and rival to Pulitzer; Hearst's newspaper, the *New York Journal,* sensationalized and distorted stories and actively promoted war with Spain.

■ **yellow journalism** The use of sensational exposés, embellished reporting, and attention-grabbing headlines to sell newspapers.

On February 15, 1898, an explosion destroyed the U.S.S. *Maine* at Havana, Cuba. Many Americans blamed the Spanish government, although there was no evidence to suggest who was responsible.

Library of Congress.

STRIDING BOLDLY IN WORLD AFFAIRS: MCKINLEY, WAR, AND IMPERIALISM, 1898–1902

☆ *What led the United States into war with Spain?*

☆ *What new attitudes about America's role in world affairs appeared in the debate over acquiring new possessions?*

In 1898 the United States went to war with Spain over Cuba. John Hay, the American ambassador to Great Britain, celebrated the conflict as "a splendid little war," and the description stuck. Some envisioned a quick war to save the suffering Cubans and establish a Cuban republic. Others saw war with Spain as an opportunity to acquire an American empire.

Enrique Dupuy de Lôme Spanish minister to the United States whose letter criticizing President McKinley was stolen and printed in the *New York Journal,* increasing anti-Spanish sentiment.

▪ **U.S.S. *Maine*** American warship that exploded in Havana Harbor in 1898, inspiring the motto "Remember the Maine!," which spurred the Spanish-American War.

McKinley and War

William McKinley became president amid increasing demands for action regarding Cuba. He moved cautiously, stepping up diplomatic efforts to resolve the crisis. In response, Spain softened the reconcentration policy and offered limited self-government but not independence. In February 1898, however, events scuttled progress toward a negotiated solution.

First, Cuban insurgents stole a letter from **Enrique Dupuy de Lôme**, the Spanish minister to the United States, and released it to the *New York Journal.* In it, de Lôme criticized President McKinley as "weak and a bidder for the admiration of the crowd." The letter also implied that the Spanish government's commitment to reform in Cuba was not serious. Although de Lôme immediately resigned, the letter aroused intense anti-Spanish feeling among many Americans.

A few days later, on February 15, an explosion ripped open the **U.S.S. *Maine***, anchored in Havana Harbor. The battleship sank, killing more than 260 Americans. The yellow press accused Spain of sabotage but without evidence. An official inquiry blamed a submarine mine but could not determine its source. Years later, an investigation indicated that the blast was probably of internal origin, resulting from a fire. Regardless of how the explosion occurred, those advocating intervention now had a rallying cry: "Remember the *Maine!*"

McKinley extended his demands: an immediate end to the fighting, an end to reconcentration, measures to relieve the suffering, and **mediation** by McKinley. He specified that one possible outcome of mediation might be Cuban independence. In reply, the Spanish government promised reforms, agreed to end reconcentration, and consented to cease fighting if the insurgents asked for an **armistice**—but said nothing about mediation or independence for Cuba.

On April 11, McKinley sent a message to Congress stating that "the war in Cuba must stop" and asking for authority to act. Congress answered on April 19 with four resolutions: (1) declaring that Cuba was and should be independent, (2) demanding that Spain withdraw "at once," (3) authorizing the president to use force to accomplish Spanish withdrawal, and (4) disavowing any intention to annex the island. The first three resolutions amounted to a declaration of war. The fourth is usually called the **Teller Amendment** for its sponsor, Senator Henry M. Teller, a Silver Republican from Colorado. In response, Spain declared war.

Most Americans wholeheartedly approved what they understood to be a war undertaken to bring independence and aid to the long-suffering Cubans. Some, however, distrusted the McKinley administration's motives. The Teller Amendment reflected this concern that the McKinley administration might try to make Cuba an American possession rather than granting it independence.

The "Splendid Little War"

Americans' attention had been riveted on Cuba. Many were surprised that the first engagement in the war occurred in the **Philippine Islands**—nearly halfway around the world from Cuba. The Philippines had been a Spanish colony for three hundred years, but had rebelled repeatedly, most recently in 1896.

Some Americans understood the islands' strategic location with regard to eastern Asia—including Assistant Secretary of the Navy **Theodore Roosevelt**. In February 1898, six weeks before McKinley's war message to Congress, Roosevelt drew upon planning exercises by the Naval War College when he cabled George Dewey, the American naval commander in the Pacific, to crush the Spanish fleet at Manila Bay if war broke out.

At sunrise on Sunday, May 1, Dewey's squadron steamed into the harbor and quickly destroyed or captured a larger Spanish fleet. The Spanish lost 161 men and 210 were wounded. The Americans lost one, a victim of heat prostration, and nine were wounded. Dewey instantly became a national hero.

Dewey's victory at Manila focused public attention on the western Pacific, raising the prospect of a permanent American presence there. This possibility, in turn, revived interest in the Hawaiian Islands as a base halfway to the Philippines. Anti-imperialist sentiment in the Senate made approval of an annexation treaty unlikely, so McKinley revived the joint-resolution precedent by which Texas had been annexed in 1844. Only a majority vote in both houses of Congress was required to adopt a joint resolution, rather than the two-thirds vote of the Senate needed to approve a treaty. Annexation of Hawai'i was accomplished on July 7.

Dewey's victory clearly demonstrated American naval superiority. However, the Spanish army in Cuba outnumbered the entire American army by five to one and had years of experience on the island. When McKinley called for volunteers, nearly a million men responded—five times as many as the army needed. Next the army began to train and supply the new recruits.

Sent to training camps in the South, the new soldiers found chaos and confusion. Food, uniforms, and equipment arrived at one location while the intended recipients stood hungry and idle at another. Disease raged through some camps, killing many men. Others died from tainted food, called "embalmed beef" by the troops. Some African American soldiers refused to comply with racial segregation, and many white southerners objected to the presence in their communities of uniformed and armed black men. Congress declared war in late April, but not until June did the first troop transports head for Cuba.

When they finally arrived in Cuba, American forces tried to capture the port city of Santiago, where the Spanish fleet had taken refuge. Inexperienced, poorly equipped, and unfamiliar with the terrain, the Americans landed some distance from Santiago and assaulted the fortified hills surrounding the city.

mediation An attempt to bring about the peaceful settlement of a dispute through the intervention of a neutral party.

armistice An agreement to halt fighting.

■ **Teller Amendment** Senate resolution in 1898 promising that the United States would not annex Cuba; introduced by Senator Henry Teller.

Philippine Islands A group of islands in the Pacific Ocean southeast of China that came under U.S. control in 1898; an independent nation since 1946.

■ **Theodore Roosevelt** (1858–1919) Twenty-sixth president of the United States. Politician and writer who advocated war against Spain in 1898; elected vice president in 1900; became president in 1901 upon McKinley's assassination.

African American troops, organized into segregated, all-black units, played a significant role in the battles that gave U.S. troops control of the heights overlooking Santiago Bay. All four black regiments, the 9th and 10th Cavalry and the 24th and 25th Infantry, were ordered to Cuba. The four regiments were later sent to the Philippines to help suppress the Philippine insurrection.

© IMAGE ASSET MANAGEMEN/AGE Fotostock.

Theodore Roosevelt had resigned as assistant secretary of the navy to organize a cavalry unit known as the Rough Riders. At Kettle Hill, near Santiago, he led a successful charge of Rough Riders and regular army units, including parts of the Ninth and Tenth Cavalry, made up of African Americans. All but Roosevelt were on foot because their horses had not yet arrived. Driving the Spanish from the crest of Kettle Hill cleared a serious impediment to the assault on nearby San Juan Heights and San Juan Hill. Journalists loved Roosevelt—and newspapers all over the country declared him the hero of the Battle of San Juan Hill.

Once American troops gained control of the high ground around Santiago harbor, the Spanish fleet tried to escape. A larger American fleet met them and duplicated Dewey's rout at Manila—every Spanish ship was sunk or run aground. The Spanish suffered 323 deaths, the Americans one.

Their fleet destroyed, surrounded by American troops, the Spanish in Santiago surrendered on July 17. A week later American forces also occupied Puerto Rico. Spanish land forces in the Philippines surrendered when the first American troops arrived in mid-August. The "splendid little war" lasted only sixteen weeks. More than 306,000 men served in the American forces. Only 385 of them died in battle, but more than 5,000 died of disease and other causes.

The Treaty of Paris

On August 12, the United States and Spain agreed to stop fighting and hold a peace conference in Paris. The major question centered on the Philippines. Finley Peter Dunne, a popular humorist, parodied the national debate in a discussion between his fictional characters, Mr. Dooley (a Chicago saloonkeeper) and a customer named Hennessy. Hennessy insists that McKinley should take the islands. Dooley retorts that "it's not more than two months since you learned whether they were islands or canned goods," then confesses his own indecision: "I can't annex them because I don't know where they are. I can't let go of them because someone else will take them.... It would break my heart to think of giving people I've never seen or heard tell of back to other people I don't know.... I don't know what to do about the Philippines. And I'm all alone in the world. Everybody else has made up his mind."

McKinley voiced almost as many doubts as Mr. Dooley. At first, he seemed to favor only a naval base, leaving Spain in control elsewhere. However, by mid-August, Filipinos seeking independence had taken charge everywhere but in Manila. Britain, Japan, and Germany watched carefully, and one or another seemed likely to step in if the United States withdrew. McKinley and his advisers decided that a naval base on Manila Bay would require control of the entire island group. No one seriously considered the Filipinos' desire for independence.

McKinley understood the political and strategic importance of the Philippines for eastern Asia (see Map 18.3). He invoked other reasons, however, when he explained his decision to a group of visiting Methodists. He repeatedly prayed for guidance on the Philippine question, he told them. Late one

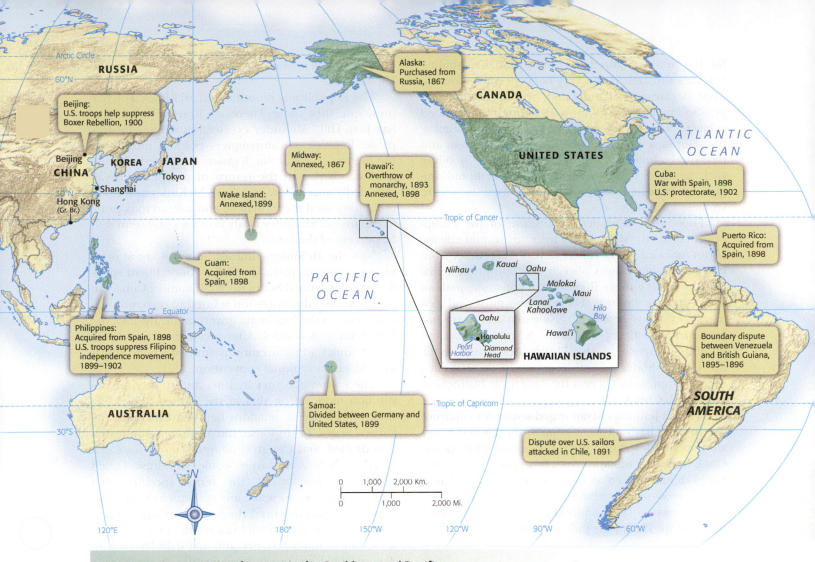

MAP 18.3 American Involvement in the Caribbean and Pacific
As a result of the war with Spain, the United States acquired possessions stretching nearly halfway around the world, from Puerto Rico to the Philippines. Note how the acquisition of various Pacific islands and island groups provided crucial "stepping stones" from the American mainland to eastern Asia. © Cengage Learning.

Labels on map:

Beijing: U.S. troops help suppress Boxer Rebellion, 1900

Alaska: Purchased from Russia, 1867

Midway: Annexed, 1867

Hawai'i: Overthrow of monarchy, 1893 Annexed, 1898

Cuba: War with Spain, 1898 U.S. protectorate, 1902

Puerto Rico: Acquired from Spain, 1898

Wake Island: Annexed, 1899

Guam: Acquired from Spain, 1898

Philippines: Acquired from Spain, 1898 U.S. troops suppress Filipino independence movement, 1899–1902

Samoa: Divided between Germany and United States, 1899

Boundary dispute between Venezuela and British Guiana, 1895–1896

Dispute over U.S. sailors attacked in Chile, 1891

HAWAIIAN ISLANDS: Niihau, Kauai, Oahu, Molokai, Maui, Lanai, Kahoolawe, Hilo Bay, Hawai'i, Oahu, Honolulu, Pearl Harbor, Diamond Head

---

night, he said, it came to him that "there was nothing left for us to do but to take them all, and to educate the Filipinos, and uplift and civilize and Christianize them and by God's grace do the very best we could by them." In fact, most Filipinos had been Catholics for centuries, but no one ever expressed more clearly the concept of the "white man's burden."

Spain resisted giving up the Philippines, but McKinley insisted. The Treaty of Paris, signed in December 1898, required Spain to surrender Cuba, cede Puerto Rico and Guam to the United States, and sell the Philippines for $20 million. For the first time in American history, a treaty acquiring new territory failed to confer U.S. citizenship on the residents. Nor did the treaty mention future statehood. Thus these acquisitions represented a new kind of expansion—America had become a colonial power.

The **Treaty of Paris** dismayed Democrats, Populists, and some conservative Republicans, sparking a debate over acquisition of the Philippines in particular and **imperialism** in general. An anti-imperialist movement quickly formed, with William Jennings Bryan, Andrew Carnegie, Grover Cleveland, Carl Schurz, and Mark Twain among its outspoken proponents. They argued that the treaty denied self-government

Treaty of Paris An 1898 treaty ending the Spanish-American War, under which Spain granted independence to Cuba, ceded Puerto Rico and Guam to the United States, and sold the Philippines to the United States for $20 million.

imperialism The practice by which a nation acquires and holds colonies and other possessions, denies them self-government, and usually exploits them economically.

for the newly acquired territories and that holding colonies threatened the very concept of democracy. "The Declaration of Independence," warned Carnegie, "will make every Filipino a thoroughly dissatisfied subject." Others voiced racist arguments, claiming that Filipinos were incapable of self-government and that the United States would be corrupted by ruling such people. Labor leaders, fearing Filipino migration, repeated arguments once used to secure Chinese exclusion.

Those who defended acquisition of the Philippines echoed McKinley's lofty pronouncements about America's duty. Albert Beveridge, senator from Indiana, among others, also cited economic benefits: "We are raising more than we can consume, making more than we can use. Therefore we must find new markets for our produce." "New markets" were not limited to the new possessions. A strong naval and military presence in the Philippines would make the United States a leading power in eastern Asia, thereby supporting access for American business to markets in China.

William Jennings Bryan urged senators to approve the treaty. That way, he reasoned, the United States alone could determine the future of the Philippines. Once the treaty was approved, he argued, the United States should immediately grant them independence. By a narrow margin, the Senate approved the treaty on February 6, 1899. Soon after, senators rejected a proposal for Philippine independence.

The New American Empire

Bryan hoped to make independence for the Philippines the central issue in the 1900 presidential election. He easily won the Democratic nomination for a second time, and the Democrats' platform condemned the McKinley administration for its "imperialism." Bryan found, however, that many conservative anti-imperialists would not support his candidacy

because he still insisted on silver coinage and attacked big business.

The Republicans renominated McKinley. For vice president, they chose Theodore Roosevelt, "hero of San Juan Hill." McKinley's reelection seemed unstoppable. Republican campaigners pointed proudly to the highly successful war, legislation on the tariff and gold standard, and the return of prosperity. Bryan repeatedly attacked imperialism. McKinley and Roosevelt never used the term at all and instead took pride in expansion. McKinley easily won a second term with 52 percent of the vote.

Now the McKinley administration set about organizing its new empire. The Teller Amendment specified that the United States would not annex Cuba, but the McKinley administration refused to recognize the insurgents as the legitimate government. Instead, the U.S. Army took control. After two years of army rule, the McKinley administration permitted Cuban voters to hold a constitutional convention.

The convention met in 1900 and drafted a constitution modeled on that of the United States. Nowhere did it define relations between Cuba and the United States. In response, the McKinley administration drafted, and Congress adopted, terms for Cuba to adopt before the army would withdraw. Called the **Platt Amendment**, the terms specified that (1) Cuba was not to make any agreement with a foreign power that impaired the island's independence, (2) the United States could intervene in Cuba to preserve Cuban independence and maintain law and order, and (3) Cuba was to lease facilities to the United States for naval bases and coaling stations. Cubans reluctantly agreed, changed their constitution, and signed a treaty with the United States stating the Platt conditions. In 1902 Cuba thereby became a protectorate of the United States.

The Teller Amendment did not apply to Puerto Rico. There, the army provided a military government until 1900, when Congress approved the **Foraker Act**. That act made Puerto Ricans citizens of Puerto Rico, not American citizens. Puerto Rican voters could elect a legislature, but final authority rested with a governor and council appointed by the president of the United States. In 1901, in the **Insular Cases**, the Supreme Court confirmed the colonial status of Puerto Rico and, by implication, the other new possessions. The Court ruled that they were not equivalent to earlier territorial acquisitions and that their people did not possess the constitutional rights of citizens.

Establishment of civil government in the Philippines took longer. Between Dewey's victory and arrival of the first American soldiers three months later, a Philippine independence movement led by **Emilio Aguinaldo** established a provisional government and took control everywhere but Manila.

■ **Platt Amendment** An amendment to the Army Appropriations Act of 1901, sponsored by Senator Orville Platt; set terms for the withdrawal of the U.S. Army from Cuba, effectively making the island an American protectorate.

■ **Foraker Act** A 1900 law establishing civilian government in Puerto Rico; provided for an elected legislature and a governor appointed by the U.S. president.

Insular Cases Supreme Court decision (1901) concerning Puerto Rico; held that people in new island territories did not automatically receive the constitutional rights of U.S. citizens.

■ **Emilio Aguinaldo** Leader of unsuccessful struggles for Philippine independence, first against Spain, then against the United States.

The Granger Collection, NYC—All rights reserved.

The Spanish banished Emilio Aguinaldo from the Philippines because of his opposition to Spanish rule. American naval officials returned him to the islands, where he helped to establish an independent Filipino government. This photograph was taken in 1900, when Aguinaldo was leading what many Filipinos considered a war for independence.

Aguinaldo and his government wanted independence. When the United States determined to keep the islands, the Filipinos resisted.

Quelling what American authorities called the "Philippine insurrection" required three years (1899–1902), took the lives of 4,196 American soldiers, and perhaps 700,000 or more Filipinos (most through disease and other noncombat causes), and cost $400 million (twenty times the price of the islands). When some Filipinos resorted to guerrilla warfare, U.S. troops adopted practices similar to those Spain had used in Cuba. Both sides committed atrocities, and anti-imperialists pointed to brutal behavior by American troops as proof that a colonial policy was corrupting American values. American troops captured Aguinaldo in 1901, but resistance continued into mid-1902.

Congress set up a government for the Philippines similar to that of Puerto Rico. Filipinos became citizens of the Philippine Islands, but not of the United States. The president of the United States appointed the governor. Filipino voters elected one house in the two-house legislature, and the governor appointed the other. Both the governor and the U.S. Congress could veto laws passed by the legislature. William Howard Taft, governor from 1901 to 1904, tried to build local

support for American control, secured limited land reforms, and started to build public schools, hospitals, and sanitary facilities. However, when the first Philippine legislature met, in 1907, more than half of its members favored independence.

The Open Door and the Boxer Rebellion in China

Late in 1899, Britain, Germany, and the United States signed the Treaty of Berlin, which divided Samoa between Germany and the United States. The new Pacific acquisitions of the United States—Hawai'i, the Philippines, Guam, and Samoa—contained excellent sites for naval bases. Combined with the modernized navy, these acquisitions greatly strengthened American ability to assert power in the region and protect Americans' commercial access to eastern Asia. The United States now began to participate in the East Asian balance of power.

Weakened by war with Japan in 1894–1895, the Chinese government could not resist European nations' demands for territory. Britain, Germany, Russia, and France had carved out spheres of influence—areas where they claimed special rights, usually a monopoly over trade, and sought to exclude other powers. The United States argued instead for the "Open Door"—the principle that citizens of all nations should have equal status in seeking trade. American observers, however, began to fear the breakup of China into separate European colonies and the exclusion of American commerce.

In 1899 Secretary of State John Hay circulated a letter to Germany, Russia, Britain, France, Italy, and Japan, asking them to preserve Chinese sovereignty within their spheres of influence and not to discriminate against citizens of other nations engaged in commerce within their spheres. Hay wanted both to prevent the dismemberment of China and to maintain commercial access for American business throughout China. Some replies proved less than fully supportive, but Hay announced in a second letter that all had

■ **William Howard Taft** Governor of the Philippines, 1901–1904; president of the United States, 1909–1913; chief justice of the Supreme Court, 1921–1930.

Samoa A group of volcanic and mountainous islands in the South Pacific.

balance of power In international politics, the notion that nations may restrict one another's actions because of the relative equality of their naval or military forces, either individually or through alliance systems.

sphere of influence A region where a foreign nation exerts significant authority.

A Deeper Understanding of History

The Decision to Annex the Philippine Islands

Historians frequently analyze the way that people in past times have made decisions. In doing so, historians often think in terms of expectations (what the people wanted to accomplish), the choices they faced, constraints they perceived on their actions (which limited their choices), and the various outcomes of the choice they made.

At the end of the war with Spain, as a result of Dewey's victory over the Spanish fleet in Manila Bay, President McKinley and his advisers had to choose among several alternatives regarding the Philippine Islands. Hanging over their decision was the expectation among many members of the administration that the United States should take a larger role in the east Asian balance of power so as to prevent other nations from restricting future American commerce in the region, especially in China. Each choice, however, carried a constraint.

- **Choice** The United States could leave the Philippines alone.
  Constraint Spanish authority had collapsed everywhere in the Philippines except Manila. A U.S. departure might well mean that an expansive power in east Asia—most likely Japan or Germany—might take control in the Philippines. This choice was seen as losing the opportunity to bolster the U.S. position in east Asia.
- **Choice** The United States could take only a site for a naval base and leave the rest of the Philippines to Spain or, alternatively, let the rest of the islands establish a republic.

Constraint Spanish authority had collapsed everywhere except Manila, and the ability of a Philippine republic to defend itself was unclear. This choice too might mean that Japan, Germany, or another power would take control in the Philippines, leaving a U.S. base vulnerable to attack.
- **Choice** The United States could take all of the Philippines and maintain a significant naval and military presence there, thereby establishing itself as a major player in the east Asian balance of power.
  Constraint The Filipinos might resist American authority and seek to maintain their independent republic.

The McKinley administration chose the third alternative and insisted on taking all of the Philippines, as the surest way to provide security for a major U.S. naval base and also as the way most likely to make the United States a major player in the east Asian balance of power. Little or no consideration was given to the first alternative, nor to a version of the second alternative in which the United States would protect the independence of a Philippine republic.

Other short-term outcomes included

- A war with those Filipinos who wanted independence
- A major U.S. naval and military presence in East Asia
- The Open Door Notes
- U.S. participation in suppressing the Boxer Rebellion

In an unanticipated outcome, significant numbers of Filipinos migrated to work in Hawai'i and the western United States, where some of them took leading roles in organizing unions of farmworkers and cannery workers in the 1930s and after.

Over the long run, after regaining control of the islands following World War II, the United States granted independence to the Philippines but negotiated a lease on military bases and a mutual defense treaty. Because of growing opposition to the presence of U.S. military personnel in the Philippines, the last base was closed in 1992.

The Granger Collection, NYC.

WELL, I HARDLY KNOW WHICH TO TAKE FIRST!

This cartoon appeared in the Boston *Globe* on May 28, 1898, after Dewey's victory at Manila Bay on May 1, but months before the annexation of Hawai'i (called the Sandwich Islands in the cartoon) or U.S. victories in Cuba and Puerto Rico. What does this suggest to you about the ways some Americans were viewing the war?

A FAIR FIELD AND NO FAVOR!
UNCLE SAM: "I'M OUT FOR COMMERCE, NOT CONQUEST!"

In this 1899 cartoon celebrating the Open Door policy, Uncle Sam insists that other nations must compete fairly for China's commerce and not seize Chinese territory. In the background, John Bull (Britain) lifts his hat in approval. Library of Congress.

agreed to his "Open Door" principles. Hay's letters have usually been called the Open Door notes.

In 1900, a Chinese secret society tried to expel foreigners from China. Because the rebels used a clenched fist as their symbol, westerners called them Boxers. The Boxers laid siege to the section of Beijing, the Chinese capital, that housed foreign legations. Hay feared that other powers might use the rebellion as a pretext to take control and divide China permanently. To block such a move, the United States took full part in an international military expedition to rescue the besieged foreign diplomats and to crush the Boxer Rebellion.

Although China did not lose territory, the intervening nations required it to pay an indemnity. After compensating U.S. citizens for their losses, the U.S. government returned the remainder of its indemnity to China. The Chinese government, in turn, used the money to send Chinese students to study in the United States.

Open Door notes Diplomatic messages in 1899–1900 by which Secretary of State John Hay announced American support for Chinese autonomy and opposed efforts by other powers to carve China into exclusive spheres of influence.

legation Diplomatic officials representing their nation to another nation, and their offices and residences.

Boxer Rebellion Uprising in China in 1900 directed against foreign powers attempting to dominate China; suppressed by an international army including Americans.

indemnity Payment for damage, loss, or injury.

Individual Voices

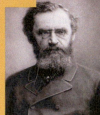

CARL SCHURZ

Comments on America's Changing Role in World Affairs, 1896–1899*

Schurz maintained a strong interest in world affairs throughout his political career, serving on the Senate Foreign Relations Committee and later helping organize the Anti-Imperialist League. The following three selections, addressing major changes in America's role in world affairs during the 1890s, brought Schurz acclaim from other Mugwump types and from many Democrats. Such primary sources assist historians in understanding opposition to the McKinley administration's policies.

akg-images/The Image Works.

1 *Jingo*, a term in general use in the 1890s, was applied to mindless, outspoken patriots, especially those advocating war.

2 Do you think that Schurz had any particular events or individuals in mind when making this statement? Given the date, what are the possibilities?

3 What action was pending in Congress at the time? How did Schurz hope to influence Congress?

4 To whom is Schurz most likely referring here?

5 Stephen Decatur, a naval officer, following the War of 1812, offered an after-dinner toast: "Our Country! In her intercourse with foreign nations may she always be in the right; but right or wrong, our country!" This has often been quoted as, "My country, right or wrong!"

6 Do these selections help you to understand Schurz's reputation for putting principle before party? What principles does he enunciate in these selections?

From a speech, January 2, 1896:

What is the rule of honor to be observed by a power so strongly and so advantageously situated as this Republic is?…it should not, as our boyish jingoes **1** wish it to do, swagger about among the nations of the world, with a chip on its shoulder, shaking its fist in everybody's face…it should not, whenever its own notions of right or interest collide with the notions of others, fall into hysterics and act as if it really feared for its own security and its very independence. **2** …With all its latent resources for war, it should be the great peace power of the world.…Is not this peace with honor? There has, of late, been much loose speech about "Americanism." Is not this good Americanism? It is surely today the Americanism of those who love their country most.

From Harper's Weekly, April 16, 1898:

The man who in times of popular excitement boldly and unflinchingly resists hot-tempered clamor for an unnecessary war, **3** and thus exposes himself to the opprobrious imputation of a lack of patriotism or of courage, to the end of saving his country from a great calamity, is, as to "loving and faithfully serving his country," at least as good a patriot as the hero of the most daring feat of arms, and a far better one than those who, with an ostentatious pretense of superior patriotism, cry for war before it is needed, especially if then they let others do the fighting. **4**

From a speech, October 17, 1899:

I confidently trust that the American people will prove themselves…too wise not to detect the false pride or the dangerous ambitions or the selfish schemes which so often hide themselves under that deceptive cry of mock patriotism: "Our country, right or wrong!" **5** They will not fail to recognize that our dignity, our free institutions and the peace and welfare of this and coming generations of Americans will be secure only as we cling to the watchword of true patriotism: "Our country— when right to be kept right; when wrong to be put right." **6**

*Taken from Harper's Weekly.

Study Tools

SUMMARY

In the late nineteenth century, political parties dominated politics. All elected public officials were nominated by party conventions and elected through party campaigns. Nearly all government jobs came through the spoils system. Republicans used government to promote rapid economic development, but Democrats argued for minimal government. Voters divided between the major parties largely along lines of region, ethnicity, and race.

The presidency of Ulysses S. Grant was plagued by scandals. Thereafter, the closely balanced strengths of the two parties contributed to a long-term political stalemate. In 1889–1890, however, Republicans wrote most of their campaign promises into law.

Grangers, Greenbackers, and silverites challenged the major parties, appealing most to debt-ridden farmers. Mugwumps argued for the merit system in the civil service, accomplished through the Pendleton Act of 1883. By the late nineteenth century, a well-organized woman suffrage movement had emerged. A wide range of reform groups sought both structural changes and policy changes.

The 1890s saw major, long-lasting changes in American politics. A political upheaval began when western and southern farmers joined the Farmers' Alliances, then launched a new political party, the Populist Party. Elected in 1892, President Grover Cleveland failed to meet the political challenges of the depression that began in 1893; his party, the Democrats, lost badly in the 1894 congressional elections. In 1896 the Democrats nominated for president William Jennings Bryan, a supporter of silver coinage. The Republicans chose William McKinley, who favored the protective tariff. McKinley won, beginning a period of Republican dominance in national politics that lasted until 1930. Under Bryan's leadership, the Democratic Party promoted government action against monopolies and other powerful economic interests.

From 1865 to 1889, few Americans expected their nation to be significantly involved in world affairs outside North America. The United States did acquire Alaska, pressured the French to withdraw from Mexico, and took actions to encourage trade with eastern Asia. The kingdom of Hawai'i became closely integrated with the American economy. During the early 1890s, the United States moved toward a new role in world affairs. Presidents Harrison and Cleveland asserted American power in Latin America.

A revolution in Cuba led the United States into a one-sided war with Spain in 1898, resulting in acquisition of the Philippines, Guam, and Puerto Rico. Congress annexed Hawai'i in the midst of the war, and the United States acquired part of Samoa in 1899. Filipinos resisted American authority, leading to a three-year war. With the Philippines and an improved navy, the United States gained new prominence in eastern Asia, especially in China, where the United States promoted the Open Door policy and American troops helped suppress the Boxer Rebellion.

CHRONOLOGY
Politics and Foreign Relations, 1865–1902

1867	French troops leave Mexico United States purchases Alaska
1868	Ulysses S. Grant elected president
1869	National Woman Suffrage Association and American Woman Suffrage Association formed Wyoming Territory adopts woman suffrage
1872	Crédit Mobilier scandal Grant reelected
1872–1874	Granger laws
1873–1879	Depression
1877	Rutherford B. Hayes becomes president
1878	Greenback Party peaks
1880	James A. Garfield elected president
1881	Garfield assassinated Chester A. Arthur becomes president
1883	Pendleton Act
1884	Grover Cleveland elected president
1887	Interstate Commerce Act
1888	Benjamin Harrison elected president
1890	Sherman Anti-Trust Act Sherman Silver Purchase Act McKinley Tariff Significant increase in naval appropriation Lodge's federal elections bill defeated Populist movement begins
1892	Cleveland elected president again
1893	*Haole* planters and businessmen proclaim Hawaiian republic
1893–1897	Depression
1895–1896	Venezuelan boundary crisis
1896	William Jennings Bryan's "Cross of Gold" speech William McKinley elected president
1898	War with Spain United States annexes Hawai'i
1899	Treaty of Paris ratified Open Door notes
1899–1902	Philippine insurrection
1900	McKinley reelected
1902	Civil government in the Philippines Cuba becomes a protectorate

Study Tools

FOCUS QUESTIONS

If you have mastered this chapter, you should be able to answer these questions and explain the terms that follow the questions.

1. What was the significance of political parties in the late nineteenth century?

2. Compare the presidencies from Grant through Cleveland. Which do you consider successful? Why?

3. What were the major goals of the various reform groups?

4. Why were some reformers more successful than others?

5. Which groups and issues led to the formation of the Populist Party?

6. What were the issues in the 1896 presidential election, and what were the short-term and long-term results?

7. How did American policymakers define the role of the United States in North America and other parts of the world during 1865–1889?

8. How and why did some Americans' attitudes about the U.S. role in world affairs begin to change between 1889 and 1897?

9. What led the United States into war with Spain?

10. What new attitudes about America's role in world affairs appeared in the debate over acquiring new possessions?

KEY TERMS

patronage system   *p. 468*

Crédit Mobilier   *p. 470*

Tweed Ring   *p. 470*

Interstate Commerce Commission   *p. 472*

William McKinley   *p. 472*

McKinley Tariff   *p. 473*

Sherman Anti-Trust Act   *p. 474*

Grange   *p. 475*

Granger laws   *p. 476*

gold standard   *p. 476*

Sherman Silver Purchase Act   *p. 477*

Mugwumps   *p. 477*

Pendleton Act   *p. 477*

National Woman Suffrage Association   *p. 478*

American Woman Suffrage Association   *p. 478*

Australian ballot   *p. 481*

Populists   *p. 481*

Farmers' Alliances   *p. 481*

antimonopolism   *p. 481*

William Jennings Bryan   *p. 484*

William H. Seward   *p. 486*

Monroe Doctrine   *p. 487*

Benito Juarez   *p. 487*

Alfred Thayer Mahan   *p. 489*

Lili'uokalani   *p. 490*

reconcentration   *p. 491*

yellow journalism   *p. 491*

U.S.S. Maine   *p. 492*

Teller Amendment   *p. 493*

Theodore Roosevelt   *p. 493*

Platt Amendment   *p. 496*

Foraker Act   *p. 496*

Emilio Aguinaldo   *p. 496*

William Howard Taft   *p. 497*

Open Door notes   *p. 499*

SUGGESTED RESOURCES

Robert L. Beisner. *From the Old Diplomacy to the New, 1865–1900,* 2nd ed. (Wheeling, IL: Harlan Davidson, 1986). A concise introduction to American foreign relations in this period.

Charles W. Calhoun. *From Bloody Shirt to Full Dinner Pail: The Transformation of Politics and Governance in the Gilded Age* (Lawrence, KS: University Press of Kansas, 2011). The most recent, and highly readable, treatment of Gilded Age politics.

Charles Postel. *The Populist Vision* (Hew York: Oxford University Press, 2007). A meticulously researched and prize-winning treatment of the Populists of the 1890s.

David Silbey. *A War of Frontier and Empire: The Philippine-American War, 1899–1902* (New York: Hill and Wang, 2007). The most recent treatment of the U.S. conquest of the Philippines.

19

The Progressive Era, 1900–1917

CHAPTER OUTLINE

Organizing for Change
The Changing Face of Politics
"Spearheads for Reform":
The Settlement Houses
Women and Reform
Moral Reform
Organizing Against Racism
Challenging Capitalism: Socialists and Wobblies

The Reform of Politics, the Politics of Reform
Exposing Corruption: The Muckrakers
Reforming City Government
Reforming State Government
The Weakening of Parties and Rise of Organized Interest Groups

Roosevelt, Taft, and Republican Progressivism
Roosevelt: Asserting the Power of the Presidency
The Square Deal in Action: Creating the Regulatory State
Regulating Natural Resources
Taft's Troubles

"Carry a Big Stick": Roosevelt, Taft, and World Affairs
Taking Panama
Making the Caribbean an American Lake
Roosevelt and Eastern Asia
The United States and World Affairs, 1901–1913

Wilson and Democratic Progressivism
Debating the Future: The Election of 1912
Wilson and Reform, 1913–1916

New Patterns in Cultural Expression
Realism, Impressionism, and Ragtime
Mass Entertainment in the Early Twentieth Century
Celebrating the New Age

Progressivism in Perspective

INDIVIDUAL VOICES: *Jane Addams Explains Her Participation in the 1912 Presidential Campaign*

Study Tools

INDIVIDUAL CHOICES

Jane Addams

On August 7, 1912, Jane Addams stood onstage at the Chicago Coliseum, facing thousands of delegates and guests at the convention of the new Progressive Party. They had come to nominate Theodore Roosevelt for president, and Addams was there to second Roosevelt's nomination. The *New York Times* reported that "Miss Addams fired her sentences at the crowd like bullets, and every one of them provoked a furious demonstration." The first woman to take such a prominent role at a party convention, Addams defined the new party as part of a worldwide movement for social justice, and she rejoiced that the party had "pledged itself to the protection of children, to the care of the aged, to the relief of overworked girls, to the safeguarding of burdened men" (see the Individual Voices feature at the end of this chapter). As she finished her speech, she grabbed a banner proclaiming "Votes for Women" and carried it off the stage as the delegates cheered wildly.

For a generation, Jane Addams was the most prominent woman in public life. Born in Cedarville, Illinois, in1860, the daughter of a banker and entrepreneur who helped to found the Republican Party, she graduated from a nearby school for

Hulton Archive/Getty Images.

women in 1881, the same year her father died, leaving her quite wealthy. For a time, she lived the life of an affluent young woman, including a two-year tour of Europe, but she found it unsatisfying. She had hoped, since childhood, to assist the poor, and in 1887 she read about Toynbee Hall, the first settlement house, established in 1884 in London's slums, where idealistic university graduates lived among and assisted the poor. When she and several friends, including Ellen Gates Starr, toured Europe again, Addams made certain to visit Toynbee Hall. Inspired there, she and Starr determined to create a settlement house in Chicago.

In 1889, they opened **Hull House** in a working-class, immigrant neighborhood in Chicago. Addams moved easily among wealthy Chicagoans and soon found generous donors to Hull House, which expanded to a dozen nearby buildings. Addams and Starr lived at Hull House for most of their lives, along with a changing group of impressive associates, mostly young, idealistic, female college graduates. For neighborhood families, Hull House offered a nursery, childcare, classes for mothers, a playground, a gymnasium, adult education classes, and more. Hull House activists challenged Chicago's political bosses and lobbied state legislators, seeking cleaner streets, the abolition of child labor, health and safety regulations for workers, compulsory school attendance, and more. Their efforts attracted national attention and helped to establish the settlement houses as what one historian called "spearheads for reform." Addams also lectured and wrote widely on the problems of the slums and working people. Hull House became the most prominent settlement house, and Addams became synonymous with settlement work and reform more generally.

After the campaign of 1912, Addams continued to work for the reforms she had long advocated and also for international peace. In 1931, she became the first woman to receive the Nobel Peace Prize. She died in 1935.

Addams became a prominent advocate for reform during what historians call the Progressive Era—a time when "reform was in the air," as one newspaper editor recalled. Reform was "in the air" almost everywhere, and many individuals and groups joined in, often with quite different expectations. Progressivism took shape through many decisions by voters and political leaders, but one question loomed behind many of those decisions: Should government play a larger role in the lives of Americans? This question lay behind debates over proposals to limit working hours of women factory workers and prohibit alcoholic beverages, as well as regulation of railroads and banking.

Time after time, Americans chose a greater role for government. Often the consensus favoring government intervention was so broad that the only debate was over the form of intervention. As Americans gave government more power, they also tried to make government more responsive to ordinary citizens. They put limits on political parties and introduced ways for people to participate more directly in politics. The political changes of the Progressive Era, following on the heels of the political realignment of the 1890s, fundamentally altered American politics and government in the twentieth century and marked the birth of many aspects of modern American politics.

ORGANIZING FOR CHANGE

☆ *What important changes transformed American politics in the early twentieth century?*

☆ *What did women and African Americans seek to accomplish by creating new organizations devoted to political change?*

During the early twentieth century, politics expanded to embrace wide-ranging concerns raised by a complex

▫ **Hull House** Settlement house founded by Jane Addams and Ellen Gates Starr in 1889 in Chicago.

assortment of groups and individuals. In the swirl of proponents and proposals, politics more than ever before came to reflect the interaction of organized interest groups.

The Changing Face of Politics

As Americans entered the twentieth century, their lives were changing in important ways. The railroad, telegraph, and telephone transformed concepts of time and space and fostered formation of new organizations. Executives of new industrial corporations now thought in terms of regional or national markets. Union members allied with others of their trade in distant cities. Farmers in Kansas and Montana studied grain prices in Chicago and Liverpool. Physicians organized nationwide to establish higher standards for medical schools.

Manufacturers, farmers, merchants, carpenters, teachers, lawyers, physicians, and many others established or reorganized national associations to advance their economic or professional interests. Sometimes that meant seeking governmental assistance. As early as the 1870s, for example, associations of merchants and farmers had pushed for laws to regulate railroad freight rates.

Some graduates emerged from the recently transformed universities with the conviction that their knowledge and skills could improve society, and they formed professional associations to advance those objectives. Long-established church organizations sometimes fostered the emergence of new associations devoted to moral reform, especially prohibition. Some people formed groups with humanitarian goals such as ending child labor. Members of ethnic and racial groups set up societies to further their groups' interests. Reformers organized to limit the power of corporations or to defeat party bosses. Overlapping with many of these new associations were the organizational activities of women, including middle-class women, new college graduates, and factory and clerical workers.

Sooner or later, many of the new associations looked to government to help them reach their objectives. Increasing numbers of citizens related to politics through such organized **interest groups**, even as the traditional political parties found they could no longer count on the voter loyalty typical of the Gilded Age.

Many of these new groups optimistically believed that responsible citizens, acting together, assisted by technical know-how, and sometimes drawing on the power of government, could achieve social progress—improvement of the human situation. As early as the 1890s, some had begun to call themselves "progressive citizens." By 1910, many were simply calling themselves "progressives."

Historians use the term *progressivism* to signify three related developments during the early twentieth

century: (1) the emergence of new concepts about the purposes and functions of government, (2) changes in government policies and institutions, and (3) the political agitation that produced those changes. A progressive was a person involved in one or more of these activities. Many individuals and groups promoted their own visions of change, making progressivism a complex phenomenon. Nonetheless, many aspects of progressivism reflected concerns of the urban middle class, especially urban middle-class women. The new **Progressive Party**, which Jane Addams embraced in 1912, sputtered for a brief time after, but failed to capture the allegiance of all who called themselves progressives.

Progressivism appeared at every level of government—local, state, and federal. And progressives promoted a wide range of new government activities: regulation of business, moral revival, consumer protection, conservation of natural resources, educational improvement, tax reform, and more. Through all these avenues, they brought government more directly into the economy and more directly into the lives of most Americans.

"Spearheads for Reform": The Settlement Houses

Hull House was not the first American **settlement house**. In 1886, young male college graduates had opened a settlement house in New York City modeled after London's Toynbee Hall, and several women, graduates of Smith College (a women's college), opened another settlement house in New York in 1889, the same year that Jane Addams and Ellen Gates Starr opened Hull House in Chicago.

Other settlement houses were organized across the country to provide assistance to poor urban families: cooking and sewing classes, public baths, English lessons, and housing for unmarried working women. Some settlement houses were church sponsored. Nearly all tried to minimize class conflict because they agreed with Addams that "the dependence of classes on each other is reciprocal." Like Addams, many settlement house workers became forces for urban reform, promoting better schools, improved public health and sanitation, and honest government. Historians have suggested that settlement house workers tried to

> ■ **interest group** A coalition of people identified with a particular cause, such as an industry or occupational group, a social group, or a policy objective.
> ■ **Progressive Party** Political party formed in 1912 with Theodore Roosevelt as its candidate for president; it collapsed when Roosevelt returned to the Republicans in 1916.
> **settlement house** Community center operated by resident social reformers in a poor urban neighborhood.

bridge the gap between urban economic classes by imparting middle-class values to the poor and persuading the wealthy to help mitigate poverty and that such efforts reflected urban middle-class anxieties over growing extremes of wealth and poverty. Historians have also noted that settlement house workers drew on the bonds of gender solidarity to appeal to upper- and middle-class women for funds to assist working-class and poor women and children.

Settlement houses spread rapidly, with some four hundred operating by 1910. Three-quarters of settlement house workers were women, and settlement houses became the first institutions created and staffed primarily by college-educated women. They led to a new profession—social work. When universities began to offer study in social work (first at Columbia, in 1902), women tended to dominate that field, too. Women college graduates thus created a new and uniquely urban profession at a time when many careers remained closed to them.

Many settlement houses also reflected the influence of the **Social Gospel**, a movement popularized by Protestant ministers concerned about urban social and economic problems. Washington Gladden, of Columbus, Ohio, called for "Applied Christianity," by which he meant the application to business of Christ's injunctions to love one another and to treat others as you would have them treat you. A similar strain of social activism appeared among Catholics, especially those inspired by Pope Leo XIII's 1891 *Rerum Novarium* ("Of New Things"), an **encyclical** urging greater attention to the problems of the industrial working class.

Women and Reform

The settlement houses are among the many women's organizations that burst onto the political scene during the Progressive Era. By 1900 or so, a new ideal for women had emerged from the women's clubs, women's colleges, and settlement houses, and from discussions on national lecture circuits and in the press. The "New Woman" stood for self-determination rather than unthinking acceptance of the concepts of domesticity and separate spheres. By 1910, this attitude, sometimes called **feminism**, was accelerating the transition from the nineteenth-century movement for suffrage to the twentieth-century struggle for equality and individualism.

Women's increasing control over one aspect of their lives appeared in the birth rate, which fell steadily throughout the nineteenth and early twentieth centuries as couples (or perhaps women alone) chose to have fewer children. However, abortion was illegal, and state and federal laws banned distribution of information about contraception. In 1915 a group of women formed the National Birth Control League to oppose laws prohibiting contraceptive information. In 1916 **Margaret Sanger**, a nurse practicing among the poor, attracted wide attention when she went to jail for informing women about birth control.

Other organizations also advanced specific causes. The National Consumers' League (founded in 1890) and the Women's Trade Union League (1903) tried to improve the lives of working women. Such efforts received a tragic boost in 1911 when fire roared through the Triangle Shirtwaist Company's clothing factory in New York City, killing 146 workers—nearly all young women—who were trapped in a building with no outside fire escapes and locked exit doors. The public outcry produced a state investigation and, in 1914, a new state factory safety law.

Some states passed laws to protect working women. In *Muller v. Oregon* (1908), the Supreme Court approved the constitutionality of one such law, limiting women's hours of work. Louis Brandeis, a lawyer working with the Consumers' League, defended the law by arguing that women needed special protection because of their roles as mothers. Such arguments ran contrary to the New Woman's rejection of separate spheres and ultimately raised questions for women's drive for equality. At the time, however, the decision was hailed as a necessary protection for women wage earners. By 1917, laws in thirty-nine states restricted women's working hours.

Though prominent in reform politics, most women could neither vote nor hold office. Support for suffrage grew, however, as more women recognized the need for political action to bring social change. By 1896, four western states had extended the vote to women (see pages 478–479). No other state did so until 1910, when Washington approved female suffrage. Seven more western states soon followed. In 1916 **Jeannette Rankin** of Montana—born on a ranch, educated as a social worker, experienced

---

■ **Social Gospel** A reform movement of the late nineteenth and early twentieth centuries, led by Protestant clergy who drew attention to urban problems and advocated for the poor.

encyclical A letter from the pope to Roman Catholic bishops, intended to guide them in their relations with the churches under their jurisdiction.

feminism The conviction that women are and should be the social, political, and economic equals of men.

■ **Margaret Sanger** Birth-control advocate who believed so strongly that information about birth control was essential to help women escape poverty that she violated laws against its dissemination.

■ *Muller v. Oregon* Supreme Court case in 1908, upholding an Oregon law that limited the hours of employment for women.

■ **Jeannette Rankin** Montana reformer and, in 1916, first woman elected to Congress; she worked for woman suffrage and to protect women in the workplace.

These union members carry banners mourning the deaths of the young women who died in the Triangle fire. They were both grieving and demanding action to prevent any such disaster in the future. Among the witnesses to the fire was Frances Perkins, a settlement house worker who later became secretary of labor—and the first woman to serve in the president's cabinet—during the administration of Franklin D. Roosevelt. Perkins considered the fire an important turning point in her life.

as a suffrage campaigner—became the first woman elected to the U.S. House of Representatives. Suffrage scored few victories outside the West, however.

Convinced that only a federal constitutional amendment would gain the vote for all women, the **National American Woman Suffrage Association** (NAWSA), led by Carrie Chapman Catt and Anna Howard Shaw, focused on lobbying in Washington, D.C. Alice Paul advocated public demonstrations and civil disobedience, tactics she learned from suffragists in England, where she had been a settlement house worker. Some white suffragists tried to build an interracial movement for suffrage—NAWSA, for example, condemned lynching in 1917—but most feared that attention to other issues would weaken their position.

Although its leaders were mostly white and middle-class, the suffrage cause became a mass movement during the 1910s, mobilizing women of all ages and socioeconomic classes. Their opponents argued that voting would bring women into the male sphere, expose them to corrupting influences, and render them unsuitable as guardians of the moral order. Suffrage advocates turned that argument on its head, claiming that women would make politics more moral

and family oriented. Others, especially feminists, argued that women should vote because they deserved full equality with men.

Moral Reform

Moral reformers, including many women, focused especially on banning alcohol—Demon Rum. The temperance movement dated to the 1820s. Early temperance advocates worked to persuade individuals to give up strong drink. By the 1890s, they looked to government to prohibit production, sale, or consumption of alcoholic beverages. Many saw prohibition as a progressive reform and expected government to safeguard what they saw as the public interest.

The drive against alcohol developed a broad base during the Progressive Era. Some old-stock Protestant churches—notably the Methodists—termed alcohol a significant obstacle to a better society. Adherents of

■ **National American Woman Suffrage Association** (NAWSA) Organization formed in 1890 that united the two major women's suffrage groups of that time.

THE AWAKENING

Library of Congress.

This cartoon, entitled "The Awakening," shows a western woman, draped in a golden robe, bringing the torch of woman suffrage from the western states that had adopted suffrage to the eastern states that had not done so. In the dark eastern states, women eagerly reach toward the light from the West. Yellow had become a symbol of the suffrage movement.

the Social Gospel urged that prohibition could save many victims of industrialization and urbanization. Others emphasized protecting the family and home from the destructive influence of alcohol. Sociologists demonstrated links between liquor and prostitution, sexually transmitted diseases, poverty, crime, and broken families. Other evidence pointed to alcohol as contributing to industrial accidents, absenteeism, and inefficiency on the job.

By the late 1890s, the **Anti-Saloon League** became the model for successful interest-group politics. Proudly describing itself as "the Church in action against the saloon," the Anti-Saloon League usually operated through old-stock Protestant churches and focused on the saloon as corrupting not only individuals—men who neglected their families—but also politics. Saloons, where political cronies struck deals and mingled with voters, had long been identified with big-city political machines.

The League endorsed only politicians who opposed Demon Rum, regardless of party or other issues.

As the prohibition cause demonstrated growing political clout, more politicians lined up against the saloon. Between 1900 and 1917, voters adopted prohibition in nearly half of the states, including nearly all of the West and the South. Elsewhere, many towns and rural areas voted themselves "dry" under **local option laws**.

Opposition to prohibition came from immigrants and their American-born descendants from Ireland, Germany, and southern and eastern Europe who did not regard alcohol as inherently sinful. For them, beer or wine was an accepted part of social life. Alcohol manufacturers, especially beer brewers, also organized to fight the prohibitionists. "Personal liberty" became the slogan for these "wets."

The drive against alcohol, ultimately successful at the national level, was not the only target for moral reformers. Reformers—including many women—tried to eliminate prostitution through state and federal legislation. Other moral reform efforts—to ban gambling or make divorces more difficult, for example— also represented attempts to use government power to regulate individual behavior.

Organizing Against Racism

During the Progressive Era, racial issues generally drew less attention than other causes. Southern white progressives often took the lead in enacting disfranchisement and segregation, and only a few white

■ **Anti-Saloon League** Political interest group advocating prohibition, founded in 1895; it organized through churches.

local option laws A state law that permitted the residents of a town or city to decide, by an election, whether to ban liquor sales in their community.

progressives actively opposed such discriminatory laws. When Jane Addams argued to add black rights to the Republican and Progressive Party platforms in 1912, she lost. In his book *Following the Color Line* (1908), Ray Stannard Baker examined the situation of African Americans and asked, "Does democracy really include Negroes as well as white men?" For most white Americans, the answer appeared to be no.

Lynchings and violence remained frightening realities for African Americans. Between 1900 and World War I, lynchings claimed more than 1,100 victims, nearly all black and most in the South. During the same years, race riots wracked several cities. In 1906 in Atlanta, whites randomly attacked African Americans, killing four, injuring many more, and vandalizing property. In 1908, in Springfield, Illinois (where Abraham Lincoln had lived), a white mob lynched two black men, injured others, and destroyed black-owned businesses.

This postcard shows the lynching of Laura Nelson and her son, L. D., both African Americans. They were being held in Okemah, Oklahoma, for trial for the murder of a deputy sheriff when a group of people removed them from their cells and hanged them from this bridge. Photographs of this lynching, and many more lynchings, were made into postcards, which participants often sent to their friends and relatives. Although the photographs showed the faces of those present at the lynchings, local law enforcement officials always insisted that it was impossible for them to determine those responsible for the crimes.

George Henry Farnum Collection, Oklahoma Historical Society Research Division, Oklahoma Historical Society.

Some African Americans challenged the accommodationist leadership of Booker T. Washington. **W. E. B. Du Bois**, the first African American to receive a Ph.D. degree from Harvard, wrote some of the first scholarly studies of African Americans. He emphasized the contributions of black men and women, disproved racial stereotypes, and used his book *Souls of Black Folk* (1903) to criticize Washington and exhort African Americans to struggle for their rights "unceasingly." "The hands of none of us are clean," he argued, speaking to both whites and blacks, "if we bend not our energies to a righting of these great wrongs."

African American leaders organized to support black rights. In 1905 Du Bois and others met in Canada, near Niagara Falls, and drafted demands for racial equality. In 1910 black and white delegates formed the **National Association for the Advancement of Colored People** (NAACP), which provided important leadership in the fight for racial equality. Du Bois became the NAACP's director of publicity and research.

Ida B. Wells provided important leadership for the struggle against lynching. Born in Mississippi in 1862, she attended a school set up by the Freedmen's Bureau and worked as a teacher. Later, in Memphis, Tennessee, she began to write for a black newspaper and attacked lynching, arguing that several local victims had been targeted to eliminate successful black businessmen. When a mob destroyed the newspaper office, she moved north. During the 1890s and early 1900s, Wells attacked lynching on speaking tours and in print. Eventually she persuaded some white northerners to recognize and condemn the horror of lynching. After the mid-1890s, she lived in Chicago; there she promoted black women's clubs and a black settlement house and worked with Jane Addams against local school segregation. Initially a supporter of the NAACP, she came to regard it as too cautious.

Challenging Capitalism: Socialists and Wobblies

Many progressive-era organizations reflected middle- and upper-class concerns, such as businesslike government and greater reliance on experts. Not so the

■ **W. E. B. Du Bois** African American intellectual and civil rights leader, author of important works on black history and sociology, who helped form and lead the NAACP.

■ **National Association for the Advancement of Colored People** (NAACP) Racially integrated civil rights organization founded in 1910; it continues to work to end discrimination.

■ **Ida B. Wells** African American reformer and journalist, prominent opponent of lynching and advocate for racial justice and woman suffrage; upon marrying in 1895, she became Ida Wells-Barnett.

Socialist Party of America (SPA), formed in 1901. Proclaiming themselves the political arm of workers and farmers, the Socialists argued that industrial capitalism had produced "an economic slavery which renders intellectual and political tyranny inevitable." They rejected most progressive proposals as inadequate and called instead for workers to control the means of production. Most looked to the political process to accomplish this transformation.

The Socialists' best-known national leader was Eugene V. Debs, leader of the Pullman strike and virtually the only person able to unite the many socialist factions. Strong among immigrants, some of whom had become socialists in their native lands, the SPA attracted some trade unionists, municipal reformers, and intellectuals, including W. E. B. Du Bois, Margaret Sanger, and Upton Sinclair. The party also attracted some former Populists and drew some support from farmers, especially in Oklahoma and Kansas.

Hundreds of cities and towns—ranging from Reading, Pennsylvania, to Milwaukee, Wisconsin, to Berkeley, California—elected Socialist mayors or council members. Socialists won election to state legislatures in several states. Districts in New York City and Milwaukee sent Socialists to the U.S. House of Representatives. Most Americans, however, had no interest in eliminating private property. Most progressive reformers looked askance at the Socialists and sometimes tried to undercut their appeal with reforms that addressed some of their concerns but stopped short of challenging capitalism.

In 1905 a group of unionists and radicals organized the **Industrial Workers of the World** (IWW, or "Wobblies"). IWW organizers boldly proclaimed, "We have been naught, we shall be all," as they set out to organize the most exploited unskilled and semiskilled workers. Unlike the American Federation of Labor, which focused on skilled workers, most of them white males, the IWW aimed their message at **sweatshop** workers in eastern cities, **migrant** farm workers who harvested western crops, southern sharecroppers, women workers, African Americans, and immigrants from southern and eastern Europe. The Wobblies' objective was simple: when most workers had joined

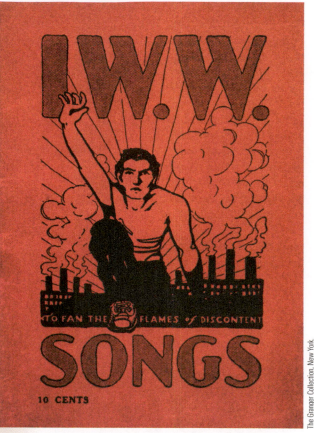

The Granger Collection, New York.

The famous "little red songbook" of the IWW began with an effort by some IWW members in Spokane, Washington, in 1909 who created a pocket-sized collection of songs entitled *Songs of the Workers, on the Road, in the Jungles, and in the Shops—Songs to Fan the Flames of Discontent*. The songbook went through many editions; this one was published in 1932.

the IWW, they would call a general strike, labor would refuse to work, and capitalism would collapse.

The IWW organized a few dramatic strikes and demonstrations and scored a handful of significant victories but made few lasting gains. More often, the IWW met brutal suppression by local authorities.

THE REFORM OF POLITICS, THE POLITICS OF REFORM

★ *What did the muckrakers contribute to reform?*

★ *What characterized reforms of city and state government and what role did organized interest groups play?*

Progressivism emerged at all levels of government as cities elected reform-minded mayors and states swore in progressive governors. In their quest for change, reformers sometimes came up against the entrenched leaders of political parties and therefore sought to limit the power of those parties.

□ **Socialist Party of America** (SPA) Political party formed in 1901 and committed to socialism—that is, government ownership of most industries.

Industrial Workers of the World (IWW) Radical workers' organization formed in 1905 to unite all wage-earners regardless of race, ethnicity, or gender, and committed to the destruction of capitalism.

sweatshop A shop or factory in which employees work long hours at low wages under poor conditions.

migrant Traveling from one area to another.

A NAUSEATING JOB, BUT IT MUST BE DONE

(President Roosevelt takes hold of the investigating muck-rake himself in the packing-house scandal.)

U.S. INSP'D AND CONDEMNED

Upton Sinclair's novel *The Jungle* (1906) prompted President Theodore Roosevelt to order an investigation of Sinclair's allegations about unsanitary practices in the meatpacking industry. Roosevelt then pressured Congress to approve new federal legislation to inspect meatpacking, including a stamp such as the one shown here.

Exposing Corruption: The Muckrakers

Journalists prepared the ground for reform. By the early 1900s, magazine publishers discovered their sales boomed when they presented exposés of political corruption, corporate wrongdoing, and other scandalous offenses. Such journalists acquired the name **muckrakers** in 1906 when President Theodore Roosevelt compared them to "the Man with the Muck-rake," a character in John Bunyan's classic allegory *Pilgrim's Progress.* Roosevelt intended the comparison as a criticism, but journalists proudly claimed the label.

McClure's Magazine led the way beginning in 1902, when the magazine began a series by Lincoln Steffens on corruption in city governments. Soon, *McClure's* added a series by Ida Tarbell on Standard Oil and a piece revealing corruption and violence in labor unions. Sales of *McClure's* soared, and other journals—including *Collier's* and *Cosmopolitan*—copied its style, publishing exposés on patent medicines, fraud by insurance companies, child labor, and more.

Muckraking soon extended to books. Many muckraking books were investigations into social problems. The most famous muckraking book, however, was a novel: *The Jungle,* by **Upton Sinclair** (1906). Sinclair, a socialist, intended his novel as an indictment of industrial capitalism. In following the experiences of fictional immigrant laborers in Chicago, Sinclair

exposed in disgusting detail how the meatpacking industry misled consumers about the quality of meat products. He chillingly described the afflictions of packinghouse workers—severed fingers, tuberculosis, blood poisoning. The nation was shocked to read of men who "fell into the vats" and "would be overlooked for days, till all but the bones of them had gone out to the world as Durham's Pure Leaf Lard!"

The Jungle horrified Americans. President Roosevelt appointed a commission to investigate its allegations, and the report confirmed Sinclair's charges. Congress soon passed the **Pure Food and Drug Act**, banning impure and mislabeled food and drugs (a law not directly related to the outcry over

- **muckrakers** Progressive Era journalists who wrote articles exposing corruption in city government, business, and industry. In John Bunyan's *Pilgrim's Progress,* "the Man with the Muck-rake" is so preoccupied with raking through the filth at his feet that he didn't notice he was being offered a celestial crown in exchange for his rake.
- **Upton Sinclair** Socialist writer and reformer whose novel *The Jungle* exposed unsanitary conditions in the meatpacking industry and advocated socialism.
- **Pure Food and Drug Act** A 1906 law forbidding sale of impure and improperly labeled food and drugs.

The Jungle), and the **Meat Inspection Act**, requiring federal inspection of meatpacking—something the industry itself welcomed to reassure nauseated consumers. Sinclair, however, was disappointed that his revelations produced regulation rather than converts to socialism. "I aimed at the public's heart," Sinclair complained, "and by accident I hit it in the stomach."

Reforming City Government

By the time of Lincoln Steffens's first article (1902) on corruption in city government, advocates of **municipal reform** had already won office and brought changes to some cities. Other municipal reformers soon appeared elsewhere.

Municipal reformers argued that eliminating corruption and inefficiency required changes in the structure of city government. City councils usually consisted of members elected from **wards** corresponding roughly to neighborhoods. Middle and working-class wards usually dominated city councils. Reformers condemned this system as producing city council members unable to see beyond their own neighborhoods. Reformers also recognized that poor immigrant neighborhoods supported political bosses and machines despite their corruption. They argued that citywide elections, in which all city voters chose from one list of candidates, would produce city council members better qualified to address the problems of the whole city—men with citywide business interests, for example—and would undercut the influence of ward bosses and machines.

James Phelan of San Francisco was an early structural reformer. Son of a pioneer banker, he attacked corruption in city government and won election as mayor in 1896. He then spearheaded adoption of a new charter strengthening the mayor's power and requiring citywide election of supervisors (equivalent to city council members).

Some municipal reformers proposed more fundamental changes in the structure of city government, notably the **commission system** and the **city manager plan**. Both reflected many progressives' distrust of political parties and desire for expertise and efficiency. The commission system was first tried in Galveston, Texas, after a devastating hurricane and tidal wave in 1900. Typically, in commission systems, the city's voters elected a few commissioners, each of whom managed a specific city function. The city manager plan—an adaptation of corporate decision-making structures—featured a professional city manager (similar to a corporate executive) appointed by an elected city council (similar to a corporate board of directors) to handle most municipal administration. In 1913 a serious flood prompted the citizens of Dayton, Ohio, to adopt a city manager plan, and other cities followed.

A few reformers went beyond structural reform to advocate social reforms. Hazen Pingree, a successful businessman, was elected mayor of Detroit in 1889. He took on the city's gas, electric, and streetcar companies for overcharging customers and providing poor service and responded to the depression of 1893 with community vegetable gardens and work projects for the unemployed. Samuel "Golden Rule" Jones, a successful manufacturer, won election as mayor of Toledo, Ohio, in 1897. He promoted free concerts, free public baths, childcare for working mothers, and the eight-hour workday for city employees. Phelan, Pingree, Jones, and a few others also advocated city ownership of utilities—the gas, water, electricity, and streetcar systems.

Reformers also produced early efforts at city planning by designating separate zones for residential, commercial, and industrial use (first in Los Angeles, in 1904–1908). By 1910, a few cities had created city planning departments. The emergence of **city planning** represents an important transition in thinking about government and the economy, for it emphasized expertise and presumed greater government control over use of private property.

The emergence of public health, mental health, social work, and other new professions produced efforts to use local government to solve the problems of an urban industrial society. The new professionals wanted to use scientific and social scientific knowledge to control social forces and thereby shape the future. New medical knowledge presented an opportunity to reduce disease on a significant scale. Public health emerged as a new medical field, combining the knowledge of the medical doctor with the insight of the social scientist and the skills of the corporate manager. New public health programs sought to wipe out **hookworm** in the South, **tuberculosis** in the slums, and sexually transmitted infections. Social workers often joined with public health professionals in efforts to use local government to improve urban health and safety.

■ **Meat Inspection Act** A 1906 law requiring federal inspection of meatpacking.

■ **municipal reform** Political activity intended to bring about changes in the structure or function of city government.

ward A division of a city or town, especially an electoral district, for administrative or representative purposes.

commission system System of city government in which executive and legislative powers are vested in a small elective board, each member of which supervises some aspect of city government.

city manager plan System of city government in which the city council hires a city manager who exercises broad executive authority.

city planning The policy of planning urban development by regulating land use.

In 1909, John D. Rockefeller, Sr., contributed $1 million to create the Rockefeller Sanitary Commission for the Eradication of Hookworm Disease. The commission launched a public-health campaign in eleven southern states, including education and medical dispensaries to provide treatment. This photograph shows the dispensary and some of the patients in Greenbrier, Tennessee, in May 1914.

Public education also attracted reformers. As university programs began graduating teachers and school administrators, these new professionals sought greater control over education. They often advocated greater centralization and professionalization in school administration by reducing the role of local, usually elected, **school boards** and replacing elected school superintendents with appointed professionals. Professional educators also began to use recently developed intelligence tests to identify children unable to perform at average levels, and then to isolate them in special classes.

Reforming State Government

As reformers launched changes in many cities and new professionals considered ways to improve society, **Robert M. La Follette** pushed Wisconsin to the forefront of reform. A Republican, he entered politics soon after graduating from the University of Wisconsin. He served three terms in Congress in the 1880s but found his political career blocked by the leader of the state Republican organization. He was firmly convinced of

the need for reform when he finally won election as governor in 1900.

Conservative legislators, mostly Republicans, defeated La Follette's proposals to regulate railroad rates and reduce the power of party bosses by replacing nominating conventions with the **direct primary**.

hookworm A parasite, formerly common in the South, that causes loss of strength.

tuberculosis An infectious disease that attacks the lungs; spread by unsanitary conditions and practices, such as spitting in public, it was common and often fatal in the nineteenth and early twentieth centuries and is reappearing today.

school board Policymakers who oversee the public schools of a local political unit.

■ **Robert M. La Follette** Progressive governor of Wisconsin; instituted direct primaries, tax reform, and anticorruption measures; later U.S. senator.

direct primary Election in which voters who identify with a specific party choose that party's candidates to run later in the general election.

La Follette threw himself into an energetic campaign to elect reformers to the state legislature. He earned the nickname "Fighting Bob" as he traveled the state to make his arguments. Most of his candidates won, and La Follette built a strong following among Wisconsin's farmers and urban wage earners, who reelected him in 1902 and 1904.

Under La Follette's leadership, Wisconsin won acclaim as a "laboratory of democracy." The state adopted the direct primary, regulated railroads, increased taxes on corporations, enacted a merit system for state employees, and restricted lobbyists. In many of his efforts, La Follette drew on the expertise of faculty members at the University of Wisconsin. These reforms, along with reliance on experts, came to be called the **Wisconsin Idea**. La Follette won election to the U.S. Senate in 1905 and remained a leading progressive voice there until his death in 1925.

La Follette's success prompted imitation elsewhere. In 1901 Iowans elected Albert B. Cummins governor, and Cummins launched a campaign against railroad corporations similar to La Follette's. He too went on to the Senate. Reformers won office in other states as well, but few matched La Follette's legislative and political success.

Progressivism came to California relatively late. Reformers accused the Southern Pacific Railroad of running a political machine that controlled the state by dominating the Republican Party. In 1910, **Hiram Johnson** ran for governor as a reformer and won. California progressives produced a volume of reform that rivaled that of Wisconsin—regulation of railroads and public utilities, restrictions on political parties, protection for labor, conservation, and woman suffrage. Johnson appointed union leaders to state positions and promoted measures to benefit working people. California progressives in both parties, however, condemned Asian immigrants and Asian Americans, and progressive Republicans in 1913 pushed through a law that prohibited Asian immigrants from owning land in California.

Like La Follette, Johnson moved on to national politics. In 1912 he was the vice-presidential candidate of the new Progressive Party. Reelected governor in 1914, he won election to the U.S. Senate in 1916 and served there until his death in 1945.

Southern progressivism took up concerns similar to those that motivated reformers elsewhere and blended them with that region's racial politics. Often inspired by northern models of reform and by

Hiram Johnson on the campaign trail. Johnson was elected governor of California in 1910, was Theodore Roosevelt's running mate in the 1912 presidential election, was reelected governor in 1914, and was elected to the US Senate in 1916.

Library of Congress.

northern reform organizations or philanthropists, southern progressives promoted school and public health reforms, limits on child labor, prohibition, and woman suffrage. Southern progressives could point to success in some states, especially on railroad regulation, prohibition, improved schools, and child labor laws. However, some southern reformers ran up against a long-standing insistence on local control. Given the South's one-party politics, the Democratic Party sometimes became the battleground between progressives and conservatives. Some southern reformers were also among the most demagogic advocates of white supremacy, pushing both corporate regulation and racist policies.

The Weakening of Parties and Rise of Organized Interest Groups

Like Wisconsin and California, other states moved to restrict political parties. Reformers charged that bosses and machines manipulated nominating conventions and public officials, and that bosses, in return

▣ **Wisconsin Idea** Program of reform sponsored by La Follette in Wisconsin.

▣ **Hiram Johnson** Governor of California; promoted many reforms, including regulation of railroads and measures to benefit labor.

for payoffs, used their influence on behalf of corporate interests. Articles by muckrakers and some highly publicized bribery trials convinced many voters that the reformers were correct. The mighty party organizations that had dominated politics during the nineteenth century came under attack along a broad front.

Progressives nearly everywhere proposed measures to enhance the power of individual voters and reduce the power of party organizations. State after state adopted the direct primary, and reformers sought to replace state patronage systems with the merit system. In many states, judgeships, school board seats, and educational offices were made nonpartisan.

A number of cities and states adopted the **initiative** and **referendum**. The initiative permitted voters to adopt a new law directly: if enough voters signed a petition, the proposed law would be voted on at the next election; if approved by the voters, it became law. The referendum permitted voters, through a petition, to reject a law adopted by the legislature. Oregon voters approved these reforms in 1902, and Oregon reformers used the initiative to create new laws, giving the initiative and referendum so much national attention that they were sometimes called the Oregon System. Some states also adopted the **recall**, permitting voters, through petitions, to initiate a special election to remove an elected official from office. The direct primary, initiative and referendum, and recall are known collectively as **direct democracy** because they remove intermediate steps between the voter and final political decisions.

With the switch to direct primaries and the weakening of party organizations, campaigns focused more on individual candidates and less on parties. Candidates now appealed directly to voters rather than to party leaders and convention delegates. Individual candidates' personal organizations and advertising replaced the armies of party retainers who had mobilized voters in the nineteenth century. At the same time, new voter registration procedures disqualified some voters, especially transient workers. Voter turnout fell. Ironically, the emergence of new channels for political participation created the illusion of an outpouring of public involvement in politics—but proportionally fewer voters actually cast ballots.

New avenues of political participation opened not only through direct democracy but also through organized interest groups that used politics to advance their agendas. Groups could cooperate when their political objectives coincided, as when merchants and farmers both favored regulation of railroad rates. Other times, they found themselves in conflict, perhaps over tariff policy. Within the many groups that advocated change, participants sometimes fought among themselves over which reform goals were most important and how to achieve them. Many groups adopted the tactics of the Anti-Saloon League—they ignored parties, pressured candidates to accept their group's position, and urged their members to vote only for approved candidates. In 1904, for example, the National Association of Manufacturers (NAM) targeted and defeated two prolabor members of Congress, one in the House and one in the Senate. The American Federation of Labor (AFL) responded in 1906 with a similar strategy and elected six union members to the House of Representatives.

Organized interest groups often focused on the legislative process. They retained **lobbyists** who urged legislators to support their group's position on pending legislation, reminded lawmakers of their group's electoral clout, and arranged campaign backing for those who supported their cause. Thus, as political parties became weaker, organized interest groups gained strength. Pushed one way by the AFL and the other by the NAM, under opposing pressure from the Anti-Saloon League and liquor interests, some elected officials came to see themselves less as loyal members of a political party and more as mediators among competing interest groups.

ROOSEVELT, TAFT, AND REPUBLICAN PROGRESSIVISM

☆ What did Theodore Roosevelt mean by a "Square Deal"? Do his accomplishments fit this description?

☆ How did Roosevelt's presidency change the federal role in the economy and alter the presidency itself?

When Theodore Roosevelt became president upon the death of William McKinley, he fascinated Americans—one visitor reported that the most exciting things he saw in the United States were "Niagara Falls and the President…both great wonders of nature!" "TR" quickly became recognizable everywhere, as cartoonists delighted in sketching his bristling mustache, thick glasses, and toothy grin.

initiative Procedure allowing voters to petition to have a new law placed on the ballot to be voted up or down, bypassing the legislature.

referendum Procedure whereby voters petition to have a legislative act submitted to the voters, who can overturn it.

recall Provision that permits voters, through petition, to hold a special election to remove an elected official from office.

■ **direct democracy** Provisions that permit voters to make political decisions directly, including the direct primary, initiative, referendum, and recall.

lobbyist A person who tries to influence the opinions of legislators or other public officials for or against a specific cause.

Roosevelt later wrote, "I cannot say that I entered the Presidency with any deliberately planned and far-reaching scheme of social betterment." Nonetheless, Americans soon saw Roosevelt as the embodiment of progressivism. In seven years, he changed the nation's domestic policies more than any president since Lincoln—and made himself a legend.

Roosevelt: Asserting the Power of the Presidency

Roosevelt was unlike most politicians of his day. He had inherited wealth and added to it from the many books he wrote. He saw politics as a duty to the nation, and he defined his politics in terms of character, morality, hard work, and patriotism. Uncertain whether to call himself a "radical conservative" or a "conservative radical," he considered politics the tool for forging an ethical and stable society. Confident in his own personal principles, Roosevelt did not hesitate to wield all the powers of the presidency. He especially liked to use the office as what he called a "bully pulpit" to publicize his concerns.

In his first message to Congress, in December 1901, Roosevelt sounded a theme that he repeated again and again: the growth of powerful corporations was "natural," but some exhibited "grave evils" that required correction. As Roosevelt later explained, "When I became President, the question as to the method by which the United States Government was to control the corporations was not yet important. The absolutely vital question was whether the Government had power to control them at all." He determined to establish that power.

The chief obstacle to regulating corporations was a Supreme Court decision, *United States v. E. C. Knight* (1895), preventing the Sherman Anti-Trust Act from being used against manufacturers. Roosevelt looked for an opportunity to challenge the *Knight* decision. In 1901, some of the nation's most prominent business leaders joined forces to form the Northern Securities Company, a railroad monopoly in the Northwest. The *Knight* case involved manufacturing; the Northern Securities Company provided interstate transportation. If any industry fit the constitutional language authorizing Congress to regulate interstate commerce, Roosevelt believed, the railroads did.

Roosevelt's attorney general filed suit against the Northern Securities Company for violating the Sherman Act. Wall Street leaders condemned Roosevelt's action, but most Americans applauded to see

the federal government finally challenge a powerful corporation. In 1904 the Supreme Court agreed that the Sherman Act could be applied to the Northern Securities Company and ordered it dissolved.

Bolstered by this confirmation of federal power, Roosevelt launched additional antitrust suits, but he used **trustbusting** selectively. Large corporations, he thought, were potentially beneficial. He thought regulation was preferable to breaking them up. Companies that met Roosevelt's standards of character and public service—and that acknowledged the power of the presidency—had no reason to fear antitrust action.

Roosevelt's willingness to act boldly was not limited to trustbusting. In time of crisis, he felt, the president should "do whatever the needs of the people demand, unless the Constitution or the laws explicitly forbid him to do it." In 1902, coal miners went on strike. Mine owners refused to negotiate with the union and also refused Roosevelt's request to submit the dispute to mediation. J. P. Morgan had an interest in some of the recalcitrant companies, and when Roosevelt's representative let Morgan know that Roosevelt was considering using the army to open the mines, the companies agreed to mediation. As Roosevelt illustrated in the coal miners' strike, he preferred to use his authority to produce what he called a **Square Deal**, fair treatment for all parties.

The Square Deal in Action: Creating the Regulatory State

Roosevelt's trustbusting and handling of the coal strike brought him great popularity. In 1903 Congress approved several measures he requested or endorsed: an act to speed up antitrust suits; creation of a cabinet-level Department of Commerce and Labor, including a bureau to investigate corporate activities; and the Elkins Act, which penalized railroads that paid rebates.

When Roosevelt sought election in 1904, he won by one of the largest margins up to that time—more than 56 percent of the popular vote. Elected in his own right, with a powerful demonstration of public approval, Roosevelt set out to secure regulation of the railroads, largest of the nation's big businesses.

Roosevelt and reformers in Congress wanted to regulate railroads' prices for both freight and passengers. In late 1905, he asked Congress for legislation to regulate railroad rates, open the financial records of railroads to government inspection, and increase federal authority in strikes involving interstate commerce. At the same time, the attorney general filed suits against some of the nation's largest corporations. Muckrakers (some of them Roosevelt's friends) fired off scathing exposés of railroads and attacks on Senate conservatives.

Although Roosevelt compromised a bit, he got most of what he wanted. On June 29, 1906, Congress

trustbusting Use of antitrust laws to prosecute and dissolve big businesses ("trusts").

■ **Square Deal** Theodore Roosevelt's term for his efforts to deal fairly with all.

The Reductive Fallacy

In both formal logic and historical analysis, the reductive fallacy occurs when one reduces complexity to simplicity, an error probably seen most often in explaining causation. Historians generally assume that complex events have multiple causes, but the very act of writing history forces historians to select some causes as most important and others as too trivial to require attention. This process of simplifying may become a fallacy, however, when the historian attributes a complex outcome to a single cause.

The role of Upton Sinclair's novel, *The Jungle*, in the passage of the Pure Food and Drug Act provides an example of the pitfall of focusing on a single cause. Some claim that the stomach-churning descriptions of meat preparation in this book prompted the passage of the Pure

Dr. Harvey W. Wiley, nicknamed "the Father of the Pure Food and Drug Act," probably around 1910. Wiley continued his campaign for pure foods and drugs throughout his life. In 1912, he left the federal government and took charge of the laboratories at *Good Housekeeping* magazine, where he continued his research and publicizing of dangerous additives to food and drugs.

Food and Drug Act. But did it? Or were a more complex set of circumstances at work?

Though Sinclair's novel had been published in serial form in a socialist newspaper between February and November 1905, it did not create a major public reaction until it appeared in book form on February 28, 1906. By then, the Senate had already passed a bill to require that food and drugs (not including meat) clearly state their ingredients. Such bills had been introduced before, but drew more attention and more support partly as a result of exposés of patent medicines and impure foods, published in such popular periodicals as *Collier's* and the *Ladies' Home Journal.* Dr. Harvey Wiley of the Bureau of Chemistry in the federal Department of Agriculture conducted extensive research on adulterated and mislabeled food and drugs over many years, and persistently prodded Congress to act. The American Medical Association and other organized interest groups also favored pure food and drug legislation. Even manufacturers of patent medicines realized, by mid-1905, that legislation was inevitable in the near future.

President Theodore Roosevelt, in a message to Congress on December 5, 1905, recommended action on pure food and drug legislation, and the Senate approved the bill on February 21 (before publication of *The Jungle* in book form) by a vote of 63 to 4. Newspaper accounts of the Senate vote said nothing about *The Jungle* playing any role. The House of Representatives did not take action on the bill until June, and the final House version of the bill was weaker than the Senate version. Though *The Jungle* had been in print for months and had generated a great public outcry, the newspaper reports on the House passage of the Pure Food and Drug Act make no mention of meat; instead the major discussion in the House seems to have focused on impure whiskey!

Because the Pure Food and Drug Act did not cover meat, and as a direct result of the revelations in *The Jungle*, Senator Albert Beveridge of Indiana, a progressive Republican, proposed separate legislation requiring federal inspection of meat. The Meat Inspection Act was given final approval in the House on the same day as the Pure Food and Drug Act. The Meat Inspection Act clearly did owe a great deal to *The Jungle,* but lumping the two bills together and asserting that passage of both resulted from the public outcry over *The Jungle* is an example of the reductive fallacy.

© Bettmann/Corbis.

Gifford Pinchot believed in careful management of natural resources, including the preservation of some wilderness areas and carefully planned use of other resources. Head of the Forestry Service under Roosevelt, Pinchot influenced Roosevelt's conservation and preservation policies.

passed the **Hepburn Act**, allowing the Interstate Commerce Commission (ICC) to establish maximum railroad rates and regulate other forms of transportation. The act also limited railroads' ability to issue free passes, a practice that reformers had long considered bribery. The next day, on June 30, Congress approved the Pure Food and Drug Act and the Meat Inspection Act. Taken together, these three measures can be considered the beginning of the federal regulatory state.

Regulating Natural Resources

An advocate for strenuous outdoor activities, Roosevelt took pride in establishing five national parks and some

fifty wildlife preserves to save what he called "beautiful and wonderful wild creatures whose existence was threatened by greed and wantonness." **Preservationists**, such as John Muir of the Sierra Club, applauded these actions and urged that such wilderness areas be kept forever safe from developers. Parks and wildlife refuges, however, were only part of Roosevelt's **conservation** agenda.

Roosevelt and **Gifford Pinchot**, the president's chief adviser on natural resources, believed conservation required not only preservation of wilderness but also carefully planned use of resources. Trained in scientific forestry in Europe, Pinchot combined scientific expertise with a managerial outlook. He and Roosevelt withdrew large tracts of federal timber and grazing land from public sale or use. By careful management of these lands, they hoped to provide for the needs of both the present and the future. Roosevelt removed nearly 230 million acres from public sale, more than quadrupling the land under federal protection.

Roosevelt strongly supported the Reclamation Act of 1902, which set aside proceeds from federal land sales in sixteen western states to finance irrigation projects. The act established a commitment later greatly expanded: the federal government would construct western dams, canals, and other facilities to support agriculture in areas of scant rainfall. Thus water,

■ **Hepburn Act** A 1906 law authorizing the Interstate Commerce Commission to set maximum railroad rates and regulate other forms of transportation.

preservationist One who advocates reserving natural areas so as to protect them against human disturbance.

conservation The careful management of natural resources so that they yield the greatest benefit to present generations while maintaining their potential to meet the needs of future generations.

■ **Gifford Pinchot** Head of the Forestry Service from 1898 to 1910; promoted conservation and urged careful planning in the use of resources.

WHITE HOUSE

G.O.P.

TAFT

·HE'S·A·
·GOOD·THING·
·PUSH·HIM·ALONG·

Collection of David J.and Janice L. Frent.

This postcard depicts Roosevelt, in command of the Republican Party, persuading his friend William Howard Taft to run for president in 1908. Taft was not eager for that office, but Roosevelt convinced him to seek it. Taft was elected but proved a disappointment to Roosevelt.

perhaps the most important natural resource in the West, came to be managed. Far from preserving the western landscape, federal water projects profoundly transformed it, vividly illustrating the vast difference between Muir's goal of preserving wilderness and Pinchot's careful management of resources.

Taft's Troubles

When Roosevelt won the election of 1904, he announced he would not seek reelection in 1908. He remained immensely popular, however, and virtually named his successor. Republicans nominated William Howard Taft. A Yale graduate and former federal judge, Taft had been governor of the Philippines before joining Roosevelt's cabinet in 1904.

William Jennings Bryan, leader of the progressive wing of the Democratic Party, won his party's nomination for the third time. Roosevelt's popularity and strong endorsement of Taft carried the day. Taft won 52 percent of the vote, and Republicans kept control of the Senate and the House. Roosevelt turned over the presidency to Taft, then set off to hunt big game in Africa.

Taft's legalistic approach often appeared timid when compared with Roosevelt's boldness. But Taft's attorney general initiated some ninety antitrust suits in four years, twice as many as during Roosevelt's seven years. And Taft approved legislation to strengthen regulatory agencies.

Roosevelt had left Taft a Republican Party divided between progressives and conservatives. Those divisions grew, and Taft increasingly sided with the conservatives. In 1909, he called on Congress to reform the tariff. The resulting Payne-Aldrich Tariff retained high rates on most imports, but Taft signed it despite protests from Republican progressives. Republican progressives also attacked the high-handed exercise of power by Joseph Cannon, the conservative Speaker of the House of Representatives. Taft first favored the progressives, then backed off and made his peace with Cannon. Republican progressives then joined Democrats in a "revolt against Cannonism" that reduced the Speaker's powers.

A dispute over conservation further damaged Republican unity. Gifford Pinchot, still head of the Forest Service, charged that Taft's secretary of the interior, Richard A. Ballinger, had weakened the conservation program. Taft supported Ballinger; when Pinchot persisted, Taft fired him. By 1912, when Taft faced reelection, the Republican Party was in serious disarray, and he faced opposition from most progressive Republicans.

"CARRY A BIG STICK": ROOSEVELT, TAFT, AND WORLD AFFAIRS

☆ *What were Roosevelt's objectives for the United States in world affairs?*

☆ *How did Roosevelt reshape American foreign policy?*

Theodore Roosevelt not only remolded the presidency and established new federal regulatory authority, he also significantly expanded America's role in world affairs. Few presidents have had so great an influence.

He once expressed his fondness for what he called a West African proverb: "Speak softly and carry a big stick; you will go far." As president, however, Roosevelt seldom spoke softly. Well read in history and current events, Roosevelt entered the presidency with definite ideas on the place of the United States in the world.

As he advised Congress in 1902, "The increasing interdependence and complexity of international political and economic relations render it incumbent on all civilized and orderly powers to insist on the proper policing of the world." The United States, Roosevelt made clear, stood ready to do its share of "proper policing."

TOWARD A MORE PERFECT UNION

The Sixteenth and Seventeenth Amendments

Reformers long advocated a graduated income tax as the fairest means of raising federal revenues. The **Sixteenth Amendment**, permitting a federal income tax, was proposed in 1909 and ratified in 1913, with strong support in the West and opposition centered in the northeast. Without the income tax, it is impossible to imagine the many activities the federal government has since assumed—from vast military expenditures to social welfare to support for the arts. Since the 1930s, the income tax has sometimes been an instrument of social policy, by which the federal government has redistributed income.

The **Seventeenth Amendment**, proposed in 1912 and ratified early in 1913, changed the method of electing U.S. senators. Previously, senators were chosen by state legislatures; in many states, U.S. Senators devoted so much attention to the election of members of the state legislature that the Senator became known as "boss" of the state party organization. Reformers long claimed that corporate influence and outright bribery often swayed state legislatures, making the Senate highly conservative. The Seventeenth Amendment, an aspect of direct democracy, provided that U.S. Senators were to be elected directly by voters.

□ **Sixteenth Amendment** (1913) Constitutional amendment authorizing the federal government to establish an income tax.

□ **Seventeenth Amendment** (1913) Constitutional amendment requiring election of U.S. senators directly by the voters of each state, rather than by state legislatures.

□ **Philippe Bunau-Varilla** Chief planner of the Panamanian revolt against Colombia and minister to the United States from the new Republic of Panama.

□ **Hay–Bunau-Varilla Treaty** A 1903 treaty with Panama that granted the United States sovereignty over the Canal Zone in return for $10 million plus annual rent.

□ **Roosevelt Corollary** A 1904 extension of the Monroe Doctrine announced by Theodore Roosevelt, in which he proclaimed the right of the United States to police the Caribbean area.

Taking Panama

While McKinley was president, American diplomats began efforts to create a canal through Central America. Many people had shared the dream of such a passage between the Atlantic and Pacific. A French company actually began construction in the late 1870s, but abandoned the project when the task proved too great.

During the Spanish-American War, the battleship *Oregon* took over two months to steam from the West Coast around South America to join the rest of the fleet off Cuba. A canal would have cut the time to three weeks. McKinley pronounced an American-controlled canal "indispensable."

Experts identified two possible locations, Nicaragua and Panama (then part of Colombia). The Panama route was shorter, and the French company had completed some work there. **Philippe Bunau-Varilla**—formerly chief engineer for the French project, now a major stockholder—did his utmost to sell the French company's interests to the United States. Building through Panama, however, meant overcoming formidable mountains and fever-ridden swamps. Previous studies had preferred Nicaragua, where geography posed fewer natural obstacles and much of the route lay through Lake Nicaragua.

In 1902, shortly before Congress was to choose between the two routes, Bunau-Varilla distributed to senators a Nicaraguan postage stamp showing a smoldering volcano looming over a lake. Bunau-Varilla's lobbying—and his stamps—reinforced efforts by prominent Republican senators. The Senate approved the route through the Colombian state of Panama.

Negotiations with Colombia bogged down. When the Colombian government offered to accept limitations on its sovereignty in return for more money, an outraged Roosevelt called the offer "pure bandit morality." Bunau-Varilla and his associates then encouraged and financed a revolution in Panama. Roosevelt ordered U.S. warships to prevent Colombian troops from crushing the uprising. The revolution quickly succeeded, Panama declared its independence, and the United States immediately extended diplomatic recognition. Bunau-Varilla became Panama's minister to the United States and promptly signed a treaty giving the United States much the same arrangement earlier rejected by Colombia.

The **Hay–Bunau-Varilla Treaty** (1903) granted the United States perpetual control over the Canal Zone, a strip of Panamanian territory 10 miles wide, for

$10 million initially and annual rent of $250,000; it also made Panama the second American protectorate (Cuba was first; see Map 19.1). The United States purchased the assets of the French company and began construction. Roosevelt considered the canal his crowning deed in foreign affairs. "When nobody else could or would exercise efficient authority, I exercised it," he wrote in his *Autobiography* (1913). He always denied any part in the revolution but once bluntly claimed, "I took the canal zone."

Construction proved difficult. Over 40 miles long, the canal took ten years to build and cost nearly $400 million. Completed in 1914, just as World War I began, it was considered one of the world's great engineering feats.

Making the Caribbean an American Lake

With canal construction under way, American policymakers considered how to protect it. Roosevelt determined to establish American dominance in the Caribbean and Central America, where the many harbors might permit a foreign power to prepare a strike against the canal or even the Gulf Coast of the United States. Acquisition of Puerto Rico, protectorates over Cuba and Panama, and naval facilities in all three locations as well as on the Gulf Coast made the United States a powerful presence.

However, several Caribbean nations had borrowed large amounts of money from European bankers, raising the prospect of intervention to secure loan payments. In 1902, Britain and Germany declared a blockade of Venezuela over such debts. In 1904, when several European nations hinted they might intervene in the Dominican Republic, Roosevelt presented what became known as the **Roosevelt Corollary** to the Monroe Doctrine. He warned European nations against any intervention in the Western Hemisphere. If intervention by what he termed "some civilized nation" became necessary in the Caribbean or Central America to correct "chronic wrongdoing," Roosevelt insisted that the United States would handle it, acting as "an international police power."

Roosevelt acted forcefully to establish his new policy. In 1905 the Dominican Republic agreed that the United States would collect customs (taxes on

MAP 19.1 The United States and the Caribbean, 1898–1917

Between 1898 and 1917, the United States expanded into the Caribbean by acquiring possessions and establishing protectorates. As a result, the United States became the dominant power in the region.

© Cengage Learning

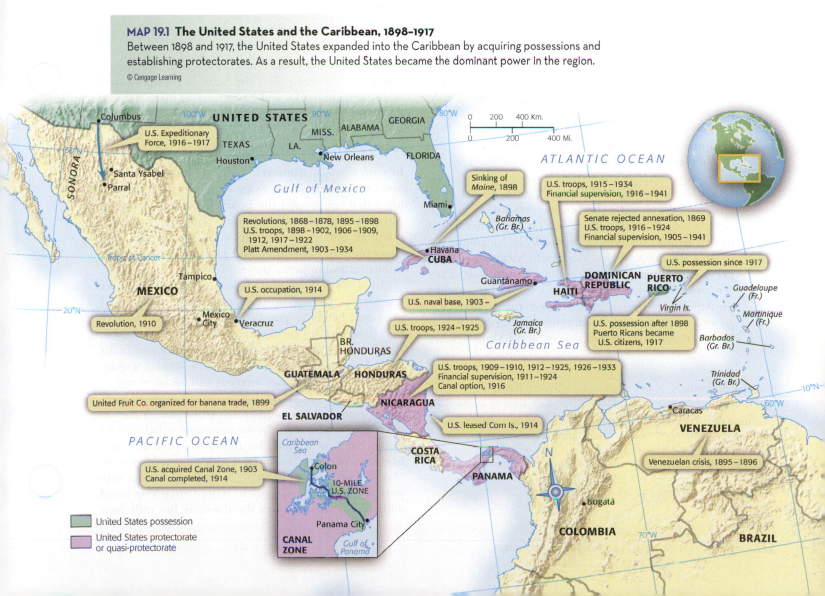

THE BIG STICK IN THE CARIBBEAN SEA

Theodore Roosevelt, in his 1904 Corollary to the Monroe Doctrine, asserted that the United States was dominant in the Caribbean. Here a cartoonist capitalized on Roosevelt's boyish nature, depicting the Caribbean as Roosevelt's pond.

The Granger Collection, New York-0008504.

imports, the major source of governmental revenue) and supervise government expenditures, including debt repayment, thereby becoming the third U.S. protectorate.

Roosevelt's successor, William Howard Taft, continued to expand American domination in the Caribbean. The Taft administration encouraged investments there, hoping that American investments would block investment by other nations and also stabilize and develop the Caribbean economies. Taft supported such "**dollar diplomacy**" (as his critics called it) throughout the region, especially in Nicaragua.

In 1912 Taft sent U.S. Marines to Nicaragua to suppress a rebellion against President Adolfo Díaz. They remained after the turmoil settled, ostensibly to guard the American legation but actually to prop up the Díaz government—making Nicaragua the fourth U.S. protectorate. A treaty was drafted giving the United States

responsibility for collecting customs, but the Senate rejected it. At that point, the State Department, several American banks, and Nicaragua set up a **customs receivership** through the banks.

Roosevelt and Eastern Asia

In eastern Asia, Roosevelt built on the Open Door notes and American participation in the international force that suppressed the Boxer Rebellion. Aware of Alfred Thayer Mahan's warnings that Japan posed a potential danger in the Pacific, Roosevelt was both concerned and hopeful about Japan's rise as a major industrial and imperial power.

In 1904 Russia and Japan went to war over **Manchuria**, part of northeastern China. Russia had pressured China to grant so many concessions there that it seemed to be turning into a Russian colony. Russia seemed also to have designs on Korea, nominally an independent kingdom. Japan saw Russian expansion as a threat to its own interests and declared war.

Roosevelt concluded that American interests were best served by reducing Russian influence in the region. He hoped thereby to maintain a balance of power. Such a balance, he thought, would be most likely to preserve nominal Chinese sovereignty in Manchuria. Early in the war, he indicated some support for Japan. The Japanese scored smashing naval and military victories over the Russians, but with their

▪ **dollar diplomacy** Name applied by critics to the Taft administration's policy of supporting U.S. investments abroad.

customs receivership An agreement whereby one nation takes over the collection of another nation's customs and exercises some control over that nation's expenditures of customs receipts, thus limiting the autonomy of the nation in receivership.

Manchuria A region of northeastern China.

"The Nations Pride"

This picture was issued as a penny postcard, expressing the nation's pride in the "Great White Fleet." The Post Office approved penny postcards in 1902, and the years 1905–1915 are sometimes considered the "golden age" for penny postcards. The one-penny price for postage made them highly affordable, and the wide variety of subjects available made them popular.

Collection of Picture Research Consultants and Archives.

resources running low, they asked Roosevelt to act as mediator. The president agreed, concerned that a Japanese victory would prove as dangerous as Russian expansion. The peace conference took place in Portsmouth, New Hampshire. The **Treaty of Portsmouth** (1905) recognized Japan's dominance in Korea and gave Japan the southern half of Sakhalin Island and Russian concessions in southern Manchuria. Russia kept its railroad in northern Manchuria. China remained responsible for civil authority in Manchuria. For his mediation, Roosevelt received the 1906 Nobel Peace Prize.

In 1906–1907, Roosevelt mediated another dispute. The San Francisco school board ordered students of Japanese parentage to attend the city's segregated Chinese school. The Japanese government protested this as a national insult, and Japanese newspapers even hinted at war. Roosevelt convinced the school officials to withdraw the order in return for his commitment to seek restrictions on Japanese immigration. He then negotiated the so-called **gentlemen's agreement** by which Japan agreed to limit the departure of laborers to the United States.

In 1908 the American and Japanese governments further agreed to respect each other's territorial possessions (the Philippines and Hawai'i for the United States; Korea, Formosa, and southern Manchuria for Japan) and to honor as well "the independence and integrity of China" and the Open Door.

The United States and World Affairs, 1901–1913

Before the 1890s, the United States had few clear or consistent foreign-policy commitments or objectives. By 1905, the Philippines, Hawai'i, Puerto Rico, eastern Samoa, and the Canal Zone were highly visible evidence of a dramatic change in America's role in world affairs.

Central to the new role was a large, modern navy, without which every other commitment was merely a moral pronouncement. Roosevelt was so proud of the navy that in 1907 he dispatched sixteen battleships—painted white to signal their peaceful intent—on an around-the-world tour. Though Roosevelt claimed that he sent the Great White Fleet "to impress the American people," he was clearly interested in impressing other nations, especially Japan, and in demonstrating that the American navy could move quickly to distant parts of the globe.

The need to protect the canal led the United States to dominate the Caribbean and Central America, but the new American role also focused on the Pacific. As Mahan and others pointed out, the Pacific Ocean was a likely theater of twentieth-century conflict. Thus commercial considerations, such as the China trade, coincided with naval strategy and led the United States to acquire possessions at key locations in the Pacific.

American policymakers' new vision seemed to divide nations into broad categories: the "civilized" nations, and those that Roosevelt described, at various times, as "barbarous," "impotent," or unable to meet their obligations. When dealing with "civilized" countries—the European powers, Japan, the large, stable nations of Latin America, Canada, Australia, New Zealand—American diplomats focused on realizing mutual objectives, especially arbitration of disputes. In eastern Asia, McKinley, Roosevelt, and Taft

■ **Treaty of Portsmouth** A 1905 treaty, mediated by Roosevelt at a conference in Portsmouth, New Hampshire, ending the Russo-Japanese War.

gentlemen's agreement An agreement rather than a formal treaty; in this case, Japan agreed in 1907 to limit Japanese emigration to the United States.

In the Wider World

The Scramble for the Last Colonies

As the United States was consolidating its control over the Philippines and establishing its dominance in the Caribbean, other nations were scrambling for the last areas that could be claimed as colonies.

Britain and France had constructed worldwide empires during the eighteenth and nineteenth centuries, and the Spanish and Portuguese empires were even older, though both lost their Latin American colonies in the nineteenth century. The Russian empire gained control over Central Asia during the nineteenth century and took concessions in northeastern China in the 1890s. Germany was unified as a nation only in 1871, and did not embark on colonialism until the 1880s. By then, little was left—a few areas in Africa and the Pacific and some concessions in China. Japan, too, came late to the scramble for colonies, taking Taiwan from China in the Sino-Japanese War (1894) along with parts of the Chinese mainland and Korea (previously independent), and fighting the Russo-Japanese War (1905) over control of Manchuria.

looked to a balance of power among the contending "civilized" powers as most likely to realize the American objective of maintaining the "open door" for American commerce in China.

A conviction was widespread that arbitration was the appropriate means to settle disputes among "civilized" countries. An international conference in 1899 created a **Permanent Court of Arbitration** in the Netherlands, which provided neutral arbitrators for international disputes. Roosevelt and Taft both tried to negotiate arbitration treaties with major powers, but the Senate refused, fearing arbitration might diminish the Senate's role in foreign relations.

The United States and Great Britain repeatedly used arbitration to settle disputes. Throughout the late nineteenth and early twentieth centuries, American relations with Britain improved steadily, mostly due to British initiatives. The more Germany expanded its army and navy, the more British policymakers worked to improve relations with the United States, the only nation besides Britain with a navy comparable to Germany's. During America's war with Spain, Britain alone among the major European powers sided with the United States. Britain reduced its naval forces in the Caribbean, thereby signaling that it not only accepted American dominance there but now depended on the United States to protect British holdings in the region.

■ **Permanent Court of Arbitration** Organization of about fifty member nations, created in the Netherlands in 1899 for the purpose of peacefully resolving international conflicts; also known as the Hague Court from its location.

■ **New Nationalism** Reform program that Theodore Roosevelt advocated before and during his unsuccessful bid to regain the presidency in 1912.

WILSON AND DEMOCRATIC PROGRESSIVISM

★ *What choices confronted American voters in the presidential election of 1912?*

★ *How did Wilson's views on reform evolve from 1912 through 1916 and how did his administration change the federal government's role in the economy?*

In 1912, Americans actively and seriously debated their future. The three presidential nominees were well educated and highly literate. Roosevelt and Wilson had written respected books on American history and politics. They approached politics with a sense of destiny and purpose, and they talked frankly to the American people about their ideas for the future.

Debating the Future: The Election of 1912

As Taft watched the Republican Party unravel, Theodore Roosevelt was hunting in Africa and then hobnobbing with European leaders. When he returned in 1910, he undertook a speaking tour and proposed a program of reform he labeled the **New Nationalism**. In the 1910 congressional elections, Republicans fared badly, plagued by intraparty divisions and an economic downturn. For the first time since 1892, Democrats won a majority in the House of Representatives. Many Republican progressives now looked to Robert La Follette to wrest the Republican nomination from Taft in 1912. Roosevelt had lost confidence in Taft, but he considered La Follette too radical. Finally, in February 1912, Roosevelt announced he would seek the Republican presidential nomination.

Thirteen states held direct primaries to choose delegates to the national nominating convention.

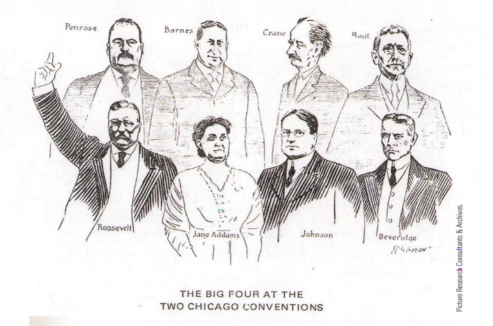

THE BIG FOUR AT THE TWO CHICAGO CONVENTIONS

This drawing from 1912 contrasts the dominant figures in the Republican nominating convention in the back row, all conservative reputed "bosses" whom the Progressives blamed for Taft's nomination, with the dominant figures of the Progressive nominating convention, former president Theodore Roosevelt, Jane Addams, California governor Hiram Johnson, and U.S. Senator Albert Beveridge.

There, Roosevelt won 278 delegates to 48 for Taft and 36 for La Follette. Taft, however, had the advantages of an incumbent president in control of the party machinery. Many states sent rival delegations to the Republican convention, one pledged to Taft and one to Roosevelt. Taft's supporters controlled the **credentials committee** and gave most contested seats to Taft delegates. Roosevelt's supporters stormed out, complaining that Taft was stealing the nomination. The remaining delegates nominated Taft on the first ballot.

Roosevelt refused to accept defeat. "We stand at Armageddon," he thundered, invoking the biblical prophecy of a final battle between good and evil. "And," he continued, "we battle for the Lord." His supporters quickly formed the Progressive Party, nicknamed the **Bull Moose Party** after Roosevelt's boast that he was "as fit as a bull moose." They issued a platform based on the New Nationalism, including tariff reduction, regulation of corporations, a minimum wage, prohibition of child labor, woman suffrage, the initiative, referendum, and recall, and more. Women were prominent at the Progressive convention and helped draft the platform—especially the sections dealing with social and industrial justice.

Democrats were overjoyed, certain that the Republican split provided their best chance at the presidency in twenty years. Their nomination was hotly contested, and they took forty-six ballots to nominate Woodrow Wilson. Their platform attacked monopolies, favored limits on corporate campaign contributions, and called for tariff reductions. Wilson labeled his program the **New Freedom**.

Much of the campaign focused on Roosevelt and Wilson. Roosevelt argued that the behavior of corporations was the problem, not their size, and that regulation was the solution. Wilson followed the lead of **Louis Brandeis** and depicted monopoly itself as the problem. Breaking up monopolies and restoring competition, Wilson argued, would bring consumers better products and lower prices. Wilson also argued that monopolies facing regulation would seek to control the regulator—the federal government—and that only antitrust actions could protect democracy from this threat. Taft was the most conservative of the candidates. Eugene V. Debs, the Socialist candidate, rejected both regulation and antitrust actions and argued for government ownership of monopolies.

credentials committee Party convention committee that settles disputes arising when rival delegations from the same state demand to be seated.

■ **Bull Moose Party** Popular name given to the Progressive Party in 1912.

■ **New Freedom** Reform program that Woodrow Wilson advocated during his 1912 presidential campaign, including reducing tariffs and prosecuting trusts.

■ **Louis Brandeis** Lawyer and reformer who opposed monopolies and defended individual rights; in 1916 he became the first Jewish justice on the Supreme Court.

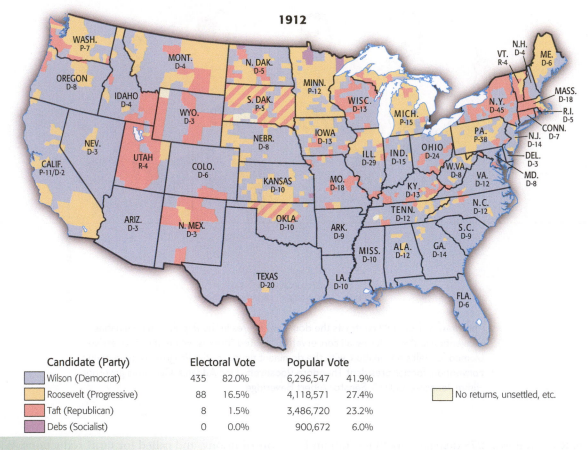

1912

Candidate (Party)	Electoral Vote		Popular Vote	
Wilson (Democrat)	435	82.0%	6,296,547	41.9%
Roosevelt (Progressive)	88	16.5%	4,118,571	27.4%
Taft (Republican)	8	1.5%	3,486,720	23.2%
Debs (Socialist)	0	0.0%	900,672	6.0%

No returns, unsettled, etc.

MAP 19.2 Election of 1912, by Counties
The presidential election of 1912 was complicated by the campaign of former president Theodore Roosevelt, running as a Progressive. Roosevelt's campaign split the usual Republican vote without taking away much of the usual Democratic vote. © Cengage Learning.

The real contest was between Roosevelt and Wilson. In the end, Wilson received nearly all the usual Democratic vote and won with 42 percent of the total. Democrats also won sizable majorities in both houses of Congress. Roosevelt and Taft split the traditional Republican vote, 27 percent for Roosevelt and 23 percent for Taft. Debs, with 6 percent, placed first in a few counties and city precincts (see Map 19.2).

Wilson and Reform, 1913–1916

Born in Virginia in 1856, Woodrow Wilson grew up in the South during the Civil War and Reconstruction. His father, a Presbyterian minister, taught him lessons in morality and responsibility that remained with him his entire life. Wilson earned a Ph.D. in political science from Johns Hopkins University, and his first book, *Congressional Government*, analyzed federal lawmaking. A professor at Princeton University after 1890, he became president of Princeton in 1902.

In 1910, conservatives who controlled the New Jersey Democratic Party picked Wilson to run for governor because of his reputation as a conservative and a good public speaker. He won the election but shocked his party's leaders by embracing reform. As governor, he led the legislature to adopt several progressive measures and thereby won support from many Democratic progressives for the 1912 presidential nomination.

Wilson firmly believed in party government and an active role for the president in policymaking. He wanted to work closely with Democrats in Congress; he succeeded to such an extent that, like Roosevelt, he changed the nature of the presidency. Confident in his oratorical skills, he became the first president since John Adams to address Congress in person.

Wilson first tackled tariff reform, arguing that high tariff rates helped breed monopolies by reducing competition. Despite opposition from manufacturers, Congress passed the **Underwood Tariff** in October 1913, establishing the most significant reductions since the Civil War. To offset federal revenue losses,

Underwood Tariff A 1913 law that substantially reduced tariffs and made up for the lost revenue by imposing a graduated income tax.

The Federal Reserve Act

The Federal Reserve Act stands as the most important domestic act of the Wilson administration, because it still provides the basic framework for the nation's banking and monetary system. Though the original act of 1913 has been amended many times, the Federal Reserve System remains an independent entity within the federal government, having both public purposes and private aspects.

Congress has charged the Federal Reserve to carry out the nation's monetary policy, including regulating the money supply and interest rates to accomplish the goals of maximum employment, stable prices, and moderate long-term interest rates. The Federal Reserve also supervises and regulates banks and financial institutions to ensure their safety and soundness. (Chapter 22's It Matters Today feature, page 600, discusses the Fed's role in recent economic events.)

- Look at a basic macroeconomics textbook for its description of the role of the Federal Reserve. How does that text present its functions? How does "the Fed" seek to control inflation?
- Look at an online newspaper and find the most recent story about the Federal Reserve Board or the chairman of "the Fed." What does the story imply about the significance of the Federal Reserve for American business?

Congress implemented the income tax recently authorized by the Sixteenth Amendment.

Wilson and the Democrats next took up banking. The national banking system dated to 1863, and periodic economic problems—most recently, a panic in 1907—had demonstrated the system's shortcomings: it had no real center to provide direction and no way to adjust the money supply (the amount of money available in the economy as cash and in bank accounts). A congressional investigation also revealed the concentration of great power in the hands of a few investment bankers. Conservatives, led by Carter Glass of Virginia, joined with bankers in proposing a more centralized system with minimal federal regulation. Progressive Democrats, especially William Jennings Bryan (now Wilson's secretary of state) and Louis Brandeis, favored strong federal regulation. The result was a compromise.

In December 1913, Wilson approved the **Federal Reserve Act**, establishing twelve regional Federal Reserve Banks. These were "bankers' banks," institutions where commercial banks kept their reserves. All national banks were required to belong to the Federal Reserve System. The participating banks owned all the stock in their regional Federal Reserve Bank and named two-thirds of its board of directors; the president named the other third. Regional banks were to be regulated and supervised by the Federal Reserve Board, a new federal agency with members chosen by the president. The Federal Reserve system was unquestionably the most important single measure to come out of the Wilson administration.

In 1913, Congress also fulfilled a Democratic campaign promise by creating a separate cabinet-level Department of Labor. In 1914, Congress passed the **Clayton Antitrust Act**, which prohibited specified business practices, including **interlocking directorates** among large companies that inhibited competition; it also exempted farmers' organizations and unions from antitrust prosecution. The act did little, however, to break up big corporations. Instead of breaking up big business, Wilson now moved closer to Roosevelt's position favoring regulation. Wilson also supported passage of the **Federal Trade Commission Act** (1914), a regulatory measure to prevent unfair methods of competition.

During his first year in office, Wilson drew sharp criticism from some northern social reformers when his appointees (especially southern Democrats) initiated racial segregation in several federal agencies. A southerner himself, Wilson clearly approved of

■ **Federal Reserve Act** A 1913 law establishing twelve regional Federal Reserve Banks to hold the cash reserves of commercial banks and a Federal Reserve Board to regulate aspects of banking.

■ **Clayton Antitrust Act** A 1914 law banning monopolistic business practices such as price fixing and interlocking directorates; also exempted farmers' organizations and unions from antitrust prosecutions.

interlocking directorates Situation in which the same individuals sit on the boards of directors of various companies in one industry.

■ **Federal Trade Commission Act** A 1914 law outlawing unfair methods of competition in interstate commerce and creating a commission appointed by the president to investigate illegal business practices.

segregation and was surprised at the swell of protest, not just from African Americans but also from some white progressives in the North and Midwest. He never designated a change in policy, but the process of segregating federal facilities slowed significantly and he resisted his party's most extreme racists.

Though many progressives applauded Wilson for tariff reform, the Federal Reserve Act, and the Clayton Act, some progressives criticized his appointees to the Federal Trade Commission and the Federal Reserve Board as being too sympathetic to business and banking. Moreover, Wilson opposed federal action to prohibit child labor as unconstitutional, and he questioned the need to amend the Constitution for woman suffrage. As the 1916 presidential election approached, Wilson reconsidered. In 1912 he had received less than half of the popular vote and had won the White House only because the Republicans split. Now Wilson joined progressives in pushing measures intended to secure his claim as the true voice of progressivism and to capture progressive voters.

In January 1916, Wilson nominated Louis Brandeis for the Supreme Court. Brandeis's reputation as a staunch progressive and critic of business aroused intense opposition from conservatives, but he was confirmed. Wilson followed with support for several reform measures: credit facilities for farmers, workers' compensation for federal employees, and the prohibition of child labor. Under threat of a railroad strike, Congress passed and Wilson signed the Adamson Act, securing an eight-hour workday for railroad employees.

The presidential election of 1916 played out against the background of war in Europe (covered in the next chapter). Wilson's shift toward social reform helped solidify his support among progressives. His support for organized labor earned him backing among unionists, and labor's votes probably ensured his victory in a few states. Where women could vote, many of them preferred Wilson, probably because he backed issues of interest to women, such as outlawing child labor and keeping the nation out of war. In a very close election, Wilson won with 49 percent of the popular vote to 46 percent for Charles Evans Hughes, a progressive Republican.

NEW PATTERNS IN CULTURAL EXPRESSION

★ *Did developments in cultural expression draw more from American sources or European sources?*

★ *How did social and technological changes contribute to new patterns in mass entertainment?*

The changes sweeping American society also affected cultural expression. Shortly after 1900, the director of the nation's leading art museum, the Metropolitan Museum of New York, observed "a state of unrest" in art, literature, and music. Unrest meant change, and Americans at that time witnessed dramatic changes in all the arts—many of them directly influenced by the new urban industrial society, and some of them reflecting the concerns of progresssives.

Realism, Impressionism, and Ragtime

At the turn of the century, American novelists increasingly turned to a realistic—and sometimes critical—portrayal of life. The towering figure of the era remained **Mark Twain** (pen name of Samuel L. Clemens), whose novel *The Adventures of Huckleberry Finn* (1885) may be read at many levels, from a nostalgic account of boyhood to profound social satire. In this masterpiece, Twain reproduced the everyday speech of unschooled whites and blacks, poked fun at social pretensions, scorned the Old South myth, and challenged racially biased attitudes toward African Americans. Twain continued as an important social commentator until his death in 1910.

The novels of William Dean Howells and Henry James, in contrast, presented restrained, realistic, and sometimes unsympathetic portrayals of upper-class men and women. Kate Chopin sounded feminist themes in *The Awakening* (1899), dealing with repression of a woman's desires. Stephen Crane, Theodore Dreiser, and Frank Norris showed the influence of Émile Zola, a prominent French novelist, as they sharpened the critical edge of fiction. In Crane's *Maggie: A Girl of the Streets* (1893), urban squalor, alcohol, and callous men drive a young woman to prostitution. Norris's *The Octopus* (1901) portrayed the abusive power of a railroad over farmers.

As American literature moved toward realism and social criticism during these years, John Sloan, Robert Henri, and other painters provided an artistic counterpart to critical realism in literature with their portrayals of everyday urban life, including working-class saloons and prize fights. Their unswerving focus on ordinary urban life led critics to label them the **Ash Can School**. Other painters looked for inspiration to French **impressionism**, which emphasized less an exact reproduction of the world and more the artist's impression of it. Mary Cassatt was the only American—and one of only two women—to rank among the leaders of impressionism, but she lived and painted mostly in France. Among prominent impressionists working in the United States was Childe Hassam, who often depicted pleasant urban scenes.

In 1913 the most widely publicized art exhibit of the era permitted Americans to view works by the most innovative European painters. Known as the Armory Show for its opening in New York's National Guard Armory (it was later displayed in Chicago

Reunion des musees Nationaux / Art Resource, New York.

Mary Cassatt created this portrait of a mother and child in 1897. Cassatt was the only American woman to have a major role in French impressionism; some of her paintings were included in the Armory Show of 1913. Unlike other leading impressionists, her work often focused on women and children.

and Boston), the exhibit presented works by Pablo Picasso, Henri Matisse, Marcel Duchamp, Wassily Kandinsky, and others. Sophisticated critics and popular newspapers alike dismissed them as either insane or anarchists. One reviewer scornfully suggested that Duchamp's cubist painting *Nude Descending a Staircase* be retitled "explosion in a shingle factory." The abstract, modernist style, however, became firmly established by the 1920s.

As with painting, many aspects of American music derived from European models, notably John Philip Sousa, the most popular American composer of the day, best known for his stirring patriotic marches. More significant in creating a uniquely American form of music, was the African American composer Scott Joplin. Born in Texas, Joplin had formal instruction in the piano, then traveled through black communities from New Orleans to Chicago where he encountered ragtime music. He soon began to write his own. In 1899 he published "Maple Leaf Rag" and quickly soared to fame as the leading ragtime composer in the country. Though condemned by some as vulgar, ragtime contributed significantly to the later development of jazz (discussed in Chapter 21).

Mass Entertainment in the Early Twentieth Century

By 1900, changes in transportation (the railroads) and communication (telegraph and telephone) combined with increased leisure time among the middle class and some skilled workers to foster new forms of entertainment.

Traveling dramatic and musical troupes had long entertained some Americans, but now booking agencies could schedule such groups into nearly every corner of the country. Traveling performers offered everything from Shakespeare to slapstick, from opera to melodrama.

Other traveling spectacles also took advantage of improved transportation and communication to establish regular circuits, including circuses and Wild West shows. A less sensational traveling show but one of the most popular was the Chautauqua, a blend of inspirational oratory, educational lectures, and entertainment.

During the late nineteenth century, a quite different form of mass entertainment appeared—professional baseball. Teams traveled by train from city to city, and urban rivalries built loyalty among fans. In 1876 team owners formed the National League as a cartel to dominate the industry by excluding rival clubs from their territories and controlling the movement of players from team to team. Because African Americans were barred from the National League, separate black clubs and Negro leagues emerged. In the 1880s and 1890s, the National League warded off challenges from rival leagues and defeated a players' union. Not until 1901 did another league—the American League—successfully organize. In 1903 the two leagues merged

■ **Mark Twain** Pen name of Samuel L. Clemens, prominent American author of the late nineteenth century; Twain wrote *The Adventures of Huckleberry Finn* and other literary classics.

■ **Ash Can School** New York artists who shared a focus on urban life.

impressionism A style of painting that developed in France in the 1870s and emphasized the artist's impression of a subject; American impressionism was prominent from the 1880s through the 1910s.

ragtime Style of popular music characterized by a syncopated rhythm and a regularly accented beat; considered the immediate precursor of jazz.

slapstick A rowdy form of comedy marked by crude practical jokes and physical humor, such as falls.

melodrama A sensational or romantic stage play with exaggerated conflicts and stereotyped characters.

Chautauqua A traveling show offering educational, religious, and recreational activities, part of a nationwide movement of adult education that began in the town of Chautauqua, New York.

This photo shows a small part of the crowd at the New York Polo Grounds, watching the final game for the 1908 National League pennant, between the Chicago Cubs and the New York Giants. The Cubs won, and went on to beat the Detroit Tigers in the World Series. How is this crowd different from the crowd at a baseball game today?

into a new, stronger cartel and staged the first World Series—in which the Boston Red Sox beat the Pittsburgh Pirates. As other professional spectator sports developed, they often imitated the organization, labor relations, and racial discrimination first established in baseball.

Celebrating the New Age

In 1893, when the World's Columbian Exposition opened in Chicago, Hamlin Garland, a writer living there, wrote to his parents in South Dakota, "Sell the cook stove if necessary and come.... You must see this fair." Between 1876 and World War I, Americans repeatedly held great expositions, beginning with one in Philadelphia in 1876 that commemorated the centennial of independence and concluding with one in San Francisco in 1915 that celebrated the opening of the Panama Canal. Others took place in Atlanta, Buffalo, Omaha, Portland (Oregon), San Diego, and St. Louis. The most impressive and influential was the Columbian Exposition in Chicago, marking the four hundredth anniversary of Columbus's voyage to the New World.

These expositions typically featured vast exhibition halls where companies demonstrated their latest technological marvels, artists displayed their creations, and farmers presented their most impressive produce.

In other halls, states and foreign nations showcased their accomplishments. Many exhibits expressed the conviction that technology and industry would inevitably improve the lives of all. After 1898, most included demeaning exhibits of "savage" or "barbarian" people from the nation's new overseas possessions.

Behind the gleaming machines in the imitation marble palaces, however, lurked troubling questions that never appeared in the exhibits glorifying "Progress." What should be the working conditions of those whose labor created such technological marvels? Were democratic institutions compatible with the concentration of power and control in industry and finance or with the acquisition of colonies?

PROGRESSIVISM IN PERSPECTIVE

★ Was progressivism successful? How do you define success?

★ How did progressivism affect modern American politics?

The Progressive Era began with municipal reforms in the 1890s and sputtered to a close during World War I. Some politicians who called themselves progressives remained in prominent positions afterward,

This painting by Charles Courtney Curran captures the drama of the center of the Columbian Exposition of 1893: a great water-filled basin, with a sculpture representing Columbus at one end and this dramatic, 65-foot-tall depiction of the republic at the opposite end. The sculptor, Daniel Chester French, represented the American republic with one hand on a pole with a liberty cap at its end and with the other hand holding a globe surmounted by an American eagle. Though the original statue was destroyed by fire, a smaller replica was created by French in 1918 and stands today in Chicago's Jackson Park.

The Granger Collection, NYC.

and progressive concepts of efficiency and expertise continued to guide government decision making. American entry into the war in 1917 diverted attention from reform, and by the end of the war political concerns had changed. By the mid-1920s, many of the major leaders of progressivism had passed from the political stage.

The changes of the Progressive Era transformed American politics and government. Before the Hepburn Act and the Federal Reserve Act, the federal government's role in the economy consisted largely of distributing land grants and setting protective tariffs. After the Progressive Era, the federal government became a significant and permanent player in the economy, regulating a wide range of economic activity and enforcing laws to protect consumers and some workers. The income tax quickly became the most significant source of federal funds.

During the Progressive Era, political parties declined in significance, and political campaigns focused increasingly on personality and advertising. These patterns accelerated in the second half of the twentieth century under the influence of television and public opinion polling. Organized pressure groups have proliferated and become ever more important. Women's participation in politics has continued to increase, especially in the last third of the twentieth century and the first two decades of the twenty-first.

The assertion of presidential authority by Theodore Roosevelt and Woodrow Wilson reappeared in the presidency of Franklin D. Roosevelt (1933–1945). The two Roosevelts and Wilson transformed Americans' expectations regarding the office of the presidency itself. Throughout the nineteenth century, Congress had dominated the making of domestic policy. During the twentieth century, Americans came to expect domestic policy to flow from forceful executive leadership in the White House.

All in all, the most important changes of the Progressive Era laid the basis for many aspects of our modern politics and government.

Individual Voices

JANE ADDAMS
Explains Her Participation in the 1912 Presidential Campaign

Jane Addams faced a storm of criticism for her prominence in the Progressive Party and her support for Roosevelt. Some claimed she was demeaning womanhood or damaging the causes of settlement work and woman suffrage by participating in party politics, and others criticized her acceptance of a platform committed to building battleships but silent on civil rights. In the following selections, Addams explains her choices.

Hulton Archive/Getty Images.

1 Here and in the *New York Times* interview, Addams implicitly answers the criticism that she was damaging the cause of settlement work by taking an active role in party politics. How does she relate party politics to the goals of settlement work?

2 One of the activities at Hull House was to investigate social legislation that existed in other advanced industrial nations. How does Addams use those studies?

3 Some of Addams's critics were prominent women philanthropists. How does she seek to link their concerns to her political activities?

4 Here Addams answers those who criticized her support for building additional battleships. How does her explanation relate to the adage that "politics is the art of compromise"? Is her argument persuasive?

From the New York Times, *September 26, 1912:*

"Why you are a Progressive?" Miss Addams was asked. "I went into the party, as I said at the time, because it was standing for many of the things I had been working for for years. The social reforms that I had been working for, and the legislation for women for which I had been working, is put at last into practical politics."

From McClure's Magazine, *November 1912:*

Aristotle is reported to have said that politics is a school wherein questions are studied, not for the sake of knowledge, but for the sake of action. **1** …During the present campaign, measures of social amelioration will be discussed up and down the land, as only party politics are discussed.…The discussion of the Progressive party platform will further surprise many a voter into the consciousness that the industrial situation in America has developed by leaps and bounds, without any of the restraining legislation which has been carefully placed about it in Europe.…Only by federal control…can great corporations be made to assume the injury of workmen as one of the risks of industry; only when human waste shall automatically involve a reduction in profits will a comprehensive system of safe-guards be developed, as Germany has clearly demonstrated.… **2**

It did not seem strange that women were delegates to this first convention of the Progressive party, and it would have been much more unnatural if they had not been there, when such matters of social welfare were being considered.… Philanthropic women, on their side, will be surprised to find that their long concern for the human wreckage of industry has come to be considered politics. **3**

[In approving the platform] we were, first and foremost, faced with the necessity of selecting from our many righteous principles those that might be advocated at the moment.…For many years I have been an advocate of international peace…[But] I voted to adopt a platform, 'as a whole,' which advocated the building of two battleships a year…I found it very difficult to swallow those two battleships…[but] when a choice was presented to me between protesting against the human waste in industry or against the havoc in warfare, the former made the more intimate appeal. **4**

SUMMARY

Progressivism, a phenomenon of the late nineteenth and early twentieth centuries, refers to new concepts of government, to changes in government based on those concepts, and to the political process by which change occurred. Those years marked a time of political transformation brought about by many groups and individuals who approached politics with often contradictory objectives. Organized interest groups became an important part of this process. Women broke through long-standing constraints to take a more prominent role in politics. The Anti-Saloon League was the most successful of several organizations that appealed to government to enforce morality. Some African Americans fought

segregation and disfranchisement, notably W. E. B. Du Bois and the NAACP. Socialists and the Industrial Workers of the World saw capitalism as the source of many problems, but few Americans embraced their radical solutions.

Political reform took place at every level, from cities to states to the federal government. Muckraking journalists exposed wrongdoing and suffering. Municipal reformers introduced new methods into city government in a quest for efficiency and effectiveness. Some tried to use government to remedy social problems by employing the expertise of new professions such as public health and social work. Reformers attacked the power of party bosses and machines by reducing the role of political parties.

CHRONOLOGY
The Progressive Era

1885	Mark Twain's *The Adventures of Huckleberry Finn*
1890	National American Woman Suffrage Association formed
1893	World's Columbian Exposition, Chicago
1895	Anti-Saloon League formed
1898	War with Spain
1899	Permanent Court of Arbitration (the Hague Court) created Scott Joplin's "Maple Leaf Rag"
1900	Robert M. La Follette elected governor of Wisconsin President William McKinley reelected
1901	Socialist Party of America formed McKinley assassinated; Theodore Roosevelt becomes president
1902	Muckraking journalism begins Antitrust action against Northern Securities Company Roosevelt intervenes in coal strike Reclamation Act
1903	W. E. B. Du Bois's *Souls of Black Folk* Hay–Bunau-Varilla Treaty; work begins on Panama Canal
1904	Roosevelt Corollary Roosevelt elected president
1905	Industrial Workers of the World organized Roosevelt mediates Russo-Japanese War Dominican Republic becomes third U.S. protectorate

1906	Upton Sinclair's *The Jungle* Hepburn Act Meat Inspection and Pure Food and Drug Acts
1908	*Muller v. Oregon* Race riot in Springfield, Illinois William Howard Taft elected president
1910	National Association for the Advancement of Colored People formed Hiram W. Johnson elected governor of California
1911	Fire at Triangle Shirtwaist factory
1912	Progressive ("Bull Moose") Party formed Wilson elected president Nicaragua becomes a protectorate
1913	Sixteenth Amendment (federal income tax) ratified Seventeenth Amendment (direct election of U.S. senators) ratified Federal Reserve Act Armory Show
1914	Clayton Antitrust Act Federal Trade Commission Act Panama Canal completed
1915	National Birth Control League formed
1916	Louis Brandeis appointed to the Supreme Court Jeannette Rankin first woman elected to House of Representatives Wilson reelected
1917	United States enters World War I

Study Tools

At the federal level, Theodore Roosevelt set the pace for progressive reform. Relishing his reputation as a trustbuster, he challenged judicial constraints on federal authority over big business and promoted other forms of economic regulation, thereby increasing government's role in the economy. He also regulated the use of natural resources. His successor, William Howard Taft, failed to maintain Republican Party unity and eventually sided with conservatives against progressives.

Roosevelt played an important role in defining America's status as a world power, as he secured rights to build a U.S.-controlled canal through Panama and established Panama as an American protectorate. The Roosevelt Corollary declared that the United States was the dominant power in the Caribbean and Central America. In eastern Asia, Roosevelt tried to bolster the Open Door policy by maintaining a balance of power. Roosevelt and others sought arbitration treaties with leading nations but failed because of Senate opposition. Faced with the rise of German military and naval power, Great Britain improved relations with the United States.

In 1912 Roosevelt led a new political party, the Progressives, making that year's presidential election a three-way contest. Roosevelt called for regulation of big business, but Wilson, the Democrat, favored breaking up monopolies through antitrust action. Wilson won the election but soon preferred regulation over antitrust actions. He helped to create the Federal Reserve System to centralize and regulate banking. As the 1916 election approached, Wilson also pushed for social reforms in an effort to unify progressives behind his leadership.

The new urban, industrial, multiethnic society contributed to critical realism in literature, new patterns in painting, and ragtime music, although many creative artists continued to look to Europe for inspiration. Urbanization and changes in transportation and communication also fostered the emergence of a mass entertainment industry.

Progressive reforms made a profound impression on later American politics. In many ways, progressivism marked the origin of modern American politics and government.

FOCUS QUESTIONS

If you have mastered this chapter, you should be able to answer these questions and to identify the terms that follow the questions.

1. What important changes transformed American politics in the early twentieth century?

2. What did women and African Americans seek to accomplish by creating new organizations devoted to political change?

3. What did the muckrakers contribute to reform?

4. What characterized reforms of city and state government and what role did organized interest groups play?

5. What did Theodore Roosevelt mean by a "Square Deal"? Do his accomplishments fit this description?

6. How did Roosevelt's presidency change the federal role in the economy and alter the presidency itself?

7. What were Roosevelt's objectives for the United States in world affairs?

8. How did Roosevelt reshape American foreign policy?

9. What choices confronted American voters in the presidential election of 1912?

10. How did Wilson's views on reform evolve from 1912 through 1916 and how did his administration change the federal government's role in the economy?

11. Did developments in cultural expression draw more from American sources or European sources?

12. How did social and technological changes contribute to new patterns in mass entertainment?

13. Was progressivism successful? How do you define success?

14. How did progressivism affect modern American politics?

KEY TERMS

Hull House   *p. 504*

interest group   *p. 505*

Progressive Party   *p. 505*

Social Gospel   *p. 506*

Margaret Sanger   *p. 506*

Muller v. Oregon   *p. 506*

Jeannette Rankin   *p. 506*

National American Woman Suffrage Association   *p. 507*

Anti-Saloon League   *p. 508*

W. E. B. Du Bois   *p. 509*

National Association for the Advancement of Colored People   *p. 509*

Ida B. Wells   *p. 509*

Socialist Party of America   *p. 510*

muckrakers   *p. 511*

Upton Sinclair   *p. 511*

Pure Food and Drug Act   *p. 511*

Meat Inspection Act   *p. 512*

municipal reform   *p. 512*

Robert M. La Follette   *p. 513*

Study Tools

Wisconsin Idea *p. 514*
Hiram Johnson *p. 514*
direct democracy *p. 515*
Square Deal *p. 516*
Hepburn Act *p. 518*
Gifford Pinchot *p. 518*
Sixteenth Amendment *p. 520*
Seventeenth Amendment *p. 520*
Philippe Bunau-Varilla *p. 520*

Hay–Bunau-Varilla Treaty *p. 520*
Roosevelt Corollary *p. 521*
dollar diplomacy *p. 522*
Treaty of Portsmouth *p. 523*
Permanent Court of
    Arbitration *p. 524*
New Nationalism *p. 524*
Bull Moose Party *p. 525*

New Freedom *p. 525*
Louis Brandeis *p. 525*
Federal Reserve Act *p. 527*
Clayton Antitrust Act *p. 527*
Federal Trade Commission
    Act *p. 527*
Mark Twain *p. 528*
Ash Can School *p. 528*

SUGGESTED RESOURCES

Jane Addams. *Twenty Years at Hull House* (1910; various publishers.) Vividly conveys the complex world of Hull House and the personality of Jane Addams.

Kathleen Dalton. *Theodore Roosevelt: A Strenuous Life* (New York: Knopf, 2002). Probably the best one-volume biography of the dominant figure of the age.

Lester D. Langley. *The Banana Wars: United States' Intervention in the Caribbean, 1898–1934,* 2nd ed. (Lanham, MD: Rowman and Littlefield, 2001). Sprightly and succinct account of the role of the United States in the Caribbean and Central America.

David Levering Lewis. *W. E. B. Du Bois: Biography of a Race, 1868–1919* (New York: Henry Holt, 1993). Powerful biography of Du Bois that delivers on its promise to present the "biography of a race" during the Progressive Era.

"The World's Columbian Exposition: Idea, Experience, Aftermath," http://xroads.virginia.edu/~ma96/wce/title.html. An elaborate website dealing with almost every aspect of the Columbian Exposition of 1893.

20

The United States in a World at War, 1913–1920

CHAPTER OUTLINE

Inherited Commitments and New Directions
Anti-Imperialism, Intervention, and Arbitration
Wilson and the Mexican Revolution

The United States and the Great War, 1914–1917
The Great War in Europe
American Neutrality
Neutral Rights and German U-Boats
The Election of 1916
The Decision for War

The Home Front
Mobilizing the Economy
Mobilizing Public Opinion
Civil Liberties in Time of War
The Great Migration and White Reactions

Planning for Peace in the Midst of War
Mobilizing for Battle
Americans "Over There"
Bolshevism, the Secret Treaties, and the Fourteen Points

The Peace Conference and the Treaty
The World in 1919
Wilson at Versailles
The Senate and the Treaty
Legacies of the Great War

America in the Aftermath of War, November 1918–November 1920
"HCL" and Strikes
Red Scare
Race Riots and Lynchings
Amending the Constitution: Prohibition and Woman Suffrage
The Election of 1920

INDIVIDUAL VOICES: *Woodrow Wilson Proposes His Fourteen Points*

Study Tools

INDIVIDUAL CHOICES

Charles Young

In 1917, Lieutenant Colonel Charles Young was the highest-ranking African American in the U.S. Army. Like other aspects of American life, the army was segregated. When the United States went to war against Germany, many African Americans expected Young to command a division, made up of the four black regular army regiments, and to take a prominent role in the war in Europe. Young also wanted to do this. He was a patriotic army officer, eager to carry out the duties for which he had prepared. But he also wanted to show that a black commanding officer and black soldiers were as capable as white troops of confronting an enemy under fire.

Growing up in Ohio, the son of former slaves, Young considered his father's Union Army service as a "heritage of honor" and secured an appointment to West Point through his academic accomplishments. After graduating, he was assigned to the 10th Cavalry, one of the army's two black cavalry units. He later taught military science at Wilberforce University in Xenia, Ohio, a leading black university.

During the war with Spain, Young commanded a battalion of black volunteers, but his unit was not sent into action. He was then assigned to the 9th Cavalry and sent to the Philippines to help suppress the resistance to American rule (see page 497). Afterward, he received diplomatic assignments in Haiti and Liberia. In 1913, he was back with

Library of Congress.

the 10th Cavalry and participated in Pershing's expedition into Mexico (discussed in this chapter). As a major, Young was superior to several white officers, some of whom complained about taking orders from an African American.

When the war with Germany came, Young, now a lieutenant colonel, hoped to command. However, all four black units in the regular army were assigned to duties far from Europe, and Young was given a medical retirement. Unwilling to accept that status, Young rode his horse nearly 500 miles to prove his physical fitness. He was returned to active duty and promoted to colonel, but too late to take part in the war. In 1919, he was again assigned to diplomatic duty, again in Liberia. He died there of a kidney infection in 1923.

Young's experience was part of larger patterns of discrimination against African Americans. Though a capable and experienced officer, he was often given teaching or diplomatic duties rather than command of troops, most likely to prevent him from giving orders to white officers. It must have seemed deeply ironic for Young and other African Americans to read that President Wilson defined the war as a struggle for "the principle of justice to all peoples and nationalities, and their right to live on equal terms of liberty and safety with one another" (see the Individual Voices feature at the end of this chapter). In 1919, when asked about plans for a monument to African Americans who had died in the military, Young may have been reflecting on Wilson's statement when he suggested that the most fitting commemoration would not be a monument but instead "liberty, justice, equal opportunities and educational facilities, the suppression of lynching by making it a federal crime and the abolition of [segregated railroad] cars."

On June 28, 1914, a Serbian terrorist killed Archduke Franz Ferdinand, heir to the throne of Austria-Hungary, and his wife, Sophie. The royal couple was visiting Sarajevo, in Bosnia-Herzegovina, which Austria had recently annexed against the wishes of the neighboring kingdom of Serbia. In response to the assassinations, Austria consulted its ally Germany, then made stringent demands on Serbia. Serbia sought help from Russia, which was allied with France. Tense diplomats invoked elaborate, interlocking alliances. Huge armies began to move. Soon most of Europe was at war.

Before those events, many Americans had concluded that war among what Theodore Roosevelt called the world's "civilized" nations had become unthinkable. Given the widely held expectation that war had become obsolete, many Americans were shocked, saddened, and repelled when the leading "civilized" nations of the world—all of which had been busily accumulating arsenals—lurched into war.

When the nations of Europe went to war, the United States was no minor player on the international scene. Between 1898 and 1908, America acquired the Philippines and the Panama Canal, came to dominate the Caribbean and Central America, and actively participated in the balance of power in eastern Asia. The three presidents of the Progressive Era—Roosevelt, William Howard Taft, and Woodrow Wilson—agreed wholeheartedly that the United States should exercise a major role in world affairs.

INHERITED COMMITMENTS AND NEW DIRECTIONS

★ In what new directions did Wilson steer U.S. foreign policy before the coming of war in Europe?

When Woodrow Wilson entered the White House in 1913, he expected to spend most of his time on domestic issues. Although well read on international affairs, he had neither significant international experience nor set foreign policies. For secretary of state he chose William Jennings Bryan, who had also devoted his political career to domestic matters and had little experience in foreign relations. Both were devout Presbyterians, sharing a confidence that God had a plan for humankind and specifically for the United States. Both hoped—perhaps naively—that they might make the United States a model among nations for peaceful settlement of international disputes. Initially, Wilson fixed his attention on the three regions of greatest American involvement: Latin America, the Pacific, and eastern Asia. There, he tried to balance the anti-imperialist principles of his Democratic Party against the expansionist practices of his Republican predecessors. He marked out some new directions but in the end extended many previous commitments.

Anti-Imperialism, Intervention, and Arbitration

Wilson's Democratic Party had opposed many of the foreign policies of McKinley, Roosevelt, and Taft, especially imperialism. Secretary of State Bryan was a leading anti-imperialist who had criticized Roosevelt's "Big Stick" in foreign affairs. During the Wilson administration, Democrats took limited action against imperialism. In 1916 Congress established a bill of rights for residents of the Philippines, provided more autonomy, and promised eventual independence. The next year, Congress made Puerto Rico an American territory and extended American citizenship to its residents.

Though Democrats had criticized Roosevelt's actions in the Caribbean, Wilson intervened more in Central America and the Caribbean than any previous administration. In Nicaragua, where Taft had sent marines to prop up the rule of President Adolfo Díaz, Wilson sought more authority for the United States. Senate Democrats rejected his efforts, reminding him of their party's opposition to further protectorates. Even so, Bryan negotiated a treaty in 1914 that gave the United States significant concessions, including the right to build a canal through Nicaragua.

Haiti's government was unstable and owed a staggering debt to foreign bankers. When a mob killed the president in 1915, Wilson sent in the marines. A treaty followed, making Haiti a protectorate in which American forces controlled most aspects of government until 1933. Wilson sent marines into the Dominican Republic in 1916, and U.S. naval officers exercised control there until 1924. In 1917, the United States bought the Virgin Islands from Denmark for $25 million. Thus, rather than changing previous policies, Wilson's administration significantly extended American dominance in the Caribbean.

Porfirio Díaz Mexican soldier and politician; became president after a coup in 1876 and ruled Mexico until overthrown in 1911.

◾ **Victoriano Huerta** Mexican general; overthrew President Francisco Madero in 1913 and established a military dictatorship until 1914.

◾ **Venustiano Carranza** Mexican revolutionary leader; helped to lead armed opposition to Victoriano Huerta, became president in 1914, and was overthrown in 1920.

Wilson and Bryan did, however, bring a new approach to the arbitration of international disputes. Roosevelt's and Taft's secretaries of state had sought arbitration treaties, but the Senate refused to accept them. Bryan drafted a model treaty and first obtained approval from the Senate Foreign Relations Committee. The Senate ultimately ratified treaties with twenty-two nations. All featured a "cooling-off" period for disputes, typically a year, during which the nations agreed to seek arbitration instead of going to war. These treaties marked the beginning of efforts by Wilson to redefine international relations, substituting rational negotiations for raw power.

Wilson and the Mexican Revolution

In Mexico, Wilson attempted to influence internal politics but eventually found himself on the verge of war. **Porfirio Díaz** had ruled Mexico for a third of a century, supported by great landholders, the church, and the military. During his rule, many American companies invested in Mexico. However, discontent among peasants, workers, and intellectuals boiled over into rebellion. Díaz resigned in 1911. Francisco Madero, a leading advocate of reform, became president but failed to unite the country. Conservatives feared Madero as a reformer, but radicals found him too timid. In some places, peasant armies demanding *tierra y libertad* ("land and liberty") attacked the mansions of great landowners. In February 1913, conservatives joined with the commander of the army, General **Victoriano Huerta**, to overthrow Madero. Huerta took control of the government and had Madero executed.

Most European governments extended diplomatic recognition to Huerta because his government clearly held power in Mexico City. Wilson faced that decision soon after his inauguration. American companies with investments in Mexico urged recognition because Huerta seemed likely to protect their holdings. Wilson, however, privately vowed "not to recognize a government of butchers." In public, Wilson announced he withheld recognition because Huerta's regime did not rest on the consent of the governed.

Wilson's addition of an ethical dimension to diplomatic recognition constituted something new in foreign policy. Previous presidents had automatically extended diplomatic recognition to governments in power. Wilson's approach, sometimes labeled "missionary diplomacy," implied that the United States would discriminate between virtuous and corrupt governments. Telling one visitor, "I am going to teach the South American republics to elect good men," Wilson waited for an opportunity to act against Huerta. In the meantime, anti-Huerta forces led by **Venustiano Carranza** made significant gains.

In April 1914, Mexican officials in Tampico arrested some American sailors (see Map 20.1). The

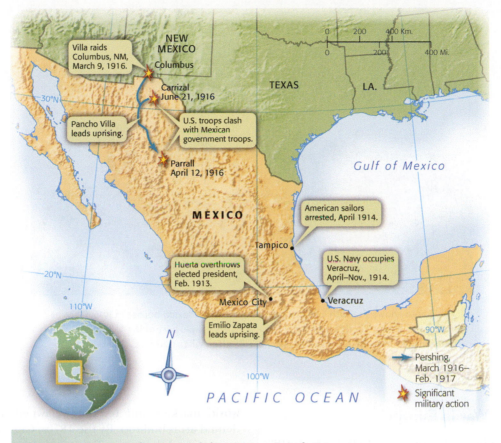

Villa raids
Columbus, NM,
March 9, 1916.

NEW
MEXICO

Columbus

Carrizal
June 21, 1916

TEXAS

LA.

Pancho Villa
leads uprising.

U.S. troops clash
with Mexican
government troops.

Parrall
April 12, 1916

Gulf of Mexico

MEXICO

American sailors
arrested, April 1914.

Tampico

U.S. Navy occupies
Veracruz,
April–Nov., 1916.

Huerta overthrows
elected president,
Feb. 1913.

Mexico City

Veracruz

Emilio Zapata
leads uprising.

Pershing,
March 1916–
Feb. 1917

Significant
military action

PACIFIC OCEAN

MAP 20.1 The United States and the Mexican Revolution © Cengage Learning.

city's army commander immediately released them and apologized, but Wilson used the incident to justify ordering the U.S. Navy to occupy **Veracruz**, the leading Mexican port and the major source of the Huerta government's revenue (from customs). The occupation cut off most government military supplies. However, it cost more than a hundred Mexican lives and turned many Mexicans against Wilson for violating their sovereignty. Without munitions and revenue, Huerta fled the country in mid-July. Wilson withdrew the last American forces from Veracruz in November.

Carranza succeeded Huerta as president, and Wilson officially recognized his government. Carranza, however, faced armed opposition from **Francisco "Pancho" Villa** in northern Mexico and Emiliano Zapata in the south. When Villa suffered setbacks, he apparently decided to involve Carranza in a war with the United States. Villa's men murdered several Americans in Mexico and then, in March 1916, raided across the border and killed several Americans in New Mexico. With Carranza's reluctant approval, Wilson sent an expedition of nearly seven thousand men, commanded by General John J. Pershing, into Mexico to punish Villa. Villa evaded the American troops, but drew them ever deeper into Mexico, alarming Carranza.

When a clash between Mexican government forces and American soldiers produced deaths on both sides,

Carranza asked Wilson to withdraw his troops. Wilson refused. Only in early 1917, when Wilson recognized that America might soon go to war with Germany, did he withdraw the troops, leaving behind resentment and suspicion toward the United States.

THE UNITED STATES AND THE GREAT WAR, 1914–1917

☆ *Why did Wilson proclaim American neutrality? How did Americans respond?*

☆ *What made neutrality difficult?*

☆ *How did Wilson justify going to war?*

At first, Americans paid little attention to the assassinations at Sarajevo. When Europe plunged into war, however, Wilson and all Americans faced difficult choices.

Veracruz Major Mexican port city on the Gulf of Mexico; in 1914, the U.S. Navy occupied the port.

■ **Francisco "Pancho" Villa** Mexican bandit and revolutionary; raided into New Mexico in 1916, prompting U.S. government to send troops into Mexico.

This photo shows the 10th Cavalry patrolling the U.S.-Mexico border in 1916. Charles Young was a major in this regiment. The 10th Cavalry was part of the U.S. expedition that entered Mexico in pursuit of Pancho Villa after Villa's raid on Columbus, New Mexico.

The Great War in Europe

Within the ethnically diverse empires of Austria-Hungary, Russia, and Turkey, many groups hoped for independence based on language and culture. Ethnic antagonisms and aspirations were especially powerful in the **Balkan Peninsula**, where the Ottoman (Turkish) Empire had lost territory as several groups had established their independence. Some of the new Balkan states were weak, attracting the neighboring Austrian and Russian empires. As Austria-Hungary sought to annex new territories, Russia claimed the role of protector of other **Slavic** peoples.

During the late nineteenth and early twentieth centuries, competition among European powers seeking world markets and territory spawned an unprecedented arms buildup. By the 1870s, Germany had the most powerful army in Europe and set out to make its navy as powerful as Britain's. Technology produced new and powerful weapons, including the machine gun, and designers quickly adapted automobiles and airplanes for combat. The major powers of Europe had avoided war with one another since 1871, but they continued to prepare for war. Eventually European diplomats constructed two major alliance systems: the Triple Entente (Britain, France, and Russia) and the Triple Alliance (Germany, Austria-Hungary, and Italy). Britain was also allied with Japan.

Called the "powder keg of Europe," the Balkans lived up to the nickname in 1914. The assassinations at Sarajevo grew out of a territorial conflict between Austria-Hungary and Serbia. Russia, alarmed over Austrian expansion into the Balkans, presented itself as the protector of Serbia. Austria assured itself of Germany's backing, then declared war on Serbia. Russia confirmed France's support, then **mobilized** its army in support of Serbia. Germany declared war on Russia on August 1 and on France soon after. German strategists planned to bypass French defenses along their border by invading **neutral** Belgium (see Map 20.2). Britain entered the war in defense of Belgium. By August 4, much of Europe was at war. Eventually Germany and Austria-Hungary combined with Bulgaria and the Ottoman Empire to form the **Central Powers**. Italy abandoned its Triple Alliance partners and joined Britain, France, Russia, Romania, and Japan as the **Allies**.

Balkan Peninsula Region of southeastern Europe; included several relatively new and sometimes unstable states in the early twentieth century.

Slavic Linguistic groups, mainly in eastern and central Europe; includes Croats, Czechs, Poles, Russians, Serbs, Slovaks, and others.

mobilize To make ready for combat or other forms of action.

neutral A nation not aligned with either side in a war; traditionally, neutral nations could engage in certain types of trade with nations at war.

▪ **Central Powers** In World War I, Germany, Austria-Hungary, Bulgaria, and the Ottoman Empire.

▪ **Allies** In World War I, Britain and its empire, France, Russia, Italy, Romania, Japan, Serbia, and Belgium.

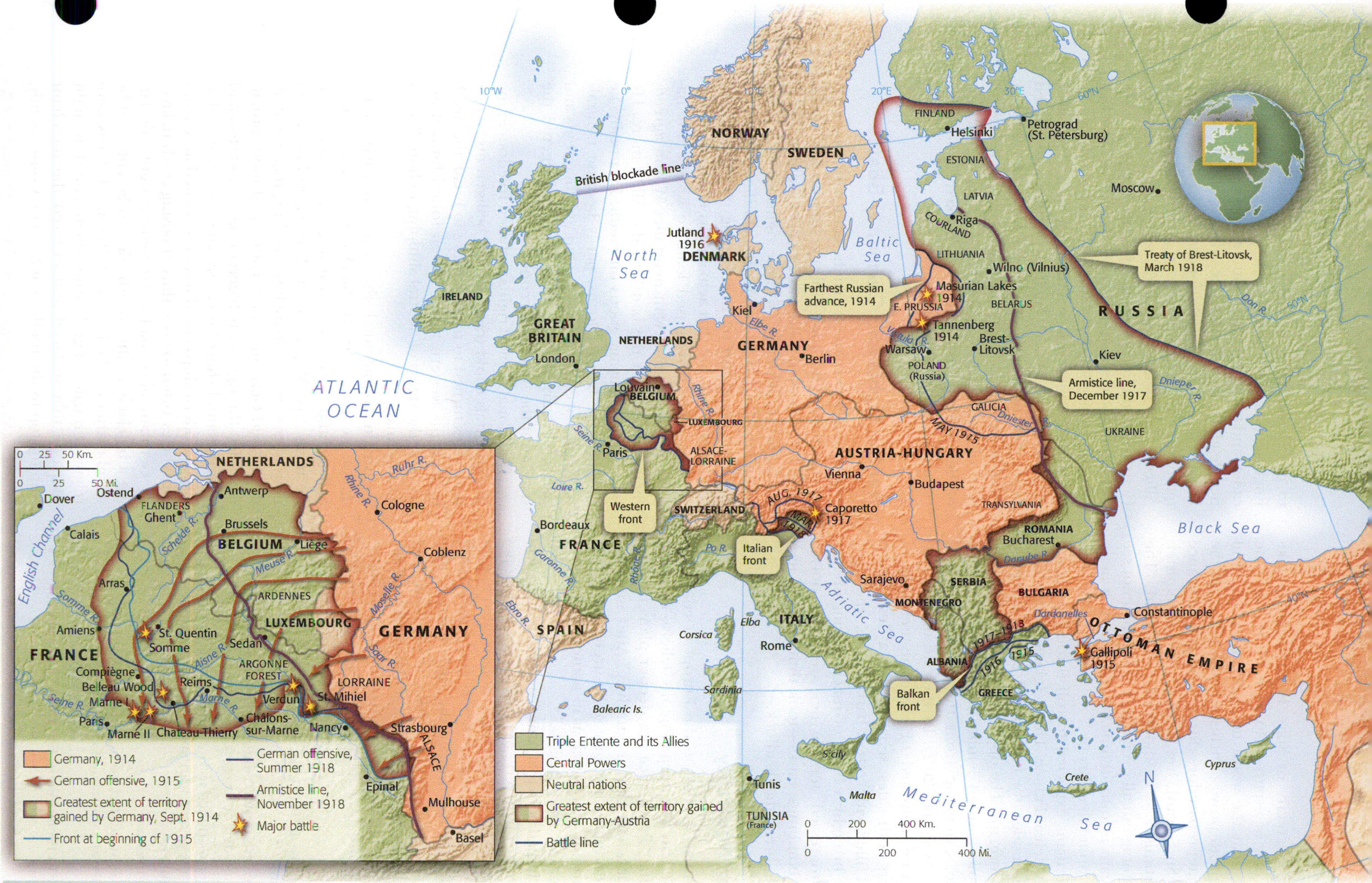
NORWAY
SWEDEN
FINLAND
Helsinki
Petrograd (St. Petersburg)
ESTONIA
LATVIA
Riga
COURLAND
LITHUANIA
Wilno (Vilnius)
Moscow
Treaty of Brest-Litovsk, March 1918
RUSSIA
Masurian Lakes 1914
E. PRUSSIA
BELARUS
Tannenberg 1914
Brest-Litovsk
Warsaw
POLAND (Russia)
Kiev
Armistice line, December 1917
Dnieper R.
Don R.
UKRAINE
GALICIA
Dniester R.
MAY 1915
Farthest Russian advance, 1914
Baltic Sea
British blockade line
Jutland 1916
DENMARK
North Sea
IRELAND
GREAT BRITAIN
London
NETHERLANDS
Kiel
Elbe R.
GERMANY
Berlin
Vistula R.
ATLANTIC OCEAN
Louvain
BELGIUM
LUXEMBOURG
Rhine R.
ALSACE-LORRAINE
Seine R.
Paris
Loire R.
Western front
Bordeaux
FRANCE
Garonne R.
Rhône R.
Ebro R.
SPAIN
SWITZERLAND
Po R.
AUG. 1917
MAR. 1918
Caporetto 1917
Italian front
AUSTRIA-HUNGARY
Vienna
Budapest
TRANSYLVANIA
ROMANIA
Bucharest
Danube R.
Black Sea
Sarajevo
SERBIA
MONTENEGRO
BULGARIA
Dardanelles
Constantinople
OTTOMAN EMPIRE
Gallipoli 1915
ALBANIA
1917–1918
1916
1915
GREECE
Balkan front
Adriatic Sea
ITALY
Rome
Elba
Corsica
Sardinia
Balearic Is.
Sicily
Malta
Tunis
TUNISIA (France)
Crete
Cyprus
Mediterranean Sea
0 200 400 Km.
0 200 400 Mi.
N
10°W
0°
10°E
20°E
30°E
40°N
50°N
60°N
Triple Entente and its Allies
Central Powers
Neutral nations
Greatest extent of territory gained by Germany-Austria
Battle line
0 25 50 Km.
0 25 50 Mi.
Dover
Ostend
Calais
English Channel
FLANDERS
Ghent
Antwerp
Brussels
Scheldt R.
BELGIUM
Liège
Meuse R.
ARDENNES
LUXEMBOURG
Cologne
Ruhr R.
Rhine R.
Coblenz
Moselle R.
GERMANY
Saar R.
Arras
Somme R.
Amiens
St. Quentin
Somme
Sedan
FRANCE
Aisne R.
ARGONNE FOREST
Compiègne
Belleau Wood
Reims
Marne I
Marne R.
Verdun
St. Mihiel
LORRAINE
Seine R.
Paris
Marne II
Chateau-Thierry
Châlons-sur-Marne
Nancy
Strasbourg
ALSACE
Epinal
Mulhouse
Basel
Germany, 1914
German offensive, 1915
Greatest extent of territory gained by Germany, Sept. 1914
Front at beginning of 1915
German offensive, Summer 1918
Armistice line, November 1918
Major battle

MAP 20.2 The War in Europe, 1914–1918

This map identifies the two great military coalitions, the Central Powers and the Allies, and charts the development of the war. Note Russia's losses by the Treaty of Brest-Litovsk as compared with the armistice line (the line between the two armies when Russia sought peace). © Cengage Learning.

At first, Secretary of State Bryan tried to take a hopeful view of events in Europe. "It may be," he suggested, "that the world needed one more awful object lesson to prove conclusively the fallacy of the doctrine that preparedness for war can give assurance for peace." Sir Edward Grey, Britain's foreign minister, was less optimistic as he mourned to a friend, "The lamps are going out all over Europe. We shall not see them lit again in our lifetime." Grey proved a more accurate prophet than Bryan.

The Germans expected to roll through Belgium and quickly defeat France. The Belgians, however, resisted long enough for French and British troops to block the Germans. The opposing armies settled into defensive lines across 475 miles of Belgian and French countryside, extending from the English Channel to the Alps (see Map 20.2). By the end of 1914, the western front consisted of elaborate networks of trenches on both sides, separated by a desolate no man's land filled with coils of barbed wire, where any movement brought a burst of machine-gun fire. As the war progressed, terrible new weapons—poison gas, aerial bombings, tanks—took thousands of lives but failed to break the deadlock.

American Neutrality

Wilson's initial reaction to the European conflagration revealed his own deep religious beliefs—he wrote privately that "Providence has deeper plans than we could possibly have laid for ourselves." After announcing U.S. neutrality on August 4, he urged Americans to be "neutral in fact as well as in name . . . impartial in thought as well as in action."

Wilson hoped both that America would remain neutral and that he might serve as peacemaker. Such hopes proved unrealistic. The warring nations wanted to gain territory, and only a decisive victory could accomplish that. The longer they fought, the more territory they wanted. So long as they saw a chance of winning, they had no interest in the appeals of would-be peacemakers.

Wilson's hope that Americans could remain impartial was also unrealistic. Though few Americans wanted

to go to war, most probably sided with the Allies. England had cultivated American friendship for decades, and trade and finance united many of their business leaders. French assistance during the American Revolution helped to fuel support for France. And the martyrdom of Belgium aroused American sympathy. Allied **propagandists** worked hard to generate anti-German sentiment, publicizing—and exaggerating—German atrocities and portraying the war as a conflict between civilized peoples and barbarian **Huns**.

Not all Americans sympathized with the Allies. Nearly 8 million of the 97 million people in the United States had one or both parents from Germany or Austria. Not surprisingly, many of them rejected depictions of their cousins as bloodthirsty barbarians. Many of the 5 million Irish Americans disliked England for ruling their ancestral homeland.

Neutral Rights and German U-Boats

Wilson and Bryan agreed that the United States should remain neutral but took different approaches to that goal. Bryan proved willing to sacrifice traditional neutral rights if insistence on those rights seemed likely to pull the United States into the conflict. Wilson, in contrast, stood firm on maintaining traditional neutral rights, a posture that actually favored the Allies.

Bryan initially opposed loans to **belligerent** nations as incompatible with neutrality. Wilson agreed, then realized that the ban hurt the Allies more. He then allowed buying goods on credit. Eventually, he dropped the ban on loans, partly because neutrals had always been permitted to lend to belligerents and partly, perhaps, because the freeze endangered the stability of the American economy.

Traditional neutral rights included freedom of the seas: neutrals could trade with all belligerents. When both sides turned to naval warfare to break the deadlock on the western front, Wilson found himself defending the rights of neutral shipping to both Britain and Germany.

Britain commanded the seas and tried to redefine neutral rights by blockading German ports and neutral ports from which goods could reach Germany (see Map 20.3), and by expanding definitions of **contraband** to include anything that might indirectly aid Germany—even cotton and food. Britain extended the right of belligerent nations to stop and search neutral ships for contraband by insisting that large, modern ships could not be searched at sea and must be escorted to port, thus imposing costly delays.

Germany also challenged neutral rights, declaring a blockade of the British Isles, to be enforced by its submarines, called **U-boats**. Because U-boats were relatively fragile, a lightly armed merchant ship might sink one that surfaced and ordered the merchant ship to stop in the traditional manner. Consequently,

---

■ western front In World War I, the zone of fighting in France and Belgium.

propagandist One who provides information in support of a cause, especially one-sided or exaggerated information.

Hun Disparaging term applied to Germans during World War I, derived from warlike people who invaded Europe in the fourth and fifth centuries.

belligerent A nation at war.

contraband Goods prohibited from being imported or exported; in time of war, contraband included materials of war.

■ U-boat A German submarine (in German, *Unterseeboot*)

MAP 20.3 The War at Sea
This map shows the contending definitions of war zones at sea by Great Britain and Germany. Both initially sought to prevent war materials from reaching enemy ports, but both soon sought to prevent virtually all shipping to enemy ports. © Cengage Learning.

Lusitania torpedoed May 7, 1915

submarines struck from below without warning. Britain began disguising its ships by flying the flags of neutral countries, so Germany declared that neutral flags no longer guaranteed protection.

Wilson issued token protests over Britain's practices but strongly denounced those of Germany. Because Germany's violations of neutrality produced loss of life, he considered them significantly different from Britain's, which caused only financial hardship. On February 10, 1915, Wilson warned that the United States would hold Germany to "strict accountability" for its actions and would do everything necessary to "safeguard American lives and property" and maintain American neutral rights. On May 7, 1915, a German U-boat torpedoed the British passenger ship *Lusitania*. More than a thousand people died, including 128 Americans. Americans reacted with shock and horror. Upon learning that the *Lusitania* carried ammunition and other contraband, Bryan urged restraint in protesting to Germany. Wilson, however, sent a strong message that stopped just short of demanding an end to submarine attacks on merchant ships. The German response was noncommittal. Wilson composed an even stronger protest. Fearing Wilson's message would lead to war, Bryan resigned as secretary of state rather than sign it.

Robert Lansing, Bryan's successor, strongly favored the Allies. Where Bryan had counseled restraint, Lansing urged a show of strength. U-boat attacks continued. Wilson sent more protests but knew most Americans opposed going to war over that issue. Finally, he warned Germany that if unrestricted submarine warfare did not stop, the United States would sever diplomatic relations—the last step before declaring war. Germany responded that U-boats would no longer strike noncombatant vessels without warning, provided Wilson convinced the Allies to obey "international law." Wilson accepted the pledge but did little to persuade the British to change tactics.

The war strengthened America's economic ties to the Allies. Exports to Britain and France soared from $756 million in 1914 to $2.7 billion in 1916. American companies exported $6 million worth of explosives in 1914 and $467 million in 1916. Even more significantly, the United States changed from a debtor to a **creditor nation**. By April 1917, American bankers had loaned the Allies more than $2 billion. However, the British blockade stifled Americans' trade with the Central Powers, which fell from around $170 million in 1914 to almost nothing two years later.

Wilson concluded that the best way to maintain American neutrality was to end the war. He sent his closest confidant, Edward M. House, to London and Berlin early in 1916 to present proposals for peace and for a league of nations to maintain peace in the future. House received no encouragement from either side and concluded that they were not interested in negotiations.

Some Americans had begun to demand "preparedness"—a military buildup. In response, in mid-1916, Congress appropriated the largest naval expenditures in peacetime history and approved the National Defense Act, which doubled the size of the army. Wilson accepted both measures.

The Election of 1916

By embracing preparedness, Wilson defused an issue that might have helped the Republicans in the 1916 presidential campaign. The Democrats nominated Wilson for a second term, and they campaigned on their domestic reforms and preparedness programs, frequently repeating the slogan "He kept us out of war."

■ *Lusitania* British passenger liner sunk by a German submarine in 1915, creating a diplomatic crisis between the United States and Germany.

creditor nation A nation whose citizens or government has loaned more money to the citizens or governments of other nations than the total amount that they have borrowed from the citizens or governments of other nations.

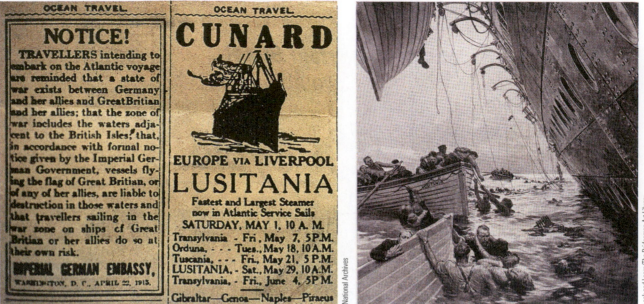

New York newspapers carried warnings from the German embassy about the dangers of trans-Atlantic travel, but passengers who boarded the *Lusitania* on May 1, 1915, probably paid little attention. The ship was sunk on May 7. Of the 1,959 passengers and crewmembers, 1,198 died, including 128 Americans.

Republicans nominated Charles Evans Hughes, a Supreme Court justice and former governor of New York with a reputation as a progressive. Hughes avoided a clear position on preparedness and neutrality, hoping for support both from German Americans upset with Wilson's harshness toward Germany and from those who wanted maximum assistance for the Allies. As a result, he failed to present a compelling alternative to Wilson.

The vote was very close. Most voters identified themselves as Republicans, and Wilson needed support from some of them. He won by uniting the always-Democratic South with the West, much of which was progressive. Wilson also received significant backing from unions, socialists, and women in states where women could vote. In the end, Wilson received 49 percent of the vote to 46 percent for Hughes.

The Decision for War

After the election, events moved quickly. In January 1917, Wilson spoke to the Senate on the need to achieve and preserve peace. The galleries were packed as he called for an international organization to keep peace in the future. He urged that the only lasting peace would be a "peace without victory" in which neither side exacted gains from the other. He called for government by consent of the governed, freedom of the seas, and reductions in armaments. Wilson aimed his speech toward "the people of the countries now at war," hoping to build public pressure on those governments to seek peace. He won praise from left-wing opposition parties in several countries, but the British, French, and German governments had no interest in "peace without victory."

In fact, the German government decided to resume unrestricted submarine warfare, fully expecting this would bring the United States into the war but gambling that they would defeat the British and French before American troops could make a difference. When Germany announced it was resuming unrestricted submarine warfare, Wilson broke off diplomatic relations. German U-boats began immediately to devastate Atlantic shipping.

A few weeks later, on March 1, Wilson released a message from the German state secretary for foreign affairs, Arthur Zimmermann, to the German minister in Mexico. Zimmermann proposed that, if the United States went to war with Germany, Mexico should join with Germany and attack the United States. Zimmermann promised that if Germany and Mexico won, Mexico would recover its "lost provinces" of Texas, Arizona, and New Mexico. Zimmermann

left-wing Not conservative; usually implies socialist or other radical leanings.

■ **Arthur Zimmermann** German foreign-affairs official who proposed in 1917 that if the United States declared war on Germany, Mexico should become a German ally, win back Texas, Arizona, and New Mexico, and persuade Japan to go to war against the United States.

A Deeper Understanding of History

A History Detective at Work

Between 1924 and 1967, more than two dozen accounts of Woodrow Wilson's decision to go to war cited a conversation between Wilson and Frank Cobb, editor of the *New York World*. In this conversation, Wilson expressed deep misgivings about going to war and was highly prophetic about what war would mean for civil liberties, progressivism, and his own political future.

In 1967, a young assistant professor, Jerald Auerbach, published an article in which he argued persuasively that such a conversation never took place. His study provides both a warning to scholars about the need to be critical of sources and an excellent example of detective work by an historian.

Auerbach began by tracking the account of the conversation to a book published in 1924. However, the account in that book was not written by Cobb but by two of his colleagues, Maxwell Anderson and Laurence Stallings, and it was written after Cobb's death, seven years after the alleged conversation. Anderson and Stallings claimed that Cobb told them the story, and that they had reproduced it—complete with long, exact quotations from Wilson—from memory. Auerbach points out that it would have been difficult for Cobb or his two colleagues to have recalled the exact words of Wilson so many years later. Auerbach also points out that there is no evidence that Cobb visited the White House within two weeks of the supposed date of the conversation.

Anderson and Stallings quote Wilson as voicing deep misgivings for civil liberties should the nation go to war. Auerbach, however, produces ample evidence that Wilson himself repeatedly took public positions that were, in Auerbach's phrase, "emphatically antilibertarian," and he points out that Wilson did nothing to protect civil liberties either before or during the war. Auerbach carefully examines the language attributed to Wilson by Anderson and Stallings and concludes that it is "so exact a statement of what actually transpired between 1917 and 1920 that one is almost forced to conclude that it was written after these years, not before." For example, he notes that Wilson supposedly predicted the general outline of the Versailles

conference. Finally, Auerbach reveals that Anderson and Stallings were, by 1924, deeply disillusioned by the war.

Auerbach presents his conclusion in the title of his article: "Woodrow Wilson's Prediction to Frank Cobb: Words Historians Should Doubt Ever Got Spoken." Not all historians accept Auerbach's conclusion, but you can read his article and decide for yourself: see the *Journal of American History,* Volume 54 (1967), pp. 608–617. A subsequent article, by Brian J. Dalton, in *The Historian*, Volume 32 (1970), pp. 545–563, presents additional information and comes to a different conclusion. Both journals are available through most college and university libraries.

This photo of Frank Cobb, the editorial chief of the *New York World*, was taken in late 1918.

also proposed that Mexico should encourage Japan to enter the war against the United States. The British intercepted the message and gave it to Wilson. Zimmermann's suggestions further outraged Americans.

By March 21, German U-boats had sunk six American ships. Wilson could avoid war only by backing down from his insistence on "strict accountability." He did not retreat. Despite his focus on neutral rights, Wilson's major objective in going to war was to defeat German autocracy and militarism and to put the United States, and himself, in a position to determine the terms of peace. On April 2, 1917, Wilson asked Congress to declare war on Germany and tried to unite Americans in a righteous, progressive crusade. Condemning German U-boat attacks as "warfare against mankind," he proclaimed, "The world must be made safe for democracy." He promised that the United States would fight for self-government, "the rights and liberties of small nations," and a league of nations to "bring peace and safety to all nations and make the world itself at last free."

Not all members of Congress agreed that war was necessary. During the debate, Senator George W. Norris, a progressive Republican from Nebraska, best voiced the opposing arguments. The nation, he argued, was going to war "upon the command of gold" to "preserve the commercial right of American citizens to deliver munitions of war to belligerent nations." In the Senate, Norris, Robert La Follette, and four others voted no, but eighty-two senators voted for war. Jeannette Rankin of Montana, the first woman in the House of Representatives, was among those who said no when the House voted 373 to 50 for war. In December, Congress also declared war against Austria-Hungary.

THE HOME FRONT

☆ How successful was the federal government in mobilizing the economy and society to support the war?

☆ How did the war affect Americans, especially women, African Americans, and opponents of war?

Historians call World War I the first "total war" because it was the first to demand mobilization of an entire society and economy. The war altered nearly every aspect of the economy as the progressive emphasis on expertise and efficiency produced unprecedented centralization of economic decision making. Mobilization extended beyond war production to people themselves and to shaping public opinion about the war.

Mobilizing the Economy

Waging war effectively depended on a fully engaged industrial economy. Thus warring nations sought to redirect economic activities toward supplying their war machines. In the United States, railway transportation delays, shortages of supplies, and the sluggish pace of some manufacturing led to increased federal direction over transportation, food and fuel production, and manufacturing. This was not unusual among the belligerents and was probably less extreme than in other nations. Even so, the extent of direct federal control over much of the economy has never been matched since World War I.

Though unprecedented, much of the government intervention was voluntary. Business enlisted as a partner with government and supplied its cooperation and expertise. Some prominent entrepreneurs volunteered their services for a dollar a year. Much of the wartime centralization of economic decision making came through new agencies composed of government officials, business leaders, and prominent citizens.

The **War Industries Board** supervised production of war materials. At first, it had only limited success in increasing productivity. Then, in early 1918, Wilson appointed Bernard Baruch, a Wall Street financier, to head the board. By pleading, bargaining, and sometimes threatening, Baruch usually persuaded companies to meet production quotas, allocate raw materials, develop new industries, and streamline operations. Though Baruch threatened steel company executives with a government takeover, he accomplished most goals without coercion—and industrial production increased by 20 percent.

Efforts to conserve fuel included the first use of daylight saving time. To improve rail transportation, the federal government consolidated the railroads and ran them during the war. The government also took over the telegraph and telephone systems and launched a huge shipbuilding program to expand the merchant marine.

The **National War Labor Board** (NWLB), created in 1918, endorsed **collective bargaining** to facilitate production by resolving labor disputes. The board also helped to settle labor disputes. Never before had a federal agency interceded this way. The board gave some support for an eight-hour workday in return for a no-strike pledge from unions.

Most unions promised not to strike for the duration of the war, and many secured contracts with significant wage increases. Union membership boomed

□ **War Industries Board** Federal agency headed by Bernard Baruch that coordinated American production during World War I.

□ **National War Labor Board** (NWLB) Federal agency created in 1918 to resolve wartime labor disputes.

collective bargaining Negotiation between the representatives of organized workers and their employer to determine wages, hours, and working conditions.

Labor shortages attracted new workers into the labor market and opened some jobs to women and members of racial minorities. In May 1918, these women worked in the Union Pacific Railroad freight yard in Cheyenne, Wyoming.

from 2.7 million in 1916 to more than 4 million by 1919. Samuel Gompers, president of the AFL, called the war "the most wonderful crusade ever entered upon in the whole history of the world." Nevertheless, many workers felt that their purchasing power was not keeping pace with increases in prices.

Demands for increased production when millions of men were marching off to war opened opportunities for women. Employment of women in factory, office, and retail jobs had increased before the war, and the war accelerated those trends. At the war's end, many women's wartime jobs returned to male hands, but in office work and some retail positions women continued to dominate after the war.

One crucial American contribution to the Allies was food, for the war severely disrupted European agriculture. Wilson appointed as food administrator **Herbert Hoover**, who had already won wide praise for directing the relief program in Belgium when America was still neutral. Now he both promoted increased food production and urged families to conserve food through Meatless Mondays and Wheatless Wednesdays and by planting "war gardens" to raise vegetables. Farmers brought large areas under cultivation for the first time. Food shipments to the Allies tripled.

Some progressives urged that the Wilson administration pay for the war by taxing the wartime profits and earnings of corporations. That did not happen, but taxes—especially the new income tax—did account for almost half of the $33 billion the United States spent on the war between April 1917 and June 1920. The government borrowed the rest, much of it through **Liberty Loan** drives. Rallies, parades, and posters pushed all Americans to buy "Liberty Bonds."

Mobilizing Public Opinion

Not all Americans supported the war. Some German Americans were reluctant to send their sons to war against their cousins. Some Irish Americans became

■ **Herbert Hoover** U.S. food administrator during World War I; later secretary of commerce (1921–1928) and president (1929–1933).

■ **Liberty Loan** One of four bond issues floated by the U.S. Treasury Department from 1917 to 1919 to help finance World War I.

James Montgomery Flagg created this poster in 1918, showing Columbia, a traditional symbol for America, sowing grain as a way of appealing to American women to contribute to victory by raising and preserving food for their families. Columbia was usually garbed in an American flag, wearing a red liberty cap, a traditional symbol of freedom.

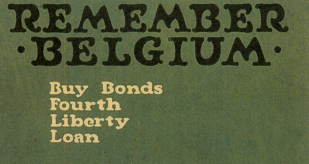

This poster by Ellsworth Young, from 1918, encouraged Americans to buy Liberty Bonds (that is, loan money to the government) by emphasizing the image of the vicious and brutal Hun, part of a larger process of demonizing the people of the Central Powers.

even more hostile to Britain after English troops brutally suppressed an attempt at Irish independence in 1916. The Socialist Party openly opposed the war, and Socialist candidates dramatically increased their share of the vote in several places in 1917—to 22 percent in New York City and 34 percent in Chicago—suggesting that their antiwar stance attracted many voters.

To mobilize public opinion in support of the war, Wilson created the Committee on Public Information, headed by George Creel. Creel determined to sell the war to Americans. The **Creel Committee** eventually counted 150,000 lecturers, writers, artists, actors, and scholars championing the war and whipping up hatred of the "Huns." Social clubs, movie theaters, and churches all joined what Creel called

"the world's greatest adventure in advertising." "Four-Minute Men"—volunteers ready to make a short patriotic speech any time and place a crowd gathered—made 755,190 speeches.

Wilson's war message had stressed that "We have no quarrel with the German people," but wartime propaganda quickly moved toward demonizing all things German, and wartime patriotism sparked extreme measures against those considered "slackers" or pro-German. "Woe to the man or group of men that seeks to stand in our way," warned Wilson. "He who is not with us, absolutely and without reserve of any kind," echoed former president Theodore Roosevelt, "is against us, and should be treated as an alien enemy."

"Americanization" drives promoted rapid assimilation among immigrants. Some states prohibited the use of foreign languages in public. Officials removed German books from libraries and sometimes publicly burned them. Some communities banned music by Bach and Beethoven and dropped German classes

□ **Creel Committee** The U.S. Committee on Public Information (1917–1919), headed by journalist and editor George Creel; used films, posters, pamphlets, and news releases to mobilize public opinion in favor of World War I.

from their schools. Even words became objectionable: sauerkraut became "liberty cabbage." Sometimes mobs hounded people with German names and occasionally attacked or even lynched people suspected of antiwar sentiments.

Civil Liberties in Time of War

Not only German Americans but also pacifists, socialists, and other radicals became targets for government repression and **vigilante** action. Congress passed the **Espionage Act** in 1917 and the **Sedition Act** in 1918, prohibiting interference with the draft and outlawing criticism of the government, the armed forces, or the war effort. Violators faced large fines and long prison terms. Officials arrested fifteen hundred people for violating these acts, including Eugene V. Debs, leader of the Socialist Party. The Espionage Act authorized the postmaster general to bar objectionable publications from the mail. By the war's end, he had denied mailing privileges to some four hundred periodicals, including, at least temporarily, the *New York Times* and other mainstream publications. When convictions under these acts were appealed to the Supreme Court, the court upheld the constitutionality of the laws.

The Industrial Workers of the World (IWW) made no public pronouncement against the war, but most Wobblies probably opposed it. IWW members and leaders quickly came under attack from employers, government officials, and vigilantes, most of whom had disliked the IWW before the war. In September 1917, Justice Department agents raided IWW offices nationwide and arrested IWW leaders, who were sent to prison for up to twenty-five years and fined millions of dollars. Deprived of most leaders and virtually bankrupted, the IWW never recovered.

Some Americans protested the abridgment of civil liberties. One group formed the Civil Liberties Bureau—forerunner of the American Civil Liberties Union. Most Americans, however, did not object to the repression, and many who did kept silent.

The Great Migration and White Reactions

In 1910, about 90 percent of all African Americans lived in the South, 75 percent in rural areas. By 1920, as many as a half-million had moved north in what has been called the **Great Migration**. Many went to industrial cities in the Midwest. New York City, Philadelphia, and Los Angeles also attracted many blacks. Several factors produced this migration, but most important were the brutality and hardships of southern life and the economic opportunities in northern cities. "Every time a lynching takes place in a community

TOWARD A MORE PERFECT UNION

Civil Liberties in Wartime

The Espionage and Sedition Acts were intended to silence critics of the war and prevent them from interfering with mobilization. Charles Schenck was convicted of violating the Espionage Act for distributing leaflets that encouraged men to refuse the draft. He appealed to the U.S. Supreme Court, arguing that his actions were protected by the First Amendment.

In 1918, the Supreme Court ruled unanimously that the First Amendment did not protect speech or writings that posed a danger to the nation. The decision, by Justice Oliver Wendell Holmes, argued from analogy: "The most stringent protection of free speech would not protect a man in falsely shouting fire in a theatre and causing a panic." In First Amendment cases, Holmes continued, the question must be whether the speech or writing in question creates "a clear and present danger" to the nation. He concluded that Schenk's leaflets fit that description.

In 1969, the Supreme Court modified the *Schenck* and related decisions when it specified that the First Amendment protected speech and writings unless they created the likelihood of "imminent lawless action."

down South," said T. Arnold Hill of Chicago's Urban League, "colored people will arrive in Chicago within two weeks."

Equally significant in the Great Migration was American industry's desperate need for workers. The labor needs of northern cities attracted hundreds of thousands of African Americans seeking better jobs and higher pay. In the North, one could earn almost as much in a day as in a week in the South. African Americans did find better wages but also racial discrimination in housing and in access to many jobs.

vigilante A person who takes law enforcement into his or her own hands, usually on the grounds that normal law enforcement has broken down.

■ **Espionage Act** A 1917 law mandating severe penalties for anyone found guilty of interfering with the draft or encouraging disloyalty to the United States.

■ **Sedition Act** A 1918 law supplementing the Espionage Act by extending penalties to anyone deemed to have abused the government.

■ **Great Migration** Movement of about a half-million black people from the rural South to the urban North during World War I.

Labor shortages and high wages drew African Americans from the South to the North. This family, including members of three generations, posed for a photographer upon their arrival in Chicago from the South as part of the Great Migration.

New black neighborhoods developed in some cities where African Americans were able to find housing.

Racial conflicts erupted in several northern cities, as whites attacked individual African Americans or tried to burn their neighborhoods. One of America's worst race riots swept through the industrial city of East St. Louis, Illinois, on July 2, 1917. Thousands of black laborers, most from the South, had settled there during the previous two years. Thirty-nine African Americans perished in the riot, and six thousand lost their homes. Incensed that such brutality could occur just weeks after the nation's moralistic entrance into the war, W. E. B. Du Bois charged, "No land that loves to lynch [black people] can lead the hosts of Almighty God," and the NAACP led a silent protest parade of ten thousand people through **Harlem**.

> **Harlem** A section of New York City in the northern part of Manhattan; one of the largest black communities in the United States.

PLANNING FOR PEACE IN THE MIDST OF WAR

☆ *What role did American ships and troops play in the war?*

☆ *How and why did Wilson keep America's participation in the war separate from the Allies?*

Some who supported the war expected that the United States would send only supplies and not soldiers, but it quickly became clear that the United States needed to mobilize troops. The army, however, was tiny compared with the armies contesting in Europe. Millions of men and thousands of women had to be inducted, trained, and transported to Europe.

Mobilizing for Battle

The navy was large and powerful after three decades of shipbuilding, and preparedness measures in 1916 further strengthened it. The American and British navies' convoy technique, in which several cargo or passenger ships traveled together under the protection of destroyers, cut shipping losses in half. By spring 1918, U-boats ceased to pose a significant danger.

In April 1917, the combined strength of the U.S. Army and National Guard stood at 372,000 men. Many volunteered but not enough. In May, Congress passed the **Selective Service Act**, requiring men ages 21 to 30 (later extended to 18 to 45) to register with local boards to determine who would be drafted (that is, called to duty). The law exempted those who opposed war on religious grounds, but such **conscientious objectors** were sometimes badly treated.

Few people demonstrated against the draft, and most seemed to accept it as efficient and fair. Twenty-four million men registered, and 2.8 million were drafted—about 72 percent of the entire army. By the end of the war, the army, navy, and Marine Corps counted 4.8 million members.

No women were drafted, but almost thirteen thousand served in the navy and marines, most in clerical capacities. For the first time, women held naval and marine rank and status. The army refused to enlist women, considering it too "radical." Nearly eighteen thousand women served as army nurses, but without army rank or pay. At least five thousand civilian women also served in France, the largest number through the Red Cross, which helped to staff hospitals and rest facilities.

Nearly 400,000 African Americans served during World War I. Emmett J. Scott, an African American and former secretary to Booker T. Washington, became special assistant to the secretary of war, responsible for African Americans. Almost 200,000 served overseas. Most were assigned to menial tasks, but nearly 30,000 fought on the front lines. Black soldiers were often treated as second-class citizens, serving in segregated units in the army, limited to food service in the navy, and excluded altogether from the marines. More than six hundred African Americans earned commissions as officers, but the army refused to put a black officer in authority over white officers. White officers commanded most black troops.

Americans "Over There"

Shortly after the United States entered the war, a new song by George M. Cohan rocketed to national popularity:

> Over there, over there,
> Send the word, send the word over there,
> The Yanks are coming, the Yanks are coming,
> And we won't come back 'til it's over over there.

A few Yanks—troops in the **American Expeditionary Force** (AEF)—arrived in France in June 1917, commanded by General John J. Pershing, recently returned from Mexico. Most American troops, however,

Nebraska State Historical Society.

About ten thousand American Indians served in the army during World War I, including John Miller (*left*) and Charlie Wolf, members of the Omaha tribe. Some Indians who went to war first underwent tribal ceremonies, long unpracticed, that prepared warriors for battle, thus helping preserve traditional customs.

were still to be inducted, supplied, trained, and transported across the Atlantic.

Throughout the war, Wilson held the United States apart from the Allies. He referred to the United States not as one of the Allies but as an Associated Power, and he insisted that American troops have their own sector of the western front. He did so because he distrusted Allied war aims and wanted to make the American contribution to victory as prominent as

■ **Selective Service Act** Law passed by Congress in 1917 establishing compulsory military service for men ages 21 to 30.

conscientious objector Person who refuses to bear arms or participate in military service because of religious beliefs or moral principles.

■ **American Expeditionary Force** (AEF) American army commanded by General John J. Pershing; served in Europe during World War I.

possible so as to maximize American influence at the peace conference.

As American troops trickled into France in mid-1917, the Allies were stretched thin. French and British offensives in 1917 failed, and the Italians suffered a major defeat later that year. After disastrous losses, Russia withdrew from the war late in 1917, permitting German commanders to shift troops to the western front (see Map 20.2). Hoping to win the war before Americans could make a difference, the Germans planned a massive offensive for spring 1918.

German troops smashed into the French and British lines in Picardy and advanced along the Marne River. By late May, the Germans were within 50 miles of Paris. As French officials considered evacuating the capital, all available troops, including AEF units, were rushed to the front. At Château-Thierry and at Belleau Wood, AEF troops took 8,000 casualties during a month-long battle over a single square mile of wheat fields and woods. Of 310,000 AEF troops who fought in the Marne region, 67,000 were killed or wounded. The German advance failed.

The Allies then launched a counteroffensive in July as American troops poured into France, topping a million. In September Pershing launched a successful offensive against the St. Mihiel salient (see Map 20.2). AEF forces then joined an Allied offensive in the Meuse River–Argonne Forest region, the last major assault of the war and one of the fiercest battles in American military history.

On October 8, Corporal Alvin York, a skilled sharpshooter from the Tennessee mountains, was in the Argonne Forest. His unit came under fire and most were wounded or killed. York, however, coolly practiced his mountaineer sharpshooting, single-handedly killing twenty-five enemy soldiers and silencing thirty-five machine guns. He and the six surviving members of his unit took 132 prisoners. York received the Congressional Medal of Honor, the Croix de Guerre (France's highest decoration), and similar awards from other nations. York's courage and coolness were not unique among the Americans in the Meuse–Argonne campaign—Harry J. Adams, with only an empty pistol, captured 300 prisoners; Hercules Korgia, captured by the Germans, persuaded his captors to become his prisoners; and Samuel Woodfill single-handedly took out five machine guns.

German military leaders now urged an armistice. Fighting ended at 11:00 A.M., November 11, 1918. Nearly 9 million combatants had died: Germany lost 1.8 million, Russia 1.7 million, France 1.4 million, Austria-Hungary 1.1 million, and the British Empire 1.1 million. Of the 4.5 million who served in the French army, 31 percent were killed and 44 percent were wounded. American losses were small in comparison—365,000 **casualties**, including 126,000 deaths. Some 800,000 civilians from the Central Powers died of famine resulting from the British blockade. Millions of other civilians, worldwide, died from war-related causes, including starvation and disease. A global **influenza** epidemic in 1918 and 1919 killed 20 to 40 million people or perhaps more—more than died in the war and including 500,000 Americans.

Some white Americans, including some military officers, worried that experiences in France might cause African American soldiers to resist segregation at home. In August 1918, AEF headquarters secretly requested that the French not prominently commend black units. The French, however, awarded the **Croix de Guerre** to several all-black units that had distinguished themselves in combat and presented awards to individual soldiers for acts of bravery and heroism. When the Allies staged a grand victory parade down Paris's Champs-Élysées, the British and French contingents included all races and ethnicities, but American commanders directed that no African American troops take part.

Bolshevism, the Secret Treaties, and the Fourteen Points

In March 1917, before the United States entered the war, war-weary and hungry Russians deposed their **tsar** and created a provisional government. In November, a group of radical socialists, the **Bolsheviks**, seized power. Soon renamed Communists, the Bolsheviks condemned capitalism and imperialism and sought to destroy them. **Vladimir Lenin**, the Bolshevik leader, initiated peace negotiations with the Germans. The **Treaty of Brest-Litovsk**, in March 1918, was harsh and humiliating, requiring Russia to surrender vast territories—Finland, its Baltic provinces, parts of Poland and Ukraine—a third of its population, half of its industries, its most fertile agricultural land, and a quarter of its territory in Europe.

salient In military usage, a portion of one's front line that projects into enemy territory. In this instance, it was a German salient that projected into the Allied line.

casualty A member of the military lost through death, wounds, injury, sickness, or capture.

influenza Contagious viral infection characterized by fever, chills, congestion, and muscular pain, nicknamed "flu"; an unusually deadly strain of the H1N1 subtype, usually called "Spanish flu," swept across the world in 1918 and 1919.

Croix de Guerre French military decoration for bravery in combat; in English, "the Cross of War."

tsar The monarch of the Russian Empire; also spelled *czar*.

■ **Bolsheviks** Radical socialists, later called Communists, who seized power in Russia in November 1917.

■ **Vladimir Lenin** Leader of the Bolsheviks; until 1924, head of the Soviet Union, the state that grew out of the revolution.

■ **Treaty of Brest-Litovsk** March 1918 treaty between Germany and Russia allowing Russia to withdraw from World War I; Russia gave up vast territories.

The Bolsheviks condemned the war as a scramble for imperial spoils. In December 1917, they published the secret treaties by which the Allies had agreed to divide colonies and territories of the defeated Central Powers among themselves. These exposés strengthened Wilson's intent to keep American war aims separate and to impose his war objectives on the Allies.

On January 8, 1918, Wilson spoke to Congress. He denounced both the secret treaties and the harsh terms the Germans were demanding from Russia. American war goals, he proclaimed, derived from "the principle of justice to all peoples and nationalities, and their right to live on equal terms of liberty and safety with one another, whether they be strong or weak." Seeking to seize the initiative, he presented fourteen objectives, soon called the Fourteen Points. Points one through five aimed to remove causes of war: no secret treaties, freedom of the seas, reduction of barriers to trade, reduction of armaments, and adjustment of colonial claims based partly on the interests of colonial peoples. Point six called for other nations to withdraw from Russian territory and to welcome Russia "into the society of free nations." Points seven through thirteen addressed particular situations: return of territories France had lost to Germany in 1871, and self-determination in Central Europe and the Middle East. The fourteenth point called for "a general association of nations" that could afford "mutual guarantees of political independence and territorial integrity to great and small states alike."

Showing little enthusiasm, the Allies accepted Wilson's Fourteen Points as starting points for discussion. When the Germans asked for an end to the fighting, however, they made clear that their request was based on the Fourteen Points.

THE PEACE CONFERENCE AND THE TREATY

☆ How successful was Wilson at the peace conference?
☆ What caused the defeat of the treaty?

With the war over, Wilson hoped that the peace process would not sow the seeds of future wars. He hoped, too, to create an international organization to keep the peace. The Allies, however, were more interested in grabbing territory or punishing Germany.

The World in 1919

In December 1918, Wilson sailed for France—the first American president to go to Europe while in office and the first to negotiate directly with other world leaders. Wilson brought reports from experts on European history, culture, ethnology, and geography who had been working since fall 1917 on plans for the postwar era. In France, Italy, and Britain, huge welcoming crowds cheered the great "peacemaker from America."

Delegates to the peace conference assembled amid the collapse of ancient empires and the birth of new republics. The Austro-Hungarian Empire had crumbled, producing the new nations of Poland and Czechoslovakia and the republics of Austria and Hungary. The German monarch, Kaiser Wilhelm, had abdicated, and a republic was forming. In January 1919, communists tried unsuccessfully to seize power in Berlin. Throughout the ruins of the Russian Empire, ethnic groups were proclaiming independent republics (most eventually incorporated into the Soviet Union, often by the Bolsheviks' Red Army). The Ottoman Empire was collapsing, too, as Arabs, with aid from Britain and France, overthrew Turkish rule in many areas.

Throughout Europe and the Middle East, national self-determination and sometimes government by the consent of the governed—part of Wilson's goal for the postwar world—seemed to be lurching into reality. Nor were the British and French colonial empires immune, for both faced growing independence movements among their many possessions.

In Russia, civil war raged between the Bolsheviks and their opponents, called Whites. When the Bolsheviks left the world war, the Allies pushed Wilson to join them in intervening in Russia, ostensibly to protect war supplies from falling into German hands. In mid-1918, Wilson sent American troops as part of Allied expeditions to northern Russia and eastern Siberia. In Siberia, his intent was primarily to head off a Japanese grab of Russian territory. Allied intervention soon changed to support for the Whites. By late 1918, Wilson was expressing concern over what he called "mass terrorism" directed by the Bolsheviks toward "peaceable Russian citizens." Before the last American troops withdrew from northern Russia in May 1919 and from eastern Siberia in early 1920, they had engaged in conflict with units of the Red Army.

▪ **Fourteen Points** President Wilson's statement of U.S. war goals, including arms reduction, national self-determination, and a league of nations.

ethnology The study of ethnocultural groups.

abdicate To relinquish a high office; usually said only of monarchs.

Red Army The Bolsheviks' army, created to defend the Communist government during the Russian civil war and to reestablish control over parts of the Russian Empire that tried to create separate republics in 1917 and 1918; it was the army of the Soviet Union throughout its existence.

self-determination The freedom of a people to determine their own political status.

In the Wider World

Civil War in Russia, 1918–1920

After the Bolsheviks took power in Russia in November 1917, the first significant opposition developed in southern Russia, led by former army officers. In January 1918, the Bolsheviks disbanded the elected Constituent Assembly and excluded from power members of the largest political party, the Socialist Revolutionaries (SRs, moderate socialists), sending many SRs into opposition. The humiliating Treaty of Brest-Litovsk pushed more Russians into opposition. By mid-1918, White (anti-Bolshevik) armies controlled much of southern Russia, all of Siberia, and small areas elsewhere and seemed to be threatening Moscow. Several nations had troops in Russia, but nearly all the fighting was by Russians against Russians. Britain provided more supplies for the Whites than any other source outside Russia.

The Bolsheviks' Red Army fought back, emerging victorious late in 1920. During the Civil War, the Bolsheviks' secret police, the Cheka, carried out a "Red terror" that included perhaps 250,000 executions of those considered "enemies of the people." The opposing armies ravaged large areas of the Russian countryside, and casualties exceeded 1.2 million on both sides. Drought and disease compounded the devastation of war, especially in southern Russia, producing an estimated 7 million homeless children.

Wilson at Versailles

The peace conference opened on January 18, 1919, just outside Paris, at the glittering Palace of Versailles, once home to French kings. Representatives attended from all nations that had declared war against the Central Powers, but major decisions were made by the Big Four: Wilson, David Lloyd George of Britain, Georges Clemenceau of France, and Vittorio Orlando of Italy. Germany was excluded. Terms of peace were to be imposed, not negotiated. Russia, too, was absent, since Lenin had withdrawn from the war and made a separate peace with Germany.

Wilson quickly realized that European leaders were focused on their own national interests, not his Fourteen Points. Clemenceau, nicknamed "the Tiger," remembered Germany's humiliating defeat of France in 1871 and hoped to disable Germany so it could never again threaten his nation. Lloyd George agreed with many of Wilson's goals but felt he carried orders from British voters to exact heavy **reparations** from Germany. Orlando and other Allies were still expecting to gain the territories promised in the secret treaties. The European Allies feared the spread of Bolshevism and intended to create buffers to keep it at bay.

Facing the insistent and acquisitive Allies, Wilson had to compromise. He did secure a **League of Nations**. Instead of "peace without victory," however, the **Treaty of Versailles** imposed harsh victors' terms,

reparations Payments as compensation for damages.

■ **League of Nations** A world organization created by the Versailles peace conference to promote peace and international cooperation.

■ **Treaty of Versailles** Treaty in 1919 ending World War I; imposed harsh terms on Germany, established territorial mandates, and created the League of Nations.

These American troops were photographed in August 1918 on parade through the streets of Vladivostok, Russia's major port on the Pacific, which was then controlled by White (anti-Bolshevik) forces. Wilson sent the U.S. troops to Russia in part to prevent the Japanese troops (some of which appear on the left side of the photo) from grabbing Russian territory.

National Archives 165-WW-558C-4.

MAP 20.4 Postwar Boundary Changes in Central Europe and the Middle East
This map shows the boundary changes in Europe and the Middle East resulting from the defeat of Austria-Hungary, Germany, Russia, and the Ottoman Empire. © Cengage Learning.

Boundaries of German, Russian, Austro-Hungarian, and Ottoman Empires in 1914
Areas lost by Austro-Hungarian Empire
Areas lost by Russian Empire
Areas lost by German Empire
Areas lost by Bulgaria
Areas lost by Ottoman Empire
Demilitarized Zones
Areas controlled under mandates from the League of Nations, 1920
Boundaries of 1926

It Matters Today

Redrawing the Map of the Middle East

Several current nations in the Middle East arose from agreements reached during World War I or at Versailles. During the war, Britain assisted Arabs to revolt against the Ottoman Empire and promised them an independent Arab state. However, at the same time, Britain and France, with the assent of Russia, secretly divided much of the Ottoman Empire between them. Further complicating matters was a wartime British promise that Palestine would be a future Jewish homeland.

Britain and France subsequently drew the boundaries of the League mandates for Iraq, Syria, Palestine, and Trans-Jordan (now Jordan), but not based on Wilson's goal of self-determination. Britain received Iraq, Palestine, and Trans-Jordan. France received Syria, which included Lebanon.

The French divided Syria into administrative regions based on the dominant religion in each area, setting up separate units for Alawite Muslims (an offshoot of Shia Islam), Sunni Muslims, Druze, and Maronite Christians, the last of which later became the core of the separate state of Lebanon. Throughout the French mandate period, the various religious groups remained anxious regarding their future relations with each other once the French left.

- How do decisions made at Versailles influence world affairs today?
- Do more research on Syria and Lebanon from 1920 onward. What do you find in that history that helps to understand the civil war that wracked Syria beginning in 2011 and the long-term civil strife in Lebanon?

---

requiring Germany to accept the blame for starting the war, pay reparations to the Allies (exact amounts to be determined later), and surrender all its colonies along with Alsace-Lorraine (which Germany had taken from France in 1871) and other European territories (see Map 20.4). The treaty deprived Germany of its navy and merchant marine and limited its army to 100,000 men. German representatives signed on June 28, 1919.

Wilson reluctantly agreed to the reparations but insisted that colonies taken from Germany and territories taken from the Ottoman Empire should not go permanently to the Allies. Called **mandates**, they were to be administered by one of the Allies on behalf of the League of Nations and were to move toward independence. In nearly every case, however, the mandate went to the nation slated to receive the territory under the secret treaties. Wilson blocked Italy's most extreme territorial demands but gave in on others.

The peace conference recognized new republics through Central Europe, thereby creating a so-called quarantine zone between Russian Bolshevism and western Europe. The treaty ignored those people—from Ireland to Vietnam—seeking self-determination for colonies held by one of the Allies. Japan tried but failed to secure a statement supporting racial equality.

Though Wilson compromised on most of his Fourteen Points, every compromise intensified his commitment to the League of Nations. The League, he hoped, would resolve future controversies without war and also solve problems created by the compromises. Even so, Wilson had to threaten a separate peace with Germany before the Allies agreed to incorporate the **League Covenant** into the treaty. Wilson was especially committed to Article 10 of the League Covenant—he called it the League's "heart." It specified that League members agreed to protect one another's independence and territory against external attacks and take joint action against aggressors.

The Senate and the Treaty

While Wilson was in Paris, opposition to his plans was brewing at home. The Senate, controlled by Republicans since the 1918 elections, had to approve any treaty.

Presented with the treaty, the Senate split into three groups. **Henry Cabot Lodge**, chairman of the

mandate A territory that the League of Nations authorized a member nation to administer and move toward independence.

League Covenant The constitution of the League of Nations, part of the 1919 Treaty of Versailles.

■ **Henry Cabot Lodge** Republican senator from Massachusetts; as chair of the Senate Foreign Relations Committee, led efforts to modify American participation in the League of Nations.

Senate Foreign Relations Committee, led the largest faction, called *reservationists* after the reservations, or amendments, to the treaty that Lodge developed. Article 10 of the League Covenant especially bothered Lodge, for he feared it might commit American troops to war without congressional approval. A small group called *irreconcilables*, mostly Republicans, opposed any American involvement in European affairs. A third Senate group, nearly all Democrats, supported the president and his treaty.

Wilson decided to appeal directly to the American people. In September 1919, he undertook an arduous speaking tour—9,500 miles with speeches in twenty-nine cities. The effort proved too demanding for his fragile health. Soon after, he suffered a serious stroke. Half-paralyzed and weak, Wilson could fulfill few duties. His wife, Edith Bolling Wilson, exercised what she later called a "stewardship," strictly limiting her ailing husband's contact with the outside world.

Lodge proposed that the Senate accept the treaty with his amendments. Some were minor, but others would have permitted Congress to block action under Article 10. Wilson refused any compromise. On November 19, 1919, the Senate defeated the treaty with the Lodge reservations by votes of 39 to 55 and 41 to 50, with the irreconcilables joining the president's supporters in opposition. Then the Senate defeated the unamended treaty by 38 to 53, with the irreconcilables joining the reservationists in voting no.

The treaty came to a vote again in March 1920. Some treaty supporters concluded that the League could never be approved without Lodge's amendments, so they joined the reservationists to produce 49 in favor to 35 opposed—still short of the two-thirds majority required. Enough Wilson loyalists—following their stubborn leader's order not to compromise—joined the irreconcilables to defeat the treaty once again. The United States did not join the League of Nations.

Legacies of the Great War

Wilson had reflected progressives' optimism and confidence in claiming that the United States was going to make the world "safe for democracy." One of his supporters even spoke of the "war to end war." Just as progressives defined their domestic policies in terms of progress, democracy, and social justice, so Wilson tried to invest his foreign policy with enlightened values. In doing so, however, he fostered unrealistic expectations that world politics might be transformed overnight.

Many Americans became disillusioned by the Allies' cynical opportunism. The war to make the world "safe for democracy" ended up with Italy annexing Austrian territory and Japan seizing German concessions in China. The "war to end war" spun off several wars in its wake: Romania invaded Hungary in 1919, Poland invaded Russia in 1920, the Russian civil war continued until late 1920, and Greece and Turkey battled until 1923.

The peace conference left many problems unresolved. Wilson's promotion of self-government and self-determination encouraged aspirations for independence throughout the Allies' colonies and among the new League mandates. Some of the new nations of Central Europe, supposedly based on ethnic self-determination, actually included different and sometimes antagonistic ethnic groups. Above all, the war and the treaty contributed to economic and political instability in much of Europe, making it a breeding ground for totalitarian and nationalistic movements that eventually generated another world war.

[AMERICA IN THE AFTERMATH OF WAR, NOVEMBER 1918–NOVEMBER 1920

☆ *How did Americans react to the outcome of the war and the events of 1919?*

☆ *How did the events of 1917–1920 affect the 1920 presidential election?*

Almost as soon as French church bells pealed for the armistice, the United States began to demobilize. Industrial demobilization occurred almost immediately, as officials canceled war contracts. In 1919, American troops came back from Europe, nearly 4 million men and women returned to civilian life, and the nation experienced raging inflation, massive strikes, bloody race riots, widespread fear of radical **subversion**, violations of civil liberties—and two new constitutional amendments that embodied important elements of progressivism: prohibition and woman suffrage.

"HCL" and Strikes

Inflation—described in newspapers as "HCL" for "High Cost of Living"—was the most pressing single problem Americans faced after the war. Between 1913 and 1919, prices almost doubled. Freed from their wartime no-strike pledge, unions made wage demands

---

subversion Efforts to undermine or overthrow an established government.

JOBS for FIGHTERS

BUREAU for RETURNING SOLDIERS and SAILORS — WALK IN

U.S. Employment Service and Co-operating Agencies

HONORABLE DISCHARGE

WELCOME

If You Need a Job
If You Need a Man
Inform the Official Central Agency
The Service is Free

The United States Employment Service
Bureau for Returning Soldiers and Sailors

United States Department of Labor—United States Employment Service

The federal Employment Service assisted returning soldiers and sailors to find jobs. Unemployment rose to nearly 12 percent by 1921.

Collection of Picture Research Consultants and Archives.

to match the soaring cost of living. In 1919, however, employers were ready for a fight.

Many companies wanted to return labor relations to prewar patterns. They blamed wage increases for inflation, and some tried to link unions to Bolshevism. In February 1919, Seattle's Central

■ **J. Edgar Hoover** Head of an antiradical unit in the Justice Department in 1919; head of the FBI from 1924 until his death in 1972.

Labor Council called out the city's unions in a five-day general strike to support shipyard workers; the mayor branded it a Bolshevik plot. Boston's police struck in September 1919 after the police commissioner fired nineteen policemen for joining a union. The governor of Massachusetts, Calvin Coolidge, called out the national guard to maintain order and break the union. "There is no right to strike against the public safety by anybody, anywhere, anytime," he proclaimed. By mid-1919, many unionists concluded that conservative politicians were joining business leaders to roll back unions' wartime gains and block new organizing.

The largest and most dramatic strike came against United States Steel. Few steelworkers were represented by unions after the 1892 Homestead strike. Steel companies often hired recent immigrants, keeping steelworkers divided by language. Most steelworkers put in twelve-hour workdays. Wages lagged far behind inflation—and company profits. In 1919 the AFL launched an ambitious unionization drive in the steel industry, and many steelworkers responded eagerly.

Steel industry leaders refused to deal with the new organization. The workers went on strike in late September, demanding union recognition, collective bargaining, the eight-hour workday, and higher wages. The company blamed the strike on radicals and mobilized public opinion against the strikers. Company guards protected strikebreakers, and U.S. military forces moved into Gary, Indiana, to help round up "the Red element." By January 1920, after eighteen workers had been killed and hundreds beaten, the strike was over and the unions were ousted.

Red Scare

The steel industry's charges of Bolshevism to discredit strikers came as many government and corporate leaders were declaiming against the dangers of Bolshevism at home and abroad. Then, in late April 1919, thirty-four bombs addressed to prominent Americans—including J. P. Morgan, John D. Rockefeller, and Supreme Court Justice Oliver Wendell Holmes—were discovered in various post offices after the explosion of two others addressed to a senator and Seattle's mayor. In June, bombs in several cities damaged buildings and killed two people. Though the work of a few anarchists, the bombs fueled fears of a nationwide radical conspiracy.

Attorney General A. Mitchell Palmer organized an anti-Red campaign, hoping that success might bring him the 1920 presidential nomination. "Like a prairie fire," Palmer claimed, "the blaze of revolution was sweeping over every American institution." He appointed **J. Edgar Hoover**, a young lawyer, to head

Alleged subversives, arrested in one of the Palmer raids in New York City in November 1919, are shown here leaving police wagons on their way to Ellis Island, where they were held pending deportation proceedings.

Bettmann/Corbis.

an antiradical unit in the Justice Department's Bureau of Investigation, the predecessor of the Federal Bureau of Investigation. In November 1919, Palmer launched what were soon called the **Palmer raids** to arrest suspected radicals. Although officials found few firearms and no explosives, they rounded up some five thousand people by January 1920, of whom several hundred radical aliens were deported. The rest were released.

State legislatures also produced antiradical measures, especially criminal syndicalism laws—measures criminalizing the advocacy of Bolshevik, IWW, or anarchist ideologies. In January 1920, the New York state legislature expelled five members elected as Socialists, solely because they were Socialists.

When a wide range of respected public figures denounced the legislature's action as undemocratic, public opinion regarding the **Red Scare** began to shift. With the approach of May 1, a day of celebration for radicals, Palmer dramatically warned of a general strike and bombings. When nothing happened, many concluded that the radical threat might have been overstated.

As the Red Scare sputtered to an end, in May 1920, police in Massachusetts arrested **Nicola Sacco** and **Bartolomeo Vanzetti**, Italian-born anarchists, and charged them with robbery and murder. Despite

inconclusive evidence and the men's protestations of innocence, a jury found them guilty, and they were sentenced to death. Many argued they had not received a fair trial and had been convicted because of their political beliefs and Italian origins. Over loud protests at home and abroad, both men were executed in 1927. Historians continue to debate the evidence, many arguing that Sacco was probably guilty and Vanzetti innocent, and others insisting both were innocent and that the state police concealed evidence.

Race Riots and Lynchings

The racial tensions of the war years continued into the postwar period. Black soldiers encountered less discrimination in Europe than they had ever known

■ **Palmer raids** Government raids on individuals and organizations in 1919 and 1920 to search for radicals.

■ **Red Scare** Wave of antiradicalism in the United States in 1919 and 1920.

■ **Nicola Sacco** and **Bartolomeo Vanzetti** Italian anarchists convicted in 1921 of murder and theft; despite public protests, they were electrocuted in 1927.

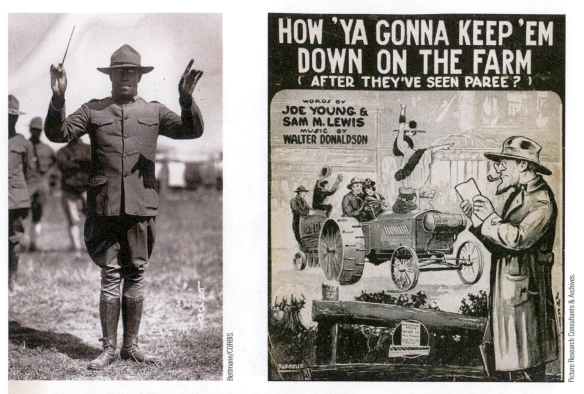

A black bandleader, James Reese Europe (*left*), went to France as a lieutenant, commanding a machine-gun company, and saw frontline action. He and other black musicians were reassigned to present musical entertainment behind the lines, becoming among the first to play jazz in France. Upon returning to the United States in 1919, he and his band recorded "How 'Ya Gonna Keep 'Em Down on the Farm After They've Seen Paree?" Many groups recorded the popular song, but black musicians may have given it a different emphasis: how can black soldiers be "kept down" after experiencing less oppressive racial patterns in France?

at home. In May 1919, the NAACP journal *Crisis* expressed what the more militant returning soldiers felt:

> We return. We return from fighting. We return fighting. Make way for Democracy! We saved it in France, and by the Great Jehovah, we will save it in the U.S.A., or know the reason why.

Some whites, however, greeted returning black troops with furious violence intended to restore prewar race relations. Southern mobs lynched ten black soldiers, some still in uniform. In all, rioters lynched more than seventy blacks in the first year after the war and burned eleven victims alive.

Rioting also struck outside the South. In July 1919, violence reached the nation's capital, where white mobs, including soldiers and sailors, attacked blacks over three days, killing several. The city's African Americans organized their own defense, sometimes arming themselves. In Chicago in late July, war raged between white and black mobs for nearly two weeks,

despite efforts by the national guard. The rioting caused thirty-eight deaths (fifteen white, twenty-three black). A thousand families—nearly all black—were burned out of their homes. In Omaha in September, a mob tried to hang the mayor when he bravely stood between them and a black prisoner accused of rape. Police saved the mayor but not the prisoner.

By the end of 1919, race riots had flared in more than two dozen places. The year saw not only rampant lynchings but also the appearance of a new Ku Klux Klan (discussed in the next chapter). Despite violence and coercion directed at African Americans, some things had changed. As W. E. B. Du Bois observed, black veterans "would never be the same again. You cannot ask them to go back to what they were before. They cannot, for they are not the same men."

Amending the Constitution: Prohibition and Woman Suffrage

At the end of the war, two of the great campaigns of the Progressive Era finally realized their goals. Both had roots in the nineteenth century, both attracted numerous supporters during the Progressive Era, and both received a boost from the war. Prohibition was adopted as the **Eighteenth Amendment** to the

■ **Eighteenth Amendment** Constitutional amendment proposed in 1919 that forbid the manufacture, sale, or transportation of alcoholic beverages.

Constitution, and woman suffrage as the Nineteenth Amendment.

Pushed by the Anti-Saloon League, Congress passed a temporary prohibition measure in 1917. A more important victory came when Congress adopted and sent to the states the Eighteenth Amendment, prohibiting the manufacture, sale, or transportation of alcoholic beverages. Intense and single-minded lobbying persuaded three-fourths of the state legislatures to ratify the amendment in 1919. It took effect in January 1920.

The cause of woman suffrage also received a boost from the war, as suffrage advocates added women's contributions to the war effort to their previous arguments (discussed in Chapters 17–19). In June 1919, by a narrow margin, Congress proposed the **Nineteenth Amendment**, to enfranchise women, and sent it to the states for ratification. After a grueling, state-by-state battle, ratification came in August 1920. Though many women by then already exercised the franchise, especially in western states, ratification meant that the electorate for the 1920 elections was significantly expanded.

The Election of 1920

Republicans confidently expected to regain the White House in 1920. Democrats had lost their congressional majorities in the 1918 elections, and postwar misgivings and disillusionment often focused on Wilson. One reporter described the stricken president as the "sacrificial whipping boy for the present bitterness."

Any competent Republican nominee was practically guaranteed election. Several candidates attracted significant support, notably former army chief of staff General Leonard Wood, Illinois governor Frank Lowden, and California senator Hiram Johnson, but no candidate counted a majority in the convention. Months earlier, Harry Daugherty, campaign manager for Ohio senator Warren G. Harding, had foreseen a deadlock and had predicted that it would be broken at about "eleven minutes after two o'clock" in the morning, when "fifteen or twenty men, bleary-eyed and perspiring profusely" pick a compromise candidate. And so it was. A small group of party leaders met late at night in a smoke-filled hotel room and picked Harding. Even some of his supporters were unenthusiastic—one called him "the best of the second-raters." For vice president, the Republicans nominated Calvin Coolidge, the governor who broke the Boston police strike.

The Democrats also suffered severe divisions. After forty-four ballots, they chose James Cox, governor of Ohio, as their presidential candidate. For vice president, they nominated Franklin D. Roosevelt, Wilson's assistant secretary of the navy and a remote cousin of Theodore Roosevelt.

Described as good natured and likable—and sometimes as bumbling—Harding had published a small-town newspaper in Ohio until his wife, Florence, and some friends pushed him into politics. Eventually winning election to the Senate, unhappy with his marriage, Harding apparently took pleasure from a series of mistresses. The press knew of Harding's liaisons but never reported them.

During the 1920 campaign, an uproar arose over a claim that Harding's ancestry included African Americans. When a reporter asked Harding, "Do you have any Negro blood?" Harding replied mildly, "How do I know, Jim? One of my ancestors may have jumped the fence." The allegation, and Harding's response to it, apparently did not hurt his cause. Most of Harding's campaign reflected his promise to "return to normalcy."

After the stress of the war and postwar years, voters enthusiastically endorsed returning to "normalcy." Harding took thirty-seven of the forty-eight states and 60 percent of the popular vote—the largest popular majority up to that time. Wilson hoped for a "solemn referendum" on the League of Nations, but the election proved more a reaction against the war launched with lofty ideals that turned sour at Versailles, the high cost of living, and the strikes and riots of 1919. Americans, it seemed, had had enough of idealism and sacrifice for a while.

■ **Nineteenth Amendment** Constitutional amendment adopted in 1920 that prohibited restrictions on voting on account of sex.

Individual Voices

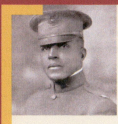

Library of Congress.

Woodrow Wilson Proposes His Fourteen Points

President Woodrow Wilson spoke to a joint session of Congress on January 8, 1918, and presented his objectives for peace, including his Fourteen Points. This is a condensed version of that speech. Historians understand that Wilson was writing to persuade many audiences: Congress, the American people, the Allies, the Central Powers—and later historians.

❶ To what events does this passage refer? To whom is it directed?

❷ How do these statements compare with the Treaty of Versailles?

❸ What are the connections among Points I through V, the causes of the war in 1914, and the reasons for American's entrance into the war?

❹ Was Wilson creating unrealistic expectations with such statements?

❺ Compare Wilson's reasons for committing America to war with Charles Young's reasons for wanting to go war.

It will be our wish and purpose that the processes of peace, when they are begun, shall be absolutely open. . . . The day of conquest and aggrandizement is gone by; so is also the day of secret [treaties]. . . . ❶

What we demand in this war . . . is that the world be made fit and safe to live in; and particularly that it be made safe for every peace-loving nation which, like our own, wishes to live its own life, determine its own institutions, be assured of justice and fair dealing by the other peoples of the world as against force and selfish aggression. All the peoples of the world are in effect partners in this interest. . . .

❷ The program of the world's peace, therefore, is our program; and that program, the only possible program, as we see it, is this:

I. Open covenants of peace, openly arrived at, after which there shall be no private international understandings of any kind but diplomacy shall proceed always frankly and in the public view.

II. Absolute freedom of navigation upon the seas, outside territorial waters. . . .

III. The removal, so far as possible, of all economic barriers and the establishment of an equality of trade conditions among all the nations.

IV. Adequate guarantees given and taken that national armaments will be reduced to the lowest point consistent with domestic safety.

V. A free, open-minded, and absolutely impartial adjustment of all colonial claims, based upon a strict observance of the principle that . . . the interests of the populations concerned must have equal weight with the equitable claims of the government whose title is to be determined. . . . ❸ [Points VI–XIII laid out specific territorial restorations or adjustments.]

XIV. A general association of nations must be formed under specific covenants for the purpose of affording mutual guarantees of political independence and territorial integrity to great and small states alike. . . .

For such arrangements and covenants we are willing to fight and to continue to fight until they are achieved; but only because we wish the right to prevail and desire a just and stable peace such as can be secured only by removing the chief provocations to war. . . .

An evident principle runs through the whole program I have outlined. It is the principle of justice to all peoples and nationalities, and their right to live on equal terms of liberty and safety with one another, whether they be strong or weak. . . . ❹

The people of the United States could act upon no other principle. . . .

The moral climax of this the culminating and final war for human liberty has come. . . . ❺

Study Tools

SUMMARY

Woodrow Wilson took office expecting to focus on domestic policy, not world affairs. He fulfilled some Democratic Party commitments to anti-imperialism but intervened extensively in the Caribbean. He also intervened in Mexico but failed to accomplish all his objectives there.

When war broke out in Europe in 1914, Wilson declared the United States to be neutral, and most Americans agreed. German submarine warfare and British restrictions on commerce, however, threatened traditional definitions of neutrality. Wilson secured a German pledge to refrain from unrestricted submarine warfare. He was reelected in 1916 on the argument that "he kept us out of war." Shortly after he won reelection, the Germans violated their pledge, and in April 1917 Wilson asked for war against Germany.

The war changed most aspects of America's economic and social life. The federal government developed a high degree of centralized economic planning, and tried to mold public opinion and restrict dissent. When the federal government backed collective bargaining, unions registered important gains. In response to labor shortages, more women and African Americans entered the industrial workforce, and many African Americans moved to northern and midwestern industrial cities.

Germany launched an offensive in 1918, hoping to achieve victory before Americans could make a difference. However, the AEF helped to break the German advance, and the Germans surrendered. In his Fourteen Points, Wilson expressed his goals for peace.

Facing opposition from the Allies, Wilson compromised at the Versailles peace conference but hoped that the League of Nations would maintain the peace. Fearing obligations that League membership might place on the United States, enough senators opposed the treaty to defeat it. Thus the United States did not become a member of the League.

The end of the war brought disillusionment and high prices, many strikes, a Red Scare, and race riots and lynchings. In 1920 the nation returned to its previous Republican majority when it elected Warren G. Harding, a mediocre conservative, to the White House.

CHRONOLOGY
The United States and World Affairs, 1913–1920

1912	Woodrow Wilson elected president
1913	Victoriano Huerta takes power in Mexico; Wilson denies recognition
1914	U.S. Navy occupies Veracruz
	War in Europe, United States declares neutrality
	Stalemate on the western front
1915	German U-boat sinks the *Lusitania*
	United States occupies Haiti
1915–1920	Great Migration
1916	U.S. troops pursue Pancho Villa into Mexico
	Wilson reelected
1917	Wilson calls for "peace without victory"
	Germany resumes submarine warfare
	Overthrow of tsar of Russia
	United States declares war on Germany
	Race riot in East St. Louis
	Bolsheviks seize power in Russia, publish secret treaties, withdraw Russia from the war
	Railroads placed under federal control
1918	Wilson presents Fourteen Points to Congress
	German offensive fails; Allies launch counter offensive that succeeds
	U.S. troops sent to northern Russia and Siberia
	Armistice in Europe
1918–1919	Worldwide influenza epidemic
1919	Signing of Treaty of Versailles
	Eighteenth Amendment (Prohibition) approved
	Race riots
	Major strikes
1919–1920	Red Scare, Palmer raids
1920	Senate defeats Versailles for second and final time
	Nineteenth Amendment (woman suffrage) approved
	Warren G. Harding elected president

Study Tools

FOCUS QUESTIONS

If you have mastered this chapter, you should be able to answer these questions and to identify the terms that follow the questions.

1. In what new directions did Wilson steer U.S. foreign policy before the coming of war in Europe?

2. Why did Wilson proclaim American neutrality? How did Americans respond?

3. What made neutrality difficult?

4. How did Wilson justify going to war?

5. How successful was the federal government in mobilizing the economy and society to support the war?

6. How did the war affect Americans, especially women, African Americans, and opponents of war?

7. What role did American ships and troops play in the war?

8. How and why did Wilson keep America's participation in the war separate from the Allies?

9. How successful was Wilson at the peace conference?

10. What caused the defeat of the treaty?

11. How did Americans react to the outcome of the war and the events of 1919?

12. How did the events of 1917–1920 affect the 1920 presidential election?

KEY TERMS

Victoriano Huerta   p. 538
Venustiano Carranza   p. 538
Francisco "Pancho" Villa   p. 539
Central Powers   p. 540
Allies   p. 540
western front   p. 542
U-boat   p. 542
Lusitania   p. 543
Arthur Zimmermann   p. 544
War Industries Board   p. 546
National War Labor Board   p. 546
Herbert Hoover   p. 547

Liberty Loan   p. 547
Creel Committee   p. 548
Espionage Act   p. 549
Sedition Act   p. 549
Great Migration   p. 549
Selective Service Act   p. 551
American Expeditionary Force   p. 551
Bolsheviks   p. 552
Vladimir Lenin   p. 552
Treaty of Brest-Litovsk   p. 552
Fourteen Points   p. 553

League of Nations   p. 554
Treaty of Versailles   p. 554
Henry Cabot Lodge   p. 556
J. Edgar Hoover   p. 558
Palmer raids   p. 559
Red Scare   p. 559
Nicola Sacco and Bartolomeo Vanzetti   p. 559
Eighteenth Amendment   p. 560
Nineteenth Amendment   p. 561

SUGGESTED RESOURCES

Kendrick A. Clements and Eric A. Cheezum, *Woodrow Wilson* (Thousand Oaks: CQ Press, 2003). Best recent treatment of Wilson's presidency.

"The Great War and the Shaping of the 20th Century," http://www.pbs.org/greatwar. An elaborate website based on a PBS series.

David P. Kilroy. *For Race and Country: The Life and Career of Colonel Charles Young* (Santa Barbara, CA: Praeger, 2003). Carefully researched and well written; puts Young's struggles for racial equality into the context of the times.

Erich Maria Remarque. *All Quiet on the Western Front,* trans. A. W. Wheen (1930; several recent editions). The classic and moving novel about World War I, seen through German eyes: some of the recent editions have useful introductions.

Richard Slotkin. *Lost Battalions: The Great War and the Crisis of American Nationality* (New York: Henry Holt, 2005). The wartime experiences of two New York state units, one of African Americans and the other largely of European immigrants.

Robert Zieger. *America's Great War: World War I and the American Experience* (Lanham, MD: Rowman and Littlefield, 2001). Excellent recent overview of the United States during World War I.

21

Prosperity Decade, 1920–1928

CHAPTER OUTLINE

The Bullish Decade
The Economics of Prosperity
Targeting Consumers
The Automobile: Driving the Economy
Changes in Banking and Business
"Get Rich Quick"
Agriculture: Depression in the Midst
of Prosperity

The "Roaring Twenties"
A People on Wheels: The Automobile
and American Life
Los Angeles: Automobile Metropolis
A Homogenized Culture Searches
for Heroes
Alienated Intellectuals
Renaissance Among African Americans
"Flaming Youth"

**Traditional America
Roars Back**
Prohibition
Fundamentalism and the Campaign
Against Evolution
Nativism, Immigration Restriction,
and Eugenics
The Ku Klux Klan

**New Social Patterns
in the 1920s**
Ethnicity and Race: North, South, and
West
Beginnings of Change in Federal
Indian Policy
Mexican Americans
Labor on the Defensive
Changes in Women's Lives
Development of Gay and Lesbian
Subcultures

The Politics of Prosperity
Harding's Failed Presidency
The Three-Candidate Presidential
Election of 1924
The Politics of Business
The 1928 Campaign and the Election
of Hoover

The Diplomacy of Prosperity
The United States and Latin America
America and Europe
Encouraging International Cooperation

INDIVIDUAL VOICES: *Sexuality and
Innuendo in Movie Advertising*

Study Tools

INDIVIDUAL CHOICES

Clara Bow

At the age of 21, Clara Bow became the "It" girl—star of the movie *It,* loosely based on Elinor Glyn's novel. "It" was sex appeal, or in Glyn's words, "an inner magic, an animal magnetism." And Clara Bow, the "It" girl, was the most popular movie star of the late 1920s.

Clara was born in Brooklyn in 1905. Her father frequently abandoned Clara and her schizophrenic mother, who showed no affection for her daughter. Clara grew up streetwise, able to defend herself with her fists. She left school at 13, began to work, and decided to become a movie actress. Clara's mother threatened to kill her if she persisted with acting, but was confined to a mental institution in 1922 and died soon after. Bow landed a contract with a Hollywood studio by the time she was 17 and appeared in thirty-five movies before reaching the age of 21. In the early 1920s, some films were emphasizing sexuality to attract audiences, as can be seen in the advertising in the Individual Voices feature at the end of this chapter. Thus, though Bow's first substantial role was as a tomboy, by 1925 her studio labeled her "the hottest jazz baby in films." The *New York Times* agreed: "She radiates an elfin sensuousness." *It*, released in 1927, clinched her fame as

Bettmann/CORBIS

the essential **flapper**. F. Scott Fitzgerald claimed that "Clara Bow is the quintessence of what the term 'flapper' signifies… pretty, impudent, superbly assured, as worldly-wise, briefly-clad and 'hard-berled' [tough] as possible." He added that thousands of young women were now "patterning themselves after her."

On the screen, Bow was flirtatious and sensuous, conscious of her sexuality and willing to use it, and aggressive in accomplishing her goal. In the process, she usually revealed as much skin as the censors permitted. She lived in much the same way, attracting Hollywood's handsomest men, making them her lovers, and discarding them for someone new. Perhaps reflecting on her parents' marriage, she told a reporter, "Marriage ain't woman's only job no more . . . . I wouldn't give up *my* work for marriage."

Despite her huge popularity and succession of famous lovers, Bow remained deeply lonely. Her working-class behavior and speech and the gossip about her sex life made her a social outcast in Hollywood. When silent films gave way to the talkies, the looming overhead microphone became her enemy, reminding her of her childhood stutter and threatening her self-confidence. She made successful talking movies, but several public scandals led to cancellation of her studio contract. At the age of 25, Clara Bow seemed a has-been.

She married actor Rex Bell and moved to a remote ranch in Nevada. She starred in two films in 1933, both successful at the box office and with the critics. But Bow was done with Hollywood. Eventually she was diagnosed with schizophrenia and depression. She later returned to live in solitude in Los Angeles and died there in 1965. In 1957, a poll of surviving silent-film directors, actors, and cameramen placed Clara Bow a close second to Greta Garbo as the greatest actress of the silent films.

Called the "Jazz Age" and the "Roaring Twenties," the 1920s sometimes seem a swirl of conflicting images. Flappers—symbolized by Clara Bow—were flaunting new freedoms for women while Prohibition, although poorly enforced, seemed an effort to preserve nineteenth-century values. The booming stock market promised prosperity to all with money to invest even as thousands of farmers abandoned the land because they could not survive financially. Business leaders celebrated the booming economy while many wage earners in manufacturing endured the destruction of their unions and saw their legal protections evaporate. White-sheeted Klansmen marched as self-proclaimed defenders of Protestant American values and white supremacy, but African American art, literature, and music were flowering.

Amid these seeming paradoxes, the economy roared along like a shiny new roadster, fueled by easy credit and consumer spending, virtually unregulated—until the fuel ran out.

THE BULLISH DECADE

☆ *What was the basis for the economic expansion of the 1920s?*

☆ *What weaknesses existed within the economy?*

By 1920, the American economy had been thoroughly industrialized, with most industry controlled by large corporations run by professional managers. During the 1920s, the growth of the automobile industry dramatized the new prominence of industries producing **consumer goods**. This significant change in direction carried implications for advertising, banking, and even the stock market.

flapper In the 1920s, a young woman with short hair and short skirts who flaunted her avant-garde dress and behavior. The origins of the term are not clear.

consumer goods Products such as clothing, food, automobiles, and radios, intended for purchase and use by individuals or households, as opposed to products such as steel beams, locomotives, and electrical generators.

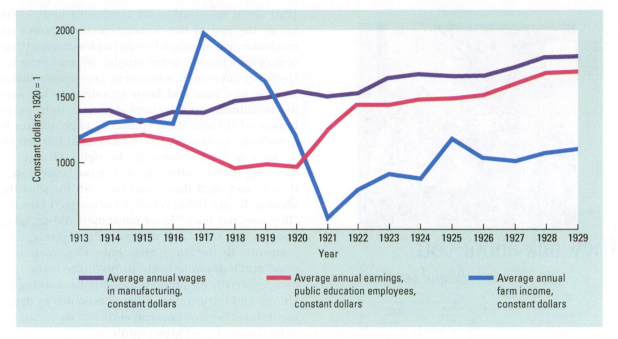

FIGURE 21.1 Patterns of Annual Income for Three Groups of Americans, 1913–1929

This graph depicts the patterns of annual income for three groups of Americans. Income has been converted to constant dollars; that is, the dollar amounts are adjusted for changes in the purchasing power of the dollar, with 1920 as the base year. Wages for manufacturing workers rose during the war years, leveled during the recession of the early 1920s, then rose again. For public education employees—mostly teachers—real earnings fell significantly with the inflation of the war years and the postwar recession, then rose to parallel those of manufacturing workers. Farmers had a boom in income during the war, then saw their earning power plunge at the end of the war with only a modest recovery after the early 1920s.

Source: U.S. Department of Commerce, Bureau of the Census, *Historical Statistics of the United States, Colonial Times to 1970,* Bicentennial edition, 2 vols. (Washington, D.C.: U.S. Government Printing Office, 1975), 1: 167, 170, 483.

The Economics of Prosperity

With the end of the war in 1918, the government cancelled most orders for war supplies. Large numbers of recently discharged military and naval personnel swelled the ranks of job seekers. Given wartime shortages and overtime pay, many Americans had been earning more than they could spend. At the end of the war, their spending helped to delay the postwar slump until 1920 and 1921. Gross domestic product dropped by 4.3 percent between 1919 and 1920, then fell by 8.6 percent between 1920 and 1921. During the war, unemployment affected only about 1 percent of the workforce. The jobless rate increased to 5 percent in 1920 and 12 percent in 1921. Some employers cut hours and wages. Figure 21.1 presents earnings for three groups of Americans and indicates the impact of recession in the early 1920s. In the end, reduced earnings, unemployment, and declining demand halted the rampaging inflation of 1918 and 1919.

The economy quickly rebounded. Gross domestic product increased by 15 percent between 1921 and 1922, a bigger jump than during the booming war years. Unemployment remained low from 1923 through 1929, and prices for most manufactured goods remained relatively stable. Thus many Americans seemed somewhat better off by 1929 than in 1920.

Targeting Consumers

By the 1920s, many business leaders understood that persuading Americans to buy their products—that is, advertising—was crucial to keeping the economy healthy. The marketing of Listerine provided a useful model. Though Listerine had originally been intended as a general antiseptic, Gerard Lambert in 1921 developed a more profitable use for it when he plucked the obscure term *halitosis* (bad breath) from a medical journal. Until then, few Americans had been concerned about their breath. Through aggressive advertising, Lambert fostered anxieties about the effect of halitosis on popularity and made millions by selling Listerine to combat the condition. Other entrepreneurs also rushed to sell products by defining needs that consumers had not previously identified. In 1924 General Mills first advertised Wheaties as the "Breakfast of Champions," tying breakfast cereal to athletic prowess. Americans responded by buying those products and many others. "We grew up founding our dreams on the infinite promises of American advertising," Zelda Sayre Fitzgerald later wrote.

Changing fashions also encouraged buying. Short hairstyles for women led to development of hair salons and stimulated sales of the recently invented bobby pin. Cigarette advertisers began to target women, as

This ad for Listerine suggests that people will discuss your breath when you leave a room. Other Listerine ads suggested that halitosis was an obstacle to romance, but this ad seems to draw upon psychological fear of being judged by others. Edward Bernays, nephew of Sigmund Freud and a leading figure in American public relations in the 1920s, pioneered the use of psychology in appealing to consumers.

when the American Tobacco Company urged women to "Reach for a Lucky instead of a sweet" to attain a fashionably slim figure. Disposable products promoted recurrent purchases, notably Kotex, the first manufactured disposable sanitary napkin, introduced in 1921, and the first disposable handkerchiefs, introduced in 1924 and later known as Kleenex.

Other technological advances contributed more prominently to the consumer-oriented economy. In

installment plan A way of paying for a purchase over time, so that the price of the product is spread over several payments, typically due monthly.

finance company Business that makes loans to clients based on some form of collateral, such as a new car, thus allowing a form of installment buying when sellers do not extend credit.

■ **Henry Ford** Inventor and manufacturer, founded the Ford Motor Company in 1903 and pioneered mass production of autos.

Model T Lightweight automobile that Ford produced from 1908 to 1927 and sold at the lowest possible price on the theory that an affordable car would be more profitable than an expensive one.

1920 about one-third of all residences had electricity. By the end of the decade, electrical power had reached nearly all urban homes but fewer than 10 percent of farm homes. As the number of residences with electricity increased, advertisers encouraged housewives to save time and labor by using electric washing machines, irons, vacuum cleaners, and toasters. Between 1919 and 1929, consumer expenditures for household appliances grew by more than 120 percent.

Increased consumption brought changes in spending habits. Before the war, most families saved their money until they could pay cash for what they needed. In the 1920s, retailers encouraged buyers to "Buy now, pay later." Many consumers did so, taking home a new radio and worrying about paying for it tomorrow. By the late 1920s, about 15 percent of all retail purchases were made through the **installment plan**, especially furniture, phonographs, washing machines, and refrigerators. Charge accounts in department stores became popular, and **finance companies** (which made loans) grew rapidly.

The Automobile: Driving the Economy

The automobile epitomized the consumer-oriented economy of the 1920s. Early automobiles were luxuries, but **Henry Ford** developed a system that drove down production costs.

Ford, a former mechanic, built his success on the **Model T**, introduced in 1908. As early as 1918, the Model T dominated the market. By 1927, Ford had produced more than 15 million of them. "Get the prices down to the buying power," Ford ordered, and his dictatorial management style combined with technological advances and high worker productivity to bring the price of a new Model T as low as $290 by 1927 (equivalent to $3,700 today). It was a dream come true for many Americans. Families came to love their ungraceful but reliable "Tin Lizzies," so named because of their lightweight metal bodies. The Model T sacrificed style and comfort for durability, ease of maintenance, and the ability to handle almost any road. It made Henry Ford a folk hero—a wealthy one. By 1925, his company showed a daily profit of some $25,000.

Ford provides an example of efforts by American entrepreneurs to reduce labor costs by improving efficiency. Work on Ford's assembly line, shown in the photo on the next page, became a thoroughly dehumanizing experience. Ford workers were prohibited from talking, sitting, smoking, singing, or even whistling while working. As one critic put it, workers were to "put nut 14 on bolt 132, repeating, repeating, repeating until their hands shook and their legs quivered."

Ford's first assembly line, in 1913, was not the first moving assembly line, but it was the one that attracted worldwide attention and imitation. It was, in many ways, an extension of the work of Frederick W. Taylor, an industrial engineer who built a national reputation

AP Photo/Ford Motor Co.

Model A Fords under production at Ford's main assembly plant in 1928. Assembly-line workers repeated the same task on car after car, as the line moved 6 feet per minute. Ford pioneered the assembly line to reduce both cost and reliance on skilled workers.

Advertising made the automobile the symbol not only of the ability of Americans to acquire material goods but also of technology, progress, and the freedom of the open road. American consumers were receptive. By the late 1920s, about 80 percent of the world's registered vehicles were in the United States. By then, America's roadways sported nearly one automobile for every five people.

The automobile industry often led the way in devising new sales techniques. By 1927 two-thirds of all American automobiles were sold on credit. GM began introducing new models every year, encouraging owners to keep up with changes in design, color, and features. Small automakers soon found they could not compete with Chrysler, Ford, and GM—the Big Three. By 1929, the Big Three were making 83 percent of all cars manufactured in the country. The industry had become an oligopoly.

on his ability to take a complex operation, requiring a high level of skill, and break it down into its component parts. Taylor redesigned complex work processes so they could be done by relatively unskilled workers, who required little training and were easy to replace. Then efficiency experts conducted time-and-motion studies to determine the ideal speed at which each task should be performed. Taylor described his system in *Principles of Scientific Management*, published in 1911. His emphasis on efficiency made that concept an important goal for manufacturers and for many Americans more generally.

Ford paid his workers well—and increased their pay if they completed Americanization classes. Ford workers earned enough to buy their own Model T! Ford's high wages pushed other automakers to increase pay for their workers, to keep them from defecting to Ford. Auto workers thus came to enjoy some of the consumer buying previously restricted to middle- and upper-income groups.

Competition helped keep auto prices low. Other automobile companies challenged Ford's predominance, notably General Motors (GM), founded by William Durant in 1908, and Chrysler, created by Walter Chrysler in 1925. GM and Chrysler adopted many of Ford's production techniques, but their cars also offered more comfort and style than the Model T. Ford stopped producing the Model T in 1927, when Chevrolet passed Ford in sales. The next year, Ford introduced the Model A, which incorporated some features promoted by his competitors.

Changes in Banking and Business

Henry Ford brought automobiles within reach of most Americans, and **A. P. Giannini** did something similar for banking. The son of Italian immigrants, Giannini founded the Bank of Italy in 1904 as a bank for shopkeepers and workers in San Francisco's Italian neighborhood. Until then, most banks had only one location, in the center of a city, and limited their services to businesses and substantial citizens. Giannini brought his bank to ordinary people by opening branches near people's homes and workplaces. Called the greatest innovator in twentieth-century American banking, Giannini broadened the base of banking by encouraging working people to open small accounts and to borrow for such purposes as car purchases. In the process, his bank—renamed the Bank of America—became the third largest in the nation by 1927.

Ford and Giannini were not the only entrepreneurs to emerge as popular and respected public figures. Perhaps the ultimate glorification of the entrepreneur came in 1925, in a book entitled *The Man*

■ **A. P. Giannini** Italian American who changed banking by opening multiple branches and encouraging small accounts and personal loans.

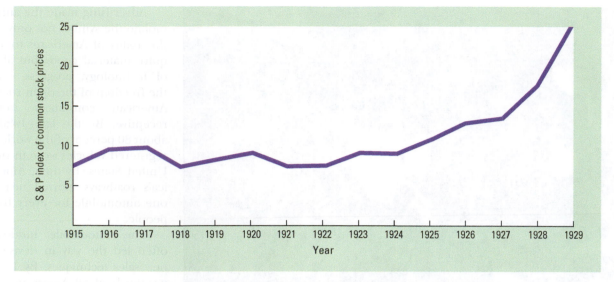

FIGURE 21.2 Stock Prices, 1915–1929
This graph shows the Standard & Poor index of common stock prices, with 1941–1942 as the base years (the index = 10 for those years). Figures for other years show stock prices in comparison to the base year. The Great Bull Market began in late 1924 and roared upward until late 1929.

Source: U.S. Department of Commerce, Bureau of Census, *Historical Statistics of the United States, Colonial Times to 1970,* Bicentennial edition, 2 vols. (Washington, D.C.: U.S. Government Printing Office, 1975), 2: 10–14.

Nobody Knows. The author, Bruce Barton, founder of a leading advertising agency, suggested that Jesus Christ could best be understood as a business executive who "had picked up twelve men from the bottom ranks of business and forged them into an organization that conquered the world." Portraying Jesus's parables as "the most powerful advertisements of all time," Barton's book led the nonfiction bestseller lists for two years.

Even though the number of corporations increased steadily throughout the 1920s, corporate mergers also accelerated, continuing earlier patterns toward greater economic concentration. By 1930, 5 percent of American corporations were receiving 85 percent of all net corporate income. Giannini's bank and Ford's company survived as relics of family management in an economy increasingly dominated by giant corporations and faceless corporate managers. For most large corporations, ownership (thousands of stockholders) and control (salaried managers) continued to grow more remote from each other, especially as large numbers of people came to see stock ownership as a short-term speculative venture—a way to "get rich quick" rather than a long-term investment.

bullish Optimistic or confident; regarding stocks, stock prices go up in a bull market and down in a bear market.

"Get Rich Quick"

During the 1920s, the stock market captured people's imagination as the fast track to riches. Speculation—buying a stock with the expectation of selling it at a higher price—ran rampant. Popular magazines proclaimed that everyone could participate and get rich quickly. By 1929, 4 million Americans owned stock, equivalent to about 10 percent of American households.

Just as Americans purchased cars and radios on the installment plan, some also bought stock on credit. Some people bought stocks "on margin"—paying part of the cost and owing the rest to the stockbroker. More people borrowed money to buy stocks. Such ventures carried a risk. If the investor paid $50 for a stock costing $100, with the remainder on margin or with borrowed money, and the stock price advanced to $150, the investor could sell, pay off the debt, and gain a profit of $50. Unfortunately, if the stock price fell to $50, the investor would still owe $50.

Driven partly by real economic growth and partly by speculation, stock prices rose higher and higher (see Figure 21.2). Common stock prices tripled between 1920 and 1929. As long as the market stayed **bullish** and stock prices kept climbing, prosperity seemed endless.

The ever-rising stock prices and corporate dividends of the 1920s encouraged creation of holding companies. Samuel Insull, for example, created an empire of electrical utilities companies, much of it consisting of holding companies, which existed solely to own the stock of other companies, some of which existed primarily to own the stock of yet others. The financial well-being of such structures rested on the ability of the **operating companies** to pay regular dividends, since those dividends enabled the holding companies to pay dividends on their bonds. An interruption in the dividends from the operating companies could bring the collapse of the entire pyramid, swallowing up the investments of speculators.

Although the stock market remained the most popular path to instant riches, other speculative opportunities abounded. A land boom developed when people poured into Florida, especially Miami, attracted by the climate, the beaches, and the ease of travel from the chilly Northeast. Speculators bought land—any land—expecting its value to soar. Stories circulated of land that increased 1,500 percent in value over ten years. Like stocks, land was bought with borrowed money. In 1926, the population influx slowed. The boom faltered, then collapsed when a hurricane slammed into Miami. By 1927, many Florida land speculators were facing bankruptcy.

Agriculture: Depression in the Midst of Prosperity

Prosperity never extended to most farmers, and farmers made up nearly 30 percent of the workforce in 1920. During the war, many farmers expanded operations in response to demands from abroad for food, and exports of farm products nearly quadrupled. After the war, European farmers resumed production, exports of farm products fell, and agricultural prices dropped. Throughout the 1920s, farmers consistently produced more than the domestic market could absorb, pushing prices down.

The average farm's net income for the years 1917 to 1920 ranged between $1,196 and $1,395 (in current dollars) per year. Farm income fell to a dreadful $517 in 1921, then slowly rose, but never reached 1917–1920 levels until World War II. Although farmers' net income never recovered to prewar levels, their mortgage payments more than doubled over prewar levels, partly because many had borrowed to expand wartime production. Tax increases, purchases of tractors and trucks—now necessities on most farms—and the cost of fertilizer and other supplies bit further into farmers' meager earnings.

As the farm economy deteriorated, the average value of an acre of farmland fell by more than half between 1920 and 1928—the average farm was actually less valuable in 1928 than in 1912! Thousands of families left farming, and the percentage of farmers in the workforce fell from nearly 30 to less than 20.

The 1920s were not the prosperity decade for rural America.

THE "ROARING TWENTIES"

☆ What groups most challenged traditional social patterns during the 1920s?

☆ What role did technology play in social change during the 1920s?

"The world broke in two in 1922 or thereabouts," wrote novelist Willa Cather, and she didn't like what came after. F. Scott Fitzgerald, another novelist, agreed with the date but believed 1922 marked "the peak of the younger generation," who brought about an "age of miracles"—that, he admitted, became an "age of excess." Evidence of dramatic social change was easy to see, from automobiles, radios, and movies to a new youth culture and an impressive cultural outpouring by African Americans.

A People on Wheels: The Automobile and American Life

The automobile profoundly changed Americans' lives. Highways significantly shortened the travel time from rural areas to cities, reducing the isolation of farm life. One farm woman, when asked why her family had an automobile but no indoor plumbing, responded, "Why, you can't go to town in a bathtub." Trucks allowed farmers to take more products to market more quickly and conveniently. Tractors expanded the amount of land a family could cultivate. By reducing the need for human labor, gasoline-powered farm vehicles stimulated migration to urban areas.

The automobile profoundly changed city life too. The 1920 census, for the first time, recorded more Americans living in urban areas (places having twenty-five hundred people or more) than in rural ones. As automobiles freed suburbanites from dependence on commuter rail lines, new suburbs mushroomed, with most of the growth in single-family houses. From 1922 through 1928, construction began on an average of 883,000 new homes each year. New home construction rivaled the auto industry as a major driving force behind economic growth.

However, the automobile soon demonstrated its ability to strangle urban traffic. In response, cities experimented with traffic lights. Various versions were

operating company A company that directly sells goods or services, as opposed to a holding company that exists to own other companies.

The prevalence of automobiles in Los Angeles meant that many car-related innovations first appeared there. Carpenter's Sandwiches was one of the first—perhaps the first— eating establishment where people were expected to eat in their cars.

tried, but Detroit's four-directional, three-color model won out. Traffic lights spread rapidly to other large cities, but traffic congestion nonetheless worsened. By 1926, during the evening rush hour in Manhattan, cars crawled along at less than 3 miles per hour— slower than a person could walk—and many commuters returned to trains and subways.

Los Angeles: Automobile Metropolis

Manhattan was not designed for automobile traffic, but the fastest-growing major city of the era—Los Angeles— was. The population of Los Angeles increased tenfold between 1900 and 1920, then more than doubled by 1930, reaching 2.2 million. Expansion of citrus-fruit raising, major oil discoveries, and the development of the motion-picture industry laid an economic foundation for rapid population growth in southern California. Manufacturing also expanded—during the 1920s, the city moved from twenty-eighth to ninth place among American cities based on manufacturing.

Lack of sufficient water threatened to limit growth until city officials diverted the Owens River to Los Angeles through a 233-mile-long aqueduct, opened in 1913. Throughout the 1920s, southern California promoters attracted many thousands of people with images of perpetual summer, tall palm trees lining wide boulevards filled with automobiles, fountains gushing water into the sunshine, and broad sandy beaches.

Los Angeles boomed as the automobile industry advocated a car for every family and real-estate developers pushed the single-family home. By 1930,

94 percent of all Los Angeles residences were single-family homes, an unprecedented level for a major city, giving Los Angeles the lowest urban population density of any major U.S. city.

Life in Los Angeles came to be organized around the automobile. The first supermarket, offering "one-stop shopping," appeared there, and the "Miracle Mile" along Wilshire Boulevard was the first large shopping district designed for automobiles. The *Los Angeles Times* put it this way in 1926: "Our forefathers in their immortal independence creed set forth 'the pursuit of happiness' as an inalienable right of mankind. And how can one pursue happiness by any swifter and surer means . . . . than by the use of the automobile?" By then, Los Angeles had one automobile for every three residents, twice the national average. Urban developers elsewhere now looked to Los Angeles for inspiration.

A Homogenized Culture Searches for Heroes

Los Angeles was the capital of the movie industry. By the mid-1920s, towns of any size boasted at least one movie theater, and movie attendance increased from a weekly average of 40 million people in 1922 to 80 million in 1929—the equivalent of two-thirds of the total population. As Americans all across the country laughed or wept at the same movie, this new medium helped to homogenize the culture, that is, make it more uniform by bridging regional or ethnic differences.

Radio also contributed to greater homogeneity. The first commercial radio station began broadcasting in 1920. Within six years, 681 were operating. By 1930, 40 percent of all families had radios, including half of urban families. Other important factors in

homogenize To make something uniform throughout.

Several of the biggest stars owed their fame to their sex appeal. Clara Bow was the "It" girl, and "It" meant sex appeal. Rudolph Valentino was the leading male sex star of the 1920s. This poster advertises *The Sheik* (1921), a movie so popular and influential that handsome young men came to be referred to for a time as sheiks.

promoting more homogeneity included the automobile, which cut travel time, and new laws that sharply reduced immigration.

Radio and film joined newspapers and magazines in creating and publicizing national trends and fashions as Americans pursued one fad after another. In 1924, crossword puzzles captured the attention of many Americans, and contract bridge, a card game, became the rage in 1926. Such fads created markets for new consumer goods, from crossword dictionaries to folding card tables.

The media also helped to make spectator sports an obsession. Baseball had long been the preeminent national sport, and radio now broadcast baseball games nationwide. Other sports competed for fans' attention—and dollars. Most Americans in the 1920s were familiar with the exploits of Lou Gehrig and Babe Ruth on the baseball diamond, Jack Dempsey and Gene Tunney in boxing, and Bobby Jones, a golfer. Gertrude Ederle won national acclaim in 1926 when she became the first woman to swim the English Channel and did so faster than any previous man.

The rapid spread of movie theaters created a new category of fame—the movie star. Charlie Chaplin, Buster Keaton, Harold Lloyd, and others brought laughter to the screen. Tom Mix was the most prominent movie cowboy. In addition to Clara Bow, sex made

a star of Theda Bara, the **vamp**. Rudolph Valentino soared to fame as a male sex symbol, with his most famous film, *The Sheik,* set in a fanciful Arabian desert.

The greatest popular hero of the 1920s, however, was neither athlete nor actor but a small-town airmail pilot—**Charles Lindbergh**. Aviation then was barely out of its infancy. A few transatlantic flights had been logged by 1926, but the longest nonstop flight before 1927 was 2,500 miles, from San Diego to New York.

Lindbergh, in 1927, set his sights on the $25,000 offered by a New York hotel owner for the first successful nonstop flight between New York and Paris—3,500 miles. Lindbergh's plane, *The Spirit of St. Louis,* was a stripped-down, one-engine craft. In a sleepless, 33½-hour flight, he earned the $25,000—and the adoration of crowds on both sides of the Atlantic. In an age devoted to materialism and dominated by a corporate mentality, Lindbergh's accomplishment suggested that old-fashioned individualism, courage, and self-reliance could still triumph over odds and adversity.

vamp A woman who uses her sexuality to entrap and exploit men.

■ **Charles Lindbergh** American aviator who made the first solo transatlantic flight in 1927 and became an international hero.

Charles Lindbergh favored photos in which he appeared alone with his plane, emphasizing the individual nature of his flight. This photo was taken before his historic solo flight across the Atlantic.

Alienated Intellectuals

Other Americans, too, went to Paris in the 1920s, but for different reasons than Lindbergh. These **expatriates** left the United States to escape what they considered America's intellectual shallowness, dull materialism, and spreading uniformity. As Malcolm Cowley put it in *Exile's Return* (1934), his memoir of life in France, "by expatriating himself, . . . the artist can break the puritan shackles, drink, live freely, and be wholly creative." Paris in the 1920s, he added, "was a great machine for stimulating the nerves and sharpening the senses."

Sinclair Lewis and H. L. Mencken became leading critics of middle-class materialism and uniformity without moving to Paris. Lewis, in *Main Street* (1920), presented small-town, middle-class existence as not just boring but stifling. In *Babbitt* (1922), Lewis depicted a suburban businessman (George Babbitt) as narrow minded and complacent, speaking in clichés and buying every new gadget. H. L. Mencken, editor of *The American Mercury*, pilloried the "booboisie," jeered at politicians, and celebrated only writers who shared his disdain for most of American life.

expatriate A person who takes up long-term residence in a foreign country.

▪ **Sinclair Lewis** Novelist who satirized middle-class America in works such as *Babbitt* (1922); the first American to win the Nobel Prize for literature.

▪ **Harlem Renaissance** Literary and artistic movement in the 1920s, centered in Harlem, in which black writers and artists celebrated African American life.

Others added to the critique of modern life. In *The Waste Land* (1922), T. S. Eliot, an American poet living in England, presented modernity as sterile and futile. F. Scott Fitzgerald, in *The Great Gatsby* (1925), portrayed the pointless lives of wealthy pleasure seekers and their careless disregard for life and values. Ernest Hemingway, in *The Sun Also Rises* (1926), depicted disillusioned and jaded expatriates.

Renaissance Among African Americans

For the most part, despair and disillusionment troubled white writers and intellectuals. Such sentiments rarely appeared in the striking outpouring of literature, music, and art by African Americans in the 1920s.

As African Americans continued to move from the South to northern cities, Harlem, the largest black neighborhood in New York City, came to symbolize the new life of African Americans. The term **Harlem Renaissance**, or Negro Renaissance, refers to a literary and artistic movement in which black artists and writers insisted on the value of black culture and drew upon African and African American traditions in their writing and art. Black actors, notably Paul Robeson, appeared in serious theaters and earned acclaim for their abilities. Earlier black writers, especially Alain Locke, James Weldon Johnson, and Claude McKay, encouraged and guided the novelists and poets of the Harlem Renaissance. Jean Toomer's novel *Cane* (1923), dealing with African Americans in rural Georgia and Washington, D.C., has been praised as "the most impressive product of the Negro Renaissance." Zora Neale Hurston began her long writing career with several short stories in the 1920s.

"Survey Graphic Magazine" cover, March 1925.

This was the cover of the March 1925 issue of *Survey Graphic*, a popular magazine of the period. *Survey Graphic* devoted the entire issue to Harlem and the emergence of new consciousness among its African American residents.

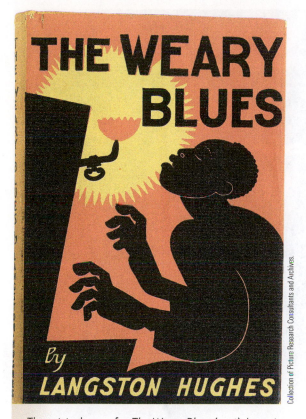

Collection of Picture Research Consultants and Archives.

The original cover for *The Weary Blues* (1926), Langston Hughes's first book of poetry, which included some of the first blues that Hughes ever heard, dating to his childhood in Lawrence, Kansas. Hughes's references to the blues and the cover design evoke the connection between music and poetry that was part of the Harlem Renaissance.

Among the movement's poets, Langston Hughes became the best known. Born in Joplin, Missouri, in 1902, Hughes began to write poetry in high school, briefly attended college, then worked and traveled in Africa and Europe. By 1925, he was a significant figure in the Harlem Renaissance. Some of his works present images from black history, vividly depict racism, or look to the future with an expectation for change, as in "I, Too" (1925):

> I, too, sing America.
> I am the darker brother.
> They send me
> To eat in the kitchen
> When company comes,
> But I laugh,
> And eat well,
> And grow strong.
> Tomorrow
> I'll sit at the table
> When company comes....*

Hughes sometimes recited his poetry to the accompaniment of **jazz**, which became so prominent during the 1920s that the decade has been called the Jazz Age. African American musicians in southern cities, especially New Orleans, developed jazz in the early twentieth century, drawing from earlier strains in African American music, particularly the blues and ragtime. Jazz moved north by the 1910s. Some attacked the new sound, claiming it encouraged people to abandon self-restraint, especially with regard to sex. Despite—or perhaps because of—such condemnation, the wail of the saxophone became as much a part of the 1920s as the roar of the roadster and the flicker of the movie projector.

The great black jazz musicians of the 1920s—Louis "Satchmo" Armstrong, Bessie Smith, Fletcher Henderson, Ferdinand "Jelly Roll" Morton, and others—drew white audiences into black neighborhoods to hear them. Harlem came to be associated with exotic nightlife and glittering jazz clubs. Edward "Duke" Ellington

* "I, Too" from *The Collected Poems of Langston Hughes* by Langston Hughes, edited by Arnold Rampersad with David Roessel, Associate Editor, copyright © 1994 by the Estate of Langston Hughes. Used by permission of Alfred A. Knopf, a division of Random House, Inc., and Harold Ober Associates.

■ **jazz** Style of music developed in America in the early twentieth century, characterized by strong, flexible rhythms and improvisation on basic melodies.

Bessie Smith was the most prominent female blues and jazz singer in the 1920s and became the most highly paid black entertainer in the country by the late 1920s. Called "the Empress of the Blues," she brought the blues and jazz to a wide audience with her recordings and her tours.

came to lead the Cotton Club band in 1927 and began to develop the works that made him one of America's most respected composers. George Gershwin, a white composer, brought jazz into the symphony halls with his *Rhapsody in Blue* (1924).

Few African Americans experienced the glitter of the Cotton Club, but one Harlem black leader influenced black people throughout the country and beyond. **Marcus Garvey**, born in Jamaica, advocated a form of **black separatism**. His Universal Negro Improvement Association (UNIA), founded in 1914, stressed racial pride, the importance of Africa, and racial solidarity across national boundaries. Garvey

■ Marcus Garvey Jamaican black nationalist active in America in the 1920s.

■ black separatism A strategy of creating separate black institutions, based on the assumption that African Americans can never achieve equality within white society.

speakeasy A place that illegally sells liquor and sometimes offers entertainment.

supporters urged blacks around the world to help Africans overthrow colonial rule and build a strong Africa. Garvey's message of racial pride and solidarity attracted wide support among African Americans, especially in the cities. Black integrationist leaders, especially W. E. B. Du Bois of the NAACP, opposed Garvey's separatism and argued that the first task facing blacks was integration and equality at home. Garvey and Du Bois each labeled the other a traitor to his race. Garvey was convicted of mail fraud in 1923 due to irregularities in his fundraising. After two years in jail, he was deported to his native Jamaica.

"Flaming Youth"

African Americans created jazz, but those who danced to it, in the popular imagination, were white—a male college student, clad in a stylish raccoon-skin coat with a flask of illegal liquor in his pocket, and his female counterpart, the uninhibited flapper, with bobbed hair and a daringly short skirt. This stereotype of "flaming youth"—the title of a popular novel—reflected changes among many white youths of middle- or upper-class background.

In the 1920s adolescence emerged as a separate subculture. The booming economy allowed more middle-class families to send their children to college. Before World War I, just over 3 percent of people ages 18 to 24 were in college. By 1930, that proportion had more than doubled, with larger increases among women. Now women were receiving 40 percent of all bachelor's degrees. Students reshaped colleges into youth centers, where football games and dances assumed as much significance as examinations and term papers.

Young women who captured public attention with their clothes and behavior were called flappers. They scandalized their elders with skirts that stopped at the knee, stockings rolled below the knee, short hair often dyed black, and generous amounts of rouge and lipstick. Many observers assumed that their outrageous look reflected outrageous behavior—that young women were abandoning their parents' moral values. In fact, women's sexual activity outside marriage began to increase before the war, especially among working-class women and radicals. "Dating," too, owed its origins to prewar working-class young people. In the 1920s, these behaviors appeared among college and high school students from middle-class families. About half of the women who came of age during the 1920s had intercourse before marriage, a marked increase from prewar patterns.

Such changes were often linked to automobiles. Automobiles brought greater freedom to young people, for there they had no chaperone and could go where they wanted. Sometimes they went to a **speakeasy** (where illegal alcohol was sold). Before

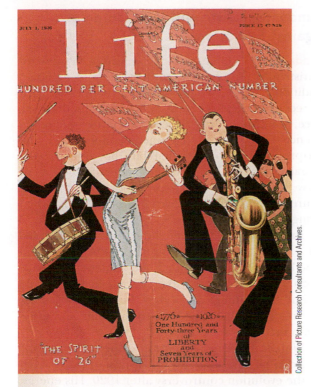

On the 150th anniversary of the Declaration of Independence, *Life* presented this cover parodying the famous painting *The Spirit of '76* by depicting "The Spirit of '26"—an uninhibited flapper with a jazz saxophonist and drummer, and banners with the snappy sayings of the day. The caption reads: "1776–1926: One Hundred and Forty three Years of LIBERTY and Seven Years of PROHIBITION."

Prohibition, few women entered saloons, but now men and women alike went to speakeasies to drink, smoke, and dance to jazz. Some adults criticized such behavior by young people, but others emulated them, launching the first American youth culture. F. Scott Fitzgerald later called the years after 1922 "a children's party taken over by elders."

TRADITIONAL AMERICA ROARS BACK

☆ *Why and how did some Americans try to restore traditional social values during the 1920s?*

Many Americans embraced cars, movies, jazz, and radios, but others felt threatened by the pace of change and what seemed to be an upheaval in social values. In nearly every case efforts to stop the tide of change appeared in both cities and rural areas, and many of those efforts dated to the prewar era. In the 1920s, several movements seeking to restore elements of an older America came to fruition at the same time as Fitzgerald's "age of excess."

TOWARD A MORE PERFECT UNION

The Eighteenth and Nineteenth Amendments

The Eighteenth and Nineteenth Amendments took effect in 1920. Both marked the culmination of decades-long advocacy, and both benefited significantly from women's political activism.

The Eighteenth Amendment, Prohibition, is unlike other amendments. First, Prohibition was designed to change Americans' behavior by prohibiting the "manufacture, sale, or transportation of intoxicating liquors." Other amendments have changed political procedures, specified individual rights, or defined governmental authority; none have attempted to modify individuals' behavior. Second, Prohibition is the only amendment ever repealed, testimony to its failure and a warning against using constitutional amendments to modify social behavior.

The Nineteenth Amendment, woman suffrage, took effect in time for women to participate in the 1920 elections, but most women did not vote. Careful analysis by recent political scientists suggests that, outside the South (where very few people voted), about 25 to 40 percent of eligible women voted in 1920, and that the proportion of women who voted was significantly and consistently lower than that of men. Not until 1980 did women's turnout rate exceed that of men, but since 1980 the gap between women's and men's voting participation rates has steadily widened. In both 2008 and 2012, 53% of eligible women actually voted, compared to 47% of eligible men.

Prohibition

The **Eighteenth Amendment** (Prohibition) came to symbolize many of the efforts to preserve white, old-stock, Protestant values. Prohibition did reduce drinking somewhat, but many Americans simply ignored it. It grew less popular the longer it lasted. By 1926, a poll indicated that only 19 percent of Americans supported Prohibition, 50 percent wanted it modified, and 31 percent favored outright **repeal**. Prohibition, however, remained the law, if not the reality, from 1920 until 1933, when the Twenty-first Amendment finally did repeal it.

■ **Eighteenth Amendment** A 1919 constitutional amendment forbidding the manufacture, sale, or transportation of alcoholic beverages.

repeal The act of canceling a law or regulation; repeal of a constitutional amendment requires a new amendment.

Prohibition was never well enforced anywhere, partly because of the immensity of the task and partly because Congress never provided enough money for serious federal enforcement. In 1923 a federal agent visited major cities to see how long it took to find an illegal drink: 35 seconds in New Orleans, 3 minutes in Detroit, and 3 minutes and 10 seconds in New York City.

Previously, neighborhood saloons had often attracted working-class and lower-middle-class men, but the new speakeasies were often more glamorous, drawing an upper- and middle-class clientele, women as well as men. **Bootlegging**—production and sale of illegal beverages—flourished. Some bootleggers made only small amounts of beer or wine and sold it to their neighbors. Large-scale bootlegging, however, provided criminals with a fresh and lucrative source of income, part of which could buy influence in city politics and protection from police.

In Chicago, **Al Capone**'s gang counted nearly a thousand members and, in 1927, took in more than $100 million (equivalent to $1.3 billion today)—$60 million from bootlegged liquor. Capone faced competition from other gangs, and gang warfare raged across Chicago, producing some five hundred slayings. In 1931 federal officials finally convicted Capone—of income-tax evasion—and sent him to prison.

Elsewhere, other gangsters—many of recent immigrant background, including Italians, Irish, Germans, and Jews—also found riches in bootlegging, gambling, prostitution, and **racketeering**. Through racketeering they gained power in some labor unions. The gangs, killings, and corruption confirmed other Americans' distrust of cities and immigrants, and they clung to the vision of a dry America as the best hope for renewing traditional values.

bootlegging Illegal production, distribution, or sale of liquor.

◼ **Al Capone** Italian-born American gangster who ruthlessly ruled the Chicago underworld until imprisoned in 1931.

racketeering Crimes such as extortion, loansharking, and bribery, sometimes behind the front of a seemingly legitimate business or union.

◼ **fundamentalism** Originally an early twentieth-century Protestant Christian religious movement that emphasized the literal truth of the Bible and opposed efforts to reconcile the Bible with scientific knowledge; applied today to any religious movement based on uncompromising adherence to a set of principles.

◼ **evolution** The central organizing principle of the biological sciences, which holds that genetic change in organisms over generations can produce new species; it includes the concept that humans evolved from nonhuman ancestors.

◼ **Clarence Darrow** A leading trial lawyer of the early twentieth century, who often defended those challenging the status quo.

Fundamentalism and the Campaign Against Evolution

Fundamentalism, a movement within Protestant Christianity, represented another effort to maintain traditional values. Where Christian modernists tried to reconcile their religious beliefs with modern science, fundamentalists rejected anything—including science—they considered incompatible with the Scriptures. Every word of the Bible, they argued, is the revealed word of God. The fundamentalist movement grew throughout the early twentieth century, led by figures such as Billy Sunday, a baseball player turned evangelist.

In the early 1920s, some fundamentalists focused on **evolution**. Biologists cite evolution to explain how living things developed over millions of years. Because the Bible states that God created the world and all living things in six days, fundamentalists saw in evolution a challenge both to the Bible and to religion itself.

William Jennings Bryan, former Democratic presidential candidate and secretary of state, fixed on the evolution controversy after 1920. His energy, eloquence, and enormous following guaranteed that his arguments received wide attention. "It is better," Bryan wrote, "to trust in the Rock of Ages than to know the age of rocks." Bryan played a central role in the most famous dispute over evolution—the Scopes trial.

In March 1925, the Tennessee legislature made it illegal for public school teachers to teach evolution. The American Civil Liberties Union (ACLU) offered to defend a teacher willing to challenge the law, and John T. Scopes, who taught biology in Dayton, accepted. Bryan volunteered to assist the local prosecutors, who faced a defense team that included the famous attorney **Clarence Darrow**. Bryan claimed that the only issue was the right of the people to regulate public education, but Darrow insisted the issue was to prevent "ignoramuses from controlling the education of the United States."

The court proceedings were carried nationwide via radio. Toward the end of the trial, in a surprising move, Darrow called Bryan to the witness stand as an authority on the Bible. Under Darrow's withering questioning, Bryan revealed that he knew little about findings in archaeology, geology, and linguistics that cast doubt on Biblical accounts. He also admitted, to the dismay of many fundamentalists, that he did not always interpret the words of the Bible literally. "Darrow never spared him," one reporter wrote. "It was masterful, but it was pitiful." Bryan died a few days later. Scopes was found guilty, but the Tennessee Supreme Court reversed his sentence on a technicality.

It Matters Today

Teaching Evolution in Public Schools

After the Scopes trial, other state legislatures also prohibited the teaching of evolution. Textbook publishers diluted or omitted treatment of evolution. Not until the 1950s, when national science education standards were developed, did a thorough treatment of evolution return to most high school textbooks.

In 1968, the U.S. Supreme Court overturned a 1928 Arkansas law prohibiting the teaching of evolution because it reflected the views of a particular religious group that considered evolution to be in conflict with the Bible, and therefore violated the First Amendment, which prohibits Congress from adopting any law that privileges one religious group, and the Fourteenth Amendment, which applies the First Amendment to state governments.

Opponents of evolution then secured laws requiring teaching "creationism." This the U.S. Supreme Court struck down in 1987, in a case involving a Louisiana law. Since then, opponents of evolution have often used the term "intelligent design." That issue continues to be hotly debated in several states.

- Search online newspapers to find examples of recent controversies over the teaching of evolution. What are the arguments?
- William Jennings Bryan argued, in part, that in a democracy elected officials should control the content of courses in the public schools. Should course content be determined by elected officials or by specialists in each discipline?

Nativism, Immigration Restriction, and Eugenics

Throughout the 1920s, nativism and discrimination were widespread. **Restrictive covenants** attached to real-estate titles prohibited future sale to particular groups, typically African Americans and Jews. Exclusive colleges placed quotas on the number of Jews admitted, and some companies refused to hire Jews. In 1920 Henry Ford accused Jewish bankers of controlling the American economy, then suggested an international Jewish conspiracy to control virtually everything from baseball to bolshevism. When Aaron Sapiro sued Ford for defamation and challenged him to prove his claims, Ford retracted his charges and apologized. Ethnic hostility sometimes turned violent, as when rioting townspeople beat and stoned Italians in West Frankfort, Illinois, in 1920.

Laws to restrict immigration resulted in significant part from nativist anxieties that immigrants, especially from southern and eastern Europe, were transforming the United States. Advocates of restriction redoubled their efforts in response to an upsurge in immigration after the war—430,000 in 1920 and 805,000 in 1921, with more than half from southern and eastern Europe. Efforts to cut off immigration were not new. However, the presence of many German Americans during the war with Germany, the Red Scare and fear of foreign radicalism, and the continued influx of poor immigrants at a time of growing unemployment bolstered

nativist arguments. Congress limited immigration with a temporary measure in 1921, then approved a permanent law in 1924, the **National Origins Act**, restricting total immigration to 150,000 per year. Quotas for each country were set at 2 percent of the number of Americans whose ancestors came from that country. In attempting to freeze the ethnic composition of the nation, the law reflected the arguments of those nativists who contended that immigrants from southern and eastern Europe and Asia made less desirable citizens than people from northern and western Europe. All Asians were excluded, but the law permitted unrestricted immigration from Canada and Latin America.

In its transparent effort to restrict immigration from southern and eastern Europe while admitting larger numbers from northern and western Europe, the National Origins Act also reflects the concerns of some **eugenics** advocates. The eugenics movement

---

restrictive covenant Provision in a property title that prohibits subsequent sale to specified groups, especially people of color and Jews.

■ **National Origins Act** A 1924 congressional act establishing quotas for immigration to the United States; it limited immigration from southern and eastern Europe and prohibited immigration from Asia.

eugenics The notion that genetic information should be used to improve the human race.

developed in the late nineteenth and early twentieth century; its proponents hoped to apply genetics to improve the human race. Some eugenicists argued that southern and eastern Europeans showed undesirable genetic traits and advocated excluding them. Other eugenicists focused on mental ability or mental illness to argue that those with "undesirable" traits should be sterilized. In 1927, the U.S. Supreme Court approved a Virginia law permitting the state to sterilize those considered mentally retarded; such state laws were widespread by the 1920s, and most continued in force until the 1960s.

The Ku Klux Klan

Nativism, anti-Catholicism, anti-Semitism, and fear of radicalism all contributed to the spectacular growth of the Ku Klux Klan in the early 1920s. The original Klan, created during Reconstruction to intimidate former slaves, had long since died out. A hugely popular film *The Birth of a Nation*, released in 1915, glorified the old Klan and led to its revival.

The new Klan claimed to be devoted to traditional American values, old-fashioned Protestant Christianity, and white supremacy. It opposed Catholics, Jews, immigrants, and blacks, along with bootleggers, corrupt politicians, and gamblers. Growth came slowly at first but surged to 5 million members nationwide by 1925.

The Klan showed strength in the South, Midwest, West, and Southwest, and in towns and cities as well as rural areas. Klan members participated actively in politics, and Klan leaders gained powerful political influence in some communities and states, notably Texas, Oklahoma, Kansas, Oregon, and Indiana. In Oklahoma, the Klan led a successful impeachment campaign against a governor who tried to restrict it. In Oregon, the Klan claimed responsibility for a 1922 law aimed at eliminating Catholic schools. (The Supreme Court ruled the law unconstitutional.) Many local and state elections in 1924 divided along pro- and anti-Klan lines.

Extensive corruption underlay the Klan's self-righteous rhetoric. Some Klan leaders joined primarily for personal gain, both legal (from recruiting) and illegal (mostly political payoffs). Some shamelessly violated the morality they preached. In 1925, D. C. Stephenson, a nationally prominent Klan leader, was convicted of second-degree murder after the death of a woman who had accused him of raping her. When the governor refused to pardon him, Stephenson produced records proving the corruption of the governor, a member of Congress, the mayor of Indianapolis, and other officials. Klan membership fell sharply amid factional disputes and further evidence of fraud and corruption.

Collection of Picture Research Consultants and Archives.

A Ku Klux Klan pamphlet published in the mid-1920s included this image. What does this image suggest about the way that the Klan was trying to present itself?

NEW SOCIAL PATTERNS IN THE 1920S

☆ *What continuities and changes characterized racial and ethnic relations during the 1920s?*

☆ *Is it appropriate to describe the 1920s as "the lean years" for working people?*

☆ *How did gender roles and definitions change in the 1920s?*

The Harlem Renaissance and Klan nightriders represent polar extremes of racial relations in the 1920s. For most people of color, the realities of daily life fell somewhere in between. For working people, the 1920s represented what one historian terms "the lean years" when earlier gains were lost and unions remained on the defensive. For women, the 1920s opened with the victory of suffrage, but the unity mustered for that measure soon broke down.

Ethnicity and Race: North, South, and West

Discrimination against Jews, violence against Italians, and the Klan's appeal to white Protestants all point

African Americans intensified their efforts to end lynching. This protest was held in Washington, D.C., in 1922. The NAACP's efforts to secure a federal anti-lynching law were repeatedly defeated by southerners in Congress.

to the continuing significance of ethnicity during the 1920s. Throughout the decade, racial relations remained deeply troubled at best, violent at worst.

The Harlem Renaissance helped produce greater appreciation for black music and other accomplishments, but racial discrimination still confronted most African Americans, wherever they lived. Some gained better jobs by moving north, but many found work only in low-paying service occupations. Nearly everywhere, social pressures and restrictive covenants limited access to desirable housing. Those who succeeded sometimes became targets for racial hostility, like the black physician whose home was attacked by a white mob when he moved into a white Detroit neighborhood in 1925. A race riot devastated Tulsa, Oklahoma, in 1921, leaving nearly forty confirmed dead (black deaths outnumbered white by more than two to one), hundreds injured, and fourteen hundred black businesses and homes burned. The NAACP continued to lobby for a federal anti-lynching law by publicizing violence against blacks, but southern legislators defeated each attempt, arguing against federal interference in the police power of the states.

East of the Mississippi River, whether North or South, race relations usually meant black-white relations. In the West, race relations were always more complex, and became more so in the years around World War I, when Filipinos began to arrive in Hawai'i and on the West Coast. Most of them worked in agriculture and aboard ships. Sikhs from India also entered the West Coast workforce, mainly as agricultural laborers.

California had long led the way with laws discriminating against Asian Americans. By the 1920s, other western states also adopted laws forbidding Asian immigrants to own or lease land. Westerners, especially Californians, also had a lengthy record of violence against Asians. In 1930, for example, a white mob killed a Filipino farm worker in Watsonville, California.

Some Asian immigrants and Asian Americans fought discrimination through the courts, but with little success. In the early 1920s, the U.S. Supreme Court reaffirmed that only white persons and persons of African descent could become naturalized citizens, denying citizenship to persons born in Asia. The Supreme Court also ruled that Mississippi could require a Chinese American schoolchild to attend a segregated school established for African Americans.

Beginnings of Change in Federal Indian Policy

During the 1920s, events began to converge in support of changes in federal policy toward American Indians. In the early 1920s, Interior Secretary Albert Fall tried to lease parts of reservations to white developers and to extinguish Pueblo Indians' title to some of their land. Fall's proposals, especially the Pueblo land issue, led to organization by John Collier, a social worker, of

These sugar-beet fieldworkers near Fort Collins, in northern Colorado, about 1928, include men, women, and boys. Unlike previous ethnic groups who worked in western agriculture, Mexicans often came as families and often worked as family units.

the **American Indian Defense Association** (AIDA), in 1923.

Collier and the AIDA soon emerged as prominent advocates for changes in federal Indian policy. They sought better health and educational services on reservations, creation of tribal governments, tolerance of Indian religious ceremonies and other customs, and an end to land allotments—changes intended to move toward a policy of recognizing Indian cultures and values rather than a policy that forced assimilation. Political pressure by AIDA and similar groups, along with political efforts by Indians themselves, secured several favorable new laws, including full citizenship for all Native Americans. These efforts laid the basis for a significant shift in federal policy in the 1930s.

Mexican Americans

California and the Southwest have been home to many Mexican and Mexican American families since the region was part of Mexico. Those states, especially Texas and California, attracted growing numbers of Mexican immigrants after 1910, when many went north to escape the revolution and civil war that was devastating their nation. Nearly 700,000 Mexicans legally entered the United States between 1910 and 1930, and probably the same number came illegally.

□ **American Indian Defense Association** (AIDA) Organization founded in 1923 to defend the rights of American Indians; it sought an end to land allotment and a return to tribal government.

The agricultural economies of the Southwest were changing. By 1925, the Southwest was relying on irrigation to produce 40 percent of the nation's fruits and vegetables, crops that were highly labor intensive. By the late 1920s, Mexicans made up more than 80 percent of farm laborers there. The southwestern states also experienced large increases in their Anglo populations. These changes in population and economy reshaped relations between Anglos and Mexicans.

In south Texas, many Anglo newcomers looked on Mexicans as what one Anglo called a "partly colored race" and tried to import elements of southern black-white relations, including disfranchisement and segregation. Disfranchisement was unsuccessful, but some schools were segregated despite Mexican opposition. The League of United Latin American Citizens (LULAC) could sometimes halt discrimination by businesses—but only occasionally.

In California, Mexican workers' efforts to organize for better pay and working conditions were often broken quickly and brutally by local authorities or growers' private guards. Leaders were often deported. Mexican labor had become vital to agriculture, however, and growers opposed any restrictions on immigration from Mexico, so the National Origins Act of 1924 permitted unlimited immigration from the Western Hemisphere.

As the doors to European immigration closed with the new immigration law, midwestern manufacturers began to recruit Mexican workers to work in steel mills, meatpacking plants, and auto factories. By 1930, significant numbers of Mexican Americans were to be found in such industrial cities as Chicago, Detroit, and Gary.

Labor on the Defensive

Difficulties in establishing unions among Mexican workers mirrored a larger failure of unions in the 1920s. When unions tried to recover lost purchasing power by calling strikes in 1919 and 1920, nearly all failed. After 1921, employers increasingly challenged Progressive Era legislation benefiting workers. The Supreme Court responded by limiting workers' rights, voiding laws that prohibited child labor, and striking down minimum-wage laws.

Many companies undertook anti-union drives. Arguing that unions were unnecessary and either corrupt or radical, some employers used the term **American Plan** to describe their refusal to deal with unions. Some companies began to provide workers with programs such as insurance, retirement pensions, cafeterias, paid vacations, and stock purchase plans, an approach sometimes called **welfare capitalism**. Such innovations stemmed from both genuine concern for workers' well-being and the expectation that such improvements would increase productivity and discourage unionization.

The 1920s marked the first period of prosperity since the 1830s when union membership declined, falling from 5 million in 1920 to 3.6 million in 1929, a 28 percent decline at a time when the total workforce increased by 15 percent. AFL leaders, insisting on separate unions for each skill group, made no efforts to organize the great mass-production industries. Some unions suffered from internal battles—the International Ladies' Garment Workers' Union lost two-thirds of its members during power struggles between Socialists and Communists.

The Communists sought power within other unions, but the membership of the **Communist Party of the United States** (CP) never approached the numbers claimed by the Socialist Party before World War I. In 1929 the CP counted only 9,300 members. Always closely tied to the leadership of the Soviet Union, the CP labored strenuously to organize workers throughout the 1920s but had little success.

Changes in Women's Lives

Attention given to flappers should not detract from important changes in women's gender roles during these years. Significant changes occurred in two arenas: family and politics.

Marriage among white middle-class women and men began to be valued increasingly as companionship between two partners. Although the ideal of marriage was often expressed in terms of a man and woman taking equal responsibility for a relationship, the actual responsibility for the smooth functioning of the family typically fell on the woman. Many women in the 1920s seem to have increased their control over decisions about childbearing. Usually in American history, prosperity brings increases in the birth rate. In the 1920s, however, changing social values together with more options for birth control resulted in fewer births (see A Deeper Understanding of History).

This declining birth rate reflected, in part, some success for efforts to secure wider availability of birth-control information and devices, for example, diaphragms. The birth-control movement gained the backing of some male physicians and became a more respectable, middle-class reform movement. By 1925, the American Medical Association had come to support birth control, and the Rockefeller Foundation began to fund medical research into contraception methods. Nevertheless, until 1936, federal law restricted public distribution of contraceptive information, and many women still relied on illegal abortions to terminate unwanted pregnancies. In Clara Bow's Hollywood, abortions became almost routine as a way for actresses to meet their contractual obligations to perform in films and to avoid public scandal.

As before, working-class women struggled to stretch their finances to cover their families' needs. As before, some women and children worked outside the home to earn additional family income. The proportion of women working for wages remained stable during the 1920s, at about one in four. The proportion of married women working for wages increased, though, from 23 percent of the female labor force in 1920 to 29 percent in 1930.

After the implementation of the Nineteenth Amendment (woman suffrage) in 1920, the unity of the suffrage movement disintegrated in disputes over the proper role for women voters. Both major political parties welcomed women as voters and modified the structure of their national committees to provide that each state be represented by both a national committeeman and a national committeewoman. Some suffrage activists joined the League of Women Voters, a nonpartisan group committed to social and political reform. The Congressional Union, led by Alice Paul, converted itself into the National Woman's Party and, after 1923, focused its efforts on securing an **Equal Rights Amendment** to the Constitution. The League

■ **American Plan** Term used by some employers in the 1920s to describe their policy of refusing to negotiate with unions.

■ **welfare capitalism** Program adopted by some employers to provide employee benefits such as lunchrooms, paid vacations, bonuses, and profit-sharing plans.

■ **Communist Party of the United States** (CP) Party organized in 1919, devoted to replacing capitalism and private property with its version of socialism.

■ **Equal Rights Amendment** Proposed constitutional amendment, first advocated by the National Woman's Party in 1923, to give women in the United States equal rights under the law.

Using Statistics in Historical Analysis

When studying the behavior of prominent individuals—politicians, corporate leaders, leaders of broadly based social movements—or events involving such individuals, historians usually have access to a wealth of primary sources, including eyewitness accounts, memoirs, newspaper reports, official papers, and the like. It is a different situation when historians study changes in the behavior of large groups of people, few of whom left any records.

How, for example, can historians analyze long-term patterns in family size? As a crucial first step, it is necessary to identify those patterns. Fortunately, the federal census provides important evidence. For several successive censuses, census-takers asked women the number of children to whom they had given birth. Census publications, in turn, present statistical data on the number of children ever born to women ever married, by the birth date of the mothers. Graphing this data makes clear long-term patterns of change.

The graph here summarizes three data series related to family size. Childbearing ages are considered to be between 15 and 45. This graph allows a comparison of women who were ever married and came of childbearing age in the 1910s and 1920s (shaded on the graph) with women of earlier and later periods. Women who reached the age of 15 in those years differ in three ways: (1) they had fewer children on average (purple line), (2) more of them had no children at all (blue bars), and (3) far fewer had large families (green bars).

To understand *why* families, and particularly women, were making these choices, census statistics provide no answers. To answer the *why* question, historians must look to other sources—memoirs, reports and interviews from the time, and the like. Such *why* questions most interest historians, and those questions may also produce differing answers, depending on the sources that different historians have used to develop their answers.

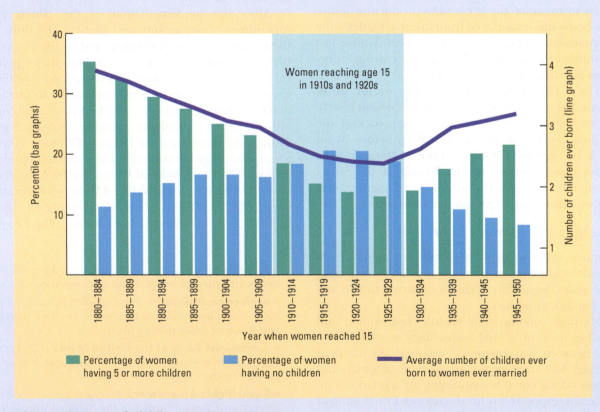

Women reaching age 15 in 1910s and 1920s

Percentile (bar graphs) / **Number of children ever born (line graph)**

Year when women reached 15

■ Percentage of women having 5 or more children   ■ Percentage of women having no children   ▬ Average number of children ever born to women ever married

Changing Patterns of Childbearing Among Women

Sources: Series B42–48, U.S. Bureau of the Census, *Historical Statistics of the United States, Colonial Times to 1970*, Bicentennial edition, 2 vols. (Washington, D.C.: U.S. Government Printing Office, 1975), 1: 53; Table 270, U.S. Bureau of the Census, *1980 Census of Population* (Washington, D.C.: U.S. Government Printing Office, 1984), 1–103.

of Women Voters disagreed, arguing that such an amendment would endanger laws providing protection for women.

Development of Gay and Lesbian Subcultures

In the 1920s, gay and lesbian subcultures became more established and relatively open in several cities. *The Captive,* a play about lesbians, opened in New York in 1926, and some movies included unmistakable homosexual references. Novels with gay and lesbian characters were published in the late 1920s and early 1930s. In Chicago, the Society for Human Rights was organized to advocate equal treatment. A relatively open gay and lesbian community emerged in Harlem, where some prominent figures of the Renaissance were gay or bisexual. The annual Hamilton Lodge drag ball in Harlem attracted as many as seven thousand revelers and spectators of all races.

At the same time, however, more and more psychiatrists and psychologists were labeling homosexuality a **perversion**. By the 1920s, the work of **Sigmund Freud** had become well known. Following Freud, psychiatrists and psychologists now labeled homosexuality a sexual disorder requiring a cure, though no "cure" proved viable. Thus Freud's theories may have been liberating for heterosexual relations but proved harmful for same-sex relations.

The new medical definitions were slow to work their way into the larger society. The armed forces, for example, made little effort to prevent homosexuals from enlisting and took disciplinary action only against behavior that violated laws against sodomy.

The late 1920s and early 1930s brought increased suppression of gays and lesbians. New state laws gave police greater authority to prosecute open expressions of homosexuality. Adam Clayton Powell, a leading Harlem minister, launched a highly publicized campaign against gays. Motion-picture studios instituted a morality code that, among its wide-ranging provisions, prohibited any depiction of homosexuality. The end of Prohibition after 1933 brought increased regulation of businesses selling liquor, and local authorities often used this power to close establishments with gay or lesbian customers. Thus, by the 1930s, many gays and lesbians were becoming more secretive about their sexual identities.

Sooner or later, the major social and economic developments of the 1920s found their way into politics, from highway construction to prohibition, from immigration restriction to the teaching of evolution, from farm prices to lynching. After 1918, the Republicans regained the national majority they had held from 1894 to 1912, and they remained the unquestioned majority throughout the 1920s. Progressivism largely disappeared, although some veteran progressives, led by Robert La Follette and George Norris, persisted in seeking to limit corporate power. The Republican administrations of the 1920s shared a faith in the ability of business to establish prosperity and benefit the American people and considered government the partner of business, not its regulator.

Harding's Failed Presidency

Elected in 1920, Warren G. Harding looked presidential—handsome, gray haired, dignified, warm, outgoing—but had little depth. For some appointments, he chose the most respected leaders of his party, including Charles Evans Hughes for secretary of state, Andrew Mellon for secretary of the Treasury, and Herbert Hoover for secretary of commerce. Harding, however, was most comfortable playing poker with his friends, and he gave many government jobs to his cronies and political supporters. They made his administration one of the most corrupt in American history. As their misdeeds began to come to light, Harding put off taking action against them. Returning from a trip to Alaska, he died on August 2, 1923, probably from a burst blood vessel in his brain.

The full extent of corruption became clear after Harding's death. Albert Fall, secretary of the interior, had accepted huge bribes from oil companies for leases on federal oil reserves at Elk Hills, California, and Teapot Dome, Wyoming. Attorney General Harry Daugherty and others pocketed payoffs to approve the sale of government-held property below its value. Daugherty may also have protected bootleggers. The head of the Veterans Bureau defrauded the government of more than $200 million. In all, three cabinet members resigned, four officials went to jail, and five men committed suicide. As if the corruption were not enough, in 1927 Nan Britton published a book claiming she had been Harding's mistress, had borne his child, and had carried on trysts with him in the White House.

As these scandals unfolded, hard-pressed farmers turned to the federal government for help. In 1921

[THE POLITICS OF PROSPERITY

☆ *Compare the economic policies of the Harding and Coolidge administrations with those of the Roosevelt and Wilson administrations.*

☆ *Compare La Follette's campaign in 1924 with those of Roosevelt in 1912 and the Populists in 1892.*

perversion Sexual practice considered abnormal or deviant.

■ **Sigmund Freud** Prominent Austrian psychoanalyst, known for his theory that the sex drive underlies much individual behavior.

No one in 1924 would have missed the significance of the teapot behind the steam roller and the would-be presidential candidates scurrying to avoid being engulfed by the Teapot Dome scandal. In the end, however, Teapot Dome seems to have played only a minor role in the 1924 elections.

farm organizations worked with senators and representatives to form a bipartisan **Farm Bloc** to support legislation that would assist farmers. In the 1922 elections, distraught farmers across the Midwest turned out conservatives and elected candidates attuned to farmers' problems. Congress passed a few assistance measures in the early 1920s, but none addressed the central problems of overproduction and low prices. By 1922, some farm organizations joined with unions, especially unions of railroad workers, to form the Conference for Progressive Political Action and agitate for a new Progressive Party.

The Three-Candidate Presidential Election of 1924

When Harding died, Vice President Calvin Coolidge became president. Fortunately for Republicans, Coolidge exemplified honesty, virtue, and sobriety. In

1924 Republicans quickly chose him as their candidate for president.

The Democratic convention, however, sank into a long and bitter deadlock. The party had long divided between southerners (mostly Protestant and committed to white supremacy) and northerners (often city-dwellers and of recent immigrant descent, including many Catholics). In 1924 the Klan was approaching its peak membership and exercised significant influence among many Democratic delegates from the South and parts of the Midwest.

Many northern Democrats wanted to nominate **Al Smith** for president. Highly popular as governor of New York, Smith epitomized urban, immigrant America. Catholic and the son of immigrants, he was everything the Klan—and most of the southern convention delegates—opposed. After nine hot days of deadlock and 103 ballots, the exhausted Democrats turned to a virtually unknown compromise candidate, John W. Davis, who had served in the Wilson administration, then became a corporate lawyer. All in all, the convention seemed to confirm the observation by the contemporary humorist Will Rogers: "I belong to no organized political party. I am a Democrat."

Surviving progressives welcomed the independent candidacy of Senator Robert M. La Follette, nominated by a new Progressive Party formed by farmers, unions, and reformers. The La Follette Progressives attacked

■ **Farm Bloc** Bipartisan group of senators and representatives formed in 1921 to promote legislation to assist farmers.

■ **Al Smith** New York governor who unsuccessfully sought the Democratic nomination for president in 1924 and was the unsuccessful Democratic candidate for president in 1928; his Catholicism and desire to repeal Prohibition were political liabilities.

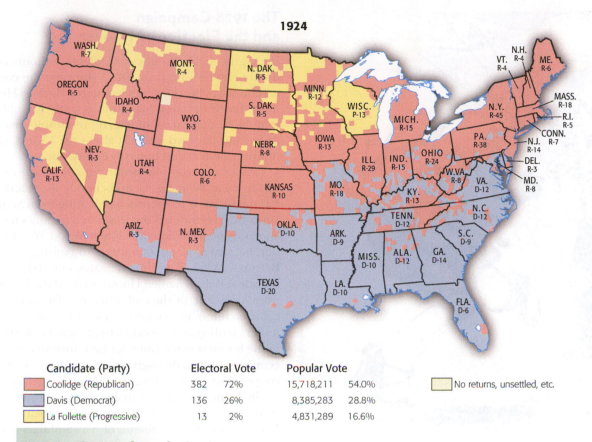

1924

Candidate (Party)	Electoral Vote		Popular Vote	
Coolidge (Republican)	382	72%	15,718,211	54.0%
Davis (Democrat)	136	26%	8,385,283	28.8%
La Follette (Progressive)	13	2%	4,831,289	16.6%

No returns, unsettled, etc.

MAP 21.1 Election of 1924, by County
In the presidential election of 1924, Senator Robert La Follette of Wisconsin ran as a Progressive. Much of his support came from the northern Midwest and parts of the West where the agricultural economy was most hard-hit. Compare this map to Maps 18.1 (page 483) and 19.2 (page 526). © Cengage Learning.

big business and promoted collective bargaining, reform of politics, public ownership of railroads and water power, and a public referendum on questions of war and peace. La Follette was the first presidential candidate to be endorsed by the American Federation of Labor.

Republican campaigners largely ignored Davis and focused on portraying La Follette as a dangerous radical. Coolidge claimed the key issue was "whether America will allow itself to be degraded into a communistic or socialistic state" or "remain American." Coolidge won with nearly 16 million votes and 54 percent of the total. Davis held on to many traditional Democratic voters, especially in the South, receiving 8 million votes and 29 percent. La Follette carried only his home state of Wisconsin but garnered almost 5 million votes, 17 percent, and did well in urban working-class neighborhoods and in parts of the Midwest and West (see Map 21.1).

The Politics of Business

Committed to limited government, Coolidge tried to reduce the significance of the presidency—and

succeeded. He announced that "the business of America is business" and believed that the free market would best sustain economic prosperity for all. As president, he set out to prevent government from interfering with business.

Coolidge had little sympathy for efforts to secure federal help for the faltering farm economy. Congress tried to resolve the problems of low prices for farm products and persistent agricultural surpluses with the **McNary-Haugen bill**, which would have created federal price supports and authorized the government to buy farm surpluses and sell them abroad. The Farm Bloc pushed the bill through Congress in 1927, but Coolidge vetoed it. The same thing happened in 1928. In contrast, the **Railway Labor Act of 1926** drew on wartime experiences to establish collective bargaining

■ **McNary-Haugen bill** Farm relief bill providing for government purchase of crop surpluses; Coolidge vetoed it in 1927 and in 1928.

■ **Railway Labor Act of 1926** Federal law guaranteeing collective bargaining for railroad employees.

This cartoon depicts Coolidge playing for big business. Big business, dressed like a flapper, wildly dances the Charleston and sings, "Yes Sir, He's My Baby."

Picture Research Consultants & Archives.

The 1928 Campaign and the Election of Hoover

In August 1927, President Coolidge announced, "I do not choose to run in 1928," stunning the country and his party. Secretary of Commerce Herbert Hoover immediately declared his candidacy, and Republicans found him an ideal candidate, representing what most Americans believed was best about the United States: individual effort and honestly earned success.

Son of a Quaker blacksmith from Iowa, Hoover was orphaned at 10 and grew up believing that hard work was the only way to success. Graduating from Stanford University, he traveled the world as a mining engineer and became a millionaire. When World War I broke out, he turned to public service, organizing relief for Belgium. When the United States entered the war, President Wilson named Hoover to head the U.S. Food Administration. By the end of the war, Hoover had become an international hero. As secretary of commerce under Harding and Coolidge, he attracted wide support in the business community for his efforts to encourage economic growth through associationalism—voluntary cooperation among otherwise competing groups.

In launching his campaign before thousands of supporters gathered in the Stanford football stadium, Hoover sounded the theme of his candidacy: "We in America today are nearer to the final triumph over poverty than ever before."

The Democrats nominated Al Smith—like Hoover, a self-made man. Unlike Hoover, who had gone to Stanford, Smith's education came from the streets of New York City and from Tammany Hall, the city's dominant Democratic machine. As a reform-minded, progressive governor of New York, Smith streamlined state government, improved its efficiency, and supported legislation to set a minimum wage and maximum hours of work and to establish state ownership of hydroelectric plants.

Smith became the main issue in the campaign. Opponents attacked his Catholic religion, his big-city background, his opposition to Prohibition, his Tammany connections, and even his New York accent. Anti-Catholic sentiment burned hotly in parts of the country, often fanned by remnants of the Klan. Evangelist Billy Sunday called Smith supporters "damnable whiskey politicians, bootleggers, crooks, pimps and businessmen who deal with them." Thus, for many voters, the choice seemed to be between a candidate who represented hard work and the pious values of small town, old-stock, Protestant America and a candidate who represented Catholics, foreigners, machine politics, and the problems of the cities.

Hoover won easily, with 58 percent. Prosperity and the nation's long-term Republican majority probably would have spelled victory for any competent

for railroad employees. Passed by overwhelming margins in Congress, the new law met most of the railway unions' demands and effectively removed them from politics.

Andrew Mellon, one of the wealthiest men in the nation, served as secretary of the Treasury throughout the 1920s. Arguing that high taxes on the wealthy stifled the economy, he secured tax breaks for the affluent, claiming they would benefit everyone through "productive investments" of the tax savings. Herbert Hoover, secretary of commerce under Harding and Coolidge, urged Coolidge to regulate the increasingly wild use of credit, which contributed to rampant stock market speculation, but Coolidge refused.

Coolidge cut federal spending and staffed federal agencies with people who shared his distaste for too much government. Unlike Harding, Coolidge found honest and competent appointees, putting probusiness figures onto regulatory commissions and naming conservative, probusiness judges to the courts. The *Wall Street Journal* described the outcome: "Never before, here or anywhere else, has a government been so completely fused with business."

Republican. Smith's religion and anti-Prohibition stance cost him in the South, where Hoover carried areas that had not voted Republican since Reconstruction. Smith brought some Democratic gains in northern cities, partly by drawing to the polls Catholic voters, especially women who had not previously voted.

The first president born west of the Mississippi River, Hoover came to the presidency with definite ideas about both domestic and foreign policy. He set out to be an active president. The role of government, he believed, was to promote cooperation. He warned that once government, especially the federal government, stepped in to solve problems directly, the people gave up some of their freedom, and government became part of the problem. Hoover recognized that the federal government had a responsibility to help find solutions to social and economic problems, but the key word was *help:* Hoover looked to the government to help but not to solve problems by itself.

THE DIPLOMACY OF PROSPERITY

★ *What role did the United States play in world affairs during the 1920s?*

★ *How successful was Hughes at the Washington Naval Conference?*

Two realities shaped American foreign policy in the 1920s: rejection of Woodrow Wilson's internationalism and a continuing quest by American business for more markets and investments. As president, Harding dismissed any American role in the League of Nations and refused to accept the Treaty of Versailles. Undamaged by the war, American firms outproduced and outtraded the rest of the world. U.S. trade accounted for 30 percent of the world's total, and American firms produced more than 70 percent of the world's oil and almost 50 percent of the world's coal and steel. American bankers loaned billions of dollars outside the United States.

With neither expertise nor interest in foreign affairs, Harding and Coolidge left most foreign policy decisions to their secretaries of state, Charles Evans Hughes and Frank Kellogg. Both very capable, they sought to expand American influence and business abroad through what historians have called "independent internationalism." Independent (or **unilateral**) internationalism had two central thrusts: avoidance of **multilateral** commitments—sometimes called **isolationism**—and expansion of economic opportunities overseas. The Commerce and State Departments promoted American business activities worldwide, for example, encouraging investments in Japan and China and securing permission for U.S. oil companies to drill throughout the Middle East. Their efforts to expand American's economic position in Latin America and Europe were quite successful. As president, Hoover and his secretary of state, Henry L. Stimson, followed a similar approach.

The United States and Latin America

When Harding took office in 1921, the United States had troops in Cuba, Panama, Haiti, the Dominican Republic, and Nicaragua (see Map 21.2). During the campaign, Harding had criticized Wilson's "bayonet rule" in Haiti and the Dominican Republic and promised to end those occupations. To maintain American dominance in the Caribbean, however, U.S. officials wanted stable and friendly local governments. Therefore, American administrators kept some control over each nation's finances and trained their military and police forces. American troops left Cuba in 1922, the Dominican Republic in 1924, Nicaragua in 1932, and Haiti in 1934. In the Dominican Republic and in Haiti, however, the United States kept control of the customs house—and tariff revenues—until the 1940s.

When American troops withdrew from the Dominican Republic and Haiti, they left better roads, improved sanitation systems, governments favorable to the United States, and well-equipped local police. But the years of occupation had not advanced the educational systems, the national economies, or most residents' standard of living. Nor had the United States promoted democracy, favoring stability instead—even if it meant accepting dictators such as Rafael Trujillo, who seized power in the Dominican Republic in 1930 and ruled brutally until his death in 1961.

In Nicaragua, American forces left in 1925 but returned in 1926 to protect the pro-American government when civil war broke out. Coolidge sent Henry L. Stimson to negotiate a peace agreement that ended most fighting in 1927. However, **Augusto Sandino**, who wanted to rid Nicaragua of American influence, rejected the peace agreement and continued guerrilla warfare.

unilateral An action taken by a country by itself, as opposed to actions taken jointly with other nations.

multilateral Involving more than two nations (when only two nations are involved, the term is *bilateral*).

■ **isolationism** The notion that the United States should avoid political, diplomatic, and military entanglements with other nations.

■ **Augusto Sandino** Nicaraguan guerrilla leader who resisted Nicaraguan and American troops from 1925 to 1933 and was murdered in 1934 by order of Anastasio Somoza, whose family remained in power until 1979, when they were ousted by rebels calling themselves Sandinistas.

ATLANTIC OCEAN

UNITED STATES

Cuba
Platt Amendment, 1902–1934
U.S. troops, 1906–1909, 1912, 1917–1922
U.S. companies invest in sugar

Havana, Cuba
U.S. upholds right of intervention at
Pan American Conference, 1928

Haiti
U.S. troops, 1915–1934
U.S. financial supervision, 1916–1941

MEXICO

Gulf of Mexico

BAHAMA IS. (Gr. Br.)

Dominican Republic
U.S. troops, 1916–1924
U.S. financial supervision, 1905–1941
Trujillo era, 1930–1961

Mexico
U.S. companies' investments, including railroads and oil
Constitution of 1917 challenges U.S. interests
Nationalization of foreign oil companies, 1938

Havana   CUBA

DOMINICAN REP.

HAITI

VIRGIN IS. (U.S./Gr. Br.)

Virgin Islands
U.S. possession since 1917

Guatemala
United Fruit Company, coffee investments

BRITISH HONDURAS (Gr. Br.)

HONDURAS

JAMAICA (Gr. Br.)

PUERTO RICO (U.S.)

Caribbean Sea

Puerto Rico
U.S. possession since 1898
Jones Act grants U.S. citizenship, 1917

GUATEMALA

NICARAGUA

TRINIDAD (Gr. Br.)

El Salvador
U.S. companies invest in coffee

EL SALVADOR

COSTA RICA

BR. GUIANA (Gr. Br.)
DUTCH GUIANA (Neth.)

Honduras
United Fruit Company investments

PANAMA

VENEZUELA

FRENCH GUIANA (Fr.)

COLOMBIA

Venezuela
U.S. companies invest in oil

Nicaragua
U.S. financial supervision, 1911–1925
U.S. troops, 1912–1925, 1927–1933
War against Sandino, 1925–1933
Somoza era, 1936–1979

ECUADOR

Equator – 0°

Amazon R.

Panama
U.S. acquired Canal Zone, 1903

PERU

BRAZIL

PACIFIC OCEAN

BOLIVIA

N

Chile
U.S. companies invest in copper mining

Parand R.

20°S

PARAGUAY

CHILE

URUGUAY

0   500   1000 Km.
0   500   1000 Mi.

ARGENTINA

40°S
40°W

FALKLAND ISLANDS (Gr. Br.)

80°W   60°W

MAP 21.2 The United States and Latin America Between the Wars
During the 1920s, the United States played an active role throughout Central America and the Caribbean and, to a lesser extent, in South America. This sometimes included military intervention, but political and economic pressures increasingly replaced military force as the means for protecting U.S. interests. © Cengage Learning.

Elsewhere in Latin America, American involvement was not military, but commercial. Throughout Central America, American firms such as the United Fruit Company purchased thousands of acres for plantations to grow produce, especially bananas and coffee, for the American and European market. United Fruit soon exercised a powerful influence in several Central American countries. In Venezuela and Colombia, American oil companies, with State Department help, negotiated contracts for drilling rights, outmaneuvering European oil companies. U.S. investments in Latin America rose from nearly $2 billion in 1919 to over $3.5 billion in 1929.

Oil played a key role in relations with Mexico. The Mexican constitution of 1917 limited foreign ownership, and Mexico moved to **nationalize** its subsurface resources, including oil. American companies strongly objected. By 1925, American oilmen and some members of the Coolidge administration were seeking military protection for American oil interests in Mexico. Coolidge instead sent Dwight W. Morrow—a college friend—as ambassador to Mexico with instructions "to keep us out of war with Mexico." Morrow knew some Spanish, understood Mexican nationalism and pride, and cultivated a personal relationship with Mexican president Plutarco Calles. He succeeded in reducing tensions and delayed nationalization of oil until 1938. Following the election of 1928, president-elect Hoover undertook a tour of eleven Latin American countries, seeking better relations.

America and Europe

World War I shattered much of Europe physically and economically. The American economy soared to unprecedented heights, however, and the United States became the world's leading creditor nation. After the war, Republican policymakers joined with business leaders to expand exports and restrict imports. The **Fordney-McCumber Tariff** of 1922 set the highest rates ever for most manufactured imports. By significantly limiting European imports, the tariff made it difficult for Europeans to acquire the dollars they needed to repay their war debts in the United States.

At the same time, Secretary of State Hughes and Secretary of Commerce Hoover worked to expand American economic interests in Europe, especially Germany. They reasoned that if Germany recovered economically and paid its $33 billion war reparations, other European nations would also recover and repay their debts. Encouraged by federal officials, Americans invested over $4 billion in Europe, doubling their investments there. General Motors purchased Opel, a German automobile firm. Ford built the largest automobile factory outside the United States in England, and constructed a tractor factory in the Soviet Union.

Dwight Morrow, U.S. ambassador to Mexico, and Mexican president Plutarco Calles (*right*), shaking hands. Morrow proved a highly successful ambassador, defusing tensions between the two countries. Morrow invited Charles Lindbergh to visit Mexico. While there, Lindbergh met Morrow's daughter Anne; they were married in 1929.

Even so, Germany could not make its reparation payments, defaulting in 1923 to France and Belgium. In response, French troops occupied Germany's **Ruhr Valley**, a key economic region, igniting an international crisis. Hughes sent Charles G. Dawes, a Chicago banker and prominent Republican, to resolve the situation. Under the **Dawes Plan**, American bankers loaned $2.5 billion to Germany for economic development. The Germans promised to pay $2 billion in reparations to the European Allies, who, in turn, were to pay $2.5 billion in war debts to the United States. Though this circular flow of capital produced jokes at the time, it worked fairly well until 1929, when the Depression ended nearly all loans and payments.

nationalize To convert an industry or enterprise from private to government ownership and control.

■ **Fordney-McCumber Tariff** Protective tariff passed by Congress in 1922 that raised tariff rates to record levels and provoked foreign reprisals.

Ruhr Valley Region surrounding the Ruhr River in northwestern Germany, containing major industrial cities and valuable coal mines.

■ **Dawes Plan** Arrangement for collecting World War I reparations from Germany; it scheduled annual payments and stabilized German currency.

In the Wider World

Hyperinflation in the Weimar Republic

In 1919, a German constitutional assembly wrote a liberal, democratic constitution in the town of Weimar, so the new government was often referred to as the Weimar Republic.

In 1921, the European Allies demanded the reparations specified by the Versailles treaty at the rate, each year, of more than 2 billion marks (the German unit of currency). Simultaneously, the Fordney-McCumber tariff policy closed American markets to German exports. Under those pressures, the German mark quickly collapsed. In early 1921, one dollar was worth about 60 marks; by late 1923, one dollar was worth 4 trillion marks. At the worst point, prices doubled every two days.

In late 1923, the German government introduced a new currency that brought inflation under control. That, together with the Dawes Plan, stabilized the Germany economy. However, the hyperinflation of 1921–1923 is often credited with undermining many Germans' confidence in democracy and aiding the rise to power of Adolf Hitler in 1933 (covered in Chapter 23).

Encouraging International Cooperation

Though committed to independent internationalism, Republican policymakers understood that some international cooperation was necessary to achieve policy goals and solve international problems. On such issues, they were willing to cooperate with other nations and enter into international agreements, but only with the understanding that the United States was not entering an alliance or otherwise agreeing to commit resources or troops in defense of another nation.

Disarmament was such an issue. The devastation of World War I had spurred calls for reducing armaments. In the United States, support for arms cuts was widespread. In early 1921, Senator William E. Borah of Idaho suggested an international conference to reduce the size of the world's navies. Fearing that naval expenditures would prevent tax cuts, Treasury Secretary Mellon joined the disarmament chorus.

American policymakers also had concerns about Japan. The United States and Britain had the largest navies, roughly equal in strength, and had no interest in expanding them. Japan, the next largest naval power, wanted to expand its navy. Americans worried that Japanese pressures on China could endanger Chinese territory and the Open Door policy.

Given these two areas of concern, Harding and Hughes agreed to host international discussions on limiting the size of navies and ensuring the status quo in China. In November 1921, Harding invited the major naval powers to Washington to discuss reducing "the crushing burdens of military and naval establishments."

When the delegates assembled for the **Washington Naval Conference**, Hughes shocked them with a radical proposal: scrap nearly 2 million tons of warships, mostly battleships. He also called for a ten-year ban on naval construction and limits on the size of navies aimed especially at the Japanese. Hughes suggested a ratio of 5 to 5 to 3 for the United States, Britain, and Japan, with Italy and France allocated 1.7 each. Hughes's plan garnered immediate support among both the American public and most of the participating nations—but not Japan. Calling Hughes's ratio an insult, the Japanese demanded equality. Discussions dragged on for two months, but the Japanese finally agreed. U.S. intelligence had broken the Japanese diplomatic code, so Hughes knew that the Japanese delegates had orders to concede if he held firm.

In February 1922, the United States, Britain, Japan, France, and Italy agreed to build no more **capital ships** for ten years and to abide by the 5:5:3:1.7:1.7 ratio for future shipbuilding. Hughes, according to a British observer, had sunk more British ships "than all the admirals of the world." The nations also agreed to prohibit the use of poison gas and not to attack one another's Asian possessions. Another treaty affirmed the sovereignty and territorial boundaries of China and guaranteed equal commercial access to China, thereby maintaining the Open Door. Hughes considered the meetings successful, though critics

■ Washington Naval Conference International conference in 1921–1922; produced agreements to limit naval armaments and prevent conflict in East Asia and the Pacific.

capital ships A navy's largest, most heavily armed ships; at the Washington Naval Conference, capital ships were those over 10,000 tons and carrying guns with at least an 8-inch bore.

Library of Congress.

Several members of the advisory committee to the U.S. delegation to the Washington Naval Conference, appointed by President Harding. The committee included a few business leaders, two labor leaders, four leaders of women's organizations, General John J. Pershing (*second from the left*), Secretary of Commerce Herbert Hoover (*far right*), and several former members of Congress. Katherine Philips Edson (*fourth from the left*) was an important leader of California progressivism.

complained that there were no enforcement provisions and no mention of smaller ships.

Other attempts to reduce armaments had mixed outcomes. In 1930, Britain, the United States, and Japan established ratios for cruisers and destroyers similar to those of the Washington Conference. By the mid-1930s, however, Japan's demands for naval equality ended British and American cooperation and spurred new naval construction by all three.

Many Americans and Europeans applauded the achievements of the Washington Naval Conference but wanted to go further to end wars. In 1923 Senator Borah proposed a Senate resolution outlawing war. In 1924 La Follette campaigned for a national referendum as a requirement for declaring war. In 1927 the French foreign minister, Aristide Briand, suggested a pact formally outlawing war between the France and the United States, privately hoping such an agreement would commit the United States to aid France if attacked. Secretary of State Kellogg instead suggested a multilateral statement opposing war, thereby removing any hint of any American commitment of aid. On August 27, 1928, the United States and fourteen other nations, including Britain, France, Germany, Italy, and Japan, signed the Pact of Paris, or **Kellogg-Briand Pact**,

renouncing war "as an instrument of national policy" and agreeing to settle disputes peacefully. Eventually sixty-four nations signed, but the pact included no enforcement provisions. Nearly every **signatory** reserved its right to self-defense.

Thus, by 1928, American independent internationalism seemed a success. Investments and loans by American businesses were fueling an expanding world economy and contributing to American prosperity. The United States had protected its Asian and Pacific interests against Japan, while protecting China and promoting disarmament and world peace. In Latin America, the United States had withdrawn some troops from the Caribbean and avoided intervention in Mexico. Foreign policies based on economic expansion and noncoercive diplomacy appeared to be launching an era of cooperation and peace in world affairs.

■ **Kellogg-Briand Pact** A 1928 treaty signed by fifteen nations, including Britain, France, Germany, the United States, and Japan, that renounced war as a means of solving international disputes.

signatory One who has signed a treaty or other document.

Individual Voices

Sexuality and Innuendo in Movie Advertising

The great popularity of movies in the 1920s means that historians are interested in ways that the films may have influenced people's behavior. The movie ads on this page and earlier in the chapter bring together three of the significant changes of the 1920s—the movies themselves, the growth of advertising as a way to attract consumers, and changing attitudes regarding sexuality.

Flaming Youth, at Loew's State theater, ad in *Los Angeles Times*, December 31, 1923.

❶ *Flaming Youth* (November 1923) was the first "flapper" movie, narrowly edging out Clara Bow's appearance in *Black Oxen* (January 1924). What does the ad suggest about the youth the film depicts?

Quo Vadis, at the Apollo theater, ad in *New York Times*, March 1, 1925.

❷ The 1925 film *Quo Vadis* was one of several based on the novel by that name by Henryk Sienkiewicz. Set in ancient Rome, the novel depicts the love between a young Christian woman and an upper-class Roman. Can you tell from this ad that the original novel was about the spiritual power of Christianity?

❸ Could these films have contributed to changing attitudes toward sexuality? Is it possible that changing attitudes toward sexuality created an audience for such films? How would you research either hypothesis?

SUMMARY

The 1920s were a decade of prosperity. Unemployment was low, productivity grew steadily, and many Americans fared well. Sophisticated advertising campaigns created bright expectations, and installment buying freed consumers from paying cash. Many consumers bought more and bought on credit—stimulating manufacturing and expanding personal debt. Expectations of continuing prosperity encouraged speculation, and the stock market boomed. Agriculture did not share in this prosperity.

During the Roaring Twenties, Americans experienced significant social change. The automobile, radio, and movies, along with immigration restriction, produced a more homogeneous culture. Many American intellectuals, however, rejected the consumer-oriented culture. During the 1920s, African Americans produced an outpouring of significant art, literature, and music. Some young people rejected traditional constraints, and one result was the emergence of a youth culture.

Not all Americans embraced change. Some tried to maintain or restore earlier cultural values. The outcomes were mixed. Prohibition was largely unsuccessful. Fundamentalism grew and prompted a campaign against the teaching of evolution. Nativism helped define significant restrictions on immigration. The Ku Klux Klan, committed to nativism, traditional values, and white supremacy, experienced nationwide growth until 1925, but declined sharply thereafter.

Discrimination and occasional violence continued to affect the lives of people of color. Federal Indian policy had long stressed assimilation and allotment, but some groups now advocated more respect for Indian cultural values. Immigrants from Mexico came especially to California, Texas, and other parts of the Southwest. Some working in agriculture tried unsuccessfully to organize unions. Nearly all unions faced strong opposition from employers. Some older gender roles for women broke down as women gained the right to vote and exercised more control over having children. A gay and lesbian subculture became more visible, especially in cities.

Politics were markedly more conservative than before World War I. Warren G. Harding was a poor judge of character, and some of his appointees were revealed as corrupt. Under Harding and his successor, Calvin Coolidge, the conservative federal government lionized business, minimized regulation, and encouraged speculation. With some exceptions, progressive reform disappeared from politics, and efforts to secure federal assistance for farmers failed. Herbert Hoover defeated Al Smith in the 1928 presidential election, in which the values of an older, rural America seemed to be pitted against those of the new, urban, immigrant society.

CHRONOLOGY
America in the 1920s

1908	Henry Ford introduces Model T
	General Motors formed
1914	Universal Negro Improvement Association founded
1914–1918	War in Europe
1920	Eighteenth Amendment (Prohibition) takes effect
	Nineteenth Amendment (women suffrage) takes effect
	Warren G. Harding elected president
1920–1921	Nationwide recession
1921	Farm Bloc formed
1921–1922	Washington Naval Conference
1922	Fordney-McCumber Tariff
	Sinclair Lewis's *Babbitt*
1923	Harding dies; Calvin Coolidge becomes president
	Jean Toomer's *Cane*
	American Indian Defense Association formed
	France occupies Ruhr Valley
1923–1927	Harding administration scandals revealed
1924	National Origins Act
	Coolidge elected
	Full citizenship for American Indians
	Dawes Plan
	U.S. forces withdraw from Dominican Republic
1924–1929	Great Bull Market
1925	Scopes trial
	F. Scott Fitzgerald's *The Great Gatsby*
	Ku Klux Klan claims 5 million members
1926	Florida real-estate boom collapses
	Railway Labor Act of 1926
1927	Charles Lindbergh's transatlantic flight
	Duke Ellington conducts jazz at Cotton Club
1928	Ford introduces Model A
	Kellogg-Briand Pact
	Herbert Hoover elected
1929	Great Depression begins

Study Tools

During the 1920s, the United States followed a policy of independent internationalism that stressed voluntary cooperation among nations, while at the same time enhancing opportunities for American business around the world. Relations with Latin America improved somewhat, and the Washington Naval Conference held out the hope for limiting naval armaments.

FOCUS QUESTIONS

If you have mastered this chapter, you should be able to answer these questions and to explain the terms that follow the questions.

1. What was the basis for the economic expansion of the 1920s?

2. What weaknesses existed within the economy?

3. What groups most challenged traditional social patterns during the 1920s?

4. What role did technology play in social change during the 1920s?

5. Why and how did some Americans try to restore traditional social values during the 1920s?

6. What continuities and changes characterized racial and ethnic relations during the 1920s?

7. Is it appropriate to describe the 1920s as "the lean years" for working people?

8. How did gender roles and definitions change in the 1920s?

9. Compare the economic policies of the Harding and Coolidge administrations with those of the Roosevelt and Wilson administrations.

10. Compare La Follette's campaign in 1924 with those of Roosevelt in 1912 and the Populists in 1892.

11. What role did the United States play in world affairs during the 1920s?

12. How successful was Hughes at the Washington Naval Conference?

KEY TERMS

Henry Ford   *p. 568*
A. P. Giannini   *p. 569*
Charles Lindbergh   *p. 573*
Sinclair Lewis   *p. 574*
Harlem Renaissance   *p. 574*
jazz   *p. 575*
Marcus Garvey   *p. 576*
black separatism   *p. 576*
Eighteenth Amendment   *p. 577*
Al Capone   *p. 578*
fundamentalism   *p. 578*

evolution   *p. 578*
Clarence Darrow   *p. 578*
National Origins Act   *p. 579*
American Indian Defense Association   *p. 582*
American Plan   *p. 583*
welfare capitalism   *p. 583*
Communist Party of the United States   *p. 583*
Equal Rights Amendment   *p. 583*
Sigmund Freud   *p. 585*

Farm Bloc   *p. 586*
Al Smith   *p. 586*
McNary-Haugen bill   *p. 587*
Railway Labor Act of 1926   *p. 587*
isolationism   *p. 589*
Augusto Sandino   *p. 589*
Fordney-McCumber Tariff   *p. 591*
Dawes Plan   *p. 591*
Washington Naval Conference   *p. 592*
Kellogg-Briand Pact   *p. 593*

SUGGESTED RESOURCES

Kareem Abdul-Jabbar with Raymond Obstfeld. *On the Shoulders of Giants: My Journey Through the Harlem Renaissance* (New York: Simon and Schuster, 2007). The former basketball superstar considers the long-term impact of the Harlem Renaissance, including its influence on his life and on basketball.

William Leuchtenburg. *The Perils of Prosperity, 1924–1932*, 2nd ed. (Chicago: University of Chicago Press, 1993). A classic account, first published in 1958, and still a valuable introduction to the period.

The Smithsonian Collection of Classic Jazz. Five compact disks (Washington: The Smithsonian Institution, 1987). An outstanding collection that reflects the development of American jazz, with annotations and biographies of performers.

David Stenn. *Clara Bow: Runnin' Wild* (New York: Cooper Square Press, 1990). The best and most carefully researched of the biographies of Bow.

Jules Tygiel. *The Great Los Angeles Swindle: Oil, Stocks, and Scandal During the Roaring Twenties* (Berkeley: University of California Press, 1996). An engagingly written account of oil speculation in Los Angeles during the 1920s.

22

The Great Depression and the New Deal, 1929–1939

CHAPTER OUTLINE

The Economic Crisis

The Crash and the Great Depression
Hoover's Response to Crisis
A Rising Tide of Discontent
The Roosevelt Landslide

The New Deal

1933—The First Hundred Days
1934—Year of Turmoil
1935—The Second Hundred Days
The Election of 1936 and the Waning of the New Deal

Changing the Face of America: The New Deal in Action

PWA and WPA
The Wagner Act and the Growth of Organized Labor
The New Deal and Agriculture

Americans Grapple with the Depression

"Making Do"
Changing Women's Roles
Race and Depression: South and West
A New Deal for All?
Cultural Expression in the Midst of Depression

The Great Depression and New Deal in Perspective

INDIVIDUAL VOICES: *Frances Perkins Explains the Social Security Act*

Study Tools

INDIVIDUAL CHOICES

Frances Perkins

On February 22, 1933, President-elect Franklin D. Roosevelt asked Frances Perkins to be secretary of labor. Trained as a social worker, Perkins had been deeply affected by the Triangle Shirtwaist tragedy in 1911. She had worked long and hard for the social justice ideals that Jane Addams had written into the 1912 Progressive Party platform, and she had served as head of the state labor department when Roosevelt was governor of New York. She agreed to Roosevelt's offer of a cabinet job only if she could push for social justice legislation, including relief for the unemployed, old-age pensions, a minimum wage, and abolition of child labor. Roosevelt agreed. He warned that she should not "expect too much help" from him but also suggested that she "nag me about this forever." She accepted, becoming the first woman to serve in a president's cabinet.

Perkins proved to be more tireless advocate than nag, giving strong support to the first federal relief program for the unemployed. She also set out to create a system of social insurance, including unemployment compensation, pensions for elderly workers, aid to dependent children, and assistance for mothers and children. To secure passage of the Social Security Act of 1935, however,

AP/Wide World Photos.

Perkins had to compromise (see the Individual Choices feature at the end of this chapter). For fiscal and political reasons, the final bill required workers to pay into the system instead of having benefits paid out of taxes. Perkins wanted medical coverage, but it was excluded. After many speeches and countless congressional committee hearings, the bill passed, and the relationship between the federal government and the people fundamentally changed.

Perkins also wanted federal standards for workers' wages and hours of work. No "self-supporting and self-respecting democracy," she argued, could justify any "economic reason for chiseling workers' wages or stretching workers' hours." The Fair Labor Standards Act of 1938 addressed these concerns and also barred industrial child labor. Shortly before Perkins left office in 1945, *Collier's* did a story on her accomplishments and concluded the previous twelve years were "not so much the Roosevelt New Deal" as the "Perkins New Deal."

In 1929, the stock market crashed and the economy plunged into a deep depression. President Herbert Hoover fought the economic collapse with policies he expected would produce recovery—but he failed.

In 1932, amid high unemployment and spreading bank failures, Franklin D. Roosevelt was elected president. He proved willing to use the federal government to combat the Depression. The New Deal, however, raised serious questions, both then and since: Should government promote human rights over property rights? Should it assist the disadvantaged by taxing the wealthy? How should the Constitution be applied to circumstances unforeseen when it was written? By its response to these questions, the New Deal set the agenda for many of the nation's political, economic, and social debates from then to now.

THE ECONOMIC CRISIS

★ *How did the stock market crash affect the American economy? What economic weaknesses contributed to the crash and the Great Depression?*

★ *How did Hoover try to deal with the Depression? How successful were his efforts?*

Campaigning for the presidency in 1928, Herbert Hoover had promised a "New Day" for America, but his sweeping victory was more a vote for the status quo. The United States had experienced almost a decade of economic growth, and people voted for Hoover expecting that trend to continue. The outcome was much different.

The Crash and the Great Depression

Hoover took office as president in the midst of rising stock prices, shiny new cars, and rapidly expanding suburbs that seemed to verify his observation about "the final triumph over poverty." But behind the rush for homes, radios, and vacuum cleaners were serious economic weaknesses, some already becoming visible. Less than eight months after Hoover took office, on "Black Thursday," October 24, 1929, the stock market crashed. As stock prices plummeted, frenzied brokers rushed to place sell orders. Few places were untouched. In the mid-Atlantic, on board the passenger liner *Berengaria*, Helena Rubenstein learned her stocks had declined by more than a million dollars in a few hours. The market rebounded a bit on Friday but crashed again on Monday. The next day—"Black Tuesday"—prices plunged again and continued to fall throughout the year.

Within the first week of the crash, stocks fell by a total of $30 billion (equivalent to about $406 billion today), a decline of about 30 percent. Thousands of speculators were ruined. Nationwide, the suicide rate increased by almost 50 percent in 1929, as compared to the previous eight years, and stories circulated of New York hotel clerks asking guests whether they wanted rooms for sleeping or jumping. The Dow Jones Industrial Average measures the stock market performance of selected major stocks. From a high point of 381.17 on September 3, 1929, the Dow fell to 41.22 on July 8, 1932, a decline of nearly 90 percent. Similar losses occurred in stock markets around the world. The Dow did not recover to pre-1929 levels until the 1950s.

The crash set off the **Great Depression**, but it was a catalyst, not the cause. The Depression resulted from uneven economic growth, overproduction, a skewed distribution of income, excessive credit buying, and a **credit crunch** resulting from serious weaknesses in the banking system. The prosperity of the 1920s had in part rested on expanding industries—especially construction, automobiles, movies, and electronics—that pushed the rest of the economy forward. By 1927, those industries were slowing down. Construction starts, for example, fell from 11 billion to 9 billion units between 1926 and 1929, causing producers of household merchandise to reduce production. The expansion of the 1920s had been uneven. Older industries, including railroads, textiles, and iron and steel had barely made a profit, while mining suffered steady losses. Workers in those industries saw little increase in wages or standards of living. The postwar economic expansion completely bypassed agriculture, and farm incomes and property values fell to about half of their wartime highs. Compounding these problems, credit had virtually dried up in rural America, as five thousand banks, many in rural areas, closed between 1921 and 1928. By the end of 1928, thousands had left their farms, and agriculture was approaching a crisis.

Another weakness of the economy lay in the skewed distribution of wealth. In 1929, the richest 5 percent of Americans received about one-third of all income, much of it as interest, dividends, and rent. Given the amount of wealth in the hands of those few, reductions in consumer spending or investment by the wealthy could have a disproportionate effect on the entire economy. Much of the $30 billion loss in stock values represented losses for the wealthiest.

The distribution of wealth affected consumer spending in other ways as well. In the late 1920s, the Brookings Institution judged that an annual salary of $2,500 provided an American family a comfortable standard of living. It also found that 70 percent of American families earned less than that amount. When Hoover took office, many people were buying on credit, especially through installment buying. Americans had used credit to spend about $100 million in 1919, but ten years later that amount had soared to over $7 billion. Still, few worried so long as the economy seemed stable, unemployment remained low, and most Americans had confidence in the economy. All that changed with the stock market crash.

The stock market crash undermined economic confidence and highlighted the weaknesses of the economy. Where the soaring stock market had symbolized a vigorous economy, the market's continued fall made investors and business leaders wary. Reduced demand led manufacturers to cut production and lay off workers or reduce hours. As more and more people found themselves out of work or with smaller

During the early years of the Great Depression, some unemployed people tried to earn money by selling fruit on the street. This photo is from New York City, in 1932.

paychecks, they cut back consumer purchases and stopped buying on credit, further reducing demand. When families could not make their installment payments, they lost their car or radio.

As the economy spiraled downward, the banking system appeared to be collapsing. Many banks had made risky loans and now found that they could not collect on them. As rumors circulated of a bank's instability, customers lined up at teller windows to empty their accounts. As such "runs" on banks intensified, more and more banks were unable to meet their obligations, declared bankruptcy, and closed their doors. Thousands lost their savings, a shock that jarred many upper- and middle-class families.

■ **Great Depression** The years 1929 to 1941 when the economy of the United States suffered a major contraction, millions were unemployed, and thousands of businesses went bankrupt; President Hoover used the term *depression* rather than the more traditional *panic* in hopes that it would reduce the public's fears.

credit crunch (or credit crisis) A significant reduction in the availability of credit, caused by changes in banks' lending policies.

It Matters Today

Preventing Another Great Depression

In September 2008, major financial institutions faced bankruptcy owing to unwise loans. Panic swept through financial markets. Fifteen banks failed, and the stock market crashed throughout the month of October, recording some of the greatest losses ever.

Benjamin Bernanke was chairman of the Federal Reserve System (see Chapter 19's It Matters Today feature, page 527). A former economics professor, Bernanke had previously researched the causes of the Great Depression. The key factor, he had concluded, had been the failure of the Federal Reserve to stop bank failures and maintain credit. In 2008, when banks began to fail and the stock market crashed, Bernanke moved quickly and worked closely with Treasury Secretary Henry Paulson to prevent some bank failures and to secure hundreds of billions of dollars of federal loans and investments in key financial institutions to keep them stable and discourage a credit crunch that could lead to another Great Depression.

- Do newspaper accounts from September and October 2008 draw comparisons to the events of 1929?
- Can you find other examples when historical analysis, such as that done by Bernanke, has affected recent governmental policies?

As some banks closed their doors and others struggled to remain open, the nation entered a credit crunch. Unable to collect on many of their current loans, bankers became reluctant to make new loans—and credit dried up. In the midst of this, the Federal Reserve *raised* interest rates, which further discouraged borrowing. Many Americans dumped their stocks for whatever they could get and refused to invest in stocks so long as the market kept falling. Because economic growth and expansion require access to credit from banks and funds from sale of stocks, the entire economy lurched toward paralysis.

By 1933, American exports were at their lowest since 1905, nearly ninety thousand businesses had failed, and corporate profits were down 60 percent. Unemployment rose from 3 percent in 1929 to 9 percent in 1930 and 25 percent in 1933, with much higher rates in manufacturing. In Gary, Indiana, for example, nearly the entire working class was out of a job. Nine thousand banks had closed, with depositors losing $2.5 billion. The drastic decline in the value of stocks, the bank failures, and actions by the Federal Reserve contributed to a serious shrinkage in the money supply, causing deflation. Average annual family income dropped 35 percent—from $2,300 to $1,500—by 1933. Prices for most products also fell, reducing income to merchants and producers, but the decline in income and uncertainties about the overall economy meant that people

were unable or unwilling to buy even at reduced prices. Automobile purchases dropped by 75 percent.

Other industrial nations also experienced economic contraction and significant unemployment. During the 1920s, the European economy was recovering from the devastation of the Great War, greatly aided by over $5.1 billion dollars borrowed from American sources. However, by the end of 1928, American investors began reducing their loans to Europe. The onset of the Depression in the United States worsened the international credit contraction. As the Depression spread, many nations, including the United States, raised tariffs to protect their industries from foreign goods. The 1930 Smoot-Hawley Tariff set the highest tariff rates in U.S. history. Such actions were intended to protect domestic markets, but they undermined world trade—including American exports. World trade slowed to a crawl by 1931.

Hoover's Response to Crisis

At first, the most common response to the plunge in stock prices was that voiced by Secretary of the Treasury Andrew Mellon, who stated that the economy remained strong, that the market plunge was temporary, and that it would actually strengthen the economy. Though many experts argued that the free-market system would eventually heal itself, Hoover summoned the nation's corporate leaders and asked them to reduce profits rather than cut jobs and wages. At the same time, he tried to stimulate the economy by urging Congress, states, and cities to spend more on **public works projects**, including government

□ **public works projects** Construction projects financed by public funds and carried out by federal, state, or local governments.

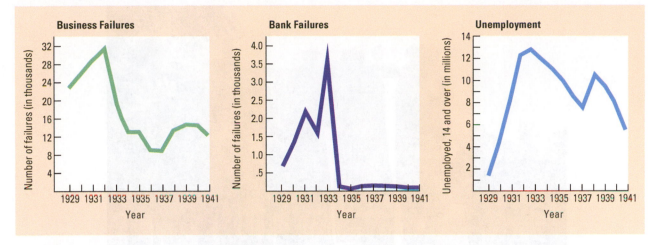

FIGURE 22.1 Charting the Economics of the Depression
Between 1929 and 1933, the number of people unemployed and of bank and business failures steadily increased. As the New Deal began, not only did the trend lines improve, but for many a sense of hope also emerged. © Cengage Learning.

buildings and highways. Hoover also called on local groups to contribute to help the unemployed. The Agricultural Marketing Act (1929) tried to address farmers' problems by creating a Farm Board to help support agricultural prices. Despite some initial successes, these efforts did little to counteract the credit crunch and produced no sustained recovery. As demand dried up, businesses cut production, reduced wages, and laid off workers. Agricultural prices continued to collapse. State, local, and private efforts to aid the unemployed were overwhelmed by the huge and growing numbers (see Figure 22.1).

As the country slipped deeper into depression, Hoover took new steps, some of which finally addressed the credit crunch. He asked Congress for banking reforms, support for home mortgages, creation of the **Reconstruction Finance Corporation** (RFC), and higher taxes to pay for it all. Congress responded in 1932 with the **Glass-Steagall Act**, which encouraged lending, and the **Federal Home Loan Bank Act**, which allowed homeowners to remortgage their homes at lower rates and payments.

Hoover intended the RFC to be the major tool to fight the Depression by pumping money into the economy. Created in 1932—several years after the beginning of the credit crunch that was producing economic paralysis—the RFC used federal funds to provide loans to banks, railroads, and large corporations to prevent their collapse and expand their operations. Hoover and his advisers hoped this funding would "trickle down" to workers and the unemployed through higher wages and new jobs. But the RFC came years too late and was slow to begin operations. It did loan over $805 million within its first five months, but with little apparent effect on the economy. Critics branded it "welfare for the rich" and insisted Hoover do something for the poor

and unemployed. Hoover opposed federal unemployment relief, however, believing that it was too expensive and eroded the work ethic. But as unemployment reached nearly 25 percent and pressure mounted from Congress and the public, he accepted an Emergency Relief Division within the RFC to provide $300 million in loans to states to pay for work relief. Yet few states wanted to put themselves more deeply in debt by borrowing, and 90 percent of the relief fund was still intact by the end of 1932. In the end, the RFC proved to be too little and too late to resolve the economic crisis.

The onslaught of the Depression changed Hoover's and the nation's fortunes. Many Americans blamed the president and the Republicans for the worsening economy and for callousness toward the hardships besetting the country. As people who lost their homes began to live in shantytowns on the outskirts of many cities, the head of publicity for the Democratic National Committee sarcastically dubbed them "**Hoovervilles**," and the name stuck.

■ **Reconstruction Finance Corporation** (RFC) Federal agency established under Hoover in 1932 to promote economic recovery; provided emergency financing for banks, life insurance companies, railroads, and farm mortgage associations; continued and expanded as part of the New Deal.

Glass-Steagall Act A 1932 law that expanded credit through the Federal Reserve System.

Federal Home Loan Bank Act A 1932 law that established twelve banks across the nation to assist institutions making home loans in an effort to reduce foreclosures and to stimulate the construction industry.

Hooverville Crudely built camp set up by the homeless on the fringes of a town or city during the Depression.

Unable to get adequate prices for their products, these dairy farmers chose to dump their milk rather than sell it.

A Rising Tide of Discontent

Some farmers began to take matters into their own hands. In October 1931, when an Iowa bank **foreclosed** on a mortgage and held an auction of the farmer's land and equipment, other farmers used their numbers and threats of violence to force a "penny auction" that returned the foreclosed farm to its owners for a fraction of its value. Penny auctions quickly spread across the Midwest. In Ohio, for example, one farmer, backed by a crowd of angry neighbors, regained his farm for a high bid of $1.90 to settle a mortgage of $800.

In the summer of 1932, some midwestern farmers joined the **Farmers' Holiday Association**, led by Milo Reno. Reno urged farmers to "stay home, buy nothing, sell nothing" and push up prices by destroying their crops rather than selling them. Many farmers responded by withholding their own produce from market and also setting up roadblocks to prevent other farmers from selling theirs.

By 1932, Communist Party organizers were signing up members among desperate farmers. Farmers were not alone. Across the nation, strikes, protest rallies, "bread marches," and rent riots took place as citizens demanded more jobs, higher wages, and relief payments. The Communist Party signed up nearly twenty thousand new members between 1931 and 1932, though most dropped out after a short time.

A major protest took place in the spring and summer of 1932 when thousands of World War I veterans, usually called the **Bonus Army**, converged on Washington, D.C., to demonstrate support for the "bonus bill," which promised early payment of veteran's bonuses originally scheduled for 1945. The marchers, some with families, set up a Hooverville at Anacostia Flats, a marshy area along the Anacostia River, about two miles from the Capitol. When the bill failed, most left, but nearly ten thousand stayed behind. In late July, Hoover ordered the army to remove them. Led by Army Chief of Staff General Douglas MacArthur, troops armed with cavalry sabers, rifles, tear gas, and fixed bayonets evicted the veterans and their families and burned their shelters. About a hundred veterans were injured and two were killed, but rumors quickly swelled those numbers and intensified the public's angry reaction. Upon hearing of the army's action, the governor of New York, Franklin D. Roosevelt, exclaimed, "This will elect me."

foreclose To confiscate property when mortgage payments are delinquent; in the 1930s, it was typical to auction off foreclosed assets.

▪ **Farmers' Holiday Association** Organization of farmers that called for direct action—such as destroying crops and resisting foreclosures—to protest the plight of agriculture and lack of government support.

▪ **Bonus Army** Unemployed World War I veterans who marched to Washington in 1932 to demand early payment of a promised bonus; Congress refused, and the army evicted protesters who remained.

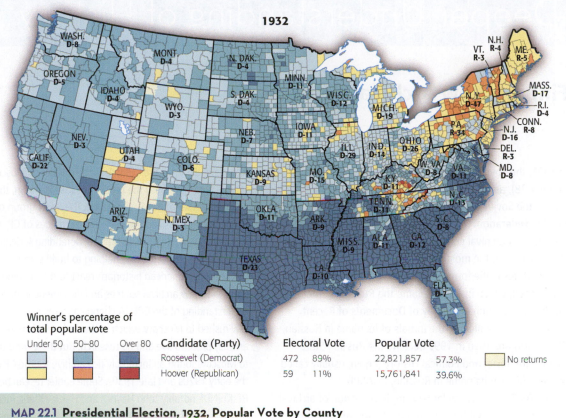

1932

Winner's percentage of total popular vote

	Under 50	50–80	Over 80	Candidate (Party)	Electoral Vote		Popular Vote	
				Roosevelt (Democrat)	472	89%	22,821,857	57.3%
				Hoover (Republican)	59	11%	15,761,841	39.6%

No returns

MAP 22.1 Presidential Election, 1932, Popular Vote by County
In the election of 1932, Franklin D. Roosevelt, promising a New Deal for Americans beleaguered by the continuing economic catastrophe, won forty-two of forty-eight states. Minor party candidates drew about 3 percent of the vote. © Cengage Learning.

The Roosevelt Landslide

Nearly any Democratic candidate could have defeated Hoover in 1932, but the Democrats nominated an exceptional politician: Franklin Delano Roosevelt, born into wealth and educated at the exclusive Groton School and Harvard College. After graduation, with a recognizable name, Roosevelt entered New York politics. Tall, handsome, charming, and an accomplished public speaker, he became assistant secretary of the navy (a position his distant cousin Theodore once held) in the Wilson administration, then won the Democratic nomination for vice president in 1920. Though he and presidential candidate James Cox lost, his political future looked bright. Then, in 1921, he was stricken with polio and paralyzed from the waist down. Greatly aided by his wife, Eleanor, he kept his political career alive and in 1928 won the governorship of New York. Roosevelt was one of the few governors to mobilize his state's limited resources to help the unemployed and poor. Although results were modest, his efforts suggested a caring and energetic leader—a champion of the "forgotten man." The opposite image stuck to Hoover, who seemed to have little concern for the 11 million unemployed Americans.

When nominated for president in 1932, Roosevelt broke with precedent and flew to Chicago to give his acceptance speech to the convention. Establishing a theme for the coming campaign, Roosevelt emphatically announced that he and the Democratic Party had no fear of breaking with "all foolish traditions" and closed by promising a "new deal for the American people." The media quickly picked up the term, and Roosevelt's campaign acquired a memorable slogan: the **New Deal**. Although his speech offered no concrete solutions to the nation's problems, it promised hope and instilled the belief that Roosevelt would move the nation along new paths.

During the campaign, Roosevelt largely avoided any commitments or policy proposals that might offend voters. He supported direct federal relief while promising to balance the budget, but mostly he stressed hope and the prospect of change. Hoover claimed that the campaign was "more than a contest between two men," that it was "a contest between two philosophies of government." The electorate chose the philosophy of Roosevelt and the Democratic Party. Across the nation, people voted for Democrats at every level, from local to national. Roosevelt won in a landslide, with 57 percent of the vote to 40 percent for Hoover, who carried only six states (see Map 22.1).

■ **New Deal** Implying a fresh start, this term became the best known name for Roosevelt's policies to combat the Depression.

Finding New Archival Sources

In 1991, the Soviet Union was dissolved (covered in Chapter 28), and most property of the Communist Party (CP) of the Soviet Union passed into the hands of the new Russian Federation. One result was the opening to western historians of archival collections that had long been closed to them. One of the most important for historians of the United States is the former Central Party Archive (located in Moscow), which in 1992 became the Russian Center for the Preservation and Study of Documents of Recent History (usually called by the initials of its name in Russian, RTsKhINDI) and then in 1999 became the Russian State Archive for Social and Political History (again, usually called by the initials of its name in Russian, RGASPI).

RGASPI contains the largest single collection of archival materials dealing with the Communist Party of the United States (CPUSA) for the years between the early 1920s and the late 1930s. During those years, the CPUSA sent many of its documents, sometimes originals and sometimes copies, to Moscow where they were saved in the archives of the Communist International (Comintern). Before these archives were opened, American historians who studied the CP had to rely on other sources.

By 1992, two different accounts of the CPUSA during the 1930s had developed. One focused on its leadership and on its domination by the Soviet Union; the other focused on the local activities of CPUSA members. The first group of historians depicted the CPUSA as the puppet of Moscow, unquestioningly doing the bidding of Joseph Stalin, the dictatorial ruler of the Soviet Union. The latter group of historians emphasized the important activities of CP members in organizing rent strikes in Harlem, defending African Americans in Alabama, and helping to build some CIO unions.

How did American historians react to the opening of these important new archival sources and did American historians' understanding of the CPUSA change as a result? Surprisingly few rushed to Moscow, which in the early 1990s was still not an easy place to live and do research. But those who did trek to Moscow found an incredibly rich archive for the CP between the early 1920s and late 1930s. Some earlier researchers at RTsKhINDI, notably John Haynes and Harvey Klehr, focused on the leadership of the CPUSA and its relation to the Soviet Union. They found that the leadership of the American Party did the bidding of the Comintern and that some of them were involved in espionage. Among other researchers at RTsKhINDI, Robert Cherny used the extensive files from local CP organizations in California and found that CP members there sometimes argued with directives from the national leadership, sometimes ignored them (and were sometimes disciplined for that), and played an important role in some union organizing and briefly in state politics. Randi Storch, who studied Chicago using RTsKhINDI materials, found CP members actively involved in efforts to halt evictions, secure relief for the unemployed, and organize workers and students, sometimes succeeding despite the rigid directives from party headquarters in New York. Vernon Pedersen, who studied Maryland, found the state CP there to be divided and ineffectual, but also found that CP members used their influence to benefit the Soviet Union and that a few CP members were involved in espionage.

So, in the end, the new archival sources did not greatly change what historians had previously concluded about the CP, but they did unearth a great deal more complexity and richness than had previously been the case.

Robert Cherny

Front entrance of the Russian State Archive for Social and Political History. The bas-relief sculptures of Marx, Engels, and Lenin are reminders that this archive was formerly the Central Party Archive—Institute of Marxism-Leninism.

THE NEW DEAL

☆ *How did the New Deal change the role of the federal government?*

☆ *How did various groups respond to New Deal measures?*

☆ *What happened to restrict expansion of the New Deal after 1936?*

Like the elections of 1860 and 1896, the election of 1932 was one of the great turning points in American political history. Since 1860, Republicans had usually been able to win the White House and set the agenda for national politics. After 1932, however, the Democrats, under the leadership of Franklin D. Roosevelt, created bold new policies and established themselves as the majority party for a generation.

1933—The First Hundred Days

In the four months between the election and Inauguration Day, the economy worsened as Americans eagerly waited for the New Deal Roosevelt

AP Photo/M.L. Suckley/FDR Library.

After his bout with polio in 1921, Roosevelt could walk using braces and supports but usually used a wheelchair—yet few pictures exist of him in a wheelchair because news photographers generally respected his wish not to be photographed that way. Here he relaxes at his family estate at Hyde Park in New York State.

had promised. Many expected that Roosevelt and his advisers, labeled by the press as the Brains Trust because the group included several college professors, were developing a plan to restore prosperity. In fact, Roosevelt's advisers were frequently at odds about which path to follow. Some, especially Rexford Tugwell and Raymond Moley, supported a collective approach, working with business through joint economic planning. Others, notably Frances Perkins, Harry Hopkins, and Eleanor Roosevelt, advocated social programs. All agreed that the worst path was doing nothing.

Roosevelt took office on March 4, as many banks seemed on the verge of closing. Millions listened to the inauguration on their radios and heard the president promise that the economy would revive and reassure them that they had "nothing to fear but fear itself." "We must act quickly," he specified, adding that he would call Congress into emergency session to deal with the banking crisis. On March 6, Roosevelt—soon widely referred to as FDR—declared a national **Bank Holiday**, closing all the banks. Three days later, as freshmen congressmen were still finding their seats, the president presented Congress with the **Emergency Banking Bill**. Without even seeing a written version of the bill, Democrats and Republicans took less than four hours to give Roosevelt what he wanted. The new law required a federal inspection before banks could reopen, thus reassuring depositors that those that reopened could be trusted, and it allowed the Federal Reserve and the RFC (held over from the Hoover administration) to prop up the nation's banking system by providing funds and buying stocks of some banks. On Sunday evening, March 12, Roosevelt took to the radio in the first of his **fireside chats**. He assured the nation that the federal government was solving the banking crisis and that banks would be safe again, adding "It is safer to keep your money in a reopened bank than under the mattress." The banks reopened the next day. Over 60 million Americans listened to the speech, and most believed him. In Atlanta, for example, deposits on March 13 outnumbered withdrawals by 3 to 1. Within a month, nearly 75 percent of the nation's banks were operating again.

The New Deal was under way. Riding a wave of popular support and great expectations, Roosevelt faced a

Bank Holiday Temporary closure of banks throughout the country by executive order of President Roosevelt in March 1933.

Emergency Banking Bill A 1933 act that permitted sound banks to reopen and allowed the government to supply funds to prop up some banks.

▫ **fireside chats** Radio talks in which President Roosevelt promoted New Deal policies and reassured the nation; Roosevelt delivered twenty-eight fireside chats.

When an industry adopted an NRA code, all the businesses in that industry were entitled to put the NRA's blue eagle on their products. The blue eagle logo carried the slogan, "We Do Our Part." In this cartoon from 1933, Uncle Sam is embracing an employee and an employer, both of whom are doing their part.

The Granger Collection, New York.

unique political climate of almost total **bipartisanship**. Some Republicans even embraced aspects of the New Deal. Within its **First Hundred Days**, the Roosevelt administration and Congress created a long list of new federal agencies and programs. A few carried out traditional Democratic Party goals, such as the repeal of Prohibition, but most were aimed at the three Rs: relief, recovery, and reform.

bipartisanship In American politics, when the two major parties work together cooperatively.

▪ **First Hundred Days** The opening period of Roosevelt's administration, during which the president and Congress developed an unprecedented number of measures aimed at relief for the unemployed and economic recovery.

▪ **Agricultural Adjustment Act** (AAA) Law passed by Congress in 1933 to bring the recovery of agriculture through planning and subsidies to reduce production.

National Industrial Recovery Act (NIRA) Law passed by Congress in 1933 establishing the National Recovery Administration to promote planning in industry and the Public Works Administration to create jobs.

▪ **National Recovery Administration** (NRA) Agency created by the NIRA to supervise the drafting and implementation of national industrial codes.

▪ **Public Works Administration** (PWA) Federal agency created to increase employment and stimulate economic recovery by constructing major public works; headed by Harold Ickes, secretary of the interior.

Roosevelt requested and Congress quickly passed the **Agricultural Adjustment Act** (AAA), intended to help agriculture recover. A new agency, the Agricultural Adjustment Administration, would pay farmers to reduce production as a way of cutting the surpluses that drove down prices for farm produce. Focusing on wheat, cotton, corn, rice, tobacco, hogs, and dairy products, a planning board determined the amount to be removed from production. All this was to be paid for by a special tax on industrial food processors. Some critics argued that the AAA gave too much power to the government. Others complained that it did nothing to help small farmers, sharecroppers, and tenant farmers, or to make surplus food available for the needy.

The AAA addressed the problems of agriculture, and the Roosevelt administration next turned to industrial recovery. The **National Industrial Recovery Act** (NIRA) was approved in June, with Roosevelt calling it the "most important and far reaching legislation passed by the American Congress." The act, a compromise among Roosevelt's advisers who had advocated two quite different approaches, incorporated both approaches by creating two new agencies, the **National Recovery Administration** (NRA) and the **Public Works Administration** (PWA).

The NRA, led by Hugh Johnson, a former army general, sought to restart the economy through national economic planning by establishing, industry by industry, codes that set prices, production levels, and

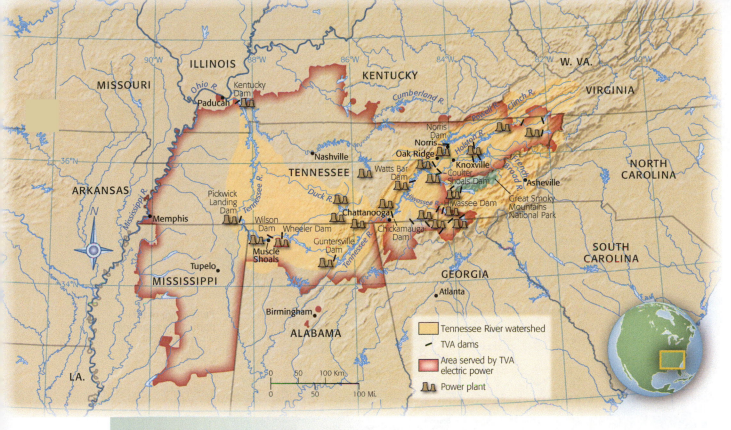

MAP 22.2 The Tennessee Valley Authority
One of the most ambitious New Deal projects was developing the Tennessee Valley. This map shows the various components of the TVA. © Cengage Learning.

wages. Business supported the NRA because it allowed **price fixing**, which raised both prices and profits. Labor was attracted by Section 7a, which gave workers the right to organize unions and bargain collectively, outlawed child labor, and established minimum wages and maximum hours of work. By early 1935, some seven hundred industries with 2.5 million workers were displaying a poster with a blue eagle that meant they were covered by NRA codes.

The PWA took a different approach: stimulating recovery by funding major construction projects, thereby directly providing jobs for construction workers and more jobs in the industries that supplied construction materials. These jobs would then stimulate demand for consumer products and create still more jobs. The PWA was, by far, the largest federal public works program up to that time and still ranks as one of the largest ever. Administered by the Department of the Interior, the PWA was slow to begin operations, partly because the projects required significant planning and partly because the secretary of the interior, "Honest Harold" Ickes, was scrupulous about preventing waste or graft. Still, over six years PWA spent some $6 billion (equivalent to about $100 billion today), usually in cooperation with state and local governments, funding some thirty-four thousand projects, including roads, bridges, giant electricity-generating dams, 70 percent of all new

school buildings, one-third of all new hospital buildings, two aircraft carriers, and much more.

One of the most innovative programs of the First Hundred Days was the **Tennessee Valley Authority** (TVA), created to develop a regional approach to planning and development for a rural and impoverished region of 40,000 square miles including parts of seven states. The most immediate benefit was jobs repairing and building dams and improving flood controls. But the TVA did much more. The TVA improved the navigability of hundreds of miles of waterways and reduced soil erosion. Its dams provided electricity through federally owned and operated hydroelectric systems (see Map 22.2), making possible the introduction of electricity to many rural areas. TVA also provided a model for other federal dam-building projects, especially in the West, that provided water and electricity for economic development. Critics of the New Deal opposed such government-owned agencies as socialist.

price fixing The artificial setting of commodity prices.

■ **Tennessee Valley Authority** (TVA) Independent public corporation created by Congress in 1933 to plan development of the Tennessee River Valley region, especially through flood control and dams that generated electricity.

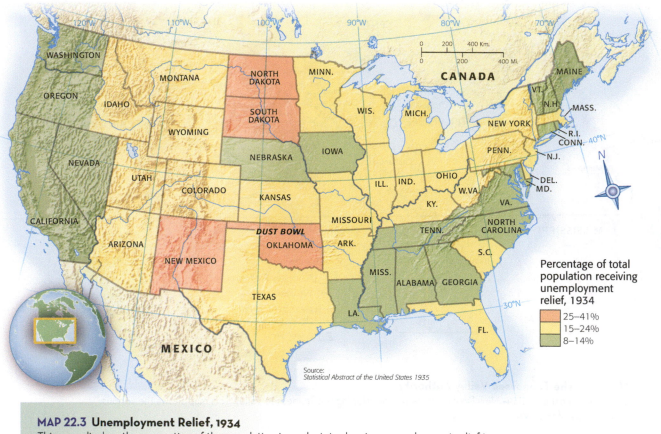

MAP 22.3 Unemployment Relief, 1934

This map displays the proportion of the population in each state drawing unemployment relief in 1934.

Source: Data: Statistical Abstract of the United States 1935; Map: © Cengage Learning.

Recovery was one thrust of Roosevelt's offensive against the Depression. He had campaigned on the slogan of helping the "forgotten man," and in March 1933 unemployment was at a historic high—25 percent of the workforce. In industrial states such as New York, Ohio, Pennsylvania, and Illinois, unemployment pushed toward 33 percent and was even higher in some manufacturing centers. Recognizing that state and private relief sources could not cope with people's needs, Roosevelt proposed and Congress enacted federal relief programs. Though all were temporary measures, they established a new role for the federal government. By the end of the decade, about 46 million people had received some form of relief support (see Map 22.3).

The first relief program was the **Civilian Conservation Corps** (CCC), passed on March 31, 1933. It established several thousand army-style camps

▪ **Civilian Conservation Corps** (CCC) Agency created in 1933 to hire young unemployed men for conservation work.

▪ **Federal Emergency Relief Administration** (FERA) Agency created in May 1933 to provide grants to states and municipalities to spend on relief.

to house, employ, and provide a healthy, moral environment for unemployed urban males ages 18 to 25. Within months it enrolled over three hundred thousand men, paying them $30 a month, $25 of which was sent to their parents. By 1941, more than 3 million men had received employment through the CCC camps. The "Conservation Army" built and improved national park facilities, constructed roads and firebreaks, worked to control erosion, dug irrigation ditches, fought forest fires, and planted trees. In the camps, thirty-five thousand men were taught to read.

The CCC reached only a small percentage of those needing relief. To widen the range of assistance, the Roosevelt administration created the **Federal Emergency Relief Administration** (FERA). FERA provided states with money for their relief needs, mostly for work relief. In some cases it bypassed state and local governments and instituted federally administered programs. One such FERA program opened special centers to provide housing, meals, and medical care for many of the homeless roaming the nation. In the program's first year of operation, it cared for as many as 5 million people. "We thought we'd gone to heaven," one man recalled years later of his experience at a transient camp where he was deloused and given a bath, a bed, and food. In other programs, half a million people attended literacy classes and 1 million received vaccinations and immunizations.

The **Civil Works Administration** (CWA) was a temporary measure to help the unemployed through the winter of 1933–34 by hiring 4 million jobless people for federal, state, and local work projects. The goal of the program was to provide work to as many unemployed people as possible, and CWA projects did result in many permanent public works.

The list of new programs approved during the "hundred days" did not end there. The **Home Owners' Loan Corporation** (HOLC), established in May 1933, permitted homeowners to refinance their mortgages at lower interest rates through the federal government. Before it stopped making loans in 1936, the HOLC refinanced 1 million homes—20 percent of all mortgaged urban homes. To correct problems within banking, the Banking Act of 1933 extended the authority of the Federal Reserve System and created the **Federal Deposit Insurance Corporation** (FDIC), which provided federal insurance for those who deposited money in member banks. In less than six months, 97 percent of all commercial banks had joined the system.

The special session and first session of the Seventy-third Congress met for 102 days, but this period quickly became known as the Hundred Days. Never before had so much major legislation been passed in so short a time. Since 1933, journalists have popularized the notion of judging a new president on the accomplishments of the first hundred days in office, and an activist president is always compared to FDR. However, such comparisons rarely take into account the seriousness of the crisis facing the nation in 1933 or the unusual degree of bipartisanship that characterized the hundred days.

1934—Year of Turmoil

The New Deal started with almost total support in Congress and among the people. However, as the economy began to improve, opposition emerged. By mid-1933, most Republicans and some conservative Democrats opposed relief programs, increased federal spending, and increased regulation of business. A few new policies were approved in 1934, notably creation of the **Securities and Exchange Commission** (SEC), to regulate stock markets, and the National Housing Act, which set up the **Federal Housing Administration** (FHA) to make home loans more available.

Also in 1934, conservative Democrats, including Al Smith, the 1928 presidential candidate, joined with representatives of several major corporations to establish the **American Liberty League**, which opposed New Deal policies through an extensive media campaign funded mostly by the Du Pont family and other corporate leaders. Conservatives fumed that Roosevelt threatened free enterprise, if not capitalism itself. The Hearst newspaper chain instructed its editors to tell the public that the New Deal was a "raw deal" and that Roosevelt was leading the nation into socialism.

The Communist Party, meanwhile, stridently attacked the New Deal as a tool of big business and charged that FDR was pushing the nation toward fascism. By late 1934, Communists claimed twenty-five thousand members and six thousand youth members; half of the members were unemployed, but the Communists also claimed an additional fifty thousand followers in Communist-controlled unions and organizations of the unemployed.

A major target of anti–New Dealers—on both the **right** and **left**—was NRA. Critics soon dubbed it the "National Run Around." Some businesses resisted the restrictions and regulations of NRA codes and questioned the government's right to impose such controls. Consumers grumbled that NRA pushed prices up without any noticeable growth in wages or jobs. Farmers griped that NRA-generated price increases ate up any AAA benefits they received. Workers complained that NRA codes set wages too low and hours too long, and that employers resisted unionization. One woman textile worker wrote to the president that her husband was "laid off, for no other reason than they got a union hear [*sic*] and My Husband became president of it."

The NRA's Section 7a set off a nationwide organizing drive by unions, but organizing drives and subsequent strikes often met stubborn resistance from

Civil Works Administration (CWA) Federal agency created to provide emergency unemployment relief in the winter of 1933–34.

Home Owners' Loan Corporation (HOLC) Federal agency created in 1933 that refinanced nonfarm home mortgages and loaned money to pay property taxes and make repairs.

Federal Deposit Insurance Corporation (FDIC) Agency created by the Banking Act of 1933 to insure deposits up to a fixed sum in banks of the Federal Reserve System and state banks that chose to participate.

Securities and Exchange Commission (SEC) Agency created by the Securities Exchange Act (1934) to license stock exchanges and supervise their activities.

Federal Housing Administration (FHA) Agency created by the National Housing Act (1934) to insure loans made by banks and other institutions for new home construction, repairs, and improvements.

■ **American Liberty League** Conservative organization established in 1934 to oppose New Deal policies; conducted an extensive media campaign funded by powerful corporations.

right, left When applied to politics, *right* refers to conservative or reactionary positions, and *left* refers to liberal or radical positions; *right-wing* and *left-wing* are common variants.

In the Wider World

The Spanish Civil War

Just as the Depression brought forth a range of new political movements in the United States, so too did the economic crisis spawn new movements and political turmoil elsewhere. In Spain, a republic had been established in 1931, but the election in 1936 of a "People's Front" government (*Frente Popular,* a coalition of left-wing parties including Communists) led to civil war when an army general, Francisco Franco, combined much of the army with support from the Catholic Church and great landowners in an effort to restore the monarchy. The republican government created an army but also relied on assistance from abroad, especially when Nazi Germany and Fascist Italy began to assist Franco. The Soviet Union supplied assistance to the republican government, as did many volunteers from abroad, who were organized into the International Brigades. About a thousand American volunteers, mostly union members and Communists, were organized into the George Washington and Abraham Lincoln battalions. Support for the Spanish republican government became a major cause for American leftists between 1936 and 1939, when Franco's forces defeated the last supporters of the republic, initiating a dictatorship that lasted until Franco's death in 1975.

employers and local officials. Between July 1 and the end of 1933 alone, the American Civil Liberties Union (ACLU) counted fifteen strikers killed, two hundred injured, and hundreds arrested along with a half-dozen deployments of National Guard troops. "Labor's rights to meet, organize and strike have been widely violated," the ACLU concluded, and added that NRA lacked "the will or the power to overcome the defiance of employers."

Further violence came in 1934, as hundreds of thousands of workers walked picket lines in nearly two thousand strikes in almost every city. Thirty thousand cab drivers shut down New York City's taxis in late January and most of February. Between January and early May, more than eighty thousand coal miners walked out in a half-dozen strikes in nine states. Nearly forty thousand autoworkers struck, sometimes only for a day, at nine plants in four states. Several hundred thousand textile workers walked out in six states, the largest of all the strikes in 1934, but failed to gain union recognition. Nearly twenty-two thousand longshore and maritime workers were more successful

after tying up shipping on the entire Pacific Coast for three months. A strike by Minneapolis Teamsters eventually gained union recognition and led to the first organization of over-the-road drivers (truckers driving between cities). In some places, notably San Francisco and Minneapolis, there were brief general strikes when all those cities' unions stopped work to protest the killing of strikers. Communists or other Marxists were prominent in some of those strikes.

By 1934, too, several figures were attracting significant attention by arguing the New Deal had not gone far enough. At three o'clock every Sunday afternoon, **Father Charles Coughlin**, a Roman Catholic priest, used the radio to preach to nearly 30 million listeners. Formerly a supporter of Roosevelt, the "radio priest" turned against the New Deal and advocated a guaranteed annual income, the redistribution of wealth, tougher antimonopoly laws, and the nationalization of banking. His attacks on Roosevelt also began to carry anti-Semitic overtones. His organization, the National Union for Social Justice, claimed 5 million members.

Huey Long, a flamboyant senator from Louisiana, proposed a dramatic "**Share Our Wealth**" plan: every family would receive an annual check for $2,000, a home, a car, a radio, and a college education for each child, all to be funded by taxing the rich, including confiscating all income over $1 million. Share Our Wealth societies signed up over 4 million members throughout the country.

Dr. Francis Townsend advocated an old-age pension plan to provide every American ages 60 and older with a monthly pension check for $200. To qualify, individuals could not work and had to spend the

Father Charles Coughlin Roman Catholic priest whose influential radio addresses in the 1930s at first emphasized social justice but eventually became anti-Semitic.

◼ **Huey Long** Louisiana governor, then U.S. senator, who ran a powerful political machine and whose advocacy of redistribution of income was gaining him a national political following at the time of his assassination in 1935.

Share Our Wealth Movement launched by Huey Long that sprang up around the nation in the 1930s urging redistribution of wealth through government taxes or programs.

© Bettmann/Corbis.

In 1934, Huey Long, a fiery politician from Louisiana, claimed that Roosevelt was not helping ordinary Americans. Long proclaimed his support for the "little man" with the slogan, "Every man a king." Before Long could become a real political threat to Roosevelt, he died of gunshot wounds, the victim of an assassin, in September 1935.

money within a month. Thousands of Townsend clubs sprang up with an estimated membership of several million, including sixty members of Congress.

Upton Sinclair, the socialist who had exposed the unsanitary conditions in meatpacking with his 1905 novel *The Jungle*, won the Democratic nomination for governor of California in 1934, arguing for a program he called "End Poverty in California," or EPIC, which proposed to take over idle factories and farmland for use by the unemployed. When Sinclair lost the election, he broadened his EPIC program to "End Poverty in Civilization" and sought to build a national movement.

Amid this turbulence, the first real measure of voter sentiment came in the 1934 state and congressional elections. Democrats had a one-vote majority in the House of Representatives after the 1930 elections, and Roosevelt's landslide victory in 1932 boosted them to a 313–117 majority. Most politicians and journalists expected the 1934 congressional elections to follow the usual off-year pattern in which the president's party lost seats. In 1934, however, Democrats made further gains, now outnumbering Republicans by 320 to 103 in the house and 60–35 in the Senate. Roosevelt, it seemed, was immensely popular despite all the criticism from the right and left.

1935—The Second Hundred Days

During the early months of 1935, the huge Democratic majorities in Congress produced little new legislation, and FDR provided little leadership beyond asking Congress to provide more **work relief**. Months later, Congress responded, allocating nearly $5 billion for relief and creating a new agency, the **Works Progress Administration** (WPA). **Harry Hopkins**, a former social worker whom FDR put in charge of the WPA, set out to put the unemployed to work. (WPA programs are discussed later in this chapter.) Beyond WPA, Roosevelt seemed uncertain where to turn next. He was anxiously watching Huey Long and the Supreme Court. He considered Long dangerous because of his contempt for democracy in Louisiana, where he completely controlled state politics, and his demagogic appeals for national support. If Long were to run as a third-party candidate in 1936 and unite the supporters of Coughlin, Townsend, and Sinclair, he might win the presidency or, at the least, throw the election to a Republican. The Supreme Court also made FDR anxious because New Deal programs were coming under challenge for their constitutionality. On May 27, 1935, in *Schechter Poultry Corporation v. United States*, the Supreme Court ruled that the NRA was unconstitutional because it improperly delegated legislative authority to the executive branch and exceeded congressional authority to regulate interstate commerce. Roosevelt furiously exclaimed that the Court still had a "horse and buggy" mentality.

Roosevelt then moved into action, calling on Congress to pass several pieces of legislation. Members of Congress had been planning to go home and avoid the steamy Washington summer but now stayed in session and, over the next three months, passed some of the most significant legislation of the twentieth century.

The establishment of a federal old-age and survivor insurance program set the tone of the **Second Hundred Days** and significantly modified the

work relief Government programs to provide paid work for the unemployed.

■ **Works Progress Administration** (WPA) Agency established in 1935 to hire the unemployed for a wide variety of programs, including construction, conservation, and art; headed by Harry Hopkins.

Harry Hopkins Close adviser to Roosevelt during his four administrations; headed several New Deal agencies, including the Works Progress Administration.

■ *Schechter Poultry Corporation v. United States* Supreme Court decision (1935) declaring the NRA unconstitutional because it improperly delegated legislative authority to the executive and regulated commerce within a state.

■ **Second Hundred Days** Period in 1935 when Roosevelt supported and Congress passed landmark legislation including the Social Security Act and National Labor Relations Act.

government's role in society. Frances Perkins was the driving force behind the **Social Security Act** (1935). She had been working on the bill since early 1933; with Roosevelt's full support now, it moved toward passage. The act's most controversial element was a pension plan for retirees age 65 or older. The program was to begin in 1937, and initial benefits were to vary depending on how much an individual paid into the system.

Compared to Perkins's original plan or to existing European systems, the Social Security system was limited and conservative. It failed to cover domestic and agricultural laborers and provided no health insurance. Roosevelt insisted that workers should pay for their pensions: "We put those payroll contributions there so as to give the contributors a legal, moral, and political right to collect their pensions and unemployment benefits. With those taxes in there, no damn politician can ever scrap my social security program."

The new Social Security program provided not only old-age pensions but also federal aid to families with dependent children and to people with disabilities, and it helped fund state-run programs of unemployment compensation. Within two years, every state was paying between $15 and $18 a week in unemployment compensation and supplying support to over 28 million people. The Social Security Act established a major new function for the federal government and is one of the most durable legacies of the New Deal. Since its inception, amendments have changed the method of payments, instituted cost-of-living increases, and added medical coverage. Millions of Americans have benefited from the system.

The next bill that Roosevelt called on Congress to approve was the National Labor Relations Act (NLRA). Largely the work of Senator Robert Wagner of New York and called the **Wagner Act**, it put the power of government behind workers' right to organize and to bargain collectively with their employers over the terms and conditions of their employment. It created the National Labor Relations Board as a new regulatory agency to oversee labor relations and ensure workers' rights, including their right to conduct elections to determine union representation and to prevent unfair labor practices, such as firing or **blacklisting** workers for union activities. Though the

act excluded workers in agriculture and service industries, the Wagner Act significantly altered the relationships among business, labor, and the government and, in a very real way, redistributed economic power from employers to unions.

The final bill that Roosevelt pushed was a revision of income tax rates for those making over $50,000 a year (equivalent to about $845,000 today). Often called the "Wealth Tax Act," it was intended to increase federal revenues to pay for such new programs as the WPA. Taken together with WPA, the Wealth Tax Act provides the first significant example of a federal redistributive policy—taxing the wealthy to provide work relief for the unemployed. Social Security also had some modestly redistributive features. Since 1935, a modest level of redistribution has been a continuing feature of federal economic policy.

The Election of 1936 and the Waning of the New Deal

By the end of 1935, Roosevelt had reasserted his leadership. The chances of a successful Republican or third-party challenge to the president were remote. Republicans nominated **Alfred Landon** of Kansas, one of the few Republican governors reelected in 1934. As governor, he had accepted and used most New Deal programs, but in keeping with party wishes he attacked Roosevelt and the New Deal as destroying the values of America. After the death of Huey Long in 1935, Townsend and Coughlin formed a third party, the Union Party, but posed no threat to Roosevelt's reelection. Roosevelt reminded voters of the New Deal's achievements and denounced big business as greedy. Roosevelt won with the largest percentage of the vote up to that time. Landon carried Maine and Vermont.

The Democratic victory demonstrated not only the personal appeal of Roosevelt but also an acceptance of an activist government that could provide social and economic benefits. Roosevelt's second inaugural address raised expectations of a Third Hundred Days. "I see millions of families trying to live on incomes so meager that the pall of family disaster hangs over them day by day," he announced. "I see one-third of a nation ill-housed, ill-clad, ill-nourished." The words seemed to promise new legislation aimed at helping the poor and the working class.

A Third Hundred Days failed to materialize. Instead of promoting new social legislation, Roosevelt first took on the Supreme Court. His anger with the Court had been growing since the Court had invalidated NRA and later AAA. As 1937 began, constitutional challenges to TVA, the Wagner Act, and Social Security were on their way to the Court. Further, there had been not a single vacancy on the Court during Roosevelt's first term, a highly unusual occurrence. Fearing the Court was determined to undo the New

□ **Social Security Act** A 1935 law creating unemployment, old-age, and disability insurance and providing for child welfare.

□ **Wagner Act** The National Labor Relations Act; law passed by Congress in 1935 that regulated labor relations and collective bargaining.

blacklisting Practice in which businesses share information to deny employment to workers known to belong to unions.

Alfred Landon Kansas governor who ran unsuccessfully for president on the Republican ticket in 1936.

Deal, Roosevelt proposed to enlarge the Court from nine to fifteen. Arguing that the Court's elderly judges were unable to keep up with their work, he asked Congress to to authorize him to nominate an additional justice for every one over age 70 who had served on the Court more than ten years. His real objective was obvious to all—he wanted to be able to add enough justices to protect the New Deal from the Court's conservative majority.

Called the **court-packing plan** by its opponents, Roosevelt's proposal proved a major political miscalculation. Several conservative Democrats, especially southerners, saw an opportunity to break with the president. Roosevelt's support weakened further when enough justices changed sides that the Court upheld a state's minimum-wage law, the Wagner Act, and the Social Security system, something since called the **Judicial Revolution of 1937**. After Justice Willis Van Devanter, a conservative, announced his retirement, Roosevelt dropped his proposal and happily appointed Hugo Black, a New Deal senator from Alabama, to the Court. Before he left office, Roosevelt had appointed every member of the Court but one.

Another setback that snagged the Roosevelt agenda was a recession, dubbed **Roosevelt's recession** by critics. As the economy stabilized by 1937, industrial outputs reached their 1929 levels, and unemployment fell to 14 percent. Secretary of the Treasury Henry Morgenthau urged Roosevelt to reduce government spending and move toward a more balanced budget. Roosevelt agreed and cut back relief programs, releasing nearly 1.5 million workers from the WPA. But the economy was not strong enough to cope with reduced government spending and thousands of people seeking jobs. At the same time, the new Social Security deductions slightly reduced the paychecks of most employed people, causing some people to cut back purchases. The recovery collapsed, and unemployment soared to 19 percent. In April 1938, Roosevelt restored spending, but the recession had tarnished his image of being able to manage recovery.

It was not just the court-packing plan and the recession that weakened the New Deal. Some wealthy Americans opposed the higher taxes approved in 1935. Labor strife during 1935 to 1938 increased concern about unions and their relation to the New Deal. The United Automobile Workers had occupied factories as part of a strike. Such "sit-down" strikes alienated many who considered them violations of property rights. The public's mood had changed. The American people, Hopkins observed, were now "bored with the poor, the unemployed, and the insecure."

Despite waning support, the administration passed two more significant pieces of legislation. In 1938, a second Agricultural Adjustment Act reestablished the principle of federally set quotas on specific commodities, acreage reduction, and subsidy payments.

TOWARD A MORE PERFECT UNION

The "Judicial Revolution" of 1937

The "Judicial Revolution" of 1937 marked the end of six decades when the Supreme Court usually interpreted the Constitution as putting severe limits on the ability of federal or state governments to regulate economic activity. But the Judicial Revolution also marked a beginning. The *U.S. v. Carolene Products* (1938) decision involved the constitutionality of a 1923 law regulating certain dairy products. The decision was by Justice Harlan Fiske Stone, who had been appointed to the court by President Coolidge. First, Stone found that such regulatory laws should be assumed to be constitutional unless they obviously violated the Constitution or were arbitrary or irrational. But he went further, in footnote 4, to present an analysis that began to define the Court's role for the next fifty years. In that famous footnote, Stone specified that the presumption of constitutionality should not apply in cases that involved the first ten amendments (the Bill of Rights, which prohibited federal restraints on rights) or the Fourteenth Amendment (which prohibited states from putting restraints on rights) or in cases that involved "prejudice" against "minorities." Such cases, he indicated, should be "subjected to more exacting judicial scrutiny." Over the following decades, the Court did exactly that, significantly extending civil liberties and protecting civil rights.

The **Fair Labor Standards Act**, also passed in 1938, addressed issues that Frances Perkins had long championed. It established forty-four hours as the standard workweek, set a minimum wage (25 cents an hour), and outlawed child labor (under age 16). With its

■ **court-packing plan** Roosevelt's effort in 1937 to expand the Supreme Court so that he could appoint more of its members; the proposal energized conservative opposition, hampering further New Deal legislation.

Judicial Revolution of 1937 Name sometimes applied to the change in direction by the Supreme Court in 1937, whereby it accepted the constitutionality of New Deal–type federal intervention in the economy.

■ **Roosevelt's recession** Economic downturn that occurred when Roosevelt, responding to improving economic figures, cut $4 billion from the federal budget, mostly by reducing relief spending.

■ **Fair Labor Standards Act** A 1938 law establishing minimum wages and maximum hours and prohibiting labor by children under 16.

minimum-wage provision, the act was especially beneficial to unskilled and nonunion workers and to workers from racial and ethnic minority groups. It was the last piece of New Deal legislation.

In the 1938 congressional elections, Roosevelt failed to get New Deal supporters elected, and Republicans increased their numbers and influence in Congress. Conservative Democrats, mostly from the South, increasingly joined Republicans in a conservative coalition that could derail new liberal programs. Roosevelt recognized political reality and asked for no new domestic programs. Though no more new legislation was forthcoming, the changes the New Deal generated remained part of the American social, economic, and political culture. By 1939, the economy was recovering, but unemployment and underemployment persisted. Eight million were still unemployed. Full "recovery" did not appear until 1942, when the United States mobilized for a second world war. Wartime spending finally propelled the American economy out of the Depression and to new levels of prosperity.

CHANGING THE FACE OF AMERICA: THE NEW DEAL IN ACTION

☆ *What were the major accomplishments of PWA and WPA ?*

☆ *How did the Wagner Act change the status of organized labor?*

☆ *How did the New Deal attempt to address the problems of agriculture?*

New Deal agencies touched the lives of a large majority of Americans and changed the United States in important ways (see Table 22.1). The activities of New Deal agencies were so widespread and various that it is possible to describe only the most prominent.

PWA and WPA

PWA was the New Deal's major stimulus project, intended to promote recovery by hiring private contractors to build a wide array of permanent public facilities. Transportation infrastructure—streets, highways, bridges—accounted for a third of all PWA projects. Next in number came school buildings, about a fifth of all PWA projects. PWA also funded huge dams, notably the massive Grand Coulee Dam on the Columbia

conservative coalition An informal cooperative relationship between conservative Democrats, mostly from the South, and Republicans; often controlled Congress during the three or four decades following 1937.

River, at the time the largest electrical power facility in the United States, providing the foundation for economic development in that region. There were, in all, about thirty-four thousand PWA projects, and they consumed about half of all concrete poured in the country between 1933 and 1943.

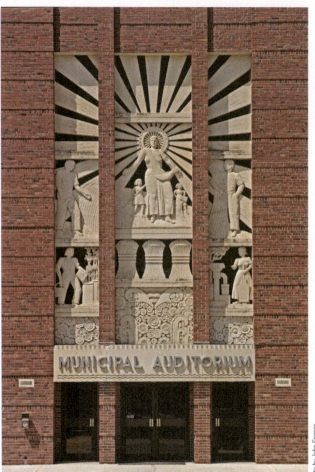

Photo by John Spence.

Some of the most visible legacies of the New Deal consist of the many public buildings and other public structures, from huge dams to city sidewalks, that were constructed by New Deal agencies. PWA structures were intended to be permanent, attractive additions to communities, and the large majority of them incorporated art. Many of the buildings were in an architectural style now often called PWA Moderne, which drew upon the Art Deco and Streamline Moderne styles of the period. This limestone bas-relief sculpture in the Art Deco style, presenting agricultural symbols, especially a woman sowing grain, forms the central decorative element for the Municipal Auditorium in Beatrice, a city of eleven thousand people (1940 census) in southeastern Nebraska. The architect was Fred Organ but the identity of the sculptor has not been established. The building was constructed between 1938 and 1940 using local and PWA funds and is now on the National Register of Historic Places. The bas-relief remains the most significant public sculpture in a several-county area.

TABLE 22.1 Selected Major Legislation of the New Deal

YEAR	NEW DEAL PROGRAMS	PURPOSE
1933	March 9–June 16: The "First Hundred Days"	
	Emergency Banking Relief Act	Stabilize banking
	Civilian Conservation Corps (CCC)	Put young men to work on conservation projects
	Federal Emergency Relief Act (FERA)	Supplement state and local relief programs
	Agricultural Adjustment Act (AAA)	Bring agricultural recovery through limiting production
	Tennessee Valley Authority (TVA)	Plan economic development of the Tennessee River Valley
	Home Owners Refinancing Act	Assist homeowners to prevent foreclosures
	Banking Act of 1933	Establish Federal Deposit Insurance Corporation (FDIC) to insure bank deposits and stabilize banking
	National Industrial Recovery Act, Title I: National Recovery Administration (NRA)	Create industry-wide codes of fair competition, plan recovery of industries
	National Industrial Recovery Act, Title II: Public Works Administration (PWA)	Stimulate economy through public works projects
1934	Securities and Exchange Act	Regulate issuance of corporate stocks and bonds
	Indian Reorganization Act	Restore tribal government, halt some forced assimilation programs
1935	Emergency Relief Appropriations Act	Establish Works Progress Administration (WPA) to work with state and local governments to provide jobs to the unemployed
	June–August: the "Second Hundred Days"	
	National Labor Relations Act (Wagner Act)	Regulate labor relations and collective bargaining
	Social Security Act	Provide old-age pensions, unemployment compensation, support for the people with disabilities
	Revenue Act of 1935 ("Wealth Tax Act")	Increase taxes on upper income groups to pay for relief and recovery programs
1937	Proposal to expand Supreme Court	Unsuccessful effort to change the direction of Supreme Court decisions
1938	Second AAA	Replace AAA; same purpose
	Fair Labor Standards Act	Establish national standards for minimum wages and maximum hours of work

© Cengage Learning.

WPA was intended to provide work to over 2.1 million unemployed workers a year between 1935 and 1938. WPA did not duplicate PWA. Only the unemployed were eligible for WPA jobs, unlike PWA projects, and WPA projects usually spent less on materials than PWA. For many WPA projects, WPA provided the wages and local governments paid for materials. WPA workers did manual labor, building roads, schools, and other public facilities in partnership with local governments. WPA sought to pay wages higher than

Michigan artist Alfred Castagne sketching WPA construction workers, 1939. The WPA provided a wide variety of jobs, from those requiring little or no previous training to jobs for artists and classical musicians. Library of Congress.

relief payments but lower than local wages. Wages for people of color and women were the exception, generally exceeding the local rate.

WPA also created jobs for professionals, writers, artists, actors and actresses, and musicians. Unemployed historians, writers, and teachers conducted oral interviews, including sessions with nearly every living ex-slave, and wrote state and local histories and guidebooks. Theater groups and orchestras toured towns and cities, performing Shakespeare and Beethoven. By 1939 an estimated 30 million people had watched a WPA production. Unemployed artists created art for public buildings. When some objected to actors, artists, and writers receiving aid, arguing that their labor was not real work, Hopkins bluntly responded, "Hell, they got to eat just like other people."

WPA also reached out to women, members of racial and ethnic minority groups, students, and young adults. Prodded by Eleanor Roosevelt, WPA employed between 300,000 and 400,000 women a year. Some were hired as teachers and nurses, but the majority, especially in rural areas, worked on sewing and canning projects. Efforts to ensure African American employment met

■ **National Youth Administration** (NYA) Program established in 1935 to provide employment for young people and help needy high school and college students.

■ **Mary McLeod Bethune** African American educator; director of the Division of Negro Affairs within the NYA; a strong and vocal advocate for equality of opportunity for African Americans during the New Deal.

■ **Congress of Industrial Organizations** Labor organization established in 1938 by a group of unions that left the AFL to unionize workers by industry rather than by trade.

with success in the northeastern states but were less successful in the South. The **National Youth Administration** (NYA), created in 1935, developed programs to aid college and high school students and young people not in school. **Mary McLeod Bethune**, an African American educator, directed NYA's Division of Negro Affairs. Through determination and constant, skillfully applied pressure, she obtained support for black schools and colleges and increased the number of African Americans enrolled in vocational and recreational programs.

The Wagner Act and the Growth of Organized Labor

While the WPA was intended primarily for relief, the Wagner Act was a major reform. It came at a time when organized labor was at a crossroads. The unions that made up the American Federation of Labor (AFL) had organized many skilled workers but not those of the major mass-production industries—steel, automobiles, rubber, textiles—and had generally avoided unskilled or less skilled workers. Some AFL unions limited their membership to whites or males.

John L. Lewis of the United Mine Workers (coal miners), an industrial union that originated in the Knights of Labor, had insisted on the inclusion of Section 7a in the NRA and had used it to launch a successful organizing drive among coal miners. He argued that the AFL should organize the large mass-production industries on an industrial model, with one union for all workers in the industry, regardless of skill. That approach violated the long-standing AFL policy of separate unions for each skill group.

When the AFL leaders turned Lewis down, in 1935, he formed the Committee on Industrial Organization (CIO) within the AFL. Composed of several AFL affiliates committed to the industrial model, the CIO launched organizing drives in the automobile, steel, rubber, electrical equipment, and textile industries. The Wagner Act gave their efforts important federal support. Most AFL craft unions opposed Lewis's efforts, and after marking important victories in the automobile and steel industries in1937, Lewis led the CIO unions out of the AFL in 1938. They formed the **Congress of Industrial Organizations** and began to charter new industrial unions. Some of the AFL unions, notably the Carpenters, Machinists, and Teamsters, launched their own organizing drives, sometimes on an industrial model. Under the Wagner Act, unions nearly doubled their membership in five years, and the percentage of the **private-sector** workforce in unions eventually reached an all-time high of 39 percent in 1958.

The New Deal and Agriculture

Like industrial workers, many farmers put their trust in Roosevelt and the New Deal. By 1935, AAA appeared to be working as farm prices climbed and the purchasing power of farmers increased (see Figure 22.2). But there was a cost. Tenant farmers and sharecroppers usually received no share of the AAA payments paid to their landlords and sometimes found themselves evicted from their farms—a million by the end of 1935—so that landlords could take the land out of production. In 1936 in *United States v. Butler*, the Supreme Court ruled that the AAA's production quotas and special tax on processing companies were unconstitutional. Quickly, the administration turned to other programs, including the **Soil Conservation and Domestic Allocation Act**, to reduce production.

In 1938, Congress approved a second Agricultural Adjustment Act that reestablished the principle of federal quotas on production, acreage reduction, and subsidies. By 1939, farm income had more than doubled since 1932, and the government had provided over $4.5 billion in aid to farmers. Since then, federal farm subsidies have continued and have significantly changed the relationship between agricultural producers and the federal government.

Nature also helped take land out of production as drought devastated a five-state region in the southern Great Plains (see Map 22.4). Above-average rainfall previously had encouraged the extension of wheat farming, but in the early 1930s reduced rainfall led to crop failure. The drought continued for several years, becoming the worst in U.S. history. High winds then created gigantic dust storms that stretched more than 200 miles across and over 7,000 feet high. A reporter labeled the region the **Dust Bowl**. Millions of tons of topsoil blew away, much of it all the way to the Atlantic Ocean. Beginning in 1937, New Deal programs planted trees in shelterbelts across the drought-ravaged region and taught farmers new farming techniques, reducing wind erosion by two-thirds.

By the mid-1930s, thousands of farm families displaced by drought, technology, depression, or the AAA headed for California, hoping to start over. Many of them found work as agricultural workers, following the crops, picking peaches and peas, grapes and plums. Few Californians greeted them warmly. The Los Angeles police chief sent police units to the state border to encourage them to turn back. Usually denigrated as Okies regardless of the state from which they came, they encountered miserable living conditions. Most migratory labor camps lacked even rudimentary sanitation, and most migratory labor families could not afford proper diets or health care. A survey of a thousand migratory children in the San

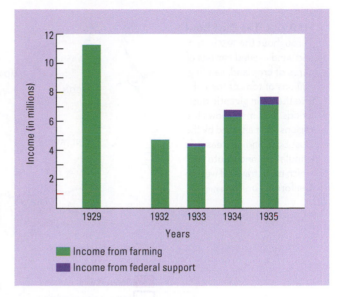

FIGURE 22.2 Farm Income, 1929–1935
Prices for farm products fell rapidly as the Depression set in, but by 1933, with support from New Deal programs, some farm incomes were rising. Some of the increase was a direct result of government payments.

Source: U.S. Department of Commerce, Bureau of the Census, *Historical Statistics of the United States, Colonial Times to 1970,* Bicentennial edition, 2 vols. (Washington, D.C.: U.S. Government Printing Office, 1975), 1: 483–484.

Joaquin valley during 1936–37 found 831 with medical problems, most caused by malnutrition or poor hygiene.

California's migratory farm workers benefited from the work of the Resettlement Administration (RA), created by executive order in 1935. The RA tried to address rural poverty everywhere in the country—western migrant farm workers, southern sharecroppers, other impoverished farm families—by helping them establish new working lives in planned

private sector Businesses owned by shareholders or individuals.

■ *United States v. Butler* Supreme Court decision (1936) declaring the Agricultural Adjustment Act invalid on the grounds that it unconstitutionally extended the powers of the federal government.

Soil Conservation and Domestic Allocation Act Legislation passed by Congress in 1935 and 1936 that sought to prevent soil erosion by paying farmers to replace soil-depleting crops with grasses and other crops that would help to hold the soil.

■ **Dust Bowl** Region devastated by drought and dust storms that began in the early 1930s; the worst years (1936–1938) saw over sixty major storms per year, seventy-two in 1937.

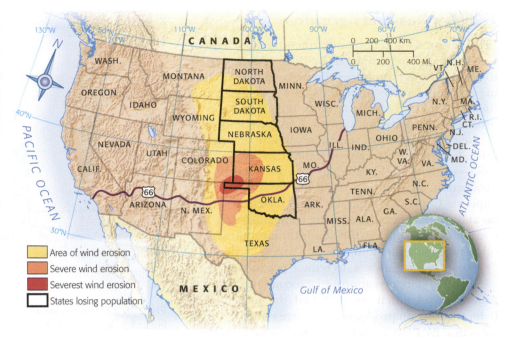

MAP 22.4 The Dust Bowl
Throughout the 1930s, sun and wind eroded millions of acres of cropland, sending millions of tons of topsoil into the air in gigantic dust clouds. This map shows the regions most affected by the Dust Bowl and decreases in population, and Route 66, which many traveled west to California. © Cengage Learning.

Area of wind erosion
Severe wind erosion
Severest wind erosion
States losing population

communities. The Resettlement Administration had just begun that work when it was absorbed by a new agency, the Farm Security Administration (FSA), in 1937. In California, the RA and FSA constructed a few migrant labor camps with adequate sanitation and housing.

Nearly all rural Americans benefited from the **Rural Electrification Administration** (REA), created in 1935. In that year, only 10.5 percent of farms had electricity. Considering rural areas unlikely to be profitable, companies had refused to extend electrical service to the countryside. REA bypassed private utility companies by helping farmers to form rural electrical cooperatives. Within just five years, REA had extended electrical service to a million farms. By 1950, 90 percent of farms were electrified. Electricity lessened the drudgery of farm life, giving families running water and access to a variety of electrical appliances. Within eight months of receiving electricity, new consumers bought an average of $180 in appliances—the two most common an electric iron and a radio. Electricity also improved rural education, health, and sanitation, encouraged greater diversification, and helped to introduce new industries.

This dust storm is approaching Stratford, Texas, on April 18, 1935. In the flat terrain of western Texas, Oklahoma, and Kansas, such a dust storm could sometimes be seen approaching from miles away, causing those in its path to hurry inside where they tried to block up all cracks around windows and doors to prevent the dust from entering. No matter how hard they tried, there was always a layer of fine dust on everything by the time the storm passed.

AP/Wide World Photos.

AMERICANS GRAPPLE WITH THE DEPRESSION

★ How did Americans cope with the many challenges presented by the Great Depression?

★ What opportunities arose for women, African Americans, Latinos, Asian Americans, and Native Americans? What challenges faced these groups during the 1930s?

★ How did the Depression and New Deal affect cultural expression?

The New Deal was able to establish new patterns of government responsibility in part because the Depression touched every segment of American life. Poverty and hardship were no longer reserved for those viewed as unworthy or relegated to remote areas and inner cities. Now poverty touched blue- and white-collar workers, and even some who were once wealthy. Most Americans worried about their futures and economic insecurity—that the next day might bring a reduction in wages, the loss of a job, or the closing of a business.

"Making Do"

To help those facing economic insecurity, magazines and newspapers provided useful hints and "Depression recipes" that stretched budgets and included information about nutrition. According to home economists, a careful shopper could feed a family of five on as little as $8 (equivalent to $138 today) a week. This was comforting news for those with that much to spend, but for many families and for relief agencies $8 a week for food was beyond possibility. Before the New Deal, New York City provided only $2.39 a week for each family on relief, and San Francisco provided only a weekly box of groceries in return for a week's work. Things were bad, comedian Groucho Marx joked, when "pigeons started feeding people in Central Park."

By 1933, most towns and cities had little ability to provide more than the smallest amount of relief and struggled unsuccessfully to maintain basic city services. Experiencing a shrinking tax base, local, county, and state governments cut back or eliminated relief and some laid off teachers, policemen, and other workers. Because state and local governments depended on property taxes, the New Deal indirectly provided assistance for local and state governments as the HOLC and the FHA saved homes, stimulated some new construction, and thereby restored property tax bases. Federal agencies, especially the PWA and the WPA, not only provided many local civic improvements—schools, hospitals, government buildings, roads, and bridges—but also reduced local relief responsibilities. Other federal programs also helped

to lessen the burdens of local and state governments. In North Dakota, for example, it was estimated that two-thirds of the people drew some form of federal assistance. Thus, the New Deal drastically altered the relationship between local and national government. Increasingly people saw the national government as having an obligation to support families and communities against economic adversity.

"Use it up, wear it out, make it do, or do without" became the motto of most American families. In working-class and middle-class neighborhoods, "making do" meant that some homes sprouted signs announcing a variety of services—household beauty parlors, kitchen bakeries, rooms for boarders. "I did baking at home," a Milwaukee woman recalled, adding, "I got 9 cents for a loaf of bread and 25 cents for an apple cake . . . . I cleared about $65 a month." A sewing machine salesman commented that he was selling more machines to people who did not previously do their own sewing. For farm families, feed sacks had long provided fabric for sewing, and companies now competed by printing attractive designs on their sacks. One woman remembered her mother making a new school dress from a sack that had "a sky-blue background with gorgeous mallard ducks on it."

Still, even with "making do," many families failed, first losing jobs, and then homes. Some families moved in with relatives. One man remembered that most Depression-era households were like his, "where father, mother, children, aunts, uncles and grandma lived together." Approximately one-sixth of America's urban families "doubled up." Many others loaded their meager possessions on their jalopies and traveled across the country looking for a better life. Some rode the rails, hitching rides in boxcars, living in Hoovervilles, begging and scrounging for food and supplies. Most American males had long expected that they would provide for their families, and many became despondent when they could not. A social worker remembered, "I used to see men cry because they didn't have a job." Many people found their families and lives torn apart. Records show increased numbers of suicides, admissions to state mental hospitals, and children placed in orphanages.

Despite the hardships, American society did not collapse, as some had predicted. The vast majority of Americans clung to traditional social norms and even expanded family togetherness. Economic necessity kept families at home. They played cards and board games, read books and magazines, and

◻ **Rural Electrification Administration** (REA) Federal agency established in 1935 to loan money to rural cooperatives to produce and distribute electricity.

Everett Collection.

Throughout the Depression, the most popular form of entertainment was probably the movies, providing escape from daily hardships into a fantasy world. At 20 cents a ticket, movies attracted as many as 75 million people a week. In this photo, from 1938, a movie theater is showing *Room Service*, one of the Marx Brothers' madcap comedies, and *Flight to Fame*, a science-fiction thriller. The tangle of bicycles in front of the theater suggests the photo was taken during a Saturday matinee. At the time, many movie theaters featured a bicycle rack in front, to accommodate their young patrons.

tended vegetable and flower gardens. The game of Monopoly, in which players won by driving the other players into bankruptcy, zoomed to popularity. Church attendance rose, and the number of divorces declined. Fewer people got married, and the birth rate fell.

Changing Women's Roles

As unemployment rose, more married women began to seek jobs, but some companies refused to hire married women. The proportion of women in the professions declined from 14.2 to 12.3 percent, with teachers particularly vulnerable. A survey of 1,500 school districts found that 77 percent did not hire married women, and 63 percent fired women if they married. By 1932, 2 million women were out of work, and an estimated 145,000 women were homeless. But employment patterns were uneven. Women in low-paying and low-status jobs were less likely to be laid off and more likely to find employment. White women also took jobs traditionally held by African Americans, especially in domestic service.

Few working women found that bringing home a paycheck changed their role within the family. Most husbands still expected to be head of the household, even if unemployed, and few helped with household work, because such work challenged their notions of masculinity. One husband helped with the laundry but refused to hang the wash outside for fear that neighbors might see him. At home women renewed and reaffirmed traditional roles: they sewed, baked bread, and canned fruits and vegetables. Even so, a woman's traditional role as mother continued to evolve—the birth rate continued to fall, as did family size, thus extending the patterns first seen in the 1920s. While some of this was due to couples agreeing they could not afford children at the time, in other cases it was due to decisions by women. The declining size of families also resulted from the postponement of marriage because of finances—the older a couple is when they marry, the fewer children they are likely to have. Through it all, women were often praised as pillars of stability in a changing and perilous society. One woman remembered, "I did what I had to do. I seemed to always find a way to make things work."

Race and Depression: South and West

The Depression's economic impact intensified economic and social difficulties for African Americans, Latinos, and Asians, who faced increased racial hostility and demands that they give up their jobs to whites. Throughout much of the Southwest, "Mexicans" were accused of "taking the bread out of our white children's mouths." Low-paying, frequently temporary jobs and high unemployment made life in Latino communities difficult. On farms in California, Mexican American workers were being replaced by Anglos, including those fleeing the Dust Bowl. Those managing to find work in the fields earned only $289 a year—about a third of what the government estimated it took to maintain a subsistence budget.

In the early 1930s, especially, the Immigration and Naturalization Service (INS) worked with local authorities to facilitate **repatriation** of Mexican nationals to Mexico. Throughout the early 1930s, some local and state agencies gave free transportation to those willing to leave. In several cities, the INS conducted sweeps of Mexican American communities to round up illegal immigrants for deportation and to scare others into leaving. In Los Angeles such sweeps resulted in nearly ten thousand people boarding trains bound for Mexico. Such actions were not limited to the Southwest. One Indiana town denied relief to Mexicans and Mexican Americans and encouraged them to board a train to Mexico. "They weren't forcing you to leave," recalled one *repatriado*; "they gave you a choice, starve or go back to Mexico." Nationally, more than half a million had left by 1937.

There was no comparable effort to repatriate Asians living on the West Coast, but Asian immigrants and Asian Americans often received inadequate relief. In San Francisco, where nearly one-sixth of the Asian population qualified for benefits, they received 10 to 20 percent less than whites, probably because relief officials accepted the stereotype that Asians could subsist on a less expensive diet. Hoping to break down economic and social barriers, some Asians intensified efforts to assimilate, becoming "200 percent Americans." The Japanese American Citizens League was organized in 1929 to overcome discrimination and oppose anti-Asian legislation, but by 1940 the group had made little headway.

Before 1929, African Americans working as sharecroppers, farm hands, and tenant farmers in the South were already experiencing depression conditions, earning only about $200 a year. Their lives worsened as farm prices continued to fall and as hard times and the AAA increased evictions during the Depression. Many left the farm for urban areas, seeking more economic security. Cities, whether South or North, provided few opportunities because whites were taking jobs previously held by African Americans. Joblessness among African Americans in

Giving Her a Lift to Town . . . . —By Knott

Franklin D. Roosevelt Library, Hyde Park, New York.

President Franklin D. Roosevelt campaigned on helping the "forgotten man." First Lady Eleanor Roosevelt did not forget women. She worked diligently to ensure that they benefited from the New Deal and had access to government and the Democratic Party.

urban areas averaged 20 to 50 percent higher than for whites.

Compounding the high unemployment, across the nation blacks faced increased racial hostility, violence, and intimidation. In 1931 the attention of the nation was drawn to Scottsboro, Alabama, where nine black men had been arrested and charged with raping two white prostitutes. Although no physical evidence linked the men to the crime, a jury of white males did not question the testimony of the women and quickly found the so-called **Scottsboro Nine** guilty. Eight

repatriation The return of people to their nation of birth or citizenship; repatriation of Mexicans from the United States during the Depression was at its height from 1929 to 1931.

Scottsboro Nine Nine African Americans convicted of raping two white women in Alabama in 1931; famous example of racism in the legal system.

were sentenced to death; the ninth, a minor, escaped the death penalty. Through appeals, intervention by the Supreme Court, retrials, parole, and escape, all those convicted were free by 1950.

A New Deal for All?

Like the Depression, the New Deal affected women and members of racial and ethnic minority groups in different ways, but generally it inspired a belief that the government cared. Eleanor Roosevelt was at the center of this image of compassion. She often acted as the social conscience of the administration and prodded her husband and other New Dealers to remember women and people of color. "I'm the agitator," she once said. "He's the politician." She criss-crossed the country, meeting and listening to people. She received thousands of letters describing people's hardships and asking for help. Although she could rarely provide direct assistance, her replies emphasized hope and pointed to the changes being made by the New Deal.

Eleanor Roosevelt helped convene a special White House conference on the needs of women in 1933. She, Frances Perkins, and other female New Dealers worked to ensure that women received more than just token consideration from government agencies. Ellen Woodward, assistant director of FERA and later WPA, succeeded in promoting a few women's programs—headed by women. Still, New Deal agencies frequently paid women less than men, and fewer women proportionately were enrolled in relief programs. Women accounted for about 10 percent of WPA workers, and the largest number were in programs focused on traditional women's skills, such as sewing. Social Security and the Fair Labor Standards Act both excluded domestic workers and similar service occupations with large proportions of women. Despite these shortcomings, the New Deal provided women with more programs and government positions than during any previous administration.

For African Americans and Latinos, the Roosevelts and the New Deal provided a large amount of hope and a smaller amount of change. More African Americans than ever before were appointed to government positions. Mary Bethune organized African Americans in the administration into a "**Black**

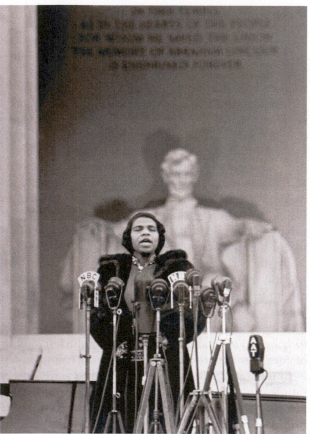

When the Daughters of the American Revolution denied opera singer Marian Anderson the use of Constitution Hall because of her race, Eleanor Roosevelt arranged a public concert at the Lincoln Memorial.

Thomas D. Mcavoy/Time Life Pictures/Getty Images.

Cabinet" that met in her home and became a semi-official advisory body on racial relations. Among the most pressing needs, the Black Cabinet argued, was access to relief and jobs. The New Deal provided both, but never to the extent needed.

Some New Deal administrators, notably Ickes and Hopkins, took steps to ensure that PWA, WPA, and other New Deal agencies included members of racial and ethnic minority groups, especially African Americans. WPA and PWA administrators eliminated much discrimination from their programs in northern cities but had less success elsewhere, where skilled African American workers were often given menial minimum-wage jobs. Other agencies were less supportive. The Civilian Conservation Corps and the Tennessee Valley Authority practiced racial segregation and wage discrimination. Still, by 1938, nearly 30 percent of African Americans were receiving some federal relief, with the WPA alone supporting almost a million African American families. But even that was

□ **Black Cabinet** Semiofficial advisory committee on racial affairs organized by Mary McLeod Bethune in 1936; made up of African American members of the Roosevelt administration.

not enough. In Cleveland, though 40 percent of PWA jobs were reserved for African Americans, black unemployment and poverty remained higher than for whites.

FDR also refused to support civil rights legislation. When confronted by black leaders over his refusal to back an anti-lynching law, Roosevelt explained, "If I come out for the anti-lynching bill now, they [powerful southern Democrats] will block every bill I ask Congress to pass....I just can't take that risk." Eleanor Roosevelt took more risks and visibly supported equality for racial and ethnic minority groups. In 1939, when the Daughters of the American Revolution refused to allow renowned black singer Marian Anderson to perform at their concert hall in Washington, the First Lady resigned her membership and, with assistance from Ickes, arranged a public concert on the steps of the Lincoln Memorial. Anderson's performance there attracted more than seventy-five thousand people.

Latinos benefited from the New Deal in much the same way as African Americans. In New Mexico and other western states, the Depression curtailed much of the migratory farm work for Mexican American workers, devastating local economies. New Deal agencies such as CCC, PWA, and WPA provided welcome jobs and income. Throughout the Southwest, federal agencies not only included Mexican Americans but also sometimes paid wages that exceeded what they received in the private sector. Discrimination, however, was still widespread, often enhanced by language differences.

New Deal legislation helped union organizers trying to assist Latino workers throughout the West. The United Cannery, Agricultural, Packing, and Allied Workers of America (UCAPAWA), chartered by the CIO in 1937, included Latinos and Latinas among its organizers. Despite some success organizing Mexican women working in California canneries, efforts to organize field workers came up against strong opposition from local growers, backed by some of the most powerful corporations in the West. UCAPAWA organizers, notably Luisa Moreno, were also active in creating El Congreso de Pueblos de Hablan Española (National Spanish-Speaking Congress), which in 1939 brought together a wide range of Latino organizations around a civil rights agenda.

Despite its limitations, the New Deal provided hope and support for many women and members of racial and ethnic minority groups, who in turn praised Roosevelt. "The WPA came along, and Roosevelt came to be a god," said one African American. "You worked, you got a paycheck, and you had some dignity." Where they could vote, many members of racial and ethnic minority groups now began to vote for Roosevelt and

Some WPA projects sought to teach new skills to the unemployed. This WPA project at Costilla, New Mexico, taught local women, many of Mexican ancestry, how to make rag rugs using a loom. Library of Congress.

John Collier worked to ensure the passage of the Indian Reorganization Act. This photo shows a group of Navajos meeting with Collier to discuss government-imposed limitations on the number of sheep each Navajo could own. Photo by Keystone-France/Gamma-Keystone via Getty Images.

the Democratic Party. In the 1936 presidential election, Roosevelt carried every black ward in Cleveland and, nationally, received nearly 90 percent of the black vote. By 1939, the Democratic Party was providing a political vehicle for the aspirations of industrial workers, people of color, and farmers.

Part of a mural depicting California agriculture, painted by Maxine Albro in 1934 as part of one of the earliest New Deal art projects, funded by the CWA, in Coit Tower, San Francisco. Note the blue eagles of the NRA on the packing crates for the oranges. The white flowers are calla lilies and are likely an homage to Diego Rivera, who often included calla lilies in his paintings and whose Rockefeller Center mural was destroyed while the Coit Tower murals were in progress.

Native Americans directly benefited from the New Deal. They had two strong supporters in Secretary of the Interior Ickes and Commissioner of Indian Affairs John Collier. Both opposed existing Indian policies that since 1887 had sought to destroy the reservation system and eradicate Indian cultures. At Collier's urging, Congress passed the **Indian Reorganization Act** in 1934. Designed to restore tribal sovereignty under federal authority, the act returned land and community control to tribal organizations, permitted Indian self-rule on a reservation if reservation residents so

decided, and ended the allocation of reservation lands in severalty (discussed in Chapter 17). Each tribe had to ratify the act to participate, and not all tribes did so. Seventy-seven rejected the changes, including the Navajos, the nation's largest tribe, although some of those who initially rejected the act later changed their decision.

To improve conditions on reservations and provide jobs, Collier organized a CCC-type agency for Indians and ensured that other New Deal agencies played a part in improving Indian lands and providing jobs. Working with tribal leaders, Collier took measures to protect, preserve, and encourage Indian customs, languages, religions, and folkways. Reservation school curricula incorporated Indian languages and customs, and Native Americans could once more openly and freely exercise their religions.

■ **Indian Reorganization Act** A 1934 law that ended Indian allotment, returned surplus land to tribal ownership, and encouraged tribal self-government.

Nonetheless, the so-called Indian New Deal did little to improve the standard of living for most American Indians. Funds were too few, and the problems created by years of poverty and government neglect were too great. Some tribal leaders complained that Collier's programs had been drafted with little or no participation by Indians themselves. At best, the programs slowed a long-standing economic decline and allowed Native Americans to regain some control over their cultures and societies.

Cultural Expression in the Midst of Depression

The homogenization of culture that began in the 1920s due to the movies and radio continued in the 1930s. At the same time, however, there were significant changes in cultural expression. During the 1920s, many American writers and artists rejected their consumer-oriented society, producing novels depicting hedonism or escapism (discussed in the previous chapter). Many writers of the 1930s changed that focus, portraying instead working people and their problems or looking for inspiration to figures in American history. Many artists turned to a more realistic style.

A generation of painters, some of whom produced works of social criticism during the 1930s, was influenced by Diego Rivera, a great Mexican muralist whose work in Rockefeller Center in New York City was destroyed in 1934 because of its Marxist politics. Other Depression-era artists, particularly those in the Federal Arts Project (FAP) of the WPA, depicted the lives of ordinary people or themes from American history, especially scenes of hardy white pioneers. By one count, FAP artists produced some 200,000 individual works of art—murals, paintings, and sculptures—nearly all intended for public display.

Prominent novels during the 1930s depicted inequities caused by capitalism, racism, and class differences. John Steinbeck defined the social protest novel of the time. Among his early works, *Tortilla Flat* (1933) portrayed the lives of Mexican Californians and *In Dubious Battle* (1936) presented an apple-pickers' strike through the eyes of an idealistic young Communist. *The Grapes of Wrath* (1939), which won the Pulitzer Prize for the best novel of the year, presented the Joad family, who lost their farm in Oklahoma and migrated to California where their family disintegrated under the strain of life as migratory farm workers. Similar social criticism appeared in Erskine Caldwell's *Tobacco Road* (1932), about Georgia sharecroppers, and Richard Wright's *Native Son* (1940), a critique of racism that became the first Book of the Month Club selection by an African American author. Ernest Hemingway's *For Whom the Bell Tolls* (1940) depicted an American fighting fascism in the Spanish

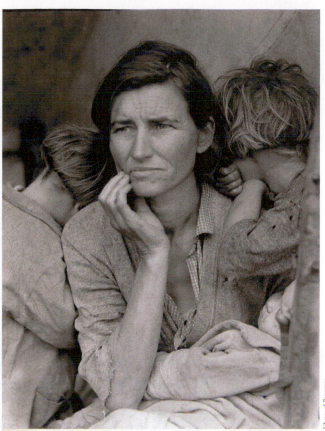

Library of Congress.

Dorothea Lange's photograph "Migrant Mother" is one of the most famous in the history of photography. Her first caption was "Destitute peapickers in California; a 32 year old mother of seven children. February 1936." Lange later recalled taking her famous picture: "I saw and approached the hungry and desperate mother, as if drawn by a magnet . . . . She said that they had been living on frozen vegetables from the surrounding fields, and birds that the children killed. She had just sold the tires from her car to buy food." Lange's subject was Florence Owens Thompson, born in Oklahoma of Cherokee Indian descent. She and her husband came to California in the late 1920s and worked as farm laborers, traveling the state picking fruit and vegetables. Her daughter—the four-year-old child on the left—later remembered her as "a hard-working disciplinarian who loved red dresses and country music, drank Lucky Lager beer and chewed Garrett snuff [tobacco]."

Civil War, in sharp contrast to the hedonism of his *The Sun Also Rises* (1926).

Dorothea Lange began photographing the victims of the Depression in the early 1930s and continued that work with the RA and FSA. She ranks among the leading figures in creating the new genre of documentary photography. Her 1936 photograph of a migratory farm worker and her children, later entitled "Migrant Mother," emerged as the most famous and perhaps the most moving photograph of the era. Margaret Bourke-White joined Lange as a pioneer in documentary photography with dramatic

Photo by Margaret Bourke-White/Time Life Pictures/Getty Images.

Margaret Bourke-White was making a strong social statement in this 1937 photograph of flood victims in Louisville, Kentucky, waiting in line for food.

photographs of the Fort Peck Dam and moving shots of the victims of the Depression.

As in the 1920s, movies remained popular, providing a welcome break from the woes of the Depression. On a national average, 60 percent of the people saw a movie a week. In the 1920s, some films had glorified gangsters or reveled in the sexuality of such stars as Clara Bow. To head off pressure for federal regulation to prevent such films, the major studios in 1930 created the Motion Picture Production Code, which specified, among other things, "the sympathy of the audience should never be thrown to the side of crime, wrongdoing, evil or sin."

Many studio heads now insisted that the public needed escapist entertainment to distract them from the Depression. Musical extravaganzas like *Forty-Second Street* (1933) and *Gold Diggers of 1933* (1933) fit the bill, as did the slapstick comedy of the Marx Brothers, whose *Duck Soup* (1933) is ranked among the best films of all time. Some disdain for the wealthy could be found in popular comedies that contrasted members of a snobby and selfish upper class with the honesty and common sense of ordinary people. Some westerns and gangster films were equally escapist, but others probed more deeply into the human condition. *Stagecoach* (1939), directed by John Ford, so defined the western genre that it inspired imitators for years after. Frank Capra directed several films that sympathized with the problems of ordinary people; *Mr. Smith Goes to Washington* (1939) showed a naïve but honest ordinary citizen battling political corruption.

Hollywood occasionally produced films of social criticism, notably an adaptation of *The Grapes of Wrath* (1940), starring Henry Fonda. Charlie Chaplin's leftist politics were apparent in two important works, *Modern Times* (1936), portraying the dehumanizing tendencies of technology, and *The Great Dictator* (1940), which mocked and criticized Adolph Hitler.

Radio also provided an escape from everyday economic woes. Nearly 90 percent of American households included a radio, suggesting that listening to the radio was nearly universal. "Gloom chasers"—that is, comedians, including Jack Benny and the comedy teams of George Burns and Gracie Allen and of Fibber McGee and Molly—filled the radio airways. Crime fighters were popular on the radio, and also in newspaper comic strips and comic books, where Dick Tracy (1931), Superman (1938), and Batman (1939) protected innocent victims from harm and oppression.

THE GREAT DEPRESSION AND NEW DEAL IN PERSPECTIVE

★ How did the Great Depression and New Deal affect Americans over the long run?

A depression—a contraction of the economy causing significant unemployment and lasting several years—was nothing new. Americans had experienced serious depressions every thirty to forty years since the 1830s. For generations, mothers had advised daughters to save up for "hard times." The Great Depression confirmed that wisdom, and left its mark on a generation. For those who lived through the 1930s, "making do" became not just a way of surviving the depression, but a way of life that many continued long after the economy revived.

The New Deal also left its mark on a generation. Some spent the rest of their lives criticizing Roosevelt for destroying free enterprise. Others proudly voted Democratic because their families had survived because of the New Deal. Democrats had been the minority from the election of Lincoln in 1860 until the election of Roosevelt in 1932. Thereafter, Democrats usually won the presidency until 1968, and usually controlled Congress until 1994. But the New Deal Democratic coalition was inherently unstable, including union members and small-scale farmers, southern white supremacists and African Americans in northern and western cities, former socialists and states-rights conservatives.

The New Deal left the permanent legacy of a more activist federal government—increased regulation of business, Social Security, the Wagner Act, the Fair Labor Standards Act, and more. For the next seventy years, no prominent politician questioned the appropriateness of a federal program benefiting the elderly or a federally defined minimum wage. Most Americans came to expect that the federal government should take prompt action to prevent depressions, reduce unemployment, and assist those most in need. Since Roosevelt, Americans have expected presidents, rather than Congress, to be the chief policymakers. In all these ways and more, the Great Depression and New Deal changed how Americans think about themselves and what they expect from their government.

Individual Voices

FRANCES PERKINS
Explains the Social Security Act

On September 2, 1935, Secretary of Labor Frances Perkins spoke over the radio to explain the importance of the recently passed Social Security Act. As the Social Security bill was being drafted and considered by Congress, it had come under attack from the right and the left. Conservatives argued that the bill imposed "big government" into an area best served by private and individual efforts. Liberals objected that it was not inclusive enough, leaving out large segments of the workforce and providing no health benefits. Because Perkins's speech gave many Americans their first explanation of how the new act would change their lives, historians find in it important information both about the thinking of New Deal policymakers and about the ways that the Roosevelt administration wanted people to understand this new program.

AP/Wide World Photos.

❶ What type of worker is most likely to receive a pension? What type of worker would be less likely?

❷ In fact, many workers were not covered because of the political compromises necessary to pass the bill.

❸ The Roosevelt administration believed that the Social Security program was an important reform in preventing another depression. Why would they believe that?

❹ In what ways does Perkins's speech respond to the criticisms from conservatives? From liberals?

People who work for a living in the United States . . . can join with all other good citizens . . . in satisfaction that the Congress has passed the Social Security Act. . . . It provides for old-age pensions which mark great progress over the measures upon which we have hitherto depended in caring for those who have been unable to provide for the years when they no longer can work. It also provides security for dependent and crippled children, mothers, the indigent disabled and the blind.

Old-age benefits in the form of monthly payments are to be paid to individuals who have worked and contributed to the insurance fund in direct proportion to the total wages earned by such individuals in the course of their employment subsequent to 1936. The minimum monthly payment is to be $10, the maximum $85. These payments will begin in the year 1942 and will be to those who have worked and contributed. **❶**

Because of difficulty of administration not all employments are covered in this plan at this time . . . but it is sufficiently broad to cover all normally employed industrial workers. . . . It is a sound and reasonable plan. . . . It does not represent a complete solution to the problems of economic security, but it does represent a substantial, necessary beginning. **❷**

This is truly legislation in the interest of the national welfare . . . its enactment into law would not only carry us a long way toward the goal of economic security for the individual, but also a long way toward the promotion and stabilization of mass purchasing power without which the present economic system cannot endure. . . . **❸**

The passage of this act . . . with so much intelligent public support is deeply significant of the progress which the American people have made in . . . using cooperation through government to overcome social hazards against which the individual alone is inadequate. **❹**

Study Tools

SUMMARY

The Great Depression brought about significant changes in American life, altering expectations of government, society, and the economy. When Hoover assumed the presidency, most believed that the economy and quality of life would continue to improve. The Depression changed that. Flaws in the economy were suddenly exposed as the stock market crashed, banks and businesses closed, unemployment soared, and people lost their homes and their hopes for the future.

More than previous presidents, Hoover expanded the role of the federal government to meet the crisis. However, Hoover's measures, including the Reconstruction Finance Corporation, failed to stimulate a worsening economy. Losing faith in Hoover, most Americans put their trust in Roosevelt and his promise of a New Deal.

Roosevelt easily won the 1932 presidential election and took office amid widespread expectations for a major shift in the role of government. The First Hundred Days witnessed a barrage of legislation, most dealing with the immediate problems of unemployment and economic collapse. The Agricultural Adjustment Administration (AAA) and the National Recovery Administration (NRA) were designed to bring economic recovery, while the Civilian Conservation Corps (CCC) and Public Works Administration (PWA) were intended both to relieve unemployment and to stimulate the economy.

In 1935, assailed by both liberals and conservatives, Roosevelt responded with a second burst of legislation that focused more on putting people to work, economic redistribution, and social legislation, especially Social Security. The overwhelming Democratic victory in 1936 confirmed Roosevelt's popularity. But FDR's ill-conceived court-packing plan, an economic downturn, labor unrest, and growing conservatism generated opposition to new legislation, and the New Deal wound down after 1938.

CHRONOLOGY
Depression and New Deal

1928	Herbert Hoover elected president
1929	Stock market crash; Mexican repatriation begins; Depression deepens
1929–1933	Thousands of banks and businesses fail; Unemployment rises to 25 percent
1931	Scottsboro Nine convicted
1932	Reconstruction Finance Corporation; Bonus Army marches on Washington; Franklin D. Roosevelt elected president
1933	Drought and wind create the Dust Bowl; Franklin D. Roosevelt inaugurated; New Deal begins; National Bank Holiday; First fireside chat; First Hundred Days (March 9–June 16): CCC, AAA, TVA, HOLC, NRA, and PWA, repeal of Prohibition, Bank Act
1934	Huey Long's Share Our Wealth plan; Indian Reorganization Act; Securities and Exchange Commission (SEC) created; American Liberty League established; Dr. Francis Townsend's movement begins; Federal Housing Administration
1935	Works Progress Administration created; NRA ruled unconstitutional in *Schechter* case; Second Hundred Days: Social Security, Wagner Act, Wealth Tax Act; Rural Electrification Administration (REA) formed; Long assassinated; Committee on Industrial Organization (CIO) established
1936	AAA ruled unconstitutional in *Butler* case; Roosevelt reelected; "Black Cabinet" organized
1937	Court-packing plan; "Roosevelt's recession"
1938	Fair Labor Standards Act; Second AAA; Congress of Industrial Organizations formed
1939	Marian Anderson's concert at Lincoln Memorial; John Steinbeck's *The Grapes of Wrath*
1940	Richard Wright's *Native Son*

Study Tools

The Depression affected all Americans, as they had to adjust their values and lifestyles to meet the economic and psychological crisis. Lives were disrupted, homes and businesses lost, but most people learned to cope with the Great Depression and hoped for better times. Gender roles were affected by the depression as men lost their jobs. Members of racial and ethnic minority groups carried the extra burdens of discrimination, sometimes by New Deal agencies. New Deal programs touched the lives of many Americans, from unemployed laborers to unemployed artists, from struggling farmers to industrial workers. During the 1930s, for the first time the federal government provided significant support to artists, writers, and musicians. While movies and radio often provided escape from daily worries, other forms of cultural expression focused on the problems faced by ordinary people.

The New Deal never fully restored the economy, but it engineered a profound shift in the nature of government and in society's expectations about the federal government's role in people's lives.

FOCUS QUESTIONS

If you have mastered this chapter, you should be able to answer these questions and to explain the terms that follow the questions.

1. How did the stock market crash affect the American economy? What economic weaknesses contributed to the crash and the Great Depression?

2. How did Hoover try to deal with the Depression? How successful were his efforts?

3. How did the New Deal change the role of the federal government?

4. How did various groups respond to New Deal measures?

5. What happened to restrict expansion of the New Deal after 1936?

6. What were the major accomplishments of PWA and WPA?

7. How did the Wagner Act change the status of organized labor?

8. How did the New Deal attempt to address the problems of agriculture?

9. How did Americans cope with the many challenges presented by the Great Depression?

10. What opportunities arose for women, African Americans, Latinos, Asian Americans, and Native Americans? What challenges faced these groups during the 1930s?

11. How did the Depression and New Deal affect cultural expression?

12. How did the Great Depression and New Deal affect Americans over the long run?

KEY TERMS

Great Depression *p. 599*

public works projects *p. 600*

Reconstruction Finance Corporation *p. 601*

Farmers' Holiday Association *p. 602*

Bonus Army *p. 602*

New Deal *p. 603*

fireside chats *p. 605*

First Hundred Days *p. 606*

Agricultural Adjustment Act *p. 606*

National Recovery Administration *p. 606*

Public Works Administration *p. 606*

Tennessee Valley Authority *p. 607*

Civilian Conservation Corps *p. 608*

Federal Emergency Relief Administration *p. 608*

American Liberty League *p. 609*

Huey Long *p. 610*

Works Progress Administration *p. 611*

Schechter Poultry Corporation v. United States *p. 611*

Second Hundred Days *p. 611*

Social Security Act *p. 612*

Wagner Act *p. 612*

court-packing plan *p. 613*

Roosevelt's recession *p. 613*

Fair Labor Standards Act *p. 613*

National Youth Administration *p. 616*

Mary McLeod Bethune *p. 616*

Congress of Industrial Organizations *p. 616*

United States v. Butler *p. 617*

Dust Bowl *p. 617*

Rural Electrification Administration *p. 619*

Black Cabinet *p. 622*

Indian Reorganization Act *p. 624*

Study Tools

SUGGESTED RESOURCES

Lizabeth Cohen. *Making a New Deal: Industrial Workers in Chicago, 1919–1939* (New York: Cambridge University Press, 1990). Detailed examination of the role of Chicago's workers, most of recent immigrant background, in transforming that city's politics.

The Dust Bowl (Public Broadcasting System, 2012), http://www.pbs.org/kenburns/dustbowl. Website for the outstanding documentary film by Ken Burns; includes additional information, as well as a link to the film.

David Kennedy. *Freedom from Fear: The American People in Depression and War, 1929–1945* (New York: Oxford University Pess, 1999). Well-written, thoroughly researched, and comprehensive.

Maury Klein. *Rainbow's End: The Crash of 1929* (New York: Oxford University Press, 2001). Compelling account of the stock market crash and the social, political, cultural, and economic events that surrounded it.

Studs Terkel. *Hard Times: An Oral History of the Great Depression* (New York: Pantheon Books, 1970). A classic example of how oral histories can provide the human dimension to history.

23

America's Rise to World Leadership, 1929–1945

CHAPTER OUTLINE

The Road to War

Diplomacy in a Dangerous World
Roosevelt and Isolationism
War and American Neutrality
The Battle for the Atlantic
Pearl Harbor

America Responds to War

Japanese American Internment
Mobilizing the Nation for War
A People at Work and War
New Opportunities and Old Constraints
Wartime Politics

Waging World War

Halting the Japanese Advance
Roads to Berlin
Stresses in the Grand Alliance
The Holocaust
Closing the Circle on Japan
Entering the Nuclear Age

INDIVIDUAL VOICES: *Justice Hugo Black Explains the Majority View in* Korematsu v. United States

Study Tools

INDIVIDUAL CHOICES

Minoru Kiyota

Located in the high desert of Utah, where temperatures ranged from 106 in the summer to minus 30 in the winter, the Topaz Relocation Center housed nearly nine thousand people of Japanese heritage interned as loyalty risks during World War II. It was a place where in April 1943, 63-year-old James Hatsuaki Wakasa was killed by a guard as he approached the barbed wire fence that surrounded the camp. In 1944, a 20-year-old Japanese American held at Topaz, Minoru Kiyota, renounced his American citizenship. He had applied to leave the camp to attend college, but an interview with an FBI agent stood in the way. During the interview, the agent was interested more in Minoru's past, because he was a *kibei*, than in his future. Minoru explained he had spent four years in Japan before returning to go to high school, but he was a loyal American. Ignoring the answer, the agent next asked what organizations Minoru had joined since his return. "None," said Minoru, but the agent accused him of lying and belonging to *Butoku-kai*.

Confused, Minoru replied he had taken *kendo* lessons but was not a member of *Butoku-kai*. The agent called him "dangerous" and demanded to know what "sabotage" Minoru was ordered to carry

Topaz Relocation Center

Picture Research Consultants & Archives.

out. Again, Minoru pleaded innocence, but was told: "You're not getting out of this camp."

Months later, an angry Minoru refused to sign the loyalty pledge, which officially made him disloyal, and he was sent to Tule, a more secure camp. There, Minoru found angry guards and gangs of ultranationalistic, pro-Japanese **Nisei** who terrorized the camp and frequently brought the army's wrath down on everyone. As his despair deepened, he renounced his American citizenship. Immediately regretting his rash decision, Minoru started efforts to undo his choice and legally challenged the **Renunciation Law**. But at the time, as illustrated in the Individual Voices feature at the end of this chapter, the courts rejected the arguments of those Japanese Americans who challenged the wartime measures.

Released from Tule in 1946, Minoru graduated from college in 1949. Using his Japanese language skills, he took a civilian position with Air Force Intelligence but lied on his application form, saying he was a U.S. citizen. He served in Korea and Japan, where, in 1954, his past caught up. He was dismissed from service and stripped of his U.S. passport. A man without a country, he enrolled at Tokyo University, majoring in Indian philosophy.

In 1955, he regained his citizenship when the Renunciation Law was nullified by the Supreme Court. He returned to the United States and in 1963 took a position as a professor of Buddhist studies at the University of Wisconsin. He retired in 1999.

The Depression shook the world, causing governments and the international system to collapse. Amid the global crisis, three nations—Japan, Italy under Benito Mussolini, and Germany under Adolph Hitler—appeared eager to use military force to achieve nationalistic goals. The result would be a European-wide and then world-wide war lasting from 1939 to 1945.

Between 1933 and 1939, Roosevelt's primary concern was restoring the American economy, but as international tensions increased he also wrestled with how best to protect U.S. interests abroad. Although he wanted more flexibility, a strongly isolationist public and Congress constrained his actions. With the onslaught of the war in Europe in 1939, Roosevelt believed the United States must provide economic and military assistance to those fighting Hitler. To check Japanese expansion, he used trade restrictions. Britain held on, but Japan's attack on Pearl Harbor indicated the failure of economic diplomacy in Asia.

The war restored American prosperity and increased presidential power. The mobilization of U.S. resources resulted in full employment and unparalleled cooperation among business, labor, and government. It also changed the lives of nearly every American, creating new challenges and opportunities both for those who marched off to war and for those who remained on the home front.

Militarily, the United States faced a global war fought on nearly every continent and ocean. Allied with Britain and the Soviet Union, the United States began its efforts to defeat Germany and Italy by invading North Africa and Italy before invading France. In the Pacific, the victory at Midway gave the United States a naval and air advantage that eventually

kibei Japanese Americans who returned to America after being educated in Japan.

Butoku-kai A philosophy started in eighth-century Japan to instill martial prowess and chivalry among the warrior class. In 1895, it became a society to promote and standardize martial arts.

kendo Literally "way of the sword," it was instruction in swordsmanship and was included in *Butoku-kai*. It became part of the Japanese physical education program and in 1939 was made mandatory training for all boys.

Nisei A U.S. citizen born in the United States of parents who emigrated from Japan.

Renunciation Law Law passed July 1, 1944, permitting American citizens to renounce their citizenship in wartime; 5,589 Japanese Americans gave up their citizenship.

allowed American forces to close the circle on Japan. Roosevelt's death in April 1945, just before Germany surrendered, left President Harry S Truman to chart the final path to victory. To end the war as soon as possible, Truman approved the use of atomic bombs, which led to Japan's surrender, the beginning of a new nuclear age, and the United States' emergence as a superpower.

THE ROAD TO WAR

☆ *How were Roosevelt's policies toward Latin America a continuation of Hoover's?*

☆ *What obstacles did Roosevelt face in trying to implement a more assertive foreign policy from 1935 to 1939?*

☆ *Following the outbreak of World War II in 1939, how did Roosevelt reshape American neutrality?*

When Herbert Hoover became president in 1929, the world appeared stable and prosperous. He saw no reason to change a foreign policy that kept the United States away from the world's political and diplomatic bickering while expanding its economic interests. The onslaught of the Depression only strengthened Hoover's and most Americans' resolve to remain focused on domestic affairs. Elsewhere, however, Japan and other countries looked abroad for possible solutions to their internal problems.

Japan's economy rested in part on international commerce, and with the collapse of world trade, many Japanese nationalists pursued other means to ensure economic vitality and power. Manchuria, a province of China situated north and west of Japanese-controlled

Korea, was rich in iron and coal, accounted for 95 percent of Japanese overseas investment, and supplied large amounts of foodstuffs. Equally important, Japan maintained an army in Manchuria to protect its interests. In September 1931, Japanese officers used the army to seize the province. The world, including the League of Nations, condemned Japan's aggression, but did little else as Japan created a new puppet nation, Manchukuo, under its control. Hoover instituted a policy of **non-recognition** of the new state. Japan's success strengthened its economy and promoted a vision of a Japanese-dominated **Greater East Asian Co-Prosperity Sphere.** It also indicated to Japan and others that the international status quo could be altered with little or no opposition.

Diplomacy in a Dangerous World

Foreign policy was hardly an issue in the 1932 election, and Roosevelt saw little reason to change Hoover's foreign policies. He maintained the Asian policies and continued non-recognition of Manchukuo. He also continued to improve relations and promote trade with Latin America by announcing a "**Good Neighbor policy,**" by which he supported the principle of non-intervention in the internal or external affairs of other countries.

When political unrest threatened the oppressive regime of Cuba's President Geraldo Machado in 1933, Roosevelt resisted calls for American armed intervention to restore stability and instead sent special envoy Sumner Wells to convince Machado to resign. He grudgingly resigned, but Wells considered his successor, Ramón Grau San Martín, too radical. The envoy asked Roosevelt for armed intervention. Roosevelt refused but allowed Wells to convince **Colonel Fulgencio Batista** to overthrow Grau. The new Batista regime was immediately recognized by the United States and received a favorable trade agreement.

Roosevelt avoided similar requests for armed intervention when Mexico nationalized and took control of foreign-owned oil properties in 1938. Instead, Roosevelt accepted the principle of nationalization and sought a fair monetary settlement for the American oil companies. A settlement was finally reached in 1941 and, as with Latin America as a whole, relations with Mexico remained cordial. Although the United States remained the dominant influence and economic power in Latin America, the Good Neighbor policy made it easier to solidify unity in the Western Hemisphere in the face of world war.

Roosevelt and Isolationism

The United States' Good Neighbor policy appeared in stark contrast to actions taken by Japan, Germany, and Italy that increasingly seemed to threaten world peace. As tensions increased between Japan and China, in Europe **fascist** Germany and Italy also

non-recognition A policy of not acknowledging changes in government or territory to show displeasure with the changes. In this way, the United States refused to accept Japan's creation of Manchukuo.

▫ **Greater East Asian Co-Prosperity Sphere** Japan's plan to create and dominate an economic and defensive union in East Asia, using force if necessary. In defending the concept, the Japanese compared it to the U.S. power in Latin America and advocated the idea of Asia for Asians.

▫ **Good Neighbor policy** An American policy toward Latin America that stressed economic ties and non-intervention; begun under Hoover but associated with Roosevelt.

▫ **Colonel Fulgencio Batista** Dictator who ruled Cuba from 1934 through 1958; his corrupt, authoritarian regime would be overthrown by Fidel Castro's revolutionary movement (see Chapter 25).

▫ **fascist** Refers to a political system led by a dictator having total control over society and the economy; fascism places the needs of the nation above those of the individual and is often characterized by racism and organized violence against members of the opposition and targeted ethnic groups.

sought to expand their influence and power. Adolf Hitler took office in 1933, promising to build up the economy and Germany's role in the world. Benito Mussolini, ruling Italy since 1921, argued that Italy needed to expand its influence abroad. As global tensions increased, U.S. isolationists were in full cry. In 1934, a congressional investigation chaired by Senator Gerald P. Nye of North Dakota alleged that America's entry into World War I had been engineered by arms manufacturers, bankers, and war profiteers—"the merchants of death." At the same time, public opinion polls revealed that a large majority of Americans believed that the nation's intervention in the war was a mistake and that the country should avoid any actions that might draw it into another conflict. Congress responded in August 1935 with the **Neutrality Act of 1935**. It prohibited the sale of arms and munitions to any nation at war, whether aggressor or victim, and warned Americans traveling on ships of belligerent nations that they sailed at their own risk. Roosevelt would have preferred **discriminatory neutrality** but, anxious to see the Second Hundred Days through Congress, he accepted political reality. When Italian troops invaded the poorly armed African nation of Ethiopia in October, Roosevelt immediately announced American neutrality. He also asked, to no avail, for a "moral embargo" against Italy to reduce American sales of nonwar goods, like coal and oil. Italy formally annexed Ethiopia in May 1936.

International tensions continued to heighten in 1936 when Japan stepped up construction of new warships, German troops violated the Treaty of Versailles by occupying the **Rhineland**, and civil war broke out between Nationalist forces led by Francisco Franco and the Republican government of Spain. Congress promptly modified the neutrality legislation (the Second Neutrality Act) to forbid U.S. involvement in civil wars and loans to countries at war.

With the peace seemingly slipping away, both political parties championed neutrality in the 1936 presidential elections. Roosevelt told an audience at Chautauqua, New York, that he hated war and that if it came to "the choice of profits over peace, the nation will answer—must answer—'We choose peace.'" The Republican candidate, Alfred Landon, was equally adamant that the Republicans were the best party to keep the nation out of war. Roosevelt easily defeated Landon. In 1937, the new Congress, with strong public support, passed another neutrality act. It required warring nations to pay cash for all "nonwar" goods and to carry them away on their own ships, and it barred Americans from sailing on belligerents' ships. Again, Roosevelt wanted more flexibility but appreciated that the law allowed him to determine which nations were at war and which goods were nonwar goods.

Roosevelt used that provision in July 1937, when Japan invaded northern China. He refused to

... and the Wolf chewed up the children and spit out their bones ... But those were <u>Foreign Children</u> and it really didn't matter."

Dr. Seuss not only produced children's books, but drew many political cartoons opposing isolationism and supporting the nation's war effort. Here he aims his pen at the America First movement that argued that Americans should not concern themselves about events in Europe and Asia.

recognize that China and Japan were at war, which allowed American trade to continue with both nations. Hoping that isolationist views had softened, on October 5 Roosevelt suggested that the United States and other peace-loving nations should quarantine "bandit nations." The "quarantine speech" was applauded in many foreign capitals, but not at home. The *Wall Street Journal* argued that Roosevelt should "stop...meddling: America Wants Peace." As Japan gobbled up Chinese territory, on December 12, 1937, Japanese aircraft sank the American gunboat *Panay*. Two Americans died, and over thirty were wounded. Outraged, Roosevelt favored retaliatory action. The *Christian Science Monitor*, expressing public and

■ **Neutrality Act of 1935** Act forbidding the sale and shipment of war goods to all nations at war and authorizing the president to warn U.S. citizens against traveling on belligerents' vessels, intended to keep America from being drawn into war.

discriminatory neutrality Withholding aid and trade from one nation at war while providing them to another.

Rhineland Region of western Germany along the Rhine River, which under the terms of the Versailles Treaty was to remain free of troops and military fortifications.

In the Wider World

Aliens in Their Own Land

Since its inception, the Nationalist Socialist Party led by Adolf Hitler described Jews as "alien" to German society and culture. Assuming power in Germany in 1932, Hitler instituted a series of anti-Jewish laws and regulations. The Nuremberg race laws stripped German Jews of their nationality and citizenship, making them aliens in their own land, while other pronouncements defined Jews by religious ancestry. If three of a person's grandparents belonged to a Jewish religious community, the person was forever Jewish. It did not matter if the person no longer practiced Judaism or had converted to Christianity. Characterizing Jews as aliens, depersonalized them, making it easier to define them as dangerous biological enemies threatening Germany and its people. This, in turn, allowed more individual and state-sponsored violence and persecution. By 1939, Jews in Germany understood that they lived as prisoners in an increasingly segregated society. What few realized was that Hitler planned a Germany free of Jews. "We are going to destroy the Jews," he told the Czech ambassador, "The day of reckoning has come."

congressional opinion, pointed out that the *Panay* was not the *Maine*. Without support for action against Japan, Roosevelt accepted Japan's apology and payment of over $2 million in damages.

As fighting raged on in China and Spain in 1938, Hitler pronounced his intentions to unify all German-speaking lands and create a new German empire, or *Reich*. He annexed Austria and then incorporated the Sudeten region of western Czechoslovakia into the German Reich (see Map 23.1). With a respectable military force and defense treaties with France and the Soviet Union, the Czechoslovakian government was prepared to resist. However, France, the Soviet Union, and Britain wanted no confrontation with Hitler. Choosing a policy of **appeasement**, in late September Britain's prime minister, Neville Chamberlain, met with Hitler in Munich and accepted Germany's annexation of the Sudetenland. France concurred. Chamberlain returned to England promising the **Munich Agreement** had secured "peace for our time."

Within Germany, Hitler stepped up the persecution of the country's nearly half-million Jews. In government-sponsored violence, synagogues and Jewish businesses and homes were looted and destroyed. Detention centers—concentration camps—at Dachau and Buchenwald soon confined over fifty thousand Jews. Thousands of German and Austrian Jews fled to other countries. Many applied to enter the United States, but most were turned away. Public opinion polls found American anti-Semitism strong. One survey found that 85 percent of Protestants, 84 percent of Catholics, and even 25.8 percent of Jews in the United States opposed more Jewish refugees entering the country. The State Department, citing immigration requirements against admitting anyone who would become "a public charge," routinely denied entry to Jews whose property and assets had been seized by the German government. Roosevelt expressed concern, but in all, only about sixty thousand Jewish refugees entered the United States between 1933 and 1938—many of them scientists, academics, and musicians.

The Munich agreement collapsed within six months as Hitler annexed the remaining parts of Czechoslovakia. Fearing a war in Europe, Roosevelt asked Congress to increase military spending for the construction of aircraft. Congress agreed and Roosevelt quickly made the money available to several aircraft companies, including Boeing and Beechcraft, which received over $11 million to build long-range bombers in Wichita, Kansas.

Events soon verified Roosevelt's fears. Hitler ominously concluded a military alliance with Italy and a **German-Soviet Nonaggression Pact** with Stalin. Peace collapsed on September 1, 1939, when Hitler invaded Poland after it refused to cede to Germany the Polish Corridor, which connected Poland to the Baltic Sea. Two days later, Britain and France declared war on Germany. Within a matter of days, German troops overran nearly all of Poland. On September 17, Soviet forces entered the eastern parts of Poland as they had secretly agreed to do in the Nonaggression Pact.

appeasement Granting concessions to potential enemies to maintain peace. Since the Munich agreement did not stop Hitler's aggression, appeasement has become a policy that most nations avoid.

■ **Munich Agreement** Agreement signed by Germany, Italy, France, and Britain in September 1938 allowing Germany to annex the part of Czechoslovakia called the Sudetenland.

■ **German-Soviet Nonaggression Pact** A 1939 agreement in which Germany and the Soviet Union pledged not to fight each other and secretly arranged to divide Poland after Germany conquered it.

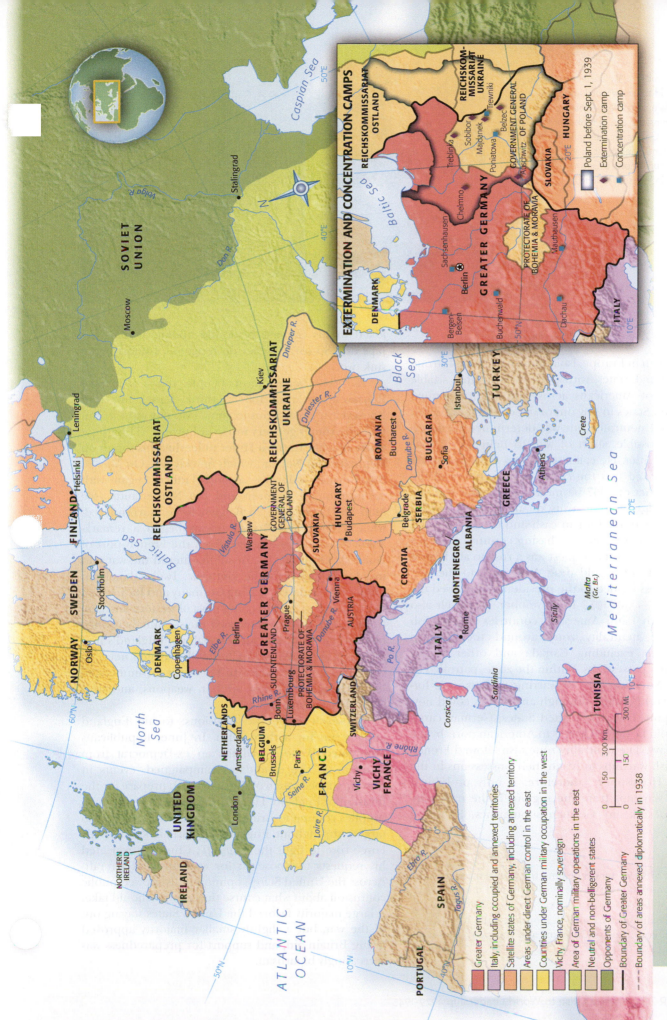

MAP 23.1 German and Italian Expansion, 1933–1942
By the end of 1942, the Axis nations of Italy and Germany, through conquest and annexation, had occupied nearly all of Europe. This map shows the political and military alignment of Europe as Germany and Italy reached the limit of their power. © Cengage Learning.

EXTERMINATION AND CONCENTRATION CAMPS

Poland before Sept. 1, 1939
Extermination camp
Concentration camp

Greater Germany
Italy, including occupied and annexed territories
Satellite states of Germany
Areas under direct German control in the east
Countries under direct German control in the west
Vichy France, nominally sovereign
Area of German military operations in the east
Neutral and non-belligerent states
Opponents of Germany
Boundary of Greater Germany
Boundary of areas annexed diplomatically in 1938

In September 1939, Germany introduced the world to a new word and type of warfare, *Blitzkrieg*—lightning war. Combining the use of tanks, aircraft, and infantry, German forces quickly overran first Poland, then most of Western Europe. This picture shows a German victory parade in Warsaw, Poland.

Hugo Jaeger/Getty Images.

War and American Neutrality

As war began in Europe, isolationism remained strong in the United States, with polls showing that sizable majorities of Americans across the country wanted the United States to stay out of the conflict. Roosevelt proclaimed neutrality but was determined to do everything possible, short of war, to help the nations opposing Hitler. He called Congress into special session and asked that the cash-and-carry policy of the Neutrality Act of 1937 be modified to allow the sale of any goods, including arms, to any nation, provided the goods were paid for in cash and carried away on ships belonging to the purchasing country. A "peace bloc" argued that the request was a ruse to aid France and Britain and would drag America into the war, but Congress yielded to the president and passed the **Neutrality Act of 1939** in November. Roosevelt also worked with Latin American countries to establish a 300-mile neutrality zone around the Western Hemisphere, excluding Canada and other British and French possessions. Within the zone, patrolled by the U.S. Navy, warships of warring nations were forbidden. So in reality, although any nation could now buy weapons from the United States, German cargo ships would be denied access to American ports by the British navy. The neutrality zone also allowed French and British warships to reach their possessions in the Western Hemisphere; therefore, it only prohibited German warships from the region. If the navy happened to sink any German submarines, Roosevelt

joked to his cabinet, he would apologize like "the Japs do, 'So sorry. Never do it again.' Tomorrow we sink two."

As 1940 began most people did not expect Roosevelt to run for a third term, nor did Roosevelt seem anxious to run: "I do not want to run unless…things get very worse in Europe." Things got worse quickly. In April Hitler unleashed his forces on Denmark and Norway, which quickly fell. On May 10 the German offensive against France began with an invasion of Belgium and the Netherlands (see Map 23.1). On May 26 Belgian forces surrendered, while French and British troops began a remarkable evacuation to England from the French port of Dunkirk. On June 10, Mussolini entered the war and invaded France from the southeast. Twelve days later, France surrendered, leaving Germany and Italy, called the **Axis powers**, controlling most of western and central Europe. Britain now faced the seemingly invincible German army and air force alone. England's new prime minister, Winston Churchill, pledged never to surrender and pleaded with Roosevelt for immediate help. He needed ships, aircraft, weapons, and steel and other raw materials.

Roosevelt made two decisions: to aid England and to run for a third term. In June, Republicans nominated Wendell Willkie, an ex-Democrat from Indiana. As the candidates campaigned, events in Europe shaped much of the debate. To prepare for the invasion of England, Hitler ordered the navy to block supplies coming to Britain and the air force to bomb targets throughout England. As Britain's Royal Air Force rose to fight the *Luftwaffe*, Churchill repeated his requests to Roosevelt for warships and aircraft. Across the United States, opinion polls showed public confusion about what course the country should take. A large majority favored the United States staying out of the war, but a slightly smaller majority approved giving Britain aid, and support for preparedness was increasingly bipartisan.

◻ **Neutrality Act of 1939** Law repealing the arms embargo and authorizing cash-and-carry exports of arms and munitions even to belligerent nations.

◻ **Axis powers** Coalition of nations that opposed the Allies in World War II, first consisting of Germany and Italy and later joined by Japan.

From 1940 to 1943, the *Unterseeboot* (U-boat) was Germany's primary weapon during the battle for the Atlantic, but by mid-1943, Allied countermeasures forced their withdrawal from most of the Atlantic. Nearly 800 of the 1,160 U-boats built during the war were sunk.

Citing preparedness, Roosevelt asked Congress to increase the military budget and supported a bipartisan bill to create the first peacetime military draft in American history. Isolationists opposed both actions, especially the draft. Senator Nye expressed the view of many, saying, "If we get into this war it will not be because the President tried to keep us out." But Nye and other isolationists were unable to prevent Congress from approving the draft and over $37 billion for military spending, more than the total cost of World War I.

In September, Roosevelt signed the **Burke-Wadsworth Act**, and the government began drafting men into the military in October. To aid Britain, he used an executive order to exchange fifty old destroyers for ninety-nine-year leases on British military bases in Newfoundland, the Caribbean, and British Guiana. The public responded favorably, contributing to a 10 percent Roosevelt lead in voter polls. Republican leaders now convinced Willkie to attack Roosevelt for pushing the nation toward war. If Roosevelt was elected, Willkie told a Baltimore audience, " expect war by April." Willkie's popularity surged. Roosevelt countered with a promise to American mothers: "Your boys are not going to be sent into any foreign wars." Roosevelt won easily, but Republicans gained seats in both the Senate and House of Representatives.

The Battle for the Atlantic

The election was barely over when Roosevelt received an urgent message from Churchill. Britain was out of money and needed credit to pay for supplies. He also asked that America help in carrying goods to England and protecting merchant ships from German submarines. Roosevelt agreed, and knowing that the requests faced tough congressional and public opposition, he turned to his powers of persuasion. In his December fireside chat, he told his audience that if England fell, Hitler would surely attack the United States next. He urged the people to make the nation the "arsenal of democracy" and to supply Britain with all the material help it needed to defeat Hitler. He then presented Congress with a bill allowing the president to lend, lease, or in any way provide goods to any country considered vital to American security.

The request drew the expected fire from isolationists. Senator Burton K. Wheeler from Montana called it a military Agricultural Adjustment Act that would "plow under every fourth American boy." Supporters countered with "Send guns, not sons." On March 11, 1941, the 60-year-old president breathed a sigh of relief when the **Lend-Lease Act** passed easily.

By the summer of 1941, the U.S. Navy's patrols of the neutrality zone overlapped Hitler's Atlantic war zone. It was only a matter of time until American and German ships confronted each other. Having called

■ **Burke-Wadsworth Act** Law passed by Congress in 1940 creating the first peacetime draft in American history.

■ **Lend-Lease Act** A 1941 law providing that any country whose security was vital to U.S. interests could receive arms and equipment by sale, transfer, or lease from the United States.

off the invasion of Britain, Hitler directed German forces into Yugoslavia, Greece, and North Africa. Breaking Germany's non-aggression pact with the Soviet Union, he also planned to crush the Soviets with the largest military force ever assembled on a single front. On June 22, 1941, German forces, supported by allied Finnish, Hungarian, Italian, and Romanian armies, opened the eastern front. Claiming he would join even the devil to defeat Hitler, Churchill made an ally of Stalin, while Roosevelt extended credits and lend-lease goods to the Soviet Union. Despite initial crushing victories in which German soldiers advanced within miles of Moscow, by November it was becoming clear that the Soviets were not going to collapse.

With the battle for the Atlantic reaching a tipping point and Germany rolling through Russia, Roosevelt and Churchill met secretly off the coast of Newfoundland on August 9–12, 1941. Churchill wanted an American declaration of war, but Roosevelt's main concern was more political than strategic. He urged Churchill to subscribe to an **Atlantic Charter** that would highlight the distinctions between the open, cooperative world of the democracies and the closed, self-serving world of fascist expansion. Championing self-determination, freedom of trade and the seas, and the establishment of a "permanent system of general security" in the form of a new world organization, Roosevelt explained, would help Americans support entry into the war. Churchill agreed but reminded Roosevelt that Britain could not fully accept the goals of self-determination and free trade within its Commonwealth and the British Empire. Returning to London, Churchill told his ministers that Roosevelt meant to "wage war, but not declare it, and that he would become more and more provocative...to force an incident...which would justify him in opening hostilities."

On September 4, 1941, in the North Atlantic near Iceland, the American destroyer *Greer* skirmished with a German U-boat. Neither ship was damaged, but Roosevelt used the skirmish to get Congress to amend the neutrality laws to permit armed U.S. merchant ships to sail into combat zones. In October, following an attack on the U.S.S. *Kearney* and the sinking of the U.S.S. *Reuben James,* Congress rescinded all neutrality laws and public opinion seemed to accept the prospect of war.

Throughout the country, FBI agents instructed local officials in how to deal with problems of a nation at war, including espionage and sabotage, air raids and blackouts, and even gas contamination. Roosevelt accepted the War Department's "Victory Program,"

◾ **Atlantic Charter** Joint statement issued by Roosevelt and Churchill in 1941 to formulate American and British postwar aims of international economic and political cooperation.

which concluded that the United States would have to fight a two-front war against Germany and against Japan. It also stated that Hitler needed to be defeated before the Japanese, and that July 1943 was about the earliest date that American troops could be ready for any large-scale operation.

Pearl Harbor

Since 1937, Japanese troops had seized more and more of China, while the United States did little but protest. By 1940, popular sentiment favored not only beefing up American defenses in the Pacific but also using economic pressure to slow Japanese aggression. In July 1940, Roosevelt began placing restrictions on Japanese-American trade, forbidding the sale and shipment of aviation fuel, steel, and scrap iron. Many Americans believed the action was too limited and pointed out that Japan was still allowed to buy millions of gallons of American oil, which it was using to "extinguish the lamps of China."

The situation in East Asia soon worsened when Japanese troops entered French Indochina (see Map 23.2), and Japan signed a defense treaty with Germany and Italy. America promptly strengthened its forces in the Philippines and tightened trade restrictions on Japan. Within the Japanese government some still hoped for an agreement with the United States and sought to negotiate. But discussions between Secretary of State Cordell Hull and Japan's ambassador, Admiral Kichisaburo Nomura, were confused and nonproductive, which convinced many in the Japanese government that war was unavoidable if Japan was to break the "circle of force" that denied its interests. High on Japan's list of interests was control over Malaysia and the Dutch East Indies (Indonesia), sources of vital raw materials, including oil. Seizing those regions, they concluded, would probably involve fighting the United States.

For Minister of War Hideki Tojo, the choice was simple: either submit to American demands, accepting a world order defined by the United States, or safeguard the nation's honor and achievements by initiating a war. In his mind, war could be averted only if the United States released frozen Japanese assets, suspended aid to China, capped its military presence in the Pacific, and resumed full trade with Japan. On November 26, after Hull made it clear there would be no American concessions

Admiral Isoroku Yamamoto dispatched part of the Japanese fleet, including six aircraft carriers, toward Hawai'i. American observers, however, focused on the activity of a larger part of the Japanese fleet, which sailed on December 5 toward the South China Sea and the Gulf of Siam. At 7:49 A.M. (Hawaiian time) on December 7, without a declaration of war, Japanese planes struck the American fleet anchored at Pearl

MAP 23.2 Japanese Advances, December 1941–1942
Beginning on December 7, 1941, Japanese forces began carving out a vast empire, the Greater East Asian Co-Prosperity Sphere, by attacking American, British, Dutch, and Australian forces from Pearl Harbor to the Dutch East Indies. This map shows the course of Japanese expansion until the critical naval battles of the Coral Sea and Midway in the spring of 1942 halted Japanese advances in the Pacific. © Cengage Learning.

Harbor. By 8:12, seven battleships of the American Pacific fleet lined up along Battleship Row were aflame, sinking, or badly damaged. Eleven other ships had been hit, nearly two hundred American aircraft had been destroyed, and twenty-five hundred Americans had lost their lives.

The attack on Pearl Harbor, however, was only a small part of Japan's strategy. Elsewhere that day Japanese planes struck Singapore, Guam, the Philippines, and Hong Kong. Everywhere, British and American positions in the Pacific and East Asia were overwhelmed. Roosevelt declared that the unprovoked, sneak attack on Pearl Harbor made December 7 "a day which will live in infamy" and asked Congress for a declaration of war against Japan. Only Representative Jeannette Rankin of Montana, a pacifist, kept the December 8 declaration of war from being unanimous. Three days later, Germany and Italy declared war on the United States. In England, Churchill

"slept the sleep of the saved and thankful." He knew that with the economic and human resources of the United States finally committed to war, the Axis would be "ground to powder."

AMERICA RESPONDS TO WAR

☆ *What actions did Roosevelt take to mobilize the nation for war and how did they affect the relationship between business and government?*

☆ *What new social and economic choices did Americans confront during the war? How were different groups affected?*

The attack on Pearl Harbor unified the nation as no other event had done. Americans were angry and full of fight, and thousands of young men rushed to enlist. On December 8, twelve hundred applicants besieged

Roosevelt called it a day of "infamy"—December 7, 1941, when Japanese planes attacked Pearl Harbor, Hawai'i, without warning and before a declaration of war. In this photo, the U.S.S. *West Virginia* sinks in flames, one of seven battleships sunk or badly damaged in the attack.

the navy recruiting station in New York City, some having waited outside the doors all night. Eventually over 16.4 million Americans would serve in the armed forces during World War II.

Japan's attack on Pearl Harbor raised fears of further attacks, especially along the Pacific Coast. On the night of December 7 and throughout the next week, panicky West Coast cities reported enemy planes overhead and practiced blackouts. Stores everywhere removed "made in Japan" goods from shelves. Alarm and anger focused on Japanese Americans, with rumors circulating wildly that they intended to sabotage factories and military installations, paving the way for the invasion of the West Coast. Within a week, the FBI had arrested 2,541 citizens of Axis countries: 1,370 Japanese, 1,002 Germans, and 169 Italians.

Issei A Japanese immigrant to the United States.

▫ **Executive Order #9066** President Roosevelt's order in 1942 authorizing the removal of "enemy aliens" from military areas; it was used to isolate Japanese Americans in internment camps.

▫ **internment camps** Camps to which more than 110,000 Japanese Americans living in the West were moved soon after the attack on Pearl Harbor; Japanese Americans in Hawai'i were not confined in internment camps.

Japanese American Internment

There were nearly 125,000 Japanese Americans in the country, about three-fourths of whom were Nisei—Japanese Americans who had been born in the United States. The remaining fourth were Japanese immigrants, or *Issei*—officially citizens of Japan, although nearly all had lived in the United States prior to 1924, when Asians were barred from the country. Reflecting long-standing anti-Japanese sentiment and the new war-based nationalism, Japanese Americans all over the West Coast were fired from their jobs, and their law and medical licenses revoked. Banks froze Japanese American assets, stores refused service, and loyal citizens vandalized Nisei and Issei homes and businesses.

On February 19, 1942, Roosevelt signed *Executive Order #9066*, which allowed the military to remove anyone deemed a threat from official military areas. When the entire West Coast was declared a military area, the eviction of those of Japanese ancestry began. By the summer of 1942, over 110,000 Nisei and Issei had been transported to ten *internment camps* (see Map 23.3). When tested in court, the executive order was upheld by the Supreme Court in *Korematsu v. United States* in 1944 (see Individual Voices, page 661). Hawai'i, with its much larger Japanese American

MAP 23.3 Internment Camps
This map shows the locations of the ten relocation centers, mostly in the West, used to house Japanese Americans during World War II. Within the West Coast military zone nearly ten thousand non-citizen Italians were also forced to leave the zone until October 1942 when the restriction was lifted. © Cengage Learning.

population, never saw the need to isolate either the Nisei or the Issei.

Once ordered to relocate, families had little time to dispose of their possessions and pack the few personal items they were allowed to take to the camps. Many had to sell their property, including homes and businesses, at ridiculously low prices. "It is difficult to describe the feeling of despair and humiliation experienced," one man recalled, "as we watched the Caucasians coming to look over all our possessions and offering such nominal amounts knowing we had no recourse but to accept." In the relocation it is estimated that Japanese American families lost from $810 million to $2 billion in property and goods.

Arriving at the relocation centers, the internees were surrounded by barbed wire and watched over by armed guards. They were assigned to 20-by-25-foot apartments in long barracks of plywood covered with tarpaper, and each camp was expected to create a community complete with farms, shops, and small factories. Within a remarkably short time, they did. Despite their treatment and humiliation, most remained loyal and patriotic citizens. One young Nisei remembered being told by one of his Japanese American teachers that their internment was "temporary" and he should not forget that "America is the greatest country." The teacher, called a "true patriot" by the young student, was later killed in action in Italy.

Some internees were able to leave the camps by working outside, supplying much-needed labor, especially farm work. By the fall of 1942, one-fifth of all males had left the camps to work. Others left for college or volunteered for military service. Japanese American units served in both the Pacific and European theaters, the most famous being the four-thousand-man 442nd Regimental Combat Team, which saw action in Italy, France, and Germany. The men of the 442nd would be among the most decorated in the army. In 2000, the federal government, citing racial bias during the war, awarded the Medal of Honor to twenty-one Asian Americans—most belonging to the 442nd Regiment, including Daniel Ken Inouye, who was elected to the U.S. Senate from Hawai'i in 1960.

Aware of anti-Japanese public opinion, Roosevelt waited until after the off-year 1943 elections to allow internees who passed a loyalty review to go home. A year later, most of the camps were empty, each internee having been given train fare home and $25. The last camp, Tule, was closed in March 1946. Returning home, the Japanese Americans discovered that nearly everything they once owned was gone. Stored belongings had been stolen. Land, homes, and businesses had been confiscated by the government for unpaid taxes. Denied even an apology from the government, Japanese Americans nevertheless began to reestablish their homes and businesses. Decades

It Matters Today

Internment

Does war or national crisis allow for the reduction and elimination of a person's rights, of a citizen's rights? During the war the government interned 110,000 people of Japanese ancestry because they were regarded as potential threats to American security. With the memory of Pearl Harbor still fresh, fears of spying and sabotage played a role; race, too was a factor. Many argued that the culture and values of Japan made the conflict a "race war" and that all Japanese, even those who were citizens, could not be trusted: "Once a Jap always a Jap!" The dissenting Justices in the *Korematsu* case believed internment was clearly a result of racism that violated the American concept of democracy and that the decision was the "legalization of racism." How a society acts in time of war often provides insights into not only the strengths of the nation but its weaknesses as well.

- Since the Al Qaeda attacks on September 11, 2001, the United States has fought a war on international terrorism and defined radical Islamic fundamentalism as a source of that terrorism. These actions have raised the issues of race, religion, and culture, and have led to comparisons to the treatment of the Nisei and the Issei during World War II. Are these comparisons valid? Why or why not?

---

later, in 1988, and after several lawsuits on behalf of victims, a semi-apologetic federal government paid $20,000 in compensation to each of the surviving sixty thousand internees.

Mobilizing the Nation for War

Like the Depression, the war touched all Americans, the 16 million who marched off to war and the many more who stayed behind. It was time to mobilize the nation, its people and its economy. To produce the goods necessary for victory, factories were to run twenty-four hours a day, seven days a week. Gone was the antibusiness attitude that characterized much New Deal rhetoric. Secretary of War Henry L. Stimson noted: "You have to let business make money out of the process or business won't work." And only big business could produce the vast amount of armaments and supplies needed; 82 percent of the over $240 billion in defense contracts went to the nation's top one hundred corporations.

Every part of the nation benefited, with the South and the coastal West seeing the largest economic gains. Higgins Industries in New Orleans developed a workable ramp and built the "Higgins Boat," a 60-foot vessel that carried tanks and men to the beaches of Africa, Europe, and the islands of the Pacific. The company grew from fifty-seven employees to over thirty thousand and produced over nine thousand landing craft. Hitler called Andrew Higgins the "new Noah." Overall, the South experienced a 40 percent increase in its industrial capacity. The West did even better. "It was," wrote one observer, "[as] if someone had tilted the

National Archives.

In February 1942, President Roosevelt signed an order sending all Japanese Americans living on the West Coast to internment camps. This photo, taken at a staging area for transportation to the internment camps, shows the quiet dignity of those waiting to be interned.

country: people, money, and soldiers all spilled west." California's Henry J. Kaiser, "Sir Launchalot," constructed massive shipyards that employed over 2 million workers. By using innovative methods that included **prefabricated** sections, he cut the time it took to build a merchant "Liberty" ship from about three hundred days to an average of forty.

By the end of the war, the United States had pumped more than $320 billion into the economy (an average of $250 million a day), and its workers and factories had constructed more than 300,000 aircraft, 88,000 tanks, and 86,000 warships. Neither Germany nor Japan came close to matching that output.

Part of the billions the government spent upgraded factories, built new industries, and supported vital research and development. When the war cut off critical supplies of raw rubber, government and business cooperated to develop and produce millions of tons of synthetic rubber. Hundreds of colleges, universities, and private laboratories, such as Bell Labs, received grants to produce improved radar and sonar technologies; new medical techniques and medicines, including penicillin; and potent pesticides to combat insects that carried typhus, malaria, and other diseases at home and overseas. "Science cities" were constructed across the country, bringing researchers and technicians together in the secret **Manhattan Project** to harness atomic energy and build an atomic bomb.

TOWARD A MORE PERFECT UNION

War and Governmental Power

War usually enhances the powers of government while diminishing the rights of citizens—and the Second World War was no exception. Though the Supreme Court generally protected a citizen's right to self-expression (the *Vireck* case), it also approved the government's nearly monopolistic control over the economy. When businessmen argued that the government had no right to determine how they conducted their businesses, the Court upheld the ability of government agencies—like the Office of Price Administration—to control business activities, including establishing prices and rents (the *Yakus, Willingham*, and *Steuart* cases) In supporting these decisions, the Court took the position that "a nation which can demand the lives of its men and women in the waging of war is under no constitutional necessity of providing a system of price control on the domestic front which will assure each landlord a 'fair return' on his property."

As the economy retooled to provide the machines of war, Roosevelt created an array of agencies and boards to provide economic planning and to regulate prices, production, and consumption. The size of the federal bureaucracy grew 400 percent. The Office of Price Administration (OPA), established in 1941, tried to limit inflation and consumption by setting prices and rationing a wide range of commodities. The War Production Board (WPB) and the National War Labor Board (NWLB), created in January 1942, tried to coordinate and plan production, allot materials, and ensure harmonious labor relations.

When these agencies failed to resolve problems and create a smoothly working economy, Roosevelt and Congress expanded their scope and created new ones, like the Office of War Mobilization (1943), which was designed to improve the effectiveness and coordination of existing agencies. Although things did not always run smoothly, by the fall of 1943, production was booming, jobs were plentiful, wages and family incomes were rising, and inflation was under control. Even farmers were climbing out of debt, as farm income had tripled since 1939.

Mobilization produced full employment, and expanding labor needs provided new opportunities for women, minorities, and even those who had retired. New workers, with NWLB encouragement, boosted union membership while unions pledged a no-strike policy in return for union recognition, collective bargaining, **closed shops**, and increased wages. The head of the Congress of Industrial Organizations (CIO) urged his members to "Work, Work, Produce, Produce, Produce." In most cases, unions and industries worked with the OPA and NWLB to hammer out acceptable agreements. Still, every year nearly 3 million workers went on strike or conducted work slowdowns. Most lasted only a brief time and did not jeopardize production, but several strikes generated the wrath of the president, Congress, and the public.

One of the most serious strikes occurred in 1943 when CIO president and head of the United Mine Workers John L. Lewis demanded higher wages and safer working conditions. An angry president threatened to take over the mines. Congress wanted Lewis jailed as a traitor and pushed through, over the president's veto, the Smith-Connally War Labor Disputes Act. It gave the president the power to seize and

prefabricated Parts of an item that are manufactured in advance, usually in standardized sections for easy shipment and quick assembly.

■ **Manhattan Project** A secret scientific research effort begun in 1942 to develop an atomic bomb.

closed shop A business or factory whose workers are required to be union members.

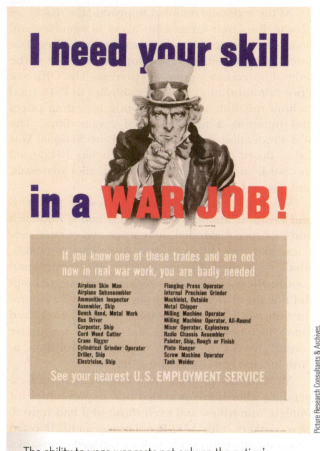

Picture Research Consultants & Archives.

The ability to wage war rests not only on the nation's raw materials and military, but on its productive labor force. In this ad, the iconic "Uncle Sam" wants those with specific skills to enlist in the production side of the war effort.

operate any strikebound industries considered vital for war production. Eventually, the parties in the mine strike compromised, giving higher wages to the miners. By the end of the war, union membership had grown from 9 million to 14.8 million, and a diversified workforce was producing an unprecedented amount of goods and receiving wages more than double their pre-war level.

To offset the cost of the war, Roosevelt turned to taxation. The 1942 and 1943 Revenue Acts increased the number of people paying taxes and raised rates. In 1939, 4 million Americans paid income taxes; by the end of the war, more than 40 million did so. Income taxes also increased. Before the war the highest tax bracket, those individuals making $5 million or more a year paid 81 percent in taxes. A year later in 1942, those individuals making over $200,000 were paying 88 percent in taxes. Corporate taxes averaged 40 percent, with a 90 percent tax on excess profits.

Even with the increases, tax revenues paid for only about half of the cost of the war. The government borrowed the rest. The largest and most publicized effort was the sale of war bonds. Movie stars and other celebrities asked Americans to "do their part" and buy bonds. The public responded by purchasing more than $40 billion in individual bonds, but the majority of bonds—$95 billion—were bought by corporations and financial institutions. Through taxes and borrowing, the country met the cost of the war, but it increased the national debt from $40 billion to almost $260 billion (see Figure 23.1).

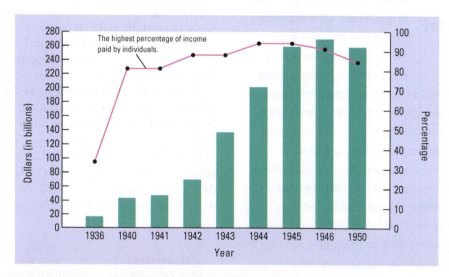

FIGURE 23.1 The National Debt and Taxes, 1936–1950
As the United States fought to defeat the Axis nations, its national debt soared (the green bars on this graph). The government raised taxes (the purple line), but still needed to borrow about 60 percent of the war's cost. By the end of the war, the debt had reached nearly $260 billion. By 1944, those with incomes over $200,000 were paying a 94 percent income tax rate. © Cengage Learning.

A People at Work and War

Buying war bonds was only one way the war changed people's activities every day. Families collected scrap metals, paper, and rubber to be recycled for the war effort. About 20 million planted victory gardens, which produced over a third of all the vegetables in the country and quickly became visible symbols of patriotism. Remembering the small plot of rock-hard soil that produced stunted carrots, a resident of Long Beach, California, said, "We all wanted to do our part....You got caught up in the mesmerizing spirit of patriotism."

There was less enthusiasm about the ration books that most Americans had by the end of 1942. They contained an array of different-colored coupons of various values that limited people's purchases of such staples as meat, sugar, and gasoline. Wartime needs also changed fashion as the War Production Board worked to conserve fabrics. Lapels were narrowed and vests and pant cuffs were eliminated on men's suits. The fabric in women's skirts was reduced and the two-piece bathing suit was introduced as "patriotic chic." When some people complained about shortages and inconveniences, more would challenge, "Don't you know there's a war on?" Nevertheless, most Americans experienced a better standard of living than ever; their incomes grew and their consumer spending increased by 12 percent.

Americans were also on the move. More than 15 million civilians—including women, African Americans, Latinos, and Native Americans—relocated to take new jobs. They went where defense industries beckoned. Over 200,000 people, many from the rural South, headed for Detroit. More went west; Southern California's population increased by over 2 million. The sudden explosion of population in areas with defense industries created needs for local services and facilities that could not be met. San Diego, California, once a small retirement community with a quiet naval base, mushroomed into a major military and defense industrial city almost overnight. Nearly fifty-five thousand people flocked there each year of the war, with thousands living in small travel trailers leased by the federal government for $7 a month. Mobile, Alabama, with its shipyards, new aluminum plant, and military bases, had too many people and too few resources. Its officials worried about diseases, housing and sanitation needs, tensions between the old and new residents, and the two thousand children skipping school each day. Some truants went to movies, but more just hung around, a potential source of mischief and crime.

Nationally, juvenile crime increased dramatically during the war, with officials putting the blame on those lockout and latchkey children who were unsupervised while their mothers worked. Particularly worrisome to local authorities were the so-called "victory girls." Nicknamed "V-girls," they were young teens, sometimes called "khaki-wacky teens," who hung around gathering spots like bus depots and drugstores to flirt with GIs and ask for dates. Their young faces thick with makeup and bright red lipstick, V-girls traded sex for movies, dances, and drinks. Going further, seventeen-year-old Elvira Taylor of Norfolk, Virginia, became an "Allotment Annie." She simply married the soldiers and collected their monthly allotment checks. Eventually, two American soldiers at an English pub showing off pictures of their wives discovered they had both married Elvira! It turned out she had wed six servicemen.

New Opportunities and Old Constraints

Adjusting to wartime realities men and women confronted new roles and accepted new responsibilities, both on the home front and in the military. Many women, like men, wanted to serve in the military. At first only female nurses were allowed in the armed forces, but in March 1942, the Army created the non-combat Women's Army Corps (WAC) to free men for combat roles. The other services soon followed: the navy's Women Appointed for Volunteer Emergency Service (WAVES) and the Marines' Women's Reserve. Women also participated as civilian Women's Airforce Service Pilots (WASPs). WASP volunteers tested planes, ferried planes across the United States and Canada, and trained male pilots. Although women were only appointed to noncombat roles and most served in safe areas, nurses and many WACS found themselves in combat zones. Nurses became prisoners of war when captured by the Japanese and five women received the silver star for valor in Italy. Overall, over 230 women died from war-related injuries. By war's end, over 350,000 women had donned uniforms, earned equal pay with men who held the same rank, and provided a new female image.

Female military service was not the only break with tradition. With over 10 million men marching off to war, civilian employers increasingly turned to women. The federal government doubled its number of female employees and supported women moving into the workforce by providing training and stressing that women could shorten the war if they joined the workforce. The image of Rosie the Riveter became the symbol of the patriotic woman doing her part.

> ■ **victory garden** Small plot cultivated by a patriotic citizen during World War II to supply household food and allow farm production to be used for the war effort.
>
> **allotment checks** Checks that a soldier's wife received from the government, amounting to a percentage of her husband's pay.
>
> ■ **Rosie the Riveter** A popular image symbolizing the patriotic woman working in industry to advance war production; the many women who entered the labor force were usually among the first let go at war's end.

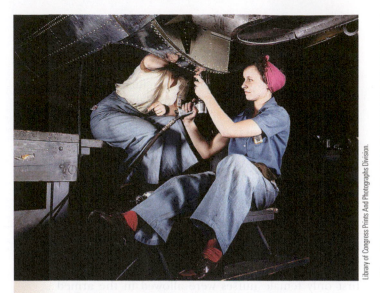

Library of Congress Prints And Photographs Division.

As during World War I, the Second World War opened up new job opportunities for women. In this picture, a real-life "Rosie the Riveter" works on the fuselage of a bomber.

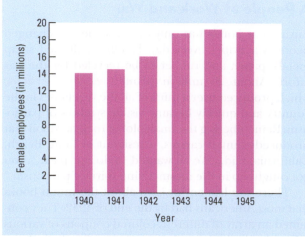

FIGURE 23.2 Women in the Workforce, 1940–1945
As men went to war, the nation turned increasingly to women to fill vital jobs. With government's encouragement, the number of women in the workforce swelled from 14 million to nearly 20 million. With the war's end, however, many women left the workplace and returned to the home. © Cengage Learning.

Increasingly, women filled jobs once held by men. As a Billings, Montana, newspaper noted, "Petticoat troops are making forced landings in businesses and industry." In Detroit, women made up 56 percent of the labor force, while in Boeing's Seattle plant, women filled 47 percent of the payroll.

Women went to work for many reasons—some because of patriotism, but most because they wanted both the job and the wages. Leaving home, Peggy Terry worked in a munitions plant and considered it "an absolute miracle.…We made the fabulous sum of $32 a week.…Before, we made nothing." Many women left menial jobs for much better-paying positions with industries and the federal government. African American Sybil Lewis left her position as a maid in Oklahoma and took a job as a riveter in California. "Hitler…got us out of the white folks' kitchen," remembered another. Neither would return to their pre-war lives. By 1944, 37 percent of all adult women were working, almost 19.4 million (see Figure 23.2). The majority (72.2 percent) were married, and over half were age 35 or older.

New opportunities did not diminish familiar constraints. Professional and supervisory positions remained dominated by men, and not all was rosy at work. Despite the labor shortage, male workers frequently resented and harassed women. "The hardest thing about the job," remembered one woman cab driver, "was the hostility of men toward women driving." Similar complaints echoed across the country even as management and the media praised women's work ethics and abilities. Edsel Ford commented that women did the hardest welding and the most delicate jobs "superbly," while a Yellow Cab manager pointed out that women drivers had more "tact" and

a "very, very low" accident rate. Keeping with tradition, women were generally paid less than men, even though the NLWB promoted the idea of the same pay for the same job.

Women with children faced the problem of daycare. Although the 1942 Lanham Act provided communities with federal funds for child care, the money, centers, and programs were never enough to meet the needs. Some women found it too difficult to balance work and family needs and left their jobs. Married or single, women realized that despite their wishes, most of their jobs would disappear when the war ended, and they would be expected to return to more traditional roles.

Those expectations proved correct. By the summer of 1945, many of the women found themselves among the unemployed. Shipyards and the aircraft plants dismissed nearly three-fourths of their women employees, automakers about a third. Those who managed to remain at work were frequently transferred to less attractive, poorly paying jobs. Thus, for most women, the war experience was mixed, with new choices cut short by changing circumstances.

The war also provided new opportunities for African Americans, but they were accompanied by long-standing racial and ethnic constraints. Like women, blacks realized that when the war ended, many of the gains and opportunities would vanish. Considering the reality of race, James Thompson wrote to the *Pittsburgh Courier* wondering if it was "too much to demand full citizenship" for being willing to sacrifice his life. He argued for a "double victory," one against the enemy abroad and the second "over our enemies from within." Among the enemies within were companies that resisted hiring nonwhite workers.

North American Aviation Company spoke for the aircraft industry when, in early 1942, it announced that it would not hire blacks "regardless of their training."

To combat racial barriers in hiring, **A. Philip Randolph**, leader of the powerful Brotherhood of Sleeping Car Porters union, in early 1941 proposed that African Americans march on Washington to demand equality in jobs and the armed forces. To avoid such an embarrassing demonstration, Roosevelt issued Executive Order #8802 in June 1941. The order forbid racial job discrimination by the government and companies holding government contracts and created the **Fair Employment Practices Commission** (FEPC) to promote compliance. Pushed by worsening labor shortages and prodded by the government, businesses and industries began to integrate their workforces by the end of 1942.

West Coast shipyards were among the first to integrate, but when Lockheed Aircraft broke the color barrier in August word soon spread that blacks could find work in California. More than 340,000 African Americans moved to Los Angeles. Thousands of others went north to cities such as Chicago and Detroit. As African Americans took new jobs, their wages rose from an average of $457 to $1,976 a year. But increased access to jobs and higher wages did not end discrimination and segregation. Wages for African Americans remained only 65 percent of those for white workers, and getting better jobs in many cases led to increased racial tensions. In several northern cities, white workers staged strikes to protest African Americans being hired or promoted to skilled positions. Detroit rapidly became a powder keg where, according to a federal agency examining racial tensions in the city, "all hell could break loose" and spread to other cities. It called for high-level intervention. None came, and in June 1943 a race riot erupted that lasted three days and cost thirty-four lives, most African American. The Detroit riot was the worst, but over fifty cities experienced racial violence.

Some "Double V" victories did occur, however. Membership in civil rights organizations increased as they continued to contest segregation and discrimination. The NAACP and Urban League stressed the necessity of racial cooperation; promoted the need for better housing, equal pay, and jobs; and called upon the government to integrate the military and pass legislation outlawing the poll tax and lynching. The newly formed **Congress of Racial Equality** (CORE), led by James Farmer, adopted a new tactic, the **sit-in**, to integrate public facilities. Sit-ins scored some successes in

For Aid and Comfort to the Enemy   Courtesy PM

Despite proclaimed opposition to the racial policies of the Axis nations, racism remained a serious problem in the United States with racial violence and race riots occurring across the country, many hampering war production.

some cities like Chicago and Washington but failed in the South. Supported by the NAACP, in 1944, Lonnie Smith challenged Texas's all-white primary before the Supreme Court in *Smith v. Alright* and won.

The opportunities and difficulties of African Americans in uniform paralleled those of black civilians. Prior to 1940, blacks generally served at the lowest ranks and in the most menial jobs in a segregated army and navy. The Army Air Corps and the Marine Corps refused to accept blacks at all. Most in the military openly agreed with Secretary of War Henry L. Stimson when he asserted, "Leadership is not embedded in the Negro race."

The manpower needs of war changed the role of the black soldier, opening up new ranks and

- **A. Philip Randolph** African American labor leader who organized a proposed 1941 march on Washington, which pressured Roosevelt to issue an executive order banning racial discrimination in government and defense industries, leading to cancellation of the march.

- **Fair Employment Practices Commission** (FEPC) Commission established in 1941 to halt discrimination in war production and government.

- **Congress of Racial Equality** (CORE) Civil rights organization founded and led by James Farmer in 1942 and committed to using nonviolent techniques, such as sit-ins, to end segregation.

sit-in The act of occupying seats or an area; a tactic used, for example, to protest segregation or strengthen the effect of a labor strike.

Archives of Labor and Urban Affairs/ Wayne State University.

occupations. In April 1942, Secretary of the Navy James Forrestal permitted black **noncommissioned officers** in the U.S. Navy, although blacks would wait until 1944 before becoming upper-rank officers. With only a small number of African American officers, in 1940 the army began to encourage the recruitment of black officers and promoted Benjamin O. Davis Sr. from colonel to brigadier general. His son, **Benjamin O. Davis Jr.**, was quickly promoted to lieutenant colonel and given command of the 99th Pursuit Squadron—the Tuskegee Airmen. Eventually six hundred African Americans were commissioned as pilots. The army also organized other African American units that fought in both the European and Pacific theaters of operations, such as the 371st Tank Battalion, which battled its way into Germany and liberated the concentration camps of Dachau and Buchenwald.

Higher ranks and better jobs for a few still did not disguise that for most blacks, even officers, military life was often demeaning and brutal, and almost always segregated. In Indiana, more than a hundred black officers were arrested for trying to integrate an officers' club. Across the country, blacks objected to the Red Cross practice of segregating its blood supply. German prisoners of war held in Salina, Kansas, could eat at any local lunch counter and go to any movie theater, but their black guards could not. One dismayed soldier wrote, "In Germany, they would break our bones. As 'colored' men in Salina, they only break our hearts." In truth, many black soldiers had their bones broken, and their lives taken, on the home front. As in the civilian world, blacks in the military resisted discrimination and called on Roosevelt and the government for help, but the response was, at best, limited. When the war ended, knowing that many would expect African Americans to return to their pre-war status, the writer and poet Maya Angelou knew that African Americans had survived the war, but wondered if they could make it through the peace to come.

---

noncommissioned officer Enlisted member of the armed forces who has been promoted to a rank such as corporal or sergeant, conferring leadership over others.

■ **Benjamin O. Davis Jr.** Army Air Corps officer who commanded the Tuskegee Airmen and in 1954 became the first African American general in the U.S. Air Force.

zoot suit A long jacket with wide lapels and padded shoulders, worn over pleated trousers pegged and cuffed at the ankle.

■ *braceros* (Spanish for "helping arms") Mexican nationals who worked on U.S. farms beginning in 1942 because of the labor shortage during World War II; despite guarantees, their housing was usually substandard and their wages kept low.

Latinos, too, found new opportunities during the war while encountering continued discrimination and hostility. Like other Americans, Latinos, almost invariably called "Mexicans" by their fellow soldiers, rushed to enlist as the war started. More than 300,000 Latinos served—the highest percentage of any ethnic community—and 17 won the nation's highest award for valor, the Medal of Honor. Although they faced some institutional and individual prejudices in the military, Latinos, unlike African Americans and most Nisei, served in integrated units and generally faced less discrimination in the military than in society.

For those remaining at home, more and better jobs were available, especially for women. The only jobs available for young Latinas before the war were "sewing and laundry work, hotel maids, and as domestics," recalled Felicia Ruiz, who left her beauty shop job and went to work for Lockheed.

Jobs drew Mexican Americans, like others, to cities. As Los Angeles's already large Latino population expanded, social and racial tensions escalated between Anglos and the Latino population, fanned by newspaper articles that highlighted a Mexican crime wave and characterized many young Mexican American men, who often wore **zoot suits**, as dope addicts and draft dodgers. In June 1943, Anglo mobs, including several hundred servicemen, descended on East Los Angeles. They dragged "zooters" out of movies, stores, even houses, beating them and tearing apart their clothes. When the police acted, it was to arrest the victims—over six hundred Mexican American youths were taken into "preventive custody." The riot lasted a week. Afterward, the Los Angeles city council outlawed zoot suits.

Zoot suiters were characterized as unpatriotic, but the opposite was true of most Mexican Americans. The war intensified their nationalism, their sense of being an American. "The Japanese attacked our country," wrote one Latina, and "[m]y generation went proudly to war…despite the discrimination." With young Latinos entering the military or moving to the cities for new jobs, there were significant shortages of farm workers across the Southwest. To resolve the problem, Washington turned to Mexico, negotiating the *bracero* program that allowed an average of fifty thousand Mexican workers into the country each year. The agreement stipulated that the **braceros** receive fair wages and adequate housing, transportation, food, and medical care. But guarantees mattered little. Ranchers and farmers praised the quality of *braceros'* work, but most paid low wages and provided substandard facilities. Although created to meet wartime need, the program benefited farmers, growers, and ranchers so much that it was not ended until 1964.

Jobs and higher wages were available to many American Indians during the war and lured more than forty thousand of them away from their reservations, many of whom never returned following the war. In addition, over twenty-five thousand Indians served in the military. Among the most famous were about four hundred Navajo code talkers in the Marine Corps, who used their native language as a secure means of communication. Although often called "chief," American Indians met little discrimination in the military. Whether in the armed forces or in the domestic workforce, those who left the reservations saw their families' average incomes rise from $400 a year in 1941 to $1,200 in 1945, and many chose to assimilate into American culture, abandoning their old patterns of life.

Nearly invisible in society, homosexuals also served in the military. The official policy was not to enlist them, but the screening process was ineffective, merely asking if a person was a homosexual and looking only for effeminate behavior. Once enlisted, many gays and lesbians discovered that the military generally tolerated them unless they were caught in a sexual act. In a circular letter sent to military commanders, the surgeon general's office asked that homosexual relationships be overlooked as long as they did not disrupt the unit. During the war, gays' war records were much like those of other soldiers. "I was super patriotic," said one gay combat veteran.

Wartime Politics

As the nation mobilized for war and employment soared, most remaining New Deal agencies were phased out. The congressional elections in November 1942 continued the trend started in 1938 and returned more Republicans and conservative Democrats to Congress. Undaunted by the conservative swing, Roosevelt reminded the public that steps would be needed to prevent postwar economic and social problems, and he asked Congress for a postwar economic bill of rights that included higher-wage jobs, home construction, and national medical care. Congress rejected Roosevelt's proposal but approved the Serviceman's Readjustment Act, the G.I. Bill. To ease the transition from a war to a postwar economy, the bill provided veterans with a year's unemployment compensation, economic support for education, and low-interest home loans.

As the presidential election approached, Roosevelt brushed aside concerns about his age and health and ran for a fourth term. Responding to conservatives within the party, he agreed to replace his liberal vice president, Henry Wallace, with a more conservative running mate. The convention chose Senator Harry S Truman from Missouri, aware that their choice might replace Roosevelt if he should die in office.

Republicans nominated 42-year-old Governor Thomas Dewey of New York, stressing his youth and undertaking a "whispering campaign," which hinted that Roosevelt, now 62, was ill. Unfazed, Roosevelt campaigned on the strong wartime economy, the successful war effort, and his leadership. The electoral vote favored Roosevelt overwhelmingly (432 to 99), and he received over 53 percent of the popular vote.

WAGING WORLD WAR

★ What factors did Roosevelt consider in shaping America's strategy for global conflict?

★ Why did Truman and his advisers choose to use the atomic bomb?

In the days following Pearl Harbor, many Americans wanted the defeat of Japan to be the country's first priority. To Churchill's and Stalin's relief, however, Roosevelt remained committed to victory first in Europe. But differences arose over the best strategy to defeat Hitler. The Soviets, fighting against 3.3 million Germans, called for a second front in northern Europe as soon as possible. The British considered an invasion across the English Channel into France too risky and promoted an easier and safer landing in western North Africa, Operation Torch, in 1942. Believing the people needed a victory anywhere, Roosevelt ignored opposition from his chiefs of staff and approved the operation.

As planning began for the invasion of North Africa, April and May 1942 saw the surrender of most American forces in the Philippines, and Japanese successes continued elsewhere in the Pacific. General Patrick Hurley admitted, "We were out-shipped, out-planed, out-manned, and out-gunned by the Japanese."

Halting the Japanese Advance

Despite the commitment to defeating Germany, the nation's first victory came in the Pacific on May 8, 1942, at the Battle of the Coral Sea (see Map 23.4). Having deciphered secret Japanese codes, American military planners deployed carrier forces to intercept and halt a Japanese invasion fleet aimed at New

■ **code talkers** Navajos serving in the U.S. Marine Corps who communicated by radio in their native language, undecipherable by the enemy.

■ **G.I. Bill** A 1944 law to provide financial and educational benefits for American veterans after World War II; *G.I.* stands for "government issue."

■ **Harry S Truman** Democratic senator from Missouri whom Roosevelt selected in 1944 to be his running mate for vice president; in 1945, on Roosevelt's death, Truman became president.

Guinea. Soon after the Coral Sea success, again reading top-secret Japanese messages, the United States learned of a Japanese aircraft carrier group advancing on **Midway Island**.

The Battle of Midway, June 4–6, 1942, helped change the course of the war in the Pacific. The air-to-sea battle was several hours old when a flight of American dive-bombers attacked the Japanese carriers in the middle of rearming and refueling their planes. Their decks cluttered with planes, fuel, and bombs, the Japanese carriers suffered staggering casualties and damage. Three immediately sank, and a fourth went down later in the battle. Although the Americans lost the U.S.S. *Yorktown*, they had destroyed the carrier-based air superiority of the Japanese. In the war of machines, the United States quickly replaced the *Yorktown* and by the end of the war had constructed fourteen additional large carriers, whereas Japan was able to build only six.

The next step in the Pacific was to begin an island-hopping campaign intended, eventually, to close in on Japan. **General Douglas MacArthur** and the army would advance toward the Philippines from the south. The navy and marines, under the direction of Admiral Chester Nimitz, would seize selected islands and atolls in the Solomon, Marshall, Gilbert, and Mariana island groups, approaching the Philippines from the east (see Map 23.4). Both forces would join for the final attack on Japan. On August 7, 1942, soldiers of the 1st Marine Division waded ashore on **Guadalcanal Island** in the Solomons. Japan, considering the invasion to be "the fork in the road that leads to victory for them or for us," furiously defended the island. Both sides suffered significant losses in the horrendous face-to-face combat that characterized the war in the Pacific. After heavy losses, the Japanese withdrew in early February.

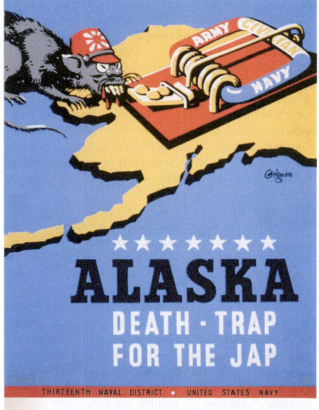

ALASKA
DEATH · TRAP
FOR THE JAP

THIRTEENTH NAVAL DISTRICT · UNITED STATES NAVY

Library of Congress Prints And Photographs Division.

War posters often used exaggerated racial and ethnic stereotypes to show the enemy in the worst possible light. In this American poster the Japanese are depicted as rats—Japanese as monkeys was also a common form. The Japanese posters frequently showed Franklin D. Roosevelt as a horned demon, accompanied by an equally demonic Churchill.

Roads to Berlin

While American marines sweated in the jungles of Guadalcanal, British and American armies closed in on German forces in North Africa. With the British driving the Germans from Egypt westward, American troops landed in Morocco in November 1942 and pushed eastward. In early May 1943, the Americans linked up with the British, forcing 300,000 German troops to surrender (see Map 23.5).

German losses in North Africa were light compared with those in Russia, where Soviet and German forces were locked in a titanic struggle. Through the summer and fall of 1942, German armies advanced steadily, but the Soviet army, led by General G. K. Zhukov, counterattacked in the dead of winter and trapped them at Stalingrad where, on February 2, 1943, 300,000 German soldiers surrendered. Both sides had taken staggering losses.

Although it was hard to predict in February, the tide of the war had turned in Europe. Soviet forces would continue to grind down the German army all the way to Berlin (see Map 23.5). But in February, Stalin knew only that the **Battle of Stalingrad** had

■ **Midway Island** Strategically located Pacific island that the Japanese navy tried to capture in June 1942; warned about Japanese plans by U.S. naval intelligence, American forces repulsed the attack and inflicted heavy losses on Japanese planes and carriers.

■ **General Douglas MacArthur** Commander of American and Filipino troops in the Philippines when Japan took the islands in 1942, he led the forces that retook the islands in 1944; in 1945, as Supreme Commander for the Allied Powers, he accepted Japan's formal surrender and subsequently oversaw the rebuilding of Japan.

■ **Guadalcanal Island** Pacific island secured by U.S. troops in February 1943, starting the process of taking strategic islands to close the circle on Japan.

■ **Battle of Stalingrad** Battle for the Russian city that was besieged by the German army in 1942 and recaptured by Soviet troops in 1943; regarded by many as the key battle of the European war.

MAP 23.4 Closing the Circle on Japan, 1942–1945
Following the Battle of Midway, American forces began the costly process of island-hopping with the invasion of Guadalcanal (August 1942). This map shows the paths of the American campaign in the Pacific, closing the circle on Japan. After atomic bombs destroyed Hiroshima and Nagasaki and the Soviet Union entered the war, Japan surrendered on August 14, 1945. © Cengage Learning.

cost the Russians dearly and that German strength was still formidable. He again demanded a second front in Western Europe. Again, he would be disappointed. Meeting with Churchill at Casablanca (January 1943), Roosevelt agreed with the British leader to invade Sicily and Italy, targets that Churchill called the "soft underbelly of the Axis." General Albert Wedemeyer expressed the U.S. military reaction to the Casablanca deal: "We lost our shirts...we came, we listened, and we were conquered."

The invasion of Sicily—Operation Husky—took place in early July 1943, and within a month the Allies controlled the island. In response, the Italians overthrew Mussolini and opened negotiations with Britain and the United States to change sides. Italy surrendered unconditionally on September 8. Immediately, German forces assumed the defense of Italy and halted the Allied advance just north of Salerno. Not until late May 1944 did Allied forces finally break through the German defenses in southern Italy, entering Rome on June 4. Two days later, the world's attention turned toward Normandy along the west coast of France. The second front demanded by Stalin had, at long last, begun (see Map 23.5).

ullstein bild / The Granger Collection, NYC. — All rights reserved.

Regarded by many as the turning point of the war in Europe, the Battle of Stalingrad lasted from July 1942 to February 1943, with much of the most brutal fighting occurring in the streets of the city during October and November 1942. Here Soviet soldiers battle in the ruins of the city in October. When German forces finally surrendered in January and February, Hitler said: "The God of War" has gone over to the other side.

The invasion of Normandy, France—**Operation Overlord**—was the grandest **amphibious** assault ever assembled: 6,483 ships, 1,500 tanks, and 200,000 men. Opposing the Allies were thousands of German troops behind the Atlantic Wall they had constructed along the coast. On D-Day, June 6, 1944, American forces landed on Utah and Omaha Beaches, while British and Canadian forces hit Sword, Gold, and Juno Beaches. At the landing sites, German resistance varied: the fiercest fighting was at Omaha Beach.

After a week of attacks and counterattacks, the five beaches were linked, and the Allied forces attacked the German positions blocking the roads to the rest of France. On July 25, American soldiers broke through at Saint-Lô. Paris was liberated on August 25, and in October, the Allies reached the west side of the Rhine River. From November 1944 to March 1945, American forces readied themselves to attack across the river.

■ **Operation Overlord** The Allied invasion of Europe on June 6, 1944—D-Day—across the English Channel to Normandy; D-Day is short for "designated day."

amphibious In historical context, a military operation that coordinates air, land, and sea military forces to land on a hostile shore.

At the same time, Allied bombers and fighter-bombers continued to bomb German-held Europe night and day. They destroyed vital industries and transportation systems as well as German cities. In one of the worst raids, during the night of February 13, 1945, three flights of British and American bombers set Dresden aflame, creating a firestorm that killed more than 135,000 civilians. Nearly 600,000 German civilians would die in Allied air raids, with another 800,000 injured.

With his cities being destroyed from the air and his forces crumbling in the east, Hitler approved a last-ditch attempt to halt the Allied advance in the west. On December 16 German troops launched an attack through the Ardennes Forest designed to split American forces. It created a 50-mile "bulge" in the Allied lines. At Bastogne, a critical crossroads within the bulge, American soldiers hung on. When asked to surrender, General A. C. McAuliffe simply told the Germans, "Nuts." After ten exhausting days, the German offensive slowed and was driven back. The Battle of the Bulge (see Map 23.5 inset) was the last major Axis counteroffensive on the western front. In March 1945, British and American forces crossed the Rhine and battled eastward. At the same time, Soviet forces began the bloody, house-to-house conquest of Berlin. On April 25, American and Soviet infantrymen shook hands at the Elbe River 60 miles south of Berlin.

MAP 23.5 The Fall of the Third Reich
In 1943 and 1944, the war turned in favor of the Allies. On the eastern front, Soviet forces drove the Germans back toward Germany. On June 6, 1944, D-Day, British, Canadian, and American forces landed on the coast of Normandy to begin the liberation of France. This map shows the course of the Allied armies as they fought their way toward Berlin. On May 7, 1945, Germany surrendered. © Cengage Learning.

Inside the city, Hitler committed suicide on April 30 and had aides burn his body. On May 8, 1945, German officials surrendered. The war in Europe was over.

Stresses in the Grand Alliance

As the Soviets pushed toward Berlin, they liberated parts of Poland, Romania, Bulgaria, Hungary, and Czechoslovakia. Soviet officials and Eastern European Communists followed the Red Army with the goal of establishing new Eastern European governments "friendly" to the Soviet Union. A Communist government (installed at the town of Lublin) was established in Poland, while in Romania and Bulgaria "**popular front**" governments, heavily influenced by local Communist Party members, took command. Only Czechoslovakia and Hungary managed to establish

non–Communist-dominated governments as the German occupation collapsed.

On February 4, 1945, the leaders of the Grand Alliance, met at the Black Sea resort of **Yalta** amid growing Western apprehension about Soviet goals in Eastern Europe. Confident that he could work with

popular front An organization or government composed of a wide spectrum of political groups; popular fronts were used by the Soviet Union in forming allegedly non-Communist governments in Eastern Europe.

■ **Yalta** Site in the Crimea of the last meeting, in 1945, between Roosevelt, Churchill, and Stalin; they discussed the final defeat of the Axis powers and the problems of postwar occupation. Among the most important issues were the Polish government, German reparations, and the formation of the United Nations.

As Allied armies fought their way closer to Berlin, Roosevelt, Churchill, and Stalin met at the Black Sea resort of Yalta in February 1945 to discuss military strategy and postwar concerns. Two months later, Roosevelt died and Harry S Truman assumed the presidency.

National Archives.

Stalin, Roosevelt wanted to ensure that the Soviet Union would enter the war against Japan and support a new United Nations. He also wanted the Soviets to show some willingness to modify their controls over Eastern Europe. Stalin's goals were Western acceptance of a Soviet sphere of influence in Eastern Europe, the weakening of Germany, and the economic restoration of the Soviet Union.

Central to Allied differences over Eastern Europe was the Lublin government in Poland, which Roosevelt and Churchill considered an undemocratic puppet of the Soviet Union. They instead supported a London-based government in exile, which Stalin viewed as hostile. After acidic haggling, the powers compromised in language so vague that Admiral William Leahy, one of Roosevelt's primary advisers, ruefully noted that the compromise could be "stretched from Yalta to Washington" without breaking. The crux was acceptance of the Lublin regime if

it were enlarged with non-Communist members. The Soviets retained eastern Poland, seized during their invasion in 1939. The agreement left Eastern Europe under Soviet control and hardly applied the ideals of the Atlantic Charter, but Roosevelt realized that little could be done to prevent the Soviet Union from keeping what it already had, or could easily take. Still Roosevelt had achieved two of his major goals: Stalin agreed to maintain Soviet support in defeating Japan and engage in a new world organization.

Roosevelt returned from Yalta exhausted and in rapidly failing health. As the 63-year-old president relaxed at Warm Springs, Georgia, a cerebral hemorrhage ended his life on April 12, 1944. Long-time political opponent Senator Robert Taft spoke for the nation: "He dies a hero of the war, for he literally worked himself to death in the service of the American people." Truman, a man few knew much about, was now president and determined to continue Roosevelt's road to victory.

The Holocaust

As Allied forces advanced into Germany, the world realized the full horror of the **Holocaust**. In 1941 the Nazi political leadership had ordered what it called the **Final Solution** to rid German-occupied Europe of Jews. In concentration camps Jews, along

■ **Holocaust** Mass murder of European Jews and other groups systematically carried out by the Nazis during World War II.

■ **Final Solution** German plan to eliminate Jews through the use of special mobile execution forces or by mass executions within concentration camps; by the end of the war, the Nazis had killed 6 million Jews.

Hitler ordered the "Final Solution"—the extermination of Europe's Jews—soon after the United States entered the war. In this picture, German troops arrest residents of the Warsaw ghetto for deportation to concentration camps. Few would survive the camps, where over 6 million Jews died.

Imagno/Getty Images.

with homosexuals, gypsies, and those with mental illnesses, were brutalized, starved, worked as slave labor, and systematically exterminated. At Auschwitz, Nazis used gas chambers—disguised as showers—to execute twelve thousand victims a day.

Reports about the camps had circulated even before the war, but Western governments and the press did little to expose or prevent the atrocities. Roosevelt, like other leaders, did not see a personal, political, diplomatic, or military need to make Holocaust information widely known; and he did not give the plight of the Jews or other refugees a high priority. Only in January 1944 did Roosevelt establish a **War Refugee Board**.

As British, American, and Soviet troops liberated the camps, reporters and photographers recorded the reality of the horrors there. Among the American units freeing Jewish survivors at Buchenwald and Dachau were the African American 761st Tank Battalion and the Japanese American 522nd Field Artillery Battalion. One survivor at first thought that the Japanese had won the war, until realizing the soldiers were Americans. "I had never seen black men or Japanese," another recalled. "They were riding in these tanks and jeeps; they were like angels who came down from heaven to save our lives." While thousands were saved, over 6 million Jews, nearly two-thirds of pre-war Europe's Jewish population, were slaughtered in the death camps.

Closing the Circle on Japan

On May 8, 1945, V-E Day—celebrating victory in Europe—touched off parades and rejoicing in the United States. But Japan still had to be defeated.

Japan's defensive strategy was simple: force the United States to pay dearly in lives and materials to secure each island invaded.

Throughout 1943, U.S. forces continued to advance toward the Philippines from the south, seizing the most strategic islands and isolating others. At the same time, far to the northeast, the U.S. Navy and the Marine Corps were establishing footholds in the Gilbert and Marshall Islands. Exemplifying the bitter fighting was "Bloody Tarawa," where in November 1943 marines overcame five thousand well-entrenched Japanese troops, nearly all of whom fought to the death. The marines suffered nearly three thousand casualties. The Mariana Islands were next (see Map 23.4 on page 653). In the battle for Saipan, the Japanese lost 243 planes and three more aircraft carriers, while nearly thirty-two thousand Japanese defenders fought to the death. Especially shocking to American troops, nearly two-thirds of the island's Japanese civilians, mostly women and children, committed suicide. By late summer of 1944, though, the southern and eastern approaches to the Philippines were in American hands.

From island bases, long-range bombers, the B-29s, began to hit military and domestic targets in Japan in February 1944. Although intended to weaken the Japanese will to resist, devastating raids against Japanese cities did little to reduce Japanese citizens' support for the war or the government, although

War Refugee Board Group belatedly created in early 1944 to rescue as many persecuted minorities of Europe as possible from Nazi oppression.

The Japanese used an estimated 2,800 kamikaze aircraft against Allied naval ships in the last months of the war, sinking 34 American ships. Here a kamikaze crashes onto the flight deck of the USS Saratoga during the battle for Iwo Jima, February 21, 1945.

Photo by Mondadori Portfolio via Getty Images.

estimated civilian deaths far exceeded the number of Japanese soldiers killed in combat.

In October 1944, American forces landed on Leyte in the center of the Philippine archipelago. The Japanese navy moved to halt the invasion, and in the largest naval battle in history, the **Battle of Leyte Gulf** (October 23–25, 1944), American forces shattered what remained of Japanese air and sea power.

After the Battle of Leyte Gulf, the full brunt of the American Pacific offensive bore down on Iwo Jima and Okinawa, only 750 miles from Tokyo. To defend the islands, Japan made large-scale use of the *kamikaze* attack—in which pilots made suicide crashes on targets in explosive-laden airplanes. The American assault on Iwo Jima began on February 19, 1945, and before it ended on March 17, virtually all of the 21,000 Japanese defenders had fought to the death, and American losses approached one-third of the landing force: 6,821 dead and 20,000 wounded.

On Okinawa, from April through June, the carnage was even worse. While American forces took heavy losses along Japanese defensive lines, Japanese planes and *kamikazes* rained terror and destruction on the American fleet. But Japan soon began to run out of planes and pilots. By the end of June, Okinawa was in American hands, but at a fearful price: 12,000 Americans, 110,000 Japanese soldiers, and 160,000 Okinawan and Japanese civilians dead.

■ **Battle of Leyte Gulf** Naval battle in October 1944 in which American forces near the Philippines crushed remaining Japanese air and sea power.

Entering the Nuclear Age

The experience of Okinawa indicated that any invasion of Japan would result in large numbers of American casualties. But by the summer of 1945, the United States had a possible alternative to invasion: a new and untried weapon—the atomic bomb. The A-bomb was the product of years of British-American research and development in the Manhattan Project. From the beginning of the conflict, science had developed and improved the tools of combat, providing radar and sonar technologies, flamethrowers, rockets, and a variety of other useful and frequently deadly products. But the most fearsome and secret of the projects was the drive started in 1941 to construct a nuclear weapon. Between then and 1945, the Manhattan Project scientists, led by physicists J. Robert Oppenheimer and Edward Teller, controlled a chain reaction involving uranium and plutonium to create the atomic bomb.

By the time Germany surrendered, the project had consumed more than $2 billion, but the bomb was born. When it was tested at Alamogordo, New Mexico, on July 16, 1945, the results were spectacular. In the words of Brigadier General Leslie R. Groves, the U.S. Army engineer who headed the project: "The effect could well be called unprecedented, magnificent, beautiful, stupendous and terrifying. . . . The whole country was lighted by a searing light. . . . Thirty seconds after the explosion came . . . the air blast . . . followed almost immediately by the strong, sustained, awesome roar which warned of doomsday." Word of the successful test was quickly relayed to Truman, who at the time was meeting with Churchill and Stalin at Potsdam, outside Berlin.

Choosing Targets for the Atomic Bomb

In mid-July 1945 President Truman approved dropping the atomic bomb on Japanese cities. Consequently on August 6 and 9, 1945, the cities of Hiroshima and Nagasaki were obliterated and thousands of people died. What made those cities targets? To help answer this question, historians, many years after the event, have examined the once highly classified records of those making the decisions to see what criteria they used.

The targeting process began in April, when a Targeting Committee reviewed seventeen potential targets and cut the number to five: Kyoto, Hiroshima, Yokohama, Kokura, and Niigata. The committee were guided by the criteria that the target:

- Be a "dual target" with some military importance but also "with homes and other buildings most susceptible to damage."
- Be the right size—a "large urban area of more than three miles in diameter" either undamaged or largely undamaged prior to the attack.
- Be "capable of being damaged effectively by the blast" and, for psychological reasons, that the damage be "sufficiently spectacular" to impress the Japanese government and the international community about "the importance of the weapon."

An evaluation followed:

- Kyoto "had a population of 100,000" and as a religious and "intellectual center" provided good psychological value; but it had little military importance and, as Japan's former capital, contained several valuable religious and historical sites.
- Hiroshima had "an important army depot . . . in the middle of an urban industrial area," and was the proper size as "a large part of the city could be extensively damaged" because its "adjacent hills" created "a focusing effect which would considerably increase the blast damage."
- Yokohama was "an important urban industrial area," but had the "disadvantage of the most important target areas being separated by a large body of water and . . . heaviest anti-aircraft concentration in Japan."
- Kokura contained "one of the largest arsenals in Japan . . . surrounded by urban industrial structures," but precise placement of the bomb was necessary to gain the maximum destructive results.
- Niigata, a smaller city, was an important port, contained war industries, and was largely untouched by bombing.

Yokohama, Kyoto, and Niigata were eliminated. Yokohama was too difficult a target and Kyoto's destruction might cause too much "bitterness" among the Japanese. Although its geography limited the destructive power of the bomb, Nagasaki, "a major shipping and industrial center," with a significant population, replaced Niigata. By August 3 a final list made Hiroshima the first target, followed by Kokura and Nagasaki. On August 9 at the last moment, Nagasaki became the second target because of cloud cover over Kokura.

Based on what you know from the chapter, how would you assess the criteria and decision-making process of the Targeting Committee? How well did the results match the committee's expectations?

Photo by Robert W.Clearny

On August 6, 1945, the world entered the atomic age when the city of Hiroshima was destroyed by an atomic bomb. "We had seen the city when we went in," said the pilot of the *Enola Gay*, "and there was nothing to see when we came back."

COUNTRY	DEAD
Soviet Union	8.6 million
China	1.3 million
Poland	130 thousand
Germany	3.6 million
Japan	1.75 million
Britain and Commonwealth	384 thousand
United States	292 thousand

FIGURE 23.3 **Military War Dead** © Cengage Learning.

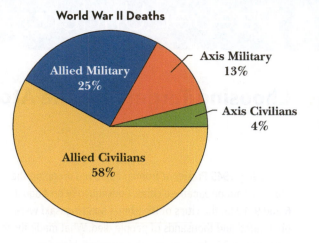

World War II Deaths

Allied Military 25%

Axis Military 13%

Axis Civilians 4%

Allied Civilians 58%

Before leaving for Potsdam, Truman had decided not to tell Stalin any details about the atomic bomb and to use the atomic bomb as soon as possible against Japan. Using the bomb, he hoped, would serve two purposes. It would force Japan to surrender without an invasion, and it would impress the Soviets and, just maybe, make them more amenable to American views on the postwar world order.

Soon after his arrival for the Potsdam Conference (July–August 1945), Truman obtained confirmation that the Soviet Union would enter the Japanese war in mid-August, so he decided to inform Stalin about a new and powerful weapon to use against Japan. Stalin, who knew from spies that it was an atomic bomb, appeared unimpressed and told Truman to go ahead and use it. Working with Prime Minister Clement Attlee of Britain (who was told of the atomic bomb), Truman released the **Potsdam Declaration**, which called on Japan to surrender by August or face total destruction.

The declaration reflected two developments—one Japan knew about, and the other it was soon to learn. Japanese officials had asked the "neutral" Soviets to try to persuade the Americans to consider negotiating a Japanese surrender. Stalin, Attlee, and Truman agreed instead to insist on unconditional surrender. In the Potsdam Declaration, the Japanese could read the rejection of their overture, but they had no way of knowing that "utter destruction" referred to the A-bomb. On July 25, Truman ordered the use of the atomic bomb as soon after August 3 as possible, provided the Japanese did not surrender.

■ **Potsdam Declaration** The demand for Japan's unconditional surrender, made near the end of the Potsdam Conference.

■ **Hiroshima and Nagasaki** Hiroshima was the target, on August 6, 1945, of the first atomic bomb, called "Little Boy"; the second, "Fat Man," devastated Nagasaki on August 9.

Flying from the island of Tinian, a B-29 bomber named the *Enola Gay* dropped the first of two available bombs over **Hiroshima** at 9:15 A.M. on August 6, 1945. Japan's eighth-largest city, Hiroshima had a population of over 250,000 and to that point had not suffered heavy bombing. In the atomic blast and fireball, almost 100,000 Japanese were killed or terribly maimed. Another 100,000 would eventually die from the effects of radiation. The United States announced that unless the Japanese surrendered immediately, they could "expect a rain of ruin from the air, the like of which has never been seen on this earth."

As Tokyo contemplated surrender, on August 8 the Soviets declared war and advanced into Japanese-held Manchuria. The next day a second atomic bomb destroyed **Nagasaki**. Nearly sixty thousand people were killed. Although some within the Japanese army argued for continuing the fight, Emperor Hirohito made the final decision. Japan must "bear the unbearable," he said, and surrender. On August 14, 1945, Japan officially surrendered, and the United States agreed to leave the position of emperor intact.

World War II was over, but much of the world lay in ruins. Some 50 million people, military and civilian, had been killed (see Figure 23.3). The United States was spared most of the destruction. It had suffered almost no civilian casualties, and its cities and industrial centers stood unharmed. In many ways, in fact, the war had been good to the United States. It had decisively ended the Depression, and although some economists predicted an immediate postwar recession, the overall economic picture was bright. Government regulation and planning for the economy that had their beginnings in the New Deal took root and flourished during the war. As the war ended, only a few wanted a return to the laissez-faire-style government that had characterized the 1920s. Big government was here to stay, and at the center of big government was a powerful presidency ready to direct and guide the nation.

Individual Voices

JUSTICE HUGO BLACK

Explains the Majority View in *Korematsu v. United States*

Japanese American Fred Korematsu did not report for internment and was arrested in May 1942 and sentenced to five years' probation. While at the Topaz Relocation Center, with the aid of the American Civil Liberties Union, he unsuccessfully appealed his conviction to the Supreme Court. In December 1944, in a split decision, the Court upheld his conviction. Justice Hugo Black, writing for the majority, found that the needs of war can abridge the rights of citizenship. Black's written majority opinion provides historians with insights into what the Court was thinking, but his arguments also reveal, and attempt to counter, ways in which some Americans might have disagreed. In 1998, President Clinton awarded Korematsu a Presidential Medal of Freedom.

1 How does Minoru Kiyota match Justice Black's definition of disloyal? In what way was Fred Korematsu disloyal?

2 Under what criteria did Justice Black dismiss race as a basis of the decision being contested by Korematsu?

3 What reasons does Justice Black use to prevent the use of hindsight? What does this view suggest about the Court's ability to reverse past decisions made by the government?

4 Why is the *Korematsu* decision important in defining limitations on civil rights and rights found in the Bill of Rights?

It should be noted . . . all legal restrictions which curtail the civil rights of a single racial group are immediately suspect. That is not to say that all such restrictions are unconstitutional0. . . . Pressing public necessity may sometimes justify the existence of such restrictions. . . .

Exclusion of those of Japanese origin was deemed necessary because of the presence of . . . disloyal members of the group, most of whom we have no doubt were loyal to this country. . . . we could not reject the finding . . . that it was impossible to . . . [segregate] the disloyal from the loyal that we sustained the validity of the curfew order. . . . That there were members of the group who retained loyalties in Japan has been confirmed. . . . Approximately five thousand American citizens of Japanese ancestry refused to swear unqualified allegiance to the United States and to renounce allegiance to the Japanese Emperor. . . . **1**

We . . . are not unmindful of the hardships imposed. . . . But hardships are part of war. . . . Compulsory exclusion of large groups of citizens from their homes . . . is inconsistent with our basic governmental institutions. But when under conditions of modern warfare our shores are threatened by hostile forces, the power to protect must be commensurate with the threatened danger. . . .

It is said [this is a] . . . case of imprisonment of a citizen . . . solely because of his ancestry, without evidence or inquiry concerning his loyalty and good disposition towards the United States. . . . To cast this case into outlines of racial prejudice, without reference to the real military dangers which were presented, merely confuses the issue. Korematsu was not excluded from the Military Area because of . . . his race. He was excluded because we are at war with the Japanese Empire, because the properly constituted military authorities feared an invasion of our West Coast and felt constrained to take proper security measures, because they decided that the military urgency of the situation demanded that all citizens of Japanese ancestry be segregated from the West Coast. . . . **2** There was evidence of disloyalty . . . the military authorities considered that the need for action was great, and time was short. We cannot—by availing ourselves of the calm perspective of hindsight **3** —now say that at that time these actions were unjustified. **4**

Study Tools

SUMMARY

In 1929 Hoover believed that he would preside over a world at peace. But he and Roosevelt faced the collapse of the international system as Japan, Italy, and Germany increased their territories, influence, and power. Japan seized Manchuria and later invaded China, while Mussolini conquered Ethiopia, and Hitler created a new German empire. In the lengthening shadow of world conflict, the majority of Americans remained isolationist, and Congress passed neutrality laws designed to keep the nation from involvement in the faraway conflicts. Even as Germany invaded Poland in 1939, most Americans were still anxious to remain outside the conflict. Roosevelt, however, chose to help those fighting Germany, linking the United States' economic might first to England and then to the Soviet Union.

Roosevelt also used economic and diplomatic pressures to halt Japan's expansion. But the pressure only heightened the crisis, convincing many in the Japanese government that the best choice was to attack the United States before it grew in strength. Japan's attack on Pearl Harbor on December 7, 1941, brought a fully committed American public and government into World War II.

Mobilizing the nation for war ended the Depression and increased government intervention in the economy. Another outcome of the war was a range of new choices for Americans in the military and the workplace. Japanese Americans, however, suffered a loss of freedom and property as the government placed them in internment camps.

CHRONOLOGY
A World at War

1929	Herbert Hoover becomes president
1931	Japan seizes Manchuria
1933	Franklin D. Roosevelt becomes president
	Hitler and Nazi Party take power in Germany
1934	Fulgencio Batista assumes power in Cuba
1935	First Neutrality Act
	Italy invades Ethiopia
1936	Germany reoccupies the Rhineland
	Italy annexes Ethiopia
	Spanish Civil War begins
1937	Sino-Japanese War begins
1938	Germany annexes Austria and Sudetenland
	Munich Conference
1939	German-Soviet Nonaggression Pact
	Germany invades Poland; Britain and France declare war on Germany
	Neutrality Act of 1939
1940	U.S. economic sanctions against Japan
	Burke-Wadsworth Act (military draft)
	Destroyers-for-bases agreement
	Roosevelt reelected
1941	Lend-Lease Act
	Fair Employment Practices Commission created
	Germany invades Soviet Union
	Atlantic Charter
	U-boats attack U.S. warships
	Japan attacks Pearl Harbor; United States enters World War II
1942	War Production Board created
	Japanese conquer Philippines
	Japanese Americans interned
	Battles of Coral Sea and Midway
	Congress of Racial Equality founded
	U.S. troops invade North Africa
1943	U.S. forces capture Guadalcanal
	Soviets defeat Germans at Stalingrad
	Detroit race riot
	U.S. and British forces invade Sicily and Italy; Italy surrenders
1944	Operation Overlord—June 6 invasion of Normandy
	G.I. Bill becomes law
	U.S. forces invade the Philippines
	Roosevelt reelected
	Soviet forces liberate Eastern Europe
	Battle of the Bulge
1945	Yalta Conference
	Roosevelt dies; Harry S Truman becomes president
	United Nations created
	Germany surrenders; Potsdam Conference
	United States drops atomic bombs on Japan
	Japan surrenders

Fighting a two-front war, American planners gave first priority to defeating Hitler. The effort began in North Africa in 1942, expanded to Italy in 1943, and to France in 1944. By the beginning of 1945, Allied armies closed in on Nazi Germany from the west and the east, and on May 8, 1945, Germany surrendered. In the Pacific theater, the victory at Midway in mid-1942 checked Japan's offensive and allowed the use of aircraft carriers to begin tightening the noose around the enemy. To bring the war to a close without a U.S. invasion, Truman elected to use the atomic bomb. Following the destruction of Hiroshima and Nagasaki, Japan surrendered on August 14, 1945, ending the war and for many Americans ushering in "America's century."

FOCUS QUESTIONS

If you have mastered this chapter, you should be able to answer these questions and to identify the terms that follow the questions.

1. *How were Roosevelt's policies toward Latin America a continuation of Hoover's?*

2. *What obstacles did Roosevelt face in trying to implement a more assertive foreign policy from 1935 to 1939?*

3. *Following the outbreak of World War II in 1939, how did Roosevelt reshape American neutrality?*

4. *What actions did Roosevelt take to mobilize the nation for war and how did they affect the relationship between business and government?*

5. *What new social and economic choices did Americans confront during the war? How were different groups affected?*

6. *What factors did Roosevelt consider in shaping America's strategy for global conflict?*

7. *Why did Truman and his advisers choose to use the atomic bomb?*

KEY TERMS

Greater East Asian Co-Prosperity Sphere *p. 634*
Good Neighbor policy *p. 634*
Colonel Fulgencio Batista *p. 634*
fascist *p. 634*
Neutrality Act of 1935 *p. 635*
Munich Agreement *p. 636*
German-Soviet Nonaggression Pact *p. 636*
Neutrality Act of 1939 *p. 638*
Axis powers *p. 638*
Burke-Wadsworth Act *p. 639*
Lend-Lease Act *p. 639*

Atlantic Charter *p. 640*
Executive Order #9066 *p. 642*
internment camps *p. 642*
Manhattan Project *p. 645*
victory garden *p. 647*
Rosie the Riveter *p. 647*
A. Philip Randolph *p. 649*
Fair Employment Practices Commission *p. 649*
Congress of Racial Equality *p. 649*
Benjamin O. Davis Jr. *p. 650*
braceros *p. 650*
code talkers *p. 651*

G.I. Bill *p. 651*
Harry S Truman *p. 651*
Midway Island *p. 652*
General Douglas MacArthur *p. 652*
Guadalcanal Island *p. 652*
Battle of Stalingrad *p. 652*
Operation Overlord *p. 654*
Yalta *p. 655*
Holocaust *p. 656*
Final Solution *p. 656*
Battle of Leyte Gulf *p. 658*
Potsdam Declaration *p. 660*
Hiroshima and Nagasaki *p. 660*

SUGGESTED RESOURCES

Simon Berthon and Joanna Potts. *Warlords* (Da Capo Press, 2006). A lively examination of the character, policies, and interactions between Roosevelt, Churchill, Stalin, and Hitler.

William O'Neill. *A Democracy at War* (Harvard University Press, 1993). A well-researched account of the United States during World War II with excellent chapters on the home front.

Smithsonian Institution. "The Price of Freedom: Americans at War," http://amhistory.si.edu/militaryhistory/collection. A collection of materials and information dealing with military history during World War II:

United States Holocaust Memorial Museum. http://www.ushmm.org. A website focusing on Holocaust studies with interesting and meaningful online exhibits and collections of archival materials.

Emily Yellin. *Our Mother's War: American Women and the Home Front During World War II* (Free Press, 2004). An often moving account of the daily lives and challenges of American women during the war, their hopes and realities, their trials and triumphs.

24

Truman and Cold War America, 1945–1952

CHAPTER OUTLINE

The Cold War Begins
Truman and Paths to Peace
The Division of Europe
The U.S. Presence in Latin America and the Middle East

The Cold War in Asia
The Chinese Civil War
Halting Communist Aggression in Korea
Seeking to Liberate North Korea

Postwar Politics
Truman and Liberalism
The 1948 Election

Cold War Politics
The Red Scare
Joseph McCarthy and the Politics of Loyalty

Homecoming and Social Adjustments
Rising Expectations
From Industrial Worker to Homemaker
Latinos and African Americans: Restrained Expectations

INDIVIDUAL VOICES: The Sporting News *Editorializes on African Americans in Baseball*

Study Tools

INDIVIDUAL CHOICES

Jackie Robinson

In high school and college Jackie Robinson proved he was a gifted athlete, but few would have thought those gifts would contribute to one of the most important choices in American sports. As this chapter's Individual Voices feature illustrates, great controversy surrounded the idea of African Americans playing in baseball's white major leagues. In 1945, Branch Rickey, the president and general manager of the Brooklyn Dodgers, asked Robinson if he was "the right man" to play baseball in the Dodgers' system—to integrate major league baseball. Rickey wanted to know whether Robinson could take abuse, be someone "with guts enough not to fight back." Robinson said he could "turn the other cheek," and the deal was set. Robinson would get $600 a month to play with the Montreal Royals, a Dodgers farm team.

At Muir Technical High School, Pasadena Junior College, and the University of California at Los Angeles, Robinson excelled in athletics—lettering in four sports: track, baseball, football,

MLB Photos/Getty Images.

and basketball. In 1941, he was drafted into the army and applied to Officer Training Corps, which was accepting applications from African Americans for the first time. He completed training in 1943, received a commission as second lieutenant, and was assigned to a segregated tank regiment. Robinson never deployed to Europe or saw combat. Involvement in an alleged racial incident and charges of insubordination resulted in a court martial that kept him stateside. Acquitted, Robinson was honorably discharged from the army in November 1944. He played professional baseball with the Kansas City Monarchs of the Negro League until he went to Montreal in 1945.

With Montreal, Robinson quickly experienced the racial hostility Rickey had predicted. The club held spring training in Florida, where he could not room at the team hotel, and some local officials cancelled games rather than let him play on their field. Robinson survived, and during the regular season led the Royals' minor league in batting and was 1946's most valuable player. The following year, he would play in the majors for the Dodgers.

On April 15, 1947, Robinson became the first African American player in major league baseball since the 1890s. He immediately faced racial tensions within the clubhouse and on the field. Team manager Leo Durocher made his views clear: "I do not care if the guy is yellow or black, or if he has stripes like a . . . zebra . . . I say he plays. What's more, I say he can make us all rich. And if any of you cannot use the money, I will see that you are all traded." When players threatened to strike rather than play against Robinson, the commissioner of baseball vowed to suspend them. These actions kept Robinson in the games but did not stop the verbal and physical abuse he received on and off the field. Robinson responded with his bat, fielding, and base-running, earning the Rookie of the Year title. The integration of major league baseball was history. Robinson played ten seasons with the Dodgers before retiring. He entered the Baseball Hall of Fame in 1962.

When World War II ended, Americans expected to return to a normal life, living in peace while they enjoyed the benefits of a consumer society. Many found jobs that allowed them to move to the suburbs and live the "American Dream." But world peace proved more elusive. By 1947, the United States and the Soviet Union were locked in a Cold War. Washington's policy was to contain Soviet power, first in Western Europe and then in Asia. When North Korea invaded South Korea, the Cold War suddenly became "hot," as President Truman committed American troops to halt Communist aggression.

The Cold War affected every aspect of American life. The growing fear of communism provided many with ammunition to attack ideas, institutions, and people they believed were too liberal. Conservatives and businesspeople asserted that unions had become too powerful—they needed to be restrained and purged of their Communist members. Southern whites charged that civil rights advocates were tainted with socialistic values. Across the nation, change and diversity were increasingly suspect. Spearheading America's defense against the dangers of communism were the House Un-American Activities Committee (HUAC) and Republican Senator Joseph McCarthy. Both claimed that American institutions were rife with disloyal Americans.

The expanding Cold War also made it more difficult for Truman to introduce or expand on New Deal–style programs. Truman had to accept the "politics of the possible," a moderate agenda that pleased neither ardent liberals nor staunch conservatives.

Despite growing concerns about communism, the majority of Americans looked forward to transitioning to a normal life. The G.I. Bill provided veterans a means to reenter civilian life with new opportunities. Those who had found new opportunities during the war, however, were expected to relinquish their wartime gains and return to their customary roles in American society. Still, a sense of optimism prevailed. The skills, experiences, and self-confidence gained during the war could not be taken away.

THE COLD WAR BEGINS

☆ *What views and actions chosen by the Soviet Union and United States contributed to the Cold War?*

☆ *How was the containment policy applied to Western Europe between 1947 and 1951?*

☆ *How did the Truman administration promote and protect American interests in Latin America and the Middle East?*

Around the globe people hoped an enduring peace would follow the defeat of the Axis powers. But could the cooperative relationship of the Allies continue into the postwar era without a common enemy to unite them? Suspicion and distrust already existed over the Soviet creation of a "zone of security" with "friendly" governments in Eastern Europe, and President Harry S Truman appeared less willing than Roosevelt to trust the Soviets. "The Soviet Union needs us more than we need them," Truman told a colleague. Although he was new to formulating foreign and domestic policies, Truman was determined to face the challenges: "The buck stops here" read a plaque in his office.

Truman and Paths to Peace

Truman and other American leaders identified two overlapping paths to peace: international cooperation and **deterrence** based on military strength.

deterrence Measures that a state takes to discourage attacks by other states, often including a military buildup.

◻ **United Nations** (UN) International organization established in 1945 to maintain peace among nations and foster cooperation in human rights, education, health, welfare, and trade.

◻ **General Assembly** Assembly of all members of the United Nations; it debates issues but neither creates nor executes policy.

◻ **Security Council** The executive agency of the United Nations; today it includes five permanent members with veto power (China, France, the United Kingdom, Russia, and the United States) and ten members elected by the General Assembly for two-year terms.

puppet governments Governments imposed, supported, and directed by an outside force, usually a foreign power.

◻ **containment** The U.S. policy of checking the expansion or influence of Communist nations by making strategic alliances, aiding friendly nations, and supporting weaker states in areas of conflict.

In 1944, as a means to achieve global cooperation and economic development, the International Monetary Fund and the World Bank were created, and at the Dumbarton Oaks conference delegates from the United States, China, Britain, and the Soviet Union mapped the basic structure of the **United Nations** (UN). In April 1945, a conference in San Francisco finished the task. It wrote the charter of the United Nations, an organization of six distinct bodies, the most important of which are the **General Assembly** and the **Security Council**. Composed of all member nations, the General Assembly was the weaker body with authority only to discuss issues, whereas resolving issues was the responsibility of the Security Council, composed of eleven nations. Six nations were elected by the General Assembly, but the real power was held by five permanent members: the United States, the Soviet Union, the United Kingdom, China, and France. To give the UN authority, the Security Council could apply economic and military pressures against other nations, but to protect their interests, each of the five permanent nations could veto Security Council decisions. When it was decided to house the headquarters of the UN in New York City, Truman noted that the center of Western civilization had shifted from Europe to the United States.

Still, most Americans did not want to rely solely on international cooperation to maintain national security or peace. They concluded that the United States must continue to field a strong military force with bases around the globe, maintain its atomic monopoly, and take the lead in creating the conditions for an enduring peace. Drawing on lessons learned from World War II, most Americans believed in halting aggressors, supporting democratic governments, and promoting a prosperous world economy. From this perspective, the Soviet Union appeared to be threatening world peace by following an "ominous course" in Eastern Europe, creating undemocratic **puppet governments** and closing the region to free trade. As 1946 began, Truman concluded that he was "tired of babying the Soviets" and the State Department asked its Russia expert, George Kennan, to evaluate Soviet policy to determine its motivations and goals.

Kennan's "Long Telegram" described Soviet totalitarianism as internally weak. Soviet leaders, he said, held Communist ideology secondary to remaining in power and needed Western capitalism as an enemy to justify their rule. But, he argued, Soviet leaders were not fanatics and would retreat when met with opposition. He recommended a policy of **containment**, meeting head-on any attempted expansion of Soviet power. His report immediately drew high praise from Washington's official circles. Soon thereafter, Truman adopted a policy designed to "set will against will, force against force, idea against idea . . . until Soviet expansion is finally worn down."

Portrait of Joseph Stalin (1879–1953) 1970 (colour litho), Chinese School, (20th century)/ Private Collection/Archives Charmet/The Bridgeman Art Library.

Joseph Stalin controlled the Soviet Union from 1926 until his death in 1953. His popular image was "Uncle Joe" during World War II, but by the time of the Truman Doctrine in March 1947, Stalin's image resembled Hitler's. Truman's first impression of the Soviet dictator, at Potsdam in July 1945, was that he was "dishonest but smart as hell" and they could work together. One of Truman's closest advisers bluntly stated that Stalin was "a liar and a crook."

By the spring of 1946, increasingly fearful of Soviet intentions, both Democrats and Republicans tried to educate the public about the Soviet threat to world stability. One of the most dramatic warnings, however, came from Winston Churchill on March 5, 1946, at Westminster College in Fulton, Missouri. With President Truman sitting beside him, the former prime minister of Britain decried Soviet expansionism and stated that an "**iron curtain**" had fallen across Europe (see Map 24.1). Churchill called for a "fraternal association of the English-speaking peoples" to halt the Russians. Truman thought it was a wonderfully eloquent speech and would do "nothing but good." Churchill, *Time* magazine pronounced, had spoken with the voice of a "lion."

As Churchill spoke, a crisis loomed in Iran. During World War II, the Big Three had stationed troops in Iran to ensure the safety of lend-lease materials going to the Soviet Union. The troops were to be withdrawn by March 1946, but as that date neared, Soviet troops remained in northern Iran. When the deadline passed and reports flashed that the Soviets were advancing rather than withdrawing, some worried that war was imminent. After Britain and the United States sent harshly worded telegrams to Moscow and petitioned the United Nations to consider an Iranian complaint against the Soviet Union, Soviet forces soon evacuated Iran. The crisis was over, but it convinced many Americans that war with the Soviets was possible. "Red Fascism" had replaced Nazi fascism, and for the sake of civilization there could be no more appeasement.

The Division of Europe

As the crisis in Iran receded, events in Europe assumed priority. A deepening economic crisis across Europe appeared to favor leftist parties and their assertion that state controls and state planning led to quicker economic recovery. But the most immediate trouble spots were in Greece and Turkey. The Soviets were pressuring Turkey to permit them some control over the Dardanelles, the straits linking the Black Sea to the Mediterranean. In Greece, a civil war raged between Communist-backed rebels and the British-supported conservative government. In February 1947, Britain informed Washington that it was unable to provide economic or military aid to the two nations and asked the United States to assume its role in the region to prevent Communist expansion. Truman eagerly assumed the responsibility of "world leadership with all of its burdens and all of its glory."

To convince Congress and gain public support for $400 million to support Greece and Turkey, Truman overstated the "crisis," presenting an image of the world under attack from the forces of evil. On March 12, 1947, he set forth the **Truman Doctrine**, offering an ideological, black-and-white view of world politics. He said it was the duty of the United States "to support free people" who resisted subjugation "by armed minorities or by outside pressure." Congress agreed and provided aid for Greece and Turkey. Bolstered by American support, Turkey resisted Soviet pressure and retained control over the straits, and the Greek government was able to defeat the Communist rebels in 1949.

Although the Truman administration asked Congress only to support Greece and Turkey, officials admitted among themselves that the request was just

■ **iron curtain** Name given to the military, political, and ideological barrier established between the Soviet bloc and Western Europe after World War II.

■ **Truman Doctrine** Anti-Communist foreign policy announced by Truman that called for military and economic aid to countries whose political stability was threatened by communism.

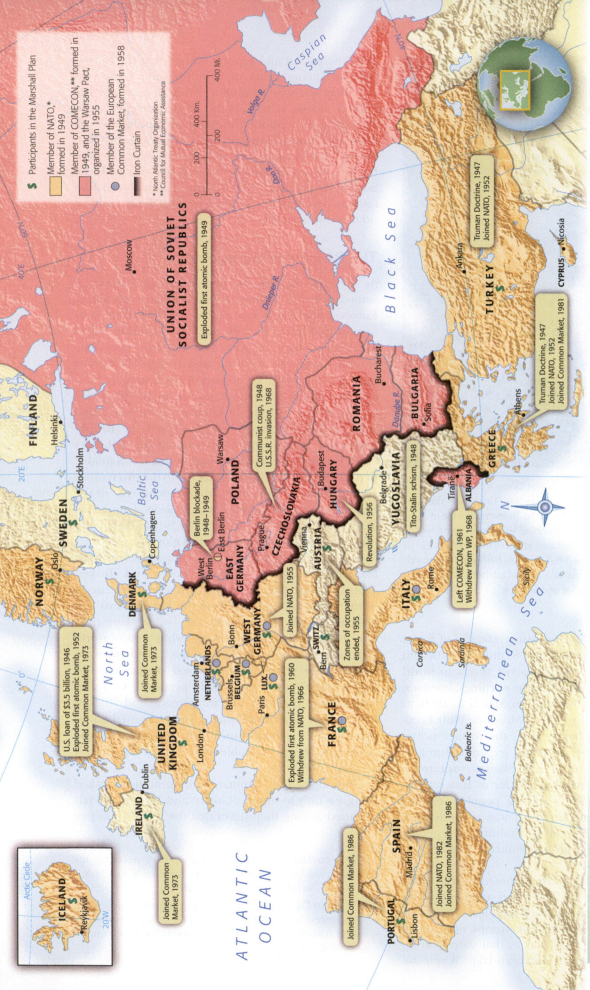

668

Map Legend

$ Participants in the Marshall Plan

Member of NATO,* formed in 1949

Member of COMECON,** formed in 1949, and the Warsaw Pact, organized in 1955

Member of the European Common Market, formed in 1958

Iron Curtain

* North Atlantic Treaty Organization
** Council for Mutual Economic Assistance

MAP 24.1 Cold War Europe
Following World War II, what Winston Churchill called the "iron curtain" split Europe, dividing most of the continent politically, economically, and militarily into an eastern bloc (the Warsaw Pact) led by the Soviet Union and a western bloc (NATO) supported by the United States. This postwar division of Europe lasted until the collapse of the Soviet Union in the early 1990s. © Cengage Learning.

Map Labels

UNION OF SOVIET SOCIALIST REPUBLICS
- Moscow
- Exploded first atomic bomb, 1949

FINLAND
- Helsinki

SWEDEN
- Stockholm
- Oslo

NORWAY

DENMARK
- Copenhagen
- Joined Common Market, 1973

ICELAND
- Reykjavik
- Joined Common Market, 1973
- Arctic Circle

IRELAND
- Dublin
- Joined Common Market, 1973

UNITED KINGDOM
- London
- U.S. loan of $3.5 billion, 1946
- Exploded first atomic bomb, 1952
- Joined Common Market, 1973

NETHERLANDS
- Amsterdam
- Joined Common Market, 1973

BELGIUM
- Brussels

LUX.

WEST GERMANY
- Bonn

FRANCE
- Paris
- Exploded first atomic bomb, 1960
- Withdrew from NATO, 1966

SWITZ.
- Bern

AUSTRIA
- Vienna
- Joined NATO, 1955
- Zones of occupation ended, 1955

SPAIN
- Madrid
- Joined NATO, 1982
- Joined Common Market, 1986

PORTUGAL
- Lisbon
- Joined Common Market, 1986

ITALY
- Rome

POLAND
- Warsaw
- Berlin blockade, 1948–1949

EAST GERMANY
- West Berlin
- East Berlin

CZECHOSLOVAKIA
- Prague
- Communist coup, 1948
- U.S.S.R. invasion, 1968

HUNGARY
- Budapest
- Revolution, 1956

ROMANIA
- Bucharest

BULGARIA
- Sofia

YUGOSLAVIA
- Belgrade
- Tito-Stalin schism, 1948

ALBANIA
- Tiranë
- Left COMECON, 1961
- Withdrew from WP, 1968

GREECE
- Athens
- Truman Doctrine, 1947
- Joined NATO, 1952
- Joined Common Market, 1981

TURKEY
- Ankara
- Truman Doctrine, 1947
- Joined NATO, 1952

CYPRUS
- Nicosia

Caspian Sea
Black Sea
Baltic Sea
North Sea
Mediterranean Sea
ATLANTIC OCEAN

Volga R.
Don R.
Dnieper R.
Danube R.

Corsica
Sardinia
Sicily
Balearic Is.

Scale: 0 200 400 Mi. / 0 200 400 Km.

the beginning. "It happens that we are having a little trouble with Greece and Turkey at the present time," stated a War Department official, "but they are just one of the keys on the keyboard of this world piano."

On June 5, 1947, Secretary of State George Marshall uncovered more of the keyboard. He offered Europe a program of economic aid to restore stability and prosperity—the **Marshall Plan**. For the Truman administration, the difficult question was whether to include the Soviets and Eastern Europeans in the invitation. To do so would seem contrary to the intent of the Truman Doctrine. But if the Soviets were excluded, the United States might be seen as dividing Europe, an image the State Department wanted to avoid. Chaired by Kennan, the State Department planning staff recommended that the United States take "a hell of a big gamble" and offer economic aid to all Europeans. Kennan believed the Soviets would reject the offer because it involved economic and political cooperation with capitalists. Thus, Marshall invited all Europeans to work together and write a program "designed to place Europe on its feet economically."

The gamble worked. At a June meeting in Paris, the Soviets rejected a British and French proposal for an economically integrated Europe, joint economic planning, and a requirement to purchase mostly American goods. The Soviets and the Eastern Europeans left the conference, and over the next ten months the Soviet Union took steps to solidify its control over its satellite states. In July 1947, Moscow announced the Molotov Plan, which further incorporated Eastern European economies into the Soviet system. Throughout the region non-Communist elements were expelled from governments, an effort that culminated in the February 1948 Soviet-engineered **coup** that toppled the Czechoslovakian government. "We are faced with exactly the same situation with which Britain and France were faced in 1938 and 1939 with Hitler," Truman announced. The Czech coup helped convince Congress to approve $12.5 billion in Marshall Plan aid to Western Europe.

In March 1948, the United States announced that the western zones of Germany were eligible for Marshall Plan aid, would hold elections to select delegates to a constitutional convention, and would adopt a standard currency. The meaning of these actions seemed clear: a West German state was being formed. Faced with the prospect of a pro-Western, industrialized, and potentially remilitarized Germany, Stalin reacted. On June 24, the Russians blockaded all land traffic to and from Berlin, which had been divided into British-, French-, Soviet-, and U.S.-controlled zones after the war. With West Berlin isolated 120 miles inside the Soviet zone of Germany (see Map 24.2), the Soviet goal was to force the West either to abandon the creation of West Germany or to face the loss of Berlin. Faced with

Americans pictured the Soviets as aggressors seeking world domination. Here the Soviet magazine *Krokodil* shows Uncle Sam armed with an atomic bomb is coercing British, French, and other European leaders to create the North Atlantic Treath Organization. Russian School, (20th century)/Private Collection/Archives Charmet/ The Bridgeman Art Library.

Soviet hostility, Americans were determined not to back down. Churchill affirmed the West's stand. We want peace, he stated, "but we should by now have learned that there is no safety in yielding to dictators, whether Nazi or Communist." "We are very close to war," Truman wrote in his diary.

American strategists confronted the dilemma of how to stay in Berlin and supply 2.4 million people without starting a shooting war. Although some recommended fighting across the Soviet zone to the city, Truman chose another option, one that would not violate Soviet-occupied territory or any international agreements. Marshaling a massive effort of men, provisions, and aircraft, British and Americans flew supply planes to three Berlin airports day after day, month after month, delivering over a ton of vital supplies daily. To drive home

■ **Marshall Plan** Program launched in 1948 to foster economic recovery in Western Europe in the postwar period through massive amounts of U.S. financial aid.

coup Sudden overthrow of a government by a group of people, usually with military support.

MAP 24.2 Cold War Germany
This map shows how Germany and Berlin were divided into temporary occupation zones, which were transformed by the Cold War into East and West Germany. In 1948, with the Berlin airlift, and again in 1961, with the erection of the Berlin Wall, Berlin became the flash point of the Cold War. With the end of the Cold War, the Berlin Wall came down in 1989, and in 1990 the two Germanys were reunified. © Cengage Learning.

to the Soviets the depth of American resolve, Truman ordered a wing of B-29 bombers, the "atomic bombers," to Britain. These planes carried no atomic weapons, but the general impression was that their presence lessened the likelihood of Soviet aggression.

The **Berlin airlift** was a victory for the United States in the Cold War and testified to America's resolve to stand firm against the Soviets and protect Western Europe. In May 1949, Stalin, finding no gains from the blockade, ended it without explanation and

■ **Berlin airlift** Response to the Soviet blockade of West Berlin in 1948 involving tens of thousands of continuous flights by American and British planes to deliver supplies.

■ **North Atlantic Treaty Organization** (NATO) Mutual defense alliance formed in 1949 among most of the nations of Western Europe and North America in an effort to contain communism.

■ **National Security Council** (NSC) Executive agency established in 1947 to coordinate the strategic and defense policies of the United States; it includes the president, vice president, and four cabinet members.

allowed land traffic to cross the Soviet zone to Berlin. The crisis swept away most congressional opposition to the Marshall Plan and the creation of West Germany and silenced those who had protested a permanent American military commitment to Western Europe. In June 1949, Congress approved American entry into the **North Atlantic Treaty Organization** (NATO), ensuring that American forces would remain in the newly created West Germany. The Mutual Defense Assistance Act, passed in 1949, provided $1.5 billion in arms and equipment for NATO member nations. By 1952, 80 percent of American assistance to Europe was military aid.

To facilitate fighting the Cold War, Congress passed the National Security Act in 1947. It created the Air Force as a separate service and unified command of the military with a new cabinet position, the Department of Defense. To improve coordination between the State Department and the Department of Defense, the **National Security Council** (NSC) was formed to provide policy recommendations to the president. The act also established the Central Intelligence Agency to collect and analyze foreign intelligence information

Photo by Walter Sanders//Time Life Pictures/Getty Images.

When the Soviets blockaded the western zones of Berlin, in one of the first confrontations of the Cold War, the United States replied by staging one of the most successful logistical feats of the twentieth century, Operation Vittles, in which vital supplies were flown into the city. During the airlift's 321 days, American planes flew more than 272,000 missions and delivered 2.1 million tons of supplies.

and carry out covert actions supporting national security. By mid-1948, covert operations included efforts to influence Italian elections (a success) and to topple the Communist Albanian government (a failure).

The U.S. Presence in Latin America and the Middle East

While the Truman administration's primary foreign-policy concern was Europe, it did not ignore the rest of the world. In Latin America, the administration encouraged private firms to develop the region and in 1947 helped organize the **Rio Pact**. The pact established the concept of collective security for Latin America and created a regional organization—the **Organization of American States** (OAS)—to coordinate common defense, economic, and social concerns.

In the Middle East, fear of future oil shortages led the United States to promote the expansion of American petroleum interests in Saudi Arabia, Kuwait, and Iran. At the same time, the United States became a powerful supporter of a new Jewish state to be created in Palestine. The area of Palestine had been administered by the British since the end of World War I and had experienced increasing tensions between the indigenous Arab population, the Palestinians, and a growing number of Jews, largely immigrants from Europe. As World War II ended, Britain faced growing pressure to create a new Jewish state in Palestine and to allow at least 100,000 displaced European Jews to migrate there. Considering the Nazi terror against Jews, he believed that they should have their own nation—a view strongly supported by a well-organized, pro-Jewish lobbying effort across the United States.

On May 14, 1948, the United Nations voted to **partition** Palestine into Arab and Jewish states. Truman recognized the nation of Israel within fifteen minutes. War quickly broke out between Israel and the surrounding Arab nations—who refused to recognize the partition. Although outnumbered, the better-equipped Israeli army drove back the invading armies, and in January 1949, UN mediator **Ralph Bunche** arranged a cease-fire. When the fighting stopped, Israel had added 50 percent more territory to its emerging nation. No Palestinian state was created, and more than 700,000 Arabs left Israeli-controlled territory, many living as refugees in the Gaza Strip, Lebanon, Jordan, and Egypt. Bitter at the loss of what they regarded as their homeland, the majority of Palestinians and other Arabs were determined to destroy the Jewish state.

THE COLD WAR IN ASIA

★ How did the Truman administration's response to Communist expansion in China differ from its response regarding Europe?

★ What events contributed to NSC 68 and how did it represent a change in strategy?

★ What were the Truman administration's goals in Korea and how did they change as the war progressed? How did the "hot war" in Korea affect American foreign policy?

If Americans were pleased with events in Latin America and the Middle East, Asia provided

■ **Rio Pact** Considered the first Cold War alliance, it joined Latin American nations, Canada, and the United States in an agreement to prevent Communist inroads in Latin America and to improve political, social, and economic conditions among Latin American nations; it created the Organization of American States.

■ **Organization of American States** (OAS) An international organization composed of most of the nations of the Americas, including the Caribbean, that deals with the mutual concerns of its members; Cuba is not currently a member.

partition To divide a country into separate, autonomous nations.

■ **Ralph Bunche** An African American scholar, teacher, and diplomat. After negotiating a settlement ending the Arab-Israeli War, he received the Nobel Peace Prize in 1950.

several disappointments. Under American occupation, Japan's government was reshaped into a democratic system and placed safely within the American orbit, but diplomatic setbacks occurred in China and Korea.

The Chinese Civil War

During World War II, the Nationalist Chinese government of Jiang Jieshi (Chiang Kai-shek) and the Chinese Communists under Mao Zedong (Mao Tse-tung) had collaborated to fight the Japanese. But when the war ended, old animosities quickly resurfaced, and civil war followed in February 1946. American supporters of Jiang, led by the "China Lobby," recommended that the United States increase its economic and military support for the Nationalist government, arguing that Soviet power threatened China and the rest of Asia as much as it did Europe. Truman and Marshall dreaded Communist success in China but questioned whether the corrupt and inefficient Nationalist government could ever effectively rule the vast country. While willing to continue some political, economic, and military support, neither wanted to commit American resources to an Asian war, which would be like "throwing money down a rat hole," Truman told his cabinet.

Jiang's overmatched forces soon disintegrated, and in December 1949 the Nationalist government fled to the island of Taiwan. Conservative Democrats and Republicans labeled the rout of Jiang a humiliating American defeat and tarred the Truman administration as soft on communism. To quiet critics and to protect Jiang, Truman refused to recognize the People's Republic of China on the mainland and ordered the U.S. 7th Fleet to the waters near Taiwan.

Adding to dismay over China, in late August 1949 the Soviets detonated their own atomic bomb, shattering the American nuclear monopoly. A joint Pentagon–State Department committee concluded that the Soviets, driven by "a new fanatic faith" whose objective was to dominate the world, might be able to launch a nuclear attack on the United States as early as 1954. The committee's report, NSC Memorandum #68, called for global containment and a massive buildup of American military force, amounting to military spending of nearly $50 billion for the next fiscal year, an increase of almost 400 percent. Truman, worried that such a mobilization of industry would choke off the manufacture of domestic consumer goods, eventually agreed to a "moderate" $12.3 billion military budget for 1950 that included building the hydrogen bomb. Proponents of NSC 68 won the final argument on June 25, 1950, when North Korean troops stormed across the 38th parallel.

Halting Communist Aggression in Korea

When World War II ended, Soviet forces occupied Korea north of the 38th parallel and American forces remained south of it, and by mid-1946, two Koreas existed (see Map 24.3). In the south was an American-supported Republic of Korea (ROK), led by Syngman Rhee, and in the north a Communist-backed Democratic People's Republic of Korea, headed by Kim Il Sung. In 1949 the Soviet and American forces withdrew, leaving behind two hostile regimes. Both claimed to be Korea's rightful government and launched raids across the border, causing more than 100,000 Korean deaths.

With approval from the Soviets, on June 25, 1950, Kim Il Sung launched a full-scale invasion of the south. Overwhelmed, South Korean forces rapidly retreated. Concluding that South Korea's survival depended on it, Truman asked the UN Security Council to intervene to protect a member nation. The Security Council complied and condemned North Korea's invasion, called for a cease-fire, and asked member nations to provide assistance to South Korea.

American forces led by General Douglas MacArthur, officially under United Nations control, arrived in Korea in July but were unable to halt the North Korean advance. By the end of July, North Korean forces occupied most of South Korea. United Nations forces, including nearly 122,000 Americans and what remained of the South Korean army, held only the southeastern corner of the peninsula—the Pusan perimeter. In September the tide turned as seventy thousand American troops landed at Inchon, near Seoul, while UN forces advanced north from Pusan. The North Koreans fled back across the 38th parallel. Seoul was liberated on September 27. The police action had achieved its purpose: the South Korean government survived, and the 38th parallel was again a real border.

Seeking to Liberate North Korea

Now, however, the South Korean leadership, MacArthur, Truman, and most Americans wanted to unify

□ **Nationalist Chinese government** The government of Jiang Jieshi, who fought the Communists for control of China in the 1940s; Jiang and his supporters were defeated and retreated to Taiwan in 1949, where they set up a separate government.

□ **NSC Memorandum #68** Report concluding that the Soviets were seeking world domination and recommending large-scale increases in military spending, increased covert operations, reduced domestic programs, and increased taxes.

hydrogen bomb Nuclear weapon of much greater destructive power than the atomic bomb.

□ **police action** Official term used by the United States for its role in the Korean conflict because there was no formal declaration of war; the North Koreans called it "the Fatherland Liberation War."

Legend:
← United States and United Nations forces
← North Korean forces
← Intervention by Chinese forces, Oct. 1950

CHINA

MANCHURIA

U.S.S.R.

Chongjin

Hyesanjin

Kanggye

Chosan

Chosin Res.

Angtung
Sinuiju

Unsan

Yalu R.

Taedong R.

Farthest U.S. advance, Oct.–Nov. 1950

Hungnam

NORTH KOREA

Sea of Japan (East Sea)

Pyongyang

Nan R.

Armistice line, July 7, 1953

Kaesong

38th Parallel

Panmunjom

Farthest Chinese/ North Korean advance, Jan. 1951

Inchon

Seoul

U.S. landing Sept. 15, 1950

Han R.

U.N. advance, Sept.–Nov. 1950

Taejon

Yongdok

Naktong R.

Pohang

36°N

Yellow Sea

SOUTH KOREA

Taegu

Farthest North Korean advance, Sept. 1950

Pusan

Korea Strait

34°N

N

0   50   100 Km.
0   50   100 Mi.

126°E   128°E

42°N

38°N

MAP 24.3 The Korean War, 1950–1953
Seeking to unify Korea, North Korean forces invaded South Korea in 1950. To protect South Korea, the United States and the UN intervened, driving North Korean forces northward, and Truman sought to unify Korea under South Korea's government. But as UN and South Korean forces pushed toward the Chinese border, Communist China intervened, forcing UN troops to retreat. This map shows the military thrusts and counterthrusts of the Korean War until it stalemated roughly along the 38th parallel. © Cengage Learning.

Deciding on War in Korea

Within days after North Korea invaded South Korea, President Truman committed American forces to the conflict, calling it a "police action" to uphold the "rule of law." It was a straightforward and simple explanation of a decision that cost millions of dollars and thousands of lives. But the terms "simple" and "straightforward" often do not apply to the way national decisions are made, and it is up to historians to examine the records of the decision-making process to better understand the how and why of it. Among the questions asked about the situation in Korea were: What alternatives to entering the conflict were available, and what considerations produced the decision to commit U.S. forces in the way it was done? The records provide the following answers.

Before the invasion, the administration considered South Korea of "no strategic value," but within minutes of the attack, Truman chose to help defend South Korea. A central consideration in that first decision was the belief, as the CIA reported, that the Soviet Union was using North Korea "to challenge the United States" and test its "resistance to Communist expansion." South Korea had suddenly become "symbolically significant," but what were the best means to meet the Communist challenge?

- One choice was to immediately commit American military forces to defend South Korea.

Truman could do this by executive order, but a declaration of war by Congress would ensure broad political support. The immediate deployment of U.S. troops could defeat North Korean forces, but this option carried the risk of enlarging the conflict from a localized one to a regional or global one.

- Another choice was to denounce the invasion, provide immediate military aid to South Korea, and seek a diplomatic solution.

This option reduced the possibility of expanding the conflict, but it would not ensure South Korea's survival and would make the United States look weak. "Europeans, to say nothing of the Asiatics, are watching to see what the United States will do," one official noted, and a weak response would encourage additional Soviet-sponsored acts of aggression.

Neither of these choices met the administration's needs, and they received little or no consideration. But the existence of the United Nations offered a third option:

- The choice the U.S. government made was to act forcefully and protect its credibility by using the "umbrella" of the United Nations.

Hours after the invasion began, Truman stated that the United States should introduce a resolution to the Security Council calling for the UN to defend South Korea, a member state, against outside aggression. By the next evening, the UN agreed to call upon its members to oppose the aggression and restore peace in Korea. Truman also deployed selected American air and naval forces to South Korea on a limited basis.

Two days later, the Security Council approved a second U.S. resolution calling for member states to provide South Korea "such assistance . . . as may be necessary to repel the armed attack and to restore international peace and security in the area." Using the UN umbrella, Truman now expanded U.S. naval and air operations and permitted a limited use of ground forces in Korea.

Three days later, June 27, as North Korean forces continued their advance and there was no sign of further Soviet or Chinese involvement, Truman ordered American ground troops into the conflict, able to tell the public and the world they were involved in a UN-sponsored "police action" to uphold the international "rule of law."

© Bettmann/Corbis.

The Korean War was one of ebb and flow, advances and retreats up and down the rugged Korean peninsula.

the peninsula under South Korean rule. Bending under American pressure, the United Nations on October 7 approved a new goal, to "liberate" North Korea from Communist rule. In mid-October, 1950, UN forces pushed northward toward the Korean-Chinese border at the Yalu River. The Chinese threatened intervention if the invaders approached the border. Relying on faulty intelligence estimates that said any intervening Chinese forces would number less than 50,000, American, British, and Korean forces advanced to within a few miles of the Yalu River—at which point nearly 300,000 Chinese soldiers entered the Korean Conflict.

Blowing their bugles, the Chinese attacked in waves, taking massive casualties and nearly trapping several American and South Korean units. In the most brutal fighting of the war, UN forces fell back. The U.S. 1st Marine Division was nearly surrounded at the Chosin Reservoir. When asked about the marines retreating, General O. P. "Slam" Smith responded, "Gentlemen, we are not retreating. We are merely advancing in another direction." Within three weeks, the North Koreans and Chinese had shoved the UN forces back to the 38th parallel. American casualties exceeded twelve thousand, but the Chinese had lost three times as many.

Truman now abandoned the goal of a unified pro-Western Korea and sought a negotiated settlement, even if it left two Koreas. The decision was not popular. Americans wanted victory. Encouraged by public opinion polls and Truman's Republican critics, General MacArthur publicly objected to the limitations his commander-in-chief had placed on him. Already displeased by MacArthur's arrogance, Truman replaced him with General Matthew Ridgeway.

The decision unleashed a storm of protest. Some called for Truman's impeachment, and Congress opened hearings to investigate the conduct of the war. MacArthur testified that expanding the war could achieve victory, while the administration argued that it might lead to a global nuclear war. In polls, Truman's approval rating plummeted. At the same time, MacArthur's hopes for a presidential candidacy collapsed because most Americans feared his aggressive policies might result in World War III. By the beginning of 1952, the vast majority of Americans were simply tired of the "useless" conflict and wanted it to end.

The Korean front, meanwhile, stabilized along the 38th parallel as four-power peace talks among the United States, South Korea, China, and North Korea began on July 10, 1951. The negotiations did not go smoothly. While the powers postured and argued about prisoners, cease-fire lines, and a multitude of lesser issues, soldiers fought and died over scraps of territory. When the Eisenhower administration finally concluded a cease-fire on July 26, 1953, the Korean conflict had cost more than $20 billion and

thirty-three thousand American lives, but it had left South Korea intact.

The "hot war" in Korea had far-reaching military and diplomatic results for the United States: increased military spending, the rearming of West Germany and Italy, and a large, permanent American presence in Asia and the Pacific. In 1951 the United States and Japan agreed that American forces would remain in Japan and on the island of Okinawa. The Australia–New Zealand–United States (ANZUS) treaty of 1951 promised American military protection to those countries. At the same time, the United States increased its military aid and commitments to Nationalist China and French **Indochina**. The containment policy had expanded—formally and financially—to cover East Asia and the Pacific.

POSTWAR POLITICS

☆ In what ways did Truman attempt to maintain and expand the New Deal? How did the fear of communism strengthen conservative opposition to his programs?

☆ Why did Truman win the 1948 election?

When Roosevelt died, many wondered if Truman would continue the Roosevelt–New Deal approach to domestic policies. Would he work to protect the social and economic gains that labor, women, and minorities had earned during the war? Conservatives and some of Truman's friends predicted that the new president was "going to be quite a shock . . . that the New Deal is as good as dead." But Truman had no intention of extinguishing the New Deal.

Truman and Liberalism

In September 1945, Truman presented to Congress what one Republican critic called an effort to "out–New Deal the New Deal." Truman set forth an ambitious program designed to ease the transition to a peacetime economy and reenergize the New Deal. To prevent inflation and a recession, he wanted Congress to continue wartime economic agencies to help control wages and prices. He also asked that the Fair Employment Practices Commission be renewed. And he recommended an expansion of Social Security, an "immediate and substantial" increase in the forty cents an hour minimum wage, the development of additional housing programs, a commitment to full employment, and a national health system.

> **Indochina** French colony in Southeast Asia, including present-day Vietnam, Laos, and Cambodia; it began fighting for its independence in the mid-twentieth century.

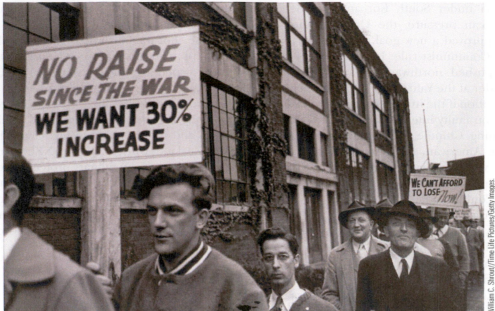

As the nation moved from a wartime to peacetime economy, workers initiated more than five thousand strikes. Pictured here are strikers in Detroit in 1945.

William C. Shrout//Time Life Pictures/Getty Images.

A conservative coalition of southern Democrats and Republicans embarked on a campaign to persuade the American public of the dangers of Truman's program, which, they argued, involved too much government, threatened private enterprise, and endangered existing class and social relations. The *Wall Street Journal* labeled Truman's program a move toward socialism. "Public sentiment is everything," wrote an officer of Standard Oil. A Truman official sadly agreed: "The consuming fear of communism fostered a widespread belief that change was subversive." Congress rejected or severely scaled back nearly all of Truman's proposals. Wartime economic controls and the Fair Employment Practices Commission quickly faded away. Congress spurned any idea of full employment and a national health program.

While Congress and Truman disagreed over the domestic agenda, the country experienced economic and social dislocations caused by the conversion to a peacetime economy. Inflation quickly emerged as a principal issue, with prices rising 25 percent within 18 months after the defeat of Germany. Inflation, cuts in hours, and layoffs cut into many workers' purchasing power, reducing it for some by as much as 30 percent. The economic changes led to nearly 4.5 million workers staging more than five thousand strikes. GM placed ads in newspapers stating that the country was at a "crossroads" and asked, "Is American business to be based on free competition, or . . . become socialized."

Many thought the nation had reached the crossroads in the spring of 1946 when coal miners and railroad workers went on strike. The earlier strikes had often been successfully ended through negotiating panels created by Truman, with settlements that usually raised workers' wages and allowed companies to raise prices. But the coal and railroad strikes brought a different response. Truman was angry and determined not to let the unions threaten the nation's economy or dictate to the government. He issued orders for the government to take control of the coal mines and railroads, ordering the workers to return. In May, Truman went to Congress to ask for power to draft strikers and put them back to work. The railroad strike was settled that same day, but labor strife continued in the coal fields for the rest of the year and ended only when the government took legal action against the United Mine Workers and John L. Lewis.

Truman's action cost him the support of many unions and workers, but the strikes had also led Congress and state and local governments to pass legislation designed to weaken unions and end work stoppages. **Right-to-work laws** banned compulsory union membership (the closed shop) and in some cases provided legal and police protection for workers crossing picket lines. In June 1947, Congress approved the **Taft-Hartley Act**, which banned the closed shop, prevented industry-wide collective bargaining, and legalized state-sponsored right-to-work

■ **right-to-work laws** State laws that make it illegal for labor unions and employers to require that all workers be members of a union. Many state laws require that all employees, even those who are not union members, must benefit from contract agreements made between the union and the employer.

laws that hindered union organizing. It also required that union officials sign **affidavits** that they were not Communists. Echoing Truman's actions in the coal strike, the law also empowered the president to use a court injunction to force striking workers back to work for an eighty-day cooling-off period. Truman vetoed the legislation knowing his veto would be overridden by Congress and hoping it would regain labors' support for his 1948 presidential run.

Amid strikes, soaring inflation, divisions within Democratic ranks, and widespread dissatisfaction with Truman's leadership—"to err is Truman" was a common quip—Republicans asked the public: "Had enough?" Voters responded affirmatively in 1946 and 1947, filling both houses of the Eightieth Congress with more Republicans and anti–New Deal Democrats. Truman refused to retreat and continued to ask Congress to pass many of the same programs he had offered in 1945. The political battle between the president and Congress reignited: Congress rejected Truman's proposals, Truman vetoed 250 bills, and Congress overrode twelve of Truman's vetoes.

Truman's veto of Taft-Hartley was an easy political decision. In contrast, the issue of civil rights was extremely complex and politically dangerous. Democrats were clearly divided. Southern Democrats opposed any mention of civil rights, while African Americans and liberals, including Eleanor Roosevelt, demanded that Truman "speak" to the issue. A central part of the issue was the racial violence in the South, where fifty-six African Americans were murdered within a year of the war's end. One of the worst incidents was in Georgia, where two African American veterans and their wives were pulled from a car and brutally murdered. A national uproar prompted an investigation by the Justice Department. No one was ever accused or convicted of the murders, but the crime and investigation increased calls for government action. The North, too, was experiencing increased racial tension and violence, including several race riots in Chicago.

Confessing that he did not know how bad conditions were for African Americans and that "the top dog in a world . . . ought to clean his own house," Truman in December 1946 appointed a presidential committee to examine race relations in the country. The December 1947 report *To Secure These Rights* described the racial inequalities in American society and called on the government to take steps to correct the imbalance. Among its recommendations were the establishment of a permanent commission on civil rights, the enactment of anti-lynching laws, and the abolition of the poll tax. The committee also called for integration of the U.S. armed forces and support for integrating housing programs and education. Truman asked Congress in February 1948 to act on the recommendations, but no civil rights legislation was forthcoming.

The 1948 Election

Republicans' hopes were high in 1948. They had done well in congressional elections in 1946 and 1947. To take on Truman they chose New York governor Thomas E. Dewey. He had lost to Roosevelt in 1944, but had earned a respectable 46 percent of the popular vote, and Truman was not Roosevelt. The Democrats were also mired in bitter infighting over the direction of domestic policy. Many Democratic liberals and minorities wished that Truman had pushed harder to sell his New Deal–type programs and civil rights to the public and Congress. Henry A. Wallace, the former vice president, entered the race as a Progressive Party candidate.

At the Democratic National Convention in July 1948, liberal Democrats forced the inclusion of civil rights recommendations in the party platform. Southern Democrats, opposing any such statement, walked out of the convention. Unwilling to support a Republican, they met in Birmingham and organized the States' Rights Democratic Party, better known as the **Dixiecrat Party**, nominating South Carolina governor J. Strom Thurmond for president. Days later, Truman ordered desegregation of the armed forces and the federal workforce. The navy and air force complied, although it took a year to implement the changes. Afterwards, the 7th Marines commander observed, "Never once did any color problem bother us. . . . It just wasn't any problem." But the Army refused until December 1949, when it agreed to integrate—but only gradually. The Korean War sped up integration, but it was not until October 1954 that the last unit was integrated. Despite his caution, Truman had done more in the area of civil rights than any president since Lincoln, a record that ensured African American and liberal support.

- **Taft-Hartley Act** Law passed by Congress in 1947 banning closed shops, permitting employers to sue unions for broken contracts, and requiring unions to observe a cooling-off period before striking.

affidavit A formal, written legal document made under oath; those signing the document state that the facts in the document are true.

- *To Secure These Rights* Created in December 1946 to investigate race relations, the President's Commission on Civil Rights issued this report a year later, making several recommendations to improve civil rights; Truman asked Congress to implement the recommendations, but Congress failed to act.

- **Dixiecrat Party** Party organized in 1948 by southern delegates who refused to accept the civil rights plank of the Democratic platform; they nominated Strom Thurmond of South Carolina for president.

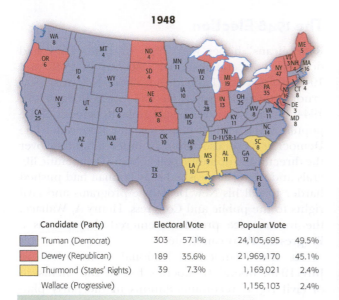

1948

Candidate (Party)	Electoral Vote		Popular Vote	
Truman (Democrat)	303	57.1%	24,105,695	49.5%
Dewey (Republican)	189	35.6%	21,969,170	45.1%
Thurmond (States' Rights)	39	7.3%	1,169,021	2.4%
Wallace (Progressive)			1,156,103	2.4%

MAP 24.4 Election of 1948
In the 1948 presidential election, Harry S Truman confounded the polls and analysts by upsetting his Republican opponent, Thomas Dewey, earning 50 percent of the popular vote and 57 percent of the electoral vote. © Cengage Learning.

Many considered Harry S Truman's 1948 victory over Thomas E. Dewey a major political upset—nearly all of the major polls had named the Republican an easy winner. Here Truman holds up the *Chicago Tribune's* incorrect headline announcing Dewey's triumph.

Confounding the pollsters, Truman defeated Dewey in a triumph for Roosevelt's New Deal coalition. Despite the Dixiecrats, most southerners did not abandon the Democratic Party. Thurmond carried only four southern states; Wallace carried none (see Map 24.4). Democrats also won majorities in Congress, and Truman hoped that in 1949 he would succeed with his domestic program, which he called the **Fair Deal**.

In his inaugural address, Truman asked for increases in Social Security, public housing, and the minimum wage, the repeal of the Taft-Hartley Act, and the creation of a national health program. He also gave civil rights and federal aid to education a place on the national agenda. Rewarding farmers for their role in his victory, Truman submitted the Brannan Plan, which included federal benefits for small farmers. Congress responded favorably to Truman's programs in areas already well established by the New Deal: a 65-cent minimum hourly wage, funds for low- and moderate-income housing, and increases in Social Security coverage and payments. Proposals going beyond the scope of the New Deal encountered effective opposition from a coalition of southern Democrats and Republicans. A national health system and

government intervention in education were communistic, said opponents, while civil rights efforts were part of a Communist conspiracy to undermine American unity. Adding their voices to the chorus, agribusiness leaders attacked the Brannan Plan as socialistic and class oriented. A frustrated and angry Truman complained that he had "kissed more SOB so-called Democrats and left-wing Republicans than all the presidents put together" to no avail.

COLD WAR POLITICS

☆ *What fears and events heightened society's worries about internal subversion, and how did politicians respond to the public's concerns?*

☆ *Why and how did Joseph McCarthy become so powerful by 1952?*

Attacks on liberal programs as socialistic or communistic were not new. But the developing Cold War intensified fears that Communists and their supporters were undermining American values and stability, leading to a second Red Scare. Some of the growing concerns were valid. The Soviets had a well-developed espionage system operating in the country, including within the atomic bomb program. Other concerns, though, arose from political opportunism and broad anti-liberalism. Tobacco giant R. J. Reynolds characterized unionism as a step toward socialism in its multimillion-dollar public ad campaign to defeat a CIO effort to organize

◼ **Fair Deal** Saying that "every segment of the population" deserved a "fair deal" from the government, President Truman hoped the Democratic majority would provide an expansion of New Deal programs, including civil rights legislation, a fair employment practices act, a system for national health insurance, and appropriations for education.

southern workers. In Pittsburgh, Pennsylvania, a local paper labeled those trying to integrate a public swimming pool "Commies." Across the country, neighborhoods and communities organized "watch groups," which screened books, movies, and public speakers and questioned teachers and public officials, seeking to ban or dismiss those considered suspect.

The Red Scare

Responding to increasing accusations, including those of the **House Un-American Activities Committee** (HUAC), that his administration tolerated Communist subversion, Truman moved to beef up the existing loyalty program by issuing Executive Order #9835 in March 1946, establishing the Federal Employee Loyalty Program. If "reasonable grounds" existed for believing a federal employee was disloyal in belief or action, the employee could, after a hearing, be fired. Soon supervisors and workers began to accuse one another of "un-American" thoughts and activities. Between 1947 and 1951, the government discharged more than three thousand federal employees because of their supposed disloyalty. In almost every case, the accused had no right to confront the accusers or to refute the evidence. While the Soviets used American citizens to conduct espionage, few of those forced to leave government service were Communists.

Truman's loyalty program intensified rather than calmed fears, especially when Federal Bureau of Investigation (FBI) director J. Edgar Hoover proclaimed that there was one American Communist for every 1,814 loyal citizens, and Attorney General Tom Clark warned that Communists were everywhere, "in factories, offices, butcher shops, on street corners, in private businesses," carrying "the germs of death for society." Grabbing headlines in 1947, HUAC targeted Hollywood, intent on removing people with liberal, leftist viewpoints from the entertainment industry and ensuring that the mass media promoted American capitalism and traditional American values. With much fanfare, HUAC called Hollywood notables to testify about Communist influence in the industry. Many of those called used the opportunity to prove their patriotism and to denounce communism. Actor Ronald Reagan, president of the Screen Actors Guild, denounced Communist methods that "sucked" people into carrying out "Red policy without knowing what they are doing" and testified that the Conference of Studio Unions was full of Reds.

Not all witnesses were cooperative. Some, including the "**Hollywood Ten**," took the Fifth Amendment and lashed out at the activities of the committee. Labeled "Fifth Amendment Communists," the ten were jailed for contempt of Congress and blacklisted by the industry. Eric Johnson, president of the Motion Picture Association, announced that Hollywood would produce no more films like *The Grapes of Wrath*,

TOWARD A MORE PERFECT UNION

The Cold War and Freedom of Speech

Passed in 1940, the Alien Registration Act, or Smith Act, made it illegal for a person or organization to advocate the overthrow of the U.S. government. It made advocacy of ideas a crime and departed from the view that words and deeds needed to constitute a real danger. Sparingly used during World War II, in 1949, the Smith Act justified the arrest of twelve leaders of the Communist Party whose words and ideology advocated the overthrow of the United States. Eleven stood trial together and were found guilty. They appealed on the grounds that advocacy of an idea constituted no "real and present danger," and that their arrest violated their First Amendment right to free speech. Their appeal, *Dennis v. United States* (1951), reached the Supreme Court, which upheld their conviction. Some 140 American Communist Party members were indicted under the Smith Act until the Supreme Court, in *Yates v. United States* (1956) and *Noto v. United States* (1961), weakened the law by requiring evidence that a real threat existed. In 1969, the Court concluded in *Brandenburg v. Ohio* that advocacy of ideas was protected by the First Amendment but did so without invalidating the Smith Act.

featuring the hardships of poor Americans or "the seamy side of American life." Moviemakers soon issued a new code—*A Screen Guide for Americans*—that demanded "Don't Smear the Free Enterprise System" and "Don't Show That Poverty Is a Virtue."

Just before the election of 1948, HUAC zeroed in on spies within the government, bringing forth a number of informants who had been Soviet agents and were now willing to name others who allegedly had sold out the United States. The most sensational revelation came from a repentant ex-Communist named Whittaker Chambers. He accused **Alger Hiss**, a New Deal liberal, one-time State Department official, and president of the Carnegie Endowment for International

■ **House Un-American Activities Committee** (HUAC) Congressional committee, created in 1938, that investigated suspected Communists during the McCarthy era.

■ **Hollywood Ten** Ten screenwriters and producers who stated that the Fifth Amendment to the Constitution gave them the right to refuse to testify before HUAC in 1947. The House of Representatives disagreed and issued citations for contempt. Found guilty in 1948, the ten served from six months to a year in prison.

■ **Alger Hiss** State Department official accused in 1948 of being a Communist spy; he was convicted of perjury and sent to prison.

Peace, of being a Communist. At first Hiss denied knowing Chambers, but under interrogation by HUAC members, especially Congressman **Richard M. Nixon** of California, Hiss admitted an acquaintance with Chambers in the 1930s but denied he was or had been a Communist. When Hiss sued Chambers for libel, Chambers escalated the charges. He stated that Hiss had passed State Department secrets to him in the 1930s, and he produced rolls of microfilm that he said Hiss had delivered to him. In a controversial and sensationalized trial, in 1949 Hiss was found guilty of **perjury** (the statute of limitations on espionage had expired) and sentenced to five years in prison.

As the nation followed the Hiss case, news of the Communist victory in China and the Soviet explosion of an atomic bomb heightened American fears. Many people believed that such Communist successes could have occurred only with help from American traitors. Congressman Harold Velde of Illinois proclaimed, "Our government from the White House down has been sympathetic toward the views of Communists and fellow-travelers, with the result that it has been infiltrated by a network of spies." Congress responded in 1950 by passing, over Truman's veto, the **McCarran Internal Security Act**, requiring all Communists to register with the attorney general. The following year the Supreme Court upheld the **Smith Act** (passed in June 1940), ruling that membership in the Communist Party was equivalent to conspiring to overthrow the American government and that no specific act of treason was necessary for conviction.

Such outcomes seemed vindicated in February 1950, when **Julius and Ethel Rosenberg** were accused of being part of a Soviet atomic spy ring. At trial in 1951, the prosecution alleged that the information the Rosenbergs passed to the Soviets was largely responsible for the successful Soviet atomic bomb. The Rosenbergs professed innocence but were convicted of espionage. (Soviet documents indicate that Julius Rosenberg was engaged in espionage but that Ethel was probably guilty only of being loyal to him. Documents concerning Hiss are inconclusive, continuing a spirited debate about his guilt or innocence.)

Joseph McCarthy and the Politics of Loyalty

Feeding on the furor over the enemy within, Republican senator **Joseph McCarthy** of Wisconsin emerged at the forefront of the anti-Communist movement. To attract votes when he ran for the Senate in 1946, he invented a glorious war record for himself that included the nickname "Tail-gunner Joe" and several wounds. In February 1950, he announced to a Republican women's group in Wheeling, West Virginia, that he knew of 205 Communists working in the State Department.

When examined by a Senate committee, McCarthy's accusations were shown to be at best inaccurate. But he ignored the findings and continued to claim he was exposing Communists. The fears generated by the Korean War increased the senator's popularity and power. Few dared to oppose him and he found many supporters, including the Senate's most powerful Republican, Robert Taft of Ohio, who slapped McCarthy on the back saying, "Keep it up, Joe."

By 1952, with the Korean Conflict stalemated, Truman's popularity was almost nonexistent, and Republicans were having a field day attacking "cowardly

At the heart of the Red Scare was Senator Joseph McCarthy. Using Inquisition-style tactics to attack his opponents, he became one of the most powerful politicians in the nation by 1952. In this picture from the 1952 presidential campaign, McCarthy waves a report on Democratic candidate Adlai Stevenson showing that he endorsed policies favoring the Soviets.

© Bettmann/Corbis.

Benard Hoffman/Time Life Pictures/Getty Images.

As World War II ended, Americans flocked to the suburbs, creating a demand for new housing—a demand matched by developers of planned communities like Levittown, Pennsylvania. Developers kept the cost of the homes down using uniformity of style and prefabricated materials.

containment," calling for victory in Korea, and labeling New Deal and administration programs socialistic. Republicans were sure voters would elect a Republican president.

HOMECOMING AND SOCIAL ADJUSTMENTS

☆ *How did suburban America reflect the social and economic expectations of many Americans?*

☆ *What adjustments did women and minorities have to make in postwar America?*

With World War II over, Americans were eager to return home and resume normal lives. Organized "Bring Daddy Back" clubs flooded Washington with letters demanding a speedy return of husbands and fathers. By November 1945, 1.25 million GIs were returning home each month. For Americans entering the postwar world, the homecoming was buoyed with expectations and fraught with anxieties. The nation had experienced dramatic economic growth, but remembering the Depression, Americans wondered if the postwar economy would remain strong. Still, most were optimistic that any recession would be short-lived and they would be able to spend savings, find jobs, and enjoy the American dream. "Consumption is the frontier of the future," chirped one economic forecast.

Rising Expectations

Owning a home was for many the symbol of the American dream. Before 1945, only about forty percent of Americans owned homes and the housing industry had focused on building custom homes or multifamily dwellings. But the postwar demand for single-family homes, together with the G.I. Bill, which provided thousands of veterans with low-interest home loans, changed the housing industry. To meet the demand, William Levitt and other developers supplied mass-produced, prefabricated houses—the suburban **tract homes**. Using building

□ **Richard M. Nixon** Republican elected in 1945 to the House of Representatives; he earned national recognition as a member of HUAC through his investigation of alleged Soviet spy Alger Hiss; elected vice president in 1952 and president in 1968.

perjury The deliberate giving of false testimony under oath.

□ **McCarran Internal Security Act** Law passed by Congress in 1950 requiring Communists to register with the U.S. attorney general and making it a crime to conspire to establish a totalitarian government in the United States.

□ **Smith Act** The Alien Registration Act, passed by Congress in 1940, which made it a crime to advocate or to belong to an organization that advocates the overthrow of the government by force or violence.

□ **Julius and Ethel Rosenberg** Wife and husband who were arrested in 1950 and tried for conspiracy to commit espionage in 1951 after being accused of passing atomic bomb information to the Soviets; they were executed in 1953.

□ **Joseph McCarthy** Republican senator from Wisconsin who in 1950 began a Communist witch hunt that lasted until his censure by the Senate in 1954; *McCarthyism* is a term associated with attacks on liberals and others, often based on unsupported assertions and carried out without regard for basic liberties.

tract homes Numerous houses of similar design built on small plots of land.

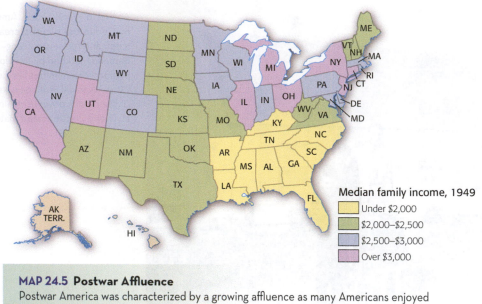

MAP 24.5 Postwar Affluence

Postwar America was characterized by a growing affluence as many Americans enjoyed the fruits of a booming economy, increasing family income, and a large variety of consumer goods. © Cengage Learning.

Median family income, 1949
- Under $2,000
- $2,000–$2,500
- $2,500–$3,000
- Over $3,000

techniques developed during the war, timber from his forests, and nonunion workers, Levitt boasted that he could construct an affordable house on an existing concrete slab in sixteen minutes. Standardized, with few frills, the two-story house had four and a half rooms. Built on generous 60-by-100-foot lots, complete with a tree or two, Levitt homes cost slightly less than $8,000, giving Levitt a $1,000 profit. The first Levittown sprang up in Hempstead, Long Island, and was a planned community with more than seventeen thousand homes, seven village greens, fourteen playgrounds, and nine swimming pools. Hundreds of look-alike suburban neighborhoods were soon built across the nation, contributing to a growing migration from rural and urban America to the suburbs (see Map 24.5).

Nowhere were tract homes more prominent than in southern California. During and after the war, networks of roads extended out from southern California cities, developing "satellite" economic centers, pulling businesses, homes, and industries away from the central cities. In Los Angeles this resulted in a 50 percent loss in sales and tax revenues, the reduction of public transportation, a loss of jobs, and a growing urban poverty rate. This pattern of development

became increasingly common across the country as suburbs multiplied.

Although part of the American dream, suburbs were not for everyone. Widespread discrimination kept some out by design. Whether it was through the official policy of developers like Levitt, individual neighborhood covenants, or denial of home loans, almost every suburb in the nation was predominately white and Christian. Even though the Supreme Court ruled in *Shelly v. Kraemer* (1948) that restrictions were illegal, the decision failed to have much effect. Neither did the Court's decision to prevent banks and the FHA from rejecting home loan applications from minorities trying to buy houses in white neighborhoods. Real-estate agents continued to abide by the Realtors' Code of Ethics, which called it unethical to permit the "infiltration of inharmonious elements" into a neighborhood. Across the nation, fewer than 5 percent of suburban neighborhoods provided nonwhites access to the American dream house.

For many veterans a cozy home was only part of the postwar dream—so too was going to college. Armed with economic support through the G.I. Bill, in September 1946 nearly 1 million veterans enrolled in college. New Jersey's Rutgers University saw its enrollment climb from seven thousand to sixteen thousand. At Lehigh University in Pennsylvania, 940 veteran students outnumbered the 396 "civilians" and refused to don the traditional freshman beanie. Schools, responding to the influx of students, not only hired more faculty and built more

■ ***Shelly v. Kraemer*** Supreme Court ruling (1948) that barred lower courts from enforcing restrictive agreements that prevented minorities from living in certain neighborhoods; it had little impact on actual practices.

It Matters Today

The G.I. Bill

Passed in 1944, the G.I. Bill took effect with the end of the war and provided benefits until 1956. Its benefits included a year's unemployment payments, loans to start businesses and farms, money for education, and inexpensive, no-money-down loans for homes. About 16 million veterans were eligible, who with their families equaled nearly one-third of the population by 1950. It was the nation's largest social welfare program, but no one called it welfare or socialistic. Those receiving the benefits had earned them by fighting for the nation. Almost half of the veterans used the education option to attend college or vocational and training schools or to complete their high school education. They also bought homes. In 1946 and 1947, veterans' mortgages represented 40 percent of all new homes purchased. In storming campuses and suburbia, vets and their families reshaped the middle class and reset the American Dream with an emphasis on education, upward mobility, and a home with a yard.

- How does the G.I. Bill era compare with today's opportunities for higher education and upward mobility and how do the differences affect America's economy and society?
- Because of its consequences, the G.I. Bill has been called the "silent revolution." What types of products, legislation, or opportunities could be promoted today that could produce similar changes in the country?

facilities but also began providing special housing, daycare centers, and expanded health clinics for married students. By the time the G.I. Bill expired in 1956, over 2 million veterans, including sixty-four thousand women, had earned their degrees under its umbrella.

Veterans expected jobs, too, and most figured that "wartime" workers would relinquish their jobs and return to traditional roles. At first jobs were scarce. The cancellation of wartime contracts and the nationwide switch to domestic production resulted in 2.7 million workers being dismissed from their jobs within a month of Japan's surrender. Fortunately for veterans, the G.I. Bill provided unemployment compensation for a year until a job was found. And within a year, jobs were becoming more and more available as American industries began producing for the domestic market. By 1947, 60 million people were working, 7 million more than at the peak of wartime production. But the workforce had changed, with noticeably fewer women and minorities.

From Industrial Worker to Homemaker

"Last hired, first fired" fit the industrial workplace as the war ended. Across the nation women, African Americans, and Latinos were told that they were no longer needed. In the aircraft and shipbuilding industries, companies drastically trimmed their workforces as wartime orders ended, dismissing most of

As World War II ended women faced the choice of remaining in the workforce or returning to the home. A majority returned home. This women states that she and her husband both preferred she "go home" and they would start a family.

Picture Research Consultants & Archives.

In the Wider World

The Condition of Women

In France, in 1949, Simone de Beauvoir wrote *The Second Sex*, one of the century's most important works on the condition of women. In it she asked, "What is a woman?" Her answer was that woman was the "Other," subordinate to man, who was the "Absolute." Rejecting that premise, she argued that women needed to live "authentic" lives rather than "necessary" lives devoted to reproduction and motherhood. Women should "dream the dreams of men" and achieve freedom. Writing the work, she discovered something that had "been staring [you] . . . in the face all the time which somehow you have never noticed." Women lived "lacerated, in a world made to put them at a disadvantage," she said, where reality offered "far more victories to be won, more prizes to be gained, more defeats to be suffered." In 1963, Betty Friedan drew upon the observations of de Beauvoir for her own controversial book *The Feminine Mystique*, discussed in Chapter 26.

the women and African Americans who had provided much-needed labor during the war. Mirroring the rest of the nation, in Seattle and Baltimore two-thirds of aircraft workers and one-third of the shipbuilding workers lost their jobs within one month after Japan's surrender. In the aircraft industry women had made up 40 percent of the workforce, but by 1948 they numbered a mere 12 percent. For most women the loss of jobs was expected. "We will work as long as they need us," stated a woman employee at Boeing, "and when we're through we will go back to our meals and dishes and children."

Indeed, most of society assumed that women would want to go back to domesticity. A *Fortune* poll in the fall of 1945 revealed that 57 percent of women and 63 percent of men believed that married women should not work outside the home. Other polls, however, found that a sizable majority of women, especially single women, wanted and needed to keep their jobs. One single woman asked simply: "What are we to do? I need a job badly." For women who did keep working, the postwar workplace became highly gender oriented again. Those women finding or keeping work took lower-paying "female" jobs. Rosie the Riveter had become Fran the File Clerk, as wages declined from about $50 to $35 a week.

While some women struggled to find or keep jobs, society stressed a renewed emphasis on femininity, family, and a woman's proper role. Psychiatrists and marriage counselors argued that men wanted their wives to be feminine and submissive, not fellow workers. Fashion designers, such as Christian Dior in his "New Look," lengthened skirts and accented waists and breasts to emphasize femininity.

Marriage was more popular than ever: by 1950, two-thirds of the population was married and having children. Factors contributing to the rush to the altar were fears of "male scarcity" caused by war losses and a new attitude that viewed marriage as the ideal state for young people. Many women's magazines and marriage experts championed the idea that men should marry at around age 20 and women at age 18 or 19. With veterans returning home, society celebrating family, and prosperity increasing, the "baby boom" began and would last for nearly twenty years. From a Depression level of under 19 births per 1,000 women per year, the birth rate rose to more than twenty-five births per thousand women by 1948 (see Figure 24.1).

Not all women accepted the role of contented, submissive wives and homemakers—the war experience had changed relationships. When one veteran informed his wife that she could no longer handle the finances because it was not "woman's work," she indignantly reminded him that she had successfully balanced the checkbook for four years and that his return had not made her suddenly stupid. Reflecting such tensions and too many hasty wartime marriages, the divorce rate rose dramatically. Twenty-five percent of all wartime marriages were ending in divorce in 1946, and by 1950 over a million GI marriages had dissolved. As the number of female heads of household rose, so also did the poverty and social stigma attached to single parenthood. Following her divorce, one suburban resident recalled that her neighbors "avoided" her and made remarks like "Why don't you get a job instead of taking tax monies?" She also noted that her children were singled out at school because they did not have a father at home.

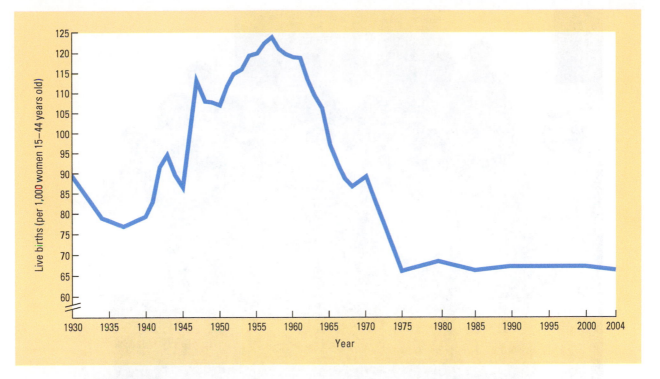

FIGURE 24.1 Birth Rate, 1930–2004
Between 1946 and 1964, rebounding from the low birth rate of the Depression, families chose to have more children. This increase is often called the "baby boom." In the 1960s, the birth rate slowed, and since the mid-1970s, it has remained fairly constant. © Cengage Learning.

Latinos and African Americans: Restrained Expectations

For Latinos the war years had brought many positive changes. Many experienced a higher degree of equality than before and, especially among Mexican Americans, there was more of a sense of being part of the United States, of "American-ness." A wounded veteran and resident of El Paso, Texas, Moises Flores recalled: "I am proud to be an American. Sometimes I even call myself gringo, which I'm not. I'm still Mexican, but I'm an American first."

The war also saw in many an increasing unwillingness to return to traditional roles. Antonio Campo, for one, had experienced a segregated life in Houston before the war. After the war he used the G.I. Bill to go to college and later ran for political office. When told in response to his activism, "If you don't like it, why don't you go back to Mexico?" he shot back: "I was born here in Texas. I went overseas and put my life on the line so you people can make decisions." He lost the election but, like many other Latinos, drew from the same desire for change that energized the League of United Latin American Citizens (LULAC) and the **American GI Forum** to attack discrimination throughout the West and Southwest.

The American GI Forum, organized in Texas in early 1948 by Mexican American veterans, worked to secure for Latino veterans the benefits provided by the G.I. Bill and to develop leadership within the Mexican American population. In California and Texas, LULAC and the American GI Forum successfully used federal courts to correct school systems that segregated Latino from white children. In *Mendez v. Westminster* (1946) and in *Delgado v. Bastrop School District* (1948), federal courts ruled that school systems could not educate Mexican Americans separately from Anglos. Despite these rulings, throughout the Southwest and West, Latino students remained in predominantly "Mexican" schools and classrooms, which perpetuated inferior educational opportunities and contributed to high dropout rates.

African Americans had experiences similar to those of Latinos and also exhibited a heightened

◾ **baby boom** Sudden increase in the birth rate that occurred in the United States after World War II and lasted until roughly 1964.

◾ **American GI Forum** Organization formed in Texas by Mexican American veterans to overcome discrimination and provide support; it led the court fight to end the segregation of Latino children in school systems in the West and Southwest.

◾ *Mendez v. Westminster* and *Delgado v. Bastrop School District* Court cases that overturned the establishment of separate schools for Mexican American children in California and Texas.

Created in 1948 by Dr. Hector Perez Garcia the American G.I. Forum was created to promote equal rights for Latinos. Private Collection/Picture Research Consultants & Archives.

degree of resistance to returning to old norms. Even as African Americans lost industrial and other higher-paying jobs as the war ended, some positive changes occurred. In the South, African American voter registration increased, primarily in the Upper South and in urban areas. In several northern cities, African Americans displayed their growing political voice by electing black representatives to local and state office and, in 1945, they sent Adam Clayton Powell Jr. to Congress from New York. That same year, Jackie Robinson gained more national recognition when he began playing in the minor leagues.

While the postwar period generally saw significant loss of income and status for women, African Americans, and Latinos, their experiences had energized many to pursue their own vision of the American dream, one that included not only improved prosperity but an unfettered role in society and an unmuzzled voice in politics.

Individual Voices

MLB Photos/Getty Images.

The Sporting News Editorializes on African Americans in Baseball

The Sporting News (TSN), established in 1886 and called the "Bible of Baseball," was for decades the most important source for those seriously interested in the sport. Its editorials and articles shaped and expressed the public's views on sports. The following editorials, separated by three years, discuss the integration of baseball. Each reflects the views of both the baseball insider and the general public and helps today's readers and historians better understand the attitudes and rationalizations regarding race in American society at the time.

① Why would the author believe that African American athletes in boxing (Lewis) and track (Owens) faced different issues than in baseball? In the first editorial, what do the editors of *TSN* believe is a primary reason why integration of baseball is a bad idea?

② What evidence does the second editorial give as to why it believes that Jackie Robinson is not a legitimate choice for the first African American to be integrated into the major leagues?

③ Does the second editorial support the integration of baseball? How is the issue of race presented in the editorials?

④ In what ways are the two editorials different in their view of the issue of the integration of baseball?

August 8, 1942: "No Good from Raising Race Issue"

There is no law against Negroes playing with white teams, nor whites with colored clubs, but neither has invited the other . . . . Other sports had their Joe Louis, Jesse Owens . . . respected and honored by all races, but they competed under different circumstances from those dominating in baseball. ①

The baseball fan is a peculiar creature . . . . it's his inalienable right . . . to criticize and jeer, in words that not always are . . . the most gentlemanly. Not even a Ted Williams . . . or a Babe Ruth is immune. It is not difficult to imagine what would happen if a player on a mixed team . . . should throw a bean ball, strike out with the bases full or spike a rival. Clear-minded men of tolerance of both races realize the tragic possibilities and have steered clear of such complications.

November 1, 1945: "Montreal Puts Negro Player on Spot"

In signing Jack Roosevelt Robinson . . . Branch Rickey . . . touched off a powder keg in the South, unstinted praise in Negro circles and a northern conviction that the racial problem in baseball is as far from a satisfactory solution as ever . . . . Robinson . . . is reported to possess baseball abilities which, were he white, would make him eligible for a trial with, let us say, the Brooklyn Dodgers' Class B farm at Newport News, if he were six years younger.

Here then is the picture which confronts the first Negro signed in Organized Ball . . . (1) He is thrown into . . . competition with a vast number of younger, more skilled and more experienced players. (2) He is . . . too old . . . . (3) He is confronted with the sweat and tears of toil, with the social rebuff and the competitive heartaches which are inevitable for a Negro trailblazer in Organized Baseball. (4) He . . . will be expected to demonstrate skills far beyond those he is reported to possess or to be able to develop . . . . ②

Granted that Robinson can "take it," insofar as points 2, 3 and 4 are concerned, the first factor alone appears likely to beat him down . . . . ③

The Sporting News believes that the attention which the signing of Robinson elicited in the press around the country was out of proportion to the actual vitality of the story . . . [and] is convinced that those players . . . who gave out interviews blasting the hiring of a Negro would have done a lot better . . . if they had refused to comment . . . . "It's all right with me, just so long as Robinson isn't on our club"—the standard reply—is unsportsmanlike and, above all else, un-American. ④

Sources: Excerpt from "No Good from Raising Race Issue" from *The Sporting News*, August 8, 1942, and "Montreal Puts Negro Player on Spot" from *The Sporting News*, November 1, 1945.

Study Tools

SUMMARY

People hoped that the end of World War II would usher in a period of international cooperation and peace. This expectation vanished with the start of the Cold War. To protect the country and the world from Soviet expansion, the United States implemented a containment policy that was first applied to Western Europe but eventually included Asia as well. By the end of Truman's presidency, the United States viewed its national security in global terms and vowed to use its resources to combat the spread of Communist power.

At home Truman sought to expand on the New Deal but found success difficult. While existing New Deal programs such as Social Security, farm supports, and a minimum wage were extended, a conservative Congress blocked new programs. Linking liberal ideas and programs with communism, moderates and conservatives—with the House Un-American Activities Committee and Joseph McCarthy leading the way—promoted their own political, social, and economic interests.

Most Americans expected to enjoy an expanding postwar economy that would bring increased prosperity and more consumer goods. For many the vision of the suburbs with its stable family structure and new-model car in every garage seemed obtainable. Women were encouraged to return to "domestic" life and raise a family. Postwar America saw a rise in marriages and the start of a baby boom. But alongside these trends were an increasing number of divorces and women dissatisfied with their traditional roles.

While white families seemed poised to achieve the American dream, African Americans and Latinos found that discrimination undid many of the economic and social gains they had made during the war. Though forced into lesser jobs and still living in a socially segregated society, many saw changes that they hoped would bring economic and educational improvement as well as full political and civil rights.

CHRONOLOGY
From World War to Cold War

1945	United Nations formed
	Potsdam Conference
1946	Kennan's "Long Telegram"
	Churchill's "iron curtain" speech
	Iran crisis
	Construction begins on first Levittown
	Vietnamese war for independence begins
1947	Truman Doctrine
	Truman's Federal Employee Loyalty Program
	Taft-Hartley Act
	HUAC begins to investigate Hollywood
	Jackie Robinson joins Brooklyn Dodgers
	To Secure These Rights issued
	Rio Pact organized
1948	Communist coup in Czechoslovakia
	State of Israel founded
	Congress approves Marshall Plan
	Shelly v. Kraemer
	Truman defeats Dewey
1949	North Atlantic Treaty Organization created
	Berlin blockade broken by Allied airlift
	Soviet Union explodes atomic bomb
	Communist forces win civil war in China
	Alger Hiss convicted of perjury
1950	U.S. hydrogen bomb project announced
	McCarthy claims Communists riddle the State Department
	NSC 68
	Korean War begins
	McCarran Internal Security Act
1951	General MacArthur relieved of command
	Rosenbergs convicted of espionage
1953	Korean War armistice signed

Study Tools

FOCUS QUESTIONS

If you have mastered this chapter, you should be able to answer these questions and to explain the terms that follow the questions.

1. What views and actions chosen by the Soviet Union and United States contributed to the Cold War?

2. How was the containment policy applied to Western Europe between 1947 and 1951?

3. How did the Truman administration promote and protect American interests in Latin America and the Middle East?

4. How did the Truman administration's response to Communist expansion in China differ from its response regarding Europe?

5. What events contributed to NSC 68 and how did it represent a change in strategy?

6. What were the Truman administration's goals in Korea and how did they change as the war progressed? How did the "hot war" in Korea affect American foreign policy?

7. In what ways did Truman attempt to maintain and expand the New Deal? How did the fear of communism strengthen conservative opposition to his programs?

8. Why did Truman win the 1948 election?

9. What fears and events heightened society's worries about internal subversion, and how did politicians respond to the public's concerns?

10. Why and how did Joseph McCarthy become so powerful by 1952?

11. How did suburban America reflect the social and economic expectations of many Americans?

12. What adjustments did women and minorities have to make in postwar America?

KEY TERMS

United Nations p. 666
General Assembly p. 666
Security Council p. 666
containment p. 666
iron curtain p. 667
Truman Doctrine p. 667
Marshall Plan p. 669
Berlin airlift p. 670
North Atlantic Treaty Organization p. 670
National Security Council p. 670
Rio Pact p. 671
Organization of American States p. 671

Ralph Bunche p. 671
Nationalist Chinese government p. 672
NSC Memorandum #68 p. 672
police action p. 672
right-to-work laws p. 676
Taft-Hartley Act p. 676
To Secure These Rights p. 677
Dixiecrat Party p. 677
Fair Deal p. 678
House Un-American Activities Committee p. 679
Hollywood Ten p. 679

Alger Hiss p. 679
Richard M. Nixon p. 680
McCarran Internal Security Act p. 680
Smith Act p. 680
Julius and Ethel Rosenberg p. 680
Joseph McCarthy p. 680
Shelly v. Kraemer p. 682
baby boom p. 684
American GI Forum p. 685
Mendez v. Westminster and Delgado v. Bastrop School District p. 685

SUGGESTED RESOURCES

Paul Boyer. *By the Bomb's Early Light: American Thought and Culture at the Dawn of the Atomic Age* (University of North Carolina Press, 1994). An insightful examination of how quickly the atomic bomb and atomic energy penetrated American optimism, fears about the future, and culture and society.

Harry S. Truman Library, http://www.trumanlibrary.org. A general source that features online information, exhibits, and documents relating to Truman's life and presidency.

Victor Navaky. *Naming Names* (Hill and Wang, 2003). A readable study of HUAC's investigation of Hollywood that examines the personal moral dilemmas of those called to testify and how their actions altered Hollywood and the country.

Wilson Center. "Cold War International History Project," http://www.wilsoncenter.org/program/cold-war-international-history-project. This is one of many subject areas that the Wilson Center explores. The Wilson Center is an excellent source for primary materials, many of which are from Communist sources.

Quest for Consensus, 1952–1960

CHAPTER OUTLINE

Politics of Consensus
Eisenhower Takes Command
Dynamic Conservatism
The Problem with McCarthy

Eisenhower and World Affairs
The New Look
The Third World
Turmoil in the Middle East
A Protective Neighbor
The New Look in Asia
The Soviets and Cold War Politics

The Best of Times
The Web of Prosperity
Suburban Culture and Consumerism
Working Wives and Rocking Kids
Rejecting Consensus
Outside Suburbia

The Civil Rights Movement
Integrating Schools
The Montgomery Bus Boycott
Ike and Civil Rights

INDIVIDUAL VOICES: Pageant
*Magazine Examines "Rock 'n' Roll
Alan Freed" (July 1957)*

Study Tools

INDIVIDUAL CHOICES

Alan Freed

It was an easy choice. As host of a classical music program for WJW radio in Cleveland, Ohio, Alan Freed had few listeners and fewer opportunities. His fortune changed in the summer of 1951, when Leo Mintz presented Freed with a unique possibility. Mintz, a record store owner, had noticed that rhythm and blues (R & B) records were selling very well and not just to African Americans. To sell more records, he offered to sponsor a late-night program of R & B music on WJW with Freed as host. Freed's acceptance began a mercurial career that brought fame and fortune before plunging him to earth in a fiery crash.

His new gig, "The Moondog Show," reached out to all the "moondog daddies" and "crazy kittens" while he rang cowbells, made pounding noises, and yelled into the microphone. To traditional listeners, it was anarchy, but to teens living in Ohio and neighboring states it was pure excitement. Realizing the profits in R & B, Freed sponsored live concerts, filling theaters, halls, and armories with screaming teens. As the music's popularity grew, so

Michael Ochs Archives/Getty Images.

too did Freed's. Soon his radio programs were being rebroadcast in larger markets, including New York City.

In 1954, the "King of the Moondoggers" left Cleveland for New York City and WINS. No longer able to use the term "Moondog" after losing a copyright suit, Freed renamed his program "Rock 'n' Roll Party." Within months he had the number one show in the New York market and the term "rock 'n' roll" was linked to a new music genre. In 1956, Freed starred with Bill Haley and His Comets and the Platters in *Rock Around the Clock*, the first rock 'n' roll movie targeting teens, which grossed $2.4 million. By 1957, Freed was hosting a nationally broadcast television show on ABC featuring teens dancing to rock 'n' roll (see this chapter's Individual Voices feature).

Although rock 'n' roll had a large number of detractors, Freed was tapping an emerging teen market estimated to spend $75 million a year on records. As the market increased, the R & B/rock 'n' roll music industry exploded, with independent record labels signing a variety of new singers and producing hundreds of records a month. For record producers, the road to success was the radio. When Freed first played "Crying in the Chapel," thirty thousand copies of the record sold the next day. Providing "scientific" proof, a study found it took only five to six radio exposures to jump-start sales of a record. With profits at stake, record companies offered gifts and monetary incentives to disc jockeys and radio stations to play their records, a long-standing technique called "payola." Freed, like most disc jockeys and radio stations, was deeply involved.

By the late 1950s, those concerned about corruption in the music industry and opponents of rock 'n' roll targeted DJs and radio stations for taking bribes and brainwashing the nation's youth. Congressional and Internal Revenue Service investigations and state-level prosecutions followed. Freed became the focus of all three. In November 1959, when he refused to sign an affidavit verifying he had never taken payola, he was dismissed from his radio and television programs. Facing the press outside the station, he announced that payola "may stink but it's here and I didn't start it," and that there was nothing wrong with receiving gifts or getting paid for promoting a song. Later, Freed pled guilty to twenty-nine cases of payola. He died penniless in 1965, shortly after the IRS claimed he owed more than $36,000 in taxes on unreported income. Although Freed disappeared from the public scene, the success of rock 'n' roll would continue to confound its detractors.

Most observers expected the Republicans to regain the White House in 1952 and to roll back the New Deal and forcefully confront Communism abroad. They got less than expected. Recognizing that most New Deal–style programs were ingrained in society, Republican president Dwight D. Eisenhower knew he could modify but not dismantle them. While he was able to cut spending and reduce regulations, he also expanded government's role into new areas. In foreign policy, Eisenhower stressed the use of nuclear weapons, alliances, and covert activities, thus maintaining his New Look strategy of containment while saving money.

Americans also expected to enjoy the benefits of a growing economy. The focus of life centered on the suburban nuclear family: Dad at work, Mom at home nurturing "baby boom" children. Between child and adult, teenagers generated their own culture, merging consumerism, conformity, and rebelliousness as reflected in the growing popularity of rock 'n' roll.

Optimists projected that most Americans had the chance to share in the American dream, even those not living in the suburbs. They promoted the image of consensus, or agreement, about the meaning and values of America.

The reality was different. Stresses existed within suburbia, and race, gender, poverty, and prejudice kept many from fulfilling their hopes. But change seemed possible as groups formed grassroots organizations to advocate equality and access to a better life. Throughout the South, African Americans, supported by Supreme Court decisions, began to batter down the walls of legal segregation. Increasingly, politics and society found it hard to ignore long-standing contradictions in the country's democratic image.

Politics of Consensus

★ What were the popular images of Eisenhower, and how did they compare with reality?

★ What constraints did Eisenhower face in trying to roll back New Deal programs?

★ How did Eisenhower alter the federal government?

"Time for a change," cried Republicans in 1952. Politically wounded by the lingering war in Korea and the soft-on-communism label, the Democrats' twenty-year hold on the White House was in jeopardy. Bypassing would-be presidential candidate Senator Robert Taft, moderate Republicans turned to General Dwight David Eisenhower. Although politically inexperienced, "Ike" was well known, revered as a war hero, and carried the image of an honest man thrust into public service. Skillfully gaining the nomination at the Republican convention, Eisenhower chose Richard M. Nixon of California as his vice-presidential running mate. Nixon was young and had risen rapidly in the party because of his outspoken anticommunism. The Democrats nominated Adlai E. Stevenson, a liberal New Dealer and governor of Illinois.

Eisenhower Takes Command

The Republican campaign took two paths. One concentrated on the popular image of Eisenhower and used "spot commercials" on television that stressed his honesty, integrity, and "American-ness." Eisenhower crusaded for high standards and good government and posed as another George Washington. A war-weary nation applauded his promise to go to Korea "in the cause of peace." McCarthy, Nixon, and others took the second path, brutally attacking the Democrats' Cold War and New Deal records, blasting the Democrats as representing "plunder at home and blunder abroad." They boasted of "no Communists in the Republican Party," promised to roll back communism, and vowed to dismantle the New Deal. Stevenson's effort to "talk sense" to the voters stood little chance.

Eisenhower buried Stevenson in popular and electoral votes (see Map 25.1), and his broad political coattails also swept Republican majorities into Congress. Republicans also won in four Southern states, breaking the Democratic "Solid South" for the first time. Four years later, the 1956 presidential election was a repeat of 1952, with Eisenhower receiving 457 electoral votes, including those from seven southern states, and again swamping Stevenson. But in 1956, the Republican victory was Eisenhower's alone, as Democrats managed to maintain the majorities in both houses of Congress that they had won in the 1954 midterm races.

During both of his administrations, Eisenhower was "Ike" to the public, a warm, friendly, grandfather figure who projected middle-class values and habits. Critics complained that he seemed almost an absentee president, often leaving the government in the hands of Congress and his cabinet while he played golf or bridge. But to those who knew and worked with him, he was far from bumbling or neglectful. In military fashion, Eisenhower relied on his staff to provide a full discussion of any issue. We had a "good growl" he would say after especially heated cabinet talks, but he made the final decisions, and he expected them to be carried out.

© Bettmann/Corbis.

In this picture, the triumphant Republican nominees for the White House pose with smiles and wives—Pat Nixon and Mamie Eisenhower. Seen as a statesman and not a politician during the campaign, Eisenhower worked hard to ensure his nomination, then chose Richard Nixon to balance the ticket because he was a younger man, a westerner, and a conservative.

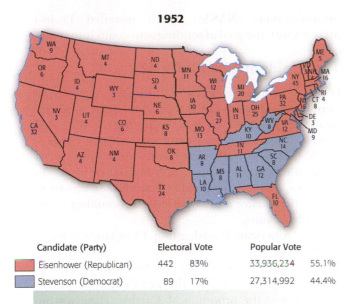

1952

Candidate (Party)	Electoral Vote		Popular Vote	
■ Eisenhower (Republican)	442	83%	33,936,234	55.1%
■ Stevenson (Democrat)	89	17%	27,314,992	44.4%

MAP 25.1 Election of 1952
Dwight David Eisenhower and the Republicans swept into office in 1952. Leading the ticket, Eisenhower swamped his Democratic opponent, Adlai Stevenson, and carried four southern states. In the 1956 presidential election, Eisenhower beat Stevenson by even larger margins—57.2 percent of the popular vote and 457 electoral votes, but Democrats retained a majority in Congress. © Cengage Learning.

Dynamic Conservatism

Eisenhower wanted to follow a "middle course" that was "conservative when it comes to money and liberal when it comes to human beings." He believed that government should be run efficiently, like a successful business, and he staffed his cabinet with a majority of businessmen, most of whom were millionaires. Among the president's key priorities was to reduce spending and the presence of the federal government. Yet, like Truman, Eisenhower recognized the politics of the practical and understood that many New Deal agencies and functions could not be attacked. He told his brother that any political party that tried "to abolish Social Security, unemployment insurance, and eliminate labor laws and farm programs" would not be heard of again.

To balance the budget, Eisenhower used a "meat ax" on Truman's projected budgets. He dismissed 200,000 government workers, cut domestic spending by 10 percent, and slashed the military budget. He and Republicans in Congress also sought to trim spending and federal responsibilities by reducing the federal government's role in the areas of energy, the environment, and trusteeship over Indian reservations. Advocating private ownership and state responsibility, he signed legislation allowing private ownership of nuclear power plants and reducing federal control over the industry, placing much of the nation's offshore

oil sources under state authority, and opening federal lands to lumber and mining companies. Eisenhower also approved legislation in 1954 that began to withdraw federal services and economic support to Native American tribes, encouraged Indians to leave the reservations, and liquidated tribal lands and resources. The Klamath tribe in Oregon, for example, sold much of their ponderosa pine lands to lumber companies. Before the policy was reversed in the 1960s, sixty-one tribes were involved. Some experienced short-term economic gains with the sale of lands and resources, but long-term benefits failed to materialize. Reservations were poorer, and the nearly half of reservation Indians who had abandoned their reservations and moved to urban areas found that few jobs or opportunities were available.

Recognizing political reality, Eisenhower stood by as Congress increased agricultural subsidies, the minimum wage (to $1.00 an hour), funds for urban development, and Social Security benefits. But he also expanded the role of government in new directions. In 1953, he created the Department of Health, Education and Welfare, although he believed that public health was best left to states and communities. In 1955, Jonas Salk developed a vaccine against polio, a disease affecting the central nervous system that in 1952 had infected fifty-two thousand people, mostly children. Many called for a nationwide federal program to inoculate children against the disease. The administration, supported by the American Medical Association, rejected the idea as too socialistic and relied on state and local vaccination programs to immunize the public.

There were also two new major government spending programs: the St. Lawrence Seaway Act (1954) and the **Federal Highway Act** (1956). The first funded joint U.S.-Canadian construction of an inland waterway connecting the Great Lakes with the Atlantic. The second provided funds to construct the initial forty-one thousand miles of an interstate highway system. In justifying the program, the administration maintained that the military needed a modern road system to effectively deploy its forces in case of war. In 1957, Eisenhower again extended federal spending after the Soviet Union launched *Sputnik I* and *Sputnik II* into space. Not only did the nation seem

■ **Federal Highway Act** Law passed by Congress in 1956, appropriating $32 billion for the construction of interstate highways.

■ ***Sputnik I*** and ***Sputnik II*** The first artificial satellite, weighing 184 pounds, launched into space by the Soviet Union in October 1957, marking the beginning of the space race. A month later, *Sputnik II*, even larger, was launched, weighing 1,120 pounds and carrying a dog named Laika.

AP Photo.

In line with his policy to reduce federal spending and controls, Eisenhower tried to turn Indian affairs over to the states and liquidate federal services and reservations. Between 1954 and 1960, sixty-one tribes were affected. This picture shows a 4-year-old Tuscarora boy protesting state and federal policies that attacked Indian rights.

vulnerable to Soviet missiles, but it appeared that the American education system was not putting enough effort into teaching mathematics and science. Eisenhower promptly asked Congress to provide money for public education and to create a new agency to coordinate the country's space program.

The **National Defense Education Act** of 1958 provided funds for public education to improve the teaching of math, languages, and science and set aside $295 million in **National Defense Student Loans** for college students. To improve the space program, Congress created the National Aeronautics and Space

■ **National Defense Education Act** A ten-part act that sought to improve instruction in science, mathematics, and foreign languages and included federally backed low-interest.

■ **National Defense Student Loans** to college students. Today those loans are known as the Federal Perkins Loans.

■ **Army-McCarthy hearings** Congressional investigations by Senator Joseph McCarthy televised in 1954; the hearings revealed McCarthy's villainous nature and ended his popularity.

demilitarized zone An area in which military forces, operations, and installations are prohibited.

Administration (NASA), which unveiled Project Mercury with the goal of sending astronauts into space.

The Problem with McCarthy

With the Democrats defeated, Eisenhower and most Republicans hoped McCarthy would fade away. Instead he continued to search for people he could label subversive and to criticize foreign policy. When, in 1954, McCarthy claimed favoritism toward known Communists in the army, anti-McCarthy forces in Congress, quietly supported by Eisenhower, moved to defang the senator and established a committee to examine his claims.

The American Broadcasting Company's telecast of the 1954 **Army-McCarthy hearings** allowed more than 20 million viewers to see McCarthy's ruthless bullying firsthand. When the army's lawyer, Joseph Welch, asked the brooding McCarthy, "Have you no sense of decency?" the nation burst into applause. McCarthy's power ebbed and several months later the Senate voted 67 to 22 to censure his "unbecoming conduct." Drinking heavily, shunned by his colleagues, and ignored by the media, McCarthy died in 1957.

EISENHOWER AND WORLD AFFAIRS

☆ *What were the weaknesses of the New Look and how did Eisenhower address them?*

☆ *What tactics did the Eisenhower administration pursue in the "third world," especially in the Middle East and Latin America, to protect American interests?*

During the 1952 campaign, Eisenhower promised to go to Korea to bring the war to an "honorable end." After his election the president kept his promise, and after a three-day visit he concluded that a negotiated peace was the only solution. To prod the North Koreans and Chinese to sign a Korean truce agreement, Eisenhower used public and private channels to suggest that the United States might use atomic weapons. By July 1953, the strategy apparently had worked. A truce signed at Panmunjom ended the fighting and brought home almost all the troops, but it left Korea divided by a **demilitarized zone**. Had the nuclear threat, "atomic diplomacy," worked? Some thought it had, but in reality it was Stalin's death in March 1953 that allowed the North Koreans and Chinese to accept resolution of key issues that had deadlocked the talks.

The New Look

Eisenhower was well qualified to lead American foreign policy, having spent years in the military and as commander of NATO. He understood the purpose of campaign slogans like "liberation" and "roll back," but he also knew that the United States could not afford to maintain its current level of military spending if the budget was to be balanced. The key was to find a policy that matched both the nation's needs and its capabilities. His approach was the **New Look**. At its core was nuclear deterrence—an enhanced arsenal of nuclear weapons and delivery systems—and the threat of **massive retaliation**. To strengthen the policy's deterrent capability, the administration intensified efforts to develop an intercontinental and intermediate-range ballistic missile system that could launch warheads from land bases and from submarines, and it introduced a new jet-powered bomber fleet of B-47s. "Rather than let the Communists nibble us to death all over the world in little wars," Vice President Nixon explained, "we will rely . . . on massive mobile retaliation." Secretary of Defense Charles E. Wilson, noting that the nuclear strategy was cheaper than conventional forces, quipped that the policy ensured "more bang for the buck." Demonstrating the country's nuclear might, the United States exploded its first hydrogen bomb in November 1952 (the Soviets tested theirs in August 1953), expanded its arsenal of strategic nuclear weapons to six thousand, and developed tactical nuclear weapons of a lower destructive power that could be used on the battlefield. It was necessary "to remove the taboo" from using nuclear weapons, Secretary of State John Foster Dulles informed the press.

The New Look was sold to the public as more positive than Truman's defensive containment policy, but insiders recognized that it had flaws. The central problem was where the United States should draw the massive-retaliation line: "What if the enemy calls our bluff? How do you convince the American people and the U.S. Congress to declare war?" asked one planner. The answer was to convince potential aggressors that the United States would strike back, raining nuclear destruction not only on the attackers but also on the Soviets and Chinese so that the bluff would never be called. This policy was called **brinkmanship**, because it required the administration to take the nation to the brink of war, trusting that the opposition would back down.

To strengthen the idea of "going nuclear" and make the possibility of World War III less frightening, the administration stressed that nuclear war was survivable. Public and private underground **fallout shelters**—well stocked with food, water, and medical supplies—could, it was claimed, provide safety against an attack. A 32-inch-thick slab of concrete, *U.S.*

To protect themselves from the effect of a nuclear explosion, the government recommended that once the flash was seen or the warning signal was given, students should "duck and cover." This picture shows elementary school children in Ohio.

© Bettmann/Corbis.

News & World Report related, could protect people from an atomic blast "as close as 1,000 feet away." Across the nation, civil defense drills were established

■ **New Look** National security policy under Eisenhower that called for a reduction in the size of the army, development of tactical nuclear weapons, and the buildup of strategic air power to deploy nuclear weapons.

■ **massive retaliation** Term that Secretary of State John Foster Dulles used in a 1954 speech, implying that the United States was willing to use nuclear force in response to Communist aggression anywhere.

brinkmanship Practice of seeking to win disputes in international politics by creating the impression of being willing to push a highly dangerous situation to the limit.

fallout shelters Underground shelters stocked with food and supplies that were intended to provide safety in case of atomic attack; *fallout* refers to the irradiated particles falling through the atmosphere after a nuclear attack.

for factories, offices, and businesses. "Duck-and-cover" drills were held in schools: when their teachers shouted "Drop!" students immediately got into a kneeling or prone position and placed their hands behind their necks.

While people were being convinced that nuclear war was survivable, movies and novels showed the possible horrors of radiation and nuclear destruction. Nevil Shute portrayed the extinction of humankind in his novel *On the Beach* (1957). In *Godzilla* (1954) and dozens of other **B movies**, hideous nuclear-mutated monsters, people, and other creatures wreaked havoc and threatened the world.

Understanding the limits of American power and that a thermonuclear war yielded no winners, Eisenhower found other ways to promote American power and influence, including an increased use of alliances and **covert operations**. Alliances would identify areas protected by the American nuclear umbrella and would protect the United States from being drawn into limited "brushfire" wars. When small conflicts erupted, the ground forces of regional allies, perhaps supported with American naval and air strength, would snuff them out.

In Asia, Eisenhower concluded **bilateral** defense pacts with South Korea (1953) and Taiwan (1955) and a **multilateral** agreement, the Southeast Asia Treaty Organization (SEATO, 1954), that linked the United States, Australia, Thailand, the Philippines, Pakistan, New Zealand, France, and Britain. In the Middle East, the United States officially joined Britain, Iran, Pakistan, Turkey, and Iraq in the **Baghdad Pact** in 1957, later called the Central Treaty Organization

(CENTO) after Iraq withdrew in 1959. In Europe, the United States approved the rearming of West Germany in 1954 and welcomed it into NATO in 1958. In all, the Eisenhower administration signed forty-three pacts to help defend regions or individual countries from Communist aggression (see Map 25.2).

The Third World

In 1946, fifty-one nations, most located in Europe and the Western Hemisphere, signed the United Nations' charter. During the next ten years, twenty-five more nations entered, about a third of them having achieved independence from European nations through revolution and political and social protests. By 1960, thirty-seven new nations existed in Africa, Asia, and the Middle East. For many of the emerging nations, independence did not bring prosperity or stability, and the so-called **third world** became part of the Cold War. Both the West and the Communist bloc competed for the "hearts and minds" of the emerging nations. Commenting on nationalistic movements in Latin America, Dulles said: "In the old days we used to be able to let South America go through the wringer of bad times . . . but the trouble is, now, when you put it through the wringer, it comes out red."

One solution to the problem was to use economic and military aid, political pressure, and the **Central Intelligence Agency** (CIA) to support governments that were anti-Communist and provide stability, even if that stability was achieved through ruthless and undemocratic means. It seemed a never-ending and largely thankless task. "While we are busy rescuing Guatemala or assisting Korea and Indochina," Eisenhower observed, the Communists "make great inroads in Burma, Afghanistan, and Egypt." To meet the growing need, the CIA expanded by 500 percent and shifted its resources to covert activities—80 percent by 1957. In its conduct of activities, the CIA, headed by Allen Dulles, operated with almost no congressional oversight or restrictions.

Turmoil in the Middle East

In the Middle East, Arab nationalism, fired by anti-Israeli and anti-Western attitudes, posed a serious threat to American interests. Iran and Egypt offered the greatest challenges. In Iran, Prime Minister Mohammad Mossadegh had nationalized British-owned oil properties and seemed likely to sell oil to the Soviets. Eisenhower considered him to be "neurotic and periodically unstable" and gave the CIA the green light to overthrow the Iranian leader and replace him with a pro-Western government. On August 18, 1953, Mossadegh was forced from office and was replaced by **Shah Mohammad Reza Pahlavi**, who awarded the United States 40 percent of Iranian oil production.

B movies Poor-quality, cheaply made films that were shown in addition to the mainstream movies.

covert operation A program or event carried out in secret.

bilateral Involving two parties.

multilateral Involving more than two parties.

▫ **Baghdad Pact** A regional defensive alliance signed between Turkey and Iraq in 1955; Great Britain, Pakistan, and Iran soon joined; the United States supported the pact but did not officially join until mid-1957.

▫ **third world** Developing nations that claimed to be independent of either the Western capitalist or Communist blocs; both sides tested this neutrality in the Cold War, as each used a variety of means to include third world nations in their camps.

▫ **Central Intelligence Agency** (CIA) An agency created in 1947 to gather and evaluate military, political, social, and economic information on foreign nations.

▫ **Shah Mohammad Reza Pahlavi** Iranian ruler who received the hereditary title *shah* from his father in 1941 and with CIA support helped oust the militant nationalist Mohammad Mossadegh in 1953.

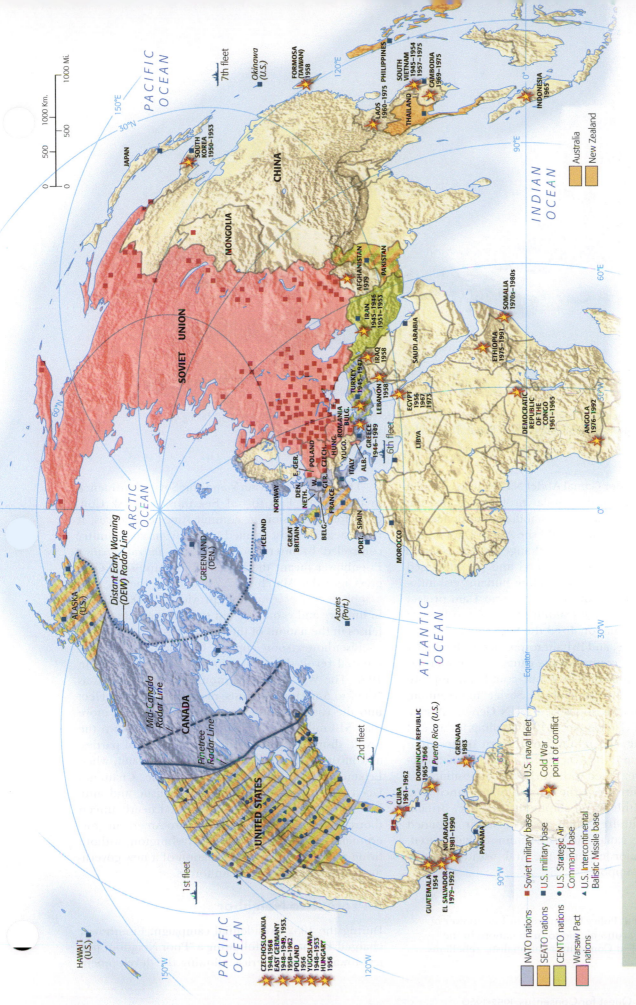

1000 Mi.
1000 Km.
500
500
0
0

PACIFIC OCEAN

30°N

150°E

JAPAN
SOUTH KOREA 1950–1953

7th fleet

Okinawa (U.S.)

FORMOSA (TAIWAN) 1958

120°E

LAOS 1960–1975
PHILIPPINES

SOUTH VIETNAM 1945–1954 1957–1975
CAMBODIA 1969–1975

THAILAND

90°E

INDONESIA 1965

INDIAN OCEAN

Australia
New Zealand

CHINA

MONGOLIA

SOVIET UNION

60°N

AFGHANISTAN 1979
PAKISTAN

IRAN 1945–1946 1951–1953

SAUDI ARABIA

SOMALIA 1970s–1980s

60°E

IRAQ 1958

ETHIOPIA 1975–1991

TURKEY 1945–1947

LEBANON 1958
EGYPT 1956 1967 1973

6th fleet

DEMOCRATIC REPUBLIC OF THE CONGO 1961–1965

ANGOLA 1976–1992

30°E

ROMANIA
BULG.
GREECE 1946–1949

LIBYA

E. GER.
POLAND
CZECH.
HUNG.
YUGO.
ITALY
ALB.

DEN.
W. GER.
FRANCE

NETH.
BELG.

NORWAY

GREAT BRITAIN

SPAIN
PORT.

MOROCCO

0°

ARCTIC OCEAN

Distant Early Warning (DEW) Radar Line

GREENLAND (DEN.)

ICELAND

Azores (Port.)

ATLANTIC OCEAN

30°W

Equator

ALASKA (U.S.)

Mid-Canada Radar Line

CANADA

Pinetree Radar Line

2nd fleet

DOMINICAN REPUBLIC 1965–1966
Puerto Rico (U.S.)

GRENADA 1983

CUBA 1961–1962

U.S. naval fleet
Cold War point of conflict

60°W

UNITED STATES

1st fleet

GUATEMALA 1954
EL SALVADOR 1979–1992

NICARAGUA 1981–1990

PANAMA

90°W

PACIFIC OCEAN

150°W

HAWAI'I (U.S.)

120°W

CZECHOSLOVAKIA 1948,1968
EAST GERMANY 1948–1949, 1953, 1958–1962
POLAND 1956
YUGOSLAVIA 1948–1953
HUNGARY 1956

NATO nations
SEATO nations
CENTO nations
Warsaw Pact nations

Soviet military base
U.S. military base
U.S. Strategic Air Command base
U.S. Intercontinental Ballistic Missile base

MAP 25.2 Cold War Confrontation

During the Cold War, the United States attempted to construct a ring of containment around the Soviet Union and its allies, while the Soviets worked to expand their influence and power. This map shows the nature of this military confrontation—the bases, alliances, and flash points of the Cold War. © Cengage Learning.

697

Implementing the Eisenhower Doctrine, American forces landed in Lebanon in July 1958, taking up positions around the city of Beirut. They landed and withdrew without incident.

Library of Congress.

Egyptian leader Gamal Abdel Nasser, who assumed power in 1954, posed a similar problem. At first the United States saw Nasser as a stabilizing influence and provided money to help build the Aswan Dam on the Nile. But the U.S. attitude changed when Nasser's relations with Israel deteriorated and he purchased arms from the Soviet bloc. Calling him an "evil influence," Eisenhower canceled the Aswan Dam project (July 1956). Days later, claiming the need to finance the dam, Nasser nationalized the Suez Canal.

Israel, France, and Britain responded with military action to regain control of the canal. Eisenhower was furious. He disliked Nasser but could not approve armed aggression. Fearful of Soviet intervention, Eisenhower quickly sponsored a UN General Assembly resolution (November 2, 1956) calling for an end to the fighting, the removal of foreign troops from Egyptian soil, and the assignment of a UN peacekeeping force there. Faced with worldwide opposition and intense pressure from the United States—including a threat to withhold oil shipments—France, Britain, and Israel withdrew their forces. Nasser regained control of the canal and, as Eisenhower had feared, emerged a major leader in the Arab world willing to accept Soviet support.

The growth of Nasser's and the Soviets' influence in the Middle East forced Eisenhower to ask Congress for permission to commit American forces, if requested, to resist "armed attack from any country controlled by internationalism" (by *internationalism* Eisenhower meant the forces of communism). Congress agreed in March 1957, establishing the so-called **Eisenhower Doctrine** and providing $200 million in military and economic aid to improve military defenses in the nations of the Middle East.

Eisenhower soon applied his doctrine when an internal revolt threatened Jordan's King Hussein in 1957. The White House announced that Jordan was "vital" to American interests, moved the U.S. 6th Fleet into the eastern Mediterranean, and supplied more than $10 million in aid. King Hussein put down the revolt, dismissed parliament and all political parties, and instituted authoritarian rule. A year later, when Lebanon's Christian president Camille Chamoun faced an uprising of Muslim nationalistic and anti-West elements, Eisenhower committed nearly fifteen thousand troops to protect the pro-American government. Within three months Washington, without firing a shot, oversaw the formation of a new government and withdrew American forces.

A Protective Neighbor

During the 1952 presidential campaign, Eisenhower charged Truman with following a "Poor Neighbor policy" toward Latin America, allowing the development

■ **Eisenhower Doctrine** Policy formulated by Eisenhower of providing military and economic aid to Arab nations in the Middle East to help defeat Communist-nationalistic rebellions.

Considering Guatemalan president Jacobo Arbenz a threat to American interests, Eisenhower approved a CIA plan to fund and direct a force commanded by Colonel Castillo Armas to invade Guatemala and topple the elected government. In this picture, a group of Armas's soldiers prepare to leave for Guatemala City in June 1954.

of economic problems and popular uprisings that had been "skillfully exploited by the Communists." He was most concerned about Guatemala's president, Jacobo Arbenz, who had instituted agrarian reforms by nationalizing thousands of acres of land, much of it owned by the American-based United Fruit Company. The administration ordered the CIA to organize and supply a rebel army led by Colonel Carlos Castillo Armas, which invaded Guatemala on June 18, 1954. Within weeks a new, pro-American government was installed in Guatemala City. Speaking after Arbenz had fled, Secretary of State Dulles announced the people of Guatemala had "cured" the problem by themselves. But social and economic inequalities continued, and the action did not foster goodwill toward the United States.

The next crisis occurred closer to home when a rebellion led by Fidel Castro toppled the Cuban government of Fulgencio Batista, who had controlled the island since the 1940s. The corrupt and dictatorial Batista had become an embarrassment to the United States, and many Americans believed that Castro could be a pro-American reformist leader. By 1959, however, with Castro's forces in control of the island, many in Washington were concerned about Castro's economic and social reforms, which endangered American investments and interests. Washington's response was to apply economic and political pressure. In February 1960, Castro reacted by signing an economic pact with the Soviet Union. Eisenhower seethed: Castro was a "madman . . . going wild and harming the whole American structure." In March, Eisenhower approved a CIA plan to overthrow the Cuban leader. Actual implementation of the plot, however, fell to Eisenhower's successor.

The New Look in Asia

Korea was not the only problem in Asia that Eisenhower faced when he took office. Chinese threats continued toward Taiwan and its offshore islands, and a "war of national liberation" raged in French Indochina.

In the Wider World

The Great Leap Forward

Concerned about the slow pace of Chinese economic growth, Mao Zedong began the Great Leap Forward in 1958 to mobilize the masses. Within a year, 700 million people were placed in more than 25,500 communes that served as centers of labor and production. Focused on grain and steel, goals were lofty, such as surpassing Britain as an industrial power in fifteen years. To expand steel production, "backyard steel furnaces" were constructed in villages, communes, and schools. Most of China's forests were destroyed to supply wood for the furnaces. From the communes, workers marched to work on farms and in factories and to build massive public works projects, like flood controls on the Yellow River. Despite claims of staggering production successes, the Great Leap Forward was an economic disaster that, combined with bad weather, resulted in "Three Hard Years" (1959–1962) of widespread starvation that claimed over 30 million victims. For Americans it was further proof that the Communist system was seriously flawed.

In both cases, he continued Truman's policies—supporting the Nationalist Chinese and the French. By 1954, the struggle between France and the **Viet Minh** was not going well for Paris. Watching the French military position worsen, Eisenhower announced the **domino theory**, warning that if Indochina fell to communism, the loss "of Burma, of Thailand, of the [Malay] Peninsula, and Indonesia" would certainly follow, endangering Australia and New Zealand. To many it meant that the United States needed to take a more direct role in the conflict.

As Viet Minh forces launched murderous attacks on the beleaguered French fortifications at Dienbienphu, the French—and some members of the Eisenhower administration—wanted American intervention to save the garrison. Eisenhower rejected the idea, saying that "no military victory" was "possible in that kind of theater." The surrender of Dienbienphu on May 7, 1954,

forced the French to negotiate an end to their control over Indochina.

The **Geneva Agreement** created three new nations out of French Indochina: Cambodia, Laos, and Vietnam. Vietnam was "temporarily" partitioned along the 17th parallel, but within two years elections were to be held to unify the nation. The three new nations were not to enter into military alliances or allow foreign bases on their territory. American strategists called the settlement a "disaster"—half of Vietnam was lost to communism, and elections were likely to favor the Communists. The United States, therefore, refused to sign the agreement and Eisenhower immediately moved to support South Vietnam's new government and prime minister, Ngo Dinh Diem. With American blessings, Diem ignored the Geneva-mandated unification elections, quashed his political opposition, and in October 1955 staged a **plebiscite** that created the Republic of Vietnam and elected him president.

The Soviets and Cold War Politics

Stalin's death in 1953 not only helped resolve the Korean War but also offered an opportunity to improve American-Soviet relations. When the new Russian premier, Georgii Malenkov, called for "peaceful coexistence," Eisenhower asked the Soviets to demonstrate their willingness to cooperate with the West. Though Malenkov responded by removing Soviets troops and control from Austria, deep-seated suspicions remained, and both nations continued to test their hydrogen bombs.

In 1955, Eisenhower agreed to a summit meeting in Geneva with the new Soviet leadership team of Nikolai Bulganin and **Nikita Khrushchev**, who had replaced Malenkov. Eisenhower expected no resolution

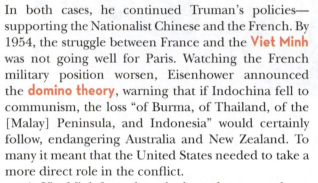

■ **Viet Minh** Vietnamese army made up of Communist and other nationalist groups led by Ho Chi Minh that fought from 1946 to 1954 for independence from French rule.

■ **domino theory** The idea that if one nation came under Communist control, then neighboring nations would also fall to the Communists.

■ **Geneva Agreement** Truce signed at Geneva in 1954 by French and Viet Minh representatives, dividing Vietnam along the 17th parallel into the Communist North and the anti-Communist South.

plebiscite Special election that allows people to either approve or reject a particular proposal.

■ **Nikita Khrushchev** Soviet leader who denounced Stalin in 1956 and improved the Soviet Union's image abroad; he was deposed in 1964, after six years as premier, for his failure to improve the country's economy.

on major issues but decided to propose a bold disarmament initiative—the Open Skies proposal. He suggested that the United States and the Soviets share information about military installations and permit aerial reconnaissance to verify the information, while also beginning work on general disarmament. Bulganin voiced official interest, but Khrushchev considered the proposal a "very transparent espionage device." The Geneva Summit ended with each side agreeing to disagree and publicly saying that the "spirit of Geneva" reduced East-West tensions.

The spirit of Geneva vanished when Soviet forces invaded Hungary in November 1956 to quell an anti-Soviet revolt. Many Americans favored supporting the Hungarian freedom fighters, but seeing no way to send aid to the Hungarians without risking all-out war, the administration only watched as the Soviets crushed the revolt. Soviet-American relations cooled, and Eisenhower and Khrushchev jousted with each other over nuclear testing, disarmament, and Germany and Berlin. Then in 1958 the simmering issue of Berlin erupted. When the Soviets stated that Berlin was to be unified under East German control, Eisenhower, joined by the British and French, declared that their forces would remain in West Berlin.

Faced with unflinching Western determination, Khrushchev backed down and suggested that he and Eisenhower exchange visits and hold a summit meeting. East-West relations seemed to improve as Khrushchev took a twelve-day tour of the United States in September 1959, and the two leaders met at a summit in Paris in May 1960. But a "thaw" in the Cold War failed to materialize. Just as the summit began, the Soviets shot down an American U-2 spy plane over the Soviet Union and captured its pilot. At first, the United States claimed the U-2 was a stray weather plane, but the Soviets' display of the captured pilot and pictures of the plane's wreckage clearly proved otherwise. In Paris, Eisenhower took full responsibility but refused to apologize for such flights, which he contended were necessary to prevent a "nuclear Pearl Harbor." Khrushchev withdrew from the summit, and Eisenhower canceled his forthcoming trip to the Soviet Union.

Eisenhower remained popular, but with the loss of the U-2, Soviet advances in missile technology and nuclear weaponry, and a Communist Cuba only 90 miles from Florida, Democrats turned the Republicans' tactics of 1952 against them. In 1960, Democrats cheerfully accused their opponents of endangering the United States by being too soft on communism.

In this cartoon, an American suburban family sits contentedly next to their cozy home with little concern about the delicate Cold War balance between peace and destruction. By 1953, both the United States and the Soviet Union had tested hydrogen bombs and seemed willing to use the A-bomb to protect national interests.

The Granger Collection, NYC.

THE BEST OF TIMES

☆ What new economic factors contributed to prosperity in the 1950s?

☆ What stresses and contradictions were at work beneath the placid surface of suburbia? Who voiced criticism and how did they express it?

☆ Why were rock 'n' roll and rebellious teens seen as threats to social norms?

According to the popular magazine *Reader's Digest*, in 1954 the average American male stood 5 feet 9 inches tall and weighed 158 pounds. He liked brunettes, baseball, bowling, and steak and French fries. In seeking a wife, he could not decide if brains or beauty was more important, but he definitely wanted a wife who could run a home efficiently. The average female was 5 feet 4 inches tall and weighed 132 pounds.

In the expanding suburbs of the 1950s, many women merged business with socializing by hosting Tupperware parties, introducing friends and neighbors to the newest ways to store leftovers.

She preferred marriage to career, but she wanted to remove the word *obey* from her marriage vows. Both man and woman were enjoying life to the fullest, according to the *Digest,* and buying more of just about everything. The economy appeared to be bursting at the seams, providing jobs, good wages, a multitude of products, and profits.

The Web of Prosperity

The expanding economy was a result of big government, big business, cheap energy, and an expanding population. World War II and the Cold War had created military-industrial-governmental linkages that primed the economy through government spending, what some have labeled "military **Keynesianism**." By 1955 national security needs accounted for half of the U.S. budget—equaling about 17 percent of the

■ **Keynesianism** The economic theories of Lord John Maynard Keynes (1883–1946), who promoted government intervention in the economy, arguing that expanding and contracting the money supply and regulating interest rates could stimulate economic growth during periods of recession and, when needed, reduce inflation.

conglomerates The combination of two or more firms engaging in entirely different businesses.

automation A process or system designed so that equipment functions automatically, often replacing workers with machines.

gross national product (GNP)—and exceeded the total net incomes of all American corporations.

The connection between government and business went beyond direct spending: millions of research and development dollars flowed into colleges and industries. The electronics industry drew 70 percent of its research money from the government, producing not only new scientific and military technology but marketable consumer goods from vinyl floors and Formica countertops to transistor radios and color televisions. By 1960, the electronics industry was the fifth largest in the nation.

In addition, a revolving door seemed to connect government and business positions. Few saw any real conflict of interest even when those from businesses to be regulated staffed regulatory agencies and cabinet positions and relaxed antitrust activity. Secretary of Defense Wilson, the ex-president of General Motors, later voiced the common view: "What was good for our country was good for General Motors and vice versa." It was an era of "new economics" where, according to the Advertising Council, "people's capitalism" was creating "the highest standard of living ever known by any people . . . at any time." Not all agreed that the connections between government and business were without risk. In his farewell address, President Eisenhower warned of the power of the "military-industrial complex" and its potential threat to the "democratic process."

However, few Americans seemed worried when corporate profits doubled between 1948 and 1958 and industrial wages steadily rose from about $55 to $80 a week. Nor was there much concern about corporations getting bigger. Throughout the 1950s over four thousand mergers occurred. Large corporations swallowed smaller companies and merged with one another to create **conglomerates**. International Telephone and Telegraph, for example, acquired construction and insurance firms, food companies, hotels, and other companies not associated with communications. By the end of the decade, 5 percent of American companies were producing 90 percent of corporate income and GNP had doubled since 1940.

The new economy also promoted changes in the workforce. Industrial jobs declined, even as salaries increased. Some of the decline resulted from increased productivity caused by larger, more efficient plants that increasingly used machines and **automation**. Another side of the decline, however, was the growth of service and consumer-related jobs. By the mid-1950s,

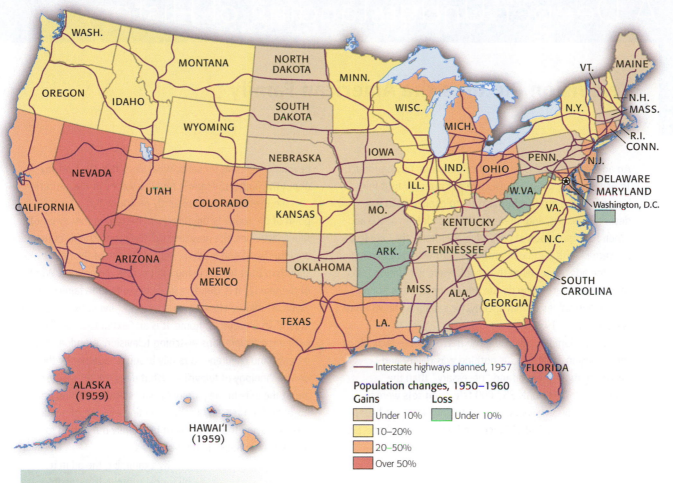

MAP 25.3 Movement Across America, 1950–1960
Americans were on the move during the 1950s. White Americans moved to the suburbs, especially in the South and West. Many African Americans left rural areas of the South; others moved against existing patterns of segregation. This map shows the web of interstate highways and population shifts during this period.
© Cengage Learning.

more white-collar jobs existed than blue-collar ones, and union membership continued to decline from wartime highs. Organized labor responded by merging the CIO and AFL in 1956, avoiding strikes, and focusing on better wages, cost-of-living raises, and pensions and health benefits.

Central to the new economy were the automobile and the industries and jobs that the car generated. By 1960, 75 percent of all Americans had at least one car and were driving millions of miles, stopping at newly constructed motels, amusement parks, shopping malls, drive-in theaters, and fast-food restaurants. The $32 billion allocated to build an interstate highway system was only a fraction of funds spent on road construction by all levels of government (see Map 25.3). New and better highways led to more cars, and more cars needed still more roads, parking lots, and places to visit. Disneyland opened in 1955, with acres of parking lots to accommodate the family cars of those who entered the "Happiest Place on Earth." Within

six months a million people had visited the "Magic Kingdom." A year earlier, Ray Kroc had opened the first McDonald's "drive-to" restaurant; within four years the chain had opened 738 locations, changed the nation's eating habits, and became an American icon.

Suburban Culture and Consumerism

The suburban housing boom continued to spark the economy and, like the automobile, to shape the American landscape. "We were thrilled to death," recalled one newly arrived suburbanite. "Everyone was arriving with a sense of forward momentum. Everyone was taking courage from the sight of another orange moving van pulling in next door, a family just like us, unloading pole lamps and cribs and Formica dining tables like our own. . . ." Many of the families were moving into new "ranch" or California-style homes, designed to match the most modern family's needs. It was a single-story rectangular or L-shaped

Television Pictures the American Family

An advertiser's goal is to convince people to buy a product. To achieve this, the most effective ads not only tout the benefits of the product but also try to connect it to the desires, concerns, and interests of those looking at the ad. When historians look at past advertisements, they are less concerned with particular products than with determining how the ads reflect what the people were like during that time in that place. How do the ads connect to the popular culture and values of that society, for example, the vision of America in the 1950s?

Here, a family is watching the newest home technology, the television. In the 1950s nothing was newer and becoming more popular and "necessary" than the television. In 1948 only 350,000 television sets were in use, but within five years over 25 million sets were being watched—nearly half of American families owned one. So, beyond competing for sales, what does this 1951 ad say about the home, the family, and the values of the period?

The television is prominently positioned as a focal point of the room. Is the television becoming the center of family activities, the new hearth? The room itself is quite well furnished and modern, very likely one of the new suburban tract homes being built across the country. What of the family? It is clearly a well-dressed white family—the "typical" middle-class American family "living the American dream" in a suburban home. It is an "extended" family with three generations watching television: grandparents, parents, and children—a family brought together by the new technology of television. What does the ad suggest about the wife in the picture? Is she standing behind her husband for a reason? Is she reflecting a vision of gender roles, enjoying the company of her family but poised to move if some household need arises?

By examining the ad in its historical context, it is possible to see that in addition to touting the product, the ad reflects a nation that is re-embracing the ideal of the traditional family as the center of social harmony and stability after two decades of social crises: depression and war. It is suggesting that achieving the American dream, or part of it, is possible, and that the television is part of that dream. It demonstrates how the new consumer world can contribute to a return to normalcy; in short, it is bridging the gap between the new and the nostalgic past.

Picture Research Consultants & Archives.

house with a simple floor plan, an attached garage, and a family room—sometimes complete with a television, now the focus of the house. Near the family room was the "modern" kitchen with its new appliances, including a refrigerator with a larger freezer to accommodate the growing number of frozen foods and "TV dinners" that made life easier for the stay-at-home housewife.

At the heart of the home was the American nuclear family. Families were considered the strength of the nation, and the number of families continued to grow, with the baby boom peaking at 4.3 million births in 1957. Within the family there were clearly defined and idealized roles. Husbands were the breadwinners and directed weekend events. Wives managed the home, cared for the children, and deferred to their husbands' decisions. "There was this pressure to be the perfect housekeeper," remembered one suburban wife. For guidance on how to raise babies and children, millions of Americans turned to Dr. Benjamin Spock's popular book *Baby and Child Care* (1946). A mother's love and positive parental guidance were keys to healthy and well-adjusted children. Strict rules and corporal punishment were to be avoided. To ensure proper gender identity, boys should participate in sports and outdoor activities, whereas girls should concentrate on their appearance and domestic skills. Toy guns and doctor bags were for boys; dolls, tea sets, and nurse kits were for girls. Conforming—being part of the group—was as important for parents as for children. Those not fulfilling those roles were suspected of being homosexual, immature, or simply irresponsible.

Television helped define suburban life. Televisions were not widely available until after the war, and then they were very expensive. But as prices fell, the number of homes with a television rocketed from about 9 percent in 1950 to nearly 90 percent by the end of the decade. At the same time, programming developed audience-oriented time slots with cartoons and westerns for children on weekend mornings and sports for dad on Saturday and Sunday afternoons. The most watched time slot, however, was after dinner and designed for family viewing. By 1960 most people watched television five hours a day.

Among the most popular shows during the family time slot were situation comedies ("sitcoms") like *Father Knows Best* (1953) and *Leave It to Beaver* (1957). They depicted "normal" middle-class families that were white with hardworking fathers and attractive, stay-at-home mothers. The children, usually numbering between two and four, did well in school, rarely worried about the future, and provided humorous dilemmas for Mom to untangle with common sense and sensitivity. After the dislocations of the Depression and the war, stable households seemed to represent the strength and future of the country.

Part of the family's strength and stability, many argued, came from religious faith. "The family that prays together stays together," announced the Advertising Council. Church attendance reached a historic high of 59.5 percent in 1953, and that did not include those who attended religious revivals or listened to religious radio and television programs. Religious leaders like the **Reverend Norman Vincent Peale** and Billy Graham were commonly rated as the most important members of society. Peale's message of Christian positive thinking as a means to improve both the individual and society found a wide audience. More conservative evangelists like Graham questioned society's materialism and stressed a higher level of personal morality. While their views on religion and the problems facing America differed, religious leaders were unanimous on the need to promote faith to prevent the spread of communism. In keeping with the spirit of the times, Congress added "under God" to the Pledge of Allegiance in 1954 and "In God We Trust" to the American currency in 1955.

Another dimension of the economy and suburbia was consumerism. Radio and television bombarded their audiences with images of products Americans supposedly needed. The average television watcher saw over five hours a week of TV with ads enticing viewers to buy goods that would improve their lives. According to one ad man, television was a "man-eating tiger," and with one commercial on television "sales would go through the roof." To sell their products, advertisers used images that resonated with the public, ones that conveyed youth, sophistication, and modernity, as well as the image of the ideal American family enjoying the fruits of a prosperous nation. Automobile companies emphasized their "modern" styles, complete with rocket-like fins, and linked the car to the idealized family that saw the "USA in their Chevrolet." The public responded enthusiastically, trading in out-of-date, but still very operable, cars for the newest models. Gone were the depression and war mottos of "use it up" and "wear it out."

Increasingly, to pay for cars, televisions, washing machines, toys, and "Mom's night out," Americans turned to credit, and a new form of credit was available—the all-purpose credit card. The Diner's Club credit card made its debut in 1950, followed by American Express and a host of other plastic cards. By 1958, credit purchases reached $44 billion, more than five times the amount bought on credit in 1946.

■ **Reverend Norman Vincent Peale** Minister who told his congregations that positive thinking could help them overcome all their troubles in life; his book *The Power of Positive Thinking* was an immediate bestseller.

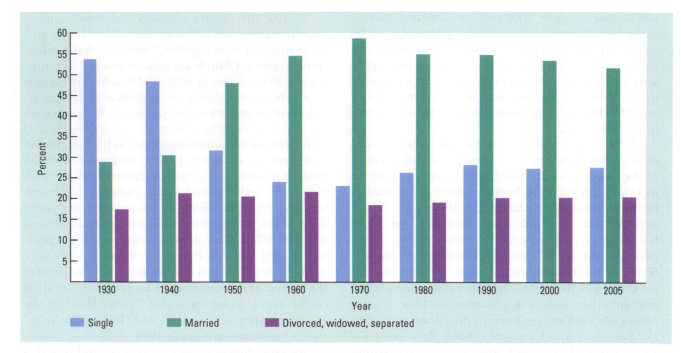

FIGURE 25.1 Marital Status of Women in the Workforce, 1930–2005
This figure shows the percentage of women in the workforce from the Great Depression through 2005. While the number of women who fell into the category of divorced, widowed, and separated remained fairly constant, a significant shift occurred in the number of single and married women in the workforce, with the number of single women declining as the number of married women increased.

Source: U.S. Department of Commerce, *Historical Statistics of the United States, Colonial Times to 1970*, Vol. 1 (Washington, D.C.: U.S. Government Printing Office, 1970), pp. 20–21, 131–132; U.S. Department of Commerce, *Statistics of the United States, 1993* (Washington, D.C.: U.S. Government Printing Office, 1993), pp. 74, 399; U.S. Department of Commerce, *Statistical Abstract of the United States: 2003* (Washington, D.C.: U.S. Government Printing Office, 2003), pp. 390–391; and Richard Smith and Susan Carlan, Eds., *Historical Statistics of the United States: Earliest Times to the Present*, Vol. 2 (Cambridge University Press, New York, 2006), pp. 131–133.

Working Wives and Rocking Kids

Unlike the families shown on television, life in the suburbs was not always idyllic or equal to expectations. "Togetherness" was more often seen on televisions than in real life. Studies found that more than one-fifth of suburban wives were unhappy with their marriages and lives. Many women complained of the drudgery and boredom of housework and a lack of understanding and affection from their husbands.

Responding to personal motives or economic needs, more married middle-class women were working outside the home, even those with young children (see Figure 25.1). While some sought self-fulfillment in careers, others worked to safeguard their family's existing **standard of living**. Most found part-time jobs or sales-clerk or clerical positions that paid low wages and provided few benefits. *Look* magazine, in a 1956 article, pointed out that about a third of the workforce

standard of living Level of material comfort as measured by the goods, services, and luxuries currently available and affordable.

were women, usually seeking to fill their "hope chest" or to buy "a new home freezer" and happily conceding "the top job rungs to men." Whether they conceded gracefully or not, in the banking sector, women made up 46 percent of the workforce but held only 15 percent of upper-level positions.

Like their mothers, children did not always match the image of the ideal family, and juvenile delinquency became a serious concern for parents and society. Juvenile crime among gangs operating in cities was not new, but as the 1950s progressed, many in the middle-class suburbs were alarmed about the behavior of their own teens who seemed to flout traditional values and behavior. At the center of the problem, many believed, was the public high school, where middle-class kids mixed with children of the "other America." The children of working-class whites, Latinos, and African Americans were attending high school in larger numbers and were thought to be a bad influence. Their clothing choices—T-shirts, jeans, leather jackets—their disrespect for authority, and their music conflicted with middle-class norms. Adding to the problem, experts said, were "improper" family environments where lax parenting and improper gender roles led to confused children and juvenile delinquents. For example, in the film *Rebel Without a Cause* (1955), with teen idol James Dean, the rebellious young characters come from suburban homes where gender roles are reversed, with dominating mothers and fathers who cook and assume many traditional housewifely duties.

The problem with kids also seemed connected to cars and "rock 'n' roll." The availability of the car allowed teens to escape adult controls and provided "a private lounge for drinking and . . . sex episodes." Rock 'n' roll, the term coined by Alan Freed, was a new American music genre that broke barriers between "black music" and "white music." Critics argued that it undermined American morals and was a tool of communism. A Catholic Youth Center newspaper asked readers to "smash" rock 'n' roll records because they promoted "a pagan concept of life." But it was a losing battle. By mid-decade, African American artists like Chuck Berry, Little Richard, and Ray Charles were successfully "crossing over" and being heard on "white" radio stations, while white singers copied and modified R&B songs to produce **cover records**.

Hosted by Dick Clark, *American Bandstand* first aired nationally in 1957, showing teens dancing to the latest top-forty records and helping to create the youth culture. Not all stations agreed that the program was "wholesome," and some refused to air it.

Paul Schutzer/Time Life Pictures/Getty Images.

Cover artists like Pat Boone sold millions of records that avoided suggestive lyrics and were heard on hundreds of radio stations that refused to play the original versions by black artists. At the same time, some white singers, including the 1950s' most dynamic star, **Elvis Presley**, were making their own contributions. Beginning with "Heartbreak Hotel" in 1956, Presley recorded fourteen gold records within two years. In concerts, he drove his audiences into frenzies with sexually suggestive movements that earned him the nickname "Elvis the Pelvis." Less controversial, Dick Clark's *American Bandstand*, a weekly television show featuring teens dancing to rock 'n' roll, was by the end of the decade one of the nation's most watched and most accepted programs.

Rejecting Consensus

Rock 'n' roll became accepted by the end of the decade, but homosexuality was another matter. **Alfred Kinsey**'s studies of sexuality found that a sizable number of gays and lesbians lived "closeted" lives throughout the United States and that an increasingly open gay subculture was centered in major cities. In a society that emphasized the traditional family and feared internal subversion, homosexuals represented behavior that could not be condoned. Some argued homosexuality was a psychological illness, but most considered

it a crime subject to legal prosecution. **Vice squads** frequently raided gay and lesbian bars, and newspapers often listed the names, addresses, and employers of those arrested. A Senate investigating committee concluded that because of a lack of moral fiber, one homosexual could "pollute a Government office." Within the government, homosexuals were barred from military service and most government jobs. In response to the attacks, many took extra efforts to hide their homosexuality, but some organized to confront the prejudice. Henry Hay formed the Mattachine Society in 1951 to fight for homosexual rights, and in 1955 Del Martin and Phyllis Lyon organized a similar organization for lesbians, the Daughters of Bilitis.

cover records A version of a song already recorded by an original artist.

■ **Elvis Presley** Immensely popular rock 'n' roll musician from a poor white family in Mississippi; many of his songs and concert performances were considered sexually suggestive.

Alfred Kinsey Biologist whose studies of human sexuality attracted great attention in the 1940s and 1950s, especially for his conclusions on infidelity and homosexuality.

vice squads Police units charged with the enforcement of laws dealing with vice—that is, immoral practices such as gambling and prostitution.

Also viewed as extreme were the **Beats**, or "beatniks," a group that rejected the morality and lifestyles of mainstream American culture. Allen Ginsberg in his poem *Howl* (1956) and Jack Kerouac in his novel *On the Road* (1957) denounced American materialism and sexual repression, and glorified a freer, natural life. A minority, especially among young college students, found the beatnik critique of "square America" meaningful, but most Americans easily rejected the Beats' message and lifestyles.

Americans could justify the suppression of beatniks and homosexuals because they appeared to mock traditional values of family and community. Other critics of American society, however, were more difficult to dismiss. Several respected writers and intellectuals claimed that the suburban and consumer culture was destructive—stifling diversity and individuality in favor of conformity. Mass-produced homes, meals, toys, fashions, and the other trappings of suburban life, they said, created a gray sameness about Americans. Sociologist David Riesman argued in *The Lonely Crowd* (1950) that postwar Americans, unlike earlier generations, were "outer-directed"—less sure of their values and morals and overly concerned about fitting into a group. Peer pressure, he suggested, had replaced individual thinking. William H. Whyte's controversial *Organization Man* (1956) echoed Riesman's concerns and found that working as a team had surpassed self-reliance as a trait of American workers. Both urged readers to resist being packaged like cake mixes and to reassert their own identities. In another vein, Holden Caulfield, the hero of J. D. Salinger's *The Catcher in the Rye* (1951), unable to find his place in society, merely concluded that the major features of American life were all phony.

Outside Suburbia

The average American depicted by *Reader's Digest* was a white, middle-class suburbanite. This portrait excluded a huge part of the population, especially minorities and the poor. Although the percentage of those living below the poverty line—set during the 1950s at around $3,000 a year—was declining, it was still over 22 percent and included large percentages of the elderly, minorities, and women heads of households. Even with Social Security payments, as 1959 ended nearly 31 percent of those over age 65 lived below the poverty line, with 8 million receiving less than $1,000 a year. Women heads of household contributed another 23 percent of those living in poverty, while throughout rural America, especially among small farmers and farm workers, poverty was common. In rural Mississippi, the annual per capita income was less than $900.

Poverty also increased in major cities as blacks and Latinos continued to migrate there. By 1960 half of all African Americans and nearly 80 percent of Latinos lived in urban centers where nonwhite unemployment commonly reached 40 percent. New York's Puerto Rican community, for example, increased more than 1,000 percent, while in cities like Atlanta and Washington, D.C., African Americans became the majority. Yet, despite their growing numbers, minorities rarely exercised any political power. At the same time, most cities were less able to provide needed services because of lost tax revenues as white middle- and working-class families moved into the suburbs and were followed by many businesses. When funds were available for urban renewal and development, many city governments, like Miami and Los Angeles, used those funds to relocate and isolate minorities in specific neighborhoods away from entertainment and upscale shopping and residential areas.

THE CIVIL RIGHTS MOVEMENT

☆ How did African Americans attack de jure segregation in American society during the 1950s?

☆ What role did the federal government play in promoting civil rights?

For many African Americans, poverty was just one facet of life. They also faced a legally sanctioned segregated society. Legal, or **de jure**, segregation existed not only in the South but also in the District of Columbia and several western and midwestern states. Changes had occurred, but most African Americans regarded them as minor victories, indicating no real shift in white America's racial views. By 1952 the NAACP had won cases permitting African American law and graduate students to attend white colleges and universities, even though the separate-but-equal ruling established in 1896 by the Supreme Court in *Plessy v. Ferguson* remained intact (see page 000). As the decade progressed, efforts against segregation intensified, but assistance from the federal government was slow in coming.

Integrating Schools

A step toward more significant integration in education came in 1954 when the Supreme Court

□ **Beats** Group of American writers, poets, and artists in the 1950s, including Jack Kerouac and Allen Ginsberg, who rejected traditional middle-class values and championed nonconformity and sexual experimentation.

de jure According to, or brought about by, law, such as "Jim Crow" laws that separated the races throughout the South until passage of the 1964 Civil Rights Act.

It Matters Today

The *Brown* Decision

The *Brown v. Board of Education* decision by the Supreme Court remains a milestone in American history. "It is doubtful that any child may reasonably be expected to succeed in life if he is denied the opportunity of an education. Such an opportunity," the Court wrote, "is a right which must be made available to all in equal terms." The ruling raised expectations in that it desegregated public schools, but it also fell short of expectations: it did not provide for effective integration or equality of education. Other cases have since tested the definitions of equality and the methods used to achieve racial diversity. Until the late 1970s, the Court's decisions upheld using race as a determining factor to achieve diversity. However, since then, several of the Court's decisions have indicated that the use of race has discriminated against Caucasians—a reverse discrimination. Is there a way, one Justice recently asked, to decide when the "use of race to achieve diversity" is benign or discriminatory?

- Some argue that the Supreme Court should apply "color-blind" criteria when deciding if institutions and businesses can use race to create diversity. How does this view reflect the view of the original *Brown* decision?
- Research the issues behind the December 2006 Supreme Court cases involving the Seattle, Washington, and Louisville, Missouri, school districts. Compare the issues to the decisions made by the Court on the issue in June 2007.

---

considered the case of **Brown v. Board of Education**, *Topeka, Kansas*. The *Brown* case had started four years earlier, when Oliver Brown sued to force the school district to allow his daughter to attend a nearby white school. The Kansas courts had rejected his suit, pointing out that the availability of a school for African Americans fulfilled the Supreme Court's separate-but-equal ruling. The NAACP appealed. In addressing the Supreme Court, NAACP lawyer **Thurgood Marshall** argued that the concept of "separate but equal" was inherently self-contradictory. He used statistics to show that black schools were unequal in financial resources and the quality and number of teachers. He also used a psychological study indicating that black children educated in a segregated environment suffered from low self-esteem. Marshall stressed that segregated educational facilities, even if physically similar, could never yield equal results.

In 1952 a divided Court was unable to make a decision, but two years later the Court heard the case again. Now sitting as chief justice was **Earl Warren**, the Republican former governor of California who had been appointed to the Court by Eisenhower in 1953. To the dismay of many who had considered Warren a legal conservative, the chief justice and the Court rejected social and political consensus and unanimously stated that "separate educational facilities are inherently unequal." Recognizing the degree of change the *Brown* decision wrought, in 1955, the Court addressed how to implement the ruling and gave primary responsibility to local school boards, ordering them to proceed

with "all deliberate speed." The justices also instructed lower federal courts to monitor progress according to this vague guideline.

Reactions to the case were predictable. African Americans and liberals hailed the decision and hoped that segregated schools would soon be an institution of the past. Southern whites vowed to resist integration by all possible means. Virginia passed a law closing any integrated school. Southern congressional representatives issued the **Southern Manifesto**, in which they proudly pledged to oppose the *Brown* ruling. Eisenhower, who believed the Court had erred, refused to support the decision publicly.

While both political parties carefully danced around school integration and other civil rights issues, the school district in Little Rock, Arkansas,

□ **Brown v. Board of Education** A 1954 Supreme Court case in which the Court ruled that separate educational facilities for different races were inherently unequal.

□ **Thurgood Marshall** Civil rights lawyer who argued thirty-two cases before the Supreme Court and won twenty-nine; he became the first African American justice of the Supreme Court in 1967.

□ **Earl Warren** Chief Justice of the Supreme Court from 1953 to 1969, under whom the Court issued decisions protecting civil rights, the rights of criminals, and First Amendment rights.

□ **Southern Manifesto** Statement issued by 106 southern congressmen in 1954, after the *Brown v. Board of Education* decision, pledging to oppose desegregation.

moved forward with "all deliberate speed." Central High School was scheduled to integrate in 1957. Opposing integration were the parents of the school's students and Governor Orval Faubus, who ordered National Guard troops to surround the school and prevent desegregation. When Elizabeth Eckford, one of the nine integrating students, walked toward Central High, National Guardsmen blocked her path as a hostile mob roared, "Lynch her! Lynch her!" Spat on by the jeering crowd, she retreated to her bus stop. Central High remained segregated.

For three weeks the black students were prevented from enrolling. Then on September 20 a federal judge ordered the integration of Central High School. Faubus complied and withdrew the National Guard. But segregationists remained determined to block integration and on Monday, September 23, 1957, when they discovered that the nine had slipped into the school unnoticed, they rushed the police lines and battered the school doors open. Inside the school, Melba Patella Beals thought, "I'm going to die here, in school." Hurriedly, the students were loaded into cars and warned to duck their heads. School officials ordered the drivers to "start driving, do not stop. . . . If you hit somebody, you keep rolling, 'cause [if you stop] the kids are dead."

Integration had lasted almost three hours and was followed by rioting throughout the city, forcing the mayor to ask for federal troops to restore order. Faced with insurrection, Eisenhower, on September 24, nationalized the Arkansas National Guard and dispatched a thousand troops of the 101st Airborne Division to Little Rock. Speaking to the nation, the president emphasized that he had sent the federal troops not to integrate the schools but to uphold the law and to restore order. The distinction was lost on most white southerners, who fumed as soldiers protected the nine black students for the rest of the school year. Even with the presence of the soldiers, threats against the nine students continued. Beals remembered that "there was no word big enough to explain her fear," fear that any day she could be killed.

The following school year (1957–1958), the city closed its high schools rather than integrate them. To prevent such actions, the Supreme Court ruled in **Cooper v. Aaron** (1959) that an African American's right to attend school could not "be nullified openly" or "by evasive schemes for segregation." Little Rock's high schools reopened, and integration slowly spread to the lower grades. But in Little Rock, as in other communities, many white families fled the integrated public schools and enrolled their children in private

■ **Cooper v. Aaron** Supreme Court decision (1958) that barred state authorities from interfering with desegregation either directly or through strategies of evasion.

Francis Miller/Time Life Pictures/Getty Images.

As Elizabeth Eckford approached Little Rock's Central High School, the crowd began to hurl curses, and a National Guardsman blocked her entrance into the school with his rifle. Terrified, she retreated down the street away from the threatening mob. Weeks later, this photograph was taken when Eckford, with army troops protecting her, finally attended—and integrated—Central High School.

schools that were beyond the reach of the federal courts. With no endorsement from the White House and entrenched southern opposition, "all deliberate speed" amounted to a snail's pace. By 1965, less than 2 percent of all southern schools were integrated.

The Montgomery Bus Boycott

While the nation responded to the *Brown* decision, other events involving civil rights grabbed national headlines, including the death of Emmett Till and the Montgomery bus boycott. In 1955, Till, an African American teenager from Chicago, visited relatives in Mississippi and was brutally tortured and murdered for speaking to a white woman without her permission. In the trial that followed, the two murderers were acquitted. It was not an unexpected verdict in Mississippi, but it and the brutality of the murder shocked much of the nation. That shock increased when the murderers sold their story to *Look* magazine for $4,000 and admitted that even after they had beaten Till, he still talked back. "I listened," said J. W. Milam, "to that nigger throw that poison at me, and I just made up my mind, 'Chicago boy', I said, 'I'm tired of 'em sending your kind down here to stir up trouble. . . . I'm going to make an example of you—just so everybody can know how me and my folks stand.'"

On December 1, 1955, Rosa Parks made a fateful choice—she refused to give up her seat to a white man on a Montgomery, Alabama, bus. Her act of defiance ignited a grassroots effort by African Americans to eliminate discrimination during which Martin Luther King Jr. emerged as a national leader for the civil rights movement. These pictures show the Montgomery Police Department's mug shots of King and Parks following their arrests. "I had no idea history was being made," Parks stated later. "I was just tired of giving in."

AP Photo/Montgomery County (Ala.) Sheriff's office.

AP Photo/Montgomery County Sheriff's office.

Later in 1955, on December 1 in Montgomery, Alabama, **Rosa Parks** set a different kind of example when she refused to give up her seat on a city bus so a white man could sit. At 42, Mrs. Parks earned $23 a week as a seamstress, and she had not boarded the bus with the intention of disobeying the seating law, although she strongly opposed it. But that afternoon, her fatigue and humiliation were suddenly too much. She refused to move and was arrested.

Hearing of her arrest, local African American community leaders saw an opportunity to contest segregation. They petitioned the city and the bus company to consider a more equitable bus seating system, and when both refused, they called for a boycott of the bus line.

On December 5, 1955, the night before the boycott nearly four thousand people filled and surrounded Holt Street Baptist Church to hear **Martin Luther King Jr.** the newly selected leader of the boycott movement—now called the Montgomery Improvement Association. King firmly believed that the church had a social justice mission and that violence and hatred, even when considered justified, brought only ruin. In shaping that evening's speech, he wrestled with the problem of how to balance disobedience with peace, confrontation with civility, and rebellion with tradition—and his words overcame the contradictions, electrifying the crowd: "We are here this evening to say to those who have mistreated us so long that we are tired of being segregated and humiliated, tired of being kicked about by the brutal feet of oppression." King asked the crowd to boycott the buses, to protest "courageously, and yet with dignity and Christian love," and when confronted with violence, to "bless them that curse you."

On December 6, Rosa Parks was tried, found guilty, and fined $10, plus $4 for court costs. She appealed,

■ **Rosa Parks** Black seamstress who refused to give up her seat to a white man on a bus in Montgomery, Alabama, in 1955, triggering a bus boycott that energized the civil rights movement.

■ **Martin Luther King Jr.** Ordained Baptist minister and civil rights leader committed to nonviolence; a brilliant orator, he led many of the important protests of the 1950s and 1960s.

Desegregation and the Supreme Court

Since the end of Reconstruction, African Americans and organizations like the NAACP have used the courts to fight segregation, but with few victories until the mid-1950s. Then the Warren Court, in the *Brown* (1954) and *Cooper* (1958) decisions utilized the equal protection clause of the Fourteenth Amendment to strike down segregation in public schools. These decisions provided a basis on which lower-level federal courts began to dismantle discrimination and segregationist practices by public service companies and state and local governments. Reflecting the *Brown* decision, the federal Fourth Circuit Court concluded in *Gayle v. Browder* (1956) "that the separate but equal doctrine can no longer be safely followed as a correct statement of the law . . . there is now no rational basis upon which the separate but equal doctrine can be validly applied. . . ."

and the boycott, 90 percent effective, stretched into days, weeks, and finally months. Police issued basketfuls of traffic tickets to drivers taking part in the car pools that provided transportation for boycotters. Insurance companies canceled their automobile coverage, and acid was poured on their cars. On January 30, 1956, someone threw a stick of dynamite that destroyed King's front porch, almost injuring King's wife and a friend. King remained calm, reminding supporters to

□ **Southern Christian Leadership Conference** (SCLC) Group formed by Martin Luther King Jr. and others after the Montgomery bus boycott; it became the backbone of the civil rights movement in the 1950s and 1960s.

□ **Civil Rights Act of 1957** Created the U.S. Commission on Civil Rights, which primarily investigated restrictions on voting, and the Civil Rights Division of the Department of Justice.

avoid violence and persevere. Finally, as the boycott approached its first anniversary, the Supreme Court ruled in *Gayle et al. v. Browser* (1956) that the city's and bus company's policy of segregation was unconstitutional. "Praise the Lord. God has spoken from Washington, D.C.," cried one boycotter.

The Montgomery bus boycott shattered the traditional white view that African Americans accepted segregation, and it marked the beginning of a pattern of nonviolent resistance. Across the South thousands of African Americans were eager to take to the streets and to use the federal courts to achieve equality. Building on the energy generated by the boycott, in 1956, King and other black leaders formed a new civil rights organization, the **Southern Christian Leadership Conference** (SCLC).

Ike and Civil Rights

As the civil rights movement continued, the White House responded with carefully selected platitudes. When asked, Eisenhower gave elusive replies: "I plead for understanding, for really sympathetic consideration of a problem. . . . I am for moderation, but I am for progress; that is exactly what I am for in this thing." Personally, Eisenhower believed that government, especially the executive branch, had little role in integration. Max Rabb, his adviser on minority affairs, thought the "Negroes were being too aggressive." On a political level, cabinet members and Eisenhower were disappointed in the low number of blacks who had voted Republican in 1952 and 1956.

But not all within the administration were unsympathetic toward civil rights. Attorney General Herbert Brownell drafted the first civil rights legislation since Reconstruction. The **Civil Rights Act of 1957** passed Congress after a year of political maneuvering, having gained the support of Democratic majority leader Lyndon B. Johnson of Texas. A moderate law, it provided for the formation of a Commission on Civil Rights and opened the possibility of using federal lawsuits to ensure voter rights. A second act passed Congress in 1960 that strengthened efforts to use the courts to gain voting rights, but like its predecessor, it was too weak to counter white opposition and violence in the South.

Individual Voices

Pageant Magazine Examines "Rock 'n' Roll Alan Freed" (July 1957)

Controversy has always surrounded rock 'n' roll. Critics called it "jungle music," "cannibalistic and tribal," rife with "leer-ics" (sexual terms and innuendo), and worst of all "a communicable disease." But less alarmist views also existed, as in this excerpt by Theodore Irwin in *Pageant*, a popular monthly magazine that mixed common interest stories with photo features.

Michael Ochs Archives/Getty Images

❶ In what ways do the critics and those supportive of rock 'n' roll suggest that part of the problem is a generation gap? Are such generation gaps to be expected when "new" ways or technologies are introduced?

❷ In what ways does the language describing Freed suggest positive or negative images or both?

❸ Given Freed's income and convictions for payola, is his statement about the music being all about the "kids" an honest or hypocritical one?

❹ Rock 'n' roll has been part of the American music scene for several generations. Has Freed's forecast proven correct? Has it become part of the mainstream of popular music? Are there forms of music today that generate the same types of criticism that rock 'n' roll received in the 1950s?

. . . getting upset over . . . teen-age behavior has . . . become a national pastime. A noisy crowd is just a crowd . . . unless it's composed of adolescents and then it's labeled a "riot" . . . when youngsters get into trouble, adults . . . have pointed an accusing finger at the new "corrupter of youth" that "awful music" rock 'n' roll. . . . Apparently rock 'n' roll has no charms to soothe the savage breast . . . over-exhilarated teenagers . . . have screeched and screamed, smashed windows, thrown beer bottles . . . wrecked theaters . . . and produced blaring headlines.

Elders have fumed . . . pontificated and legislated against the "craze." . . . [R]ock 'n' roll has been . . . banned in some public places. Eminent psychologists, sociologists and psychiatrists have characterized rock 'n' roll as everything from "adolescent rebellion" to a medieval type of spontaneous lunacy.

Yet millions of youngsters virtually live by rock 'n' roll and every day more and more . . . are becoming exponents . . . devotees will tell you that disapproving "middle-aged" people—anyone over 25—are hopeless squares . . . and . . . condemn what they don't understand. "We're having some fun before we get too old to enjoy ourselves," said one 15-year-old girl. . . ." ❶

Is rock 'n' roll . . . harmless . . . [o]r . . . dangerous?

Any serious investigation . . . inevitably runs smack into . . . Alan Freed. He coined the phrase . . . and . . . he is the acknowledged priest of the rock 'n' roll cult . . . and . . . evangelist of the teenagers' Big Beat. ❷

"Rock 'n' roll is kids," he says. . . . The music belongs to them—they had a need for it and they discovered it. . . . "Teenagers believe in me," he explains, "because they know I'm their friend and give them the music they want."

Virtually overnight, this super-salesman had parlayed rock 'n' roll to a $200,000 a year income . . . his program reaches 12 states. . . . On tape he's heard in Chicago, St. Louis, Kansas City and over . . . Radio Luxemburg throughout Europe and England. . . . On the side he writes songs . . . and is a partner in . . . a record company. . . . "In this business," he says candidly, "your career is so short you've got to get it from all angles." ❸

What is the future of rock 'n' roll?

"I think," says Freed, "it will settle itself into the mainstream of American popular music. In fact it is starting to right now . . . I expect in about ten years . . . my band will be playing at the Waldorf Astoria." ❹

Source: Theodore Irwin, "Rock 'n' Roll Alan Freed," Pageant (July 1957): 56–63.

Study Tools

SUMMARY

"Had enough?" Republicans asked voters in 1952. Voters responded by electing Eisenhower. Though promising change, Eisenhower chose foreign and domestic policies that continued the basic patterns established by Truman. Republicans reduced some domestic programs, but there was no large-scale dismantling of the New Deal. In foreign policy, the New Look relied on new tactics, but Eisenhower continued the policy of containment, expanding American influence in southern Asia and the Middle East. Although the Soviets spoke of peaceful coexistence, relations with the Soviet Union deteriorated during the decade, and Moscow seemed to score victories with *Sputnik* and in Cuba.

The 1950s spawned comforting images of American prosperity with affluent suburbs and a growing consumer culture. Yet the reality of the 1950s did not always match the image. Many people behaved contrary to the supposed norms of family and suburban culture. An increasing number of married women worked, while young adults embraced rock 'n' roll and other forms of expression that seemed to reject established norms and values. Others believed that America's middle-class culture bred too much conformity and stifled individualism.

Outside the suburbs another America existed, where economic realities, social prejudices, and entrenched politics blocked equality and upward mobility. In the South, a grassroots civil rights movement emerged to contest decades of segregation. By the end of the decade, long-established patterns of segregation were declared illegal by federal courts and civil rights had emerged as an issue that neither political party nor white America could ignore any longer.

CHRONOLOGY
The Fifties

1950	Korean War begins
1951	Mattachine Society formed
1952	Dwight David Eisenhower elected president
	United States tests hydrogen bomb
	Alan Freed's "The Moondog's Party"
1953	Death of Stalin
	Korean armistice at Panmunjom
	CIA helps overthrow Mohammad Mossadegh in Iran
	Termination programs for American Indians implemented
	Earl Warren appointed chief justice of Supreme Court
	Father Knows Best debuts on television
	Department of Health, Education, and Welfare created
1954	*Brown v. Board of Education*
	Army-McCarthy hearings
	CIA helps overthrow Jacobo Arbenz in Guatemala
	Geneva Agreement (Vietnam)
	SEATO founded
1955	Montgomery, Alabama bus boycott begins
	AFL-CIO merger
1956	Federal Highway Act
	Southern Christian Leadership Conference formed
	Eisenhower reelected
	Suez crisis
	Soviets invade Hungary
	Elvis Presley records "Heartbreak Hotel"
1957	Little Rock crisis
	Civil Rights Act
	Eisenhower Doctrine
	United States joins Baghdad Pact
	Soviets launch *Sputnik*
	Baby boom peaks at 4.3 million births
1958	United States sends troops to Lebanon
	National Defense Education Act
	NASA established
1959	Fidel Castro takes control in Cuba
	Nikita Khrushchev visits the United States
	Cooper v. Aaron
1960	Soviets shoot down U-2 and capture pilot
	Paris Summit

Study Tools

FOCUS QUESTIONS

If you have mastered this chapter, you should be able to answer these questions and to explain the terms that follow the questions.

1. *What were the popular images of Eisenhower, and how did they compare with reality?*

2. *What constraints did Eisenhower face in trying to roll back New Deal programs?*

3. *How did Eisenhower alter the federal government?*

4. *What were the weaknesses of the New Look and how did Eisenhower address them?*

5. *What tactics did the Eisenhower administration pursue in the "third world," especially in the Middle East and Latin America, to protect American interests?*

6. *What new economic factors contributed to prosperity in the 1950s?*

7. *What stresses and contradictions were at work beneath the placid surface of suburbia? Who voiced criticism and how did they express it?*

8. *Why were rock 'n' roll and rebellious teens seen as threats to social norms?*

9. *How did African Americans attack de jure segregation in American society during the 1950s?*

10. *What role did the federal government play in promoting civil rights?*

KEY TERMS

Federal Highway Act *p. 693*

Sputnik I *p. 693*

Sputnik II *p. 693*

National Defense Education Act *p. 694*

National Defense Student Loans *p. 694*

Army-McCarthy hearings *p. 694*

New Look *p. 695*

massive retaliation *p. 695*

Baghdad Pact *p. 696*

third world *p. 696*

Central Intelligence Agency *p. 696*

Shah Mohammad Reza Pahlavi *p. 696*

Eisenhower Doctrine *p. 698*

Viet Minh *p. 700*

domino theory *p. 700*

Geneva Agreement *p. 700*

Nikita Khrushchev *p. 700*

Keynesianism *p. 702*

Reverend Norman Vincent Peale *p. 705*

Elvis Presley *p. 707*

Beats *p. 708*

Brown v. Board of Education *p. 709*

Thurgood Marshall *p. 709*

Earl Warren *p. 709*

Southern Manifesto *p. 709*

Cooper v. Aaron *p. 710*

Rosa Parks *p. 711*

Martin Luther King Jr. *p. 711*

Southern Christian Leadership Conference *p. 712*

Civil Rights Act of 1957 *p. 712*

SUGGESTED RESOURCES

Glen C. Altschuler. *All Shook Up: How Rock 'n' Roll Changed America* (Oxford University Press, 2004). A readable examination of the origins and growth of rock 'n' roll and how it related to the social, sexual, and racial changes taking place in the United States in the 1950s.

Taylor Branch. *The Parting of the Waters: America in the King Years, 1954–1963* (Simon and Schuster, 1988). An interesting analysis of the beginning of the civil rights movement, focusing on the leadership of Martin Luther King.

David Halberstam. *The Fifties* (Villard Books, 1993). A well-written account of political and social changes taking place in the fifties, with excellent thumbnail sketches of important people and events.

Joanne Meyerowitz,. Ed., *Not June Cleaver: Women and Gender in Postwar America, 1945–1960* (Temple University Press, 1994). Fifteen essays that have shaped the study of women's history in the 1950s.

26

Great Promises, Bitter Disappointments, 1960–1968

CHAPTER OUTLINE

The Politics of Action
The 1960 Campaign
The New Frontier
Kennedy and Civil Rights

Flexible Response
Confronting Castro and the Soviets
Vietnam
Death in Dallas

Defining a New Presidency
Old and New Agendas
Implementing the Great Society

New Voices
Urban Riots and Black Power
Rejecting the Feminine Mystique
Rejecting Gender Roles
The Youth Movement
The Counterculture
INDIVIDUAL VOICES: *Eunice Kennedy Shriver Champions New Perspectives*

Study Tools

INDIVIDUAL CHOICES

Eunice Kennedy Shriver

In 1963, Eunice Kennedy Shriver wrote that those with severe intellectual disabilities needed a champion to change the way that people viewed them. Following her death in 2009, a commentator wrote that people with mental challenges "don't catch many breaks" but that "one island of inclusion: the Special Olympics" existed "because Eunice Shriver . . . insisted on looking differently at disability. She offered love without pity, a chance to race and win, and to win just by racing."

Unlike her brothers, Eunice Kennedy was not persuaded to enter politics. Instead, she was encouraged to take an active role in what she called "social work." Her involvement with intellectual disability arose from two sources: her experiences with her intellectually challenged sister Rosemary and a prod from her father. In the 1950s, Joseph Kennedy Sr. was considering using his Kennedy Foundation to support research on mental retardation and asked her and Sargent Shriver to investigate the possibilities. The results

UPI/Special Olympics /Landov.

were her marriage to Shriver and a commitment to bettering the lives of people with mental challenges.

Their investigation found that what was referred to as mental retardation (MR) was largely ignored by the scientific community, institutions, and governmental agencies. They discovered that families with children who had mental challenges were isolated and that such children were frequently "closeted" away from public view. They believed that MR needed to have a national priority, and Eunice Shriver was determined to see it through. In 1960, she prodded her brother, John Kennedy, who was running for president, to make children's health and MR part of his program. He agreed and over the next three years, she needled, cajoled, and lobbied him to maintain his commitment to those with mental challenges. Robert Kennedy joked that the president said, ". . . give Eunice whatever she wants so I can get her off the phone and get on with the business of government."

She also lobbied Congress, medical researchers and institutions, and the public (as illustrated in the Individual Voices feature at the end of this chapter). It was her "sense of mission" that added the weight of the federal government to improving the lives of those with mental disabilities. But government programs were only part of the solution. There was the issue of dignity. Popular perceptions needed to be changed—families needed to stop hiding their children with mental disabilities. The cycle of social isolationism had to be broken. Eunice Shriver's solution became the Special Olympics.

In 1962, Eunice Shriver created a day camp for children with mental disabilities at her Maryland home. "Camp Shriver" was a success and the idea spread. But she looked beyond localized day and summer recreational camps. She wanted a national venue that would be year-round and reach a wider public audience. In 1968, the Chicago Parks and Recreation Department sponsored a national track and field competition for children with mental retardation. Over nine hundred children from twenty-seven states and Canada competed, but only about twenty parents watched. "Parents had not yet learned they could be proud of their mentally retarded kids," observed one organizer. As the first competitions began, Eunice Shriver unexpectedly announced that the Kennedy Foundation would support "a national Special Olympics training program for all mentally retarded children everywhere," and that there would be an "international Special Olympics in 1970 and every two years thereafter." The result significantly shifted the nation's attention and perception. Today, nearly 3 million athletes of all ages participate in Special Olympics sports training and competition in more than 180 countries.

The 1960s evoke visions of change, of protest marches, demonstrations, and governmental activism. Kennedy's election provided a symbol of youth and vigor and raised expectations that the activism in the streets would be joined by that of government.

Much of Kennedy's domestic agenda faced strong political opposition in Congress, making it difficult to achieve his goals. He found more success in foreign policy, where he promised to confront global communism, especially in the developing regions of the world. Implementing a new strategy, "flexible response," he dealt with crises in Berlin, Cuba, and Vietnam.

Lyndon Johnson inherited Kennedy's agendas and added his own imprint. Prior to the 1964 presidential election, Johnson passed a civil rights bill and presented the nation with proposals for a Great Society. An onslaught of legislation that waged war on poverty and discrimination followed. Great Society measures increased education and welfare programs, expanded voting rights, and created a national system of health-care for the aged and poor. By mid-decade liberalism was at high tide.

However, unfilled expectations and increasingly controversial social and political issues brought forward new and often angry voices. Many African Americans chose confrontation over compromise as urban violence spread. Many women and young adults appeared to question, if not reject, traditional moral and social values. As the optimism that began the decade faded, many people worried about a fragmented society fraught with competing values and agendas.

THE POLITICS OF ACTION

★ *How successful was the Kennedy administration in achieving its domestic agenda?*

★ *What form of African American activism pushed the civil rights movement forward, and how did Kennedy respond to those efforts?*

Republicans had every reason to worry as the 1960 presidential campaign neared. In the last years of the 1950s, neither the president nor Republicans nor Congress appeared able to deal with the problems of the country—civil rights, a slowing economy, and Cold War setbacks. The Republican candidate for the presidency, Vice President Richard Nixon, calculated he would need the votes of practically all Republicans, more than half of independents, and about 6 million Democrats to win.

The 1960 Campaign

Facing Nixon stood John Fitzgerald Kennedy, a youthful, energetic senator from Massachusetts. A Harvard graduate, Kennedy came from a wealthy Catholic family. Some worried about his young age (43) and lack of experience. Others worried about his religion—no Catholic had ever been elected president. To offset these possible liabilities, Kennedy astutely added the politically savvy Senate majority leader Lyndon Johnson of Texas to the ticket, called for a new generation of leadership, and suggested that those who were making religion an issue were bigots. His slogan, the **New Frontier**, challenged the nation to improve the overall quality of life of all Americans and to stand fast against the Communist threat. He offered action and empowerment to the government, people, and institutions.

Nixon, too, promised an energetic presidency, vowing to improve the quality of life and support civil rights. He emphasized his executive experience and record of standing up to communism at home and abroad. Several political commentators called the candidates "two peas in a pod" and speculated that the election would probably hinge on appearances and party loyalty more than on issues.

A critical point of the campaign was the images projected by each candidate during televised debates. Kennedy appeared fresh and confident and spoke directly to the camera. Nixon appeared tired and haggard and looked at Kennedy rather than the camera. The contrasts were critical. Unable to see Nixon, the radio audience believed he won the debates, but to

The 1960 presidential race was at the time the closest in recent history, with many people believing that the outcome hinged on the public's perception of the candidates during their nationally televised debates. The majority of viewers believed that Kennedy (left) won the debates and looked more in control and presidential than Nixon.

© Bettmann/Corbis.

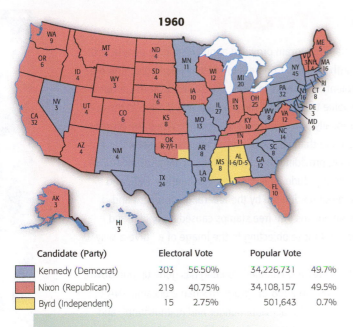

1960

Candidate (Party)	Electoral Vote		Popular Vote	
Kennedy (Democrat)	303	56.50%	34,226,731	49.7%
Nixon (Republican)	219	40.75%	34,108,157	49.5%
Byrd (Independent)	15	2.75%	501,643	0.7%

MAP 26.1 Election of 1960

Although Richard Nixon won in more states than John F. Kennedy, in the closest presidential election in the twentieth century, Kennedy defeated his Republican opponent by a slim eighty-four electoral votes and fewer than 119,000 popular votes. © Cengage Learning.

the 70 million television viewers, the winner was the self-assured Kennedy. The debates helped Kennedy, but victory depended on his holding the Democratic coalition together, maintaining southern Democratic support while wooing African American and liberal voters. Every vote was critical, but when the ballots were counted, Kennedy had secured popular and electoral victories. Congress remained in Democratic hands, although Republicans had gained twenty-two seats in the House of Representatives (see Map 26.1).

The New Frontier

The weather in Washington was frigid when Kennedy gave his inaugural address, but his speech fired the imagination of the nation. He pledged to march against "the common enemies of man: tyranny, poverty, disease, and war itself," exhorting Americans to "ask not what your country can do for you; ask what you can do for your country." Believing that most of the nation's problems were "technical" and could be solved by experts, Kennedy selected advisers from the ranks of Rhodes scholars, Harvard professors, and successful businessmen, including Ford Motor Company president Robert McNamara, who was tapped for secretary of defense. In a more controversial move, Kennedy named his brother Robert, who had never practiced law, as attorney general. Many hailed Kennedy's choices as representing "the best and the brightest." But not everyone thought so.

Referring to their lack of political background, Speaker of the House Sam Rayburn, a Democrat, remarked that he would "feel a whole lot better . . . if just one of them had run for sheriff once."

Kennedy asked Congress for a wide range of domestic programs, including a national health system and increased federal aid to education, but like Truman, he received only modest results. By 1963, Congress had approved small increases in Social Security, the minimum wage (to $1.25 an hour), a trial food stamp program, and a housing and **urban renewal** bill. Kennedy had better luck with the economy.

To spur the economy out of a recession, Kennedy implemented aggressive Keynesian monetary and **fiscal policies**. He promoted improved foreign trade and asked Congress for increased military spending and tax cuts. Congress approved a nearly 10 percent increase in defense spending and allotted more funds for NASA and the *Apollo* space program, but rejected the tax cuts. Even without the tax cuts, the economy grew by 13 percent, and by the end of the decade NASA landed a spacecraft on the moon. On July 21, 1969, Neil Armstrong became the first human to set foot on the moon.

Kennedy and Civil Rights

In 1960, the civil rights movement was continuing to expand in scope and numbers. In February 1960, four freshmen from North Carolina Agricultural and Technical College in Greensboro, North Carolina, decided to integrate the lunch counter at the local F. W. Woolworth store (see Map 26.2). They entered the store, sat down at the lunch counter, and ordered a meal. Refused service, but not arrested, they sat until the store closed. The next day twenty black A&T students sat at the lunch counter demanding service. The **sit-in** movement was born. It quickly spread to more than 140 cities, including some outside the South in Nevada, Illinois, and Ohio. In some cities, including Greensboro, integration succeeded with a minimum of resistance. But elsewhere, particularly in the Deep

New Frontier Program for social and educational reform put forward by President John F. Kennedy and largely resisted by Congress.

urban renewal Effort to revitalize rundown areas of cities by providing federal funding for the construction of apartment houses, office buildings, and public facilities.

fiscal policy The use of government spending to stimulate or slow down the economy.

sit-in The act of sitting peacefully in an establishment to protest its policies—a tactic used to protest segregation that energized civil rights activism at the start of the 1960s.

It Matters Today

Food Stamps

From 1939 to 1943, the food stamp program provided about 20 million people with government surplus food. Reauthorized by Congress in 1959, it was implemented as a pilot program in 1961. Recipients, like those in 1939, purchased a set of stamps at a discount to be used at face value to buy food. The program was limited to those on state assistance in eight traditionally poor regions of the country. When the program was made permanent in 1964, it had expanded to more than forty counties in twenty-two states.

The Food Stamp Act of 1977 made sweeping changes, providing the stamps free of charge, standardizing criteria for participation, and extending the program to include all fifty states, Washington, D.C., and overseas possessions. By the end of the 1970s the program, funded by the federal government and administered by the states, served over 20 million Americans. The free stamps caused a popular and political backlash among those opposed to welfare and those objecting to the image of a "give-a-way" welfare program.

Modifications have continued. The rules for eligibility have changed, funding has gone up and down, the stamps have been replaced with credit-like cards, and in 2008 the program's name became SNAP, Supplemental Nutrition Assistance Program, with the goal "to alleviate hunger and malnutrition" and promote healthy nutrition. In 2012, over 45 million people were served by SNAP, about 41 percent of the population. Its size, costs, and goals remain controversial. During the 2012 presidential campaign, Republicans labeled President Obama the "food stamp president" to indict his handling of the economy and to attack costly government "handout" programs.

- In the name of health, many have tried to eliminate sugary drinks and other less healthy foods from food stamp purchases. Should the government be able to tell those on food stamps what foods they can and cannot purchase?
- In 2011, food stamps formed a large part of the American "safety net." Those receiving food stamps averaged about $336 a month in take-home pay and nearly half had children. Those participating in the program were 36 percent white, 22 percent African American, 10 percent Hispanic, 4 percent Native American, 2 percent Asian, and 19 percent of unknown race or ethnicity. What do these statistics suggest about the nature of American poverty?
- Do free food stamps contribute to a culture of dependency?

South, thousands of participants were beaten and jailed.

Most of those taking part were young and initially unorganized, but as the movement grew, civil rights groups moved to incorporate the new tactic and its practitioners. In April 1960, Southern Christian Leadership Council official Ella Baker helped form the **Student Nonviolent Coordinating Committee** (SNCC), a new civil rights organization built around the sit-in movement. Although its statement advocated

nonviolence, SNCC members were anxious to confront segregation. "We do not intend to wait placidly for those rights which are already legally and morally ours," declared one SNCC member.

Although many hoped Kennedy would take an active role in promoting civil rights, once elected he acted cautiously. Needing to work with entrenched southern Democrats on other issues, Kennedy saw little reason to "raise hell" over civil rights. Instead, he relied on executive action, appointing African Americans to federal positions (more than any previous president), including NAACP lawyer Thurgood Marshall to the U.S. Court of Appeals.

Civil rights leaders applauded but were disappointed the government was not doing more. The sit-ins continued, and when the Supreme Court, in *Boynton v. Virginia* (December 1960), ruled that

■ **Student Nonviolent Coordinating Committee** (SNCC) Organization formed in 1960 to give young blacks a greater voice in the civil rights movement; it initiated black voter registration drives, sit-ins, and freedom rides.

public transportation must be desegregated, James Farmer of Congress of Racial Equality decided to test the decision with a series of **freedom rides** to integrate southern bus stations.

The freedom rides began in May 1961, despite the wishes of the Kennedy administration. Fearful of possible negative images of freedom riders being attacked while Kennedy met with Nikita Khrushchev during their summit in Vienna, the administration quietly asked that the rides be cancelled or at least delayed. Farmer refused, and as scheduled, the buses left Washington, D.C., and headed South (see Map 26.2). Trouble was anticipated, and in Anniston, Alabama, angry whites attacked some of the buses, setting them on fire and severely beating several freedom riders. "[I]t was going to be the end of me," one freedom rider recalled when his bus caught fire. Other buses proceeded on to Birmingham where the savagery continued.

As Farmer hoped, the violence forced the attorney general to place federal agents on the buses. Robert Kennedy also negotiated state and local protection for the riders through Alabama. When the buses arrived in Montgomery, Alabama, however, the police and National Guard escorts vanished, and a large mob attacked the riders and federal agents. Furious, the attorney general deputized local federal officials as marshals and ordered them to escort the freedom riders to the state line, where Mississippi forces would take over.

Battered and bloodied, the riders continued to the Mississippi state capital, Jackson. There they were peacefully arrested for violating Mississippi's recently passed **public order laws**. The jails quickly filled as more freedom riders arrived and were arrested—328 by the end of the summer. The freedom rides ended in September 1961 when the administration declared that the Interstate Commerce Commission would enforce the *Boynton* decision. Facing direct federal involvement, state and local authorities desegregated bus and train terminals.

Robert Kennedy hoped similar direct involvement would ease the integration of the University of

© Fred Blackwell/Wisconsin Historical Society.

When Kennedy took office, the sit-in movement was spreading across the South as students from colleges and universities sought to integrate places of public accommodation. In this picture, whites harass students from Tougaloo College who are participating in a sit-in at a Woolworth lunch counter in Jackson, Mississippi.

Mississippi by **James Meredith** in September 1962. A hundred federal marshals arrived to guard Meredith, but thousands of white students and nonstudents attacked Meredith and the marshals. Two people were killed, and nearly all the marshals were injured before five thousand army troops arrived and restored order. Protected by federal forces, Meredith finished the year and graduated in May 1963.

■ **freedom rides** An effort in which civil rights protesters rode buses throughout the South in 1961, despite attacks and arrests, seeking to achieve the integration of bus terminals.

public order laws Laws passed by many southern communities to discourage civil rights protests; the laws allowed the police to arrest anyone suspected of intending to disrupt public order.

■ **James Meredith** Black student admitted to the University of Mississippi under federal court order in 1962; in spite of rioting by racist mobs, he finished the year and graduated in 1963.

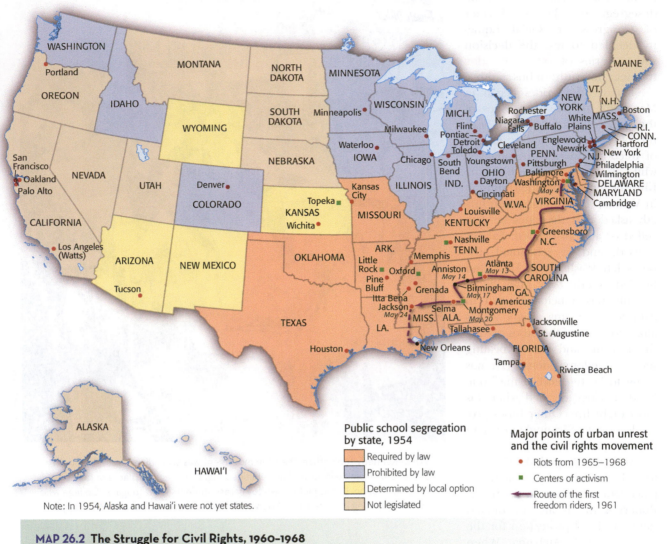

Public school segregation by state, 1954

- Required by law
- Prohibited by law
- Determined by local option
- Not legislated

Major points of urban unrest and the civil rights movement

- Riots from 1965–1968
- Centers of activism
- Route of the first freedom riders, 1961

Note: In 1954, Alaska and Hawai'i were not yet states.

MAP 26.2 The Struggle for Civil Rights, 1960–1968
In the mid-1950s, African Americans confronted the system of prejudice and segregation that existed across the country. This map shows hot spots of civil rights activism and flash points of urban unrest from 1960 to 1968. © Cengage Learning.

As Meredith prepared to graduate, Martin Luther King Jr., organized a series of protest marches to overturn segregation in Birmingham. King expected a violent reaction, which would force federal intervention and raise national awareness and support. On Good Friday, 1963, King led the first march. He was quickly arrested and, from his cell, wrote a nineteen-page "letter" defending his confrontational tactics. The "Letter from a Birmingham Jail" called for immediate and continuous peaceful civil disobedience. Freedom was "never given voluntarily by the oppressor," King asserted, but "must be demanded by the oppressed." Smuggled out of jail, read aloud in churches, and printed in newspapers across the nation, the letter rallied support for King's efforts.

In Birmingham the marches and violence continued. On May 3, as young and old alike filled the city's streets, Sheriff "Bull" Connor's police attacked the marchers with nightsticks, attack dogs, and high-pressure fire hoses. Television caught it all, including the arrest of battered and bruised children. Connor's brutality not only horrified much of the American public but caused many Birmingham blacks to reject the tactic of nonviolence. The following day, some clashed with the police, and fearing more violence, King and Birmingham's business element met on May 10. To ease tensions, business owners agreed to hire black salespeople. But neither the agreement nor King's pleading halted the violence, and two days later President Kennedy ordered three thousand troops to Birmingham to maintain order and to uphold the integration agreement. "The sound of the explosion in Birmingham," King observed, "reached all the way to Washington."

Birmingham encouraged Kennedy to make civil rights a priority. In June 1963, he sent Congress civil rights legislation that would mandate integration in public places. To pressure Congress to act on the bill, King and other civil rights leaders organized a **March on Washington**. During the August 28 march, King gave an address that electrified the throng. He warned about a "whirlwind of revolt" if black rights were denied. "I have a dream," he offered, "that my four little children will one day live . . . where they will not be judged by the color of their skin but by the content of their character" and that "all of God's children, black men and white men, Jews and Gentiles, Protestants and Catholics, will be able to join hands and sing . . . 'Free at last! Free at last! Thank God almighty, we are free at last!'" It was a stirring speech, but it did not move Congress to act. The civil rights bill stalled in committee, while in the South opposition to integration and racial violence continued. In Birmingham, within weeks of King's speech, a church bombing killed four young black girls attending Sunday school.

Paul Schutzer/Time Life Pictures/Getty Images.

In May 1961, freedom riders left Washington, D.C., for New Orleans on a mission to integrate bus terminals along the way. At stops in Alabama and Mississippi, the buses and riders were attacked. After negotiations between the Kennedy administration and Mississippi officials, it was agreed that Mississippi National Guard members, as pictured here, would guarantee the safety of the riders by escorting them on the buses. As part of the agreement, the administration allowed Mississippi officials to arrest the riders once they reached Jackson, Mississippi, on charges of traveling "for the avowed purpose of inflaming public opinion."

FLEXIBLE RESPONSE

☆ *How did Kennedy modify the strategy and tactics of Eisenhower's foreign policy?*

☆ *What actions did Kennedy take in Latin America and Vietnam to promote American interests?*

From day one, President Kennedy favored foreign over domestic policy. His inaugural address, in large part, concentrated on foreign policy, generating the powerful lines: "We shall pay any price, bear any burden, meet any hardship . . . to assure the survival and success of liberty." To back up his foreign policies, Kennedy instituted a new strategy called **flexible response** and significantly expanded military spending to pay for it. Flexible response involved maintaining existing agreements with NATO and other multilateral alliances, relying on CIA covert operations, enhancing nuclear capabilities, and completing an **intercontinental ballistic missile system**

(ICBMs). But it also included increased spending for conventional, nonnuclear weapons and for developing new strategies for fighting the Cold War in lesser developed nations.

Developing and third world nations were a special concern. Khrushchev had announced Moscow's support for "wars of national liberation" as a means to expand communism, and Kennedy meant to thwart that threat. To strengthen pro-Western governments' abilities to combat revolutionaries, Washington trained special counterinsurgency forces, such as the Green Berets. The military commitment, though, was second to wider economic strategies that provided direct government aid and private investment to "friendly" nations. This effort also included the personal involvement of American volunteers participating in the

- ■ **March on Washington** Meeting of a quarter of a million civil rights supporters in Washington in 1963, at which Martin Luther King Jr., delivered his "I Have a Dream" speech.
- ■ **flexible response** Kennedy's strategy of considering a variety of military and nonmilitary options when facing foreign-policy decisions.
- **intercontinental ballistic missiles system** (ICBMs) Missiles whose path cannot be changed once launched; their range can be from a few miles to intercontinental. In 2003 an estimated thirty-five nations had ballistic missiles.

Peace Corps. Beginning in March 1961, more than ten thousand idealistic young Americans enrolled for two years to help win the "hearts and minds" of what Kennedy called "the rising peoples" around the world. They staffed schools, constructed homes, built roads, and made other improvements.

Confronting Castro and the Soviets

Castro's success in Cuba vividly highlighted the need to succeed in the Cold War struggle for developing nations, especially those in Latin America and the Caribbean. Seeking a new approach to Latin America, in 1961 Kennedy introduced the **Alliance for Progress**, a foreign-aid package promising more than $20 billion. In return, Latin American governments were to introduce land and tax reforms and commit themselves to improving education and their people's standard of living. Kennedy believed this plan could "successfully counter the Communists in the Americas." Results did not meet expectations. United States aid fell well short of $20 billion, and Latin American governments implemented few reforms and frequently squandered the aid. Throughout the 1960s in Latin America, the gap between rich and poor widened, and the number of military dictatorships increased.

The Alliance for Progress also did not address the problem of Castro. Determined to remove the Cuban dictator, Kennedy implemented the CIA's plan approved by Eisenhower. On April 17, 1961, more than fourteen hundred Cuban exiles and mercenaries landed in Cuba at the *Bahía de Cochinos*, the **Bay of Pigs**. Within three days, Castro's forces had captured or killed most of the invaders. Kennedy took responsibility for the fiasco but indicated no regrets. Responding to his orders, U.S.

▪ **Peace Corps** Program established by President Kennedy in 1961 to send young American volunteers to other nations as educators, health workers, and technicians.

▪ **Alliance for Progress** Program proposed by Kennedy in 1961 through which the United States provided aid for social and economic programs in Latin American countries.

▪ **Bay of Pigs** Site of a 1961 CIA-sponsored invasion of Cuba by Cuban exiles and mercenaries; the invasion was crushed within three days and embarrassed the United States.

▪ **Berlin Wall** Wall between East and West Berlin that the Soviets erected during the 1961 Berlin crisis to stem the flow of refugees out of Eastern Europe.

Strategic Air Command (SAC) U.S. military unit formed in March 1946 to conduct long-range bombing operations anywhere in the world; its first strategic plan, completed in 1949, projected nuclear attacks on seventy Soviet cities. SAC was abolished in 1992 as part of the reorganization of the Department of Defense.

planners devised attempts to assassinate Castro and CIA-backed raids that destroyed roads, bridges, factories, and crops.

After the Bay of Pigs disaster, in early June 1961, Kennedy met with Khrushchev in Vienna, where their discussions focused on the status of Berlin. Khrushchev threatened to sign a peace treaty with East Germany giving the East Germans full control of all four zones of the city, leaving no room for a continued Western presence. Kennedy responded forcefully, declaring the United States' right to be there.

Returning home determined to show his resolve, Kennedy asked for massive increases in military spending, tripled the draft, and called fifty-one thousand reservists to active duty. In Moscow, Khrushchev renewed atmospheric nuclear weapons testing and reaffirmed his determination to oust the Allies from Berlin. Kennedy, in turn, resumed nuclear testing and reaffirmed his support for West Berlin. With both sides posturing, many feared armed confrontation, but in August the tension broke when the Soviets and East Germans suddenly erected a wall between East and West Berlin. Although the **Berlin Wall** blocked refugees fleeing East Germany and Eastern Europe and challenged Western ideals, it did not threaten the West's presence in West Berlin. It was "a hell of a lot better than a war," Kennedy concluded.

The Berlin crisis paled beside the possibility of nuclear confrontation over Cuba in October 1962. On October 14, an American U-2 spy plane discovered that medium-range nuclear missile sites were being built on the island. Launched from Cuba, such missiles would drastically reduce the time for mobilizing a U.S. counterattack on the Soviet Union. Kennedy promptly decided on a showdown with the Soviets and mustered a small crisis staff.

The military offered a series of recommendations ranging from a military invasion to a "surgical" air strike to destroy the missiles. These were rejected as too dangerous, possibly inviting a Soviet attack on West Berlin or on American nuclear missile sites in Turkey. President Kennedy, supported by his brother, the attorney general, decided to impose a naval blockade around Cuba until Khrushchev met the U.S. demand to remove the missiles. On Monday, October 22, Kennedy went on television and radio to inform the public of the missile sightings and his decision to quarantine Cuba. As 180 American warships got into position to stop Soviet ships carrying supplies for the missiles, army units converged on Florida. The **Strategic Air Command** (SAC) kept a fleet of nuclear-armed bombers in the air at all times. On Wednesday, October 24, confrontation and perhaps war seemed imminent as two Soviet freighters and a Russian submarine approached the quarantine line. Robert Kennedy recalled, "We were on the edge of a precipice with no way off." Voices around the world echoed his anxiety.

On October 22, 1963, at 7:00 P.M., President Kennedy addressed the nation, saying that there was "unmistakable evidence" that Moscow had placed missiles in Cuba and demanded that they be removed. For nearly two weeks the world watched and waited to see if the Cuban missile crisis would lead to nuclear war. In this political cartoon, a white-hatted Kennedy faces off against the pistol-twirling Castro who is backed up by all-in-black Khrushchev.

Library of Congress.

The Soviet vessels, however, stopped short of the blockade. Khrushchev had decided not to test Kennedy's will. After a series of diplomatic maneuvers, the two sides reached an agreement based on an October 26 message from Khrushchev: if the United States agreed not to invade Cuba, the Soviets would remove their missiles. Khrushchev sent another letter the following day that called for the United States to remove existing American missiles in Turkey. Kennedy publicly ignored the second message, but secretly agreed to remove the missiles in Turkey. The Soviets openly agreed to remove their missiles without mentioning the link to missiles in Turkey. Keeping its unpublicized promise to the Soviets, the United States withdrew its missiles in Turkey and Italy by April 1963. The world breathed a collective sigh of relief.

Kennedy basked in what many viewed as a victory in the **Cuban missile crisis**, but he recognized how near the world had come to nuclear war and concluded that it was time to improve Soviet-American relations. A "hot line" telephone link was established between Moscow and Washington to allow direct talks in case of another East-West crisis. Soviet and American negotiators also made progress on a **Limited Test Ban Treaty** to prevent further nuclear testing in the atmosphere, in space, and under the seas. Underground testing was still allowed. Completed in July, within months one hundred nations had signed the treaty, although the two newest atomic powers, France and China, refused to participate and continued to test in the atmosphere.

Vietnam

South Vietnam represented one of the most challenging issues Kennedy faced. He saw it as a place where the United States' flexible response could stem communism and develop a stable, democratic nation. But by 1961, President **Ngo Dinh Diem** was losing control of his nation. South Vietnamese Communist rebels, the **Viet Cong**, controlled a large portion of the countryside. Military advisers argued that American troops were necessary to turn the tide. Kennedy was more cautious. The South Vietnamese army (the ARVN) would have to continue to do the fighting, but more advisers would be sent. By November 1963, the United States had sent $185 million in military aid and had committed sixteen thousand advisers to Vietnam—compared with only a few hundred in 1961.

The Viet Cong were only part of the problem. Diem's administration was unpopular and unwilling to heed Washington's pleas for political and social reforms. Some feared Diem might seek an accord with North Vietnam, and by autumn of 1963, to American officials Diem seemed more a liability than an asset. Secretly, Washington informed selected Vietnamese

■ **Cuban missile crisis** Confrontation, seemingly threatening war, over Soviet missiles deployed in Cuba; the Soviets ultimately withdrew the missiles.

■ **Limited Test Ban Treaty** Treaty signed by the United States, the USSR, and nearly one hundred other nations in 1963; it banned nuclear weapons tests in the atmosphere, in outer space, and underwater.

■ **Ngo Dinh Diem** President of South Vietnam (1954–1963) who jailed and tortured opponents of his rule; he was assassinated in a coup in 1963.

Viet Cong Vietnamese Communist rebels in South Vietnam.

generals that it would support a change of government. The army acted on November 1, killing Diem and installing a new military government. The change of government, however, brought neither political stability nor improvement in the ARVN's capacity to defeat the Viet Cong.

Death in Dallas

With his civil rights and tax-cut legislation in limbo in Congress, Kennedy in late 1963 watched his popularity rating drop below 60 percent. He decided to visit Texas in November to try to heal divisions within the Texas Democratic Party. He was assassinated there on November 22, 1963. The police quickly captured the reputed assassin, Lee Harvey Oswald. Two days later a local nightclub owner, Jack Ruby, shot Oswald to death in the basement of the police station.

Many wondered whether Kennedy's assassination was the work of Oswald alone or part of a larger conspiracy. To dispel rumors, the government hastily formed a commission headed by Chief Justice Earl Warren to investigate the assassination and determine if others were involved. The commission hurriedly examined most, but not all, available evidence and announced that Oswald was a psychologically disturbed individual who had acted alone. No other gunmen were involved, nor was there any conspiracy. While many Americans accepted the conclusions of the Warren Commission, others continued to find errors in the report and to suggest additional theories about the assassination.

Kennedy's assassination traumatized the nation. Many people idealized the fallen president as an innovative chief executive who combined vitality, youth, and good looks with forceful leadership and good judgment. Lyndon B. Johnson, sworn in as president as he flew back to Washington on the plane carrying Kennedy's body, seemed very different from his Harvard-educated predecessor. He had attended public schools and graduated from a state teachers college, and he distrusted intellectuals. But Johnson had a passion for politics, and his experience was unrivaled. Having served in the House and in the Senate, where he had become Senate majority leader, Johnson knew how to wield political power and get things done in Washington.

filibuster Using obstructionist tactics, especially prolonged speechmaking, to delay legislative action.

□ **Civil Rights Act of 1964** Law that barred segregation in public facilities and forbade employers to discriminate on the basis of race, religion, sex, or national origin.

□ **War on Poverty** Lyndon Johnson's program to help Americans escape poverty through education, job training, and community development.

DEFINING A NEW PRESIDENCY

☆ In what ways did the legislation associated with Johnson's Great Society differ from New Deal programs?

☆ How did Johnson's War on Poverty and Great Society further the civil rights movement?

As president, Johnson described himself as a New Dealer and told one adviser that Kennedy was "a little too conservative to suit my taste." Johnson wanted to build a better society, "where progress is the servant of the neediest." Recognizing the political opening generated by the assassination, Johnson immediately committed himself to Kennedy's agenda, and in January 1964 he expanded on it by announcing an "unconditional war on poverty."

Old and New Agendas

Throughout 1964, wielding his considerable political skill, Johnson moved Kennedy's tax cut and civil rights bill out of committee and toward passage. The tax cut (the Tax Reduction Act) became law in February, creating over a million new jobs and increasing consumer spending by $43 million over the next eighteen months. The civil rights bill moved more slowly. To overcome a stubborn southern **filibuster** in the Senate, Johnson traded political favors for Republican votes. The filibuster lasted fifty-seven days, but the **Civil Rights Act of 1964** became law on July 2. The act made it illegal to discriminate for reasons of race, religion, or gender in places and businesses that served the public. "[W]e have just delivered the South to the Republican Party," Johnson prophetically told an aide. Putting force behind the law, Congress established a federal Fair Employment Practices Committee (FEPC) and empowered the executive branch to withhold federal funds from institutions that violated the act's provisions.

By August 1964, Johnson's **War on Poverty** had begun, aimed at benefiting the 20 percent of the population who were classified as poor. In 1962, social critic Michael Harrington published *The Other America*, which alerted the public to widespread poverty in America. Subsequently, the U.S. government, which defined the poverty line as $3,130 for an urban household of four and $1,925 for a rural family, found that almost 40 percent of the poor (15.6 million) were under the age of 18.

The War on Poverty was fought on two fronts: expanding economic opportunities and improving the social environment. The August 1964 Economic Opportunity Act established an Office of Economic Opportunity to coordinate a variety of programs that Johnson stated would "help more Americans, especially young Americans, to escape from squalor and misery." The cornerstones were education and job training. The Job Corps program enrolled unemployed teens and young adults (ages 16 to 21) lacking skills, while Head Start reached out to disadvantaged prekindergarten children to provide important thinking and social skills. Another program, called Volunteers in Service to America (VISTA), sent service-minded Americans to help improve life in regions of poverty. Among the most ambitious programs was the Community Action Program (CAP), which allowed disadvantaged community organizations to target local needs by giving them direct access to federal funds. The program never met expectations, but it helped generate local activism and led to services like legal aid and community health clinics.

As the 1964 presidential election neared, Johnson was confident. He had cut taxes, passed a civil rights bill, and started a war on poverty. Public opinion polls showed significant support for the president in all parts of the nation, except the South.

Opposing Johnson's liberal programs were conservatives and Republicans energized by the emerging **New Right**. Intellectually led by William F. Buckley and the *National Review*, conservatives cried that liberalism was destroying vital traditional American values of localism, self-help, and individualism. The Young Americans for Freedom (YAF) emerged, and their *Sharon Statement* called for the destruction of communism and emphasized a free market society and individual rights, which included the freedom to not associate with whomever one wished. Reflecting the right to not associate, one of the first "Freedom Awards" presented by YAF went to Senator Strom Thurmond, a staunch segregationist.

Conservatives were also energized by many of the decisions coming from the Warren Court. From the mid-1950s through the 1960s, the Warren Court charted new legal paths, promoting political and social equality and altering the government's obligations to its citizens at all levels. In a series of decisions, beginning in 1962 with *Baker v. Carr*, the Court concluded that the courts had an obligation to guarantee the equal apportionment of political power within states by ensuring that voting districts have similar populations, so that one person's vote in one congressional district would be equal to that of a person in another congressional district. In protecting personal and criminal rights, the Court required that states provide the same legal guarantees found in the First, Fourth, Fifth, and Sixth amendments. Between 1961 and 1969, the Court issued over two hundred criminal justice decisions that, according to critics, hampered law enforcement. Among the most important were *Gideon* v. *Wainwright* (1963), *Escobedo* v. *Illinois* (1964), and *Miranda* v. *Arizona* (1966). In those rulings the Court declared that all defendants have a right to an attorney, even if the state must provide one, and that those arrested must be informed of their right to remain silent and to have an attorney present during questioning (the *Miranda* warning).

AP Photo/Horace Cort.

For many conservatives, Chief Justice Earl Warren was one of the most despised people in the country. In this picture Georgia Governor Lester Maddox calls for the impeachment of Warren. In 1968, Governor Maddox refused to fly the Georgia flag at half-mast in honor of the death of Martin Luther King Jr. Never impeached, Warren remained chief justice until he retired in 1969.

Also angering conservatives was a series of decisions that expanded freedom of expression, separated church and state, and argued that individuals have a right to privacy in certain areas of their lives. The Court's decision to restrict prayer in public schools (*Engel v. Vitale*, 1962) produced outcries of protest across the nation from Democrats and Republicans.

■ **New Right** Conservative movement within the Republican Party that opposed liberal reforms of the 1960s, demanding less federal government interference with state and local power and a return to traditional values.

■ **Gideon, Escobedo, and Miranda** Three 1960s Supreme Court rulings declaring that the state must provide an attorney to any defendant who cannot afford one, and must inform those arrested of their rights to remain silent and to have an attorney present during questioning.

President Johnson's Great Society greatly expanded the role of society in the lives of Americans through passage of civil rights, welfare, and education legislation. In this picture, President Johnson signs legislation establishing Medicare. His wife, Lady Bird, and Vice President Hubert Humphrey watch in the background.

Congress introduced over 150 resolutions demanding that reading the Bible and praying aloud be permitted in schools. Governor George Wallace of Alabama declared: "We find the court ruling against God." Still, the Court's decisions remained law, and communities and classrooms complied.

Opponents of the Court's vision also complained that it was undermining moral values when it weakened "community standards" in favor of broader ones regarding "obscene" and sexually explicit materials in *Jacobvellis v. Ohio* (1963) and when it established that individuals had a right to privacy in certain aspects of their social behavior. The 1964 *Griswold v. Connecticut* decision declared that states could not forbid the sale of contraceptives or restrict the distribution of information on birth control.

Leading the Republican assault against the values of liberalism was Senator **Barry Goldwater** of Arizona. Plainspoken and direct, Goldwater opposed the 1964 Civil Rights Act, "Big Government," and New Deal–style programs. Riding a wave of conservative and New Right support, Goldwater seized the nomination for the presidency, launching an attack on liberalism and vowing to implement an anti-Communist crusade. When he appeared willing not only to commit American troops in Vietnam but also to use nuclear weapons against Communist nations, including Cuba and North Vietnam, Democrats quickly painted him as a dangerous radical. Johnson, meanwhile, promoted his Great Society and promised that "American boys" would not "do the fighting for Asian boys." Johnson won easily in a lopsided election.

Implementing the Great Society

Not only did Goldwater lose, but so too did many Republicans—moderates and conservatives—as more than forty new Democrats entered Congress. Armed with congressional majorities, Johnson pushed to enact his **Great Society**. He told aides that they must hurry before the natural opposition of politics returned. Between 1964 and 1968, more than sixty Great Society programs were put in place. (Table 26.1 lists some of the more important ones established between 1964 and 1966.) Most sought to provide better economic and social opportunities by removing barriers thrown up by health, education, region, and race.

One of Johnson's goals was to further racial equality. Within months of his election, he signed an

▫ **Barry Goldwater** Conservative Republican senator from Arizona who ran unsuccessfully for president in 1964.

▫ **Great Society** Social program that Johnson announced in 1964; it included the War on Poverty, protection of civil rights, and funding for education.

TABLE 26.1   War on Poverty and Great Society Programs, 1964–1966

1964	1965	1966
Tax Reduction Act	Elementary and Secondary Education Act	Demonstration Cities and Metropolitan Development Act
Civil Rights Act	Voting Rights Act	Motor Vehicle Safety Act
Economic Opportunity Act	Medical Care Act (Medicare and Medicaid)	Truth in Packaging Act
Equal Employment Opportunity Commission	Head Start (Office of Economic Opportunity)	Model Cities Act
Twenty-Fourth Amendment	Upward Bound (Office of Economic Opportunity)	Clean Water Restoration Act
Job Corps (Office of Economic Opportunity)	Water Quality Act and Air Quality Act	Department of Transportation
Legal services for the poor	Department of Housing and Urban Development	
VISTA	National Endowment for the Arts and Humanities	
Wilderness Act	Immigration and Nationality Act	

© Cengage Learning 2013.

executive order that required government contractors to practice nondiscrimination in hiring and on the job. He also appointed the first African American to the cabinet, Secretary of Housing and Urban Development Robert Weaver; the first African American woman to the federal courts, Judge Constance Baker Motley; and the first African American to the Supreme Court, Justice Thurgood Marshall.

Blacks were pleased but understood that these actions did not end discrimination or poverty and that large pockets of active opposition to civil rights remained, including denial of the right to vote. For nearly one hundred years, most southern whites had viewed voting as an activity for whites only and, through the poll tax and their control of the ballot, had maintained their political power and a segregated society. The ratification of the Twenty-Fourth Amendment (banning the poll tax) in January 1964 was a major step toward dismantling that system. Another step was to increase black voter registration. In early 1964, the SNCC's Bob Moses organized a **Freedom Summer** in Mississippi. "Freedom Schools" would teach literacy and black history, stress black pride and achievements, and help residents register to vote. In Mississippi, as in several other southern states, a voter literacy test required that

all questions be answered to the satisfaction of a white registrar. Thus a question calling for "a reasonable interpretation" of an obscure section of the state constitution could be used to block blacks from registering.

In the face of white hostility, voter registration was dangerous work. "You talk about fear," an organizer told recruits. "It's like the heat down there, it's continually oppressive. You think they're rational. But, you know, you suddenly realize, they want to kill you." Indeed, from June through August of 1964, more than thirty-five shooting incidents rocked Mississippi, and thirty buildings, many of them churches, were bombed. Hundreds were beaten and arrested, and three Freedom Summer workers were murdered. But the crusade drew national support and registered nearly sixty thousand new African American voters.

Keeping up the pressure, King announced a voter registration drive in Selma, Alabama, where only 2.1 percent of eligible black voters were registered.

■ **Freedom Summer** Effort by civil rights groups in Mississippi to register black voters and cultivate black pride during the summer of 1964.

The Twenty-Fourth Amendment to the Constitution

The Twenty-Fourth Amendment, ratified in January 1964, abolished the use of the poll tax in federal elections.

"The right . . . to vote in any primary or other election for President, Vice President, for electors . . . or for Senators or Representatives in Congress shall not be denied . . . by reason of failure to pay any poll tax or other tax."

The amendment made it unconstitutional for states to restrict the right of the poor to vote, a process used since the Civil War by many southern states to prevent African Americans from voting. It also voided the Supreme Court's 1937 decision to uphold Georgia's poll tax in *Breedlove v. Suttles*. In 1966, the Court itself declared that the poll tax could not be used to deny the vote at the state and local level (*Harper v. Virginia*).

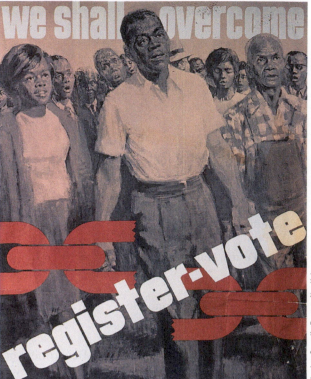

Schomburg Center/Art Resource, New York.

The summer of 1964 was called "Freedom Summer," as hundreds of civil rights volunteers—many of them college students—converged on Alabama and Mississippi to conduct voter registration drives. Many were beaten, some were jailed, and some lost their lives, but as Anne Moody wrote in her autobiography, *Coming of Age in Mississippi,* "threats did not stop them."

As expected, the police, led by Sheriff Jim Clark, confronted protesters, arresting nearly 2,000. King then called for a **freedom march** from Selma to Montgomery. On March 7, 1965, as scores of reporters watched, hundreds of freedom marchers faced fifty Alabama state troopers and Clark's mounted forces at Pettus Bridge. Firing tear gas and brandishing clubs, Clark's men chased the marchers down. Television coverage of the assault stirred nationwide condemnation of Clark's tactics and support for the marchers. When Alabama's staunch segregationist governor, George Wallace, told President Johnson that he could not provide protection for the marchers, Johnson ordered the National Guard, two army battalions, and 250 federal marshals to protect the nearly 3,200 marchers when the march resumed. By the time it arrived in Montgomery on March 27, more than 25,000 had joined.

Johnson used the violence in Selma to pressure Congress into passing the **Voting Rights Act** in August 1965. The act banned a variety of methods that states had been using to deny the right to vote, including Mississippi's literacy test, and it had immediate effect.

freedom march Civil rights march from Selma to Montgomery, Alabama, in March 1965; the violent treatment of protesters by local authorities helped galvanize national opinion against segregationists.

Voting Rights Act A 1965 law that outlawed literacy and other voting tests and authorized federal supervision of elections in areas where black voting had been restricted.

Across the South, the percentage of African Americans registered to vote rose an average of 30 percent between 1965 and 1968 (see Map 26.3). In Mississippi, it went from 7 to 59 percent, and in Selma, more than 60 percent of qualified African Americans voted in 1968, stopping Sheriff Clark's bid for reelection.

But civil rights legislation was only one of many facets of the Great Society. Several acts, like the Appalachian Regional Development Act (1965) and the Model Cities Act (1966), focused on developing economic growth in long-depressed regional and urban areas and on providing funds for housing and mass transit systems. In a related move, a cabinet-level Department of Housing and Urban Development was created in 1965.

Responding to rising environmental concerns, Johnson signed the Water Quality and Air Quality Acts in October 1965. Over the next three years, he would guide through Congress acts to expand wilderness areas, regulate waste removal, and remove billboards from federal highways.

Johnson also signed a major overhaul of the nation's immigration laws. The Immigration and

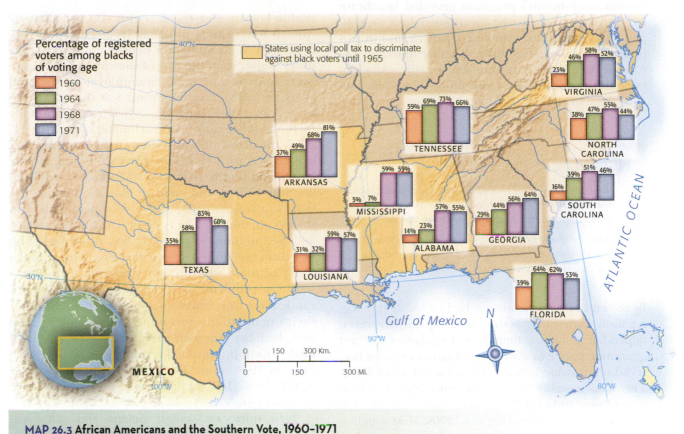

MAP 26.3 African Americans and the Southern Vote, 1960–1971
An important part of the civil rights movement was to reestablish the African American vote that had been stripped away in the South following Reconstruction. Between 1960 and 1971, with the outlawing of the poll tax and other voter restrictions, African American voter participation rose significantly across the South. © Cengage Learning.

Nationality Act of 1965 dropped the racial and ethnic discrimination in immigration policies that had been in effect since the 1920s. The act set a uniform yearly limit on immigration from any one nation, allowing for increased immigration from non-European parts of the world.

At the top of Johnson's priorities, however, were health and education. Above all, he wanted those two "coonskins on the wall." The Elementary and Secondary Education Act (1965) was the first general educational funding act by the federal government. It granted more than a billion dollars to public and parochial schools for textbooks, library materials, and special education programs. Poor and rural school districts were supposed to receive the highest percentage of federal support. But, as with many Great Society programs, implementation fell short of intention, and too often funds were diverted to affluent schools. Johnson's biggest "coonskin" was the Medical Care Act (1965), which established **Medicaid** and **Medicare** to help pay healthcare costs for the elderly and individuals on welfare.

Examining their accomplishments in 1966, many Democrats were pleased. The Great Society was becoming a reality. Their assessment, however, was overly optimistic. By the end of 1966, support for the Great Society was diminishing. Critics cited the rising costs and apparent inefficiency of many of the programs. A new, more conservative Congress generally ignored calls for new or expanded social programs. The administration, too, was less interested in domestic legislation as the war in Vietnam consumed its attention. Further, many people linked growing social and cultural turmoil and urban riots to what they considered

■ **Medicaid** Program of health insurance for the poor established in 1965; it provides states with money to buy healthcare for people on welfare.

■ **Medicare** Program of health insurance for elderly people and those with disabilities; established in 1965, it provides government payment for healthcare supplied by private doctors and hospitals.

the permissive values of liberalism. Still, despite their limitations, Johnson's programs provided healthcare for the poor and elderly, contributed to a near 10 percent decline in the number of Americans living in poverty and a one-third drop in infant mortality. For African Americans, statistics were equally encouraging: poverty declined by nearly 50 percent while family income rose about 53 percent.

New Voices

★ How did "new voices" conflict with traditional social norms, and what new organizations and agendas arose to provide a platform for those voices?

★ How did the urban riots and the emergence of the Black Power movement reflect a new agenda for the civil rights movement?

By the end of 1965, legislation had ended de jure segregation and voting restrictions. Equality, however, depended on more than laws. Legislation did not guarantee justice or end discrimination or prejudice. It did not provide jobs or a higher standard of living. This was especially true for the more than 1 million mostly poor and unskilled African Americans who left the South each year during the 1960s. Most sought a better life in northern and western cities, but too often they found soaring unemployment and cities unable or unwilling to provide adequate social services. Economics, not segregation, was the key issue: "I'd eat at your lunch counter—if only I had a job," spelled out the problem for many urban blacks. By the mid-1960s, the nation's cities were primed for racial trouble. Minor race riots occurred in Harlem and Rochester, New York, during the summer of 1964, but it was the Watts riot and militant new voices that shook the nation.

□ **Watts** Predominantly black neighborhood of Los Angeles where a race riot in August 1965 did $45 million in damage and took the lives of twenty-eight blacks.

□ **Stokely Carmichael** Civil rights activist who led SNCC and coined the term "Black Power" to describe the need for blacks to use militant tactics to force whites to accept political and social change.

□ **Black Power** Movement begun in 1966 that rejected the nonviolent, coalition-building approach of traditional civil rights groups and advocated black control of black organizations; the self-determination approach was adopted by Latinos (Brown Power) and Native Americans (Red Power).

□ **Black Muslims** Popular name for the Nation of Islam, an African American religious group founded by Elijah Muhammad, which professed Islamic religious beliefs and emphasized black separatism.

Urban Riots and Black Power

Within Los Angeles, the area of **Watts** had a largely African American population. Its 250,000-plus residents gave it a population density more than four times higher than the rest of the city. Schools were overcrowded, and male unemployment hovered at 34 percent. Patrolling Watts was the nearly all-white L.A. police force, which had a reputation for racism and brutality. In this climate, on August 11, 1965, the arrest of an African American for drunk driving led to a riot. For thirty-six hours, rioters looted and set fire to stores, and attacked firefighters and police, who were unable to put out the flames or restore order. Thirty-four people died in the riot, including twenty-eight African Americans, and $45 million in property was destroyed. The riot dismayed Johnson and shattered the complacency of those who thought civil rights was just a southern problem. It forced many African American leaders to reconsider their priorities. None of their organizations, including CORE, Farmer realized, had any "roots in the ghetto." When Martin Luther King Jr., who had received the Nobel Peace Prize in 1964, spoke after the riot he was greeted by calls like "Hell, we don't need no damn dreams. We want jobs."

New voices demanded change and called on blacks to seek power through solidarity, independence, and, if necessary, violence. **Stokely Carmichael**, after being arrested during a civil rights march in 1966, announced: "I'm not going to beg the white man for anything I deserve . . . I'm going to take it." He and others advocated Black Power, a call that resonated across much of Black America. As another marcher remarked, the gentle hymn "We Shall Overcome" should be replaced with an assertive "We Shall Overrun." Within months, SNCC and CORE changed from biracial, nonviolent organizations to **Black Power** resistance movements that stressed Black Nationalism. The violent rhetoric and insistence on independence from white allies highlighted the gap between the new and old, the moderates and the radicals. King feared that Black Power rhetoric, combined with the riots, would "confuse our allies and isolate the Black community," reducing support for civil rights.

The emergence of Black Power also increased the visibility of the Nation of Islam, or **Black Muslims**. Founded by Elijah Muhammad in the 1930s, the movement attracted mostly young males and demanded adherence to a strict moral code that prohibited the use of drugs and alcohol. Black Muslims preached black superiority and separatism from an evil white world. By the early 1960s, there were nearly a hundred thousand Black Muslims, including

Malcolm X, who by 1952 had become one of the Black Muslims' most powerful and respected leaders. A mesmerizing speaker, he promoted racial pride, preferred the term "African American" to describe black Americans, and argued that integration with a white society emasculated blacks by denying them power and personal identity. Still a Black Nationalist, in 1964 he broke with Elijah Muhammad and promoted cooperation with other civil rights groups and with some whites. The defection cost him his life when on February 21, 1965, three Black Muslims assassinated him in Harlem.

Carmichael and Malcolm X represented only two of a growing number of African American voices advocating direct—and, if necessary, violent—action. The new leader of SNCC, H. Rap Brown, told followers to grab their guns and, if necessary, "shoot the honky." Brown's rhetoric was adopted by the Black Panthers who, led by Huey P. Newton, Eldridge Cleaver, and Bobby Seale, were noted for being well armed and willing to use their weapons. FBI director J. Edgar Hoover called them "the most dangerous . . . of all extremist groups."

While the number of Black separatists remained small, the conditions that sparked the Watts riot existed in most African American urban neighborhoods. Between 1965 and 1968, more than three hundred cities experienced race riots. The summer of 1967 saw over seventy-five riots with Detroit and Newark experiencing the bloodiest confrontations. Twenty-six people died in Newark and forty-three in Detroit. Most of the dead were African Americans shot by those trying to restore order.

Conservatives blamed the riots on Communists, Black radicals, and "guerrilla bands that burn and loot," Democrats, and liberal "bearded beatnik bureaucrats." Others generally blamed social and economic inequalities. An official investigation, the Kerner Commission, appointed by Johnson in 1967, reported in February 1968 that "Pervasive discrimination and segregation in employment, education, and housing have resulted in the continuing exclusion of great numbers of Negroes from the benefits of economic progress." Urban violence would continue, the report warned, unless steps were taken to improve the lives of African Americans. King called the report a "prescription" for the health of the country.

In April 1968, King went to Memphis to support striking sanitation workers and to stress the need for social and economic justice. On April 4, James Earl Ray assassinated the reverend. Within days, 350 American cities exploded in racial unrest. After the riots, Johnson pushed through the Fair Housing Act, but a growing number of people didn't want legislation—they wanted the authorities to crack down on protestors, militants, and radicals.

From King to Black Power advocates, African Americans confronted the existing order, and by the 1960s they were not alone in demanding change. An increasing number of women and young adults were questioning social and cultural values and voicing demands for a more equitable society.

Rejecting the Feminine Mystique

By the end of the 1950s, the image of women as stay-at-home wives and mothers no longer matched reality. Increasingly, women were entering the workforce, graduating from college, getting divorces, and becoming heads of households. They also recognized that they often faced discrimination based on gender. The 1963 report of the Presidential Commission on the Status of Women confirmed that women worked for less pay than white males (on average 40 percent less), were more likely to be fired or laid off, and rarely reached top career positions. It also indicated that throughout the country divorce, credit, and property laws generally favored men, and in three states women were not allowed to serve on juries.

The president's commission provided statistics, but it was Betty Friedan's 1963 bestseller *The Feminine Mystique* that many regard as the beginning of the women's movement. After reviewing the responsibilities of the housewife, Friedan concluded that women needed to overcome the "feminine mystique" that promised them fulfillment in the domestic arts. She asked women to set their own goals and seek careers outside the home. Her book, combined with the presidential report, contributed to a renewed women's movement.

In 1963, Congress began to address women's issues when it passed the Equal Pay Act, which ended gender discrimination in pay for men and women doing the same job. It was followed a year later by Title VII of the 1964 Civil Rights Act, prohibiting discrimination based on gender as well as race, creed, religion, and place of origin. The original Civil

■ **Malcolm X** Black activist who advocated black separatism as a member of the Nation of Islam; in 1963 he converted to orthodox Islam, and two years later was assassinated.

■ **Black Panthers** Black revolutionary party founded in 1966 that endorsed violence as a means of social change.

■ **Betty Friedan** Feminist who wrote *The Feminine Mystique* in 1963 and helped found the National Organization for Women in 1966.

■ **Equal Pay Act** Forbids most employers to pay different wages, based on gender, for equal work. Some employers continued to pay lower wages to women, arguing that the jobs were not exactly equal.

■ **Title VII** Provision of the Civil Rights Act of 1964 that guarantees women legal protection against discrimination.

A Deeper Understanding of History

Using Political Cartoons: The 1960s Urban Riots

Political cartoons have been a staple of American social and political commentary since the colonial era. They have become a regular and popular feature in many magazines and newspapers, focusing the readers' attention on particular issues and problems. Like bloggers, columnists, and other political writers, the cartoonists offer a specific point of view and seek not only to inform but to sway opinion. Historians use political cartoons as primary sources. Like personal letters, official documents, interviews, and editorials, political cartoons provide a glimpse of what people thought and said at the time an event happened. But unlike many other primary sources,

political cartoons, as part of the mass media, had to reach the broadest of audiences. This was accomplished by connecting the issue to existing hopes and fears through the use of symbols, caricatures, and references, and very few words.

The political cartoons here deal with the urban violence that occurred in the last half of the 1960s. What can the historian learn from them? How are the issues being represented? What symbols and references are used, and what points are being made? What conclusions can you draw about the causes and consequences of urban violence? What is each cartoonist's perspective?

"Fiddler" 1967 Herblock Cartoon, copyright by The Herb Block Foundation," …

"…SEEMS A SHAME AFTER IT WAS SUCH A GREAT HELP TO US!"

Seems a shame after it was such a great help to us!" Atlanta Constitution,[ca. 1963] Clifford H. "Baldy" Baldowski Editorial Cartoons. Courtesy of the Richard B. Russell Library for Political Research and Studies, The University of Georgia Libraries.

An avid supporter of women's rights, Bella Abzug (1920–1998) was elected to the House of Representatives in 1970 and a year later co-founded the National Women's Political Caucus.

Rights Act had not included gender, but Representatives Martha Griffins (D.–Michigan) and Howard Smith (D.–Virginia) added the word *sex* to the bill. They did it for opposing reasons. He did it to make the bill more unpalatable; she did it to support women's rights.

Griffins and other supporters hoped that the inclusion of Title VII would mark the beginning of a serious effort by the federal government to provide equality to women. But it soon became clear that neither the Johnson administration nor the Equal Employment Opportunity Commission was interested in dealing with gender discrimination. To better promote women's rights, especially in the workplace, women began to organize to promote their interests and to persuade the government to enforce Title VII. The most prominent group was the **National Organization for Women** (NOW), formed in 1966. With Betty Friedan as president, NOW launched an aggressive campaign to draw attention to sex discrimination and redress wrongs. It demanded an Equal Rights Amendment to the Constitution to ensure gender equality and pushed for easier access to birth control and the right to have an abortion. NOW grew rapidly from about 300 members in 1966 to 175,000 in 1968. But the women's movement was larger than NOW and represented a variety of voices.

Rejecting Gender Roles

Some voices went beyond economics and politics in their critique of gender in American society. They took aim at existing norms of sex and gender roles and called for a redefinition of sexuality, family, and marriage. Some focused on male domination in American society. "We identify the agents of our oppression as men. . . . We are exploited as sex objects, breeders, domestic servants and cheap labor" declared the Redstocking Manifesto in 1969. The New York group that issued the manifesto was among the first to use "**consciousness-raising**" groups to educate women about the oppression they faced because of the sex-gender system. Author Rita Mae Brown went further, advocating lesbian rights. Her acclaimed first novel, *Rubyfruit Jungle* (1973), presented lesbianism in a positive light and provided a literary basis for discussion of lesbian life and attitudes.

Brown joined a growing chorus of voices asking society to reconsider its views toward sexuality. Since the 1950s, gay and lesbian organizations had worked quietly to promote new attitudes toward same-sex orientation and to overturn laws that punished homosexual activities. But most gays remained in the closet, fearful of reprisals by the straight community and its institutions. The Stonewall Riot in 1969, however, brought increased visibility and renewed activism to the gay community.

The police raided the Stonewall Inn in New York City because it catered to a gay clientele. The raid resulted in an unexpected riot as gay patrons fought the police and were joined by other members of the community. After the riot, a Gay Manifesto called for homosexuals and lesbians to raise their consciousness and rid their minds of "garbage" poured into them by old values. "Liberation . . . is defining for ourselves how and with whom we live. . . . We are only at the beginning."

Success came slowly. Polls in the early 1970s indicated a majority of Americans still considered homosexuality immoral and even a disease. But by the mid-1970s, new polling showed a shift as a slight majority of Americans opposed job discrimination based on sexual orientation and appeared to show more tolerance of gay lifestyles. Responding to gay rights pressure in 1973, the American Psychiatric Association ended its classification of homosexuality as a mental disorder.

■ **National Organization for Women** (NOW) Women's rights organization founded in 1966 to fight discrimination against women and improve educational, employment, and political opportunities for women.

consciousness-raising Achieving greater awareness of the nature of political or social issues through group interaction.

In the Wider World

Prague Spring, 1968

The year 1968 was "the year of the barricades" as protests and rebellions erupted around the world to challenge the status quo. One of the first occurred in January when Czech dissidents forced the resignation of the repressive government of Antonin Novotny, and Alexander Dubcek assumed the leadership of a reform movement. To put a "human face" on socialism, in April Dubcek issued the "Action Program," which began the processes of allowing more freedom of expression, emphasizing increased private ownership, releasing political prisoners, and reducing the power of the central government. Dubcek's problem was convincing the Soviet Union that the reforms did not challenge communism or Moscow's influence. In August, announcing the Brezhnev Doctrine, 200,000 Soviet and Warsaw Pact forces invaded Czechoslovakia. Despite pleas from Dubcek not to resist, seventy-two were killed and over five hundred wounded. The Prague Spring was over. Later, Dubcek was expelled from the Communist Party and assigned a job in forestry.

The Youth Movement

Within the 1960s movements for change, young adults were among the most active participants. By 1965, the baby boomers were off to college in record numbers. More than 40 percent of the nation's high school graduates were attending college, a leap of 13 percent from 1955. Although the majority of young adults remained quite traditional, an expanding number began to question the goals and nature of education. Students complained that higher education seemed sterile, an assembly line producing standardized products, not independent thinking individuals. They wanted fewer restrictions on student behavior, and a more flexible curriculum with fewer required courses. They promoted campuses as havens for free speech and social and political activism, and to achieve their goals, they organized campus protests and sit-ins in administration buildings.

A **Free Speech Movement** was part of the student "rebellion" at the University of California, Berkeley, where in 1964, students seized the administration building demanding that the university allow political activist groups on campus. The university complied in 1965. Berkeley was not alone, by the end of the decade, many colleges had relinquished their roles as guardians of student behavior, reducing the number of required courses and relaxing or eliminating dress codes and dorm curfews and restrictions on visiting hours. Reflecting the changing social culture, many institutions also introduced programs in areas like African American, Native American, and women's studies.

Some college activists looked beyond the campus, seeing it as a staging ground for promoting wider change. At the University of Michigan in 1960, Tom Hayden and Al Haber organized **Students for a Democratic Society** (SDS). SDS members insisted Americans recognize that their affluent nation was also a land of poverty and want, and that business and government chose to ignore social inequalities. In 1962 SDS issued its *Port Huron Statement*, which maintained that the country should reallocate its resources according to social needs so that all people could "live with dignity." Attacking society's materialism, SDS and other youth activists represented an emerging **New Left** movement that maintained the threat to democracy came from "corporate" liberals who were more interested in stability and profits than achieving social and economic equality. The liberal establishment could send thousands to kill in Vietnam, one New Left leader said, but would not "send 100 voter registrars . . . into Mississippi."

■ **Free Speech Movement** Protest movement led by Mario Savio that began in 1964 at the University of California, Berkeley, when the administration prevented on-campus political activities; in January 1965 the administration lifted the ban and acknowledged students' right to freedom of speech.

■ **Students for a Democratic Society** (SDS) Left-wing student organization founded in 1960 to criticize American materialism and work for social justice.

■ *Port Huron Statement* A 1962 critique of the Cold War and American materialism and complacency by Students for a Democratic Society; it called for "participatory democracy" and for universities to be centers of free speech and activism.

■ **New Left** An international movement in the 1960s primarily composed of intellectuals and college students that opposed "the Establishment" and its dominant political, economic, and social structures; in the United States it opposed the war in Vietnam and supported civil and individual rights.

To many, the counterculture was defined by "hippie" communes, where groups of young people left conventional society to establish alternative lifestyles, often close to nature, like the setting shown. In this picture, members of a commune use a bus named "The Road Hog" to participate in a Fourth of July parade in New Mexico.

The Counterculture

Another, very visible, aspect of the youth movement was the emergence of a "counterculture." Rejecting the values of traditional society, by the mid-1960s "**hippies**" were adopting lifestyles that emphasized personal freedom and opposition to materialism. Although the counterculture existed across the country, San Francisco and Northern California were seen as its center.

Across the country, members of the counterculture expressed their nonconformity in their appearance, favoring long hair and blue jeans or long flowered dresses. They advocated sexual freedom and the use of drugs, especially marijuana, as expressions of personal freedom that produced serenity and self-awareness. Many sought a higher level of understanding and well-being through non-Western mystic and religious practices like Zen Buddhism. Some groups chose to live together as extended families on communes.

Music was a prominent form of expression and defiance, linking the counterculture to the larger movements of the 1960s and to society as a whole. As Bob Dylan sang:

> *Your sons and daughters*
> *Are beyond your command . . .*
> *For the times they are a changin'!**

* FROM THE TIMES THEY ARE A-CHANGIN' Copyright © 1963 by Warner Bros. Inc. Copyright renewed 1991 by Special Rider Music. All rights reserved. International copyright secured. Reprinted by permission.

Whether Dylan's lyrics or those of the Jefferson Airplane's "White Rabbit," whose pills could "make you larger" or "small," music provided a unifying medium not only for the counterculture but for the 1960s movements in general. Across the spectrum, many musicians aimed their songs at social and cultural issues like race, alienation, war, and love. Some musicians, including Bob Dylan and Joan Baez, challenged society with protest and antiwar songs rooted in folk music, but for the majority the evolving "rock" remained dominant. In 1964, the Beatles, an English group, exploded on the American music scene. They and their music mirrored the irreverence and values of the youth movement. They soon shared the stage with other British imports such as the Rolling Stones, whose behavior and songs depicted alienation and lack of social restraints. "Music," said one writer, was a liberating and revolutionary force that could "change the world." In many ways the counterculture peaked in the summer of 1969, when musicians and an army of young adults converged on **Woodstock**, New York, for the largest free rock concert in history. For three days, through summer rains and deepening mud, more than 400,000 came together in a temporary open-air community, where many of the most popular rock 'n' roll bands performed day and night. Touted as three days of peace and love, sex, drugs, and rock 'n' roll, Woodstock symbolized the power of counterculture values to promote cooperation and happiness.

The spirit of Woodstock was fleeting. For most people, at home and on campus, the communal ideal was impractical, if not unworkable. Nor did the vast majority of young people who took up some counterculture notions completely reject their parents' society. Most stayed in school and continued to participate in the society they were criticizing. But parts of the youth movement and counterculture infiltrated into mainstream society and had a lasting impact.

■ **hippies** Members of the counterculture in the 1960s who rejected the competitiveness and materialism of American society and searched for peace, love, and autonomy.

■ **Woodstock** Free rock concert in Woodstock, New York, in August 1969; it attracted 400,000 people and was remembered as the classic expression of the counterculture.

EUNICE KENNEDY SHRIVER
Champions New Perspectives

Because she was directly involved in promoting programs for those with intellectual disabilities, Eunice Kennedy Shriver provides the public as well as historians a window on how she sought to convince the public that those once referred to as "mentally retarded" should have the same rights as everyone else and that given the opportunities their successes benefited all of society.

"Challenges of the Mentally Retarded" appeared in the New Catholic World in 1976:

UPI/Special Olympics /Landov.

❶ Is it important that here and elsewhere in this document, Shriver uses familiar phrases from famous documents in American history? What is she attempting to accomplish by using such historical references?

❷ In what ways is Shriver making the point in this article that the quality of American society is determined by how it deals with all of its people?

❸ How do the accomplishments of individuals like Billy Bosquet reflect the differences between the Special and regular Olympics?

❹ Why do you think the "smiley games" are important to the issues presented in the previous excerpt?

How can we make sure that the mentally retarded people in our midst can be guaranteed their human rights? How can we make sure that their rights to life, liberty and the pursuit of happiness are protected? **❶**

. . . we are learning that, with the proper help and by any standards of worth, the mentally retarded have great value to our society. In their naïve innocence, they believe us when we talk about love, trust and sharing. In their striving to be what they think we are, they are devoted, hard-working and trusting. In the courage with which they face their handicaps and disabilities, they inspire us all to a new standard of achievement.

Yet, we are far from being truly civilized in our response to those who deviate from our social and intellectual norms. We deal with these people as clients or cases . . . even as we attempt to deal with their problems, a dehumanization process takes place. . . .

So let us reaffirm our dedication to the rights of the handicapped, the weak and the mentally retarded in our midst. . . . Let us preserve our philosophic heritage which stated that "all men are endowed by their creator . . . with certain inalienable rights." And let us be sure . . . as for all other Americans, these inalienable rights include the right to life, education, health . . . the right to love, the right to work, the right . . . to be fully human in a humane and compassionate society. **❷**

"The Games Where Olympic Spirit Is All That Counts" was printed in the sports section of the New York Times *in August 1983:*

At a time when the ancient ideals of the Olympic Games have been obscured by politics and commercialism, many people have asked about the philosophy propelling the amazing progress of the Special Olympics.

What is the Special Olympics? It is the world's largest program of sports training and athletic competition for mentally retarded children and adults. Since its founding 15 years ago, as a single track and field event . . . it has grown to include more than a million athletes receiving year-round training and competition in 16 sports. . . .

In today's world of sports, in which winning and the rewards of winning seem to be everything, Special Olympians strive for higher value. . . . It [is] . . . in the sportsmanship of Billy Bosquet of Massachusetts, who after having been moved from first to sixth . . . for running out of his lane, said: "Don't worry, I'll do it next time." **❸**

What lessons does the Special Olympics teach about the world? . . . It is that all human beings are created equal in the sense that each has the capacity and a hunger for moral excellence, for courage, for friendship and for love. . . . "This is the smiley games." **❹**

Source: First selection: From Eunice Kennedy Shriver, "Challenges of the Mentally Retarded," New Catholic World, *219 (September 1976): 200-203. Copyright © 1976 by Special Olympics, Inc. Reprinted with permission. Second selection: From Eunice Kennedy Shriver, "The Games Where Olympic Spirit Is All That Counts,"* New York Times, *August 14, 1983. Copyright © 1983 by Special Olympics, Inc. Reprinted with permission.*

SUMMARY

Kennedy's election generated a wave of optimism that the nation's and the world's problems could be solved. This spirit fueled the New Frontier, the War on Poverty, and the Great Society. Kennedy's domestic agenda included civil rights, education, and tax legislation, but, like Truman and Eisenhower, he faced political opposition, and those measures soon were mired in congressional politics. He settled for modest legislative successes that generally expanded existing programs.

Less constrained in his foreign policy, Kennedy implemented a more comprehensive, flexible strategy to confront communism. Confrontations over Berlin and Cuba, escalating arms and space races, and expanding commitments to Vietnam were accepted as part of the United States' global role and passed intact to Johnson.

President Johnson was able to cut through politics as usual and got Kennedy's mired legislation passed. He then announced a War on Poverty and the agenda for a Great Society. Between 1964 and 1966, Johnson initiated legislation that tackled poverty and discrimination, expanded educational opportunities, revised immigration rules, and created a national system of health insurance for the poor and elderly.

The decade's emphasis on activism encouraged more Americans to push their own agendas. As the civil rights movement focused more on economic and social issues, some African Americans rejected assimilation and more militantly demanded basic institutional changes. Race riots swept the country, causing many to reassess the civil rights issue and Johnson's Great Society programs. But African Americans were not alone in calling for social and economic change; women and young adults were also challenging societal values and championing a more egalitarian and tolerant society.

CHRONOLOGY
New Frontiers

1960	Sit-ins begin
	Young Americans for Freedom formed
	SNCC formed
	Students for a Democratic Society formed
	John F. Kennedy elected president
1961	Peace Corps formed
	Alliance for Progress
	Bay of Pigs invasion
	Freedom rides begin
	Berlin Wall erected
1962	SDS's *Port Huron Statement*
	James Meredith enrolls at the University of Mississippi
	Cuban missile crisis
1963	Report on the status of women
	Betty Friedan's The Feminine Mystique
	Equal Pay Act
	Martin Luther King's "Letter from a Birmingham Jail"
	March on Washington
	Diem assassinated
	Kennedy assassinated; Lyndon Baines Johnson becomes president
1964	War on Poverty begins
	Freedom Summer
	Civil Rights Act
	Johnson elected president
1965	Malcolm X assassinated
	Selma freedom march
	Medicaid and Medicare
	Voting Rights Act
	Watts riot
	Water Quality and Air Quality Acts
1966	Black Panther Party formed
	National Organization for Women founded
1967	Urban riots in over 75 cities
1968	Martin Luther King Jr., assassinated
1969	Woodstock
	Stonewall Riot
	Neil Armstrong sets foot on moon

Study Tools

FOCUS QUESTIONS

If you have mastered this chapter, you should be able to answer these questions and to identify the terms that follow the questions.

1. How successful was the Kennedy administration in achieving its domestic agenda?

2. What form of African American activism pushed the civil rights movement forward, and how did Kennedy respond to those efforts?

3. How did Kennedy modify the strategy and tactics of Eisenhower's foreign policy?

4. What actions did Kennedy take in Latin America and Vietnam to promote American interests?

5. In what ways did the legislation associated with Johnson's Great Society differ from New Deal programs?

6. How did Johnson's War on Poverty and Great Society further the civil rights movement?

7. How did "new voices" conflict with traditional social norms, and what new organizations and agendas arose to provide a platform for those voices?

8. How did the urban riots and the emergence of the Black Power movement reflect a new agenda for the civil rights movement?

KEY TERMS

New Frontier   *p. 718*

sit-in   *p. 719*

Student Nonviolent Coordinating Committee   *p. 720*

freedom rides   *p. 721*

James Meredith   *p. 721*

March on Washington   *p. 723*

flexible response   *p. 723*

Peace Corps   *p. 724*

Alliance for Progress   *p. 724*

Bay of Pigs   *p. 724*

Berlin Wall   *p. 724*

Cuban missile crisis   *p. 725*

Limited Test Ban Treaty   *p. 725*

Ngo Dinh Diem   *p. 725*

Civil Rights Act of 1964   *p. 726*

War on Poverty   *p. 726*

New Right   *p. 727*

Gideon, Escobedo, and Miranda   *p. 727*

Barry Goldwater   *p. 728*

Great Society   *p. 728*

Freedom Summer   *p. 729*

freedom march   *p. 730*

Voting Rights Act   *p. 730*

Medicaid   *p. 731*

Medicare   *p. 731*

Watts   *p. 732*

Stokely Carmichael   *p. 732*

Black Power   *p. 732*

Black Muslims   *p. 732*

Malcolm X   *p. 733*

Black Panthers   *p. 733*

Betty Friedan   *p. 733*

Equal Pay Act   *p. 733*

Title VII   *p. 733*

National Organization for Women   *p. 735*

Free Speech Movement   *p. 736*

Students for a Democratic Society   *p. 736*

Port Huron Statement   *p. 736*

New Left   *p. 736*

hippies   *p. 737*

Woodstock   *p. 737*

SUGGESTED RESOURCES

Michael Dobbs, *One Minute to Midnight: Kennedy, Khrushchev, and Castro on the Brink of Nuclear War* (Vintage Press, 2009). A masterfully written, engrossing account of the Cuban missile crisis drawn from a wide variety of primary sources.

Daniel Horowitz, *Betty Friedan and the Making of the Feminist Movement* (University of Massachusetts Press, 2000). Uses many of Friedan's papers to examine her role as the central figure of the women's movement.

John F. Kennedy Library and Museum, http://www.jfklibrary.org. Located in Boston, Massachusetts, this library features a variety of materials on Kennedy's presidency, including issues regarding the civil rights movement and Cuba.

Sidney M. Milkis and Jerome M. Mileur, Eds., *The Great Society and the High Tide of Liberalism* (University of Massachusetts Press, 2005). An excellent collection of essays that focuses on the goals, legislation, and legacy of the Great Society.

27

America Under Stress, 1967–1976

CHAPTER OUTLINE

Johnson and the War
Americanization of the Vietnam War
The Antiwar Movement

Tet and the 1968 Presidential Campaign
The Tet Offensive
Changing of the Guard
The Election of 1968

Defining the American Dream
The Emergence of *La Causa*
Native American Activism

Nixon and the World
Vietnamization
Modifying the Cold War

Nixon and the Domestic Agenda
Nixon as Pragmatist
Building the Silent Majority
An Embattled President
An Interim President

INDIVIDUAL VOICES: *Dolores Huerta on Winning Rights for Farm Workers*

Study Tools

INDIVIDUAL CHOICES

Dolores Huerta

Seeing the poverty of farm worker children, Dolores Huerta, a schoolteacher in Stockton, California, decided it was not enough to be a good teacher and chose in 1955 to work for the Community Service Organization (CSO), an activist organization working to help the poor. There, she met César Chávez and in 1962, they formed the National Farm Workers Association. As a union organizer, Huerta and her family experienced what "farm worker families go through every day of their lives"—poverty.

Over the next forty-five years, she organized workers, led strikes, stood in picket lines, oversaw a grape boycott, and negotiated contracts with growers. In the process, she and others awakened the public and legislators to the many problems facing the farm workers (as illustrated in the Individual Voices feature at the end of this chapter). In the process Huerta was arrested twenty-two times, placed under FBI surveillance because of suspected Communist ties, and suffered a severe beating by a San Francisco police officer that ruptured her spleen.

Photo by Arthur Schatz//Time Life Pictures/Getty Images.

But there were victories. Through negotiations with growers, she improved wages and working conditions, including portable toilets, health coverage, and the restriction of pesticides, especially DDT, which was completely banned in 1974. Huerta was instrumental in getting the California Agricultural Labor Relations Act (1975) passed, giving farm workers the right to organize and collectively bargain with employers. She remains involved in *La Causa* (discussed in this chapter), working for the rights of Latinos, workers, and women. Still supporting farm workers, in July 2006 she organized a march in Lamont, California, to gain "just wages." In 2012, she was awarded the Presidential Medal of Freedom.

When Johnson ran for the presidency in 1964, he told the American public that he had no intention of sending Americans to fight in Vietnam. At the same time, however, his foreign policy advisers informed him that American air and ground forces were needed to prevent a Communist victory there. Focusing on his election and domestic agenda, Johnson chose a policy of gradual **escalation** of American forces in South Vietnam. The goal was to convince North Vietnam that the cost of the war was too high. The strategy failed. Not only did North Vietnam meet escalation with escalation, but it was the United States that grew war weary. For many then, the election of 1968 was a referendum on the war. But to others, it was a general critique of liberal policies and a socially and culturally fragmented society.

By the mid-1960s, Latinos and American Indians were among the "new" voices calling for political, economic, and social change. "Brown Power" and "Red Power" had joined "Black Power." In running against Humphrey in 1968, Nixon promised to restore national unity and global prestige by asserting conservative policies and respect for authority. He won votes from Americans tired of war, domestic unrest, and social reform. As president, he implemented pragmatic policies, including a "southern strategy," to attract largely white, middle-class Americans who accepted some governmental activism. By 1972, he could point to several successes. American troops were being withdrawn from Vietnam and he improved relations with the Soviet Union and the People's Republic of China.

Domestically, his choices showed flexibility, expanding some Great Society programs and following Keynesian guidelines to improve the economy. Nixon easily won reelection. But behind the scenes he worked to ruin his political enemies, leading to the Watergate break-in and a bitter harvest: not only the unprecedented resignation of a president, but a nationwide wave of disillusionment with politics and government. The unelected president, Gerald Ford, tried to heal the nation, but faced an uphill battle against a floundering economy and a politically cynical public. Although he reaped few political victories, he gained his party's nomination for the 1976 presidential election.

JOHNSON AND THE WAR

☆ *How did Johnson modify Kennedy's policies toward Latin America and Southeast Asia?*

☆ *What considerations led Johnson to expand America's role in Vietnam and how did the North Vietnamese respond to the changes?*

Lyndon Johnson inherited two foreign policy problems from Kennedy: Latin America and Vietnam. While not experienced in foreign affairs, Johnson was sure of one thing—he was not going to allow further erosion of American power, especially in Latin America and Southeast Asia.

In the Western Hemisphere, Castro remained the problem. Johnson continued Kennedy's economic boycott of Cuba and the CIA's efforts to destabilize the Castro regime. But he refocused Kennedy's Alliance for Progress from reform to political stability. This new approach, labeled the **Mann Doctrine**, increased American military equipment and advisers in Latin America to help various regimes suppress disruptive elements they labeled "Communist." It also led to direct military intervention in the Dominican Republic in 1965. There, supporters of deposed, democratically

□ **escalation** An increase in something; the term became associated with the steady increase in U.S. forces and the intensity of U.S. military activity in Vietnam.

□ **Mann Doctrine** U.S. policy outlined by Thomas Mann during the Johnson administration that called for stability in Latin America rather than economic and political reform.

elected president Juan Bosch rebelled against a repressive, pro-American regime. Deciding that the pro-Bosch coalition was dominated by Communists, Johnson sent in twenty-two thousand American troops to protect the Dominican people from an "international conspiracy." They restored order; monitored elections that put a pro-American president, Joaquín Balaguer, in power; and left the island in mid-1966. Johnson claimed to have saved the Dominicans from communism, but many Latin Americans saw the American intervention only as an example of Yankee interventionism.

Americanization of the Vietnam War

When Johnson assumed the presidency in 1963, his advisers told him that the South Vietnamese government remained unstable, its army ineffective, and that the Viet Cong, supported by North Vietnam, appeared to be winning the conflict. There would be no improvement, they said, without a large and direct American involvement. Johnson felt trapped: "I don't think it is worth fighting for," he told an adviser, "and I don't think we can get out." "I am not going to be the president who saw Southeast Asia go the way China went," he asserted. In formulating policy, Johnson concluded that a gradual escalation of American force against North Vietnam and the Viet Cong would be the most effective course. It would pressure the North Vietnamese to halt their support of the Viet Cong while limiting domestic opposition. He also wanted to wait until a Communist action justified U.S. retaliation before asking Congress for permission to use whatever force was necessary to defend South Vietnam.

The chance came off the coast of North Vietnam. On August 2, 1964, North Vietnamese torpedo boats skirmished with the American destroyer *Maddox* in the Gulf of Tonkin (see Map 27.1). On August 4, experiencing rough seas and poor visibility, radar operators on the *Maddox* and another destroyer, the *C. Turner Joy*, concluded that the patrol boats were making another attack. Confusion followed. Both ships fired at targets visible only on radar screens. Johnson immediately ordered retaliatory air strikes on North Vietnam and prepared a resolution for Congress. Although within hours he learned that the second incident probably had not occurred, Johnson told the public and Congress that Communist attacks against "peaceful villages" in South Vietnam had been "joined by open aggression on the high seas against the United States of America." On August 7, Congress approved the **Gulf of Tonkin Resolution**, allowing the United States "to take all necessary measures to repel" attacks against American forces in Vietnam and "to prevent further aggression." It was, in Johnson's terms, "like Grandma's nightgown, it covered everything." Public opinion polls showed strong support for the president.

The resolution gave Johnson freedom of action, but he wanted to wait until the presidential election was over and another Communist incident had occurred before escalating the war. In March 1965, following a Viet Cong attack on an American base at Pleiku, he gave the order to begin an air offensive against North Vietnam (Operation Rolling Thunder). By July, American planes were flying more than nine hundred missions a week, and a hundred thousand American ground forces had reached South Vietnam. Johnson's strategy soon showed flaws. Instead of reducing its support for the Viet Cong, as the administration had hoped, North Vietnam committed units of the North Vietnamese Army (NVA) to the fight. The U.S. commanding general in Vietnam, **William Westmoreland**, asked for more American soldiers to carry out offensive missions. Reluctantly, Johnson gave the green light. Vietnam had become an American war.

Westmoreland intended to use overwhelming numbers and firepower to destroy the enemy and planned a large-scale sweep of the Ia Drang Valley in November 1965. Ten miles from Cambodia, the Ia Drang Valley contained no villages and was a long-time sanctuary for Communist forces. Airlifted into the valley, air cavalry units soon clashed with North Vietnamese troops. "There was very vicious fighting," the North Vietnamese commander remembered, "soldiers fought valiantly. They had no choice, you were dead if not." Both sides claimed victory and drew different lessons from the engagement. Examining the losses, 305 Americans versus 3,561 Vietnamese, American officials embraced the strategy of **search and destroy** to grind down the enemy. Hanoi concluded its "peasant army" could withstand America's firepower and that over time they would wear down the Americans.

The war's intensity grew in 1966 and 1967. Both sides committed more troops, and American aircraft rained more bombs on North Vietnam and on supply routes, especially the **Ho Chi Minh Trail** (see Map 27.1).

■ **Gulf of Tonkin Resolution** A 1964 congressional action authorizing the president to take any measures necessary to repel attacks against U.S. forces in Vietnam.

William Westmoreland Commander of all American troops in Vietnam from 1964 to 1968.

search and destroy Military strategy in which U.S. ground forces attacked the enemy in their territory with the goal of destroying as many as possible; the term "body count" was used to explain the outcome of the operation.

■ **Ho Chi Minh Trail** Main route by which North Vietnamese soldiers and supplies reached South Vietnam; it ran through Laos and Cambodia.

Legend:
- Main area of confrontation
- Viet Cong base areas
- Communist supply route
- U.S. forces
- Major battle

0 50 100 Km.
0 50 100 Mi.

CHINA

MYANMAR (BURMA)

Dien Bien Phu

Hanoi
Haiphong

U.S. air raids on Hanoi 1966, 1968, 1972

NORTH VIETNAM

Red R.

Black R.

PLAIN OF JARS

Mekong R.

LAOS

Vientiane

Ca R.

Vinh

Keo Nua Pass

Mu Gia Pass

Gulf of Tonkin

Gulf of Tonkin, 1964

Hainan

20°N

THAILAND

Bangkok

Demilitarized Zone

Demarcation Line, 1954

17°N

Hue Tet Offensive 1968

Da Nang

South China Sea

My Lai Massacre 1968

15°N

Pleiku

Qui Nhon

CENTRAL HIGHLANDS

CAMBODIA

Mekong R.

Ia Drang Valley 1965

Ho Chi Minh Trail

Phnom Penh

SOUTH VIETNAM

Saigon

Tet Offensive 1968

110°E

Gulf of Thailand

10°N

CA MAU PENINSULA

Mekong Delta

N

100°E

105°E

MAP 27.1 Southeast Asia and the Vietnam War
Following the French defeat at Dienbienphu in 1954, the United States committed itself to defending South Vietnam. This map shows some of the major battle sites of the Vietnam War from 1954 to the fall of Saigon and the defeat of the South Vietnamese government in 1975. © Cengage Learning.

Despite the huge losses they suffered and the destruction caused by the bombing of North Vietnam, the enemy continued the struggle. Some in Washington began to speculate that victory would be a matter of will and feared that growing opposition to the war in the United States might be a deciding factor.

The Antiwar Movement

Throughout 1964, support at home for an American role in Vietnam was widespread. As the war escalated in 1965 a largely college-based opposition arose—with Students for a Democratic Society (SDS) the prime instigators. The University of Michigan held the first Vietnam "teach-in" to mobilize opposition to American policy on March 24, 1965. In April, SDS organized a protest march of nearly twenty thousand past the White House, and by October its membership had increased 400 percent. By mid-1966, SDS was only one of many groups and individuals demonstrating against the expanding war.

Those opposing the war fell into two major groups. Pacifists and some on the political left opposed the war for moral and ideological reasons. Others had more pragmatic reasons: the draft, the loss of lives and money, and the inability of the United States either to defeat the enemy or to create a stable, democratic South Vietnam. A University of Michigan student complained that if he were drafted and spent two years in the army, he would lose more than $16,000 in income. "I know I sound selfish," he explained, "but...I paid $10,000 to get this education."

Yet college students were not the most likely to be drafted or go to Vietnam. Far more often, minorities and the poor served in Vietnam, especially in combat roles. African Americans constituted about 12 percent of the population but in Vietnam they made up nearly 50 percent of frontline units and accounted for about 25 percent of combat deaths. Stokely Carmichael and SNCC had opposed the war as early as 1965, but it was Martin Luther King Jr.'s denunciation of the war in 1967 that made headlines. The war was immoral, King said, and it was wrong to send young blacks to defend democracy in Vietnam when they were denied it in Georgia.

Others said the war was too expensive in lives and dollars and showed, according to Senator J. William Fulbright, an "arrogance of power" that in reality weakened the United States at home and abroad. Johnson dismissed the critics, calling Fulbright "Halfbright" and King a "crackpot." But as the antiwar movement grew and public opinion polls registered increasing

National Archives.

By 1967, the antiwar movement conducted several major demonstrations with one of the largest at the entrance of the Pentagon, where over 30,000 protestors confronted soldiers protecting the Headquarters of the Department of Defense.

Opposing the War in Vietnam: Public Opinion—Who and When

Public opinion polls survey a segment of the population to understand how the larger population thinks about specific issues. They provide a snapshot of views held at a specific time, while a series of polls asking the same or similar questions can be an effective way to describe change taking place over a period of time. The number of people polled, the means of asking the questions, and the questions asked often vary, and sometimes polls provide incorrect and misleading information. Yet despite the possibility of errors and biases, public opinion polls are an important source of information for historians.

During the war in Vietnam, many polls were taken, asking people what they thought about the war, political leadership, and other related questions. The graph shown here depicts the results of opinion polls taken by Gallup (considered one of the best polling agencies) during the Vietnam War. These polls asked respondents one of two questions:

- "In view of the developments since we entered the fighting in Vietnam, do you think the U.S. made a mistake sending troops to fight in Vietnam?"
- "Do you support or oppose the war in Vietnam?"

The graph provides a summary of those who showed support for the American military effort in South Vietnam beginning in July 1965, when the first American troops arrived in a combat role, to 1971, when large numbers of American forces were coming home from Vietnam. It provides some very useful information:

- When American troops were first deployed to Vietnam in 1965 almost every group supported the decision.
- In 1965, those over age 49 were the least supportive of the war and those of college age were the most supportive of the decision.
- As the fighting continued, support for the war effort generally declined.

While the polls and the graph indicate the respondents' views about the Vietnam War, they do not explain why the responses were given. To better understand the reasons for them, historians need to consider other information, for instance, casualty rates, the number of troops being deployed, the role of the draft, and what military action was occurring when the polls were taken. With information from other sources, historians can look at public opinion and provide more complete explanations. For example, there appears to be a correlation between the Tet offensive (early 1968) and decline in support for the war.

Equally important, the information gained from public opinion polls can raise new questions and prompt reevaluations of existing understandings. Why, for example, did those in the "over 49" age group appear to respond more positively to the question in 1971 than any other group? What other evidence can confirm or explain what so many people and historians believe was a "generation gap" in support for the war? Answering such questions requires more research and analysis, which will produce new explanations and, no doubt, more questions.

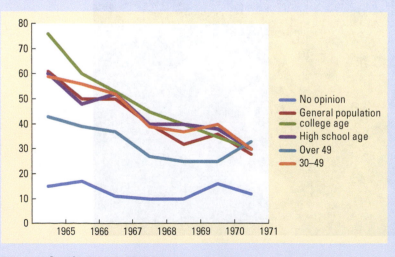

Support for the War in Vietnam © Cengage Learning.

disapproval of the war effort, the administration implemented **COINTELPRO** and **Operation Chaos** to infiltrate, discredit, and disrupt antiwar groups. Nevertheless, opposition to the war swelled. During "Stop-the-Draft Week" in October 1967 more than 200,000 people staged a massive protest march in Washington against "Lyndon's War."

Like the country, by late 1967, the administration was experiencing increasing disagreement about the course of the war. Hawks supported General Westmoreland's assertions that the war was being won but that more troops were needed to complete the job. Others, including Secretary of Defense Robert McNamara, were taking a different view, recommending a reduction in the war effort, including ending the bombing of North Vietnam. The result was the beginning of an exit strategy. Johnson agreed to initially commit more troops, intensify the bombing, and put more pressure on the South Vietnamese to make military and domestic reforms, and later he would scale back the American role and force the South Vietnamese to take a larger one. "The clock is ticking," Johnson said.

Unlike previous wars, Vietnam was a war without fixed frontlines. In this picture, marines work their way through the jungle south of the demilitarized zone (DMZ), trying to cut off North Vietnamese supplies and reinforcements moving into South Vietnam.

Larry Burrows/Time Magazine/Time & Life Pictures/Getty Images.

TET AND THE 1968 PRESIDENTIAL CAMPAIGN

☆ *What were the political, social, and military outcomes of the Tet offensive?*

☆ *What key issues shaped the 1968 campaign? What strategy did Richard Nixon use to win?*

Johnson was correct: the clock was ticking—not only for the United States but also for North Vietnam. As Westmoreland reported success, North Vietnamese leaders planned an immense campaign to capture South Vietnamese cities during **Tet**, the Vietnamese lunar New Year holiday.

The Tet Offensive

Catching American intelligence agencies and forces off guard, in January 1968, the Viet Cong struck forty-one cities throughout South Vietnam, including the capital, Saigon. In some of the bloodiest fighting of the war, American and South Vietnamese forces recaptured the lost cities and villages. It took twenty-four days to oust the Viet Cong from the old imperial city of Hue, leaving the city in ruins and costing more than 10,000 civilian, 5,000 Communist, 384 South Vietnamese, and 216 American lives. The Tet offensive was a military defeat for North Vietnam and the Viet Cong. It provoked no popular uprising, the Communists held no cities or provincial capitals, and they suffered staggering losses. Tet was, nevertheless, a "victory" for the North Vietnamese because it seriously weakened American support for the war. Amid official pronouncements

of "victory just around the corner," Tet destroyed the Johnson administration's credibility and strengthened a growing antiwar movement. The highly respected CBS news anchor Walter Cronkite had supported the war, but after Tet he announced there would be no victory in Vietnam and the United States should make peace. "If I have lost Walter Cronkite, then it's over. I have lost Mr. Average Citizen," Johnson lamented.

□ **COINTELPRO** (COunterINTELligence PROgram) Acronym for an FBI program from 1956 and until 1971 that sought to expose, disrupt, and discredit groups considered to be radical political organizations; it targeted various antiwar groups during the Vietnam War.

□ **Operation Chaos** CIA operation within the country from 1965 to 1973 that collected information on and disrupted anti–Vietnam War elements; although it is illegal for the CIA to operate within the United States, it collected files on over seven thousand Americans.

□ **Tet** The lunar New Year celebrated as a huge holiday in Vietnam; the Viet Cong–North Vietnamese attack on South Vietnamese cities during Tet in January 1968 was a military defeat for North Vietnam, but it seriously undermined U.S. support for the war.

By March 1968, Johnson and most of his advisers realized that the war was not going to be won. In the words of the new secretary of defense, Clark Clifford, four years of "enormous casualties" and "massive destruction from our bombing" had not weakened "the will of the enemy" and an exit strategy should be started. Westmoreland received fewer troops than requested, Johnson chose to begin negotiations with North Vietnam, and the South Vietnamese were told to assume a larger military responsibility.

Changing of the Guard

The first presidential primary, in New Hampshire, came two months after Tet. There, Democratic Minnesota senator Eugene McCarthy campaigned primarily on the conduct of the war. At the heart of his New Hampshire effort were hundreds of student volunteers who, deciding to "go clean for Gene," cut their long hair and shaved their beards. They knocked on doors and distributed bales of flyers and pamphlets touting their candidate and condemning the war. As McCarthy's antiwar candidacy strengthened, Johnson's advisers organized a write-in campaign for the president, who had not entered the primary. Johnson won by nearly 8 percent of the votes, but political commentators named McCarthy the real winner. The results in New Hampshire prompted New York senator Robert Kennedy to announce his candidacy in mid-March.

On March 31, 1968, a haggard-looking president delivered a major televised speech announcing changes in his Vietnam policy. The United States would seek a political settlement through negotiations in Paris with the Viet Cong and North Vietnamese. The escalation of the ground war was over, and the South Vietnamese would take a larger role in the war. The bombing of northern North Vietnam would end, and a complete halt of the air war would follow the start of negotiations. At the end of his speech, Johnson calmly announced: "I shall not seek, and I will not accept, the nomination of my party for another term as president." Listeners were shocked, and nearly everyone agreed that the Vietnam War had ended Johnson's political career and undermined his Great Society.

The Election of 1968

There were now three Democratic candidates. McCarthy campaigned against the war and the "imperial presidency." Robert Kennedy opposed the war, but not executive and federal power, and he called on the government to better meet the needs of the poor and minorities. Vice President Hubert H. Humphrey, running in the shadow of Johnson, stood behind the president's foreign and domestic programs.

By June, Kennedy was the front runner, but his assassination on June 5, by Sirhan Sirhan, a Jordanian immigrant, stunned the nation and led to Humphrey's eventual nomination. McCarthy continued his campaign but generated little support among party regulars. When the national convention met in Chicago in August, Humphrey had enough pledged votes to guarantee his nomination. Nevertheless, the convention was dramatic. Inside and outside the convention center, antiwar and anti-establishment groups demonstrated for McCarthy, peace in Vietnam, and social justice. On the second day of the convention, clashes between the police and protesters started. Protesters threw eggs, bottles, rocks, and balloons filled with water, ink, and urine at the police, who responded with tear gas and nightsticks. After four days of clashes, the police attacked protesters and bystanders alike as television cameras recorded the scene. The violence in Chicago's streets overshadowed Humphrey's nomination.

The 1968 presidential campaign soon became a three-party race. Drawing on growing dissatisfaction with liberal social policies within Democratic ranks, Governor George Wallace of Alabama left the Democratic Party and ran for president as the American Independent Party's candidate. He aimed his campaign at southern whites, blue-collar workers, and low-income white Americans. Wallace called for victory in Vietnam and gleefully attacked the counterculture and the "rich-kid" war protesters who avoided serving in Vietnam while the sons of working-class Americans died there. He also opposed federal civil rights and welfare legislation. Two months before the election, Wallace commanded 21 percent of the vote, according to national opinion polls. "On November 5," he confidently predicted, "they're going to find out there are a lot of rednecks in this country."

Richard Nixon easily won the Republican nomination. He focused his campaign on the need for effective international leadership, law and order, and the restoration of values. He denounced the four "Ps": pot, pornography, protesters, and permissiveness. On the critical issue of Vietnam, he offered no specifics but promised to "end the war and win the peace."

▣ **Eugene McCarthy** Senator who opposed the Vietnam War and made an unsuccessful bid for the 1968 Democratic nomination for president.

write-in campaign An attempt to elect a candidate in which voters are urged to write the name of an unregistered candidate directly on the ballot.

▣ **Robert Kennedy** Attorney general during the presidency of his brother John F. Kennedy, elected to the Senate in 1964; his campaign for the presidency was gathering momentum when he was assassinated in 1968.

▣ **George Wallace** Conservative Alabama governor who opposed desegregation in the 1960s and ran unsuccessfully for the presidency in 1968 and 1972.

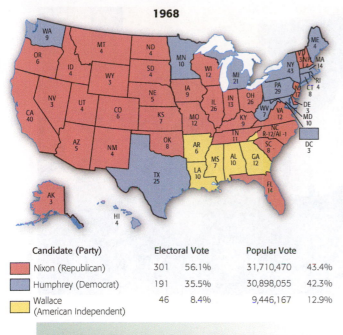

1968

Candidate (Party)	Electoral Vote		Popular Vote	
Nixon (Republican)	301	56.1%	31,710,470	43.4%
Humphrey (Democrat)	191	35.5%	30,898,055	42.3%
Wallace (American Independent)	46	8.4%	9,446,167	12.9%

MAP 27.2 Election of 1968
In winning the 1968 election against Hubert Humphrey, Richard Nixon received fewer popular votes than he did in 1960. But in the all-important electoral vote, Nixon easily defeated his Democratic rival. As they did in the 1960 election, some southerners, unwilling to vote for a Republican or a liberal Democrat, opted for a third choice, George Wallace. © Cengage Learning.

Nixon won with a comfortable margin in the Electoral College, although he received only 43 percent of the popular vote (see Map 27.2). Together, Nixon and Wallace attracted almost 56 percent of the popular vote, which conservatives interpreted as wide public support for an end to liberal programs, a return to traditional values, and a major political realignment that emphasized the suburbs and the Sunbelt.

DEFINING THE AMERICAN DREAM

☆ How did Latinos and Native Americans seek to address the problems they faced in American society?

☆ How did the federal government respond to their efforts?

By 1968, there seemed little agreement on the nature of the American dream and the role of government in helping to achieve that end. It appeared that African Americans, women, and gays and lesbians, as well as a very visible counterculture, were demanding significant alterations in the traditional American dream. They were not alone. Like blacks, Latinos and American Indians remained near society's lowest levels of income and education. As the 1960s progressed, they too organized grassroots movements and confronted the status quo, demanding change.

The Emergence of *La Causa*

Initially enthusiastic about John Kennedy, many Latino leaders were disappointed in his presidential actions. He appointed only a few Hispanics to government positions, and his administration did not show much interest in Latino issues. Meanwhile, local and state governments frequently resisted Latino activism. A Mexican American leader commented that despite being the largest minority in the western states, Mexican Americans were an "invisible minority," especially those working in the fields. Mexican American farm workers were at the bottom of the occupational ladder, not covered by Social Security or minimum-wage and labor laws, working long hours for low wages, usually under deplorable conditions.

In 1962, **César Chávez** and Dolores Huerta organized farm workers in central California, creating the National Farm Workers Association (NFWA). The union gained national recognition three years later when it struck against the grape growers. The union demanded a wage of $1.40 an hour and asked the public to buy only union-picked grapes. After five years, the strike and the nationwide boycott forced most of the major growers to accept unionization and to improve wages and working conditions. Eventually, California and other states passed legislation recognizing farm workers' unions and improving the wages and conditions of work for field workers. Still, agricultural workers, especially migrants, remain among the lowest-paid workers in the nation.

Chávez was central in promoting *La Causa* (Spanish for "the cause"), but he was not alone. Similar grassroot movements focusing on jobs, wages, and education were forming throughout the West and Southwest. Latino leaders like Rodolfo "Corky" Gonzales argued that discrimination and segregation barred their children from a decent education and that school districts needed to offer programs to meet the special needs of Hispanic students, including bilingual education.

In Los Angeles, Raul Ruiz told Mexican American students: "If you are a student you should be angry! You should demand! You should protest! You should organize for a better education!" He called for students to walk out of their classes if schools did not

Sunbelt A region stretching from Florida in a westward arc across the South and Southwest.

■ **César Chávez** Labor organizer who in 1962 founded the National Farm Workers Association; Chávez believed in nonviolence and used marches, boycotts, and fasts to bring moral and economic pressure to bear on growers.

In 1965 mostly Filipino farm workers struck Delano, California grape growers and were soon joined by Mexican American farmworkers led by Cesar Chavez and Dolores Huerta. In this picture a group of Mexican American workers and their families vote to join the strike. The strike lasted five years and ended in an agreement that covered over ten thousand farm workers.

© Farrell Grehan/CORBIS.

meet their demands. In 1968 "walkouts" spread from California across the West and Southwest. In the small South Texas school district of Edcouch-Elsa, Mexican American students walked out of the high school in November 1968. They demanded dignity, respect, and an end to "blatant discrimination," including corporal punishment—paddling—for speaking Spanish. The school board suspended more than 150 students. But as in other school districts, the protests brought results. The Edcouch-Elsa school district implemented Mexican American studies and bilingual programs, hired Mexican American teachers, and

created programs for migrant farm worker children, who moved from one school to another during picking season. Prominent in the growing grassroots militancy among Mexican Americans were young adults, who called themselves **Chicanos**. They stressed pride in their heritage and Latino culture and called for resistance to the dictates of Anglo society—"We're not in the melting pot....Chicanos don't melt."

It was not only in the West that Latinos were becoming more visible (see Map 27.3). In the urban Northeast, the Puerto Rican population had increased to about a million, but economic opportunities had declined as

MAP 27.3

Changing Latino Population

Growing rapidly, the Latino population had become the largest minority population in the United States by 2000, reaching 12.5 percent of the total population.

Source: Data from U.S. Census Bureau, *The Hispanic Population: 2010.* © Cengage Learning.

WA 11.2%
OR 11.7%
MT 2.9%
ND 2.0%
MN 4.7%
NH 2.8%
VT 1.5%
ME 1.3%
ID 11.2%
SD 2.7%
WI 5.9%
MI 4.4%
NY 17.6%
MA 9.6%
RI 12.4%
WY 8.9%
IA 5.0%
PA 5.7%
CT 13.4%
NJ 17.7%
NV 26.5%
UT 13.0%
NE 9.2%
IL 15.8%
IN 6.0%
OH 3.1%
DE 8.2%
CA 37.6%
CO 20.7%
KS 10.5%
MO 3.5%
KY 3.1%
WV 1.2%
VA 7.9%
MD 8.2%
DC 9.1%
AZ 29.6%
NM 46.3%
OK 8.9%
AR 6.4%
TN 4.6%
NC 8.4%
SC 5.1%
TX 36.7%
MS 2.7%
AL 3.9%
GA 8.8%
LA 4.2%
FL 22.5%
AK 5.5%
HI 8.9%

Percentage of population that is Hispanic, by state

25–50%
10–24.9%
5–9.9%
2–4.9%
Under 2%

MAP 27.4 American Indian Reservations
In the seventeenth century, American Indians roamed over an estimated 1.9 billion acres, but by 1990 that area had shrunk to about 46 million acres in enclaves spread across the United States. This area constitutes the federal reservation system. This map shows the location of most of the federal Indian reservations and highlights the high unemployment found on nearly every reservation. (*Note:* California is enlarged to show the many small reservations located there.) © Cengage Learning.

Labels on map:

Wounded Knee: 1890, massacre of Lakota Indians by U.S. Army. 1973, occupied by AIM for 71 days.

1. San Juan, Santa Clara, San Ildelfonso, Jemez, Zia, Sandia, Santa Ana, San Felipe, Cochiti, Santa Domingo, Tesuque, Nambe, Pojoaque, Picuris
2. Laguna, Acoma, Isleta, Canoncito

Percentage of reservation population unemployed, 1989
- Over 64%
- 55–64%
- 40–54%
- 24–39%
- States having no reservations
- Major reservation

---

manufacturing jobs, especially in the garment industry, relocated to the Sunbelt or overseas. The Puerto Rican Forum attempted to coordinate federal grants and to find jobs, while the more militant Young Lords organized younger Puerto Ricans in Chicago and New York with an emphasis on their island culture and Hispanic heritage. "Brown Power" had joined Black Power, soon to be joined by "Red Power."

Native American Activism

Native Americans, responding to poverty, federal and state termination policies, and efforts by state government to seize land for development, organized and asserted their rights with new vigor in the 1960s

(see Map 27.4). In 1961, Indian leaders met in Chicago and produced the "Declaration of Indian Purpose." It called for the end of the termination policies and for improved educational, economic, and health opportunities. Presidents Kennedy and Johnson responded positively, ensuring that Indians benefited from New Frontier and Great Society programs. Johnson, in 1968, declared that Native Americans should have the same "standard of living" as the rest of the nation and

■ **Chicano** A variation of *Mexicano,* a man or boy of Mexican descent. The feminine form is Chicana. Many Mexican Americans used the term during the late 1960s to signify their ethnic identity.

Oscar Bear Runner was one of two hundred Sioux organized by the American Indian Movement (AIM) who took over Wounded Knee, South Dakota, the site of the 1890 massacre, holding out for seventy-one days against state and federal authorities. Following the end confrontation, the federal government agreed to examine the treaty rights of the Oglala Sioux.

signed the Indian Civil Rights Act. It officially ended the termination program and gave more power to tribal organizations.

Kennedy's and Johnson's support was a good beginning, but many activists wanted to redress old wrongs. The National Indian Youth Council called for "Red Power"—for Indians to use all means possible to resist further loss of their lands, rights, and traditions. They began "fish-ins" in 1964 when the Washington state government, in violation of treaty rights, barred Indians from fishing in certain areas. Protests, arrests, and violence continued until 1975, when the state complied with a federal court decision (*United States v. Washington*) upholding treaty rights. Native American leaders also demanded the protection and restoration of their water and timber rights and ancient burial grounds. Museums were asked to return for proper burial the remains and grave goods of Indians on display. But for most, the crucial issue was self-determination, which would allow Indians control over their lands and over federal programs that served the reservations.

In 1969 a group of San Francisco Indian activists, led by **Russell Means**, gained national attention by seizing **Alcatraz Island** and holding it until 1971 when, without bloodshed, federal authorities regained control. Two years later, in a more violent confrontation, **American Indian Movement** (AIM) leaders Means and Dennis Banks led an armed occupation of Wounded Knee, South Dakota, the site of the 1890 massacre of the Lakotas by the army (see page **420**). AIM controlled the town for seventy-one days before surrendering to federal authorities. Two Indians were killed, and over 230 activists arrested, in the "Second Battle of Wounded Knee."

President Nixon opposed AIM's actions at Wounded Knee but agreed that tribal and individual lives needed to be improved. He doubled funding for the Bureau of Indian Affairs, promoted tribal economies, and signed bills that returned 40 million acres of Alaskan land to Eskimos and other native peoples. In 1974 Congress passed the **Indian Self-Determination and Education Assistance Act**, giving tribes control and operation of many federal programs on their reservations. Tribal and pan-Indian movements sparked cultural pride and awareness. Indian languages were revived and on

▪ **Russell Means** Indian activist who helped organize the seizures of Alcatraz and Wounded Knee.

Alcatraz Island Rocky island, formerly a federal prison, in San Francisco Bay occupied by Native American activists who demanded that it be made available to them as a cultural center.

▪ **American Indian Movement** (AIM) Militant Indian movement founded in 1968 that was willing to use confrontation to obtain social justice and Indian treaty rights; organized the seizure of Wounded Knee.

Indian Self-Determination and Education Assistance Act A 1974 law giving Indian tribes control over federal programs carried out on their reservations and increasing their authority in reservation schools.

Richard Nixon and Secretary of State Henry Kissinger sought to end the Vietnam War through a negotiated peace treaty with the North Vietnamese. In this picture, Nixon and Kissinger are meeting with Nguyen Phu Duc, a high ranking South Vietnamese official, to consider terms for a possible ceasefire in Vietnam. Their effort failed, resulting in the Christmas bombings of North Vietnam. Further negotiations followed, and on January 27, 1973 the Paris Peace Accords were signed.

© Bettmann/Corbis.

many reservations disease and mortality rates declined, leading to population growth. "We're a giant that's been asleep," stated a Navajo leader. "But now that's ending, and . . . no one knows what we're capable of." Economic growth, however, has been less than hoped, even with the 1988 Indian Gaming Regulatory Act that allowed reservations to open gaming casinos. By 2011, nearly half of the 562 federally recognized tribes operated casinos, earning nearly $23 billion a year. Those near urban areas, like Mohegan Sun in Connecticut and Pechango in California, do well, but many in rural areas often struggle to break even. Consequently, the economic benefits from casinos vary greatly, and overall Indians remain the nation's most impoverished peoples with an average yearly income of about $33,300.

NIXON AND THE WORLD

☆ How did Richard Nixon plan to achieve an "honorable" peace in Vietnam?

☆ How did Nixon's Cold War policies differ from those favored by earlier administrations?

In 1969 Nixon achieved the presidency denied him in 1960. Determined to be the center of decision making, he relied primarily on a few close advisers. For domestic affairs, he looked to John Mitchell, his attorney general, and longtime associates H. R. "Bob"

Haldeman and John Ehrlichman. In foreign affairs, he tapped Harvard professor **Henry Kissinger** as his national security adviser and later made him secretary of state. In both domestic and foreign affairs, Nixon wanted to institute policies that would consolidate his presidency and strengthen the Republican Party.

Vietnamization

Vietnam was the foremost issue; it influenced nearly all others—the budget, public and congressional opinion, foreign policy, and domestic stability. Nixon needed a solution before he could move ahead on other fronts. The central question was how best to withdraw American troops while ensuring America's international credibility and the viability of Nguyen Van Thieu's government.

The outcome was **Vietnamization**. Better trained and better equipped South Vietnamese units would assume the bulk of the fighting as American troops left (see Figure 27.1). Changing the "color of bodies" and

■ **Henry Kissinger** German-born American diplomat who was President Nixon's national security adviser and secretary of state; he helped negotiate the cease-fire in Vietnam.

■ **Vietnamization** U.S. policy of scaling back American involvement in Vietnam and helping Vietnamese forces fight their own war.

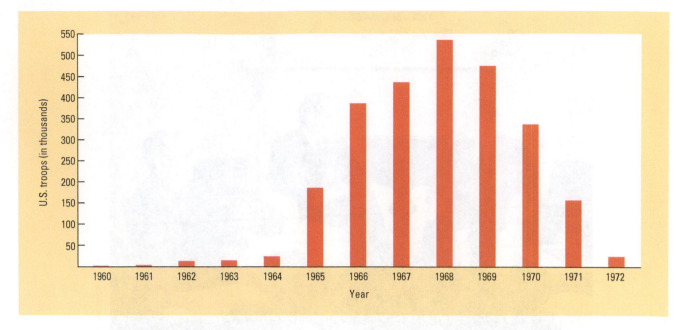

FIGURE 27.1 Troop Levels by Year, 1960–1972

For America, the Vietnam War went through two major phases: Americanization from 1960 to 1968 and Vietnamization from 1969 to 1972. © Cengage Learning.

bringing American soldiers home, Nixon believed, would rebuild public support and undermine the antiwar protesters. In the spring of 1969, Nixon announced that 25,000 American soldiers were coming home and called on the nation to rally behind Vietnamization. To discredit protestors, Nixon declared, "North Vietnam cannot defeat or humiliate" us . . . "[o]nly Americans can do that." In July, he unveiled the **Nixon Doctrine**, which promised that countries fighting communism would receive American political and economic support but only limited military support. By the end of the 1969, American forces in Vietnam had declined by over 110,000, public opinion polls indicated support for Nixon's policy, and it appeared that the antiwar movement was losing momentum.

While Nixon's Vietnam policy gained support, he and Kissinger quietly worked to improve relations with the Soviets and Chinese and to encourage the North Vietnamese to resume negotiations in Paris.

To accomplish the latter, Nixon resumed the air war against North Vietnam and began secret air attacks (Operation Menu) on enemy bases inside Cambodia and Laos. Nixon wanted Hanoi "to believe . . . I might do anything to stop the war." "We'll just slip the word," he said, "that 'for God's sake, you know Nixon. . . . We can't restrain him when he's angry—and he has his hand on the nuclear button.'" When North Vietnam failed to satisfactorily respond, in April 1970 Nixon ordered American troops to cross the border into Cambodia to destroy Communist bases and supply areas. The mission destroyed enemy bases and large amounts of supplies, but it also created a firestorm of protest in the United States.

In over 350 universities and colleges, demonstrations against the war broke out. At Kent State (Ohio) and Jackson State (Mississippi) clashes with troops and police resulted in six student deaths. Nixon tried to rally support, but the sentiment favoring the war, even with Vietnamization, only declined.

In January 1971, the Senate repealed the Gulf of Tonkin Resolution, which had provided the legislative foundation for the war, and forbade the further use of American troops in Laos or Cambodia. Three months later, half a million people marched in Washington, D.C., calling for an end to the war, while the *New York Times* began to print classified documents, the **Pentagon Papers**, showing that American officials from Truman to Nixon had misled the public about Vietnam. In November 1973, trying to prevent a future Vietnam-like war, Congress passed the **War Powers Act** to limit the

□ **Nixon Doctrine** Nixon's policy of requiring countries threatened by communism to shoulder most of the military burden, with the United States offering mainly political and economic support.

Pentagon Papers Classified government documents on policy decisions leaked to the press by Daniel Ellsberg and printed by the *New York Times* in 1971.

□ **War Powers Act** A 1973 law to prevent the president from involving the United States in war without authorization by Congress.

president's war-making abilities. It requires the president to inform Congress of the overseas deployment of troops within forty-eight hours, and unless Congress authorizes the deployment, to withdraw those forces within sixty days.

Another factor contributing to expanding opposition to the war was concern about the effect it was having on American soldiers. In late 1969 came the shocking news that Americans were involved in the massacre of over five hundred men, women, and children in and around the village of **My Lai** in March 1968. For two years the nation witnessed the court martials of Lieutenant William Calley and others accused of the killings. While only Calley was found guilty of murder, the trial, combined with stories of widespread drug use and **fragging**, confirmed to many that the war was corrupting the moral values of American soldiers. "This is not what the American soldier does," explained a helicopter pilot who had rescued some of the My Lai villagers.

Aware of declining support for the war in the United States and the weakness of South Vietnamese forces, North Vietnam in March 1972 launched its "Easter Offensive." Pushing aside South Vietnamese (ARVN) troops, Communist forces advanced toward Saigon. Nixon ordered massive bombing raids against North Vietnam and Communist forces in South Vietnam that blunted the advance and enabled ARVN forces to drive the North Vietnamese back. The Easter Offensive's failure also renewed the peace talks in Paris, and in October, Kissinger announced that "peace is at hand."

South Vietnamese president Thieu, however, rejected the plan. Reluctantly, Nixon supported Thieu and he ordered the Christmas bombing of Hanoi and North Vietnam. After eleven days the bombing stopped. When the Paris talks resumed, Washington advised Thieu to accept the next peace settlement or fend for himself. On January 27, 1973, he accepted a peace settlement that did not differ significantly from the one offered in October. Nixon proclaimed peace with honor.

The peace settlement imposed a cease-fire, removed the twenty-four thousand remaining American troops, and promised the return of American prisoners of war. The peace permitted the United States to end its role in the war. But because the settlement left North Vietnamese troops in South Vietnam, it did little to ensure the existence of Thieu's government or nation. When asked how long the South Vietnamese government could last, Kissinger replied, "If they're lucky, they can hold out for a year and a half." In March 1975, North Vietnam renewed the war, and a month later, North Vietnamese troops entered Saigon. The Vietnam War ended as it had started, with Vietnamese fighting Vietnamese. The war had killed an estimated 2 million Vietnamese and over 58,000 Americans, with about 40 percent of those being Hispanics and African Americans (see Table 27.1). It also had eroded respect for the military and the government and undermined support for the U.S. Cold War role as global policeman.

Modifying the Cold War

Ending the Vietnam War was part of Nixon's larger plan to reshape the Cold War by pursuing **détente**. An "era of confrontation" must give way to an "era of negotiation," Nixon announced. China was the key to the strategy. The United States had not recognized the Beijing government since the end of the Chinese civil war in 1949. Reopening relations with Communist China, in Nixon's and Kissinger's view, would provide several positive results. It would create new trade opportunities, encourage the North Vietnamese to negotiate in Paris, and pressure the Soviets to improve their relations with the United States. The Soviets and Chinese had engaged in several bloody clashes along their border, and the Chinese hoped that better relations with the United States would help deter Soviet aggression. They also wanted access to American technology.

Sending a signal to China, Nixon lowered restrictions on trade. The Chinese responded by inviting an American ping-pong team to tour China in April 1971. Three months later, Kissinger secretly met with Premier Zhou Enlai in Beijing. On Kissinger's return, Nixon stunned the world when he announced he would meet with Communist Party chairman Mao Zedong and Zhou in Beijing in February 1972.

The first step in moving toward détente was in place. The second occurred in May when Nixon had a successful meeting with Soviet President **Leonid Brezhnev** that produced the **Strategic Arms Limitation agreement** (SALT I). The product of

---

■ **My Lai** Site of a massacre of South Vietnamese villagers by U.S. infantrymen in 1968. Of those brought to trial for the atrocity, only Lieutenant William Calley was found guilty of murder.

fragging An effort to kill fellow soldiers, frequently officers, by using a grenade. It may have accounted for over a thousand American deaths in Vietnam.

détente Relaxing of tensions between the superpowers in the early 1970s, which led to increased diplomatic, commercial, and cultural contact.

■ **Leonid Brezhnev** Leader of the Soviet Union (first as Communist Party secretary, and then also as president) from 1964 to his death in 1982; he worked to foster détente with the United States during the Nixon era.

■ **Strategic Arms Limitation agreement** (SALT I) Treaty between the United States and the Soviet Union in 1972 that limited offensive nuclear weapons and defensive antiballistic missile systems.

As North Vietnamese forces entered Saigon in April 1975, the last American evacuees left by helicopter. Here, they scramble to the roof of the Pittman apartments in Saigon; others left from the roof of the American embassy. Henry Kissinger asked the nation "to put Vietnam behind us."

© Bettmann/Corbis.

TABLE 27.1 **The Vietnam Generation, 1964–1975**

	MEN	WOMEN
Total in military service	8,700,000	250,000
Served in Vietnam	2,700,000	6,431
Killed in Vietnam	58,219	8
Wounded	303,000*	
Missing in action	2,330	1
Draft resisters (estimate)	570,000	—
Accused	210,000	—
Convicted	8,750	—

*Combined men and women.
Source: Department of Defense and Veterans Administration.

prolonged negotiations, SALT I restricted antimissile sites and established a maximum number of intercontinental ballistic missiles (ICBMs) and submarine-launched ballistic missiles (SLBMs) for each side. The Cold War was not over, but détente reduced big power tensions.

Although Nixon pursued détente with China and the Soviet Union, in Latin America the administration continued its efforts to isolate Cuba and

prevent the spread of socialist governments. Of special concern was Chile, with the democratically elected socialist-Marxist government of **Salvador Allende**. Kissinger believed Chile represented another Cuba and that the administration should not "let a country go Marxist just because its people are irresponsible," and from 1970 to 1973, the United States worked both openly and covertly to bring down the Allende government. In September 1973, when a military coup in which Allende was killed toppled his government, the Nixon administration denied any role in the coup but quickly recognized the repressive dictatorship of General Augusto Pinochet. Other Latin American dictators and the repressive governments of Iran and South Africa also received economic and military aid.

NIXON AND THE DOMESTIC AGENDA

☆ *How did Nixon's policies dealing with the economy, welfare, and the environment reflect his pragmatic approach? What did he do to increase the base of the Republican Party?*

☆ *What actions led to the Watergate investigation and Nixon's resignation?*

Nixon had no plan for domestic affairs that equaled his grand scheme for changing foreign policy. Nixon was the first president since 1858 to take office without his own party controlling either house of Congress, which clearly complicated implementing traditional

◾ **Salvador Allende** Chilean president who was considered the first democratically elected Marxist to head a government; he was killed in a coup in 1973.

In the Wider World

The Sino–Soviet Split

Since the Communist Revolution in 1917, the Soviet Union assumed the dominant role as the leader of the global Communist movement. But by the 1960s a rift was growing between the leaders of Communist China and the Soviet Union. Their disagreements ranged from ideological to differences over social, cultural, economic, and foreign policies.

In 1961, the Chinese officially denounced the ideology practiced by the Soviet Union as reactionary and accused Moscow of being too friendly to the West. By the mid-1960s, the Soviets supported India in the Sino–Indian War and the widening split forced other Communist nations to choose sides. Most remained loyal to the Soviet Union. In 1969, an increasingly volatile border conflict along the Ussuri River resulted in a major military engagement between the two powers and raised worldwide concern about a Sino–Soviet nuclear war. The tensions declined, but the widening Sino–Soviet split encouraged the Chinese to improve relations with the United States.

Republican agendas. Consequently, Nixon adopted a complex and pragmatic approach that balanced his desire to expand the Republican Party with an unexpectedly progressive social agenda.

In efforts to redirect the Cold War, Nixon became the first president to visit China, meeting with Mao Zedong and Zhou Enlai, seen here, in 1972. With regard to Chinese–Soviet relations, Nixon confided to Zhou that if Moscow marched either east or west, he was ready to "turn like a cobra on the Russians." Nixon's visit to China began the process of normalizing relations with the People's Republic of China that was finalized under Carter.

John Dominis/Time Life Pictures/Getty Images.

Nixon as Pragmatist

Shocking many conservatives, between 1969 and 1971, Nixon's administration adopted a surprisingly liberal agenda. It expanded the federal government's regulatory functions by creating the Occupational Safety and Health Administration (OSHA), the **Environmental Protection Agency** (EPA), and the National Oceanic and Atmospheric Administration (NOAA). Nixon's principal economic adviser noted that no administration had passed so much regulatory legislation since the New Deal.

Nixon was not an environmentalist, but he understood that the environmental movement had momentum and was becoming a political issue. Rachel Carson had alerted the nation to the dangers of DDT in her book *Silent Spring* (1962), which touched off a wave of environmental concerns. By 1969, it was impossible to ignore the health problems caused by air pollution, the ecological death of Lake Erie, and growing mountains of garbage everywhere. A national response came in April 1970, when communities and thousands of schools and colleges hosted Earth Day activities. It was the largest single-day demonstration in American history and reflected deep public concern about a worsening environment.

Correctly gauging the public's attitude, in July 1970 Nixon asked Congress to create a central executive branch agency, the EPA, to set, monitor, and implement national pollution standards. The EPA

■ **Environmental Protection Agency** (EPA) Agency created to consolidate all major governmental programs controlling pollution and other programs to protect the environment.

It Matters Today

Banning DDT

In 1972, the United States banned the use of the pesticide DDT. Widely used in agriculture to protect crops from insects, it entered the food chain, creating medical problems in animals and humans. Momentum for the ban began with Rachel Carson's publication of *Silent Spring* (1962), which examined the effects of the chemical on nature and questioned societies' blind faith in technological progress. Since 1972, many other nations have stopped the use of DDT, and in 2008 the United Nations announced its goal to halt its worldwide use by 2020. Carson's views and the banning of DDT were, and continue to be, strongly criticized. Some have claimed that following her logic would mean returning to the "Dark Ages" when "insects and diseases . . . would . . . again inherit the earth" and that she is responsible for more deaths than Hitler.

- Should developed nations be able to dictate the ban of chemicals like DDT to countries that might benefit economically from using such toxic chemicals?
- The reference to Carson's killing of millions of people refers to deaths from malaria—a disease linked to mosquitoes—because DDT has been banned. Research the spread of malaria and the use of DDT since 1972 to determine if this accusation is valid.

was formed in December and there followed a wide variety of environmental legislation, including restrictions on the use of pesticides and automobile emissions, a Clean Air Act, a Safe Drinking Water Act, and an Endangered Species Act.

Nixon's social programs also surprised many. He expanded Job Corps and the food stamp programs and increased benefits for those receiving Social Security, Medicare, and Medicaid. He also accepted Congress's extension of the Voting Rights Act to give those between ages eighteen and twenty-one the right to vote in federal, local, and state elections, although he did question the provision's constitutionality. But it was his effort to develop an affirmative action program and to alter the welfare system that dismayed most conservatives.

Nixon's plan for affirmative action, the Philadelphia Plan, required companies receiving federal contracts to hire minority and women workers and unions to open membership to more women and minorities. To fix the "welfare mess," Nixon wanted to replace "millions on welfare rolls" with "millions on payrolls" by enacting the Family Assistance Plan. It was designed to eliminate most existing welfare agencies by providing to low-income families a direct monetary payment ($1,600)

from the government as long as recipients worked or enrolled in job training programs. The plan was defeated in 1969 by a coalition of conservatives and liberals and again in 1971. Nixon blamed the first defeat on Congress, conservatives, and "damn social workers." By 1971, the wily Nixon told Haldeman that the bill was too expensive and that for political purposes he wanted "it killed by Democrats."

Nixon's ideological flexibility also showed in his actions on the economy. When he took office the country faced a budget deficit of nearly $25 billion and a climbing rate of inflation. In keeping with a fiscally conservative policy, Nixon cut spending, increased interest rates, and balanced the budget in 1969. But economic recovery failed to follow, and inflation rose as economic growth slowed—giving rise to a new phenomenon, **stagflation**. By 1971, the economy was in its first serious recession since 1958. Unemployment and bankruptcies increased, and still inflation climbed.

Fearing that stagflation would cost votes in the next presidential election of 1972, Nixon shifted his approach and asked for increased federal spending to boost recovery and for a wage and price freeze to stall inflation. Shocked conservatives complained bitterly at the betrayal of their economic values. But the economy responded positively as inflation and unemployment declined through the 1972 elections.

Nonetheless, Nixon's battle with inflation was a losing one. Wages and prices climbed when the president lifted the wage and price freeze, and they soared in 1973 when the **Organization of Petroleum Exporting Countries** (OPEC) raised oil prices and

stagflation Persistent inflation combined with stagnant consumer demand and relatively high unemployment.

■ **Organization of Petroleum Exporting Countries** (OPEC) Economic alliance of oil-producing countries, mostly Arab, formed in 1960 to influence the world price of oil by controlling oil supplies; in 1973 OPEC members embargoed the sale of oil to countries supporting Israel.

TOWARD A MORE PERFECT UNION

The Twenty-Sixth Amendment to the Constitution

The Twenty-sixth Amendment was adopted on July 1, 1971. It contains two short sentences:

Section 1. The right of citizens of the United States, who are eighteen years of age or older, to vote shall not be denied or abridged by the United States or by any State on account of age.

Section 2. The Congress shall have the power to enforce this article by appropriate legislation.

The need for the constitutional amendment followed a Supreme Court decision (*Oregon v. Mitchell*, December 1970) that invalidated those parts of the 1970 renewal of the Voting Rights Act of 1965 that permitted those ages eighteen and over to vote in federal, state, and local elections. The Court ruled that Congress had no power to legislate criteria for voting in state and local elections. The Senate passed the proposed amendment (94–0) on March 10, 1971, followed by the House (401–19) on March 23. It took only four months for the requisite three-fourths of the states to ratify it, the shortest ratification time for any amendment.

limited oil sales to the United States because of Washington's support for Israel in the **Yom Kippur War**. Nixon reinstituted wage and price controls, but with declining results, and by 1974 inflation was over 12 percent and the nation's economy slumped into a

recession. Pat Buchanan, Nixon's speechwriter, concluded that the president was not a true conservative.

Building the Silent Majority

Conservatives may have disliked Nixon's social and economic policies, but they applauded his effort to expand and strengthen the Republican Party. To do this he looked at two regions, the Sunbelt and the South. He adopted a "**southern strategy**" to shatter the once solid Democratic South by bringing white Southerners into the Republican fold. In the Sunbelt, he hoped that his **New Federalism**, which returned more revenue, power, and responsibilities to state and local governments, would attract more voters to the Republican Party. By opposing forced integration and supporting neighborhood schools, Nixon hoped to attract not only white southerners but many blue-collar workers in the north. He candidly told Haldeman to "go for the Poles, Italians, Irish" but not "Jews or Blacks."

Responding to a 1969 effort by Mississippi to postpone court-ordered integration of its school systems, Attorney General John Mitchell petitioned the Supreme Court for a delay. The Supreme Court ignored the

▫ **Yom Kippur War** On October 6, 1973, Egypt and Syria suddenly invaded Israel; after initial losses, the Israeli military defeated the Arab armies; peace terms were agreed to on October 22.

▫ **southern strategy** A plan to entice southerners into the Republican Party by appointing white southerners to the Supreme Court and resisting the policy of busing to achieve integration.

New Federalism A political term introduced during the Nixon Administration that advocated transferring federal power and responsibilities back to state governments, providing states more autonomy.

AP Photo.

On January 29, 1969, six miles off the coast of Santa Barbara, California, an oil spill from a Union Oil Co. platform released over 200,000 gallons over more than eleven days. The oil spill spread 800 square miles and washed ashore along the California coast. In this picture, workers and volunteers work to clean up the oil-soaked beaches, and others sought to save oil-coated wildlife. President Nixon said the spill at Santa Barbara "touched the conscience of the American people."

requests and in October 1969 unanimously decreed in *Alexander v. Holmes* that it was "the obligation of every school district to terminate dual school systems at once." The White House suffered another loss in 1971 when the Burger Court reaffirmed the use of busing to achieve integration in a North Carolina case, *Swann v. Charlotte-Mecklenburg.* The administration criticized the decisions but agreed to "carry out the law."

The Court's decision had by 1973 completed the legal process of integrating public schools in the South, but across the country protests, demonstrations, and lawsuits sought to reverse court-ordered busing. In many cities from Los Angeles to South Boston, angry parents took direct action to halt "forced busing" and the loss of neighborhood schools. In Pontiac, Michigan, anti-busing forces used dynamite to destroy ten school buses. "Pontiac is the new South," lamented one state legislator.

Another aspect of Nixon's political strategy was to stress his administration's support for law and order and to appoint more conservative judges and justices who would be tougher on criminals and more narrowly interpret the Constitution. In 1969, Chief Justice Earl Warren retired, and to replace him, Nixon nominated Warren Burger, a respected, conservative federal judge who was easily confirmed by the Senate. Within months, another resignation gave Nixon a second opportunity to alter the Court. Merging his desire for a conservative judge with his southern strategy, Nixon first chose South Carolinian Clement Haynsworth and then G. Harrold Carswell of Florida for the position. The Senate rejected both nominees because of their lack of support for integration. On his third try, Nixon abandoned his southern strategy and chose Harry Blackmun, a conservative from Minnesota. Blackmun was confirmed easily. In 1971 Nixon appointed two more justices, Lewis Powell of Virginia and William Rehnquist of Arizona, creating a more conservative Supreme Court.

An Embattled President

By the end of Nixon's first term, nearly 60 percent of respondents in national opinion polls approved of the president's record. The South was no longer solidly Democratic, and Sunbelt and blue-collar worker voters seemed to be supporting Republican issues and candidates. The economy, while still a worry, seemed under control. Diplomatically, Nixon had scored major successes with China and the Soviets, and a peace agreement in Paris seemed possible. Nixon projected an easy reelection in 1972.

Meanwhile, Democrats were in disarray. Their most enthusiastic members appeared to be migrating to either the liberal Senator **George McGovern** or the conservative George Wallace. The newest category of voter, those ages 18 to 21 who were voting for the first time as a result of the Twenty-sixth Amendment (ratified in 1971), seemed to be in McGovern's camp. When Senator McGovern won the nomination, George Wallace—confined to a wheelchair following an assassination attempt that left him paralyzed—again bolted the party to run as a third-party candidate on the American Independent ticket.

Despite almost certain victory, Nixon obsessed about enemies surrounding him. Repeatedly, as president, he spoke about "screwing" his domestic enemies before they got him and how the press hated him. He warned his cabinet and staff that the press would "run lies about you . . . and the cartoonists will depict you as ogres." To combat his foes, Nixon kept an "enemies list," used illegal wiretaps and infiltration to spy on anti-administration organizations and people, and instructed the FBI, the Internal Revenue Service, and other governmental organizations to intimidate and punish his opponents. As the 1972 campaign began, Nixon and the **Committee to Re-elect the President** (CREEP), directed by John Mitchell, wanted to humiliate and crush the Democrats and were willing to step outside the bounds of normal election behavior to do so. A Special Investigations Unit, known informally as the "Plumbers," conducted "dirty tricks" to disrupt Democratic activities. CREEP also approved a burglary at the Democratic National Committee headquarters in the **Watergate** building in Washington, D.C., to copy documents and tap phones.

On June 17, 1972, a Watergate security guard detected the burglars and notified the police. Five men were arrested carrying "bugging" equipment and two others were apprehended across the street. The burglars were soon linked to CREEP, which along with the White House denied any connection to the burglary, while Nixon told Mitchell to "stonewall it" and "cover it up." The furor soon passed, and in November, Nixon buried McGovern in an avalanche of electoral votes, winning every state except Massachusetts.

Despite Democrats still holding majorities in Congress, Nixon was overjoyed. But his optimism faded as the Watergate cover-up unraveled. In January, the burglars were convicted and two *Washington Post* reporters, Bob Woodward and Carl Bernstein, helped by a secret

■ **George McGovern** South Dakota senator who opposed the Vietnam War and was the unsuccessful Democratic candidate for president in 1972.

■ **Committee to Re-elect the President** (CREEP) Nixon's campaign committee in 1972, headed by John Mitchell, which enlisted G. Gordon Liddy and others to spy on the Democrats and break into the offices of the Democratic National Committee.

■ **Watergate** Apartment and office complex in Washington, D.C., where CREEP "Plumbers" broke into the headquarters of the Democratic National Committee; its name became synonymous with the Nixon administration's involvement and the president's part in the cover-up that followed.

The Supreme Court's decisions to require busing as a means to integrate school districts resulted in demonstrations and protests in both the North and the South. In this picture a Pontiac, Michigan, woman stopped a school bus to try and prevent busing. The bus driver said he tried to get around her but finally had to pull off the road to avoid hitting her.

informer inside the FBI called "Deep Throat," had uncovered a trail of "hush money" leading to CREEP and the White House. Three separate investigations of the Watergate affair followed. The most public was by a Special Committee of the Senate chaired by a Democrat, Senator Sam Ervin, Jr., of North Carolina, but the federal grand jury investigation led by Judge John Sirica and a Justice Department investigation conducted by Archibald Cox would result in criminal prosecutions.

Throughout the spring and summer, testimony linked the break-in and cover-up to CREEP and the executive branch. Trying to limit the damage, Nixon accepted the resignations of Haldeman, Ehrlichman, and others on his staff, while denying his own role. His denials became less and less credible as the testimony unfolded. When it was revealed that Nixon had secretly recorded meetings in the Oval Office, Cox, Sirica, and Ervin each demanded to examine the tapes. Nixon refused, claiming executive privilege, and when Cox persisted Nixon had him fired. A firestorm of protest erupted, Nixon's popularity dropped to under 30 percent, and the House Judiciary Committee started to gather evidence for impeachment proceedings. Adding to Nixon's woes, in October, Vice President **Spiro Agnew** was forced to resign for accepting bribes while governor of Maryland. In keeping with the Twenty-fifth Amendment, Nixon selected Representative Gerald R. Ford of Michigan to replace Agnew.

In March 1974, the Sirica grand jury **indicted** Mitchell, Haldeman, and Ehrlichman and named Nixon as an "unindicted coconspirator" in the Watergate break-in and cover-up. Nixon, under tremendous pressure, released transcripts of selected tapes. The outcome was devastating. The transcripts contradicted some official testimony, and Nixon's apparent callousness, lack of decency, and profane language shocked the nation. In July, the Supreme Court rejected Nixon's executive privilege position and ordered him to hand over all the tapes. Having ample evidence, the House Judiciary Committee charged Nixon with three impeachable crimes: obstructing justice, abuse of power, and defying subpoenas. Nixon's choices were to either resign or be impeached and removed from office. He resigned on August 9, 1974. Eventually, twenty-nine people connected to the White House were convicted of crimes related to Watergate and the 1972 campaign.

An Interim President

Gerald Ford assumed the presidency with Nixon's resignation and faced a resurgent Democratic-controlled Congress, a slumping economy, and growing concerns about Nixon's foreign policies. Though most saw Ford as a well-intentioned, able administrator, to many he was just an interim president. What goodwill he had with Democrats and much of the public quickly eroded after he pardoned Nixon for any crimes he might have committed as president. Nor did his domestic and foreign policies provide a picture of effective leadership.

When he assumed office, the nation was experiencing a deepening recession along with spiraling

■ **Spiro Agnew** Vice president under Richard Nixon; he resigned in 1973 amid charges of illegal financial dealings during his governorship of Maryland.

indict To make a formal charge of wrongdoing against a person or party.

Despite his efforts to keep his role in the Watergate break-in hidden, the Watergate tapes and other testimony clearly indicated Nixon's direct role in the affair. When it became evident that he would be removed from office through impeachment, he chose to resign from the presidency. In this picture taken on August 9, 1974, in the East Room of the White House, surrounded by his family, President Nixon informs his staff and others of his resignation.

inflation that led to 9 percent unemployment and inflation above 10 percent. His ineffective response was to trim spending and name inflation "public enemy number one." To fend off Democrat-sponsored legislation to increase spending and expand government services, Ford resorted to the veto, using it over fifty times. His foreign policy was seen as a weaker version of Nixon's. He relied heavily on Kissinger as his secretary of state, but was criticized by many within his own party for not better supporting the South Vietnamese when North Vietnam resumed the war in 1975. Conservative Republicans also criticized

the results of his summit meetings with Soviet leader Brezhnev, which they believed yielded approval of the Soviet domination of Eastern Europe. One of the most outspoken critics was Ronald Reagan, who attacked Ford's lack of toughness in foreign policy and his ineffectiveness in dealing with domestic issues.

As the presidential campaign began in 1976, many Republicans moved to support Reagan for the nomination. In a series of hard-fought primary battles, Ford emerged with the nomination, but many wondered if he could defeat the Democratic candidate, Georgia governor James Earl Carter, Jr.

Individual Voices

DOLORES HUERTA
on Winning Rights for Farm Workers

Union organizer Dolores Huerta spoke in 1978 to an audience at the University of California–Los Angeles, explaining the problems faced by farm workers and how the farm workers union she and César Chávez created managed to gain benefits for the workers. In this document, she presents an insider's view of the nature of the effort and why it was successful, but readers and historians need to be aware of how the university audience might have shaped the content and tone of the speech and her request.

Arthur Schatz//Time Life Pictures/Getty Images.

1 What types of benefits did unionization obtain for the workers and how did they compare to Chávez's and Huerta's goals for *La Causa*?

There was a time when farm workers couldn't get any kind of welfare . . . if they were out of work. . . . Back in 1963, we did a big campaign and we got farm workers covered under welfare so if farm workers were out of work they could at least get welfare. . . . We have come a long way in the changes that have been made. The minimum wage for farm workers . . . in the places that we don't have the union are two dollars and fifty cents an hour and . . . where we have union contracts . . . farm workers' wages are three dollars and fifty-five cents an hour. **1**

How were these change made? . . . The changes . . . were made by people that were like the poorest of all, people that didn't know how to read or write, people who had no resources, and when we think of the changes that we were able to make . . . it's really kind of a mindblower. About this time ten years ago, César Chávez started his first fast. . . . We had been on strike . . . for about . . . three years, and we still didn't have any contract. He . . . didn't eat for twenty-five days. And of course a lot of people thought he was crazy. . . . We sort of picked up on . . . César's fast, and then we thought, why couldn't the whole country do a little fast? Let's ask everyone not to eat grapes. That's kind of a simple thing, right? It doesn't take a lot, just don't eat grapes. **2** And so we asked the whole country and the whole world not to eat grapes and they didn't. And as a result of . . . people not eating grapes, we had our first big national grape boycott and we got our first contract. That was a really simple thing, but it had tremendous impact. Because we were going to the heart of the growers, and that is their pocketbook. . . . They respond to only one thing and that is economic power. So, somehow, you have to hit them in that pocketbook where they have their heart and their nerves and then they feel the pain. . . . This is why . . . the Montgomery Bus Boycott was effective. . . . Because it hit them . . . [in] the pocketbook. **3**

2 According to the document, what contributed to the decision to turn to the national boycott of grapes?

3 Why do you think that Huerta connects the efforts of the farm workers to those of the bus boycott?

4 How does the phrase "*Sí se puede*" reflect the goal of the speaker and the nature of the farm workers' struggle?

This country needs a lot of changes and we have to make them. . . . In Spanish, in our union, we have a saying. . . . We always say, "*Sí se puede.*" It can be done, right? *Sí se puede* means it can be done. **4**

Source: Speech by Dolores Huerta at the University of California, Los Angeles, February 22, 1978. From Mario T. Garcia, ed., A Dolores Huerta Reader, *University of New Mexico Press, 2008. UCLA Chicano Studies Research Center Library and Archive.*

763

Study Tools

SUMMARY

Adopting Kennedy's policies, President Johnson worked to oppose communism around the world. In South Vietnam he implemented a series of planned escalations that Americanized the war. North Vietnam kept pace and showed no slackening of resolve or resources. Within the United States, however, as the American commitment grew, a significant antiwar movement developed. The combination of the Tet offensive and presidential politics divided the Democratic Party and compounded the divisions in American society.

By 1968, the country seemed aflame with urban riots and protests. Hispanics and Native Americans joined their voices with other groups demanding more recognition of their needs and calling on the federal government for support. Those advocating social change, however, faced a resurgence of conservatism that helped elect Nixon. Seeking a strategy for withdrawing from Vietnam, Nixon implemented a policy of Vietnamization. To restructure the Cold War, he worked to improve relations with the Soviet Union and China. At home, Nixon charted a pragmatic course, switching between government activism and more traditional Republican policies, hoping to cement the Sunbelt and the South to the Republican Party.

Despite Nixon's domestic and foreign-policy successes, his desire to crush his enemies led to the Watergate scandal and his resignation. President Ford tried to restore confidence in government but faced too many obstacles. As the 1976 bicentennial election approached, the nation seemed mired in a slowing economy and public cynicism toward government and politics. Many wondered if the optimism that began the 1960s would ever return.

CHRONOLOGY
A Nation Under Stress

1962	César Chávez and Dolores Huerta form National Farm Workers Association
1963	Lyndon B. Johnson becomes president
1964	Gulf of Tonkin Resolution
	Johnson elected president
1965	U.S. air strikes against North Vietnam begin
	American combat troops arrive in South Vietnam
	Anti-Vietnam "teach-ins" begin
	Dominican Republic intervention
1967	Antiwar march on Washington
1968	Tet offensive
	My Lai massacre
	Johnson withdraws from presidential race
	Robert Kennedy assassinated
	Mexican American student walkouts
	American Indian Movement founded
	Richard Nixon elected president
1969	Secret bombing of Cambodia
	First American troop withdrawals from Vietnam
	American Indians occupy Alcatraz
1970	U.S. troops invade Cambodia
	Kent State and Jackson State killings
	First Earth Day observed
	Environmental Protection Agency created
1972	Nixon visits China and Soviet Union
	Attempted assassination of George Wallace
	Watergate break-in
	Nixon reelected
	SALT I treaty
1973	Vietnam peace settlement
	"Second Battle of Wounded Knee"
	Watergate hearings
	Salvador Allende overthrown in Chile
	War Powers Act
	Arab oil boycott
1974	Nixon resigns
	Gerald Ford becomes president
1975	South Vietnam government falls to North Vietnamese

FOCUS QUESTIONS

If you have mastered this chapter, you should be able to answer these questions and to explain the terms that follow the questions.

1. How did Johnson modify Kennedy's policies toward Latin America and Southeast Asia?

2. What considerations led Johnson to expand America's role in Vietnam and how did the North Vietnamese respond to the changes?

3. What were the political, social, and military outcomes of the Tet offensive?

4. What key issues shaped the 1968 campaign? What strategy did Richard Nixon use to win?

5. How did Latinos and Native Americans seek to address the problems they faced in American society?

6. How did the federal government respond to their efforts?

7. How did Richard Nixon plan to achieve an "honorable" peace in Vietnam?

8. How did Nixon's Cold War policies differ from those favored by earlier administrations?

9. How did Nixon's policies dealing with the economy, welfare, and the environment reflect his pragmatic approach? What did he do to increase the base of the Republican Party?

10. What actions led to the Watergate investigation and Nixon's resignation?

KEY TERMS

escalation *p. 742*

Mann Doctrine *p. 742*

Gulf of Tonkin Resolution *p. 743*

Ho Chi Minh Trail *p. 743*

COINTELPRO *p. 747*

Operation Chaos *p. 747*

Tet *p. 747*

Eugene McCarthy *p. 748*

Robert Kennedy *p. 748*

George Wallace *p. 748*

César Chávez *p. 749*

Chicano *p. 750*

Russell Means *p. 752*

American Indian Movement *p. 752*

Henry Kissinger *p. 753*

Vietnamization *p. 753*

Nixon Doctrine *p. 754*

War Powers Act *p. 754*

My Lai *p. 755*

Leonid Brezhnev *p. 755*

Strategic Arms Limitation agreement *p. 755*

Salvador Allende *p. 756*

Environmental Protection Agency *p. 757*

Organization of Petroleum Exporting Countries *p. 758*

Yom Kippur War *p. 759*

southern strategy *p. 759*

George McGovern *p. 760*

Committee to Re-elect the President *p. 760*

Watergate *p. 760*

Spiro Agnew *(p. 761)*

SUGGESTED RESOURCES

Stephen Ambrose. *Nixon: The Triumph of a Politician, 1962–1973* (Simon and Schuster, 1989). An excellent examination of the Nixon presidency and its policies—the second volume of a three-volume series.

Edward Berkowitz. *Something Happened: A Political and Cultural Overview of the Seventies* (Columbia University Press, 2006). An introduction to the seventies that indicates it was a period of activism and change as people and institutions debated the issues facing the nation.

Philip Caputo. *Rumor of War* (Holt Paperbacks, 1996). The author's engaging account of his service in Vietnam and how his perspective toward the war changed.

Farmworkers Movement. http://www.farmworkermovement.us. César Chávez and the farm workers' movement are the focus of this website.

Nguyen T. Lien-Hang. *Hanoi's War: An International History of the War for Peace in Vietnam* (University of North Carolina Press, 2012). Using North Vietnamese sources, the author examines the Vietnam War from the North's perspective.

28

New Economic and Political Alignments, 1976–1992

CHAPTER OUTLINE

The Carter Presidency
New Directions in Foreign Policy
Domestic Priorities

Resurgent Conservatism
The New Right
Reaganism

A Society and Economy in Transition
A Shifting Economy
New Immigrants

Asserting World Power
Cold War Renewed
The Middle East and Terrorism
Reagan and Gorbachev

In Reagan's Shadow
Bush Assumes Office
Bush and a New International Order
The Election of 1992

INDIVIDUAL VOICES: *Phyllis Schlafly Opposes the Equal Rights Amendment*

Study Tools

INDIVIDUAL CHOICES

Phyllis Schlafly

Phyllis Schlafly became a nationally recognized conservative figure with the publication of *A Choice, Not an Echo* in 1964. She claimed that since the 1930s, grassroots conservative Republicans—those who were truly dedicated to small government and anticommunism—had been subverted by the eastern, more liberal Republican establishment. Republican "kingmakers" had bypassed real conservatives (like Senator Robert Taft of Ohio) in selecting presidential candidates. She argued that grassroots Republicans should assert themselves and choose Barry Goldwater, an authentic conservative, to run for president. Many credit the book for ensuring Goldwater's nomination. Goldwater lost the election, but Schlafly remained an active and dedicated advocate of true conservatism.

In 1967, she created the Eagle Trust to raise money for conservative causes and published a monthly newsletter, the *Phyllis Schlafly Report,* to expose the evils of communism and liberalism. Three years later, following an unsuccessful attempt to unseat a long-term Illinois Democratic congressman, she concentrated on the feminist movement and the Equal Rights Amendment as

Bettmann/Corbis.

major threats to the nation. She said the country needed to be saved from "the little clique of women's libbers" who wanted to reverse the "moral vision" and the traditional and respectable values that were the foundations of American stability and strength (see this chapter's Individual Voices feature). She mobilized a grass-roots movement which stressed that women, especially housewives, were the guardians of social and moral order. By 1972, Schlafly had created two organizations. "Stop Taking Our Privileges" (STOP-ERA) emerged to prevent ratification of the Equal Rights Amendment (ERA), and the Eagle Forum was designed to support a broader range of conservative causes.

Stopping ratification of the ERA looked like a daunting, if not impossible, task. Support seemed high, and in 1972 twenty-eight of the needed thirty-eight states had approved the amendment. Schlafly was confident of the righteousness of her crusade, but more importantly, she was politically experienced, had an existing organization, and was able to attract other women who were also politically astute and active in conservative causes. By stressing the extreme and radical aspects of the feminist movement, Schlafly linked the ERA to several separate but related issues ranging from homosexuality to women being drafted and sent into combat, unisex toilets, and fears that existing privileges and protections for women would be stripped away. STOP-ERA spread rapidly, rallying a growing number of women to lobby and pressure state legislators to reject ratification. Schlafly testified in over forty legislative hearings, made hundreds of speeches, and wrote dozens of articles.

After losing a hard-fought battle in Indiana in 1977 that left the ERA only three states short of ratification, Schlafly's movement turned the tide. ERA supporters were unable to win approval from any of the remaining states. By defeating the ERA, Schlafly and STOP-ERA not only gave conservative women political legitimacy, but also significantly contributed to the rise of the New Right and the election of Ronald Reagan, as conservatives recognized the effectiveness of social issues. Today, Schlafly and the Eagle Forum continue to mobilize conservatives against liberal social, political, and economic policies they believe constitute an attack on vital American values.

Across the country in 1976, Americans celebrated the bicentennial of the American Revolution, but a sluggish economy and rising unemployment made some wonder if the future would be worth celebrating. The government activism associated with Johnson and New Deal–style liberalism no longer seemed to provide answers for the problems facing the nation. Even the Democratic presidential candidate, Jimmy Carter, admitted that government could not solve every problem. In office, Carter seemed unable to reverse the slowing economy or to fulfill liberal expectations on social issues. His foreign policy appeared incapable of projecting American power or protecting the nation's interests.

A hopeful nation chose Ronald Reagan as president in 1980. Reagan promised changes that would restore American power and prosperity. His policies implemented a conservative agenda to replace liberal economic and social policies and to restore an assertive Cold War foreign and military policy. Critics charged his policies benefited the wealthy and abandoned support for minorities and the poor, and they warned of a growing national debt. But most Americans embraced Reagan's policies as the economy rebounded and the country assumed a preeminent role in the world with the decline of the Soviet Union.

In 1988, Americans elected George H. W. Bush. He promised experienced and fiscally sound leadership and continued American strength abroad. Taking office as the Soviet Union collapsed, he charted a foreign policy in a new international setting, cautiously supporting democratic change in Eastern Europe and Central America. When Iraq invaded Kuwait, he organized an international coalition, committed American forces, and liberated Kuwait. At home, however, he was unable to improve a deteriorating economy or meet the expectations of either liberals or conservatives. Focusing on the economy, Democrat William (Bill) Clinton swept into the presidency.

THE CARTER PRESIDENCY

☆ *What new directions in foreign policy did Carter take, especially in Central America and the Middle East?*

☆ *What problems did Carter face in implementing his domestic policies, and why were many Democrats unhappy with his approach?*

In 1976, amid the bicentennial festivities lurked a deepening sense of cynicism and uncertainty. President Gerald Ford's efforts to restore faith in government and the economy had not succeeded. For the first time since the Depression, many parents worried that their children would not enjoy a higher standard of living than their own. The optimism that had characterized the 1960s had faded into frustration and apathy.

When the two presidential contenders began their race for the White House, polls showed that people liked Ford but considered him ineffective. His Democratic opponent, James Earl Carter, Jr., who preferred to be called "Jimmy," had little political experience—aside from being a one-time governor of Georgia—but argued that being an outsider to the Washington system was a positive attribute. Both men voiced good intentions but were vague on specifics. Their televised debates were dull and in an election where only 54.4 percent of eligible voters cast ballots Carter won by 56 electoral votes. Explaining why he had decided not to vote, a Californian simply said he did not want "to force a second-class decision on my neighbors."

Jimmy Carter arrived in the nation's capital in January 1977 brimming with enthusiasm. He stressed

human rights Basic rights and freedoms to which all human beings are entitled, such as the right to life and liberty, to freedom of thought and expression, and to equality before the law.

◻ **Camp David Accords** Treaty, signed at Camp David in 1978, under which Israel returned territory captured from Egypt and Egypt recognized Israel as a nation; most of the Arab world denounced the agreement and Egyptian leader Sadat.

he was free of Washington politics and the lures of special interests. He pledged honesty and hard work and a more moral approach to tackling foreign and domestic problems. With majorities in Congress, Democratic congressional leaders also were eager to assert their leadership. The problem was that Carter had little intention of playing politics as usual, and he frequently ignored Congress. Objecting to Carter's approach, Democratic congressional leaders announced that Congress had no intention of "rolling over and playing dead." The results were repeated conflicts between Congress and the president that left few satisfied.

New Directions in Foreign Policy

Carter hoped to reshape American foreign policy, which he believed focused too much on Europe and an "inordinate fear of communism." He wanted the United States to recognize the economic and social needs of the world's non-European and non-Communist nations and to foster **human rights**, which he considered the "soul of our foreign policy."

Carter's new tone in foreign policy became evident in his effort to complete a new treaty with Panama and to promote peace between Israel and its Arab neighbors. Overcoming public and bipartisan opposition, in 1978 Carter shepherded two treaties through the Senate, one giving the United States the right to defend the Panama Canal if freedom of transit was threatened and the other returning the canal to Panamanian sovereignty on December 31, 1999.

Carter showed even more persistence in convincing Egyptian president Anwar Sadat and Israeli prime minister Menachem Begin to accept a set of carefully crafted agreements by which Egypt recognized Israel's right to exist and Israel returned the Israeli-occupied Sinai Peninsula to Egypt (see Map 28.1). After the two leaders met with Carter in September 1978 at the presidential retreat at Camp David in Maryland, it took several months to finalize the **Camp David Accords**. But on March 26, 1979, Carter looked on as Begin and Sadat signed the first peace treaty between an Arab state and Israel.

In promoting human rights, Carter received mixed reviews. He was generally applauded when he denounced, applied sanctions against, and reduced aid to repressive governments in El Salvador, Guatemala, Chile, Nicaragua, Uganda, the Soviet Union, and the minority white governments in southern Africa. Some, however, questioned his human rights emphasis when, after American aid to Nicaragua ended, forces of the Marxist Sandinista Liberation Front overthrew the government of Anastasio Somoza in 1979. Other critics pointed out that Carter declined to denounce human rights violations by the governments of the Philippines and Iran, and by the People's Republic of

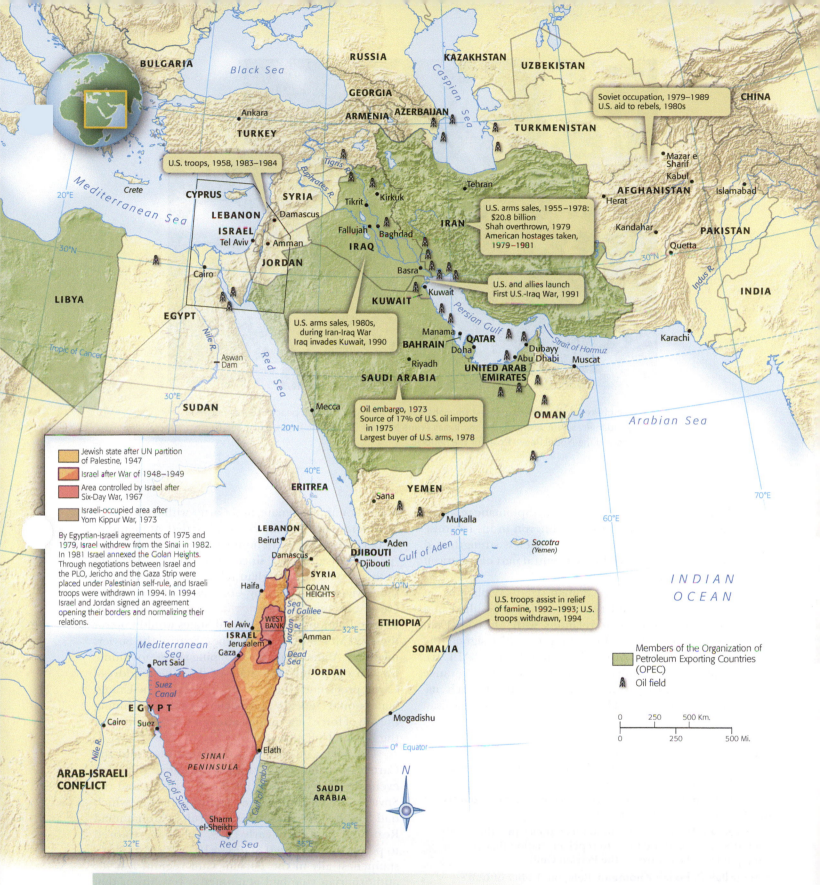

Soviet occupation, 1979–1989
U.S. aid to rebels, 1980s

U.S. troops, 1958, 1983–1984

U.S. arms sales, 1955–1978:
$20.8 billion
Shah overthrown, 1979
American hostages taken,
1979–1981

U.S. and allies launch
First U.S.-Iraq War, 1991

U.S. arms sales, 1980s,
during Iran-Iraq War
Iraq invades Kuwait, 1990

Oil embargo, 1973
Source of 17% of U.S. oil imports
in 1975
Largest buyer of U.S. arms, 1978

U.S. troops assist in relief
of famine, 1992–1993; U.S.
troops withdrawn, 1994

Members of the Organization of
Petroleum Exporting Countries
(OPEC)

Oil field

ARAB-ISRAELI CONFLICT

Jewish state after UN partition
of Palestine, 1947

Israel after War of 1948–1949

Area controlled by Israel after
Six-Day War, 1967

Israeli-occupied area after
Yom Kippur War, 1973

By Egyptian-Israeli agreements of 1975 and
1979, Israel withdrew from the Sinai in 1982.
In 1981 Israel annexed the Golan Heights.
Through negotiations between Israel and
the PLO, Jericho and the Gaza Strip were
placed under Palestinian self-rule, and Israeli
troops were withdrawn in 1994. In 1994
Israel and Jordan signed an agreement
opening their borders and normalizing their
relations.

MAP 28.1   The Middle East
Since 1946, the United States has tried to balance its support for Israel with its need for oil from the Arab states.
To support its interests in this volatile region, the United States has provided large amounts of financial and
military aid to some nations while also seeking to create peace talks between Israel and its Arab neighbors and
the Palestinians. © Cengage Learning.

One of President Carter's greatest triumphs was the signing of the 1978 peace accords between Egyptian President Anwar Sadat and Israeli Prime Minister Menachem Begin. Sadat and Begin received the Nobel Peace Prize for their efforts.

China, with which he restored full diplomatic relations in 1979. Although Carter was uneven in his response to brutal governments, he nonetheless strengthened the role of human rights as a central part of American foreign policy.

Carter's focus on human rights violations in Eastern Europe and the Soviet Union resulted in a noticeable cooling of relations with Moscow. Even so, Carter and Brezhnev in June 1979 signed the second Strategic Arms Limitation Treaty (SALT II), which placed limits on the number of long-range bombers, missiles, and nuclear warheads each nation could deploy. The treaty faced strong bipartisan opposition in the Senate, and Carter withdrew it from consideration when the Soviets invaded Afghanistan in December. Carter denounced the invasion as the "gravest threat to peace since 1945," and approved aid to the **mujahedeen**, Afghan rebels who were fighting the Soviets. Supported by Congress and the public, Carter also imposed **economic sanctions** on the Soviets and announced the United States would boycott the 1980 Moscow Olympic Games. Fearful the Soviets might use Afghanistan as a "stepping stone" to Middle Eastern oil, in his 1980 State of the Union address, Carter proclaimed the "**Carter Doctrine**." The United States would "repel by any means necessary, including the use of force" any outside attempt to take control of the Persian Gulf region.

The Soviet intervention in Afghanistan and the Carter Doctrine were responses to more than just events in Afghanistan. Both the Americans and the Soviets were reacting to the revolution in Iran, which had toppled the pro-American ruler, Mohammad Reza Shah Pahlavi, in early 1979. The shah, restored to power by the United States in 1953, was America's staunchest ally in the Persian Gulf region. But his authoritarian rule had generated a revolution that brought to power Iran's religious leaders, led by the **Ayatollah Ruhollah Khomeini**, who established an Islamic fundamentalist state and denounced the United States as the main source of evil in the world.

- **mujahedeen** Afghan resistance group supplied with arms by the United States for its fight against the Soviets following their 1979 invasion of Afghanistan.

economic sanctions Trade restrictions imposed on a country that has violated international law.

- **Carter Doctrine** Carter's announced policy that the United States would use force to repel any nation that attempted to take control of the Persian Gulf.

- **Ayatollah Ruhollah Khomeini** Religious leader of Iran's Shiite Muslims; after toppling the shah in 1979, the ayatollah (a title of respect given to a high-ranking Shiite religious authority) established a new constitution that gave him supreme power.

Tensions between Iran and the United States reached a crisis after the exiled shah entered a New York hospital for cancer treatment. On November 4, an angry mob stormed the American embassy in Tehran taking sixty-six American hostages.

As the world watched televised pictures of the hostages, Carter first used negotiations and covert operations to free some of the hostages, but with further negotiations failing and his popularity falling, Carter ordered an April 1980 military rescue mission. It failed, losing three helicopters in a violent dust storm in Iran. Finally, in late 1980, Canadian and Algerian diplomatic efforts obtained the release of the remaining hostages, who were set free on January 20, 1981, the day Carter left the presidency, ending 444 days of captivity.

Domestic Priorities

Throughout his presidency Carter, like Ford, struggled with an economy characterized by high unemployment and inflation and increasing energy costs. His solutions pleased few. For those focused on stimulating the economy and creating jobs, especially congressional Democrats, his efforts were inadequate. They called him a southern Ford and pushed legislation to expand social programs and government spending. When Carter asked for a 20-cent increase in the minimum wage, congressional Democrats pushed through a much larger increase, raising it from $2.30 per hour in1976 to $3.35 in 1981. At the same time, business groups, Republicans, and fiscal conservatives complained that Carter was spending too much and not dealing effectively with inflation, and they demanded deeper budget cuts.

Energy costs represented another issue that everyone agreed should be addressed. When Carter announced the nation's need to reduce its dependence on foreign oil and declared solving the **energy crisis** the "moral equivalent of war," he drew widespread support. But once he began to lay out solutions, the support quickly faded. Rather than stress the production of more American-based gas and oil, he called on the nation to use less energy and to develop nuclear and other **alternative fuels**. Proponents of oil and gas production argued that alternative fuels were too expensive and could not meet the nation's demands. Nuclear energy lost its viability in March 1979 when a serious accident at **Three Mile Island** in Pennsylvania released a cloud of radioactive gas and

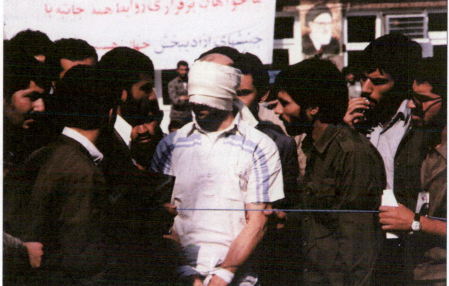

In November 1979, Iranians seized the American embassy in Tehran and took sixty-six hostages. Thirteen were soon released through the efforts of Palestinian leader Yasir Arafat, but negotiations to release more failed. Held for more than a year, the hostages were set free as Ronald Reagan was being sworn in as president. When one hostage was asked if he would ever return to Iran, he said yes, but only in an American bomber.

Photo by Alain MINGAM/Gamma-Rapho via Getty Images.

nearly caused a **meltdown**. No one was injured, but the accident made nuclear power less attractive and more than thirty companies canceled their nuclear energy projects.

Overall, Carter offered more than a hundred energy proposals that Congress mostly ignored. It did approve a cabinet-level Department of Energy and the Energy Policy and Conservation Act, which provided some funds to develop alternative sources of energy. Carter's pleas to reduce energy consumption by wearing sweaters, lowering thermostats in winter, and using public transportation carried little weight. When the Iranian revolution and a war between Iraq and Iran (1979–1980) sparked higher oil prices, it was

energy crisis Vulnerability to dwindling oil supplies, wasteful energy consumption, and potential embargoes by oil-producing countries.

alternative fuels Sources of energy other than coal, oil, and natural gas, such as solar, wind, geothermal, hydroelectric, and nuclear energy.

■ **Three Mile Island** Site of a nuclear power plant near Harrisburg, Pennsylvania; an accident at the plant in 1979 led to a release of radioactive gases and almost caused a meltdown.

meltdown Severe overheating of a nuclear reactor core, resulting in the melting of the core and the escape of life-threatening radiation.

The Twenty-Seventh Amendment to the Constitution

The Twenty-seventh amendment, ratified in May 1992, states: "No law, varying the compensation for the services of the Senators and Representatives, shall take effect, until an election of Representatives shall have intervened."

The intent was to prevent Congress from voting itself an increase in salary every year by allowing voters the option of not reelecting those who approved the pay increase. It was proposed to Congress in 1789—202 years before its ratification—as one of the proposals for the Bill of Rights. It fell four states short of the required ten needed for ratification, but unlike later proposed amendments, it had no deadline established for its ratification. Although Ohio (1873) and Wyoming (1978) approved the amendment to protest congressional pay increases, few paid it any attention until a University of Texas student began lobbying for it in 1982? by writing letters to state legislatures. In a period of broad opposition to government spending and tax increases, the campaign took root. When Michigan ratified it in 1992, the so-called James Madison amendment became part of the Constitution.

clear that the United States had yet to find an effective energy strategy.

It was also evident that Carter's handling of the economy had brought neither growth nor stability. By1980, unemployment was nearly 7.6 percent, and inflation hovered at 14 percent—the highest rate since 1947. The only thing that seemed to decline was Carter's popularity—it stood at 19 percent.

affirmative action Policy that seeks to redress past discrimination through active measures to ensure equal opportunity, especially in education and employment.

▫ **Alan Bakke** Student who filed a lawsuit against the University of California at Davis for reverse discrimination; the Supreme Court agreed in 1978.

▫ **Equal Rights Amendment** (ERA) Proposed constitutional amendment giving women equal rights under the law; Congress approved it in 1972, but it failed to achieve ratification by the required thirty-eight states.

▫ *Roe v. Wade* Supreme Court ruling that women have an unrestricted right to choose an abortion during the first three months of pregnancy.

Many Democrats and those who helped Carter win the presidency were unhappy not only with his economic policies but also with what they believed was his tepid support for programs to help minorities, women, and the poor, disagreeing with his view that the government could not "eliminate poverty or provide a bountiful economy." In particular, liberals pushed Carter to support **affirmative action**.

Since the mid-1960s, many businesses and colleges, in an effort to implement affirmative action, had set aside positions for minorities. Many opponents argued that such programs constituted preferential treatment for minorities, or "reverse discrimination." Using that argument, in 1974 **Alan Bakke** sued the University of California at Davis Medical School claiming he was denied admission because he was white, and that less-qualified African American students were enrolled in his place. When the case reached the Supreme Court, the Justice Department did petition the Court on the university's behalf, but to the dismay of liberals Carter publicly stated that he disliked "[endorsing] the proposition of quotas." The Supreme Court in 1978 in a 5-to-4 decision agreed with Bakke, ruling that the university's admissions program was a quota system and violated the Constitution. Bakke graduated from the medical school in 1982.

Nor were some liberals pleased with Carter's positions on women's issues, especially the **Equal Rights Amendment** and abortion. The amendment was sent to the states for ratification in 1972, and thirty-three of the needed thirty-eight states had approved it when opposition stiffened under the leadership of **Phyllis Schlafly.** By 1974, under pressure from Schlafly's STOP-ERA movement, seventeen states had rejected the amendment and its passage was stalled. As the 1979 deadline for ratification approached, pro-ERA groups pressured Carter to endorse the amendment and an extension for ratification. Although Carter agreed and Congress extended the ratification process by thirty-nine months, many ERA supporters felt the president had not supported the amendment vigorously enough. In the end, the amendment fell three states short of ratification.

Part of STOP-ERA's success resulted from linking the ERA to abortion and other social issues, creating a wider "pro-family" movement. In 1973, the Supreme Court in a 5-to-2 decision on the *Roe v. Wade* case, invalidated a Texas law that prohibited abortion. Justice Harry Blackmun, writing for the majority, held that "the right to privacy" allowed women to choose to have an abortion during the first three months of pregnancy. The controversial ruling struck down laws in forty-six states that had made abortions nearly impossible to obtain legally, except in cases of rape or to save the life of the mother.

Although most public opinion polls indicated that a majority of Americans favored giving women

During the 1970s the debate over the Equal Rights Amendment became a major point of conflict between liberals and conservatives. Here, women rally in support of the amendment in New York City in 1974. In 1972, New York was among the first of thirty-five states to ratify the amendment. For the proposed amendment to become part of the Constitution, thirty-eight states needed to ratify it.

the right to choose an abortion, many religious organizations worked with conservative groups to organize a **Right to Life movement** "opposing abortion rights on moral and legal grounds." It found common cause with the pro-family and anti-ERA movements in voicing a multifaceted critique of American society, feminism, and liberalism. Pointing out that the Medicaid program in 1973 paid out more than $45 million for abortion services, in 1976 anti-abortion forces successfully lobbied Congress to prohibit the use of federal funds to pay for abortions by attaching the Hyde Amendment to the annual funding bill for the Department of Health and Human Services. Abortion supporters who hoped that Carter would work against anti-abortion efforts were disappointed. Personally opposed to abortion, Carter agreed to uphold *Roe v. Wade* but was unwilling to increase funding for abortion services or oppose the Hyde Amendment, which needs to be reattached to the budget every year.

RESURGENT CONSERVATISM

☆ *What issues contributed to the emergence of the New Right, and how did the New Right help shape the 1980 election?*

☆ *What is "Reaganomics," and what were the consequences of Reagan's economic policies?*

While many Democrats disagreed with Carter's view that liberalism had its limits, growing numbers of people were going even further and agreeing with the ex-governor of California, Ronald Reagan, that the federal government was too big, too inefficient, and too expensive, and that liberal programs harmed those who worked hard, saved their money, and paid their taxes. His message resonated across the country, especially in the Sunbelt with its growing population and political importance. Reagan's message also found favor with an emerging New Right that emphasized social and moral issues.

The New Right

The New Right emerged as a coalition of conservative grassroots movements that believed the social and governmental liberal activism of the 1960s had weakened the national identity, contributing to a moral breakdown. Like Schlafly, the New Right passionately claimed that liberalism sought to alter the foundation of the American family by promoting social equality, abortion rights, feminism, the ERA, and

◼ **Right to Life movement** Anti-abortion movement that favors a constitutional amendment to prohibit abortion; some adherents grew increasingly militant during the 1980s and 1990s; also called the pro-life movement.

In the 1970s, the "electronic church" began to draw audiences of over 100 million viewers and listeners. Televangelists like Jerry Falwell, pictured here, shaped the "moral majority" by damning liberalism, feminism, homosexuality, and the teaching of evolution. The media pulpit, he stated, not only allowed explaining "the issues" but permitted endorsing "candidates, right there in church on Sunday morning."

homosexuality; to save America, true conservative values needed to triumph in the 1980 election.

Highly visible among New Right groups were evangelical Christian sects, many of whose ministers were **televangelists**—preachers who used radio and television to spread the gospel. Receiving donations that exceeded a billion dollars a year, they did not hesitate to mix religion and politics. Jerry Falwell's **Moral Majority** promoted New Right views on more than five hundred television and radio stations. Reaching millions of Americans, Falwell called on listeners to wage political war against liberal government officials whose views on the Bible, homosexuality, prayer in school, abortion, and communism were too liberal. Falwell told his listeners to get people "saved, baptized, and registered."

The New Right's message not only generated new levels of political activism, but successfully linked this activism to traditional conservative economic issues revolving around taxes and government spending. Throughout the 1970s, state and local taxes had risen. At the federal level, Social Security taxes, now including a Medicare component, grew by 30 percent at the same time that income taxes, pushed by an inflation-fueled "**bracket creep**," increased by as much as 20 percent. Taxes and government spending, especially for social programs, became powerful broad-based issues. In California, Republicans and Democrats joined forces in 1978 to pass **Proposition 13**, which placed limits on property taxes and state spending. It "isn't just a tax revolt," observed a Carter official, "it is a revolution against government."

In his campaign for the presidency, Reagan embraced the New Right's social positions and promised to restore America by reducing government spending and activism. He attacked welfare cheats, affirmative action, and forced busing while vowing to take a tougher stance toward the Soviet Union. Embracing the image of the "citizen politician, speaking out for

televangelist Protestant evangelist minister who conducts televised worship services; many such ministers used their broadcasts as a forum for promoting conservative values.

■ **Moral Majority** Conservative religious organization led by televangelist Jerry Falwell; it had an active political lobby opposing abortion, homosexuality, and the Equal Rights Amendment.

bracket creep Inflation of salaries that pushes individuals into higher tax brackets.

■ **Proposition 13** A 1978 measure adopted by referendum in California that cut local property taxes by more than 50 percent.

the . . . common sense of everyday Americans," Reagan quipped, "A recession is when your neighbor loses his job. A depression is when you lose yours. A recovery is when Jimmy Carter loses his."

As the November election approached, the central question was the size of Reagan's victory and how many Republicans his **political coattails** would carry into office. When the votes were counted, Reagan had received an impressive 51 percent of the popular vote, an even more impressive 91 percent of the electoral count, and his coattails had worked well. Republicans kept their majority in the Senate and substantially narrowed the Democratic majority in the House of Representatives.

Reaganism

Called the "Great Communicator" by the press, Reagan brought to the White House an unusual ability to convey his views and agenda to the American public. The New Right and conservatives were expectant as he took office. He had campaigned not just on restoring prosperity and cutting intrusive government, but also on promoting traditional American values and strengthening the family. In office, however, Reagan disappointed the New Right by choosing to concentrate on the economy and foreign policy. The administration's economic plan was simple: cut the number and cost of social programs, increase military spending, and reduce taxes and government restrictions. "If we can do that, the rest will take care of itself," Reagan's chief of staff, James A. Baker III, argued.

Calling the formula for restoring economic vitality **supply-side economics**, the Reagan administration fought inflation by keeping interest rates high—they spiked to 18 percent, the highest in the twentieth century. To promote economic growth, the goals were to reduce federal regulations, taxes, and social programs. Privately, Reagan admitted wanting to dismantle the Great Society, which he thought caused the nation's current "mess." Budget Director David Stockman proposed a package that would significantly reduce individual and business taxes and included large-scale budget cuts to avoid increasing the **federal deficit** and to reduce the size and scope of government. His formula did not survive Reagan's review. The president increased military spending levels and restored the cuts to Social Security, Medicaid, and Medicare, confident that a revived economy would produce enough revenue to balance the budget by 1984. Consequently, the final budget found most of its savings in reduced funding for social programs like food stamps, housing, and **Aid to Families with Dependent Children**. By August, Congress approved both the budget and

A former radio sports announcer, movie star, and host of television shows, Ronald Reagan used television and radio very effectively to outline his visions of American domestic and foreign policies. Because of his communication style, he was called "the Great Communicator."

the **Economic Recovery Tax Act**, which lowered income taxes and most business taxes by an average of 25 percent.

political coattails Term referring to the ability of a presidential candidate to attract voters to other office seekers from the same political party.

■ **supply-side economics** Theory that reducing taxes on the wealthy and increasing the money available for investment will stimulate the economy and eventually benefit everyone.

■ **federal deficit** The total amount of debt owed by the national government during a fiscal year.

■ **Aid to Families with Dependent Children** A program created by the Social Security Act of 1935; it provided states with matching federal funds and became one of the states' main welfare programs.

■ **Economic Recovery Tax Act** A 1981 law passed by Congress that cut income taxes over three years by 25 percent across the board and lowered the rate for the highest bracket from 78 percent to 28 percent.

Another part of **Reaganomics** reduced federal controls over business and deregulated oil and gas, banking, and communications industries. To further stimulate growth, Secretary of the Interior James Watt opened federally controlled land, coastal waters, and wetlands to mining, lumber, oil, and gas companies—a policy strongly advocated by many in the West. At the same time, to help business growth, the Environmental Protection Agency relaxed enforcement of federal guidelines for reducing air and water pollution. Reagan's economic policies were not immediately effective. The economy worsened, unemployment climbed to over 12 percent, the **trade deficit** soared, and bankruptcies for small businesses and farmers increased. The deficit, pushed by declining tax revenues and increases in military spending and entitlement programs like Social Security, was growing with alarming speed. Reagan called for patience, assuring the public that his economic programs eventually would work.

As Reagan predicted, in 1983, the economy recovered. Inflation dropped to 4 percent and unemployment fell to 7.5 percent. Many, especially corporate leaders, loudly cheered Reaganomics. Deregulation of financial institutions was heralded as especially positive because it spurred investment, which drove the stock market upward—the Great Bull Market. "I think we hit the jackpot," Reagan announced when in 1982 he signed the Garn–St. Germain Act, which expanded the types of loans that the **savings and loan industry** (S & Ls) could make beyond those for single-family homes.

The recession ended just in time for the 1984 election. Reagan's campaign projected continued economic growth and affirmed his commitment to a strong America abroad. Democrats nominated Carter's vice president, traditional liberal Walter Mondale, whom Republicans immediately defined as a "tax and spend" liberal. Hoping to energize voters, Mondale selected New York Representative Geraldine Ferraro as the nation's first female vice

presidential nominee. His choice made political history but had no effect on the election. President Reagan scored an overwhelming victory, taking 59 percent of the popular vote and carrying every state except Mondale's Minnesota.

Reagan continued to push Reaganomics during his second term, but the results were mixed, and by 1987 the economy was showing important weaknesses. Concerns grew about the size of the federal deficit and a **national debt** that had reached new records, requiring 14 percent of the annual budget to pay the interest. Others feared that the recently deregulated savings and loan industry, because of its aggressive and risky investment and loan policies, was tottering on the verge of collapse, and indeed, in 1989 many S & Ls, especially in the Southwest, faced bankruptcy and asked the federal government to provide more than $500 billion to cover the losses. By that time, in less than ten years, the United States went from the world's biggest lender to the world's biggest borrower.

A SOCIETY AND ECONOMY IN TRANSITION

☆ How was the changing U.S. economy affecting Americans?

☆ Who were the "new immigrants," and how were they received?

In the first decades after 1946, the nation experienced the longest era of consistent economic growth in its history, with the gross national product rising at an average annual rate slightly higher than 2.5 percent. This expansion was based on industrial growth and robust sales in foreign markets. At home, it meant higher-paying jobs, more home ownership, accessible college education, and overall an expanding consumer society with rising expectations. But in the early 1970s, economic growth slowed, dipping to slightly over 1 percent, while the cost of living increased over 200 percent. This contraction resisted conventional solutions and, in personal terms, the changing economy resulted in higher prices, fewer jobs, and for many, shattered expectations.

A Shifting Economy

Many of the economic problems had roots in the shift from a manufacturing base to a service-based, **postindustrial economy** and increasing **globalization**. Since the late 1960s, the expanding economies of West Germany, Japan, Korea, and Taiwan had begun to compete successfully for American domestic and foreign markets. Japanese goods and automobiles were beginning to dominate the electronics industry and cut deeply into the American automobile market. American companies that in 1946 had produced two-thirds of

□ **Reaganomics** Economic beliefs and policies of the Reagan administration, including the belief that tax cuts for the wealthy and deregulation of industry benefit the economy.

trade deficit Amount by which the value of a nation's imports exceeds the value of its exports.

savings and loan industry (S & Ls) Network of financial institutions originally founded to provide home mortgage loans; deregulation allowed S & Ls to provide loans for office buildings, shopping malls, and other commercial properties.

□ **national debt** The total amount of money owed by the United States to domestic and foreign creditors.

□ **postindustrial economy** An economy whose base is no longer driven by manufacturing but by service and information industries.

globalization Interaction among countries worldwide in the free flow of trade, capital, ideas and information, and people.

Part of the globalization made possible by advanced telecommunications is the establishment of customer service centers in India that provide 24/7 answering and information services for American and British companies. In this picture dozens of Indians answer toll-free calls from English-speaking customers for a variety of American companies.

the world's steel by 1980 made only 15 percent. Aggravating the problem were higher oil prices and a growing national dependence on foreign oil.

To maintain profitability and survive in the changing economy, corporations devised new strategies and embraced new technologies. Many rid themselves of less profitable manufacturing operations and invested more heavily in service industries. General Electric, for example, once one of the largest manufacturing firms in America, sold off most of its manufacturing divisions and moved its resources into the service sector by buying the entertainment giant RCA as well as a number of investment and insurance firms. Other companies closed less-productive plants and shifted their production to locales with lower operating costs. Many moved to southern and western states, but an increasing number of companies relocated overseas.

Across the country, but especially in the northeast, as American companies lost money, shed workers, and closed plants, an expanding "Rust Belt" formed. Philadelphia, from 1969 to 1981, lost 14 percent of its population and 42 percent of its factory jobs. Pittsburgh, Cleveland, Detroit, and other Rust Belt cities also faced staggering economic losses as plants closed. But changes were felt everywhere. Suburban Lakewood, California, which had seen economic success for three decades after World War II, experienced economic decline when nearby defense-related and other industries relocated and downsized and stores like Wal-Mart replaced higher-end department stores like Macy's.

With higher-paying manufacturing jobs on the decline, many Americans found new jobs in the service industry—which paid about one-third less and used more part-time help. Suddenly, McDonald's was one of the largest employers in the nation. Between 1980 and 1992, the average hourly wage of the American worker declined from $10.59 to $9.87. But the shift away from industry brought new opportunities for some, especially those able to participate in the expanding sector linked to advances in technology.

Technological developments by the mid-1970s were opening new fields and business opportunities, especially in communications and electronics. With Apple and IBM leading the way, office and personal computers restructured the process of handling information and communications, spawning a new wave of "tech" companies and a new crop of millionaires such as Bill Gates. A Harvard dropout, Gates developed computer software, founded Microsoft in 1975, and eventually became America's youngest billionaire.

■ **Rust Belt** Industrialized Middle Atlantic and Great Lakes region whose old factories are barely profitable or have closed.

In the Wider World

The European Union and the Euro

Since the end of the Second World War, many European leaders have envisioned the integration of Europe (Eurofederalism) into an organization that would provide a system of political, social, and economic unity and would make another European war "not only unthinkable but materially impossible." The process began with the European Coal and Steel Community in 1951. Composed of six countries, it developed into the European Economic Community (EEC) in 1957, which further integrated economic, defensive, and political activities. In 1992, the twelve members of the EEC removed all national barriers to business activities, as well as border controls. They initiated a common travel area with a uniform EEC passport. With the signing of the Maastricht Treaty in 1994, the EEC became the European Union (EU) and instituted a common currency, the Euro, which replaced members' national currencies. In 2013, the "Eurozone" comprised seventeen member states (Austria, Belgium, Cyprus, Estonia, Finland, France, Germany, Greece, Ireland, Italy, Luxembourg, Malta, the Netherlands, Portugal, Slovakia, Slovenia, and Spain) and six nonmember states (Andorra, Kosovo, Monaco, Montenegro, San Marino, and Vatican City).

Gates was not alone. It seemed that thousands of people were riding the expanding economy to wealth and power, from inventors to financial "wizards" who brokered mergers. Stories of economic success filled the news media and the plots of television shows and movies, creating a money culture. "Buy high, sell higher," *Fortune* magazine proclaimed. The pursuit of wealth and the goods that it could buy became a life-style sought after by many young Americans, particularly the baby boomers, who were reaching their peak earning and spending years. Income-conscious college graduates hoping to become highly paid professionals eagerly applied to law, business, and other postgraduate schools. Consequently, the number of doctors, lawyers, and MBAs (those with degrees as master's of business administration) swelled, while in the business world, many executive salaries broke $40 million. The 1980s were called by some the "Me Decade," and *Newsweek* declared 1984 the "Year of the Yuppie"—the young, upwardly mobile urban professional who was on the leading edge of the new economic vitality.

But for every Gates or successful yuppie, there seemed to be many more Americans whose economic realities were going in the other direction. Society seemed to be settling into a two-tiered structure with a widening gap separating rich and poor. Between 1980 and 1990, the percentage of the nation's wealth held by the richest 1 percent of American families climbed, but the other 99 percent of families saw their share of the nation's wealth decline. Put simply, the rich got richer

and everyone else, on average, got poorer. The ranks of those in economic and social distress grew. Across the country, the number of homeless increased, placing more pressure on social programs even as their budgets were reduced. The employed were not immune. With 15 percent blue-collar unemployment in Los Angeles, Juan Sanchez, who was employed in a furniture factory, was happy to have a good job even though he and his wife and three children were unable to afford a home and had to live in his brother-in-law's garage. Contributing to stresses on the two-tiered society was a new wave of immigrants who entered the United States following the passage of the 1965 Immigration and Nationality Act.

New Immigrants

The 1965 Immigration Act ended the national quota system that began in the 1920s and established new criteria that favored those with family members in the United States and with desired occupational skills. It set general annual immigration totals by nation and hemispheric limits, which were eliminated in subsequent legislation.

The immediate result was a change in the place of origin of those coming to the United States. Before the 1965 act, three of every four immigrants came from Europe, but within two decades, more than half of all immigrants arrived from the Caribbean and Latin America, with Asian immigrants becoming the second largest group, surpassing those arriving from Europe. Most came for the traditional reasons: jobs and security. Because the new immigration laws favored those with education and skills, many filled the ranks of professionals and technicians, found well-paying jobs, and merged into American society. By 2010, immigrants represented 40 percent of new American entrepreneurial activity,

□ **yuppie** Young, upwardly mobile urban professional with a high-paying job and a materialistic lifestyle.

A Deeper Understanding of History

Immigration Since 1965: Unintended Consequences

In 1965, President Johnson signed the Hart-Celler Act, which replaced the old national origin quota system for immigration. The new law initially divided quotas between the Western and Eastern Hemispheres and established a limit of twenty thousand on immigration from any one nation. Although the act allowed fifty thousand more immigrants from the Eastern Hemisphere than from the Western Hemisphere, supporters argued that the preference given to adults who had family in the United States would ensure the majority would continue to be Europeans. Emanuel Celler, who sponsored the legislation, maintained that "Since people of . . . Asia have very few relatives here . . . few could immigrate from those countries because they have no family ties in the U.S." President Johnson echoed that view, saying: "it is not a revolutionary bill. It will not reshape the structure of our daily lives."

Johnson and Celler were very, very mistaken. Without knowing or intending to, they and others had launched a measure that began changing the nation from a homogeneous, mainly white society to a more socially, religiously, and culturally diverse heterogeneous one. Since 1965, more than 23 million people have entered the United States—the second largest period of immigration since 1880 to 1910—and unlike previous immigrants, most did not come from Europe. The majority arrived from Asia, Africa, and Latin America, in large part from Mexico. The graph here provides a visual way to examine post-1965 immigration and, when compared with Figure 17.3 on page 447, provides a clear picture of the changes in immigration patterns.

Why were those touting the 1965 immigration act so wrong? There is no single answer. Part of the explanation is that low numbers came from Europe. Unexpectedly, most of those eligible to come from Western Europe had little pushing them from their homelands, and until the 1990s those in Communist-dominated Eastern Europe were restrained from immigrating. The opposite was true for many living in Asia and Latin America, beset by expanding populations, war and internal turmoil, and lack of economic opportunities. Another part of the explanation is that by the early to mid-1970s "chain migration" emerged as a contributing factor, especially for those coming from Asia. Because of the preference given to those with needed skills and occupations and the granting of student visas, many individual Asians were allowed to enter the country, found employment, and obtained permanent resident status or citizenship. They then used the family preference provision to bring over other family members. Similarly, when Reagan signed the 1986 Immigration Act granting amnesty to undocumented aliens currently living in the United States, he significantly added to the chain of migration coming primarily from Mexico and Central America.

Just as the "New Immigrants" of 1880–1910 changed the face of America, so too has the unintended consequence of the post-1965 immigrants. Recent immigrants are quietly and not-so-quietly reshaping the country. From politics, to businesses, education, and even the foods we eat, the evidence is all around, in every state and neighborhood. All we have to do is look.

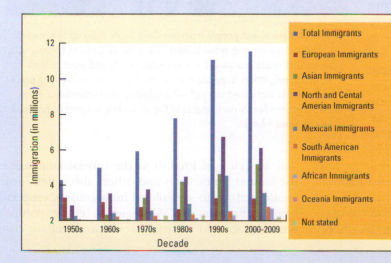

Immigration to the United States by Origin, 1950–2009 © Cengage Learning.

It Matters Today

Illegal Immigrants

For most of the twentieth century, American farmers have relied on migrant workers to harvest crops. The life of migrant workers is one of long hours, low wages, and little respect. Working conditions are not much different from those described by John Steinbeck in *The Grapes of Wrath* (see page 645). A majority of migrant families live near or below the poverty line and face more health risks and shorter life expectancy than any other occupational group in the United States. Since the 1970s, the number of illegal immigrants working as migrants has increased steadily, but illegal immigrants are not just farm workers.

By 2005, an estimated 12 million undocumented immigrants resided in the United States, prompting additional calls for legislation to tighten border security, to exclude them and their children from state and federal social services, and to hasten their deportation. Dissatisfied with a lack of federal response, Arizona, followed by several other states, passed its own immigration control acts. The controversial Arizona law of April 2010 stated that all aliens must carry their federal registration papers with them while in Arizona and, if stopped by local law enforcement officers for "reasonable" cause, could be required to produce those papers or face arrest. Two months later the Supreme Court ruled in a split decision that parts of the Arizona law were invalid because they encroached on federal authority. But it upheld the right of local law enforcement officials to ask for proof of citizenship or of legal resident status.

- California has the highest percentage of foreign-born residents, causing a state senator to say: "We have the best benefit package . . . for illegal immigrants, so they come here." Do you think illegal immigrants should receive federal and state benefits like access to education, health care, and welfare?

---

especially in the electronics and communication industries—companies like Google, eBay, Garmin, Yahoo, and YouTube were founded by immigrants. Immigrants from Japan, China, Korea, and India had and continue to have among the highest income and education levels in the country.

But other Asians, especially those coming from the Philippines, Vietnam, Laos, and Cambodia, along with many immigrants from Latin America, arrived with fewer educational and occupational skills. Working at low-paying and frequently part-time or seasonal jobs in the service and agriculture sectors, they were often mired in poverty. Many had difficulty assimilating into American society. Unless new immigration laws are passed, patterns of immigration that began in the late twentieth century are expected to continue, and by 2050 the Census Bureau estimates that non-Hispanic white Americans will be around 46 percent of the total population.

As the number of non-European immigrants shrank by the mid-1980s, some critics of immigration, especially conservatives, voiced fears about the expanding cultural diversity that threatened their vision of an America centered on European culture. They pushed for Protestant Christian prayer in school

Latinos, Asians, and people from the Caribbean make up the majority of immigrants arriving in the United States today. Critics of immigration worry that these groups will not assimilate easily and want to limit further immigration. Supporters argue that assimilation is taking place and point to increased rates of nationalization and citizenship. Here, a Vietnamese family participates in the all-American sport of baseball (in this case, T-ball).

and adoption of English as the official language of the United States. They and others also called for increased efforts to stop illegal immigration, especially from Latin America. Opponents, citing competition for jobs and increased social and welfare costs, called on Congress to reduce the flow of undocumented immigrants. Congress responded with the **Immigration Reform and Control Act** (1986), which strengthened the U.S. Border Patrol and established stiffer punishments for employing illegal immigrants. But rather than deportation, the act offered amnesty and possible citizenship to undocumented immigrants who had arrived in the United States before 1982. Except for those who thereby became American citizens, few found much merit in the act, and as undocumented immigration continued, so too did the calls for more assertive actions to prevent it.

ASSERTING WORLD POWER

☆ *What did the Reagan administration view as the main issue in world affairs, and how did it try to implement a more assertive foreign policy?*

☆ *How and why did Reagan shift U.S.-Soviet policy during his second term?*

Reagan's victories in 1980 and 1984 resulted not only from the popularity of his domestic agenda but also from public support for his views on the role of the United States in world affairs. Throughout the 1980

"ON TO CENTRAL AMERICA!"

A 1984 Herblock Cartoon, ©The Herb Block Foundation.

In this political cartoon, Herblock, indicates that President Reagan did not learn the lesson of his intervention in Lebanon (discussed on the next page), which cost over two hundred and eighty American lives, and was now seeking to intervene in Central America.

presidential campaign, the Republicans had hammered at Carter's ineffective foreign policies and promised to restore American power and influence. Although he had little expertise in foreign policy, Reagan firmly believed that the Soviets were the "focus of evil" in the world and would use any means, "commit any crime . . . lie . . . cheat," to achieve their "evil empire." He also understood that the United States was stronger than the Soviet Union, and when "we turn our full industrial might into an arms race, they cannot keep pace." Unable to keep pace, when faced with strength, Reagan believed the Kremlin would negotiate.

Cold War Renewed

To get the Soviets to recognize that reality, Reagan needed to expand America's offensive and defensive capabilities and confront Soviet expansionism. He told the Pentagon it would have whatever it needed, and a compliant Congress quickly added more than $100 billion a year to the military budget, including funding to install a new missile system in Europe and to develop a system of defense against Soviet missiles: the Strategic Defense Initiative (SDI). These initiatives, Reagan explained to those critics of the spending, would force the Soviets to spend more, which they could not afford to do without weakening their economy.

To add more pressure on Soviet capabilities, Reagan implemented the "Reagan Doctrine" to support "freedom fighters" and governments confronting communism, especially in the third world. In these "battles," the administration supplied economic and military aid, including covert operations, in Afghanistan, Angola, Ethiopia, El Salvador, and Nicaragua. In the Caribbean, a Marxist government on **Grenada** allowed the Soviets and Cubans to build an extended airport runway that could be used as a staging area for Soviet and Cuban aircraft. When the government, called by the Reagan administration "a brutal gang of leftist thugs," appeared to threaten the freedom of nearly five hundred American students attending medical school on the island, Reagan ordered an invasion. On October 25, 1983, American soldiers quickly overcame minimal opposition, brought home the American students, and installed a pro-American government on the island. The administration basked in public approval.

In Central America, the administration took a less direct path (see Map 28.2). Linking the Marxist

▫ **Immigration Reform and Control Act** Law passed in 1986 that prohibits the hiring of illegal aliens; it offered amnesty and legal residence to any who could prove that they had entered the country before January 1982.

▫ **Grenada** Country in the West Indies that achieved independence from Britain in 1974 and was invaded briefly by U.S. forces.

Sandinista Nicaraguan government to Communist efforts to export revolution to El Salvador, which it called a "textbook case of indirect armed aggression by Communists," the Reagan administration increased its economic and military aid to the non-Communist government of El Salvador and ignored valid reports of human rights violations by "death squads" connected to the Salvadoran military. It also organized and funded a covert military force, the **Contras**, to overthrow the Nicaraguan government. However, when in 1984 the press uncovered large-scale covert American aid to the Contras, Congress passed the **Boland Amendment**.

■ **Contras** Nicaraguan rebels, many of them former followers of Anastasio Somoza, fighting to overthrow the leftist Sandinista government.

■ **Boland Amendment** Motion, approved by Congress in 1984, that barred the CIA from using funds to give direct or indirect aid to the Nicaraguan Contras.

■ **Palestine Liberation Organization** (PLO) Political and military organization of Palestinians, originally dedicated to opposing the state of Israel through terrorism and other means.

Designed to prevent the executive branch from creating another Vietnam-like scenario, it prohibited the CIA and other U.S. intelligence agencies from "directly or indirectly" supporting any military operations in Nicaragua. The administration ignored the amendment and found creative ways to aid the Contras until the Iran-Contra scandal broke in 1986.

The Middle East and Terrorism

Reagan also worked to establish a stronger position for the United States in the Middle East to support Israel and to confront the growing problem of terrorism in the Mediterranean region. Associated with the **Palestine Liberation Organization** (PLO), Syria, Iran, and Libya, terrorists had kidnapped and killed Americans and Europeans, hijacked planes and ships, and attacked airports and other public places. In April 1983 in Beirut, Lebanon, terrorists attacked the American embassy, killing 63 people. Six months later, they attacked a Marine barracks, killing 241 Marines who were part of a United Nations (UN) peacekeeping force. Reagan vehemently denounced the attacks and Hezbollah, the Iranian-sponsored terrorists

MAP 28.2 The United States and Central America and the Caribbean
Geographical proximity, important economic ties, security needs, and the drug trade continue to make Central America and the Caribbean a critical region for American interests. This map shows some of the American economic, military, and political actions taken in the region since the end of World War II. © Cengage Learning.

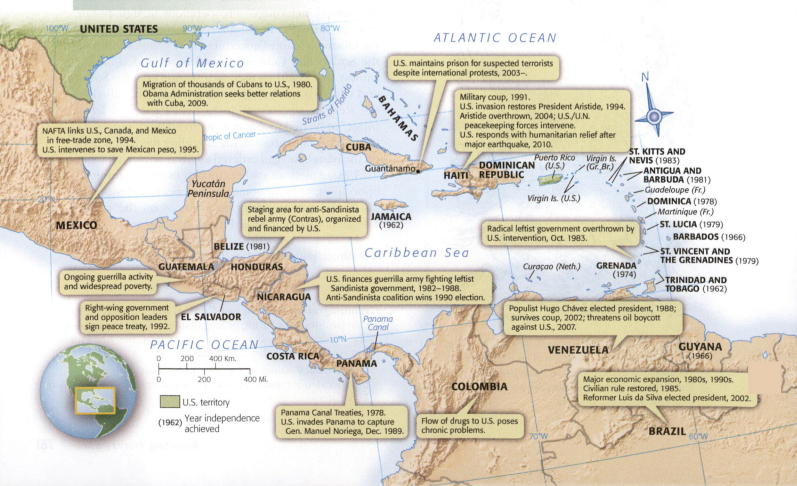

who claimed responsibility, but took no other action except to remove American troops from Lebanon in January 1984.

A year later in an effort to secure the release of hostages held by Hezbollah in Lebanon, the Reagan administration took the unusual path of offering to sell weapons to Iran. In return, Iran would help gain the release of the hostages. The money from the sale would then be transferred to the Contras. When news of this **Iran-Contra Affair** became public, the administration and Reagan denied they were trying to do business with Iran or secretly fund the Contras. But two reports by investigatory committees in 1987 determined otherwise and found that members of the CIA and the National Security Council (NSC) had violated the Boland Amendment and lied to Congress to hide their operation. Eventually eleven, including several top-level advisers to Reagan, were convicted of violating a variety of federal laws and sentenced to prison terms. Reagan claimed, "I just didn't know," but both committees concluded that he had encouraged such illegal activities. A final report in 1994 found that Reagan and Vice President Bush had direct knowledge of the program and had given instructions to mislead Congress. During the hearings, the three American hostages were released, but three others were taken and two other Americans were killed by terrorists.

The administration found a more satisfying response to terrorist activities in April 1986 when it bombed targets in Libya after intelligence sources linked Libyan ruler Muammar Qaddafi to a bombing in West Berlin that killed two American soldiers. Undeterred, in December 1988 a Libyan-Syrian-Iranian sponsored terrorist exploded a bomb on Pan Am Flight 103 over Scotland, killing all 259 passengers.

Reagan and Gorbachev

Until 1985, Reagan's foreign policy had focused on combating the power of the Soviet Union around the globe. But his actions had seemed only to make the Soviet leadership more combative until **Mikhail Gorbachev** assumed power in 1985. Gorbachev was committed to making fundamental changes in the Soviet Union and improving relations with the West and the United States. He released political prisoners, and with his policy of **perestroika** ("restructuring"), he began to restructure an economy that was stagnating under the weight of military spending and state planning. His policy of **glasnost** ("openness") initiated reforms that provided increased political and civil rights to the Soviet people. He told American officials he wanted to move beyond détente and to demonstrate he was a new type of Soviet leader; Gorbachev unilaterally stopped nuclear testing and deployment of missiles in Eastern Europe and informed Reagan that he wanted to work "vigorously" to improve relations

©Bettmann/Corbis.

After declaring the Soviet Union an "evil empire" responsible for nearly all the world's problems, President Reagan reversed course in 1988 and opened productive discussions with Soviet reformer Mikhail Gorbachev. The outcome was an intermediate-range nuclear force treaty that helped to end the Cold War as well as to reduce the overall number of nuclear missiles. Here, the two superpower leaders pose in front of St. Basil's Cathedral in Moscow.

■ **Iran-Contra Affair** A secret effort by the Reagan administration to use arms sales to Iran to help free American hostages held in Lebanon and to fund the Contras in violation of the Boland Amendment; the program became public in 1986 and was terminated.

■ **Mikhail Gorbachev** Soviet General Secretary of the Communist Party who introduced political and economic reforms and then presided over the breakup of the Soviet Union; in 1991 he was forced from office.

perestroika Organizational restructuring of the Soviet economy and bureaucracy that began in the mid-1980s.

glasnost Official policy of the Soviet government under Gorbachev emphasizing freedom of thought and candid discussion of social problems.

with the United States. A CIA report informed Reagan that the Soviet Union was "an economic basket case" unable to compete with the United States.

Reagan, too, wanted to improve relations, and he met with Gorbachev seven times between 1985 and 1989, with arms control the central issue. When the two leaders met in Reykjavik, Iceland, in October 1986, differences over SDI prevented an agreement to reduce strategic weapons. Both left the summit disappointed, but they agreed to keep working on arms limitations and in December 1987, they signed the **Intermediate Nuclear Force Treaty**, which removed their intermediate-range missiles from Europe. Soviet-American relations continued to improve as Gorbachev withdrew Soviet forces from Afghanistan and Reagan visited Moscow. Assessing the changes, Secretary of State George Shultz noted that the Cold War "was all over but the shouting."

In Reagan's Shadow

☆ *What constraints hampered Bush in developing a domestic agenda?*

☆ *What foreign-policy choices did Bush face in protecting American global interests?*

Despite some concerns over the economy and the Iran-Contra revelations, most Republicans believed that the Reagan years had cemented a conservative ascendancy and that Vice President George Herbert Walker Bush would be able to defeat any Democratic candidate. Although some in the New Right worried that he was not conservative enough, most Republicans believed that Bush had earned the nomination. He had served the party faithfully, holding important posts under Presidents Nixon and Ford, including chair of the Republican National Committee and director of the Central Intelligence Agency. He would, they believed, defeat the Democratic candidate, Governor Michael Dukakis of Massachusetts, and continue the Reagan revolution.

Bush Assumes Office

The 1988 campaign followed a familiar pattern. Republicans labeled Dukakis weak on defense and too liberal, especially on fighting crime and drugs. Bush emphasized his foreign policy experience and promised to wage war on drugs and crime and not to raise taxes: "Read my lips . . . no new taxes." Dukakis had no effective answer to the Republican attacks and Bush sailed to an easy victory. With 79.2 percent of the electoral vote and 54 percent of the popular vote, he became the first sitting vice president to be elected president since Martin Van Buren in 1836. Although Bush trounced Dukakis, the victory was not as sweet as he had hoped. Democrats maintained large majorities in the House and the Senate.

During the campaign, Bush had rested largely on Reagan's policies, saying that changes and "new directions" were not needed. As president, he kept many of Reagan's advisers and announced his goal was not "to remake society" but to "see that government doesn't get in the way." It was a realistic goal, given that he faced a Congress in which Democrats had a ten-vote majority in the Senate and an eighty-nine-vote majority in the House. By the end of his first years in office, Bush and his advisers believed they were managing well, although the economy remained a problem. Domestically, he had increased federal efforts to curtail the drug trade, effectively used the veto to block or modify Democratic-sponsored legislation, and signed the Clean Air Act (1990), which reduced smokestack and auto emissions and set standards for a wide variety of pollutants in the air. He had also strongly supported passage of the **Americans with Disabilities Act** of 1990 despite opposition from many business groups and the high cost of the bill.

If Bush was pleased about his limited domestic agenda, he was increasingly concerned about the nation's economic condition. The country was in a recession, businesses were downsizing and facing bankruptcy while unemployment rose, and the federal budget deficit and long-term debt were growing. Families watched their savings shrink and their incomes drop below 1980 levels, to $37,300 from a 1980 high of $38,900. Focusing on the deficit, Bush reduced spending and agreed to increase taxes. His decision violated his campaign pledge and brought immediate condemnation from many Republicans. Bush's popularity dropped 25 percent and in the 1990 congressional elections, Democrats gained ten more Senate seats and twenty-five more seats in the House. The recession lingered and political gridlock followed.

Bush and a New International Order

Bush found international affairs more satisfying than dealing with budget and other domestic issues. The world was changing rapidly, and Bush considered the management of international relations to be one of his strengths. As he assumed office, Gorbachev's

□ **Intermediate Nuclear Force Treaty** A 1987 treaty that provided for the destruction of all U.S. and Soviet medium-range nuclear missiles and for verification with on-site inspections.

□ **Americans with Disabilities Act** A 1990 act that prohibits private employers from discriminating against individuals with disabilities; it defines a disability as a physical or mental impairment that substantially limits one or more major life activities.

MAP 28.3 The End of the Cold War Changes the Map of Europe
As the Soviet Union collapsed and lost its control over the countries of Eastern Europe, the map of Eastern Europe and Central Asia changed. The Soviet Union disappeared into history, replaced by fifteen new national units. In Eastern Europe, West and East Germany merged, Czechoslovakia divided into two nations, and Yugoslavia broke into five feuding states. © Cengage Learning.

reforms touched off a series of political changes that rocked the Soviet Union and its Eastern European satellites. Nationalism and the rejection of Communist rule resulted in new democratic governments in Poland, Hungary, and Czechoslovakia, as well as the unification of Germany and the fragmentation of Yugoslavia (see Map 28.3). In 1989, the Berlin Wall was torn down, and Gorbachev and Bush, meeting on the island of Malta in the Mediterranean Sea, had declared that the Cold War was over.

In 1990, the Soviet Union began to disintegrate when the Baltic States—Latvia, Estonia, and Lithuania—declared their independence. Fearful that Gorbachev would allow the further fragmentation of the Soviet Union, in August 1991 conservatives staged a coup. The poorly planned coup failed when **Boris Yeltsin**, the president of the Russian Republic, called for a popular uprising against it. The aborted coup encouraged other Soviet republics to seek their independence. Faced with the collapse of the Soviet

Union, on Christmas, Gorbachev resigned and the following day the Soviet Union ceased to exist. In its place the **Commonwealth of Independent States** (CIS) emerged, a federation of once-Soviet republics led by Yeltsin, who moved into Gorbachev's offices in the Kremlin.

Central and Eastern Europe were not the only sites of democratic reform. In South Africa, the one-time apartheid (white supremacist) government freed opposition leader Nelson Mandela after twenty-seven

■ **Boris Yeltsin** Russian parliamentary leader who was elected president of the new Russian Republic in 1991 and provided increased democratic and economic reforms.

■ **Commonwealth of Independent States** (CIS) Weak federation of the former Soviet republics; it replaced the Soviet Union in 1992 and soon gave way to total independence of the member countries.

AP Photo/Lionel Cironneau.

With the collapse of the Soviet Union and communism across Eastern Europe, the symbol of the iron curtain and the Cold War came tumbling down in Berlin. Jubilant Berliners sit atop the Berlin Wall, which had divided the city from 1962 to November 1989.

years in prison, and in a 1992 election white voters officially ended apartheid and moved to allow non-whites to vote. The political changes in South Africa and much of Eastern Europe were relatively peaceful, but in parts of Yugoslavia religious and ethnic differences led to horrific violence.

In Yugoslavia, ethnic separatist movements demanded the dismantling of Yugoslavia and called for independence for the regions of Slovenia, Croatia, Bosnia-Herzegovina, and Macedonia. Representing a united Yugoslavia, Serbia fought to maintain its control, but by 1992 all but Bosnia-Herzegovina had

achieved independence. In Bosnia-Herzegovina a religious and ethnic civil war continued until 1995 as Serb forces instituted a policy of "ethnic cleansing" to remove the Muslim population (as discussed further in the next chapter).

Democratic reformers were not always successful. In several Communist countries, like Cuba, Romania, and the People's Republic of China, the existing leadership maintained control. In China, thousands of people filled the massive expanse of Tiananmen Square in 1989 calling for political, social, and economic reforms, only to be attacked by Chinese troops who killed hundreds of protesters as the world watched on television. Bush condemned the attacks, but stuck to his policy of nonintervention and verbal support for the growth of democracy.

The collapse of the Soviet Union, in Bush's view, did not mean that the United States should reduce its global role. The world was still a dangerous place, Bush insisted, and American power must continue to protect national interests and world stability. Iraq's invasion of neighboring oil-rich Kuwait in August 1990 seemed to verify his position.

When Iraq's forces overran Kuwait, the Bush administration feared that Iraqi dictator Saddam Hussein sought to dominate the Persian Gulf and thereby control more than 40 percent of the world's oil supply. Bush decided to intervene and organized a UN response. A multinational coalition deployed more than 500,000 troops, including 200,000 Americans, to Saudi Arabia in Operation Desert Shield to protect the Saudi nation and its oil and to pressure Iraq to withdraw from Kuwait. Bush and coalition leaders set January 15, 1991, as the deadline for Iraq to withdraw from Kuwait. Otherwise, the coalition would use force.

Eighteen hours after the deadline expired, with Iraq making no move to pull out, the UN coalition began devastating air attacks on Iraqi positions in Kuwait and on Iraq itself, beginning what many called the **Persian Gulf War**. On February 23, 1991, American General Norman Schwarzkopf loosed coalition ground forces against Iraqi positions, launching what Saddam had said would be the "mother of all battles" (see Map 28.4).

Within a hundred hours, the war against Iraq, which U.S. forces called Operation Desert Storm, was over. Coalition forces liberated Kuwait, capturing thousands of demoralized Iraqi soldiers. It was the "mother of all victories," quipped many Americans. As the architect of the coalition, President Bush saw his approval rating soar above 90 percent. Some, less euphoric, speculated that the offensive had ended too soon and should have continued until all, or nearly all, of the Iraqi army had been destroyed and Hussein ousted from power.

Bush also gained applause for his policies in Central America, where he helped end the violence in Nicaragua and El Salvador. Reversing Reagan's policy, he ended support for the Contras and with Gorbachev's aid convinced Nicaraguan leader Daniel Ortega to hold free elections, which took place in 1990 and resulted in the defeat of the Ortega government. In neighboring El Salvador, American-supported peace negotiations helped end the civil war.

Bush relied on diplomacy to reduce conflict in Nicaragua and El Salvador, but Panama required a different approach. There, Manuel Noriega ruled the

©Peter Turnley/Corbis.

In Operation Desert Storm, American and coalition forces drove Iraqi forces from Kuwait. In this picture an American soldier stands atop an Iraqi tank. In the background, Kuwaiti oil wells burn.

country with an iron hand. Once useful to the United States as a supporter of the Contras, Noriega had become increasingly dictatorial and an embarrassment to Washington, culminating when he was linked to the torture and murder of political opponents and to facilitating shipments of drugs to the United States. When he ignored American pressure to step down, Bush, referring to the war on drugs, ordered American troops into Panama to arrest Noriega on drug-related charges. On December 20, 1989, in

■ **Persian Gulf War** War in the Persian Gulf region in 1991, triggered by Iraq's invasion of Kuwait; a U.S.-led coalition defeated Iraqi forces and liberated Kuwait; the American operation was called Operation Desert Storm.

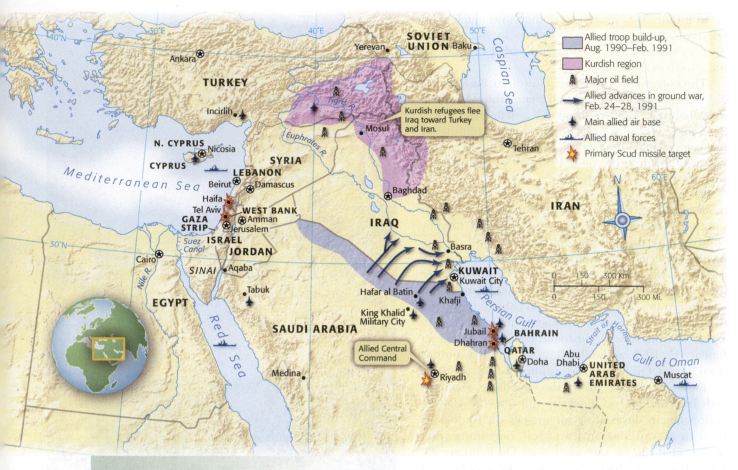

MAP 28.4 The Gulf War
On August 2, 1990, Iraq invaded Kuwait, threatening Saudi Arabia and the Persian Gulf region. In response, the United States and other nations formed an international coalition to restore Kuwait's independence. In January 1991, the coalition forces of Operation Desert Storm began to attack the forces of Saddam Hussein. The outcome was the destruction of most of the Iraqi army and the liberation of Kuwait, but Saddam Hussein maintained control of Iraq. © Cengage Learning.

Operation Just Cause, American forces invaded Panama. Within seventy-two hours—at the cost of three thousand, mostly civilian, Panamanians lives—Noriega was in custody. In 1992, a Miami court found him guilty of drug-related offenses and sentenced him to prison.

The Election of 1992

As the presidential election season approached, many Republicans were still angry over Bush's tax hike, which had raised the highest tax rates from 28 to 31 percent. Contesting Bush's nomination was social conservative

▫ **cultural war** A conflict over the nation's liberal and conservative values that stresses moral issues as an important part of the political debate.

Patrick Buchanan, who claimed to represent true conservatives and middle, moral America. Buchanan roused the convention by calling for a "**cultural war** . . . for the soul of the nation," but Bush and party regulars fought off his challenge. Nonetheless, the social agenda championed by conservatives like Buchanan and Schlafly was written into the party platform. It attacked permissiveness in American society, opposed abortion and alternative lifestyles, advocated less government, and stressed the "traditional American values" that emphasized family and religion." Bush accepted the platform, but his campaign chose to emphasize his experience and foreign policy victories.

The Democratic nominee, Governor William (Bill) Clinton of Arkansas, was an unknown to many Americans. A 46-year-old baby boomer, he had gained support throughout his primary campaign and easily won the nomination. Joining Clinton and Bush was a third presidential candidate,

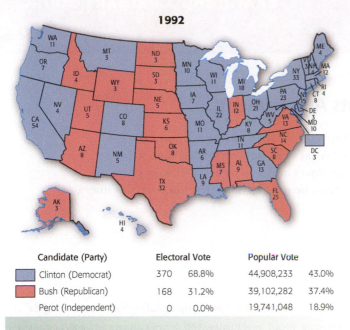

1992

Candidate (Party)	Electoral Vote		Popular Vote	
Clinton (Democrat)	370	68.8%	44,908,233	43.0%
Bush (Republican)	168	31.2%	39,102,282	37.4%
Perot (Independent)	0	0.0%	19,741,048	18.9%

MAP 28.5 Election of 1992, by State
Bill Clinton received almost 69 percent of the Electoral College votes—about double the electoral votes received by George Bush. Nevertheless, Clinton received only 43 percent of the popular vote—the lowest popular vote percentage since Woodrow Wilson's victory in 1912. Third-party candidate H. Ross Perot drew votes from both Democrats and Republicans in equal numbers and had no impact on the electoral vote.

© Cengage Learning.

the millionaire **H. Ross Perot**. Perot's messages were simple: politicians had messed up the nation, Congress was ineffective, the deficit needed to be reduced, and his election would return control to the people. By June, Perot led in the polls but as the election neared Bush and Clinton passed Perot in the polling. Clinton and his advisers stressed one basic message, the economy. James Carvell, Clinton's chief political adviser, tacked reminders over his own desk reading, "It's the Economy, Stupid." While Bush stressed his foreign policy successes, other Republicans focused on their cultural agenda and attacked Clinton's character. They claimed that he had avoided the draft during Vietnam, had smoked marijuana, and was a known womanizer.

On Election Day, Clinton swept to victory with 370 votes in the Electoral College, 100 more than he needed to win (see Map 28.5). While Democrats still held the majority in Congress, Republicans had gained nine seats in the House of Representatives. In both parties, a record number of women and minorities were elected to Congress.

■ **H. Ross Perot** Texas billionaire who used large amounts of his own money to run as an Independent candidate for president in 1992 and who created the Reform Party for his 1996 bid for the presidency.

Individual Voices

PHYLLIS SCHLAFLY

Opposes the Equal Rights Amendment

In blocking the Equal Rights Amendment, Phyllis Schlafly gave hundreds of speeches and wrote dozens of articles. "What's Wrong with 'Equal Rights' for Women" appeared in the *Phyllis Schlafly Report* in February 1972. It voices many of the reasons why opponents thought that the ERA should be rejected and that the women's liberation movement was a threat to American society.

Bettmann/Corbis.

❶ How do Schlafly's descriptions of the supporters of the Equal Rights Amendment shape her arguments?

❷ What threats does Schlafly claim the ERA represents for American women and the moral values of the country?

❸ Asked why Missouri did not support the ERA, its governor replied: "Do you mean the old ERA or the new ERA? ...I was for equal pay for equal work, but after those women...got tangled up with the abortionists and the lesbians, I can tell you ERA will never pass in the Show-Me State." How does this statement reflect the message and the success of the approach taken by the STOP-ERA movement?

In the last couple of years, a noisy movement has sprung up agitating for "women's rights" . . . with aggressive females . . . yapping about how mistreated American women are, suggesting that marriage has put us in some kind of "slavery," that housework is menial and degrading, and . . . that women are discriminated against. ❶ New "women's liberation" organizations are popping up . . . purporting to speak for some 100,000,000 American women. It's time to set the record straight. The claim that American women are downtrodden and unfairly treated is the fraud of the century. The truth is that American women never had it so good. Why should we lower ourselves to "equal rights" when we already have the status of special privilege? . . . The proposed Equal Rights Amendment . . . will absolutely and positively make women subject to the draft . . . it will abolish a woman's right to child support and alimony, and substitute what the women's libbers think is a more "equal" policy, that "such decisions should be within the discretion of the Court. . . . Why should women abandon . . . good laws . . . for something so nebulous . . . as the "discretion of the Court"? . . . By law . . . in case of divorce, the mother always is given custody of her children unless there is . . . evidence of mistreatment. . . . Do women really want to give up this special privilege . . . so that the mother gets one child and the father gets the other? ❷

The women's libbers are radicals who are waging a total assault on the family, on marriage, and on children. Don't take my word for it—read their own literature . . . *Women* tells the American woman that she is a prisoner in the "solitary confinement" . . . of marriage. The magazine promises . . . that it will break the barriers . . . that separate wife, mistress and secretary...heterosexual and homosexual women.

The "women's lib" movement is *not* an honest effort to secure better jobs for women who want or need to work outside the home. This is just . . . sweet-talk to win broad support . . . [it] is a total assault on the role of the American woman as wife and mother, and on the family as the basic unit of society. . . . Women's libbers are promoting free sex instead of the "slavery" of marriage. They are promoting Federal "day-care centers" for babies instead of homes. They are promoting abortions instead of families.

If the women's libbers want to reject marriage and motherhood, it's a free country. . . . But let's not permit these . . . libbers to get away with pretending to speak for the rest of us. ❸

Source: Phyllis Schlatly Report 5, no. 7 (February 1972).

Study Tools

SUMMARY

The years between Carter's inauguration and Clinton's election saw important changes to the American economy. The economic growth that had characterized the postwar period was slowing, making the American dream harder to attain. During Carter's presidency the nation experienced several blows to its domestic prosperity and international status that neither Carter nor Congress was able to solve. These problems contributed to a conservative resurgence that blamed liberal policies for most of the nation's troubles.

During the 1980 campaign Reagan rejected Carter's view that the nation faced limits and argued that American greatness was constrained only by the government's excessive regulation and interference in society. He promised to restore prosperity and reassert American power and prestige in the world. It was a popular message and as president, Reagan fulfilled many conservative expectations by reducing support for social programs, easing and eliminating some government regulations, and exerting American power around the world—altering the structure of Soviet-American relations. Supporters claimed that Reagan's choices had restored prosperity and pride and that the administration had worked to "change a nation, and instead . . . changed a world."

Bush used Reagan's legacy to win the presidency in 1988 but found that unlike Reagan, he was unable to project an image of strong and visionary leadership. Although he gained public approval for his handling of world affairs, those successes seemed only to highlight his inability to overcome a nagging recession that sapped the public's confidence in Republican leadership and the economy. Confident that his foreign policy successes would propel him to another term, Bush lost to Clinton when the Democrat stressed the poor economy and the need for change.

CHRONOLOGY
New Directions, New Limits

1976	Jimmy Carter elected president
1977	Department of Energy created
	Panama Canal treaties
1978	Camp David Accords
1979	Ayatollah Khomeini assumes power in Iran
	United States recognizes People's Republic of China
	Nuclear accident at Three Mile Island, Pennsylvania
	Egyptian-Israeli peace treaty signed in Washington, D.C.
	Hostages seized in Iran
	Soviet Union invades Afghanistan
1980	Carter applies sanctions against Soviet Union
	Carter Doctrine
	Ronald Reagan elected president
1981	Iran releases American hostages
	Economic Recovery Tax Act
1983	United States invades Grenada
1984	Withdrawal of U.S. forces from Lebanon
	Boland Amendment
	Reagan reelected
	Newsweek's "Year of the Yuppie"

1985	Mikhail Gorbachev assumes power in Soviet Union
	Secret arms sales to Iran to obtain funds for the Contras
1986	U.S. bombing raid on Libya
	Gorbachev-Reagan summit in Reykjavik, Iceland
1987	Iran-Contra hearings
	Intermediate Nuclear Force Treaty
1988	George Bush elected president
1989	Berlin Wall pulled down
	United States invades Panama
1990	Recession begins
	Clean Air Act
	Iraq invades Kuwait
	Americans with Disabilities Act
1991	Breakup of the Soviet Union
	Gorbachev resigns
	First Iraqi War
1992	Clinton elected

Study Tools

FOCUS QUESTIONS

If you have mastered this chapter you should be able to answer these questions and to explain the terms that follow the questions.

1. What new directions in foreign policy did Carter take, especially in Central America and the Middle East?

2. What problems did Carter face in implementing his domestic policies, and why were many Democrats unhappy with his approach?

3. What issues contributed to the emergence of the New Right, and how did the New Right help shape the 1980 election?

4. What is "Reaganomics," and what were the consequences of Reagan's economic policies?

5. How was the changing U.S. economy affecting Americans?

6. Who were the "new immigrants," and how were they received?

7. What did the Reagan administration view as the main issue in world affairs, and how did it try to implement a more assertive foreign policy?

8. How and why did Reagan shift U.S.-Soviet policy during his second term?

9. What constraints hampered Bush in developing a domestic agenda?

10. What foreign-policy choices did Bush face in protecting American global interests?

KEY TERMS

Camp David Accords   *p. 768*

mujahedeen   *p. 770*

Carter Doctrine   *p. 770*

Ayatollah Ruhollah Khomeini   *p. 770*

Three Mile Island   *p. 771*

Alan Bakke   *p. 772*

Equal Rights Amendment   *p. 772*

Roe v. Wade   *p. 772*

Right to Life movement   *p. 773*

Moral Majority   *p. 774*

Proposition 13   *p. 774*

supply-side economics   *p. 775*

federal deficit   *p. 775*

Aid to Families with Dependent Children   *p. 775*

Economic Recovery Tax Act   *p. 775*

Reaganomics   *p. 776*

national debt   *p. 776*

postindustrial economy   *p. 776*

Rust Belt   *p. 777*

yuppie   *p. 778*

Immigration Reform and Control Act   *p. 781*

Grenada   *p. 781*

Contras   *p. 782*

Boland Amendment   *p. 782*

Palestine Liberation Organization   *p. 782*

Iran-Contra Affair   *p. 783*

Mikhail Gorbachev   *p. 783*

Intermediate Nuclear Force Treaty   *p. 784*

Americans with Disabilities Act   *p. 784*

Boris Yeltsin   *p. 785*

Commonwealth of Independent States   *p. 785*

Persian Gulf War   *p. 787*

cultural war   *p. 788*

H. Ross Perot   *p. 789*

SUGGESTED RESOURCES

Hal Brands, *From Berlin to Baghdad* (University of Kentucky Press, 2008). An understandable overview of American foreign policy after the collapse of the Soviet Union.

George Washington University http://www.gwu.edu/~nsarchiv/. The university has created a collection of essays and primary materials on the end of the cold war and other national security issues.

Migration Policy Institute, http://www.migrationinformation.org. The MPI provides a wide range of essays and data on American immigrants and immigration policy.

Jules Tygiel, *Ronald Reagan and the Triumph of American Conservatism* (Pearson Longman, 2006). Part of the Library of American biography series, this is a brief, very readable, and balanced biography of Reagan with an excellent bibliography.

29

Entering a New Century, 1992–2013

CHAPTER OUTLINE

The Clinton Years
The Opening Round
The Comeback
Clinton's Second Term
Clinton's Foreign Policy

Economy and Society in the 1990s
A Revitalized Economy
Rich, Poor, and In Between
Women, Family, and the Culture War
The Judicial Arena

New Agendas and Challenges
The 2000 Election
The Bush Agenda
Charting New Foreign Policies
An Assault Against a Nation

War and Politics
The War on Terrorism
Iraq and Politics
Bush's Second Term
Economic Crises and Obama

Obama's Presidency
Shifts in Foreign Policy
Change and the Politics of Filibuster
Republican Resurgence
Gridlock and the Election of 2012

INDIVIDUAL VOICES: *Nicholas Carr Asks, "Is Google Making Us Stupid?"*

Study Tools

INDIVIDUAL CHOICES

Evan Williams

For Evan Williams the choices were not difficult; he just allowed himself to follow his interests. That included leaving the University of Nebraska in his sophomore year when he concluded that college was not for him. He took jobs in Florida and Texas, becoming aware of his interests and opportunities in the emerging field of computer technology connected to the Internet. In 1994, he returned to Nebraska and, with his father, formed a company that produced CD-ROMs and videos instructing people how to use the Internet. The company failed. Later, he admitted that he had no idea or interest in running a company and that he was more interested in starting new projects than finishing old ones. Leaving angry employees behind, Williams moved to northern California where he worked for various computer-related industries, mostly in areas associated with Web development.

Wanting to work on his own schedule and pursue his ideas, in 1999, he and Meg Houghton formed Prya Labs, which produced various marketing programs. Williams and his group tinkered with the process and developed a new application for general use on the Internet. He named the program the Blogger. It allowed people to create their own websites without knowing how to program. The blog allowed unlimited communications through the Internet with

© Jonathan Sprague/Redux.

anyone wanting to log on to the site. Its use exploded, creating new forms of publishing and journalism. Some used it to keep not-so-personal diaries and journals, while others created specialized newsletters and information and opinion pieces. Many fully embrace the new technology and see the Internet, blogs, and texting as a positive, even liberating means of communication; but others, as shown in this chapter's Individual Voices feature, offer a different vision.

In 2003, with blogging reaching millions, Williams sold the company to Google, making him and his partners rich. They went to work for the corporate giant, but Williams found the corporate climate at Google stifled his curiosity and creativeness. After two years, he left Google, saying that he needed freedom to scratch new "itches." One itch produced a new company, Obvious, and a brainstorming session brought a new variation of the blog—a mini blog—called Twitter. Although it limits text to only 140 characters and was designed to answer questions like "What are you doing now?" Twitter users have expanded its function, changing the nature of social networking and modern communications. By the spring of 2009, well over 15 million people were "twittering," "tweeting," or sending "tweets." Most carried personal messages, but Twitter also emerged as an immediate source of information. During protests in Iran over disputed elections, protesters used Twitter to communicate to the world when the government blocked other modes of communication. "We think of Twitter," Williams explained, "not [as] a social network, but…an information network."

In implementing his domestic agenda, President Bill Clinton balanced between social activism and fiscal conservatism. By 1994, his policies and personal behavior had led to a series of Republican congressional victories, political gridlock, and a partisan effort to impeach him. Clinton survived the Republican efforts and by 2000 had balanced the budget as the economy soared.

The year 2000 saw no lessening of divisions in the nation as Republican George W. Bush narrowly defeated Al Gore in an election decided by the Supreme Court. Bush's effort to implement his domestic policy, however, was overwhelmed on September 11, 2001, when terrorists crashed airliners into New York's World Trade Center and the Pentagon in Washington, D.C. The nation immediately united behind Bush, who declared a global war on terrorism that focused on Afghanistan and Iraq. Both appeared to be easy victories as the Taliban regime collapsed in Afghanistan and Saddam Hussein fled Baghdad. Replacing the two regimes with stable and democratic governments, however, proved more difficult. By the time of Bush's reelection, the Taliban was conducting a guerrilla war against the Afghan government, and Iraq was mired in a civil war.

As the violence in Iraq heightened, an increasing number of people questioned the American presence there. In 2006, opposition to the war contributed to Democrats gaining control of Congress. The 2008 Democratic presidential primaries made political history with a woman and an African American emerging as the leading candidates for the nomination. Barack Obama secured the nomination and faced off against Senator John McCain. As the candidates debated policy on Iraq and Obama's political experience, an economic crisis shifted political priorities and contributed to an Obama victory.

Faced with two wars and an economic emergency, President Obama hoped for bipartisan support but found increasingly partisan opposition. Though Republicans vowed to oppose his domestic and foreign agendas, Obama successfully pushed through legislation to stimulate the economy and implement a national healthcare system. Neither program found much support among voters who, energized by the newly formed Tea Party movement, in 2010 elected a majority of Republicans to the House of Representatives. The result was political gridlock and a budget crisis that threatened the slowly recovering economy. In foreign policy, Obama oversaw the withdrawal of American forces from Iraq and increased the military effort in Afghanistan.

In 2012, Republicans selected Mitt Romney to run against Obama. Romney promised to repeal Obama's healthcare package, restore conservative values, and use his business expertise to improve the economy. Democrats argued that Romney represented the wealthy and that his policies would harm the majority of Americans socially and economically. With women, African American, and Latino voters playing key roles and with large numbers of Democrats turning out to vote, Obama won reelection with more than 51 percent of the popular vote.

THE CLINTON YEARS

☆ *In what ways did President Clinton's centrist agenda and personal behavior shape his presidency?*

☆ *How did the Contract with America represent a conservative critique of liberalism and Democratic policies?*

☆ *What actions did Clinton take to expand trade and support global stability?*

"I want to get something done," William Jefferson Clinton told a press conference as he entered office. With that, he dove into an ambitious agenda that included an economic recovery plan, support for gay rights, and development of a national healthcare system.

The Opening Round

Signing the **Family and Medical Leave Act**, earlier vetoed by Bush, was one of Clinton's first acts. It allowed workers to take up to twelve months of unpaid leave because of illness or family needs and guaranteed they would be able to return to the same job. While the medical leave act drew widespread support, much of Clinton's agenda met with bipartisan opposition. Citing statistics about the soaring costs of healthcare and the over 40 million Americans who could not afford any health insurance, Clinton made enacting a national healthcare program a primary goal. In September, he appointed First Lady Hillary Rodham Clinton to lead a task force to draft legislation. Many working in health-related industries, Republicans, and even Democrats attacked both the goal and the emerging plan. After a year of heated debate, Clinton admitted defeat and dropped the plan. His efforts to support gay rights by having Congress lift the ban against homosexuals in the military also met bipartisan and public opposition and resulted in a compromise policy of "Don't Ask, Don't Tell" that pleased no one. It required the military not to ask about soldiers' sexual preferences and expected soldiers to refrain from open homosexual activities.

But the movement for gay rights continued and strengthened. During the next decades many states, counties, and cities, including the District of Columbia, passed antidiscrimination laws and sexual preference laws that protected jobs, provided work-related benefits for partners, and allowed same-sex marriages and adoptions. In 2003, the Supreme Court in *Lawrence v. Texas* declared that consenting adults had the right to sexual privacy and declared sodomy laws unconstitutional. In September 2012, the military discarded the "Don't Ask" policy and allowed homosexuals to openly serve in the military.

Clinton had more success in increasing financial support to fight the AIDS epidemic. AIDS (**acquired immune deficiency syndrome**) was first noticed in American cities in the early 1980s, but because it infected mostly gay men and drug users, governmental and public responses were at first largely apathetic. The Reagan administration did little to fight the disease, and many suggested it was more of a moral than a medical problem. Some, like Pat Buchanan and Senator Jesse Helms (R.–North Carolina), even suggested that those with the disease were being punished for their lifestyles.

As the number of victims climbed and the disease spread to the heterosexual population, the public's awareness and fear of AIDS grew, as did governmental and private support for AIDS education, prevention programs, and research. By 2007, AIDS had claimed more than half a million American lives and had killed over 20 million people worldwide, but significant advances in research were also taking place. Combinations of drugs now appear to slow the advance of the disease.

Clinton also faced bipartisan opposition to his plans for dealing with the national debt, which had risen ominously under Reagan, and the still struggling economy. His solutions angered both Republicans and Democrats. Many Democrats criticized his trimming of federal spending and his failure to cut middle-class taxes. They also refused to support the **North American Free Trade Agreement** (NAFTA) and the **General Agreement on Tariffs and Trade** (GATT). Both had been initiated by Bush but blocked by Senate Democrats who claimed they would harm the economy by encouraging U.S. factories

■ **Family and Medical Leave Act** Law that permits an employee to take job-protected unpaid leave owing to a serious health condition or to care for sick family members or a new child.

acquired immune deficiency syndrome (AIDS) Gradual and eventually fatal breakdown of the immune system caused by the human immunodeficiency virus (HIV); HIV/AIDS is transmitted by the exchange of body fluids through such means as sexual intercourse or needle sharing.

■ **North American Free Trade Agreement** (NAFTA) Agreement approved by the Senate in 1993 that eliminated most tariffs and other trade barriers between the United States, Mexico, and Canada.

■ **General Agreement on Tariffs and Trade** (GATT) First signed in 1947, the GATT sought to encourage free trade among member states by regulating and reducing tariffs and resolving trade disputes; in 1995 its functions were assumed by the World Trade Organization.

In 1987, the San Francisco-based Names Project started to make quilts in memory of those who had died of AIDS in the United States. In 1992, the quilts were exhibited on the Mall in Washington, D.C., displaying the names of twenty-six thousand people.

and in 1994, led by Newt Gingrich (R.–Georgia), Republicans seized the initiative with a political agenda called the "**Contract with America**." It called for support for family values, large cuts in federal spending, and a balanced budget by 2002. The public responded by giving the Republicans nine new senators, fifty-two new representatives, and majorities in both houses of Congress for the first time in forty years. The new conservative majority was "going to change the world," predicted Gingrich, now the Republican Speaker of the House.

The Comeback

The Republican surge in the 1994 election encouraged congressional Republicans to assume the political offensive with a legislative and economic plan that slashed spending on education, welfare, Medicare, Medicaid, and the environment. "You cannot sustain the old welfare state" with a balanced budget, Gingrich proclaimed. In response, Clinton emphasized his centrism. He agreed that reducing the deficit and balancing the budget should be priorities, but argued that the Republican cuts were too drastic, harmful to most people's lives, and mean spirited. He complained that those who argued that welfare programs created a class of morally impoverished welfare-dependent people did not understand the realities of those on welfare or the number of children receiving aid.

The battle lines were clear when in 1995 Republicans drafted their budget bill with large cuts in welfare programs. Clinton sent it back to Congress, where overconfident Republicans refused to pass a spending measure to keep the government operating unless their budget was accepted. Unmoved, Clinton shut down all nonessential government functions first for six days in November, then for twenty-one days in December. Because the public blamed Republicans for the budget impasse, they were forced to compromise with the president on the budget and accept most of his spending proposals.

In the following months, Clinton and Congress agreed to raise the minimum wage, increase spending for education, job training, and child care, and pass welfare reform. In July, Clinton signed the 1996 Welfare Act (Personal Responsibility and Work Opportunity Reconciliation Act), saying that it ended "welfare as we know it." The act gave states more responsibility for running welfare programs, reduced access to food stamps, and required those receiving assistance to have a job, seek employment, or enroll in job training or educational programs.

In 1996, Republicans selected Kansas Senator Robert Dole to run against Clinton and attacked Clinton for his liberal policies, which they contended were out of step with the American people. The problem for Republicans was that a majority of

to relocate to nations with lower costs and standards. To pass both bills, Clinton had to twist Democratic arms and rely on Republican votes.

Republicans also opposed Clinton's economic stimulus package and proposed budget, claiming that tax increases would harm the economy. Finally, after weeks of heated debate, the budget passed the House by two votes and was approved in the Senate only when Vice President Al Gore cast the tie-breaking vote. For the first time since World War II, a bill had passed Congress even though every member of the opposition party had voted against it.

The bitter fights over the budget, healthcare, and gays in the military boosted Republican popularity,

◻ **Contract with America** Pledge taken in 1994 by some three hundred Republican candidates for the House, who promised to reduce the size and scope of the federal government and to balance the federal budget by 2002.

© Robert Giroux/AFP/Getty Images.

The North American Free Trade Agreement eliminated many trade barriers between the United States, Canada, and Mexico. Here, a Mexican worker sews garments to be shipped and sold north of the border. American supporters of the agreement argue that it has led to an overall increase in trade, while critics argue that it cost American jobs as American companies used Mexican plants and workers to produce goods that were once made in the United States.

the public thought Clinton was doing a good job and that the economy was improving. Clinton's popularity and Dole's often lackluster campaign resulted in Clinton becoming the first Democratic president to be reelected since Franklin D. Roosevelt, capturing 379 electoral votes and 49 percent of the popular vote.

Clinton's Second Term

In his 1997 State of the Union address, Clinton set a centrist agenda for his second term. He spoke about ending the "bickering and extreme partisanship" and finding common ground to balance the budget and put "an end to decades of deficits that have shackled our economy." Over the next years, enough common ground was found to balance the budget and achieve surpluses from 1998 to 2001. But on most issues, the bitter partisanship continued, culminating in an effort to impeach Clinton in 1998.

In 1997, Republicans learned of the president's sexual involvement with White House intern Monica Lewinsky and decided to use the affair to try to remove him from office. Clinton denied the allegations, but an investigation confirmed that the affair had gone on between 1995 and 1997. Clinton then admitted to "inappropriate relations" with Lewinsky and to "misleading" Congress and the public. His supporters argued that the affair was a private matter and did not affect how he ran the government. Republicans

disagreed and cited two offenses, perjury and obstruction of justice. In December 1998 the House voted to impeach Clinton who became the second president to face a trial in the Senate that could remove him from office. (The first, Andrew Johnson, was acquitted in 1868, covered in Chapter 15.)

The Republicans had a 55-to-45 majority in the Senate, but in a five-week trial, they failed to find the two-thirds majority needed to remove Clinton from office. By February 19, 1999, the drama of impeachment was over. Clinton expressed his sorrow for the burden he had placed on the nation, and the government returned to business. Clinton's popularity remained high, while that of Congress dipped.

Clinton's Foreign Policy

Clinton's foreign policy on economic and trade issues generally followed the path set by President Bush. He oversaw passage of the NAFTA and GATT agreements and the formation of the **World Trade Organization** to expand international trade. He

■ **World Trade Organization** Geneva-based organization that oversees world trading systems; founded in 1995 by 135 countries to replace the 1948 General Agreement on Tariffs and Trades (GATT).

On August 5, 1997, Bill Clinton signed the Balanced Budget Act. Applauding the president are Vice President Al Gore (*left*) and House Speaker Newt Gingrich (*right*). In the fall of 1998, Clinton announced a federal budget surplus of $70 billion, the first surplus since 1969.

A Balanced Budget
That Protects Our Families, Invests in Our People and Cuts Taxes for Middle Class Families

AP Photo/Ron Edmonds.

also worked with the **G-8 nations** to promote global economic stability and growth.

Moving beyond Bush's policies, Clinton took a more active diplomatic and military role in seeking to resolve international issues. He actively supported the peace process in Northern Ireland that ended thirty years of sectarian violence. He also brokered an accord that established Palestinian self-rule in some Israeli-occupied areas and a treaty of cooperation between Jordan and Israel. Working with the United Nations, Clinton intervened in Haiti to encourage the military junta that ousted democratically elected President Jean-Bertrand Aristide to restore democracy, and in October 1994, Aristide returned to Haiti.

To restore peace and stability in the Balkans, Clinton dispatched American forces to join with the United Nations in protecting "safe areas" for refugees displaced by the fighting. In the fall of 1995, the United States sponsored peace talks resulting in the **Dayton Agreement**, which ended the fighting and partitioned the country into a Bosnian-Croat federation and a Serb republic.

Stability in the Balkans was tested again in 1998 when Serbian President Slobodan Milosevic tried to crush insurgent forces in the province of Kosovo and began a program of **ethnic cleansing** aimed at the majority Muslim population. Unable to halt the bloodshed with diplomacy, NATO leaders and U.S. Secretary of State Madeleine Albright called for "humanitarian intervention" and autonomy for Kosovo within Serbia. Unwilling to use ground forces, U.S. and NATO planes unleashed a bombing campaign in March 1999. After the Serbian capital of Belgrade was bombed in June, Milosevic agreed to withdraw his troops, recognize Kosovo's autonomy, and allow UN peacekeeping forces into the area to ensure the peace. When the war was over Milosevic was charged with crimes against humanity by the International War Crimes Tribunal at The Hague, and in 2001 he stood trial for his war crimes, dying in prison before the trial was completed.

G-8 nations The leading industrial nations (Canada, China, France, Germany, Italy, Japan, the United Kingdom, and the United States), which meet annually to discuss economic and other global issues facing their countries and the international community.

Dayton Agreement Agreement signed in Dayton, Ohio, in November 1995 by the three rival ethnic groups in Bosnia that pledged to end the four-year-old civil war there.

ethnic cleansing An effort to eradicate an ethnic or religious group from a country or region, often through mass killings.

ECONOMY AND SOCIETY IN THE 1990S

☆ *What changes were taking place in the American economy as the country headed toward the twenty-first century?*

☆ *How did economic changes shape society and politics?*

Clinton's election in 1992 and 1996 rested in part on the economy, which after the recession of 1990

American forces played a key role in the United Nations (UN) and North Atlantic Treaty Organization (NATO) peacekeeping effort in Bosnia and Kosovo. In this picture, an American patrol greets Albanian children from a Kosovo village.

rebounded into a period of economic growth. Clinton and Democrats gave their policies credit for the economic surge, the balanced budget, and renewed economic and social opportunities for all Americans. While there is some truth in the claim, the economic surge that occurred throughout the 1990s and into the twenty-first century was also a product of a changing national and global economy.

A Revitalized Economy

The economy that climbed out of the recession in 1992 (see Figure 29.1) started one of the longest periods of sustained economic growth in the nation's history. Until it slowed in 2001, it averaged a growth rate of about 3 percent per year. The revitalized "New Economy" benefited from increased productivity by American workers after the downsizing, restructuring, and continuing automation of industries during the previous two decades. Globalization and expanding markets for foreign trade also contributed. But the most important reason was the rapid growth in **information technology** industries and the service sector (see Figure 29.2 on page 801).

The broad-based service industry, which in the 1990s included everyone from highly paid professionals to minimum-wage workers in retail, expanded from about 50 percent to over 75 percent of the workforce. At the same time, new technology and computer industries boomed, pushing stock market prices upward,

especially those listed on the **NASDAQ** index, which tracked the stocks in many new high-tech industries. Suddenly, the ranks of the very rich included "dot-com" millionaires, men and women who owned or invested in companies associated with the new technology and telecommunications industries, such as Microsoft and Internet-based businesses. Northern California's Silicon Valley drew entrepreneurs like Evan Williams and Apple's Steve Jobs and emerged as a center of the computer and microprocessing industries. Merging the new technology with retail, Amazon, an online bookstore, was created in 1995, and soon was followed by an ever-increasing number of other services doing business over the Internet. Venture capitalists provided funding for many new Internet businesses, connecting the financial system to the "vein of gold" the technological boom seemed to be.

In 2000, the dot-com bubble burst, contributing to a short recession in 2001. But it was only a brief setback. Worldwide, electronics and tech industries continued to produce new products and furthered global economic growth. With each passing year, computers and

information technology A broad range of businesses concerned with managing and processing information, especially with the use of computers and other forms of telecommunications.

NASDAQ A stock exchange, launched in 1971, that focuses on companies in technological fields; NASDAQ stands for National Association of Securities Dealers Automated Quotations.

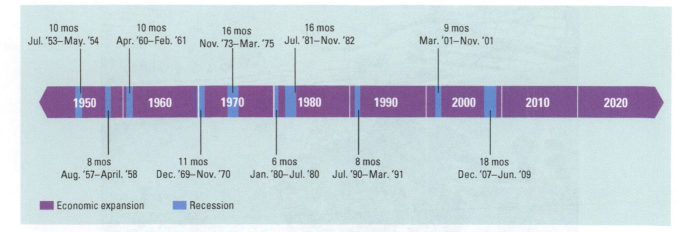

10 mos
Jul. '53–May. '54

10 mos
Apr. '60–Feb. '61

16 mos
Nov. '73–Mar. '75

16 mos
Jul. '81–Nov. '82

9 mos
Mar. '01–Nov. '01

1950   1960   1970   1980   1990   2000   2010   2020

8 mos
Aug. '57–April. '58

11 mos
Dec. '69–Nov. '70

6 mos
Jan. '80–Jul. '80

8 mos
Jul. '90–Mar. '91

18 mos
Dec. '07–Jun. '09

■ Economic expansion   ■ Recession

FIGURE 29.1 **Periods of Expansion and Recession in the United States, 1950–2013**
Economists define a recession as a contraction in the economy that is characterized by rising unemployment and decreasing production. Since the end of World War II, the average recession has lasted about ten months. As this figure shows, the period of economic expansion that ended in March 2001 was the longest period of growth since the end of World War II. The recession that began in December 2007 and was officially declared over in June 2009 was the worst and longest U.S. economic decline since the Great Depression of 1929.

Source: Data from Bureau of Economic Analysis.

© David Brabyn/Corbis.

Since the 1980s, laptop computers, cell phones, and Wi-Fi have made communications and acquisition of information nearly global and instantaneous. Here, two recent additions to the global network of "connectivity" are highlighted as a man snaps a picture of an iPad with his iPhone.

electronic and communications devices grew smaller, faster, more powerful, and less expensive. The outcome was a revolution that affected everything from politics and military and espionage activities to social chit-chat, information sharing, and online education to the way we do our jobs and live our daily lives. Words like "flat screens," "googling," "apps," and "tweeting" have become universally used vocabulary.

Rich, Poor, and in Between

The economic boom also meant more jobs; the number of new jobs rose by 12 million and unemployment dropped to 4 percent—the lowest level since the

1960s. Wages increased by about 4 percent, with low-income workers' incomes growing by 6 percent between 1993 and 1998. Hispanic and African American household incomes rose, and the number of Americans living in poverty in 2000 fell to 11.3 percent, the lowest rate since 1979.

Hidden within the statistics, however, were grim realities. As the economy developed, the continued loss of manufacturing jobs moved many people into service industries, where wages were lower and benefits scarce, and the income gap between the rich and everyone else continued to widen. For more than 15 percent of Americans who lived below the official poverty level of $15,150 (for a family of four in 1995), good paying jobs seemed harder to find. Many middle and working class families' incomes were barely holding steady as medical and fuel costs continued to rise. As the baby boom generation grew older, healthcare costs climbed. In 1990, Americans spent $714 billion on healthcare, only to watch costs mushroom to over $2.2 trillion in 2007, an average of $7,421 per person.

Women, Family, and the Culture War

Many also worried about the growing feminization of poverty as the number of single women heading households and of children living in poverty increased. A contributing factor was that too often, women experienced inequalities in positions and pay. In California, a female manager discovered that her pay was less than half that of the male assistant managers. When she confronted the company, she was told that the assistant manager had a wife and two children. She pointed out that she was a single mother with a child to support. Beset by

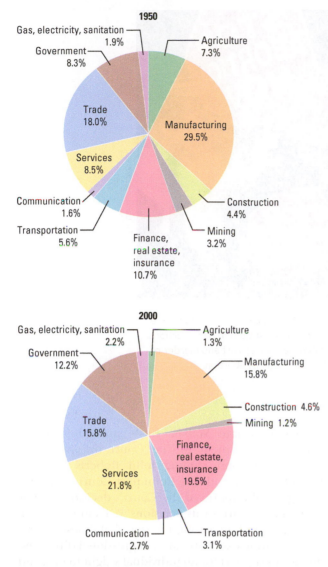

1950

- Gas, electricity, sanitation 1.9%
- Government 8.3%
- Agriculture 7.3%
- Trade 18.0%
- Manufacturing 29.5%
- Services 8.5%
- Communication 1.6%
- Transportation 5.6%
- Finance, real estate, insurance 10.7%
- Mining 3.2%
- Construction 4.4%

2000

- Gas, electricity, sanitation 2.2%
- Government 12.2%
- Agriculture 1.3%
- Trade 15.8%
- Manufacturing 15.8%
- Construction 4.6%
- Mining 1.2%
- Services 21.8%
- Finance, real estate, insurance 19.5%
- Communication 2.7%
- Transportation 3.1%

FIGURE 29.2 Main Sectors of U.S. Economy
A comparison of the 1950 and 2000 graphs shows that many of the economic sectors that deal with the production and marketing of goods—such as manufacturing, agriculture, transportation, and trade—have declined, while those sectors that mainly provide services have increased, especially government, services, and finance. © Cengage Learning 2013.

such inequalities, she and other women brought class action lawsuits against a variety of companies, including the Publix chain of supermarkets and Wal-Mart.

The feminization of poverty was only one trend among women throughout the 1990s and into the twenty-first century. More women were entering college than men and continuing on to professional and graduate programs. More than three-fourths of women worked outside the home, and they made up about one-half of the workforce. By the end of the 1990s, women also made up about one-fourth of all doctors and lawyers and held nearly 30 percent of managerial and executive positions. Despite such gains, most women still earned only 73 cents for every dollar a man made, and many encountered a "**glass ceiling**" that kept them out of the highest positions.

Some turned to the courts, contesting job discrimination and **sexual harassment**, which women complained were pervasive throughout the workforce. Supporting an expanded view of sexual harassment, in 1993 the Supreme Court, in *Harris v. Forklift Systems*, ruled that sexual harassment involved not only "verbal and physical conduct" but also the creation of a "hostile environment."

A changing and more diverse society and women's expanding roles further fueled the culture wars. In the debate over women's rights and the future of the family, conservatives and groups like the Eagle Forum and Concerned Women of America claimed that liberalism and feminism endangered the traditional American family. They argued, too, that even "mommy-friendly" workplaces were not a replacement for full-time mothers. "It all comes down to values," an antifeminist explained. "Traditional values work because they are the guidelines most consistent with human nature."

Among those protecting "traditional values" were groups opposing abortion and gay rights. In 1992, conservatives cheered a small victory when the Supreme Court, in *Planned Parenthood of Southeastern Pennsylvania v. Casey*, ruled that, in some cases, states could modify the right to an abortion. At the same time, some within the Right to Life movement opted for intimidation and violence and targeted abortion clinic doctors, staff, and patients. By 1994, more than half of all abortion clinics reported varied cases of one or both, and nearly a hundred clinics had been targets of arson or bombings. In response, in 1994 the Clinton administration supported the Freedom of Access to Clinic Entrances Act, which restricted the tactics of intimidation that pro-life supporters could use.

Supporting the traditional view of marriage, conservatives championed the passage of the 1996 **Defense of Marriage Act** following a Hawaiian state court decision that determined that laws barring same-sex marriages were unconstitutional in that state. The Defense of Marriage Act barred federal recognition of same-sex marriages and allowed states to ignore such marriages performed in other states.

The Judicial Arena

By the end of the Bush administration in 1992, conservatives increasingly hoped they had an ally in the Supreme

- **glass ceiling** An intangible barrier within the hierarchy of a company that prevents women or minorities from rising to upper-level positions.
- **sexual harassment** Unwanted sexual advances, sexually derogatory remarks, gender-related discrimination, or the existence of a sexually hostile work environment.
- **Defense of Marriage Act** A 1996 law that defines marriage as between a man and a woman for the purpose of federal law and prevents other jurisdictions (states, counties, cities) from being forced to accept any other definition of marriage. In June 2013 the Supreme Court declared this act unconstitutional.

Photo by Diana Walker//Time Life Pictures/Getty Images.

Ever since the controversial *Roe v. Wade* decision in 1973, opponents of abortion have petitioned the Supreme Court, lobbied Congress, and demonstrated to ban abortions. Some radical pro-life supporters have even advocated violence against and murder of those performing abortions as a moral choice in the "war" against abortion.

Court. In selecting Supreme Court justices and federal judges, Reagan and succeeding Republican presidents sought to appoint those who advocated **judicial restraint**, reductions in the authority of the federal government, and a return of executive and legislative power to the states (federalism). By 1990, it appeared that the Court, led by Chief Justice William Rehnquist, had a narrow, although not always stable, conservative majority willing to reverse many of the Court's earlier positions on social issues and federal regulatory power. While an associate justice, Rehnquist had stated that the Warren and Burger Courts had erred by "reflecting society's changing and expanding values" and had incorrectly acted as a legislative body. He believed that Congress and the state legislatures should determine policies, not the Court.

Although conservatives were disappointed with some of the Court's decisions, they praised the more restricted view of federal power taken by the Rehnquist Court. They applauded the 1992 *DeKalb County, Georgia* decision that ruled busing could not be used to integrate schools segregated by de facto housing patterns, and a ruling upholding the use of a state voucher system to provide public funds for religious schools (*Zelman v. Simmon-Hart*, 2002).

In 2005, following the resignation of Justice O'Connor and the death of Justice Rehnquist,

President George Walker Bush strengthened the conservative element in the Court by appointing Samuel Alito and naming John Roberts the new Chief Justice. As with the Rehnquist Court, conservatives generally approved the Court's decisions. They praised the Court for its decisions weakening affirmative action and increasing the states' abilities to resist implementing executive and congressional directives, and for its support for an individual's right to own and carry a firearm (*District of Columbia v Heller*, 2008), its removal of restrictions on campaign contributions from corporations and groups in the Citizens United case (2010), and its nullification of part of the Voting Rights Act in the Shelby County, Alabama, case in 2013. Conservatives were less pleased with the Court's 2012 decision upholding the administration's health-care program and loudly denounced the Court's 2013 five to four decision that declared the Defense of Marriage Act unconstitutional (*US v Windsor*).

NEW AGENDAS AND CHALLENGES

★ *What issues contributed to Bush's election and why was the election so controversial?*

★ *How did Bush's domestic and foreign policy agenda differ from those of the Clinton years?*

Americans welcomed the twenty-first century with celebrations and optimism. With the economy expanding,

■ **judicial restraint** Refraining from using the courts to interpret laws in ways that implement social change but instead deferring to Congress, the president, and the consensus of the people.

it was an upbeat and popular President Clinton who told the American people: "We have restored the vital center, replacing outdated ideologies with a new vision anchored in basic enduring values: opportunity for all, responsibility from all, and a community for all Americans." He set forth an agenda that included improving Social Security, healthcare, and the quality of education. It was an agenda that Vice President Al Gore, as the Democratic candidate for the presidency, could embrace. Republicans labeled the agenda typically liberal and focused on the dangers of big government and the need to cut taxes and restore integrity to the White House.

The 2000 Election

Leading the Republican hopefuls was George W. Bush, governor of Texas and son of the former president. He won the nomination and announced a policy of "compassionate conservatism," which stressed the use of private sector initiatives to improve education, Social Security, and healthcare. At the heart of this campaign, however, was a promise to reduce taxes.

The campaign generated a lot of spending and little excitement or sharp debates. On the issues, the candidates' differences were largely matters of "how to," reflecting party ideologies. To improve education, Bush supported state initiatives and more stringent testing, whereas Gore wanted federal funds to hire more teachers and repair school facilities. On how to spend the budget surplus, Bush advocated a tax cut to give money back to the people. Gore said he would use the surplus to reduce the national debt and fund government programs.

The two candidates ran a dead heat. Bush was strong in the less populated states and was particularly popular with white males, who voted for him 5 to 3. Gore's strength was in urban areas (he received over 70 percent of the vote in large metropolitan areas), in the Northeast and Pacific Coast, and among Latinos and African Americans. On election day Gore received a minuscule majority of popular votes—half a million more than Bush out of the 10.5 million votes cast—but Bush appeared to have won the Electoral College vote with 271 votes to 267, one vote more than necessary to win (see Map 29.1).

But when Americans awoke the next day, they found that the election was not yet settled—there was a question over Florida's twenty-five electoral votes. Bush carried Florida by less than 1,000 popular votes and Florida law required a recount. As the recount proceeded, Gore supporters claimed voting irregularities and asked the Florida Supreme Court to set aside certification of the vote until hand counts were completed in several largely Democratic counties. When the court agreed, Bush supporters filed their own suit in federal court. Ultimately, on December 4, a special

TOWARD A MORE PERFECT UNION

Federalism and the Supreme Court

Since 1995, the Rehnquist and Roberts Courts have used the Tenth and Eleventh Amendments to limit federal authority over the states, reversing over thirty-five years of legal precedent. In reinforcing the concept of federalism, the Court has taken the position that states hold joint sovereignty with the federal government and that in some areas their sovereignty is immune to federal controls. In a series of decisions (for example, *United States v Lopez*, *1995*; *Printz v. the United States*, *1997*; *Alden v. Maine*, *1999*; *United States v Morrison*, *2000*), the Court ruled that states and their institutions did not have to abide by specific federal laws and mandates. In explaining the Court's position, Chief Justice Rehnquist declared a distinction between what is "truly national" and "truly local." Within this context, for example, when the Court ruled in the *Kimel* case (1999) that Florida did not have to comply with federal age discrimination rules for its employees, Justice O'Connor said that the federal goal of eliminating age discrimination "must yield" to state sovereignty. Justice Thomas simply declared that the Eleventh Amendment precluded federal courts from hearing lawsuits against a state unless the state consented.

session of the U.S. Supreme Court decided, 5 to 4, that the outcome favoring Bush should be certified. Bush had won Florida's electoral votes and the presidential election. Gore conceded, and an hour later President-elect Bush stated, "Whether you voted for me or not, I will do my best to serve your interest, and I will work to earn your respect."

The Bush Agenda

Despite the controversial election, George Walker Bush entered the presidency determined to implement his campaign promises. He had a Republican majority in the House of Representatives and a 50–50 tie in the Senate (which, if necessary, could be broken by the vote of the vice president). Among Bush's highest priorities were tax cuts and education reform. Bush's tax cut, $1.6 trillion over a six-year period, had two objectives: to stimulate the economy and to force a reduction in government spending. Many Democrats rejected the projected tax cut, arguing that it was too large and favored the rich, with the largest reductions given to the top two income brackets. Others found it difficult to oppose a tax cut, and in June

2000

Candidate (Party)	Electoral Vote		Popular Vote	
Bush (Republican)	271	50.4%	50,465,169	47.79%
Gore (Democrat)	266	49.4%	50,996,062	48.29%
Nader (Green)	0	0.0%	2,529,871	2.40%

* One elector from the District of Columbia abstained.

MAP 29.1 Election of 2000
In a tight race, Gore won the popular vote, but Bush gained the electoral victory. Many believe that although Ralph Nader's Green Party won less than 3 percent of the popular vote, his votes in Florida may have reduced the Gore tally, helping Bush win that state's critical electoral votes.

© Cengage Learning.

Congress voted to cut taxes for the second time since World War II. Bush praised the vote as expanding "individual freedom."

Bush also moved to reduce federal regulations and standards for many industries and businesses, especially those in the energy sector, and pushed forward his education bill. Passed in June 2001, the No Child Left Behind Act required states to set proficiency standards in math and reading and financially penalized schools whose students did not meet the standards.

Charting New Foreign Policies

During the presidential campaign, Bush had called for a more "humble" foreign policy that focused on national needs. As president, he appointed a recognized advocate of international cooperation, General Colin Powell, as secretary of state, but he relied more on National Security Adviser Condoleezza Rice, Secretary of Defense Donald Rumsfeld, and Vice President Dick Cheney, all

global warming The gradual warming of the surface of the Earth; most scientists argue that during the past few decades, the Earth's temperature has risen at an unnaturally rapid rate because of industrial emission of gases that trap heat; the consequence of continued emissions, they argue, could be major ecological changes.

of whom favored a more unilateral approach. Bush quickly reversed Clinton's policies supporting measures to fight **global warming** and create international controls on biological and chemical weapons. He also broke off discussions with the Russians on a nuclear nonproliferation agreement and considered reenergizing Reagan's antiballistic missile defense system. Many, including the Russians, feared that Bush could start a new arms race with Russia and China. European newspapers denounced the American go-it-alone policy, calling the president the "Toxic Texan."

An Assault Against a Nation

However, an event that no one thought possible would characterize Bush's foreign policy and alter his presidency. On the morning of September 11, 2001, a group of five terrorists led by Mohammed Atta hijacked four airplanes that became flying bombs aimed at symbols of American financial and military power. At 8:48 A.M., American Airlines Flight 11 crashed into the North Tower of the World Trade Center. As New York fire and police departments responded, a second airliner struck the South Tower of the World Trade Center at 9:06 A.M. The second crash confirmed that the United States was being attacked by terrorists.

The September 11, 2001, terrorist attack on the World Trade Center left the nation stunned, angry, and determined to bring those who had orchestrated the attack to justice.

The scope of the attack expanded when a third hijacked plane slammed into the Pentagon, just outside Washington, D.C., at 9:45 A.M. A fourth plane crashed into a field southeast of Pittsburgh, Pennsylvania, after passengers, learning about the other hijackings by cell phone, battled the terrorists, causing the plane to go down short of its Washington, D.C., target.

In New York City the tragedy was soon magnified when the twin towers of the World Trade Center, the tallest structures in the city, collapsed, engulfing and killing thousands, including many of the firefighters and police officers who had rushed into the towers to provide help. Over three thousand people died that morning. President Bush, speaking to a stunned nation, declared that Americans had witnessed "evil, the very worst of human nature" and vowed to track down those responsible and bring them to justice.

WAR AND POLITICS

☆ *How did the events of September 11, 2001, affect the public and change Bush's foreign policy?*

☆ *What considerations and events led to the United States' invasion of Iraq?*

☆ *How did the war in Iraq shape the issues Republicans wanted to highlight in the presidential elections of 2004?*

Patriotism and support for the president swept across the country after September 11, but there was also a feeling of vulnerability. Sales of guns and gas masks increased. Assaults and threats targeted Arab Americans and those who looked Middle Eastern. In Congress, battles over domestic issues were set aside. "The war we have now is against terrorism," said Democrat John Breaux of Louisiana, and Congress quickly appropriated $40 billion for disaster relief and support for the effort to fight terrorism. Lawmakers passed the **USA Patriot Act** in October, giving law enforcement agencies wider discretion in dealing with those suspected of terrorism. The act loosened restrictions on the use of searches, wiretaps, and monitoring the Internet. Further, it gave the attorney general's office the power to detain and deport noncitizens thought to be a security risk. While some criticized the Patriot Act for restricting civil liberties, most Americans supported actions that might prevent further acts of terrorism, including the Justice Department's detention of over twelve hundred people, mostly Arab immigrants.

To defend against terrorism at home, in November, Congress agreed to form a new cabinet department, Homeland Security, whose function would be to coordinate and direct various governmental agencies in preventing further acts of terrorism against the United States. The president also asked Congress for large increases in spending for the military and for homeland defense. Bush accepted that the spending would create a deficit, maintaining that the price of freedom was "never too high."

The War on Terrorism

While Americans grappled with the enormity of the terrorist attacks, the Bush administration named **al Qaeda**, a worldwide Islamic militant organization led by **Osama bin Laden**, as the organization responsible for the September 11 attacks. The son of a wealthy Saudi Arabian family, bin Laden had dedicated himself to freeing Muslim nations from outside control, especially American capitalist control. He announced in 1996 that it was the "duty of every Muslim" to "kill Americans and their allies." He and al Qaeda were responsible for a series of strikes against American targets, including attacks on American embassies in Kenya and Tanzania in 1988 and a car bombing in front of the World Trade Center that killed six people. Responding to the car bombing, President Clinton had ordered missile strikes against al Qaeda training camps in Afghanistan, but they did not deter further terrorism. Seventeen sailors died on board the *U.S.S. Cole* when in October 2000 al Qaeda–linked terrorists struck the American warship in the Yemen.

President Bush quickly defined the new war on terrorism as a global effort, aimed not only against the "network of terrorists" but at any person or country that supported them. "Every nation in every region," he announced, had a choice to be "with us, or you are with the terrorists." Inside the White House, plans were being made for a military response against the **Taliban**, the Islamic fundamentalist government of Afghanistan, which supported bin Laden's operations. At the same time, the administration constructed a global coalition to fight terrorism. On October 7, 2001, the United States and others in

▫ **USA Patriot Act** (Uniting and Strengthening America by Providing Appropriate Tools Required to Intercept and Obstruct Terrorism) Legislation passed by Congress in 2001 that reduced constraints on the Justice Department and other law enforcement agencies in dealing with individuals having suspected links to terrorism.

▫ **al Qaeda** Terrorist network established by Saudi.

Osama bin Laden In 1989 to organize the activities of militant Islamic groups seeking to establish a global fundamentalist Islamic order; has orchestrated terrorist attacks against American targets and others.

▫ **Taliban** An organization of Muslim fundamentalists that gained control over Afghanistan in 1996 after the Soviets withdrew and that established a strict Islamic government.

It Matters Today

Islamic Fundamentalism

When the shah of Iran was overthrown, most Americans were introduced to Islamic fundamentalism for the first time. It appeared to many Americans that Islamic fundamentalism was anti-American, antidemocratic, and militant, advocating violence, even the use of terrorism, to accomplish its goals. Since 1979, that belief has been hardened by terrorist attacks against the United States, including those against the World Trade Center and Pentagon. Some argue that fundamentalists' "objective is nothing less than the total destruction of the West" and there can be "no peaceful coexistence." Others respond that the extremists within the Islamic fundamentalist movement are a small minority and that most Muslims are neither antidemocratic nor anti-Western. Whether it is benign or hostile, it is clear that Islamic fundamentalism has become a powerful force in international politics and American politics.

- More Americans than ever before have negative views toward Islam and believe that it promotes violence more than other religions. Are these views based on their perceptions of terrorism, of fundamentalism, or of Islam?
- With Islam the fastest growing religion in the United States, should schools and institutions recognize Muslim religious holidays and dress codes?

---

the coalition began the Afghan campaign to destroy al Qaeda and remove the Taliban from power (see Map 29.2). In early November, American Special Forces units working with a collection of existing anti-Taliban forces, the Afghan Northern Alliance, captured the capital of Kabul.

The Taliban no longer ruled Afghanistan. Within weeks, the coalition formed an interim government headed by Hamid Karzai. Suffering large losses, al Qaeda and bin Laden fled into the mountains bordering Pakistan and Afghanistan, where they continued to conduct their efforts.

With the threat from bin Laden reduced, the Bush administration shifted its focus to Iraq. In January 2002, Bush described an "axis of evil," composed of Iraq, Iran, and North Korea that threatened world security. He also announced a new strategy against terrorists and others who threatened world peace, the **preemptive strike**. The Bush Doctrine, Rumsfeld explained, rejected Clinton's "reflexive" policy. In the war against

terrorism, the nation could not wait until it was attacked but would take whatever action was needed to prevent such attacks.

The first preemptive strike was against Iraq. The reasons were varied. In part, it was personal. Saddam Hussein represented unfinished business left over from the war to liberate Kuwait. He was also a vile dictator who, the administration said, possessed chemical and biological weapons (classified as **weapons of mass destruction**, WMDs) and supported al Qaeda and terrorism. The administration designated his regime a threat to American security and world peace that needed to be removed from power. Others, especially in the international community, discounted Iraq's immediate threat and resisted the use of force. They recommended diplomacy and economic sanctions to force Saddam Hussein's regime to allow UN inspectors to verify whether it had or was building WMDs.

When, over the next months, diplomacy and inspections proved frustrating and inconclusive, the Bush administration intensified its efforts to obtain UN support for using force. The administration claimed that it had proof that Saddam Hussein had WMDs and was reviving his "nuclear weapons program." When pressed on Iraq's nuclear capability, Condoleezza Rice admitted that the status of Saddam Hussein's nuclear weapons was unknown, but added, "We don't want the smoking gun to be a mushroom cloud."

Not waiting for the UN, in October Congress passed a resolution permitting a preemptive strike

◻ preemptive strike Policy adopted by the Bush administration allowing the United States to use force against suspected threats before the threats occur.

weapons of mass destruction (WMDs) Nuclear, chemical, and biological weapons that have the potential to injure or kill large numbers of people—civilians as well as military personnel.

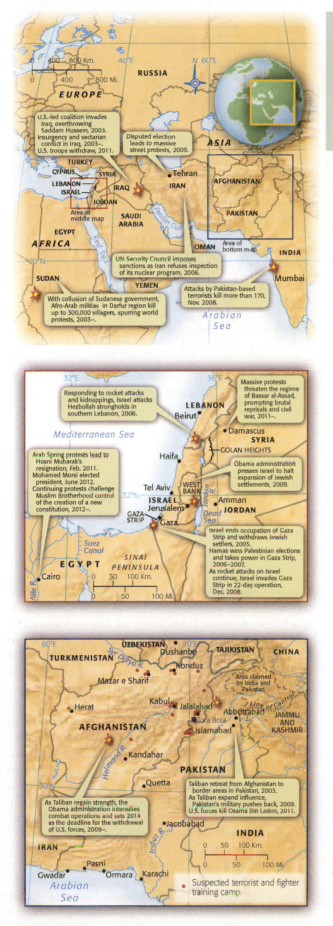

MAP 29.2 The Middle East and Afghanistan
These maps highlight events in the Middle East and southwestern Asia in the first decade of the twenty-first century. The bottom map shows Afghanistan, where Taliban leaders refused to turn over bin Laden and other al Qaeda leaders, and the United States and its allies joined with anti-Taliban forces in a military action in 2001. Taliban and al Qaeda leaders eluded capture. © Cengage Learning.

against Iraq (see Map 29.3). In November, the UN issued a less forceful resolution ordering Iraq to give up its WMDs or face "serious consequences."

Iraq and Politics

On March 17, 2003, as American troop strength in the Persian Gulf region grew, Bush was tired of playing "patty-cake" with the UN and Iraq. He gave Saddam Hussein notice to leave the country within forty-eight hours or face a military onslaught that would "shock and awe" those who witnessed it. When Saddam showed no sign of leaving, on March 19, before the ultimatum expired, American and British forces launched an offensive to capture Baghdad. It met only moderate resistance and on April 9, Baghdad was in American hands and Saddam and his government were in hiding. On May 1, Bush announced that combat operations in Iraq were over and proclaimed "mission accomplished." The president's approval rating soared.

Removing Saddam Hussein proved simple, but it was soon apparent that remaking Iraq would be no easy task. Most Iraqis thanked the United States for removing Saddam, who was later found hiding in a small "spider hole" in the ground on December 2003 and taken into custody. But the Iraqis quickly grew impatient with the U.S. occupation. They complained about the slow restoration of electricity, water, and other necessities, and they criticized the ominous lack of internal security. Impatience turned to anger as bitter divisions within the Iraqi population erupted into violence and rebellion.

Iraq became a new kind of war zone as occupation forces faced rapidly expanding violence not only from those resisting the occupation and the U.S.–sponsored interim government, but from those fighting a sectarian civil war between Sunni and Shiite religious factions. Over the next two years, terrorism and violence rose dramatically, resulting in thousands of American and tens of thousands of Iraqi casualties. The administration admitted that what it had projected would be a short-term American occupation was going to be much longer and much more expensive. Nonetheless, Bush often explained, it was necessary "to stay the course" and refashion Iraq into a

MAP 29.3 Second Iraq War
Saddam Hussein's regime collapsed within weeks of the beginning of the invasion north along the Tigris and Euphrates Rivers. Although the official hostilities ended, insurgents continued to resist the American occupation and the control of the interim Iraqi government, especially in the Sunni Triangle. © Cengage Learning.

stable democratic state, which would promote peace and stability in the Middle East. The reality was quite different, as anti-American sentiment across much of the Arab world increased.

At home and abroad, support for Bush's Iraq policies ebbed as American casualties increased and the Bush administration admitted it could find no weapons of mass destruction. Over the next two years, various investigatory commissions established to evaluate the intelligence reports and decisions leading to the war determined that the information claiming Saddam possessed such weapons and had links to al Qaeda was wrong. With critics blaming the administration for manipulating the nation into military action, it seemed like the United States was trapped in an expensive war with no plans to end the conflict or withdraw American troops.

Amid growing questions about the Iraq war, Bush ran for reelection. Although he received positive public approval ratings for combating terrorism, the public gave him lower marks on conducting the Iraq war, dealing with the economy, and controlling the deficit. Accordingly, the Democratic presidential candidate, Senator John Kerry of Massachusetts, focused on the economy and the war. Bush attacked Kerry and the Democrats as too liberal and claimed that their opposition to the war undermined the American effort and encouraged terrorism. When critics pointed to the misinformation on WMDs used to justify the invasion, Bush stressed the need to end Saddam Hussein's brutal dictatorship and his decisive leadership. "We acted. We led," stated Bush. Bush argued, too, that the economy was improving, spurred by the administration's low interest rates, tax cuts, and military spending. Democrats replied that the administration's "declared victory over the recession" was premature as many were still losing their jobs and seeing their wages drop.

Republicans also attacked Democrats over a variety of social issues, including gay marriage. In November 2003, the Massachusetts Supreme Court had ruled that banning same-sex marriage violated

Left: Joseph Sohm; Visions of America/CORBIS. Right: ATEF HASSAN/Reuters/Corbis.

On March 20, 2003, U.S. and British forces crossed from Kuwait into Iraq in the second Iraq war. (*Left*) By May 1, on board the U.S.S. *Abraham Lincoln,* President Bush declared the war in Iraq over. But for thousands of American soldiers in Iraq, the conflict continued as insurgents fought on. (*Right*) An Iraqi armed with a rocket-propelled grenade launcher stands by a burning vehicle in Basra. Between May 2003 and October 2004, more Americans had been killed in Iraq than during the "official" war.

the state's constitution. The court gave the state legislature 180 days to act on its decision. The following April, the Massachusetts legislature approved a constitutional amendment that permitted same-sex **civil unions** but defined marriage as a union only between a man and a woman. The amendment, however, could not be ratified until 2006, which meant that until it was ratified Massachusetts would issue marriage licenses to same-sex couples.

Across the country, the response to the Massachusetts court's decision was generally negative, and thirty-five states hurried to strengthen their prohibitions of same-sex marriage. In addition, many opponents of same-sex marriage believed that civil unions should also be banned. In February 2004, President Bush endorsed the idea of a constitutional amendment that would disallow same-sex marriage. When pressed for his view, Kerry opposed such an amendment and argued that the issue should be left to the states to legislate. He also said that he personally opposed same-sex marriages but approved of civil unions.

Targeting "battleground" swing states, both parties poured vast amounts of time and campaign money into a few states, along with venomous campaign ads. Both also took new approaches to campaigning using the Internet to woo supporters. "Bloggers" created their own websites providing news, political analysis, and ads for and against the candidates. Days before the election, most polls showed the candidates tied in popular support.

On November 2, 2004, more Americans voted than ever before. They reelected Bush, giving him 51 percent of the vote. Bush had effectively mobilized his party's loyalists and won most of the battleground states. To the surprise of most observers, a majority of Bush supporters stated that moral issues and family values were critical reasons for how they voted. Supporting this observation, in Ohio—which was critical to the president's reelection—and ten other states, voters affirmed their support for amendments to their state constitutions to prohibit same-sex marriages and civil unions. "Make no mistake—conservative Christians and 'value voters' won this election," stated one conservative observer.

Bush's Second Term

Referring to his victory as a public mandate for action and with Republican majorities in Congress, President Bush was eager to use his "political capital" to implement domestic goals that promoted an "ownership society," putting control in the hands of individuals. "Now comes the revolution," voiced some conservatives when the president announced that strengthening family values and reforming Social Security, tax codes, and education were agenda priorities. In foreign affairs, Bush said the election showed support for creating a democratic Iraq and his war against terrorism. Bush's political capital fell apart within months when Congress and the public rejected his efforts to privatize Social Security and further reduce taxes. His

civil union Term for a civil status similar to marriage, allowing same-sex partners access to legal, medical, financial, and other benefits enjoyed by married heterosexuals.

Among the areas most devastated by Hurricane Katrina when it struck the Gulf Coast in August 2005 was New Orleans' Ninth Ward, where waters from Lake Pontchartrain engulfed the area after levees were breached.

Marko Georgiev/Contributor/Getty Images.

leadership, which he had touted during the election campaign, suffered a serious blow following his lethargic response to the devastation caused by a category-four hurricane.

On August 29, 2005, **Hurricane Katrina** devastated areas of the Gulf Coast and battered New Orleans, much of which is below sea level. When the levees protecting the city broke, flood waters poured in and submerged some sectors of New Orleans under 20 feet of water. When television crews broadcast the horrific conditions and widespread destruction, especially in New Orleans, it became clear that government agencies were, at best, slow to deal with the crisis. To many it appeared that both President Bush and the Federal Emergency Management Agency (FEMA) were ignoring the stricken city and downplaying the magnitude of the disaster. The administration's slow response caused significant damage to its aura of efficient management and was a blow to the public's confidence in Bush's leadership and policies. "The rich escaped," conservative writer David Brooks editorialized, "while the poor were abandoned. . . . Leaving the poor in New Orleans was the moral equivalent of leaving the injured on the battlefield."

■ **Hurricane Katrina** Formed in the Caribbean on August 23, 2005, it travelled over southern Florida as a weak hurricane before slamming into the coastline of Louisiana on August 29 as the sixth strongest Atlantic hurricane in history; from Florida to Texas it caused over eighteen hundred confirmed deaths and over $81 billion in damages; most of the damage and deaths occurred in Louisiana and the city of New Orleans, where over 80 percent of the city and surrounding areas were flooded.

Katrina pushed Bush's popularity rating below 50 percent, and criticism of the administration's domestic and war policies intensified. The Iraq war was not going well. The civil war between religious factions continued, and the death tolls for both Americans and Iraqis soared—over 3,000 American soldiers had died since the occupation started. For Iraqis, exact numbers are unknown, but estimates range from over half a million to less than 100,000. At home, gasoline prices and the national debt continued to rise, and Bush's popularity continued to fall as the 2006 congressional elections neared.

With all 435 House seats and 33 Senate seats up for grabs, Democrats, sensing an opportunity to regain control of Congress, called for a "New Direction for America." The results were better than Democrats had hoped. In a rout, Democrats won 31 additional seats in the House and 6 seats in the Senate, gaining a majority in both bodies. In the House, triumphant Democrats selected Congresswoman Nancy Pelosi from California as the first woman to hold that position. It was, she said, "a historic moment," one that broke the "marble ceiling," and one that women had been waiting more than two hundred years for.

Some thought the election results ended the Reagan revolution and that the Bush administration would have to moderate its policies, especially on Iraq. Bush admitted he and Republicans had taken a "thumpin'" but showed little willingness to change his agenda. Denying the election was a "call to change" his policy toward Iraq, Bush announced a 21,500-troop "surge" to boost security, reduce the violence, and allow the Iraqi forces to complete the training they were receiving from U.S. troops. It was the way to win the war, according to the administration, and Vice President Cheney stressed that efforts to block the president's plan would "undermine"

AP Photos.

In the congressional elections of 2006, Democrats regained control of both houses of Congress. Nancy Pelosi (D.-Calif.) became the first woman Speaker of the House of Representatives. In this picture, she is accompanied by her grandchildren and other members' children and grandchildren at the podium of the House.

the troops. Most Democrats opposed the surge and called for a time frame for the removal of American forces. Republicans rejected any timeline and argued that the surge was working, reducing violence and stabilizing the Iraqi government.

Economic Crises and Obama

With the battle lines drawn over the war in Iraq, the 2008 presidential campaign started a year and a half before the election. The leading Democratic candidates, Senators Hillary Clinton of New York and Barack Obama of Illinois, were breaking historical traditions of gender and race, since neither a woman nor an African American had ever been nominated for the presidency by a major party. After a series of hard-fought primaries, Obama secured the nomination and selected Senator Joseph Biden of Delaware as his running mate. In a less bruising series of primaries, Arizona Senator John McCain overcame his Republican challengers and captured the nomination. Hoping to consolidate his support from conservative Republicans and to attract women voters, McCain surprised everyone by naming Alaska governor Sarah Palin as his running mate. Many expected the war in Iraq and Obama's lesser political experience to dominate the campaign issues.

The campaign began nearly as expected. McCain touted his decades of government service and attacked Obama as inexperienced, too liberal, weak on foreign policy, and wrong in his position on the Iraq war. Obama countered by offering innovation and change, asking the nation if they wanted four more years of

the same failed Bush policies. Obama argued that Bush had fought the wrong war and should instead have continued the effort in Afghanistan to destroy al Qaeda. Afghanistan, Obama asserted, should be the priority, to hunt down terrorists, bring bin Laden to justice, and establish a stable country. But the central issue of the election campaign soon shifted away from comparative experience and the war on terror to who could best deal with a growing economic crisis. A mid-June Gallup Poll discovered that more than 56 percent of voters thought fixing the economy was more important than fighting terrorism, and believed Obama was more qualified on economic issues than McCain.

Signs of an unsteady economy were visible, for those choosing to see them, as early as 2006. At the center of the brewing economic storm were extremely low interest rates, a boom in the housing market, inattentive government regulators, and greed. Banks and other lending institutions made housing loans, including **subprime loans**, to thousands of people who could normally not afford them. In many cases, profit-seeking lenders actively marketed subprime and other special loan arrangements to high-risk borrowers. In one case a worker at McDonald's who earned $35,000 a year was able to get a half-million-dollar loan for a home.

■ **subprime loan** A loan that carries a higher-than-normal interest rate, generally used to make a loan to someone with a history of bad credit and default; between 2005 and 2006 such loans represented 20 percent of all housing loans.

Then, in 2007, housing values began to drop; within a short time an alarming number of homeowners were "underwater," owing more than their house was worth. A cascade of foreclosures followed, starting a financial crisis. Institutions that had either directly or indirectly invested in mortgages, once considered a safe investment, found themselves short of capital and unable to pay their investors, depositors, and creditors. By September 2008, the stock market tumbled and banks and insurance and investment corporations teetered on the edge of bankruptcy. Secretary of the Treasury Henry Paulson and Federal Reserve Chairman Ben Bernanke convinced the fiscally conservative Bush administration that a massive infusion of money was needed to prop up some of the nation's largest financial institutions. They were "too big" to fail, said one government official. Bush asked Congress for $700 billion for the **Troubled Asset Relief Program** (TARP); the alternative, he said, was to watch "this sucker [the economy] go down."

Congress approved the complex and controversial bill and Bush signed it on October 3. Responses to the TARP were mixed. Many people complained that it rewarded "Wall Street"—those who had caused the economic crisis—and did nothing for "Main Street," the hard-working Americans who were losing their jobs or homes or both. Others voiced concerns about the TARP's effectiveness and cost and about the level of government intervention in buying the assets of private financial institutions. Even more controversial was the administration's request in December for more funds, $17.4 billion in loans to support failing American automobile manufacturers General Motors and Chrysler.

By November, the economic crisis, now officially a recession, had intensified and spread to Europe and Asia. Obama offered change, and on Election Day more people voted than in any other presidential election, providing him a decisive victory (see Map 29.4). Obama received 53 percent of the popular vote, and 365 electoral votes. Democrats also added eight seats to their majority in the Senate and twenty-one to their margin in the House.

On January 20, 2009, President Obama gave his inaugural address to over a million people who braved cold weather to watch the inauguration ceremonies. He acknowledged the serious problems the

2008

Candidate (Party)	Electoral Vote		Popular Vote	
Obama (Democrat)	365	68%	69,498,459	52.9%
McCain (Republican)	173	32%	59,948,283	45.6%

MAP 29.4 Election of 2008, by State
In a spirited and historic election, Democrat Barack Obama more than doubled the electoral count of Republican John McCain (365 to 173) and earned nearly 53 percent of the popular vote. In a county-by-county analysis, most counties showed larger Democratic votes than in 2004, except in Alaska, Arizona, Arkansas, Louisiana, Kentucky, and Tennessee. © Cengage Learning.

nation confronted: "Our nation is at war against a far-reaching network of violence and hatred. Our economy is badly weakened, a consequence of greed and irresponsibility on the part of some but also our collective failure to make hard choices and prepare the nation for a new age." He added that the challenges would not be easily overcome but that "the work of remaking America" would be done, and he voiced the hope that the bitter polarization that had characterized politics would be laid aside for the common good.

OBAMA'S PRESIDENCY

☆ *What major issues contributed to Barack Obama's election in 2008, and what constraints did he face in implementing his policies?*

☆ *In what ways were Obama's goals different from the Bush administration's, and what events led to the formation of the Tea Party?*

☆ *How did political gridlock shape the debate over economic policy, and what major issues contributed to Barack Obama's reelection in 2012?*

Over the next months, Obama unfolded an ambitious agenda that emphasized the theme of change

◻ **Troubled Asset Relief Program** (TARP) A 2008 act allowing the government to buy $700 billion of "troubled assets" from selected financial institutions to reduce their level of debt and to infuse capital into the system; the TARP's primary goal was to help deal with the economic crisis caused by subprime loans.

ROMEO GACAD/AFP/Getty Images.

In the war on terrorism, American forces joined with NATO and other anti-Taliban forces in Afghanistan to attack Taliban, Al Qaeda, and other insurgent forces. In this picture, NATO, U.S., and Afghan forces patrol an Afghanistan village in Kandahar Province.

voiced during his campaign. He sought to restore the economy; improve education, energy, and environmental policies; implement a national healthcare system; and change the tone and direction of U.S. foreign policy. Despite Democratic majorities in Congress and Obama's popularity, it was not an agenda that reduced political polarization. Republican leaders in the Congress called for solid opposition to Obama's domestic programs and argued that his foreign policy approach would weaken American security and influence. Senator George Voinovich (R.–Ohio) summed it up by saying, "If Obama was for it . . . we had to be against it."

Shifts in Foreign Policy

During the campaign Obama had criticized the Bush administration for the war in Iraq and its unilateral approach to most international problems. He and Secretary of State Hillary Rodham Clinton meant to reverse that approach, improve relations with Arab states, and hold international discussions to deal with a wide range of global issues, including the global recession, nuclear proliferation, sanctions against Iran and North Korea, and saving the environment. One of the early results was a new **Strategic Arms Limitation Treaty** (START) between the United States and Russia, which reduced the number of both countries' nuclear warheads from six thousand to fifteen hundred.

The administration also shifted the focus of the war against terrorism from Iraq to Afghanistan. Fulfilling his campaign pledge, Obama oversaw the final withdrawal of American forces from Iraq by the end of December 2011. The Iraqi war had cost more than $800 billion and taken more than 4,000 American and 100,000 Iraqi lives. It produced neither a

unified nor an economically and politically stable country. But most Americans were just pleased that the war was over. The war in Afghanistan, however, continued as Obama deployed twenty-one thousand additional troops to "dismantle and defeat al Qaeda." The administration hoped that the troop surge would strengthen the Afghan government's effectiveness and control over its country before American troops were withdrawn by the end of 2014. As part of the war against terrorism, Obama increased the use of Special Forces units and drone attacks against terrorist targets across the Middle East, including in Yemen and Pakistan. In one such mission, on May 1, 2011, a Navy SEAL unit covertly entered Pakistan, where they found and killed the elusive Osama bin Laden, generating celebrations across the United States.

But the Middle East remained volatile, with continuing concerns about Iran's suspected efforts to build nuclear weapons and new challenges caused by a wave of popular revolts, the **Arab Spring** (see Map 29.5). The unrest started in Tunisia in December 2010, when police confiscated street vendor Mohamed

■ **Strategic Arms Limitation Treaty** (START) Modifying the original treaty signed in 1991 that expired in 2009, the new treaty reduced the number of nuclear war heads to fifteen hundred and the number of operationally deployed delivery systems to seven hundred; other START agreements in 1993 and 1997 were never implemented.

■ **Arab Spring** Beginning in December 2010 in Tunisia, a series of popular protests and uprisings demanding widespread reforms and change that swept across North Africa and the Middle East.

In the Wider World

The Arab Spring

In December 2010 popular protests erupted throughout the Arab world as citizens demanded widespread democratic reforms. While many governments implemented various reforms and maintained control, in Tunisia, Egypt, Libya, and Yemen, the existing governments were removed and new, less authoritarian ones formed. In a few countries, the government responded with enough force to remain in power. Below are some of the major outcomes of the Arab Spring.

In December 2010, protests
- in Tunisia forced the president from office and created a new government.
- in Algeria forced the government to lift a 19-year-old state of emergency.

In January 2011, protests
- in Mauritania were stopped by the government.
- in Egypt toppled the government and created a new government.
- in Sudan forced the president not to run for a third term.
- in Lebanon forced a 40 percent increase in wages.
- in Saudi Arabia, Oman, and Jordan, forced political and economic reforms.

In February 2011, protests
- in Morocco, forced political concessions.
- in Yemen, forced the president to resign.
- in Bahrain, forced economic reforms.
- in Kuwait, forced the cabinet to resign.
- in Libya, led to civil war, removal of the government, and the death of Libyan leader Muammar Qaddafi.

In March 2011, protests
- in Syria, led to government repression and civil war, which continued as of mid-2013.

Bouazizi's vegetable cart—his only means of making a living. In protest, he set himself on fire. His protest exploded into larger protests against the status quo, the authoritarianism, corruption, and political and social conditions that characterized many Middle Eastern governments. In two weeks, the Tunisian regime had crumbled and the movement spread. Within months, similar protests forced reforms on several governments and toppled others. In Egypt and Yemen, authoritarian rulers were forced out with slight violence, but in Libya and Syria the governments ordered the military to crush the protesters and civil war followed.

Although most Americans cheered the changes taking place, the Obama administration's response was mixed and cautious. In Egypt, the United States reluctantly abandoned a long-time ally, authoritarian leader Hosni Mubarak, and rallied behind efforts to establish a democratic government. In Libya, the United States along with a coalition of other nations agreed to support the rebels and to use air power to aid in ousting autocrat Muammar Qaddafi. In Syria,

where by the end of 2012 the civil war had destroyed much of the country and cost over forty thousand lives, the Obama administration remained cautious, limiting its response to political pressure in trying to remove dictator Bashar al-Assad from power. By the end of his first administration, most Americans gave Obama high marks in the conduct of American foreign policy, but that was not the case when it came to domestic affairs.

Change and the Politics of Filibuster

Obama had emphasized change during the campaign and in the first weeks of his presidency, prospects for a political honeymoon appeared promising. Congress quickly approved acts supporting equal pay for women (the Lilly Ledbetter Fair Pay Act) and expanding children's health insurance, both previously vetoed by Bush. But the political honeymoon never fully materialized. By February, when the administration introduced a bill to provide over $700 billion in increased

MAP 29.5 The Arab Spring and Change
In December 2010 demands for political, economic, and social change swept across much of the Arab world. It continues to the present as the general public seeks to express its political power. In Egypt public demonstrations in mid-2013 forced the removal of the president elected as a result of the Arab Spring demonstrations in February 2011, while the civil war in Syria continued into the summer of 2013 with no end in sight. © 2013 Cengage Learning.

federal spending combined with tax relief to stimulate the economy, Republicans baulked. They called it an expensive government handout and connected it to the unpopular TARP passed by Bush. Consequently, the **American Recovery and Reinvestment Act** passed in the House without any Republican votes and in the Senate only when three Republican Senators broke party unity. It provided money for states to help balance their budgets and pay for infrastructure projects, and it extended unemployment benefits. Despite being the largest economic stimulus bill in American history, it had little effect on what was being termed "the Great Recession." As Republicans claimed that businesses created jobs, not the government, unemployment rose, and the economy and Obama's popularity continued to decline. In their determination to block further Obama programs, Republicans in the Senate used the filibuster to force Democrats to muster sixty votes to pass legislation.

When Obama established his agenda, many recommended that he focus on the economy, but he argued that many issues should not be delayed, especially creating a national healthcare system. He believed that such a program was necessary to contain the soaring costs of medical care threatening to bankrupt families, businesses, and the government, and to improve the health of the nation. The Obama administration worked with Congress to craft a program to require that all Americans be covered by health insurance and to establish rules of coverage for insurance companies. It required that most businesses offer health

■ **American Recovery and Reinvestment Act** A 2009 act that increased federal spending for healthcare, infrastructure, education, various tax programs, and direct assistance to individuals to be spent over several years.

A Deeper Understanding of History

Evaluating *The National Federation of Independent Business v. Sebelius Case*

Historians, like the rest of the nation, waited for the Supreme Court's decision regarding President Obama's Patient Protection and Affordable Care Act. A split decision was expected from a Court that was seen as ideologically and politically divided. The Court's conservative, Republican-appointed justices were expected to oppose parts or all of the law, while the liberal, Democrat-appointed justices were expected to uphold it.

Although forecasting any of the Court's decisions is difficult, most observers projected a conservative decision making the president's landmark legislation null and void. They supported their prediction by pointing out that the Supreme Court was moving toward a more conservative view of the federal government's power, reversing the approach of the Warren Court. They also noted that most of the twenty-eight legal challenges to the law took the position that the government had overreached its power in creating a national health system that forced people and states to comply with its dictates, especially the "mandate" that all citizens have health insurance or face a penalty. They argued against supporters' position that the commerce clause could be used to force people to purchase specific products or face a penalty. Others, taking a more political perspective, emphasized that public opinion polls showed a majority of

the people disapproved of the law and, in an election year, nearly every Republican was calling for its repeal.

On its last day in session, June 28, 2012, the Court gave its ruling. As expected the outcome was a 5-to-4 decision. But to nearly everyone's surprise, the Court upheld the constitutionality of the law. Even more surprising was the composition of the majority. As expected the conservative justices (Thomas, Scalia, Kennedy, Alito) had rejected the law, holding the mandate as unconstitutional and exceeding the power of the federal government. The liberal members of the Court (Ginsberg, Breyer, Sotomayor, Kagan), as predicted, approved it as a necessary function of the government. What was unexpected was that Chief Justice John Roberts, regarded as a conservative, had joined with his liberal colleagues to validate the law. President Obama and Democrats praised the decision. Disappointed Republicans reaffirmed their opposition to the law and stressed that the decision underlined the importance of electing Mitt Romney president.

In determining the importance of the case, historians will take very different approaches. Some will focus on the politics of healthcare. The Court's decision was a historical moment, culminating an effort reaching back to the Progressive Era to institute a national health system. Many presidents had called for such a program and, finally, President Obama had overcome many obstacles to succeed. Others, especially legal historians, are likely to see the importance of the case not in establishing a national system of healthcare, but in the nature of the decision and what it suggests for the future. Roberts, they could point out, walked a legal tightrope. In his decision, he wrote that the government could enforce the mandate by imposing "a tax on those without health insurance," but it did "not have the power to order people to buy health insurance." Thus, he validated the long-held liberal goal of a healthcare system, while shrewdly advancing the conservative vision of the Constitution by limiting the power of the federal government to use the commerce clause.

In your opinion, which result of the case was more important—the validation of the law and the establishment of a national system of healthcare or the precedent set by denying use of the commerce clause to compel citizens to make consumer decisions?

Photo by Alex Wong/Getty Images.

In this photo, supporters of the administration's national healthcare program demonstrate before the Supreme Court, linking the conservative opposition to "Obamacare" with a general attack on women's rights.

insurance to their employees and that those who were uninsured buy health insurance or pay a penalty. After a complex series of debates and compromises over House and Senate versions of the bill, the Senate and the House approved the **Patient Protection and Affordable Care Act**, without Republican support, and Obama signed it in March 2010. With its provisions to be implemented over a four-year period, the United States had joined most of the world in having a national healthcare system.

Republicans immediately denounced "Obamacare" and called for its repeal. At the same time, officials in eighteen states filed motions in federal court arguing the acts were unconstitutional and infringed on states' rights. "The Constitution," their motion read, "nowhere authorizes the United States to mandate, either directly or under threat of penalty, that all citizens and legal residents have qualifying healthcare coverage." President Obama dismissed the constitutional challenges as pure politics and argued that as the provisions of national healthcare took effect, public support for the system would increase. In June 2012, the Supreme Court upheld the act's constitutionality in a 5-to-4 decision. The Court's decision only strengthened Republican resolve to win the 2012 election and repeal it.

If the economy and the debate over healthcare were not challenges enough, in April 2010, a British Petroleum (BP) drilling rig, the *Deepwater Horizon*, exploded and sank in the Gulf of Mexico, killing eleven workers. It spewed millions of gallons of oil into the Gulf, generating a major ecological and economic disaster along the coastlines of Louisiana, Alabama, Mississippi, and Florida. BP finally capped the gushing well and accepted "full responsibility for the spill," agreeing to pay for the costs of the cleanup and to financially compensate those affected by the disaster. Although some argued that Obama was not assertive enough in dealing with the disaster, the public generally credited him for getting BP to take financial responsibility.

In July, the administration won another congressional victory when three Republican Senators broke ranks and voted for the Wall Street Reform and Consumer Protection Act (the Dodd-Frank Act). It placed new and increased regulations on financial and investment institutions and created a new government agency, the Consumer Financial Protection Bureau. Opponents blasted the act, contending that it would harm the banking system. Obama responded that only those institutions that depended on "cutting corners or bilking... customers" needed to fear it.

Republican Resurgence

The faltering economy combined with the acidic debates over the economy and healthcare sparked a conservative political insurgency, the **Tea Party movement**, that swept the country. It began as an antitax movement, but by the midterm elections of 2010, it had become a larger conservative movement. Composed of largely white middle-class Republicans over the age of forty, Tea Partiers saw themselves as victims of a tax structure that stripped them of their hard earned money to pay for wasteful liberal programs. They focused not only on taxes but on the intrusive "un-American nature of Big Government," and on Obama's programs, especially Obamacare.

Tea Partiers leapt into state and congressional political races supporting those Republicans who were the most conservative, further polarizing the political debate. The results were stunning. Several moderate Republicans lost congressional seats in primaries to Tea Party candidates, who formed a large portion of the Republican gain of sixty-four seats in the House of Representatives and six seats in the Senate. The 2010 election results gave Republicans a majority in the House, whereas in the Senate their 47 votes made their use of the filibuster more effective. The outcome was political gridlock.

Gridlock and the Election of 2012

As the new Congress met in 2011, Republicans and Democrats agreed on two basic goals—the economy needed to be fixed and the deficit reduced—but there was little agreement on how to accomplish either. Many of the newly elected Republicans had campaigned on not raising taxes and on reducing the size of government and the deficit. They vowed to slash government spending, repeal Obamacare, and make permanent the Bush tax cuts that expired at the end of 2012. Obama and most Democrats took an opposite stance. While they agreed spending needed to be reduced, they wanted fewer budget cuts, opposed changes in Social Security and Medicare, and sought to end the Bush tax cuts for those making more than $200,000 per year. These opposing positions created heated debates and gridlock on economic and budget issues. In 2012, congressional Republicans refused to raise the debt ceiling unless the White House and Democrats accepted their spending cuts.

■ **Patient Protection and Affordable Care Act** Act passed in 2010 that established a complex governmental and private system of national healthcare that will include nearly all Americans by 2014; it included provisions preventing health insurance companies from denying or canceling coverage to those with preexisting conditions.

■ **Tea Party movement** Arising in early 2009 in protest to the bailout and stimulus packages, the movement calls for limited government, a balanced budget, and a free market economy, attracting those who distrust Washington and seem most worried about the future. Polls taken in 2010 showed they represented about 18 percent of the electorate.

As 2009 primary and general elections neared, the Tea Party movement organized and sponsored rallies against Obama's programs and liberal policies, vowing to help elect those candidates holding similar conservative goals. In this picture thousands of people protest big government, federal spending, Obama's administration, and liberal policies in a September 2009 demonstration in Washington, D.C. As the November off-year election approached in 2010, Tea Partiers credited their movement for the unexpected success of several conservative Republican candidates running for state and national offices.

For months the two sides postured, debated, and grew increasingly exasperated with each other. In June, Obama stated that he was willing to reduce spending to get an agreement to raise the debt ceiling, provided Republicans agreed to increase tax revenues. "You can't reduce the deficit to levels it needs to be," he said, "without having some revenue in the mix." House Majority Speaker John Boehner (R.–Ohio) replied, "The American people will not accept, and the House cannot pass, a bill that raises taxes on job creators." On August 2, a last-minute compromise was struck, and Congress passed the Budget Control Act. It raised the debt ceiling for six months, cut federal spending without additional revenue from raising taxes, and created a special congressional committee to find agreement on the budget. To force Congress and the White House to reach common ground, the act specified that deep across-the-board spending cuts would be triggered—establishing a "fiscal cliff"—unless an agreement was reached by the end of December. It was an imperfect solution that did nothing to resolve the gap between Republicans and Democrats over the budget, tax cuts, and other outstanding issues. As the country entered the 2012 presidential election campaign, politics remained polarized and deadlocked.

Willard Mitt Romney, businessman, millionaire, and ex-governor of Massachusetts, emerged as the Republican candidate, although many conservatives questioned his conservative credentials and initially had supported an array of more conservative but weaker candidates. To solidify his conservative base, Romney chose fiscally conservative representative Paul Ryan as his vice presidential candidate. Romney touted his business background and the free market's ability to energize the economy and put people back to work. He promised to cut the size of government, balance the budget, and repeal Obamacare.

Democrats, in turn, attacked Romney as a protector of the wealthy with little concern for the middle and working classes. They pointed out that Romney had several foreign bank accounts and paid extremely low income taxes. In the spring, however, a new set of cultural and social issues emerged involving gay and women's rights, immigration, and Latino and African American voters. President Obama announced that he now supported same-sex marriage and also removed the last barrier to gays serving openly in the military. Conservatives and Romney quickly proclaimed their ardent opposition to gay marriage and claimed that gays in the military reduced combat effectiveness and harmed morale. In June, the president issued an executive order allowing children brought to the United States by undocumented immigrants to remain in the

This photo was taken on election night in 2008. Having won the Democratic nomination for president, Barack Obama easily defeated the Republican candidate John McCain. Receiving news of his victory, President-elect Obama addressed his supporters gathered in Chicago's Grant Park. On stage with him was the new first family: his wife Michelle and their two daughters Sasha and Malia.

Ralf-Finn Hestoft/Ralf-Finn Hestoft/CORBIS.

country and pursue a path to citizenship. This measure conflicted sharply with views held by most conservatives, who argued for widespread immigration restrictions and supported state-based legislation like that passed in Arizona and Georgia to deny undocumented immigrants public services and facilitate their deportation.

Further reshaping the political debate, many Republican-dominated state legislatures approved or promoted legislation to deny or limit abortions and women's access to reproductive services. Democrats, many women, and various other groups assailed these efforts as being part of a Republican "war on women" designed to interfere with women's rights and healthcare needs. Meanwhile, in many states, Republicans led efforts to implement restrictive procedures regarding voter registration, to limit when voting could take place, and to require those without state-issued IDs, like a driver's license, to obtain special voter identification cards before being allowed to vote. Democrats and other critics claimed the measures were efforts to suppress the Latino and African American vote.

By the end of October, in what was the most expensive election campaign in American history, most national polls indicated Obama had a small lead with his support coming from urban areas, younger voters, women, African Americans, and Latinos. Romney, whose in-house polls showed him leading Obama, was running well ahead in rural and less populated areas and was getting the majority of the white, male vote. Most predicted a close race with the results hinging on which campaign could turn out the most voters.

On Election Day, a much better organized Obama campaign succeeded in mobilizing the most voters, many of whom were willing to stand in line for many hours at the polls, especially in the key swing states of Florida and Ohio. Many Latinos and African Americans explained that they were motivated to vote because they thought Republicans were trying to deny them the opportunity. When the votes were counted, President Obama had received over 51 percent of the popular vote, and his electoral margin doubled that of Romney (see Map 29.6). The balance of power in the new 113th Congress remained the same; Democrats retained a majority in the Senate and Republicans did so in the House, but the new Congress was notable for having the largest number of women in history, 101 members. When asked if the number of women made a difference, Senator Kay Hagan (D.–N.C.) replied: "Women have a tendency to work in partnerships, and that's something I think the American public would really appreciate us doing, working across the aisle."

However, before the new Congress convened, the outgoing Congress had unfinished business—avoiding the "fiscal cliff." The congressional committee created to propose a budget reported that after "months of hard work and intense deliberations" it was unable to find a bipartisan solution. With both sides fearing that the draconian automatic budget cuts and ending the Bush tax cuts for all tax brackets would plunge the economy back into recession, the House and Senate and the White House began frantic negotiations. Obama, reelected with a pledge to raise taxes on the wealthiest Americans, demanded those making over $200,000 a year pay more taxes. House Republicans continued to reject any tax increases and demanded larger spending cuts.

By Christmas it was clear that the White House and the House of Representatives could not reach

The November 2012 elections not only re-elected President Obama but produced five additional women senators, raising the number of women in the Senate to a historical record of twenty.

ABC via Getty Image.

an agreement, and it was left to the Senate to find a compromise. Going beyond the last minute, the Senate and the White House forged an agreement, the American Taxpayer Relief Act, which was approved by the Senate on New Year's Day at 2 o'clock in the morning. It delayed the automatic budget cuts, raised taxes on Americans making more than $400,000 a year, and extended federal unemployment benefits for a year. Twenty-one hours later, the House also agreed. The fiscal cliff had been avoided, but the deep differences over taxes and spending between Democrats and Republicans remained. Dealing with the looming automatic budget cuts and finding an agreement on the budget would be the job of the new Congress.

In the months following Obama's reelection, the new Congress proved hardly more willing to compromise than the previous one. Although Republicans agreed to not block debt ceiling extensions, no agreement on the budget was reached and on March 1, 2013, the one trillion dollars in the automatic across the board budget cuts took effect while Democrats and Republicans blamed each other for playing politics with it. On other issues, especially on enhanced gun control measures and immigration, there was initial hope that Congress and the White House could work effectively together, but the White House – backed legislation on gun control and immigration reform faced strong and effective opposition, preventing or delaying their passages in Congress. By the summer of 2013, many liberals were criticizing the White House for a lack of leadership and direction while many conservatives argued that the Obama administration was stifling individual rights. Critics of Congress

and especially the Republican-controlled House pointed out that internal politics as well as political gridlock had resulted in Congress approving the fewest bills in recent history. Despite denial from Republicans and Democrats, hope for political cooperation remained elusive as the political and public debate over the function of the federal government in the making of America intensified.

Candidate (Party)	Electoral Vote		Popular Vote	
Obama (Democrat)	332	62%	65,899,660	51.1%
Romney (Republican)	206	38%	60,932,152	47.2%

MAP 29.6 Election of 2012, by State
The November 2012 elections not only re-elected President Obama but produced five additional women senators, raising the number of women in the Senate to a historical record of twenty.
© 2013 Cengage Learning.

© Jonathan Sprague/Redux.

NICHOLAS CARR
Asks, "Is Google Making Us Stupid?"

Historians are constantly reminded that some of the most important results of change are not always expected, or even beneficial. In this document a journalist comments on what he believes may be one of the most important and long-lasting outcomes of using new technologies to research and write.

❶ In what ways has the Internet changed the way in which people do research?

❷ How does the author believe technologies like the Internet have affected the brain and people's reading and comprehension skills?

❸ What evidence does Carr use to support his views? Is this really evidence? Should such evidence be accepted? Should historians rely on it?

Over the past few years, I've had an uncomfortable sense that someone, or something, has been tinkering with my brain, remapping the neural circuitry, reprogramming my memory. My mind isn't going—so far as I can tell—but it is changing. I'm not thinking the way I used to think. I can feel it most strongly when I'm reading.... Now my concentration often starts to drift after two or three pages. I get fidgety, lose the thread, begin to look for something else to do.

I think I know what's going on.... I've been spending a lot of time online, searching and surfing.... Research that once required days in ... libraries can now be done in minutes. For me, as for others, the Net is becoming a universal medium, the conduit for most of the information that flows through my eyes and ears and into my mind.... And what the Net seems to be doing is chipping away my capacity for concentration and contemplation. My mind now expects to take in information the way the Net distributes it: in a swiftly moving stream of particles. Once I was a scuba diver in the sea of words. Now I zip along the surface like a guy on a Jet Ski. ❶

Thanks to the ubiquity of text on the Internet, not to mention the popularity of text-messaging on cell phones, we may be reading more today than we did in the 1970s and 1980s.... But it's a different kind of reading, and behind it lies a different kind of thinking—perhaps even a new sense of self.

Reading ... is not an instinctive skill.... We have to teach our mind how to translate the ... characters we see ... the media or other technologies we use in learning.... [R]eading plays an important part in shaping the ... circuits inside our brain. ❷

Maybe I'm just a worrywart. Just as there's a tendency to glorify technological progress, there's a countertendency to expect the worst of every new tool.... Socrates bemoaned the development of writing. He feared that, as people came to rely on the written word ... they would "cease to exercise their memory and become forgetful" and would be "filled with the conceit of wisdom instead of real wisdom."

... [Y]ou should be skeptical of my skepticism.... Perhaps ... [from] the Internet ... will spring a golden age of intellectual discovery and universal wisdom. Then again the Net isn't the alphabet, and although it may replace the printing press, it produces something altogether different. ❸

... [A]s we come to rely on computers to mediate our understanding of the world, it is our own intelligence that flattens into artificial intelligence.

Source: Nicholas Carr, "Is Google Making Us Stupid?" The Atlantic (July/August 2008). Copyright © 2008 by Nicholas Carr. Reprinted with permission of the author.

821

Study Tools

SUMMARY

During the past three decades, the changing economy has shaped many of the nation's political and social issues. It contributed to Clinton's 1992 and Obama's 2008 presidential victories. President Clinton placed the nation on a firm financial footing, balanced the budget, and reduced the national debt. The 2000 presidential election between Gore and Bush was very close and was decided only when the Supreme Court awarded Florida's electoral votes to Bush. President Bush began by implementing a tax cut, but the events of September 11, 2001, when terrorists affiliated with al Qaeda attacked the United States, eclipsed other issues. As the nation rallied around the administration, it established a Department of Homeland Security, and the United States joined forces with others in a war in Afghanistan that brought down the Taliban government and destroyed much of al Qaeda's organization.

In 2003, the Bush administration shifted its attention to Iraq. Claiming that Saddam Hussein possessed weapons of mass destruction and was linked to al Qaeda, the United States led an invasion in March that toppled the Iraqi government. However, as the U.S. occupation of Iraq dragged on and American casualties increased, a growing number of Americans came to oppose Bush's conduct of the war. In 2004, Kerry used the war issue to mobilize his unsuccessful presidential campaign to defeat Bush. Bush won reelection in 2004, but by 2006, amid increasing public frustration over the war in Iraq and Bush's response to the damage caused by Hurricane Katrina, Democrats managed to regain a majority in Congress.

CHRONOLOGY
A New Century with New Challenges

1992	Bill Clinton elected president
1993	Congress ratifies North American Free Trade Agreement
1994	U.S. troops sent to Haiti "Contract with America"
1995	Dayton Agreement
1996	Welfare reform passed Clinton reelected
1998	Terrorists attack U.S. embassies in Kenya and Tanzania
1999	NATO bombs Serbia over Kosovo crisis Effort to impeach Clinton fails
2000	George W. Bush elected president
2001	Terrorists associated with Al Qaeda attack World Trade towers and Pentagon Department of Homeland Security established U.S. launches operations in Afghanistan USA Patriot Act
2002	Taliban regime in Afghanistan collapses; replaced by interim government
2003	U.S. invades Iraq, removes Saddam Hussein regime Massachusetts Supreme Court permits same-sex marriage
2004	George W. Bush reelected
2005	Hurricane Katrina strikes Gulf Coast
2006	Democrats regain majorities in Congress
2007	Nancy Pelosi becomes first woman Speaker of the House of Representatives
2008	Congress passes the Troubled Asset Relief Program Barack H. Obama elected
2009	Congress passes economic stimulus bill. Congress approves financial aid package for American automobile manufacturers General Motors and Chrysler
2010	Congress passes a national healthcare bill Strategic Arms Limitation Treaty signed Ecological disaster caused by the *Deepwater Horizon* oil drilling platform in Gulf of Mexico Congress passes Wall Street financial regulation bill
2011	Arab Spring: Tunisian, Egyptian, Libyan governments toppled; Syrian civil war Osama bin Laden killed Don't Ask, Don't Tell repealed Budget Control Act Last American troops leave Iraq
2012	Affordable Care Act upheld by Supreme Court Obama reelected American Taxpayer Relief Act
2013	Automatic spending cuts implemented Supreme Court declares the federal Defense of Marriage Act unconstitutional; nullifies part of the 1965 Voting Rights Act.

Study Tools

In the 2008 presidential race, John McCain faced off against Barack Obama. Beset by an economic crisis, more Americans believed Obama would be better at fixing the economy than McCain and elected the first African American president.

In office, Obama advanced an ambitious agenda to fix the economy, create a national healthcare system, defeat al Qaeda, and end the American presence in Iraq. Republicans vowed to oppose his programs, arguing that they were too expensive and expanded the size and power of the federal government. The ensuing acidic debates led to a newly energized conservative movement, the Tea Party.

The 2010 Congressional elections were a disaster for Democrats, who lost control of the House of Representatives. Political gridlock followed as the White House and Republicans faced off on economic policies with neither side willing to compromise. Republicans nominated Mitt Romney for president in 2012. Romney centered his campaign on his business expertise and ability to fix the economy. As the election neared, the economy was slowly improving and much of the political debate highlighted social issues that favored Democrats and Obama. Obama won the election, but Republicans still controlled a majority in the House, continuing the formula for gridlock as Obama began his second term.

FOCUS QUESTIONS

If you have mastered this chapter, you should be able to answer these questions and to explain the terms that follow the questions.

1. In what ways did President Clinton's centrist agenda and personal behavior shape his presidency?

2. How did the Contract with America represent a conservative critique of liberalism and Democratic policies?

3. What actions did Clinton take to expand trade and support global stability?

4. What changes were taking place in the American economy as the country headed toward the twenty-first century?

5. How did economic changes shape society and politics?

6. What issues contributed to Bush's election and why was the election so controversial?

7. How did Bush's domestic and foreign policy agenda differ from those of the Clinton years?

8. How did the events of September 11, 2001, affect the public and change Bush's foreign policy?

9. What considerations and events led to the United States' invasion of Iraq?

10. How did the war in Iraq shape the issues Republicans wanted to highlight in the presidential elections of 2004?

11. What major issues contributed to Barack Obama's election in 2008, and what constraints did he face in implementing his policies?

12. In what ways were Obama's goals different from the Bush administration's, and what events led to the formation of the Tea Party?

13. How did political gridlock shape the debate over economic policy, and what major issues contributed to Barack Obama's reelection in 2012?

KEY TERMS

Family and Medical Leave Act   p. 795

North American Free Trade Agreement   p. 795

General Agreement on Tariffs and Trade   p. 795

Contract with America   p. 796

World Trade Organization   p. 797

Dayton Agreement   p. 798

glass ceiling   p. 801

Defense of Marriage Act   p. 801

judicial restraint   p. 802

USA Patriot Act   p. 805

al Qaeda   p. 805

Taliban   p. 805

preemptive strike   p. 806

Hurricane Katrina   p. 810

subprime loans   p. 811

Troubled Asset Relief Program   p. 812

Strategic Arms Limitation Treaty   p. 813

Arab Spring   p. 813

American Recovery and Reinvestment Act   p. 815

Patient Protection and Affordable Care Act   p. 817

Tea Party movement   p. 817

Study Tools

SUGGESTED RESOURCES

Peter Baldwin. *Disease and Democracy: The Industrial World Faces AIDS* (University of California Press, 2005). A compelling, readable, and useful look at the spread of the disease and how Western nations have responded to the AIDS epidemic.

James MacGregor Burns and George J. Sorenson. *Dead Center: Clinton-Gore Leadership and the Perils of Moderation* (Scribner, 1999). A readable account of the politics of the Clinton revival of the Democratic Party and his administration.

Michael Gordon and Bernard Trainor. *Endgame: The Inside Story of the Struggle for Iraq from George W. Bush to Barack Obama* (Pantheon, 2012). Written from a military perspective, it provides an account of the Iraq war that examines the decisions of those in power and the lives of those doing the actual fighting.

Michael Lewis. *The Big Short* (W. W. Norton and Company, 2010). A well-written and perceptive view of the short-and long-term origins of the Great Recession.

Documents

Declaration of Independence in Congress, July 4, 1776

When, in the course of human events, it becomes necessary for one people to dissolve the political bonds which have connected them with another, and to assume, among the powers of the earth, the separate and equal station to which the laws of nature and of nature's God entitle them, a decent respect to the opinions of mankind requires that they should declare the causes which impel them to the separation.

We hold these truths to be self-evident: That all men are created equal; that they are endowed by their Creator with certain unalienable rights; that among these are life, liberty, and the pursuit of happiness; that, to secure these rights, governments are instituted among men, deriving their just powers from the consent of the governed; that whenever any form of government becomes destructive of these ends, it is the right of the people to alter or to abolish it, and to institute new government, laying its foundation on such principles, and organizing its powers in such form, as to them shall seem most likely to effect their safety and happiness. Prudence, indeed, will dictate that governments long established should not be changed for light and transient causes; and accordingly all experience hath shown that mankind are more disposed to suffer, while evils are sufferable, than to right themselves by abolishing the forms to which they are accustomed. But when a long train of abuses and usurpations, pursuing invariably the same object, evinces a design to reduce them under absolute despotism, it is their right, it is their duty, to throw off such government, and to provide new guards for their future security. Such has been the patient sufferance of these colonies; and such is now the necessity which constrains them to alter their former systems of government. The history of the present King of Great Britain is a history of repeated injuries and usurpations, all having in direct object the establishment of an absolute tyranny over these states. To prove this, let facts be submitted to a candid world.

He has refused his assent to laws, the most wholesome and necessary for the public good.

He has forbidden his governors to pass laws of immediate and pressing importance, unless suspended in their operation till his assent should be obtained; and, when so suspended, he has utterly neglected to attend to them.

He has refused to pass other laws for the accommodation of large districts of people, unless those people would relinquish the right of representation in the legislature, a right inestimable to them, and formidable to tyrants only.

He has called together legislative bodies at places unusual, uncomfortable, and distant from the depository of their public records, for the sole purpose of fatiguing them into compliance with his measures.

He has dissolved representative houses repeatedly, for opposing, with manly firmness, his invasions on the rights of the people.

He has refused for a long time, after such dissolutions, to cause others to be elected; whereby the legislative powers, incapable of annihilation, have returned to the people at large for their exercise; the state remaining, in the mean time, exposed to all the dangers of invasions from without and convulsions within.

He has endeavored to prevent the population of these states; for that purpose obstructing the laws for naturalization of foreigners; refusing to pass others to encourage their migration hither, and raising the conditions of new appropriations of lands.

He has obstructed the administration of justice, by refusing his assent to laws for establishing judiciary powers.

He has made judges dependent on his will alone, for the tenure of their offices, and the amount and payment of their salaries.

He has erected a multitude of new offices, and sent hither swarms of officers to harass our people and eat out their substance.

He has kept among us, in times of peace, standing armies, without the consent of our legislatures.

He has affected to render the military independent of, and superior to, the civil power.

He has combined with others to subject us to a jurisdiction foreign to our constitution, and unacknowledged by our laws, giving his assent to their acts of pretended legislation:

For quartering large bodies of armed troops among us;

For protecting them, by a mock trial, from punishment for any murders which they should commit on the inhabitants of these states;

For cutting off our trade with all parts of the world;

For imposing taxes on us without our consent;

For depriving us, in many cases, of the benefits of trial by jury;

For transporting us beyond seas, to be tried for pretended offenses;

For abolishing the free system of English laws in a neighboring province, establishing therein an arbitrary government, and enlarging its boundaries, so as to render it at once an example and fit instrument for introducing the same absolute rule into these colonies;

For taking away our charters, abolishing our most valuable laws, and altering fundamentally the forms of our governments;

For suspending our own legislatures, and declaring themselves invested with power to legislate for us in all cases whatsoever.

He has abdicated government here, by declaring us out of his protection and waging war against us.

He has plundered our seas, ravaged our coasts, burned our towns, and destroyed the lives of our people.

He is at this time transporting large armies of foreign mercenaries to complete the works of death, desolation, and tyranny already begun with circumstances of cruelty and perfidy scarcely paralleled in the most barbarous ages, and totally unworthy the head of a civilized nation.

He has constrained our fellow-citizens, taken captive on the high seas, to bear arms against their country, to become the executioners of their friends and brethren, or to fall themselves by their hands.

He has excited domestic insurrection among us, and has endeavored to bring on the inhabitants of our frontiers the merciless Indian savages, whose known rule of warfare is an undistinguished destruction of all ages, sexes, and conditions.

In every stage of these oppressions we have petitioned for redress in the most humble terms; our repeated petitions have been answered only by repeated injury. A prince, whose character is thus marked by every act which may define a tyrant, is unfit to be the ruler of a free people.

Nor have we been wanting in our attentions to our British brethren. We have warned them, from time to time, of attempts by their legislature to extend an unwarrantable jurisdiction over us. We have reminded them of the circumstances of our emigration and settlement here. We have appealed to their native justice and magnanimity; and we have conjured them, by the ties of our common kindred, to disavow these usurpations, which would inevitably interrupt our connections and correspondence. They, too, have been deaf to the voice of justice and of consanguinity. We must, therefore, acquiesce in the necessity which denounces our separation, and hold them, as we hold the rest of mankind, enemies in war, in peace friends.

We, therefore, the representatives of the United States of America, in General Congress assembled, appealing to the Supreme Judge of the world for the rectitude of our intentions, do, in the name and by the authority of the good people of these colonies, solemnly publish and declare, that these United Colonies are, and of right ought to be, FREE AND INDEPENDENT STATES; that they are absolved from all allegiance to the British crown, and that all political connection between them and the state of Great Britain is, and ought to be, totally dissolved; and that, as free and independent states, they have full power to levy war, conclude peace, contract alliances, establish commerce, and do all other acts and things which independent states may of right do. And for the support of this declaration, with a firm reliance on the protection of Divine Providence, we mutually pledge to each other our lives, our fortunes, and our sacred honor.

JOHN HANCOCK
and fifty-five others

Articles of Confederation

Whereas the Delegates of the United States of America in Congress assembled did on the fifteenth day of November in the Year of our Lord One Thousand Seven Hundred and Seventy seven, and in the Second Year of the Independence of America agree to certain articles of Confederation and perpetual Union between the States of Newhampshire, Massachusetts-bay, Rhodeisland and Providence Plantations, Connecticut, New-York, New-Jersey, Pennsylvania, Delaware, Maryland, Virginia, North-Carolina, South-Carolina and Georgia in the Words following, viz. "Articles of Confederation and perpetual Union between the states of Newhampshire, Massachusetts-bay, Rhodeisland and Providence Plantations, Connecticut, New-York, New-Jersey, Pennsylvania, Delaware, Maryland, Virginia, North-Carolina, South-Carolina and Georgia.

Article I The Stile of this confederacy shall be "The United States of America."

Article II Each state retains its sovereignty, freedom and independence, and every Power, Jurisdiction and right, which is not by this confederation expressly delegated to the United States, in Congress assembled.

Article III The said states hereby severally enter into a firm league of friendship with each other, for their common defence, the security of their Liberties, and their mutual and general welfare, binding themselves to assist each other, against all force offered to, or attacks made upon them, or any of them, on account of religion, sovereignty, trade, or any other pretence whatever.

Article IV The better to secure and perpetuate mutual friendship and intercourse among the people of the different states in this union, the free inhabitants of each of these states, paupers, vagabonds and fugitives from Justice excepted, shall be entitled to all privileges and immunities of free citizens in the several states; and the people of each state shall have free ingress and regress to and from any other state, and shall enjoy therein all the privileges of trade and commerce, subject to the same duties, impositions and restrictions as the inhabitants thereof respectively, provided that such restriction shall not extend so far as to prevent the removal of property imported into any state, to any other state of which the Owner is an inhabitant; provided also that no imposition, duties or restriction shall be laid by any state, on the property of the united states, or either of them.

If any Person guilty of, or charged with treason, felony, or other high misdemeanor in any state, shall flee from Justice, and be found in any of the united states, he shall upon demand of the Governor or executive power, of the state from which he fled, be delivered up and removed to the state having jurisdiction of his offence.

Full faith and credit shall be given in each of these states to the records, acts and judicial proceedings of the courts and magistrates of every other state.

Article V For the more convenient management of the general interests of the united states, delegates shall be annually appointed in such manner as the legislature of each state shall direct, to meet in Congress on the first Monday in November, in every year, with a power reserved to each state, to recall its delegates, or any of them, at any time within the year, and to send others in their stead, for the remainder of the Year.

No state shall be represented in Congress by less than two, nor by more than seven Members; and no person shall be capable of being a delegate for more than three years in any term of six years; nor shall any person, being a delegate, be capable of holding any office under the united states, for which he, or another for his benefit receives any salary, fees or emolument of any kind.

Each state shall maintain its own delegates in a meeting of the states, and while they act as members of the committee of the states.

In determining questions in the united states, in Congress assembled, each state shall have one vote.

Freedom of speech and debate in Congress shall not be impeached or questioned in any Court, or place out of Congress, and the members of congress shall be protected in their persons from arrests and imprisonments, during the time of their going to and from, and attendance on congress, except for treason, felony, or breach of the peace.

Article VI No state without the Consent of the united states in congress assembled, shall send any embassy to, or receive any embassy from, or enter into any conference, agreement, or alliance or treaty with any King, prince or state; nor shall any person holding any office of profit or trust under the united states, or any of them, accept of any present, emolument, office or title of any kind whatever from any king, prince or foreign state; nor shall the united states in congress assembled, or any of them, grant any title of nobility.

No two or more states shall enter into any treaty, confederation or alliance whatever between them, without the consent of the united states in congress assembled, specifying accurately the purposes for which the same is to be entered into, and how long it shall continue.

No state shall lay any imposts or duties, which may interfere with any stipulations in treaties, entered into by the united states in congress assembled, with any king, prince or state, in pursuance of any treaties already proposed by congress, to the courts of France and Spain.

No vessels of war shall be kept up in time of peace by any state, except such number only, as shall be deemed necessary by the united states in congress assembled, for the defence of such state, or its trade; nor shall any body of forces be kept up by any state, in time of peace, except such number only, as in the judgment of the united states, in congress assembled, shall be deemed requisite to garrison the forts necessary for the defence of such state; but every state shall always keep up a well regulated and disciplined militia, sufficiently armed and accoutred, and shall provide and constantly have ready for use, in public stores, a due number of field pieces and tents, and a proper quantity of arms, ammunition and camp equipage.

No state shall engage in any war without the consent of the united states in congress assembled, unless such state be actually invaded by enemies, or shall have received certain advice of a resolution being formed by some nation of Indians to invade such state, and the danger is so imminent as not to admit of a delay, till the united states in congress assembled can be consulted: nor shall any state grant commissions to any ships or vessels of war, nor letters of marque or reprisal, except it be after a declaration of war by the united states in congress assembled, and then only against the kingdom or state and the subjects thereof, against which war has been so declared, and under such regulations as shall be established by the united states in congress assembled, unless such state be infested by pirates, in which case vessels of war may be fitted out for that occasion, and kept so long as the danger shall continue, or until the united states in congress assembled shall determine otherwise.

Article VII When land-forces are raised by any state for the common defence, all officers of or under the rank of colonel, shall be appointed by the legislature of each state respectively by whom such forces shall be raised, or in such manner as such state shall direct, and all vacancies shall be filled up by the state which first made the appointment.

Article VIII All charges of war, and all other expences that shall be incurred for the common defence or general welfare, and allowed by the united states in congress assembled, shall be defrayed out of a common treasury, which shall be supplied by the several states, in proportion to the value of all land within each state, granted to or surveyed for any Person, as such land and the buildings and improvements thereon shall be estimated according to such mode as the united states in congress assembled, shall from time to time direct and appoint. The taxes for paying that proportion shall be laid and levied by the authority and direction of the legislatures of the several states within the time agreed upon by the united states in congress assembled.

Article IX The united states in congress assembled, shall have the sole and exclusive right and power of determining on peace and war, except in the cases mentioned in the sixth article—of sending and receiving ambassadors—entering into treaties and alliances, provided that no treaty of commerce shall be made whereby the legislative power of the respective states shall be restrained from imposing such imposts and duties on foreigners, as their own people are subjected to, or from prohibiting the exportation or importation of any species of goods or commodities whatsoever— of establishing rules for deciding in all cases, what captures on land or water shall be legal, and in what manner prizes taken by land or naval forces in the service of the united states shall be divided or appropriated.— of granting letters of marque and reprisal in times of peace—appointing courts for the trial of piracies and felonies committed on the high seas and establishing courts for receiving and determining finally appeals in all cases of captures, provided that no member of congress shall be appointed a judge of any of the said courts.

The united states in congress assembled shall also be the last resort on appeal in all disputes and differences now subsisting or that hereafter may arise between two or more states concerning boundary, jurisdiction or any other cause whatever; which authority shall always be exercised in the manner following. Whenever the legislative or executive authority or lawful agent of any state in controversy with another shall present a petition to congress, stating the matter in question and praying for a hearing, notice thereof shall be given by order of congress to the legislative or executive authority of the other state in controversy, and a day assigned for the appearance of the parties by their lawful agents, who shall then be directed to appoint by joint consent, commissioners or judges to constitute a court for hearing and determining the matter in question: but if they cannot agree, congress shall name three persons out of each of the united states, and from the list of such persons each party shall alternately strike out one, the petitioners beginning, until the number shall be reduced to thirteen; and from that number not less than seven, nor more than nine names as congress shall direct, shall in the presence of congress be drawn out by lot, and the persons whose names shall be so drawn or any five of them, shall be commissioners or judges, to hear and finally determine the controversy, so always as a major part of the judges who shall hear the cause shall agree in the determination: and if either party shall neglect to attend at the day appointed, without shewing reasons, which congress shall judge sufficient, or being present shall refuse to strike, the congress shall proceed to nominate three persons out of each state, and the secretary of congress shall strike in behalf of such party absent or refusing; and the judgment and sentence of the court to be appointed, in the manner before prescribed, shall be final and conclusive; and if any of the parties shall refuse to submit to the authority of such court, or to appear to defend their claim or cause, the court shall nevertheless proceed to pronounce sentence, or judgment, which shall in like manner be final and decisive, the judgment or sentence and other proceedings being in either case transmitted to congress, and lodged among the acts of congress for the security of the parties concerned: provided that every commissioner, before he sits in judgment, shall take an oath to be administered by one of the judges of the supreme or superior court of the state, where the cause shall be tried, "well and truly to hear and determine the matter in question, according to the best of his judgment, without favour, affection or hope of reward:" provided also that no state shall be deprived of territory for the benefit of the united states.

All controversies concerning the private right of soil claimed under different grants of two or more states, whose jurisdictions as they may respect such lands, and the states which passed such grants are adjusted, the said grants or either of them being at the same time claimed to have originated antecedent to such settlement of jurisdiction, shall on the petition of either party to the congress of the united states, be finally determined as near as may be in the same manner as is before prescribed for deciding disputes respecting territorial jurisdiction between different states.

The united states in congress assembled shall also have the sole and exclusive right and power of regulating the alloy and value of coin struck by their own authority, or by that of the respective states—fixing the standard of weights and measures throughout the united states.—regulating the trade and managing all affairs with the Indians, not members of any of the states, provided that the legislative right of any state within its own limits be not infringed or violated—establishing and regulating post-offices from one state to another, throughout all the united states, and exacting such postage on the papers passing thro' the same as may be requisite to defray the expences of the said office—appointing all officers of the land forces, in the service of the united states, excepting regimental officers.—appointing all the officers of the naval forces, and commissioning all officers whatever in the service of the united states—making rules for the government and regulation of the said land and naval forces, and directing their operations.

The united states in congress assembled shall have authority to appoint a committee, to sit in the recess of congress, to be denominated "A Committee of the States," and to consist of one delegate from each state; and to appoint such other committees and civil officers as may be necessary for managing the general affairs of the united states under their direction—to appoint one of their number to preside, provided that no person be allowed to serve in the office of president more than one year in any term of three years; to ascertain the necessary sums of Money to be raised for the service of the united states, and to appropriate and apply the same for defraying the public expences—to borrow money, or emit bills on the credit of the united states, transmitting every half year to the respective states an account of the sums of money so borrowed or emitted,—to build and equip a navy—to agree upon the number of land forces, and to make requisitions from each state for its quota, in proportion to the number of white inhabitants in such state; which requisition shall be binding, and thereupon the legislature of each state shall appoint the regimental officers, raise the men and cloath, arm and equip them in a soldier like manner, at the expence of the united states, and the officers and men so cloathed, armed and equipped shall march to the place appointed, and within the time agreed on by the united states in congress assembled: But if the united states in congress assembled shall, on consideration of circumstances judge proper that any state should not raise men, or should raise a smaller number than its quota, and that any other state should raise a greater number of men than the quota thereof, such extra number shall be raised, officered, cloathed, armed and equipped in the same manner as the quota of such state, unless the legislature of such state shall judge that such extra number cannot be safely spared out of the same, in which case they shall raise, officer, cloath, arm and equip as many of such extra number as they judge can be safely spared. And the officers and men so cloathed, armed and equipped, shall march to the place appointed, and within the time agreed on by the united states in congress assembled.

The united states in congress assembled shall never engage in a war, nor grant letters of marque and reprisal in time of peace, nor enter into any treaties or alliances, nor coin money, nor regulate the value thereof, nor ascertain the sums and expences necessary for the defence and welfare of the united states, or any of them, nor emit bills, nor borrow money on the credit of the united states, nor appropriate money, nor agree upon the number of vessels of war, to be built or purchased, or the number of land or sea forces to be raised, nor appoint a commander in chief of the army or navy, unless nine states assent to the same: nor shall a question on any other point, except for adjourning from day to day be determined, unless by the votes of a majority of the united states in congress assembled.

The congress of the united states shall have power to adjourn to any time within the year, and to any place within the united states, so that no period of adjournment be for a longer duration than the space of six Months, and shall publish the Journal of their proceedings monthly, except such parts thereof relating to treaties, alliances or military operations as in their judgment require secresy; and the yeas and nays of the delegates of each state on any question shall be entered on the Journal, when it is desired by any delegate; and the delegates of a state, or any of them, at his or their request shall be furnished with a transcript of the said Journal, except such parts as are above excepted, to lay before the legislatures of the several states.

Article X The committee of the states, or any nine of them, shall be authorised to execute, in the recess of congress, such of the powers of congress as the united states in congress assembled, by the consent of nine states, shall from time to time think expedient to vest them with; provided that no power be delegated to the said committee, for the exercise of which, by the articles of confederation, the voice of nine states in the congress of the united states assembled is requisite.

Article XI Canada acceding to this confederation, and joining in the measures of the united states, shall be admitted into, and entitled to all the advantages of this union: but no other colony shall be admitted into the same, unless such admission be agreed to by nine states.

Article XII All bills of credit emitted, monies borrowed and debts contracted by, or under the authority of congress, before the assembling of the united states, in pursuance of the present confederation, shall be deemed and considered as a charge against the united states, for payment and satisfaction whereof the said united states, and the public faith are hereby solemnly pledged.

Article XIII Every state shall abide by the determinations of the united states in congress assembled, on all questions which by this confederation are submitted to them. And the Articles of this confederation shall be inviolably observed by every state, and the union shall be perpetual; nor shall any alteration at any time hereafter be made in any of them; unless such alteration be agreed to in a congress of the united states, and be afterwards confirmed by the legislatures of every state.

AND WHEREAS it hath pleased the Great Governor of the World to incline the hearts of the legislatures we respectively represent in congress, to approve of, and to authorize us to ratify the said articles of confederation and perpetual union. Know Ye that we the undersigned delegates, by virtue of the power and authority to us given for that purpose, do by these presents, in the name and in behalf of our respective constituents, fully and entirely ratify and confirm each and every of the said articles of confederation and perpetual union, and all and singular the matters and things therein contained: And we do further solemnly plight and engage the faith of our respective constitutents, that they shall abide by the determinations of the united states in congress assembled, on all questions, which by the said confederation are submitted to them. And that the articles thereof shall be inviolably observed by the states we respectively represent, and that the union shall be perpetual. In Witness whereof we have hereunto set our hands in Congress. Done at Philadelphia in the state of Pennsylvania the ninth Day of July in the Year of our Lord one Thousand seven Hundred and Seventy-eight, and in the third year of the independence of America.

Constitution of the United States of America and Amendments*

Preamble

We the people of the United States, in order to form a more perfect union, establish justice, insure domestic tranquillity, provide for the common defense, promote the general welfare, and secure the blessings of liberty to ourselves and our posterity, do ordain and establish this Constitution for the United States of America.

Article I

Section 1 All legislative powers herein granted shall be vested in a Congress of the United States, which shall consist of a Senate and a House of Representatives.

Section 2 The House of Representatives shall be composed of members chosen every second year by the people of the several States, and the electors in each State shall have the qualifications requisite for electors of the most numerous branch of the State Legislature.

No person shall be a Representative who shall not have attained to the age of twenty-five years, and been seven years a citizen of the United States, and who shall not, when elected, be an inhabitant of that State in which he shall be chosen.

Representatives and direct taxes shall be apportioned among the several States which may be included within this Union, according to their respective numbers, *which shall be determined by adding to the whole number of free persons, including those bound to service for a term of years and excluding Indians not taxed, three-fifths of all other persons.* The actual enumeration shall be made within three years after the first meeting of the Congress of the United States, and within every subsequent term of ten years, in such manner as they shall by law direct. The number of Representatives shall not exceed one for every thirty thousand, but each State shall have at least one Representative; *and until such enumeration shall be made, the State of New Hampshire shall be entitled to choose three, Massachusetts eight, Rhode Island and Providence Plantations one, Connecticut five, New York six, New Jersey four, Pennsylvania eight, Delaware one, Maryland six, Virginia ten, North Carolina five, South Carolina five, and Georgia three.*

When vacancies happen in the representation from any State, the Executive authority thereof shall issue writs of election to fill such vacancies.

The House of Representatives shall choose their Speaker and other officers; and shall have the sole power of impeachment.

Section 3 The Senate of the United States shall be composed of two Senators from each State, *chosen by the legislature thereof,* for six years; and each Senator shall have one vote.

Immediately after they shall be assembled in consequence of the first election, they shall be divided as equally as may be into three classes. The seats of the Senators of the first class shall be vacated at the expiration of the second year, of the second class at the expiration of the fourth year, and of the third class at the expiration of the sixth year, so that one-third may be chosen every second year; *and if vacancies happen by resignation or otherwise, during the recess of the legislature of any State, the Executive thereof may make temporary appointments until the next meeting of the legislature, which shall then fill such vacancies.*

No person shall be a Senator who shall not have attained to the age of thirty years, and been nine years a citizen of the United States, and who shall not, when elected, be an inhabitant of that State for which he shall be chosen.

The Vice-President of the United States shall be President of the Senate, but shall have no vote, unless they be equally divided.

The Senate shall choose their other officers, and also a President *pro tempore,* in the absence of the Vice-President, or when he shall exercise the office of President of the United States.

The Senate shall have the sole power to try all impeachments. When sitting for that purpose, they shall be on oath or affirmation. When the President of the United States is tried, the Chief Justice shall preside: and no person shall be convicted with-out the concurrence of two thirds of the members present.

Judgment in cases of impeachment shall not extend further than to removal from the office, and disqualification to hold and enjoy any office of honor, trust or profit under the United States: but the party convicted shall nevertheless be liable and subject to indictment, trial, judgment and punishment, according to law.

Section 4 The times, places and manner of holding elections for Senators and Representatives shall be prescribed in each State by the legislature thereof; but the Congress may at any time by law make or alter such regulations, except as to the places of choosing Senators.

The Congress shall assemble at least once in every year, and such meeting *shall be on the first Monday in December, unless they shall by law appoint a different day.*

Section 5 Each house shall be the judge of the elections, returns and qualifications of its own members, and a majority of each shall constitute a quorum to do business; but a smaller number may adjourn from day to day, and may be authorized to compel the attendance of absent members, in such manner, and under such penalties, as each house may provide.

Each house may determine the rules of its proceedings, punish its members for disorderly behavior, and with the concurrence of two-thirds, expel a member. Each house shall keep a journal of its proceedings, and

---

* Passages no longer in effect are printed in italic type.

from time to time publish the same, excepting such parts as may in their judgment require secrecy; and the yeas and nays of the members of either house on any question shall, at the desire of one-fifth of those present, be entered on the journal.

Neither house, during the session of Congress, shall, without the consent of the other, adjourn for more than three days, nor to any other place than that in which the two houses shall be sitting.

Section 6 The Senators and Representatives shall receive a compensation for their services, to be ascertained by law and paid out of the treasury of the United States. They shall in all cases except treason, felony and breach of the peace, be privileged from arrest during their attendance at the session of their respective houses, and in going to and returning from the same; and for any speech or debate in either house, they shall not be questioned in any other place.

No Senator or Representative shall, during the time for which he was elected, be appointed to any civil office under the authority of the United States, which shall have been created, or the emoluments whereof shall have been increased, during such time; and no person holding any office under the United States shall be a member of either house during his continuance in office.

Section 7 All bills for raising revenue shall originate in the House of Representatives; but the Senate may propose or concur with amendments as on other bills.

Every bill which shall have passed the House of Representatives and the Senate, shall, before it become a law, be presented to the President of the United States; if he approve he shall sign it, but if not he shall return it with objections to that house in which it originated, who shall enter the objections at large on their journal, and proceed to reconsider it. If after such reconsideration two-thirds of that house shall agree to pass the bill, it shall be sent, together with the objections, to the other house, by which it shall likewise be reconsidered, and, if approved by two-thirds of that house, it shall become a law. But in all such cases the votes of both houses shall be determined by yeas and nays, and the names of the persons voting for and against the bill shall be entered on the journal of each house respectively. If any bill shall not be returned by the President within ten days (Sundays excepted) after it shall have been presented to him, the same shall be a law, in like manner as if he had signed it, unless the Congress by their adjournment prevent its return, in which case it shall not be a law.

Every order, resolution, or vote to which the concurrence of the Senate and House of Representatives may be necessary (except on a question of adjournment) shall be presented to the President of the United States; and before the same shall take effect, shall be approved by him, or being disapproved by him, shall be repassed by two-thirds of the Senate and House of Representatives, according to the rules and limitations prescribed in the case of a bill.

Section 8 The Congress shall have power

To lay and collect taxes, duties, imposts, and excises, to pay the debts and provide for the common defense and general welfare of the United States; but all duties, imposts and excises shall be uniform throughout the United States;

To borrow money on the credit of the United States;

To regulate commerce with foreign nations, and among the several States, and with the Indian tribes;

To establish an uniform rule of naturalization, and uniform laws on the subject of bankruptcies throughout the United States;

To coin money, regulate the value thereof, and of foreign coin, and fix the standard of weights and measures;

To provide for the punishment of counterfeiting the securities and current coin of the United States;

To establish post offices and post roads;

To promote the progress of science and useful arts by securing for limited times to authors and inventors the exclusive right to their respective writings and discoveries;

To constitute tribunals inferior to the Supreme Court;

To define and punish piracies and felonies committed on the high seas and offenses against the law of nations;

To declare war, grant letters of marque and reprisal, and make rules concerning captures on land and water;

To raise and support armies, but no appropriation of money to that use shall be for a longer term than two years;

To provide and maintain a navy;

To make rules for the government and regulation of the land and naval forces;

To provide for calling forth the militia to execute the laws of the Union, suppress insurrections, and repel invasions;

To provide for organizing, arming, and disciplining the militia, and for governing such part of them as may be employed in the service of the United States, reserving to the States respectively the appointment of the officers, and the authority of training the militia according to the discipline prescribed by Congress;

To exercise exclusive legislation in all cases whatsoever, over such district (not exceeding ten miles square) as may, by cession of particular States, and the acceptance of Congress, become the seat of government of the United States, and to exercise like authority over all places purchased by the consent of the legislature of the State, in which the same shall be, for erection of forts, magazines, arsenals, dockyards, and other needful buildings;—and

To make all laws which shall be necessary and proper for carrying into execution the foregoing powers, and all other powers vested by this Constitution in the government of the United States, or in any department or officer there of.

Section 9 The migration or importation of such persons as any of the States now existing shall think proper to admit shall not be prohibited by the Congress prior to the year 1808; but a tax or duty may be imposed on such importation, not exceeding $10 for each person.

The privilege of the writ of habeas corpus shall not be suspended, unless when in cases of rebellion or invasion the public safety may require it.

No bill of attainder or ex post facto law shall be passed.

No capitation, or other direct, tax shall be laid, unless in proportion to the census or enumeration herein before directed to be taken.

No tax or duty shall be laid on articles exported from any State.

No preference shall be given by any regulation of commerce or revenue to the ports of one State over those of another; nor shall vessels bound to, or from, one State, be obliged to enter, clear, or pay duties in another.

No money shall be drawn from the treasury, but in consequence of appropriations made by law; and a regular statement and account of the receipts and expenditures of all public money shall be published from time to time.

No title of nobility shall be granted by the United States: and no person holding any office of profit or trust under them, shall, without the consent of the Congress, accept of any present, emolument, office, or title, of any kind whatever, from any king, prince, or foreign state.

Section 10 No State shall enter into any treaty, alliance, or confederation; grant letters of marque and reprisal; coin money; emit bills of credit; make anything but gold and silver coin a tender in payment of debts; pass any bill of attainder, ex post facto law, or law impairing the obligation of contracts, or grant any title of nobility.

No State shall, without the consent of Congress, lay any imposts or duties on imports or exports, except what may be absolutely necessary for executing its inspection laws: and the net produce of all duties and imposts, laid by any State on imports or exports, shall be for the use of the treasury of the United States; and all such laws shall be subject to the revision and control of the Congress.

No State shall, without the consent of Congress, lay any duty of tonnage, keep troops or ships of war in time of peace, enter into any agreement or compact with another State, or with a foreign power, or engage in war, unless actually invaded, or in such imminent danger as will not admit of delay.

Article II

Section 1 The executive power shall be vested in a President of the United States of America. He shall hold his office during the term of four years, and, together with the Vice-President, chosen for the same term, be elected as follows:

Each State shall appoint, in such manner as the legislature thereof may direct, a number of electors, equal to the whole number of Senators and Representatives to which the State may be entitled in the Congress; but no Senator or Representative, or person holding an office of trust or profit under the United States, shall be appointed an elector.

The electors shall meet in their respective States, and vote by ballot for two persons, of whom one at least shall not be an inhabitant of the same State with themselves. And they shall make a list of all the persons voted for, and of the number of votes for each; which list they shall sign and certify, and transmit sealed to the seat of government of the United States, directed to the President of the Senate. The President of the Senate shall, in the presence of the Senate and House of Representatives, open all the certificates, and the votes shall then be counted. The person having the greatest number of votes shall be the President, if such number be a majority of the whole number of electors appointed; and if there be more than one who have such majority, and have an equal number of votes, then the House of Representatives shall immediately choose by ballot one of them for President; and if no person have a majority, then from the five highest on the list said house shall in like manner choose the President. But in choosing the President the votes shall be taken by States, the representation from each State having one vote; a quorum for this purpose shall consist of a member or members from two-thirds of the States, and a majority of all the States shall be necessary to a choice. In every case, after the choice of the President, the person having the greatest number of votes of the electors shall be the Vice-President. But if there should remain two or more who have equal votes, the Senate shall choose from them by ballot the Vice-President.

The Congress may determine the time of choosing the electors and the day on which they shall give their votes; which day shall be the same throughout the United States.

No person except a natural-born citizen, *or a citizen of the United States at the time of the adoption of this Constitution,* shall be eligible to the office of President; neither shall any person be eligible to that office who shall not have attained to the age of thirty-five years, and been fourteen years a resident within the United States.

In cases of the removal of the President from office or of his death, resignation, or inability to discharge the powers and duties of the said office, the same shall devolve on the Vice-President, and the Congress may by law provide for the case of removal, death, resignation, or inability, both of the President and Vice-President, declaring what officer shall then act as President, and such officer shall act accordingly, until the disability be removed, or a President shall be elected.

The President shall, at stated times, receive for his services a compensation, which shall neither be increased nor diminished during the period for which he shall have been elected, and he shall not receive within that period any other emolument from the United States, or any of them.

Before he enter on the execution of his office, he shall take the following oath or affirmation:—"I do solemnly swear (or affirm) that I will faithfully execute the office of the President of the United States, and will to the best of my ability preserve, protect and defend the Constitution of the United States."

Section 2 The President shall be commander in chief of the army and navy of the United States, and of the militia of the several States, when called into the actual service of the United States; he may require the opinion, in writing, of the principal officer in each of the executive departments, upon any subject relating to the duties of their respective offices, and he shall have power to grant reprieves and pardons for offenses against the United States, except in cases of impeachment.

He shall have power, by and with the advice and consent of the Senate, to make treaties, provided two-thirds of the Senators present concur; and he shall nominate, and by and with the advice and consent of the Senate, shall appoint ambassadors, other public ministers and consuls, judges of the Supreme Court, and all other officers of the United States, whose appointments are not herein otherwise provided for, and which shall be established by law: but Congress may by law vest the appointment of such inferior officers, as they think proper, in the President alone, in the courts of law, or in the heads of departments.

The President shall have power to fill up all vacancies that may happen during the recess of the Senate, by granting commissions which shall expire at the end of their next session.

Section 3 He shall from time to time give to the Congress information of the state of the Union, and recommend to their consideration such measures as he shall judge necessary and expedient; he may, on extraordinary occasions, convene both houses, or either of them, and in case of disagreement between them, with respect to the time of adjournment, he may adjourn them to such time as he shall think proper; he shall receive ambassadors and other public ministers; he shall take care that the laws be faithfully executed, and shall commission all the officers of the United States.

Section 4 The President, Vice-President and all civil officers of the United States shall be removed from office on impeachment for, and on conviction of, treason, bribery, or other high crimes and misdemeanors.

Article III

Section 1 The judicial power of the United States shall be vested in one Supreme Court, and in such inferior courts as the Congress may from time to time ordain and establish. The judges, both of the Supreme and inferior courts, shall hold their offices during good behavior, and shall, at stated times, receive for their services a compensation which shall not be diminished during their continuance in office.

Section 2 The judicial power shall extend to all cases, in law and equity, arising under this Constitution, the laws of the United States, and treaties made, or which shall be made, under their authority;—to all cases affecting ambassadors, other public ministers and consuls;—to all cases of admiralty and maritime jurisdiction;—to controversies to which the United States shall be a party;—to controversies between two or more States;—*between a State and citizens of another State;*—between citizens of different States;—between citizens of the same State claiming lands under grants of different States, and between a State, or the citizens thereof, and foreign states, citizens or subjects.

In all cases affecting ambassadors, other public ministers and consuls, and those in which a State shall be party, the Supreme Court shall have original jurisdiction. In all the other cases before mentioned, the Supreme Court shall have appellate jurisdiction, both as to law and fact, with such exceptions, and under such regulations, as the Congress shall make.

The trial of all crimes, except in cases of impeachment, shall be by jury; and such trial shall be held in the State where said crimes shall have been committed; but when not committed within any State, the trial shall be at such place or places as the Congress may by law have directed.

Section 3 Treason against the United States shall consist only in levying war against them, or in adhering to their enemies, giving them aid and comfort. No person shall be convicted of treason unless on the testimony of two witnesses to the same overt act, or on confession in open court.

The Congress shall have power to declare the punishment of treason, but no attainder of treason shall work corruption of blood, or forfeiture except during the life of the person attainted.

Article IV

Section 1 Full faith and credit shall be given in each State to the public acts, records, and judicial proceedings of every other State. And the Congress may by general laws prescribe the manner in which such acts, records, and proceedings shall be proved, and the effect thereof.

Section 2 The citizens of each State shall be entitled to all privileges and immunities of citizens in the several States.

A person charged in any State with treason, felony, or other crime, who shall flee from justice, and be found in another State, shall on demand of the executive authority of the State from which he fled, be delivered up, to be removed to the State having jurisdiction of the crime.

No person held to service or labor in one State, under the laws thereof, escaping into another, shall, in consequence of any law or regulation therein, be discharged from such service or labor, but shall be delivered up on claim of the party to whom such service or labor may be due.

Section 3 New States may be admitted by the Congress into this Union; but no new State shall be formed or erected within the jurisdiction of any other State; nor any State be formed by the junction of two or more States, or parts of States, without the consent of the legislatures of the States concerned as well as of the Congress.

The Congress shall have power to dispose of and make all needful rules and regulations respecting the territory or other property belonging to the United States; and nothing in this Constitution shall be so construed as to prejudice any claims of the United States, or of any particular State.

Section 4 The United States shall guarantee to every State in this Union a republican form of government, and shall protect each of them against invasion; and on application of the legislature, or of the executive (when the legislature cannot be convened), against domestic violence.

Article V

The Congress, whenever two-thirds of both houses shall deem it necessary, shall propose amendments to this Constitution, or, on the application of the legislatures of two-thirds of the several States, shall call a convention for proposing amendments, which, in either case, shall be valid to all intents and purposes, as part of this Constitution, when ratified by the legislatures of three fourths of the several States, or by conventions in three-fourths thereof, as the one or the other mode of ratification may be proposed by the Congress; provided *that no amendments which may be made prior to the year one thousand eight hundred and eight shall in any manner affect the first and fourth clauses in the ninth section of the first article;* and that no State, without its consent, shall be deprived of its equal suffrage in the Senate.

Article VI

All debts contracted and engagements entered into, before the adoption of this Constitution, shall be as valid against the United States under this Constitution, as under the Confederation.

This Constitution, and the laws of the United States which shall be made in pursuance thereof; and all treaties made, or which shall be made, under the authority of the United States, shall be the supreme law of the land; and the judges in every State shall be bound thereby, anything in the Constitution or laws of any State to the contrary notwithstanding.

The Senators and Representatives before mentioned, and the members of the several State legislatures, and all executive and judicial officers, both of the United States and of the several States, shall be bound by oath or affirmation to support this Constitution; but no religious test shall ever be required as a qualification to any office or public trust under the United States.

Article VII

The ratification of the conventions of nine States shall be sufficient for the establishment of this Constitution between the States so ratifying the same.

Done in Convention by the unanimous consent of the States present, the seventeenth day of September in the year of our Lord one thousand seven hundred and eighty-seven and of the Independence of the United States of America the twelfth. In witness whereof we have hereunto subscribed our names.

GEORGE WASHINGTON
and thirty-seven others

Amendments to the Constitution*

Amendment I

Congress shall make no law respecting an establishment of religion, or prohibiting the free exercise thereof; or abridging the freedom of speech, or of the press; or the right of the people peaceably to assemble, and to petition the government for a redress of grievances.

Amendment II

A well-regulated militia being necessary to the security of a free State, the right of the people to keep and bear arms shall not be infringed.

Amendment III

No soldier shall, in time of peace, be quartered in any house without the consent of the owner, nor in time of war, but in a manner to be prescribed by law.

Amendment IV

The right of the people to be secure in their persons, houses, papers, and effects, against unreasonable searches and seizures, shall not be violated, and no warrants shall issue but upon probable cause, supported by oath or affirmation, and particularly describing the place to be searched, and the persons or things to be seized.

Amendment V

No person shall be held to answer for a capital, or otherwise infamous crime, unless on a presentment or indictment of a grand jury, except in cases arising in the land or naval forces, or in the militia, when in actual service in time of war or public danger; nor shall any person be subject for the same offense to be twice put in jeopardy of life or limb; nor shall be compelled in any criminal case to be a witness against himself, nor be deprived of life, liberty, or property, without due process of law; nor shall private property be taken for public use without just compensation.

---

* The first 10 amendments (the Bill of Rights) were adopted in 1791.

Amendment VI

In all criminal prosecutions, the accused shall enjoy the right to a speedy and public trial, by an impartial jury of the State and district wherein the crime shall have been committed, which district shall have been previously ascertained by law, and to be informed of the nature and cause of the accusation; to be confronted with the witnesses against him; to have compulsory process for obtaining witnesses in his favor, and to have the assistance of counsel for his defense.

Amendment VII

In suits at common law, where the value in controversy shall exceed twenty dollars, the right of trial by jury shall be preserved, and no fact tried by a jury shall be otherwise reexamined in any court of the United States, than according to the rules of the common law.

Amendment VIII

Excessive bail shall not be required, nor excessive fines imposed, nor cruel and unusual punishments inflicted.

Amendment IX

The enumeration in the Constitution, of certain rights, shall not be construed to deny or disparage others retained by the people.

Amendment X

The powers not delegated to the United States by the Constitution, nor prohibited by it to the States, are reserved to the States respectively, or to the people.

Amendment XI

[Adopted 1798]

The judicial power of the United States shall not be construed to extend to any suit in law or equity, commenced or prosecuted against one of the United States by citizens of another State, or by citizens or subjects of any foreign state.

Amendment XII

[Adopted 1804]

The electors shall meet in their respective States, and vote by ballot for President and Vice-President, one of whom, at least, shall not be an inhabitant of the same State with themselves; they shall name in their ballots the person voted for as President, and in distinct ballots the person voted for as Vice-President, and they shall make distinct lists of all persons voted for as President, and of all persons voted for as Vice-President, and of the number of votes for each, which lists they shall sign and certify, and transmit sealed to the seat of government of the United States, directed to the President of the Senate;—the President of the Senate shall, in the presence of the Senate and House of Representatives, open all the certificates and the votes shall then be counted;—the person having the greatest number of votes for President shall be the President, if such number be a majority of the whole number of electors appointed; and if no person have such majority, then from the persons having the highest numbers not exceeding three on the list of those voted for as President, the House of Representatives shall choose immediately, by ballot, the President. But in choosing the President, the votes shall be taken by States, the representation from each State having one vote; a quorum for this purpose shall consist of a member or members from two-thirds of the States, and a majority of all the States shall be necessary to a choice. And if the House of Representatives shall not choose a President whenever the right of choice shall devolve upon them, before the fourth day of March next following, then the Vice-President shall act as President, as in the case of the death or other constitutional disability of the President.

The person having the greatest number of votes as Vice-President shall be the Vice-President, if such number be a majority of the whole number of electors appointed; and if no person have a majority, then from the two highest numbers on the list the Senate shall choose the Vice-President; a quorum for the purpose shall consist of two-thirds of the whole number of Senators, and a majority of the whole number shall be necessary to a choice. But no person constitutionally ineligible to the office of President shall be eligible to that of Vice-President of the United States.

Amendment XIII

[Adopted 1865]

Section 1 Neither slavery nor involuntary servitude, except as a punishment for crime whereof the party shall have been duly convicted, shall exist within the United States, or any place subject to their jurisdiction.

Section 2 Congress shall have power to enforce this article by appropriate legislation.

Amendment XIV

[Adopted 1868]

Section 1 All persons born or naturalized in the United States, and subject to the jurisdiction thereof, are citizens of the United States and of the State wherein they reside. No State shall make or enforce any law which shall abridge the privileges or immunities of citizens of the United States; nor shall any State deprive any person of life, liberty, or property, without due process of law; nor deny to any person within its jurisdiction the equal protection of the laws.

Section 2 Representatives shall be apportioned among the several States according to their respective numbers, counting the whole number of persons in each State, excluding Indians not taxed. But when the right to vote at any election for the choice of Electors for President and Vice-President of the United States, Representatives in Congress, the executive and judicial officers of a State, or the members of the legislature thereof, is denied to any of the male inhabitants of such State, being twenty-one years of age and citizens of the United States, or in any way abridged, except for participation in rebellion, or other crime, the basis of representation therein shall be reduced in the proportion which the number of such male citizens shall bear to the whole number of male citizens twenty-one years of age in such State.

Section 3 No person shall be a Senator or Representative in Congress, or Elector of President and Vice-President, or hold any office, civil or military, under the United States, or under any State, who, having previously taken an oath, as a member of Congress, or as an officer of the United States, or as a member of any State legislature, or as an executive or judicial officer of any State, to support the Constitution of the United States, shall have engaged in insurrection or rebellion against the same, or given aid or comfort to the enemies thereof. Congress may, by a vote of two-thirds of each house, remove such disability.

Section 4 The validity of the public debt of the United States, authorized by law, including debts incurred for payment of pensions and bounties for services in suppressing insurrection or rebellion, shall not be questioned. But neither the United States nor any State shall assume or pay any debt or obligation incurred in aid of insurrection or rebellion against the United States, or any claim for the loss or emancipation of any slave; but all such debts, obligations, and claims shall be held illegal and void.

Section 5 The Congress shall have power to enforce, by appropriate legislation, the provisions of this article.

Amendment XV

[Adopted 1870]

Section 1 The right of citizens of the United States to vote shall not be denied or abridged by the United States or by any State on account of race, color, or previous condition of servitude.

Section 2 The Congress shall have power to enforce this article by appropriate legislation.

Amendment XVI

[Adopted 1913]

The Congress shall have power to lay and collect taxes on incomes, from whatever source derived, without apportionment among the several States, and without regard to any census or enumeration.

Amendment XVII

[Adopted 1913]

Section 1 The Senate of the United States shall be composed of two Senators from each State, elected by the people thereof, for six years; and each Senator shall have one vote. The electors in each State shall have the qualifications requisite for electors of [voters for] the most numerous branch of the State legislatures.

Section 2 When vacancies happen in the representation of any State in the Senate, the executive authority of such State shall issue writs of election to fill such vacancies: Provided, that the Legislature of any State may empower the executive thereof to make temporary appointments until the people fill the vacancies by election as the Legislature may direct.

Section 3 This amendment shall not be so construed as to affect the election or term of any Senator chosen before it becomes valid as part of the Constitution.

Amendment XVIII

[Adopted 1919; Repealed 1933]

Section 1 After one year from the ratification of this article the manufacture, sale, or transportation of intoxicating liquors within, the importation thereof into, or the exportation thereof from the United States and all territory subject to the jurisdiction thereof, for beverage purposes, is hereby prohibited.

Section 2 The Congress and the several States shall have concurrent power to enforce this article by appropriate legislation.

Section 3 This article shall be inoperative unless it shall have been ratified as an amendment to the Constitution by the legislatures of the several States, as provided by the Constitution, within seven years from the date of the submission thereof to the States by the Congress.

Amendment XIX

[Adopted 1920]

Section 1 The right of citizens of the United States to vote shall not be denied or abridged by the United States or by any State on account of sex.

Section 2 The Congress shall have power to enforce this article by appropriate legislation.

Amendment XX

[Adopted 1933]

Section 1 The terms of the President and Vice-President shall end at noon on the 20th day of January, and the terms of Senators and Representatives at noon on the 3rd day of January, of the years in which such terms would have ended if this article had not been ratified; and the terms of their successors shall then begin.

Section 2 The Congress shall assemble at least once in every year, and such meeting shall begin at noon on the 3d day of January, unless they shall by law appoint a different day.

Section 3 If, at the time fixed for the beginning of the term of the President, the President-elect shall have died, the Vice-President-elect shall become President. If a President shall not have been chosen before the time fixed for the beginning of his term, or if the President-elect shall have failed to qualify, then the Vice-President-elect shall act as President until a President shall have qualified; and the Congress may by law provide for the case wherein neither a President-elect nor a Vice-President-elect shall have qualified, declaring who shall then act as President, or the manner in which one who is to act shall be selected, and such persons shall act accordingly until a President or Vice-President shall have qualified.

Section 4 The Congress may by law provide for the case of the death of any of the persons from whom the House of Representatives may choose a President whenever the right of choice shall have devolved upon them, and for the case of the death of any of the persons from whom the Senate may choose a Vice-President whenever the right of choice shall have devolved upon them.

Section 5 Sections 1 and 2 shall take effect on the 15th day of October following the ratification of this article.

Section 6 This article shall be inoperative unless it shall have been ratified as an amendment to the Constitution by the Legislatures of three-fourths of the several States within seven years from the date of its submission.

Amendment XXI

[Adopted 1933]

Section 1 The eighteenth article of amendment to the Constitution of the United States is hereby repealed.

Section 2 The transportation or importation into any State, Territory, or Possession of the United States for delivery or use therein of intoxicating liquors, in violation of the laws thereof, is hereby prohibited.

Section 3 This article shall be inoperative unless it shall have been ratified as an amendment to the Constitution by conventions in the several States, as provided in the Constitution, within seven years from the date of submission thereof to the States by the Congress.

Amendment XXII

[Adopted 1951]

Section 1 No person shall be elected to the office of President more than twice, and no person who has held the office of President, or acted as President, for more than two years of a term to which some other person was elected President shall be elected to the office of President more than once. But this article shall not apply to any person holding the office of President when this article was proposed by the Congress, and shall not prevent any person who may be holding the office of President, or acting as President, during the term within which this article becomes operative from holding the office of President or acting as President during the remainder of such term.

Section 2 This article shall be inoperative unless it shall have been ratified as an amendment to the Constitution by the legislatures of three-fourths of the several States within seven years from the date of its submission to the States by the Congress.

Amendment XXIII

[Adopted 1961]

Section 1 The District constituting the seat of Government of the United States shall appoint in such manner as the Congress may direct:

A number of electors of President and Vice-President equal to the whole number of Senators and Representatives in Congress to which the District would be entitled if it were a State, but in no event more than the least populous State; they shall be in addition to those appointed by the States, but they shall be considered for the purposes of the election of President and Vice-President, to be electors appointed by a State; and they shall meet in the District and perform such duties as provided by the twelfth article of amendment.

Section 2 The Congress shall have the power to enforce this article by appropriate legislation.

Amendment XXIV

[Adopted 1964]

Section 1 The right of citizens of the United States to vote in any primary or other election for President or Vice-President, for electors for President or Vice-President, or for Senator or Representative in Congress, shall not be denied or abridged by the United States or any State by reason of failure to pay any poll tax or other tax.

Section 2 The Congress shall have the power to enforce this article by appropriate legislation.

Amendment XXV

[Adopted 1967]

Section 1 In case of the removal of the President from office or of his death or resignation, the Vice-President shall become President.

Section 2 Whenever there is a vacancy in the office of the Vice-President, the President shall nominate a Vice-President who shall take office upon confirmation by a majority vote of both Houses of Congress.

Section 3 Whenever the President transmits to the President pro tempore of the Senate and the Speaker of the House of Representatives his written declaration that he is unable to discharge the powers and duties of his office, and until he transmits to them a written declaration to the contrary, such powers and duties shall be discharged by the Vice-President as Acting President.

Section 4 Whenever the Vice-President and a majority of either the principal officers of the executive departments or of such other body as Congress may by law provide, transmit to the President pro tempore of the Senate and the Speaker of the House of Representatives their written declaration that the President is unable to discharge the powers and duties of his office, the Vice-President shall immediately assume the powers and duties of the office as Acting President.

Thereafter, when the President transmits to the President pro tempore of the Senate and the Speaker of the House of Representatives his written declaration that no inability exists, he shall resume the powers and duties of his office unless the Vice-President and a majority of either the principal officers of the executive department[s] or of such other body as Congress may by law provide, transmit within four days to the President pro tempore of the Senate and the Speaker of the House of Representatives their written declaration that the President is unable to discharge the powers and duties of his office. Thereupon Congress shall decide the issue, assembling within forty-eight hours for that purpose if not in session. If the Congress, within twenty-one days after receipt of the latter written declaration, or, if Congress is not in session, within twenty-one days after Congress is required to assemble, determines by two-thirds vote of both Houses that the President is unable to discharge the powers and duties of his office,

the Vice-President shall continue to discharge the same as Acting President; otherwise, the President shall resume the powers and duties of his office.

Amendment XXVI

[Adopted 1971]

Section 1 The right of citizens of the United States, who are eighteen years of age or older, to vote shall not be denied or abridged by the United States or by any State on account of age.

Section 2 The Congress shall have power to enforce this article by appropriate legislation.

Amendment XXVII

[Adopted 1992]

No law, varying the compensation for the services of the Senators and Representatives, shall take effect, until an election of Representatives shall have intervened.

Presidential Elections

Year	Number of States	Candidates	Parties	Popular Vote	% of Popular Vote	Electoral Vote	% Voter Participation[a]
1789	11	**George Washington**	No party designations			69	
		John Adams				34	
		Other candidates				35	
1792	15	**George Washington**	No party designations			132	
		John Adams				77	
		George Clinton				50	
		Other candidates				5	
1796	16	**John Adams**	Federalist			71	
		Thomas Jefferson	Democratic Republican			68	
		Thomas Pinckney	Federalist			59	
		Aaron Burr	Democratic Republican			30	
		Other candidates				48	
1800	16	**Thomas Jefferson**	Democratic Republican			73	
		Aaron Burr	Democratic Republican			73	
		John Adams	Federalist			65	
		Charles C. Pinckney	Federalist			64	
		John Jay	Federalist			1	
1804	17	**Thomas Jefferson**	Democratic Republican			162	
		Charles C. Pinckney	Federalist			14	
1808	17	**James Madison**	Democratic Republican			122	
		Charles C. Pinckney	Federalist			47	
		George Clinton	Democratic Republican			6	
1812	18	**James Madison**	Democratic Republican			128	
		DeWitt Clinton	Federalist			89	
1816	19	**James Monroe**	Democratic Republican			183	
		Rufus King	Federalist			34	
1820	24	**James Monroe**	Democratic Republican			231	
		John Quincy Adams	Independent Republican			1	

Year	Number of States	Candidates	Parties	Popular Vote	% of Popular Vote	Electoral Vote	% Voter Participation[a]
1824	24	**John Quincy Adams**	Democratic Republican	108,740	30.5	84	26.9
		Andrew Jackson	Democratic Republican	153,544	43.1	99	
		Henry Clay	Democratic Republican	47,136	13.2	37	
		William H. Crawford	Democratic Republican	46,618	13.1	41	
1828	24	**Andrew Jackson**	Democratic Republican	647,286	56.0	178	57.6
		John Quincy Adams	National Republican	508,064	44.0	83	
1832	24	**Andrew Jackson**	Democratic Republican	688,242	54.5	219	55.4
		Henry Clay	National Republican	473,462	37.5	49	
		William Wirt	Anti-Masonic	101,051	8.0	7	
		John Floyd	Democratic			11	
1836	26	**Martin Van Buren**	Democratic	765,483	50.9	170	57.8
		William H. Harrison	Whig			73	
		Hugh L. White	Whig			26	
		Daniel Webster	Whig	739,795	49.1	14	
		W. P. Mangum	Whig			11	
1840	26	**William H. Harrison**	Whig	1,274,624	53.1	234	80.2
		Martin Van Buren	Democratic	1,127,781	46.9	60	
1844	26	**James K. Polk**	Democratic	1,338,464	49.6	170	78.9
		Henry Clay	Whig	1,300,097	48.1	105	
		James G. Birney	Liberty	62,300	2.3		
1848	30	**Zachary Taylor**	Whig	1,360,967	47.4	163	72.7
		Lewis Cass	Democratic	1,222,342	42.5	127	
		Martin Van Buren	Free-Soil	291,263	10.1		
1852	31	**Franklin Pierce**	Democratic	1,601,117	50.9	254	69.6
		Winfield Scott	Whig	1,385,453	44.1	42	
		John P. Hale	Free-Soil	155,825	5		
1856	31	**James Buchanan**	Democratic	1,832,955	45.3	174	78.9
		John C. Frémont	Republican	1,339,932	33.1	114	
		Millard Fillmore	American	871,731	21.6	8	
1860	33	**Abraham Lincoln**	Republican	1,865,593	39.8	180	81.2
		Stephen A. Douglas	Democratic	1,382,713	29.5	12	
		John C. Breckinridge	Democratic	848,356	18.1	72	
		John Bell	Constitutional Union	592,906	12.6	39	
1864	36	**Abraham Lincoln**	Republican	2,206,938	55.0	212	73.8
		George B. McClellan	Democratic	1,803,787	45.0	21	
1868	37	**Ulysses S. Grant**	Republican	3,013,421	52.7	214	78.1
		Horatio Seymour	Democratic	2,706,829	47.3	80	

Year	Number of States	Candidates	Parties	Popular Vote	% of Popular Vote	Electoral Vote	% Voter Participation[a]
1872	37	**Ulysses S. Grant**	Republican	3,596,745	55.6	286[b]	71.3
		Horace Greeley	Democratic	2,843,446	43.9		
1876	38	**Rutherford B. Hayes**	Republican	4,036,572	48.0	185	81.8
		Samuel J. Tilden	Democratic	4,284,020	51.0	184	
1880	38	**James A. Garfield**	Republican	4,453,295	48.5	214	79.4
		Winfield S. Hancock	Democratic	4,414,082	48.1	155	
		James B. Weaver	Greenback-Labor	308,578	3.4		
1884	38	**Grover Cleveland**	Democratic	4,879,507	48.5	219	77.5
		James G. Blaine	Republican	4,850,293	48.2	182	
		Benjamin F. Butler	Greenback-Labor	175,370	1.8		
		John P. St. John	Prohibition	150,369	1.5		
1888	38	**Benjamin Harrison**	Republican	5,477,129	47.9	233	79.3
		Grover Cleveland	Democratic	5,537,857	48.6	168	
		Clinton B. Fisk	Prohibition	249,506	2.2		
		Anson J. Streeter	Union Labor	146,935	1.3		
1892	44	**Grover Cleveland**	Democratic	5,555,426	46.1	277	74.7
		Benjamin Harrison	Republican	5,182,690	43.0	145	
		James B. Weaver	People's	1,029,846	8.5	22	
		John Bidwell	Prohibition	264,133	2.2		
1896	45	**William McKinley**	Republican	7,102,246	51.1	271	79.3
		William J. Bryan	Democratic	6,492,559	47.7	176	
1900	45	**William McKinley**	Republican	7,218,491	51.7	292	73.2
		William J. Bryan	Democratic; Populist	6,356,734	45.5	155	
		John C. Wooley	Prohibition	208,914	1.5		
1904	45	**Theodore Roosevelt**	Republican	7,628,461	57.4	336	65.2
		Alton B. Parker	Democratic	5,084,223	37.6	140	
		Eugene V. Debs	Socialist	402,283	3.0		
		Silas C. Swallow	Prohibition	258,536	1.9		
1908	46	**William H. Taft**	Republican	7,675,320	51.6	321	65.4
		William J. Bryan	Democratic	6,412,294	43.1	162	
		Eugene V. Debs	Socialist	420,793	2.8		
		Eugene W. Chafin	Prohibition	253,840	1.7		
1912	48	**Woodrow Wilson**	Democratic	6,296,547	41.9	435	58.8
		Theodore Roosevelt	Progressive	4,118,571	27.4	88	
		William H. Taft	Republican	3,486,720	23.2	8	
		Eugene V. Debs	Socialist	900,672	6.0		
		Eugene W. Chafin	Prohibition	206,275	1.4		
1916	48	**Woodrow Wilson**	Democratic	9,127,695	49.4	277	61.6
		Charles E. Hughes	Republican	8,533,507	46.2	254	
		A. L. Benson	Socialist	585,113	3.2		
		J. Frank Hanly	Prohibition	220,506	1.2		

Year	Number of States	Candidates	Parties	Popular Vote	% of Popular Vote	Electoral Vote	% Voter Participation[a]
1920	48	**Warren G. Harding**	Republican	16,143,407	60.4	404	49.2
		James M. Cox	Democratic	9,130,328	34.2	127	
		Eugene V. Debs	Socialist	919,799	3.4		
		P. P. Christensen	Farmer-Labor	265,411	1.0		
1924	48	**Calvin Coolidge**	Republican	15,718,211	54.0	382	48.9
		John W. Davis	Democratic	8,385,283	28.8	136	
		Robert M. La Follette	Progressive	4,831,289	16.6	13	
1928	48	**Herbert C. Hoover**	Republican	21,391,993	58.2	444	56.9
		Alfred E. Smith	Democratic	15,016,169	40.9	87	
1932	48	**Franklin D. Roosevelt**	Democratic	22,809,638	57.4	472	56.9
		Herbert C. Hoover	Republican	15,758,901	39.7	59	
		Norman Thomas	Socialist	881,951	2.2		
1936	48	**Franklin D. Roosevelt**	Democratic	27,752,869	60.8	523	61.0
		Alfred M. Landon	Republican	16,674,665	36.5	8	
		William Lemke	Union	882,479	1.9		
1940	48	**Franklin D. Roosevelt**	Democratic	27,307,819	54.8	449	62.5
		Wendell L. Wilkie	Republican	22,321,018	44.8	82	
1944	48	**Franklin D. Roosevelt**	Democratic	25,606,585	53.5	432	55.9
		Thomas E. Dewey	Republican	22,014,745	46.0	99	
1948	48	**Harry S Truman**	Democratic	24,105,695	49.5	303	53.0
		Thomas E. Dewey	Republican	21,969,170	45.1	189	
		J. Strom Thurmond	States' Rights	1,169,021	2.4	39	
		Henry A. Wallace	Progressive	1,156,103	2.4		
1952	48	**Dwight D. Eisenhower**	Republican	33,936,234	55.1	442	63.3
		Adlai E. Stevenson	Democratic	27,314,992	44.4	89	
1956	48	**Dwight D. Eisenhower**	Republican	35,590,472	57.6	457	60.6
		Adlai E. Stevenson	Democratic	26,022,752	42.1	73	
1960	50	**John F. Kennedy**	Democratic	34,226,731	49.7	303	62.8
		Richard M. Nixon	Republican	34,108,157	49.5	219	
1964	50	**Lyndon B. Johnson**	Democratic	43,129,566	61.1	486	61.7
		Barry M. Goldwater	Republican	27,178,188	38.5	52	
1968	50	**Richard M. Nixon**	Republican	31,710,470	43.4	301	60.6
		Hubert H. Humphrey	Democratic	30,898,055	42.7	191	
		George C. Wallace	American Independent	9,446,167	13.5	46	
1972	50	**Richard M. Nixon**	Republican	47,169,911	60.7	520	55.2
		George S. McGovern	Democratic	29,170,383	37.5	17	
		John G. Schmitz	American	1,099,482	1.4		
1976	50	**Jimmy Carter**	Democratic	40,830,763	50.1	297	53.5
		Gerald R. Ford	Republican	39,147,793	48.0	240	

Year	Number of States	Candidates	Parties	Popular Vote	% of Popular Vote	Electoral Vote	% Voter Participation[a]
1980	50	**Ronald Reagan**	Republican	43,899,248	50.8	489	52.6
		Jimmy Carter	Democratic	35,481,432	41.0	49	
		John B. Anderson	Independent	5,719,437	6.6	0	
		Ed Clark	Libertarian	920,859	1.1	0	
1984	50	**Ronald Reagan**	Republican	54,455,075	58.8	525	53.1
		Walter Mondale	Democratic	37,577,185	40.6	13	
1988	50	**George Bush**	Republican	48,901,046	53.4	426	50.2
		Michael Dukakis	Democratic	41,809,030	45.6	111[c]	
1992	50	**Bill Clinton**	Democratic	44,908,233	43.0	370	55.0
		George Bush	Republican	39,102,282	37.4	168	
		Ross Perot	Independent	19,741,048	18.9	0	
1996	50	**Bill Clinton**	Democratic	47,401,054	49.2	379	49.0
		Robert Dole	Republican	39,197,350	40.7	159	
		Ross Perot	Independent	8,085,285	8.4	0	
		Ralph Nader	Green	684,871	0.7	0	
2000	50	**George W. Bush**	Republican	50,465,169	47.79	271	50.7
		Albert Gore, Jr.	Democratic	50,996,062	49.4	266[d]	
		Ralph Nader	Green	2,529,871	2.40	0	
2004	50	**George W. Bush**	Republican	62,040,610	51	286	60.7
		John F. Kerry	Democratic	59,028,109	48	252	
		Ralph Nader	Independent	463,653	1	0	
2008	50	**Barack Obama**	Democratic	69,498,459	52.9	365	61.7
		John McCain	Republican	59,948,283	45.7	173	
2012	50	**Barack Obama**	Democratic	65,455,010	51	332	58.2
		Mitt Romney	Republican	60,771,703	47	206	

Candidates receiving less than 1 percent of the popular vote have been omitted. Thus the percentage of popular vote given for any election year may not total 100 percent.

Before the passage of the Twelfth Amendment in 1804, the Electoral College voted for two presidential candidates; the runner-up became vice president.

Before 1824, most presidential electors were chosen by state legislatures, not by popular vote.

[a]Percent of voting-age population casting ballots (eligible voters).
[b]Greeley died shortly after the election; the electors supporting him then divided their votes among minor candidates.
[c]One elector from West Virginia cast her Electoral College presidential ballot for Lloyd Bentsen, the Democratic Party's vice-presidential candidate.
[d]One elector from the District of Columbia abstained.

Index

Abdication: of Kaiser Wilhelm, **553**

Abolitionists, 371

Abortion, 506, 583, 735, 772, 773, 801, 802 (illus.), 819

Abraham Lincoln (ship), 809 (illus.)

Abzug, Bella, 735 (illus.)

Accommodationists, 509

Acquired immune deficiency syndrome (AIDS), **795,** 796 (illus.)

Activism. *See* Civil rights movement; specific movements and groups

Adams, Harry J., 552

Adams, Henry, 470

Adamson Act, 528

Addams, Jane, 503–504, 503 (illus.), 505, 509, 525 (illus.); on her participation in 1912 presidential campaign, 532

Adolescents: in 1920s, 576. *See also* Young people

Advance Thresher Company, 425 (illus.)

Advertising, 431; consumer culture and, 412–413, 412 (illus.), 567–568; farm equipment, 425 (illus.); of Listerine, 567, 568 (illus.); movie, 594, 594 (illus.); for railroad land grants, 448 (illus.); television, 704, 704 (illus.), 705; World War I and, 548

Advertising Council, 702, 705

Affidavit, 677

Affirmative action, 758, **772,** 774

Affluence: after World War II, 681–682, 682 (map)

Afghanistan, 807 (map); NATO and Afghan forces in, 813 (illus.); Obama and, 813; Soviet intervention in, 770; terrorism and, 805; U.S. coalition in, 806–807, 807 (map); U.S. covert operations in, 781

AFL. *See* American Federation of Labor

Africa: immigrants from, 779, 779 (figure)

African Americans, 722 (map); in baseball, 529, 664–665, 664 (illus.), 686, 687; benevolent societies, 377; black codes and, 379; civil rights movement and, 708–712, 710 (illus.), 711 (illus.), 722 (map); Colored Farmers' Alliance, 481; as cowboys, 422, 422 (illus.); Croix de Guerre awarded to, 552; desegregation of schools and, 708–710, 710 (illus.); fraternal orders, 377; in Great Depression, 616, 621; Great Migration and, 549–550, 550 (illus.), 563; Harlem Renaissance and, 574–576; illiteracy among, 444; in Knights of Labor, 459, 460; in Korean War, 674 (illus.); Ku Klux Klan and, 380; labor unions and, 458; lynchings and, 447, 509, 509 (illus.), 581, 581 (illus.); Lyndon Johnson and, 728–732; Nazi concentration camps liberated by, 650, 657; in New Deal, 622; as office holders, 369–370, 369 (illus.); population and duration of Reconstruction, 386 (map); post-World War II, 683, 685–686, 688; as president, 812–813; race riots and, 559–560; Reconstruction and, 375, 385–388, 385 (illus.), 392; in Republican Party of the South, 386–387; restrictive housing covenants and, 579; rock 'n roll and, 707; Southern vote, 1960-1971 and, 731 (map); in Spanish-American War, 493, 494, 494 (illus.), 536; in sports, 664–665; Truman and, 677; in Vietnam War, 745, 755; voting rights of, 384–385, 385 (illus.), 393; women's clubs, 440; women workers, 456; World War I and, 536–537, 536 (illus.), 551; World War II and, 647, 648–650. *See also* Affirmative action; Civil rights; Civil rights movement; Discrimination; Emancipation; Freed people; Segregation; Slaves and slavery

African Methodist Episcopal Church: Atlanta, 446

Agnew, Spiro, 761

Agribusiness, 424

Agricultural Adjustment Act (AAA): first, **606;** second, 613, 617

Agricultural Adjustment Administration, 606, 629

Agricultural Marketing Act (1929), 601

Agriculture, 399; expansion of, 1860-1900, 400–401, 400 (map); farm workers in, 780; in Great Depression, 599, 601; Indians and, 415; labor and, 456; New Deal and, 606; in 1920s, 571; rainfall and (1890), 423 (map), 424; sharecropping and, 378; subsidies to, 695. *See also* Crops; Farms and farming; Farm workers; specific crops

Aguinaldo, Emilio, 496–497, 497 (illus.)

AIDS. *See* Acquired immune deficiency syndrome

Aid to Families with Dependent Children, 775

Aircraft industry: women workers in, 684

Air force: in World War II, 657

Airplane: as terrorist weapon, 804–805, 804 (illus.)

Air pollution, 757, 784

Air Quality Act, 729 (table), 730

Alabama: freedom riders in, 721; pig iron production in, 415

Alabama (ship), 487

Alaska: purchase of, 486

Alawite Muslims, 556

Albright, Madeleine, 798

Albro, Maxine, 624 (illus.)

Alcatraz Island, Indian seizure of, **752**

Alcohol and alcoholism: prohibition and, 507, 577–578; temperance movement and, 440. *See also* Prohibition

Alden v. Maine, 803

Alexander v. Holmes, 760

Algiers, 814

Alito, Samuel, 802

Allen, Gracie, 627

Allende, Salvador, 756

Alliance for Progress, 724

Allies (World War I), **540,** 541 (map), 543, 552; food shipments to, 547; Paris Peace Conference and, 554, 556. *See also* World War I

Allies (World War II): defeat of Germany, 654–655; post-War, 655–656. *See also* Cold War; World War II

Allotment checks, 647

"Aloha 'Oe" (Lili'uokalani), 490 (illus.)

Al-Qaeda, 644, **805,** 807 (map), 813

Alsace-Lorraine, 556

Alternating current (AC), 412
Alternative fuels, 771
Altgeld, John Peter, 461
Amazon.com, 799
Amendments: to Constitution, A11–A15. *See also* specific amendments
American Academy of Arts and Sciences, 439
American Apparel, 407
American Bandstand, 707, 707 (illus.)
American Broadcasting Company, 694
American Civil Liberties Union (ACLU), 549, 610; *Korematsu v. United States,* 642, 644; Scopes trial and, 578
American Dream: defining, 749–753; post–World War II, 665, 681–682, 681 (illus.)
American Expeditionary Force (AEF), 551, 552, 563
American Express, 705
American Federation of Labor (AFL), **461,** 462, 515, 616; La Follette endorsed by, 587; merger with CIO, 703; World War I and, 547
American GI Forum, 685, 686 (illus.)
American Indian Defense Association (AIDA), **582**
American Indian Movement (AIM), **752,** 752 (illus.)
American Indians: activism by, 742, 751–753, 752 (illus.); buffalo and, 415, 417 (illus.), 418; changes in federal Indian policy, 581–582; forced assimilation of, 452–454; Medicine Lodge Creek conference, 416–417; Navajo code talkers, 651; in New Deal, 623 (illus.), 624–625; in 1950s, 693, 694 (illus.); war for the West and, 415–420; war of attrition against, 417–420; women doctors, 453 (illus.); in World War I, 551 (illus.); in World War II, 647, 650–651; at Wounded Knee, 419 (illus.), 420. *See also* Reservations; specific battles and treaties; specific groups and leaders
"Americanization" drives: World War I and, 548
American League, 529
American Liberty Party, 609
American Medical Association, 517, 693; birth control and, 583
American Mercury, The (magazine), 574
American Plan, 582
American Protective Association (APA), **449,** 485
American Psychiatric Association: homosexuality classified by, 735

American Railway Union, Debs and, 461, 462
American Recovery and Reinvestment Act, 815
American Revolution: bicentennial of, 767
American Sugar Refining Company, 413, 476
Americans with Disabilities Act, 784
American Taxpayer Relief Act, 820
American Tobacco Company, 413, 568
American Woman Suffrage Association (AWSA), **478,** 479
Ames, Adelbert, 390
Amnesty: Andrew Johnson and, 374
Amphibious assault, 654
Anarchists, 449, 559; Haymarket bombing and, 461
Anderson, Marian, 622 (illus.), 623
Anderson, Maxwell, 545
Angelou, Maya, 650
Anglos, 454
Anglo-Saxonism, 490
Anglo Saxons: glorification of, 449–450
Angola: U.S. covert operations in, 781
Annexation: of Hawai'i, 493; of Texas, 454
Anthony, Susan B., 381, 384, 478
Anti-Catholicism, 449, 580, 588
Anti-imperialism, 538
Anti-Imperialist League, 500
Antimonopolism, 481
Anti-Saloon League, 508, 515, 533, 561
Anti-Semitism, 580; of Father Coughlin, 610; of Henry Ford, 579. *See also* Jews and Judaism; in United States, 636
Antiwar movement, 737; in Vietnam War, 745, 745 (illus.), 747, 748, 754
APA. *See* American Protective Association
Apartheid (South Africa), 446, 785–786
Apollo space program, 719
Appalachian Regional Development Act, 730
Appeasement, 636
Apple Computer, 777
Appliances, 568, 618
"Applied Christianity," 506
Aqueducts, 426
Arab Americans: after September 11, 2001, 805
Arab Spring, 813, **814;** change and, 815 (map); protests in, 814
Arab world: Camp David Accords and, 768, 770 (illus.); nationalism in, 696; partition of Palestine

and, 671. *See also* Islam; Israel; Middle East; Muslims
Arbenz, Jacobo, 699
Arbitration, 460 (illus.), **487,** 491, 523, 524; British-U.S. Civil War claims, **487;** of international disputes, 538; Venezuela boundary dispute and, 491; under Wilson, 554, 556
Architecture: PWA Moderne, 614 (illus.); skyscrapers and, 435 (illus.), 436, 437
Ardennes Forest, 654
Argentina: migration to, 448
Aridity, 422
Aristide, Jean-Bertrand, 798
Arkansas, 372
Arkansas National Guard: school desegregation and, 710
Armas, Carlos Castillo, 699
Armed forces: discrimination in, 649–650; integration of, 677; in Spanish-American War, 493; in World War I, 536, 551
Armistice, 493
Armory Show of 1913, 528
Armstrong, Louis "Satchmo," 575
Armstrong, Neil, 719
Army-McCarthy hearings, 694
Art Deco, 614 (illus.)
Arthur, Chester A., 471, 472
Articles of Confederation: document, A3–A6
Articles of Constitution. *See* Constitution (U.S.)
Artisans, 399, 412; dignity of labor and, 457
Art(s): Harlem Renaissance and, 574–576; Impressionism, 528, 529 (illus.); in New Deal, 624 (illus.); WPA sponsorship of, 616, 616 (illus.). *See also* specific arts and artists
ARU. *See* American Railway Union
Ash Can School of painters, 528
Asia: Cold War in, 671–675; Eisenhower and, 699–700; immigrants from, 450, 452, 778, 779, 779 (figure); Open Door policy and, 497, 501; Southeast Asia Treaty Organization, 696. *See also* specific countries
Asian Americans: discrimination against, 433–434, 452, 579, 581; in Great Depression, 621; in World War II, 643. *See also* specific groups
Assad, Bashar al-, 814
Assassinations: of Garfield, 471, 477; of John Kennedy, 726; of Martin Luther King, Jr., 733; of Robert Kennedy, 748

Assembly line, 568–569, 569 (illus.)
Assimilation, 448–449; of
    American Indians, 452–454; of
    immigrants, 434, 780 (illus.)
Associationalism, Hoover and, 588
Aswan Dam, 698
Atlanta: in New South, 414 (illus.)
Atlanta Compromise, 445, 446
Atlanta Constitution, 414
Atlantic Charter, 640, 656
Atlantic Ocean region: in
    World War II, 639–640
Atomic bomb, 634, 645, 658, 659,
    660, 701 (illus.); fallout shelters
    and, 695; Soviet, 672, 680
Atomic power. *See* Atomic
    bomb; Nuclear power
Atta, Mohammed, 804
Attlee, Clement, 660
Auerbach, Jerald, 545
Auschwitz, 657
Australia: migration to, 448
Australian ballot, 481, 485
Australia-New Zealand-United
    States (ANZUS) treaty, 675
Austria, 553
Austria-Hungary: in Triple
    Alliance, 540; World War I and,
    540, 541 (map), 546, 552
Austro-Hungarian Empire,
    end of, 553
Autobiographies, 408
*Autobiography of Andrew
    Carnegie, The,* 408
Automation, 702
Automobiles and automobile
    industry, 411, 566; American
    lifestyle and, 571–572, 576; Europe
    and, 591; in Great Depression,
    600; lifestyle and, 568–569; loans
    to, 812; in 1950s, 703, 705
Autonomy, 375
Aviation: Lindbergh and,
    573, 574 (illus.)
Awakening, The (Chopin), 528
Axis of evil, 806
Axis powers, 638, 654, 666

Babbitt (Lewis), 574
Babe Ruth, 573
Baby and Child Care (Spock), 705
Baby boom, 688; Reagan and,
    778; in 1950s, 684, **685,** 685
    (figure), 691, 705; youth
    movement and, 736–737
Baez, Joan, 737
Baghdad: attack on, 807
Baghdad Pact, 696
Bahrain, 814

Baker, Ella, 720
Baker, James A., III, 775
Baker, Ray Stannard, 509
Baker v. Carr, 727
Bakke, Alan, 772
Balaguer, Joaquín, 743
Balanced Budget Act
    (1997), 798 (illus.)
Balance of power: East Asian, **497**
Balkan Peninsula, 540, 798
Ballinger, Richard A., 519
Baltic region, independence in, 785
Baltimore, 435
Baltimore & Ohio Railroad:
    strike, 458
Bank Holiday, 605
Banking Act of 1933, 609
Bank of America, 569
Bank of Italy, 569
Bank runs, 598, 599
Bankruptcy: under Nixon, 758; of
    railroads, 428; under Reagan, 776
Banks, Dennis, 752
Banks and banking: cooperative,
    475; in depression of 1890s, 428;
    in Great Depression, 599, 600,
    601 (figure), 605; innovations
    in, 569; investment banks, 405;
    mobilization of capital and,
    399; reform of, 527. *See also*
    Savings and loan industry
Bara, Theda, 573
Barbed wire, 424
Barrios, 454
Barton, Bruce, 570
Baruch, Bernard, World
    War I and, 546
Baseball, 529–530, 530 (illus.), 573;
    integration of, 664–665, 686
Bastogne, battle at, 654
Batista, Fulgencio (Colonel), 634, 699
Battles: at Belleau Wood, 552; of
    the Bulge, 654, 655 (map); at
    Chateau-Thierry, 552; of the
    Coral Sea, 651; of Iwo Jima, 658;
    of Leyte Gulf, 658; at Manila
    Bay, 493; at Marne River, 552;
    at Meuse-Argonne Forest, 552;
    of Midway Island, 633, **652;** of
    Okinawa, 658; of Saipan, 657; St.
    Mihiel salient, 552; **of Stalingrad,
    652**–653, 654 (illus.); at Tarawa,
    657; **at Wounded Knee Creek,**
    419 (illus.), **420.** *See also* Wars and
    warfare; specific battles and wars
Battleships, 489, 489 (illus.)
Bay of Pigs operation, **724**
Beals, Melba Patella, 710
Bear Runner, Oscar, 752 (illus.)
Beatles, 737

Beats (beatniks), **708**
Beauvoir, Simone de, 686
Begin, Menachem, 768, 770 (illus.)
Beirut: Muslim terrorists in, 782
Belgium, 540, 542, 547, 638
Belknap, William, 471
Bell, Rex, 566
Belleau Wood, battle at, 552
Belligerent nations: in
    World War I, **542**
Bell Labs, 645
Benevolent societies: for blacks,
    377; for Chinese, 450
Benny, Jack, 627
Berlin: blockade, 669, 670,
    671 (illus.); World War II
    conquest of, 654
Berlin: Treaty of (1899), 497
Berlin airlift, 670, 670 (map)
Berlin Wall, 670 (map), **724;**
    fall of, 785, 786 (illus.)
Bernanke, Ben, 600, 812
Bernstein, Carl, 760
Berry, Chuck, 707
Bessemer, Henry, 406
Bethune, Mary McLeod, 616, 622
Beveridge, Albert, 490, 496,
    517, 525 (illus.)
Bible: fundamentalists and, 578;
    in public schools, 727. *See also*
    Fundamentalism; Scopes trial
Biden, Joseph: 2008 election and, 811
Big business: Coolidge and, 588, 588
    (illus.); investment banking
    and, 429; prosperity of 1950s
    and, 702; railroads and,
    401–405; Rockefeller on, 430; steel
    industry and, 405–407; in World
    War II, 644. *See also* Business
Big Three (auto manufacturers), 569
Bilateral defense pacts, **696**
Bilingual education, 749
Bill of Rights, 381, 382, 613
Bin Laden, Osama, 805, 806, 813
Biographies, 408
Biological weapons, 804, 806
Bipartisanship: New Deal and, **606**
Birmingham: civil rights marches in,
    722–723; freedom riders in, 721
Birth control, 506, 583, 728, 735
Birth of a Nation, The (film), 393, 580
Birth rate: 1930-2004, 685 (figure);
    in Great Depression, 620
Black, Hugo, 613; on *Korematsu
    v. United States,* 661
"Black Cabinet": of Franklin
    Roosevelt, **622**
Black codes, 379, 380, 388
Black Hills: gold in, 418;
    Indians and, 419

Blacklisting, 612; of
   Hollywood Ten, 679
Blackmun, Harry, 760, 772
Black Muslims, 732–733
Black Nationalism, 732
Black Panthers, 733
Black Power, 732
**Black Reconstruction,
   385–388,** 385 (illus.)
Black Reconstruction in America
   (Du Bois), 392
Blacks. *See* African Americans;
   Free blacks
Black separatism, 576
"Black Thursday" (October
   24, 1929), 598
"Black Tuesday," 598
Blackwell, Elizabeth, 440
Blaine, James G., 471, 472
Bland-Allison Act, 477
Blitzkrieg (lightning war), 638 (illus.)
Blockade: of Berlin, 669, 671
   (illus.); in World War I, 543
Blockade runners: in Civil War, 369
Blogger program, 793
Blogging: political
   campaigns and, 809
Blue-collar jobs: in 1950s, 703
Blue-collar workers: Nixon
   and, 759, 760
B movies, 696
Boas, Franz, 452
Boehner, John, 818
Boeing, 684
Boer republics (South Africa), 446
Bohemia, 423
Boland Amendment, 782, 783
Bolsheviks (Russia), **552**–553, 554
Bombs and bombings: of abortion
   clinics, 801; by Al Qaeda, 805;
   of Dresden, 654; of Hiroshima
   and Nagasaki, 659, 659 (illus.),
   660; of Pearl Harbor, 633,
   640–641, 642, 642 (illus.); Red
   Scare and, 558; of Serbia, 798; in
   World War II, 654, 657. *See also*
   Hydrogen bomb; Nuclear power
Bonanza farms, 425
Bonds: railroads and, 388,
   405. *See also* War bonds
Bonus Army, 602
Boone, Pat, 707
Bootlegging, 578
Borah, William E., 592
Border Patrol, 781
Borders: North and South Korea, 672,
   673 (map). *See also* Boundaries
Bosch, Juan, 743
Bosnia, 798
Bosnia-Herzegovina, 537, 786

Boston, 399, 435; police
   strike in, 558, 561
Boston Red Sox, 530
Bouazizi, Mohamed, 813–814
Boundaries: Europe and Middle
   East after World War I, 555
   (map); Venezuela/British Guiana
   dispute, 491. *See also* Borders
Bourke-White, Margaret,
   625–626, 626 (illus.)
Bow, Clara, 565–566, 565 (illus.),
   573, 573 (illus.), 583, 626
Boxer Rebellion, 499, 501, 522
Boycotts: of grape growers, 741,
   749; of 1980 Olympics, 770
Boynton v. Virginia, 720–721
BP: deep-water drilling rig
   explosion and oil spill, 817
Braceros, 650
Bracket creep, 774
Brains Trust, 605
Brandeis, Louis, 506, **525,** 527, 528
Branding, 420, 421
Brannan Plan, 678
Breaux, John, 805
Breedlove v. Suttles, 730
Brest-Litovsk, Treaty of,
   541 (map), **552**
Brezhnev, Leonid, 755, 762, 770
Brezhnev Doctrine, 736
Briand, Aristide, 593
Bribery: Harding administration
   and, 585; machine politics and,
   469; by railroads, 403–404, 518
Bridges, 436
Brinksmanship, 695
Bristow, Benjamin, 470, 471
British Guiana: Venezuela's
   boundary dispute with, 491
Britton, Nan, 585
Brookings Institution, 599
Brooklyn Bridge, 436
Brooklyn Dodgers: integration
   of, 664–665
Brooks, David, 810
Brown, H. Rap, 733
Brown, Oliver, 709
Brown, Rita Mae, 735
Brownell, Herbert, 712
"Brown Power," 742
***Brown v. Board of Education,* 709,** 712
Bryan, William Jennings, 501; anti-
   imperialism of, 495, 538; 1896
   election and, 484–485, 484 (illus.),
   486 (map); 1908 election and,
   519; Philippines and, 495, 496;
   political button, 485 (illus.);
   Scopes trial and, 578; as secretary
   of state, 527, 537, 542, 543; World
   War I and sentiments of, 538

Buchanan, Pat, 759, 788, 795
Buchenwald, 636, 657
Buckley, William F., 727
Budget: Clinton and, 797; Eisenhower
   and, 693; national security needs
   in, 702; Nixon and, 758. *See
   also* Economy; Federal deficit
Budget Control Act, 818
Buffalo: hunting of, 417, 417 (illus.),
   418; Plains Indians and, 415
Buffalo, New York, 435
Building codes: urban, 443
Bulganin, Nikolai, 700, 701
Bulge, Battle of. *See* Bastogne, battle at
Bull Moose Party, 525
Bunau-Varilla, Philippe, 520
Bunche, Ralph, 671
Bunyan, John, 511
Bureau of Indian Affairs, 752
Bureau of Labor Statistics, 457
Burger, Warren: Burger
   Court and, 760
Burke-Wadsworth Act, 639
Burlington and Missouri
   Railroad: farmland advertising
   poster, 448 (illus.)
Burns, George, 627
Bus boycott: in Montgomery,
   Alabama, 710–712, 711 (illus.)
Bush, George H. W., 767, 783; 1988
   election and, 784; 1992 election
   and, 788–789, 789 (map);
   foreign policy of, 784–788
Bush, George W., 794; domestic
   agenda of, 803–804; foreign
   policy of, 804; Great Recession
   and, 811–812; Hurricane Katrina
   and, 810, 810 (illus.); Iraq and,
   806–808, 808 (map); second term
   of, 809–811; September 11, 2001,
   attacks and, 804–805, 804 (illus.);
   Supreme Court and, 802; 2000
   election and, 803, 804 (map); 2004
   election and, 809; war on terrorism
   and, 805–807, 809 (illus.)
Bush Doctrine, 806
Business: government and, 702; in
   Great Depression, 601 (figure);
   politics of, 586, 587–588, 588
   (illus.); in World War II, 644.
   See also Big business; Economy
Busing, 760, 774
Butcher, Solomon, 424 (illus.)
Butoku-kai, **632, 633**

C. Turner Joy (ship), 743
Cabinet (presidential): Black
   Cabinet of Roosevelt, 622
Caldwell, Erskine, 625

California: Chinese immigrants in, 450; economic growth in, 572; ethnic groups in, 581; farm workers in, 749–750; gold in, 399, 454; Mexican Americans in, 582; migratory labor camps in, 617; Progressivism in, 514; race riots in, 732; tract homes in, 681–682; wheat farms in, 425, 425 (illus.); in World War II, 647, 649. *See also* specific cities

California Agricultural Labor Relations Act, 742

Californios, 454

Calles, Plutarco, 591, 591 (illus.)

Calley, William, 755

Cambodia, 700, 743; immigrants from, 780; Vietnam War and, 754

Campaigns (political). *See* Election(s); Political campaigns

Campbell, John, 380 (illus.)

Camp David Accords, 768, 770 (illus.)

Campo, Antonio, 685

Canada: immigrants from, 447; migration to, 448

Canals, 490, 522, 538; agricultural growth and, 400

Cane (Toomer), 574

Cannon, Joseph, 519

Capital (financial): for economic development, 429; for industrialization, 399; for railroads, 402, 405; in South after Civil War, 378

Capitalism: challenges to, 509–510

Capital ships, 592

Capone, Al, 578

Capra, Frank, 626

Captive, The (play), 585

Caribbean region: American involvement in, 495 (map); immigrants from, 778; United States and, 521–522, 521 (map), 522 (illus.), 782 (map); U.S. and, 589; Wilson and, 538

Carmichael, Stokely, 732, 733, 745

Carnegie, Andrew, 398, 410, 413, 429, 431, 455; anti-imperialism and, 495; competition and, 398, 406; on "Gospel of Wealth," 408, 409; Philippines and, 495, 496; steel industry and, 405, **406**

Carnegie Endowment for International Peace, 679–680

Carnegie Hall, New York City, 409

Carnegie Steel, 406 (illus.), 407, 413, 461

Carpenter's Sandwiches, Los Angeles, 572 (illus.)

Carpetbaggers, 386, **387,** 387 (illus.), 391, 393

Carr, Nicholas, 821

Carranza, Venustiano, 538, 539

Cars. *See* Automobiles and automobile industry

Carson, Rachel, 757, 758

Carswell, G. Harrold, 760

Cartels: Rockefeller and, **398,** 409, 411

Carter, James Earl ("Jimmy"), 762, 767; domestic policy of, 771–773; human rights and, 768; Iran and, 770–771, 771 (illus.); Middle East and, 768; 1976 election and, 768

Carter Doctrine, 770

Cartoons: Dr. Seuss, 635 (illus.); McKinley and protective tariff, 474 (illus.); in political propaganda, 470 (illus.); Theodore Roosevelt in, 522 (illus.)

Carvell, James, 789

Casinos, Indian, 753

Cassatt, Mary, 528, 529 (illus.)

Castagne, Alfred, 616 (illus.)

Castro, Fidel, 699, 724; Lyndon Johnson and, 742. *See also* Cuba

Casualties: from atomic bomb at Hiroshima, 660; in Korean War, 675; in "Philippine insurrection," 497; in Second Iraq War and occupation, 807, 808, 809 (illus.), 810; in Serbia-Kosovo conflict, 798; in Vietnam War, 756 (table); in World War I, 552; in World War II, 654, 657, 658, 660 (figure). *See also* specific battles and wars, 660 (table)

Catcher in the Rye, The (Salinger), 708

Cather, Willa, 571

Catholicism: immigrants and, 449; of Kennedy, 718; Klan and, 580; nativism and, 449; social activism and, 506. *See also* Religion

Catt, Carrie Chapman, 507

Cattle and cattle industry: in West, 420–422

Cattle towns, 421

Caucuses, 468

Celler, Emanuel, 779

Census, 451, 451 (illus.)

Central America: George H. W. Bush and, 787–788; Reagan and, 781–782; United States and, 782 (map). *See also* Latin America; specific countries

Central Intelligence Agency (CIA), 670, **696,** 783; covert operations and, 696, 781, 782; Cuba and, 699, 724, 742; Guatemala and, 699

Central Pacific Railroad, 402, 420

Central Park, New York City, 437

Central Powers, 554; in World War I, **540,** 541 (map)

Central Treaty Organization (CENTO), 696

Century of Dishonor, A (Jackson), 452

"Challenges of the Mentally Retarded" (Shriver), 738

Chamberlain, Neville, 636

Chambers, Whitaker, 679, 680

Chamoun, Camille, 698

Chaplin, Charlie, 573, 626

Charity Organization Society (COS), 443

Charles, Ray, 707

Chateau-Thierry, battle at, 552

Chattel slavery, 374

Chautauqua, 529

Chávez, César, 741, 749, 763

Cheka (Russia), 554

Chemical weapons, 804, 806

Cheney, Dick, 804, 810

Cherokee Indians, 453

Chevrolet, 569

Cheyenne Indians, 416, 418

Chicago: Democratic National Convention in 1968, 748; Great Fire in, 438; Haymarket bombing and, 461; Hull House in, 504, 505; mail-order sales in, 404; meatpacking in, 404–405; Obama family in, 819 (illus.); paved streets in, 438; Pullman strike in, 462, 462 (illus.); railroads and, 404–405, 404 (illus.); shopping district, circa 1910, 437 (illus.); stockyard workers in, 443; World's Columbian Exposition in, 530, 531 (illus.)

Chicanos/Chicanas, **750, 751.** *See also* Mexican Americans

Chief Joseph, 419

Childbearing: women and, 583, 584, 584 (illus.)

Child labor, 456, 464; abolition of, 476; Fair Labor Standards Act and, 598; farm workers and, 582 (illus.); outlawing of, 460, 607, 613; in textile industry, 444, 444 (illus.)

Children: health insurance for, 814; in industrial workforce, 456; polio vaccine and, 693; school attendance laws and, 439. *See also* Child labor; Families

Chile: Allende and, 756; Benjamin Harrison and, 491

China: Boxer Rebellion in, 499, 501; Carter and, 768, 770; civil war in, 672; communism in, 755;

China (continued)
Eisenhower and, 694; Great Leap Forward in, 700; immigrants from, 420, 433, 450, 452, 780; investment in, 589; Japanese invasion of, 635; Korean War and, 675; Nixon and, 755; Open Door policy and, 497, 499, 592; Soviet Union and, 755, 757; spheres of influence in, 497; Tiananmen Square, 786–787; in UN, 666; war with Japan (1894), 524

China Lobby, 672

Chinatowns, 450, 451

Chinese Americans: segregation of, 433–434, 452. *See also* Asian Americans

Chinese Consolidated Benevolent Association, 450

Chinese Exclusion Act, 452

Chiricahua Apache Indians, 419

Chlorination: of water, **437**

Choctaw Indians, 453

Choice, Not an Echo, A (Schlafly), 766

Chopin, Kate, 528

Christianity: Scopes trial and, 578

Christian Science Monitor, 635

Chrysler, Walter, 569

Chrysler Corporation, 569, 812

Church(es): African American, 376, 377 (illus.). *See also* specific churches and religions

Churchill, Winston, 638, 639, 641; Atlantic Charter and, 640; at Casablanca, 653; iron curtain speech of, 667; at Yalta, 656, 656 (illus.)

CIA. *See* Central Intelligence Agency

Cigarette manufacturing: in New South, 414

Cigarettes: advertising of, 412, 567–568

Cigarmakers' Union, 461

CIO. *See* Congress of Industrial Organizations

Cities and towns: architecture in, 435 (illus.), 436; automobiles and, 571–572; in Gilded Age, 434–438; homosexuals and lesbians in, 441–442, 464, 707; machine politics in, 469; in Rust Belt, 777; utilities and services in, 438; walking, 435

Citizenship: Fourteenth Amendment and, 381–382, 384; illegal immigrants and, 780, 781; Insular Cases and, 496; Treaty of Paris and, 494–495

Citizens United case, 802

City councils, 512

City government, reforms of, 512–515

City manager plan, 512

City planning, 512

Civil disobedience, 722

Civilian Conservation Corps (CCC), **608,** 622, 629

Civil liberties: after September 11, 2001, 805; World War I and, 545. *See also* Civil rights, 549

Civil Liberties Bureau, 549

Civil rights, 381; Eleanor Roosevelt and, 677; Kennedy and, 719–723; Truman and, 677; voting rights and, 384–385. *See also* Civil rights movement

Civil Rights Act, 391; of 1866, 380–381, 395; **of 1875, 370, 385,** 395, 445; **of 1957, 712;** of 1964, 729 (table); **of 1964, 726**

Civil Rights Cases (1883), 445

Civil rights movement, 392; in 1950s, 708–712, 710 (illus.), 711 (illus.); in 1960s, 719–723, 721 (illus.), 722 (map), 723 (illus.)

Civil service: classified positions, 478; merit system for, 477

Civil unions: same-sex, **809**

Civil War: constitutional revolution and, 384

Civil war(s): in China, 672; in Greece, 667; in Iraq, 807; in Spain, 635

Civil War (U.S.), 487

Civil Works Administration (CWA), 609

Clansman, The (Dixon), 393

Clark, Dick, 707, 707 (illus.)

Clark, Jim, 730

Clark, Tom, 679

Classes: settlement houses and, 506. *See also* Middle class; Working class

Classified civil service positions, **478**

Clayton Antitrust Act, 527, 528

Clean Air Act, 758, 784

Clean Water Restoration Act (1966), 729 (table)

Cleaver, Eldridge, 733

Clemenceau, Georges, 554

Clemens, Samuel. *See* Twain, Mark

Cleveland, Grover, 472, 482, 501; anti-imperialism and, 495; depression of 1890s and, 428; 1892 election and, 483; Latin America and, 491; Philippines and, 495; Pullman strike and, 462

Clinton, Hillary Rodham: healthcare and, 795; as secretary of state, 813; 2008 election and, 811

Clinton, William Jefferson ("Bill"): Congress and, 796–797; domestic policy of, 794; economy and, 795–796, 798–802; first term

of, 795–796; foreign policy of, 797–798, 805; healthcare and, 795; impeachment of, 797; 1992 election and, 788–789, 789 (map); 1996 election and, 797; second term of, 797

Closed shop, 645

Clothing: of freed people, 375 (illus.), 376; for women in 1950s, 684; in World War II, 647; zoot suits, 650

Coalition, 389

Coal mines: strikes in, 516, 610

Cobb, Frank, 545, 545 (illus.)

Code talkers: Navajo, **651**

Coercion, 378

Cohan, George M., 551

COINTELPRO, 747

Cold War, 665, 688; in Asia, 671–675; beginning of, 666–667, 669–671; Carter and, 768; confrontations in, 697 (map); containment and, 666; end of, 785, 785 (map); in Europe, 668 (map); Nixon and, 755–756, 757 (illus.); politics of, 678–681; Reagan and, 781–782; third world and, 696. *See also* Kennan, George F.

Collective bargaining, 563; farm workers and, 742; National Recovery Administration and, 607; Taft-Hartley Act and, 676; World War I and, **546**

Collier, John, 581, 582, 623 (illus.), 624, 625

Collier's magazine, 511, 517

Colombia, 591

Colonies and colonization: after Spanish-American War, 495–496; last scramble for, 524; Monroe Doctrine and, 521

Colored Farmers' Alliance, 481

Comanche Indians, 418

Combines, 425

Comedy: during 1930s, 627

Comic strips: in 1930s, 627. *See also* Cartoons

Coming of Age in Mississippi (Moody), 730 (illus.)

Commerce Department, 516, 589

Commission on Civil Rights, 712

Commission system, 512

Committee on Industrial Organization, 616

Committee to Re-elect the President (CREEP), 760, 761

Commodity markets, 475

Commonwealth of Independent States (CIS), **785**

Communications: computer and digital devices for, 799–800,

800 (illus.); information technology, 777

Communist Party (CP): of Soviet Union, 604

Communist Party of the United States, 582, 604; in Great Depression, 602, 609; Red Scare, 679–680

Communists and communism, 552; in Eastern Europe, 655; Korean War and, 674; in Latin America, 699; McCarthyism and, 694; Reagan and, 781–782; second Red Scare and, 678, 679–680; in third world, 696. *See also* Cold War; Red Scare; Vietnam War

Communities: ethnic, 449; of freed people, 376–377

Community Action Program (CAP), 727

Community Service Organization (CSO), 741

Commuter rail lines, 436

Compassionate conservatism: of George W. Bush, 803

Competition: in automobile industry, 569; Carnegie and, 398, 406; "merger movement" (1895-1905), 428–429, 429 (figure); railroads and, 402, 405; Rockefeller and, 398

Compromise of 1877, 390, 391

Computers, 799–800, 800 (illus.)

Concentration camps: Nazi, 636, 637 (map), 650, 656, 657 (illus.)

Concerned Women of America, 801

Confederacy, 416

Conference for Progressive Political Action, 586

Conference of Studio Unions, 679

Conglomerates, 702

Congress: First Hundred Days and, 606; Truman and, 677

Congressional Medal of Honor: in World War I, 552

Congressional Reconstruction, 380–385

Congressional Union, 583

Congress of Industrial Organizations (CIO), **616**; merger with AFL, 703; World War II and, 645

Congress of Racial Equality (CORE), **649,** 732

Congress (U.S.): Clinton and, 796; Contract with America and, 796; scandal in, 470, 471; TARP and, 812

Conkling, Roscoe, 471

Connor, "Bull," 722

Conscientious objectors, 551

Consciousness-raising groups, **735**

Consensus: rejecting, 707–708; in 1950s, 692–694

Conservation, 518. *See also* Preservationists; Roosevelt, Theodore

Conservative coalition, 614

Conservatives and conservatism: Buchanan and, 788; New Right and, 773–775; in 1980s, 775; in 1990s, 796; Supreme Court and, 802; Tea Party movement and, 794, 817, 818 (illus.); 2004 election and, 809. *See also* specific groups and presidents

Constitution (U.S.), 381, 382; Articles of, A7–A11; document, A7–A15. *See also* Amendments; specific Amendments

Consumer culture, 439

Consumer Financial Protection Bureau, 817

Consumer goods, 566; advertising of, 412–413, 412 (illus.)

Consumer-goods industries: economic concentration in, 413

Consumers and consumerism: in 1920s, 567–568; in 1950s, 681, 702–703, 705

Consumers' cooperatives: Grange and, 475

Containment policy, **666,** 675

Contraband: World War I and, **542**

Contraception. *See* Birth control

Contract bridge (game), 573

Contraction (economic), **426,** 427. *See also* Depression(s); Recessions

Contract with America, 796

Contras, 782, 787

Conventions: party, 468. *See also* specific parties

Coolidge, Calvin, 558; assumption of presidency, 586; Boston police strike and, 561; and business, 587, 588, 588 (illus.); foreign affairs and, 589

Cooperatives, 460

Cooper v. Aaron, **710,** 712

Coral Sea, Battle of, 651

CORE. *See* Congress of Racial Equality

Corporate personhood, 413

Corporations: in 1920s, 570; in 1950s, 702; Theodore Roosevelt and, 516

Corruption, 391; under Grant, 389, 390, 470–471; Harding and, 585; muckrakers and exposing of, 511–512; in music industry, 691; patronage system and, 468; Reconstruction officials and, 388; reform of

city government and, 512; Tweed Ring, 470–471. *See also* Bribery; specific scandals

COS. *See* Charity Organization Society

Cosmopolitan magazine, 511

Cost analysis, 413

Cotton and cotton industry: increased output and, 400; in New South, 414, 444. *See also* Textile industry

Cotton Club, 576

Cotton States and International Exposition, 446

Coughlin, Father Charles, 610, 611

Counterculture, 737, 737 (illus.)

Counterinsurgency forces, 723

Coups: in Chile, 756; in Czechoslovakia, **669**

Court-packing plan, 613

Cover records, 707

Covert operations, 696; Eisenhower and, 696; under Reagan, 781

Cowboys, 422 (illus.); in dime novels, 421; Mexican American, 420; in movies, 422

Cowley, Malcolm, 574

Cox, Archibald, 761

Cox, James, 561, 603

Coxey, Jacob S., 483

Craft unions, 457, 458

Crane, Stephen, 528

Crazy Horse, 418, 419

Creationism, 579

Credentials committee, 525

Credit: depression of 1890s and, 428; before Great Depression, 599; installment plans and, 568; lend-lease and, 639; sharecropping and, 378; stocks and, 570

Credit cards, 705

Credit crunch: Great Depression, 599, 600, 601

Crédit Mobilier scandal, 404, **470**

Creditor nation: U.S. as, **543,** 591

Creek Indians, 453

Creel, George, 548

Creel Committee, 548

Crime: in 1950s, 706; in World War II, 647, 650

Criminal syndicalism laws, 559

Crisis, The, 392

Crisis (journal), 560

Croatia, 786

Croix de Guerre: awarded to African Americans, **552**

Croker, Richard, 469

Cronkite, Walter, 747

Crop liens, 378

Crops: increased production in, 400. *See also* Agriculture; Farms and farming; specific crops

"Cross of gold" speech (Bryan), 484
Crow Indians, 417
Cuba, 501, 786; Castro in, 699; Lyndon Johnson and, 742; *Maine* and, 492–493; Platt Amendment and, 496; Spain and, 491, 492–494; Spanish American War in, 492–494, 494 (illus.); sugar industry in, 490, 491; U.S. intervention in, 589
Cuban missile crisis, 724–**725,** 725 (illus.)
Cubism, 528
Cultural war, 788
Culture(s): consumer, 567–568; in Great Depression, 625–627; homogenized, 572
Culture wars: gay marriage and, 808–809; women and, 800–801
Cummins, Albert B., 514
Currier and Ives cartoon, 401 (illus.)
Custer, George A., 418
Customs receivership, 522
Cuyahoga River, 437
Czechoslovakia, 553; after collapse of Soviet Union, 785 (map); coup in, 669; democratic government in, 785; Nazi Germany and, 636; Prague Spring in, 736

Dachau, 636, 657
Dairy farmers: milk dumping in Great Depression, 602 (illus.)
Dakota (Lakota) Indians, 416
Dakotas: Homestead Act and, 400
Dakota Territory: bonanza farms in, 425
Dams, 426; in West, 614. *See also* Tennessee Valley Authority
Dardanelles, 667
Darrow, Clarence, 578
Darwin, Charles, 407
Daugherty, Harry, 561, 585
Daughters of Bilitis, 707
Daughters of the American Revolution: Marian Anderson and, 622 (illus.), 623
Davis, Alexander, 390
Davis, Benjamin O., Jr., 650
Davis, John W., 586, 587
Dawes, Charles G., 591
Dawes Plan, 591, 592
Dawes Severalty Act, 453, 472
Dayton Agreement, 798
D-Day, 654, 655 (map)
DDT: banning of, 742, 758
Dean, James, 707
Death squads: in El Salvador, 782

Debs, Eugene V., 461, 462, 510; 1912 election and, 525, 526; Sedition Act and, 549
Debt: farmers in, 475, 476, 481; sharecropping and, 378
Declaration of Independence (U.S.): document, A1–A2
"Declaration of Indian Purpose," 751
"Deep Throat": in Watergate scandal, 761
Deepwater Horizon, 817
Defense Department: NSC and, 670
Defense industries: in World War II, 644–645
Defense of Marriage Act, 801
Defense spending. *See* Military spending
Defensive containment policy, 695
Deflation, 476, 477
De jure segregation, **708**
DeKalb County, Georgia decision, 802
Delaware, 373
Delgado v. Bastrop School District, **685**
Demilitarized zone (DMZ), **694**
Democratic Party: Bryan and, 485–486; characteristics of, 469; donkey symbol of, 470 (illus.); 1868 election and, 383; 1894 election and, 483–484; in Great Depression, 603, 623; New Departure and 1872 election, 388–389; Populists and, 482; post-World War II, 677–678; 2000 election and, 803; 2006 election and, 810, 811 (illus.)
Demon Rum, 507, 508
Demonstration Cities and Metropolitan Development Act, 729 (table)
Dempsey, Jack, 573
Denmark: Hitler and, 638
Department of Energy, 771
Department of Health, Education, and Welfare: creation of, 693
Department of Housing and Urban Development, 729 (table), 730
Department of the Interior, 607
Department of Transportation, 729 (table)
Departments of government. *See* Cabinet; specific departments
Department stores, 412, 413
Deportation: after Palmer raids, 559
Depression(s), 627; of 1870s, **390,** 391, 428, 458; of 1890s, 428, 462, 483. *See also* Great Depression
Deregulation: under Reagan, 776
Desegregation: of armed forces and federal workforce, 677; of

schools, 708–710, 710 (illus.); Supreme Court and, 712
Détente policy, **755,** 756
Detroit: race riots in, 733; strike in, 676 (illus.)
Dewey, George, 493, 494, 498
Dewey, Thomas E., 651, 677, 678, 678 (illus.), 678 (map)
Díaz, Adolfo, 522, 538
Díaz, Porfirio, 538
Dictators: in Latin America, 699; U.S. support for, 696
Diem, Ngo Dinh, 700, 725, 726
Dienbienphu, 700
Dime novels, 421
Diner's Club credit card, 705
Dior, Christian, 684
Dip, Jeu. *See* Tape family
Diplomacy: with China, 755–756; in Mexico, 538; of prosperity, 592–593; before World War II, 634. *See also* Foreign policy
Direct current (DC), 412
Direct democracy, 515
Direct primary, 513
Disabled Americans: workplace accidents and, 457
Disarmament: in 1920s, 592
Discrimination, 384, 685; against African Americans, 445, 537, 649; in armed forces, 649–650; against Catholics, 449; against children of Chinese descent, 433; disability, 716–717; in Great Depression, 621–622; against Jews, 449; against Latinos, 650, 749, 750; in 1920s, 579; segregated schools and, 387; sexual, 795; in suburbs, 682. *See also* specific groups
Discriminatory neutrality, 635
Disease: Spanish-American War and, 493. *See also* Health; Medicine
Disfranchise, 445
Disfranchisement, 384
Disneyland, 703
District of Columbia v. Heller, 802
Dividends, 413, 429, 571
Divorce, 508, 733; after World War II, 684, 688
Dixiecrat Party, 677
Dixon, Thomas, 393
DMZ. *See* Demilitarized zone
Doctors: women as, 440, 453 (illus.)
Documentary photography: in 1930s, 625
Dodd-Frank Act, 817
Dole, Robert, 796, 797
Dollar diplomacy, 522
Domesticity, 439–440

Dominican Republic: intervention in, 589, 742–743; as protectorate, 521; U.S. troops in, 538

Domino theory, 700

"Don't Ask, Don't Tell" policy, 795

Dot-coms, 799

Douglass, Frederick, 377; Black Reconstruction and, 385 (illus.); on Emancipation Proclamation, 371; on separate black schools, 387

Dow Jones Industrial Average: in Great Depression, 598

Draft (military): Vietnam War and, 745; World War I and, 551; World War II and, 639

Dred Scott decision, 384

Dreiser, Theodore, 528

Dresden: bombing of, 654

Drinking. *See* Alcohol and alcoholism

Drone warfare, 813

Drugs (illegal): counterculture and, 737; Noriega and trade in, 787, 788

Dry farming, 424

Dubcek, Alexander, 736

Du Bois, W. E. B., 392, 392 (illus.), **509,** 510, 533, 550, 576; on black veterans, 560

Duc, Nguyen Phu, 753 (illus.)

Duchamp, Marcel, 529

Duck Soup, 626

Dukakis, Michael: 1988 election and, 784

Duke, James B., 413

Dulles, Allen, 696

Dulles, John Foster, 695, 696, 699

Dumbarton Oaks conference, 666

Dunkirk, evacuation from, 638

Dunne, Finley Peter, 494

Dunning, William Archibald, 392, 392 (illus.)

Durant, William, 569

Durocher, Leo, 665

Dust Bowl, 617, 618 (illus.), 618 (map), 621

Dylan, Bob, 737

Dynamic conservatism: of Eisenhower, 693–694

Eagle Forum, 767, 801

Eagle Trust, 766

Earp, Wyatt, 421

Earth Day (1970), 757

East Asia: containment policy and, 675; Japan in, 634; Roosevelt and, 522–523; trade with, 487

East Berlin, 701

Eastern Europe: end of Cold War and, 785, 785 (map),

786; immigration from, 579; Soviet Union and, 655, 656

Eastern Hemisphere: national origin quota system and, 779

"Easter Offensive": in Vietnam, 755

East Germany, 670 (map)

eBay, 780

Eckford, Elizabeth, 710, 710 (illus.)

Ecology: BP oil spill and, 817; Dust Bowl and, 617, 618. *See also* Environment; Pollution

Economic development: during Reconstruction, 388

Economic Opportunity Act (1964), 726, 729 (table)

Economic Recovery Tax Act, 775

Economic sanctions, 770

Economy: Carter and, 771–772; of China, 700; from Civil War to World War I, 426–429; Clinton and, 789, 795–796, 798–800; dot-com stock collapse and, 799; federal spending for, 812; George H. W. Bush and, 784; globalization of, 776–778; industrialization and, 399; of Japan, 634, 776–777; main sectors of, 801 (figure); measures of growth, 1865-1900, 427 (figure); "merger movement" (1895-1905), 428–429, 429 (figure); in New South, 414–415; in 1920s, 567; in 1950s, 702–703; in 1960s, 719; Nixon and, 758–759; Obama and, 794, 811, 815; in post-Civil War South, 378; postindustrial, 776; in postwar Europe, 667; post-World War I, 557–558; post-World War II, 676–677; prosperity and, 681–683; public works projects and, 600–601; Reagan and, 775–776; World War I and, 546–547. *See also* Depression(s); Great Depression; Industrialization; Inflation; Labor; New Deal; Panics (financial)

Ecosystem, 422

Edcouch-Elsa school district (Texas), 750

Ederle, Gertrude, 573

Edison, Thomas A., 410, **411**–412, 411 (illus.), 415

Edson, Katherine Philips, 593 (illus.)

Education: bilingual, 749; Black Reconstruction and, 387–388; *Brown* decision and, 709; George W. Bush and, 803; for Indians, 452; Land-Grant College Act and, 439; Lyndon Johnson and, 731; in math and science, 694; of middle class,

439; in New South, 444; online, 800; for women, 439, 440

Egypt: Arab Spring and, 814; Israel and, 768, 770 (illus.); Nasser in, 698

Ehrlichman, John, 753, 761

Eighteenth Amendment, 560, 577, A13

Eighth Amendment, A12

Eight-hour workday, 458, 460, 476, 482, 512, 528, 546

Eisenhower, Dwight D.: Asia and, 699–700; civil rights and, 712; Cuba and, 699; domestic policy of, 693; dynamic conservatism of, 693–694; foreign policy of, 694–701; Korean War and, 675, 692, 694; Latin America and, 698–699; McCarthy and, 694; Middle East and, 696, 698; on "military-industrial complex," 702; New Look national security policy and, 695–696; 1952 election and, 692 (illus.), 693 (map); 1956 election and, 692; school desegregation and, 710; Soviet Union and, 700–701; Third World and, 696

Eisenhower Doctrine, 698

Elbe River, 654

Election(s): of 1866, 382; of 1868, 383–384; of 1872, 388–389, 389 (map); of 1874, 390; of 1876, 390–391, 391 (map), 393; of 1884, 472; of 1896, 484–486, 484 (illus.), 486 (map); of 1900, 496; of 1904, 516; of 1908, 519; of 1912, 503, 524–526, 525 (illus.), 526 (map); of 1916, 528, 543–544; of 1920, 561; of 1924, 586–587, 587 (map); of 1928, 588–589; of 1932, 603, 603 (map); of 1934, 611; of 1936, 612, 635; of 1938, 614; of 1940, 638; of 1942, 651; of 1948, 677–678, 678 (illus.), 678 (map); of 1952, 692; of 1956, 692; of 1960, 718–719, 719 (map); of 1964, 728; of 1968, 742, 747, 748–749, 749 (map); of 1972, 760; of 1976, 768; of 1980, 775; of 1984, 776; of 1988, 784; of 1992, 788–789, 789 (map); of 1994, 796; of 1996, 796–797; of 2000, 803, 804 (map); of 2004, 809; of 2006, 810; of 2008, 794, 811, 812 (map), 819 (illus.); of 2012, 794–795, 817–820, 820 (map); of 1890 and 1892, 482–483, 483 (map); of 1952 (map), 693 (map); presidential, A16–A20. *See also* Initiative; Referendum

Electoral College: 1876 election and, 390; 1968 election and, 749; 2000 election and, 803, 804 (map)

Electric appliances, 568

Electricity: consumer culture and, 568; Edison and, 411–412, 411 (illus.); in Great Depression, 607, 618; urban transit and, 436

Electronics industry, 780, 799; Japan and, 776–777; in 1950s, 702

Elementary and Secondary Education Act, 729 (table), 731

Eleventh Amendment, A12

Eliot, T. S., 574

Elkins Act (1903), 516

Ellington, Edward "Duke," 575

Ellsberg, Daniel, 754

El Salvador: death squads in, 782; George H. W. Bush and, 787; U.S. covert operations in, 781, 782

Emancipation, 370

Emancipation Proclamation, 370, 371, 372

Emergency Banking Bill, 605

Employment: post-World War I, 558 (illius.); of women, 547, 620; World War II and, 645

Empower, 374

Encyclicals, 506

Endangered Species Act, 758

"End Poverty in California" (EPIC) program: of Upton Sinclair, 611

Energy crisis, 771

Energy Policy and Conservation Act, 771

Enforcement Acts, 384

Enfranchise, 381, 481. *See also* Voting and voting rights

Engel v. Vitale, 727

England (Britain): immigrants from, 447; Iraq and, 807; sphere of influence of, 497; in Triple Entente, 540; in UN, 666; Venezuela/ British Guiana boundary dispute and, 491; in World War I, 552; in World War II, 633, 636, 638, 639

Enola Gay (B-29 bomber), 659 (illus.), 660

Entertainment: in Great Depression, 620 (illus.), 626; mass, in early twentieth century, 529–530

Entrepreneurs, 398, 409, 431; city services and, 438; competition and, 402, 406; Ford as, 568; inventions by, 411; in manufacturing, 398–399; philanthropy of, 409; railroads and, 402, 404, 405

Environment: DDT ban and, 758; Earth Day and, 757;

global warming and, 804; Nixon and, 757–758

Environmental Protection Agency (EPA), 757, 776

Equal access: to public transportation and accommodations, **388**

Equal Employment Opportunity Commission, 729 (table), 735

Equality: for women, 506. *See also* Women's rights

Equal Pay Act, 733

Equal Rights Amendment (ERA), **583,** 735, 766–767, **772,** 773 (illus.), 790

Ervin, Sam, Jr., 761

Escalation, 742

Escobedo v. Illinois, **727**

Espionage Act, 549

Estonia, 785

Ethiopia: Italian invasion of, 635; U.S. covert operations in, 781

Ethnic cleansing: in former Yugoslavia, 786; in Kosovo, 798

Ethnic groups: of immigrants, **449;** in 1920s, 580–581. *See also* specific groups

Ethnicity: political party and, 485

Ethnology, 553

Eugenics, 579

Euphrates river region, 808 (map)

Euro, 778

Eurofederalism, 778

Europe: America and, post-World War I, 591; Cold War in, 668 (map); end of Cold War and, 785, 785 (map); immigrants from, 447–449; postwar division of, 667, 668 (map), 669–671; in World War I, 537, 540, 541 (map), 542; in World War II, 636, 652–655, 655 (map). *See also* specific countries

Europe, James Reese, 560 (illus.)

European Economic Community (EEC), 778

European Union (EU), 778

Eurozone, 778

Evangelicalism, 578, 705; televangelists and, 774, 774 (illus.)

Evolution, 578; teaching in public schools, 579

Executive Order # 8802, 649

Executive Order # 9066, 642

Executive Order # 9835, 679

Exile's Return (Cowley), 574

Expansion (economic), **426,** 427

Expatriate intellectuals, in 1920s, **574**

Exports: in Great Depression, 600; in World War I, 543

Expositions, 530

Extermination camps, German, 636, 637 (map)

Factories: in World War II, 644, 645. *See also* Manufacturing

Fair Deal, 678

Fair Employment Practices Commission (FEPC), **649,** 675, 676, 726

Fair Housing Act, 733

Fair Labor Standards Act (1938), 598, **613,** 622, 627

Faith Memorial Church, 377 (illus.)

Fall, Albert, 581, 585

Fallout shelters, 695

Falwell, Jerry, 774, 774 (illus.)

Families: abortion rights and, 772; in Great Depression, 619, 620; in Great Plains, 424, 424 (illus.); middle class, 439; suburban culture and, 705; "togetherness" of, 706; women, culture war and, 800–801; in World War II, 647. *See also* Baby boom; Women

Family and Medical Leave Act, 795

Family Assistance Plan, 758

Famine: Chinese immigrants and, 450; immigration and, **448**

Farm Bloc, 586, 587

Farm Board, 601

Farmer, James, 649, 721

Farmers' Alliances, 481, 501

Farmers' Holiday Association, 602

Farms and farming: American Indians and, 415; bonanza farms, 425; dry farming, 424; Grange and, 475–476, 477 (illus.); immigrants and, 448; income, 1929-1935, 617 (figure); increased output and, 400–401; irrigation and, 426; mechanization of, 401; Mexican American workers and, 582, 582 (illus.); monetary policy and, 476; New Deal and, 606, 617; in New South, 414–415; in 1920s, 571, 585–586, 599; Populists and, 481–482; sharecropping and, 378; in West, 422–425; wheat farming, 424–425; World War II and, 645. *See also* Agriculture; Crops; Grange; Rural areas

Farm Security Administration (FSA), 618

Farm workers, 741, 780; strikes by, 749, 750 (illus.); winning rights for, 763; in World War II, 650

Fascism, 667

Fascists, 634

Fashion: "New Look" in, 684; in 1920s, 567, 573, 576. *See also* Clothing

Father Knows Best, 704, 704 (illus.), 705

Fathers. *See* Families; Men
Faubus, Orval, 710
FBI. *See* Federal Bureau of Investigation
Federal Arts Project (FAP), 625
Federal Bureau of Investigation (FBI), 679, 760, 761
Federal deficit: under Reagan, **775**
Federal Deposit Insurance Corporation (FDIC), **609**
Federal Emergency Management Agency (FEMA): Hurricane Katrina and, 810
Federal Emergency Relief Administration (FERA), **608–609**
Federal Employee Loyalty Program, 679
Federal Highway Act, 693
Federal Home Loan Bank Act, 601
Federal Housing Administration (FHA), **609**
Federalism: Supreme Court and, 803
Federal old-age and survivor insurance program. *See* Social Security Act (1935)
Federal receipts and expenditures, 1865-1901, 473 (figure)
Federal Reserve Act, 527, 528, 531
Federal Reserve Banks, 527
Federal Reserve Board, 528
Federal Reserve System, 527, 534; in Great Depression, 600, 605, 609; Wilson and, 527
Federal Trade Commission, 528
Federal Trade Commission Act, 527
Federal workforce: desegregation of, 677
FEMA. *See* Federal Emergency Management Agency
Feminine Mystique, The (Friedan), 686, 733
Feminism, 506, 507, 733; antifeminism and, 767, 801; self-determination and, **506**
Ferraro, Geraldine, 776
Fertilizers, 401
Fifteenth Amendment, 384, 391, 393, 395, A13
Fifth Amendment, A11
"Fifth Amendment Communists," 679
Filibuster, 726; politics of, 814–815, 817
Filipinos: in Hawai'i, 581
Final Solution, 656–657
Finance companies, 568
Financial and investment institutions: TARP and, 812. *See also* Savings and loan industry
Financial panic, 428

Firefighters: urban, 438
Fireside chats: of Franklin Roosevelt, **605,** 639
First Amendment, 382, A11
First Hundred Days, 629; of New Deal, **606,** 615 (table)
"Fiscal cliff," 818
Fiscal policies, 719
Fish, Hamilton, 470
Fish-ins, 752
Fitzgerald, F. Scott, 571, 574, 577
Fitzgerald, Zelda Sayre, 567
Fixed costs, 402
Flagg, James Montgomery, 548 (illus.)
"Flaming Youth," 576–577
Flappers, 566, 576, 577 (illus.), 583
Flexible response policy, 717, **723**
Flores, Moises, 685
Florida: land speculation in, 571; 2000 election and, 803
Florida (ship), 487
Following the Color Line (Baker), 509
Fonda, Henry, 626
Food(s): World War I and, 546, 547, 548 (illus.), 588; World War II and, 647. *See also* Crops
Food Stamp Act of 1977, 720
Food stamps, 720, 758, 796
Foraker Act, 496
Ford, Edsel, 648
Ford, Gerald R., 761; foreign policy of, 762; 1976 election and, 768; as president, 761–762; as vice president, 761
Ford, Henry, 568, 569, 570; Anti-Semitism of, 579
Ford, John, 626
Ford Motor Company, 568–569, 569 (illus.), 591
Fordney-McCumber Tariff, 591, 592
Foreclosure: Great Recession and, 812; on mortgages, **602**
Foreign aid. *See* Economic aid
Foreign policy: of Carter, 768, 770–771; of Clinton, 797–798, 805; of Eisenhower, 694–701; of Ford, 762; of George H. W. Bush, 784–788; of George W. Bush, 804; of Kennedy, 723–726; of Lyndon Johnson, 742–743, 745, 747; in 1920s, 592–593; of Obama, 813–814; of Reagan, 781–784; Schurz on, 500; of Theodore Roosevelt, **520, 521;** of Truman, 671; of Wilson, 538. *See also* Cold War; Diplomacy; Treaties; specific countries; specific presidents and issues
Forrestal, James, 650

Fortune magazine, 778
Forty-Second Street, 626
For Whom the Bell Tolls (Hemingway), 625
Fourteen Points, 553, 556, 562, 563
Fourteenth Amendment, 375, 384, 391, 393, 395, 413, 445, 613, A12–A13; citizenship and, 381–382; defining meaning of, 452; women's rights and, 382
Fourth Amendment, A11
Fragging, 755
France: in Indochina, 675, 679, 700; Mexico and, 487; sphere of influence of, 497; in Triple Entente, 540; in UN, 666; in World War I, 551, 552; in World War II, 633, 636, 638, 653–654. *See also* World War I; World War II; specific wars
Franchises, 438
Franchise (voting rights). *See* Voting and voting rights
Franco, Francisco, 610, 635
Franz Ferdinand (Austria), World War I and, 537
Fraternal orders: for blacks, **377;** for men, 440
Freed, Alan, 690–691, 690 (illus.), 707
Freedman's Aid Societies, 376–377
Freedmen's Bureau, 376, 377, 386, 387, 509; land redistribution and, 377; schools and, 378 (illus.)
Freedom: for former slaves, 375–376
Freedom fighters, in Hungary, 701
Freedom of Access to Clinic Entrances Act, 801
Freedom rides, 721, 723 (illus.)
Freedom Summer, 729–730, 730 (illus.)
Freed people, 370. *See also* Slaves and slavery
Free love: counterculture and, 737
Free Speech Movement, 736
Free trade, 795
French, Daniel Chester, 531 (illus.)
French Indochina, 675, 699, 700
Freud, Sigmund: homosexuality and, **585**
Frick, Henry Clay, 461
Friedan, Betty, 686, 733, 735
Frontier: Great Plains, 424, 424 (illus.)
Fruit raising, 425
Fulbright, William J., 745
Fundamentalism, 578; in Iran, 770–771; Islamic, 770, 806; Scopes trial and, 578

Galveston, Texas, city
  manager plan in, 512
Gambling, 508
Gangsters, in 1920s, 578
GAR. *See* Grand Army of
  the Republic
Garbo, Greta, 566
Garfield, James A., 468, 471, 472, 477
Garland, Hamlin, 530
Garmin, 780
Garn-St. Germain Act, 776
Garvey, Marcus, 576
Gary, Indiana: unemployment
  in (1933), 600; U.S.
  Steel strike in, 558
Gates, Bill, 777, 778
GATT. *See* General Agreement
  on Tariffs and Trade
Gauges, 402
Gayle et al. v. Browser, 712
Gay Manifesto, 735
Gay rights, 801
Gays and lesbians. *See* Homosexuals
  and homosexuality
Gaza Strip, 671
Gehrig, Lou, 573
G-8 nations, 798
Gender: changes in roles and,
  464; in Gilded Age, 439–442;
  in 1920s, 583, 595; in suburban
  families, 704, 704 (illus.), 705;
  wage differential and, 456;
  in World War II workforce,
  647–648. *See also* Men; Women
**General Agreement on Tariffs
  and Trade** (GATT), 795
General Assembly (U.N.), 666
General Electric, 412, 777
General Managers Association, 462
General Mills, 567
General Motors (GM),
  569, 591, 702, 812
General Pass Regulations Bill, 446
General strike, 459
Geneva Agreement, 700
Geneva Summit (1955), 700–701
Gentlemen's agreement, 523
George, David Lloyd, 554
George, Henry, 409, 443
Georgia: maps of plantation
  in, 379 (illus.)
German Americans: World
  War I and, 548–549
Germans: World War II and, 563
**German-Soviet Nonaggression
  Pact, 636**
Germany: army in, 540; cartels
  in, 411; Cold War in, 670;
  expansion of, 1933-1942, 637
  (map); immigrants from, 423,

447, 466; reparations and, 591;
  sphere of influence of, 497; in
  Triple Alliance, 540; U-boats
  and, 542–543, 546; unification
  of, 785; in World War I, 540,
  542–543, 544, 546, 548, 552, 552.
  See also Cold War; Nazi Germany;
  World War II; specific wars
Geronimo, 419, 452
Gershwin, George, 576
Ghost Dance, 419
Ghouls, 380
G.I. Bill (1944), **651,** 665,
  681, 682, 683, 685
Giannini, A. P., 569, 570
Gideon vs. Wainwright, **727**
Gilbert Islands, 652, 657
Gilded Age, 433–465; ethnicity
  and race in, 447–450, 452–455;
  federal economic policy
  debate and, 479; middle class
  in, 437, 438–439; redefining
  gender roles in, 439–442
Gilded Age, The: A Tale of Today
  (Clemens and Warner), 434
Gingrich, Newt, 796, 798 (illus.)
Ginsberg, Allen, 708
Gladden, Washington, 506
Glasnost, 783
Glass, Carter, 527
Glass ceiling, 801
Glass-Steagall Act, 601
Globalization, 776–778,
  795–796, 797 (illus.), 799
Global warming, 804
GMA. *See* General Managers
  Association
Godzilla (1954), 696
Gold, 420, 422; in Black Hills,
  418; in California, 399,
  454; in Montana, 422
Gold Beach, 654
Gold Democrats, 485
Gold Diggers of 1933, 626
Golden Gate Park, San Francisco, 437
Gold Rush: Chinese
  immigrants and, 450
Gold standard, 476; *vs.* silver, 484–485
Goldwater, Barry, 728, 766
Gompers, Samuel, 461, 462, 547
Gonzales, Rodolfo "Corky," 749
Good Neighbor policy, 634
Google, 780, 794, 821
Gorbachev, Mikhail, 783, 783 (illus.)
Gore, Al, 794; 2000 election
  and, 803, 804 (map); as vice
  president, 796, 798 (illus.)
Gospel of Wealth, 408, 409
Government: business and,
  702; economic development

and, 399; railroads and, 403;
  Republican shutdown of, 818;
  war and power of, 645. *See also*
  Constitution (U.S.); Politics
Government contracts, 468
Graduated income tax, 476
Grady, Henry, 414
Graham, Billy, 705
Grand Alliance: in World
  War II, 655–656
Grand Army of the Republic, 469
Grand Coulee Dam, 614
Grandfather clause, 446
Grand Passenger Station
  (Chicago), 404 (illus.)
Grange, 475–476, 481, 501;
  political cartoon, 478 (illus.)
Granger laws, 472, 476
Granger Parties, 475–476,
  477 (illus.), 479
Grant, Ulysses S., 467; 1868
  election and, 383; as General
  of the Army, 382; Mississippi
  Plan and, 390; presidency of,
  384, 470–471; Reconstruction
  and, 391; scandals and, 390
Grape industry: strike against,
  749, 750 (illus.)
Grapes of Wrath, The (film), 626, 679
Grapes of Wrath, The
  (Steinbeck), 625, 780
Grau San Martín, Ramon, 634
Great American Desert, 422
Great Chicago Fire of 1871, 438
Great Depression, 599, 629, 634;
  culture in, 625–627; discrimination
  during, 621–622; economics of,
  599, 601 (figure); in Europe, 600;
  Herbert Hoover and, 600–601;
  lifestyle during, 619–620; in
  perspective, 627; prevention of
  recurrence, 600; prices during,
  600, 609; protests during, 602;
  public works projects during,
  600–601; relief during, 606–609,
  611; strikes during, 602, 610,
  613; unemployment in, 600, 601,
  608–609, 608 (map), 613, 614,
  621; women's roles during, 620;
  year of turmoil in 1934, 609–611.
  See also New Deal; Roosevelt,
  Franklin D.; Stock market crash
Great Dictator, The (movie), 626
**Greater East Asian Co-Prosperity
  Sphere, 634,** 641 (map)
Great Gatsby, The (Fitzgerald), 574
Great Leap Forward (China), 700
Great Migration: of African
  Americans from South,
  549–550, 550 (illus.), 563

Great Northern Railroad, 405
Great Plains region, **415**; cattle and, 420–422; farming in, 422–425; in Great Depression, 617; Indians of, 415–420, 431; rainfall in, 423 (map), 424; water and, 426
Great Railway Strike of 1877, 459, 459 (illus.), 464
Great Recession (2007-), 811–812, 815
Great Sioux Reservation, 417, 419; gold in, 418
Great Sioux War, 418, 452
Great Society, 728–732, 729 (table)
Great White Fleet, 523, 523 (illus.)
Greece, 557; civil war in, 667
Greeley, Horace, 389
Greenback Party, 476, 479, 481, 482, 501
Greenbacks, 476, 479
Green Berets, 723
Green Party, 804 (map)
Greer (ship), 640
Grenada, invasion of, **781**
Grey, Edward, 542
Griswold v. Connecticut, 728
Gross national product (GNP), 702
Groves, Leslie R., 658
Guadalcanal Island: invasion of, **652,** 653 (map)
Guadalupe Hidalgo, Treaty of, 454
Guam, 495, 497, 501
Guatemala: human rights in, 768; intervention in, 699, 699 (illus.)
Guerrilla warfare: of Plains Indians, **417**
Guiteau, Charles, 471
Gulf of Mexico region: oil spill in, 817
Gulf of Tonkin Resolution, 743, 754

Hagan, Kay, 819
Hague, The: International War Crimes Tribunal at, 798
Haiti: Clinton and, 798; as protectorate, 538; U.S. intervention in, 589; U.S. troops in, 538
Haldeman, H. R. ("Bob"), 753, 758, 759, 761
Hamilton Lodge drag ball, Harlem, 585
Hanoi, 743, 754
Haole community (Hawai'i), 488, 490, 491
Harding, Warren G., 563, 589, 592, 595; failed presidency of, 585–586; League of Nations and, 561, 589
Harlem: protest in, **550**
Harlem Renaissance, 574–576, 581
Harper's Weekly, 385 (illus.)

Harper v. Virginia, 730
Harrington, Michael, 726
Harrison, Benjamin: Congress and, 472–474; 1892 election and, 482; Latin America and, 491
Harris v. Forklift Systems, 801
Hart-Celler Act, 779
Harvard University, 439
Hassam, Childe, 528
Havana Harbor, *Maine* at, 492, 492 (illus.)
Hawai'i, 487–488, 497, 501; annexation of, 493; revolution in, 490–491; sugar industry in, 488. *See also* Pearl Harbor
Hay, Henry, 707
Hay, John, 492, 497, 499
Hay-Bunau-Varilla Treaty, 520
Hayden, Tom, 736
Hayes, Rutherford B., 390, 391, 395, 458, 459, 466, 467, 471, 477
Haymarket bombing, 461
Haynsworth, Clement, 760
Head Start, 727, 729 (table)
Health: local government and, 512; of migratory workers, 617. *See also* Disease; Medicine
Healthcare: Clinton and, 795; costs of, 800; Hillary Rodham Clinton and, 795; Lyndon Johnson and, 731–732; Obama and, 813, 815–817
Hearst, William Randolph, 485, **491**
Helms, Jesse, 795
Hemingway, Ernest, 574, 625
Hemispheres. *See* Eastern Hemisphere; Western Hemisphere
Henderson, Fletcher, 575
Henri, Robert, 528
Hepburn Act (1906), 472, **518,** 531
Hetch Hetchy Valley, damming of, 426
Hezbollah, 782, 783
Hickok, James B. "Wild Bill," 421
Higgins, Andrew, 644
"Higgins Boat," 644
Higgins Industries, New Orleans, 644
"High Cost of Living" (HCL): after World War I, 557–558
Higher education. *See* Universities and colleges; specific schools
High schools, 439
Hill, James J., 420
Hill, T. Arnold, 549
Hine, Lewis, 444 (illus.)
Hippies, 737, 737 (illus.)
Hirohito, Emperor, 660
Hiroshima, 659, 659 (illus.), **660**
Hispanics: in Vietnam War, 755. *See also* Latinos
Hispanos, 455
Hiss, Alger, 679, 680

Hitler, Adolf, 592, 626, 633, 635, 636, 639, 651, 669; on Battle of Stalingrad, 654 (illus.); "Final Solution" of, 656–657, 657 (illus.); suicide by, 655; in World War II, 640. *See also* Nazi Germany; World II; specific countries
Ho Chi Minh Trail, 743, 744 (map)
Holding company, 410, 411, 571
Hollywood. *See* Movies and movie industry
Hollywood Ten, 679
Holmes, Oliver Wendell: bomb sent to, 558
Holocaust, 656–657
Homeland Security, Department of, 805
Homelessness, 428; in Great Depression, 608, 620; in 1980s, 778
Home Owners' Loan Corporation (HOLC), 609
Homestead Act (1862), **399,** 400, 415; Great Plains region and, 422, 423; immigrants and, 448
Homestead strike, 408, 461
Homestead Works, 406 (illus.)
Homogenized culture, **572**
Homosexuals and homosexuality: AIDS and, 795, 796; Clinton and, 795; gay and lesbian subculture and, 441–442, 585; lesbian rights and, 735; medical classification and, 735; in military, 795; in 1950s, 707; during World War II, 651
Hookworm, 512, 513 (illus.)
Hoover, Herbert, 547, 585, 595, 629, 634; as commerce secretary, 588, 593 (illus.); as food administrator, 588; Great Depression and, 600–601; 1928 election and, 588–589, 598; 1932 election and, 603, 603 (map)
Hoover, J. Edgar, 558, 679, 733
Hoovervilles, 601, 602, 619
Hopkins, Harry, 605, **611,** 613, 616, 622
Horizontal integration: in consumer-goods industries, 413; of oil industry, **409,** 410 (figure)
Horse culture, 415, 416
Horses: Indians and, 415–416, 417 (illus.)
Hostage crisis: in Iran, 771, 771 (illus.)
Houghton, Meg, 793
House, Edward M., 543
House of Morgan, 410
House of Representatives: first African American to serve in, 369–370, 369 (illus.)

House Un-American Activities Committee (HUAC), 665, **679**–680

Housing: for middle class, 438, 438 (illus.); in 1920s, 571; in 1950s, 681–682, 681 (illus.); restrictive covenants in, 449, 579; sod houses, 423–424, 424 (illus.); suburban, 703, 705; tenements, 443; tract homes, 681–682

Housing market: Great Recession and, 811–812

Howard, Oliver O., 377

Howells, William Dean, 528

Howl (Ginsberg), 708

How the Other Half Lives (Riis), 442, 442 (illus.)

Huckleberry Finn (Twain), 434, 528

Huerta, Dolores, 741–742, 741 (illus.), 749, 763

Huerta, Victoriano, 538, 539

Hughes, Charles Evans, 528, 544, 585, 589, 591, 592

Hughes, Langston, 575, 575 (illus.)

Hull, Cordell, 640

Hull House, 504, 505

Human rights: Carter and, **768**

Humphrey, Hubert, 728 (illus.); 1968 election and, 742, 748, 749 (map)

Hungary, 553, 557; democratic government in, 785; Soviet invasion of, 701

Huns, 542, 548 (illus.)

Hunting, 44

Huntington, Collis P., 404

Hurley, Patrick, 651

Hurricane Katrina, 810, 810 (illus.)

Hurston, Zora Neale, 574

Husbands. *See* Families; Men

Hussein, King (Jordan), 698

Hussein, Saddam. *See* Saddam Hussein

Hyde Amendment, 773

Hydrogen bomb, 695, 700

"I, Too" (Hughes), 575

Ia Drang Valley, 743

IBM, 777

ICBMs. *See* Intercontinental ballistic missiles (ICBMs)

ICC. *See* Interstate Commerce Commission

Ice-making machine, 411

Ickes, Harold, 607, 622, 623, 624

Icon, 422

Idaho: woman suffrage in, 479

Illegal immigrants, 780, 781

Illiteracy: in New South, 444

Immigrants and immigration: from Asia, 450; Chinese as, 450, 452; ethnic groups and, 449; from Europe, 447–449; in farming, 423; gangsters and, 578; in Gilded Age, 433; illegal immigrants, 780; from Japan, 452, 523, 642; Jewish refugees in World War II and, 636; from Mexico, 454, 455; National Origins Act (1924) and, 579; nativism and, 579; in 1980s, 778, 780–781; Obama and, 818–819; prohibition and, 508; railroad land grant advertising, 448 (illus.); Sapiro, Aaron, 579; urbanization and, 435, 436 (map); to U.S. by origin, 1950-2009, 779 (figure). *See also* Migrants and migration; Slaves and slavery

Immigration Act of 1986, 779

Immigration and Nationality Act (1965), 729 (table), 730–731, 778

Immigration and Naturalization Service (INS), 621

Immigration Reform and Control Act, 781

Impeachment: of Andrew Johnson, 383, 383 (illus.); of Clinton, 797; Nixon and, 761

Imperialism, 495, 496

Import(s): Fordney-McCumber Tariff and, 591; protective tariffs and, 399

Impressionism, 528, 529 (illus.)

Income: of farmers, 571; in Great Depression, 600; median, 1949, 682 (map); for three groups of Americans, 1913-1929, 567 (figure); in World War II, 647

Income gap: growth of, 800

Income inequality: in 1980s, 778

Income tax, 483, 485, 527, 531, 547, 646, 774

Indemnity, 499

India: customer service centers in, 777 (illus.); immigrants from, 780; Sino-Indian War, 757

Indian Civil Rights Act, 752

Indian Gaming Regulatory Act, 753

Indian Reorganization Act, 623 (illus.), **624**

Indians. *See* American Indians

Indian Self-Determination and Education Assistance Act, 752

Indian Territory, 418, 419, 421

Indigenous peoples: Hawaiians as, 488. *See also* American Indians

Indochina, 675; Japanese troops in, 640; "war of national liberation" in, 699. *See also* Cambodia; Laos; Vietnam

Indonesia: Japan and, 640

In Dubious Battle (Steinbeck), 625

Industrial accidents, 457

Industrial cartels: in Europe, 411

Industrial economy: expansion of, 409–415

Industrialization: interchangeable parts and, 399; resources, skills, capital and, 398–399; workers and, 455–457, 456 (figure)

Industrial union, 461

Industrial Workers of the World (IWW, Wobblies), 510, 510 (illus.), 533, 549

Industry, 399; average annual earnings for men, women, and children in, 457 (figure); in Great Depression, 600, 608; Great Migration and, 549; post-World War II, 683; World War I and, 546, 547; World War II and, 644–645. *See also* Labor; Manufacturing; specific industries

Inflation: Carter and, 771, 772; Ford and, 762; George H. W. Bush and, 784; Nixon and, 758–759; post-World War I, 557–558; post-World War II, 676, 677; Reagan and, 775; World War II and, 645

Influence of Sea Power upon History, The (Mahan), 489

Influenza epidemic (1918), **552**

Information: Twitter and, 794

Information technology, 799

Infrastructure: urban, **437**

Ingalls, John J., 482

Initiative, 515

Injunction: against Pullman strikers, **462**

Inouye, Daniel Ken, 643

Installment buying, 599

Installment plans, 568, 570

Insular Cases, 496

Insull, Samuel, 570

Insurgents, 491

Integration: of baseball teams, 664–665, 686; *Brown* decision and, 709, 712; of military, 677; Nixon and, 759–760; of schools, 708–710; during World War II, 649, 650. *See also* Desegregation

"Intelligent design," 579

Interchangeable parts, 399

Intercontinental ballistic missiles system (ICBMs), 695, **723, 756**

Interest groups, 505; rise of, 514–515

Interest rates: in Great Depression, 600

Interlocking directorates, 527

Intermarriage: racial, 445
Intermediate Nuclear Force Treaty, 784
Intermediate-range ballistic missiles, 695
Internal Revenue Service, 760
International affairs. *See* Diplomacy; Foreign policy; International relations
International Brigades, 610
International Code Council, 443
International cooperation, 666–667
Internationalism: independent, 592–593
International Ladies' Garment Workers' Union, 582
International Monetary Fund, 666
International Telephone and Telegraph, 702
International War Crimes Tribunal (Hague), 798
Internet, 793, 799, 821
Internment camps: for Japanese Americans, 632–633, 632 (illus.), 642–644, 643 (map), 644 (illus.), 662
Interstate commerce: railroads and, 516
Interstate Commerce Act (1887), 472
Interstate Commerce Commission, 472, 518, 721
Intervention: in Haiti, 538
Inventors and inventions: Edison and, 410–412, (illus.). *See also* Technology; specific inventors and inventions
Investment: in Japan, 634; in Mexico, 538
Investment banks and bankers: industrial reorganizations and, 429; railroads and, 405; steel industry and, 406
Iowa Pool, 402
iPad, 800 (illus.)
iPhone, 800 (illus.)
Iran, 782; Carter and, 768, 770–771, 771 (illus.); crisis in, 667; oil interests in, 696; Twitter and protests in, 794
Iran-Contra Affair, 782, 783
Iraq, 556; Kuwait invaded by, 787, 788 (map); Obama and, 813; Persian Gulf War and, 787, 788; politics and, 807–809; weapons inspections in, 806–807
Iraq War: Second, 807, 808 (map); troop surge in, 810–811
Ireland: immigrants from, 420, 447, 448. *See also* Northern Ireland

Iron and iron industry: development of, 399
Iron curtain, 667, 668 (map)
Iron curtain speech: of Churchill, 667
Irreconcilables, 557
Irrigation: in Great Plains, 426; in Southwest, 582
"Is Google Making Us Stupid?" (Carr), 821
Islam: bin Laden, Al-Qaeda and, 805. *See also* Islamic fundamentalism; Muslims
Islamic fundamentalism, 770, 806
Isolationism, 589, 634–636
Isolationists, 639
Israel: Camp David Accords and, 768, 770; Clinton and, 798; creation of, 671; Egypt and, 768, 770 (illus.)
Issei, **642,** 643
Italy, 635; Ethiopia invaded by, 635; expansion of, 1933–1942, 637 (map); immigrants from, 449; treaty with Nazi Germany and Japan, 640; in Triple Alliance, 540; in World War II, 633, 641, 653. *See also* World War II
Iwo Jima, Battle of, 658, 658 (illus.)
IWW. *See* Industrial Workers of the World

Jackson, Andrew, 482
Jackson, Helen Hunt, 452
Jackson State: student deaths at, 754
Jacobvellis v. Ohio, 728
James, Henry, 528
James Madison amendment, 772
Japan, 540; advances by, December 1941-1942, 641 (map); as Allies in World War I, 540; China invaded by, 635; electronics industry and, 776–777; halting advances by, in World War II, 651–652; immigrants from, 452, 523, 780; investment in, 589; Manchuria and, 522, 634; navy of, 592, 593; Pearl Harbor and, 633, 640–641, 642, 642 (illus.), 662; trade with, 487; treaty with Nazi Germany and Italy, 640; war with China (1894), 524; World War I and, 540, 546; World War II and, 652 (illus.), 657–658. *See also* World War II
Japanese American Citizens League, 621
Japanese Americans: Nazi concentration camps liberated by, 657; relocation and

internment in World War II, 632–633, 632 (illus.), 642–644, 643 (map), 644 (illus.), 662
Jazz, 528
Jazz Age: 1920s as, 566, 575
Jefferson, Thomas: Populists and quoting of, 481–482
Jefferson Airplane, 737
Jenney, William LeBaron, 436
Jews and Judaism: anti-Semitism and, 636; Final Solution and, 656–657; Hitler and, 636; Holocaust and, 656–657; immigrants and, 449; Israel and, 671; nativism and, 579. *See also* Israel; Religion
Jiang Jieshi (Chiang Kai-shek), 672
Job Corps, 726, 729 (table), 758
Jobs: in service industries, 800. *See also* Employment; Unemployment
Johnson, Andrew, 390; impeachment of, 383, 383 (illus.); Reconstruction and, 373–375, 380, 381
Johnson, Eliza McCardle, 373
Johnson, Eric, 679
Johnson, Hiram, 514, 514 (illus.), 525 (illus.), **561**
Johnson, Hugh, 606
Johnson, James Weldon, 574
Johnson, Lady Bird, 728 (illus.)
Johnson, Lyndon B., 712, 726, 728 (illus.), 779; Great Society and, 728–732; Medicare and, 729 (table), 731; 1960 election and, 718; 1964 election and, 728; 1968 election and, 742; presidency of, 726–728; Tet offensive and, 747–748; Vietnam War and, 742–743, 745, 747; War on Poverty and, 726–727
Jones, Bobby, 573
Jones, Samuel ("Golden Rule"), 512
Joplin, Scott, 528
Jordan, 556, 698, 798
Jordan Marsh (store), 412
Journalism: yellow, 491. *See also* Newspapers
Journalists: muckrakers, 511–512
Juarez, Benito, 487
Jubilee, 376
Judicial restraint, 802
Judicial Revolution of 1937, 613
Jungle, The (Sinclair), 511–512, 511 (illus.), 517, 611
Juno Beach, 654
Justice Department: Palmer raids and, 559
Juvenile crime: in 1950s, 706; during World War II, 650

Kaiser, Henry J., 645
Kalakaua, David, 488, 490
Kamikaze, 658, 658 (illus.)
Kandinsky, Wassily, 529
Kansas: Homestead Act and, 400
Karzai, Hamid, 806
Kearney (ship), 640
Keaton, Buster, 573
Kellogg, Frank, 589, 593
Kellogg-Briand Pact, 593
Kelly, William, 406
Kem, Omer M., 424 (illus.)
Kendo lessons, **632, 633**
Kennan, George, 669; "Long
    Telegram" of, 666
Kennedy, John F., 717; assassination
    of, 726; Bay of Pigs invasion
    and, 724; civil rights and,
    719–723; Cuban missile crisis
    and, 725; foreign policy of,
    723–726; Hispanics and, 749; New
    Frontier of, 719; 1960 election
    and, 718–719, 718 (illus.), 719
    (map); Vietnam and, 725–726
Kennedy, Joseph, Sr., 716
Kennedy, Robert, 717; assassination
    of, 748; as attorney general,
    719; on Cuban missile crisis,
    724; freedom riders and, 721;
    1968 election and, 748
Kennedy, Rosemary, 716
Kennedy Foundation, 716, 717
Kent State University: student
    deaths at, 754
Kentucky, 373
Kenya: embassy attacked in, 805
Kerner Commission, 733
Kerouac, Jack, 708
Kerry, John, 808, 809
Keynesianism, 702
Khomeini, Ruhollah (Ayatollah), 770
Khrushchev, Nikita, 700, 701,
    721, 723, 724, 725
Kibei, **632, 633**
Kickbacks, 470, 471
Kimel case, 803
Kim Il Sung, 672
King, Martin Luther, Jr., 711, 711
    (illus.), 712; assassination of,
    733; Birmingham marches
    and, 722–723; March on
    Washington, 723; Nobel Peace
    Prize awarded to, 732; Vietnam
    War opposed by, 745; voter
    registration and, 729–730
Kinsey, Alfred, 707
Kiowa Indians, 418
Kipling, Rudyard, 490
Kissinger, Henry, 753, 753
    (illus.), 762; Chile and, 756;

China relations and, 755;
    Vietnam War and, 755
Kiyota, Minoru, 632–633
Klamath tribe (Oregon), 695
Klan. *See* Ku Klux Klan
Kleenex tissues, 568
Klehr, Harvey, 604
Knights of Labor, 459, 460, 460
    (illus.), 461, 481, 616
Korea, 524, 776; immigrants
    from, 780; trade with, 487.
    See also Korean War
Korean War, 672, 673 (map),
    674–675, 674 (illus.), 680, 700;
    Eisenhower and, 692, 694;
    integration of military during, 677
Korematsu v. United States, 642, 644, 661
Korgia, Hercules, 552
Kosovo, 798, 799 (illus.)
Kotex, 568
Kroc, Ray, 703
Krokodil, 669 (illus.)
Ku Klux Klan, 380, 384, 388, 390,
    395, 560, 580, 586, 595; 1868
    election and, 383; portrayals
    of, 380 (illus.), 580 (illus.)
Ku Klux Klan Act: of 1871, 370;
    Rainey's speech in support of, 394
Kuwait, 814; Iraq invasion
    of, 787, 788 (map)

Labor: African American migration
    and, 549–550; in agriculture, 456;
    Chinese immigrant, 450, 452; in
    1890s, 461–462; farm workers,
    741–742; in Great Depression,
    612, 613; industrial, 510; Japanese,
    452, 523; manufacturing and,
    399; in 1920s, 583; in 1950s, 703;
    in postwar South, 377–378; for
    railroads, 420, 421 (illus.); skilled
    workers and, 458; in southern
    textile industry, 414; wheat farms,
    425; Wilson and, 528; World War I
    and, 546; World War II and, 645,
    646, 646 (illus.), 647–648. *See also*
    Factories; Labor unions; Slaves
    and slavery; Strikes; Workers
Labor Department, 516, 527
Labor organizations: competing,
    in 1880s, 459–461
Labor unions: blacklisting and, 612;
    Debs and, 510; Fair Labor Standards
    Act and, 598; farm workers in, 742,
    749; in Great Depression, 609–610;
    Mexican Americans and, 582; in
    1920s, 582; origins of, 457–459;
    post-World War I, 595; post-World
    War II, 676–677; racketeering

and, 578; trade unions as, 457;
    Wagner Act and, 616; World
    War I and, 546–547, 557–558.
    See also Strikes; specific unions
La Causa, 742, 749–751
Ladies' Home Journal, 439, 517
La Flesche, Francis, 415
La Flesche, Susan, 453 (illus.), 454
La Follette, Robert M., 513,
    514, 524, 525, 585; 1912
    election and, 514; in 1920s,
    586–587, 587 (map); Wisconsin
    government reform and,
    514; World War I and, 546
Laissez faire, 407, 409
Lake Erie, 757
Lakota Indians: horse culture
    and, 416, **417;** Wounded
    Knee and, 419 (illus.), 420
Lambert, Gerard, 567
Land-Grant College Act
    (1862), **399,** 439
Land grants: railroads and, 402
Landon, Alfred, 612, 635
Land redistribution, 377
Land(s): boom in Florida, 571;
    conservation, 518; Dawes Act
    and, 453; in Great Plains region,
    415, 422, 423; Homestead
    Act and, 399, 400, 422, 423;
    in postwar South, 377–378;
    of southwestern Mexican
    Americans, 454–455; speculation
    in, 571. *See also* Land grants
Lange, Dorothea, 625, 625 (illus.)
Lanham Act, 648
Lansing, Robert, 543
Laos, 700; immigrants from, 780;
    Vietnam War and, 754
Latin America, 638; crises in, 491;
    Eisenhower and, 698–699;
    immigrants from, 778, 779;
    Kennedy and, 724; Lyndon
    Johnson and, 742; Nixon and,
    756; Truman and U.S. presence
    in, 671; United States and,
    487, 589, 590 (map), 591
Latinos: activism by, 742; changing
    population of, 2000, 750 (map);
    in Great Depression, 621;
    New Deal and, 622, 623, 623
    (illus.); post-World War II, 683,
    685–686, 686 (illus.), 688; rights
    for, 749–751; in Southwest,
    455; World War II and, 647
Latvia, 785
Lawrence, Massachusetts:
    industrial economy in, 456
Lawrence v. Texas, 382, 795
Lawyers, women as, 440

League Covenant, **556,** 557
League of Nations, 554, 556, 557, 561, 563, 634; Wilson and, 556
League of United Latin American Citizens (LULAC), 582, 685
League of Women Voters, 583
Leahy, William, 656
Leave It to Beaver, 704, 704 (illus.), 705
Lebanon, 556, 814; Muslim terrorists in, 782; U.S. intervention in, 698, 698 (illus.)
Left (political), 609
Left-wing parties: Wilson and, **544**
Legation, 499
Legislation: civil rights, 729 (table); New Deal, 605–609, 615 (table); for workers, 598, 613
Leisure: mass entertainment in early twentieth century, 529–530, 534; in 1920s, 573
Lend-lease, 667
Lend-Lease Act, 639
Lenin, Vladimir, 552, 554
Leo XIII (pope): encyclical of, 506
Lesbians. *See* Homosexuals and homosexuality
"Letter from a Birmingham Jail" (King), 722
Levitt, William, 681, 682
Lewinsky, Monica, 797
Lewis, John L., 616, 645, 676
Lewis, Sinclair, 574
Lewis, Sybil, 648
Leyte Gulf, Battle of, 658
Liberalism: antifeminism *vs.,* 787, 801; New Deal and, 627; New Right on, 773; Reagan on, 775; Truman and, 675–677
Liberal Republican movement, 389
Liberty Loan drives, 547, 548 (illus.)
Libya, 782, 783, 814
Life magazine, 577 (illus.)
Lifestyle: automobiles and, 571, 572; in Great Depression, 600; suburban, 681–682, 703, 705; in World War II, 647. *See also* Society
Lili'uokalani (queen of Hawai'i), 490, 490 (illus.), 491
Lilly Ledbetter Fair Pay Act, 814
Limited Test Ban Treaty, 725
Lincoln, Abraham, 371; assassination of, 373; Emancipation Proclamation and, 372; Reconstruction plans of, 372
Lindbergh, Charles, 573, 574 (illus.), 591 (illus.)
Listerine: advertising for, 567, 568 (illus.)
Literacy test: voting rights and, 729, 730

Literature: Harlem Renaissance and, 574–576; Realism in, 528; in 1920s, 574; in 1950s, 708. *See also* specific writers and works
Lithuania, 785
Little Bighorn River: battle at, **418**
Little Richard, 707
Little Rock: integration in, 709–710, 710 (illus.)
Livestock, 404. *See also* Cattle and cattle industry
Lloyd, Harold, 573
Loans: subprime, 811
Lobby: railroads and, **403**
Lobbyists: interest groups and, **515**
Local option laws, 508
Locke, Alain, 574
Lockheed Aircraft, 650
Locomotives, 401, 401 (illus.). *See also* Railroads
Lodge, Henry Cabot: force bill and, 473, 475, 482; Treaty of Versaille and, **556–557**
Lodgers, 443
Lôme, Enrique Dupuy de, 492
Lonely Crowd, The (Riesman), 708
Long, Huey, 610, 611 (illus.), 612
Longhorn cattle, 421
"Long Telegram" (Kennan), 666
Look magazine, 706, 710
Loomis, Samuel Land, 435
Los Angeles: anti-Chinese riots in, 450; automobiles and, 572, 572 (illus.); Chinese in, 450; housing in, 682; water management and, 426; Watts riot in, 732
Los Angeles Times, 572
Lost Cause: myth of, 445; in South, **445**
Louisiana, 35, 372; grandfather clause in, 446; oil in, 415
Lowden, Frank, 561
Lublin government (Poland), 655, 656
Luftwaffe, 638
Lumbering: in West, 425–426
Lumber mills, 425
Lusitania (ship), 543, 544 (illus.)
Lynchings, 549; of African Americans, 447, 509, 509 (illus.); attacks against, 509, 581, 581 (illus.); post–World War I, 559–560
Lyon, Phyllis, 707

MacArthur, Douglas, 652, 672; Bonus Marchers and, 602; Korean War and, 672, 675
Macedonia, 786
Machado, Geraldo, 634

Machine politics, 469, 512
Machinery: farm, 401
Macy's, R. H. (store), 412, 777
Maddox, Lester, 727 (illus.)
Maddox (ship), 743
Madero, Francisco, 538
Magazines, 439; advertisements in, 412; in 1920s, 573
Maggie: A Girl of the Streets (Crane), 528
Mahan, Alfred Thayer, 489–490, 522
Mahone, William, 388 (illus.), 389
Mail-order houses: railroads and, 413
Mail-order sales, 404
Maine (ship), 489 (illus.), 492, 492 (illus.)
Main Street (Lewis), 574
"Making do": Great Depression and, 619–620, 627
Malcolm X: assassination of, **733**
Malenkov, Georgii, 700
Malta: Gorbachev-Bush meeting on, 785
Manchukuo, 634
Manchuria: Japan and, 634; Russo-Japanese war over, 522, 524
Mandates, 556
Mandela, Nelson, 785
Manhattan Project, 645, 658
Manila Bay, Spanish-American War and, 493
Mann Doctrine, 742
Man Nobody Knows, The (Barton), 569–570
Mansfield, Arabella, 440
Manufacturing: in California, 572; mergers in, 412, 413, 415; mergers in, 1895-1905, 429 (figure); postindustrial, 776; skills and problem solving in, 399; steel, 406; urban expansion and, 435; vertical integration and, 406–407; World War I and, 546. *See also* Factories
Mao Zedong (Mao Tse-tung), 672, 700, 755
March on Washington: of 1963, **723**
Marcy, William, 468
Mariana Islands, 652
Marines: in Beirut, 782; in Haiti, 538; in Korean War, 675; in Nicaragua, 522. *See also* Armed forces; Intervention; Military
Marines' Women's Reserve, 647
Marne River region, battles at, 552
Marriage: in Great Depression, 620; in middle class, 583; in 1950s, 702; post–World War II, 684, 688; same-sex, 795, 801, 808–809, 818; suburban, 706
Married women: in work force, 456, 620, 648, 706 (figure)

Marshall, George, 669, 672
Marshall, Thurgood, 709, 720, 729
Marshall Field (store), 412
Marshall Islands, 652, 657
Marshall Plan, 669, 670
Martial law: Grant and, 384
Martin, Del, 707
Marx, Groucho, 619
Marx Brothers, 626
Maryland, 373
Masculinity: in Gilded Age, 440–441
Masons, 440
Massachusetts: same-sex
     marriage and, 808–809
Mass entertainment: in early
     twentieth century, 529–530, 534
Massive retaliation policy, **695**
Matisse, Henri, 529
Mattachine Society, 707
Mauritania, 814
Maximilian, Archduke of Austria, **487**
McAuliffe, A. C., 654
McCain, John, 794; 2008 election
     and, 811, 812 (map)
McCarran Internal Security Act, 680
McCarthy, Eugene, 748
McCarthy, Joseph, 665, 680,
     680 (illus.), **681,** 688; and
     McCarthyism, 694
McClure's Magazine, 511
McDonald's, 703, 777
McGladery, Mary, 433
McGovern, George, 760
McKay, Claude, 574
McKinley, William, 472, 498, 501; East
     Asia and, 523; 1896 election and,
     484–486, 484 (illus.), 486 (map);
     political button, 485 (illus.);
     presidency of, 486; Spanish-
     American War and, 492–494
McKinley Tariff, 473, 474, 482, 483;
     sugar industry and, 490, 491
McNamara, Robert, 747; as
     secretary of defense, 719
McNary-Haugen bill, 587
Means, Russell, 752
Meat Inspection Act (1906),
     512, 517, 518
Meatpacking industry, **404,** 413;
     Sinclair and, 511–512, 511 (illus.)
Medal of Honor: for Latinos, 650
Media: in 1920s, 572–573; in 1960s,
     704, 707. *See also* specific media
Mediation, 493
Medicaid, 731; Nixon and, 758
Medical Care Act, 731
Medicare, 731; Nixon and, 758
Medicine: women in, 440,
     453 (illus.), 454

Medicine Lodge Creek
     treaties, 416–417, 418
Mellon, Andrew, 585, 588, 592, 600
Melodrama, 529
Meltdown, 771
Memoirs, 408
Memory, new understanding of, 408
Men: changing gender roles of,
     440; in 1950s, 701; in suburban
     families, 705; wages of, 456.
     See also Gender; Women
Mencken, H. L., 574
Mendez v. Westminster, **685**
Mental health, 512
Mental retardation: Special
     Olympics and, 716–717
Meredith, James, 721
"Merger movement" (1895-1905),
     428–429, 429 (figure)
Mergers, 412; in manufacturing,
     413, 415; in 1920s, 570
Meridian, 422
Merit system: for civil service,
     477; Progressives and, 515
Mestizos, 454
Metropolis: San Francisco as, **426**
Metropolitan Museum, New York, 528
Meuse-Argonne campaign,
     in World War I, 552
Mexican Americans: as cowboys,
     420, 422; as farmworkers,
     582, 582 (illus.); in Great
     Depression, 621; *La Causa and,*
     749–751; post-World War II,
     685; repatriation of, 621; section
     hands, 455 (illus.); in Southwest,
     454–455; in World War II, 650
Mexican Revolution: United
     States and, 528–539, 539
     (map), 540 (illus.)
Mexican War, 454
Mexico: American oil interests
     in, 589, 591; immigrants from,
     582, 779; Maximilian of Austria
     in, 487; nationalization of,
     634; Zimmerman telegram
     and, 544, 546. *See also* Mexican
     Americans; Mexican War
Microsoft, 777, 799
Middle class: Chinese American,
     433–434; marriage and, 583; men's
     role in, 705; in 1920s, 576–577;
     in 1950s, 701–705, 702 (illus.),
     704 (illus.); suburban, 437;
     urban, 438–439. *See also* Classes
Middle East: Arab-Israeli conflict in,
     769 (map); Carter and, 768, 770
     (illus.); Clinton and, 798; drone
     warfare in, 813; Eisenhower and,

696, 698; Persian Gulf War (1991)
     in, 787, 788 (map); post-World
     War I, 555 (map), 556; terrorism
     in, 782–783, 805, 806; Truman
     and U.S. presence in, 671
Midway Island, Battle of, 633, **652**
Midwest: family farms in, 424;
     Farmers' Alliances in, 481; Grange
     in, 474–476; Ku Klux Klan in, 580
"Migrant Mother" (Lange), 625
Migrants and migration, **510;** farm
     workers and, 621, 749–750, 780;
     in Great Depression, 617, 625
     (illus.); in World War II, 647. *See
     also* Immigrants and immigration
Milam, J. W., 710
Military: American Indians in,
     650–651; "Don't Ask, Don't Tell"
     policy in, 795; homosexuals in,
     795; Mexican Americans in,
     650; segregation in, 493. *See also*
     Armed forces; Disarmament;
     Navy; Soldiers; Weapons;
     specific wars and battles
"Military-industrial complex":
     Eisenhower on, 702
Military Reconstruction Act, 382
Military spending: under Reagan, 781
Militia: Great Railway Strike and, **458**
Miller, John, 551 (illus.)
Miller and Lux, 425
Milosevic, Slobodan, 798
Mineral resources, 399
Minimum wage, 607, 613,
     614, 675, 695, 719, 771
Mining and mining industry: mergers
     in, (1895-1905), 429 (figure);
     strikes in, 645, 646, 676, 677; in
     West, 422. *See also* Gold; Silver
Minneapolis, 420; strike against
     Teamsters Union, 610
Minnesota: Homestead Act and, 400
Minorities: affirmative action
     for, 758, 772; in New Deal,
     621–622; unemployment for
     (1990s), 800. *See also* Affirmative
     action; specific groups
Mintz, Leo, 690
Miranda v. Arizona, **727**
Missiles: Cold War and, 756. *See also*
     Intercontinental ballistic missiles
Missions and missionaries: Anglo-
     Saxonism and, 490; in Hawai'i, 487
Mississippi: civil rights movement
     in, 721; freedom riders in,
     721; Freedom Summer in,
     729–730, 730 (illus.); National
     Guard in, 723 (illus.)
Mississippi Plan, 390

Missouri, 373
Mitchell, John, 753, 759, 760
Mitchell, Maria, 439
Mix, Tom, 573
Mobilization: for World War I, **540**
Model Cities Act, 729 (table), 730
Model T Ford, 568, 569
Moderates: during Reconstruction, 282, **372,** 381
Modern Times (movie), 626
Moley, Raymond, 605
Molotov Plan, 669
Mondale, Walter: 1984 election and, 776
Monetary policy, 476; Federal Reserve System and, 527
Money: greenbacks as, 476
Monopoly, 525; Grange political cartoon, 478 (illus.); Sherman Anti-Trust Act and, 474; by Standard Oil, **409–410**
Monroe Doctrine, 487, 491; Roosevelt Corollary to, 520, 521, 522 (illus.)
Montana: gold in, 422
Montgomery, Alabama: bus boycott in, 710–712, 711 (illus.); freedom riders in, 721
Montgomery Improvement Association, 711
Montgomery Ward, 412
Montreal Royals, 664, 665
Moody, Anne, 730 (illus.)
Moon, first man on, 719
Moral Majority, 774
Moral reforms, 507–508
Moreno, Luisa, 623
Morgan, John Pierpont, 405, 405 (illus.), 412, 413, 431; bomb sent to, 558; coal miner strike and, 516; mergers and, 429; southern railroads and, 414; U.S. Steel and, 415
Morgan, Lewis Henry, 452
"Morganization," 405
Morgenthau, Henry, 613
Mormons: woman suffrage and, 479
Morocco, 814
Morrill, Lot, 381, 384
Morrill Act, 399
Morrow, Dwight W., 591, 591 (illus.)
Mortgages: foreclosures, 601, 602; refinancing, 609
Morton, Ferdinand ("Jelly Roll"), 575
Moses, Bob, 729
Mossadegh, Mohammed, 696
Most-favored-nation status: of China, **487**
Mothers and motherhood: antifeminists on, 767,

801; in 1950s, 705. *See also* Families; Women
Motion Picture Association, 679
Motion Picture Production Code, 626
Motley, Constance Baker, 729
Motor Vehicle Safety Act (1966), 729 (table)
Movies and movie industry: B movies, 696; in Great Depression, 620 (illus.), 626; HUAC investigation of, 679; in 1920s, 572–573; sex and sexuality in, 565, 565 (illus.), 573, 573 (illus.), 594, 594 (illus.)
MR. *See* Mental retardation
Mr. Smith Goes to Washington, 626
Mubarak, Hosni, 814
Muckrakers, 511–512, 515, 516
Muckraking, 533
Mugwumps, 477, 479, 501
Muhammad, Elijah, 732, 733
Muir, John, **518,** 519
Mujahedeen, 770
Muller v. Oregon, **506**
Multilateral agreements, **589, 696**
Munich Agreement, 636
Munn v. Illinois, 476
Music: of counterculture, 737; Harlem Renaissance, 575–576, 575 (illus.); jazz, 528; rock 'n roll, 690–691
Muslims: ethnic cleansing of, 786, 798; as terrorists, 782, 805. *See also* Arab world; Islam
Mussolini, Benito, 633, 635, 638, 653, 662
Mutual Defense Assistance Act, 670
Mutual insurance companies, 475
My Lai, 755

NAACP. *See* National Association for the Advancement of Colored People
Nader, Ralph: 2000 election and, 804 (map)
NAFTA. *See* North American Free Trade Agreement
Nagasaki, 659, **660**
Names Project, 796 (illus.)
Napoleon III, 487
NASDAQ, 799
Nasser, Gamal Abdel, 698
Nast, Thomas, 470 (illus.)
National Aeronautics and Space Administration (NASA), 694
National Association for the Advancement of Colored People (NAACP), 392, **509,** 560, 581, 649, 709

National Association of Manufacturers (NAM), 515
National Birth Control League, 506
National City Bank of New York, 410
National Consumers' League, 506
National debt: Clinton and, 795; Reagan and, **776,** 795; taxes and, 1936-1950, 646 (figure)
National Defense Act (1916), 543
National Defense Education Act (1958), **694**
National Defense Student Loans, 694
National Endowment for the Arts and Humanities, 729 (table)
National Farm Workers Association (NFWA), 741, 749
National Guard Armory, New York, 528
National Guard (U.S.): freedom march and, 722, 723 (illus.), 730
National Housing Act, 609
National Indian Youth Council, 752
National Industrial Recovery Act (NIRA), **606**
National Irrigation Association, 426
Nationalist Chinese government, 672. *See also* China
Nationalize, 591
National Labor Reform Party, 458
National Labor Relations Act (NLRA), 612
National Labor Relations Board (NLRB), 612
National Labor Union, 458
National League, 529, 530 (illus.)
National Oceanic and Atmospheric Administration (NOAA), 757
National Organization for Women (NOW), **735**
National Origins Act, 579, 582
National parks, 518
National Recovery Administration (NRA), 606, 606 (illus.), 607, 609, 629
National Review, 727
National security: George W. Bush and, 805; Truman and, 695
National Security Act, 670
National Security Council (NSC), **670,** 783
National Union for Social Justice, 610
National War Labor Board (NWLB), **546, 645**
National Woman's Party, 583
National Woman Suffrage Association (NWSA), **478,** 479, 507
National Youth Administration (NYA), 616
Nation of Islam, 732

Native American Church, 454

Native Son (Wright), 625

Nativism, 449–450, 464, 579, 595

Nativity, 384

NATO. *See* North Atlantic
   Treaty Organization

Natural resources, 399;
   regulating, 518–519

Navajo Indians, 417, 623 (illus.);
   as code talkers, 651

Navy: expansion of, 490; Japanese,
   592, 593; Mahan and, 489; Pacific
   bases for, 497; Washington
   Naval Conference and, 592,
   593; in World War I, 550–551;
   in World War II, 650, 658

Nazi Germany: bombing of, 654;
   extermination and concentration
   camps of, 636, 637 (map); Jews
   and, 636; nonaggression pact with
   Soviet Union, 636; treaty with
   Japan and Italy, 640; in World
   War II, 641, 652–655. *See also*
   Germany; World War II, 662

Nebraska: Homestead Act and, 400

Negro American Baseball League, 665

Nelson, L. D. (son), 509 (illus.)

Nelson, Laura (mother), 509 (illus.)

Netherlands: Hitler's invasion of, 638;
   Permanent Court of Arbitration
   in, 524; in World War II, 638

Neutrality: in World War I, **540,** 542;
   before World War II, 638–639

Neutrality Act of 1935, 635

Neutrality Act of 1937, 638

Neutrality Act of 1939, 638

Nevada: silver mines in, 422

Newark: race riots in, 733

New Deal, 598, **603,** 627, 629;
   agriculture and, 617–619;
   American Indians in, 624–625;
   Bank Holiday during, 605;
   election of 1936 and waning of,
   612–614; First Hundred Days,
   605–609; Latinos in, 622, 623,
   623 (illus.); major legislation
   of, 615 (table); in perspective,
   627; Second Hundred Days,
   611–612; Social Security
   and, 612; women in, 622

New Departure: 1872 presidential
   election and, **388–389,** 395

New England: textile mills in, 414

New Federalism, 759

New Freedom, 525

New Frontier, 718, 719

"New immigrants", 449

New Left, 736

"New Look": in 1950s fashion, 684

New Look national security
   policy, **695**–696

New Nationalism, 524, 525

New Orleans: Hurricane Katrina in,
   810, 810 (illus.); jazz in, 575

New Orleans Tribune, 377

New Right, 727, 767, 773–775

New South, 431; economic base
   for, 414–415; illiteracy in,
   444; society in, 444–445

Newspapers: advertisements in, 412;
   black, 377; foreign language, 449;
   middle class families and, 439;
   New South, 414; political parties
   and, 468; political role of, 485; in
   1920s, 573; Spanish language, 454

Newsweek, 778

Newton, Huey P., 733

"New Woman," 506

New York Central Railroad, 405

New York (city), 435; capital for
   industrialization and, 399; Puerto
   Ricans in, 708; Riis on, 442, 443;
   Tammany Hall in, 468, 469,
   471; tenements in, 442–443,
   442 (illus.); terrorist attack on
   (2001), 804, 804 (illus.), 805;
   Tweed Ring in, 470–471

New York Daily Tribune, 389

New York Journal, 491, 492

New York Stock Exchange, 413;
   railroad stocks and, 405

New York Times, 503, 549, 754

New York World, 491

Nez Perce Indians, 419, 452

Ngai, Mae, 434

Nicaragua: George H. W. Bush
   and, 787; human rights and,
   768; intervention in, 522, 589;
   Sandinistas in, 768; U.S. and, 538;
   U.S. covert operations in, 781

Nimitz, Chester, 652

Nineteenth Amendment, 561, 577,
   A13; woman suffrage and, 583

Ninth Amendment, A12

Nisei, 633, 642, 643, 650

Nixon, Richard M., 680, **681,** 753
   (illus.); China relations and, 755,
   757 (illus.); Cold War policy of,
   695, 755–756; domestic policy
   of, 756–759; environment and,
   757–759; foreign policy of,
   753–756; New Federalism and,
   759; 1952 election and, 692;
   1960 election and, 718–719,
   718 (illus.), 719 (map); 1968
   election and, 742, 748–749, 749
   (map); 1972 election and, 760;
   resignation of, 761, 762 (illus.);
   on Santa Barbara oil spill, 759
   (illus.); as vice president, 692;
   Vietnam War and, 753–755, 753
   (illus.); Watergate and, 760–761

Nixon Doctrine, 754

NLU. *See* National Labor Union

NOAA. *See* National Oceanic and
   Atmospheric Administration

Nobel Peace Prize: to Jane
   Addams, 504; to Martin
   Luther King, Jr., 732; to Sadat
   and Begin, 770 (illus.); to
   Theodore Roosevelt, 523

No Child Left Behind Act, 804

Nomura, Kichisaburo, 640

Noncommissioned officers, 650

Non-recognition policy, **634**

Nonviolent resistance, 712

Noriega, Manuel, 787

Normal schools: black, 387, **446**

Normandy: Allied invasion of,
   653–654, 655 (map)

Norris, Frank, 528

Norris, George W., 546, 585

North: distribution of population
   in, by race, 1900, 450 (figure);
   Great Migration to, 549

North Africa: World War II
   in, 633, 640, 651, 652

**North American Free Trade
   Agreement** (NAFTA),
   795, 797 (illus.)

North Atlantic Treaty Organization
   (NATO), 670, 723; in Afghanistan,
   813 (illus.); Serbian conflict with
   Kosovo and, 798, 799 (illus.);
   West Germany and, 696

North Carolina Agricultural
   and Technical College,
   sit-ins and, 719–720

Northeast: family farms in, 424;
   Irish immigrants in, 448;
   manufacturing in, 399; Puerto
   Rican activism in, 750–751

Northern Europe:
   immigration from, 579

Northern Ireland: peace
   process in, 798

Northern Pacific Railroad, 405, 418

Northern Securities Company, 516

North Korea, 665, 672, 673 (map),
   674, 675; Eisenhower and, 694

North Vietnam, 742, 743, 744
   (map), 747, 748, 754

North Vietnamese Army (NVA), 743

Norway: Hitler and, 638

Novels: dime novels, 421;
   in 1920s, 574

Novotny, Antonin, 736

NOW. *See* National Organization for Women
NSC. *See* National Security Council
NSC Memorandum, 672
Nuclear deterrence, 695
Nuclear family: in 1950s, 705
Nuclear power: bombings of Hiroshima and Nagasaki, 659, 659 (illus.), 660; "duck and cover" drills, 695 (illus.), 696; fallout shelters and, 695; massive retaliation policy and, 695; Three Mile Island and, 771; weapons testing and, 725. *See also* Hydrogen bomb
Nude Descending a Staircase (Duchamp), 528
Nuremberg race laws, 636
Nurses: in World War I, 551; in World War II, 647
Nye, Gerald P., 635, 639

Obama, Barack, 720, 819 (illus.); BP oil spill and, 817; foreign policy of, 813–814; healthcare and, 813, 815–817; inaugural address of, 812; Middle East, Afghanistan and, 813–814; politics of filibuster and, 814–815, 817; 2008 election and, 794, 811, 812 (map); 2012 election and, 795, 817–820, 820 (map)
Obama, Michelle, Sasha, and Malia, 819 (illus.)
"Obamacare," 817
Obvious (company), 794
Occupational Safety and Health Administration (OSHA), 757
Occupation zones: in Berlin, 669, 670 (map)
O'Connor, Sandra Day, 802, 803
Octupus, The (Norris), 528
Office of Price Administration (OPA), 645
Office of War Mobilization, 645
Office work: women and, 456
Offshoring, 777
Oil and oil industry, 777; Latin America and, 591; Mexico and, 634; Middle East and, 696, 771–772; in New South, 415; Rockefeller and, 397–398, 397 (illus.), 409–410; vertical and horizontal integration in, 409, 410, 410 (figure)
Oil spill: in Gulf of Mexico, 817; off coast of Santa Barbara, California, 759 (illus.)
Okies, 617

Okinawa, 658, 675
Oklahoma: oil in, 415
"Old immigrants", 449, 450
Old South: myth of, 444, **445**
Old stock, 448
Oligopoly, 413, 431
Olney, Richard, 462, 491
Olympic Games: in 1980, 770
Omaha Beach, 654
On the Beach (Shute), 696
On the Origin of Species (Darwin), 407
On the Road (Kerouac), 708
OPEC. *See* Organization of Petroleum Exporting Countries
Open Door notes, 499
Open Door policy, 497, 499 (illus.), 522, 534, 592; in China, 497, 501
Open-range system, **420**
Open Skies proposal, 701
Operating companies, 571
Operation Chaos, 747
Operation Desert Shield, 787
Operation Desert Storm, 787, 787 (illus.), 788 (map)
Operation Husky, 653
Operation Just Cause, 788
Operation Menu, 754
Operation Overlord, 654
Operation Rolling Thunder, 743
Operation Torch, 651
Operation Vittles, 671 (illus.)
Oppenheimer, J. Robert, 658
Oregon (ship), 520
Oregon System, 515
Oregon v. Mitchell, 759
Organ, Fred, 614 (illus.)
Organization Man (Whyte), 708
Organization of American States (OAS), **671**
Organization of Petroleum Exporting Countries (OPEC), **758**–759
Orlando, Vittorio, 554
Ortega, Daniel, 787
OSHA. *See* Occupational Safety and Health Administration
Oswald, Lee Harvey, 726
Other Americans, The (Harrington), 726
Ottoman (Turkish) Empire, 540, 541 (map); collapse of, 553; World War I and, 555 (map), 556
Owens, Furman, 444 (illus.)
Owens River region, 426

Pacheco, Romualdo, 454
Pacific Northwest: lumbering in, 425–426
Pacific Ocean region: American involvement in, 495 (map);

Asian immigrants in, 451–452; containment policy and, 675; Hawai'i and, 487–488; in World War II, 651–652, 653 (map). *See also* Pacific Northwest
Pacific Railway Act, 402, 415, 420
Pacifism: after World War I, 592–593; in Vietnam War, 745
Pact of Paris. *See* Kellogg-Briand Pact
Pageant magazine, 713
Pahlavi, Mohammad Reza (Shah), 696, 770, 771
Painting: cubist, 528; in Great Depression, 625; Impressionism, 528, 529 (illus.)
Pakistan: Al Qaeda and, 807 (map); death of Osama bin Laden in, 813; terrorism and, 806
Palestine, 556, 798; partitioning of, 671
Palestine Liberation Organization (PLO), **782**
Palin, Sarah, 811
Palmer, A. Mitchell, 558
Palmer raids, 559, 559 (illus.)
Panama: George H. W. Bush and, 787–788; U.S. intervention in, 520, 589
Panama Canal: Carter and, 768; McKinley and, 520; Roosevelt and, 521
Pan Am Flight 103: terrorism and, 783
Panay (gunboat), 635, 636
Panics (financial): of 1907, 527
Pardons: after Civil War, 374
Paris: expatriates in, 574
Paris: liberation in World War II, 654; **Treaty of** (1898), 494–**495**; Vietnam War peace talks in, 755
Parks, Rosa, 711, 711 (illus.)
Parks: urban, 437
Partition: of Palestine, **671**
Party convention, 467
Party politics, 467. *See also* Political parties
Pass system, 376
Patent medicines, 412
Patent Office, 412
Patents: Edison and, **411**
Patient Protection and Affordable Care Act (2010), 816–**817**
Patriotism: after September 11, 2001, 805; in World War I, 548–549; in World War II, 647
Patrollers, 376
Patronage system, 468; critics and defenders of, 468–469; reform and, 477–478
Patrons of Husbandry, 475

Paul, Alice, 507, 583
Paulson, Henry, 600, 812
Payne-Aldrich Tariff, 519
Payola, 691
Peace: Truman and paths to, 666–667
Peace Corps, 724
Peacekeeping: in Balkans, 798; in Kosovo, 799 (illus.)
Peale, Norman Vincent (Reverend), 705
Pearl Harbor: Japanese attack on, 633, 640–641, 642, 642 (illus.), 662; U.S. use of, 488
Pedersen, Vernon, 604
Pelosi, Nancy, 810, 811 (illus.)
Pembina Silver Mining Co. v. Pennsylvania, 413
Pendleton, George, 477
Pendleton Act, 477, 481, 501
Pennsylvania: iron industry in, 399; plane crash in (September 11, 2001), 805; Three Mile Island, 771
Pennsylvania Railroad, 397, 398, 405
Penny auctions: in Great Depression, 602
Pensions, 597; old-age, 610
Pentagon: terrorist attack on, 794, 805
Pentagon Papers, 754
People's Party. *See* Populists
People's Republic of China. *See* China
Perestroika, 783
Perjury, 680
Perkins, Frances, 507, 597–598, 597 (illus.), 605, 612, 622; on Social Security Act, 628
Permanent commission on civil rights: Truman and, 677
Permanent Court of Arbitration, 524
Perot, H. Ross, 789, 789 (map)
Pershing, John J., 593 (illus.); in Mexico, 539; World War I and, 551, 552
Persian Gulf War (1991), **787,** 788 (map)
Personal computers, 799–800
Perversion, 585
Pesticides, 757, 758
Petroleum industry. *See* Oil and oil industry
Peyote cult, 453
Phelan, James, 512
Philadelphia, 399; exposition of 1876 in, 530
Philadelphia Plan, 758
Philanthropy, 409
Philippine Islands, 497, 501; Aguinaldo in, 496–497, 497 (illus.); annexation and, 498; Carter and, 768; immigrants

from, 780; independence and, 496–497; insurrection in, 497; Spanish-American War and, **493**–496; U.S. control of, 495, 498; in World War II, 657, 658
Phonograph, 411
Photography: in 1930s, 625–626, 625 (illus.)
Phyllis Schlafly Report, 766, 790
Physicians. *See* Doctors; Medicine
Picasso, Pablo, 529
Piecework, 456
Pig iron: in Alabama, 415
Pilgrim's Progress (Bunyan), 511
Pinchback, P. B. S., 386
Pinchot, Gifford, 518, 518 (illus.), 519
Pingree, Hazen, 512
Pinkerton National Detective Agency, 461
Pinochet, Augusto, 756
Pioneers: on Great Plains, 424, 424 (illus.)
Pittsburgh, 435
Pittsburgh Courier, 648
Pittsburgh Pirates, 530
Plains Indians: horses and, 415
Plains region. *See* Great Plains region
Planned Parenthood of Southeastern Pennsylvania v. Casey, 801
Planters and plantations: in Central America, 591; in Georgia, 379 (illus.); in Hawai'i, 488, 490
Platform (political), **468;** of Populists, 481–482
Platt Amendment: Cuba and, 496
Plebiscite, 700
Pledge of Allegiance, 705
Plessy v. Ferguson, **446,** 708
PLO. *See* Palestine Liberation Organization
Plunkitt, George W., 468
Poets and poetry: in Harlem Renaissance, 574, 575, 575 (illus.)
Poland, 553, 557; democratic government in, 785; Hitler's invasion of, 636, 638 (illus.); immigrants from, 449
Poland Corridor, 636
Police action: Korean War and, **672,** 673
Police force: in New York City, 438
Policy, 479
Polio vaccine, 693
Political buttons: Bryan-Sewall and McKinley buttons, 485 (illus.)
Political campaigns, 468, 515; in 1896, 484–486
Political cartoons: on 1960s urban riots, 734, 734 (illus.)

Political coattails, 775
Political parties: caucus of, 468; patronage and, 467–469, 468. *See also* Party politics; Platform (political); specific parties
Politics: of action, 718–723; bipartisanship in, 606; of business, 586, 587–588, 588 (illus.); Carl Schurz in, 466–467; of Cold War, 678–681; of consensus, 692–694; Farmers' Alliances in, 481, 501; of filibuster, 726, 814–815, 817; in Gilded Age, 479; Grange and, 475–476; Iraq and, 807–809; of loyalty, Joseph McCarthy and, 680, 680 (illus.), **681;** patronage system and, 468–469; Populists and, 482–483; post-World War II, 675–678; in Progressive Era, 504, 505; of prosperity, 585–589; of reform, 510–515; religion and, 774; stalemate in, 1876-1889, 471–472; structural change in, 479, 481; in World War II, 651. *See also* Conservatives and conservatism; Government; Liberalism; Machine politics; Political parties
Poll tax, 445, 730
Pollution, 757. *See also* Environment
Polygamy: among Mormons, **479**
Pontiac, Michigan: anti-busing forces in, 760
Pools: railroad, **402**
Popular front, 655
Population: foreign-born, U.S., 1870-1920, 447 (figure); of immigrants, 447–448, 447 (figure); Latino, 2000, 750 (map); measures of economic growth and, 427 (figure); movement across America, 1950-1960, 703 (map); regional distribution of, by race, 1900, 450 (figure); urban and rural, 1860-1910, 435 (figure); in World War II, 647
Populists, 481, 501; Bryan and, 485; 1890 and 1892 elections and, 482–483, 483 (map); 1896 election and, 484–485; platform of, 482; political cartoon, 482 (illus.); woman suffrage and, 479, 482
Port Huron Statement, **736**
Postindustrial economy, 776
Potsdam Conference, 658, 660
Potsdam Declaration, 660
Poverty: farm workers and, 741; feminization of, 800–801; Great Depression and, 619; of migrant workers, 780; in 1950s, 708;

in 1960s, 726; rural, 617–618; urban, 442–443, 442 (illus.); urban politics and, 468–469. *See also* War on Poverty
Powderly, Terence, 460, 460 (illus.)
Powell, Adam Clayton, Jr., 585, 686
Powell, Colin, 804
Powell, Lewis, 760
Prague Spring, 1968, 736
Prayer: in schools, 727, 780
Preemptive strike, 806
Prefabricated sections, **645**
Preservationists, 518, 519
President: popular vote for, 1892, 483 (map); war-making abilities of, 755. *See also* specific presidents
Presidential Commission on the Status of Women, 733
Presidential elections, A16–A20. *See also* Election(s); specific presidents
Presidential Medal of Freedom: for Dolores Huerta, 742
Presley, Elvis, 707
Press. *See* Newspapers
Price fixing: NRA and, **607**
Price(s): in Great Depression, 600, 609; steel industry, 406; wartime and, 645
Primary sources, 408
Principles of Scientific Management (Taylor), 569
Printz v. the United States, 803
Prisoners of war: American nurses captured by Japanese, 647; Vietnam War, 755
Private-sector workforce, 616
Pro-choice supporters, 772–773. *See also* Abortion
Proclamation of **Amnesty** and Reconstruction, **372**
Producers' cooperatives, 475
Professional organizations, 505
Progress and Poverty (George), 409, 443
Progressive Era, 504
Progressive Party, 505; as Bull Moose Party, 525; in 1912, 524
Progressives and progressivism, 504; city government reform and, 512–513; interest groups and, 514–515; moral reform and, 507–508; muckrakers and, 511–512; organizing for change and, 504–510; perspective on, 530–531; racial issues and, 508–509; southern, 514; state government reform and, 513–514; Theodore Roosevelt and, 515–516, 518; use of terms, 505; Wilson and, 526–528; World War I and, 547, 557

Prohibition, 469, 507, 508, 566, 595; Eighteenth Amendment and, 561, 577–578
Prohibition Party, 479
Project Mercury, 694
Pro-life supporters, 802 (illus.)
Promontory Summit, transcontinental railroad and, 420, 421 (illus.)
Propagandists, 542
Proposition 13, 774
Prospect Park, Brooklyn, 437
Prosperity: in 1920s, 567; in 1950s, 702–703; politics of, 585–589
Prostitution, 508
Protective tariffs, 399, 472; Democrats and, 469
Protectorates, 491; Cuba as, 521; Dominican Republic as, 521; Haiti as, 538; Nicaragua as, 522; Panama as, 521
Protestants and **Protestantism:** fundamentalism and, 578; reform movements and, 440. *See also* Religion
Protest(s): in Arab Spring, 814; in China's Tiananmen Square, 786–787; in Great Depression, 602; against lynchings, 581, 581 (illus.); Twitter and, 794; against Vietnam War, 745, 745 (illus.), 747, 748
Provisional, 375
Public accommodations, 385; equal access to, 368
Publications. *See* specific types
Public domain, 399
Public education: reform of, 513. *See also* Education; School(s)
Public health, 512
Public opinion: Vietnam War and, 743, 745, 746, 746 (figure); World War I and, 547–549; before World War II, 638
Public order laws, 721
Public Works Administration (PWA), **606,** 607, 614, 622, 629
Public works project, 600–601. *See also* New Deal
Publix chain of supermarkets, 801
Pueblo Indians: land issue, 581
Pueblos, 454
Puerto Ricans, 750–751; in New York city, 708
Puerto Rico, 494, 495, 501; Foraker Act and, 496; as territory, 538; as U.S. colony, 521
Pulitzer, Joseph, 485, **491**
Pullman Palace Car Company: strike, 462, 462 (illus.)
Pullman Strike, 484

Puppet governments, 666
Pure Food and Drug Act (1906), 511, 517, 518
PWA Moderne, 614 (illus.)
Pyra Labs, 793

Qaddafi, Muammar, 783; death of, 814
Quarantine speech: of Franklin Roosevelt, 635

Rabb, Max, 712
Race and racism: Anglo-Saxonism and, 449–450, 490; eugenics movement and, 579; Great Depression and: South and West, 621–622; in housing, 449, 579; Japanese American internment and, 632–633, 640–641, 642–644, 643 (map), 644 (illus.); in New Deal, 622–623; in 1920s, 580–581; post-World War II, 677; in Progressive Era, 508–509; regional distribution of population by, 1900, 450 (figure); in sports, 664–665; Truman and, 677, 678; in World War II, 649–650. *See also* African Americans; Discrimination; Segregation; Slaves and slavery; specific groups and issues
Race riots, 509; after Civil War, 381–382; after King assassination, 733; in Chicago, 677; in Detroit, 581, 733; Great Migration and, 550; in Newark, 733; political cartoons on, 734, 734 (illus.); post-World War I, 559–560; school desegregation and, 710; in Watts, 732. *See also* Riots
Racial equality, Lyndon Johnson and, 728–729
Racial integration, 372
Racial intermarriage, 445
Racketeering, 578
Radical Republicans: congressional Reconstruction and, 380, 382; Johnson's impeachment and, 383; Reconstruction and, 381; voting rights and, 384–385; war aims of, 371–372
Radio, 572–573; consumerism and, 705; in Great Depression, 605, 610; in 1930s, 626–627; rock 'n roll on, 690–691
Ragtime music, 528
Railroads: agriculture and, 400, 401; antimonopolism and, 481; as big business, 401–405; Chicago and,

Railroads (continued)
404–405, 404 (illus.); Chinese
workers on, 450; Civil War and,
401–402; depression of 1890s and,
428; eight-hour workday and, 528;
expansion of, 404; farming and,
422; farmland advertising, 448
(illus.); free passes, 518; freight
rates and, 475, 505; investment
banking and, 405; land grants
and, 388, 399, 402, 403 (map);
lumber industry and, 425; mail-
order houses and, 413; Mexican
American section hands and,
455 (illus.); mining expansion
and, 416; in New South, 414;
petroleum refining business and,
397, 398; pools and, 402; rate
discrimination and, 402–403;
rebates and, 516; strikes against,
458–459, 459 (illus.), 484, 676;
subsidies, 420; track gauges
of, 402; transcontinental, 402,
420, 421 (illus.); unions for,
587–588; in West, 220, 402, 405;
World War I and, 546. See also
Great Railway Strike of 1877
Railway Labor Act of 1926, 587
Rainey, Joseph, 369–370, 369
(illus.), 386, 394; Black
Reconstruction and, 385 (illus.)
Rainey, Susan, 369
Rainfall: agriculture and, 1890, 423
(map); in Great Plains, 424
Ramona (Jackson), 452
Randolph, A. Philip, 649
*Random Reminiscences of Men and
Events* (Rockefeller), 408, 430
Rankin, Jeannette, 506, 641;
World War I and, 546
Rationing: World War II and, 645, 647
Raw materials: industry and, 399; in
New South, 414; in West, 420
Ray, James Earl, 733
Rayburn, Sam, 719
RCA, 777
Reader's Digest, 701, 702, 708
Reading Railroad, 428
Reagan, Ronald, 679, 762, 767;
foreign policy of, 781–784;
immigration and, 779; intervention
in Lebanon and, 782–783; New
Right and, 774; 1980 election
and, 775; 1984 election and,
776; Reaganism and, 775–776;
Soviet Union and, 783–784, 783
(illus.); Supreme Court and, 802
Reagan Doctrine, 781
Reaganomics, 776

Realism: in American literature, 528
Realtors' Code of Ethics, 682
Rebel Without a Cause (film), 707
Recall, 515
Recessions, 426–427; dot-com bubble
and, 799; under Nixon, 759; periods
of expansion and, 1950-2013,
800 (figure); Roosevelt's
recession, 613; of 2008, 600
Reclamation Act (1902), **426,** 518
Reclamation Service, 426
Reconcentration policy, **491,** 492, 493
Reconstruction, 370, 395; African
American population and
duration of, 386 (map); Andrew
Johnson and, 373–375, 380,
382; Black, **385–388,** 385
(illus.); congressional, 380–385;
constitutional revolution and,
384; end of, 388–389, 445; history
of, 392; Lincoln's plans for, 372;
perspectives on, 392, 393
*Reconstruction: Political & Economic,
1865-1877* (Dunning), 392
Reconstruction Finance Corporation
(RFC), **601,** 605, 629
Red Army, 553, 554
Redeemers, 389
"Red Fascism," 667
"Red Power," 742, 752
Red River Valley: wheat farms in, 424
Red Scare, 563; in 1950s, 678, 679–680;
post-World War I, 558–559
Redstocking Manifesto, 735
Reductive fallacy, 517
Reed, Thomas B., 472
Referendum, 515
Refinery: of Rockefeller, **409**
Reform(s): of city government,
512–513; muckrakers and, 511–512;
of politics, 510–515; Progressive,
504; of public education, 513;
settlement houses and, 504,
505–506; of spoils system, 477–478;
of state government, 513–514;
structural, 479, 481; of welfare and
welfare programs, 796; Wilson
and, 526–528; women and, 440,
506–507. See also Progressives
and progressivism; specific
movements and individuals
Rehnquist, William, 760;
Rehnquist Court and, 802
Reich: Hitler and, 636
Relief programs: in Great Depression,
606–609, 608 (map). See also
Welfare and welfare programs
Religion: of counterculture,
737; ethnic groups and, 449;

Ghost Dance, 419; New Right
and, 774; in 1950s, 705
Relocation: of Japanese Americans,
633, 640–641, 642–644,
643 (map), 644 (illus.)
Reno, Milo, 602
Rent riots, 602
Renunciation Law, 633
Reparations, 591; after World
War I, **554,** 556
Repatriation: of Mexican
nationals, 621
Repeal: of Prohibition, **577**
Republican Party: after Civil War,
371–372; Carl Schurz in, 466, 467;
characteristics of, 469; Clinton
and, 796–797; Contract with
America and, 796; 1872 election
and, 389; elections between 1896
and 1932, 486; elephant symbol
of, 470 (illus.); fifty-first Congress
and, 472–474; in 1950s, 692;
Obama presidency and, 813, 817,
820; post-Reconstruction, 383;
in South, 386–387; under Taft,
519, 524. See also Election(s);
Radical Republicans; specific
candidates and presidents
Republic of Korea (ROK), 672
Repudiate, 375
Repudiation, 491
Rerum Novarium (Leo XIII), 506
Research and development (R&D):
of Edison, 411, 411 (illus.)
Reservationists, 557
Reservations, 695, 751 (map), 753;
Dawes Act and, 453; Navajo,
417; western Indian, 418 (map).
See also American Indians;
Bureau of Indian Affairs
Resettlement Administration
(RA), 617
Restrictive covenants: in
housing, **449, 579**
Return, 405
Reuben James (ship), 640
Revenue Acts (1942 and 1943), 646
Reykjavik, Iceland: summit
meeting at, 784
Reynolds, R. J. (company), 678
Rhapsody in Blue (Gershwin), 576
Rhee, Syngman, 672
Rhineland, 635
Rice, Condoleezza, 804, 806
Richmond, Virginia: electric
streetcars in, 436
Rickey, Branch, 664, 665
Ridgeway, Matthew, 675
Riesman, David, 708

Rifle clubs: Democratic, 390

Right (political), 609

Rights: Eleanor Roosevelt and, 621 (illus.) 622, 623; for farm workers, 763; of women, 773, 773 (illus.). *See also* Civil rights

Right to Life movement, 773, 801

Right-to-work laws, **676**

Riis, Jacob, 442, 442 (illus.), 443

Rio Pact, 671

Riots: anti-Chinese, 450, 452; Zoot Suit, 650. *See also* Race riots

Rivera, Diego, 624 (illus.), 625

Roads and highways: interstate highway system, 703, 703 (map). *See also* Automobiles and automobile industry

"Roaring Twenties," 566

Roberts, John, 802

Robeson, Paul, 574

Robinson, Jackie, 664–665, 664 (illus.), 686, 687

Rock Around the Clock (movie), 691

Rockefeller, John D., 397–398, 397 (illus.), 407, 415, 431; on big business, 430; bomb sent to, 558; competition and, 398; hookworm eradication and, 512, 513; Standard Oil and, 409–410, 413; vertical and horizontal integration by, 409, 410

Rockefeller Foundation: contraception research and, 583

Rockefeller Sanitary Commission for the Eradication of Hookworm Disease, 513 (illus.)

Rock 'n roll, 690–691, 707

Roe v. Wade, 382, **772,** 773

Rogers, Will, 586

Rolling Stones, 737

Romania, 557, 786

Romney, Willard Mitt: 2012 election and, 794–795, 818, 819

Roosevelt, Eleanor, 603, 605, 621 (illus.); civil rights and, 622, 623; New Deal and, 616

Roosevelt, Franklin D., 531, 561, 597, 627, 629, 662; Bonus Army and, 602; death of, 634, 656; isolationism and, 634–636; New Deal and, 603, 605–618; 1932 election and, 598, 603, 603 (map); 1936 election and, 612, 635; 1940 election and, 638; 1944 election and, 651; 1933-first hundred days, 605–609; stricken with polio, 605 (illus.); at Yalta, 656, 656 (illus.). *See also* New Deal; World War II

Roosevelt, Theodore, 441, **493,** 531, 534, 537; antitrust actions and, 516; "bully pulpit" and concerns of, 516; coal mine strike and, 516; conservation agenda of, 518–519; East Asia and, 522–523; foreign policy of, 521–522; Japanese immigration and, 452; meatpacking industry and, 511, 511 (illus.); muckrakers and, 511, 516; 1900 election and, 496, 515; 1912 election and, 503, 524, 525, 525 (illus.), 526; on presidential powers, 519–520; Spanish-American War and, 493, 494; Square Deal of, 516; trustbusting by, 516; White Fleet and, 523

Roosevelt Corollary, 520, 521, 522 (illus.), 534

Roosevelt's recession, 613

Rosenberg, Julius and Ethel, 680, **681**

Rosie the Riveter, 647, 648 (illus.)

Rough Riders, 494

Roundups, 420, 421

Rubenstein, Helena, 598

Ruby, Jack, 726

Rubyfruit Jungle (Brown), 735

Ruhr Valley, 591

Ruiz, Felicia, 650

Ruiz, Raul, 749

Rumsfeld, Donald, 804, 806

Rural areas: poverty in, 571, 617–618

Rural Electrification Administration (REA), **618**

Russia, 557; civil war in, 1918-1920, 554; immigrants from, 423; Manchuria and, 522; sphere of influence of, 497; in Triple Entente, 540; U.S. troops in, 554 (illus); World War I and, 540, 552, 552. *See also* Soviet Union

Russian State Archive for Social and Political History, 604, 604 (illus.)

Russo-Japanese War (1905), 524

Rust Belt, 777

Ryan, Paul, 818

Sacco, Nicola, 559

Sadat, Anwar, 768, 770 (illus.)

Saddam Hussein, 787, 806, 807, 808

Safe Drinking Water Act, 758

Saigon: in Vietnam War, 744 (map), 747, 755, 756 (illus.)

Saint-Lô, 654

Saipan, battle of, 657

Salient, 552

Salinger, J. D., 708

Salk, Jonas, 693

SALT agreements: SALT I, 755–756; SALT II, 770

Same-sex civil unions, 809

Same-sex marriage, 795, 801, 808–809, 818

Same-sex relationships, 441, 442

Samoa, 497, 501

Sanborn insurance maps, 451, 451 (illus.)

Sanchez, Juan, 778

Sandinista Liberation Front, 768

Sandino, Augusto, 589

San Francisco: Chinese in, 450; discrimination against Asian Americans in, 621; economic dominance of, 426; exposition of 1915 in, 530

Sanger, Margaret, 506, 510

Sanitation: in cities, 437–438; urban, 438

Santa Barbara: oil spill at, 759 (illus.)

Santa Fe Railroad, 405

Santiago, Cuba, 493, 494

Sapiro, Aaron, 579

Sarajevo, assassinations in, 537, 539, 540

Saturday Evening Post, 439

Saudi Arabia, 814

Savings and loan industry (S & Ls), **776**

Scalawags, 386, **387,** 391, 393

Scandinavia: immigrants from, 423, **447**

Schechter Poultry Corporation v. United States, **611**

Schlafly, Phyllis, 766–767, 766 (illus.), **772,** 773, 788, 790

School boards, 513

School(s): attendance laws, 439; creationism taught in, 579; for freed people, 376, 378 (illus.); integration of, 708–710, 759–760; Native American children in, 453; in New South, 444; prayer in, 727, 780; segregated, 387; segregation of Chinese in, 433, 452; segregation of Latinos in, 685, 686 (illlus.), 749–750. *See also* Education; Universities and colleges

Schurz, Carl, 466–467 (illus.), 468, 477; on America's role in world affairs, 500; anti-imperialism and, 495; Philippines and, 495

Schwarzkopf, Norman, 787

Science: education in, 694

"Science cities": World War II and, 645

Scopes, John T., 578

Scopes trial, 578

Scott, Emmett J., 551
Scott, Tom, 397
Scottsboro Nine, 621
Screen Actors Guild, 679
Screen Guide for Americans, A, 679
Scribner's Monthly, 379 (illus.)
Seale, Bobby, 733
Search and destroy, 743
Sears, Roebuck and Co.,
    412–413, 412 (illus.)
Seattle: strike of 1919 in, 558
Second Amendment, A11
"Second Battle of Wounded
    Knee," 752
Second Hundred Days,
    611–612, 615 (table), 635
Second Iraq War, 807, 808 (map), 810
Second Mississippi Plan, 445
Second Sex, The (de Beauvoir), 686
Section hands: Mexican
    American, 455 (illus.)
Securities and Exchange
    Commission (SEC), **609**
Security Council (UN), 666;
    Korean War and, 672, 674
Sedition Act, 549
Segregated schools, **387**
Segregation: of African Americans,
    445; in armed forces, 493; of
    blood supply, 650; of Chinese,
    452, 463; of Mexican American
    children, 749–750; in New Deal
    agencies, 622; separate but
    equal facilities, 446; in World
    War I, 536; World War I and,
    551. *See also* Integration
Selective Service Act: in
    World War I, **551**
Self-determination, 553, 556;
    feminism and, 506; post-
    World War I, 557
Self-employed women, 456
Semiskilled workers, 616
Senate: women in, 820 (illus.)
Senate Foreign Relations
    Committee, 487, 557
Seneca Falls, New York: Women's
    Rights Convention at, 478
Separate but equal facilities, 446, 709
Separate spheres: colleges and,
    440; women and, **440,** 478
September 11, 2001, terrorist attacks,
    794, 804–805, 804 (illus.)
Serbia, 786; Kosovo and, 798;
    World War I and, 537, 540
Settlement houses, 504,
    505–506; black, 509
Settlements: European
    immigrants and, 448

Seuss, Dr.: political cartoons
    of, 635 (illus.)
Seventeenth Amendment, 520, A13
Seventh Amendment, A12
Severalty, 453
Sewage systems: in cities, 437
Seward, William H.: Alaska
    and, **486**–487
Sex and sexuality: counterculture and,
    737; movies and, 565, 565 (illus.),
    573, 573 (illus.), 594, 594 (illus.);
    in 1920s, 576; in 1950s, 707; in
    1960s, 735–736. *See also* Gender;
    Homosexuals and homosexuality
Sexual discrimination, 795
Sexual harassment, 801
"Sexuality and Inuendo in Movie
    Advertising," 594, 594 (illus.)
Sexually transmitted infections, 512
Seymour, Horatio, 383
Sharecroppers, 424
Sharecropping, 378, 379 (map)
"Share Our Wealth" plan:
    of Huey Long, **610**
Sharon Statement, 727
Shaw, Anna Howard, 507
Sheik, The (film), 573, 573 (illus.)
Shelly v. Kraemer, **682**
Sheridan, Philip: Plains
    Indians and, 417–418
Sherman, John, 473
Sherman, William Tecumseh, 377,
    414; Plains Indians and, 417
Sherman Anti-Trust Act,
    462, **474,** 476, 516
Sherman Silver Purchase Act,
    473, 474, **477,** 483
Shiite faction, Iraq, 807
Ships and shipping: capital ships
    and, 592; strikes against, 558;
    Washington Naval Conference
    and, 592, 593; in World War I,
    542–543, 543 (map); in World
    War II, 644–645. *See also*
    Blockade; Navy; specific ships
Shriver, Eunice Kennedy,
    716–717, 716 (illus.), 738
Shultz, George, 784
Shute, Nevil, 696
Siberia, 554
Sicily: Allied invasion of, 653
Sierra Club, 426, 518
Signatory: to Kellogg-Briand Pact, 593
Sikhs, 581
Silent Majority, 759–760
Silent Spring (Carson), 757, 758
Silicon Valley, 799
Silver, 420; *vs.* gold standard, 476–477
Silverites, 477, 501

Silver mines: in Nevada, 422
Silver movement, 482
Silver Republicans, 484,
    484 (illus.), 485
Sinclair, Upton, 510, **511,**
    512, 517, 611
Single-family houses, 681, 681 (illus.)
Single parenthood: after
    World War II, 684
Sino-Indian War, 757
Sino-Japanese War (1894), 524
Sioux Indians: Lakotas/
    Dakotas as, 416; at Wounded
    Knee, 419 (illus.), 420
Sirhan, Sirhan, 748
Sirica, John, 761
Sit-down strikes, 613
Sit-in: labor movement
    and, **649**; lunch counter,
    719–720, 721 (illus.)
Sitting Bull, 418, 419
Situation comedies, on television,
    704, 704 (illus.), 705
Six Companies. *See* Chinese
    Consolidated Benevolent
    Association
Sixteenth Amendment, 520, 527, A13
Sixth Amendment, A12
Skilled workers: organized labor and,
    616. *See also* Labor; Labor unions
Skyscrapers, 435 (illus.),
    436, 437 (illus.)
Slapstick, 529
Slaves and slavery: abolition
    of, around the world,
    374; chattel slavery, 374;
    Emancipation Proclamation
    and, 370; freedom and legacy
    of slavery, 375–376; Thirteenth
    Amendment and, 372–373
Slavic peoples, Russia and, **540**
SLBMs. *See* Submarine-launched
    ballistic missiles (SLBMs)
Sleepers, 478 (illus.)
Sleeping Car Porters union, 649
Sloan, John, 528
Slovenia, 786
Smith, Al, 586, 588, 589, 595, 609
Smith, Bessie, 575, 576 (illus.)
Smith, Lonnie, 649
Smith, O. P. "Slam," 675
Smith Act, 680, 681
Smith-Connally War Labor
    Disputes Act, 645
Smith v. Alright, 649
Smoking. *See* Cigarettes
Smoot-Hawley Tariff (1930), 600
SNCC. *See* Student Nonviolent
    Coordinating Committee

Social activism, 506
Social Darwinism, 407, 409, 490
Social Gospel, 508; settlement houses and, 506
Socialist Party of America (SPA), 485, **510**; opposition to World War I, 548
Socialist Revolutionaries (Russia), 554
Socialists, 533; Red Scare and, 559
Social networking, 794
Social patterns: reconstructing, 451, 451 (illus.)
Social protest novel, of the 1930s, 625
Social Security: Eisenhower and, 695; Kennedy and, 719; Nixon and, 758; privatization and, 809; Truman and, 675, 678
Social Security Act (1935), 622, 627; Frances Perkins and, 597–598, 628; passage of, 612
Social work, 506, 512
Society: Clinton and, 800–801; male and female characteristics in 1950s, 701–702; in New South, 444–445; post-World War II, 681–686
Society for Human Rights, 585
Sod houses, **423**–424, 424 (illus.)
Sodomy, 441; laws on, 585, 795
Soil: farming and, 424
Soil Conservation and Domestic Allocation Act, 617
Solomon Islands, 652
Somoza, Anastasio, 768
Songs: post-World War I, 560 (illus.)
Souls of Black Folk (Du Bois), 509
Sousa, John Philip, 528
South: African American population and duration of Reconstruction in, 385, 386 (map); Alliance voters in, 482; civil rights movement in, 708–712; Democrats in, 469; distribution of population in, by race, 1900, 450 (figure); Farmers' Alliances in, 481; freedom rides in, 721, 723 (illus.); Grange in, 475; Great Migration of African Americans from, 549–550, 550 (illus.); Ku Klux Klan in, 580; New Departure Democrats in, 388–389; post-Civil War, 370–371, 377–380; post-Reconstruction, 376; progressivism in, 514; race and Great Depression in, 621–622; Redeemers in, 389; Republican Party in, 386–387; restoring civil government in, 372, 373 (illus.); sit-in movement in, 719–720, 721 (illus.); white supremacy in, 390, 393. *See*

also Civil rights movement; New South; Reconstruction
South Africa: disfranchisement and segregation in, 446; end of apartheid in, 785, 786 (illus.)
South America: Cold War and, 696. *See also* Latin America
South Carolina: freed families in, 377
Southeast Asia: Vietnam War and, 744 (map). *See also* Asia; Vietnam War; specific countries
Southeast Asia Treaty Organization (SEATO), 696
Southern Alliance, 481
Southern Christian Leadership Conference (SCLC), **712**
Southern Europe: immigration from, 579
Southern Manifesto, 709
Southern Pacific Railroad, 404, 405, 420
Southern strategy: of Nixon, **759**
South Improvement Company, 397, 398
South Korea, 665, 672, 673 (map), 674, 675; bilateral defense pact with, 696. *See also* Korean War
South Vietnam, 700, 742, 744 (map), 747, 748; Kennedy and, 725–726
South Vietnam army (ARVN), 725, 726
Southwest: Ku Klux Klan in, 580; Mexican Americans in, 454–455
Soviet Union: Afghanistan and, 770; American image of, 669 (illus.); atomic bomb of, 672, 680; Battle of Stalingrad and, 652–653; China and, 755, 757; Cold War politics and, 665, 678, 700–701; collapse of, 604, 768, 785; Cuba and, 699, 724–**725**, 725 (illus.); Eisenhower and, 700–701; Hungary and, 701; Iran and, 667; lend-lease to, 640; Middle East and, 698; Reagan and, 774–775, 781, 783–784, 783 (illus.); Sputnik I and II launched by, 693; in UN, 666; in World War II, 633. *See also* Cold War; Russia; World War II, 640, 651
Space exploration: Kennedy and, 719; *Sputnik* and, 693
Spain: Cuba and, 491, 492–494. *See also* Spanish Civil War
Spanish-American War, 492–496, 492 (illus.), 494 (illus.), 501; African Americans in, 536
Spanish Civil War, 610, 625, 635
Speakeasy, 576–577, 578

Special Olympics, 716–717, 716 (illus.)
Speculators: in 1920s, 570
Speed-up, 457
Spencer, Herbert, 407, 409
Spending: consumer, 439; under Nixon, 758; to stimulate economy, 815, 816; TARP, 812. *See also* Economy; Government; Military spending
Spheres of influence, 497
Spindletop Pool, 415
Spirit of St. Louis, The (airplane), 573, 574 (illus.)
Spock, Benjamin, 705
Spoilsman, 468
Spoils system, 468, 471, 472, 479; reforming, 477–478
Sporting News, The, 687
Sports: men and, 440–441, 464; in 1920s, 573; racism in, 665; Special Olympics, 716–717
Sprague, Frank, 436
Spreckels, Claus, 488 (illus.)
Sputnik I, 693
Sputnik II, 693
Square Deal: of Theodore Roosevelt, **516**
St. Lawrence Seaway Act (1954), 693
St. Louis, 435
St. Mihiel salient, battle at, 552
Stagecoach, 626
Stagflation, 758
Stalemate, 471
Stalin, Joseph, 604, 640, 667 (illus.); Berlin blockade and, 669, 670; death of, 694, 700; German Nonaggression Pact with, 636; at Potsdam, 658, 660; at Yalta, 656, 656 (illus.). *See also* Soviet Union; World War II
Stalingrad, Battle of, 652–653, 654 (illus.)
Stallings, Laurence, 545
Stalwarts, 471
Standard of living, 706; in 1920s, 567–568; in 1950s, 702–703, 705
Standard Oil, 398, 408, 415; IdaTarbell's series on, 511; model for monopoly, 409–410; Rockefeller and, 413; Sherman Anti-Trust Act and, 476
Stanley, John Mix, 417 (illus.)
Stanton, Edwin, 383
Stanton, Elizabeth Cady, 381, 384, 478
Starr, Ellen Gates, 504, 505
State Department, 589, 591; NSC and, 670
State government: reform of, 513–514

States: Thirteenth Amendment and, 375

States' rights, 374; Andrew Johnson and, 375

States' Rights Democratic Party (Dixiecrat Party), 677

Statistics: in historical analysis, 584, 584 (figure)

Steel industry, 431; Carnegie and, 398, 405–406; reorganization of, 429; strike against, 558

Steffens, Lincoln, 511, 512

Steinbeck, John, 625, 780

Stephenson, D. C., 580

Sterilization: of mentally retarded persons, 580

Steuart case, 645

Stevens, Harry, family, 375 (illus.)

Stevens, John L., 491

Stevens, Thaddeus, 371, 371 (illus.), 372, 377, 380, 383

Stevenson, Adlai E.: 1952 election and, 692, 693 (map)

Stimson, Henry L., 589, 644, 649

Stock exchanges, 399

Stockman, David, 775

Stock market: Great Recession and, 812; in 1920s, 570–571, 570 (figure); Reagan and, 776; technology stocks and, 799

Stock market crash: of 1929, 598, 599, 600

Stocks: railroad, 405

Stone, Harlan Fiske, 613

Stone, Lucy, 478

Stonewall Riot (1969), 735

STOP-ERA movement, 767, 772

Strategic Air Command (SAC), 724

Strategic Arms Limitation agreement (SALT I), 755–756

Strategic Arms Limitation Treaty (SALT II), 770

Strategic Arms Limitation Treaty (START), 813

Strategic Defense Initiative (SDI), 781, 784

Streamline Moderne style, 614 (illus.)

Stream of commerce doctrine, 476

Streetcars, 436

Streetcar suburbs, 436–437

Strikebreakers, 558

Strikes, 457, 459, 459 (illus.); AFL and, 461; coal miners, 516; by farm workers, 749, 750 (illus.); in Great Depression, 602, 610, 613; Great Railway Strike (1877), 458–459; Homestead, 461; IWW, 510; Knights of Labor and, 460–461; post-World War I,

558; post-World War II, 676, 676 (illus.), 677; Pullman, 462, 462 (illus.), 484; against U. S. Steel, 558; World War II and, 645–646. *See also* Labor; Labor unions

Strong, Josiah, 490

Structural reforms, 479, 481

Student Nonviolent Coordinating Committee (SNCC), **720**

Students for a Democratic Society (SDS), **736,** 745

Subculture: adolescence as, 691, 736–737; gay and lesbian, 441–**442,** 464, 585, 595, 707

Submarine-launched ballistic missiles (SLBMs), 756

Submarines: missiles for, 695

Subprime loans, 811

Subsidies: to agriculture, 617, 695; for railroads, 420

Suburbs, 436, 437; automobiles and, 571; lifestyle in, 703, 705; in 1950s, 681–682, 681 (illus.), 691

Subversion, 557

Sudan, 814

Sudetenland, 636

Suez Canal: nationalization of, 698

Suffragists, 507

Sugar and sugar industry: in Cuba, 490, 491; in Hawai'i, 488; vertical integration of, 488 (illus.)

Sugar-beet fieldworkers, Colorado, 582 (illus.)

Suicides: in depression of 1890s, 428; in Great Depression, 598, 619

Sullivan, Louis, 435 (illus.)

Sumner, Charles, 372, 379, 384, 487

Sumner, William Graham, 407, 409

Sun Also Rises, The (Hemingway), 574, 625

Sunbelt, 749, 759, 760; conservatism and, 773

Sunday, Billy, 578

Sunni Muslims, 556, 807

Supplemental Nutrition Assistance Program (SNAP), 720

Supply-side economics, 775

Supreme Court: on abortion rights, 772; African Americans on, 803; *Boynton v. Virginia,* 720–721; *Brown v. Board of Education,* 709; on corporate personhood, 413; desegregation and, 712; *Dred Scott* decision and, 384; federalism and, 803; Fourteenth Amendment interpreted by, 382; Franklin Roosevelt and, 611, 612–613; judicial restraint, 802; Nixon and, 760; Obama's Affordable Care Act

and, 816, 817; *Plessy v. Ferguson,* 708; Rehnquist Court, 802; on separate but equal facilities, 709; sexual harassment ruling by, 801; on sodomy laws, 795; stream of commerce doctrine and, 476; 2000 election and, 803. *See also* specific cases and justices

Survey Graphic (magazine), 575 (illus.)

Survival of the fittest, 407, 409

Swann v. Charlotte-Mecklenburg, 760

Sweatshops, 510

Swift, Gustavus, 413

Sword Beach, 654

Sylvis, William, 458

Syria, 556, 782, 814

Taft, Robert, 656, 680, 692, 766

Taft, William Howard, 497, 534, 537; Caribbean region and, 522; East Asia and, 523; 1908 election and, 519, 519 (illus.); 1912 election and, 524, 525, 526

Taft-Hartley Act, 676, 677, 678

Taiwan (Formosa), 524, 776; bilateral defense pact with, 696

Taliban, 794, **805,** 806, 807 (map)

Tammany Hall, 468, 469, 472; Al Smith and, 588

Tanneries, 417

Tanzania: embassy attacked in, 805

Tape, Joseph, 433, 434, 451

Tape, Mamie, 433, 434, 452, 463

Tape, Mary: challenge to San Francisco Board of Education, 463

Tape family, San Francisco, 433–434, 451, 451 (illus.)

Tarawa, battle at, 657

Tarbell, Ida, 511

Tariffs: Fordney-McCumber Tariff, 591, 592; McKinley Tariff, 473, 474, 482, 483, 491; protective, 399, 469, 472; Smoot-Hawley Tariff, 600; Underwood Tariff, 526. *See also* Protective tariffs; Trade

TARP. *See* Troubled Asset Relief Program

Taxation: Clinton and, 796; George H. W. Bush and, 788; George W. Bush and, 803; Obama and, 817, 819–820; Reaganism and, 775; World War I and, 547; World War II and, 646, 646 (figure)

Tax Reduction Act (1964), 726, 729 (table)

Taylor, Elvira, 647

Taylor, Frederick W., 568–569

Teaching: in freedmen schools, 377

Teach-ins, 745
Tea Party movement, 794,
   817, 818 (illus.)
Teapot Dome scandal, 585, 586 (illus.)
Technology, 431; advancements in,
   777; consumer-oriented economy
   and, 568; for farming, 424,
   425 (illus.); Great Plains and,
   424; information, 799; in steel
   industry, 406–407; World War II
   and, 645. *See also* Factories
Tehran: hostage crisis and,
   771, 771 (illus.)
Tejanos, 454, 455
Telecommunications:
   industries in, 777
Telegraph, 406
Telephone, 411
Televangelists, 774
Television: consumerism and,
   705; in 1950s, 694, 704, 704
   (illus.), 705; presidential debates
   on, 718–719, 718 (illus.)
Teller, Edward, 658
Teller, Henry M., 453, 493
Teller Amendment, 493, 496
Tenements, 443
Tennessee, 372; teaching
   of evolution in, 578
Tennessee Coal, Iron, and
   Railroad Company, 415
Tennessee Valley Authority,
   607, 607 (map), 622
Ten-Percent Plan, 372
Tenth Amendment, A12
Tenth Cavalry: Charles Young and,
   536, 536 (illus.), 540 (illus.)
Tenure of Office Act, 383
Terrorism: against American
   embassies, 805; bin Laden,
   Al-Qaeda and, 805; Islamic
   fundamentalism and, 806;
   Mississippi Plan and, 390;
   Reagan and, 782; September
   11, 2001 attacks, 794, 804–805,
   804 (illus.); war on, 805–807
Terrorists, 383
Terry, Peggy, 648
Tesla, Nikola, 412
Tet offensive: during Vietnam
   War, **747–748**
Texas: annexation and, 454; cattle
   industry in, 420; oil in, 410, 415
Texas Alliance, 481
Textile industry: child labor
   in, 444, 444 (illus.); in New
   South, 414; women in, 456
Thieu, Nguyen Van, 755
Third Amendment, A11

Third Reich, 655 (map)
Third World: Eisenhower and, 696
Thirteenth Amendment, 370,
   372–**373,** 375, 376, 384, A12
38th parallel, 672, 673 (map), 675
Thomas, Clarence, 803
Thompson, Florence
   Owens, 625 (illus.)
Thompson, James, 648
"Three Hard Years" (China), 700
Three Mile Island: nuclear
   accident at, **771**
Thurmond, J. Strom, 677, 678
Tiananmen Square: protests
   in, 786–787
Tigris river region, 808 (map)
Tilden, Samuel J., 390, 391
Till, Emmett, 710
Time magazine, 667
Tipis, 415
Title VII: of 1964 Civil
   Rights Act, **733,** 735
Tobacco Road (Caldwell), 625
Tojo, Hideki, 640
Tom Sawyer (Twain), 434
"Too big to fail," 812
Toomer, Jean, 574
Topaz Relocation Center,
   632, 632 (illus.)
Tortilla Flat (Steinbeck), 625
To Secure These Rights, 677
Total war: World War I as, 546
Townsend, Francis, 610–611
Toynbee Hall (London), 504, 505
Tract homes, 681–682
Tractors, 571
Tracy, Benjamin F., 490
Trade: with Eastern Asia, 487;
   globalization of, 795–796, 797
   (illus.); Japanese-American, 640;
   Open Door policy and, 497; U.S.,
   interwar years, 589. *See also* Tariffs
Trade deficit, 776
Trademark, 412
Trade unions, 461, 464; banners,
   458 (illus.); labor unions as, **457.**
   See also Labor; Labor unions
Traffic: in 1920s, 571–572
Transcontinental railroad,
   420, 421 (illus.)
Transportation: agricultural
   growth and, 400; in cities,
   436; World War I and, 546
Treaties: Australia-New Zealand-
   United States (ANZUS), 675;
   of Berlin, 497; **of Brest-Litovsk,**
   541 (map), **552; of Guadalupe**
   Hidalgo, 454; **Hay-Bunau-Varilla,**
   520–521; Intermediate Nuclear

   Force, 784; Limited Test Ban, 725;
   Medicine Lodge Creek, 416–417,
   418; of Paris, 1898, 494–495; **of**
   Portsmouth, 523; SALT I and
   SALT II, 755–756, 770; **Strategic**
   Arms Limitation Treaty, 813;
   of Versailles, 554, 555 (map)
Triangle Shirtwaist Company, fire
   at, 506, 507 (illus.), 597
Tribes. *See* American Indians;
   specific groups
Triple Alliance, 540
Triple Entente, 540
Troubled Asset Relief
   Program (TARP), 812
Trujillo, Rafael, 589
Truman, Harry S., 651, 665, 688;
   atomic bomb and, 634, 658, 659;
   civil rights and, 677, 678; defensive
   containment policy, 695; Korean
   War and, 672, 674–675, 680;
   liberalism and, 675–677; loyalty
   program of, 679; 1948 election
   and, 677–678, 678 (illus.), 678
   (map); Potsdam Conference and,
   658, 660; United Nations and, 666
Truman Doctrine, 667, 669
Trumbull, Lyman, 382
Trust, 411; Standard Oil as, **409**
Trustbusting, 516
Truth in Packaging Act
   (1966), 729 (table)
Tsar, 552
Tuberculosis, 512
Tugwell, Rexford, 605
Tule relocation camp, 633, 643
Tunisia: Arab Spring and, 813
Tunney, Gene, 573
Tupperware parties, 702 (illus.)
Turkey, 557; Cuban missile crisis
   and, 724, 725; post-World War II,
   667; World War I and, 540
Turner, Henry M., 446
Tuskegee Airmen, 650
Tuskegee Normal and
   Industrial Institute, 446
Twain, Mark, 434, 445, **528;**
   anti-imperialism and, 495;
   Philippines and, 495
Tweed, William Marcy, 471
Tweed Ring, 470–471
Tweeting, 794
Twelfth Amendment, A12
Twentieth Amendment, A13–A14
Twenty-fifth Amendment, A14–A15
Twenty-first Amendment, 577, A14
Twenty-fourth Amendment,
   729, 729 (table), 730, A14
Twenty-second Amendment, A14

Twenty-seventh Amendment, 772, A15
Twenty-sixth Amendment,
    759, 760, A15
Twenty-third Amendment, A14
Twitter, 794
Tyler, John, 487

U-boats, 542–543, 544, 546,
    551, 639 (illus.), 640
Underwood Tariff, 526
Underwrite, 388
Undocumented
    immigrants, 780, 781
Unemployment, 483, 598; Carter
    and, 771, 772; in depression of
    1890s, 428; in 1870s, 427–428; in
    Great Depression, 599 (illus.),
    600, 601, 601 (figure), 608–609,
    608 (map), 613, 614, 621; Lyndon
    Johnson and, 727; in 1990s,
    800; under Nixon, 758; women
    after World War II and, 648
Unemployment compensation, 506,
    507 (illus.), 597; G.I. Bill and, 683
Unilateral internationalism, **589**
Union Pacific Railroad, 402, 420;
    Crédit Mobilier scandal and, 470;
    women workers for, 547 (illus.)
Unions. *See* Industrial union;
    Labor unions; Trade
    unions; specific groups
United Automobile Workers
    (UAW), 613
United Brotherhood of Carpenters
    and Joiners, 457, 458 (illus.)
United Cannery, Agricultural,
    Packing, and Allied Workers of
    America (UCAPAWA), 623
United Fruit Company, 591, 699
United Mine Workers, 461,
    616, 676; strike, 645
United Nations, 666; Iraq and, 806;
    Korean War and, 672, 674, 675;
    Kosovo and, 798, 799 (illus.)
United States: Caribbean region
    and, 521–522, 521 (map), 522
    (illus.); European immigrants in,
    447–449; foreign-born population
    of, 1870-1920, 447 (figure);
    Latin America and, 487, 589, 590
    (map), 591; in UN, 666; world
    affairs and, 1901-1913, 523–524
United States Steel Corporation,
    415, 429; strike against, 558
United States v. Butler, **617**
United States v. E. C. Knight, 476, 516
United States v. Lopez, 803

United States v. Morrison, 803
United States v. Washington, 752
Universal Negro Improvement
    Association (UNIA), 576
Universities and colleges: antiwar
    movement and, 754; enrollments
    in, 439; first degrees awarded
    by, 1870-1920, 439 (figure);
    post-World War II attendance
    in, 682–683; women in, 576. *See
    also* School(s); specific schools
University of Michigan:
    teach-in at, 745
University of Mississippi: James
    Meredith at, 721, 722
Unskilled workers, 616
Upward Bound, 729 (table)
Urban areas: automobile and,
    572; population of, 1860-1910,
    435 (figure); poverty in,
    442–443, 442 (illus.), 708.
    See also Cities and towns
Urban League, 549, 649
Urban renewal bill, 719
U.S. v. Carolene Products, 613
USA Patriot Act (2001), **805**
U.S.S. Cole, 805
USS Maine. See Maine (ship)
Utah: woman suffrage in,
    479. *See also* Mormons
Utah Beach, 654
U-2 spy planes: incident over, 701;
    missiles in Cuba and, 724

Vaccination, for polio, 693
Vacuum cleaners, 411
Vagrancy, 379
Valentino, Rudolph, 573
Vamp, 573
Van Devanter, Willis, 613
Vanzetti, Bartolomeo, 559
Vaqueros (cowboys), 420
Vassar College, 439
V-E Day, 657
Velde, Harold, 680
Venezuela, 591; boundary dispute
    with British Guiana, 491
Venture capitalists, 799
Veracruz, 539
Versailles, Treaty of, 554, 555 (map)
Vertical integration, 406–407, 431;
    in consumer-goods industries,
    413; consumer products and,
    412; in lumber industry, 425; in
    oil industry, 409, 410 (figure);
    steel industry and, 429; in sugar
    and sugar industry, 488 (illus.)

Veterans: in Bonus Army, 602; G.I. Bill
    and, 683, 651, 665, 681, 682, 685
Vetoes: by Andrew Johnson,
    381; by Cleveland, 472; by
    Coolidge, 587; by Ford, 762; by
    Hayes, 477; by Truman, 677
V-girls (victory girls), 647
Vice president: Ferraro nominated
    for, 776. *See also* specific individuals
Vice squads, 707
Victory gardens, 647
"Victory Program," 640
Viereck case, 645
Viet Cong, 725, 743, 747; TET
    offensive and, 747–748
Viet Minh, 700
Vietnam, 744 (map); division of,
    700; immigrants from, 780
Vietnamization policy,
    753, 754 (figure)
Vietnam War: Americanization of,
    743, 745; antiwar movement in,
    745, 745 (illus.), 747; generation
    affected by, 1964-1975, 756 (table);
    Johnson and, 742–743, 745, 747;
    media coverage of, 747, 748; Nixon
    and, 753–755; public opinion on,
    745, 746, 746 (figure); Southeast
    Asia and, 744 (map); Tet Offensive
    during, 747–748; troop levels by
    year, 1960-1972, 754 (figure)
Vigilantes: during World War I, **549**
Villa, Francisco ("Pancho"), 539
Violence: against abortion clinics,
    801, 802 (illus.); in Birmingham,
    722; in civil rights movement,
    710, 712; in former Yugoslavia,
    786; against freedom riders,
    721; during Freedom Summer,
    729; in Iraq, 807–808; Watts riot,
    732. *See also* Race riots; Riots;
    Slaves and slavery; Terrorism
Virginia, 373
Virgin Islands: purchase of, 538
Voinovich, George, 813
Volunteers in Service to America
    (VISTA), 727, 729 (table)
Voting and voting rights, 819;
    African Americans and, 377,
    378, 381, 385 (illus.), 393, 686;
    Australian ballot and, 481; civil
    rights and, 384–385; Fourteenth
    Amendment and, 446; Freedom
    Summer and, 729–730, 730
    (illus.); party lines and, 468
Voting Rights Act (1965), 475,
    729 (table), **730,** 802;
    25-year extension of, 758

Wage and price controls: Nixon and, 758, 759

Wages: for African Americans in World War II, 649; for auto workers, 569; for *braceros,* 650; in depression of 1870s, 428; of farm workers, 749; in Great Depression, 609; in Lawrence, Massachusetts factories, 456; for men *vs.* women, 456; of miners, 646; in New South, 414; in 1920s, 567; in 1950s, 702; in 1990s, 777, 800; under Nixon, 758; post-World War I, 558; post-World War II, 676, 676 (illus.); in service economy, 777; of women workers, 456, 648, 684; World War II and, 645; WPA, 616

Wagner, Robert, 612

Wagner Act (1935), **612,** 616, 627; organized labor and, 616

Wainwright Building, 435 (illus.)

Wakasa, James Hatsuaki, 632

"Walking cities", 435

Wallace, George, 728, 730, **748,** 749, **760**

Wallace, Henry A., 651, 677, 678

Wall Street Journal, 588, 635, 676

Wall Street Reform and Consumer Protection Act (Dodd-Frank Act), 817

Wal-Mart, 777, 801

War bonds, 646, 647

Ward, Lester Frank, 409

Wards, 512

War Industries Board, 546

Warner, Charles Dudley, 434

War of attrition, 418

War on drugs, 787

War on Poverty, 726–727, 729 (table)

War on terrorism, 805–807, 813, 813 (illus.)

War Power Act, 754–755

War Production Board (WPB), 645, 647

War Refugee Board, 657

Warren, Earl: calls for impeachment, 727 (illus.); retirement of, 760; Warren Commission and, 726; Warren Court and, 727

Warren, Earl, 709

Wars and warfare: governmental power and, 645. *See also* specific battles and wars

Washington, Booker T., 445, 445 (illus.), 446, 509, 551

Washington Naval Conference, 592, 593, 593 (illus.)

Washington Post, 760

Waste Land, The (Eliot), 574

Water: chlorination of, 437; Western development and, 426

Watergate scandal, **760**–761

Water Quality Act, 729 (table), 730

Water table, 424

Waterways, 693

Watt, James, 776

Watts (Los Angeles): riot in, **732**

WCTU. *See* Woman's Christian Temperance Union

Wealth and wealthy, 409; Great Depression, 599; in 1980s, 778. *See also* Gospel of Wealth; Social Darwinism

"Wealth Tax Act," 612

Weapons: biological, 804, 806; chemical, 804, 806. *See also* Disarmament; Missiles; Nuclear power

Weapons of mass destruction (WMDs), **806**

Weary Blues, The (Hughes), 575 (illus.)

Weaver, James B., 476, 482

Weaver, Robert, 729

Wedemeyer, Albert, 653

Weimar Republic: hyperinflation in, 592

Welch, Joseph, 694

Welfare Act (1996), 796

Welfare and welfare programs: reform on, 796

Welfare capitalism, 582

Wells, Ida B., 509

Wells, Sumner, 634

Wells-Barnett, Ida, 440

West: cattle industry in, 420–422; dams in, 614; distribution of population in, by race, 1900, 450 (figure); farming in, 422–425; incorporating into national economy, 415–426; Japanese in, 642; Ku Klux Klan in, 580; in late nineteenth century, 416 (map); lumbering in, 425–426; mining industry in, 422; race and Great Depression in, 621–622; railroads in, 402, 405, 420; segregation against Chinese in, 452; water in, 426, 431; woman suffrage in, 479. *See also* specific cities and states

West Berlin, 669, 701, 724. *See also* Berlin entries

Western Europe: immigration from, 579

Western front: in World War I, **542**

Western Hemisphere: Castro in, 742; national origin quota

system and, 779; United Nations' charter and, 696

West Germany, 670, 670 (map), 696, 776; Marshall Plan and, 669

Westmoreland, William, 743, 747, 748

West Virginia: Great Railway Strike, 458–459, 459 (illus.)

West Virginia (ship), 642 (illus.)

Weyler, Valeriano, 491

Wheat: farms, 423, 424–425

Wheeler, Burton K., 639

Whiskey Ring, 471

White-collar jobs: in 1950s, 703

"White man's burden," 490, 495

Whites: in post-Civil War South, 378

Whites (Russia), 553, 554

White supremacy, 380, 390, 393, 580, 595

Whitney, William C., 489

Whyte, William H., 708

Wilderness Act (1964), 729 (table)

Wildlife preserves, 518

Wiley, Harvey W., 517, 517 (illus.)

Wilhelm, Kaiser, abdication of, 553

Wilkie, Wendell, 638

Willard, Frances, 440, 479

Williams, Evan, 793–794, 793 (illus.)

Willingham case, 645

Wilson, Charles E., 695

Wilson, Edith Bolling, 557

Wilson, Woodrow, 531, 534; democratic progressivism and, 524–528; foreign policy of, 538; Fourteen Points and, 553, 556, 562, 563; illness of, 557; Mexican Revolution and, 528–539; neutrality and, 542; 1912 election and, 525; 1916 election and, 543; 1920 election and, 561; Paris Peace Conference and, 554, 556; presidency and, 537; reform and, 526–528; World War I and, 542, 544, 545, 546

Wisconsin: reforms in, 513, 514

Wisconsin Idea, 514

Wives. *See* Families; Women

Wobblies. *See* Industrial Workers of the World

Wolf, Charlie, 551 (illus.)

Woman's Christian Temperance Union (WCTU), **440,** 441 (illus.), 479

Woman suffrage, 381, 384, 478–479, 506–507, 508 (illus.), 595; around the world, 480 (table); Bull Moose Party and, 525; Greenbackers and, 476; Nineteenth Amendment

Woman suffrage *(continued)* and, 561, 577, 583; Populists and, 479, 482; ratification of, 583; WCTU and, 440. *See also* Voting and voting rights; Women

Women: Carter and, 772; in cattle towns, 421; childbearing and, 583, 584, 584 (illus.); cigarette advertising and, 567–568; college graduates, 439; conservative, 766–767; as consumers, 412; culture war and, 800–801; education for, 439, 440; equal pay for, 814; gender roles of, 439–441, 464; G.I. Bill and, 683; Grange and, 475; in Great Depression, 616, 620, 622; high school graduates, 439; homesteading by, 423; Impressionists, 528, 529 (illus.); in industrial workforce, 456; labor unions and, 458, 460; as lawyers, 440; marital status in workforce, 1930-2005, 706 (figure); in medicine, 440; in 1950s, 684, 691, 701–702, 702 (illus.), 704, 704 (illus.), 705; Nobel Peace Prize recipients, 504; in Populist campaigning, 481; post-World War II, 683–684, 683 (illus.); in presidential race, 811; Progressive convention of 1912 and, 525; reform and, 506–507; in Senate, 820 (illus.); separate spheres for, 440, 478; and settlement house movement, 504; in social work, 506; as Speaker of the House, 810, 811 (illus.); Tupperware parties, 702 (illus.); in universities and colleges, 576; as vice presidential nominee, 811; Wilson and, 528; World War I and, 547, 547 (illus.), 551; in World War II, 647–648, 648 (figure). *See also* Gender; Voting and voting rights; Women's rights, 648 (illus.)

Women Appointed for Volunteer Emergency Service (WAVES), 647

Women's Airforce Service Pilots (WASPs), 647

Women's Army Corps (WAC), 647

Women's clubs, 440

Women's rights: Eleanor Roosevelt and, 621 (illus.); movements for, 506–507, 733, 735

Women's Rights Convention: at Seneca Falls, 478

Women's Trade Union League, 506

Wood, Leonard, 561

Woodfill, Samuel, 552

Woodstock: rock concert in, **737**

Woodward, Bob, 760

Woodward, Ellen, 622

Woolworth lunch counter, sit-in at, 719–720, 721 (illus.)

Workday: eight-hour, 458, 460, 476, 482, 512, 528, 546; in late nineteenth century, 457

Workers: assembly line, 568–569, 569 (illus.); Fair Labor Standards Act and, 598, 613; industrial, 455–457, 456 (figure), 510; women as, 801; WPA, 616. *See also* Labor; Work force; Working class

Worker safety, 506

Work force: alternation between expansions/contractions and, 427; industrial distribution of, 1870, 1890, 1910, 456 (figure); integration of, 649; marital status of women in, 1930-2005, 706 (figure); married women in, 733; in "New Economy," 799; in 1950s, 702–703; women in, 1940-1945, 648 (figure). *See also* Industrialization; Labor; Women; Workers

Working class: in 1920s, 576; tenement living and, 442–443, 442 (illus.). *See also* Labor; Workers

Workplace fatalities, 457

Work relief program, of New Deal, **611**

Works Progress Administration (WPA), **611,** 615–616, 616 (illus.), 622, 623, 623 (illus.), 625

Workweek: forty-four hour, 613

World Bank, 666

World's Columbian Exposition (1893), 530, 531 (illus.)

World Series, 530

World Trade Center: car bombing in front of, 805; terrorist attack on (2001), 794, 804, 804 (illus.), 805

World Trade Organization (WTO), **797**

World War I: alliances in, 540; Alvin York and, 552; America in aftermath of, 557–561; American neutrality in, 542; American troops in, 551–552; armistice for, 541 (map); casualties in, 552; Charles Young and, 536–537; civil liberties during, 549; in Europe, 537, 540, 541 (map), 542; as first "total war," 546; home front in, 546–550; legacies of, 557; mobilizing the economy and, 546–547; naval

warfare in, 542–543, 543 (illus.); pacifism after, 592–593; Paris Peace Conference after, 553–554; postwar boundary changes and, 555 (map), 556; progressivism and, 547, 557; public opinion and, 547–549; U.S. entry into, 546

World War II: African Americans during, 648–650; in Atlantic Ocean region, 639–640; Casablanca meeting in, 653; casualties in, 654, 657, 658, 660 (figure), 660 (table); in Europe, 636, 638, 652–656; events leading to, 634–636, 638–641; Japanese Americans during, 632–633, 642–644, 643 (map); Japanese American units in, 643; Latinos during, 650; lifestyle in, 647; mobilization for, 644–651; Pearl Harbor attack and, 633, 640–641, 642, 642 (illus.); politics after, 675–678; politics during, 651; society after, 665–666, 681–686; women and, 647–648; Yalta Conference and, 655–656, 656 (illus.). *See also* Cold War; Hitler; Italy; Nazi Germany

Wounded Knee, South Dakota: AIM seizure of, 752

Wounded Knee Creek: battle at, 419 (illus.), **420**

WPA. *See* Works Progress Administration

Wright, Richard, 625

Write-in campaign: in 1968 election, **748**

Writers. *See* Literature; Poets and poetry; specific individuals

WTO. *See* World Trade Organization

Wyoming: woman suffrage in, 478, 479 (illus.)

Yahoo, 780

Yakus case, 645

Yale University, 439

Yalta Conference, **655**–656, 656 (illus.)

Yalu River, 675

Yamamoto, Isoroku, 640

Yankee ingenuity, 399

Yellow journalism, 491

Yeltsin, Boris, 785

Yemen, 805, 814

Yick Wo v. Hopkins, 452

YMCA. *See* Young Men's Christian Association

Yom Kippur War, 759

York, Alvin, 552
Yorktown (ship), 652
Young, Charles, 536–537, 536 (illus.)
Young, Ellsworth, 548 (illus.)
Young Americans for
    Freedom (YAF), 727
Young Men's Christian
    Association (YMCA), 441
Young people: in 1920s,
    576–577; in 1950s, 691

Youth culture: youth movement
    of 1960s and, 736–737
YouTube, 780
Yugoslavia: breakup of, 786
Yuppies, 778

Zapata, Emiliano, 539
Zavala, Lorenzo de, 454
Zelman v. Simmon-Hart, 802

Zen Buddhism, 737
Zhou Enlai, 755, 757 (illus.)
Zhukov, G. K., 652
Zimmerman, Arthur, 544, 546
Zola, Émile, 528
Zones of occupation. *See*
    Occupation zones
Zoning: city planning and, 512
Zoot suits, 650